D0565447

BEST of the BEST
from
NORTH CAROLINA

Selected Recipes from North Carolina's
FAVORITE COOKBOOKS

BEST
of the BEST
from
NORTH
CAROLINA

Selected Recipes from North Carolina's
FAVORITE COOKBOOKS

EDITED BY
Gwen McKee
AND
Barbara Moseley

Illustrated by Tupper Davidson

QUAIL RIDGE PRESS

Recipe Collection © 1990 Quail Ridge Press, Inc.

Reprinted with permission and all rights reserved under the name of the cookbooks or organizations listed below.

Bill Neal's Southern Cooking © 1989 William F. Neal; *Bravo* © 1984 The Greensboro Symphony Guild, Greensboro, N.C.; *Coastal Carolina Cooking* © 1986 The University of North Carolina Press; *A Cookbook of Pinehurst Courses* © 1980 Moore Regional Hospital Auxiliary; *A Cook's Tour of the Azalea Coast* © 1982 The Auxiliary to the Medical Society of New Hanover, Pender and Brunswick Counties; *A Dash of Down East* © 1986 The Junior Guild of Rocky Mount, Inc.; *Even More Special* © 1986 The Junior League of Durham and Orange Counties, Inc.; *The Fearrington House Cookbook* © 1987 by Jenny Fitch; *Goodness Grows in North Carolina Cookbook* © 1989 North Carolina Department of Agriculture, Marketing Division; *The Grecian Plate* © 1984 The Hellenic Ladies Society, St. Barbara Greek Orthodox Church; *Heart of the Mountains* © 1987 Buncombe County Extension Homemakers; *High Hampton Hospitality* © 1970 Lily Byrd; *In Good Taste* © 1983 Department of Nutrition, School of Public Health of the University of North Carolina; *I Remember: A Collection of Old-Time Recipes and Memories from the Past* © 1988 Hank Kellner; *Island Born and Bred* © 1987 Harkers Island United Methodist Women; *Korner's Folly Cookbook* © 1977 Beth Tartan and Fran Parker; *Love Yourself Cookbook* © 1987 Edie Low; *Mama's Recipes and Others Cookbook* © 1976 June Thompson Medlin; *Marion Brown's Southern Cook Book* © 1980 The University of North Carolina Press; *Market to Market* © 1983 The Service League of Hickory, North Carolina, Inc.; *The Microwave Touch* © 1984 The Microwave Touch; *Mountain Elegance* © 1982 The Junior League of Asheville, Inc.; *Mountain Potpourri* © 1979 The Haywood County Hospital Auxiliary; *Mushrooms, Turnip Greens and Pickled Eggs* © 1971 Frances Carr Parker; *North Carolina and Old Salem Cookery* © 1955 Elizabeth Hedgecock Sparks; *North Carolina's Historic Restaurants and their recipes* © 1990 Dawn O'Brien; *Nothing Could Be Finer* © 1982 The Junior League of Wilmington, Inc.; *Out Of Our League* © 1978 Junior League of Greensboro, Inc.; *Pass the Plate* © 1984 Pass the Plate, Inc.; *Recipes From Our Front Porch* © 1982 by Ella Jo and John Shell, Hemlock Inn; *Sea to Shore* © 1988 Ship to Shore, Inc.; *Ship to Shore I* © 1983 Ship to Shore, Inc.; *Ship to Shore II* © 1985 Ship to Shore, Inc.; *Sip to Shore* © 1986 Ship to Shore, Inc.; *Stirring Performances* © 1988 The Junior League of Winston-Salem, Inc.; *Taste Buds* © 1985 Winslow, Woverton, Komegay; *A Taste of History* © 1982 The North Carolina Museum of History Associates, Inc.; *Vegetarian Masterpieces* © 1988 Carol Tracy and Julie Bruton; *What Is It? What Do I Do With It?* © 1978 Beth Tartan and Fran Parker; *What's New in Wedding Food* © 1985 Marigold P. Sparks and Beth Tartan.

Library of Congress Cataloging-in-Publication Data
Best of the Best from North Carolina: selected recipes from North
Carolina's favaorite cookbooks / edited by Gwen McKee and Barbara
Moseley: illustrated by Tupper Davidson.
p. cm.
Includes index.
ISBN 0-937552-32-0 : $14.95
1. Cookery--North Carolina. I. McKee, Gwen. II. Moseley, Barbara.
TX715.B48456416 1990   90-45535

Copyright © 1990
Quail Ridge Press, Inc.
First printing, October 1990
Second printing, September 1991
Third printing, February 1993
Manufactured in the United States of America
Chapter opening photos and cover photo courtesy of
North Carolina Division of Travel and Tourism
Quail Ridge Press 1-800-343-1583

CONTENTS

The North Carolina mountains.

PREFACE

North Carolina constantly impresses us with her sheer beauty, her prideful history, her industrious people...and her wonderful cuisine.

Entering the state from the southwest, the mountains greet you with their awesome beauty. From the valley, they rise majestically above you, beckoning you upward. And you go, with both excitement and serenity, feeling at times that you are totally away from civilization. And when you get up very high and can see only mountain peaks piercing the "Smoky" clouds beneath them, you feel you have surely reached heaven!

In further contrast to the bustling of her thriving cities, her seashores offer a peacefulness that deepens with the sound of the waves and the squawks of the seagulls. And from her cobble-stoned streets in well-preserved places of history, there swells in you a patriotic pride that comes from the realization that so much of our American history began right here.

We find North Carolina's food heritage to be as varied as the landscape. In the East, much of the food comes from the sea, where every imaginable sea creature ends up in the pot along with Irish potatoes and onions to produce a muddle or a stew. And into the hot broth goes dumplings of some sort, usually cornmeal. Farming in the West yields an abundance of vegetables, fruits, cows, chickens and hogs. All of this brings food, fun, fellowship and friends to a variety of occasions—clambakes, oyster roasts, pit-cooked barbecues, and hunt breakfasts with dishes made from whatever is being celebrated or is available. There might be Liver Dumplings, Persimmon Puddings, and Rock Muddles from the past, as well as new and innovative dishes like Veal à la Cardinal, Almond Champagne Chicken, Original Dirigibles, Tarheel Crocks, and Butter Dips—to name but a few of the superb recipes between these pages.

We are so pleased to have forty-eight North Carolina contributors to this tenth volume in our "Best of the Best" series, who have lent us their favorite recipes along with their enthusiasm and support. We are indeed grateful to the authors, editors, and publishers for their cooperation in making this book possible. Each contributing cookbook has its own special features—recipes, pictures, artwork, anecdotes, history, cooking hints, calorie counts, etc.—and we have attempted to retain their flavors by reproducing the recipes as they appear in each book, changing only for clarity and uniformity of type style. The complete catalog showing and describing each book, along with ordering information, begins on page 269. Further study into the cuisine of North Carolina is available to cooks and collectors by ordering these individual books. There are included recipes from a few classic cookbooks that are no longer in print; we are privileged to make available again the favorite recipes of these cookbooks. We do beg forgiveness for any books that might have been included that we inadvertently overlooked.

Tupper Davidson does all the artwork for our "Best" series, and though we run out of ways to thank her, she never runs out of ways to catch the spirit of the state with her drawings. We are grateful to the food editors from newspapers across the state who helped us with our research. And also to the book and gift store managers who answered our many questions and lent us their knowledge of area cookbooks. We thank the state tourism department for graciously providing us with pictures and information. All along the way, we met people who were so enjoyable to chat with, eagerly telling us of their personal favorite foods and cookbooks. And finally, we thank our special customers and friends from all over the country, who send us their always welcome ideas and suggestions.

It is with great pleasure and pride that we present these North Carolina cookbooks and their outstanding recipes. Perhaps our enjoyment and enthusiasm in working on this book have spilled over into the pages for all to enjoy the unique and wonderful cuisine of the beautiful state of North Carolina.

Gwen McKee and Barbara Moseley

Contributing Cookbooks

Bill Neal's Southern Cooking
Bravo
Centenary Cookbook
Christmas Favorites
Coastal Carolina Cooking
A Cookbook of Pinehurst Courses
A Cook's Tour of the Azalea Coast
A Dash of Down East
Even More Special
Favorite Recipes of the Lower Cape Fear
The Fearrington House Cookbook
Goodness Grows in North Carolina Cookbook
The Grecian Plate
Have Fun Cooking With Me
Heart of the Mountains
High Hampton Hospitality
In Good Taste
I Remember: A Collection of Old-Time Recipes
Island Born and Bred
Jarrett House Potpourri
Knollwood's Cooking
Korner's Folly Cookbook
Love Yourself Cookbook
Mama's Recipes and Others Cookbook

Contributing Cookbooks

Marion Brown's Southern Cook Book
Market to Market
The Microwave Touch
Mountain Elegance
Mountain Potpourri
Mushrooms, Turnip Greens and Pickled Eggs
North Carolina and Old Salem Cookery
North Carolina's Historic Restaurants and their recipes
Nothing Could Be Finer
Out Of Our League
Pass the Plate
Queen Anne's Table
Recipes From Our Front Porch
Seafood Sorcery
Sea to Shore
Ship to Shore I
Ship to Shore II
Sip to Shore
Stirring Performances
Taste Buds
A Taste of History
Vegetarian Masterpieces
What Is It? What Do I Do With It?
What's New in Wedding Food

Appetizers

Chimney Rock, a unique rock formation overlooking Hickory Nut Gorge
and Lake Lure.

Sunday Punch

1 (46-ounce) can pineapple
  juice
2 (46-ounce) cans apple
  juice

3 quarts ginger ale

Chill juices and ginger ale. Make ice ring of apple juice with cherries and orange slices. So easy and very good!!
    Can do ahead. Serves: 40.

Mountain Elegance

Holiday Punch

1 cup sugar
1 cup water
1 teaspoon whole cloves
3 sticks of cinnamon

2 quarts orange juice
1 quart cranberry cocktail
1/4 cup lemon juice

Combine sugar, water, cloves, cinnamon sticks in a large saucepan. Simmer 15 minutes and remove spices. Add juices. Heat but do not boil. Float lemon and orange slices on top. Serve hot.

Mountain Potpourri

Champagne Nectar Punch
The Best!

2 (12-ounce) cans apricot
  nectar
1 (6-ounce) can frozen
  orange juice concentrate
3 cups water

1/4 cup lemon juice
1/8 teaspoon salt
3 (4/5-quart) bottles
  champagne, chilled

Mix all ingredients except champagne; chill. Add champagne just before serving. Makes about 42 servings in champagne glasses.

What's New in Wedding Food

Kiwi Colada
A New Creation!

1 1/2 ounces light rum
1 1/2 ounces Midor liqueur
2 ounces cream of coconut
2 kiwi fruit, peeled
1/4 cup pineapple juice

1 ounce whipping cream
1 1/2 cups small cubes or
   crushed ice
Garnish: 1 slice kiwi fruit,
   1/4 slice pineapple

Pour ingredients into blender with ice. Blend until smooth. Garnish with kiwi and pineapple slices cut to fit over rim of collins glasses. Serves 2.

Sip to Shore

Country Syllabub
(North Carolina Style)

1/2 cup sugar
1/2 cup Scuppernong wine
1 quart whipping cream

1/2 cup brandy
Nutmeg

Mix sugar and wine in a bowl until sugar is dissolved. Add a small amount of cream; mix well. Whip remaining cream in large bowl until thickened. Add wine mixture and brandy gradually, beating well. Pour into large pitcher; pour back into bowl. Repeat process until mixture is frothy. Garnish with nutmeg. Yield: 10 servings.

Approx. Per Serving: Calories 403; Protein 2.0g; Carbohydrates 17.0g; T Fat 35.2g; Cholesterol 130.5mg; Potassium 152.0mg; Sodium 36.9mg.

Goodness Grows in North Carolina

Grandmother's Eggnog

6 eggs	**2 cups whipping cream**
4 tablespoons sugar	**1/2 teaspoon salt**
5 tablespoons bourbon	**Nutmeg**
1 tablespoon rum	

Separate eggs, keeping whites cold until used. Beat the yolks until light. Add the sugar, a little at a time, beating well as you add it. Then add the whiskeys a teaspoon at a time. It is important to add whiskey slowly so that the egg yolks get well cooked and won't have a raw taste. Whip the cream, add to mixture, then the well-beaten whites—a grating or two nutmeg according to taste, and the vanilla. Allow to ripen for at least 12 hours, which improves the taste. Keep in cool place 'till ready to use and mix well before serving. (It was thought whiskey "cooked" eggs in the way vinegar cooks raw fish in seviche.)

Korner's Folly Cookbook

Korner's Folly in Kernersville is a 22-room house constructed in 1880 on seven different levels. The top floor was converted into a theatre in 1897, and was the first "Little Theatre" in the United States.

Cancun Coffee
Best Coffee Drink Ever!

1 lime
Sugar
1/2 ounce kahlua
1/2 ounce anisette
  (liquorish liqueur)

1 ounce Bailey's Irish Cream
2 or 3 ounces coffee, brewed
Garnish: whipped cream

Wet lip of coffee mug with lime and dip rim in sugar. Pour liqueurs into mug and fill with coffee. Top with whipped cream. Makes one mug.

Note: This was made for me in Cancun by an aspiring young waiter. Great for a sore throat instead of a hot toddy. Best coffee drink ever. A smooth blend that doesn't taste liquorish!

Sip to Shore

Homemade Irish Cream
A Bailey's Irish Cream Substitute!

1 cup Irish whiskey
1 (14-ounce) can sweetened
  condensed milk
4 eggs, slightly beaten
2 tablespoons vanilla
  extract

2 tablespoons chocolate
  extract
1 tablespoon coconut extract
1 tablespoon powdered
  espresso or coffee
Ice

Blend all ingredients together in blender or food processor. Refrigerate 12-16 hours before serving to allow flavors to mellow. Serve over ice in Old Fashion glasses. Serves 4-6.

Note: In places where Bailey's Irish Cream is expensive—like in the states—or people don't have it with them, the Homemade Irish Cream is fantastic and even richer than Bailey's. Try it out and I think you'll agree.

Sip to Shore

Raspberry Mint Chiller

1/4 cup sugar
1/2 cup fresh mint leaves,
  lightly packed
1 cup boiling water
10 ounces frozen red
  raspberries

6 ounces frozen lemonade
  concentrate
2 cups cold water

Combine sugar, mint leaves, and boiling water; let stand 5 minutes. Add raspberries and lemonade concentrate; stir until thawed. Add cold water and stir. Serve over ice. Serves 8.

In Good Taste

Executive Mansion Russian Tea

This Russian tea is served often for state and social parties at the North Carolina Executive Mansion.

3 tablespoons tea (leaves)
6 whole cloves
3 (1-inch) sticks cinnamon
3 cups boiling water

1/2 cup orange juice
3 tablespoons lemon juice
1 scant cup sugar
3 extra cups boiling water

Place the tea, cloves, and cinnamon sticks in a teapot; cover with the 3 cups of boiling water. Cover and let steep for 5 minutes. Strain into another vessel; add the orange and lemon juices and sugar; stir to dissolve sugar. Just before serving, add 3 cups of boiling water. Serves 15.

Marion Brown's Southern Cook Book

Lush Slush

1 (8 1/2-ounce) can crushed
  pineapple
2 bananas, mashed

1 (6-ounce) can frozen
  orange concentrate, thawed
2 cups ginger ale

Blend all ingredients and turn into a metal pan (about 11x7). Freeze for about 1 hour. Spoon into sherbet glasses and serve. If prepared ahead of time, let stand until slushy before serving. Makes about 10-12 servings.

This is very good with those after-Christmas cookies you try to get rid of. Also, I use for breakfast and as a fruit cup for first course dinner.

Knollwood's Cooking

Hot Dip with Sliced Apples

6 slices bacon, cooked
1 (8-ounce) package cream
  cheese
2 cups Cheddar cheese,
  grated
6 tablespoons cream
1 teaspoon Worcestershire
  sauce

1/4 teaspoon dry mustard
1/4 teaspoon onion powder
4 dashes Tabasco sauce
Wedges of red and green
  apples, unpeeled

Crumble bacon. Melt cream cheese in double boiler. Stir in grated cheese and cream. Add remaining ingredients. Add crumbled bacon in melted cheese mixture. Serve in chafing dish to keep warm. Serve with alternating slices of Granny Smith and Red Delicious apples. Serves 8-10.

Sip to Shore

Most Requested Men's Dip

Treat your guests to an absolutely delicious dip. Serve with a thin wheat cracker and watch it disappear.

1 (8-ounce) package cream
  cheese
1 (8-ounce) carton sour
  cream
2 (.75-ounce) packages dry
  Italian salad dressing mix

2 (4 1/2-ounce) cans tiny
  shrimp
2 tablespoons lemon juice
1 green pepper, finely
  minced

Combine all ingredients. Allow the flavors to blend for a day if possible prior to serving. Serve with wheat crackers.
  Yield: 2 1/2 cups.

Taste Buds

 Carl Sandburg's 240-acre farm in Flat Rock is a national historic site open to visitors. The famed poet called the home "Connemara." Thomas Wolfe's boyhood home is in Asheville.

Tomato Cheese Spread

8 ounces Cheddar cheese,
  grated
1 cup tomatoes, peeled and
  chopped
1 (8-ounce) package cream
  cheese, softened
4 ounces margarine, softened

1 small onion, grated
1 teaspoon salt
1/2 teaspoon cayenne pepper
Garlic powder to taste
1 1/2 cups pecans or
  walnuts, chopped

Combine all ingredients, except nuts, in mixing bowl or food processor. Process until combined. May at this point shape into a log or ball and roll in nuts. Or, stir in nuts and serve as spread for crackers.

Best if prepared a day ahead. May be frozen up to two months. Makes 12 servings.

Stirring Performances

Tarheel Crocks

1/2 pound sharp New York
  cheese (black rind)
2 hard-cooked eggs, mashed
3/4 cup mayonnaise
1 teaspoon Worcestershire
  sauce
8 stuffed green olives,
  chopped

1/2 teaspoon salt
1/4 teaspoon paprika
1 teaspoon minced fresh
  parsley
3/4 teaspoon onion, grated

Allow cheese to soften. Combine all ingredients and blend together by hand. (A food processor will purée the chopped ingredients.) Put in a crock and chill until ready to serve. Serve with crackers, Melba toast, or black bread rounds. Yield: 1 large or 2 small cheese crocks.

Hint: You may want to grate the cheese before trying to blend with other ingredients.

Even More Special

 The Carolinas' only cheese factory, The Ashe County Cheese Factory, is in West Jefferson.

Boursin Cheese

2 cloves garlic
8 ounces unsalted whipped
  butter
16 ounces cream cheese
1/2 teaspoon salt
1/2 teaspoon basil

1/2 teaspoon marjoram
1/2 teaspoon chives
1/4 teaspoon thyme
1/4 teaspoon pepper
1 teaspoon dill

Crush garlic in blender or food processor; add butter, softened cheese and spices. Mix and store in refrigerator overnight before serving. Mix can be stored in refrigerator or frozen.

Pass the Plate

Pumpkin Cheese Ball

1 (8-ounce) package cream
  cheese, softened
1/2 cup cooked pumpkin,
  mashed
1 (2 1/2-ounce) jar dried
  beef slices, chopped

2 cups (8 ounces) shredded
  sharp Cheddar cheese
1/4 cup crushed pineapple,
  well drained
1 tablespoon chopped onion

Combine cream cheese and pumpkin, mixing until well blended. Stir in beef, cheese, pineapple and onion; mix well. Chill at least one hour. Form into large ball. Score sides with knife to resemble pumpkin. Serve with crackers. Yield: About 2 1/2 cups.

Heart of the Mountains

Ten Thousand Dollar Contest Winner

1 pound sharp Cheddar cheese
1 small onion
4 slices bacon
1/4 teaspoon mustard

1 teaspoon Worcestershire sauce
1 egg
48 bread rounds
  (approximately)

Preheat broiler. Put first 3 ingredients through a meat grinder. Add mustard and Worcestershire sauce. Add egg and mix well. Toast one side of bread rounds under broiler. Put cheese mixture on soft side and put under broiler until brown.

A Cookbook of Pinehurst Courses

Cheese Mold with Apricot Topping

1 1/2 pounds sharp Cheddar
cheese, shredded
1 cup walnuts, finely
chopped
1 cup mayonnaise

1 1/2 medium onions, finely
chopped
1/2 teaspoon hot pepper
sauce
Apricot topping

Grate cheese; but do not put in food processor, then combine with other ingredients and mix well. Grease a 1 1/2-quart ring mold and pack cheese mixture into mold. Chill 24 hours before unmolding. Do not put in hot water to unmold. Spread Apricot Topping on top and serve with crackers.

APRICOT TOPPING:
1 (6-ounce) package dried
apricots
1/2 cup water
1/4 cup sugar

2 tablespoons butter
2 tablespoons sherry (or
more to taste)

Put apricots and water in a saucepan and simmer until apricots are thick like jam. Mash as it cooks and add more water to prevent burning. Add sugar and butter; taste to adjust sweetness. Take off heat and add sherry. Cool and put in a glass jar. Can be stored in refrigerator about 1 week. Yield: 25-30 servings.

Market to Market

Black-Eyed Susans

1 pound sharp cheese
2 sticks margarine
2 cups flour
1/4 teaspoon cayenne pepper
  (optional)

1 teaspoon salt
2 pounds pitted dates
1 pound pecan halves
1/2 cup sugar

Cream grated cheese and margarine together well. Have both at room temperature. Add flour, pepper and salt. Mix well. This will make a very stiff dough. Put in cookie press. Using box plate, squeeze out in long strips. Cut 2-3 inches long. Wrap around dates which have been stuffed with pecan half. Roll in the sugar. Place on cookie sheet and bake at 300° until lightly browned. This is a Christmas must at this house. Very pretty and good. Yield: About 100.

Have Fun Cooking With Me

Hot Crab Antojito
(Microwave)

1 pound white crabmeat,
  flaked
3/4 cup Monterey Jack cheese
  with hot peppers, grated
1/4 cup sour cream
1/2 cup mayonnaise
1 tablespoon green onion,
  minced

1 tablespoon fresh lemon
  juice
1 tablespoon white wine
1/2 teaspoon salt
1/4 teaspoon cayenne pepper
1/4 teaspoon Tabasco
Melba rounds

Mix all ingredients, except Melba rounds, and toss lightly. Spoon mixture on Melba rounds. Place 15 rounds on a paper plate. Microwave on Full power for 45 seconds. Repeat with remaining rounds. Serve hot. Serves 45.

A Taste of History

Swiss Crab Bites

1 (7 1/2-ounce) package crabmeat, drained
1 tablespoon green onion,
chopped
1 cup Swiss cheese, shredded
1/2 cup mayonnaise
1 teaspoon lemon juice

1/4 teaspoon curry powder
1 (10-ounce) package flake-style
refrigerator rolls
Garnish: sliced water chestnuts, red pepper slices,
parsley

Preheat oven to 400°. Combine first six ingredients. Separate rolls
and divide each into three pieces. Place on ungreased baking
sheet. Spoon mixture on rolls. Top with water chestnuts. Bake
until golden at 400° for 10-12 minutes. Garnish with sliced water
chestnuts, red pepper slices, and parsley. Makes 30.

Sea to Shore

Crab-Potato Nibblers

1 (2-serving size) package
instant mashed potatoes
1 teaspoon minced onion
1 1/4 teaspoons
Worcestershire sauce

1/8 teaspoon garlic powder
Dash pepper
8 ounces crab meat
1 egg, slightly beaten
1/2 cup fine bread crumbs

Prepare potatoes as directed *except* use 2 tablespoons less milk than
specified. Add minced onion to amount of water specified in
directions. Stir in Worcestershire sauce, garlic powder and pepper. Add crab meat. Shape into bite-size balls. Dip into beaten
egg; roll in bread crumbs. Fry in deep fat at 375° about 1 minute
until golden brown. Drain; serve hot. Yield: 36 nibblers.

Island Born and Bred

Mushroom or Shrimp Turnovers

CREAM CHEESE PASTRY:

1 (8-ounce) package cream
cheese, softened
1/2 pound butter or
margarine, softened

Dash of salt
2 cups presifted flour
1 egg yolk
2 teaspoons cream or milk

Combine cheese, butter, and salt. Work in the flour with a fork or your fingers until a smooth dough is formed. Refrigerate for several hours or overnight before using. Roll dough on a floured surface to about 1/8 inch thickness and cut into 3-inch round circles. Place a teaspoon of filling just off center on each circle. Fold dough over filling and crimp edges with a floured fork. Freeze turnovers uncovered on a tray. Place them in a plastic bag for freezer storage. When ready to serve, brush tops with beaten egg yolk and cream. Bake frozen turnovers in 375° oven for 15-20 minutes. Yields 40.

MUSHROOM FILLING:

1/2 pound fresh
mushrooms
3 tablespoons butter
1 onion, minced
2 teaspoons flour

1/2 teaspoon salt
Pepper to taste
1 teaspoon dried dill
1/2 cup sour cream

Wash mushrooms, trim off toughest stems and chop finely. Sauté onions and mushrooms in butter until tender. Add flour, salt and pepper. Cook for 1-2 minutes. Remove from heat and stir in sour cream and dill. Cool.

SHRIMP FILLING:

2 (4 1/2-ounce) cans,
shrimp
3 green onions, chopped
2 teaspoons spicy
prepared mustard

Salt to taste
1/2 teaspoon tarragon
6 tablespoons sour cream

Drain and finely chop the shrimp. Thoroughly combine all ingredients.

Out Of Our League

Shrimp Stuffed Celery

1 (4 1/2-ounce) can washed
  and drained broken shrimp
1 teaspoon dried chives
3 tablespoons onion, finely
  chopped
5 black olives, pitted,
  finely chopped

2 tablespoons slivered
  almonds
Dash of lemon juice
Enough mayonnaise for
  consistency
Celery stalks, cut in 3-inch
  pieces

Mix all ingredients thoroughly. Stuff celery and arrange on platter. Good quickie hors d'oeuvre. Also good when serving several hors d'oeuvres.

Sip to Shore

Daddy's Pickled Shrimp

2 pounds broiled shrimp,
  shelled and deveined
3 medium sweet onions,
  sliced in rings
1 cup salad oil
1/2 cup red wine vinegar
1/2 cup catsup

4 bay leaves
2 tablespoons Worcestershire
  sauce
1 teaspoon salt
1/2 teaspoon dry mustard
Dash of red pepper

Place shrimp and onions in glass container, preferably a half-gallon wide mouth jar with lid. Mix together all other ingredients in a medium-sized mixing bowl, then pour mixture over shrimp and onions. Close container and place in refrigerator at least 24 hours before serving. Turn several times during refrigeration period. Pour entire contents in serving bowl. Remove bay leaves. Serve with crackers, if desired. Serves 10-12.

    Note: The onions are as good as the shrimp.

A Dash of Down East

Stuffed Cream Cheese Roll, with Oysters or Clams

The original version of this recipe called for smoked oysters instead of minced clams as a filling. I definitely prefer my oysters prepared in other ways, so I experimented and came up with the following. Actually, the night I was introduced to this oyster roll, I never hesitated to help myself; so, you decide!

2 (8-ounce) packages cream
   cheese
2 tablespoons mayonnaise
2 teaspoons Worcestershire
   sauce
Dash hot pepper seasoning
1 tablespoon grated onion

1/2 teaspoon salt
Garlic salt
6 1/2 ounces smoked oysters
   or minced clams
Lots of fresh parsley,
   minced

Combine cheese, mayonnaise and seasonings. Spread into a rectangle 1/2-inch thick on a large piece of foil spread on a baking sheet. Drain clams well and mash slightly (same with oysters). Spread over cheese rectangle. Chill thoroughly. Roll up jelly roll fashion. Refrigerate. Cover generously with fresh minced parsley. Serve with crackers. Serves 8-10.

Taste Buds

Oyster Filling for Patty Shells

3/4 stick butter
1 bunch spring onions,
   minced
3 tablespoons minced parsley
2 cloves garlic put through
   press

5 tablespoons flour
1 pint oysters, drained on
   paper towel and cut in half

Sauté onions in butter; add garlic, stir in flour til smooth. Add oysters (will get thinner as they cook, but a little water may be added if too thick). Season with salt and pepper. This fills 3 dozen small shells.

High Hampton Hospitality

The Elms's Fleur De Lis Viennese Triangles

PASTRY:

2 sticks unsalted butter
1/3 cup sugar
1 teaspoon vanilla
1 egg

2 1/2 cups all-purpose
  flour, unsifted
1/3 cup raspberry-apricot
  jam

TOPPING:

5 egg whites
1 cup sliced almonds
1 1/2 cups sugar
3 tablespoons flour
1 tablespoon light corn
  syrup

1 teaspoon cinnamon
1/2 teaspoon almond extract
1/4 teaspoon baking powder

Grease a 10x15-inch jelly roll pan and set it aside. Cream butter with sugar. Add vanilla; beat in egg; blend in flour. Pat pastry evenly into pan; refrigerate one hour to let set.

Spread raspberry-apricot jam over entire surface of pastry. Position rack in lower third of oven and preheat to 350°.

In 2 1/2-quart saucepan, combine all ingredients for topping except extract and baking powder. Place over very low heat; stir constantly until mixture reaches 200°. Remove from heat; stir in extract and baking powder. Pour over crust, spreading evenly. Bake until golden brown, about 30 minutes. Cool in pan on rack.

When cool, cut into 1 1/2-inch squares, then cut each diagonally to make triangles. Yields 50.

North Carolina's Historic Restaurants

Burgundy Meatballs

1 pound ground beef (very lean)
1 tablespoon parsley flakes
1 cup dry grated bread crumbs
1 tablespoon instant minced onion
1 teaspoon monosodium glutamate
1 egg
1 teaspoon salt
Pepper to taste
1 (10 3/4-ounce) can cream of chicken soup or cream of mushroom soup
2/3 soup can Burgundy

Combine first 8 ingredients, blend well. Form into small balls. Brown in electric skillet. Add Burgundy to soup gradually, pour sauce over meatballs. Simmer, covered, for 30 minutes.

Mountain Potpourri

Pungent Chicken Wings

1 1/2 pounds broiler-fryer wings (8-10)
2 teaspoons cornstarch
1 1/2 teaspoons 4-spice powder*
2 tablespoons sugar
1 tablespoon peanut oil
2 tablespoons dry, medium or sweet sherry
1/4 teaspoon pepper flakes
1 tablespoon minced fresh ginger root
1/2 cup soy sauce
1/2 cup water

Wash wings, drain and dry; cut into two parts at joints. (Do not use tips.) In a medium saucepan, stir together the cornstarch, spice powder, sugar, oil and sherry until blended; stir in all ingredients but wings. Bring to a boil stirring constantly. Add wings and boil; cover and simmer 20 minutes. Leave in sauce and reheat just before serving.

*4-spice powder: 1/4 teaspoon each: cinnamon, ginger, cloves, and nutmeg.

Favorite Variation: Add garlic powder, if desired. Wings are also delicious marinated in only Kikkoman Soy Sauce; then, bake at 325° for 30 minutes (baste often with marinade).

Christmas Favorites

Bambinos

PASTRY ROUNDS:

2 cups flour

1 teaspoon salt

2/3 cup shortening

1/4 cup water

To make pastry rounds, heat over to 475°. Mix flour and salt; cut in shortening. Sprinkle with water and mix with fork. Divide in half and roll each to 1/8-inch thick. Cut into 1 1/2 to 2-inch circles. Place on foil-covered baking sheet and prick with fork. Bake 8 to 10 minutes or until lightly browned.

6 ounces tomato paste

1 teaspoon garlic salt

1/4 teaspoon oregano

1/4 pound American or
  mozzarella cheese, cubed

1/8 pound salami or
  pepperoni, cut into rounds

Before serving, heat oven to 400°. Combine tomato paste, garlic salt and oregano. Spoon a small amount onto a pastry round. Top with small cube of cheese and a piece of the meat. Sprinkle with oregano. Bake 3 to 5 minutes. Serve hot. Makes about 4 dozen.

Jarrett House Potpourri

Stuffed Mushrooms

8 ounces fresh mushrooms
  (approximately 30-35)
Butter to dot
1 1/2 tablespoons onions,
  chopped
1/2 stick margarine
1 egg, beaten

1 1/2 teaspoons lemon juice
1 teaspoon parsley
5 slices bacon, fried and
  crushed
1/2 cup herb croutons,
  finely crushed
Salt and pepper

Preheat oven to 400°. Remove stems from mushrooms. Place caps in baking dish, dot with butter, and bake in a 400° oven for 10 minutes. Chop stems finely. Sauté stems and onion in margarine. Add egg, lemon juice and parsley. Add bacon and enough crumbs to absorb liquid. Add salt and pepper to taste. Fill caps with mixture in mound shape. Bake in 350° oven until warmed.

Note: May be done ahead and refrigerated, then baked before serving.

A Cook's Tour of the Azalea Coast

Mary's Artichokes

2 (6-ounce) jars marinated
  artichokes
1 small onion, chopped fine
1 clove garlic, minced
2 eggs
1/4 cup fine bread crumbs
1/8 teaspoon salt

1/8 teaspoon pepper
Tabasco to taste
1/4 teaspoon oregano
1/2 pound sharp Cheddar
  cheese, grated
2 tablespoons parsley

Drain marinade from 1 jar of artichokes into a frying pan. Chop artichokes. To liquid add onion and garlic, and sauté. Beat eggs in bowl; add bread crumbs and seasonings. Stir in cheese, parsley, artichokes and sautéed mixture. Turn into greased 7x11-inch baking dish and bake at 325° for 30 minutes. Let stand 5 minutes after baking and cut into small squares. May be wrapped in foil and frozen at this point for later use. To serve when frozen, thaw and reheat in foil 15 minutes at 325°.

Pass the Plate

Parmesan Toast Strips

4 slices toasted bread
1/4 cup melted margarine
1/2 teaspoon onion salt
   (optional)

1 cup corn chips, finely
   crushed
1/4 cup grated Parmesan
   cheese

Remove crust from bread, cut each slice in 5 strips, toast. When cool, roll in mixture of butter and salt. Combine corn chips and cheese; dip sticks in this and bake at 400° for 5-8 minutes until crisp. Makes 20.

Mushrooms, Turnip Greens & Pickled Eggs

Rumaki

1 (8-ounce) can whole water
   chestnuts
1/2 teaspoon sugar

3 - 4 tablespoons soy sauce
2 strips bacon, cut into
   thirds

Drain the water chestnuts, reserving the liquid. Count out 6 water chestnuts. (Store the rest in the reserved liquid for another use, such as in a salad.)

Combine the sugar and soy sauce, stirring to dissolve the sugar. Marinate the water chestnuts in the mixture for 30 minutes. Drain, then wrap each water chestnut in a piece of bacon. Secure with a toothpick.

Place the water chestnuts in a pie pan. Broil until the bacon is crisp on all sides, turning as necessary. Watch them carefully, as they burn easily. Makes two servings.

Variation: Instead of cutting the bacon into thirds, cut each piece in half. Add a chunk of pineapple to each water chestnut, then wrap in bacon and cook as directed. You will need an extra slice of bacon to do it this way.

Love Yourself Cookbook

Potato Peels With Caviar Dip

POTATO PEELS:

2 tablespoons unsalted
  butter, melted
1/2 teaspoon seasoning salt
1/4 teaspoon pepper

Peelings from 6 scrubbed baking potatoes, 1/4-inch thick
  (leave some potato on peel),
  3/4-inch wide, 2 inches long

Preheat oven to 425°. In a bowl, combine melted butter, seasoning salt and pepper. Brush peels with mixture. Arrange skin side down on a buttered baking sheet. Bake in a preheated 425° oven 15-20 minutes until lightly browned. Turn them and bake 10-15 minutes more or till golden brown. Serves 8-10.

Sip to Shore

Dilly Brussels Sprouts

2 (10-ounce) packages frozen
  Brussels sprouts
Dash of salt

1 cup Italian dressing
1 teaspoon dillweed
2 tablespoons chives

Cook Brussels sprouts in seasoned water according to package directions. Do not over cook. Drain and place in a plastic container. Add remaining ingredients and chill at least overnight before serving. Lift from dressing into serving dish. Supply toothpicks. Serves 8-10.

Bravo

Party Mix

1 stick margarine	1 tablespoon seasoned salt
3 tablespoons Worcestershire sauce	1/2 teaspoon garlic salt
	1/4 teaspoon salt

Melt margarine and add Worcestershire sauce, seasoned salt, garlic salt, and salt. Blend well and pour over:

2 cups Rice Chex	2 cups Wheat Chex
2 cups Corn Chex	1 cup salted peanuts

You can also add Bugles, pretzels, and Cheerios. Put in large deep pan and bake at 250° for about 45 minutes. Stir twice while cooking. Store in an airtight container. We always have these at Christmas time.

Have Fun Cooking With Me

 Many of the waterfalls in the western tip of the state have names to match their splendor, like Bridal Veil, Looking Glass, Dry, Whitewater, and Rainbow Falls. On the Blue Ridge Parkway, double level Linville Falls plunge spectacularly into Linville Gorge, whose steep walls enclose the Linville River.

Soups

*Whitewater Falls in the Nantahala National Forest near Cashiers,
said to be the highest waterfall in the Eastern United States.*

Zesty Gazpacho

4 large ripe tomatoes,
 peeled and chopped
1/3 green bell pepper
1/3 cucumber, peeled
1/4 onion, chopped
2 garlic cloves
3 tablespoons red wine
 vinegar

2 tablespoons olive oil
1 tablespoon salt
3 cups French bread, (crust
 removed), soaked in water
Garnish: minced onion, green
 pepper, cucumber, sour
 cream, black olives

In processor/blender purée tomatoes, green pepper, cucumber, onion, and garlic. Blend in vinegar, oil, salt, and bread crumbs in batches. Transfer to a bowl, thin it to desired consistency with ice water. Chill covered.

Garnish with minced onion, green pepper, cucumber and a dollop of sour cream with black olive curls. Makes 6 cups and serves 4-6. Yum!

Ship to Shore II

Chilled Zucchini Soup

2 large zucchini, unpeeled
 and sliced
1 green pepper, finely
 chopped
1/2 cup finely chopped
 onions
3 cups chicken stock

1 cup sour cream
1 tablespoon parsley
1/2 teaspoon fresh chopped
 dill or 1/4 teaspoon dry
 dill
Salt and pepper to taste

Combine zucchini, green pepper, onions and chicken broth in a saucepan. Cover and simmer for 20 minutes. Strain vegetables and reserve stock. In blender or food processor, put sour cream, parsley, dill, and cooked vegetables. While blending, add stock. Season with salt and pepper and shill. Garnish with a dab of sour cream. Serve in long-stem crystal champagne glasses.

A Cookbook of Pinehurst Courses

Watercress Soup

1/2 stick butter
1 clove minced garlic
2 1/2 cups chopped onion
3/4 cups boiling water
4 1/2 cups diced raw
  potatoes
1/2 teaspoon salt

1/2 teaspoon black pepper
1 1/2 bunches chopped
  watercress (include stems)
2 cups strong chicken broth
1 1/2 cups milk
3/4 cup coffee cream

Melt the butter in a large saucepan and add the garlic and onion. Sauté gently for about 6 minutes. Add the boiling water, potatoes, salt and pepper. Simmer about half an hour. Add 3/4 of the watercress and the chicken stock. Cook 5 minutes on medium heat. Add the 1 1/2 cups milk and cook about 10 more minutes (it may need some water added). Pureé in food mill or blender and return to pan. Add the cream. Stir until thick and hot and garnish with watercress on top. This is superb hot and equally good when served cold with a dollop of sour cream topped by red caviar on top. Worth the effort! Also freezes well.

High Hampton Hospitality

Cream of Spinach Soup

2 pounds fresh spinach,
  washed and ribbed
6 cups salted water
3 teaspoons granulated
  chicken or beef bouillon
3 cups milk
1/2 cup butter

1 teaspoon salt
1 teaspoon nutmeg
2 thick slices onion
3 tablespoons flour
Hard-boiled eggs, grated
Paprika

Place spinach in salted water. Bring to a boil, simmer 5 minutes. Drain; reserve 3 cups of cooking liquid. Set aside. Blend spinach in food processor or blender to make a coarse paste (approximately 2 cups). Add bouillon to hot spinach stock. When bouillon is dissolved, add milk.

In heavy saucepan, melt butter. Add salt and nutmeg. Sauté onion in butter 3 minutes. Remove onion. Add flour to butter while stirring. Gradually add milk, stock mixture, stirring vigorously. Continue to stir over medium heat until well blended. Add spinach paste. Beat well. Serve hot with grated hard boiled eggs and paprika on top for garnish. Makes 2 quarts.

From Zevely House Restaurant in *Heritage of Hospitality*, a cookbook published in 1975 by the Junior League of Winston-Salem, which is no longer in print.

Stirring Performances

Cream of Asparagus Soup

Easy and tasty.

2 cups asparagus	3 cups Basic Cream Sauce
1 cup water	1/4 teaspoon nutmeg

Cut asparagus in small pieces. Cook in water until soft; save tips for garnish. Press asparagus and liquid through a sieve or whirl in blender. Combine with cream sauce and nutmeg; heat. Sprinkle with a few tips over each serving. Yield: 12 1/2-cup servings.

BASIC CREAM SAUCE:

6 tablespoons butter	1 teaspoon salt
1 medium onion, sliced	Pinch of white pepper
3 tablespoons flour	3 cups milk

Melt butter and sauté onions until soft (about 5 minutes). Discard onion. Stir in flour, salt and pepper. Add milk slowly, stirring constantly over low heat. Bring to a boil, but do not boil. The cream sauce thickens slightly as it cools. All cream soups may be thinned by adding milk or water as they are heated.
  Can do ahead. Can freeze. Yield: 3 cups.

Mountain Elegance

Creamy Broccoli Soup

1 small onion, minced	3 cups light cream
4 tablespoons butter or	1 - 2 cups chicken broth
margarine	2 (10-ounce) packages
5 tablespoons all-purpose	frozen chopped broccoli,
flour	slightly thawed
1 teaspoon salt	1/2 teaspoon nutmeg

Sauté onion in butter until tender; stir in flour and salt. Gradually add cream, stirring constantly. Add broth according to desired thickness of soup. Add broccoli and nutmeg. Cook over low heat 25 minutes. Stir occasionally. Yield: 6-8 servings.
  Variation: 1/8 teaspoon mace may be substituted for nutmeg. Cauliflower can be used in lieu of broccoli.

Market to Market

French Onion Soup

5 medium-size onions thinly
  sliced
2 tablespoons margarine
3 (10 1/2-ounce) cans beef
  consommé
2 (10 1/2-ounce) can water
1 tablespoon Worcestershire
  sauce
1/2 teaspoon salt
1/8 teaspoon pepper
8 slices French bread, cut
  3/4-inch thick, toasted
3 thin slices mozzarella
  cheese the size of the bread
1/3 cup grated Parmesan
  cheese

Separate onions into rings and cook in melted margarine until glossy. Add consommé, water, Worcestershire, salt and pepper. Bring to boil, cover tightly and cook over low heat 15 minutes.

Pour into 6 to 8 oven-worthy bowls; top with toasted bread, slice of mozzarella; sprinkle with Parmesan. Heat in a 400° oven for 15 minutes or until bubbly. Makes 6 to 8 servings.

What Is It? What Do I Do With It?

Mushroom Onion Soup

1 pound fresh mushrooms,
  sliced
1 very large onion, sliced
1 clove garlic, minced
1/4 cup margarine
3 tablespoons tomato paste
8 cups water, boiling
8 chicken bouillon cubes
1/4 cup Parmesan cheese,
  grated
1 cup dry white wine
Salt and pepper to taste
Grated Parmesan cheese for
  garnish

Sauté mushrooms, onions, and garlic in margarine in heavy saucepan until onions are tender. Stir in tomato paste. Dissolve bouillon cubes in boiling water. Add broth, 1/4 cup Parmesan cheese, wine, salt, and pepper to saucepan. Simmer 1 hour. Serve with additional Parmesan cheese. Serves 10-12.

A Cook's Tour of the Azalea Coast

Plantation Stew

1/2 leg of lamb
Salt and pepper
1/2 cup olive oil or
  1/2 stick butter
2 quarts stock
6 Idaho potatoes, diced
6 onions, diced
6 green olives, chopped
2 red pepper pods, diced
1 tablespoon sugar
2 teaspoons thyme

3 tablespoons vinegar
2 thin slices lemon
2 tablespoons dry mustard
1 tablespoon Worcestershire
  sauce
4 bay leaves
2 sprigs parsley, chopped
2 teaspoons sage
2 thin slices orange
Sherry

Cut lamb in cubes; salt and pepper well. Brown in iron frying pan with 1/2 cup olive oil or 1/2 stick butter. Have stock boiling in Dutch oven on top of stove. Add contents of frying pan, diced potatoes, diced onions, olives, and all of the seasonings.

Let simmer with top on for 3 hours. Just before serving add 1 tablespoon of sherry. Season to taste with salt. Serve hot. Serves 6-8.

Favorite Recipes of the Lower Cape Fear

 Historic Oakwood in Raleigh is one of the finest examples of intact Victorian neighborhoods remaining in the United States.

Skier's Chowder

1 pound roll of hot pork
  sausage
2 (1-pound) cans kidney
  beans
1 (1-pound 13-ounce) can
  tomatoes, broken up
1 quart water
1 large onion, chopped

1 bay leaf
1 1/2 teaspoons seasoning
  salt
1/2 teaspoon garlic salt
1/2 teaspoon thyme
1/8 teaspoon pepper
1 cup potatoes, diced
1/2 green pepper, chopped

Cook sausage until brown and drain thoroughly. In a large pot combine beans, tomatoes, water, onion, bay leaf, seasoned salt, garlic salt, thyme and pepper. Add sausage and simmer, covered, for 1 - 1 1/2 hours. Add potatoes and green pepper. Cook covered, 15-20 minutes, until potatoes are tender. Remove bay leaf. Makes 8 servings.

Christmas Favorites

Mushroom Chowder

This mushroom chowder is the best.

1 pound fresh mushrooms
1/2 cup butter or margarine
1/2 cup chopped onions
1 cup diced potatoes
1 cup finely chopped celery
1/2 cup diced carrots
1 3/4 teaspoons salt or to
  taste

1/4 teaspoon ground black
  pepper
1 tablespoon flour
2 tablespoons cold water
3 cups chicken stock
1 cup milk or light cream
1/4 cup grated Parmesan
  cheese

Rinse, pat dry and slice mushrooms; set aside.

In a large saucepan heat butter, add onions and sauté until golden brown. Add mushrooms, vegetables, salt and black pepper. Cover and simmer 15 to 20 minutes or until vegetables are tender. Combine flour with cold water; slowly stir into vegetable mixture. Add chicken stock; simmer 10 more minutes. Just before serving, stir in milk and cheese. Heat only until hot. Do not boil. Sprinkle with additional Parmesan. Serves 6.

What Is It? What Do I Do With It?

Corn and Cheese Chowder

2 cups water
2 cups potato, diced
1/2 cup onion, chopped
1/2 cup celery, diced
2 tablespoons butter
1/2 teaspoon dried whole
  basil
1 large bay leaf
1 (17-ounce) can cream corn
  or 1 (10-ounce) package
  frozen

2 cups milk
1 cup tomatoes, chopped
1/8 teaspoon pepper
1/2 cup Cheddar cheese,
  grated
1 tablespoon fresh parsley,
  minced

Combine water, potatoes, onion, celery, butter, basil, and bay leaf in large kettle and bring to a boil. Reduce heat and simmer 10 minutes or until potatoes are tender. Discard bay leaf. Stir in corn, milk, tomatoes, and pepper and heat thoroughly. Add cheese and cook over low heat, stirring constantly until cheese is melted. Sprinkle parsley over chowder in bowls and serve. Serves 8-10.

In Good Taste

Ginger Crab and Corn Soup

1 (16-ounce) package frozen
  whole kernel corn, thawed
  and divided
1 tablespoon cornstarch
1/4 cup water
3 (10 3/4-ounce) cans
  no-salt-added chicken broth
1 teaspoon peeled, minced
  ginger root

1/2 pound fresh crab meat
1/2 cup green onions,
  chopped
1/4 teaspoon white pepper
1 teaspoon rice vinegar,
  optional

Position knife blade in food processor bowl; add half of corn. Top with cover, and process until finely chopped. Add remaining corn; stir well and set aside. Combine cornstarch and water in a small bowl; stir well and set aside.

   Combine chicken broth and ginger root in a large saucepan; bring to a boil. Add corn, cornstarch mixture, crab meat and remaining ingredients; return to a boil. Reduce heat and simmer, uncovered, 3 minutes. Yields 7 cups; serves 4-6.

Sip to Shore

Muddle

A muddle is a very thick fish stew celebrated in eastern Virginia and North Carolina, particularly on the long isolated barrier islands known as the Outer Banks. The customs and foods of the earliest English colonists have been maintained in these Atlantic outposts; linguists study the dialect for its Elizabethan overtones, and anthropologists record the raucous Twelfth Night celebrations. Muddle is the traditional feast of the region whose poor soil yields a meager harvest. The simple vegetables—potatoes, onions, tomatoes—in perfect proportion with the freshest fish achieve the satisfaction sought in all good peasant cooking.

Recommended equipment: A blender or mortar and pestle, Dutch oven. Preheat oven to 325°.

1 1/2 teaspoons dried thyme
2 bay leaves
2 whole cloves
1 1/2 teaspoons (or more)
  red pepper flakes
Water
1/2 pound sliced bacon, cut
  into 1-inch squares
3 pounds onions, thinly sliced
3 pounds boiling potatoes,
  peeled, thinly sliced
1/2 cup chopped, fresh
  parsley

3 pounds large, firm
  white-fleshed non-oily
  fish fillets, cut into cubes
  1 1/2 inches on each side
Salt
Freshly ground black pepper
1 pound canned whole
  tomatoes, chopped with
  liquid
2 tablespoons apple cider
  vinegar
1 dozen very fresh eggs at
  room temperature

Pulverize the thyme, bay, cloves, and red pepper flakes to a fine, regular powder, either in a blender or by hand in the mortar, and reserve. Render the bacon gently in the bottom of the casserole until lightly browned. Remove one-half of the bacon and reserve. Divide the onions, potatoes, parsley, fish, pulverized seasonings, and tomatoes with their liquid in two equal portions. Assemble by layering the ingredients in the following order, lightly sprinkling each layer with salt and freshly ground black pepper: onions, potatoes, parsley, fish, seasonings, tomatoes, bacon, onions, potatoes, parsley, fish, seasonings, and tomatoes. Add just enough cold water to cover, but not swamp, the ingredients. Finally, add

CONTINUED

CONTINUED

the cider vinegar. Bring to a gentle boil on top of the stove over medium heat. Cover tightly and place in the preheated oven. Bake for 1 hour or until the ingredients are just tender.

When the top layer of potatoes is done, the whole will be ready. Return to the top of the stove over medium heat. Break the eggs over the surface as it bubbles. Cover and cook for 4 minutes. The eggs should be lightly poached, the whites set and the yolks still liquid. Serve warmed bowls with one egg per serving. Accompany with hushpuppies and coleslaw. Yields 12 servings.

Bill Neal's Southern Cooking

Harbour House Cream of Crab Soup

6 tablespoons butter	White pepper, dash
6 tablespoons flour	1 quart milk
1/2 tablespoon chicken base	1/2 pound backfin crabmeat

Melt butter; add flour, chicken base and pepper. Stir and simmer for 2 minutes. Add milk and simmer until thickens, stirring constantly. Add crabmeat and remove from heat. Add a little sherry before serving if you would like. (Served at Annapolis Harbour House). Yield: 3-4 servings.

Nothing Could Be Finer

Old Drum Stew

4 medium irish potatoes,
  quartered
Water
2 pounds old drum fillets

1/4 pound salt pork
1 medium onion, diced
Cornmeal dumplings (opposite
  page)

In a large saucepan, place quartered potatoes and cover with water. Bring to a boil, reduce heat, and simmer for 20 minutes. Meanwhile cut drum fillets into chunks. In a skillet, render fat from salt pork. Remove meat and save drippings.

Over potatoes, add a layer of diced onions and then a layer of chunked drum. Pour pork drippings over stew. Shake saucepan gently from side to side to mix ingredients. Continue simmering 30 to 45 minutes or until broth thickens. Add cornmeal dumplings and simmer 10 more minutes. Serves 6 to 8.

Note: Lucille says there are three types of drum: puppy drum, yearling drum, and old drum. Using her hands, she shows that a puppy drum measures about 10 to 12 inches in length, a yearling about 18 to 20 inches, and an old drum 28 to 30 inches. Lucille prefers old drum for her stew. To clean the large fish, she "Nails their tails to a board and scales 'em with a hoe."

Coastal Carolina Cooking

Conch Stew

1 quart conch meat, frozen
4 cups water
2 to 3 slices salt pork
3 medium Irish potatoes,
  diced
1 large onion, diced

2 tablespoons flour
1/2 teaspoon thyme
2 tablespoons Worcestershire
  sauce
1/2 teaspoon black pepper
Cornmeal dumplings

Allow conch meat to thaw partially. Chop into small pieces. Place conch meat and water in a heavy pot. Cover pot and simmer over medium heat for 2 1/2 to 3 hours. Additional water may be needed. In a skillet, fry salt pork until crisp and brown. Remove meat, chop, and set aside. Add potatoes, onions, flour and thyme to the drippings. Sauté until potatoes and onions are almost done,

CONTINUED

CONTINUED

but not brown. Add this mixture to the conch meat. Add Worcestershire sauce, pepper, and browned pork meat. Continue simmering until potatoes are done and flavors are blended. Add cornmeal dumplings the last 5 minutes. Serves 6 to 8.

CORNMEAL DUMPLINGS:

1 cup cornmeal	1/2 teaspoon salt
1 tablespoon plain flour	1/2 cup water

In a mixing bowl, combine dry ingredients. Add enough water to hold the mixture together. Pat dough in hands into small patties. Drop around the side of the pot of conch stew, chowder, or greens during the last 5 minutes of cooking. The dumplings will float to the top when done.

Coastal Carolina Cooking

Shrimp Bisque

2 or 3 fresh mushrooms, sliced	3/4 cup cooked shrimp, peeled and deveined
1 tablespoon butter	Dash of pepper
1 (10 3/4-ounce) can condensed cream of shrimp soup	2 - 4 tablespoons sherry (optional)
3/4 cup milk or light cream	Paprika

Sauté the mushrooms in butter until tender, 3 to 4 minutes. Combine the soup and milk in a large saucepan, blending until smooth. Set aside 2 whole shrimp, and chop the rest and add to the soup. Stir in the mushrooms and pepper.

Cook over low heat until just below the boiling point; it must not boil. Remove from the heat and stir in the sherry. Ladle into hot bowls and garnish with a dusting of paprika and the reserved shrimp. Makes 2 servings.

Love Yourself Cookbook

Oyster and Artichoke Soup

1/4 cup butter
1 1/2 cups chopped green
  onion
2 garlic cloves (minced)
3 tablespoons flour
2 (14-ounce) cans artichokes
3 cups chicken stock or
  broth

3 cups milk
1 teaspoon crushed red
  pepper
1 teaspoon salt
1/2 teaspoon anise seed
1 quart oysters

Melt butter in a large and heavy pot. Add onions and garlic, sauté 5 minutes. Add flour and cook 5 minutes, stirring constantly. Drain and rinse artichokes. Cut into quarters and add to the pot. Add chicken and broth, milk and seasonings. Cook 20 minutes. Add oysters and their liquor. Simmer 10 minutes. Top with a lemon slice to serve. Serves 12.

Seafood Sorcery

Catfish and Shrimp Soup

2 cups chopped onions
2 cloves of garlic, crushed
2 tablespoons oil
1 large (16-ounce) can
  tomatoes
3 tablespoons tomato paste
1/2 teaspoon salt
1/4 teaspoon freshly ground
  black pepper

1 bay leaf
3 cups water
1 cup dry white wine
1 cup chicken broth
4 catfish fillets, cut into
  1-inch pieces
1/2 pound shelled shrimp
2 tablespoons chopped fresh
  parsley

Sauté onions and garlic lightly in oil in saucepan. Stir in tomatoes, tomato paste, salt, pepper and bay leaf. Simmer, covered, for 15 minutes. Add water, wine and broth. Simmer, uncovered, for 45 minutes. Add catfish and shrimp. Cook for 10 minutes or until fish flakes easily. Remove bay leaf. Ladle into soup bowls. Sprinkle with parsley. Yield: 8 servings.

Approx. Per Serving: Calories 246; Protein 28.5g; Carbohydrates 7.1g; T Fat 9.0g; Cholesterol 121.0mg; Potassium 744.0mg; Sodium 464.0mg.

Goodness Grows in North Carolina

Salads

Duke University Chapel. Durham.

Wedding Bell Pear Salads

12 canned Bartlett pear
  halves
1 (5-ounce) jar Old English
  cheese
1 (3-ounce) package cream
  cheese, softened
2 tablespoons finely chopped
  celery

1 tablespoon minced green
  onion
1 tablespoon minced parsley
1/8 teaspoon tarragon
Green onion for garnish
Salad greens

Drain pears and place cut-side down on absorbent paper. Cream together Old English and cream cheeses, celery, green onion, parsley and tarragon. Spread on cut sides of pear halves; place halves together in pairs to form whole pears. Garnish with piece of green onion to resemble stem. Chill. To serve, place pears upright on greens on a platter. Makes 6 salads.

What's New in Wedding Food

Cool Carrots

2 bunches carrots, peeled
  and thinly sliced,
  or baby carrots
1/2 teaspoon salt
1 (10 1/2-ounce) can tomato
  soup, undiluted
3/4 cup vinegar
3/4 cup sugar

1/2 cup vegetable oil
1 teaspoon dry mustard
1 bell pepper (green or
  red), chopped
1 jar sour pickled onions,
  cocktail small size (pearl)
1 teaspoon herb seasonings
  (optional)

Boil carrots 10 minutes in water with 1/2 teaspoon salt. Drain. Boil the next 6 ingredients for 5 minutes. Remove from stove and add drained sour pickled onions and herb seasonings. Pour over carrots. Marinate 6-8 hours. Serve hot or cold.

  Favorite Variation: Use canned baby carrots, drained.

Christmas Favorites

Fruit Salad

2 packages frozen blueberries
2 packages frozen or fresh
  strawberries
1 cantaloupe, cut up

3 or 4 peaches, cut in
  pieces
2 cans chunk pineapple
  drained

Let fruit marinate about 2 hours before serving.

MARINADE:
2 cups orange juice
1 cup sugar
1/2 teaspoon almond extract

1/2 teaspoon vanilla
1/4 cup cream sherry

Mountain Elegance

Bombay Aspic

1 (16-ounce) can sliced
  peaches, drained
1 (3-ounce) package lemon
  gelatin

1 cup hot water
3/4 cup peach syrup
1/2 cup, or less, chutney

Dissolve gelatin in water; mix with remaining ingredients. Chill until firm. Yield: 4-6 servings.
  Note: Excellent with fowl.

Nothing Could Be Finer

Modified Waldorf Salad

4 large red delicious
  apples, unpared
Lemon juice
1 honey-dew melon, peeled
  and cubed
1 cantaloupe, peeled and
  cubed

2 stalks celery, cleaned and
  chopped
1/2 cup pecans
1/2 cup walnuts
1/2 cup coconut

Cube unpared apples and sprinkle with lemon juice. Combine apples, melon, cantaloupe, celery, nuts and coconut. Pour cooled sauce over mixture; toss. Chill. Toss again before serving. Yield: 8-10 servings.

SAUCE:
1/2 cup sugar
1/2 cup water

1 cup mayonnaise

Blend sauce ingredients over low heat until smooth. Set aside to cool.

Island Born and Bred

Cherry Salad I
(An Old Quaker Recipe)

1 can sour red pie cherries
1 cup sugar
1 small package cherry Jello
1 package (1 tablespoon)
  Knox gelatin

1/2 cold water
2 oranges
1 small can crushed
  pineapple, undrained
1/2 cup pecans

Bring cherries and sugar to boil. Add Jello. Dissolve gelatin in cold water and add to Jello mixture. Cool. Add grated rind of 1 orange and sections and juice of 2 oranges. Stir in pineapple and chopped nuts. Pour into mold or oblong Pyrex and put into refrigerator to congeal.

Mama's Recipes

Emerald Salad

1 (6-ounce) package lime
  Jello
3/4 cup boiling water
1 1/2 cups grated cucumber
  and rind

2 tablespoons grated onion
1 (8-ounce) carton cottage
  cheese
1 cup mayonnaise
3/4 cup slivered almonds

Mix real well Jello with boiling water. Let cucumbers drain until they don't even drip. Mix cucumbers and onion with Jello mixture. Fold in cottage cheese and mayonnaise. Add almonds. Serves 12.

Recipes From Our Front Porch

Orange-Avocado Toss

1 medium head lettuce, torn
  in bite-size pieces
1 small cucumber, thinly
  sliced
2 tablespoons green
  onions, sliced

1 avocado, seeded, peeled
  and sliced
1 (11-ounce) can mandarin
  oranges, drained

DRESSING:
1/4 cup orange juice
1/2 cup salad oil
2 tablespoons sugar
2 tablespoons red
  wine vinegar

1 tablespoon lemon
  juice
1/4 teaspoon salt

In large salad bowl, combine lettuce, cucumber, avocado, mandarin oranges and green onions. In a screw-top jar combine dressing ingredients. Cover tightly and shake well. Just before serving, pour over salad. Toss lightly. Serves 8.

Out Of Our League

 The University of North Carolina at Chapel Hill was the first state university in the nation to open its doors to students (1795).

Ham Mousse Salad

4 cups ground ham, finely
  chopped
2 cups consommé
2 envelopes plain gelatin
1 teaspoon Worcestershire
  sauce

1 cup mayonnaise
1/2 pint whipping cream,
  whipped
1/4 cup pimentos

Put plain gelatin in 1/2 cup cold consommé. Heat 1 1/2 cups consommé to boiling and dissolve gelatin. Add Worcestershire sauce and let cool. Add ham and mayonnaise and fold in whipped cream. Mold and refrigerate. Serves 6-8.

A Taste of History

Chicken Salad Habañera

Easy, everything is done ahead except the mixing.

2 cups chicken, cooked and
  diced
1/2 cup green pepper, cut
  in 1 x 1/4-inch strips
1/4 cup onion, chopped
1/4 cup ripe olives, sliced

1 avocado, cut in crescents
Lettuce leaves
3 medium tomatoes, cut in
  wedges
4 slices bacon, cooked crisp
  and crumbled

DRESSING:
1/3 cup salad oil
1/4 cup red wine vinegar
1 tablespoon lemon juice
2 teaspoons sugar

1 teaspoon salt
1/2 teaspoon dry mustard
1/4 teaspoon pepper
1/8 teaspoon garlic powder

Mix together, chicken, green pepper, onion and olives. Cover and chill. Combine dressing ingredients in jar and shake well. Refrigerate. Just before serving add avocado to salad ingredients. Shake dressing and pour over salad; toss lightly. Serve on bed of lettuce. Place tomato wedges around salad. Sprinkle with crumbled bacon. Yield: 4 servings.

Pass the Plate

Baked Chicken Salad

2 (6-ounce) cans boned
  chicken, broken apart
1 cup macaroni shells,
  cooked and drained
1 cup diced celery
2 tablespoons minced onion
1/2 teaspoon salt
1/4 teaspoon pepper

1 tablespoon white vinegar
1/2 cup broken pecans
3 hard cooked eggs, chopped
3/4 cup crushed potato chips
3/4 cup mayonnaise
1 cup condensed cream of
  chicken soup

Put all ingredients except mayonnaise and soup in a large mixing bowl. Mix gently. Add mayonnaise and soup; toss until mixed. Bake in a 350° oven for 30-35 minutes or until thoroughly heated. Makes 8 servings.

Korner's Folly Cookbook

Incorporated in 1705, historic Bath is North Carolina's oldest town and first meeting place of the Colonial Assembly of the Province. Several historic structures have been restored and are open for public viewing.

Cobb Salad

1/2 medium head leaf lettuce	6 strips bacon, cooked
1/2 bunch watercress	1 ripe avocado
1/2 head Romaine lettuce	3 hard boiled eggs
1 small bunch endive	1 bunch green onions
2 large tomatoes	1/2 cup crumbled bleu cheese
2 chicken breasts, cooked	1 cup Cobb Salad Dressing

Wash thoroughly, dry all greens so dressing will cling. Remove most of watercress stems. Tear up greens and arrange in salad bowl. Cut tomatoes in small pieces and add. Dice chicken, crumble bacon and arrange both in center of greens. Slice avocado into strips and arrange around edge of bowl. Chop eggs and onion, being sure to include green ends of onion. Decorate salad by sprinkling eggs, onion and crumbled bleu cheese over top of salad. Chill until ready to serve. Just before serving, toss with dressing. Serves 4 as a meal, 6 as a salad.

COBB SALAD DRESSING:

1 cup water	1 tablespoon Worcestershire
1 cup red wine	sauce
1 teaspoon sugar	1 tablespoon Dijon mustard
Juice of 1/2 lemon	1 clove garlic, chopped
2 1/2 tablespoons salt	1 cup olive oil
1 tablespoon ground black	3 cups vegetable oil
pepper	

Blend all ingredients except oils in blender. Add oils very slowly and blend well in blender. Chill. Shake thoroughly before serving. Yield: 1 1/2 quarts.

Note: Bottles of this make an excellent gift. Original recipe made the Brown Derby Restaurant famous in the heydays of Hollywood. Legend has it that a famous but demanding actress ordered chef salad and the frantic chef, finding himself short of the traditional ingredients, created this "make-do" salad which became the rage of Hollywood. Excellent for a luncheon served with crackers or for supper with French onion soup.

A Dash of Down East

Avocado Mousse

1 package lime Jello
1 cup hot water
1/2 cup cold water
1 tablespoon vinegar
1/2 cup mayonnaise
1/4 teaspoon salt
Dash pepper

1/2 teaspoon minced onion
1 tablespoon green pepper, minced
3/4 cup grapefruit segments, halved
1 small or 1/2 large avocado, cubed

Dissolve Jello in hot water. Add cold water, vinegar, mayonnaise, salt, and pepper. Blend thoroughly with fork or rotary beater. Turn into 1-inch deep freezing tray 15 or 20 minutes until fairly firm. Turn into bowl and beat until fluffy. Add onion, green pepper, grapefruit and avocado cubes; fold carefully into mixture. Pour into melon mold and chill until firm. Unmold and garnish with sliced chicken. Serve with watercress and Sour Cream Dressing.

SOUR CREAM DRESSING:
1 teaspoon rosemary
3 tablespoons boiling water
1 cup mayonnaise

2 scallions, chopped
Pinch salt
2-3 tablespoons vinegar

Pour the boiling water over the rosemary leaves and let it steep for 5 minutes. Strain and add the sour cream mixed with the mayonnaise. Then add the scallions, salt and vinegar to taste. If you want it tart, add the 3 tablespoons; otherwise 2 is enough. Makes 1 pint.

High Hampton Hospitality

 Monks built the Belmont Abbey Church from 1891 to 1894 with bricks made from local clay. The Benedictine Monastery building was, from 1910 until 1977, the only Abbey Cathedral in the U.S.

Mexican Cauliflower Salad
A Real Winner!

4 cups raw cauliflower,
  thinly sliced
1 cup ripe olives, pitted
  and chopped

1 cup green pepper, finely
  chopped
1/2 cup pimiento, chopped
1/3 cup onion, chopped

Combine 5 salad ingredients in a large bowl.

DRESSING:
1/2 cup salad oil
3 tablespoons lemon juice
3 tablespoons wine vinegar

2 teaspoons salt
1/2 teaspoon sugar

Mix dressing ingredients with beater until well-blended. Pour over the cauliflower mixture, cover and chill at least 3 hours. Yield: 6-8 servings.

Pass the Plate

Artichoke Salad

Must prepare ahead.

1 (8-ounce) package
  chicken-flavored rice
2 (6-ounce) jars marinated
  artichokes, drained and cut
  in pieces
1 tablespoon onion, finely
  chopped

3 rings green pepper,
  finely chopped
15 stuffed green olives,
  sliced
3/4 teaspoon curry powder
1/3 cup mayonnaise

Cook rice according to package directions, leaving out butter. Cool completely. Drain artichokes and save liquid. Add onion, pepper, and olives to cooled rice. Mix one half of artichoke liquid with curry powder and mayonnaise. Add artichokes to rice mixture; pour marinade mixture over all and refrigerate overnight. Yield: 8-10 servings.

  Note: This is attractive served in a glass bowl or platter on a bed of lettuce.

Market to Market

Fresh Broccoli Salad

1 bunch fresh broccoli,
  chopped
1/2 cup raisins
1/2 cup Spanish peanuts
2 stalks celery, chopped
1 carrot, grated

1 tablespoon Parmesan cheese
1/2 jar real bacon bits
1 cup mayonnaise-type salad
  dressing
2 tablespoons sugar
1 tablespoon vinegar

Combine broccoli, raisins, peanuts, celery, carrot, Parmesan cheese and bacon bits in bowl; toss to mix. Combine salad dressing, sugar and vinegar in small bowl; mix until sugar dissolves. Pour over broccoli mixture. Marinate for 12 hours or longer before serving. Yield: 6 servings.

Approx. Per Serving: Calories 332; Protein 7.6g; Carbohydrates 31.6g; T Fat 21.6g Cholesterol 14.2mg; Potassium 483.0mg; Sodium 447.0mg.

Goodness Grows in North Carolina

Mixed Pasta Salad

Mixed pasta salad is indeed a treat for a hot summer evening meal. This dish has the added attraction of needing to be prepared early in the day in order for the flavors to mingle. Serve on a bed of lettuce with crusty rolls and butter.

1 (8-ounce) bottle of oil
  and vinegar salad dressing
2 cups fresh broccoli
  florets, blanched
1 cup sliced pitted ripe
  olives
1 1/2 cups cherry tomatoes,
  sliced in half
1/2 cup canned mushrooms
2 green onions, thinly
  sliced

4 ounces fettucini noodles,
  cooked, drained and chilled
4 ounces spinach fettucine
  noodles, cooked, drained,
  and chilled
4 ounces boiled ham, sliced
  in strips
1/2 cup grated Parmesan
  cheese
1/2 cup crumbled, fried
  bacon

Marinate broccoli, olives, tomatoes, mushrooms and onions in the salad dressing at least 5 hours.

Drain, reserving the dressing. Combine the vegetables with the noodles, ham, cheese and bacon. Toss with the reserved dressing. Serve on lettuce leaves. Sprinkle with additional cheese, bacon and parsley flakes, if desired. Serves 6.

Taste Buds

Tortellini Liberty Oak

1/2 pound egg tortellini
1/2 pound spinach tortellini
1/2 pound smoked ham,
  julienne
1 (8-ounce) can artichoke
  hearts, cut in quarters
1/4 pound cherry tomatoes,
  cut in quarters

2 green peppers, julienne
Fresh parsley, chopped fine
1 purple onion, diced
Salt and freshly ground
  pepper

DRESSING:
2 cloves garlic
1 tablespoon lemon juice
3 tablespoons balsamico
  vinegar
1/2 cup virgin olive oil

1/2 cup vegetable oil
2 teaspoons Dijon mustard
1 teaspoon basil
1 teaspoon oregano
1/2 teaspoon thyme

Cook both tortellinis for 8 minutes in boiling water. Strain. Cool off with cold water. Add remaining ingredients. Mix well.

Mix together all dressing ingredients in food processor or blender. Add to tortellini. Mix again and serve. Recipe shared by Liberty Oak Restaurant. Serves: 6.

Bravo

Salata Meh Kritharaki
Orzo Salad

1 cup orzo or converted rice
3/4 cup crumbled feta cheese
3 tablespoons minced fresh
  parsley
3 tablespoons minced fresh
  basil or dill

1 tomato, cut into wedges
1/3 cup olive oil
1/4 cup lemon juice
1/2 teaspoon salt
1/4 teaspoon pepper

Cook orzo in a quart of salted, boiling water about 15 minutes until tender, stirring frequently to prevent sticking. Drain in colander, rinse with cold water and drain again. Add feta cheese, parsley, basil and tomato. In a jar, combine remaining ingredients and shake well. Pour over salad and toss until well coated. Refrigerate to chill and toss again before serving. Serves 6.

The Grecian Plate

Asheville Salad

1 can Campbell's tomato soup
1 (8-ounce) package cream
  cheese
1 1/2 packages Knox gelatin
1/2 cup cold water

1 tablespoon grated onion
1/2 cup finely chopped
  pecans
1 cup finely cut celery
1/2 cup mayonnaise

Heat tomato soup. Add cream cheese and stir until dissolved. Mix gelatin with cold water and add to hot mixture. Cool. Stir in onion, pecans, celery and mayonnaise. Pour into mold and congeal. Serves 8-10 people.

Mama's Recipes

Christmas Aspic—Cucumber Mold

1 envelope gelatin
1 3/4 cups V8 juice
1/2 cup onion, finely minced
1/4 cup green olives,
  chopped
1/2 teaspoon salt
1 tablespoon lemon juice
Dash Worcestershire
1 (3-ounce) package lime
  Jello

3/4 cup boiling water
1/4 cup mayonnaise
2 teaspoons cider vinegar
1/2 teaspoon salt
1 (8-ounce) carton sour
  cream
2 medium cucumbers, seeded
  and chopped very small

Soften gelatin in a little V8 juice; dissolve in remainder of heated juice. Add onion, olives, salt, lemon juice and Worcestershire; mix thoroughly. Pour into a mold and refrigerate until set.

Meanwhile, dissolve Jello in boiling water. Remove from stove and mix thoroughly with mayonnaise, vinegar, salt, sour cream and cucumber. When first layer has congealed, pour this on top for a second layer. Refrigerate until congealed. Serves 12. Colorful red and green salad!

Christmas Favorites

Chicken N' Tomato Aspic

1 (6-ounce) package lemon
  Jello
1 cup boiling water
1 (24-ounce) can V8 juice
1 1/2 tablespoons
  creamy-style horseradish
  sauce
2 tablespoons vinegar
1 teaspoon Worcestershire
  sauce

1/2 teaspoon salt
2 (5-ounce) cans chunk white
  chicken, chopped
1/2 cup green pepper,
  chopped fine
1/2 cup celery, chopped fine
1/4 cup stuffed green
  olives, sliced (optional)

TOPPING:
1/2 cup mayonnaise
1 teaspoon curry powder
1 tablespoon creamy-style
  horseradish sauce

Paprika for color, if
  desired

Dissolve Jello in boiling water. Mix together V8 juice and horse-radish sauce until smooth. Slowly add Jello mixture, blending well. Stir in vinegar, Worcestershire sauce and salt. Pour into a 9x9-inch dish and chill mixture until slightly thickened. Carefully fold in chicken, green pepper, celery and olives. Chill until set. Cut into squares and serve on a bed of lettuce. If desired, garnish with a spoonful of topping, blended well, and sprinkled with paprika. Serves: 8-10.

Bravo

New Potato Salad

8-10 new potatoes
1 bunch green onions, sliced

3 stalks celery, chopped
3 boiled eggs, chopped

Make a day ahead. Boil new potatoes and mix in large bowl with onions, celery and eggs.

DRESSING:
1 teaspoon salt
1 teaspoon basil
1/2 teaspoon pepper
1 tablespoon Dijon mustard
2 cloves garlic, minced

3 tablespoons red wine
 vinegar
1/2 cup mayonnaise
1/3 cup olive oil

Combine salt, pepper, basil, Dijon mustard, garlic and vinegar in small bowl, stirring in mayonnaise and whisk in oil. Pour over potatoes and let sit overnight.

Knollwood's Cooking

Cole Slaw

1 medium-size cabbage,
 grated
1 small onion, finely diced
1 apple, finely cubed
1 tablespoon sweet pickle
 relish and juice

1/2 cup mayonnaise
1 heaping tablespoon sugar
1/4 teaspoon salt
1 teaspoon celery seed

In a large mixing bowl, combine cabbage, onion, and apple. Add relish, mayonnaise, sugar and seasonings. Combine. Serves 6-8.

Coastal Carolina Cooking

Wilted Lettuce and Onion Salad

8 slices bacon
1/2 cup vinegar
1/2 cup water
2 teaspoons sugar

2 quarts torn leaf lettuce
8 green onions (cut into
 small pieces)

Fry, cool, and crumble the bacon into pieces. In the skillet, add vinegar, water, and sugar to the bacon drippings. Bring to boil. Pour over lettuce and onions, and top with crumbled bacon bits.

I Remember

Pork 'N Bean Salad

1 (1-pound) can pork and	1 small onion, chopped
beans	3 small dill pickles,
3 tablespoons mayonnaise	chopped
Dash of salt	2 hard cooked eggs, chopped

Drain beans. Add mayonnaise, salt, onion, pickles, and eggs. Mix well and chill for an hour or longer, if desired. Great for a picnic or cookout. It is better when it is 2 days old. Yield: 4 servings.

Have Fun Cooking With Me

Nu-Wray Smothered Lettuce

This fine ole-fashioned salad is know in some regions as "Mountain Salad" or "Wilted Lettuce."

Lettuce	Salt to taste
3 green onions	2 tablespoons vinegar
1 teaspoon sugar	5 slices cured country bacon

Select fresh spring lettuce before it heads. Chop enough lettuce to fill bowl. Add 3 young onion heads and onion tops chopped fine. Add 1 teaspoon sugar, and salt to taste. Pour over 2 tablespoons of vinegar. Fry 5 slices of cured country bacon crisply, and place strips upon lettuce. Pour hot bacon grease over all. Serve immediately. Serves 4.

From *Ole-Time Recipes* from the Nu-Wray Inn at Burnsville.

Marion Brown's Southern Cook Book

 Designated the North Carolina State Theatre, the Flat Rock Playhouse is one of the top ten summer theatres in the United States.

Hemlock Inn Salad Dressing

1 teaspoon salt
6 tablespoons sugar
1 teaspoon garlic powder
1/2 teaspoon oregano

1/2 teaspoon basil
1/2 teaspoon parsley flakes
1/2 cup vinegar
1 1/2 cups mayonnaise

Mix all ingredients together really well. Yield: approximately 2 1/2 cups.
   Note: May add ketchup for French dressing.

Recipes From Our Front Porch

Low-Calorie Roquefort Dressing

Make this in a blender.

1 package bleu or Roquefort
   cheese dressing mix
1 (12-ounce) carton cottage
   cheese
3/4 cup milk
1/2 cup mayonnaise

1 tablespoon lemon juice
1 tablespoon Worcestershire
   sauce
1/4 pound Roquefort cheese,
   crumbled fine

Combine all ingredients except Roquefort cheese in the blender container; blend at medium speed until mixture is smooth. Stir in the crumbled Roquefort cheese. Blend a second or two to further crumble the Roquefort, or remove from container before blending in the cheese. Store in a glass jar with screw top. Refrigerate. Will keep for several weeks. About 3 cups.

Marion Brown's Southern Cook Book

 America's top brand cigarettes are made by the R. J. Reynolds Tobacco Company in Winston-Salem.

**Bread
and
Breakfast**

Old Salem at Winston-Salem.

Never-Fail Pan Rolls

3/4 cup sugar
3/4 cup shortening
1 cup boiling water
2 packages dry yeast
1 cup warm water

2 eggs, slightly beaten
6 to 7 cups plain flour
1 teaspoon salt
1 teaspoon baking powder
1/2 teaspoon baking soda

In a large mixing bowl, cream sugar and shortening until light and fluffy. Add boiling water. Mix thoroughly and let cool. In a small mixing bowl, dissolve yeast in warm water and set aside.

Add eggs to cooled shortening mixture and mix well. Stir in yeast mixture. Combine 5 cups flour with salt, baking powder, and soda. Add to yeast mixture and mix well. Turn out dough on well-floured surface. Knead in enough remaining flour until dough is no longer sticky. Roll into 1 1/2-inch balls. Place balls, nearly touching, in greased 9-inch round cake pans. Cover and let rolls rise in warm place until doubled. Bake at 400° for 20 minutes. Makes 3 dozen.

Note: Mae says this dough will keep in refrigerator for a week.

Coastal Carolina Cooking

Mama's Rolls

8 level tablespoons Crisco
1/2 cup sugar
3 1/4 teaspoons salt
2 cups milk, scalded
8 - 8 1/4 cups plain flour
   (White Lily or Red Band)

2 envelopes yeast (dissolve
   in 1/2 cup tepid water
   to which 1 teaspoon sugar has
   been added)
2 eggs, beaten

In large bowl place Crisco, sugar and salt. Pour scalded milk over these ingredients and let cool until warm. To cool milk, add 4 cups flour and mix well. Next, add dissolved yeast and mix well. Now add beaten eggs and mix. Last, add remaining flour. Let rise one hour. Stir down and place dough on floured board. Roll out to 1/4-inch thick, cut with biscuit cutter, and then dip circles in melted butter. Fold over to make pocketbook. Place in pans to rise for 2 hours. Bake at 450° for 6 minutes.

Note: With Red Band or White Lily flour (or any soft wheat flour) use 8 - 8 1/4 cups. With a hard wheat flour like Pillsbury or Gold Medal, Mama used only 7 - 7 1/4 cups.

Mama's Recipes

Hemlock Inn Yeast Rolls

3/4 cup scalded milk	3 tablespoons oil
1 tablespoon yeast	1 slightly beaten egg
1/4 cup lukewarm water	3 1/2 cups flour
1/8 cup sugar	1 teaspoon salt

Put milk on to warm. Put yeast and lukewarm water in bowl. Make rounded spoonfuls—be generous. Put sugar and oil in mixing bowl. Beat egg in small bowl. Mix milk, yeast and egg with sugar and oil. Mix well! Put in a small amount of flour and add salt. Beat until air bubbles appear. Gradually add more flour until stiff. Cover with melted butter and let rise until double. *Don't let set after dough rises!* Roll and cut; fold over. Butter and let rise again. (We use melted margarine.) Bake at 500-550° for about 10 minutes. Yield: 6 dozen rolls.

To make whole wheat rolls, use 1/3 whole wheat to 2/3 white flour.

Recipes From Our Front Porch

Buttermilk Rolls

There are no rolls like buttermilk rolls.

2 cups buttermilk	1 teaspoon salt
1 package dry granular yeast	1/4 teaspoon baking powder
5 cups sifted flour	1/4 teaspoon soda
3 tablespoons sugar	4 tablespoons shortening

Heat a portion of the buttermilk to lukewarm and use for dissolving yeast. Allow to stand a few minutes and then mix with remaining buttermilk.

Sift flour with remaining dry ingredients. Cut in shortening. Add buttermilk and blend well. Grease top with butter. Cover and store in refrigerator.

About 2 hours before serving, take out and make into rolls. Allow to rise in warm place until double in bulk. Bake at 400° for 12-15 minutes or until done.

North Carolina and Old Salem Cookery

Butter Dips

1/3 cup butter	3 1/2 teaspoons baking powder
2 1/4 cups sifted Gold Medal flour	1 1/2 teaspoons salt
1 tablespoon sugar	1 cup milk

Heat oven hot (450º). Melt butter in oven in oblong pan, 13x9 1/2x2 inches. Remove pan when butter is melted. Sift together flour, sugar, baking powder, salt. Add milk. Stir slowly with fork until dough just clings together. Turn onto well-floured board. Roll over to coat with flour. Knead lightly about 10 times. Roll out half-inch thick into rectangle, 12x8 inches. With floured knife, cut dough in half lengthwise, then cut crosswise into 16 strips. Pick up strips in both hands and dip each strip on both sides in melted butter. Next lay them close together in two rows in same pan in which butter is melted. Bake 15-20 minutes until golden brown. Serve hot. Makes 32 sticks.

Variations: (1) Add 1/2 cup grated sharp Cheddar cheese to dry ingredients. (2) Add 1/2 clove finely minced garlic to butter before melting. (3) Sprinkle paprika, celery seed or garlic salt over dips before baking.

High Hampton Hospitality

Capital Landmarks Cheese Biscuits

1/2 pound sharp Cheddar
  cheese, grated
1/2 stick butter or
  margarine
2 cups Bisquick
6 drops Tabasco

1/4 teaspoon pepper
1/2 teaspoon salt
1 teaspoon mustard powder
1/4 teaspoon dill
1/2 cup water

Mix cheese and butter until soft. Coat with Bisquick. Add seasonings. Moisten to pie crust consistency with 1/2 cup water. Roll into small balls (approximately 7 dozen). Bake on ungreased cookie sheet in preheated oven for 20 minutes at 375° or until lightly brown.

These will be slightly puffed and have a flaky texture. They freeze and reheat well. Serve at room temperature. Can make ahead and freeze. Serves 30.

A Taste of History

Buttermilk Yeast Biscuits

5 cups plain flour
5 teaspoons baking powder
1 teaspoon salt
1/2 teaspoon baking soda
3 tablespoons sugar

1 cup shortening
2 cups buttermilk
1 package yeast dissolved in
  5 tablespoons lukewarm
  water

In a large mixing bowl, sift together flour, baking powder, salt baking soda and sugar. Cut in shortening. Stir in buttermilk. Add yeast mixture. Knead lightly. Roll dough onto a floured surface using a rolling pin. Cut with biscuit cutter. Bake on greased baking sheet 10 to 12 minutes at 450°. Makes 60 biscuits.

Instead of baking all 60 biscuits at once, Mae freezes some of the uncooked biscuits on cookie sheets lined with wax paper. When they are frozen, she stores them in plastic bags.

Coastal Carolina Cooking

Mattie's Sweet Potato Biscuits

For a special treat take biscuits hot from oven and fill with butter and a thin slice of sharp Cheddar cheese and/or ham. Keep hot in oven (door ajar and heat off) until cheese is melted. I served these to a hungry crowd after a mixed doubles tennis tournament and they were the hit of the day. The men stood by the kitchen door ready to pounce each time a tray came through.

2 cups sweet potatoes (3
  medium sweet potatoes or
  the canned equivalent)
1/3 cup butter or margarine
1/3 cup sugar

4 cups self-rising flour
1 cup shortening
1 - 2 tablespoons water, if
  needed

Boil peeled and cut sweet potatoes about 20 minutes. Preheat oven to 450°. Drain potatoes, mash and add butter and sugar while still hot. Sift flour into mixture. Cut in shortening. Add water, if needed for right consistency. Roll out and cut to size and thickness you like. Bake about 10 minutes or until lightly browned. May be partly done ahead. Stores well. Yield: 4-5 dozen medium-sized biscuits.

Pass the Plate

Cutie's Fried Corn Bread

8 tablespoons bacon drippings
2/3 cup self-rising cornmeal
2 tablespoons plain flour

1 egg
Water

Preheat electric skillet to 380°. Add bacon drippings. Combine the flours and mix in the egg and enough cold water to make a thick batter. Place a big tablespoon of batter in the skillet, repeat, do not let sides touch. Brown on each side, remove and eat . . . delicious. Teaspoonful size makes great hors d'oeuvres. Serves 6.

Note: Preheat skillet before adding water to flour.

Ship to Shore I

Sweet Potato Love Buns

1 cup mashed sweet potatoes
1/2 cup scalded milk
1 cup sugar
1/2 cup butter
1/2 teaspoon salt
3 packages yeast softened in
   1/2 cup warm water
2 beaten eggs

1 tablespoon grated orange
   rind
1 teaspoon grated orange
   juice
1 teaspoon lemon juice
1/4 teaspoon nutmeg
5-6 cups flour

Scald milk; combine sugar, butter and salt. Into sugar mix add lukewarm milk, potatoes, yeast, eggs, rinds, juices and nutmeg. Stir in 2 1/2 cups flour, beat until smooth. Add more flour to make a soft dough. Knead. Let rise to double; punch down; let rest 10 minutes. Shape into buns about 2 inches in diameter. Place 1 inch apart on greased baking pan. Let rise to double. Bake at 350° for 15-20 minutes. Freezes well. Yields 4-5 dozen buns.

A Taste of History

Bunker Hill Brown Bread

An easy bread with a delicious flavor. Spread with cream cheese or serve plain.

1 1/2 cups flour
1 1/2 teaspoons salt
2 teaspoons baking soda
1 cup wheat germ
1 cup graham cracker crumbs

2 eggs
1/2 cup vegetable oil
1 cup molasses
2 cups buttermilk

Preheat oven to 350°. Sift flour, salt, and soda into a mixing bowl. Add wheat germ and graham cracker crumbs. Stir to combine. In a second bowl combine eggs, vegetable oil, molasses, and buttermilk. Blend.

Add liquid ingredients to dry ingredients. Stir until well blended. Pour batter into 2 well-greased and floured tall one-pound coffee cans (or prepared Bundt pan). Bake for 50-55 minutes or until bread tests done. Makes 2 loaves or 1 Bundt pan.

Stirring Performances

Pineapple Crunch Coffee Cake

2 cups flour	1/4 cup packed brown sugar
1 1/2 cups sugar	1 (1-pound 4-ounce) can
1 teaspoon soda	crushed pineapple
1/2 teaspoon salt	1 cup chopped walnuts

Combine flour, sugar, soda, salt, brown sugar and pineapple with juice and nuts. Mix well. Pour into ungreased 9x13-inch loaf pan. Bake at 350° for 35 minutes.

ICING:

2/3 cup sugar	1/2 cup margarine or butter
1/4 cup milk	

Combine the above in a small saucepan and boil 2 minutes. Pour over warm cake. Sprinkle with coconut if desired. Serves 6.

Ship to Shore I

Butterscotch Breakfast Ring

This is a good recipe to have for holidays.

1 cup butterscotch morsels	1/2 cup chopped pecans
2 tablespoons butter	1 (10-ounce) package
2 tablespoons flour	refrigerated crescent rolls
1/8 teaspoon salt	7 teaspoons corn syrup

Preheat the oven to 375°. Melt half the butterscotch morsels and the butter in the top of a double boiler over hot, not boiling, water. Remove from the heat. Stir in the flour, salt, and nuts, mixing gently with a fork. Set aside.

Separate the rolls into triangles. Arrange on a greased cookie sheet so the triangles form a circle. The edges should overlap slightly and the long ends point outward.

Spread 2 teaspoonfuls of butterscotch mixture on each triangle. Roll up, jelly roll fashion, toward the center. Slash the inside half of each roll. Bake for 15 minutes, or until golden brown.

Meanwhile, combine the remaining 1/2 cup butterscotch with the corn syrup. Melt over hot water, stirring to blend. Let cool slightly, then drizzle over the breakfast ring. Serve hot or cold. Makes 1 ring.

Love Yourself Cookbook

Orange Date Nut Bread

This is served with tea in the lobby of the High Hampton Inn.

2 cups sifted all-purpose
　flour
1 1/2 teaspoon baking powder
1/2 teaspoon soda
1/2 teaspoon salt
3/4 cup sugar
1/2 cup chopped nuts
1/4 cup grated orange rind
　(2 medium oranges)

1/2 cup hot water
1 cup chopped dates
1/3 cup orange juice
2 teaspoons lemon juice
2 tablespoons melted butter
　or shortening
1 teaspoon vanilla
1 egg, beaten

Sift flour, baking powder, soda, salt and sugar together. Add nuts and orange rind. Mix well. Pour hot water over chopped dates in small mixing bowl and add orange juice, lemon juice and melted butter, vanilla and beaten eggs. Mix. Pour liquid mix all at once into sifted dry ingredients and mix lightly. Pour batter into a well-greased 9x5x3-inch pan and bake in a preheated oven at 350°. Bake for one hour or until done.

　Cream cheese softened with 2 tablespoons of frozen, undiluted orange juice is good to serve with this.

High Hampton Hospitality

Hawaiian Banana-Nut Bread

3 cups all-purpose flour
2 cups sugar
1 teaspoon soda
1 teaspoon salt
1 teaspoon ground cinnamon
1 cup chopped nuts

3 eggs, beaten
1 1/2 cups vegetable oil
2 cups mashed ripe bananas
1 (8-ounce) can crushed
　pineapple, drained
2 teaspoons vanilla

Combine dry ingredients; stir in nuts and set aside. Combine remaining ingredients; add to dry ingredients, stirring just until batter is moistened. Spoon batter into two greased and floured 9x5x3-inch loaf pans. Bake at 350° for 65 minutes, or until done. Cool 10 minutes before removing from pans.

Island Born and Bred

Cream Cheese Braids

1 cup sour cream
1/2 cup sugar
1 teaspoon salt
1/2 cup butter or margarine, melted

2 (1/4-ounce) packages yeast
1/2 cup warm water (105 to 115°)
2 eggs, beaten
4 cups all-purpose flour

Heat sour cream over low heat; stir in sugar, salt, and butter. Cool to lukewarm. Sprinkle yeast over warm water in a large mixing bowl, stirring until yeast dissolves. Add sour cream mixture, eggs, and flour. Mix well. Cover tightly and refrigerate overnight.

The next day, divide dough into four equal parts. Roll out each part on a well floured board into a 12x8-inch rectangle. Spread one fourth of cream cheese filling on each rectangle. Roll up jelly roll fashion, beginning at long sides. Pinch edges together and fold ends under slightly. Place the rolls, seam side down, on greased baking sheets. Slit each roll at 2-inch intervals about two thirds of way through dough to resemble a braid. Cover and let rise in a warm place, free from drafts, until doubled in bulk. (About 1 hour.) Bake at 375° for 12-15 minutes. Spread with glaze while warm. Yield: four 12-inch loaves.

CREAM CHEESE FILLING:
2 (8-ounce) packages cream cheese, softened
3/4 cup sugar

1 egg, beaten
1/8 teaspoon salt
2 teaspoons vanilla extract

Combine cream cheese and sugar in a small mixing bowl. Add egg, salt, and vanilla. Mix well. Yield: 2 cups.

GLAZE:
2 cups powdered sugar
4 tablespoons milk

2 teaspoons vanilla extract

Combine all ingredients in a small bowl. Mix well. Yield: about 1 cup.

Market to Market

 Biltmore Estate is an elegant 250-room French Renaissance chateau built in the 1890s by George W. Vanderbilt. It is the largest private home in America. Surrounded by formal gardens, the 12,000-acre estate is a national historic landmark.

Skillet-Popover

Delight your family with this fancy giant-size popover for breakfast. I serve it with a light sprinkling of cinnamon sugar. You may choose syrup or warmed fruit preserves or lemon juice and powdered sugar. At any rate, it is sure to please. Be careful to follow the directions carefully and be certain to heat the frying pan.

1/2 cup butter	**1/2 cup all-purpose flour**
1/2 cup milk	**2 eggs**

Place butter in a heavy iron 9-inch skillet. Place the pan in a preheated oven set at 475°. Mix the milk, flour and eggs lightly to make a batter. After the butter has melted, tilt pan so that the entire surface will be coated with butter. Add batter and bake for 12 minutes. Remove from the oven and invert onto a large plate. Drizzle the butter in the pan over the popover. Sprinkle with cinnamon sugar. Roll it over in loose jelly roll fashion. Slice and serve. Serves 2-4.

Taste Buds

Applesauce Puffs

Best when served warm with coffee.

2 cups packaged biscuit mix	1/4 cup milk
1/4 cup sugar	1 egg, slightly beaten
1 teaspoon cinnamon	2 tablespoons salad oil
1/2 cup applesauce	

TOPPING:

2 tablespoons melted margarine	1 teaspoon cinnamon
	1/2 cup sugar

Combine biscuit mix, 1/4 cup sugar and 1 teaspoon cinnamon. Add applesauce, milk, egg and oil. Beat vigorously for 30 seconds. Grease 2 small muffin tins and fill two-thirds full (yields 24) or 1 regular muffin tin (yields 12). Bake in 400° oven for 12 minutes. Dip tops in melted butter and then into sugar mixed with cinnamon. Can be frozen. Yield: 24.

Bravo

Any light object tossed from Blowing Rock will be returned by the wind; and snow falls up! The rock overhangs John's River Gorge hundreds of feet below.

Pineapple Muffins

A small tasty muffin, attractively baked in a tiny muffin tin is a nice change. Serve with lots of whipped butter.

2 cups all-purpose flour
1 1/2 teaspoons baking
 powder
1/8 teaspoon salt
1/4 cup butter

2 tablespoons sugar
1 large egg
1 (8 1/4-ounce) can crushed
 pineapple in heavy syrup,
 undrained

Stir together the flour, baking powder and salt. Cream butter and sugar. Beat in egg until blended. Add flour mixture and pineapple. Stir only until moistened. Turn into paper lined muffin tins. Bake at 350° for 30 minutes. Yield: 12 large muffins or 24-36 tiny muffins.

Taste Buds

Tavern Pumpkin Muffins

1 1/4 cups flour
2 cups sugar
1 1/2 tablespoons baking
 powder
1 teaspoon salt
3/4 tablespoon cinnamon

1 cup raisins
1 (16-ounce) can pumpkin
2 tablespoons butter, melted
4 eggs
1 tablespoon vanilla
1/2 cup milk

Mix dry ingredients with raisins. Mix pumpkin, butter, eggs, and vanilla. Blend dry ingredients into this mixture. Slowly add milk, stirring constantly. Pour batter into greased muffin tins and bake at 375° until golden brown. Makes 12-18 muffins (24 small size). This recipe is used at the Zevely House and Salem Tavern.

Knollwood's Cooking

North Carolina Yam Muffins

1 cup yams, mashed	3 cups self-rising flour
1 - 2 cups sugar	1 cup raisins
1 cup oil	1 cup pecans, broken
4 eggs, beaten	

Combine yams, sugar, oil, and eggs. Add flour and blend until just moistened. Fold in raisins and nuts. Spoon batter into greased muffin tins. Bake 15-20 minutes at 350°. Batter may be refrigerated and used as needed. Makes 24 muffins.

In Good Taste

Apricot Ice Box Muffins

1 1/4 cups Crisco	1 teaspoon ground ginger
1 1/2 cups sugar	1/2 teaspoon ground allspice
4 eggs	1 teaspoon salt
1 cup buttermilk	1 cup chopped nuts
2 teaspoon soda	1 cup raisins
1/2 cup Grandma's molasses	1 cup dried apricots, ground
4 cups (sift and measure) plain flour	or cut into small bits

Blend Crisco and sugar. Add eggs, one-at-a-time, blending after each. Mix soda with buttermilk and add to mixture. Add molasses and mix. Mix flour, ginger, allspice, and salt and add to mixture. Remove bowl from mixer and stir in the nuts, raisins and apricots. Bake in tiny muffin tins at 400° for 12-15 minutes. Batter will keep for weeks in refrigerator in tightly covered containers.

Mama's Recipes

 Mellowed by time, and rolling gracefully into the distance like great blue waves, the mountains of North Carolina have a quiet, introspective majesty. They are older than the Andes and more ancient than the Alps.

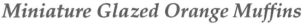

Miniature Glazed Orange Muffins

1 egg
3/4 cup buttermilk
1 orange rind, grated
1/4 cup orange juice
4 ounces butter, melted
1 3/4 cups unbleached flour

1/3 cup sugar
1 teaspoon baking powder
1/2 teaspoon salt
1/2 teaspoon baking soda
1 recipe Orange Glaze

Preheat oven to 400°. Beat egg lightly. Stir in buttermilk, orange rind, orange juice, and melted butter. Sift dry ingredients together, add to the liquid ingredients, and stir until just mixed. The batter should be lumpy; do not overmix.

Fill greased muffin cups (or use muffin liners) 2/3 full. Bake 20-25 minutes at 400°. Prepare glaze while muffins are baking. Remove muffins from oven. Run knife around edges of muffin cups. While the muffins are still warm, prick the tops lightly and pour glaze over. Remove from pan when cool. Yields 3 dozen muffins.

ORANGE GLAZE:
3/4 cup sugar
3/4 cup orange juice

1 teaspoon lemon juice
1 orange rind, grated

Combine all ingredients; cook and stir until the sugar is dissolved. The mixture should come to a soft simmer and make a light syrup.

The Fearrington House Cookbook

Orange Breakfast Treat

1 tablespoon butter
6 ounces orange marmalade
1/4 cup chopped nuts
1 cup brown sugar, firmly
  packed

1/2 teaspoon cinnamon
2 (10-ounce) cans Hungry
  Jack Buttermilk Biscuits
1 stick melted butter

Grease a tube pan with butter. Drop marmalade in by teaspoons evenly around bottom. Sprinkle with nuts.

Mix sugar and cinnamon together in a small bowl. Dip biscuits in melted butter and then in sugar mixture one at a time. Stand them up close together around pan in two rows. Sprinkle any left over sugar or butter over top. Bake at 350° for 30 - 40 minutes or until golden brown. Cool 5 minutes. Invert onto plate.

Jarrett House Potpourri

French Toast with Orange Butter

12 (1-inch thick) slices
  French bread
6 eggs
4 cups milk
1/2 teaspoon salt

1/2 teaspoon ground nutmeg
1/2 teaspoon vanilla
2 tablespoons butter,
  divided

Place bread in 13x9x2-inch pan. Combine eggs, milk, salt, nutmeg and vanilla; beat well. Pour mixture over bread. Cover and refrigerate overnight.

Melt 1 tablespoon butter in an electric skillet at 300°. Remove 6 slices bread from dish and cook in butter 10 to 12 minutes on each side or until cooked through. Repeat procedure with remaining butter and bread. Serve hot with Orange Butter. Makes 6 servings.

ORANGE BUTTER:
1 cup softened butter
1/2 cup orange juice

1/2 cup powdered sugar

Cream butter until light and fluffy. Add orange juice and powdered sugar. Beat until thoroughly blended. Makes about 2 cups.

Jarrett House Potpourri

Frances' Fancy Breakfast

3 English muffins, split in half
1/4 cup butter
2 green onions (or 1 small onion), chopped
1 small green pepper, chopped
6 - 8 large fresh (or canned) mushrooms, sliced

4 eggs, beaten with a small amount of milk
Salt and pepper to taste
6 slices Canadian bacon
1 (10-ounce) can cream of mushroom soup, undiluted
1 cup Cheddar cheese, grated

Lightly butter and toast English muffin halves. Sauté in butter the onions, green peppers and mushrooms until softened. Add the beaten eggs, season, and scramble. Top each muffin half with a slice of Canadian bacon. Mound some of the egg mixture on the bacon and then place a tablespoon of mushroom soup on top. Add grated cheese on top of the soup and heat under the broiler until the cheese is melted and browned. This makes a delightful breakfast or brunch when served with spiced apple rings or fresh fruit. Yield: 6 servings.

Pass the Plate

Brunch Casserole

4 cups day-old white or French bread, cubed
2 cups Cheddar cheese, shredded
10 eggs, lightly beaten
1 quart milk
1 teaspoon dry mustard
1 teaspoon salt

1/4 teaspoon onion powder
Freshly ground pepper to taste
8-10 slices bacon, cooked and crumbled
1/2 cup mushrooms, sliced
1/2 cup tomatoes, peeled and chopped

Generously butter a 9x13-inch baking dish. Arrange bread cubes in baking dish and sprinkle with cheese. In a bowl, add the next six ingredients and mix. Pour evenly over bread. Sprinkle mixture with bacon, mushrooms, and tomatoes. Cover and chill up to 24 hours. To bake, preheat oven to 325° and bake, uncovered, for 1 hour or until set. Tent with foil if top begins to over brown. Makes 12 servings.

Stirring Performances

Potato Scramble

1/4 cup butter
1/2 large package frozen
  grated potatoes
1 small onion, grated
8 eggs, beaten

3 tablespoons cream
1 cup chopped bacon or ham
Salt and pepper to taste
1 cup grated Cheddar cheese

Melt butter in sauté pan and add potatoes and onion. Cook over medium heat until lightly browned. Combine next 4 ingredients. Pour over potatoes and cook as for scrambled eggs. Add cheese. Heat until melted. To serve, cut in pie wedges.

Bravo

Spinach Scrambled with Eggs

3 pounds spinach, washed
2 cups salted water
1 tablespoon butter

Black pepper to taste
2 eggs, beaten

Cook spinach in salted water just until tender. Remove from stove and pour out as much liquor as possible. Chop spinach. Lightly brown 1 tablespoon butter in skillet, then add spinach. Sprinkle with black pepper and cook until there is no remaining juice. Add eggs and scramble until eggs are done. Will serve 6.

Queen Anne's Table

"Top Hat" Cheese Soufflé

4 tablespoons butter or
  margarine
4 tablespoons flour
1 teaspoon salt
Dash of cayenne

1 1/2 cups milk
1/2 pound Old English sliced
  pasteurized process cheese
6 egg yolks, beaten
6 egg whites, stiffly beaten

Preheat oven to 300°. Melt butter in top of double boiler placed over boiling water. Remove from boiling water and blend in flour, salt and cayenne. Gradually add milk, blending well. Return to boiling water and cook, stirring constantly until the sauce is thick and smooth. Add the sliced or grated cheese and continue cooking, stirring frequently until the cheese has melted. Remove from heat and slowly add the beaten egg yolks, blending them in well.

Slightly cool the mixture, then pour it slowly onto the stiffly beaten egg whites, cutting and folding the mixture thoroughly together. Pour into an ungreased 2-quart casserole. Run the tip of a teaspoon around the mixture one inch from the edge of the casserole, making a slight "track" or depression. This forms the "Top Hat" on the soufflé as it bakes and puffs up. Bake 1 1/4 hours in 300° oven. Serve immediately. Serves 6.

A Cookbook of Pinehurst Courses

Incredible Pimiento Cheese

1 pound Velveeta cheese
1 pound medium Cheddar
  cheese
1 pound sharp Cheddar cheese
1 pint Miracle Whip salad
  dressing

8 ounces pimiento, drained
  and chopped
3 tablespoons sugar
Salt to taste
Pepper to taste

Grate cheeses or cut into small pieces. Allow to soften at room temperature. Combine all ingredients and blend using mixer, blender or food processor. It may be necessary to divide ingredients into two batches unless you have an exceptionally large mixing container. Can be frozen. Yield: 2 quarts.

Pass the Plate

Monte Cristo Club

6 slices whole-wheat bread
4 tablespoons strawberry
  preserves
4 slices boiled ham
4 slices cooked turkey

4 slices Swiss cheese
1 egg
1/4 cup milk
Salt to taste
Butter for grilling

Spread each of 4 slices of bread with 1 tablespoon preserves. Top each of 2 of these slices with a slice of ham, turkey, and cheese and a plain slice of bread. Place another slice of ham, turkey and cheese on the plain slice.

Place the remaining preserve-coated bread, preserve side down, on top. Beat together the egg, milk, and salt. Dip the sandwiches in the egg mixture, then grill in a buttered skillet until golden brown and hot enough. Serve at once. Makes 2 servings.

Love Yourself Cookbook

Baked Asparagus and Cheese Sandwich

1 pound fresh asparagus,
  blanched, or 1 package
  thawed frozen asparagus
12 slices bread, trimmed
6 slices Swiss cheese
4 eggs
2 1/2 cups milk

1/4 teaspoon nutmeg
1 3/4 teaspoons salt
1/8 teaspoon pepper
2 tablespoons finely chopped
  onion
3/4 cup shredded Cheddar
  cheese

If asparagus are large, cut spears in half lengthwise. Arrange 6 slices of bread on bottom of a 13x9x2-inch baking dish; cover each with asparagus spears. Top each with a slice of Swiss cheese, and cover with other piece of bread. In a bowl, beat eggs until light. Add milk, nutmeg, salt, pepper, and onion; blend thoroughly. Pour this mixture over the sandwiches and bake in a moderate oven 350° for 25 minutes. Sprinkle with the Cheddar and continue to bake 10-15 minutes, or until custard is set. Allow to stand 10 minutes before serving. Cut into squares. Serves 6.

Mushrooms, Turnip Greens & Pickled Eggs

Stuffed French Rolls

4 French rolls
1/2 pound nippy cheese
1/4 - 1/2 pound minced ham
Stuffed olives
1/2 large onion, chopped

1/4 cup tomato sauce
2 teaspoons chopped green
 pepper
1/4 cup salad oil

Cut tops from French rolls and hollow out the centers. Mix all the ingredients together thoroughly and refill the centers of the rolls. Wrap in foil and bake for 20 minutes at 350°.

Mushrooms, Turnip Greens & Pickled Egg

Josephinas
For Soups!

1 cup butter, softened
1 cup green chilis, rinsed
 and chopped
1 clove garlic, crushed

1 cup mayonnaise
1/2 pound Jack cheese (or
 Cheddar), grated
Hard dinner rolls

Combine the first five ingredients. Split the rolls; toast lightly on the hard side. Spread the split sides with the chili mixture. Broil a few inches from broiler flame until brown and puffy. Serve with soup. Store this mixture in a jar in refrigerator, use as required. Makes about 1 3/4 pints.

Marion Brown's Southern Cook Book

Grits Casserole

Great with jalapeño cheese instead of Cheddar, too!

1 cup grits
1 stick butter
1 package garlic cheese (or
 8 ounces sharp Cheddar and 1
 teaspoon garlic powder)

2 beaten eggs
3/4 cup milk

Cook grits in 4 1/2 cups salted water. When done, add butter, garlic cheese, eggs and milk. Stir until melted. Pour into greased casserole and sprinkle buttered bread crumbs on top. Bake 45 minutes (or until center is done) in 350° oven. Serves 6.

Mountain Elegance

Shrimp and Grits, Crook's Corner Style

Shrimp and Grits is undoubtedly the most requested recipe I have yet created. In 1985 Craig Claiborne visited Crook's Corner in Chapel Hill for dinner and sampled many dishes. After dinner he asked me to prepare Shrimp and Grits for him in my kitchen the next morning. Mr. Claiborne, who is a champion of southern foods, especially grits, later published this and several other recipes from my book in the New York Times, and the craze was on. Now we serve over 10,000 plates of Shrimp and Grits a year at Crook's Corner. Here is the "real" recipe.

1 recipe (6 servings) basic boiled grits	**Peanut oil**
3/4 cup grated sharp Cheddar cheese	**2 cups sliced mushrooms**
Tabasco sauce	**1 cup finely sliced scallions**
Freshly grated nutmeg	**1 large garlic clove, peeled**
White pepper	**4 teaspoons lemon juice**
1 pound fresh shrimp	**Tabasco sauce**
6 slices bacon	**2 tablespoons fresh, chopped parsley**
	Salt and pepper

Recommended equipment: A 10-inch skillet, garlic press.

Prepare the grits according to the recipe using the full amount of cheese. Season to taste, but lightly, with Tabasco, a very little nutmeg, and white pepper. Hold in a warm place or in the top of a double boiler over simmering water.

Peel the shrimp, rinse, and pat dry.

Dice the bacon and sauté lightly in the skillet. The edges of the bacon should brown, but the bacon should not become crisp.

Add enough peanut oil to the bacon fat in the skillet to make a layer of fat about 1/8-inch deep. When quite hot, add the shrimp in an even layer. Turn the shrimp as they start to color, add the mushrooms, and sauté about 4 minutes. Turn occasionally and add the scallions. Add the garlic through the press and stir around. Then season with lemon juice, a dash or two of Tabasco, and parsley. Add salt and pepper to taste.

Divide the grits among four plates. Spoon the shrimp over and serve immediately. Yields 4 servings.

Bill Neal's Southern Cooking

Vegetables

The Market House in Fayetteville, built as a produce market in 1838, is now headquarters of the Chamber of Commerce.

Pea and Asparagus Casserole

1 (17-ounce) can green
  peas, drained (I use
  Le Sueur brand)
1 (10-ounce) can asparagus
  tips, drained (I use Le
  Sueur brand)

3 hard boiled eggs, grated
1/2 pound sharp cheese,
  grated
1 can cream of mushroom
  soup, undiluted

In round or rectangular casserole, place a layer of peas and asparagus; then a layer of grated egg; then a layer of grated cheese. Repeat the process, placing a layer of peas and asparagus, layer of egg, layer of casserole. Spoon mushroom soup over top of whole casserole. Bake for 30 minutes at 350° or until bubbly. Remove from oven and sprinkle remaining grated cheese over top. Return to oven to melt.

Mama's Recipes

Asparagus Venetian

2 pounds fresh or
  2 (10-ounce) packages frozen
  asparagus (if fresh, cook
  and drain)
1/3 cup onion butter, melted
  (mix 1 envelope dried onion
  soup with 1 cup butter)

1 cup mozzarella cheese,
  diced
2 tablespoons Parmesan
  cheese, grated

Preheat oven to 450°. Arrange asparagus in 8-inch baking dish. Drizzle with onion butter, then sprinkle with both cheeses. Bake 10 minutes or until cheese is melted. Yield: 4-6 servings.

Nothing Could Be Finer

Asparagus Casserole

4 tablespoons margarine
4 tablespoons flour
2 cups milk
Salt and pepper
1 can asparagus, drained
1 can sliced water chestnuts

1 (4-ounce) jar pimento,
  chopped
1 small can mushrooms
4 hard-cooked eggs
Bread crumbs
3 tablespoons margarine

Mix a thick white sauce of the first four ingredients. Alternate vegetables and eggs in a casserole dish with the white sauce. Sprinkle top with bread crumbs and dot with margarine. Bake at 325° for 30 to 40 minutes.

Jarrett House Potpourri

 Within the Cape Hatteras National Seashore is the Pea Island National Wildlife Refuge. The area is the winter home to Greater Snow Geese and dozens of other species of birds. Its 5,880 acres are closed to all hunting.

Creamed Jerusalem Artichokes

2 cups Jerusalem artichokes	1 teaspoon winter savory
2 tablespoons margarine or vegetable oil	1 - 2 teaspoons lovage or celery leaves, chopped
1 onion, chopped	1/8 - 1/4 teaspoon salt
2 garlic cloves, pressed	

Slice artichokes about 1/4-inch thin and boil in water until fork tender, about 7-10 minutes. Melt margarine in a skillet and add onion and garlic. Sauté until light brown. Add the savory, lovage and salt. Stir and remove from heat. Drain artichokes and add to onion mixture. Preheat oven to 325°.

CREAM SAUCE:

1 cup milk	1 cup grated mozzarella cheese*
1/4 cup flour	
1 tablespoon butter or margarine	

Stir milk and flour together. In a small pot, melt the butter and add the milk/flour mixture. Stir constantly until the sauce thickens. Remove from heat and add sauce and cheese to the artichokes. Stir until mixed, and spoon into a greased casserole dish. Bake at 350° for about 20 minutes or until the cheese melts. Serves 4-5.

   *Try using 1/2 cup soy mozzarella and 1/2 cup mozzarella.

Vegetarian Masterpieces

Broccoli-Onion Deluxe

1 pound fresh broccoli or 2
  (10-ounce) packages frozen
  broccoli
2 cups frozen small whole
  onions or 2 medium onions,
  quartered
4 tablespoons butter
2 tablespoons all-purpose
  flour

1 cup milk
1/4 teaspoon salt
Dash of pepper
1 (3-ounce) package cream
  cheese
2 ounces sharp Cheddar
  cheese, shredded (1/2 cup)
1 cup soft bread crumbs

Cook broccoli. Drain. Cook onions. Drain. In saucepan, melt 2 tablespoons butter; blend in flour, salt, and dash of pepper. Add milk; cook and stir until thick and bubbly. Reduce heat; blend in cream cheese until smooth.

Place vegetables in a 1 1/2-quart casserole. Pour sauce over and mix lightly. Top with cheese. Melt 2 tablespoons butter, toss with crumbs. Bake casserole about 30 minutes at 350°, then sprinkle crumbs around edge and continue baking uncovered until heated (about 20 minutes more). Serves 6.

Knollwood's Cooking

Snow-Capped Broccoli Spears

2 (10-ounce) packages frozen
  broccoli spears
1 tablespoon butter or
  margarine, melted
2 egg whites

1/4 teaspoon salt
1/2 cup mayonnaise or salad
  dressing
Parmesan cheese, grated

Preheat oven to 350°. Cook broccoli according to package directions and drain well. Arrange stem ends toward center of an oven proof platter or 9-inch pie plate. Brush with butter. In a small bowl, beat egg whites and salt until stiff peaks form. Gently fold in mayonnaise. Spoon mixture in center of broccoli and sprinkle with Parmesan cheese. Bake at 350° for 12-15 minutes. Yield: 6 servings.

Market to Market

Broccoli Casserole

1 package frozen chopped
  broccoli
1/2 can mushroom soup
Dash of red pepper
1/2 cup sharp cheese, grated

1 egg, beaten
1 tablespoon grated onion
1/2 cup mayonnaise
1/2 cup cheese crackers
1 tablespoon melted butter

Cook broccoli for 10 minutes; drain. Mix with other ingredients, except cheese crackers and butter. Pour into casserole and top with crumbled crackers mixed with butter. Bake at 300° until bubbly.

Have Fun Cooking With Me

Blender Carrot Ring "Quickie"

Crumble 1 slice of bread in blender. Set aside.

2 1/2 cups diced, cooked
  carrots
3 eggs
1 slice of onion
4 sprigs parsley

1 tablespoon melted butter
1 teaspoon salt
1/4 teaspoon pepper
1 tablespoon brown sugar

Place in blender container. Blend until carrots are finely cut. Fold in bread crumbs and turn into a buttered 8-inch mold. Set in shallow pan of water and bake in moderately hot oven, 375° for 30 minutes or until firm. Unmold and fill with creamed peas. Serves 6.

High Hampton Hospitality

 Stalactites and stalagmites along an underground river are lighted, and accessible by marked passageways at the Linville Caverns.

Zesty Cheezy Cauliflower
(Microwave)

1 medium head cauliflower
2 tablespoons water
1/4 cup sour cream
1/4 cup mayonnaise

2 teaspoons spicy mustard
1 cup shredded Cheddar
    cheese

Break cauliflower up into flowerettes. Put in 2-quart round casserole dish. Add 2 tablespoons water. Cover. Microcook on High 6-8 minutes or until almost tender. Let stand. Drain.

Mix sour cream, mayonnaise and mustard. Toss gently with cauliflower. Sprinkle with cheese. Microcook on Medium (50%) 2-4 minutes. Serve. Serves 4-6.

Note: Cauliflower can be cooked whole. Add 1 or 2 tablespoons of water and microcook, covered, on High 8-10 minutes. Let stand. The above mixture can be spread over the whole cauliflower.

The Microwave Touch

Cheese and Almond Cauliflower

1 small head cauliflower,
    cut into florets
2 tablespoons butter
2 tablespoons flour
1 cup milk
3/4 cup grated sharp Cheddar
    cheese

1/2 cup blanched almonds,
    lightly toasted
Salt and freshly ground
    pepper to taste
Butter

Steam or boil cauliflower florets until crisp-tender. While cauliflower is cooking, melt butter in a small saucepan over low heat. Add flour, stirring constantly until smooth. Blend in milk and continue stirring until sauce thickens. Add cheese, stirring until melted. Remove sauce from heat.

Preheat oven to 200°. Drain cooked cauliflower and place in a deep casserole dish. Pour cheese sauce over it and top with almonds. Sprinkle salt and freshly ground pepper over all. Dot with butter. Stir several times. Bake for 30 minutes. Yield: 4 servings.

Even More Special

Great Corn on the Cob

6 ears fresh or frozen sweet
  corn
1 tablespoon parsley flakes
1/2 teaspoon garlic powder
1 teaspoon oregano

Salt to taste
Pepper to taste
1/4 cup butter
Parmesan cheese

Add corn to boiling water and cook 15 minutes. Remove from water and place in rectangular dish. Sprinkle with spices and add butter. Sprinkle corn with Parmesan cheese. Cover dish with foil and place in warm oven until ready to serve. Serves 6.

Note: Remember when salting corn that Parmesan cheese is also salty.

A Dash of Down East

Corn Soufflé

1 1/2 tablespoons butter
1/4 cup flour
2 cups milk
1 tablespoon chopped green
  pepper

1 cup scalded green corn
1 cup grated cheese
1 teaspoon prepared mustard
2 egg yolks
3 egg whites

Melt butter and add flour, blending well. Add milk slowly and cook over low heat, stirring constantly, until mixture thickens. Add green pepper which has been sautéed in butter. Stir in corn, grated cheese, mustard, and egg yolks. Fold in stiffly beaten egg whites. Place in buttered soufflé dish and set dish in pan of water. Bake 30-40 minutes in 350° oven. Serve immediately. Serves 4-6.

Favorite Recipes of the Lower Cape Fear

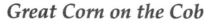 Gold City is a reconstructed mining village in Franklin which includes a restored miner's cabin, a mile-high chair lift, and a four-state view from its overlook. There are precious and semi-precious stones still mined near Franklin, and many gem and craft shops in the area.

Lima Bean and Corn Casserole Supreme

1 1/2 cups milk	1/4 cup Parmesan cheese
1/2 cup butter	1 small onion, chopped
1/2 teaspoon salt	1/4 cup pimento, chopped
1/4 teaspoon pepper	2 cups whole kernel corn
1/4 cup flour	1/2 cup bread crumbs
2 cups cooked limas	1 tablespoon melted butter

Make white sauce using the first 5 ingredients. Cook 3 minutes after it thickens. Add remaining ingredients, and top with bread crumbs mixed with the melted butter. Bake at 350° for 30 minutes.

Mama's Recipes

Collards

7 quarts water	1/4 pound country ham fat or
4 tablespoons salt	fat back
1/4 pound streak-of-lean	6 pounds collards
salt pork	10 small, new, red potatoes

Put water, salt and salt pork in large cooking pot (10-12-quart size). Bring to boil and cook 1 - 1 1/2 hours. Fry-out ham fat and add to pot; reserve cracklings.

Prepare collards for cooking by stripping the large leaves from the main collard stalk. Reserve the buds to add during the last increment of cooking. Wash leaves thoroughly and add to pot of prepared boiling water. After all leaves are in pot, turn heat down to medium and cook until collards begin to get tender. Cooking time may vary for summer collards (3 hours) to winter collards (1 1/2-2 hours. Add reserved collard buds and potatoes; continue cooking for 1/2 hour.

Add small cornmeal dumplings on top of collards, cooking for an additional 15 minutes.

CORNBREAD DUMPLINGS:

2 cups plain corn meal	1 teaspoon salt
1/2 cup plain flour	Warm water

Mix dry ingredients. Add enough warm water to reach a consistency that is easy to handle and pat into a dumpling. Place in pot last 10-12 minutes of cooking time. Yield: 6-8 dumplings.

Island Born and Bred

Eggplant and Tomato Casserole

1/4 cup salad oil
1 medium onion, chopped
Optional: 3/4 pound
  mushrooms, sliced
1/2 medium green pepper,
  chopped
1 medium eggplant, peeled
  and cut into 1-inch cubes

1 (1-pound) can tomatoes
1 teaspoon salt
1 tablespoon parsley
Pinch of basil and oregano
1 cup each, grated Parmesan
  and shredded mozzarella
  cheeses
2 eggs, beaten

Sauté onion in oil in large frying pan; add mushrooms and green pepper and sauté until limp. Stir in eggplant, tomatoes, salt, parsley, basil and oregano. Cover and simmer until eggplant is tender, stirring often. Uncover and reduce liquid if necessary. Combine cheeses with eggs. Spoon half of eggplant mixture in a 2 1/2-quart casserole and top with half of cheese mixture. Repeat. Bake uncovered at 350° for 25 minutes.

Mountain Elegance

Green Beans and Zucchini Bundles

1 1/2 pounds green beans,
  stringed
2 zucchini squash, two
  inches in diameter
1/2 cup vegetable oil

1/4 cup white wine vinegar
2 tablespoons Dijon mustard
2 tablespoons honey
2 cloves garlic, minced
2 teaspoons fresh basil

Cook beans in salted water until crisp tender, about 7 minutes. Cool beans in ice water and drain. Set aside. Cut zucchini into eight 1 1/2-inch slices. Carve out the centers so that you have rings with 1/4-inch rims.

Steam zucchini rings for 2-3 minutes until crisp tender. Immerse rings in ice water and drain well. Poke 8-12 beans through each zucchini ring. Arrange bundles in a 13x9-inch casserole dish.

Combine the remaining ingredients in a blender and pour over the beans. Cover and refrigerate for 24 hours. Makes 8 servings.

Stirring Performances

Boiled Butter Beans—Lima Beans

Butter beans and lima beans are cooked in the same manner. The lima bean is larger and more mealy. They may be seasoned with butter, ham, or salt meat.

**2 cups fresh butter beans,
  or lima beans
4 cups water
1 teaspoon salt
1 teaspoon sugar
2 tablespoons butter, or
  piece of boiling meat about
  2 inches square, 1-inch
  thick**

**1/2 cup milk or cream
  (optional)
Pepper to taste**

Wash and pick over the beans; cover with water in a saucepan with lid. Add salt and sugar. Boil for about 10 minutes, then add the butter; or if meat is to be used, add the meat. Boil slowly until beans are tender, about 45 minutes to 1 hour. If pan becomes too dry, add a little warm water. There should be a little broth left with the beans. If desired, just before serving, add the milk or cream and season to taste with pepper; reheat. Serves 4-6.

Marion Brown's Southern Cook Book

Bootleg Beans

**3 strips bacon, diced
1 small onion, chopped
1 (16-ounce) can pork and
  beans**

**1 tablespoon brown sugar
2 tablespoons vinegar
2 tablespoons catsup**

Fry bacon until half cooked; add onion. When onion is lightly browned, pour off excess fat. Add pork and beans, brown sugar, vinegar and catsup. Stir well and cover. Let simmer for 30-45 minutes, or bake slowly at 300° for 2 hours. Yield: 4 servings.

Note: Add hot dogs last 10 minutes, if desired. Great for picnics or barbecues.

Heart of the Mountains

Spanish Onion Quiche
(A no-egg quiche)

CRUST:

1 1/4 cups unsifted flour	3 - 4 tablespoons ice water
1/2 teaspoon salt	
1/2 cup (1 stick) Fleischmann's corn oil margarine	

Combine flour and 1/2 teaspoon salt in a bowl. Cut in 1/2 cup margarine with pastry blender or two knives until mixture resembles coarse meal. Stir in ice water; mix lightly. Form dough into ball.

On lightly floured board, roll out dough to fit a 13x9x2-inch pan. Transfer to pan; trim edge. Carefully line pastry with aluminum foil; add dried beans to weigh down.

Bake at 400° 10 minutes. Remove foil and beans; set pastry aside. Reduce over to 375°.

1 1/2 cups chopped onion	2 cups skim milk
3 tablespoons Fleischmann's corn oil margarine	1 teaspoon salt
2 (10-ounce) packages frozen chopped spinach, cooked and drained	1/4 teaspoon white pepper
	1/8 teaspoon ground nutmeg
2 cups Egg Beaters Cholesterol-free Egg Substitute	

Sauté onion in remaining 3 tablespoons margarine until transparent but not browned. Stir in spinach. Spread spinach-onion mixture on bottom of prepared pastry.

Combine Egg Beaters, skim milk, remaining 1 teaspoon salt, pepper and nutmeg; pour over spinach mixture.

Bake at 375° 30 minutes, or until knife inserted in center comes out clean. Let stand for 10 minutes before serving. Makes 12 servings.

What Is It? What Do I Do With It?

Herbed Onions

Leaves from 3 sprigs of
  fresh thyme or 1/2 teaspoon
  dried thyme

1/4 cup butter
2 large Vidalia onions,
  thinly sliced

Sauté thyme in butter in skillet for 5 minutes. Add onions. Cook, covered, for 15 minutes or until tender. Serve with meats. Yield: 4 servings.

Approx. Per Serving: Calories 231; Protein 1.2g; Carbohydrates 6.0g; T Fat 23.2g; Cholesterol 62.1mg; Potassium 133.0mg; Sodium 195.0mg.

Goodness Grows in North Carolina

Gourmet Potatoes

2 cups shredded Cheddar
  cheese
1/2 cup butter
1 1/2 cups sour cream at
  room temperature
1/2 cup chopped green onions

1 teaspoon salt
1/2 teaspoon pepper
8 medium potatoes, peeled,
  coarsely shredded
2 tablespoons butter

Heat cheese and 1/2 cup butter in saucepan over low heat until partially melted, stirring occasionally; remove from heat. Stir in sour cream, green onions, salt and pepper. Fold in potatoes. Spoon into greased 8-inch glass baking dish. Dot with 2 tablespoons butter. Bake at 350° for 25 minutes or microwave, covered, on High for 12 minutes. Yield: 8 servings.

Approx. Per Serving: Calories 480; Protein 11.7g; Carbohydrates 36.2g; T Fat 33.0g; Cholesterol 87.7mg; Potassium 722.0mg; Sodium 594.0mg.

Goodness Grows in North Carolina

Snowy Mashed Potatoes

12 medium potatoes
1 (8-ounce) package cream
  cheese
1 (8-ounce) carton sour cream
2 teaspoons salt

1/8 teaspoon pepper
Garlic salt
1/4 cup chives
1/2 teaspoon paprika
1 tablespoon butter

Preheat oven to 350°. Cook potatoes until tender; drain, and beat with electric mixer. Add cream cheese, sour cream, salt, pepper, garlic salt, and chives; beat until light. Pour into a 9x13x2-inch casserole; sprinkle with paprika and dot with butter. Bake at 350° for 30 minutes. Yield: 12 servings.

Note: May add 1 tablespoon beef bouillon granules, 3 tablespoons grated cheese and additional cheeses on top.

Market to Market

Potato-Onion Fans

1 medium baking potato	1 tablespoon butter
1 small onion, sliced	1 tablespoon sour cream
Salt and pepper to taste	1 teaspoon chopped chives

Scrub the potato, but do not peel. Cut into 1/4-inch slices, being careful not to cut all the way through; the potato should open out rather like a fan. Place a slice of onion between each potato slice. Don't push too hard, or you will break the potato. Preheat the oven to 400°.

Sprinkle the potato with salt and pepper and dot with butter, a little on each cut. Wrap loosely in heavy-duty foil. Bake for 1 hour or until done.

Open the foil carefully. Remove the potato to a serving plate, add the sour cream and chives, and serve at once. Makes 1 serving.

Love Yourself Cookbook

Baked Potato Sauce

1 cup Hellman's mayonnaise	1/4 cup butter, softened
1/2 cup grated Parmesan cheese	1/2 teaspoon hot pepper sauce
1/4 cup grated onion	

Combine all ingredients. This mixture will keep indefinitely under refrigeration. Yield: 2 cups.

Note: A great alternative to sour cream.

A Dash of Down East

 More than 100 factory and discount stores offer reduced prices in the Burlington outlet area.

Clawson's Emporium's Original Dirigible

1 (1-pound) potato
1 tablespoon butter
1 tablespoon chopped onion
1 tablespoon chopped green
  pepper
1/8 cup diced ham
1/8 cup diced turkey
1/8 cup shredded provolone
  cheese

1/8 cup shredded Cheddar
  cheese
1/4 cup sour cream
Pinch of chives
2 slices cooked bacon,
  crumbled

Bake potato at 400° for 1 hour or until done. Split open and rake with fork. Work in butter, onion, and pepper; work in diced ham, turkey, and cheeses. Close potato and heat until cheese melts. Remove and top with sour cream, chives, and bacon.

For a seafood Dirigible, substitute cooked, minced crab and shrimp for ham and turkey. Serves 1.

North Carolina's Historic Restaurants

Seasoned Potato Slices
(Microwave)

2 baking potatoes (1 1/4
  pounds)
1/4 cup margarine
1/2 teaspoon seasoned salt

1 tablespoon parsley
1 small onion, sliced
  in rings
1 tablespoon Parmesan cheese

Scrub potatoes and slice 1/4-inch thick slices. Melt margarine in 2-quart casserole on Medium High (70%) 1 minute. Stir in seasoned salt and parsley. Add potatoes and stir gently to coat. Put onion rings on top. Cover. Microcook on High 9-11 minutes, stirring after 5 minutes. Potatoes should be almost tender when you remove them from oven. Let stand 5 minutes. Sprinkle with cheese. Serves 4.

The Microwave Touch

Sweet Potato Cups

4 to 6 medium size sweet
  potatoes
1 stick butter
1 can (about 14-ounces)
  crushed pineapple

3 eggs, beaten
1/2 cup dark rum
1/2 cup chopped walnuts
1 cup miniature marshmallows
Orange shells

Boil unpeeled potatoes until soft; drain, peel and mash. To hot potatoes, add butter, undrained pineapple, eggs, rum, nuts and marshmallows. Blend well. Mound into 6-8 orange shells. This can be done ahead of time. Heat in a 325° oven for 30 minutes or until heated through. Makes 6-8 servings.

Korner's Folly Cookbook

Grated Potato Pudding

1/2 cup butter (or butter
  and lard)
1 1/2 cups sugar
2 eggs, well beaten

3 cups grated sweet potatoes
1 1/2 cups milk
1/2 teaspoon salt
Pinch allspice

Cream butter and sugar. Add eggs. Gradually add potatoes and milk. Add water, salt, and spice. Bake at 350° about 1 hour until crusty. May be made ahead and reheated.

Queen Anne's Table

Porgie's Squash

3 cups grated squash (yellow
  crookneck or zucchini)
1 small onion, grated or
  chopped
1/2 cup oil

1/2 teaspoon oregano
1 cup Bisquick
4 eggs, lightly beaten
4 ounces Parmesan cheese

Grease small 8x8-inch casserole. Blend all ingredients. Pour into casserole dish and bake at 325° for 40-45 minutes. Should there be any leftover, slice in finger-sized pieces and freeze. Makes a great quick hors d'oeuvre—pop in hot oven, heat quickly and serve. Also good served as a light vegetable lunch accompanied by a crisp green salad and rolls. Serves 4-6.

Ship to Shore I

Spinach-Stuffed Squash

8 yellow, crooked-neck
  squash
Salt, pepper, butter
1 small onion, chopped
1/2 cup butter or margarine
3 (10-ounce) packages frozen
  chopped spinach, cooked
  and drained

1 (8-ounce) package cream
  cheese
Salt and pepper
Herb stuffing mix
Butter to dot

Split squash and boil or steam for about 10 minutes or until tender. Scoop out seeds. Sprinkle with salt, pepper and butter. Sauté onion in butter until tender. Add spinach, cream cheese, salt and pepper to taste. Fill each squash with spinach mixture. Sprinkle each with herb stuffing mix and dot with butter. Bake for 15-20 minutes at 350° until thoroughly hot. Yield: 16 servings.

Nothing Could Be Finer

 Visit with zebras, elephants, lions and other animals at the 1,300-acre first natural habitat zoo in the country at Asheboro.

Zucchini Deluxe

6 large zucchini
1 cup fresh bread crumbs
1/4 cup onion, chopped
1 tomato, chopped
1/2 teaspoon salt
1/4 teaspoon pepper

2 tablespoons margarine
  melted
1/2 pound Cheddar cheese,
  grated
1/4 cup milk

Wash and trim ends of zucchini. Cook, covered, in boiling salted water for 5-8 minutes. Drain. Cut in half lengthwise. Scoop out center of each. Chop up and combine with bread crumbs, onion, tomato, seasonings, and margarine. Toss lightly. Fill shells and place in dish. Heat cheese and milk in saucepan over low heat, stirring until sauce is smooth. Pour sauce over stuffed zucchini. Bake in 350° oven for 25-30 minutes. Serves 6-12.

In Good Taste

Spinach and Mushroom Quiche

1 (10-ounce) box frozen
  chopped spinach
4 tablespoons butter
2 teaspoons lemon juice
2 cloves minced garlic
1/2 cup light cream
1 cup heavy cream
4 eggs

1 tablespoon salt
1 teaspoon pepper
4 ounces Swiss cheese,
  grated
1 (2 1/2-ounce) can mushroom
  pieces, drained
1 (10-inch) pastry shell,
  partially baked

Preheat oven to 375°. Thaw and drain spinach. Sauté the spinach in the butter. Add lemon juice and garlic. Make a batter by beating creams, eggs, salt and pepper together. Add cheese and mix well.

To assemble, line partially baked pie shell with mushrooms and spinach. Pour batter over all and bake for 25-30 minutes.

Serves 6.

Bravo

Anita's Spinach Quiche

PIE CRUST: (10-INCH)

1 cup flour

1/8 teaspoon salt

Scant 1/3 cup vegetable oil
  (4 1/2 tablespoons)

2 1/2 tablespoons milk

Preheat oven to 400°. Place the flour and salt in a medium bowl and add the oil and milk. Stir with a fork until just mixed. Roll out the dough between two sheets of waxed paper until you have a 10-inch in diameter circle. Place the crust into a 9 1/2 x 1-inch deep quiche dish and bake in a preheated oven for 5-10 minutes at 400°. Remove and place on a rack.

SPINACH LAYER:

2 tablespoons margarine or
  vegetable oil

1 large onion, finely
  chopped

2 - 3 garlic cloves, minced

1 teaspoon crumbled sage
  leaves

1 teaspoon thyme

20 ounces fresh spinach,
  chopped (or 20 ounces
  frozen chopped spinach,
  thawed and drained)

While the crust is prebaking, melt margarine in a frying pan. Add onion and sauté until clear. Add garlic, sage and thyme to the pan. When the onion and garlic are brown, add spinach and salt, stir well and remove from heat.

CHEESE LAYER:

1 cup grated gruyère cheese

1 tablespoon primary yeast

Mix the gruyère with the primary yeast.

CREAM SAUCE:

2 tablespoons butter or
  margarine

2 tablespoons flour mixed in
  1 - 1 1/2 cups milk

Over medium heat, melt margarine in a small saucepan. When melted add the milk/flour mixture and stir constantly until thickened. Remove pan from heat. Preheat oven to 375°.

Place half spinach mixture into crust; top with half cream sauce, then half cheese and yeast. Repeat layers. Put quiche into a 375° oven and bake 20 minutes. Remove from oven and let sit 5 minutes, then slice and serve. Serves 4-6.

Vegetarian Masterpieces

Spinach Lasagne

1/2 pound fresh spinach	1 teaspoon basil
1/2 onion, chopped	1/2 teaspoon oregano
1 garlic clove, minced	2 tablespoons parsley,
1 tablespoon olive oil	chopped
1 cup low-fat cottage cheese	1/2 pound lasagne noodles
1 egg, beaten	1/2 pound mozzarella cheese
Salt and pepper to taste	3 cups tomato sauce

Wash spinach carefully, tearing out stems, and chop coarsely. Sauté chopped onion and minced garlic in oil. Combine sautéed onion and garlic with spinach, cottage cheese, and beaten egg. Mix well. Season with salt, pepper, basil, oregano and parsley.

Cook lasagne noodles until tender. Coarsely grate mozzarella cheese. In a buttered oblong baking dish, layer noodles, cottage cheese mixture, mozzarella cheese, and tomato sauce, in order listed. Repeat layering three times, making sure tomato sauce is on top. Cover with aluminum foil. Bake at 350° for 40 minutes. Remove foil and bake 10 minutes more. Serve with garlic bread and green salad. Serves 4.

In Good Taste

Spinach Soufflé

2 packages chopped frozen	1 pint sour cream
spinach	1 cup Pepperidge Farm crumbs
1 package Lipton's dry onion	3 tablespoons melted butter
soup	

Boil spinach, drain well. Reserve juice and use as needed to keep dish from becoming too dry. Mix sour cream and onion soup together and let stand 1/2 hour. Then add to spinach with 3/4 of bread crumbs (mixed with melted butter). Bake in a greased dish at 275° for 30 minutes or until hot. Add rest of soaked crumbs sprinkled on top. Makes 6 servings.

Centenary Cookbook

Broccoli-Stuffed Tomatoes

6 medium tomatoes
Salt and pepper
1 bunch fresh broccoli
1 cup grated Swiss cheese
1 cup fresh bread crumbs
1/2 cup mayonnaise

2 tablespoons minced onion
2 tablespoons freshly grated
  Parmesan cheese
Green onion fans for
  garnish, optional

Wash tomatoes, cut off tops and scoop out pulp, leaving shells intact. Sprinkle cavities of tomatoes with salt and pepper, and invert on wire rack to drain 30 minutes.

Preheat oven to 350°. Remove tough stems from broccoli. Blanch florets in boiling water until crisp-tender (3-4 minutes). Drain and chop coarsely. Combine broccoli, Swiss cheese, bread crumbs, mayonnaise, and minced onion; mix well.

Stuff tomato shells with broccoli mixture; sprinkle with Parmesan cheese. (May be prepared ahead to this point and refrigerated.)

Place tomatoes in ovenproof dish and bake 30 minutes. Serve with green onion fans, if desired. Yield: 6 servings.

Hint: Substitute Monterey Jack or Dilled Havarti for Swiss cheese.

Even More Special

Fried Green Tomatoes

1/3 cup flour
1/3 cup cornmeal
1 teaspoon cornstarch
3/4 - 1 cup milk

Salt and pepper to taste
2 - 3 large green tomatoes
Vegetable oil to fry
  tomatoes

Mix flour, cornmeal, cornstarch, milk, salt and pepper in a medium bowl. Batter should be fairly thick. Slice tomatoes into 1/4 - 1/3-inch thick slices. Fry in oil on medium to medium-high heat until golden brown on both sides. Serves 3 as a side dish.

Vegetarian Masterpieces

Scalloped Tomatoes

2 cups thinly sliced onion
2 tablespoons margarine
1 (20-ounce) can tomatoes
3 slices toasted bread, cubed

1/4 teaspoon pepper
1/2 teaspoon celery salt
2 tablespoons brown sugar
1 cup shredded Cheddar cheese

Sauté onions in margarine until transparent; remove from pan and drain. Combine tomatoes with bread cubes and add seasonings, sugar and onions. Pour into buttered casserole. Top with cheese and bake uncovered at 350° for 1 hour. Yield: 6 servings.

Heart of the Mountains

Provençal Pie

2/3 cup bread crumbs,
  divided
1/4 cup freshly grated
  Parmesan cheese
3 or 4 medium tomatoes
1 medium onion, thinly
  sliced
1/2 cup grated mild Cheddar
  cheese

2 eggs
1/2 teaspoon salt
1/4 teaspoon dried oregano
Pepper to taste
3 strips bacon, partially
  cooked

Preheat oven to 350°. Put 1/3 cup bread crumbs in bottom of a 9-inch pie pan. Mix Parmesan cheese with remaining crumbs. Layer half the tomatoes, onion, and Cheddar cheese in pie pan atop crumbs. Repeat for second layer. Beat eggs with salt, oregano, and pepper; pour over layers. Sprinkle with rest of bread crumbs-Parmesan mixture. Top with 3 strips bacon. Bake 30 minutes. Yield: 6 servings.

Even More Special

Garden Vegetable Medley
(Microwave)

1 small cauliflower	1 - 2 tablespoons diced red
1 large bunch broccoli	pepper
1 crookneck squash, cut	1/2 cup butter
into 1/4-inch rounds	Garlic salt
1 zucchini, cut into	Seasoned pepper
1/4-inch rounds	

Break cauliflower into flowerets; cut flowerets in half. Slice flowerets from broccoli, leaving 2 inches of stem. Arrange broccoli in circle around edge of 12-inch round platter with flowerets resting on rim. Arrange cauliflower in inner circle. Arrange squash, then zucchini, in circle in center. Place red pepper in center. Place butter in 1 cup measuring cup and cook on High for 45 seconds. Pour melted butter over vegetables. Sprinkle with garlic salt and seasoned pepper. Cover with plastic wrap and cook on High 7-8 minutes or until crisp but tender. Let stand, covered, 3 minutes. Yield: 4-6 servings.

Heart of the Mountains

Lahanika Plaki
(Baked Vegetables)

6 potatoes, thinly sliced	1/2 cup each vegetable and
1 (10-ounce) package frozen	olive oil
cut green beans, thawed	1/2 cup water
3 yellow squash, thinly	2 tablespoons chopped fresh
sliced	parsley
1 (8-ounce) can tomato sauce	Salt and pepper to taste

Arrange the potatoes, beans, and squash in a 13x9-inch baking pan. Combine tomato sauce, oil and water; pour over the vegetables. Sprinkle with parsley, salt and pepper. Cover with aluminum foil; bake at 350° about 1 1/2 hours. Remove foil the last 30 minutes. Serve warm. Serves 8-10.

The Grecian Plate

Bicycle Wreck

3 tablespoons olive oil
1 garlic clove, minced
1 medium onion, chopped
1 green pepper, chopped
1 medium carrot, sliced
2 medium zucchini, sliced
1 1/2 cups bulgur wheat

1 (16-ounce) can stewed
  tomatoes
1/2 cup water
1 teaspoon paprika
1/8 teaspoon cayenne pepper
1/2 teaspoon salt
1 pound tofu, cut up

Sauté vegetables in oil. After 3 minutes, add bulgur and cook until it crackles. Add tomatoes, water, and seasonings. Cover and cook for 25 minutes over low heat. Add more water if necessary. Stir in tofu just before serving. Serves 4.

In Good Taste

Company Rice

1 cup regular rice,
  uncooked
1 cup onion,
  chopped
1/2 cup butter or
  margarine, melted
1/2 cup seedless
  raisins

1 (4-ounce) can sliced
  mushrooms, drained
2 (10 1/2-ounce)
  cans consommé
1/2 cup peanuts,
  chopped
1/2 cup celery,
  chopped

Lightly brown rice and onion in butter. Combine rice mixture, raisins, mushrooms, consommé, peanuts, and celery; mix well. Pour into a 2-quart casserole. Bake uncovered at 350° for 50-60 minutes or until rice is done. Serves 8-10.

Out Of Our League

Green Rice Casserole

3 cups cooked rice
3 eggs (well beaten)
1 1/2 cups chopped parsley
1 small clove garlic
  (mashed)
3 tablespoons melted butter

3 tablespoons grated Swiss
  cheese
2/3 cup milk
Salt and pepper to taste
1/2 cup sliced stuffed olives
1 medium onion, chopped

Combine and pour into greased 1 1/2 or 2-quart casserole. Bake at 350° for 35-40 minutes or until top browns . Serves 4-6.

Mountain Potpourri

Brazilian Rice

3 cups boiled rice
1/4 cup butter or margarine
4 eggs, beaten
1 pound grated sharp Cheddar
  cheese
1 cup milk
1 (10-ounce) package frozen
  chopped spinach, cooked and
  drained

1 tablespoon chopped onion
1 tablespoon Worcestershire
  sauce
2 teaspoons salt
1/2 teaspoon marjoram, thyme
  and rosemary

Prepare boiled rice. Melt butter and add eggs, cheese, milk and spinach. Add onion, Worcestershire sauce, salt and seasonings to sauce. Mix sauce well and stir in rice. Pour into a 2-quart baking dish and bake in pan of water at 350° for 35 minutes. Serves 8-12.

A Cookbook of Pinehurst Courses

Rice Pilaf

PLAIN PILAF:
1 cup uncooked rice
4 tablespoons butter
1 large onion, sliced

2 cups bouillon (beef or
  chicken)

Brown sliced onions in butter. Add rice. Cook in butter and onion mixture over low heat for 4-5 minutes, stirring often. Rice will be lightly colored. Heat liquid bouillon to boiling point and pour over rice. Cover dish or pan tightly and bake in 350° oven for 25-30 minutes or until liquid is absorbed. Yield: 8 servings.

Variations:
    1. Add 1 (6-ounce) can of mushrooms.
    2. Add sliced green peppers.
    3. Add chopped onions.
Note: I always add mushrooms to my rice pilaf!

Nothing Could Be Finer

Pasta Primavera

1/4 cup butter
1 small onion, chopped
1 clove garlic, minced
3 ounces cauliflower, in
  pieces
1/2 carrot, sliced
1/2 zucchini, sliced
1/2 pound fresh asparagus,
  cut in 1/4-inch pieces
1/4 pound fresh mushrooms,
  sliced

1/2 cup heavy cream
1/4 cup chicken stock
1 teaspoon dried basil
Salt and pepper to taste
1/2 cup frozen peas, thawed
2 scallions, thinly sliced
12 ounces vermicelli or
  linguine, cooked al dente
Freshly grated Parmesan
  cheese

In large skillet, melt butter and sauté onion and garlic. Add cauliflower and carrot; cook 3 minutes. Add zucchini, asparagus, and mushrooms to skillet and cook 2 minutes more. Add cream, stock, and seasonings, and cook until liquid is slightly reduced. Add peas and scallions and cook briefly. Serve sauce over cooked and drained noodles. Sprinkle with lots of fresh Parmesan cheese. Yield: 4 servings.

Even More Special

Apple and Cheese Casserole

1/2 cup all-purpose flour
1/2 cup sugar
1/4 teaspoon salt
1/4 cup butter
7 apples, peeled, sliced

6 tablespoons water
1 tablespoon lemon juice
1 cup shredded sharp Cheddar
  cheese

Mix flour, sugar and salt in small bowl. Cut in butter until crumbly. Toss apples with water and lemon juice in bowl. Spoon into greased 8-inch baking dish. Sprinkle with flour mixture. Bake at 350° for 35 minutes. Sprinkle with cheese. Bake for 5 minutes longer. Yield: 8 servings.

Approx. Per Serving: Calories 255; Protein 4.6g; Carbohydrates 37.1g; T Fat 10.9g; Cholesterol 30.4mg; Potassium 165.0mg; Sodium 204.0mg.

Goodness Grows in North Carolina

Samosas

Samosas are the spicy vegetable pastries sold everywhere on the streets in India.

PASTRY:

1/2 pound plain flour	4 tablespoons vegetable oil
1/2 teaspoon salt	4 tablespoons water

To make pastry, sift flour and salt. Dribble the oil and rub onto mixture until it resembles bread crumbs. Slowly add water. Make a stiff ball of dough and knead for 5 minutes until smooth. Put aside in refrigerator.

FILLING:

1 onion, finely chopped	1 pound potatoes, cooked and diced
1 (6-ounce) package frozen peas	
1 small piece of ginger, finely grated	1 teaspoon ground coriander seed
1 hot chili or local pepper, finely chopped	1 teaspoon ground cumin
	1/4 teaspoon cayenne pepper
3 tablespoons cilantro or parsley	2 tablespoons lemon juice
	Oil for deep frying

Make filling by frying chopped onion in a little hot oil until brown. Add peas, ginger, hot pepper, cilantro, and add a little water if it looks as though it is drying out. Simmer until peas are cooked. Then add cooked potatoes, coriander, cumin, cayenne, and lemon juice. Stir to mix and heat through for 3-4 minutes. Roll out pastry into 3-inch rounds. I use a wine glass as a cutter. Lay a teaspoon of filling in each circle, fold in half and seal with water. Flute the edge with a fork. Deep fry in hot oil until golden brown. Serve warm with mango chutney. Serves 8.

Try to find cilantro, a wonderful pungent herb. If you cannot, use parsley.

Sip to Shore

Sarah's Apple-Pepper Relish

6 green bell peppers	6 medium onions
6 red bell peppers	1/2 cup salt
6 apples (don't peel)	

Take core out of peppers and apples. Grind peppers, apples and onions coarsely in meat grinder and add 1/2 cup salt. Soak overnight in 2 or 3 gallons of water.

Next morning: Drain well.

SYRUP:

4 cups vinegar	1 tablespoon mustard seed
6 cups sugar	1 tablespoon celery seed

Bring syrup to boil. Add drained apple-pepper-onion-mixture to syrup and cook 30-40 minutes. Pack in hot jars and seal.

Note: Most any apple will do, but red delicious are wonderful in it.

Mama's Recipes

Bread and Butter Pickles

1 gallon cucumbers	5 cups sugar
(medium-sized)	1 1/2 teaspoons tumeric
8 small white onions	1/2 teaspoon ground cloves
1 green pepper	2 tablespoons mustard seed
1 red pepper	2 teaspoons celery seed
1/2 cup salt	5 cups vinegar
Cracked ice	

Slice cucumbers crosswise. Add sliced onions and pepper cut into strips. Add salt; cover with ice and mix thoroughly. Let stand 3 hours; drain. Combine remaining ingredients and pour over cucumber mixture. Bring to boiling; seal in 8 sterilized pint jars. (This is a recipe for people who do not make pickles. They can be done in odd moments on a busy day and they are always just perfect.)

Centenary Cookbook

Meats

Popularly known as the "Three Presidents" statue, this bronze sculpture on
Capitol Square at Raleigh honors native sons, Andrew Jackson (seventh),
James Knox Polk (eleventh), and Andrew Johnson (seventeenth).

Lobster-Stuffed Tenderloin of Beef

1 (3 to 4-pound) whole beef
  tenderloin
2 (4-ounce) frozen lobster
  tails
1 tablespoon butter or
  margarine, melted

1 1/2 teaspoons lemon juice
6 slices bacon, partially
  cooked

Preheat oven to 425°. Cut beef tenderloin lengthwise to within 1/2 inch of bottom to butterfly.

Place frozen lobster tails in boiling salted water to cover. Return to boiling. Reduce heat and simmer 5-6 minutes. Carefully remove lobster from shells. Cut in half lengthwise. Place lobster, end to end, inside beef. Combine the 1 tablespoon melted butter or margarine and lemon juice. Drizzle on lobster. Close meat around lobster. Tie roast together securely with string at intervals of 1 inch. Place on rack in shallow roasting pan. Roast in 425° oven for 45-50 minutes for rare doneness. Lay bacon slices on top. Roast 5 minutes more.

WINE SAUCE:
1/2 cup sliced green onions
1/2 cup butter or margarine

1/2 cup dry white wine
1/8 teaspoon garlic salt

Meanwhile, prepare wine sauce. In saucepan, cook green onions in the remaining butter over very low heat until tender, stirring frequently. Add wine and garlic salt and heat through, stirring frequently. To serve, slice roast, and spoon on wine sauce. Garnish platter with fluted whole mushrooms and watercress or parsley, if desired. Serves: 8-10.

Bravo

 The first Patriot victory of the American Revolution was fought at the battle of Moores Creek Bridge on February 27, 1776.

Prime Rib Roast

A prime rib roast (or what Granny used to call a standing rib) should be started in a hot oven at 450° for 20-30 minutes. This browns the outside and keeps the inside juicy. Then turn the oven down to 350° and continue roasting for about 20 minutes per pound for a medium doneness.

Note: Because this cut of meat has become outrageously expensive, it doesn't pay to take chances. Always use a meat thermometer to help determine how well the meat is cooked.

YORKSHIRE PUDDING:

1 cup flour
2/3 cup milk
1/3 cup water

2 eggs, beaten
1/2 teaspoon salt

After the rib roast is done, take enough drippings and a little fat from the bottom of the roasting pan and pour enough of them into a 9x5x3-inch loaf pan to cover the bottom.

While you mix the above ingredients to form a batter, preheat the pan containing the drippings at 450°. The secret of a high, fluffy pudding is that the batter must be poured into a very hot preheated pan.

After you have poured the batter into the preheated pan, quickly put it back into the oven and bake at 450° for 15-20 minutes. Yield: 4-6 servings.

I Remember

Marinated Beef Tenderloin

1 cup catsup
2 teaspoons prepared mustard
1/2 teaspoon Worcestershire
  sauce
1 1/2 cups water

2 envelopes Italian salad
  dressing mix
1 (6-pound) beef tenderloin,
  trimmed

Combine catsup, mustard, Worcestershire sauce, water and salad dressing mix in bowl; mix well. Pierce beef in several places. Combine with marinade in heavy duty sealable plastic bag; seal. Marinate in refrigerator for 8 hours, turning occasionally. Drain, reserving marinade.

Place beef on rack in baking pan; insert meat thermometer. Bake at 425° for 30-45 minutes or to 140° on meat thermometer for rare, 150° for medium-rare or 160° for medium, basting occasionally with reserved marinade. Place on serving plate. Garnish with watercress and grapes. Serve with remaining marinade. Yield: 12 servings.

Approx. Per Serving: Calories 420; Protein 45.5g; Carbohydrates 5.8g; T Fat 22.5g; Cholesterol 144.0mg; Potassium 527.0mg; Sodium 326.0mg.
(Nutritional information includes entire amount of marinade).

Goodness Grows in North Carolina

Drip Beef

3 (5-pound) chuck roasts,
   trim fat, or use rump or
   sirloin tip
2 cloves garlic, minced
1 1/2 teaspoons oregano

3/4 teaspoon rosemary
2 1/4 teaspoons Lawry's
   seasoned salt
3 cubes beef bouillon

Combine all ingredients in a large roaster, almost covering beef with water. Bake at 300° for 5 hours. Cool, tear apart with fork until literally shredded. Serve on plate with a heated hard roll and a small bowl of the broth for each person. Instruct guests to break bite-size pieces of bread on plate with fork. Or, place shredded beef on/in the roll for each person and instruct them to dip bread into broth.

Pass the Plate

Stuffed Eye of Round Roast

Eye of round roast,
   approximately 5 pounds
1 cup red wine
1 cup water
2 bunches of green onions,
   finely chopped
4 fresh tomatoes, finely
   chopped

1 cup ripe olives, finely
   chopped
2 green peppers, finely
   chopped
3 teaspoons salt
2 tablespoons wine vinegar
1 stick margarine

Simmer roast in wine and water for 3-4 hours, covered, until tender. Mix together onions, tomatoes, olives and peppers with salt and vinegar; cover and refrigerate. When roast is tender, cut in 3/4 to 1-inch slices while hot. Place on foil and spoon chopped vegetables between slices. Melt margarine and pour over meat. Wrap tightly in foil and let stand for 1 hour. Place in warm oven to reheat, if necessary, before removing foil. Serves 8-10.

A Cook's Tour of the Azalea Coast

Deerpark's Veal a la Cardinale

3 veal cutlets	3 slices Prosciutto ham
2 eggs	3 slices mozzarella cheese
Bread crumbs	2 cups sliced mushrooms
4 tablespoons oil	1 teaspoon chopped fresh
4 tablespoons butter	basil or parsley

Pound veal to less than 1/4-inch thick. Dip veal into beaten eggs, then into bread crumbs. Sauté in butter until golden brown on each side. Remove to baking dish. On each piece of veal, place 1 slice ham and 1 slice cheese. Bake at 400° until cheese melts. Meanwhile, in same frying pan used for veal, sauté mushrooms with herbs. Put mushrooms over veal. Serve with wild rice. Serves 3.

North Carolina's Historic Restaurants

Noodles and Veal in Wine Sauce

1/2 pound egg noodles	1/2 cup dry red wine
1/2 pound thin veal slices	1 tablespoon lemon juice
Seasoned salt and pepper to	Dash of oregano
taste	Dash of basil
1 tablespoon oil	1/4 cup grated Parmesan
3 tablespoons butter	cheese
1/2 small onion, chopped	
4 - 6 mushrooms, chopped or	
sliced	

Cook the noodles according to package directions, drain, and keep hot. Meanwhile, sprinkle the veal with seasoned salt and pepper. Heat the oil and 1 tablespoon butter in a skillet. Sauté the veal on both sides until golden brown. Drain on paper towels.

Add the onion to the skillet, along with the mushrooms. Cook, stirring, for 3 minutes. Stir in the wine, lemon juice, oregano, and basil. Return the veal to the pan and simmer 3 minutes, turning the veal once.

Toss the hot noodles with the remaining 2 tablespoons butter and the Parmesan cheese. Turn onto a serving platter. Top with the veal and sauce. Serve at once. Makes 2 servings.

Love Yourself Cookbook

Stuffed Round Steak

4 slices bacon, diced	3 - 3 1/2 pounds thin round
1 onion, chopped	steak, cut into 6's
2 cups toasted bread crumbs	1/2 teaspoon salt
2 1/2 tablespoons minced	1/4 teaspoon pepper
parsley	1 cup bouillon
1/2 teaspoon celery salt	1 - 2 (8-ounce) cans tomato
1/2 teaspoon sage	sauce

To make stuffing: Sauté bacon with onion; mix in bread crumbs; add parsley, celery salt, and sage. Sprinkle steak with salt and pepper. Spread each portion of steak with dressing and roll up. Hold together with toothpicks. Place in a large skillet; pour bouillon over; cover and simmer 1 hour. Pour on tomato sauce; recover and simmer another 45 minutes or until done. If gravy is thin, uncover and cook until it thickens. Serves 6.

Mushrooms, Turnip Greens & Pickled Eggs

La Strata

1 (10-ounce) package frozen
  chopped spinach, cooked and
  well-drained
1 pound ground beef
1/2 cup onion, minced
1 (8-ounce) can tomato sauce
1 teaspoon basil
1 teaspoon parsley, chopped
1/4 teaspoon oregano

Dash garlic salt
Dash pepper
1 (4-ounce) can mushrooms,
  drained
1 (8-ounce) container
  cottage cheese
4 ounces mozzarella cheese,
  shredded

Preheat oven to 375°. Cook spinach as directed on package. In medium skillet, sauté ground meat and onion until onion is tender and meat is browned. Add tomato sauce, basil, parsley, oregano, garlic salt, pepper and mushrooms. Combine spinach and cottage cheese. In 8-inch square casserole, arrange in layers the spinach mixture, meat mixture, then mozzarella cheese. Repeat layering ending with cheese. Bake 15-20 minutes or until hot and bubbly. Yield: 4 servings.

Pass the Plate

Grandfather Mountain near Linville, dated as one of the oldest mountains on earth, is named for its bearded face looking toward the sky. It features a mile-high swinging bridge connecting two peaks, and hang gliding exhibitions daily, weather permitting.

Quick Beef Skillet

1/2 pound boneless beef,
  sliced thin
3 tablespoons flour
Salt and pepper to taste
2 tablespoons shortening
1 small onion, chopped
1 garlic clove, minced

1/4 cup dry red wine
  (optional)
3/4 cup beef broth
1 (4-ounce) can mushroom
  stems and pieces, undrained
2 hot baked potatoes

Pound the beef with a mallet to tenderize it. Cut it into 1-inch strips. Combine the flour with salt and pepper, then dredge the meat in the seasoned flour. Brown the meat in hot shortening. Add the onion and garlic. Cook 3 minutes, stirring often. Add the wine, broth, and mushrooms with their liquid. Cover, reduce the heat, and simmer 20-30 minutes, or until the meat is tender. There should be about 1/4 cup of liquid left in the pan.

Split the potatoes and fluff with a fork. Spoon the beef mixture over the potatoes. Serve at once. Makes 2 servings.

Love Yourself Cookbook

Calf's Liver and Apples

This is a German recipe and very, very excellent!

2 pounds calf's liver
1/2 cup bread crumbs
1 teaspoon white pepper
1/2 pound butter
2 1/2 cups thinly sliced
  onions

3 apples, peeled and sliced
  1/2-inch thick
4 tablespoons sugar

Rinse liver; cut into pencil-thin 2-inch pieces and dry on paper towels. Toss the meat with a mixture of bread crumbs, salt and pepper. Melt 3 tablespoons butter in a skillet and sauté the liver 3 minutes until just browned. Remove and keep warm. Now sauté the onions until brown. In another pan, sauté the apples until golden, sprinkling with sugar. Arrange the apples and onions over the liver. Serves 6.

Mushrooms, Turnip Greens & Pickled Eggs

Liver Pudding

Liver pudding is a dish that one has to be born to. What I mean is that it never appears on restaurant menus, nor is it likely to be served outside the family. Some might say it is too low a dish, too much an economy item to be served to a guest when one can afford more elegant fare, but I suspect it is just too good to waste on anyone who might fail to appreciate its gusto. Sliced and browned, it is too often accompanied by tomato catsup these days, a further mask of its charms. Golden sautéed onions and a slice of lemon will elevate this simple loaf into another realm. Its commercial counterpart runs heavily to cereal and water; this recipe yields a correspondent to the finest regional French charcuterie.

FOR THE PAN:

2 tablespoons lard	1/2 teaspoon dried thyme
1/2 teaspoon whole black peppercorns	1/2 teaspoon dried sage
	4 whole allspice corns
1 bay leaf	

Thoroughly grease the interior of a loaf pan with the lard, being sure that all surfaces are coated. Crack all the herbs and spices together in a mortar and pestle until the bay is pulverized. Coat the greased sides and bottom of the loaf pan with the flavorings.

FOR THE PUDDING:

1 3/4 pounds pork or calf's liver, trimmed of all gristle and veins, and cut into 1-inch cubes	1/2 cup cornmeal
	3/4 teaspoon whole black peppercorns
	3/4 teaspoon dried sage
4 ounces fresh pork fat, finely chopped	1/2 teaspoon dried thyme
2 cups chopped onion	1/4 - 1/2 teaspoon dried red pepper flakes
2 eggs	1/2 teaspoon freshly grated nutmeg
1/2 cup hot cooking liquid from the liver or chicken or beef stock	1 1/2 teaspoons salt

The liver may be prepared in one of two ways, both of which are used throughout the South. Either precook the liver by covering it with cold water in a 4-quart saucepan, bringing it to a boil,

CONTINUED

CONTINUED

draining it and reserving 1/2 cup of the cooking liquid, or grind it raw. In both instances it must be thoroughly cleaned of all gristle and veins before proceeding to the next step.

Preheat oven to 375°. Add the liver (raw or cooked) to a bowl in which the pork fat, onion, and eggs are combined. Add the hot stock or cooking liquid to the cornmeal, stir well, and let cool before adding to the liver. Crack the peppercorns roughly in a mortar and pestle, adding them to the bowl along with the sage, thyme, red pepper flakes, nutmeg, and salt. Mix thoroughly and pass through a food grinder (using the fine blade) or a food processor. Pack into the loaf pan and cover tightly with aluminum foil. Set the loaf pan in the larger pan and add 1 inch of boiling water. Set on the middle level of the preheated oven and bake for about 1 hour if using precooked liver or about 1 3/4 hours if using raw liver. In either case, the center of the pudding will be set when done, the sides will pull away slightly, and a meat thermometer should read 165°.

Let cool at room temperature and turn out of the pan. Wrap well in plastic and refrigerate.

To serve: Slice 1/2-inch thick, dredge in flour seasoned with salt and freshly ground black pepper and fry in your preferred fat (bacon, butter, lard, or vegetable oil) until lightly crisp on both sides. Yields about 20 slices.

Bill Neal's Southern Cooking

Liver Dumplings

3 pounds calf liver	**Flour**
2 - 3 onions	**Beef broth**
7 eggs	

Grind calf liver with onions. Add eggs and enough flour to make mixture stick together when shaped into balls and cooked in beef broth. Make test balls to determine proper amount of flour.

Drop balls into rich beef stock and cook until done. Serve in soup bowls with broth.

North Carolina and Old Salem Cookery

Salisbury Steaks
(Microwave)

A family favorite.

1 pound lean ground beef	1/8 teaspoon garlic powder
1/2 cup soft bread crumbs	1 teaspoon Worcestershire
1/4 cup chopped onion	sauce
1/2 teaspoon salt	1 egg

Combine all meat ingredients in bowl. Divide into 4 portions and form into 4 oval patties. Place in 2-quart casserole. Cover with lid. Microcook on Medium High (70%) for 6 minutes. Drain liquid and turn steaks over.

SAUCE:

1 (10 1/2-ounce) can beef	1 tablespoon Worcestershire
bouillon	sauce
2 tablespoons flour	1 (2-ounce) can sliced
1/4 cup catsup	mushrooms, drained
1/4 teaspoon basil	

Add bouillon slowly to flour, stirring until smooth. Add catsup, basil, Worcestershire sauce and mushrooms. Pour over steaks. Cover. Microcook on Medium High (70%) for 6-8 minutes. Stir. Let stand covered 3-5 minutes. Serve with rice or mashed potatoes. Serves 4.

    Note: This recipe freezes well.

The Microwave Touch

Hamburger-Potato Bake

2 pounds ground chuck
2 eggs, beaten
2 cups bread crumbs

2 tablespoons catsup
4 teaspoons salt
4 teaspoons pepper

Combine meat, eggs, bread crumbs, catsup, salt and pepper. Mix well, adding more crumbs if needed to make mixture firm. Put in an ungreased oblong glass baking dish and bake at 350° for 20 to 30 minutes or until brown.

TOPPING:
8 medium potatoes
1 carton sour cream
1 stick butter or margarine
3 ounces cream cheese

Garlic salt to taste
Salt and pepper to taste
8 ounces grated sharp
   Cheddar cheese

Cook potatoes until done. Mash, adding sour cream, butter, cream cheese, garlic salt, salt and pepper. Whip. Spread over meat mixture. Sprinkle with Cheddar cheese. Return to oven and bake until cheese melts and is slightly browned.

Jarrett House Potpourri

Hobo Stew

1 cup thinly sliced onion
1 cup green pepper, coarsely
   chopped
1/4 cup olive oil
1 pound ground beef
1 (1-pound) can red kidney
   beans, drained
1 (1-pound) can whole kernel
   corn, drained

1 (32-ounce) can Italian
   style tomatoes
2 (8-ounce) cans tomato
   sauce
1 tablespoon steak sauce
Dried basil, dry mustard,
   salt and pepper to taste

Cook onion and green pepper in oil in large skillet until golden brown. Add beef and cook, stirring. Add rest of ingredients and mix well. Cover and simmer 15 to 20 minutes. Serves 8 - 10.

Jarrett House Potpourri

Chamber's Meat Loaf

1 1/2 pounds ground beef
3/4 cup quick Quaker Oats
1 - 1 1/2 teaspoons salt
1/4 teaspoon pepper
1/4 cup onion or 1
  tablespoon minced onion
1 egg, well-beaten

3/4 cup milk
1 tablespoon Worcestershire
  sauce
1/2 teaspoon Accent
2 tablespoons ketchup
2 tablespoons margarine

Mix all ingredients together and place in loaf pan. Mix topping and put on meat loaf. Bake at 350° for 1 hour.

TOPPING:
1/3 cup ketchup
1 tablespoon mustard

2 tablespoons brown sugar

Mama's Recipes

Cornbread Meat Loaf

1 pound ground beef
1/2 pound sausage
1 egg
1 cup cornbread crumbs
1 chopped onion
1 1/2 teaspoons salt

1/4 teaspoon pepper
1 cup tomato sauce
1 cup water
2 tablespoons vinegar
2 tablespoons mustard
2 tablespoons brown sugar

Mix ground beef, sausage, egg, cornbread crumbs, onion, salt, pepper and 1/2 cup tomato sauce. Mold into mound and put in greased baking dish. Combine water, vinegar, 1/2 cup tomato sauce, mustard and brown sugar. Pour over meat loaf. Bake in 325° oven for about 45 minutes. Baste several times while baking. Yields 6 servings.

Recipes From Our Front Porch

Swiss Meat Loaf

2 pounds ground chuck
1 1/2 cups grated Swiss
  cheese
2 beaten eggs
1 medium grated onion
  (sautéed in little butter)
1/2 cup chopped green pepper

1 1/2 teaspoons salt
1/2 teaspoon pepper
1 teaspoon celery salt
2 1/2 cups milk
1 cup dry bread crumbs
1/2 teaspoon paprika

Mix all together. Press into large, greased loaf pan. Bake, uncovered, in 350° oven, approximately 1 hour.

High Hampton Hospitality

Best Italian Meatballs

3/4 pound ground beef
1/4 pound ground pork
1/3 cup dried bread crumbs,
  finely rolled
4 tablespoons Parmesan
  cheese
3 eggs
3 sprigs fresh parsley,
  minced

1 teaspoon salt or to taste
1 teaspoon pepper
1 clove minced garlic
3 tablespoons chopped canned
  tomatoes
Salad oil

Place meat in bowl; add all remaining ingredients except salad oil and mix thoroughly. Shape into balls; brown lightly in a small amount of salad oil in a heavy skillet. Add to spaghetti sauce and do not stir for first 20 minutes after adding. Serves 6.

What Is It? What Do I Do With It?

The Guilford Courthouse National Military Park (Greensboro) is the site of the first battleground area in the nation to be preserved as a national military park.

Divine Casserole

1 (16-ounce) package small
  egg noodles
2 (10-ounce) packages frozen
  spinach
2 pounds ground chuck
2 (6-ounce) cans tomato
  paste
2 teaspoons Worcestershire
Few drops Tabasco
Salt to taste
1/2 teaspoon oregano leaves

1 (12-ounce) carton creamed
  cottage cheese
1 (8-ounce) package cream
  cheese, softened
1 (8-ounce) carton sour
  cream
2 onions, chopped
2 sticks butter, melted
1 cup sharp Cheddar cheese,
  grated

Boil noodles by package directions; drain and rinse under hot water. Cook spinach according to package directions and drain. Brown meat and drain. Add tomato paste, Worcestershire, Tabasco, salt and oregano to meat. Mix well. Mix cottage cheese, cream cheese, sour cream and onions. Grease 2 (2-quart) casseroles. Layer ingredients in casserole in following order: noodles, butter, cheese mixture, spinach, noodles, butter and meat layer on top. Sprinkle 1/2 cup grated cheese on each casserole. Bake at 350° for 40 minutes or until bubbly. Freezes well. Serves 10-12.

Christmas Favorites

Mexican Casserole

1/4 cup onion, chopped
1/2 pound ground beef
2 tablespoons vegetable oil
1/2 pound kidney beans,
  drained
1 can mild enchilada sauce

8 ounces tomato sauce
1 1/2 cups sour cream or
  plain yogurt
2 cups Cheddar cheese,
  grated
10 ounces tortilla chips

Brown onion and beef in oil, then drain. Add beans and sauces. Place in a 2-quart casserole dish. Bake in 375° oven uncovered 1/2 hour. Cover top with sour cream, sprinkle with cheese and place chips around edge. Return casserole to the oven until cheese melts. Serves 4.

In Good Taste

Eggplant Parmigiana Barbara

This recipe may be altered for a meatless meal by eliminating ground beef and doubling or tripling the amount of mozzarella.

2 tablespoons butter or margarine	**1/4 teaspoon pepper**
1/2 cup onion, chopped	**1/2 cup water**
1 clove garlic, minced	**1 tablespoon brown sugar**
1 pound ground beef	**1 large eggplant**
1 (16-ounce) can tomatoes	**2 eggs, beaten slightly**
1 (6-ounce) can tomato paste	**1/2 cup dry bread crumbs**
2 teaspoons dried oregano	**1/4 cup salad oil**
1 teaspoon basil	**1 1/4 cups Parmesan cheese**
1 1/2 teaspoons salt	**6 - 8 ounces mozzarella, shredded**

In large skillet sauté onion, garlic and ground beef in butter until meat is no longer red. Add tomatoes, tomato paste, oregano, basil, salt and pepper. Stir well. Add 1/2 cup water and brown sugar. Bring all ingredients in skillet to a boil. Simmer uncovered 20 minutes.

Heat oven to 350°. Spray baking dish with non-stick product. Peel eggplant and cut into 1/2-inch slices. Combine eggs and 1 tablespoon water; mix well. Dip eggplant in egg; coat well. Dip in crumb mixture and coat well. Sauté eggplant in oil until brown and arrange in bottom of baking dish; sprinkle with half Parmesan; top with half of mozzarella cheese and cover with half of tomato sauce. Repeat. Bake uncovered 20 minutes. Arrange mozzarella cheese over top and bake 20 minutes longer or until mozzarella is melted and slightly brown. Yield: 6 servings.

Pass the Plate

Chili
(Microwave)

1 pound lean ground beef
1/2 cup chopped onion
1/2 cup chopped green pepper
1/4 cup chopped celery
1 (15-ounce) can pinto,
  chili, or kidney beans
1 (16-ounce) can stewed
  tomatoes
1 (6-ounce) can tomato paste

1 teaspoon beef bouillon
  granules, dissolved in 3/4
  cup water
1 tablespoon chili powder
1/2 teaspoon ground cumin
  (optional)
1/2 teaspoon salt
1 small bay leaf

Crumble meat and arrange in a circle around outside edge of 4-quart cooker. Spoon onion, green pepper and celery into the center. Cover. Microcook on High 5-7 minutes or until meat is brown. Drain.

Add remaining ingredients. Cover. Microcook on High 5 minutes. Stir. Cover. Reduce to Medium (50%) and microcook 25-30 minutes. Let stand. Serves 4.

The Microwave Touch

Spiro's Chili for Hot Dogs

In the 1930's a Greek named Spiro Carello came to the Village, and following an old Greek custom, he opened a café almost on the square. This was in the era of the "blue plate special," a lunch of meat, vegetables, dessert and beverage but "no substitutions" for 25 cents.

For some 40 years, with the help of his wife, he served plate lunches, hot dogs and hamburgers, and provided a setting for early morning gatherings of the men who discussed the issues of the day over coffee before beginning their day's work. Spiro made chili for the hot dogs which were the best in the world.

1 medium onion, chopped	1 tablespoon Worcestershire
1 pound ground beef	sauce
1/4 pound good pork sausage	1 teaspoon chili powder or
1 (6-ounce) can tomato sauce	more to taste

Cook onion, beef and sausage together in a heavy skillet, stirring, until lightly browned. Add remaining ingredients and simmer for about 15 minutes. The mixture is quite thick. For a thinner mixture, add a little water.

Korner's Folly Cookbook

Frankfurter-Bean-Cornmeal Casserole

1 pound hot dogs	1 teaspoon salt
2 (1-pound) cans baked beans	1 1/2 teaspoons baking powder
1/2 cup catsup	2/3 cup corn meal
1/2 cup water	1 egg, slightly beaten
1 tablespoon prepared	2/3 cup milk
mustard	1/4 cup melted shortening
3/4 cup flour	1/3 cup chopped onions
1 tablespoon sugar	

Cut hot dogs into 1/2-inch pieces. Put in baking dish (12x8) with beans, catsup, water and mustard. Combine flour, sugar, salt and baking powder in large bowl. Stir in corn meal. Add egg and rest of ingredients. Stir just enough to combine. Spread evenly over beans. Bake at 400° for 35 to 40 minutes. Makes 8 to 10 servings.

Jarrett House Potpourri

Kosher Corned Beef

This beef may be served as a "boiled dinner," for sandwiches, hash, etc.

1 (5-pound) kosher brisket of corned beef	6 cloves garlic, sliced (less if desired)
1/4 cup vinegar	Vegetables for the dinner:
Cold water	whole potatoes, peeled;
1 teaspoon each of thyme, rosemary, caraway seeds, salt, and pepper	cabbage, quartered; carrots, scraped; whole onions, peeled
1 tablespoon dill seeds	

In a large kettle place the beef, vinegar, and enough cold water to well cover the brisket. Bring to a boil and scoop off the foam. Add all the seasonings; reduce heat to simmer. Simmer beef for 3 1/2 hours. Remove beef from liquid.

If beef is to be served as a boiled dinner dish, place the beef in a baking dish and pour over it 1 cup of the liquid it was boiled in. Set aside. Meanwhile prepare the vegetables. Allow 1 potato, 1 carrot, 1 onion, and 1/8 head cabbage per person. Boil in the liquid until potatoes, onions, and carrots are tender. Boil the cabbage only 20 minutes. One-half hour before serving time, put the beef in a 350° oven and bake for 1/2 hour. Serve it hot, sliced, with the hot vegetables. Serves 10-12 for dinner.

If beef is to be served for sandwiches, remove it from liquid and chill thoroughly. With a sharp knife, slice across the grain into paper thin slices.

Marion Brown's Southern Cook Book

Corned Beef Hash

Kosher Corned Beef (see
previous recipe)
8 medium potatoes, peeled,
diced

3 medium o
Bacon dripp
Poached egg

Prepare the corned beef as directed in recipe. Slice beef very thin, allowing several slices for each person. In a large frying pan, fry the potatoes and onions in bacon fat until vegetables are tender. Place the slices of corned beef on top of vegetables. Simmer on low heat until thoroughly heated. Stir meat and vegetables together. Serve hot; top each serving with a soft poached egg (or an easy-over fried egg). Serves 6-8.

Marion Brown's Southern Cook Book

Unsandwich Reuben Casserole

1 (12-ounce) can corned beef
1 (16-ounce) can sauerkraut,
drained
2 cups Swiss cheese,
shredded
1/2 cup Thousand Island
dressing

1 large tomato, sliced
1 cup pumpernickel bread
crumbs
2 tablespoons butter
Salt and pepper
2 tablespoons caraway seeds

Layer each ingredient in a 2-quart casserole in order given. Bake at 350° for 30 minutes. Let set 5 minutes before serving.

A Cookbook of Pinehurst Courses

The World Golf Hall of Fame is in the charming village of Pinehurst, known for its lush green golf courses, with over two dozen of them in a 20-mile radius.

Shredded Barbeque Beef
Makes terrific leftovers!

1 (3-pound) chuck roast
1 large onion, chopped
1 stalk celery, cut into
   pieces
1 large green pepper, chopped
2 cloves garlic, minced
1 1/2 quarts water
1 teaspoon salt
1 small bottle catsup
2 tablespoons brown sugar

2 tablespoons vinegar
1/2 teaspoon chili powder
2 - 3 drops hot sauce
1 teaspoon Worcestershire
1 bay leaf
1/4 teaspoon garlic salt
1/4 teaspoon paprika
1 teaspoon allspice
1 teaspoon dry mustard

Place roast and vegetables in a large pot and add water. Cook covered for 4 hours. Remove meat. Cool and shred. Return meat to top of stove with 1 1/2 cups of broth from cooking pot. Add remaining ingredients. Slowly boil uncovered for 1 hour. Add additional broth if needed. Serve on party rolls from a chafing dish. Serves: 12 - 15.

Bravo

Fresh Brisket

1 (4 - 5-pound) brisket
2 (5-ounce) bottle liquid
   smoke
Onion salt

Celery salt
Garlic salt
1/2 (2 3/4-ounce) bottle
   Worcestershire sauce

Place brisket in baking dish. Pour liquid smoke over meat. Sprinkle with onion salt, celery salt and garlic salt. Cover and refrigerate overnight. Discard marinade. Pour one-half bottle Worcestershire sauce over meat, fat side up in baking pan. Cover tightly with foil and bake 5 hours at 275° degrees.

BARBECUE SAUCE:

1 (46-ounce) can tomato
   juice
1 medium onion, grated
1 (8-ounce) can tomato sauce
2 tablespoons brown sugar
1 teaspoon dry mustard

1 (20-ounce) bottle catsup
2 tablespoons Worcestershire
   sauce
2 teaspoons lemon juice
2 teaspoons chili powder

CONTINUED

CONTINUED

Combine ingredients of barbecue sauce and simmer slowly until desired thickness. Uncover meat and pour half of barbecue sauce over and bake uncovered for 1 hour longer. Baste occasionally. Freeze remaining sauce. Brisket also freezes well.

Knollwood's Cooking

Barbequed Country Style Pork Ribs

5 pounds country-style pork
  ribs
2 tablespoons butter
1/2 cup chopped onions
1 tablespoon paprika
1/2 teaspoon pepper

4 tablespoons sugar
1 teaspoon prepared mustard
2 teaspoons Tabasco sauce
1/4 cup catsup
3 tablespoons vinegar

Melt butter, add chopped onions and cook until clear. Add rest of ingredients and simmer 5 minutes. Pour over ribs and bake at 350° for 1 hour. Test for doneness. Sauce is also good to make barbeque chicken.

Jarrett House Potpourri

Barbecue Pig, Scotland Neck Style

Scotland Neck in Halifax County, North Carolina, is famous for superior Southern Barbecue. This authentic recipe is for "pit cooked" barbecue, cooked over oak coals.

1 (65-pound) pig   A bit of lard
1 1/2 quarts vinegar   A bit of salt
Red pepper pods

PREPARATION:
Dig a hole or pit sufficiently large so that when the pig is placed over it there well be a 4-5-inch margin at both ends and at one side; the other side should have a margin of at least 20 inches so that coals can be easily placed under the pig when cooking. The depth of the spit should be such that the pig will be 8-10 inches from the coals when cooking. Put 3-4 iron rods across the pit to put pig on. Since coals (only) are used in cooking, a fire will have to be built in a separate location. This should be on an elevated wire grating with a 2 to 3-inch mesh so that the coals cannot drop through. Hardwoods, preferably oak, make the best coals.

Select a pig which will weigh approximately 65 pounds when dressed. Cut off head and slit down entire length of belly. Open up so that pig will lie flat.

SAUCE:
A sauce for mopping (basting), while cooking, is made by using 1 1/2 quarts of vinegar seasoned to taste with red pepper pods. A simple mop can be made by tying a rag around the end of a stick.

COOKING:
Place the pig on the iron rods across pit with the skin up, and it stays in this position until it is nearly finished cooking. Put a thin layer of live coals in the pit under the entire surface of the pig, and replenish coals from time to time. Cook slowly—it should take from 6-7 hours. Mop the skin side with the sauce 3 or 4 times while cooking. In this position the pig should cook practically done and to a beautiful brown on the under side. However, be careful not to put the coals under it too fast or too freely as it will burn. When it is determined that it is done, rub the skin side with a thin coat-

CONTINUED

CONTINUED

ing of lard and turn the pig over so that the skin side will be over the coals. Let stay long enough for the skin to become brown and crisp. While skin is browning, add some salt to the vinegar sauce and mop freely the cooked side. This is for the purpose of seasoning.

When the cooking process is completed, take the pig off and allow to cool only long enough to be handled. Cut up into small pieces with a knife; *do not* run it through meat chopper. When it is cut up, put it into a large container and season it to taste using the same sauce as for the cooking, but with salt added. The seasoning should be worked into meat thoroughly.

This should be served with cole slaw and real corn bread. Serves 40-50.

Marion Brown's Southern Cook Book

Streak-o-Lean

We buy the best of streak-o-lean, or fatback, or salt pork, or whatever you call it in your part of the country. It is sliced very thin and placed in sugar water the night before we serve the next day. Small amount of sugar—approximately 1 teaspoon to 2 quarts of water. The morning of serving, the streak-o-lean is drained well, dipped in a small amount of flour, and fried very slowly in hot peanut oil that barely covers the meat. The streak-o-lean is fried until golden crisp. It has been called: Georgia Chicken, Sawmill Chicken, Tennessee Chicken, Bryson City T-Bone, Country Bacon, or you may call it something else; but when served with country gravy, it surely is popular!

COUNTRY GRAVY:

1/2 cup grease from streak-o-lean	2 tablespoons flour
	1 1/2 - 2 cups milk

Pour off all but about 1/2 cup grease. Stir in 2 tablespoons of flour and stir constantly until brown. Slowly add about 1 1/2 to 2 cups milk to flour mixture and stir constantly until thick as desired. We do not add salt because grease will be pretty salty—you may add if you want. Yields about 2 cups.

Recipes From Our Front Porch

Oven-baked Spareribs

For most of the South, barbecue means pork, and it is a centuries-old tradition.

4 pounds pork
  spareribs
3 quarts water
1/2 cup Barbecue Sauce
  (see below)

1/2 cup water
More sauce for basting
Salt and pepper

Put the spareribs in a 6-quart pot, cover with cold water, and bring to a boil. Drain and remove to a large bowl.

Pour the barbecue sauce over all sides of the ribs. Pour 1/2 cup water in the bottom of an 11x15-inch baking dish and put the ribs on top. Let sit 30 minutes.

Preheat the oven to 300°. Roast the ribs until very tender and brown—about 2 hours—basting occasionally. Use more sauce if desired. Season with salt and pepper upon serving. Pass extra sauce with the ribs. Yields 4 servings.

Bill Neal's Southern Cooking

North Carolina Barbecue Sauce

In North Carolina the most traditional barbecue sauce is a straightforward mix of vinegar and red pepper. To my taste, it is a classic, hardly interfering with the smoky roast and just setting it off. Ketchup and mustard sauces make a thick, sticky coating. The vinegar sauce gives the roast a crisp coat and cuts the fat.

1 cup apple cider
  vinegar
1/2 - 3/4 cup water
2/3 cup minced
  onion
1 garlic clove, crushed
1/2 teaspoon salt
1 teaspoon ground black
  pepper

1 - 2 teaspoons red pepper
  flakes
1 teaspoon sugar
1 bay leaf
2/3 teaspoon thyme
3 tablespoons peanut oil
2 - 3 teaspoons dry mustard
4 - 6 teaspoons cold water

CONTINUED

CONTINUED

Combine all the ingredients except the last two in a small stainless steel or enamel saucepan. Bring to a rapid boil, then simmer five minutes. Remove from heat. Dissolve the mustard in the cold water, then thin it out with some of the hot vinegar sauce. Stir the mustard into the sauce. Let cool, bottle, and store in the refrigerator. Yields about 2 cups.

Bill Neal's Southern Cooking

Spicy Glazed Pork with Vegetables

2 thick pork cutlets or
  chops
1 tablespoon oil
2 tablespoons sugar
1/2 cup spicy brown mustard
2 tablespoons dry white wine
1 teaspoon powdered
  bouillon

1 1/2 teaspoons molasses
1/2 teaspoon celery salt
1/4 teaspoon crushed thyme
1 package frozen mixed
  vegetables, thawed

Preheat the oven to 350°. Brown the pork in oil. Arrange the pieces in a single layer in a baking dish. Combine the sugar, mustard, wine, bouillon, molasses, celery salt, and thyme, mixing well. Spread a tablespoon of mixture on each chop. Cover and bake for 35 minutes.

Meanwhile, set aside 2 tablespoons of sauce. Combine half the package of vegetables with the remaining sauce and spoon over the partially cooked chops. (Store the rest for another dish, such as soup.)

Bake, uncovered, for an additional 10-15 minutes, or until the vegetables are done and the chops are tender. Garnish with dollops of the reserved sauce and serve at once. Makes 2 servings.

Love Yourself Cookbook

Baked Ham with Peach and Brandy Glaze

1 (10-pound) ready-to-eat
   (slightly smoked) ham,
   bone-in
Whole cloves
1/4 cup Dijon mustard

3/4 cup dark brown sugar
2 1/2 cups apple juice
1 cup peach preserves
1/4 cup brandy

Preheat oven to 350°. Peel the skin from the ham, leaving a collar around the shank bone. If necessary, trim the fat so that you have layer 1/4-inch thick. Score the fat in a diamond pattern, and stick whole cloves everywhere the lines criss-cross. Put the ham in a shallow baking pan. Pat the mustard all over the top and sides of the ham, coating it evenly, then cover with brown sugar. (You might just find it easier to do this with your fingers!) Pour the apple juice into the bottom of the pan and put the ham in the oven. Bake, basting frequently with pan juices, for 1 1/4 - 1 1/2 hours, depending on how dry you want your ham to be. Remove from oven and allow to stand until ham is cool enough to glaze (almost room temperature).

To prepare the glaze: spoon peach preserves into a saucepan, and bring to a boil. Add brandy, stir to blend, and cook about 3 minutes. Spoon or brush glaze all over the top and sides of the ham. Let the glaze set a little before you carve and serve with some sweet, hot mustard, or Dijon, on the side.

What's New in Wedding Food

Best Baked Ham Ever

1 (10-15-pound) semi-
 boneless, fully cooked
 ham
2 cups sugar
1 cup cider vinegar
1 stick cinnamon
12 whole cloves

6 allspice berries
Additional cloves to stud
 ham
White pepper to taste
1 1/2 cups brown sugar
1 cup sherry

Preheat oven to 350°. Wash ham and place in large roasting pan with lid. Add sugar, vinegar, cinnamon stick, cloves, and allspice berries. Fill pan with water, cover, and place in oven. Cook 15 minutes per pound, turning ham often. Remove from oven and cool.

Lower oven temperature to 250°. Remove top skin, but leave fat on ham. Place ham in washed and dried roasting pan and stud at intervals with cloves. Sprinkle liberally with white pepper and spread brown sugar all over. Pour sherry into pan and bake, uncovered, for 1 hour. After 30 minutes of cooking time, baste every 10 minutes with pan juices. Remove from oven and keep covered and warm until serving time. Makes 20 servings.

MUSTARD SAUCE:
2 teaspoons dry mustard
1/4 teaspoon salt
1 teaspoon sugar
2 tablespoons flour
3/4 cup water

2 tablespoons vinegar,
 warmed
2 egg yolks, beaten
2 tablespoons butter, melted

Combine mustard, salt, sugar, and flour. Place in top of double boiler. Add water and vinegar, stirring until smooth and creamy. Add egg yolks and butter, stirring until thickened. Do not boil or eggs will curdle. Can be prepared one day ahead and reheated to serve.

Stirring Performances

 Dublin Wine Cellars in Rose Hill produces more than 120,000 gallons of wine per season using America's first cultivated grape, the muscadine.

Souvlakia

Souvlakia are sold on street corners throughout Greece.

1 (3-pound) leg of lamb, boned

MARINADE SAUCE:

1 cup olive oil	**3 tablespoons minced parsley**
2 tablespoons lemon juice	**3 green peppers, quartered**
1 teaspoon salt	**1 large onion, quartered and**
1 teaspoon pepper	**separated into slices**
2 teaspoons dried oregano	**12 cherry tomatoes**
3 bay leaves	**Lemon juice (optional)**
4 cloves garlic, crushed	**Olive oil (optional)**

Cut meat into 1 1/2-inch cubes. Place in a deep bowl. Combine all marinade ingredients in a jar; shake well. Pour over lamb. Cover and refrigerate overnight.

Remove meat; reserve marinade for basting, if desired. Skewer on a 12-inch metal rod the lamb, pepper, onion and cherry tomatoes; repeat ending with lamb. Baste with reserved marinade, or beat a little lemon juice and olive oil together and brush on lamb and vegetables. Broil on broiler rack 3 inches from flame for 15-20 minutes or until done. Turn frequently. Serve with rice. Serves 6.

The Grecian Plate

 The Blue Ridge Parkway was designed solely for vacation travel and no commercial vehicles are allowed. It skims the crest of the mountains between the North Carolina-Virginia line and the entrance to the Great Smoky Mountains National Park near Cherokee. With numerous scenic overlooks, trails, campgrounds, picnic areas and recreation areas, it is considered America's most popular scenic parkway.

Cap'n Barky's Lamb Chops

12 lamb chops　　　　　　　　**1/4 cup rosemary leaves**
1 tablespoon ground thyme

Separate lamb chops and rub ground thyme over all surfaces. Sprinkle rosemary over hot barbeque coals, and cook chops for 3-4 minutes per side with barbeque cover on. Serve with Mint Jelly.

MINT JELLY:
3/4 cup apple mint jelly　　　**1 tablespoon white sugar, or**
2 tablespoons plain vinegar　　　**to taste**
2 tablespoons chopped fresh　　**1/8 cup mint syrup**
mint or 1 tablespoon mint
flakes

Blend all ingredients in small saucepan over low heat. Transfer to serving dish and table.

　　Note: Mint Jelly can ruin the taste of good red wines. Ask your wine cellar for advice. Serves 6.

Ship to Shore II

Sausage Lasagna Roll Ups

1 pound hot Italian link
  sausage, cut into 1/2-inch
  pieces
3/4 cup onion, chopped
1 clove garlic, minced
1 (24-ounce) can tomato
  juice
1 (6-ounce) can tomato paste
1/2 cup water
2 teaspoons sugar
1/2 teaspoon salt

1 bay leaf
2 cups cottage cheese
1 egg, slightly beaten
1/2 cup grated Parmesan
  cheese, divided
2 cups (8 ounces) shredded
  mozzarella cheese, divided
1/2 teaspoon salt
1/4 teaspoon white pepper
8 lasagna noodles

Cook sausage in large, heavy skillet until browned; remove sausage, reserving 1/4 cup drippings in skillet. (If sausage does not yield 1/4 cup drippings, add oil to make 1/4 cup.) Sauté onion and garlic in drippings until onion is crisp-tender. Add sausage, tomato juice, tomato paste, water, sugar, 1/2 teaspoon salt, and bay leaf; simmer, uncovered, one hour, stirring occasionally. Remove bay leaf.

Combine cottage cheese, egg, 1/4 cup Parmesan cheese, one cup mozzarella cheese, 1/4 teaspoon salt, and pepper. Chill thoroughly.

Cook lasagna noodles according to package directions; drain. Rinse noodles and cool.

Spread about 1 cup meat sauce in a lightly greased 13x9x2-inch baking dish. Spread 1/4 cup cheese mixture on each lasagna noodle; roll up jelly roll fashion from narrow end. Arrange lasagna rolls, seam side down, in pan. Pour remaining meat sauce over rolls; top with remaining Parmesan and mozzarella cheese. Bake at 350° for 30-40 minutes, until bubbly. Yield: 8 servings.

Knollwood's Cooking

The Cherokee Indian Reservation, spanning over 56,000 acres at the eastern edge of the Great Smoky Mountains National Park, is the home of 8,000 Eastern Cherokees.

Poultry and Game

A Cherokee woman weaves baskets at the Ocoanluftee Indian Village,
a recreated Cherokee community of 200 years ago.

Breast of Chicken Queen Elizabeth

3 chicken breasts	Flour
6 thin slices ham	3 tablespoons butter
6 slices Swiss cheese	1/2 pound mushrooms
1 teaspoon chopped shallot	1/2 cup dry white wine
or onion	1 cup heavy cream
1 beaten egg	

Remove the breasts from 3 chickens and trim off the skin. Separate the top fillet section of each breast from the smaller one lying beneath. Flatten each fillet. The smaller, thicker one should be flattened until it spreads to the same size as the upper one. (A friendly butcher will do this for you if properly approached and instructed.) Cut ham and cheese slices the same size as fillets. Sandwich the fillets with 1 slice each of ham and cheese. Moisten the edges of the fillets with beaten egg to hold them together. Roll the breasts in flour and shake off the excess.

Melt 3 tablespoons butter in shallow pan. Sauté the fillets for 10-12 minutes. Turn and continue to sauté for 5 minutes on each side. Remove to serving platter and keep warm. To butter in pan, add 1/2 pound mushrooms, 1 teaspoon shallots, and 1/2 cup dry white wine. Cook until liquid is reduced by half. Add 1 cup heavy cream and cook 'til mixture is fairly thick. Correct seasoning, pour sauce over chicken and serve.

Bon appetit!

High Hampton Hospitality

Honey French Chicken

This recipe won second prize in the North Carolina Chicken Cooking Contest.

6 chicken breasts
1 teaspoon flavor enhancer
1/2 cup corn oil
1/2 cup honey
1/4 cup cider vinegar
1/4 cup chili sauce

1 tablespoon Worcestershire sauce
1/2 (1 3/8-ounce) envelope onion soup mix
1/4 teaspoon salt

Sprinkle chicken with flavor enhancer. In a jar, place corn oil, honey, vinegar, chili sauce, Worcestershire sauce, soup mix and salt. Shake well. Place chicken in single layer in large shallow baking pan. Pour sauce over chicken. Baste, uncovered, in 350° oven about 35-40 minutes or until fork can be inserted with ease. Serves 6.

Sauce can be made a week ahead. Keep in refrigerator and pour over chicken when ready to cook the chicken. Boning of chicken is optional. Serve with Oriental rice.

Mountain Elegance

Almond Champagne Chicken

4 chicken breasts, boned and halved
1/2 cup butter
2 tablespoons finely chopped shallots
1/4 pound chopped fresh mushrooms

2 tablespoons flour
1 cup champagne, or dry white wine
Salt and pepper
1/2 cup whipping cream
1/2 cup sliced toasted almonds

Put chicken breasts in a shallow baking dish and pour 1/4 cup melted butter over them. Bake at 350° for 30 minutes until tender. Melt remaining 1/4 cup butter in a saucepan. Add shallots and chopped mushrooms and sauté over low heat until soft but not brown. Sprinkle with flour; add the wine, stirring constantly over medium heat until sauce is thickened and alcohol is evaporated from wine. Season with salt and pepper. Transfer chicken breasts to a heated serving platter to keep them warm. Stir pan drippings into the sauce and add cream. Heat through over low heat. Spoon sauce over chicken and sprinkle with toasted almonds. Serves 6.

A Cookbook of Pinehurst Courses

Boned Chicken Breast with Plum Sauce

1/4 cup butter
1 medium onion, chopped
1 (1-pound) can purple plums
1 (6-ounce) can frozen
  lemonade
1/3 cup chili sauce
10 - 12 boned chicken
  breasts

1/4 cup soy sauce
1 teaspoon Worcestershire
  sauce
1 teaspoon ginger
2 teaspoons prepared mustard
2 drops Tabasco

Melt butter, add onions and cook until tender. Pit plums and put through strainer or in blender with most of the juice to purée. Add to onion. Blend in remaining ingredients and simmer 15 minutes. Put chicken breasts in shallow pan. Bake at 350° for 30-45 minutes. Baste with sauce the last 30 minutes. The sauce may be made the day before using. Sauce also good on pork tenderloin.

Centenary Cookbook

Crab Stuffed Chicken Breasts

6 boned chicken breasts
1/2 cup onion, chopped
1/2 cup celery, chopped
3 tablespoons butter
3 tablespoons white wine
1 (7-ounce) can crabmeat, or
  fresh

1/2 cup Pepperidge Farm
  stuffing
2 tablespoons flour
1/2 teaspoon paprika

Salt and pepper chicken breasts and pound. Cook onion and celery in butter. Remove from heat and add wine, crabmeat, and stuffing. Put inside chicken breasts and secure with toothpicks. Combine flour and paprika and coat chicken. Drizzle with butter and bake uncovered at 375° for 40 minutes. Pour sauce over when serving. Serves 6.

SAUCE:
1 envelope Hollandaise Sauce
  Mix
3/4 cup milk

2 tablespoons white wine
1/2 cup Swiss cheese

Heat ingredients and spoon over chicken.

A Taste of History

Chicken in a Package

1 large chicken breast,
  halved, skinned, and boned
Salt and pepper to taste
Spicy mustard
2 small potatoes, thinly
  sliced
2 small onions, thinly
  sliced

2 carrots, cut into julienne
  strips
4 - 6 mushrooms, sliced
2 tablespoons butter
Paprika

Preheat the oven to 350°. Sprinkle the chicken with salt and pepper. Spread each breast half lightly with mustard; set aside.

On a large square of heavy-duty foil, alternate slices from one potato and one onion so that they overlap slightly. Repeat with the remaining, onion and potato on another square of foil. Sprinkle half of the carrot strips over one, the rest over the other. Divide the mushrooms between the pieces of foil. Cut the butter into bits and sprinkle over the vegetables. Lay a chicken breast half on each pile of vegetables. Sprinkle both liberally with paprika.

Seal the foil and lay the packets on a cookie sheet. Bake for 25-30 minutes, or until the chicken is done and vegetables are tender. Serve at once. Makes 2 servings.

Love Yourself Cookbook

Chicken Cranberry Casserole

1 (6-ounce) package long
  grain and wild rice with
  herb seasoning
1 (16-ounce) bag frozen
  French-style green beans
8 chicken breast halves,
  skinned and boned
Paprika
1 cup freshly grated
  Parmesan cheese
1/2 cup butter or margarine
1/2 cup chopped onion
1 cup chopped celery
1 cup sliced mushrooms
1 1/2 cups fresh cranberries
  or 2 (16-ounce) cans whole
  berry cranberry sauce
1 cup dry white wine
1/2 cup slivered almonds
1/4 cup butter or margarine

Preheat oven to 350°. Prepare rice according to package directions. Cook green beans in small amount of boiling water for 4-5 minutes; drain. If using canned cranberry sauce, drain in colander until most of liquid is drained, leaving berries. Sprinkle chicken with paprika. Roll in cheese.

Melt 1/2 cup butter in large skillet. Add onion, celery, and mushrooms; sauté until soft. Stir in rice and cranberries. Place green beans and almonds in shallow 3-quart casserole. Place chicken breasts on top in single layer in the center. Spoon rice mixture around edge of casserole. Pour wine over all. Dot chicken with 1/4 cup butter or margarine. (May be prepared ahead to this point and refrigerated.) Bake 45-50 minutes. Yield: 6-8 servings.

Even More Special

Lazy Man's Fried Chicken

2 - 3 pounds frying chicken,
  cut up
1/4 cup shortening
1/4 cup butter
1/2 cup flour
1 teaspoon salt
1 teaspoon paprika
1/4 teaspoon pepper

Wash and dry chicken. In oven melt shortening and butter in 13x9x2-inch pan. Mix flour, salt, paprika and pepper. Coat chicken thoroughly with flour mixture. Place chicken, skin side down, in melted shortening. Bake uncovered for 30 minutes. Turn chicken and cook 30 minutes more. Serves 4.

Ship to Shore I

Chicken in Pastry

6 whole chicken breasts,
  boned and split
Seasoned salt and pepper to
  taste
1/4 cup grated orange peel
1 (6-ounce) package long
  grain and wild rice, cooked

3 (8-ounce) cans
  refrigerated crescent dinner
  rolls
2 eggs, separated
1 tablespoon water

Pound chicken with mallet to flatten; sprinkle with seasoned salt and pepper. Add orange peel to cooked rice. Beat egg whites until soft peaks form; fold into rice mixture.

On a floured surface roll 2 triangular pieces of roll dough together to form a circle. Repeat until there are 12 circles. Place a chicken breast in the center of each circle. Spoon 1/4 cup of the rice mixture over the chicken; roll the chicken jelly roll fashion. Spoon 1/4 cup of the rice mixture over. Bring dough up around stuffed breast; moisten edges of the dough with water and press together to seal. Place seam side down on a large baking sheet. Lightly beat egg yolks with water, brush over dough. Bake at 375° for 45-50 minutes. Cover loosely with foil if dough browns too quickly. Serve with sauce.

SAUCE:
2 (10-ounce) jars red
  currant jelly
1 tablespoon prepared
  mustard

3 tablespoons port wine
1/4 cup lemon juice

Heat currant jelly; gradually stir in mustard, wine and lemon juice. Serve warm with chicken. Serves 6-8.

A Dash of Down East

 The world's largest natural gardens of crimson-purple rhododendron are located on Roan Mountain near Bakersville in the Pisgah National Forest recreation area. Peak bloom is mid-June.

Tarragon Chicken Oven Baked Potatoes

4 potatoes, baked
4 - 5 green onions, sliced
1 1/2 cups mushrooms, sliced
5 tablespoons margarine
3 - 4 tablespoons flour
2 cups milk
1 pound chicken, stewed
2 - 3 teaspoons tarragon, ground

1/4 teaspoon coarsely ground pepper
Salt to taste
3/4 cup slivered almonds, toasted
3/4 cup parsley, snipped

Clean and bake potatoes until done. While potatoes are baking, sauté onions and mushrooms in 1 tablespoon margarine. To make cream sauce, melt 4 tablespoons margarine, add flour and blend. Stir in slowly 2 cups milk. Cook and stir the sauce with a wire whisk or wooden spoon until thickened and smooth. To cream sauce add stewed chicken (deboned and cut in chunks), tarragon, pepper, onions and mushrooms, and salt to taste. Simmer for 20-30 minutes. Split potatoes and fill with chicken mixture. Top with almonds and parsley when served. Serves 4.

In Good Taste

North Carolina Chicken

8 ounces butter or margarine
2 envelopes Italian Salad Dressing mix

1/2 cup lime juice
1 teaspoon salt
5 pounds chicken pieces

Melt butter in saucepan. Stir in salad dressing mix, lime juice and salt. Marinate chicken 3-4 hours or overnight. Bake at 350° for 1 hour or until done. Or cook on outdoor grill for 1 hour turning and basting every 10-15 minutes. Serves 6.

Ship to Shore I

Marinated Chicken with Brown Rice

2 pounds boned chicken
  breasts, cut bite size

MARINADE:

1 (5-ounce) bottle soy sauce
5 ounces water
2 tablespoons lemon juice
1 tablespoon brown sugar

1/4 cup sherry
1/4 teaspoon onion powder
1/4 teaspoon garlic powder

Marinate chicken overnight. Bake on foil-lined cookie sheet in 350° oven for 1 hour.

BROWN RICE:

1 1/2 cups cooked rice
1 medium onion, chopped
1/2 to 1 stick butter

2 cans consommé or chicken
  stock

Brown rice and onion in butter or margarine and pour into casserole dish. Add consommé or stock. Cover and bake at 325° for 1 to 1 1/4 hours.

Jarrett House Potpourri

Barbecued Chicken

1 frying-size chicken,
  quartered

One onion, sliced

Place chicken in roasting pan with slice of onion on top of each piece.

SAUCE:

3/4 cup catsup
4 tablespoons Worcestershire
  sauce
2 teaspoons prepared mustard
3/4 cup vinegar

2 bay leaves
1/2 cup water
1 tablespoon sugar
1/4 teaspoon salt
Tabasco

Combine ingredients for sauce and pour over chicken and cook at 350° for 2 hours. Baste frequently.

Queen Anne's Table

Chicken-Wild Rice Casserole

1 (1 3/8-ounce) package
  dehydrated onion soup
1 pint commercial sour cream
3 (2 1/2-pound) frying
  chickens, (cooked and
  chopped)
2 cups dry sherry
1 cup water
1 teaspoon salt
Dash pepper

1/2 teaspoon dried basil
Pinch thyme
1 teaspoon curry powder
6 tablespoons minced fresh
  parsley
1 (10 1/2-ounce) can cream
  of mushroom soup
1 1/2 cups uncooked wild
  rice

Blend dry onion soup into sour cream in a bowl and allow to stand for 2 hours. Place chicken in roasting pan; pour sherry and water over it; sprinkle with all seasonings and parsley; cover roaster tightly. (If lid doesn't fit securely, place a sheet of aluminum foil over pan before covering.) Bake at 300° for 1 1/2 hours, or until meat falls off bones. Remove chicken from roaster, cover loosely and set aside to cool. Strain pan juices from roaster into saucepan and simmer until reduced to 1 1/2 cups.

Blend in mushroom soup until smooth and heat together a few minutes. (This is better if you blend by pouring liquid into canned soup.) Slowly combine with sour cream mixture. The cream will not curdle if you blend slowly, pouring hot liquid into cream mixture a little at a time.

Cook rice according to package instructions. Skin and bone cooled chicken; cut into bite-size pieces. Combine with rice and turn into buttered casserole. Pour sauce over and toss lightly. When ready to serve, heat uncovered at 250° for about 30 minutes. Yields 12 servings.

Mountain Potpourri

Beverly Hall Broiled Chicken

Butter
6 chicken breasts or whole
  fowl
Worcestershire sauce
1/3 cup vinegar
1 teaspoon salt
2 bay leaves

Dot each piece of fowl with butter. Cover entire fowl with Worcestershire sauce. Place chicken in small roaster with vinegar, salt, bay leaves, and enough water to almost cover. Bake at 350° for about 1 hour. Remove top of roaster, dot with butter again and broil until golden brown. Thicken gravy slightly.

Queen Anne's Table

Chicken Chow Mein

1/2 cup butter*
1 cup chopped onion
2 cups chopped celery
Salt and pepper
1 cup chicken stock
1 can chop suey vegetables
1 can bean sprouts
1 can water chestnuts,
  sliced (optional)
2 cups diced chicken

Cook onion in melted butter about ten minutes. Add celery, salt and pepper. Add chicken stock, cover and cook ten minutes. Add drained chop suey vegetables, bean sprouts, water chestnuts and diced chicken. Mix thoroughly and heat to boiling. Add sauce.

SAUCE:
2 tablespoons butter*
3 tablespoons flour
1 cup chicken stock
2 teaspoons soy sauce
2 teaspoons sugar

Add flour to butter to make a paste. Add chicken stock and seasoning and cook until thickened. Add to chicken mixture. Serve on rice or chow mein noodles. Serves 6-8. I triple this recipe and freeze.

  *Fat skimmed from chicken stock may be used.

Mountain Potpourri

Chicken Salad in a Cream Puff

CHICKEN SALAD:

2 cups cubed, cooked chicken
1 cup seedless green grapes, halved
1/2 cup (2 ounces) shredded Swiss cheese
1/2 cup sliced celery

3 tablespoons sliced green onions
1/2 cup dairy sour cream
1/4 cup mayonnaise
1/4 cup toasted sliced almonds

Combine chicken, grapes, cheese, celery, onions, sour cream, and mayonnaise. Chill until ready to serve.

CREAM PUFF:

1/2 cup margarine
1 cup boiling water
1 cup all-purpose flour

1/4 teaspoon salt
4 eggs
Leaf lettuce, garnish

Preheat oven to 400°. Add margarine to boiling water and stir until melted; add flour and salt all at once. Stir until well blended and a ball forms. Set aside to cool for 10 minutes. Add eggs to flour mixture, one at a time. Stir after each addition until thoroughly blended. Butter a 9-inch pie pan. Spread batter evenly in bottom and on sides. Bake 30-35 minutes, or until puffed and lightly browned.

When ready to serve, line pastry with lettuce leaves and fill with chicken salad. Sprinkle toasted almonds on top. To serve, cut into wedges. Yield: 4-6 servings.

Hints: Cream puff may be made one day ahead and re-crisped in moderate (325°) oven for 5 minutes. Chicken salad may be prepared one to three days ahead.

Even More Special

The Tyron Palace Restoration and Gardens Complex in New Bern is the restoration of elegant Georgian buildings completed in 1770 as the residence of the royal governor and the meeting place of the colonial assembly. Later it was the first state capitol.

Garden Chicken Pie

4 tablespoons butter
1/2 cup onion, finely
  chopped
6 tablespoons flour
2 teaspoons instant chicken
  bouillon
1/2 teaspoon salt
1/4 teaspoon pepper
1 1/2 cups half-and-half
1/2 cup water

4 cups cooked chicken,
  chopped
1 cup carrots, thinly sliced
1 (9-ounce) package frozen
  peas, thawed
1 (4-ounce) jar sliced
  mushrooms, drained
1 stick butter, melted
10 sheets phyllo pastry

Preheat oven to 375°. Melt butter in a saucepan. Add onion and sauté until wilted. Blend in flour, chicken bouillon, salt, pepper, half-and-half, and water. Cook, stirring, until slightly thickened. Add chicken, carrots, peas, and mushrooms. Stir to combine. Remove from heat.

Brush baking dish lightly with melted butter. Layer 5 sheets of phyllo in baking dish, brushing each sheet with butter. Keep phyllo sheets that you are not working with under a damp cloth to keep from drying out. Spread chicken filling over pastry sheets. Layer remaining 5 sheets of phyllo over chicken, brushing each sheet with butter. Bake pie for 25-35 minutes or until golden. Serve. Makes 10-12 servings.

Note: If phyllo sheets are 14 inches by 18 inches, only use 5 sheets and cut each sheet in half.

Stirring Performances

Oriental Chicken

4 pieces of chicken
1/2 cup flour
1 teaspoon salt
1/4 teaspoon pepper
1/3 cup cooking oil
1 (1-pound 4-ounce)
  can sliced pineapple,
  reserve syrup

1 large green pepper, cut
  crosswise into 1/4-inch
  circles

Wash chicken parts. Coat chicken with flour, salt and pepper. Heat oil in skillet; brown the chicken on all sides. Remove when browned and place in a shallow baking dish. Pour sauce over chicken and bake at 350° for 30 minutes. Garnish with pineapple slices and green peppers. Bake additional 30 minutes or until chicken is tender. Serve with rice. Yield: 4 servings.

SAUCE:
Reserved pineapple syrup
1 cup sugar
2 tablespoons cornstarch
3/4 cup white vinegar

1 tablespoon soy sauce
1/4 teaspoon ginger
1 cube chicken bouillon

Pour syrup into 2-cup measure. Add water to make 1 1/4 cups. In a medium saucepan, combine sugar, cornstarch, pineapple syrup, vinegar, soy sauce, ginger and bouillon cube. Bring to boil, stirring constantly. Boil 2 minutes and pour over chicken.

A Cookbook of Pinehurst Courses

Oriental-Broiled Turkey Steaks

Must prepare ahead.

1 turkey breast
1 tablespoon ground ginger
1 teaspoon dry mustard
1 teaspoon monosodium
  glutamate (optional)

1 tablespoon honey
1/2 cup soy sauce
1/4 cup salad oil
1/2 teaspoon garlic, minced

Ask butcher to cut turkey breast crosswise into 1-inch steaks. Combine all remaining ingredients in glass bowl, allow to stand overnight at room temperature. Pour over turkey steaks, cover and refrigerate for several hours or overnight. Drain steaks and cook over hot coals, allowing about 8 minutes on each side. Brush with marinade if desired. Yield: 4-6 servings.

Market to Market

Stuffing for Turkey
(Microwave)

1/2 cup margarine
1 cup chopped celery
3/4 cup chopped onion
3/4 cup chopped green pepper
2 teaspoons chicken bouillon
  granules or 2 chicken
  bouillon cubes
2 cups water
1 teaspoon salt

1 tablespoon parsley
1 teaspoon poultry seasoning
2 cups herb seasoning
  stuffing mix
1 (9-ounce) package corn
  bread mix, cooked and
  crumbled
1/2 cup chopped walnuts or
  pecans, optional

Combine margarine, celery, onion, and green pepper in 3-quart casserole. Cover. Microcook on High 4-6 minutes. Add bouillon granules, water, salt, parsley, and seasoning. Cover. Microcook on High 5-7 minutes. Add stuffing mix, corn bread, and nuts. Add more moisture if it seems too dry.

Stuff turkey, or cook stuffing in casserole. If turkey is stuffed it will not change microcook time or temperature setting for the probe. To bake in casserole, cover dish with wax paper. Microcook on Medium High (70%) 8-10 minutes. Let stand. Yield: To stuff a 10-12-pound turkey.

The Microwave Touch

Grilled Stuffed Quail

The flavorful stuffing and wood grilling puts a little of the taste of the wild back into farm-raised quail. My favorite accompaniment for this recipe is the Sweet Potato and Pear Soufflé.

8 quail, cleaned and split down the backbone (approximately 2 ounces each)

4 tablespoons chopped pork sidemeat

2 large garlic cloves

2 tablespoons mixed green herbs such as parsley, sage, thyme, or parsley alone

2 1/2 tablespoons stale white bread crumbs

2 tablespoons finely chopped carrot

2 tablespoons finely chopped celery

Freshly ground black pepper

1 tablespoon bacon fat

Note: Build and light charcoal fire approximately 45 minutes before cooking is to begin.

Wash, drain, and dry the quail. Set aside. Chop the pork sidemeat with the garlic and herbs into a fine paste. Add the bread crumbs, carrot, celery, and black pepper, mixing thoroughly. Stuff the quail, trying not to tear the skin (don't panic if you do). Gently separate the skin from the breast and work the stuffing in between the two. Pack extra stuffing between the thigh and the breast and into any other cavities, using all the stuffing.

Brush the birds with a little of the melted bacon fat and grill over hot coals until golden brown and crisp (or cook under a hot broiler about 4 minutes on each side). Yield 4 servings.

Bill Neal's Southern Cooking

 North Carolina residents have been known as "Tar Heels" since Civil War days. Legend has it that one of the state's regiments, disgusted by the lack of support they received from other states' troops, said that Jeff Davis had bought all the tar up to make the other troops hold their ground. Later General Lee, hearing of the story, remarked, "God Bless the Tar Heel Boys."

Quail Baked in Vermouth

8 plump quail, dressed and
  split down the back
1 teaspoon salt
1/4 teaspoon freshly ground
  black pepper
1 cup butter, divided
3 tablespoons corn oil

3 tablespoons lemon juice
1 tablespoon Worcestershire
  sauce
1/2 cup dry vermouth
8 slices melba toast
3 cups cooked wild rice

Salt and pepper quail. Heat 3 tablespoons butter and corn oil in a 12-inch iron skillet over high heat. Brown quail quickly, turning from one side to the other. (Long-handled tongs do the best job.) When birds are brown, remove skillet from heat; pour lemon juice, Worcestershire sauce, and vermouth over the sides of each bird. Melt remaining buter. Place quail breast side down in skillet and pour melted butter over all. Cover with foil and bake in a preheated 325° oven for 1 hour and 15 minutes. Test with fork in thick part of breast to be sure birds are tender. Remove to a heated platter and place on melba toast. Serve hot with cooked wild rice. Serves 6-8.

A Dash of Down East

165

Wild Duck Stroganoff

8 duck breasts, cleaned, skinned, and sliced thinly	1 medium onion, grated 3 tablespoons butter

In a large skillet, melt butter. Add meat and onions. Stir and cook over medium heat until just cooked. Remove to bowl.

1 pound fresh mushrooms, sliced	1 onion, sliced 3 tablespoons butter

Melt butter in skillet. Add mushrooms and onions and cook over high heat, stirring constantly until moisture has evaporated. Add to duck breasts.

6 tablespoons flour 2 cups half-and-half 1 cup sour cream 1 teaspoon salt	1/2 teaspoon freshly ground pepper 1/4 teaspoon nutmeg 2 tablespoons white wine

Combine flour with 1/4 cup cooled juice from ducks. Cook for 2 minutes over medium heat. Add half-and-half, salt and pepper and nutmeg. Cook and stir until thickened. Simmer for 5 minutes. Add wine and sour cream to hot mixture just before serving. Keep hot but do not boil. Serve with wild rice.

A Taste of History

Seafood

Cape Hatteras Lighthouse at Buxton, the tallest lighthouse in North America.

Mountain Trout with Bacon and Scallions

Bacon frying is almost always irresistible. In mountain forest, by a limpid stream, at sunset, over an open fire, it beckons more seductively than Circe. When coupled with the reward of an honest fisherman—fresh trout fried till crisp, ash-roasted baby potatoes, and, in the spring, perhaps a handful of freshly chopped ramps tossed into the sputtering fat—it creates my idea of a great meal: strong, fresh flavors in equal combat, food that sustains, not just entertains. This recipe for trout is a bit of a refinement on such camp cooking, but not too much so. A light cornmeal dusting adds flavor and crispness to the fish, and the scallions will permit a quicker re-entry to society than their obstreperous wild cousin, the ramp, but the essence of the dish remains the same.

With simple equipment, an indoor fireplace can become a camp fire, too. Beyond a good bed of coals, you'll need four to eight bricks to support an oven rack above the heat source. Use an unscented soap bar to coat the rack and the bottom of the skillet—afterwards any blackening washes away quickly. Roast potatoes in their jackets covered well in hot ashes, not coals.

Beyond mountain trout, you may use any flavorful ocean fish: drums, blues, channel bass, even mackerel, and they may be filleted or cut into steaks. The delicacy of a sole or flounder will be obscured by the bacon and scallions. Small, whole fish will re-create the original nature of the dish best, though, like that of the fisherman's repast. Leave the heads on; their presence prevents moisture loss and provides an additional delicacy: the cheek. To placate squeamish diners, replace the eyes after cooking with a whole caper or a bit of black olive.

4 mountain trout, cleaned
  but left with head intact
  (12 ounces each,
  dressed weight)
1/4 teaspoon salt and
  freshly ground black pepper
3/4 cup yellow
  cornmeal
1/4 cup flour
1 teaspoon salt
6 tablespoons peanut oil

6 slices bacon, diced
  (approximately 5 ounces)
2 cups sliced scallions
2 tablespoons apple cider
  vinegar or lemon juice
2 tablespoons freshly
  chopped parsley
1/2 teaspoon salt
Freshly ground black pepper
Black olives or capers
  (optional)

CONTINUED

CONTINUED

Recommended equipment: One or two 12-inch cast-iron skillets or enameled cast-iron sauté pans, brown paper bag. Wash the fish well under running cold water. Dry the cavity and outside thoroughly with paper towels. Make 2 diagonal slashes 1/4-inch deep and 1-inch long on each side of the fish at the thickest point. Sprinkle the 1/4 teaspoon of salt and a dash of freshly ground black pepper inside each one. Combining the cornmeal, flour, and salt, coat each fish lightly but thoroughly and reserve.

Add the peanut oil and bacon to the cold skillet or sauté pan. Heat slowly to moderate, browning the bacon. Remove the bacon and reserve. Ensuring that the pan is hot, place two trout in it and brown well on each side, about 10-12 minutes in all. (If you have two skillets that will accommodate two fish each, divide fat and bacon between them and cook all four at once.) If you have any doubts as to doneness, check the spine at the center of the abdominal cavity: it should be opaque. Drain fish on brown paper bag and hold in a warm oven while you fry the remaining fish and prepare the sauce.

Increase heat to high. Add the scallions and stir until just wilted. Pour in vinegar or lemon juice and boil down rapidly. Stir in bacon and parsley; check for seasoning. Transfer fish to a warm serving platter, pour the bubbling sauce over all, and serve immediately. Yields 4 servings.

Bill Neal's Southern Cooking

Vegetable Stuffed Rainbow Trout

6 pan-dressed rainbow trout,
  fresh or frozen
2 teaspoons salt
Vegetable Stuffing

6 slices bacon, cut in
  thirds
Paprika

Thaw frozen fish. Sprinkle inside and out with salt. Stuff fish and place in a well-greased baking pan, approximately 11x14-inch. Place 3 pieces of bacon on each fish. Sprinkle with paprika. Bake at 350° for 25-30 minutes or until fish flakes easily when tested with fork. Turn oven control to broil. Place fish about 3 inches from source of heat and broil for 2-3 minutes or until bacon is crisp. Yield: 6 servings.

VEGETABLE STUFFING:

1 cup grated carrot
3/4 cup chopped celery
1/2 cup chopped onion
1/3 cup vegetable oil
2 cups soft bread crumbs

1 tablespoon lemon juice
1/2 teaspoon salt
1/4 teaspoon white pepper
1/4 teaspoon thyme

Cook vegetables in oil until tender, stirring occasionally. Add remaining ingredients and mix lightly.

Heart of the Mountains

Blackened Catfish

1 tablespoon paprika
1 teaspoon onion powder
1 teaspoon garlic powder
3/4 teaspoon freshly ground
  black pepper
1 teaspoon cayenne pepper
3/4 teaspoon white pepper

1/2 teaspoon thyme
1/2 teaspoon oregano
6 (8-ounce) skinless catfish
  fillets
6 tablespoons melted
  margarine

Combine paprika, onion powder, garlic powder, black pepper, cayenne pepper, white pepper, thyme and oregano in shallow dish. Dip fillets in margarine; coat well with seasoning mixture. Heat large cast-iron skillet over very high heat for 10 minutes or until it is beyond the smoking stage and has a white ash in the bottom. Place fillets in single layer in skillet. Cook over high heat for 2 minutes on each side or until fish is blackened and flakes easily with fork. Unless you have a very good exhaust fan for blackening fish, cook it outside. Yield: 6 servings.

Approx. Per Serving: Calories 374; Protein 41.8g; Carbohydrates 2.1g; T Fat 21.3g; Cholesterol 132.0mg; Potassium 846mg; Sodium 278mg.

Goodness Grows in North Carolina

Mama's Baked Bluefish

1 fresh bluefish, 4 - 5
  pounds
Salt and pepper to taste
12 thin slices of fat back
6 medium potatoes cut into
  3/4-inch chunks

2 large onions cut into
  3/4-inch chunks
2 or 3 bay leaves

Score the fish every few inches along both sides. Add salt and pepper. Stuff the slices of fat back into the scores.

Put the fish into a large baking pan. Place the potatoes, onions, and bay leaves around the fish. Add just enough water to cover the vegetables.

Cover the pan and bake at 350° for 30-45 minutes or until the fish flakes easily. Serve with baked corn bread and collards. Yield: 6 servings.

I Remember

Sole with Black Butter and Capers

1 1/2 pounds fillet of sole
Flour for dredging
3 tablespoons unsalted
  butter

2 tablespoons light
  vegetable oil
1/3 cup olive oil
1/3 cup tiny capers

Cut the fillet of sole in half lengthwise. Dredge lightly with flour. Heat butter and vegetable oil in a large skillet. Sauté the fish for 2 or 3 minutes on each side, or until firm and golden. Remove the fish to a heated platter. Keep warm.

In a small skillet heat olive oil until very hot. Drop in the capers and fry until they puff open like flowers. Drain well and sprinkle over fish.

BLACK BUTTER SAUCE:

6 tablespoons unsalted
  butter

2 tablespoons balsamic or
  sherry vinegar

Melt the butter in a small skillet over medium heat until it becomes a nutty brown. Add the vinegar and stir well. Pour over the fish. Serve immediately. (Our favorite fish dish.)

Knollwood's Cooking

Savory Baked Fish

1 teaspoon instant minced
  onion
1/2 teaspoon powdered
  mustard
1/4 teaspoon tarragon
  leaves, crushed
1/16 teaspoon ground black
  pepper

2 teaspoons warm water
1 1/2 pounds filet flounder,
  whitefish, halibut or cod
Salt to taste
1 teaspoon freshly squeezed
  lemon juice
1/2 cup mayonnaise
Paprika

Preheat oven to 425°. Combine instant onion, mustard, tarragon and pepper with warm water; let stand 10 minutes for flavors to blend. Wipe fish and arrange in greased 9x11-inch baking dish. Sprinkle with salt. Add lemon juice and mayonnaise to tarragon mixture. Spread on fish. Bake for 25-30 minutes until browned and fish flakes easily. Garnish with paprika. Serves 6.

A Cook's Tour of the Azalea Coast

Fish Almandine
(Microwave)

1/4 cup margarine or butter	1 pound fish fillets (sole,
1/3 cup sliced almonds	trout)
1/4 teaspoon salt	1 teaspoon parsley
2 teaspoons lemon juice	Lemon slices

Microcook almonds and margarine in 2-quart rectangular dish on High 4-6 minutes, stirring twice. They should be golden brown. Remove almonds and set aside.

Add salt and lemon juice to margarine. Rinse fish fillets and pat dry with paper towel. Add fish to seasoned margarine, turning to coat. Place thickest part of fillets to outside of dish.

Cover with wax paper. Microcook on High 6-8 minutes or until fish flakes when touched with a fork. Let stand 3 minutes.

Sprinkle almonds and parsley over the top when ready to serve. Garnish with lemon slices. Serves 4.

The Microwave Touch

Fish Filets Elegante

1 (1-pound) package frozen or fresh fish filets (filets of sole, haddock, halibut, flounder, cod or trout may be used)	1 (10 1/2-ounce) can condensed cream of shrimp soup
	1/4 cup Parmesan cheese, grated
1/2 teaspoon pepper	1/2 teaspoon paprika
2 tablespoons butter or margarine	1 lemon, cut into wedges

Preheat oven to 400°. Butter a 9x13-inch baking dish. Separate filets. Place in baking dish. Dash with pepper; dot with butter. Spread soup over filets; sprinkle with Parmesan cheese and paprika. Bake for 25 minutes. Garnish with lemon wedges. Serves 2-4.

A Cook's Tour of the Azalea Coast

Oven-Fried Fish Fillets

3/4 pound fish fillets
1/4 cup frozen orange juice
  concentrate
Salt and lemon pepper to
  taste

1/4 cup dry bread crumbs
1 tablespoon melted butter
Parsley
Lemon slices

If the fillets are large, cut them into small portions. Combine the orange juice concentrate with salt and lemon pepper. Dip the fish in it, then roll in bread crumbs, coating well. Preheat the oven to 500°.

Place the fish in a single layer in a greased baking dish. Drizzle on melted butter. Bake for 10 minutes. Reduce the heat to 350° and continue cooking for 5 minutes, or until the fish flakes when pierced with a fork. Serve on a heated platter, garnished with parsley and lemon slices. Makes 2 servings.

Love Yourself Cookbook

Fish Fillets with Sweet Sour Sauce

1 pound fish fillets (white
  fish sole, bass, haddock or
  sturgeon)
1/4 cup corn oil
Salt to taste
1/2 cup chopped onions
1 green pepper, cut in thin
  strips

1/4 cup firmly packed brown
  sugar
1/4 teaspoon dry mustard
2 tablespoons water
1 tablespoon cornstarch
1 tablespoon soy sauce
1/3 cup lemon juice

Brush fillets with 2 tablespoons corn oil, sprinkle with salt. Cook until done under broiler. Arrange on warm platter and keep warm. Meanwhile cook onions in 2 tablespoons corn oil in skillet until light golden brown. Stir in green pepper. Mix together remaining ingredients, add to mixture in skillet. Cook until sauce is thick. Spoon over fish.

Centenary Cookbook

Fish in Wine Sauce

Salt and pepper
2 pounds haddock fillets (or
  other firm white fish)
Flour
1 stick butter

1 can artichoke hearts
1 cup dry white wine
Paprika
Lemon wedges

Salt and pepper fillets and dredge in flour. Place overlapping in a greased pan. Cut butter in chunks and place on fillets. Cut artichoke hearts in half and place on fillets. Pour wine over all. Bake in 400° oven, basting once or twice, for about 1/2 hour or until fish flakes. Sprinkle with paprika and serve with lemon wedges.

Queen Anne's Table

Drunken Flounder

1/2 cup butter
2 cloves garlic, crushed
4 flounder fillets
1/2 cup light rum
1/2 cup sweet vermouth
1/2 cup chopped onions

1/2 cup chopped green pepper
1/2 teaspoon oregano
1/4 cup toasted almond
  slivers
1/2 cup sherry
Lemon wedges for garnish

Preheat oven to 400°. Melt butter in shallow baking dish and sprinkle with garlic. Cut fish into 3-inch pieces and marinate in rum and vermouth mixture for 20 minutes.

Arrange fish in pan on melted butter and top with onions and green pepper. Pour over the remaining rum/vermouth marinade. Sprinkle with oregano, then with toasted almond slivers and bake 10 minutes at 400°. Douse with sherry and broil 2 minutes to brown. Serves 4.

Sea to Shore

Broiled Catfish Steaks

8 (2-ounce) catfish steaks*
1/4 cup tomato sauce
1/4 cup vinegar
1 1/2 teaspoons sugar
3/4 teaspoon minced fresh
   dill
1/4 teaspoon paprika

Fresh ground black pepper
1/2 teaspoon Worcestershire
   sauce
1 teaspoon vegetable oil
Vegetable cooking spray
Garnish: lemon slices and
   fresh dill sprigs

Rinse catfish steaks under cold, running water. Pat dry, set aside. Combine tomato sauce and next 7 ingredients in a small bowl. Stir well. Brush half of mixture over one side of steaks. Coat rack of a broiler pan with cooking spray. Place steaks on rack; broil 4-5 inches from heat for about 6 minutes. Carefully turn fish over. Brush with remaining tomato mixture. Broil an additional 6 minutes or until fish flakes easily when tested with a fork. Garnish. Serves 4.

   *Preferably farm-raised. Alternative: Black Sea Bass.

Sea to Shore

Salmon Cakes

1 large (16-ounce) can pink
   salmon
1 egg, beaten
1 small (5.3-ounce) can
   evaporated milk
1 small onion, minced
1/2 cup minced green pepper

1/2 teaspoon salt
1/4 teaspoon black pepper
3 - 4 slices fresh bread,
   torn into small bits
1 cup all-purpose flour
Oil to fry cakes in a
   10-inch skillet

Drain and pick over salmon, removing skin and bones. In a large bowl, mix together all ingredients except flour and oil. Shape into hamburger-sized patties, about 1/2-inch thick, dip in flour and fry in oil over medium heat until lightly browned. Drain on paper towels. Yields 4-6 servings.

Seafood Sorcery

Grilled Fresh Tuna with Herbs

2 pounds fresh tuna,
  preferably from the belly
  portion
Freshly ground black pepper
1/3 cup olive oil
6 sprigs fresh thyme
4 cloves garlic, crushed
3 tablespoons freshly
  squeezed lemon juice

4 strips lemon rind
1/4 teaspoon red pepper
  flakes
2 tablespoons melted butter
Garnish: lemon wedges and
  parsley flakes

Heat charcoal, gas grill or broiler to high. Sprinkle tuna with pepper on both sides. Place oil in a flat dish and add thyme, garlic, lemon juice, lemon rind and hot red pepper flakes. Add tuna and coat on both sides. Marinate for about 15 minutes. Remove tuna from the marinade. Add butter to marinade and place the dish in a warm place.

If the tuna is to be cooked on a charcoal or gas grill, place it directly on the grill, fatty side down, and cook, turning often, 5-6 minutes. If it is to be cooked under a broiler, arrange tuna on a rack, fatty side up. Broil about 2 inches from heat, leaving broiler door partly open. Cook 3 minutes and turn; continue cooking 2 minutes. Transfer tuna to marinade. Turn tuna to coat on both sides. Cut into thin slices and serve. Garnish. Serves 4-6.

Serve with Maître D'Hôtel Butter and new small red boiled potatoes, along with a tomato and onion salad.

MAÎTRE D'HÔTEL BUTTER:

2 ounces softened butter
1 tablespoon finely chopped
  parsley

Fresh lemon juice
Freshly ground black pepper

Blend softened butter with parsley. Then add a squeeze of lemon juice and freshly ground black pepper. Roll butter into a tube shape, wrap tightly in wax paper, chill or freeze. Slice off as needed.

Sea to Shore

Small Fry Crab Cakes with Tarragon-Chive Mayonnaise

8 ounces lump crabmeat
1/4 cup celery, finely
  chopped
1/4 cup green or red pepper,
  finely chopped
4 scallions, minced
1 teaspoon lemon juice
1/4 teaspoon salt
Freshly ground white pepper
1 1/2 tablespoons mayonnaise
1 1/2 tablespoons butter,
  melted

1 1/4 cups bread crumbs
2 tablespoons egg, beaten
1 teaspoon Dijon mustard
1/2 teaspoon Worcestershire
  sauce
1 tablespoon chives, chopped
1 tablespoon butter
1 recipe Tarragon-Chive
  Mayonnaise

Carefully pick over the crabmeat to remove any pieces or cartilage. Squeeze crabmeat in small batches to remove excess water. Add the remaining ingredients except for the last two, mix, and shape into 1 1/2 x 2 1/2 x 1/2-inch thick cakes. Sauté in butter until lightly browned. Serve with Tarragon Chive Mayonnaise. Makes 12 portions.

TARRAGON-CHIVE MAYONNAISE:
1 whole egg
1/2 teaspoon Dijon mustard
1/4 teaspoon salt
1 tablespoon fresh chives,
  minced
1 tablespoon fresh tarragon,
  minced

1/2 lemon rind, grated
1/2 small clove garlic,
  minced
2 tablespoons lemon juice
1/2 cup vegetable oil
1/2 cup olive oil

Place the egg in a blender and process for about 2 minutes until the mixture is thick and sticky. Add mustard, salt, herbs, lemon rind, garlic, and lemon juice and blend. With the machine still running, use a baster to add the oil, drip by drip, until over half the oil has been added and the mixture thickens. Add the rest of the oil in a steady stream. Yields approximately 1 cup.

The Fearrington House Cookbook

Edge Hill Crab Cakes

1/2 cup milk
1 pound crab meat
1 slightly beaten egg
1 teaspoon dry mustard
2 teaspoons mayonnaise
1/8 teaspoon pepper

1 teaspoon Worcestershire
  sauce
1 teaspoon bitters
1 teaspoon chopped parsley
1 teaspoon salt

Make into cakes. Dip in milk and then in cracker crumbs. Place on baking sheet in 375° oven for 20 minutes. Serve with Caper Sauce. Makes 8 crab cakes.

CAPER SAUCE:
1 tablespoon butter
1 tablespoon flour
1 1/2 cups chicken broth

1/2 teaspoon salt
1/2 cup capers

Melt butter. Add flour and broth slowly. Add salt and capers.

Favorite Recipes of the Lower Cape Fear

Crab Meat Casserole I

2 tablespoons butter
2 tablespoons flour
1 1/4 cups half-and-half
  cream
Salt
White pepper
4 tablespoons sherry

1 (8 1/2-ounce) can
  artichoke hearts
1 pound fresh mushrooms,
  sautéed in butter
1/2 pound lump crab meat
Paprika
Parmesan cheese

Melt butter and whisk in flour. Slowly stir in half-and-half, salt and pepper. When sauce thickens, remove from heat and add sherry. Put artichoke hearts, sautéed mushrooms, and crab meat in buttered casserole dish. Cover with white sauce and sprinkle with paprika and Parmesan cheese. Bake at 350° for 20-30 minutes until heated thoroughly. Can do ahead. Serves 6.

Serve with salad (Romaine, mandarin oranges, almonds), French bread, and Pinot Chardonnay wine.

Mountain Elegance

Stewed Hard Crabs

2 dozen hard crabs, backed
  and cleaned
6 - 8 medium white potatoes,
  diced or cubed
1 large onion, diced

Salt and pepper to taste
6 - 8 thin slices salt
  fat-back, fried-out, or 2
  tablespoons oil, if desired
Corn meal dumplings

Place crabs in large pot. Add potatoes, onion, salt and pepper, grease from fat-back or oil, and water to cover. Cook over medium heat for approximately 15 minutes after full-boil begins.

CORN MEAL DUMPLINGS:
2 cups fine or medium-ground
  white corn meal
2/3 cup plain flour

1 - 1 1/2 teaspoons salt
Water to mix to desired
  consistency

Form dumplings in hands; place around sides of pot. Break-up at least 1 dumpling and stir-in to thicken gravy. Cook another 20-30 minutes, or until potatoes and dumplings are well-cooked and gravy is desired thickness. Yield: 4-6 servings.

Note: Never stir ingredients. Use a long fork to lift crabs occasionally. Use a long spoon to loosen dumplings from sides of pot and allow gravy to cover dumplings. Wetting hands before putting dumplings around sides of pot proves helpful.

Island Born and Bred

Crabmeat Casserole

1 (20-ounce) can artichoke
  hearts
1 pound crabmeat
1/2 pound fresh mushrooms,
  sautéed
4 tablespoons butter
2 1/2 tablespoons flour
1 cup cream
1/2 teaspoon salt

1 teaspoon Worcestershire
  sauce
1/4 cup medium dry sherry
Paprika to taste
Cayenne o taste
Pepper to taste
1/4 cup Parmesan cheese,
  grated

Preheat oven to 375°. Place artichokes in bottom of 2 1/2-quart baking dish; spread a layer of crabmeat. Add a layer of sautéed mushrooms. Melt butter in a saucepan; add flour, cream, salt, Worcestershire sauce, sherry, paprika, cayenne and pepper. Stir well after each addition to form a smooth sauce. Pour sauce over artichoke-crab layer and sprinkle with cheese on top. Bake 20 minutes. Serves 8.

Nancy Reagan's. (Ronald Reagan participated in Azalea Festival in 1969.)

A Cook's Tour of the Azalea Coast

Crabmeat Au Gratin

1 pound white crabmeat
1 tablespoon butter
1 tablespoon flour
1 cup heavy cream

Salt and pepper to taste
1 cup sherry (or to taste)
1/2 pound New York sharp
  cheese, sliced

Carefully pick crabmeat and remove all pieces of shell. Melt butter in a double boiler. Add flour and stir until smooth; add cream and continue stirring until mixture dissolves. Salt and pepper to taste. Add sherry and mix thoroughly. Add crabmeat to sauce, and stir gently until crab is hot. Place in casserole or ramekins and cover generously with slices of cheese. This much may be done ahead. Place in the refrigerator. Before serving, place under broiler until cheese has melted and is browned. Yields 4-6.

Seafood Sorcery

Creamed Crab

1 pound fresh crabmeat
1/4 cup margarine
1/4 cup all-purpose flour
2 cups milk or half-and-half

Salt and pepper to taste
Worcestershire sauce to
 taste
Herbed toast points

Remove and discard cartilage from crabmeat; set aside. Melt margarine in a large saucepan over low heat. Add flour; cook, stir in milk, crabmeat and seasonings. Transfer to a chafing dish. Serve over herbed toast points. Yields 8-10 servings.

Seafood Sorcery

Crabmeat-Sauced Pasta

This sauce is delightful over any pasta, but especially favored in my home over linguine.

1 (5 1/2-ounce) package
 frozen crabmeat, thawed
2 tablespoons butter
1 green onion, including
 green stem, sliced
2 or 3 mushrooms, sliced
2 tablespoons flour
Salt to taste

1/4 tablespoon dry mustard
Pepper to taste
1 cup milk
1 tablespoon lemon juice
2 tablespoons dry white wine
 (optional)
1 tablespoon catsup
2 cups hot cooked pasta

Drain the crab and cut into small pieces. Combine the butter, onion, and mushrooms in a skillet. Sauté until the onion is opaque but not browned, about 3 minutes.

Stir the flour into the butter in the pan. Blend in the salt, mustard, and pepper. Slowly add the milk, whisking until smooth. Cook, stirring, until the mixture thickens slightly. Stir in the crab, lemon juice, wine, and catsup. Stirring often, continue to cook over medium heat until the crab is done and the mixture is about to boil. Serve steaming hot over pasta. Makes 2 servings.

Love Yourself Cookbook

Baked Crab Casserole

1 pound crab
4 hard boiled eggs, chopped
1 cup Pepperidge Farm
  stuffing
Milk

1/2 teaspoon cayenne
1 cup mayonnaise
1 teaspoon Worcestershire
1 teaspoon lemon juice

Pick over crab to remove any shell. Put dry stuffing in a measuring cup and add milk over stuffing to the 1 cup line. Mix with the remaining ingredients and put in a buttered casserole. Top with bread crumbs and dot with butter. Bake at 350° for 20-30 minutes. Serves 8.

Seafood Sorcery

Crab Meat Dressing

The following recipe is the result of combining three which I picked up on the coast of North Carolina. It is the most delicious I have ever tasted. It is delicious stuffed into the fish and baked and is simply wonderful baked separately in a shallow pan and then cut into squares to serve with baked fish.

1 (6 1/2-ounce) can crab
  meat
2 eggs, beaten
2 tablespoons melted butter
1/2 small onion, finely
  diced
1/4 medium green pepper,
  finely diced
1/2 cup diced celery

1/4 cup chopped parsley
3/4 cup fine corn bread
  crumbs
1 slice white bread, rubbed
  into crumbs
1/2 teaspoon Worcestershire
  sauce
Salt and pepper
1/4 teaspoon dry mustard

Open crab meat and pick out any pieces of cartilage or shell which are present. Mix with all remaining ingredients and stuff fish or spread out in a greased shallow pan. Bake with the fish. If baked separately, bake at 400° for about 25 minutes.

North Carolina and Old Salem Cookery

Shrimp and Cashews with Rice

1 1/2 tablespoons cornstarch
1/4 teaspoon sugar
1/4 teaspoon baking soda
1 1/4 teaspoons salt,
  divided
1/8 teaspoon pepper
2 pounds raw shrimp, peeled
  and deveined
1 cup regular rice, uncooked
1/2 cup vegetable oil
1 cup chopped onion
1 clove garlic, minced
1 teaspoon minced fresh
  ginger
1 cup cubed, unpeeled
  zucchini
1/2 cup diced sweet red or
  green pepper
1/2 cup salted cashews

Combine cornstarch, sugar, baking soda, 1/4 teaspoon salt, and pepper in medium bowl. Cut shrimp in half lengthwise. Stir shrimp into cornstarch mixture, toss to coat, and let stand at room temperature 15-20 minutes.

While shrimp is marinating, prepare rice according to package directions.

Heat oil in wok or skillet until very hot. Add shrimp gradually. Cook and stir over high heat until shrimp turn pink (2-3 minutes). Remove and reserve shrimp. Drain all but 2-3 tablespoons of oil. Sauté onion, garlic, and ginger in oil until transparent. Add zucchini and pepper. Cook and stir 2 minutes. Stir in cooked rice, cashews, and shrimp. Toss gently until heated. Serve immediately. Yield: 4-6 servings.

Even More Special

Shrimp in Lemon Butter

1 cup butter
1/4 cup lemon juice
1 clove garlic, minced
1 teaspoon parsley flakes
1 teaspoon Worcestershire
  sauce
1 teaspoon soy sauce
1/2 teaspoon coarsely ground
  black pepper
1/4 teaspoon salt
2 pounds large shrimp,
  peeled and deveined
Lemon wedges (optional)

Melt butter in large skillet. Add next 7 ingredients; bring to a boil. Add shrimp. Cook over medium heat 5 minutes, stirring occasionally. Garnish shrimp with lemon wedges if desired. Yield: 4-6 servings.

Knollwood's Cooking

Deviled Crab and Shrimp

This combination of crabmeat and shrimp is attractive served in individual scallop shells. Preparation is simple and may be done in advance and refrigerated. Serve with an individual tomato aspic molded around an artichoke heart and fresh steamed broccoli drizzling with lemon butter. Add hot cheese biscuits to complete a memorable meal.

1 medium green pepper, finely chopped
1 medium onion, finely chopped
1/2 cup finely diced celery
1 1/2 cups crabmeat
1 1/2 cups shrimp, cleaned and chopped
1/2 teaspoon salt
1/8 teaspoon pepper (preferably white)
1 tablespoon Worcestershire sauce
1 teaspoon dill weed
1 tablespoon parsley
1 cup mayonnaise
1 cup buttered bread crumbs

Combine all ingredients except crumbs. Place in individual shells. Sprinkle with crumbs. Bake at 350° for 30 minutes. Serves 8.

Taste Buds

Spaghetti with Shrimp

1/4 cup butter or margarine
3 tablespoons all-purpose
  flour
1/2 teaspoon salt
2 cups milk
1 (3-ounce) can sliced
  mushrooms, undrained
1/3 cup sliced, pitted, ripe
  or stuffed green olives

1 tablespoon lemon juice
1/2 to 3/4 teaspoon dill
  weed
1 1/2 pounds shrimp, cooked,
  peeled and deveined
4 - 6 servings hot, seasoned
  spaghetti
2 teaspoons chopped parsley
Parmesan cheese, to taste

Melt butter, blend in flour and salt. Add milk and cook, stirring constantly until thickened. Add undrained mushrooms, olives, lemon juice, dill weed and shrimp. Stir carefully and heat well. Serve over hot spaghetti. Sprinkle with parsley and cheese. Yield: 4-6 servings.

Nothing Could Be Finer

Tahitian Skillet Shrimp

1 (1-pound 4-ounce) can
  pineapple chunks
2 tablespoons oil
1 cup celery, chopped
2 medium green peppers,
  cubed
2 pounds large shrimp,
  parboiled

1/2 cup green onion, chopped
4 tablespoons soy sauce
2 tablespoons, cornstarch
1 tablespoon fresh ginger,
  minced
2 cloves garlic, crushed
10 cherry tomatoes, cut in
  halves

Drain pineapple reserving syrup. Heat oil in skillet. Add celery and pepper, sauté until pepper turns bright green; do not over cook. Add shrimp, and toss with vegetables until heated through. Add pineapple chunks and green onions. Combine syrup, soy sauce, cornstarch, ginger and garlic. Stir into shrimp mixture and heat until thickened and bubbly. Add cherry tomatoes and serve at once over rice or noodles. Serves 6.

Sea to Shore

Garithes Bakatsias
(Shrimp Bakatsias)

A delicious gourmet meal by one of the Triangle area's best-known chefs, George Bakatsias.

3 pounds fresh spinach,
  trimmed and washed
5 ounces fine noodles,
  cooked and drained

6 tablespoons butter, melted
Shrimp-Tomato Sauce (below)
Romano cheese, grated

Blanch spinach in boiling, salted water; drain well. Briefly sauté spinach in 3 tablespoons hot butter. In another pan, sauté cooked noodles briefly in remaining butter. Spread spinach in a circle on a plate. Place a mound of noodles in the center; top with Shrimp-Tomato Sauce. Sprinkle top with Romano cheese. Serves 4.

SPRIMP-TOMATO SAUCE:

6-8 whole green onions,
  chopped
1/2 cup butter
1 ripe tomato, finely
  chopped
1/2 cup chopped fresh
  parsley
2 ounces dry white wine
1/2 ounce brandy

1 cup chicken stock
1/2 teaspoon dried basil
Juice of 1/2 lemon
Salt and pepper
1/2 pound medium shrimp,
  peeled and deveined
2 cloves garlic, minced
4 ounces feta cheese,
  crumbled

Sauté onions in 1/4 cup hot butter until tender. Add the next 8 ingredients and cook down (uncovered) over medium-high heat for 15-20 minutes or until sauce thickens. In another pan, sauté shrimp and garlic in remaining butter for 2 minutes; season lightly with salt and pepper. Drain. Add shrimp and feta cheese to tomato mixture; simmer 1 minute. Pour sauce over spinach and noodles.

The Grecian Plate

 The little coastal village of Calabash is famous for its 22 fine seafood restaurants. The term "Calabash style" is a familiar expression heard up and down the Atlantic Coast when referring to fried seafood.

All-Time Favorite Shrimp with Artichokes

1 (20-ounce) can artichoke
  hearts
3/4 pound raw shrimp, boiled
  and cleaned
1/4 pound fresh or canned
  mushrooms, sliced
5 tablespoons butter
1/4 cup onions, chopped

4 tablespoons flour
1 1/2 cups half-and-half
1 tablespoon Worcestershire
Salt and pepper to taste
3 tablespoons dry sherry
1/4 cup grated Parmesan
  cheese
Paprika

Drain artichokes, slice in half and arrange in buttered 9x13-inch baking dish. Spread the cooked shrimp over these. Sauté mushrooms in butter for about 5 minutes, lift out and sprinkle over shrimp and artichokes. Cook onions in same butter until transparent. Add flour and cook a minute or two longer. Add half-and-half and stir until thickened. Add Worcestershire, salt (lightly, as Parmesan cheese is salty), pepper and sherry to cream sauce and pour over contents of baking dish. Sprinkle with Parmesan cheese and paprika. Bake at 375° for 20 minutes. Serves 6.

Christmas Favorites

Shrimp Scampi Sensation

4 pounds jumbo shrimp,
  shelled

4 ounces melted butter
1 cup fresh bread crumbs

Split shrimp down the middle, and arrange on a baking tray. Brush with butter, and sprinkle with bread crumbs. Broil 5 minutes. Arrange on a platter and pour the sauce over.

SAUCE:

4 scallions
1 clove garlic
1 tablespoon Worcestershire
  sauce
1 cup lemon juice

Salt
3/4 cup cream sherry
3/4 pound butter (12 ounces)
3/4 cup Dijon mustard

Chop the scallions finely, and press garlic. Add Worcestershire sauce, lemon juice, salt, and sherry. Mix the butter with the mustard until soft and smooth. Add to the rest of the sauce. Boil for 5 minutes, stirring constantly. This sauce is also excellent over chicken breasts and all fish. Serves 8.

Ship to Shore II

Garithes Meh Karithia
(Shrimp with Walnuts)

An unusually good combination.

1 tablespoon butter
20 large shrimp, peeled and
  deveined
Juice of 1/2 lemon

Salt and pepper
4 tablespoons chopped
  walnuts

Melt butter in shallow baking dish or in 4 individual small baking dishes. Arrange shrimp in single layer and turn to coat both sides with butter. Sprinkle with lemon juice, salt and pepper. Pack chopped walnuts around and on top of shrimp. Bake at 350° for 10-20 minutes, depending upon desired firmness of shrimp. Serves 4.

The Grecian Plate

Casserole Saint Jacques
Excellent!

16 ounces scallops
1 cup dry white wine
1 small onion, sliced
2 teaspoons lemon juice
1/2 teaspoon salt
4 tablespoons margarine, or
  butter
4 tablespoons flour
1 cup evaporated milk
2 ounces or more Gruyére
  cheese, grated

1 (7 1/2-ounce) can crab
  meat, drained and flaked
1 (4 1/2-ounce) can shrimp,
  drained
1 (3-ounce) can sliced
  mushrooms
1 1/2 cups soft bread crumbs
1 tablespoon melted butter

Combine scallops, wine, onion, lemon juice and salt. Bring to a boil, simmer 5 minutes. Drain, reserving 1 cup liquid.

In a saucepan, melt butter; stir in flour. Add evaporated milk and reserved scallop liquid. Cook and stir over medium heat until mixture thickens and bubbles. Remove from heat; add cheese and dash of pepper. When cheese melts, add scallops, crab, shrimp and mushrooms. Spoon into individual casseroles. Combine bread crumbs and melted butter and sprinkle over casseroles. Bake at 350° for 25 minutes. Can do ahead. Serves 6.

Mountain Elegance

Langoustines in Porto

30 langoustines or 3 medium-
size lobsters
Salt and cayenne, to taste
Pinch of celery seeds
4 tablespoons butter
1/3 glass of fine champagne
or white wine

1 tablespoon shallot,
chopped
1/2 cup of porto (port)
2 egg yolks
3/4 cup of heavy cream
1 tablespoon of mustard,
Dijon or English

Boil the lobsters or langoustines in a lot of water, salted and spiced with some celery seeds. Cook for 10 minutes. Put the butter in a pan and add langoustines (lobsters) and sauté for about 5 minutes on each side until golden brown. Pour the fine champagne in a saucepan, heat it and flambé it. Pour it over the lobsters. Make sure the alcohol burns completely. Add the chopped shallot. Add the port and cook it for 8-10 minutes. Beat the egg yolks with the heavy cream and mustard. Pour over lobsters. Don't boil. Season with salt and a pinch of cayenne. Stir over a very low fire. Place the lobsters into a shallow serving dish. Pour the sauce over in horizontal lines. Serve immediately. Serves 6. This dish goes well with some Riesling.

Sea to Shore

Scallop Kabob

3 pounds scallops
6 limes, cut in slices
8 ounces Canadian bacon,
sliced

1/2 cup butter, melted
6 tablespoons Parmesan
cheese, grated

Alternate scallops, lime slices and bacon slices on skewers. Squeeze several lime slices over the scallops. Coat scallops generously with melted butter and sprinkle with Parmesan. Place skewers on hot grill, 4 inches from the fire, for about 6-7 minutes. Turn and brush with remaining butter and cheese. Broil 6-7 minutes longer. Yields 6 servings.

Seafood Sorcery

Lobster Thermidor

2 (2-pound) lobsters, cooked
1/2 cup butter
2 small onions, finely
  chopped
1/2 cup all-purpose flour
1 1/4 cups milk
1/2 cup grated Cheddar
  cheese

2 1/2 tablespoons dry white
  wine
1/4 teaspoon paprika
Salt and pepper
Grated Parmesan cheese
Lettuce, watercress, lemon
  slices for garnish

Cut boiled lobsters in half carefully and remove meat. Discard intestines. Twist off claws and remove meat. Clean shells thoroughly and rub with oil to make them shiny. Cut meat into pieces 1/2-inch long. Heat half the butter in a skillet and sauté meat. Meanwhile, in another pan heat remaining butter and sauté onions till soft. Stir in the flour and cook over low heat for about 30 seconds. Remove from heat and stir in milk. Cook over medium heat, stirring constantly, to a boil and gently simmer for 2 minutes. Remove from heat and stir in cheese, wine and paprika. Season. Cook over low heat, stirring, for about 1 minute. Pour the cheese sauce over the hot lobster in the skillet. Cook over low heat for a few minutes. Remove from heat.

Place the cleaned lobster shells on a broiler rack and fill them with the lobster mixture. Sprinkle heavily with grated Parmesan. Broil in a preheated broiling compartment, about 4 inches from broiler, until sauce is bubbling and top is golden brown. Serve immediately garnished with lettuce, watercress, and lemon slices. Serves 4.

Ship to Shore I

Clambake

1 large (12-quart) canning
  pot
1 1/2 pecks clams (little
  neck or cherry stone)
12 medium/white potatoes,
  scrubbed
4 sweet potatoes,
  cut in half lengthwise
6 - 8 large carrots,
  cut in half

2 medium-size rutabagas,
  cut in fourths (optional)
2 fryers, cut-up
Salt, pepper, paprika
6 ears corn, shucked and
  silked
12 - 15 small onions
1 - 2 pounds shrimp,
  unpeeled

Scrub clams with vegetable brush and allow to set in sink of clean, salt water while preparing vegetables—this will eliminate grit. Scrub potatoes and carrots with vegetable brush. Peel and cut rutabagas. Wash chicken; pat dry with paper towel; salt, pepper and paprika to taste. Set aside. Prepare corn.

Remove clams from salt water and place in bottom of canning pot. Layer vegetables on top of clams, beginning with onions; then white potatoes, rutabagas, carrots, sweet potatoes and corn. Place chicken parts on top of vegetables. Add 1 pint of water to pot; cap with aluminum foil and lid.

Turn heat on high—until steam gets up—then reduce heat to low or simmer, depending on individual range. Cook 3 - 3 1/2 hours. Uncover and add unpeeled shrimp; cook for an additional 10 minutes.

Note: Melt butter to use on vegetables or as a dip for clams. Or serve with Clambake Sauce, if desired.

CLAMBAKE SAUCE:

8 ounces ketchup
4 ounces hot pepper vinegar
1 tablespoon salt

1 teaspoon pepper
2 teaspoons Worcestershire
  sauce

Combine ingredients; mix thoroughly; serve with baked clams.

Island Born and Bred

 The first forestry school in the United States was opened in Brevard in 1898. It is located in the Pisgah National Forest.

Downeast Clam Bake

Cheesecloth
1 fryer chicken, cut up
4 carrots
4 onions
4 medium Irish or sweet
  potatoes, whole

4 ears of corn, in the
  shucks
2 dozen cherrystone clams
Kitchen string
Water

In a large piece of cheesecloth, place 1 or 2 pieces of chicken, 1 carrot, 1 onion, 1 whole Irish or sweet potato, 1 ear of corn, and 1/2 dozen clams. Gather edges of cheesecloth together and tie with kitchen string to make a bag. Allow 1 bag per person. Pour two inches of water in the bottom of a 12-quart steamer. Place bags in steamer basket. Steam 1 hour. Additional water may be needed. Serves 4.

Coastal Carolina Cooking

Trent Shores Panned Oysters

1 pint oysters, drained
1/4 cup butter
2 tablespoons dry white wine
1 tablespoon lemon juice
1 teaspoon Worcestershire
  sauce

1/2 teaspoon salt
Toast points, or rounds of
  Holland Rusk
Lemon wedges

Sauté oysters gently in butter for 8-10 minutes. Remove oysters; add wine and seasonings; heat to a boil. Pour over oysters. Serve on toast with lemon wedges. Great! Yield: 6 servings.

Pass the Plate

Oysters Parmesan

3 English muffins, split, or
  patty shells, or toast
  points
1/2 pint oysters, drained
1 tablespoon chopped onion
1 cup milk, divided
1 1/2 tablespoons butter

2 tablespoons flour
1/4 teaspoon salt
Dash pepper
1/4 teaspoon celery salt
1/4 cup Parmesan cheese
1 teaspoon chopped parsley

Combine oysters, onion and 1/2 cup milk and cook over medium heat 15 minutes. (Do NOT over cook oysters.) Melt butter and blend in flour and seasonings and rest of milk and cook until thick, stirring constantly. Add Parmesan and parsley and stir well. Add oyster mixture and cook 5 minutes. Serve over lightly toasted and buttered muffins, toast points or patty shells. You may also serve oysters in a chafing dish for added elegance.

A Taste of History

Oyster Pie

1 quart oysters
Flour
Large slice bacon
1 small onion, minced
1 tablespoon minced parsley
1 tablespoon chopped green
  pepper

1 teaspoon salt
1/4 teaspoon pepper
1/2 teaspoon paprika
Few grains cayenne
Juice 1 lemon
1/2 cup fine cracker crumbs
1 tablespoon butter or cream

Butter a shallow baking dish. Wash oysters and dry between towels. Roll in flour and place half in a layer in a dish. Cut bacon fine and cook with onion until browned.

Sprinkle half the onion and bacon with fat over the oysters. Sprinkle half the parsley, green pepper and seasoning over oysters. Add 1/2 the lemon juice. Add another layer and seasonings in the same manner. Top with crumbs and cream or butter. Bake 450° for 20 minutes . . . marvelous first course or for lunch.

High Hampton Hospitality

Cakes

Somerset Place, a State Historical Site plantation on the shore
of Lake Phelps near Creswell.

Company Pecan Cheesecake

This is a very special Christmas dessert. Top with a sprig of holly. It will serve a crowd.

1 cup graham cracker crumbs
3 tablespoons sugar
3 tablespoons melted butter
1/2 cup finely chopped
  pecans
3 (8-ounce) packages cream
  cheese, softened
1 1/4 cups dark brown sugar,
  firmly packed

2 tablespoons all-purpose
  flour
3 eggs
1 1/2 teaspoons vanilla
3/4 cup chopped pecans
Maple syrup
Pecan halves

Combine crumbs, sugar, butter, and pecans. Press into the bottom of a 9-inch springform pan. Bake at 350° for 10 minutes. Set aside to cool. Combine cheese, sugar, and flour and mix well. Add eggs one at a time, beating after each addition. Blend in vanilla and chopped pecans. Pour into crust and bake at 350° for 50-55 minutes. Cool. Remove from pan. Chill. Brush with syrup and garnish with pecan halves. Yield: One 9-inch cheesecake.

Taste Buds

Chocolate Cheesecake with Raspberry Sauce

CRUST:
3 cups graham cracker crumbs
2 ounces semi-sweet chocolate

1 1/2 sticks butter, melted
3 tablespoons sugar

Pulverize the crackers in a food processor with quick on and off turns. Grate 2 ounces chocolate in the same work bowl and combine with the crumbs, melted butter, and 3 tablespoons sugar. Press the mixture into two 8 1/2-inch springform pans, spreading it evenly on the bottom and partially up the sides. Set aside.

FILLING:
3 eggs
1 cup sugar
3 (8-ounce) packages cream
  cheese, softened
12 ounces semi-sweet
  chocolate

1 1/2 sticks butter
1 cup sour cream
1 teaspoon vanilla
1 cup pecans, coarsely
  chopped
1 recipe Raspberry Sauce

CONTINUED

CONTINUED

Preheat oven to 325°. Beat the eggs with the sugar until the mixture is thick and ribbons when the beater is lifted. Add the softened cream cheese and whip until the mixture is smooth. Melt the chocolate with the butter by setting in a saucepan over the lowest possible flame on a gas stove (otherwise use a double boiler). Add the sour cream and vanilla and blend with the cream cheese-egg mixture.

Divide the cheesecake mixture between the 2 crusts and bake at 325° for 2 hours. Let the cakes cool, remove them from the springform pans, and chill for several hours.

To serve, slice one cheese cake (freeze the other) and cap with 2-3 tablespoons of the Raspberry Sauce. Garnish with fresh raspberries, if available. Yields two 8 1/2-inch cheesecakes, each serving 8-10 people.

RASPBERRY SAUCE:

2 (10-ounce) packages frozen
  raspberries
1/4 - 1/2 cup sugar

2 tablespoons raspberry
  liqueur (Framboise) or
  Grand Marnier

Bring the raspberries to room temperature and push the pulp through a drum sieve or strainer with a large spoon to remove the seeds. Season to taste with sugar and liqueur. The sauce may be kept in the refrigerator for several weeks. Yields approximately 1 cup.

The Fearrington House Cookbook

Strawberry Glazed Cream Cheese Cake

CRUST:

3/4 cup (3 ounces) coarsely
  ground walnuts
3/4 cup finely ground graham
  crackers

3 tablespoons melted
  unsalted butter

Preheat oven to 350°. Place rack in center of oven. Lightly butter 9-inch or 10-inch springform pan. Combine above ingredients and press onto bottom of springform pan.

FILLING:

4 (8-ounce) packages cream
  cheese
4 eggs

1 1/4 cups sugar
1 tablespoon lemon juice
2 teaspoons vanilla

Beat cream cheese by electric mixer or processor until smooth. Add eggs, sugar, lemon juice and vanilla. Beat thoroughly. Spoon over crust. Set pan on baking sheet to catch any butter that may drip out. Bake 10-inch cake 40-45 minutes or 9-inch cake 50-55 minutes. Remove from oven. Let stand at room temperature 15 minutes.

TOPPING:

2 cups sour cream
1/4 cup sugar

1 teaspoon vanilla

Combine above ingredients and blend well. Cover and refrigerate. When cake finishes baking, spoon topping over, return to oven and bake 5 minutes longer. Let cool and refrigerate cake at least 24 hours or preferably 2-3 days.

GLAZE:

1 quart strawberries
1 (12-ounce) jar raspberry
  jelly

1 tablespoon cornstarch
1/4 cup orange liqueur
1/4 cup water

Wash and dry strawberries. Combine a little jelly with cornstarch in saucepan and mix well. Add remaining jelly, orange liqueur and water and cook over medium heat, stirring until thickened and clear—about 5 minutes. Cool to lukewarm. Loosen cake from pan. Remove springform. Arrange berries on top, pointed end up. Spoon glaze over. Return to refrigerator until glaze is set. Yield: 10-12 servings.

Nothing Could Be Finer

Velvet Cake

This recipe came from a woman 90 years old who said it belonged to her mother. It is the moist crumbly type of cake that really does just disappear in the mouth. There is no better cake recipe in my book.

I like to bake it in a large pan about two inches deep and then frost it with chocolate frosting and cut it into squares.

1 cup butter	1 cup buttermilk
2 cups sugar	3/4 teaspoon soda
2 egg yolks	2 1/2 cups sifted flour
2 whole eggs	1 teaspoon vanilla

Cream butter. Add sugar and cream well together. Beat in egg yolks and mix well. Add eggs, one at a time, beating well after each.

Stir soda into buttermilk and add to creamed mixture alternately with flour, blending well. Add vanilla.

Pour into three greased layer cake pans and bake at 375° for 20-25 minutes or until done. Cool and frost with white frosting made from the egg whites left from the 2 yolks used in the recipe.

If baked in a loaf, bake at 325° until done.

North Carolina and Old Salem Cookery

Seafoam Frosting

Seafoam frosting is often used on spice or devil's food cake. This is the best recipe I have ever tried.

2 egg whites	Dash of salt
1 1/2 cups brown sugar,	1/3 cup of water
firmly packed	1 teaspoon vanilla

Combine egg whites, sugar, salt and water in top of double boiler. Place over rapidly boiling water and beat at high speed for seven minutes, or until mixture will stand in stiff peaks. Add vanilla and beat until thick enough to spread.

North Carolina and Old Salem Cookery

Fresh Apple Pound Cake

3 eggs
2 cups sugar
1 cup vegetable oil
3 cups all-purpose flour
1 teaspoon cinnamon
1 teaspoon nutmeg
1 teaspoon baking soda
1/2 teaspoon salt

1 teaspoon vanilla
1/2 teaspoon orange extract
 (optional)
1/2 teaspoon lemon extract
 (optional)
3 cups tart apples, chopped
 and unpeeled
1 cup pecans, chopped

In a large bowl, combine and beat eggs, sugar, and vegetable oil. Sift together the dry ingredients and stir into the egg mixture until batter is smooth. Stir in flavorings and fold in chopped apples and nuts. Spoon into a greased and floured tube pan. Bake 1 hour and 20 minutes at 325°. Allow to cool slightly in the pan (about 10 minutes). Remove from pan and brush outside of cake lightly with melted margarine. Keep covered until served.

SAUCE:
1 stick margarine
1/2 cup light brown sugar,
 packed

2 tablespoons milk
1 - 2 tablespoons rum
 extract

Combine margarine, sugar, and milk in a small saucepan. Bring to low boil and simmer gently about 2 minutes, until clear and syrupy. Add rum extract. While hot, spoon over warm cake. Keep covered until served.

This cake freezes well, and will keep unfrozen one week in the refrigerator if tightly covered.

In Good Taste

5 Flavor Pound Cake

CAKE:
2 sticks butter
1/2 cup vegetable shortening
3 cups sugar
5 eggs, well beaten
3 cups all-purpose flour
1/2 teaspoon baking powder

1 cup milk
1 teaspoon coconut extract
1 teaspoon rum extract
1 teaspoon lemon extract
1 teaspoon vanilla extract
1 teaspoon butter extract

CONTINUED

CONTINUED

Cream butter, shortening and sugar until lightly fluffy. Add eggs which have been beaten until lemon colored. Combine flour and baking powder and add to creamed mixture alternately with milk. Stir in flavorings. Spoon into a greased and papered 10-inch tube pan and bake at 325° for 1 hour and 30 minutes.

GLAZE:

1 cup sugar	1 teaspoon butter extract
1/2 cup water	1 teaspoon lemon extract
1 teaspoon coconut extract	1 teaspoon vanilla extract
1 teaspoon rum extract	1 teaspoon almond extract

Combine ingredients in heavy saucepan. Bring to a boil and stir until sugar is melted; pour over cake just out of oven. Let sit in pan until cake is cool.

Can freeze. Serves 12-15.

Mountain Elegance

C's Pound Cake

1 stick margarine	1/2 teaspoon baking powder
1 cup Crisco	1/2 teaspoon salt
3 cups sugar	1 cup milk
6 eggs	1 tablespoon butternut
3 1/2 cups flour	flavoring

Blend margarine, Crisco and sugar until creamy. Add eggs, one at a time. Sift dry ingredients. Add alternately with milk. Add in flavoring. Pour in a greased and floured tube pan. Bake at 325° for about 1 hour and 15 minutes or until done. This is a really good cake.

CHOCOLATE GLAZE:

1 cup semi-sweet chocolate pieces	1/4 cup white corn syrup
	2 tablespoons water

Melt chocolate pieces in double boiler. Stir in syrup and water. Stir until smooth. Drizzle over cake.

Have Fun Cooking With Me

White Chocolate Mousse Cake

CAKE:

2 cups sugar
3 eggs
1 1/4 cups oil
4 teaspoons vanilla
1 1/3 cups boiling water
1 cup cocoa

1 1/3 teaspoons baking soda
1 1/3 teaspoons baking
  powder
2/3 teaspoon salt
2 1/2 cups unsifted
  all-purpose flour

In a large mixing bowl beat sugar and eggs until creamy; blend in oil and vanilla and beat for 2 minutes. Combine water and cocoa. Add to egg mixture, blend thoroughly. Stir in baking soda, powder and salt; mix well. Add flour and blend until smooth. Pour into three 9-inch greased cake pans. Bake for 25-30 minutes at 350°. Remove from oven, cool 5 minutes in pan and turn onto racks; cool completely.

FILLING I:
1 1/2 cups strawberry preserves (preferably homemade)

FILLING II: WHITE CHOCOLATE MOUSSE

1/2 pound white chocolate,
  grated
1/4 cup sugar

1/8 cup water
2 egg whites
1 cup whipping cream

Place white chocolate in top of double boiler over simmering, not boiling water. Heat, stirring constantly until chocolate melts. Remove from heat and set aside. Combine sugar and water in small saucepan. Cook over medium heat, stirring frequently, until candy thermometer registers soft ball stage (234°). Beat egg whites (at room temperature) in a large mixing bowl until soft peaks form. Slowly pour hot syrup in a thin stream over beaten egg whites while beating at medium speed of electric mixer. Continue beating at medium speed while slowly adding reserved white chocolate. Turn mixer to high speed and continue beating until mixture is thick. Cool to room temperature. Beat whipping cream in a medium bowl until stiff peaks form; gently fold into egg mixture. Refrigerate.

To assemble cake cut each layer in half with very sharp knife. Take first layer and lay (cut side up) on serving plate. Spread with 1/2 cup strawberry preserves and top with remaining half of first

CONTINUED

CONTINUED

layer (smooth side up); spread white chocolate mousse over this half. Repeat above procedure once. With remaining halves, lay cut side up and again spread with preserves. Top with last half (smooth side up).

FROSTING:

1/2 cup butter or margarine
1 (1-pound) box
  confectioners' sugar

1/2 cup cocoa
1/2 cup evaporated milk
1 teaspoon vanilla

Combine all ingredients. Beat on high speed until smooth and creamy. Frost top and sides of cake. If desired, pipe or attractively spoon remaining white chocolate mousse on borders of cake. Serves 16.

A Dash of Down East

Sour Cream Chocolate Chip Cake

Who can ever resist a chocolate chip? This recipe for a sour cream cake with nuts and chocolate chips is sure to please your family or guests as well. I bake it in a Bundt pan.

1 cup butter, soft
1 1/4 cups sugar
3 eggs, lightly beaten
1/2 pint sour cream
2 cups cake flour, sifted
1 teaspoon baking powder

1/2 teaspoon baking soda
1 teaspoon vanilla
1 (12-ounce) package
  chocolate chips
1 cup pecans, chopped

Preheat oven to 350°. Grease and flour a 10-inch Bundt pan. Cream butter and sugar. Beat in eggs and sour cream. Sift together dry ingredients and add to sugar mixture. Add vanilla, chips, pecans. Pour into pan. Bake 1 hour. Yield: One 10-inch Bundt cake.

Taste Buds

Julie's Bridge Meringue Torte

MERINGUE:

6 egg whites
2 teaspoons vanilla
1/2 teaspoon cream
  of tartar

Dash salt
2 cups sugar

Have egg whites at room temperature. Add vanilla, cream of tartar, and dash of salt; beat to soft peaks. Gradually add sugar, beating to very stiff peaks. Cover 2 cookie sheets with pastry paper (ungreased paper). Draw a 9-inch circle on each and spread meringue evenly within circles. Bake in very slow oven 275° for 1 hour. Turn off heat; let dry in oven with door closed at least 2 hours or overnight.

TOPPING AND FILLING:

6 (3/4-ounce) chocolate-
  coated English Toffee
  Bars, chilled and crushed

Dash salt
2 cups whipping
  cream, whipped

Fold crushed candy and dash of salt into whipped cream. Spread one-third of the whipped cream between layers. Frost top and sides with remainder. Chill 8 hours or overnight. Garnish with additional crushed candy. Serves 16.

Out Of Our League

Chocolate Torte

1 stick butter
1 cup flour
3/4 cup chopped pecans
1 (8-ounce) package cream
  cheese
1 cup powdered sugar

1 (9-ounce) carton prepared
  whipped topping
1 (family-size) package
  instant chocolate pudding
1 teaspoon almond flavoring

Melt butter in 9x13-inch baking dish. Sprinkle in flour and nuts and spread until smooth with spoon. Bake in 350° oven for 15 minutes. Let cool. Cream the cheese and sugar. Mix together 1 cup whipped topping and cheese mixture. Spread over crust as first layer. Prepare instant chocolate pudding as directed and add flavoring. Spread over first layer. Top with remaining whipped topping. Yields 12 servings.

Recipes From Our Front Porch

Sensational Chocolate Cake

1 cup cocoa	1/2 teaspoon baking powder
2 cups boiling water	1 cup butter, softened
2 3/4 cups flour	2 1/2 cups sugar
2 teaspoons baking soda	4 eggs, room temperature
1/2 teaspoon salt	1 1/2 teaspoons vanilla

Mix cocoa and boiling water. Mix with whisk until smooth. Cool completely. Mix dry ingredients; set aside. In large bowl, beat at high speed the butter, sugar, eggs and vanilla. Beat until light, about 5 minutes. Add dry ingredients alternately with cocoa mixture in halves—beginning and ending with flour. Beat only until well mixed; do not over beat. Pour into 3 greased and floured 9-inch layer cake pans. Bake at 350° for 25-30 minutes. Cool on racks for 10 minutes; then carefully remove from pans. Cool completely.

FILLING:

1 cup heavy cream	1 teaspoon vanilla
1/4 cup confectioners' sugar	

Whip cream with sugar and vanilla and refrigerate. To assemble cake, place cake layer top side down on cake plate. Spread with half the whipped cream. Place second layer top side down. Spread with remainder of whipped cream. Place third layer top side up. Frost sides and top with chocolate frosting. Keep refrigerated. Serves 12 or more. This cake is moist, light and sinfully rich, but well worth the effort. Follow the recipe exactly. Make no substitutions.

FROSTING:

1 (6-ounce) package semi-sweet chocolate morsels	3 1/2 cups confectioners' sugar
1/2 cup light cream	1 teaspoon vanilla
1 cup butter	

Combine chocolate morsels, cream and butter in medium saucepan. Stir over medium heat until smooth. Remove from heat. Blend in sifted confectioners' sugar and vanilla. Beat until it holds its shape (set bowl in ice if necessary).

Christmas Favorites

Anita's Chocolate Cake

2 cups flour
1 cup sugar
1 1/2 teaspoons soda
1 1/2 teaspoons baking
 powder
1 teaspoon salt
4 tablespoons Nestle Quik
 (chocolate)

1/3 - 1/2 cup chocolate
 syrup
1/2 cup plain yogurt
1/2 cup water
2 teaspoons vanilla
1 cup eggless mayonnaise

Preheat oven to 350°. Measure all ingredients into a large bowl and mix just enough to blend well with the mayonnaise. Pour into 2 greased 9-inch pans and bake at 350° for 20-25 minutes or when centers test done with a tester. Let stand for 5 minutes, then remove from the pans and cool on racks.

ANITA'S CHOCOLATE ICING:

6 ounces semi-sweet
 chocolate chips
1/2 cup butter

1/2 cup half-and-half
1 1/2 cups confectioners'
 sugar

Combine chocolate chips, butter and half-and-half in saucepan over low heat and stir until the chocolate is melted. Remove from heat and blend in sugar until smooth. Frosts a two layer cake.

Vegetarian Masterpieces

Pineapple Carrot Cake
(Microwave)

1 cup sugar	2 eggs, slightly beaten
1 cup flour (all-purpose)	1/2 cup oil
1 teaspoon cinnamon	1 1/2 cups grated carrots
1 teaspoon baking powder	1 (8-ounce) can crushed
1 teaspoon baking soda	pineapple, well drained
1/4 teaspoon salt	

In a large bowl, combine sugar, flour, cinnamon, baking powder, baking soda and salt. Stir in eggs, oil, carrots and pineapple. Line bottom of 9x9-inch glass baking dish or ring pan with wax paper. Pour batter into pan. Invert a glass pie plate in the oven. Set cake pan on pie plate. Microcook on Medium (50%) 9-10 minutes. Increase power to High 3-5 minutes. Test cake for doneness with a toothpick. Cake will begin to pull away from sides of pan when done. Let stand 10 minutes. Invert onto serving plate. Serves 8.

CREAM CHEESE FROSTING:

1 (3-ounce) package cream	2 cups confectioners' sugar
cheese	1 teaspoon vanilla
4 tablespoons margarine or	
butter	

Place cream cheese and margarine in 4-cup measure. Microcook on Medium (50%) 1 - 1 1/4 minutes, or until softened. Stir in sugar and vanilla until smooth and creamy. Frost cool cake.

The Microwave Touch

E-Z Apple Pie

3/4 cup sugar	1 egg
1/2 cup flour	1/2 teaspoon vanilla
1/4 teaspoon salt	1/2 cup chopped walnuts
1 teaspoon baking powder	1 cup diced apples (2
1/2 teaspoon cinnamon	apples)

Preheat oven to 350°. Combine sugar, flour, salt, baking powder, and cinnamon. Stir well. Beat in egg and vanilla with whisk or spoon. Stir in nuts and apples. Mixture becomes thick. Spoon into a buttered 8-inch pie plate, and spread evenly. Bake for 30 minutes at 350°. Delicious served warm with ice cream or whipped cream. Serves 6. A rich apple "cake" consistency.

Ship to Shore II

Blueberry Cake

1 cup plain flour	1 cup chopped pecans
1 stick butter or margarine, softened	1/4 cup brown sugar

In a large mixing bowl, mix all ingredients, using a potato masher. When well-blended, pat mixture into an ungreased 9x12-inch baking pan. Bake at 350° until brown on top. Cool.

FILLING:

2 1/2 cups blueberries	1/4 cup plain flour
1 cup sugar	1 tablespoon lemon juice

In a medium saucepan, combine ingredients and simmer over low heat until thickened. Cool.

TOPPING:

1 cup whipping cream	3/4 cup sugar
6 ounces cream cheese, room temperature	1 teaspoon vanilla

In a large mixing bowl, beat cream until it forms a soft peak. Add cream cheese, sugar and vanilla and continue to beat until well blended. To assemble, place cake on large platter. Spread with filling. Top with whipped cream mixture. Chill and cut into squares for serving.

Coastal Carolina Cooking

Orange Blossoms

GLAZE:

2 oranges	1 box powdered sugar
2 lemons	

Prepare Glaze first: grate rind of oranges and lemons; squeeze juice from both. Sift sugar into mixture of peel and juice, saving enough of powdered sugar to dust over glazed cakes. If mixture is too dry, add small amount of additional orange juice. This mixture should be of glaze consistency.

CAKES:

1 1/3 cups sugar	1/2 teaspoon salt
3 eggs	1 teaspoon vanilla
1 1/2 cups all-purpose flour	1/2 cup water
1 1/2 teaspoons baking powder	

CONTINUED

CONTINUED

Grease and flour tea-cake pans (tiny muffin-size pans). Preheat oven at 350°. Cream sugar and eggs; add sifted flour, baking powder and salt. Add vanilla and water. Fill tea-cake pans no more than half-full. Bake for 12-15 minutes. Take out of pan while hot; dip into Glaze mixture. Drain on rack; place wax paper under rack to catch Glaze dripping.

Note: This recipe is especially attractive on table when lightly dusted with powdered sugar and garnished with mint leaves. Great for spring weddings and parties. Yield: 6 dozen.

Island Born and Bred

Cherry "Upside-Down" Cake

1/2 cup firmly packed brown
  sugar
1 (No. 2) can sour pie
  cherries, drained; reserve
  juice
1 3/4 cups sifted flour
2 teaspoons baking powder

1/2 teaspoon salt
1 cup sugar
1/3 cup shortening (liquid)
3/4 cup milk
1 teaspoon vanilla
1 egg

All must be at room temperature.

Grease a 12x8x2-inch pan with butter. Sprinkle brown sugar over bottom of pan. Add drained cherries. Sift together flour, baking powder, salt and sugar. Add to shortening and milk and vanilla. Beat for 1 1/2 minutes until batter is well blended. Add egg, unbeaten, and beat for another 1 1/2 minutes. Pour over cherries in pan.

Bake in moderate oven (350°) for 35-45 minutes.

CHERRY SAUCE:
1/2 cup sugar
2 tablespoons cornstarch
1 1/2 cups juice (juice
  reserved from cherries plus
  water)

1/8 teaspoon almond extract

Combine sugar, cornstarch and juice. Cook until thickened, stirring constantly. Remove from heat and add almond extract. Serve warm over warm cake. A fluff of whipped cream for decoration may be added. Serves 12.

A Taste of History

Hurricane Oatmeal Cake

Good to have on hand for "hurricane watches."

1 cup oatmeal	1/2 cup vegetable oil
1 1/4 cups boiling water	1 1/2 cups flour
2 eggs	1 teaspoon soda
1 cup brown sugar	1 teaspoon salt
1 cup granulated sugar	1 teaspoon cinnamon

Combine oatmeal and boiling water; set aside. Beat together eggs, sugars and oil until blended. Add sifted flour, soda, salt and cinnamon; add oatmeal mixture.

Pour into greased 9x13-inch baking pan. Bake at 350° for 30-35 minutes.

TOPPING:

1 cup coconut	1/2 cup chopped pecans
1 cup brown sugar	1/4 cup evaporated milk
6 tablespoons melted margarine	

Mix together topping ingredients until moist. Spread over cake; broil until topping is light brown and crunchy—about 2 minutes.

Island Born and Bred

Gingerbread with Peach Sauce

1 package gingerbread mix   1/2 cup mincemeat

Cook gingerbread mix with 1/2 cup mincemeat as directed on package.

PEACH SAUCE:

1 (13-ounce) can sliced
  peaches
1/4 cup sugar
1 1/2 tablespoons cornstarch
1/4 teaspoon salt

1 tablespoon lemon juice
1/2 teaspoon lemon rind
2 tablespoons butter
1/2 cup mincemeat

Drain peaches. To syrup (add water if necessary to make one cup), add sugar, cornstarch, and salt and cook until clear and thick. Add lemon juice, rind and butter, then fold in peaches and mincemeat. Serve warm over gingerbread. Makes 7 or 8 servings.

Knollwood's Cooking

Pantespani
(Lemon Sponge Cake)

A light melt-in-your-mouth cake.

5 eggs, separated
1 cup sugar
1 cup cake flour
1 1/4 teaspoons baking
  powder

1 lemon rind, grated
1 teaspoon vanilla
1/2 cup butter, melted

Beat egg yolks and sugar several minutes until light and creamy. Sift dry ingredients together and gradually add to batter. Add lemon rind and vanilla. Beat egg whites until stiff and fold gently into batter. Pour into greased and floured 13x9-inch pan. Spoon melted butter evenly over top. Bake at 350° for 25-30 minutes. Slowly spoon cooled syrup over hot cake. Serves 24.

SYRUP:

1 1/2 cups sugar
1 1/4 cups water

Juice of 1 lemon

Combine all ingredients and gently boil for 5-7 minutes, or until candy thermometer reaches 205°.

The Grecian Plate

Spice Cake

1 cup quick oatmeal	1 1/3 cups flour
1 1/4 cups boiling water	1 teaspoon soda
1/2 cup shortening	1/2 teaspoon salt
1 cup brown sugar	1/2 teaspoon cinnamon
1 cup sugar	1/2 teaspoon nutmeg
2 eggs	1 teaspoon vanilla

Pour boiling water over oatmeal. Let stand 10 minutes. Cream shortening, brown sugar and white sugar. Add to oatmeal mixture. Add eggs one at a time. Sift flour, soda, salt, cinnamon, nutmeg and add to mixture. Stir just enough to mix. Add vanilla. Pour into greased 9x13-inch pan and bake in 325° for 35-40 minutes. Yield: 18 servings.

TOPPING:

1 stick margarine	1 cup well-drained crushed
1 cup brown sugar	pineapple
2 egg yolks	1 cup nuts

Cream margarine, sugar and egg yolks together. Add pineapple and nuts (if desired, use one or the other). Spread on cooked cake. Brown under broiler. Serve warm.

Recipes From Our Front Porch

Meringue Spice Cake

3/4 cup shortening	1 teaspoon soda
2 cups brown sugar	1 teaspoon cinnamon
2 beaten egg yolks	1 teaspoon cloves
2 1/3 cups flour	1 1/4 cups sour milk
1 teaspoon baking powder	1 teaspoon vanilla
3/4 teaspoon salt	

Thoroughly cream shortening and sugar; add egg yolks and beat until fluffy. Add sifted dry ingredients, alternating with milk and vanilla. Beat vigorously after each addition. Pour into greased 9x13-inch pan. Cover with Brown Sugar Meringue. Bake at 325° about 50 minutes.

CONTINUED

CONTINUED

BROWN SUGAR MERINGUE:

1 cup brown sugar	1/2 cup broken nut meats
2 stiffly beaten egg whites	

Slowly add sugar to egg whites; beat until smooth. Fold in nuts. Spread over batter and bake as directed.

From Margaret D. Tomlinson's *What's Cookin'?*

Marion Brown's Southern Cook Book

Date and Nut Cake

This recipe makes an excellent cake. Personally, I like the combination of dates, nuts and cherries a lot more than the combination of the other candied fruits usually found in fruit cakes.

2 pounds pitted dates, chopped	1/2 cup butter
4 cups nuts, slightly broken	1 cup sugar
1 cup candied cherries, cut in half	4 eggs
1/2 teaspoon soda, dissolved in 1/2 cup boiling water	1 cup sifted flour
	1/2 teaspoon salt
	1 teaspoon baking powder
	1 teaspoon vanilla

Mix dates, nuts and cherries. Pour soda and boiling water over them and allow to stand while mixing remaining ingredients.

Cream butter and sugar together. Add eggs one at a time and mix well after each. Sift flour with salt and baking powder. Add with vanilla to creamed mixture and blend well.

Add date mixture and mix well—use hands if necessary. Pour batter into large tube pan which has been greased and lined with greased and floured brown paper. Cover top with aluminum foil squeezed around edges. Place a pan of water in the bottom of the oven. Bake at 275° for 3 1/2 hours or until cake tests done. Remove foil the last 30 minutes of baking.

North Carolina and Old Salem Cookery

Crumb Cake

An absolutely delicious and simple-to-prepare dessert is the crumb cake recipe to follow. The original version calls for a topping of whipped cream and then a refrigeration period. When I first tried the recipe, it was still warm and I served it with large scoops of vanilla ice cream. Another alternative, add 1 cup chopped apples.

1 1/4 cups graham cracker
  crumbs
1 3/4 cups sugar
2 teaspoons baking powder
5 eggs, lightly beaten

2 cups chopped walnuts
3 teaspoons vanilla
2 cups heavy cream, whipped
1 cup chopped apples (optional)
Vanilla ice cream

Mix dry ingredients and add eggs, nuts and vanilla. Pour into greased 10-inch deep dish pie pan. Bake in a 350° preheated oven for 30-35 minutes. Allow to cool, cut into wedges and top with vanilla ice cream and serve. If desired, top with whipped cream and place in the refrigerator until ready to serve. Yield: One 10-inch deep dish pie.

Taste Buds

Sally White Cake I

Original recipe brought from Petersburg in 1830 by Mrs. Kate Walker Whiting.

1 pound butter
2 1/2 cups sugar
10 eggs
4 cups flour
1 whole nutmeg (grated)
Mace to taste

3 pounds citron
1 1/2 pounds almonds
2 medium coconuts, grated
  (or 1 pound grated coconut)
3 ounces each of brandy and
  sherry

Cream well the sugar and butter. Add the beaten yolks. Sift the spices into the flour and mix all of the fruit into this. Mix this alternately with the wine into the sugar and butter mixture, and lastly fold in the beaten whites of eggs. Bake at 250° for 3 hours.

Favorite Recipes of the Lower Cape Fear

Box Wedding Cake

You won't believe it is a cake made from a box of cake mix.

1 (regular size) package
   yellow cake mix for pound
   cake supreme
1 (4-serving size) package
   instant vanilla pudding mix
4 eggs

1/2 cup butter, melted and
   cooled
1 cup water
1 tablespoon coconut extract
   (yes, 1 tablespoon)

Combine all ingredients, blending together well. (In the recipe the 1/2 cup of melted and cooled butter is substituted for the 1/2 cup oil called for in some recipes.)

One package of cake mix prepared as suggested in the foregoing is sufficient to make two layers in greased and floured tiered wedding cake pans—one pan 6 x 1 3/4-inches deep, and one layer 8 x 1 3/4-inches deep.

A second package of cake mix prepared as suggested in the foregoing is sufficient to make a layer in a greased and floured tiered layer pan that is 10 x 1 3/4 inches deep.

Do not fill the pans much more than half full, or the batter will run over in the oven, smoke, and even burn in the oven.

After baking the layers of cake, turn out. Place pan back immediately over the layer to allow the cake to sweat: this makes for a more moist cake. Freezing the layers before frosting also helps make the cake more moist.

Frost cake and decorate as desired.

What's New in Wedding Food

Fresh Coconut Cake
with Rum and Orange Filling

A coconut cake is a traditional holiday dessert in the South. This cake's delicious flavor comes from including grated orange rind in the batter, orange juice and rum on the layers, and an orange filling between the layers. It may be made well in advance and frozen.

3/4 cup butter, softened	1/4 teaspoon salt
1 1/2 cups sugar	3/4 cup milk
2 egg yolks	3 egg whites
2 cups flour	1 orange rind, grated
2 teaspoons baking powder	

Preheat oven to 350°. Grease the bottoms of two 9-inch cake pans. Cut wax paper to fit the bottoms, and grease and flour the wax paper. Cream the butter and sugar until light and fluffy. Beat in egg yolks one at a time. Sift the flour, baking powder, and salt together. Add alternately with milk, beginning and ending with dry ingredients. Whip egg whites until stiff but not dry. Fold into the cake batter along with the grated orange rind. Pour the batter into the pans and bake at 350° for about 25 minutes or until a toothpick inserted in the middle comes out clean. Let the cakes cool in the pans for a few minutes, invert onto rack, and peel off the wax paper.

1/4 cup orange juice	1/2 cup rum

Slice the layers in half to get 4 thin layers, prick with a fork, and drizzle with the mixture of orange juice and rum. Set aside.

1 cup sugar	2 tablespoons butter
1/4 teaspoon salt	1 orange rind, grated
4 tablespoons cornstarch	2 tablespoons lemon juice
1 cup orange juice	

Blend 1 cup sugar with salt and cornstarch until the mixture is smooth. Gradually add orange juice and bring to a boil on top of stove. Boil 1-2 minutes, remove from the heat, and stir in butter, orange rind, and lemon juice. Cool. Spread 1/3 of the mixture on the first layer; stack the second and third layers and repeat the process. Add the fourth layer.

CONTINUED

CONTINUED

8 ounces heavy cream
2 teaspoons rum
1/3 cup sugar

Grated meat of 1 fresh
coconut

Whip the cream until soft peaks form and add the rum and sugar. Continue to whip until stiff. Spread over the cake and pat shredded coconut onto the sides and top. Yields one 4-layer 9-inch cake.

The Fearrington House Cookbook

Rave Review

CAKE:

1 package yellow cake mix
1 package instant coconut
  pudding
1 1/3 cups water

4 eggs
1/4 cup oil
2 cups coconut
1 cup nuts (toasted)

Combine and mix well. Put into 3 greased and floured pans. Bake 35 minutes at 350°.

COCONUT ICING:

4 tablespoons butter
1 (8-ounce) package cream
  cheese
1 box powdered sugar

2 cups coconut
2 teaspoons milk
1 teaspoon vanilla

Cream butter and cream cheese. Add to sugar, coconut, milk and vanilla. Mix well and ice between layers.

Ship to Shore I

Rum Squares

1 cup powdered sugar	1/2 pound candied red
1 cup sifted flour	cherries, finely chopped
1/2 teaspoon salt	1 pound pitted dates, finely
1 teaspoon baking powder	chopped
1/2 pound candied green	4 eggs
pineapple, finely chopped	1 teaspoon vanilla

Sift together 1 cup powdered sugar, flour, salt and baking powder. Add candied fruits and dates.

Beat eggs with vanilla and pour over fruit mixture. Turn into a greased and floured pan about 11x7 inches. Bake in a 325° oven (300° if pan is Pyrex) for 45 minutes, or until done.

FROSTING:

1/3 cup soft butter	1 teaspoon instant coffee
1 1/2 cups powdered	powder
sugar	Rum

Cool in pan and then cover with layer of frosting made by blending butter with 1 1/2 cups powdered sugar and coffee powder. Add sufficient rum to make a mixture of proper spreading consistency. Cut into 1-inch squares.

What's New in Wedding Food

The Mast General Store in Valle Crucis was founded in 1883 and is listed in the National Register of Historic Places as one of the best examples of an old general store.

Cookies
and Candies

The Mast General Store at Valle Crucis.

Granny Lail's Sugar Cookie

2 1/2 cups all-purpose
  flour, sifted
2 cups powdered sugar
1 cup butter, softened
1 teaspoon baking soda

1 teaspoon cream of tartar
1 large egg
1/4 teaspoon salt
1 teaspoon vanilla

Mix all ingredients with a wooden spoon and knead dough. Chill dough overnight. Roll out small portion of dough and cut into desired shapes. Bake 5-8 minutes at 375°. (Stores well in the refrigerator for several weeks.) Yield: 5-6 dozen.

Note: Important to chill the dough before cutting the shapes. Also, it helps to release the cookie from the cutter if you dip the cookie cutter in powdered sugar first.

Variations: Add lemon flavoring for lemon cookies, pecans for pecan flavor.

Heart of the Mountains

"Big Mama" Coldough's Old-Fashioned Tea Cakes

1 stick butter, room
  temperature
1 egg

1 tablespoon vanilla
1 1/2 cups flour, sifted
1 cup sugar

Preheat oven to 350°. Mix all ingredients by hand in large mixing bowl, rolling into loaf of even consistency. Lift dough to sprinkle additional flour on sides of mixing bowl because dough will be sticky. Pinch off a teaspoon-size piece of dough and, with floured hands, roll into small ball. Place on ungreased cookie sheet, leaving room for expansion. Cook for 9-10 minutes or until just starting to brown at edges. Best when served hot, as the generations will all attest.

Knollwood's Cooking

Tasty Thin/Cinnamon Thins

1 stick butter
1 stick margarine
1 cup sugar
1 egg yolk (save white to
  brush top of cookie)

2 cups flour
1 teaspoon vanilla
Ground or finely chopped
  pecans

Cream butter, margarine and sugar. Add egg yolk, flour and vanilla. Mix well. Use one 18x12x1-inch pan or two 15x10x1-inch pans. Use teflon pans, if possible. Spray pans with Pam, then grease well.

Spread dough very thin, brush top of cookies with egg white. Then sprinkle nuts on top and gently press. Bake at 300° for 30 minutes. Cut into small rectangles (1x3 inches) while hot, and remove from pan.

Note: For Cinnamon Thins, add 4 teaspoons (yes, 4 teaspoons) cinnamon to dough.

Mama's Recipes

Benne Cookies

1 cup benne (sesame) seeds
10 tablespoons butter,
  softened
10 tablespoons margarine,
  softened
1 1/2 cups sugar

3 cups flour
6 tablespoons milk
2 cups coconut
1/2 cup chopped almonds
2 teaspoons vanilla
Dash salt

Toast benne seeds until light brown; do not burn seeds. Cream butter, margarine and sugar together until fluffy. Add flour and milk, stir until just combined. Add benne seeds, coconut, almonds, vanilla and salt. Mix well.

Preheat oven to 325°.

Take up about 1 tablespoon of dough for each cookie and roll into a 1-inch ball. Flatten slightly and place 1 inch apart on lightly greased cookie sheet. Bake at 325° on ungreased cookie sheet for 15-20 minutes. Cool on racks. Makes about 6 dozen cookies.

Vegetarian Masterpieces

Fruit Cake Cookies

6 slices candied pineapple
8 ounces candied cherries
8 ounces dates
All-purpose flour for
  dredging
6 cups pecans
1 cup butter
1 cup brown sugar, firmly
  packed

2 eggs
2 1/4 cups self-rising flour
1 1/2 tablespoons milk
1/2 teaspoon baking soda
1/2 teaspoon vanilla
1 cup pineapple preserves

Preheat oven to 325°. Grease several cookie sheets. Chop pineapple, cherries, and dates; dredge with flour. Chop pecans. Cream butter and sugar together. Add eggs, flour, milk, soda, vanilla, and preserves. Mix well. Stir in floured, chopped fruit and pecans.

Drop batter by the teaspoonful onto cookie sheets and bake for 15 minutes. Remove to wire racks to cool. Yield: 6 dozen.

Hints: This recipe can be doubled. Use 3 eggs when doubling. Chop fruit ahead of time—this makes the process shorter.

Even More Special

Unique Date Cookies

1 cup butter	1 tablespoon vanilla
1 cup sugar	4 cups flour
1 cup brown sugar	1 teaspoon salt
3 eggs	1 teaspoon baking soda

Cream together butter and sugars. Add eggs and beat until fluffy. Add vanilla. Sift together flour, salt and baking soda and add to mixture. Mix well and chill. Before taking dough out of refrigerator, combine filling ingredients. Roll out dough on floured board and spread with filling. Roll up like a jelly roll and chill overnight. Slice 1/8-inch thick pieces and place on lightly greased baking sheets. Bake at 375° for 12 minutes.

FILLING:

1 pound dates, chopped	1/2 cup water
1/2 cup sugar	

Combine filling ingredients in saucepan and boil for 1 minute. Set aside to cool. Spread dough with cooled filling.

A Cookbook of Pinehurst Courses

Tryon Palace Ginger Crinkle Cookies

This recipe was provided in answer to many requests.

2/3 cup Wesson oil	2 teaspoons baking soda
1 cup sugar	1/2 teaspoon salt
1 egg	1 teaspoon cinnamon
4 tablespoons molasses	1 teaspoon ginger
2 cups sifted flour	1/4 cup sugar for dipping

Preheat oven to 350°. Mix oil and sugar thoroughly. Add egg and beat well. Stir in molasses. Sift dry ingredients together and add. Drop by teaspoonfuls into sugar and form into balls coated with sugar. Place on ungreased cookie sheet 3 inches apart. Bake for 15 minutes. Cookies will flatten and crinkle. Remove to wire rack. Yield: 5 dozen.

Pass the Plate

Black Walnut Drop Cookies

These squares are rich but make luscious use of Carolina's full-flavored black walnuts.

1/2 cup shortening	1/4 teaspoon salt
1/2 cup butter	1/2 teaspoon soda
2 1/2 cups dark brown sugar	1/8 teaspoon walnut
2 eggs	flavoring
2 1/2 cups sifted flour	1 cup crushed black walnuts

Cream shortening and butter. Add sugar and mix well. Add eggs and mix.

Sift flour with salt and soda and add to creamed mixture with nuts and flavoring. Don't add any more flavoring because 1/8 teaspoon gives a fine walnut taste.

Drop by half teaspoons onto a greased cookie sheet. Bake in a moderate oven, 350°, for about 10 minutes or until lightly browned. Makes about 5 dozen cookies.

North Carolina and Old Salem Cookery

Chocolate-Filled Snowballs

1 cup soft butter	1 cup finely chopped pecans
1/2 cup sugar	1 (5 3/4-ounce) package
1 teaspoon vanilla	chocolate kisses
2 cups sifted flour	Confectioners' sugar

Cream butter, sugar and vanilla until very light and fluffy. Add sifted flour and nuts, blending well. Cover bowl with plastic wrap and chill dough about 1 hour. Remove foil wrappers from kisses. Preheat oven to 375°. Shape dough around kisses, using about 1 tablespoon of dough for each roll to make a ball. Cover completely. Bake 12 minutes until set, not brown. Remove from cookie sheet onto absorbent paper and cool slightly. While still warm, roll in confectioners' sugar. Cool completely before storing. Roll in confectioners' sugar again, if desired. Yield: 5 dozen.

Bravo

Sweetheart Cookies

1 cup butter, softened
1 1/3 cups sugar
1 1/3 cups packed brown
  sugar
2 eggs
1 teaspoon vanilla extract
1 1/2 cups all-purpose flour

1 teaspoon soda
3 cups oats
1 1/2 cups chopped roasted
  peanuts
1 cup semi-sweet chocolate
  chips

Cream butter, sugar and brown sugar in mixer bowl until light and fluffy. Add eggs and vanilla; mix well. Combine flour and soda in medium bowl; mix well. Add oats; mix well. Add to creamed mixture 1 cup at a time, beating well after each addition. Stir in peanuts and chocolate chips. Drop by teaspoonfuls onto cookie sheet. Bake at 375° for 10-12 minutes or until light brown. Remove to wire rack to cool. Yield: 72 cookies.

Approx. Per Cookie: Calories 98; Protein 1.6g; Carbohydrates 12.5g; T Fat 5.2g; Cholesterol 14.5mg; Potassium 54.2mg; Sodium 66.0mg.

Goodness Grows in North Carolina

Cathedral Cookies

1 (12-ounce) package
  chocolate chips
4 tablespoons butter
2 eggs
1/2 teaspoon vanilla

1/4 teaspoon salt
1 (10 1/2-ounce) package
  miniature colored
  marshmallows
1 cup chopped pecans

Melt chocolate chips in top of double boiler over hot water. Add butter and mix well. Beat eggs well for 2 minutes and add to chocolate mixture. Add vanilla and salt. Cook for 2 minutes. Take top pan off and let cool. Add marshmallows and nuts. Cover waxed paper with powdered sugar. Divide batter into thirds. Roll into long rolls 2 inches in diameter. Chill overnight. Slice off when needed. Keeps indefinitely in refrigerator. Freezes well. Yields 3 dozen.

Recipes From Our Front Porch

Hermit Bars

1/3 cup margarine, softened
1/3 cup brown sugar
1 egg, beaten
2 tablespoons milk
1/2 cup molasses
2 cups all-purpose flour
1/4 teaspoon baking soda

1 teaspoon baking powder
1/2 teaspoon cinnamon
1/2 teaspoon ginger
1/2 teaspoon ground cloves
1/2 cup nuts, chopped
1 cup raisins

Blend margarine and brown sugar together. Add beaten egg, milk, and molasses. Blend well. Sift together flour, baking soda, baking powder, and spices. Stir into liquid ingredients. Add chopped nuts and raisins and blend well.

Spread cookie mixture evenly on pans that have been greased and lined with waxed paper. Bake at 350° for 30-40 minutes (until firm). Turn immediately out of pan onto board or other flat surface. Remove wax paper liner. Cut into square or bars while still warm. Makes 32 bars.

In Good Taste

Layer Cookies
High Hampton Inn

FIRST LAYER:
1/2 cup Crisco
1 cup sugar
2 eggs

1/2 teaspoon salt
1 1/2 cups flour
1 teaspoon baking powder

Cream Crisco and sugar and add eggs well-beaten. Add salt and vanilla. Sift baking powder with flour and add. Spread in long shallow pan and cover with second layer.

SECOND LAYER:
1 cup brown sugar
1/2 teaspoon vanilla

2 egg whites, beaten stiff
3/4 cup chopped nuts

Spread this mixture over first layer and bake in medium oven. Cut into squares when cool. They freeze well.

High Hampton Hospitality

Orange Chocolate Chip Bars

1 cup shortening
1/2 cup brown sugar
3/4 cup sugar (1/2 cup at
 first)
2 eggs
2 tablespoons vanilla

1/2 teaspoon salt
1 cup flour
1 cup dry oatmeal
1/2 cup chocolate chips
1/2 cup orange juice

Cream shortening, add brown sugar, 1/2 cup sugar, eggs, vanilla and salt. Add flour, oatmeal and chocolate chips. Turn into greased 9x9-inch pan. Bake 40 minutes at 350°.

Combine remaining sugar and orange juice. Bring to boil and pour over hot bars. (Doubled recipe fills 9x13-inch pan.)

A Taste of History

Snowbird Trail Bars

1 cup butter
1/2 cup sugar
1/2 cup brown sugar
2 eggs
1 teaspoon vanilla
1 1/4 cups flour

1 teaspoon soda
1 1/2 cups rolled oats,
 uncooked
1 (6-ounce) package
 chocolate chips
1 cup pecans, broken

Cream butter and sugars well. Blend in eggs and vanilla. Sift flour and soda together and add to first mixture. Stir in oats, chocolate chips and pecans. Bake 25-30 minutes at 375° in a well-greased 9x13-inch pan.

Nestled in the mountains of North Carolina near Robinsville, "Trail Bars" are a special treat packed in picnic lunches for all-day hikers . . . lots of added energy and oh-so-good!

Christmas Favorites

 Mount Mitchell, at 6,684 feet, is the highest peak in Eastern America. There is an observation tower on top.

Summit Lemon Squares

2 sticks butter, softened
2 cups flour
1/2 cup powdered sugar
4 eggs, beaten slightly
2 cups sugar

6 tablespoons lemon juice
1 tablespoon flour
1/2 teaspoon baking powder
1 cup pecans (optional)

Preheat oven to 325°. Mix first three ingredients and press into a 10x4-inch pan. Bake for 15 minutes. Mix together remaining ingredients and pour on top of pastry. Bake at 325° for 40-50 minutes. Sprinkle with additional powdered sugar. Makes 2-3 dozen. From *Heritage of Hospitality*.

Stirring Performances

Cheese Cake Bars
... a hit with everyone!

1/3 cup butter
1/3 cup brown sugar

1 cup flour
1/2 cup chopped nuts

Cream butter with brown sugar in small mixing bowl, add flour and nuts. Mix to make a crumb mixture. Reserve 1 cup for topping. Press remainder into bottom of 8-inch square pan.

FILLING:
1/4 cup sugar
1 egg
1/2 teaspoon vanilla
1 (8-ounce) package cream
   cheese

2 tablespoons milk
1 tablespoon lemon juice

Mix well and beat until creamy. Pour over crumb mixture. Sprinkle remaining crumbs over filling. Bake at 350° for 12-15 minutes.

Mountain Potpourri

Cranberry Crunchy Squares

1 cup quick-cooking rolled
  oats
1/2 cup sifted flour (plain)
3/4 cup brown sugar
1/2 cup coconut

1/3 cup butter or margarine
1 can whole berry cranberry
  sauce
1 tablespoon lemon juice

Mix oats, flour, brown sugar and coconut. Cut in butter with 2 knives, fork or pastry blender until butter is in small pea-size lumps. Spread half of this mixture over bottom of 8 or 9-inch square baking dish. Add lemon juice to cranberry sauce, mix well and pour over mixture in pan. Sprinkle remaining dry mixture over top of cranberry sauce. Bake at 350° for 40 minutes. Serve plain or with whipped cream or ice cream.

Centenary Cookbook

Orange Sticks

This is a distinctive cookie.

2 tablespoons butter
1 cup brown sugar, firmly
  packed
2 eggs
2 tablespoons grated orange
  rind
1 1/4 cups sifted flour
1/2 teaspoon baking powder

1/2 pound orange candy (the
  kind which looks like orange
  sections)
1/3 cup chopped nuts
2 tablespoons orange juice
Juice of 1 large orange
4 tablespoons granulated
  sugar

Cream butter and sugar. Add eggs and mix well. Add orange rind and blend. Sift flour and baking powder together. Mix with orange candy which has been cut into small pieces, and nuts. Add to creamed mixture with 2 tablespoons orange juice.

Pour into 8 1/2 x 11-inch pan which has been greased with wax paper. Bake at 350° about 30 minutes or until done. Turn out.

Mix juice of one large orange with granulated sugar and pour over hot cake. Cool and cut into finger-like pieces. Roll in additional granulated sugar.

North Carolina and Old Salem Cookery

Chocolate Bars

3 squares unsweetened
  chocolate
1 1/2 sticks butter
3 eggs

1 1/2 cups sugar
3/4 cup flour
3/4 cup chopped pecans

Preheat oven to 350°. Melt chocolate and butter over very low heat. Cool. Beat eggs and sugar together and add to chocolate mixture. Add flour and nuts. Mix well. Spread into a 9x13-inch pan and bake 20 minutes, no more. Cool.

ICING:

6 tablespoons butter,
  softened
3 cups powdered sugar

3 tablespoons evaporated
  milk
1 teaspoon vanilla

Mix butter, sugar, milk, and vanilla. Spread over cool cake.

GLAZE:

1 square unsweetened
  chocolate

1 tablespoon butter

Melt chocolate. Add butter. Drizzle over cake. Refrigerate. Makes 15 squares.

A Cook's Tour of the Azalea Coast

Butterscotch Brownies

1 stick (1/2 cup) butter
2 cups light brown sugar
2 eggs
1 cup cake flour

1 teaspoon baking powder
1/2 teaspoon salt
1 teaspoon vanilla
1 cup chopped pecans

Cream butter and sugar; add eggs, one at a time. Add flour to which baking powder has been added, then salt; add vanilla and lastly the nuts. Pour in greased pan (approximately 8x12). Bake at 350° for 30 minutes. Cut in squares while still warm and sprinkle powdered sugar over them.

Favorite Recipes of the Lower Cape Fear

Dream Bars

Quick, easy and melts in your mouth.

CRUMB LAYER:

1/2 cup butter	1 cup flour
1/2 cup brown sugar	

Combine butter, sugar, and flour until the texture of coarse meal. Pat into a buttered 9x9-inch pan. Bake approximately 10 minutes at 350° or until slightly browned.

BAR MIXTURE:

1 cup brown sugar	2 tablespoons flour
1 teaspoon vanilla	2 eggs
1/2 teaspoon baking powder	1/4 teaspoon salt
1 cup coconut	1/2 - 1 cup nuts, chopped

Mix all ingredients together. Pour over baked crumb layer. Bake again at 350° for 20-25 minutes or until brown. Cool. Cut into bars. Can do ahead and freeze. Yields 24.

Out Of Our League

Tiger Stripes

1 pound white chocolate	2 (8-ounce) packages
1 (12-ounce) jar chunky peanut butter	semi-sweet chocolate, melted

Combine white chocolate and peanut butter in top of double boiler above water heated to boiling. Reduce heat and stir constantly until mixture is melted and well blended. Spread mixture onto a waxed paper lined 10x15-inch jelly roll pan. Pour semi-sweet chocolate over first layer and swirl through with a knife. Chill until firm. Cut into small squares. Store in refrigerator. Yield: 6 dozen squares.

Note: Chocolate may be melted in a microwave.

Heart of the Mountains

Peppermint Rounds

1 cup butter or
  margarine, softened
1/2 cup sugar
1 egg, beaten
1 teaspoon vanilla
2 1/2 cups flour,
  sifted

1/2 teaspoon salt
1 cup rolled oats
1/3 cup peppermint
  candy, crushed

Preheat oven to 350°. Cream butter; add sugar gradually. Blend in egg and vanilla. Sift flour and salt and add to creamed mixture gradually. Stir in oats and candy; chill. Roll out to 1/8-inch thickness on board lightly dusted with confectioners' sugar and cut with floured cutter. Place on greased, foil-covered cookie sheets. Bake 8-10 minutes, then cool.

FROSTING:

4 cups powdered
  sugar
4 - 8 tablespoons
  light cream

Dash of salt
1 teaspoon peppermint
  extract
Red food coloring

Sift sugar and mix with enough cream to make spreadable. Add salt and extract. Take out a small portion and color with red food coloring and thin with water. When cookies have cooled, frost with white frosting. Make several lines across each frosted cookie with red frosting before the white frosting sets. Draw a toothpick lightly back and forth across lines to give a swirled look. Can do ahead and freeze. Yields 4 dozen.

Out Of Our League

Pecan Caramel Cream Squares

16 vanilla caramels
24 large marshmallows
1/2 cup milk
1 cup toasted pecan pieces, chopped

1 cup heavy cream, whipped
1 cup graham cracker crumbs
4 tablespoons melted butter

In top of double boiler place caramels, marshmallows, and milk, being careful not to let the bottom touch the boiling water. Cook, stirring occasionally until all is melted and smooth (about 25 minutes). Remove and cool. Stir in pecans. Carefully fold in whipped cream. Combine graham cracker crumbs and butter. Reserve 1/4 cup. Press the remainder into an oiled 10x6x2-inch pan. Pour caramel mixture over. Sprinkle with remaining graham cracker crumbs. Chill overnight. Serves 6-8.

A Taste of History

Date Balls

MIXTURE ONE:
1 cup margarine
1 beaten egg
Pinch of salt

1 cup sugar
1 cup chopped dates (1 box)

MIXTURE TWO:
1 teaspoon vanilla
2 cups Rice Krispies

1 cup chopped pecans

Combine mixture #1 ingredients and cook for 10 minutes. Stir constantly. Remove from heat and stir in mixture #2 ingredients. Drop by teaspoon on waxed paper. While hot, roll in powdered sugar or very fine grated coconut. May be shaped in logs or balls.

Mountain Potpourri

Over 60 percent of the nation's entire furniture production is crafted within a 200-mile radius of High Point, the furniture capital of the world. There are more than 125 manufacturing plants in the area, many of which are the largest factories in the world.

English Toffee

1 pound sugar
1 pound butter
1/2 pound chopped pecans
2 tablespoons light Karo
  syrup

Pinch of salt
2 (6-ounce) bags chocolate
  bits
1/2 pound pulverized pecans

Place sugar, butter, pecans, Karo syrup, and a pinch of salt in a saucepan. Keep on low heat stirring constantly until butter and sugar have melted. Increase heat and cook rapidly continuing to stir until candy has reached 310° on candy thermometer (wait as long as possible to insert thermometer). Pour in flat buttered pan, spread out into a thin sheet. Let cool and get hard.

In the meantime melt one small package chocolate bits. Spread over candy. Press half of pulverized nuts into the chocolate firmly so that they stick. When this is hardened, turn candy over and repeat the process with the other package of chocolate bits and remainder of pulverized nuts. Let this harden and break. Yield: 40-50 pieces.

Centenary Cookbook

Incredible Toffee

2 cups almonds, sliced
1 pound butter
1 box light brown sugar

1 (6-bar) package Hershey's
  milk chocolate bars

Grease a 10 1/2 x 15 x 1-inch cookie sheet. Spread 1 cup almonds evenly on cookie sheet. Melt butter and sugar in a heavy saucepan. Stir constantly with a wooden spoon until candy thermometer reaches 290°. Remove from heat immediately. Pour toffee back and forth evenly over cookie sheet. Put chocolate bars on hot toffee; spread evenly over mixture. Sprinkle with remaining almonds. Makes 1 1/2 pounds.

Stirring Performances

Cherry Divinity

3 cups granulated sugar
1/2 cup light corn syrup
Dash of salt
1/2 cup cold water

2 egg whites
1 teaspoon vanilla
1/2 cup candied red cherries
1/2 cup chopped nuts

Place sugar, syrup, salt and water in pan over low heat. Stir until sugar is dissolved. Cook until a small amount forms a soft ball in cold water—a candy thermometer takes the guesswork out of the job.

Beat egg whites until stiff and continue beating while pouring half of the syrup in gradually. Cook remaining syrup until it forms a hard ball in cold water. Beat egg whites slowly until remaining syrup cooks. Add remaining syrup gradually.

Continue beating until candy is thick enough to drop. Add vanilla, cherries and nuts. A few drops of red vegetable coloring gives a prettier pink color. Drop on waxed paper.

What Is It? What Do I Do With It?

Easy Candy

2 cups sugar
1 small can milk
12 marshmallows

1 stick margarine
6 ounces chocolate chips
1 cup nuts, chopped

Combine sugar, milk and marshmallows in heavy saucepan and boil hard for 6 minutes. Remove from heat and stir in margarine, chocolate chips and nuts. Continue to stir until chocolate chips have melted. Pour quickly onto greased platter and allow to cool before cutting into squares.

Have Fun Cooking With Me

 The Fireman's Museum in historic New Bern was founded by the two oldest continuously operating fire companies in the nation.

Chocolate Sticks

2 cups vanilla wafers,
  crushed
2 cups nut meats
4 squares Baker's Chocolate
1 can Eagle Brand condensed
  milk

1 teaspoon vanilla
1/8 teaspoon salt
Powdered sugar

Crush vanilla wafers and add chopped nuts. Toss as you would a salad. Melt chocolate in milk until it coats spoon. Add vanilla and salt. Pour over nuts and vanilla wafers. Place in buttered bread pan about 1/2-inch thick and chill. Cut in fingers as you would fudge. Roll in powdered sugar. Will keep well for 2 weeks. Makes 48.

Centenary Cookbook

Peanut Butter Sticks

1 king-size loaf white
  thin-sliced bread
1 (12-ounce) jar smooth
  peanut butter

1/2 cup vegetable oil
1 package cornflake crumbs

Trim crust from bread. Cut slices into 5-6 strips. Place on cookie sheet and dry in oven at 200° for 3 hours. Combine peanut butter and oil in top of double boiler; heat until thoroughly blended and smooth. Remove from heat, but keep mixture over hot water. Drop a few sticks at a time into mixture, tossing lightly until coated. Remove sticks. Toss in cornflake crumbs. Place on waxed paper to dry. Store in heavy plastic bags or airtight tins. Yield: 6 dozen sticks.

Variation: Dry crusts of bread; process into bread crumbs in blender (about 3 cups of crumbs). Add cinnamon and sugar to taste. Substitute for cornflake crumbs.

Heart of the Mountains

 Near Kitty Hawk and Kill Devil Hills is a monument that marks the spot where Wilbur and Orville Wright made the world's first powered aircraft flight on December 17, 1903.

Pies and Desserts

Wright Brothers National Memorial at Kill Devil Hills.

Peanut Butter Pie

PIE:

1 (8-ounce) package cream
  cheese, softened
1 (14-ounce) can Eagle
  sweetened condensed milk
  (not evaporated milk)
1 cup peanut butter

1 teaspoon vanilla
1 (4-ounce) carton Cool Whip,
  thawed
1 Chocolate Crunch Crust
1 (6-ounce) jar Smuckers
  Chocolate Fudge Sauce

In large bowl, beat cream cheese until fluffy, beat in condensed milk, peanut butter and vanilla until smooth. Fold in whipped cream. Turn into crust. Top with fudge sauce (it helps to place in freezer for a time to make spreading easier). Chill in freezer for about two hours. This is delicious and similar to a peanut butter cheesecake. Serves 8.

CHOCOLATE CRUNCH CRUST:

1/3 cup butter
1 (6-ounce) package
  chocolate chips

2 1/2 cups Rice Krispies

In heavy saucepan, over low heat, melt 1/3 cup butter and 1 small package chocolate chips. Remove from heat and gently stir in cereal until completely coated. Press into bottom and side of greased 9-inch pie plate. Chill 30 minutes.

Ship to Shore I

Cantaloupe Cream Pie

1 cup granulated sugar
2 tablespoons all-purpose
  flour
3 eggs, beaten
1 cup puréed cantaloupe
1 teaspoon vanilla extract

2 tablespoons butter
1 (8-inch) pastry shell,
  baked
1 cup whipping cream,
  whipped

Combine sugar and flour in saucepan; add eggs, mixing well. Stir in cantaloupe purée and cook over medium heat 8-10 minutes, stirring constantly until mixture boils and thickens. Remove from heat; stir in vanilla and butter. Cool. Pour filling into pastry shell; spread evenly with whipped cream. Chill. Yield: 6 servings.

Heart of the Mountains

Tanglewood Manor House Restaurant's
Tar Heel Pie

12 ounces cream cheese,
  softened
1/2 cup sugar
1/2 pint whipping cream

1 1/2 medium bananas, sliced
1 (9-inch) deep-dish pie
  shell, baked

Mix softened cream cheese with sugar. Whip cream until stiff peaks form. Carefully fold cream into cheese mixture and mix until thoroughly blended. Slice bananas and place in bottom and sides of pie shell. Pour cheese mixture over bananas and chill until firm.

BLUEBERRY GLAZE:
1 package frozen blueberries
1/3 cup sugar

1 tablespoon cornstarch

Combine all ingredients and cook over low heat until thick. Be careful not to break up the berries. Cool to room temperature. Spoon glaze evenly over cheese mixture and chill several hours or overnight.

North Carolina's Historic Restaurants

Caramel Chiffon Pie

1 cup vanilla caramel sauce
1/2 cup water
1 envelope unflavored
  gelatin
1/4 cup cold water

1/4 teaspoon salt
1/4 teaspoon vanilla
1 (6-ounce) can evaporated
  milk, chilled until ice cold
1 cup chopped nuts

Place the caramel sauce and water in top of a double boiler. Heat, stirring, until the mixture is blended. Soften the gelatin in cold water and dissolve in the hot caramel sauce; add the salt and vanilla. Chill until slightly thickened. Whip the chilled milk until fluffy; fold in the caramel mixture and 1/2 cup chopped nuts. Pour into pastry shell and sprinkle with the remaining nuts. Chill until firm.

Mushrooms, Turnip Greens and Pickled Eggs

Fresh Strawberry Pie
(Microwave)

3/4 cup sugar
3 tablespoons cornstarch
1 1/2 cups water
1 (3-ounce) package
 strawberry gelatin

1 (9-inch) pie shell, baked
4 cups sliced strawberries
 (1 quart)
Whipped cream

Combine sugar, cornstarch, and water in cup. Stir until smooth. Microcook, uncovered, in 8-cup measure, on High 6-7 minutes. Stir every 2 minutes until mixture boils and thickens. Add gelatin and stir until dissolved.

While gelatin mixture is cooling (about 5 minutes) place strawberries in cooled pie shell. Pour gelatin mixture over berries. Refrigerate. Serve with whipped cream. Serves 8.

Variation: For fresh peach pie, use peach gelatin and 4 cups fresh peaches instead of strawberries.

The Microwave Touch

Glazed Strawberry Pie

1 1/2 quarts fresh
 strawberries
1 (9-inch) pie crust, baked,
 or graham cracker pie crust
1 cup sugar
2 1/2 tablespoons cornstarch

Pinch of salt
1/2 cup water
1 tablespoon butter
Few drops of red food
 coloring
Whipped cream

Wash and hull berries. Put 1 quart of berries into prepared pie crust. Combine sugar, cornstarch and salt in saucepan. Crush remaining 1/2 quart of berries and place in saucepan with sugar and water. Bring mixture to a boil, stirring constantly and cook until thick and clear. Remove from heat; add butter and enough food coloring to make the color pronounced but not too red. Strain glaze and pour carefully over the berries in the pie shell. Cool before serving. Pipe edges around pie with whipped cream.

A Cookbook of Pinehurst Courses

Cay Lime Pie

FILLING:

4 egg yolks
1 (14-ounce) can condensed
  milk
1/2 cup lime juice
4 egg whites

1/4 cup sugar
1 teaspoon vanilla
Gratings from 1 lime
1 Yummy Pie Crust

Beat egg yolks until soft and lemon colored. Beat in sweetened condensed milk and lime juice. Beat with electric mixer for 2-3 minutes or by hand a long time. Pour in cooled 9-inch pie crust. Beat egg whites until nearly stiff.* Add sugar and vanilla while beating a few seconds longer (not too much). Pour over filling. Make peaks with spoon and sprinkle grated lime over top. Chill as long as possible before serving. *The fresher eggs make a stiffer meringue.

YUMMY PIE CRUST:

1 cup flour
1/4 cup brown sugar
1/3 cup butter (softened)

1/4 teaspoon salt
4 - 5 tablespoons cold milk

Mix flour, brown sugar, butter and salt with fork or pastry blender. Add milk little by little. Form into ball of dough and chill if possible before rolling out. Bake at 425° for 10-15 minutes.

Ship to Shore I

Harkers Island Lemon-Milk Pie

1 can condensed milk
3 eggs, separated (save
  whites for meringue)
1/4 cup plus 1 tablespoon
  freshly-squeezed, strained
  lemon juice

1 package section Ritz
  crackers

Stir together milk and egg yolks, vigorously, until well mixed; add lemon juice and stir until smooth. Pour into Ritz cracker-lined pie dish. Top with meringue. Bake at 400° until golden brown.

Island Born and Bred

Lemon Frost Pie with Blueberry Sauce

This pie was made for the first time for my sister-in-law's rehearsal dinner many years ago. It has always been a family favorite, and has since become a favorite on the summer menu at Fearrington House. When it is served, we garnish each slice with scented geranium leaves and white petunias.

1 pre-baked (9-inch) pie shell	1 tablespoon lemon rind,
2 egg whites	grated
2/3 cup sugar	1 cup heavy cream, whipped
1/4 cup lemon juice	1 recipe Blueberry Sauce

In the bowl of an electric mixer, whip whites and sugar until thick and frothy. Slowly add lemon juice combined with the grated lemon rind, and whip until the mixture forms soft peaks. Blend in the whipped cream. Spread onto cooled pre-baked pie shell and chill or freeze. Serve with Blueberry Sauce.

BLUEBERRY SAUCE:

2/3 cup sugar	2/3 cup water
1 tablespoon cornstarch	1 lemon rind, grated
Pinch of salt	2 cups fresh blueberries

Combine sugar with cornstarch and salt and mix until completely blended, with no lumps. Add water and grated lemon rind. Cook and stir until the mixture comes to a boil and is thick. Add blueberries and let return to boiling point. Remove from the stove and cool. Chill. Yields approximately 2 cups.

The Fearrington House Cookbook

Strawberry-Cheese Tarts

1 cup grated cheese	1/8 teaspoon salt
1 stick butter, softened	1/8 teaspoon cayenne pepper
2 cups flour	Strawberry preserves

Mix all ingredients except preserves (no liquid is used). Roll and cut into squares about 2 inches square. Place in center of each square 1 teaspoon of strawberry preserves or jam and fold over at corners. Bake at 375° until slightly brown on top. These are delightful tea accessories or may be filled with anchovies, caviar, tuna fish, meat paste, and served as appetizers. About 30.

Marion Brown's Southern Cook Book

English Lemon Tarts

1 cup sugar
2 tablespoons flour
Pinch salt
3 whole eggs
Juice of 1 1/2 lemons, rind
  of one

1 stick butter
1 (9-inch) baked pie shell
  or tart shells
Whipped cream

Put sugar, flour and salt in top of double boiler. Mix well. Add 3 whole beaten eggs and lemon juice and rind. Stir constantly until thickened. Add butter. Pour into 9-inch baked pie shell or tart shells. Top with whipped cream.

Centenary Cookbook

Lemon Custard in Meringue Tarts

MERINGUE SHELLS:
3 egg whites
1/4 teaspoon vanilla

Dash salt
1 cup sugar

Beat whites until frothy. Add salt and add sugar, 1 tablespoon at a time. Continue beating until meringue is stiff. Add vanilla. Prepare baking sheet with brown paper and place 6 globs of meringue on paper. With the back of a spoon, shape the shells 4 inches wide and 1 1/2 inches high. Bake at 225° for 1 - 1 1/4 hours. Cool. Fill with chilled custard.

LEMON CUSTARD:
1 cup sugar
5 tablespoons cornstarch
Dash salt
1 1/2 cups boiling water

3 yolks
1/4 cup fresh lemon juice
2 tablespoons grated lemon
  rind

Combine sugar, cornstarch and salt. Stir in water. Cook over low heat stirring constantly until mixture thickens. Combine yolks with lemon juice and rind. Stir some of the hot mixture into the yolks, then add it all back. Cook, stirring constantly until mixture thickens and is smooth (about 10 minutes). Chill. Serves 6.

A Taste of History

Mud Pie

1 box Famous Chocolate
  Wafers or 1 (15-ounce)
  package Oreos, crushed
2/3 cup butter, melted
1/2 gallon coffee ice cream
4 squares unsweetened
  chocolate

1 cup sugar
1 (13-ounce) can evaporated
  milk
2 tablespoons butter
Whipped cream
Nuts for topping

This makes 2 pies or can be put in one 9x13-inch pan. Make crust with chocolate cookies and 2/3 cup melted butter. Press in pan. Top with coffee ice cream. Freeze hard.

Make chocolate sauce in double boiler. Mix the unsweetened chocolate, sugar, evaporated milk and butter. Cook until thick. Cool and pour over ice cream. Freeze. Serve pie with whipped cream and nuts.

Make your own coffee ice cream: Soften 1/2 gallon ice cream or ice milk. Add 2-3 tablespoons powdered instant coffee dissolved in 1 tablespoon vanilla and 1-2 tablespoons rum flavoring. Mix well. Refreeze in sealed container or use to make pie.

Christmas Favorites

Chess Pie II

1 stick butter
1 cup sugar
1 whole egg
2 egg yolks

4 tablespoons graham cracker
  crumbs
1/4 cup evaporated milk
1/4 cup lemon juice

Cream butter and sugar. Add whole egg and egg yolks. Mix. Add graham cracker crumbs, milk and lemon juice. Pour in very short, unbaked pie crust. Bake at 300° for 45 minutes or until firm. This can also be cooked in tart shells. Serves 6-8.

Favorite Recipes of the Lower Cape Fear

German Chocolate Angel Pie

SHELL:

2 egg whites
1/8 teaspoon salt
1/8 teaspoon cream
  of tartar

1/2 cup sugar
1/8 teaspoon vanilla
1/2 cup finely
  chopped nuts

Beat egg whites with salt and cream of tartar until foamy. Add sugar, 2 tablespoons at a time, beating well after each addition; continue beating until stiff peaks form. Fold in vanilla and nuts. Spoon into lightly greased 8-inch pie pan to form nest-like shell, building sides up to 1/2 inch above edge of pan. Bake at 300° 50-55 minutes. Cool.

CHOCOLATE CREAM FILLING:

1 (4-ounce) bar
  Baker's German sweet
  chocolate
3 tablespoons water

1 teaspoon vanilla
1 cup heavy cream,
  whipped

Stir chocolate in water over low heat until melted; cool until thick. Add vanilla. Fold whipped cream into chocolate mixture. Pile into cooled shell. Chill 2 hours. Serves 6-8.

    Substitute: 5 ounces Hershey chocolate bar for German chocolate.

    Variation: Double amounts of egg whites, sugar, cream of tartar and vanilla for deeper meringue crust. Use larger pie pan.

Out Of Our League

Two-Berry Ambrosia

For some time after World War II, Miss Dore continued to have someone raise red raspberries on the place in Oak Ridge. She was a familiar figure on Main Street (in Kernersville) dressed in one of her purple or lavender outfits, going to call on someone carrying a basket of red raspberries.

1 cup (1/2 pint) fresh red
  raspberries
1 cup (1/2 pint) fresh
  strawberries
1/4 cup sifted
  confectioners' sugar

1/2 pound seedless green
  grapes
1/2 cup flaked coconut
1/2 pint whipping cream,
  whipped

Wash berries, drain well. Reserve 6 raspberries for garnish. Cap and half strawberries, reserving 6 halves for garnish. Carefully combine raspberries, strawberries and confectioners' sugar. Fold in grapes, coconut and whipped cream. Spoon into serving dishes. Garnish with reserved berries. Makes 6 servings.

Korner's Folly Cookbook

Irene's Lemon Freeze

1 (13-ounce) can evaporated
  milk
1 cup sugar

Juice and rind from 3 lemons
1/2 box vanilla wafers

Chill evaporated milk real well. Whip milk, adding sugar slowly. Add lemon juice and rind slowly. Crush vanilla wafers. Place half of the crumbs in the bottom of a 9x13-inch pan. Spread whipped milk over crumbs. Sprinkle remaining crumbs evenly over whipped milk. Freeze until firm. Serves 8.

Recipes From Our Front Porch

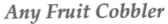

Any Fruit Cobbler

1/2 cup butter, melted	2 teaspoons baking powder
3/4 cup flour	1/2 teaspoon cinnamon
1 cup sugar	1/2 teaspoon nutmeg
3/4 cup milk	Your favorite fruit

Melt butter in saucepan. Mix in bowl, flour, sugar, milk, baking powder, and spices. Pour batter in 9x9-inch pan. Pour butter on top. *Do not stir.* Add your favorite fruit: peaches, apples, berries, etc. Bake at 350° for 1 hour.

Mountain Potpourri

Gingerbread Apple Cobbler
(Microwave)

4 medium apples, peeled and sliced (4 cups)	2 tablespoons water
	1 tablespoon lemon juice
1/2 cup packed brown sugar	1/2 teaspoon cinnamon
1 teaspoon cornstarch	

GINGERBREAD TOPPING:

1 egg	1/4 cup sugar
1/2 cup buttermilk or sour milk	1/2 teaspoon soda
	1/2 teaspoon ginger
1/4 cup molasses	1/2 teaspoon salt
2 tablespoons cooking oil	1/4 teaspoon baking powder
1 cup unsifted all-purpose flour	1/4 teaspoon nutmeg

Combine apples, brown sugar, cornstarch, water, lemon juice and cinnamon in an 8-inch round glass cake dish. Microwave, covered, 4-5 minutes or until apples are tender-crisp, stirring once.

Beat together egg, buttermilk, molasses and oil in mixing bowl. Add remaining ingredients; beat until smooth. Pour over apples. Microwave, uncovered, 6-7 minutes or until toothpick inserted near center comes out clean, rotating dish once or twice. Serve warm or cold, plain or with whipped cream. Serves 6-8.

A Taste of History

Country Apple Tart with Lemon Zest and Vanilla Ice Cream

This is the simplest possible tart, and one of the best. Be sure to use a cooking apple such as Granny Smith, Winesap, or McIntosh. Keep the vanilla ice cream in a bucket surrounded by ice so that guests may help themselves when it's time for dessert.

1 recipe all-purpose pastry
  (for double crust pie)
1/4 cup apricot preserves
2 tablespoons sugar
5 - 6 apples
1/2 cup sugar

2 lemon rinds, finely grated
Freshly grated nutmeg
1 teaspoon cinnamon
2 tablespoons butter
1 quart vanilla ice cream

Preheat oven to 400°. Roll out pastry to fit a 12x16-inch pan. Sprinkle a cookie sheet with cold water before putting pastry in place to help keep it from shrinking. Fold in the edges 3/8 inch to make a flat rim. Dock the edge with a knife to make a decorative mark all the way around (do not cut all the way through the pastry).

Heat apricot preserves in a saucepan and brush over surface of pastry. Sprinkle with 2 tablespoons sugar. Peel and core apples and slice them very thin (1/8 inch). Arrange in a pattern. Sprinkle again with sugar, lemon rind, nutmeg, and cinnamon. Dot with paper-thin pieces of butter. Bake at 400° for 25 minutes. Cut into rectangles roughly 2 1/2 x 2 inches and serve with ice cream. Yields 30 small portions.

The Fearrington House Cookbook

Coffee Toffee Ice Cream Cake

28 Oreo cookies
6 large Heath candy bars
 (coffee-toffee bars)
1/2 gallon coffee ice cream

1/2 gallon chocolate ice
 cream
8 ounces Hershey chocolate
 syrup

Put 14 Oreo cookies in one plastic bag and 14 Oreo cookies in another plastic bag. Crush with a rolling pin or mallet. Do not use food processor. Place 6 Heath candy bars in a plastic bag and crush. Lightly oil a 10-inch springform pan. Sprinkle bottom of pan with one bag of cookies. Add 1/2 gallon softened chocolate ice cream. Drizzle 4 ounces of Hershey syrup over ice cream. Sprinkle second bag of cookies over syrup. Add 1/2 gallon softened coffee ice cream. Drizzle with 4 ounces of Hershey syrup. Sprinkle top with bag of crushed Heath bars. Cover with foil. Freeze until hard. Serves 25.

Bravo

Dody's Banana Split Pie

3 bananas
1 tablespoon lemon juice
1 (9-inch) graham cracker
 crust
1 pint strawberry ice cream

1 cup whipped topping
1 (8-ounce) jar whole
 maraschino cherries, drained
2 tablespoons finely chopped
 nuts

Slice bananas thinly, sprinkle with lemon juice and arrange on bottom of pie crust. Stir ice cream to soften slightly—spread over bananas. Freeze.

Spread thawed whipped topping over ice cream. Top with cherries. Sprinkle with nuts. Freeze again. Let stand 30 minutes at room temperature before serving. Pour Chocolate Quick Sauce over each serving. Serves 8.

CHOCOLATE QUICK SAUCE:
1 (6-ounce) package
 chocolate chips

2/3 cup evaporated milk
1 cup marshmallow creme

Cook chocolate chips and milk together over low heat. Beat in marshmallow cream until blended. Serve warm or cold.

Recipes From Our Front Porch

Apple Crisp
(Microwave)

5 cups apples, sliced
3/4 cup quick-cooking rolled
  oats
1 cup all-purpose flour
1 cup brown sugar

1/2 teaspoon salt
1 teaspoon cinnamon
1/2 cup butter, cut into 8
  pieces

Slice apples with medium slicing disk of food processor and place in a 2-quart glass casserole. In work bowl of food processor, combine oats, flour, brown sugar, salt, cinnamon, and butter pieces; pulse until mixture is crumbly. Sprinkle evenly over apples. Microwave on High for 15 minutes. Rotate dish every 2 minutes. Yield: 6 servings.

Market to Market

 Founded in 1766, Old Salem, an 18th century Moravian congregational town, is a treasury of fine old buildings, many of which have been restored and opened as exhibit buildings. Other buildings have been in continuous use since the 18th and 19th centuries. Winston-Salem.

Dody's Apricot-Cheese Delight

1 (20-ounce) can drained
  crushed pineapple
1 (20-ounce) can drained and
  cut apricots
2 (3-ounce) packages orange
  Jello

2 cups boiling water
1 cup juice from pineapple
  and apricots
1 cup marshmallows

Drain pineapple and apricots, reserving 2 cups juice, divided. Mix Jello with boiling water and add 1 cup juice (save remaining cup for topping). Add marshmallows and stir until they are melted. Chill in large, flat baking dish. When this mixture starts to jell, add pineapple and apricots. Put topping on.

TOPPING:
1/2 cup sugar
3 tablespoons flour
1 beaten egg
1/4 teaspoon salt
1 cup juice from pineapple
  and apricots

2 tablespoons butter
1 cup whipping cream
2 cups grated Cheddar cheese

Mix well the first 4 ingredients and add the remaining cup of juice. Cook over low heat until thick. Remove from heat and add butter. Cool thoroughly. Fold in whipping cream. After fruit mixture is congealed, spread this evenly over it and sprinkle with cheese. Refrigerate for 24 hours before serving. Serves 18.

Recipes From Our Front Porch

Lime Angel Dessert

1 package lime gelatin
1 cup sugar
1 1/4 cups boiling water
1/3 cup lime juice

1 can (1 cup) flaked coconut
1 cup heavy cream, whipped
1 small angel food cake,
  torn into pieces

Dissolve gelatin and sugar in boiling water. Add juice and chill until thickened. Fold in coconut and whipped cream. Make layers of cake bits and gelatin mixture in 9x13-inch pan. Chill overnight and cut into squares. Serves 12.

Mushrooms, Turnip Greens and Pickled Eggs

Chocolate Mousse

When you want a dessert that is just a little bite of something...
this one is extra easy and has the taste of mousses that take hours.

1 (6-ounce) package of
  chocolate chips
2 tablespoons granulated
  sugar
1 teaspoon vanilla

1 egg
Pinch of salt
3/4 cup milk
Whipped cream or whipped
  topping

Put chocolate chips, sugar, vanilla, egg and pinch of salt in container of electric blender. Heat milk just to boiling; pour into container. Blend 1 minute or until thoroughly blended. Pour into six demi-tasse cups. Chill and serve topped with whipped cream or topping. Makes 6 servings.

What Is It? What Do I Do With It?

Mystery Dessert

1 stick margarine, melted
1 cup plain flour
1/2 cup chopped nuts
1 (8-ounce) package cream
  cheese, softened
1 cup Cool Whip (from large
  size container)

1 cup confectioners' sugar
2 small packages instant
  chocolate pudding
3 cups milk
Bitter chocolate for garnish

Mix together margarine, flour and nuts. Press into 9-inch pie pan and bake at 350° for about 15 minutes. Watch closely! Cool. Combine cream cheese, 1 cup Cool Whip and confectioners' sugar. Mix until smooth and spread gently over crust. Mix chocolate pudding and milk. Spread over cream cheese mixture. Cover pudding with the remaining Cool Whip and grate bitter chocolate over top. Put into refrigerator for several hours or overnight. Delicious!

Mama's Recipes

Pineapple Mint Supreme

1 cup flour
1/2 cup walnuts, chopped (or pecans)

1/4 cup firmly packed brown sugar
1/2 cup butter

Combine flour, chopped walnuts, and brown sugar in bowl. Cut in 1/2 cup butter until fine. Press into bottom of greased 12x8x2-inch (or larger) baking dish. Bake at 400° for 12-15 minutes. Cool.

PINEAPPLE MINT FILLING:

1 (1-pound 4-ounce) can crushed pineapple
1 (3-ounce) package lime gelatin
1 (8-ounce) package cream cheese

1 cup sugar
2/3 cup evaporated milk, chilled
1/8 teaspoon peppermint extract

Drain can of crushed pineapple into saucepan. Bring juice to boiling point. Dissolve gelatin in hot juice. Cool. Beat cream cheese with 1 cup sugar. Blend in gelatin mixture. Stir in pineapple. Chill until thick but not set. Chill evaporated milk with peppermint extract (or 2 drops of oil of peppermint) in small bowl until ice crystals form. Beat until thick. Fold into pineapple-cheese mixture. Spoon over baked crust. Refrigerate while preparing glaze. Spread glaze carefully. Chill at least 4 hours. Serves 12.

CHOCOLATE MINT GLAZE:

1/2 cup semi-sweet chocolate morsels
1/3 cup evaporated milk

1 tablespoon butter
1/4 teaspoon peppermint extract

Melt—stirring occasionally over low heat—1/2 cup chocolate morsels in 1/3 cup evaporated milk. Add 1 tablespoon butter and 1/4 teaspoon peppermint extract (or 2 drops oil of peppermint.) Spread over filling while warm.

Centenary Cookbook

The Gwyn Staley Memorial Auto Race and the Wilkes 400 Grand National Stock Car Race are hosted by North Wilkesboro Speedway each year.

Banana Pudding

North Carolina natives think of banana pudding as a dessert served everywhere. It was not until I received a request for the recipe from New York City that I began to realize, it is distinctive to this section.

1/2 cup sugar	2 cups milk
Pinch of salt	Vanilla wafers
3 tablespoons flour	Bananas
4 eggs	6 tablespoons sugar

Blend sugar, salt and flour. Add 1 whole egg and 3 yolks and mix together. Stir in milk. Cook over boiling water, stirring, until thickened. Remove from heat and cool.

In a baking dish, arrange a layer of whole vanilla wafers, a layer of sliced bananas and a layer of custard. Continue, making three layers of each.

Make a meringue of remaining three egg whites and 6 tablespoons sugar. Spread over banana mixture and brown in 375° oven. Makes 8 servings. Serve cold, not chilled.

North Carolina and Old Salem Cookery

Ice Box Pudding

1 1/2 cakes German sweet chocolate	1 teaspoon vanilla or almond flavoring
3 tablespoons water	1 teaspoon powdered coffee
3 tablespoons confectioners' sugar	2 packages lady fingers
5 eggs	1 cup whipped cream

Melt the chocolate in the water and confectioners' sugar. Separate the eggs, adding the yolks to the chocolate mixture. Beat the whites until stiff and fold into mixture. Flavor with almond and the powdered coffee.

In plate used to serve (must have sides at least 3 inches deep), place the lady fingers around in upright position. Then cover bottom of dish with lady fingers. Pour mixture into dish. Refrigerate 24 hours. Before serving, cover with whipped cream.

This is a great favorite with men!

High Hampton Hospitality

Persimmon Pudding

The first frost was anticipated because a good nip takes the "pucker" out of the persimmon and makes it sweet and ready to be put into a pudding.

2 1/2 cups persimmon pulp	1 teaspoon cinnamon
4 cups flour	3 eggs, beaten
2 cups milk	3/4 stick butter
1 teaspoon soda	1 cup granulated sugar
1 teaspoon baking powder	1 cup brown sugar
1/2 teaspoon salt	

Mix all ingredients together; pour into two greased baking dishes. Bake in 300° oven for 1 hour or until firm.

Korner's Folly Cookbook

Saucy Lemon Pudding

1/2 cup margarine	1 tablespoon grated lemon
1 cup sugar	rind
3 eggs, separated	1/3 cup flour
2 tablespoons lemon juice	1 cup milk

Beat the margarine and 3/4 cup of sugar until light and fluffy. Blend in the egg yolks, lemon juice, and lemon rind. Being sure to mix well, add the flour. Then stir in the milk.

In a separate bowl, beat the egg whites and the remaining 1/4 cup of sugar until stiff peaks form. Fold beaten egg whites into the batter. Pour the batter mixture into eight 6-ounce custard cups, or into a 1-quart casserole dish.

Set the cups or dish into a baking pan, and pour boiling water into the pan to a depth of 1/2 inch. Bake at 350° for 35-40 minutes. Remove from water, cool custard cups 10 minutes or casserole 20 minutes. Invert on dessert dishes.

Note: Because it separates into a sponge layer and creamy lemon sauce, this recipe needs no additional topping.

I Remember

Puffs of Mountain Air

2 eggs, separated
6 tablespoons sugar
1 tablespoon flour
1 teaspoon vanilla

2 egg whites
Pinch salt
2 tablespoons butter
Powdered sugar

Preheat oven to 325°. Beat yolks and 2 tablespoons sugar until forms a ribbon; add flour, beat again. Add vanilla. Beat 4 whites with salt until stiff peaks; add sugar 1 tablespoon at a time. Beat stiff. Fold whites into yolks. Spoon into buttered oval dish, making three large mounds. Bake 12 minutes until golden. Dust with powdered sugar.

Serve and listen to the ooh's and ah's. This literally melts in your mouth.

Ship to Shore II

Snow Cream

In the 1920s teachers let kids make snow cream at school when it snowed. It all came under the heading of putting-first-things-first because it didn't snow that often and lessons could wait.

1 egg
1/2 cup sugar
1 cup milk

1 teaspoon vanilla
1 quart fluffy snow

Beat an egg until fluffy; add sugar, milk and vanilla. Keep in cold while you run outside and get snow. Stir snow gently into milk mixture.

Korner's Folly Cookbook

Chocolate Dipped Strawberries

1 quart strawberries, washed and unstemmed

SAUCE:

2 tablespoons butter
1 (6-ounce) package
  semi-sweet chocolate morsels
1 teaspoon vanilla or orange
  extract (try it both ways!)

1 (14-ounce) can Eagle Brand
  sweetened condensed
  milk

Arrange strawberries on doilied plate. Place sauce ingredients in top of double boiler, and stir until blended. Serve in bowl over hot water and let guests hand dip the strawberries. If there is any sauce left over, freeze and re-use as fudge sauce for ice cream. Serves 4. Wonderfully easy—wonderfully delicious!

Ship to Shore II

Coffee Tortoni

2 eggs
1/4 cup sugar
1/8 teaspoon salt
1 teaspoon powdered coffee
  (not granules)
1 cup whipping cream

2 tablespoons sugar
1 teaspoon vanilla
1/4 teaspoon almond extract
1/3 cup chopped almonds,
  toasted

Beat eggs, 1/4 cup sugar and salt at high speed in small bowl of electric mixer. Beat until very light and fluffy; the mixture should more than half fill the bowl. Toward the end of beating, add powdered coffee. In another bowl beat whipping cream with two tablespoons sugar. When stiff, fold in vanilla and almond extracts. Fold into egg mixture, blending well. Stir in toasted almonds and pour into paper muffin cups or spoon into parfait glasses to freeze. A few chopped nuts may be used to garnish top if desired. Yields 8 (4-ounce) paper muffin cups or 6 parfait glasses.

Note: Freezes well.

A Dash of Down East

The Lamp Lighter's Tartufi

10 maraschino cherries
2 tablespoons rum
1 cup superfine sugar
2/3 cup Dutch process cocoa
2 teaspoons instant espresso
  powder

1/3 cup water
4 egg yolks
1 cup whipping cream
1/3 cup chopped toasted
  almonds
Shaved chocolate for garnish

Stem and pit cherries; rinse them, then soak in rum.

Sift sugar, cocoa, and espresso into a heavy to medium saucepan. Whisk in the water. Place over medium heat and bring to a boil, stirring constantly until all sugar is dissolved and mixture is smooth, about 10 minutes. In a large bowl, beat egg yolks with electric mixer on high speed. When yolks are light and fluffy, reduce to medium speed and add hot chocolate mixture in a slow, steady stream. Continue to beat until cool. Chill one hour.

Remove cherries from rum with slotted spoon and set aside. Mix rum into cooled chocolate. Whip cream until stiff peaks form. Stir one large spoonful into chocolate mixture to loosen, blending well. Gently fold in remaining whipped cream and chopped almonds, being careful not to deflate whipped cream. Fill ten individual serving cups less than half full with chocolate mixture. Place a cherry in the center; fill to within half an inch of the top. Sprinkle shaved chocolate lightly on top. Cover with plastic and then with foil. Freeze a minimum of four hours.

Thaw 5-10 minutes before serving. Will keep for a month. Serves 10.

North Carolina's Historic Restaurants

Peanut Butter Ice Cream Balls

1 cup sugar honey
  graham cracker crumbs
1/4 cup creamy or chunk-style
  peanut butter

2 tablespoons sugar
1/4 teaspoon cinnamon
1 quart vanilla ice cream
Chocolate syrup

Blend crumbs, peanut butter, sugar and cinnamon. Scoop ice cream into large balls and roll in crumb mixture until well coated. Freeze until serving time. Serve with chocolate syrup. Makes 6-8 servings.

What Is It? What Do I Do With It?

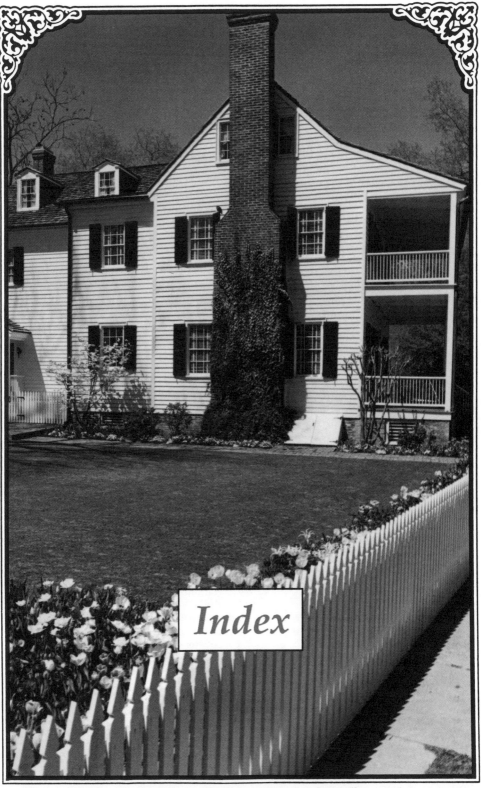

Index

The Jones House at New Bern, c. 1818, is a Federal style dwelling used as a guest house for the Tryon Palace Commission.

INDEX

INDEX

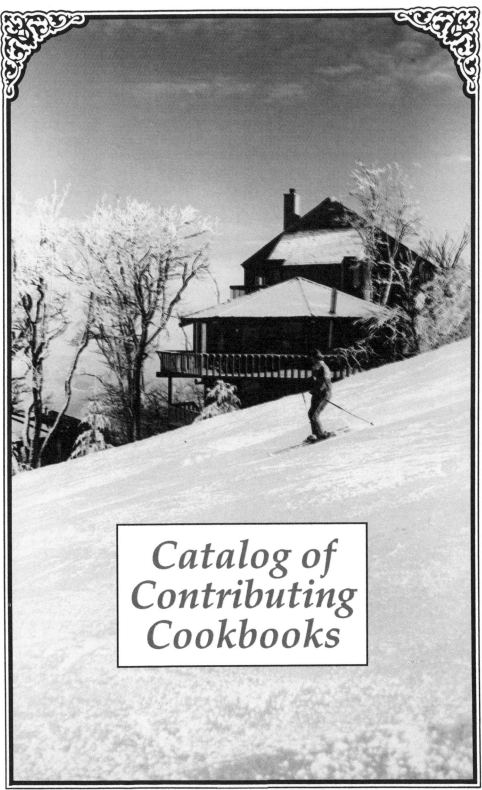

Catalog of
Contributing
Cookbooks

Beech Mountain Ski Resort near Banner Elk.

CATALOG OF CONTRIBUTING COOKBOOKS

All recipes in this book have been submitted from the North Carolina cookbooks shown on the following pages. Individuals who wish to obtain a copy of any particular book can do so by sending a check or money order to the addresses listed. Prices are subject to change. Please note the postage and handling charges that are required. North Carolina residents add tax only when requested. Retailers are invited to call or write to same address for wholesale information.

BILL NEAL'S SOUTHERN COOKING
by William F. Neal
The University of North Carolina Press
P. O. Box 2288
Chapel Hill, NC 27514   800/848-6224

Surveying the cooking of twelve southern states, Bill Neal presents a cookbook that reveals something more than just what is consumed by hungry people in the southeastern US. From the fiery gusto of Louisiana Cajun to the refined cooking of Maryland plantations, he presents southern recipes surrounded by his marvelous tales of history and culture. 210 pages.

$19.95 Retail price, cloth; $12.95 paper
5% Tax for North Carolina residents
$ 1.50 Postage and handling
Make check payable to University Press of NC
ISBN 0-8078-1859-3 cloth; 0-8078-4255-9 paper

BRAVO
Greensboro Symphony Guild
P. O. Box 29224
Greensboro, NC 27408   919/274-6899

Bravo is an attractive 254-page cookbook, with 450 recipes, and into its second printing. Many chapters contain quick ideas such as blender yeast rolls and short cut coq au vin. One section is on picnics with five types of outdoor meals, including a North Carolina pig picking and a Southwestern patio fiesta. Proceeds benefit educational projects.

$11.95 Retail price
$ .60 Tax for North Carolina residents
$ 1.50 Postage and handling
Make check payable to Greensboro Symphony Guild

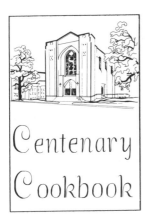

CENTENARY COOKBOOK

United Methodist Women
Centenary United Methodist Church
P. O. Box 608
Winston-Salem, NC 27102   919/724-6311

Hundreds of Winston-Salem Methodist Women contributed 922 recipes in their 400-page *Centenary Cookbook* offering a wide variety of culinary classics. Included are favorites for entertaining, family, youth, men and a special collection of "Heritage Recipes." "Tips for the Bride" chapter is fun to read and provides practical advice for all!

$12.00 Retail price
$ 2.00 Postage and handling
Make check payable to Centenary United Methodist Church
ISBN 56-0552783

CHRISTMAS FAVORITES

by Mary Ann Crouch and Jan Stedman
P. O. Box 15162
Charlotte, NC 28211

Over 120,000 copies in print! Christmas decorating ideas, entertainment suggestions and tasty recipes make this 120-page book a complete Christmas handbook. Includes wreath and bow-making instructions, party notebook with helpful reminders, imaginative menus and creative planning. Dedicated to the spirit of Christmas!

$ 5.95 Retail price
$ 1.00 Postage and handling
$ .30 Tax for North Carolina residents
Make check payable to *Christmas Favorites*

COASTAL CAROLINA COOKING

by Nancy Davis and Kathy Hart
The University Press of North Carolina
P. O. Box 2288
Chapel Hill, NC 27514   800/848-6224

Thirty-four cooks from Currituck County to Brunswick County and everywhere in between have shared dishes you do not find on restaurant menus or fancy cookbooks. These people tell about their families, their traditions, their way of life—all in the context of food. 180 pages. Paperback.

$ 8.95 Retail price
$ .45 Tax for North Carolina residents
$ 1.50 Postage and handling
Make check payable to University Press of NC
ISBN 0-8078-4152-8

271

A COOKBOOK OF
PINEHURST COURSES

Moore Regional Hospital Auxiliary
P. O. Box 704
Pinehurst, NC 28374

This delightful cookbook features outstanding recipes
from auxiliary members and friends. The book also
features menus and recipes from some of the outstanding hotels and country clubs of the area. Line drawings are scattered throughout the 320 pages of this
lovely spiral-bound book.

$11.95 Retail price
$ .60 Tax for North Carolina residents
$ 1.50 Postage and handling
Make check payable to Moore Regional Hospital
Auxiliary
ISBN 0-918544-48-3

A COOK'S TOUR OF
THE AZALEA COAST

New Hanover, Pender, Brunswick County
Medical Auxiliary
P.O. Box 5303
Wilmington, NC 28403   919/791-6030

A Cook's Tour combines 430 outstanding, tested recipes,
original photographs, and drawings to capture the special charm and beauty of the Azalea Coast. The 246
pages are in eleven sections ranging from appetizers to
desserts. A special seafood section with 47 recipes is a
collection by local physicians, area restaurants, and
Azalea festival celebrators and their families.

$10.95 Retail price
$ .55 Tax for North Carolina residents
$ 2.00 Postage and handling
Make check payable to *A Cook's Tour*
ISBN 9-39114-36-4

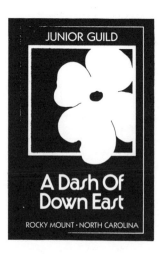

A DASH OF DOWN EAST

Junior Guild of Rocky Mount
P. O. Box 7912
Rocky Mount, NC 27804   919/442-1274

A Dash of Down East contains 338 pages with about
1400 recipes. The cookbook represents the basic every-
day recipes to gourmet recipes. It includes ideas for
gift giving to grilled dove for hors d'oeuvres to Party
Gumbo to Hunter's Chili to Cobb Salad. *A Dash of
Down East* has something for everyone.

$11.00 Retail Price
$ .55 Tax for North Carolina residents
$ 2.00 Postage and handling
Make check payable to Junior Guild of Rocky Mount
ISBN 0-9616940-0-9

EVEN MORE SPECIAL

Junior League of Durham and Orange Counties
900 South Duke Street
Durham, NC 27707   919/682-2325

From the Research Triangle of North Carolina comes a cookbook that's a perfect blend of southern hospitality and cosmopolitan panache. With over 400 triple-tested recipes and numbered, easy-to-follow instructions, this 316-page carefully crafted cookbook is sure to become your favorite cooking companion.

$14.95 Retail Price
$ .75 Tax for North Carolina residents
$ 1.75 Postage and handling
Make check payable to Special Publications
ISBN 0-9615845-0-5

FAVORITE RECIPES OF THE LOWER CAPE FEAR

The Ministering Circle
P. O. Box 3862
Wilmington, NC 28406   919/763-6998

The book is bound in red with illustration on front of Cape Fear River. It has 218 pages, is illustrated, and has a history of the ministering circle. The recipes were donated by members and people of the community. Now in its sixth printing.

$ 7.00 Retail Price (Tax and postage included)
Make check payable to Ministering Circle Cook Book

THE FEARRINGTON HOUSE COOKBOOK

by Jenny Fitch
Ventana Press
P. O. Box 2468
Chapel Hill, NC 27515   919/942-0220

The Fearrington House Cookbook contains the flavors and charm of the highly-acclaimed Fearrington House, one of the South's finest restaurants. Arranged by season, the book features menus for special occasions with tips on cooking, gardening, and flower arranging. 269 pages. Beautifully illustrated with line drawings. Over 500 recipes and tips for entertaining.

$19.95 Retail Price
$ 1.00 Tax for North Carolina residents
$ 3.60 Postage and handling
Make check payable to Ventana Press
ISBN 0-9400-87-23-5

GOODNESS GROWS IN NORTH CAROLINA COOKBOOK

North Carolina Department of Agriculture
P. O. Box 27647
Raleigh, NC 27611   919/733-7912

A sizzling success! This new 350-recipe collection features the finest fare from our state's food producers and companies. We've included special tables and charts, a Celebrity Section, and a nutritional analysis of each recipe. A must for every bookshelf and a perfect gift any time, for any occasion. One taste from this book and you'll know why *Goodness Grows in North Carolina*!

$10.00 Retail Price
$ .50 Tax for North Carolina residents
$ 2.00 Postage and handling
Make check payable to NC Department of Agriculture
ISBN 0-87197-262-X

THE GRECIAN PLATE

Hellenic Ladies Society
P. O. Box 1149
Durham, NC 27705   919/682-1414

Winner of the 1985 Tastemaker Award! The book features 300 tested traditional recipes from appetizers to desserts with easy to follow instructions. *The Grecian Plate* was featured in "The Cookbook Corner" of Good Housekeeping Magazine in March, 1988.

$11.95 Retail Price
$ .60 Tax for North Carolina residents
$ 2.05 Postage and handling
Make check payable to *The Grecian Plate*
ISBN 0-9613856-0-X

HAVE FUN COOKING WITH ME

by Lela J. Clarke
451 Kings Grant Court
Statesville, NC 28677   704/872-6999

Includes many very old recipes. There are some new ones, too. As a rule you will have the ingredients in your kitchen already.   120 pages and 400 recipes and some I originated myself. I have collected these recipes for over fifty years. Some come from friends, and they were great cooks.

$ 7.00 Retail Price
$ 1.25 Postage and handling
Make check payable to Lela J. Clarke

HEART OF THE MOUNTAINS

Buncombe County Extension Homemakers
P. O. Box 7667
Asheville, NC 28802   704/255-5522

Heart of the Mountains features a collection of recipes from the hearts of the Buncombe County Extension Homemakers, a volunteer organization which promotes education, leadership development and community service projects. These home-tested recipes are made from ingredients a homemaker usually has on the shelf and are wonderful to eat.

At the time of this printing, *Heart of the Mountains* is being reprinted.

HIGH HAMPTON HOSPITALITY

by Lily Byrd
c/o High Hampton Inn and Country Club
Cashiers, NC 28717

High Hampton Hospitality gives a wonderful description of the history and heritage of the High Hampton, beginning with Colonel Hampton's hunting lodge in 1830. With photographs, legends, "yarbs," etc., the book contains menus and excellent recipes from those who live in the high lands. 220 pages. Fifth printing.

$ 7.50 Retail Price
$ .38 Tax for North Carolina residents
$ 1.00 Postage and handling
Make check payable to *High Hampton Hospitality*

IN GOOD TASTE

Department of Nutrition
CB7400, Rosenau Hall Room 2202
Chapel Hill, NC 27599   919/966-7212

This book contains 177 recipes and nutrition tips from the Department of Nutrition. The cookbook represents the Department's major effort to raise scholarship funds to help support the training of public health nutritionists at the Master's degree level.

$ 5.00 Retail Price
$ 1.00 Postage and handling
Make check payable to Nutrition MPH Scholarship Fund

I REMEMBER: A COLLECTION OF OLD-TIME RECIPES AND MEMORIES FROM THE PAST

Edited by Hank Kellner
Simmer Pot Press
Route 3 Box 973A
Boone, NC 28607   704/262-3289

This beautifully illustrated collection features 29 authentic handed down recipes; 13 personal memories from the past; 9 nostalgic childhood tales; and 24 fascinating historical vignettes. In *I Remember* "You'll discover priceless old-time recipes...you'll be rewarded by happy memories." Carole Currie, *The Asheville Citizen-Times*. First printing 8/88; second printing 8/90.

$ 6.95 Retail Price
$ .35 Tax for North Carolina residents
$ 1.25 Postage and handling
Make check payable to Simmer Pot Press
ISBN 0-944010-01-06

ISLAND BORN AND BRED: A COLLECTION OF HARKERS ISLAND FOOD, FUN, FACT AND FICTION

Harkers Island United Methodist Women
P. O. Box 625
Harkers Island, NC 28531   919/728-4644

A unique blend of recipes, local history, and folklore from a small island between the Outer Banks and mainland of North Carolina. It characterizes the lifestyle of a community once dominated by the water surrounding it. A treasured keepsake of the Island's past as it struggles against the "progress" taking place around it. 378 pages. 625 recipes. 7th printing.

$12.95 Retail Price
$ .65 Tax for North Carolina residents
$ 1.55 Postage and handling
Make check payable to H.I. United Methodist Women

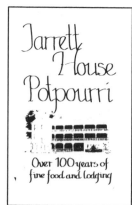

JARRETT HOUSE POTPOURRI

The Jarrett House
P. O. Box 219
Dillsboro, NC 28725

The Jarrett House has been known for its "home cooking" for 100 years. People from across the nation have dined in the friendly atmosphere inherent to the House, which is now on the National Register of Historic Places. Jean and Jim Hartbarger welcome you to visit, whether in person or through the wonderful recipes that are recreated within this cookbook. Ringbound. 90 pages.

$ 6.50 Retail price
$ .33 Tax for North Carolina residents
$ 1.25 Postage and handling
Make check payable to The Jarrett House

276

KNOLLWOOD'S COOKING

Knollwood Baptist Church
330 Knollwood Street
Winston-Salem, NC 27104   919/725-1343

A collection of recipes from the members of Knollwood Baptist Church designed to relate our daily menus to the growth of our lives within the church. Using the section artwork to correlate the areas of spiritual nourishment to the equivalent area of physical nourishment from Beginnings to Endings, the book abounds with food for the body and soul.

$10.00 Retail Price
$ 1.00 Postage and handling
Make check payable to Knollwood Baptist Church

KORNER'S FOLLY COOKBOOK

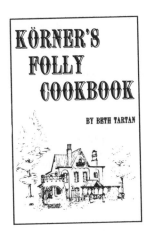

by Beth Tartan
TarPar Ltd.
P. O. Box 3
Kernersville, NC 27284   919/993-2037

It would only be folly *not* to add this delightful book to your collection. The book about Korner's Folly, a restoration project of a castle-like structure in Kernersville, is described as a "culinary counterpane." You will find it reads like a novel about life in the South from the early 1800s up to the present. Spiral bound. 152 pages.

$ 4.00 Retail Price
$ .20 Tax for North Carolina residents
$ 1.25 Postage and handling
Make check payable to TarPar

LOVE YOURSELF COOKBOOK

by Edie Low
P. O. Box 35152
Charlotte, NC 28235   704/535-0103

This award-winning, all-purpose cookbook features almost 400 quick, easy recipes for 1 or 2 servings of tasty food, plus hints on shopping for 1 or 2; how to make the most of your purchases; definitions of cooking terms; spices and food each enhances; substitions; etc. Outstanding recipes. Hardcover with jacket. Color illustrations. A gift for anyone...especially yourself.

$23.00 Retail Price (Tax and postage included)
Make check payable to *Love Yourself Cookbook*

277

MAMA'S RECIPES AND OTHERS
by June Thompson Medlin
P. O. Box 866
Lake Junaluska, NC 28745   704/452-5488

Mama's Recipes and Others, a 210-page volume, is not
only a book of recipes, but it is also interspersed with
nostalgic "chapterettes" about the author's mother and
her childhood in the mountains of Western North
Carolina.

$ 9.95 Retail price (Tax and postage included)
Make check payable to *Mama's Recipes*

MARION BROWN'S SOUTHERN COOK BOOK
by Marion Brown
The University of North Carolina Press
P. O. Box 2288
Chapel Hill, NC 27514   800/848-6224

Featuring treasured old recipes from southern house-
holds, favorite dishes from hotels and restaurants with
a tradition of southern cuisine, and newer recipes that
take advantage of prepared products, this popular regional cook book has sold more than a half million copies. 1,000 recipes. 489 pages. Paperback.

$12.50 Retail price
$ .63 Tax for North Carolina residents
$ 2.00 Postage and handling
Make check payable to University Press of NC
ISBN 0-8078-4078-5

MARKET TO MARKET
Service League of Hickory, NC, Inc.
P. O. Box 1563
Hickory, NC 28603   704/324-0201

Country fare or city flair, *Market to Market* offers it all.
Presented by the Service League of Hickory, NC, this
time-tested recipe collection features unique menus,
local favorites, sumptuous desserts, international cuisine and microwave delights. Its cosmopolitan blend
of food offerings makes it a cookbook of distinction.
428 pages. 700+ recipes.

$14.50 Retail Price
$ .73 Tax for North Carolina residents
$ 1.50 Postage and handling
Make check payable to *Market to Market*
ISBN 0-9611356-0-3

THE MICROWAVE TOUCH

by Galen N. Hill
942 Greenwood Drive
Greensboro, NC 27410   919/294-0767 or 852-9774

A different microwave cookbook....the format and step-by-step instructions take the guesswork out of microwaving. Recipes are favorites, delicious and quick. Recipes tested many times in different ovens for accuracy. Over 100 tips indexed for easy reference.

$ 9.95 Retail Price
$ .50 Tax for North Carolina residents
$ 1.50 Postage and handling
Make check payable to *The Microwave Touch*
ISBN 0-9614205-0-2

MOUNTAIN ELEGANCE

Junior League of Asheville
P. O. Box 8723
Asheville, NC 28814   704/254-5608

Over 300 treasured recipes (on more than 300 pages) from members and friends of the Asheville Junior League, including many of the best professional chefs in this popular resort area. For picnics, Blue Ridge Mountain style, to romantic candlelight dinners, this book will enhance any cookbook collection.

$11.95 Retail Price
$ .48 Tax for North Carolina residents
$ 1.50 Postage and handling
Make check payable to Junior League of Asheville
ISBN 0-9608444

MOUNTAIN POTPOURRI

Haywood County Hospital Auxiliary
90 Hospital Drive
Clyde, NC 28721

Mountain Potpourri is a 254-page, picturesque and unique cookbook, blending old and new and bringing together this party-flavored concept of cookery. The blending of generations of "local folks" and "summer people" creates a festive potpourri of ideas colored by multi-flavored cultures.

$ 8.95 Retail Price
$ .45 Tax for North Carolina residents
$ 2.00 Postage and handling
Make check payable to Haywood County Hospital Auxiliary
ISBN 0-918544-27-0

MUSHROOMS, TURNIP GREENS AND PICKLED EGGS

by Frances Carr Parker
TarPar Ltd.
P. O. Box 3
Kernersville, NC 27284   919/993-2037

How to save grocery money, and your time, is done for you with three meals a day planned...for 365 days of the year. Holidays, parties, and festive events. This standby cookbook has proven its worth in gold to many new homemakers, as well as veteran housekeepers. Hard cover with jacket. 288 pages.

$ 6.00 Retail Price
$ .30 Tax for North Carolina residents
$ 1.25 Postage and handling
Make check payable to TarPar

NORTH CAROLINA AND OLD SALEM COOKERY

by Beth Tartan
TarPar Ltd.
P. O. Box 3
Kernersville, NC 27284   919/993-2037

What fine tables our Tarheel grandmothers used to set! Here is a book that preserves that part of our North Carolina heritage which deals with food. (Our foremothers in the kitchen are just as important to our history as our forefathers on the battlefield.) Here are recipes that will evoke the response, "My, that tastes the way grandma used to make it." Hardcover.
8th printing.

$ 7.95 Retail Price
$ .40 Tax for North Carolina residents
$ 1.25 Postage and handling
Make check payable to TarPar

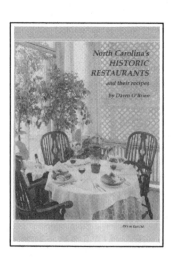

NORTH CAROLINA'S HISTORIC RESTAURANTS AND THEIR RECIPES

John F. Blair, Publisher
1406 Plaza Drive
Winston-Salem, NC 27103   919/768-1374

This book features fifty restaurants in North Carolina housed in buildings at least fifty years old. It also includes two or three recipes from each restaurant. This North Carolina entry is part of a series featuring seven southeastern states.

$14.95 Retail Price
$ .45 Tax for North Carolina residents
$ 1.50 Postage and handling
Make check payable to John F. Blair
ISBN 0-89587-067-3

280

NOTHING COULD BE FINER

The Junior League of Wilmington, Inc.
The Carriage House—Cottage Lane
Wilmington, NC 29401

The diversity of this outstanding collection features menus and recipes that range from Croustades Aux Champignons to Gun Club Sauce! Currently out of print, the proceeds from its sale and their current *Seafood Sorcery* help fund educational and charitable projects within the community.

OUT OF OUR LEAGUE

The Junior League of Greensboro, Inc.
c/o Julia Milton
1216 Briarcliff Road
Greensboro, NC 27408   919/275-7402

One to the top cookbooks in the country with more than 100,000 copies in print. *Out of Our League* was first printed in October 1978 and had five printings. Currently out of print, this award-winning cookbook has 400 illustrated pages of kitchen-tested recipes, tips, metric measures on every recipe, and "all time favorites."

ISBN 09605788-0-3

PASS THE PLATE: THE COLLECTION FROM CHRIST CHURCH

by Alice G. Underhill and Barbara S. Stewart
P. O. Box 836
New Bern, NC 28563   919/633-2270 or 638-8610

Over 50,000 copies of *Pass the Plate* exist as the "delicious menu" resource for both novice and experienced cooks. Over 900 easy-to-read recipes within this attractive 516-page hard-cover spiral-bound volume are punctuated by 25 illustrations and historical information about restored 18th century homes and Tryon Palace, the original seat of Colonial government for the Carolinas.

$16.95 Retail Price
$ .85 Tax for North Carolina residents
$ 3.05 Postage and handling
Make check payable to *Pass the Plate*
ISBN 0-939114-13-5

QUEEN ANNE'S TABLE

Edenton Historical Commission
P. O. Box 474
Edenton, NC 27932   919/482-3663

Queen Anne's Table features a collection of tried and true recipes original to 26 historic Edenton homes pictured in the book. The pen and ink drawings are by local artists.

$ 6.00 Retail Price
$ 1.50 Postage and handling
Make check payable to Edenton Historical Commission

RECIPES FROM OUR FRONT PORCH

By Ella Jo and John Shell
Hemlock Inn
P. O. Drawer EE
Bryson City, NC 28713   704/488-2885

Wonderful recipes from the front porch of the Hemlock Inn. There are 150 pages, with lithograph photos. We share some of the blessings that are said at our Inn throughout the book, along with the history of our Inn. Hard back, spiral binding.

$ 8.75 Retail Price
$ .35 Tax for North Carolina residents
$ 1.25 Postage and handling
Make check payable to *Recipes From Our Front Porch*
ISBN 0-939-11465-8

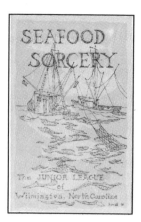

SEAFOOD SORCERY

Junior League of Wilmington, NC
3803 Wrightsville Avenue Unit 9
Wilmington, NC 28403   919/799-7405

In *Seafood Sorcery*, there are 77 pages of wonderful recipes and information on seafood, including details on how to choose, store and prepare fish, crabs, oysters, and shrimp.

$ 6.00 Retail Price
$ .30 Tax for North Carolina residents
$ 1.00 Postage and handling
Make check payable to Junior League of Wilmington, Inc.

SEA TO SHORE

by Jan Robinson
10500 Mount Holly Road
Charlotte, NC 28214   704/392-4740

More than 65 species of fish and shellfish are suc-
culently prepared in recipes for appetizers, soups,
chowders, entrees, casseroles, and souffles. Features a
valuable cook's guide to identifying, buying, cleaning,
cutting, cooking, and serving bounty from the sea.

$14.95 Retail Price
$ .75 Tax for North Carolina residents
$ 1.50 Postage and handling
Make check payable to Ship to Shore, Inc.
ISBN 0-921686-3-8

SHIP TO SHORE I

by Jan Robinson
10500 Mount Holly Road
Charlotte, NC 28214   704/392-4740

Sixty-five Caribbean charter yacht chefs reveal to you
a fabulous collection of closely guarded and treasured
recipes that have enticed and tantalized guests year
after year. Ease in preparation and simple ingredients
ensure every chef success... whether on land or at sea!

$14.95 Retail Price
$ .75 Tax for North Carolina residents
$ 1.50 Postage and handling
Make check payable to Ship to Shore, Inc.
ISBN 0-961686-0-3

SHIP TO SHORE II

by Jan Robinson
10500 Mount Holly Road
Charlotte, NC 28214   704/392-4740

A second collection of all new mouth-watering recipes
that continues the tradition of offering a taste of the
good life on the high seas. New features include individual menus for more than 100 entrees, French and
California wine suggestions, and a potpourri of helpful measurement equivalents.

$14.95 Retail Price
$ .75 Tax for North Carolina residents
$ 1.50 Postage and handling
Make check payable to Ship to Shore, Inc.

SIP TO SHORE

by Jan Robinson
10500 Mount Holly Road
Charlotte, NC 28214   704/392-4740

Recreate your own Caribbean cocktail hour! Discover the taste of tropical splendor in a glass—be it alcoholic, non-alcoholic, or deliciously dietetic! Serve your luscious liquid refreshments with several hot and cold island hors d'oeuvres.

$10.95 Retail Price
$ .55 Tax for North Carolina residents
$ 1.50 Postage and handling
Make check payable to Ship to Shore, Inc.
ISBN 0-921686-2-X

STIRRING PERFORMANCES

Junior League of Winston-Salem, Inc.
c/o Timothy Vogler
909 South Main Street
Winston-Salem, NC 27101   919/722-9681 or 773-0675

A must-have collection of over 500 recipes that blend a contemporary cuisine and Southern hospitality with a twist of uptown and a dash of down home. Stunning and sophisticated, it also features the arts in Winston-Salem, known as the cultural center of the Southeast. Unique grilling section features appetizers, entrees, and desserts—all prepared completely on the grill.

$16.95 Retail Price
$ .85 Tax for North Carolina residents
$ 2.00 Postage and handling
Make check payable to Junior League of Winston-Salem, Inc.
ISBN 0-9615429-2-6

TASTE BUDS

Winslow, Wolverton, Komegay
P. O. Box 83
Hertford, NC 27944   919/426-5663, 5443, 7665

Our book contains seasonal recipes and gardening tips. It is based on a monthly format and subdivided by weeks. The gardening and cooking are oriented toward holidays and appropriate food in season. 303 pages, 166 recipes, delightful short stories, gardening advice and numerous detailed pen and ink illustrations.

$12.95 Retail Price
$ .65 Tax for North Carolina residents
$ 2.00 Postage and handling
Make check payable to Taste Buds
ISBN 0-9614874-0-2

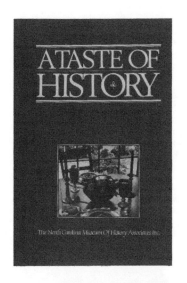

A TASTE OF HISTORY

North Carolina Museum of History Associates
109 East Jones Street
Raleigh, NC 27601   919/733-3076

Since 1898 the North Carolina Museum of History has had the official responsibility of preserving North Carolina's social, economic and political hisotry for millions of visitors and school children who come to historic sites all over the state. Currently out of print, this beautiful cookbook of menus and recipes has helped preserve the state's history.

VEGETARIAN MASTERPIECES

by Carol Tracy and Julie Bruton
2122 Forest Drive
Charlotte, NC 28211   704-365-4505

Highly nutritious, delicious, and easy-to-prepare dishes that will help those going through the transition from meat-eating to vegetarianism. The more than 300 recipes are gourmet dishes that just happen to be strictly lacto-vegetarian! A healthy choice in cook-books.

$12.95 Retail Price
$ .65 Tax for North Carolina residents
$ 2.00 Postage and handling
Make check payable to *Vegetarian Masterpieces*
ISBN 0-9622168-2-8

WHAT IS IT? WHAT DO I DO WITH IT?

by Beth Tartan and Fran Parker
TarPar Ltd.
P. O. Box 3
Kernersville, NC 27284   919/993-2037

A dictionary for the novice in a non-equipped kitchen, and a blessing for those who have everything...but don't have the foggiest idea how to use it. From Aeble-skiver pans to Zesters, this little book will explain what it is while providing delicious recipes utilizing every imaginable culinary houseware. Spiral bound. 138 pages.

$ 4.00 Retail Price
$ .20 Tax for North Carolina residents
$ 1.00 Postage and handling
Make check payable to TarPar

WHAT'S NEW IN WEDDING FOOD

by Marigold P. Sparks and Beth Tartan
TarPar Ltd.
P. O. Box 3
Kernersville, NC 27284   919/993-2037

The renowned food editor of the Winston-Salem Journal and her daughter (the bride) have collaborated in
authoring this collection of recipes and helpful ideas
about the festivities surrounding a trip to the altar. A
delightful blending of tradition and trend, it is a valuable reference for anybody who might ever have any
role in a wedding. Spiral bound. 102 pages.

$ 7.95 Retail Price
$ .40 Tax for North Carolina residents
$ 1.00 Postage and handling
Make check payable to TarPar
ISBN 0-933-193-00-9

THE QUAIL RIDGE PRESS
"BEST OF THE BEST" COOKBOOK SERIES

The cookbooks in the Quail Ridge Press "Best of the Best" series are considered the most complete survey available of a state's particular cooking style and flavor. They are compiled by searching out a comprehensive cross-section of the leading cookbooks written and published within the state, and then requesting the authors, editors, and publishers of these books to select their most popular recipes. A sampling of these recipes are selected to create that state's Best of the Best edition. A catalog section in each volume lists the contributing cookbooks with descriptive copy and ordering information on each book. This section is of particular interest and value to cookbook collectors. The volumes listed below have been completed as of January, 1993.

Best of the Best from Alabama
288 pages, (28-3) $14.95

Best of the Best from Florida
288 pages, (16-X) $14.95

Best of the Best from Georgia
320 pages, (30-5) $14.95

Best of the Best from Kentucky
288 pages, (27-5) $14.95

Best of the Best from Louisiana
288 pages, (13-5) $14.95

Best of the Best from Mississippi
288 pages, (19-4) $14.95

Best of the Best from North Carolina
288 pages, (38-0) $14.95

Best of the Best from South Carolina
288 pages, (39-9) $14.95

Best of the Best from Tennessee
288 pages, (20-8) $14.95

Best of the Best from Texas
352 pages, (14-3) $14.95
Hardbound, (34-8) $16.95

Best of the Best from Virginia
320 pages, (41-0) $14.95

Best of the Best from Arkansas
288 pages, (43-7) $14.95

Best of the Best from Missouri
288 pages, (44-5) $14.95

Best of the Best from Pennsylvania
(Available Fall '93)

All books plastic-ring bound, unless noted otherwise. ISBN Prefix: 0-937552-; suffix noted in parentheses under each title. *See next page for complete listing of Quail Ridge Press Cookbooks.*

"Best of the Best" Cookbook Series:

	ISBN SUFFIX
Best of the Best from Alabama $14.95	28-3
Best of the Best from Arkansas $14.95	43-7
Best of the Best from Florida $14.95	16-X
Best of the Best from Georgia $14.95	30-5
Best of the Best from Kentucky $14.95	27-5
Best of the Best from Louisiana $14.95	13-5
Best of the Best from Mississippi $14.95	09-7
Best of the Best from Missouri $14.95	44-5
Best of the Best from North Carolina $14.95	38-0
Best of the Best from Pennsylvania $14.95	47-X
Best of the Best from South Carolina $14.95	39-9
Best of the Best from Tennessee $14.95	20-8
Best of the Best from Texas $14.95	14-3
Best of the Best from Texas (hardbound) $16.95	34-8
Best of the Best from Virginia $14.95	41-0

The Quail Ridge Press Cookbook Series:

	ISBN SUFFIX
The Little New Orleans Cookbook (hardbound) $8.95	42-9
The Little Gumbo Book (hardbound) $6.95	17-8
The Little Bean Book (hardbound) $9.95	32-1
Gourmet Camping $9.95	45-3
Lite Up Your Life $14.95	40-2
Hors D'Oeuvres Everybody Loves $5.95	11-9
The Seven Chocolate Sins $5.95	01-1
A Salad A Day $5.95	02-X
Quickies for Singles $5.95	03-8
Twelve Days of Christmas Cookbook $5.95	00-3
Country Mouse Cheese Cookbook $5.95	10-0

ISBN Prefix: 0-937552-. All books are plastic-ring bound unless noted otherwise. To order by mail, send check, money order, or Visa or MasterCard number with expiration date to:

QUAIL RIDGE PRESS
P. O. Box 123 / Brandon, MS 39043

Please add $1.50 postage and handling for first book; 50¢ per additional book. Gift wrap with enclosed card add $1.00. Mississippi residents add 7% sales tax. Write or call for free catalog of all QRP books and cookbooks.

Phone orders call toll free: 1-800-343-1583

Guide to the Manuscript Collections of the New England Historic Genealogical Society

Timothy Salls, Editor

New England Historic Genealogical Society
2002

Copyright © 2002 by New England Historic Genealogical Society

Cover Design: Carolyn Sheppard Oakley

All rights reserved. No part of this publication may be reproduced or transmitted in any form or by any means, electronic or mechanical, including photocopying, recording, or any information storage or retrieval systems, without permission in writing from the copyright holder, except for the inclusion of brief quotations in a review.

International Standard Book Number: 0-88082-144-2
Library of Congress Control Number: 2002108455

Published by
New England Historic Genealogical Society
101 Newbury Street
Boston, MA 02116-3007
www.NewEnglandAncestors.org

Printed by: McNaughton-Gunn, Inc. Saline, Michigan.

Table of Contents

The Manuscript Collections

Dedication

To the memory of R. Stanton Avery and in honor of his family for their support of the Society's special collections

Introduction

Two of the first ten items donated to NEHGS in 1845 were manuscripts. Today, 157 years later, the R. Stanton Avery Special Collections Department holds one of the most extensive manuscript collections dedicated to genealogical material in the country. Yet, a recent marketing survey indicates that many NEHGS members are unfamiliar with the Society's extensive manuscript holdings and how to access them. This guide was created as an easy means to identify the individual bible records, diaries, account books, research notes, etc., that collectively constitute our manuscript collections.

Although this guide contains over 5,500 entries, representing hundreds of thousands of individual items or records, entries exist only for manuscripts cataloged as of April 2002. As a result, this guide describes just a portion of our total holdings — probably somewhere between fifty to seventy-five percent of the entire collection. Subsequent editions will document the manuscripts still to be cataloged.

Each entry contains at least one of the following fields from the manuscript's catalog record: title, author/corporation, call number, physical description, restrictions, additional form, and scope. The catalog record does contain additional fields not included here such as the historical and provenance notes. Some of the entries in this guide consist of only a title and call number. These "skeleton" catalog records were added into our library database by copying the information directly from the catalog card, and are part of a two-year initiative to ensure at least a basic catalog record for every manuscript in the collections.

We hope that the Guide to the Manuscript Collections of the New England Historic Genealogical Society will encourage greater use of the resources in these unique collections. As you examine the individual entries, you will begin to appreciate the tremendous wealth of material available here. Who knows how many genealogical mysteries might be solved by using these items? For far too long, the NEHGS manuscripts collections were a hidden treasure — the publication of this guide assures that this treasure will be hidden no longer.

Acknowledgements

Even a simple book like this one represents the work of numerous people who deserve my thanks and appreciation.

Ralph J. Crandall, Pamela P. Swain, and D. Brenton Simons for being strong advocates for the special collections department and for promoting the department through articles, lectures, etc.

Gabrielle Stone for her help in the production of this book.

Linda McGuire for her help in editing the text and Valerie Beaudrault for her help in proofreading.

Lynne Burke and Jean Maguire who are always willing to share their cataloging expertise and their knowledge of the library database.

David C. Dearborn, Marshall Kirk, David Allen Lambert, Julie Otto, Gary Boyd Roberts, and George F. Sanborn Jr. for their work on project entry, pulling and re-shelving manuscripts, and sharing their genealogical knowledge.

Peter Cameron, John Carney, William Deane, Polly Furbush, Bill Larson, Mary McCarl and the other volunteers who have helped to process collections.

Timothy Hughes, my assistant, for his efforts to catalog the collections among all his other assignments.

Finally, I want to thank the donors for their tremendous generosity without which, obviously, our collection would not exist. I hope that individuals with manuscript material that matches our acquisition policy (see page xii) will consider donating to NEHGS so this material can be preserved and made accessible to current and future researchers.

Timothy Salls
Archivist
R. Stanton Avery Special Collections Department
July 31, 2002

Using this catalog

The indexes are the keys to using this catalog. The guide contains name, place, and subject indexes, which provide complete access to the content of each manuscript item.

The individual entries are arranged by call number, which groups the items according to format. As you browse through the guide, you will find the different manuscript formats on the following pages:

typescripts — pp. 1–178
large collections — pp. 179–304; 405–471; 521–522; 537–574
individual items (letter-size) — pp. 305–464
individual items (legal-size) — pp. 471–521
oversized typescripts — pp. 522–537

Abbreviations:
ALS – autograph letter(s) signed (letter written and signed by the author)
ADS – autograph document(s) signed (document written and signed by the author)
DS – document(s) signed (only the signature is in the hand of the author)

Access policy for manuscript collections

Access to the NEHGS manuscript collections is a benefit of NEHGS membership. NEHGS members may view manuscripts during normal reference library hours of operation. Manuscripts held by NEHGS can be used only at 101 Newbury Street — they do not circulate. However, patrons who are unable to visit 101 Newbury Street should note the services offered by the NEHGS Research Services Department described on page ix. In addition, NEHGS has microfilmed several collections, including the Walter Corbin Papers. NEHGS members may borrow duplicate microfilm copies from the circulating library. The Society has released several CD-ROMs for sale with transcribed records from the manuscript collections, including Bible Records from the manuscript collections of the *New England Historical Genealogical Society and New England Marriages Prior to 1700* [from the Clarence A. Torrey Papers]. Several manuscript records have been transcribed for publication in *The New England Historical and Genealogical Register* (available to NEHGS members on the www.NewEnglandAncestors.org website); members may also access online databases created from manuscripts in our collection.

In addition to using this printed guide, patrons can locate manuscripts by author, title, and subject searches with our online public access catalog, which is available at *www.newenglandancestors.org/libraries/sydneyplus.asp.*

Manuscript finding aids
Inventories are available for many of the larger collections. The catalog record will note if there is an inventory for that collection. Each inventory contains a general overview of the collection; a short history or biography of the collection's creator/compiler; a description of the contents, including its strengths and weaknesses; and a folder-by-folder listing of the collection contents. NEHGS is currently working to place these finding aids on our website.

Using the manuscript collections at the NEHGS research library

All manuscript material is housed in closed stacks. Patrons may access materials by completing a manuscript request form (available at the local history reference desk on the fifth floor) to facilitate retrieval from the stacks and to establish responsibility for use. Patrons should note that unprocessed or partially processed collections may not be immediately available to patrons.

To safeguard the unique materials found in the R. Stanton Avery Special Collections Department, please observe the following rules:
- Request only one collection at a time
- Use one box, and only one folder from the box at a time
- Maintain the existing order of material within each folder and box. (If there appears to be a problem, please notify the librarian on duty.)

- While in the reading room, store coats and personal belongings (briefcases, knapsacks, purses etc.) in the lockers provided; keys are available.
- No food or beverages are allowed on the floor. Smoking is prohibited.
- Researchers may be required to use microfilm or printed copies of manuscripts when available.
- Patrons using manuscripts are expected to take notes in pencil to avoid making permanent marks (stray or otherwise). Laptop computers can be used.
- All material must be handled with care. Turn pages carefully. Materials should be kept flat on the reading table — nothing (including elbows) should be placed on them and marks may neither be added nor erased. Please do not touch the surface of photographic prints.
- Manuscripts may not be removed from the table by the patron, except to return a collection to the reference desk.

Using the manuscript collections from a distance

As noted previously, some manuscripts are accessible to NEHGS members on microfilm through the circulating library, on NEHGS CD-ROMs, or as databases on *www.NewEnglandAncestors.org*. In addition, all manuscript items can be accessed through NEHGS Research Services. The research services staff will review the manuscripts in which you are interested, determine whether they contain relevant information, and provide documentation of their findings.

NEHGS Research Services Department
NEHGS Research Services offers in-depth research in the NEHGS manuscript collections (as well as in the research library collections, and in collections and sources outside of NEHGS).
To submit an in-depth research request, members should:
• state the specific question to be answered
• provide the information currently known about the person(s)
• cite the resources already searched
• authorize the number of hours to be spent researching the request

Fees for this service are as follows:
    $40 per hour + $3.50 shipping and handling for members
    $60 per hour + $3.50 shipping and handling for non-members
    Payment is by credit card.

    Fees are subject to change.

Orders can be placed online at *www.NewEnglandAncestors.org* or mailed (with your authorization for the number of hours and credit card information) to: NEHGS Research Services, 101 Newbury Street, Boston, MA 02116. Our staff will search relevant sources carefully to locate the name(s) you have provided. We cannot guarantee that the information you seek is, in fact, in these sources.

Manuscript collections use policies

Copyright
All patrons accept full legal responsibility for observing copyright law, as well as legislation concerning libel, invasion of privacy, property rights, and fair use.

Photocopying
NEHGS seeks a careful balance between our obligation for the long-term preservation of collections entrusted to our care and our desire to make our collections accessible to our members. NEHGS members who cannot visit the Society in person may use NEHGS Research Services to obtain photocopies of manuscript material.

Patrons should note that our Society reserves the right to decline any photocopy request that, in our opinion, jeopardizes the physical condition of the material, violates copyright law, or involves a collection with restricted access. If the condition is questionable, the decision rests with the archivist. No more than twenty-five pages from a single manuscript item will be copied for any patron for any reason without specific permission from the Archivist. Hand-held copiers are not permitted. The reproduction of any collection in its entirety is prohibited; however, the department will try to cooperate with other institutions in joint microform projects as well as undertaking its own microform/digitalization projects whenever feasible.

Permission to reproduce does not constitute permission to publish. A request to publish any information found in the manuscripts collections must be made in writing to the Archivist. There is no charge for permission to publish brief excerpts in most cases. The R. Stanton Avery Special Collections Department requests a copy of any publication that uses information taken from our collection.

Requests for information
The special collections staff will answer all written and telephone requests for information about the manuscript collections. The special collections staff is not able to conduct research on behalf of a patron. Patrons can engage NEHGS Research Services Department to perform research — see page ix.

Image use
Image reproduction fees
Black and white print (8" x 10")
[Additional sizes and color prints also available — contact the special collections department for fees.]

	In stock	New print
NEHGS members	$10	Cost + $10
Non-profit	$25	Cost + $25
Commercial	$50	Cost + $50

Fees are subject to change.

All on-site film, video, or photographic work must be arranged in advance.

Image use fees

	Non-profit	**Commercial**
Advertisement		
Half-page	$50/image/use	$50/image/use
Full-page	$100/image/use	$100/image/use
Cover (book/magazine)	$50/image/use	$100/image/use
Interior (book/magazine)	$25/image/use	$50/image/use
Video/film	$50/image/use	$100/image/use
Website	$50/image/use	$100/image/use

Fees are subject to change.

Fees for use on calendars, postcards, notecards, posters, CD-ROM/DVDs, etc., will be determined based on quantity, size, distribution, and price.

No image may be reproduced in any form without written permission of NEHGS. Each use must be requested in writing and include a complete and detailed citation for each item requested and a complete description of where and how the image will be used. All uses are non-exclusive and are for one-time use only.

Acquisition policy for manuscripts

The R. Stanton Avery Special Collections department complements the print, microform, and electronic collections of the NEHGS reference library by collecting, preserving, and providing access to manuscripts that support the research of New England families.

The categories of material sought for the NEHGS manuscript collections include:
- Handwritten or typed (unpublished) genealogies, research notes, or charts of professional or amateur genealogists and family associations;
- Transcriptions or other copies of town and church records;
- Family papers, including bible records, correspondence, diaries, deeds, photographs, and wills;
- Corporate or professional records that contain valuable genealogical or historical records;
- Transcriptions or other copies of documents concerning naturalization, immigration, census, military service, etc.

The bulk of the collection is in English, but relevant material is not excluded if it is in a foreign language. Although the preferred format is paper, electronic records are accepted. The department does not collect objects.

Donors of original manuscripts are asked to sign a deed of gift document that will transfer the physical and intellectual ownership of the collection to NEHGS. This is requested so the Society may, at its sole discretion, exhibit, reformat, or reproduce (for either preservation or publication) all or part of the collection in the media of our choice, without further approval by the donor or donor's representatives.

Large donations should include a financial donation, if possible, to offset the cost of processing and caring for the collection. Loans are discouraged. All loans must have a defined time limit after which they become the property of NEHGS. In accordance with federal tax laws, representatives of NEHGS cannot provide monetary appraisals.

For information about donating manuscript material to NEHGS, please contact the special collections department at 101 Newbury Street, Boston, MA 02116, at 617-536-5740, ext. 232, or at *manuscripts@nehgs.org*.

Guide to the Manuscript Collections of the New England Historic Genealogical Society

Notes on central Alabama families
England, Flora D.
ALA 4 20
1956
Typescript

New Englanders in the Alabama census of 1850
Hawes, Frank Mortimer, 1850-1941.
ALA 7
Typescript

Vital statistics from cemeteries in Dallas County, Alabama
England, Flora D.
ALA 123 10
Typescript

Index to earliest marriage record book of Dallas County, Alabama, 1818-1845
England, Flora D.
ALA 123 5
1955
Typescript

Index to Will Book A, Dallas County, Alabama
England, Flora D.
ALA 123 8
Typescript

Index to Will Book B, Dallas County, Alabama
England, Flora D.
ALA 123 8A
Typescript

Heads of families in Marengo County, Alabama, in 1830
England, Flora D.
ALA 145 30
Typescript

Notes on some families of Perry County, Alabama
England, Flora D.
ALA 152 10
Typescript

Heads of families in Perry County, Alabama, in 1830, alphabetically arranged; taken from the United States census
England, Flora Dainwood.
ALA 152 12
13 p.
Typescript

Perry County [Alabama] marriage record, 1820-1839
ALA 152 14
Typescript

Index to marriage record book, Perry County, Alabama, 1839-1851
England, Flora D.
ALA 152 18
21 p.
1955
Typescript

Index to Will Book A, Perry County, Alabama
England, Flora D.
ALA 152 8
Typescript

Index to Will Book B, Perry County, Alabama
England, Flora D.
ALA 152 18A
Typescript

Boshell Cemetery records, Walker Co., Alabama. Chickasaw Cemetery records, Walker Co., Alabama. Coal City Cemetery records, Walker Co., Alabama. Fike Cemetery records, Walker Co., Alabama. Holy Grove Cemetery record, Walker Co., Alabama. Manasco Cemetery records, Walker Co., Alabama
ALA 163 5
9, 4, 8, 3, 2, 3p.
Typescript

Manasco Cemetery records, Walker County, Alabama
King, Albert P.
ALA 165 5
Typescript

Cemetery records, Selma, Dallas Co., Alabama
ALA SEL 10
37 p.
Typescript

Cemetery records: Clarkdale, Yavapai, Arizona
ARI CLA 10
Typescript

Cemetery records of St. Joseph, now Joseph City [Navajo Co.], Arizona, completed as nearly as possible from ward clerk's records
ARI JOS 5
Typescript

List of names of prominent families of Mesa [Arizona] and vicinity
ARI MES 40
Typescript

Literal copy of all the gravestone inscriptions in the old cemetery at Barrington Head, Nova Scotia [Canada]
Doane, Alfred A. (Alfred Alder), 1855-1918.
CA 20 BAR
1905
Typescript

Records taken from gravestones in Little Harbor, Louis's Head, Osborne, Port L'Herbert, Rockland villages in the County of Shelburne, Nova Scotia [Canada]
CA 20 SHE 1
1958
Typescript

Cemetery inscriptions, Shelburne County, Nova Scotia [Canada]
Smith, George Hathorn.
CA 20 SHE
1928
Typescript

Inscriptions copied in cemetery of North Bedeque Presbyterian Church, Prince Edward Island, Canada
Schurman, V.L.
CA 22 18
1950
Typescript

Three pioneer cemeteries in Lobo Township, Ont. [Canada]
Miller, H. Orlo
CA 28 LOB
1939
Typescript

Some pioneer churchyards and cemeteries of London Township, Ont. [Canada]
Miller, H. Orlo
CA 28 LON
Typescript

Cemetery records in Westminster Township, County of Middlesex, Ont. [Canada]
Miller, H. Orlo
CA 28 WES
1939
Typescript

Two pioneer churchyards in Woodhouse Township, County of Norfolk, Ont. [Canada]
Miller, H. Orlo
CA 28 WOO
1939
Typescript

Some Elgin County [Ontario] cemetery records [Canada]
Miller, H. Orlo
CA 28 YAR
1939
Typescript

Cemetery records, village of Delaware, Middlesex Co., Ont. [Canada]
Miller, H. Orlo
CA DEL 28
1939
Typescript

San Francisco, California. Yerba Buena Cemetery, epitaphs 1850-1855
CALIF SAN 10
2 vols.
1921
Typescript

*San Francisco, Calif. Lone Mountain Cemetery
epitaphs 1859-1860*
CALIF SAN 11
4 vols.
Typescript

San Francisco, California epitaphs 1850-1859
CALIF SAN 11A
Typescript

*Cemetery records from Santa Paula Cemetery,
Santa Paula, California*
Cummings, Ada B.
CALIF SAN 2250
1931
Typescript

Cemetery at Old Shasta, Shasta Co., California
Morse, Theoda Mears, b. 1876.
CALIF SHA 225
1936
Typescript

*The Jewett family of America: notes and
corrections to "History and genealogy of the
Jewetts of America"*
Jewett, Everett D., Mrs.
CS71/J5/1908
1972?
Typescript

*Thomas Simmons (Symons or Simons) of
Plymouth, Scituate, Braintree (Quincy), Hingham,
and Boston [Massachusetts] ....*
Simmons, Frederick Johnson, b. 1884.
CS 71 S586 1936
45 p.
1936
Typescript

*List of Connecticut Revolutionary soldiers
mentioned in Beckwith's Almanac, New Haven,
1850 to 1870 inclusive; also War of 1812; 1856
to 1889 inclusive*
Weed, Clara L.
CT 42 31
16 p.
1927
Typescript

*Some Connecticut marriages: 1820-1837. Items
from the Norwich Courier, and other Connecticut
newspapers*
Bowman, John Elliot, 1866-1933.
CT 70 28
31 p.
1928
Typescript

*Connecticut deaths: from files of Massachusetts
Spy, Hartford Gazette, and New Hampshire &
Vermont Journal, 1792-1800*
Bowman, John Elliot, 1866-1933.
CT 70 29
1931
Typescript

*Connecticut deaths; 1820-1837; assembled from
various issues of Norwich Courier, and other
Connecticut newspapers*
Bowman, John Elliot, 1866-1933.
CT 70 30
1930
Typescript

*Connecticut deaths, 1801-1810, alphabetically
arranged from files of the Columbian Centinel,
Boston*
Bowman, John Elliot, 1866-1933.
CT 70 31
74 p.
1931
Typescript

*Connecticut deaths: 1821-1825. Alphabetically
arranged from files of The Columbian Centinel,
Boston, with some items from other newspapers of
the period*
Bowman, John Elliot, 1866-1933.
CT 70 32
27 p.
1931
Typescript

*Connecticut deaths: from file of the Connecticut
Observer, 1826*
Bowman, John Elliot, 1866-1933.
CT 70 33
99 p.
1931
Typescript

Connecticut deaths: including all reported in obituary columns of the Connecticut Observer, Hartford, 1825
Bowman, John Elliot, 1866-1933.
CT 70 34
99 p.
1931
Typescript

Connecticut deaths: items alphabetically arranged from files of Connecticut Observer 1827-1828
Bowman, John Elliot, 1866-1933.
CT 70 35
1 + 126 p.
1932
Typescript

Connecticut deaths: from file of The Connecticut Observer: 1829
Bowman, John Elliot, 1866-1933.
CT 70 36
1 + 66 p.
1932
Typescript

Connecticut deaths: file of The Connecticut Observer. 1830
Bowman, John Elliot, 1866-1933.
CT 70 37
1932
Typescript

Connecticut deaths: file of the Connecticut Observer, 1831
Bowman, John Elliot, 1866-1933.
CT 70 38
About 600 items. 1 + 57 p.
1932
Typescript

Connecticut deaths: from file of the Connecticut Observer, 1832
Bowman, John Elliot, 1866-1933.
CT 70 39
41 p.
1932
Typescript

Connecticut deaths: file of The Connecticut Observer, 1833
Bowman, John Elliot, 1866-1933.
CT 70 40
1 + 41 p.
1833
Typescript

List of Revolutionary soldiers' graves located by Daughters of the American Revolution. From the 22nd report of the National Society of the D.A.R., 1 March 1918-1 March 1919
Daughters of the American Revolution
CT 70 60
1 + 28 p.
1919
Typescript

Revolutionary Graves in the church yard at Westminster Hill [Connecticut]
Dorrance, Sarah F.
CT 70 65
6 p.
Typescript

Connecticut records
CT 70 80
22 p.
Mounted newspaper clippings.

Fairfield County, Conn. Superior Court records. First volume, 1702-1734
Card, Lester.
CT 81 10
222 + 1 p.
1941
Typescript

Deaths in Fairfield Co., Conn., as given in the U.S. census for year[s] 1850-1860
Card, Lester.
CT 81 20
14 p.
1942
Typescript

The cemeteries of Hartford County, Connecticut, and the location and identification in the same of the veterans of the twelve wars in which Connecticut has participated
Hale, Charles R.
CT 82 25
17 p.
Typescript

Tomb stone inscriptions on some back roads in Litchfield County, Connecticut
Huntley, Elsie M.
CT 83 25
9 + 1 p.
1956
Typescript

Cemetery records of New London County, Connecticut.
Ellsberry, Elizabeth Prather, 1923-.
CT 86 6
2 vols.
1968
Typescript

Deaths in Tolland County, Conn., 1830-1832. Copied from the People's Advocate, published at Tolland, Conn. on Wednesdays
Barlow, Claude W. (Claude Willis), 1907-1976.
CT 87 3
5 p.
1949

Inscriptions from the cemetery on Main Street, Bethel, Conn.
Taylor, W. O.
CT BET 9
10 p.
1891
Typescript

Congregational Church record of marriages 1767 to 1781 inclusive, Brooklyn, Windham County, Conn.
CT BRO 20
8 p.
Typescript

Inscriptions from the Cleaveland Cemetery, Canterbury, Conn.
Dorrance, Sarah F.
CT CAN 1
2 p.
1923
Typescript

Canton, Conn. epitaphs, Collinsville Cemetery
Barbour, Lucius Barnes, 1878-1934.
CT CAN 12
31 p.
1915
Typescript

Genealogical data from Connecticut cemeteries: Chester, Conn. All gravestones in the town (except Catholic cemetery), standing July 1931
Barbour, Lucius Barnes, 1878-1934.
CT CHE 20
1931
Typescript

Genealogical data from Connecticut cemeteries: Columbia, Conn. Old, Center and West St. cemeteries and a private yard
Barbour, Lucius Barnes, 1878-1934.
CT COL 14
13 + 15 + 4 p.
1933
Typescript

Genealogical data from Connecticut cemeteries: Colchester, Conn. Westchester Center, Ponemah and Linwood, Scott Hill cemeteries and private yard, Babcock farm
Barbour, Lucius Barnes, 1878-1934.
CT COL 4
10 + 6 + 46 + 2 p.
1933
Typescript

Coventry, Connecticut. Genealogical data from Connecticut cemeteries: North, Center and South cemeteries, North Coventry; Nathan Hale Cemetery and Babcock yard, South Coventry
Barbour, Lucius Barnes, 1878-1934.
CT COV 11
11 + 14 + 7 + 41 + 1 p.
1933
Typescript

Genealogical data from Connecticut cemeteries: Cromwell, Connecticut: Old Cemetery; Kelsey Cemetery (West Cromwell); East Side and West Side cemeteries
Barbour, Lucius Barnes, 1878-1934.
CT CRO 19
25 + 7 + 20 + 2 p.
1933
Typescript

Danbury Methodist Episcopal Church, Conn.: church records 1848-1851
Card, Lester.
CT DAN 4
28 p.
1942
Typescript

Cemetery inscriptions from Danbury and New Fairfield, Conn.
Frost, Josephine C., 1864-1942.
CT DAN 5
54 p.
1915
Typescript

Danbury, Conn. "vital records."
CT DAN 6
Mounted newspaper clippings.

Abstract of church records of the town of Darien, county of Fairfield, and State of Connecticut, from the earliest records extant to 1850
Mead, Spencer Percival, b. 1863.
CT DAR 5
2, 2-135 leaves
1920
Typescript

Derby, Conn. -- epitaphs
Bassett, Anne B.
CT DER 10
31 p.
Typescript

Genealogical data from Connecticut cemeteries: Durham, Conn. New Cemetery
Barbour, Lucius Barnes, 1878-1934.
CT DUR 8
30 p.
Typescript

East Windsor, Conn. graveyard inscriptions ["East Windsor Hill Graveyard dates back to 1708"]
CT EAS 1650
6 p.
Mounted newspaper clippings.

Genealogical data from Connecticut cemeteries: East Windsor, Connecticut. All gravestones in the town except Catholic cemetery, Broad Brook.
Barbour, Lucius Barnes, 1878-1934.
CT EAS 1660
1931
Typescript

Eastford, Connecticut, Methodist Episcopal Church. Excerpted from the Souvenir History of the N[ew] E[ngland] Southern Conference, vol. 2, Norwich district, 1897
Chapman, Grace Olive.
CT EAS 310
3 p.
Typescript

Inscriptions in the North Ashford Cemetery, Eastford, Windham County, Connecticut
Chapman, Grace Olive.
CT EAS 325, 325A
2 + 26 + 8 p.
1938
Typescript. The "A" version includes annotations.

Eastford, Connecticut: Old cemetery inscriptions
Chapman, Grace Olive.
CT EAS 330
1 + 19 p.
1939

Eastford, Conn., Congregational Church or Ashford Third Parish, baptisms and communicants, 1778-1868
Barlow, Claude W., (Claude Willis), 1907-1976.
CT EAS 336
20 p.
1949
Includes index.
Typescript

Latham - Bullard Cemetery, Phoenixville, Eastford, Connecticut
Chapman, Grace Olive.
CT EAS 339
9 p.
1949
Typescript.

Spaulding - Snow Cemetery, Eastford, Windham County, Connecticut [with genealogical notes]
Chapman, Grace Olive.
CT EAS 341
14 p.: ill.
1949
Typescript.

Eastford, Connecticut: General Lyon Cemetery inscriptions [with genealogical notes]
Chapman, Grace Olive.
CT EAS 345
60 p.
1950
Typescript.

Genealogical data from Connecticut cemeteries: East Granby, Elmwood Cemetery
Barbour, Lucius Barnes, 1878-1934.
CT EAS 540
4 p.
1932
Typescript.

Book of records containing an account of the rise and progress of the First Baptist Church in East Haddam, Conn.
Huntington, Edna.
CT EAS 710
Typescript.

East Haddam, Conn. cemetery inscriptions: North Granby Cemetery inscriptions
CT EAS 713
Typescript.

Records of the First Congregational Church at East Haddam, Connecticut, 1704-1802
CT EAS 715
Typescript.

Genealogical data from Connecticut cemeteries: East Hampton, Conn. All stones standing in the town.
Barbour, Lucius Barnes, 1878-1934.
CT EAS 840
1931
Typescript.

East Hartford, Conn. records of the Rev. Samuel Woodbridge, East Hartford, Connecticut
Wood, W. Herbert (William Herbert), 1888-1953.
CT EAS 980
23 p.
1933
Typescript.

Ellington, Connecticut: Crystal Lake Cemetery inscriptions, with added genealogical notes
Barlow, Claude W., (Claude Willis), 1907-1976.
CT ELL 10
11 p.
1950
Typescript.

Square Pond Methodist Episcopal Church, Ellington, Connecticut. Excerpt from the Souvenir History of the New England Southern Conference, vol. 2, Norwich district, 1897
Chapman, Grace Olive.
CT ELL 6
5 p.
Typescript.

Genealogical data from Connecticut cemeteries: Ellington. From cemeteries near Crystal Lake
Barbour, Lucius Barnes, 1878-1934.
CT ELL 8
1931
Typescript.

Genealogical data from Connecticut cemeteries: Enfield, Conn.: Thompsonville Cemetery (Protestant section), King Street Cemetery
Barbour, Lucius Barnes, 1878-1934.
CT ENF 8
1931
Typescript.

Old Fairfield [clippings from The Fairfield News, 14-28 Feb. 1947]
The Fairfield News (Fairfield, Conn.)
CT FAI 20
6 p.
1947
Mounted newspaper clippings

Abstract of probate records at Fairfield, county of Fairfield, and State of Connecticut, 1704-1757
Mead, Spencer Percival, b. 1863.
CT FAI 29
365 p.
1934
Typescript. Includes index.

Families of our Revolutionary ancestors, Eunice Dennie Burr chapter, Daughters of the American Revolution, Fairfield, Connecticut
Chatfield, Florence M. Van Tine
CT FAI 48
1 + 151 p.
1956
Mimeograph typescript.

A list of those persons in the town of Fairfield [Conn.] only, who suffered in the late war between Great Britain and America, and proprietors of the land south of Lake Erie. [Fairfield, Conn. fire victims from British raids, given grants of land south of Lake Erie.] Copied from records in Fairfield Historical Society
Card, Lester.
CT FAI 50
11 p.
1942
Typescript.

Granby, Connecticut: Genealogical data from Connecticut cemeteries
Barbour, Lucius Barnes, 1878-1934.
CT GRA 15
1932
Typescript.

Abstract of records and tombstones of the town of Greenwich, county of Fairfield, and State of Connecticut
Mead, Spencer Percival, b. 1863.
CT GRE 16
2 vols.
1913
Typescript. Part 1: Abstract of births, marriages and deaths from the earliest town and land records to June, 1847. Part 2: Abstract of every known tombstone in the town of Greenwich, also in the cemetery at Middle Patent, Westchester County...

Abstract of records and tombstones of the town of Greenwich, county of Fairfield, and State of Connecticut ... part II
Mead, Spencer Percival, b. 1863.
CT GRE 17
275 p.
1913
Typescript

Abstract of church records of the town of Greenwich, county of Fairfield, and State of Connecticut
Mead, Spencer Percival, b. 1863.
CT GRE 18
1913
Typescript.

Griswold cemeteries: Historical and descriptive sketches of twenty-two burial places in Griswold, Conn., and St. Mary's Cemetery in Lisbon, Conn.
Phillips, Daniel L.
CT GRI 15
1918
Typescript.

First book of First Church of Christ, Groton, Conn., 1727-1810
CT GRO 30
Typescript.

Record of deaths in Guilford, 1883-1890
Palmer, Alvan B.
CT GUI 8
6 p.
Typescript.

*Genealogical data from Connecticut cemeteries.
Hampton: Old and New Litchfield cemeteries*
Barbour, Lucius Barnes, 1878-1934.
CT HAM 10
3 + 3 p.
1933
Typescript.

*Gravestone inscriptions in the cemetery in the
town of Hamden, Conn.*
Hotchkiss, Frank E.
CT HAM 4
46 p.
1894
Typescript.

*Hebron, Connecticut. Genealogical data from
Connecticut cemeteries: Gilead Cemetery, St.
Peter's Church and Cemetery*
Barbour, Lucius Barnes, 1878-1934.
CT HEB 2
18 + 16 p.
1933
Typescript.

*Oblong - Anno Domini 1769. The names of early
residents of Kent, Connecticut. Copied from an
old account book ... 1769-1800*
CT KEN 105
9 p.
Typescript.

Kent, Connecticut, names of early residents
CT KEN 5
Typescript.

Killingly[Conn.] church records.
Larned, E. D.
The Putnam Patriot (Putnam, Conn.)
CT KIL 1
26 p.
1894
Newspaper clippings.

*Genealogical data from Connecticut cemeteries:
Killingworth, Conn. All gravestones standing in
the town*
Barbour, Lucius Barnes, 1878-1934.
CT KIL 7
1931
Typescript.

*Genealogical data from Connecticut cemeteries:
Lebanon, Connecticut: Lebanon Center, South
[West], Liberty Hill, Scovell-Buckingham,
Goshen, Exeter and private yards*
Barbour, Lucius Barnes, 1878-1934.
CT LEB 7
1933
Typescript.

*A supplementary index of John Avery's history of
Ledyard, Conn., 1560-1900*
Gallup, Jennie Tefft.
CT LED 1A
29 p.
Typescript.

*Genealogical data from Connecticut cemeteries:
Lisbon, Conn. headstone records from Ames
Cemetery, Newent; Read - Herskell Cemetery;
and Perkins Lovett Yard, Sprague near Versailles*
Barbour, Lucius Barnes, 1878-1934.
CT LIS 10
1932
Typescript.

*Genealogical data from Connecticut cemeteries:
Lisbon, Connecticut Kinsman Cemetery,
Versailles [in Lisbon]*
Barbour, Lucius Barnes, 1878-1934.
CT LIS 11
3 p.
1914
Pub. in *NEHG Register* 1932.
Typescript.

*Genealogical data from Connecticut cemeteries:
Madison, Conn. records from all cemeteries in
Madison: West or Center; Hammonasset; East
and West, North Madison; Summer Hill and
Rockland cemeteries*
Barbour, Lucius Barnes, 1878-1934.
CT MAD 12
1932
Typescript.

Madison, Conn. town records
Allen, Louise R.
CT MAD 14
1935
Typescript.

Early church records of Madison, Conn.
Allen, Louise R.
CT MAD 15
19 + 46 p.
1935
Typescript.

Genealogical data from Connecticut cemeteries: Marlborough, Conn. All gravestone records in the town of Marlborough: Old Center; New; North, Jones Hollow; and South, Fawn Brook, cemeteries
Barbour, Lucius Barnes, 1878-1934.
CT MAR 5
1932
Typescript.

Baptisms in the First Church of Milford; baptisms and marriages in Milford Second Society Church records
CT MIL 8
126 p.
Typescript.

Inhabitants of Monroe, Fairfield County, Connecticut. The within contained names, gathered from all sources ... fairly represent all the dwellers in New Stratford (now Monroe) ... 1762-1809
Swan, Benjamin Lincoln.
CT MON 1
37 p.
Typescript.

Genealogical data from Connecticut cemeteries: Montville, Conn. Raymond Hill, Uncasville, Private, Chesterfield, Chapman and Private cemeteries
Barbour, Lucius Barnes, 1878-1934.
CT MON 16
1931-1932
Typescript.

Genealogical data from Connecticut cemeteries: New London, Gardner Cemetery
Barbour, Lucius Barnes, 1878-1934.
CT NEW 1543
4 p.
1932
Typescript.

Marriages and deaths in New York State from New Canaan, Conn. "Era," 1865-1871
Card, Lester.
CT NEW 171
14 p.
1941
Typescript.

New Canaan, Conn. first library, 1811, membership list and similar data
Card, Lester.
CT NEW 176
6 p.
1942
Typescript.

Note book of Joel Wells Northrop of New Milford, Conn.: New Milford, Conn. records 1709-1801
Northrop, Joel W.
CT NEW 1815
32 p.
1834
Photostat copy of mss.

Old New Milford, Connecticut, records
Sherman, Thomas Townsend, b. 1853.
CT NEW 1820
Typescript.

The New Canaan, Conn. Methodist Episcopal Church [history, records, lists of members, etc.]
Card, Lester.
CT NEW 188
134 p.: ill.
1947
Typescript.

Census of New Canaan, Conn., 1820
Card, Lester.
CT NEW 190
17 p.
1947
Typescript.

New Canaan, Conn. cemetery records
Card, Lester.
CT NEW 192
87 p.
1947
Typescript.

Vital records of Newtown, Connecticut, 1704-1850
CT NEW 2050
153 p.
Typescript.

New Fairfield, Conn., church records
CT NEW 320
6 p.
Typescript.

First Congregational Church, New Fairfield, Conn.; New Fairfield, Connecticut 1790 U.S.Census
CT NEW 325
11 p.
Typescript.

An index of persons in North Haven Annals, State of Connecticut, 1680-1886, by Sheldon B. Thorpe, New Haven, Conn., 1892
Brown, Nelson K.
CT NOR 1150A
1965
Typescript.

St. Paul's Episcopal Church. Norwalk, Conn. Marriages, 1830-1850
Card, Lester.
CT NOR 1850
19 p.
Typescript.

Court records of Theophilus Fitch, J. P., Norwalk, Conn., 1755 to 1768
Card, Lester.
CT NOR 1912
5 p.
1946
Typescript.

Record of the Church of Christ, Norfolk, Connecticut
CT NOR 20
10 p.
Typescript.

Vital statistics of Norwich, New London and Montville, Conn. [1733-1790], from the Boston Evening Transcript, 12 and 22 May 1912.
CT NOR 2126
5 p.
1912
Mounted newspaper clippings.

Records of baptisms, marriages, deaths and church admissions of the First Church of Norwich, Connecticut, from 1739 to 1824, kept by Joseph Murdock, pastor of the church
Murdock, Joseph.
CT NOR 2130
88 p.
Typescript.

Abstracts of the first probate records of Norwich, Conn., 1740-1770
Gallup, Jennie Tefft.
CT NOR 2134
3 vols.
Typescript. Vol. 1: 1748-1757. Vol. 2: 1749-1761. Vol. 3: 1761-1770.

Genealogical data from Connecticut cemeteries: North Branford, Conn. Old, Congregational, Episcopal, Bare Plain and Northford cemeteries.
Barbour, Lucius Barnes, 1878-1934.
CT NOR 315
1932
Typescript.

Unidentified stones in the town cemetery, Plainfield, Conn., with probable identification from town and church records
Dorrance, Sarah F.
CT PLA 1
6 p.
Typescript.

Genealogical data from Connecticut cemeteries, Plainville (formerly a part of Farmington): all gravestone records from the Old or East and New or West cemeteries
Barbour, Lucius Barnes, 1878-1934.
CT PLA 7
1932
Typescript.

Catalogue of the members of the First Church in Pomfret, Conn., from May 5, 1802 to July 1, 1832
MacLea, Florence
CT POM 15
17 p.
1927
Typescript.

Genealogical data from Connecticut cemeteries: Portland, Connecticut: Old Cemetery, Trinity Church Cemetery, Center Cemetery
Barbour, Lucius Barnes, 1878-1934.
CT POR 4
8, 31, 41 p.
1933
Typescript.

Redding, Connecticut baptisms
Card, Lester.
CT RED 6
9 p.
Typescript.

Ridgefield, Conn. inscriptions from the graveyards with notes and index.
Spies, Francis F. (Francis Ferdinand), 1871-1934.
CT RID 74
1, 150 p.
1934

Genealogical data from Connecticut cemeteries: Salem. All stones standing in the town, copied August 1931 [and 1932]
Barbour, Lucius Barnes, 1878-1934.
CT SAL 5
1931-1932
Typescript.

Saybrook, Conncticut, probate records. Index to volume 1, 1780.
Card, Lester.
CT SAY 10
4 p.
Typescript.

Genealogical data from Connecticut cemeteries: Saybrook, Connecticut: cemetery at Winthrop, Conn., Town of Saybrook; Essex Street Cemetery, Deep River; Fountain Hill Cemetery, Deep River
Barbour, Lucius Barnes, 1878-1934.
CT SAY 15
16 + 1 + 47 p.
1907-1932
Typescript.

Cemetery inscriptions from Sherman, Connecticut
Frost, Josephine C., 1864-1942.
CT SHE 5
118 p.
1912
Typescript.

Genealogical data from Connecticut cemeteries: Simsbury, Connecticut: All gravestone records in the town of Simsbury (except St. Barnard's Roman Catholic Cemetery, Tariffville). Simsbury, Bushy Hill and Tariffville cemeteries.
Barbour, Lucius Barnes, 1878-1934.
CT SIM 15
1932
Typescript.

Genealogical data from Connecticut cemeteries: Sprague, Connecticut: Headstone records from the Old and New Cemeteries. Hanover; Lovett Cemetery, near Versailles (see also Lisbon)
Barbour, Lucius Barnes, 1878-1934.
CT SPR 15
1932
Typescript.

Cemetery inscriptions: Stafford Street, Stafford, Tolland County, Connecticut
Chapman, Grace Olive.
CT STA 11
44 + 13 p.
1938
Typescript with mounted photos.

Inscriptions. West Cemetery, Village Hill, Stafford, Tolland County, Connecticut
Chapman, Grace Olive.
CT STA 12
4 + 4 p.
1938
Typescript.

Crystal Lake cemeteries. Stafford, Tolland County, Connecticut
Chapman, Grace Olive.
CT STA 16
33 + 1 p.
1940
Typescript with mounted photos.

First settlers of Stafford, Connecticut
Chapman, Grace Olive.
CT STA 17
59 p. + 3 p.
1940
Typescript.

Inscriptions in an old cemetery, Stafford, Connecticut
CT STA 2
4 p.
Typescript.

Stafford Street Cemetery Association's records: Stafford, Tolland County, Connecticut
Chapman, Grace Olive.
CT STA 21
18 p.
1949
Typescript.

Inscriptions: small burial plot, Stafford Springs, Connecticut
Chapman, Grace Olive.
CT STA 30
19 + 2 p.
1944
Typescript.

Stafford Springs, Connecticut, Methodist Episcopal Church
Chapman, Grace Olive.
CT STA 31
Typescript.

Gravestone inscriptions, Leonard District Cemetery, Stafford, Connecticut
Corbin, Walter E., 1885-1960.
CT STA 4
1 + 13 + 2 p.
1933
Typescript.

Brief history of Stafford. Stafford Springs, Conn. (Supplement to "The Press," April 27, 1910, vol. 53, no. 4.)
CT STA 4
8 p.
1910
Typescript.

Staffordville, Connecticut cemetery inscriptions.
Chapman, Grace Olive.
CT STA 40
4 + 18 + 9 p.
1937
Typescript.

Cemetery inscriptions: Hall District, Staffordville, Tolland County, Connecticut
Chapman, Grace Olive.
CT STA 41
11 + 1 p.
1938
Typescript with mounted photos.

Staffordville, Connecticut, Methodist Episcopal Church. Excerpted from the Souvenir history of the N[ew] E[ngland] Southern Conference, Vol. 2, Norwich District, 1897
Chapman, Grace Olive.
CT STA 46
4 p.
Typescript.

Genealogical collection, no. ___: Stratfield [Conn.] Congregational Church records [marriages, baptisms, 1695-1770]; Census of Norwalk, Conn., 1850
Card, Lester.
CT STR 1
160 + 1 p.
1945
Typescript.

Genealogical data from Connecticut cemeteries. Suffield, Conn.: Old Center, Hastings Hill, West Suffield, Phelps - Warner and two family yards
Barbour, Lucius Barnes, 1878-1934.
CT SUF 16
1933
Typescript.

Thompson, Conn. Congregational Church records, 1730-1795.
CT THO 10
Typescript.

Genealogical data from Connecticut cemeteries: Union, Connecticut: Old, New, North and East cemeteries
Barbour, Lucius Barnes, 1878-1934.
CT UNI 2
8 + 2 + 8 + 5 p.
1933
Typescript.

Mashapaug Methodist Episcopal Church, Union, Connecticut. Excerpted from The souvenir history of the N[ew] E[ngland] Southern Conference, and Lawson's History of Union, Conn.
Chapman, Grace Olive.
CT UNI 5
12 p.
Typescript.

Union, Conn. cemetery inscriptions copied by Lucius B. Barbour, 1933, typed from his record and genealogical notes added. Old Cem., New Cem., Armour Cem., East Cem., North Cem., Union, Conn.
Chapman, Grace Olive.
CT UNI 7
63 p.
1949
Typescript.

Genealogical data from Connecticut cemeteries: Waterford, Conn. Headstone records from East Neck, West Neck, Mullen Hill, Durfey Hill, Quaker Hill and Jordan cemeteries, and two family yards
Barbour, Lucius Barnes, 1878-1934.
CT WAT 9
1932
Typescript.

Inscriptions. Town of Westbrook, Conn., Saybrook Third Society
Barbour, Lucius Barnes, 1878-1934.
CT WES 22
2 + 75 p.
1907-1910
Typescript.

Weston, Fairfield Co., Conn. Inscriptions copied from the graveyards, arranged with genealogical and historical notes and an index.
Spies, Francis F. (Francis Ferdinand), 1871-1934.
CT WES 40
1 + 112 p.
1934
Typescript.

Cemetery inscriptions. West Stafford, Tolland County, Connecticut - the newer cemetry on the Myron Kemp road [with genealogical notes]
Chapman, Grace Olive.
CT WES 55
24 p.
1938
Typescript.

Inscriptions, Old Cemetery, West Stafford, Tolland County, Connecticut [with genealogical notes]
Chapman, Grace Olive.
CT WES 56
41 p.
1939
Typescript.

West Stafford, Connecticut cemetery inscriptions. West Stafford Center; Woodworth, Davis-Blodgett family plots; genealogical notes
Chapman, Grace Olive.
CT WES 57
1 + 38 p. (1 p. added Aug. 1951).
1940
Typescript.

Deaths in West Stafford, Conn. Copied from records of the Chase family in the possession of Claude W. Barlow. (1851-1890)
Barlow, Claude W., (Claude Willis), 1907-1976.
CT WES 58
14 p.
1946
Typescript.

*Record of Burials, 1775-1808, Wethersfield
[Connecticut]*
Boardman, William Francis Joseph, 1828-1912.
CT WET 6
54 p.
1910
Typescript.

Inscriptions in the cemetery at Wilsonville, Conn.
Clarke, Avis Gertrude, 1902-.
CT WIL 15
1 + 136 p.
1931
Typescript.

*Wilton, Fairfield County, Conn. inscriptions
copied from graveyards with notes*
Spies, Francis F. (Francis Ferdinand), 1871-1934.
CT WIL 50
1 + 267 p.
1934
Typescript.

*Cemetery inscriptions: Village Hill, Willington,
Tolland County, Connecticut*
Chapman, Grace Olive.
CT WIL 6
23 p.
1939
Typescript.

*Moose Meadow Cemetery, Willington,
Connecticut. Copied by Joel N. Eno, 1915,
additions and corrections by Claude W. Barlow
1948, typed and genealogical notes by Grace
Olive Chapman 1948*
Eno, Joel Nelson
CT WIL 7
34 p.
1948
Typescript.

*Moose Meadow Methodist Episcopal Church,
Willington, Connecticut. Excerpt from The
Souvenir History of the N[ew] E[ngland]
Southern Conference, vol. 2, Norwich District,
1897*
Chapman, Grace Olive.
CT WIL 8
5 p. Typescript.
1949

*Genealogical data from Connecticut cemeteries:
Windsor Locks, Grove Cemetery*
Barbour, Lucius Barnes, 1878-1934.
CT WIN 184
21 p.
1932
Typescript.

*Woodbridge, Conn., baptisms, marriages, and
births, 1742-1846 [recorded in the old records of
the church of Woodbridge, Conn.]*
Marvin, S. P.
CT WOO 1
106 p.
Typescript.

*Genealogical data from Connecticut cemeteries:
Woodstock, Conn. Inscriptions: Woodstock Hill;
West Woodstock, Bungee Hill; East Woodstock;
West Woodstock, New Cemetery; and Central
Cemetery, Woodstock*
Barbour, Lucius Barnes, 1878-1934.
CT WOO 26
160 p.
1908-1911
Typescript.

Woodstock ancient records
Paine, Royal
CT WOO A
1888
Typescript.

*Address by Gov. Henry B. Harrison at
Woodstock, July 4th, 1885 (reprint from The
Independent). Bound with* Woodstock ancient
records *from The Putnam Patriot, Jan. - June
1888 [copied by Royal Paine of Brooklyn, N.Y.]
Bound with* Map of Woodstock by John S. Lester,
1883, with topographical and historical names
added by G. C. Williams, 1886. *Bound with*
Thompson, Conn. church records, 1730-1773,
from The Putnam Patriot, Aug. 1885 - Dec. 1888,
copied by Royal Paine of Brooklyn, N.Y. *Bound
with* Rev. Amos Throop's record of marriages at
New Roxbury (Woodstock), Conn.
Harrison, Henry B., Gov.
The Putnam Patriot (Putnam, Conn.)
CT WOO A
188 p.

*Grace Protestant Episcopal Church, Georgetown,
D. C. [1863-1895]*
DC GEO 30
60 + 49 p.
1939
Typescript

*New Englanders in the census of 1850 for the
District of Columbia, comprised in two volumes*
Hawes, Frank Mortimer, 1850-1941.
DC WAS 28
13 p.
Typescript.

New Englanders in the Delaware census of 1850
Hawes, Frank Mortimer, 1850-1941.
DEL 6 3
6 p.
Typescript.

*Thomas, Dragoo, Hollis, Adams, Edgell, Graham
families' Bible records, Delaware*
Bell, Albert Dehner, 1911-.
DEL 42 30
Typescript transcription.

*Index to wills, Georgetown, Sussex County,
Delaware, up to 1850, inc. A-L*
DEL GEO 3
23 p.
Typescript.

Cemetery records; Seaford, Sussex Co., Delaware
DEL SEA 10
32 p.
Typescript.

Cemetery records. Florida [1846-1944]
FLA 100 5
85 p.
Typescript.

*Dyal Cemetery records, Bradford County,
Florida*
FLA 104 5
10 p.
Typescript.

*Elum Cemetery records, Columbia County,
Florida. Copied by Oak Grove branch, Southern
States Mission*
FLA 112 5
9 p.
Typescript.

*Royal Palms Cemetery records, Dade County,
Florida. Woodlawn Cemetery records, West Palm
Beach, Palm Beach, Florida*
FLA 113 5
12 + 32 p.
Typescript.

*Duval Co., Florida, epitaphs. Chaseville
Cemetery records, Jacksonville, Duval Co.,
Florida. Dixie Pythian Cemetery records, Duval
Co., Florida. Dunns Creek Cemetery records,
Duval Co., Florida. Ogilvie Cemetery records,
Duval Co., Florida. Rest Lawn Cemetery records,
Duval County, Florida. Turner Cemetery records
(near Jacksonville), Duval Co., Florida.*
FLA 116 5
2 + 19 + 3 + 3 + 8 + 2 p.
Typescript.

*Ealom Cemetery records, Escambia County,
Florida*
FLA 117 5
9 p.
Typescript.

*Gadsden Co., Florida, epitaphs. Mt. Pleasant
Cemetery, Philadelphia Cemetery*
FLA 120 5
2 + 3 p.
Typescript.

*Jackson Heights Cemetery records, Tampa,
Hillsborough Co., Florida: Lake Carroll
Cemetery records, Tampa... Oak Grove Cemetery
records, Tampa... Tampa, Hillsborough Co.,
Florida, cemetery records. Cemetery records,
Thonotosasso, Hillsborough Co., Florida*
FLA 129 5
7 + 6 + 5 + 2 + 5 p.
Typescript.

Lake Co., Florida, epitaphs. Shiloh Cemetery, Fruitland Park, Lake Co., Florida. Glendale Cemetery records, Umatilla, Lake Co., Florida
FLA 135 5
4 + 15 p.
Typescript.

Cemetery records (Fifteenth Street, Manatee, Manatee Co., Florida. Cemetery records (Fifth Street), Palmetto, Manatee Co., Florida
FLA 141 5
4 + 3 p.
Typescript.

Marion Co., Florida epitaphs: cemetery records of Anthony (near Ocala) and Belleview. Evergreen and Greenwood cemeteries, Osceola
Genealogical Society of Utah.
FLA 142 5
3 + 3 + 4 + 6 p.
Typescript.

Buford Grove Cemetery records, Nassau County, Florida
FLA 145 5
3 p.
Typescript.

Okaloosa Co., Florida epitaphs: Kennedy Cemetery records. Peryon Chapel Cemetery records. Pilgrim Rest Cemetery records, Baker. Cemetery records, Crestview. Travelers Rest Cemetery records, Laurelhill. Cemetery records, Milligan
FLA 146 5
2 + 4 + 4 + 6 + 2 + 3 p.
Typescript.

Bardin Cemetery records, Putnam Co., Florida. Federal Point Cemetery records, Federal Point, Putnam Co., Florida. Fruitland Cemetery records (near Crescent City), Putnam Co., Florida. Mt. Olivet Cemetery records, Putnam Co., Florida. Oak Hill Cemetery records, Palatka, Putnam Co., Florida. West View Cemetery records, Palatka... Cemetery records, San Mateo, Putnam Co., Florida. Satsuma Cemetery records, Satsuma, Putnam Co., Florida. Welaka Cemetery records, Welaka, Putnam Co., Florida
FLA 154 5
4 + 5 + 2 + 5 + 2 + 10 + 12 + 4 + 8 p.
Typescript.

Union Co., Florida, epitaphs: New Zion Cemetery records, Union Co., Florida. Tuscanooga Cemetery records, Union Co., Florida. Sapp Cemetery records, Raiford, Union Co., Florida
Genealogical Society of Utah.
FLA 162 5
7 + 6 + 9 p.
Typescript.

Volusia Co., Florida epitaphs
FLA 163 5
Typescript.

Cemetery records: Brooksville, Hernando Co., Florida
FLA BRO 10
18 p.
Typescript.

Cemetery records: Clarksville, Calhoun Co., Florida
FLA CLA 10
3 p.
Typescript.

Cemetery records: Clearwater, Pinellas Co., Florida
FLA CLE 10
47 p.
Typescript.

Cemetery records: Espanola, Flagler Co., Florida
FLA ESP 10
6 p.
Typescript.

*Parian Cemetery records: Grandin, Putnam Co.,
Florida*
FLA GRA 10
9 p.
Typescript.

*Cemetery records of Jacksonville, Duval Co.,
Florida. Lone Star Road Cemetery. Oak Lawn
Cemetery. Old City Cemetery. Pickett Cemetery.
Riverside Memorial Cemetery. St. Mary's
Cemetery*
Genealogical Society of Utah.
FLA JAC 10
5 + 66 + 8 + 12 + 36 + 1 p.
1946

Cemetery records: Marco, Lee Co., Florida
FLA MAR 10
2 p.
Typescript.

*[Persons] cremated in Orlando, Orange Co.,
Florida. Greenwood Cemetery records, Orlando,
Florida*
FLA ORL 10
3 + 24 p.
Typescript.

*Cemetery records (old cemetery on Tallahassee
Road), Salem, Taylor Co., Florida*
Gleaton, Grace N.
FLA SAL 10
Typescript.

*Oakland Cemetery records, Tallahassee, Leon
Co., Florida*
FLA TAL 10
4 p.
Typescript.

*Cemetery records; Zephyrhills, Pasco Co.,
Florida*
FLA ZEP 10
4 p.
Typescript.

*Descent from William Adams of Ipswich,
Massachusetts*
Holman, Winifred Lovering, 1899-1989.
G ADA 130
63p.
1931
Typescript.

Adams notes
Holman, Winifred Lovering, 1899-1989.
G ADA 176
17p.
1951
2nd ed.
Typescript.

*The Albee family of Berkeley California. One line
of descent from Benjamin Albee of Braintree
Mass. and Benjamin Cooley of Springfield Mass.
with ancestral charts of each. 1640-1940*
Albee, George C.
G ALB 15
1943
Typescript.

*Ancestor David Alexander of Topsham Me. and
his descendants*
Sinnett, Charles Nelson, 1847-1928.
G ALE 820
124 p.
1922
Typescript.

David Alexander and descendants
Sinnett, Charles Nelson, 1847-1928.
G ALE 830
122, 38 p.
1929
2d ed.
Typescript. Includes index.

*Descendants of Amos son of Ebenezer Allen &
Tabitha Fulham*
Allen, Gladys.
G ALL 1514A
5 p.
Typescript

The Allbee family in England [and in America]
Allbee, Harold J.
G ALL 1613
13 p.
1949
Typescript.

Allen [genealogical data Vermont and Michigan]
G ALL 4420
4 p.
Typescript.

William Allen of Kingstown R.I. and some of his descendants
Russell, Alice R.
G ALL 4438
19 p.
Typescript.

The Allen family of Braintree
Jackson, Edward Evarts, b. 1868.
G ALL 4525A
10 p.
1903
Typescript.

Allen ancestry of Robert Francis Allen (1884-1934)
Chapman, Grace Olive.
G ALL 4612
26p.
1950
Typescript.

James Allen of Burlington County New Jersey and some of his descendants
Atkinson, Alan W.
G ALL 4628
17 p.
1955
Typescript.

A Sandwich - Dartmouth - North Kingston Allen line
Clark, Bertha W. (Bertha Winifred), 1875-1965.
G ALL 4630; G ALL 4630A
35p.; 33p.
1954; 1955
1st ed.; 2nd ed.
Typescript.

Some descendants of George^1 Allen of Sandwich Mass. and of his son Samuel^2 Allin of Braintree Mass.
Brewster, Margaret Isabel Fraser, b. 1886.
G ALL 4640
41 p.
1961-1962
Typescript.

Ancestry of Walter Scott Allerton descent from early settlers of America 1620-1720
G ALL 4879
18 p.
1909
Typescript.

A dream that came true [romance of Mary & Rebecca Alleyne of Barbados in 1740]
Allen, Louise R.
G ALL 5252
5 p.
1935
Typescript.

Descendants of Richard Alsop who came from England to Newtown Long Island about 1664
G ALS 1
Typescript.

The Alston family [N.C.]
G ALS 6
9, 6 p.
Typescript.

Ambrose of England. Ambrose of America
G AMB 60
9, 4 p.
1964
Typescript.

Ames Eames Eimes Ams family of Essex Co. Mass.
Sharples, Stephen Paschall, 1842-1923.
G AME 13
2, 30, 6 p.
1903
Typescript.

Additional information to the Samuel Ames family
Graves, John Kimball, 1912-.
G AME 7A
5 p.
1961
Typescript.

Amory [genealogy descendants of Jonathan of Eng. and Ire. and his descendants in America]
G AMO 10
15 p.
[1897?]
Typescript.

Estate of Thomas Andrews of Dorchester
G AND 1975
3 p.
Typescript.

Andrews - Bardwell genealogy notes made by Andrew Earl Hitchcock as told to him by his grandmother Experience Bardwell Andrews
Hitchcock, Andrew Earl.
G AND 1977
5 p.
Typescript.

Supplemental records for the Andrews Memorial a genealogical history of John and Mary Andrews by Alfred Andrews ...
Balch, Samuel W. (Samuel Weed), b. 1862.
G AND 2000A
6 p.
1935
Typescript.

The descendants of Abraham Tourtellotte Andrews and his wife Miriam Lurinda Guild
Shiner, Harry Lawrence.
G AND 2060
6 p.
1918
Typescript.

The ancestry of Martha Susan Andrews Elliott Seabury Andrews Christopher Blake Andrews Amy Elizabeth Andrews
Andrews, Elliott Morrison, 1886-1970.
G AND 2105
1957
Typescript.

Andrews - Maxwell families
Stewart, Mary L.
G AND 534
5 p.
1915
Typescript.

The Angell line compiled for Mrs. J. M. Morrison, May 1944
Holman, Winifred Lovering, 1899-1989.
G ANG 22
65p.
1944
Typescript.

Annis Lurvey and allied families
Gathemann, Mabel S.
G ANN 45
1946
Typescript.

[Antrim collection.] Ancestors of Caleb D. Antrim 1866- in collection of pamphlets [as follows] Crozier Hancock Harding Stockton Nichol(l)s Fisher Butcher Antrim Hodgkins Shreve Conaroe Ridg(e)way Jeffery Blessing families. Newby Clare Phelps Bundy Winslow Boque Thoms Needham Chilton Albert Hare Hooker Baird Griffin Latham. Wood or Woods Bruen Allen or Allan Combs Harlan Younger Messer Ashby Wright Baker Greenup Schwartz Herlocker Ladd Edwards Bridges Dillon Ruckman Stanley Ballinger Ellison White
Media Research Bureau, Washington, D.C.
G ANT 398, 398A, 398B, 398C
4 v.
Typescript.

Information on people and places named Antrobus
Yeager, Lyn Allison Antrobus.
G ANT 510
2 v.
1969
Typescript.

*Notes on the Appletons, including some data on
the Isaacke, Everard, Wiseman, Josselyn families*
Holman, Winifred Lovering, 1899-1989.
G APP 65
59p.
1934
Typescript.

*Descendants of David and Elizabeth (Elliott) of
Londonderry Ire. and Truro N.S.*
Hough, Benjamin Kent, 1875-1948.
G ARC 52
1 chart; 22 x 196.5 cm.
1933

*Descendants of John Arew of Accomac County
Virginia who now spell their family name Rew
Rue and Rhue*
Rhue, George N. (George Noble), b. 1893.
G ARE 710
60 p.
1955
Typescript.

*A genealogical table of the ancestors of Lewis
Addison Armistead of Boston Mass.*
G ARM 1
Typescript.

*Arthur Trader of August(a) County Virginia with
the Armitrading family of Accomac County
Virginia*
Newman, Harry Wright, b. 1894.
G ARM 201
20 p.
1959
Typescript.

Armstrong
Armstrong, Addie.
G ARM 710
22, 11 p.
Typescript.

*The Arnold line compiled for Mrs. J. M.
Morrison, Sept 1950*
Holman, Winifred Lovering, 1899-1989.
G ARN 460
24 p.
1950
Typescript.

Baird family record and history
G BAI 2620
28, 7 p.
Typescript.

*Descendants of William and Mary Baker of
Concord Mass.*
Baker, Amos.
G BAK 10
221 p.
Typescript.

*The Rosenberger family. An addition to the Baker
genealogy*
Baker, Robert Helsley, b. 1895.
G BAK 110A
1956
Typescript.

*Thomas Baker of Roxbury Massachusetts and
some of his descendants*
G BAK 12
Typescript.

*The family of James Alexander Baker (2-9-1815 /
10-12-1885)*
Baker, Ruth Virginia.
G BAK 129
8 p.
1967
Typescript.

*Genealogies of the following families: Baker ...
Steel ... Sturges ... Shepard ... Hall ... Hatch ...
Lytle ...*
Baker, Francis Asbury.
G BAK 41
119, 12 p.
1909
Typescript.

Ancestry of Charles Chaney Baker
G BAK 5
13 p.
Typescript.

Ancestor Barnabas Baker of Yarmouth Mass. and Litchfield Me. ancestry and descendants
Sinnett, Charles Nelson, 1847-1928.
G BAK 62
41 p.
1922
Typescript.

Nathaniel [1764-1839] and Sarah (Garrison) Baker family of Schodack Rensselaer Co. N.Y.
Huftalen, Sarah G.
G BAK 84
4, 128 p.
1945
Typescript.

Baker family Bible record from Bible of Joseph b. 1838 and Lucinda Baker Mt. Jackson Va.
Baker, Charles A., Mrs.
G BAK 88
6 p.
1947
Typescript.

A Baker - Swett line from Francis Baker 1611-1692-6
Melvin, Jeneve M.
G BAK 9
1966?
Typescript.

Nathaniel Baker 1764-1839 ancestry and descendants
Huftalen, Sarah G.
G BAK 90
3, 105 p.
1947
Typescript.

Baldwins of Chester Pa.
G BAL 2568
18 p.
Typescript.

Baldwin
Arthur, Robert
G BAL 2652
16 p.
1952
Typescript.

Abigail Baldwin's journal 1853 and supplement genealogy of the Baldwin - Pollard families
Maverick, Lewis A.
G BAL 2661
24, 12 p.
1961
Typescript.

Thomas and Eva Baldwin their ancestors and descendants
Stembel, Ruth Willis (Baldwin) 1884-.
G BAL 2665
341 p.
1965
Typescript.

The Balestiers of Beechwood
Ireland, Gordon.
G BAL 3080
vi, 77 p.
1948
Typescript.

Edward Ball the son of Alling
G BAL 4220
3, 7 p.
Typescript.

Genealogy of Beulah Ball Cass: Descendants of William Ball of Wiltshire England William Towne of Yarmouth England
Cass, Earle Millard, 1901-.
G BAL 4297
3, 8 p.
1939
Typescript.

Brief Ball notes
Holman, Winifred Lovering, 1899-1989.
G BAL 4312
2, 18 p.
1950
Typescript

The Ball family descended from Francis Ball of Springfield Massachusetts died 1648
Druse, Joseph L.
G BAL 4329
28 p.
1968
Typescript.

Henry Ballinger of New Jersey and his descendants
G BAL 5625
Typescript.

Genealogy of the Balch family
G BAL 698 1
Typescript.

Bancroft family descendants of John and Jane of Lynn Mass
Bancroft, J. M. (John M.)
G BAN 15
106 x 46.5 cm.
1903
Bound blueprint chart

Bang [descendants of Johann Peter Bang]
Craig, Robert D.
G BAN 301
3, 46 p.
Typescript.

Edward Banges the pilgrim a narrative ...
Bangs, Charles Howard, 1861-.
G BAN 402
16 p.
1916
Typescript.

Derbyshire - genealogy Bancroft family
Drury, Gertrude.
G BAN 44
17 p.
1953
Typescript.

Thomas Bancroft and his descendants
Bancroft, J. M. (John M.)
G BAN 9
11 p., geneal. table.
1876
Typescript.

How our little family grew [Barclay family]
Warrell, Mary Margaret.
G BAR 1080
7, 97 p.
1964
Typescript.

Four Fulton County families Bard Carmichael Carpenter MacGregor
Jones, Edward Thomas.
G BAR 1449
1962
Typescript.

Genealogies of the Barden families and their descendants in the United States to the present generation ...
Potter, Ezra Cornelius, b. 1866.
G BAR 1850; G BAR 1860
Various pagings.
1927
Typescript.

Genealogies of the Potter families and their descendants in the United States to the present ...
Potter, Ezra Cornelius, b. 1866.
G BAR 1850A
Various pagings.
1928; 1936
2nd ed.
Typescript.

The ancestry and descendants of Isaac Barden of Middleborough and Attleborough Mass. and Scituate R.I.
Eddy, Ruth Story Devereux, 1875-1958.
G BAR 1870
1945
Typescript.

Descendants of Milton Bond Bardwell 1821-1899
Walrod, C.R.
G BAR 1938
16, vi p.
1966
Typescript.

Genealogy. Family of Baret Margaret wife of Simon Huntington
Porter, George S.
G BAR 2150
15 p.
Typescript.

Peter Barger and Ann Pettigrew IXth family of Natural Bridge Va. Bargers
Barger, Gervase.
G BAR 2408
1962
Typescript.

Barker [descendants of Lieut. Stephen Barker of Methuen Mass.]
G BAR 2787
3 p.
Typescript.

Genealogical notes of the Barker family
Bowman, Sumner Eli.
G BAR 2824
4 p.
1902
Typescript.

Barker papers: deeds, surveyor's reports, tax list, division of real estate, bonds etc. Copied from the original documents...
Morse, Elizabeth G.
G BAR 2860
3, 136, 8 p.
1938-1939
Typescript.

Barker family [descendants of Francis of Concord Mass.]
Barker, John Herbert, 1870-1951.
G BAR 2866
261 p.
1941
Typescript.

Descendants of Thomas Barnes of Connecticut
Barnes, Rodney.
G BAR 4444
59 p.
1877-1913
Typescript.

A history of John Barns and his descendants
Barnes, John Albert, b. 1847.
G BAR 4452
2, 81, 7 p.
1927
Typescript.

Family records of Barnes Brown Lair and Wilson with references to Crays Fee Sherrill Stark and Thornton
Barnes, Clair Elmer.
G BAR 4485
1963
Typescript.

Barnes - King families of Chenango County New York.
Barnes, Raymond Curtis, b. 1899.
G BAR 4486
117 p.
1964
Typescript.

The saga of George Newton Barnes
Whipple, Florence Julia.
G BAR 4489
21 p.
1965
Typescript.

Barnes the western migration of one line of the descendants of Thomas Barnes of Hartford and Farmington Connecticut including the vital records of the descendants of Julius Elizer Barnes and Sylvina Harriet Vought
Barnes, Clair Elmer.
G BAR 4491
13 p.
1966
Typescript.

Barnes a tabulation of all known descendants of Thomas Barnes who came to Marlborough Mass. ... in 1656 ...
Fisk, Edward Ray.
G BAR 4492
2, 41 p.
1967
Typescript.

The Barney generations in America together with ... some reminiscences [of] Jeffrey A. and Harriet Ewing Barney
Ludens, Gertrude Ross.
G BAR 4790
31 p.
1937
Typescript.

Ebenezer Barnum 1749-1830 of Monkton Vt.
Eldridge, William Henry, 1873-1943.
G BAR 4972
2 p.
1932
Typescript.

Copy of letter written in 1898 ... descendants of John Barber of Exeter Rhode Island
Barber, Paul M.
G BAR 541
5 p.
1898
Typescript.

The Barrackman - Barrickman families of West Virginia
Barekman, June Beverly, 1915-.
G BAR 5628
1 v.
1960
Typescript.

The Barrackman - Barkman - Barekman family of Knox County Indiana
Barekman, June Beverly, 1915-.
G BAR 5630
1 v.
1961
Typescript.

Family history records of the name of Barrack or Barrick
Barrick, Vincent P.
G BAR 5650
134 p.
Typescript.

Barrett data Boston family
Calder, Philip R.
G BAR 5800
1932
Typescript.

Genealogy of a branch of the Barrett family of the Connecticut Valley.
Barrett, Robert E. Jr.
G BAR 5820
78 p.
1966
Typescript.

One branch of the Connecticut Valley Barretts
Lacy, Ruth Barrett.
G BAR 5824
32, 2 p.
1967
Typescript.

A few Barrett kin
Reeves, Emma Barrett, 1901-.
G BAR 5828
93 p.
[c1971]
Typescript.

The genealogy of the Barrickman family of Franklin Ripley and Marion Counties of Indiana
Shoemaker, Vivian Barrickman, 1903-1959.
G BAR 5870; G BAR 5870A
22 p.
1961; 1967
Typescript.

Barrows genealogy descendants of John of England and Salem Mass.
Barrows, Chester Willard.
G BAR 6400
5 p.
1927
Typescript.

History of the Barrys...
Barry, Michael Henry.
G BAR 6644
92 p.
1930
Typescript.

Descendants of Thomas Barry and Mary Nagel Barry in America
Dwyer, Mary Frances.
G BAR 6664
1953
Typescript.

Ancestor Joshua Barstow of Scituate Mass. and Harpswell Me. his ancestry and descendants...
Sinnett, Charles Nelson, 1847-1928.
G BAR 7385
19 p.
1922
Typescript.

Bartlett family data
G BAR 7950 pamphlet box
12 p.
Typescript.

Photostat copy of death record of Wright Bartlett drowned in Boston Harbor 16 March 1747
G BAR 7957
1 p.
Typescript.

Ancestors of Lydia Bartlett
G BAR 7959 pamphlet box
Typescript.

[Bartlett family] Parson Porter with a printed program of a reunion of the descendants of John and Lucinda Miller of Ludlow Mass. Nov. 28 1878...
Osborne, Percy E.
G BAR 8018
4 p.
1933
Typescript.

Additions to Genealogy of the descendants of Joseph Bartlett of Newton Mass. by Aldis Everard Hibner 1934
Warner, Frederick C. (Frederick Chester), 1886-.
G BAR 8023A
5 p.
Typescript.

Descendants of Samuel Bartlett of Stafford Conn.
Barlow, Claude W., (Claude Willis), 1907-1976.
G BAR 8052
13 p.
1953
Typescript.

Material concerning the Bartlett family [which] appeared in the Newburyport Daily Herald (Massachusetts) ... May 21 1881 ...
Bartlett, Ralph Sylvester.
G BAR 8058
7 p.
1957
Typescript.

The Bartlett family in America descent of Ralph Sylvester Bartlett from Richard Bartlett his earliest paternal ancestor in America
Bartlett, Ralph Sylvester.
G BAR 8059
15 p.
1957
Typescript.

Ensign Eleazar Barton and his descendants...
McLaren, Grace Helen (Barton) 1874-.
G BAR 8784
Various pagination.
1941
Typescript.

The family of Capt. David Barton of early Granby Mass.
Hook, James W. (James William), 1884-1957.
G BAR 8788
32 p.
1951
Typescript.

Barton - Green and related families
Kaye, Ruth Lincoln
G BAR 8803
ii, 83 p.
1969
Typescript.

Our family records [desc. of Silas and Ruth Luce Bartoo]
Bartoo, Eli.
G BAR 8820
4, 133 p.
1938
Typescript.

Bass family of Windham and Ashford, Connecticut
Chapman, Grace Olive.
G BAS 459
71 p.
1943
Typescript.

Bassett genealogy
Copeland, Maynard Bassett.
G BAS 1000
22, 93, 1 p.
1940
Typescript.

Bassetts of Chatham and Harwich, Massachusetts
Chapman, Grace Olive.
G BAS 1005
68 p.
1944
Typescript.

Bass family
G BAS 440
5 p.
Typescript.

Bass family of Windham and Ashford Connecticut
Chapman, Grace Olive.
G BAS 459
70 p.
1943
Typescript.

Bass families of the South...
Bell, Albert Dehner, 1911-.
G BAS 465
1 v.
1961
Typescript.

Report of the proceedings of the 1st - 4th reunions [of the Bassett Family Association] 1897-1902
Bassett Family Association of America.
G BAS 965, 965A, 965B, 965C
4 v.
1897-1902
Typescript.

Descendants of Nathaniel Josiah and David Batchelder
G BAT 310
4 p.
1882
Typescript.

Some notes on the descendants of Joseph Bates of Middleborough Mass.
Bates, Frank Amasa.
G BAT 832
10, 12 p.
Typescript.

Ichabod Bates 1757-1804 of Kent Conn. and Monkton Vt.
Eldridge, William Henry, 1873-1943.
G BAT 880
8 p.
1937
Typescript.

Bates Selleck and allied families of Stamford Norwalk and Fairfield Connecticut
Gorham, Henry S.
G BAT 883A-C
3 v.
1938-1939
Typescript.

The family of Daniel Bates of Hanover N.J. Cincinnati and Sandusky County Ohio
Smith, Edward Church, b. 1877.
G BAT 894
11 p.
1949-1950
Typescript.

Notes on the history of the Bauch (Bouck) family
Forshee, Archibald A.
G BAU 220
Typescript.

The Baxters of New England a family history...
Baxter, James Phinney, 1831-1921.
G BAX 13
344, 13, 14, 2 p.
1921
Typescript. Another copy, Mss C 4950; "this material compiled from Baxter-Proctor genealogical records, SG BAX 9."

[Baxter family] a collection of genealogies
Baxter, James Phinney, 1831-1921.
G BAX 2
1, 128 p.
Typescript.

The Bayleys & Baileys
Bayley, Warren Chester.
G BAY 68
29 p.
1945
Typescript.

Beal notes [John Beal probably born in Hingham England about 1590 died in Hingham Mass. 1688]
Holman, Mary Lovering, 1868-1947.
G BEA 2320
Various pagination.
1928
Typescript.

Beale geneal. and history supplement to N.E. Hist. Geneal. Register 86:455-460 91:372-373
G BEA 2528
11 p.
Typescript.

The ancestors and descendants of Charles Brewster Beach...
Atwell, Charles Beach, b. 1855.
G BEA 29
26 p.
1932
2nd ed.
Typescript.

Jonathan Beadle family...who came to Ovid Seneca County New York about 1805...
Beadle, Walter J.
G BEA 326
Various pagings.
1972
Typescript.

Gamaliel Beaman family of Lancaster and Sterling Mass
Cheever, Herbert M.
G BEA 3568
2 p.
1955
Typescript.

Beadon Bedon family of Suffolk and Bristol Counties Mass.
Holman, Winifred Lovering, 1899-1989.
G BEA 360
1959
Typescript.

The Beach Radway Mattice and Williams ancestors of Mary Electa Beach Brownyard
Brownyard, Theodore Lucius, 1905-.
G BEA 45
46 p.
1967
Typescript.

Pedigree of the descendants of John Bean Exeter N.H. 1660
Bean, Jacob.
G BEA 5203
43 x 55.6 cm.
1903
Bound tabular pedigree chart

Some of the descendants of John Bean of Exeter N.H. 1660...
Miller, Edna Mae (Bean).
G BEA 5230
8, 68 p.
1938
Typescript.

Beardsley genealogy ... William Lincoln Beardsley and his descendants
Rogers, Wilmot Polk, 1889-.
G BEA 8430
12 p.
1958
Typescript.

Genealogical records of Austin Bearse (or Bearce) Barnstable Cape Cod Massachusetts U.S.A. A.D. 1638 to A.D. 1933.
Meadows, Fanny Louisa Steed.
G BEA 8910 [mss project entries]
390 p.
1933
Typescript.

Supplement to genealogical records of Austin Bearse (or Bearce) Barnstable Cape Cod Massachusetts U.S.A. A.D. 1638 to A.D. 1933. A record of his descendants ...
Meadows, Fanny Louisa Steed.
G BEA 8910A
2, 49, 17 p.
1939
Typescript.

Bearus - Darlington family and its branches
Darlington, James Henry, 1856-1930.
G BEA 9400
63 p.
1893?
Typescript.

Beath - Pelham families
Potter, Margaret R. Beath.
G BEA 9940
13 p.
1870
Typescript.

Bebb genealogy the descendants of William Bebb and Martha Hughes of Llanbrynmair Wales
Bebb, Herbert, 1887-.
G BEB 225
1, 69 p.
1944
Typescript.

Persons of the name of "Bebee" (spelled that way) listed in the master index to the Vermont Vital Records (early file to 1870) State House Montpelier [Vt]
G BEB 350
2 p.
Typescript.

Beckford & Bickford families
Upham, Anna Bickford.
G BEC 645
35, 120 p.
1948
Typescript.

Beecher genealogy descendants of Isaac of New Haven Conn.
McGraw, Helen M.
G BEE 133
Various pagings.
Typescript.

The Beers - Fox families notes from published records and Beers epitaphs in Fairfield Conn.
G BEE 1735
18 p.
Typescript.

Descendants of Munson Hoyt Beers who originated in Fairfield Connecticut
Gault, Charles Beers, 1911-.
G BEE 1750
3 p.
1968
Typescript.

Beeson family Bible records of Helen Beeson Stuckey Loomis including family names of Beeson Stuckey Loomis Moore Wooldridge Foster Thompson Skeels Madden Cain & Engler
Meyer, Harold I.
G BEE 2212
2, 9 p.
1954
Typescript.

Ancestry of Alexander Beebe and Sarah (Bowker) Beebe
Seger, Adah Beebe, 1881-.
G BEE 50
4 p.
Typescript.

Some ancestors and descendants of Alexander Beebe
Seger, Adah Beebe, 1881-.
G BEE 50A
9 p.
Typescript.

Beebe data [N.Y.]
Whelan, Florence Spencer
G BEE 78
1951-1953
Typescript

Ancestors and descendants of David Belcher of Staffordville, Connecticut
Chapman, Grace Olive.
G BEEL 283
31 p.
1939
Typescript.

The descendants of Peter Beghtol of Pennsylvania Kentucky and Illinois by his first wife Polly Bruner his second wife Catherine Bruner and his third wife Sarah Ann Evans ...
Maes, Virginia (Ingles), 1913-.
G BEG 725
4, 22 [i.e. 24], 1 p.
1942
Typescript.

The Beitzel family
Beitzell, Edwin Warfield, 1905-.
G BEI 725
19, 2 p.
1948
Typescript.

John Bell of Barree township Huntingdon County Pennsylvania a record of his ancestors and descendants
Bell, Raymond Martin, 1907-1999
G BEL 1787
5 p.
1937
Typescript.

The Bell family descendants of John Bell of Beverley Yorkshire England and Shrigley Melancthon Ontario
Daniels, Olive Bell, b. 1891.
G BEL 1789
1, 47 p.
1939
Typescript.

The Bells of Stony Creek Middle Paxton Twp. Dauphin Co. Penn.
Bell, Raymond Martin, 1907-1999
G BEL 1815
6 p.
1966
Typescript.

Belcher notes [Jeremiah Belcher born about 1612 England died in Ipswich Mass. in March 1892-3 {sic}]
Holman, Mary Lovering, 1868-1947.
G BEL 281
3 p.
1928
Typescript.

Ancestors and descendants of David Belcher of Staffordville Connecticut
Chapman, Grace Olive.
G BEL 283
30 p.
1939
Typescript.

The Belden genealogy ... of Wethersfield Conn. and ... Hadley Hatfield [and] Deerfield Mass.
Hinman, R. R. (Royal Ralph), 1785-1868.
G BEL 415
4, 74 p.
1884
Typescript.

The family history of Judge Ellsworth B. Belden and collateral families
Belden, Stanley R. (Stanley Raymond), 1892-1976.
G BEL 425
10, 224 p.
1969
Typescript.

A genealogical study [Bell family]
Bell, Winthrop Pickard, 1884-1965.
G BELL 1810
viii, 292 p.
1962
Typescript.

Ancestral lines of Angela Brown Bemis
G BEM 175
32 p.
Typescript.

The Bemis family in Maine
Sinnett, Charles Nelson, 1847-1928.
G BEM 179
6 p.
1922
Typescript.

*History of the Benedicts descended from Thomas
Benedict b. 1617 Nottinghamshire Eng. d. abt.
1690 in Norwalk Conn. with special reference to
Byron Kingsbury Benedict b. 1834 Southport N.Y.
d. 1902 at Monroetown Pa.*
G BEN 1925
13 p.
1953
Typescript.

*Benjamin genealogy England Cambridge Mass.
Preston Conn. Worthington Mass. Bloomington
Ill. 1632-1952 also Pease genealogy*
Benjamin, Edith.
G BEN 2346
26, 1, 8 p.
1953
Typescript.

*Benner notes [Henry from Germany to Maine
1753]*
Barker, John Herbert, 1870-1951.
G BEN 2945
52, 34, 30 p.
Typescript.

*Benner family some notes of the Benner family
1753-1940 also records of Barker Castner and
Eames families*
Barker, John Herbert, 1870-1951.
G BEN 2954
2, 30 p.
1940
Typescript.

*Some descendants of William Adrianse Bennet of
Long Island 1636*
Chidsey, Andrew Dwight, b. 1879.
G BEN 3282
1931
Typescript.

Bennett Lufkin and allied Ipswich families
Andrews, Charles Herbert.
G BEN 3472
21 p.
Typescript.

Bennett genealogy of Wrentham Mass.
Hawes, George O.
G BEN 3514
5 p.
1941
Typescript.

Ben Oliel and Seeley
Ewers, Dorothy Wood, 1910-.
G BEN 4300
203 p.
1966
Typescript.

*The ancestry and posterity of Alanson Benson of
Tiskilwa Bureau Co. Ill.*
Benson, Fred Harvey, b. 1853.
G BEN 4435
36 p.
Typescript.

*Stephen and Mary (Holbrook) Benson of Mendon
Massachusetts and Skaneateles N.Y. with some of
their ancestry and many of their descendants*
Benson, Fred Harvey, b. 1853.
G BEN 4454
2, 50 p.
1920
Typescript.

*The Benson genealogy arranged by the
descendants of Stephen and Mary (Holbrook)
Benson of the town of Skaneateles N.Y.*
Benson, Fred Harvey, b. 1853.
G BEN 4456
32 p.
1923
Typescript.

Some of the descendants of Captain Isaac Benson of Richmond New Hampshire
Benson, Mrs. Julia A.S.
G BEN 4458
1, 39 p.
1925
Typescript.

William Benson of Barbour County Virginia
Grant, Howard Brooke.
G BEN 4464
5 p.
1934
Typescript.

A pioneer family ... John Benson of Hull Massachusetts
Benson, Ernest Leon, b. 1867.
G BEN 4466
Various pagings.
1938
Second printing
Typescript.

William Bentley of Lebanon Conn. 16__ - 1751 and his descendants
Bentley, Edward M., Mrs.
G BEN 5795
26, 4 p.
1925
Typescript.

The Bentley family
Gandrud, Pauline Myra Jones, 1904-1980.
G BEN 5798
61, 7 p.
1931
Typescript.

A line of descent from William Bentley Jr.
Bentley, E.T.
G BEN 5800
1, 8, 1 p.
1941
Typescript.

Bentley notes
Holman, Winifred Lovering, 1899-1989.
G BEN 5814
115-116 p.
1955
Typescript.

Ancestry of Harriet Maria Drown Benton
Benton, Charles E. (Charles Edward), b. 1841.
G BEN 8248
106, 7 p.
1914
Typescript.

The Benton & Butler family record
Keller, Gertie B.
G BEN 8275
2, 53, 18 p.
1958
Typescript.

Han Hansen Bergen and his descendants 1633-1793 [2nd part] genealogy of our branch of the Bergen family 1793-1946
Bergen, Margaret.
G BER 25
1946
Typescript.

Betty genealogy, Cheek history
Betty, L.P.
G BET 1101
1, 33 p.
Typescript.

Some of the descendants of Richard Betts of Ipswich Mass and Newtown L.I.
Corwin, Edna Betts.
G BET 889
7, 9 p.
1933
Typescript.

Genealogical lists of the descendants of Christopher Bewer (Baver)
Baver, Russell S.
G BEW 325
Various pagings.
1955
Typescript.

*Prospectus and personal and surname index to
"The Beyer - Miller family" including ancestry of
the author*
Miller, Charles.
G BEY 25
Various pagings.
1955
Typescript.

*A record of that branch of the New Hampshire
Bickfords from one John Bickford of Bloody Point
(Newington) N.H. down thru Harriet Elenor
Bickford Mueller of Council Bluffs Iowa*
Mueller, Ralph Scott, b. 1877.
G BIC 10
1, 24, 1 p.
1934
Typescript.

Bickley genealogy descendants of John
Bickley, W.P.
G BIC 20
6 p.
1928
Typescript.

The Bickford family
Mueller, Ralph S.
G BIC 8
41 p.
1933
Typescript.

*The Bierer - Berry family ... descendants of John
and Barbara ... with brief accounts of the
Holtzinger - Holtzer family and the Mull family*
Berry, Charles Jerome, b. 1892.
G BIE 525
iv, 128 p.
1933
Typescript.

*Biggs - McGrew and allied lines (Swartwout Hall
Munday Howell Finley McFerran) ... ancestors
and descendants of Llewellyn Biggs and Martha
McGrew married ... 1827 ... New York New
Jersey Maryland Virginia and Pennsylvania*
Hathaway, Bernice FitzSimmons, 1903-.
G BIG 122
249, xlix p.
1963
Typescript.

Biggs - McGrew and allied lines ... [supplement]
Hathaway, Bernice FitzSimmons, 1903-.
G BIG 122A
47 p.
Typescript.

*Letters from Melville M. Bigelow of Cambridge
Mass. to Emma Frances Van Ness Richmond of
Lodi Wisc. (1896-1904) Bigelow genealogy
included.*
G BIG 3
28 p.
Typescript.

*Bigelow lineage ancestors and descendants of
Solomon Bigelow soldier of the American
Revolution*
Webster, W. Burton.
G BIG 45
1956
Typescript.

*The Bigler family descendants of Mark Bigler
who immigrated to America in 1733*
Burns, Norman, 1905-.
G BIG 750
2, 138 p.
1960
Typescript.

Billington - Whelan families
Whelan, Florence Spencer
G BIL 1258
8 p.
1946
Typescript.

Descent and descendants of the brothers Otis and Jason Bills of Knox County Maine (being a continuation-in-part of the "History of the Bill family" by Ledyard Bill 1867)
Bills, Charles Everett.
G BIL 1525
41 p.
1964
Typescript.

Jonathan Biles [of] Beverly Mass.
G BIL 280
24 p.
Typescript.

A part of genealogical and ancestral notes series 2 ancestors of Mary Elizabeth Billard
Edwards, William Hopple
G BIL 605
27, 2 p.
1959
Typescript.

Descendants in Maine of Joseph[4] Billings of Concord Mass.
G BIL 740
Typescript.

Prospectus of an unpublished genealogy in two volumes of Roger Billings Richard Billings William Billings and Nathaniel Billings ...
Billings, Charles.
G BIL 745
Various pagings.
1903
Typescript.

The Billing family of Concord Mass. first five generations with chart
MacLea, Florence
G BIL 772
17 p.
1927
Typescript.

Some notes on the Binkley Shackleford Steele Shane Markham Carver Beadle & Cooper families
Hollinshead, W. H., Mrs.
G BIN 675
9 p.
Typescript.

A partial genealogy of the American descendants of Joseph and Elizabeth Birch
Burch, George Bosworth.
G BIR 104
2, 30 p.
1970
Typescript.

The descendants of James Birdsall
Perry, Harold George.
G BIR 325
13 p.
1962
Typescript.

The Birdsall family genealogy and history ...
Birdsall, George A.
G BIR 328
3, 105, 45 p.
1964
Typescript.

Bishop genealogy James Bishop and Partheena Sheldon
Bishop, Ira Elmore.
G BIS 454
Typescript.

Bishop families in Maine. Ancestor Luke Bishop of Harpswell Me. ... and descendants. Bishop families of Wayne and Monmouth Me.
Sinnett, Charles Nelson, 1847-1928.
G BIS 475
13 p.
1922
Typescript.

Some descendants of Revd. John Bishop (1643-1694) of Stamford Conn.
Wait, John Cassan, 1860-1936.
G BIS 482
1930
Typescript.

Bishop genealogy
Bishop, Loren C.
G BIS 484
7, 173, 4 p.
1932-1933
Typescript.

Genealogy: Edward Bishop and John Young
Clarke, Leone G.
G BIS 486
2, 75 p.
1938
Typescript.

Descendants of Israel Bissell
Smith, Edward Church, b. 1877.
G BIS 961
17 p.
1932
Typescript.

Bither - Byther genealogy some descendants of the Revolutionary soldier Peter Bither of Maine
Boyd, Janice.
G BIT 310
41, 13 p.
1957
Typescript.

Blanding of Upton on Severn Worcester England genealogical chart
Roberts, H. Weeks.
G BLA 10225
Chart 41 x 34.5 cm, folded & bound.
1895
Typescript.

Some descendants of William and Phoebe Blanding of Upton-on-Severn England and Boston Mass.
Blanding, Edward M., Mrs.
G BLA 10234
7, 1, 2 p.
1932
Typescript.

Blaney genealogy
Drollinger, Ziba L.
G BLA 10437
6, 3 p.
1930
Typescript.

Brewster Prence Freeman Tracy Merrick Ashley Pond Bouton Laury the ancestors of Clarisssa Laury Blankienship [sic]
Gaut, Ida Belle Blankienship.
G BLA 10932
42 p.
1951
Typescript.

The Blauvelt family genealogy from 1636
Ackerman, Herbert Stewart, b. 1875.
G BLA 15466
1, 228, 38 p.
1955
Typescript.

Genealogical records of Blackledge Burson Carter families
Leckey, Howard Louis, b. 1892.
G BLA 2854
1936
Typescript.

History of the Blacklidge family
Blacklidge, W.E.
G BLA 3850
16 p.
1921
Typescript.

Blair genealogy [descendants of Alexander]
G BLA 6326
Typescript.

Some descendants of Charles and Easter Robinson Blair
Blair, Charles Robert.
G BLA 6382
31 p.
1962
Typescript.

Line of descent from Ralph Blisdale 1640
Blaisdell, Harper.
G BLA 6500
Typescript.

Ancestor William Blaisdell of North Yarmouth and Lewiston Me.
Sinnett, Charles Nelson, 1847-1928.
G BLA 6708
8 p.
1929
Typescript.

Elijah Blaisdell of Amesbury Mass. 1740-1769 (fifth generation from Ralph the original ancestor in America) and his descendants to 1949
Blaisdell, James Arnold.
G BLA 6716
Various pagings.
1949
Typescript.

Record of the ancestors of Sarah Olcott Murdock Blake
G BLA 7064
1 v.
In Whitmore Ancestral Tablet.

William Blake of Harpswell Me. ancestry and descendants
Sinnett, Charles Nelson, 1847-1928.
G BLA 7100
54 p.
1922
Typescript.

An account of the Blakeney family of Westmoreland County New Brunswick Canada
Blakeney, R.V.
G BLA 7708
26 p.
1940
Typescript.

David Blakeslee his ancestors and descendants
McCray, Fred W.
G BLA 7960
69, 12 p.
1947
Typescript.

Blanchard family records. Part 1 men descended from Thomas (1) Blanchard of Charlestown. Part 2 women descended from Thomas (1) ... Part 3 men and women whose Blanchard ancestry is uncertain
Bethune, Louise.
G BLA 8910
Typescript.

Genealogy of the descendants of Dea. John [Blanchard] of Dunstable Mass.
Bethune, Louise.
G BLA 8913
Typescript.

Brief notes on Silvanus and Caleb Blanchard of Malden and Medford Massachusetts
Reed, Marion Charlotte, 1906-1966.
G BLA 8918
16 p.
Typescript.

History of the Blanchard family from 1636 to the present time
Hunt, Jonathan.
G BLA 8925
15, 10 p.
1898
Typescript.

Blanchard family [Jean or John of Kingston N.Y.]
G BLA 8935
8 p.
1916
Typescript.

The Blanchard - Buker - Brown genealogy 1639-1948
Gatenby, Ethel M. Blanchard.
G BLA 8956
12 p.
1948
Typescript.
Ancestral register of Frederick J. Bliss and Mrs. Clara A. Bliss
Stenberg, Algot G.
G BLI 140
4, 132 p.
1938
Typescript.

*Ancestors and descendants of Minerva Arthur
Bliss with data on related families Dunning - Lee
- Tenney - Wise*
Brehm, Elsie Lee.
G BLI 164
1, 47 p.
1963
Typescript.

[Blood family]
G BLO 2050
17 p.
1938
Typescript.

*Blount - Blunt [descendants of William of
Andover Mass.]*
Taylor, George Frederick.
G BLO 3743
4, 33 p.
1951
Typescript.

*Family record of Henry Boardman of
Williamstown Mass.*
Shepard, Elmer I. (Elmer Irwin), 1878-1966.
G BOA 150
4 p.
1945
Typescript.

*The Bobb family and associated families of Hoge
Armstrong Naggle Longsdorf and Waugh early
settlers in Cumberland County Pennsylvania*
Ellis, Luella May (Waggoner).
G BOB 50
24, 4 p.
1963
Typescript.

*Report concerning Hugh Boden of Cumberland
County Pennsylvania and concerning the Kelso
family of Cumberland and Dauphin Counties
Pennsylvania*
Adams, Arthur, 1881-1960.
G BOD 1020
2, 10 p.
1942
Typescript.

Bodurtha family of Agawam Mass.
NSDAR Mercy Warren Chapter.
G BOD 4090
5 p.
Copies of Bible records and family papers.

*Boggs ancestry of Rubie Ray Boggs wife of James
Ellsworth Ewers and other Boggs records*
Ewers, Dorothy Wood, 1910-.
G BOG 310
Various pagings.
1965
Typescript.

Annetje Webber Jans Bogardus
G BOG 95
6, 2 p.
Typescript.

*The German Bohne - Bohn - Boon - Boone family
descendants of Johann Diel Bohne of Maryland
1711-1764*
Whedon, Nellie Eva (Woods).
G BOH 2
iv, 40 "(i.e., 41)" p.
1945
Typescript.

*The Boice line ... [Dea. David Boice of Hopkinton
Mass.]*
Holman, Winifred Lovering, 1899-1989.
G BOI 10
23 p.
1943
Typescript.

*Notes on the Peter Bolton family of Yorkshire
Eng. and Nauvoo Ill.*
Bolton, Thaddeus Lincoln, b. 1865.
G BOL 1664
5 p.
1918
Typescript.

Bolles - Bowles notes
Byrne, Daniel, Mrs.
G BOL 750
76 p.
1968
Typescript.

*Genealogy of the Bonar family of Scotland
Pennsylvania and Virginia*
Bonar, Everett W.
G BON 100
10 p.
1953
Typescript.

*Notes [on] the English sources and connections
of Nicholas Bond ... of York - Agamenticus
Gorgiana a freeman in 1652*
Bond, Arthur Thomas.
G BON 190
5 p.
Typescript.

The Bond Eshelman Longacre and allied families
Jenkins, John Gill Jr.
G BON 242
69 p.
1962
Typescript.

Notes on the Hill and Bone families [in the South]
Jones, Kathleen Paul.
G BON 400
22, 5 p.
1931
Typescript.

Bone connections.
Herring, Dorothy Holland, 1937-.
G BON 406
40 p.
1970
Typescript.

Bonner genealogy descendants of Capt. John.
G BON 600
Typescript.

Bonney family genealogy
Hunt, Roberta Lee.
G BON 735
20, 7, 2 p.
1965
Typescript.

The ancestry (in America) of Dr. Daniel Bontecou
G BON 895
Typescript.

Four generations of Boone genealogy
Buchanan, J. H., Mrs.
G BOO 138
5 p.
1955
Typescript.

Booher - Shepard and collateral
Shepard, Gracie (Booher), b. 1890.
G BOO 35
6, 10, 1, 14 p.
1954
Typescript.

The Booker family in Maine
Sinnett, Charles Nelson, 1847-1928.
G BOO 50
31 p.
1922
Typescript.

*Ambrose Boots and his wife Elizabeth Bull ... who
came to America from Sussex County England in
... 1830 and settled in Beaver County
Pennsylvania*
Boots, John R., 1939-.
G BOO 500
47 p.
1970
Typescript.

Boone family Maryland and Delaware
Chance, Hilda.
G BOO 95
6 p.
Typescript.

*The descendants of John Boreing Maryland
planter*
Hecklinger, Roger S.
G BOR 1120
42 p.
1950
Typescript.

The New Jersey Bos Bosch Bush family
Pryor, William Y.
G BOS 125
8, 97, a-o p.
1949
Typescript.

The Bossemeyer family and allied lines
Weniger, Myrtle Elizabeth (Knepper), 1886-.
G BOS 2215
2, 31 p.
1944
Typescript.

Ancestry of Charles Frederick Bosworth and George Frederick Bosworth
Bosworth, George Frederick.
G BOS 3798
9, 14 p.
1946-1947
Typescript.

The Bottum collection records used in compiling Bottum (Longbottom) family album
Oliver, Rebekah (Deal), 1901-.
G BOT 525
4, 139 p.
1967
Typescript.

Boughton - Bouton families ...
Bouton, Eugene.
G BOU 1040
Various pagings.
Typescript.

Boughton - Bouton names in the Detroit city directories of 1855 through 1941 with years of first mention
Boughton, Willis A. (Willis Arnold), 1885-1977.
G BOU 1045
2 p.
Typescript.

Descendants of Myron and Jane F. Boughton
Boughton, Willis A. (Willis Arnold), 1885-1977.
G BOU 1060
13 p.
1965
Typescript.

Family record of George & Marcia Boulton
Boulton, Frederick William.
G BOU 1250
1903
Typescript.

Bourn - Boorn family. Jared Bourn who settled in Boston Mass. abt. the year 1630 and many of his Providence R.I. and Richmond N.H. descendants
Julian, Jennie Bowen (Bourn).
G BOU 1785
30 p.
1949
Typescript.

Boutell - Boutelle or Boutwell [James[1] Boutell of Salem Mass. 1639]
Driscoll, Marion Lang.
G BOU 2000
33 p.
1947
Typescript.

The Boutelle family of Lynn Reading Leominster (and other places)
G BOU 2175
10 p.
Typescript.

Elias Boudinot an account of his life ...
Church, Mary Brinsmade.
G BOU 925
25 p.
1913
Typescript.

Letters of Eliza Southgate Mrs. Walter Bowne ...
Bowne, Eliza (Southgate), 1783-1809.
G BOW 1050
Typescript.

Descendants of Charles Pickering Bowditch and Cornelia Rockwell Bowditch [a continuation in one branch of Harold Bowditch's 1936 "Bowditch family of Salem Massachusetts"]
Balch, Henry G.
G BOW 150A
17 p.
1960
Typescript.

Journey to Wales an account of a visit to the Welsh home of Griffith Bowen
Bowen, Georgene B.
G BOW 292
21 p.
Typescript.

Descendants of John Bowen of Old Rappahannock County Va.
Wheatley, A. E. B., Mrs.
G BOW 335
7 p.
1924
Typescript.

Genealogical leaflet of the Consider Bowen family...
King, Isaac Fenton.
G BOW 338
7 p.
1892
1925 reprint
Typescript.

Thomas Bowen Richmond N.H. and many of his descendants
Cady, Alice Bowen.
G BOW 359
20 p.
1949
Typescript.

Genealogical notes of the Bowerman family
Bowman, Sumner Eli.
G BOW 600
3 p.
1892
Typescript.

Bower family of England
Bowers, A.B.
G BOW 710
59 p.
1911
Typescript.

The Bowers family
Bowers, Beatrix.
G BOW 718
1963
Typescript.

Bowie family of Maine [copied from notes and records ... of Angela F. Bowie ...]
Bowie, Harold Sanford.
G BOW 775
6 p.
1951
Typescript.

Copy of family records from the Bible belonging to Capt. Benj. Bowlend 1769-1812 and ... genealogy of the Bowlend Goodwin and Crosby families.
Hodgman, Arthur Winfred, b. 1869.
G BOW 790
18 p.
1929
Typescript.

Bowles family history and record of the Bowles family ...
Bowles, David.
G BOW 895
7 p.
Typescript.

The genealogical record of one branch of the Boyce family in America
Boyce, Earnest.
G BOY 30
55, 8, 6 p.
1972
Typescript.

Boykin
Arthur, Robert, 1886-.
G BOY 325
34 p.
1964
Typescript.

The Boylston family some descendants of Thomas of Watertown
Brook, Hazel P.
G BOY 378
1, 7, 1 p.
1956
Typescript.

A bit of Boynton genealogy and ancestry of Ann (Boynton) Batt
G BOY 420
4, 5 p.
Typescript.

Concise genealogical history of several families being those from whom the Eleazer Boynton family of Rockport claim their descent ...
Pool, Ebenezer.
G BOY 425
15 p.
1900
Typescript.

Notes on the Thomas Boyd family
Voorhees, Edward Kinsey, b. 1862.
G BOY 48
1, 11 p.
1930
Typescript.

Genealogy of the Canadian and American descendants of John Brand (1757-1841) and his wife Margaret Head both of Acton Suffolk County England
Brand, Robert Franklin, 1904-.
G BRA 14606
1, 84 p.
1943
Typescript.

The Brandt family of the early days
Fellers, Forest S. (Forest Stanley), b. 1896.
G BRA 15650
19 p.
Typescript.

The descendants of James and Dorcas (Quint) Brann.
Towle, Lloyd K.
G BRA 16120
103 p.
1971
Typescript.

The Bradbury lineage English descent New England descent
Holman, Mary Campbell (Lovering), 1868-1947.
G BRA 2249
1, 23 p.
Typescript.

Bracey family descendants of John
Banks, Charles Edward, 1854-1931.
G BRA 239
2 p.
Typescript.

The genealogy of the Braytons
Brayton, George M.
G BRA 24830
1, 68 p.
1914
Typescript.

The ancestry of Harry F. Bradford
G BRA 3230
5, 58 p.
Typescript.

Some Bradfords
McElwain, Mrs. Edgar.
G BRA 3256
22 p.
Typescript.

Daniel Bradley of Haverhill & Dea. Amos Bradley his descendants [sic] who removed to Dracut abt. 1761 being mainly Bradleys of Dracut
Bradley, Asa Mayo.
G BRA 4147
50 p.
1909
Typescript.

Documentary evidence concerning John Brahan (about 1725-1775) of Fauquier County Virginia and some of his descendants
Lane, (Elise Denison Brown)
G BRA 6982
25 p.
1946
Typescript.

Brackenbury of Lincolnshire volume one wills etc.
Brackenbury, K.F.
G BRA 750
68, 15 p.
1954
Typescript.

To direct descendants of Richard Brackett of Braintree now Quincy, Mass.
Brackett, Jeffrey R.
G BRA 970
4 p.
1935
Typescript.

Brackett family from England to New England in 1630
Cheever, Herbert Milton.
G BRA 980
4 p.
1956
Typescript.

Brewster - Martin lineage Brewster - Malburn lineage Kellogg - Webster lineage
Ravenscroft, Ruth Thayer, 1903-1991.
G BRE 11772
29, 23 p.
1961
Typescript.

What I know about the Breyfogle family through the first five generations in America
Breyfogle, Lewis W., b. 1889.
G BRE 11925
59, 9, 34 p.
1963
Typescript.

Breed - Ormsby family notes includes family lines of Blanchard Chapin Coburn Hendrix McFarland Porter Wightman
Ormsby, Jennie Eliza (Breed), 1872-.
G BRE 342
48 p.
1952
Typescript.

The ancestry of the Breese family
Batchelder, Charles Hull, 1876-1948.
G BRE 410
2, 14, 8 p.
1934
Typescript.

Breitborde genealogy (Breitbord - Breitboard - Brietborde - Brietbord) and allied families of Burstein - Feldman - Kavitsky (Kovitsky - Gavitt)
Nickerson, Vernon Roscoe, 1933-.
G BRE 520
6, 1 p.
1967

An incomplete genealogy of the family of John Bretz of Fairfield Co. Ohio with a partial history of one line of descent ...
Bretz, J. Harlen, 1882-.
G BRE 8630
65, 2 p.
1949
Typescript.

The Britt family in Maine
Sinnett, Charles Nelson, 1847-1928.
G BRI 12700
7 p.
1923
Typescript.

The Bridges story
Bullock, Joseph Floyd.
G BRI 1498
11 p.
1963
Typescript.

Briers. Jackson. [John Briers of Saco - Biddeford John Jackson of Gloucester Mass. and related families]
Gathemann, Mabel S.
G BRI 2865
1, 30, 19 p.
1935
Typescript.

*Paris Maine soldier in the Revolutionary War and
desendents [sic]*
G BRI 3195
107-116 p.
Typescript.

*Ansel Briggs the first governor of Iowa his
ancestry and descendants*
Sinnett, Charles Nelson, 1847-1928.
G BRI 3198
14 p.
Typescript.

*Some descendants of William Briggs of Taunton
Mass. who married Sarah Macomber*
Briggs, Charles Harold, 1878-1953.
G BRI 3225
Various pagings.
1917
Typescript.

*Descendants of Freeman Briggs and Abigail
(French) Briggs originally of Berkley Mass.*
Briggs, Fletcher.
G BRI 3228
51 p.
1918-1919
Typescript.

*A genealogy of ten generations of the Briggs
family of Rhode Island and county Essex England
with their New York descendants and records of
ten allied families*
Heck, Pearl Leona.
G BRI 3232
73 p.
1932
Typescript.

*A genealogy of the descendants of Daniel Briggs
of Turner Maine and of his brother William
Briggs of Poland (Minot) Maine*
Alexander, Winthrop, 1861-1941.
G BRI 3239
139 p.
1937

*Ancestors and descendants of Henry Delos Briggs
of Oak Grove Louisiana*
Johnson, Charles Owen.
G BRI 3258
1957
Typescript.

*Brimhall family story from where we are in 1698
[1968?] back toward the Garden of Eden*
Brimhall, Logan.
G BRI 4675
1969
Typescript.

*Ancestor Thomas Brimigion of Bowdoin Me. and
descendants*
Sinnett, Charles Nelson, 1847-1928.
G BRI 4800
3 p.
1922
Typescript.

Brimmer family of Rensselaer Co. N.Y.
Fellner, Itta Allen.
G BRI 5150
8 p.
1913
Typescript.

*Family lines of my [Brinckerhoff] children with
the earliest known ancestor in each family given
first*
Brinckerhoff, Dana Gilbert.
G BRI 5500
17 p.
Typescript.

*Horatio Gates[6] Bronson of Waterbury Conn. and
some of his descendants*
Jones, Roderick Bissell, 1898-.
G BRO 1370
6 p.
1947
Typescript.

Brookfield family
Brookfield, Henry Morgan, b. 1871.
G BRO 1710
159 p.
1946
Typescript.

*Genealogy of one branch of the Richard
Brownson family 1631-1951*
Brownson, Ernest Ray, b. 1870.
G BRO 17125
335, 8, 7, 27 p.
1951
Typescript.

Genealogical record of the Brooks family
Brooks, Ella Augusta.
G BRO 2042
19 p.
Typescript.

*Genealogy of the Brooks family continuation of
direct line from William Brooks born in England
in 1610 came to Virginia from London in 1635 on
the Speedwell*
Brooks, Virrell I. Harris.
G BRO 2088A
12 p.
1944
Typescript.

*Brooks genealogy ancestors and descendants of
Nathaniel Brooks of Vernon Vermont*
Priest, Alice L. (Alice Lucinda), 1866-1954.
G BRO 2103
9 p.
1930
Typescript.

Descendants of Charlotte Field Brooks
Nodine, Lillie I.
G BRO 2123
1959
Typescript.

Our heritage
Adair, Caroline (Brooks), 1876-.
G BRO 2125
37, 33, 20 p.
1954
Typescript.

Genealogy of Lawrence Leland Browne
Browne, Lawrence Leland.
G BRO 2174
1970
Typescript.

*Brocklebank - one line of descent from Jane
Brocklebank of Rowley Massachusetts*
Pease, Marietta.
G BRO 225
4 p.
1940
Typescript.

Brossman pioneers in America
Brossman, Schuyler C.
G BRO 2720
9 p.
1964
Typescript.

*Amos Broughton 1743-1837 of Hoosic Rensselaer
County New York and some of his descendants.
The Puritan manuscripts...*
Phillips, Vernon Sirvilian, b. 1871.
G BRO 3258
1, 8, 1 p.
1932
Typescript.

Brower family notes
Kerr, John C.
G BRO 3925
8 p.
1925
Typescript.

*Brockways in vital records of Mass. Maine New
Hampshire Vermont*
Brockway, Florence M. (Florence May), b. 1869.
G BRO 530
114, 27 p.
Typescript.

*Descendants of Stephen-3 Williams Brown
(Merlin-4 Josiah-5 Josiah-6 Tristram-7 Tristram-
8 Joshua-9 Richard-10)*
G BRO 5592
14 p.
Typescript.

*Brown abstracts all the abstracts of Brown
estates on file in Saratoga Co. N.Y. to about 1860*
G BRO 5599
8, 7 p.
Typescript.

Descendants of Richard and Edith Brown and of Stephen Williams Brown
Brown, F.N.M.
G BRO 5606
3 p. each
Typescript.

Brown [descendants of Daniel of Madison Co. N.Y.]
Prindle, Paul Wesley, 1903-1991.
G BRO 5610
3 p.
Typescript.

A record of some of the descendants of Thomas Brown of Concord Mass.
Lines, Maxine Phelps, 1909-
G BRO 5611
22, 526 p.
Typescript.

Brown family descendants of Oliver soldier of the Revolution [Conn.]
Brown, James C.
G BRO 5776
14 p.
1928
Typescript.

David Arms Brown and Cleora Augusta Towne their ancestry and descendants
Grobel, William Kendrick, 1908-.
G BRO 5838
2, 40 p.
1940
Typescript.

Lineage of the children of Edmund Woodward Brown and Martha Coit Brown
Elliott, Ellen Coit Brown.
G BRO 5841
125 p.
1942
Typescript.

The Brown line [John Brown of Mass. & Me. d. 1696]
Holman, Winifred Lovering, 1899-1989.
G BRO 5842
1, 42 p.
1942
Typescript.

Family of Sylvanus Brown b. 1749 Augusta N.Y. and Kezia Cushman b. 1754
G BRO 5855
1 p.
1945
Typescript.

The grave of Salmon Brown and wife Abbie C. Hinckley
Cheever, Herbert Milton.
G BRO 5863
1, 7 p.
1949
Typescript.

The Brown genealogy
McConnell, Margaret Wallace Brown, b. 1897.
G BRO 5864
6 p.
1951
Typescript.

The ancestry and descendents [sic] of George Everett Brown and Abbie Putnam Brown Billerica Mass. So. Lyndeboro N.H. Woburn Mass. Washington Co., Colo.
Brown, Dexter P.
G BRO 5865
81 p.
1952
Typescript.

300 American ancestors of Leon R. Brown
Brown, Leon R. (Leon Robertson), b. 1886.
G BRO 5870
85 p.
1952
Typescript.

Ancestors and descendants of Hannah Twitchell Phillbrook Brown and George W. Brown. With charts by Madge Anderson and Roy B. Earling
Anderson, Mary Brown.
G BRO 5888
1, 194, 1 p.
1959
Typescript.

Family of Abraham Brown his descendants of New Jersey and Ohio with some allied names Fitz Randolph Holden Haywood Groome Newbold and others
Ravenscroft, Ruth Thayer, 1903-1991.
G BRO 5892
7, 87, 1 p.
1959
Typescript.

Chad Brown of Providence (genealogy)
Brown, Leland P.
G BRO 5903
Various pagings.
1966
Typescript.

Early generations of the Browne family of Sudbury Massachusetts
Weis, Frederick Lewis, 1895-1966.
G BRO 6798
1, 57B p.
1931
Typescript.

The Brown line, compiled for Mrs. S. Westray Battle of Asheville, NC.
Holman, Winifred Lovering, 1899-1989.
G BRO 6848
Typescript, 50p.
1943
Typescript.

The Browne line [James Browne of Charlestown Newbury and Salem Mass.]
Holman, Winifred Lovering, 1899-1989.
G BRO 6848
2, 49 p.
1943
Typescript.

John Browne gentleman of Wannamoisett. Edited and enl. from the ms. notes of Benjamin William Brown Northbridge Mass.
Eck, Aimee May (Huston), 1907-.
G BRO 6852
xvi, 170 p.
1951
Typescript.

The genealogy of John Browne of Kansas and Harpers Ferry
Cheever, Herbert Milton.
G BRO 6854
2, 7 p.
1954
Typescript.

1777 military census of Rhode Island which show [sic] the names [sic] of Brownell
Brownell, Elijah Ellsworth, b. 1872.
G BRO 8150
9 p.
Typescript.

The genealogy and history of the Bruns families of Portland Me. & vicinity & Brons families of the west coast 1819-1954 giving the descendants of Jens Nielsen Bruns [and others].
McCann, Kenneth S. (Kenneth Sutherland), b. 1893.
G BRU 3625
104 p.
1954
Typescript.

Genealogy and history of the Portland Me. Bruns families including the Brons variation in Denmark and America 1739-1956 ... a new issue
McCann, Kenneth S. (Kenneth Sutherland), b. 1893.
G BRU 3627
14, 194, 5 p.
1956
Typescript.

Brush and others families included Barbour Beeler Brown Conkling Corey Crispel...
Brush, Grace L.
G BRU 3838
Various pagings.
1930
Typescript.

Bruyn family of Ulster County New York
Roney, Lila James.
G BRU 4800
2, 84 p.
Typescript.

Ancestry of Myrtle Palfrey Brumby including families of Cossitt Du Bose Gates Gorham Howland McKerall Murphy Palfrey Wall Winans
Brumby, Myrtle Palfrey.
G BRU 825
23 p.
1960
Typescript.

Descendants of David Bryant of Bristol Maine
Hatch, Frederick A.
G BRY 216
15 p.
Typescript.

Copy of Bible records of the family of Nathaniel Bryant of Scituate, Mass.
Bryant, Percy.
G BRY 240
6 p.
1928
Typescript.

A historical and genealogical record of Lawrence Bryant and Pattie Sessoms' five other sons of Nash County North Carolina
Bryant, Lawrence Chesterfield.
G BRY 264
iv, 144 p.
1968
Typescript.

Bryan wills and deeds with genealogical notes
Brien, Lindsay M. (Lindsay Metcalfe)
G BRY 40
5, 114, 1 p.
Typescript.

Ancestor Thomas Bryeryhurst of Bowdoin Me. and descendants
Sinnett, Charles Nelson, 1847-1928.
G BRY 475
10 p.
1923
Typescript.

John Neely and Margaret Beeman Bryan of Dallas Texas
Cockrell, Monroe F. (Monroe Fulkerson), b. 1884.
G BRY 80
9 p.
c1961
Typescript.

Pedigree of Sir John Bucke
Buck, George.
G BUC 100
5 p.
1646
Typescript.

Genealogy of the family of Philander Buck
Buck, George M.
G BUC 124
106 p.
1907
Typescript.

Descendants of William Buckingham of Chester Co. Pa.
Whitcomb, William Arthur, 1873-1946.
G BUC 288
20 p.
Typescript.

Bonnell - Buckingham family additions to Buckingham genealogy [G BUC 288]
Hollingshead, Margaret B.R.
G BUC 288A
Typescript.

Squire Bucklin of Foster R.I. his ancestors back to William Hingham Buckland of Hingham Mass. 1635 and his descendants
Cooper, Hattie B.
G BUC 350
45, 5 p.
1944
Typescript.

Buecher family history Millstadt St. Clair County Illinois 1734-1971
Buecher, Robert.
G BUE 70
112 p.
1971
Typescript.

Partial record of the Buffum family in New England
Buffum, Charles Hudson.
G BUF 10
4, 171, 13 p.
1910
Typescript.

Record of some of the descendants of Edward Bugby who settled in Roxbury Mass. in 1634
Bugbee, Edwin Holmes, 1820-1900.
G BUG 25
4, 17 p.
1877
Typescript.

Descendants of Captain Thomas Bull (1610-1684) original proprietor of Hartford Connecticut
Pope, Virginia Buell, 1903-.
G BUL 144
1, 17 p.
1939
Typescript.

An outline of the descendants of Captain Thomas Buell (1610-1684) of Hartford Connecticut
Pope, Virginia Buell, 1903-.
G BUL 148
28 p.
1962
Typescript.

History of the Thomas Bulla family
G BUL 175
3 p.
Typescript.

A genealogy of the ancestors and descendants of Charles Bulfinch famous architect of Boston Massachusetts 1640 to 1964
Diem, Francis Ernest.
G BUL 24
27 p.
1964
Typescript.

A Bullard family including Fisher Pond Jones Rockwood Corey Richmond Chamberlain Edson Hathaway Newton etc.
Krechniak Helen Bullard, 1902-.
G BUL 250
74, 1, 4 p.
1966
Typescript.

The Bullock story
Bullock, Joseph Floyd.
G BUL 375
16 p.
1963
Typescript.

Bulkeley notes [Rev. Edward Bulkeley born at Woore Shropshire 1550]
Holman, Mary Campbell (Lovering), 1868-1947.
G BUL 58
17 p.
1928
Typescript.

The Bumpus family
Bumpus, H.C.
G BUM 250
Various pagings.
Typescript.

The Bumstead family
Brook, Hazel P.
G BUM 375
13 p.
Typescript.

Bundys in America [John Bundy of Plymouth Mass. 1635 Boston 1643 Taunton 1665]
Driscoll, Marion Lang.
G BUN 1300
29 p.
1947
Typescript.

The Bunker family
Bunker, Charles Waite Orville.
G BUN 1630
7 p.
Typescript.

Ancestry of William Jenkins Bunker 1795-1875 - Bunker Jenkins & allied families
Matthews, Nathan Jr.
G BUN 1640
16, 7 p.
1882
Typescript.

Extracts from the Proceedings of the Bunker Family Association of America...
Bunker Family Association of America.
G BUN 1674
20 p.
1931-1933
Typescript.

Report of a genealogical excursion into Canada and Maine ... Oct. 3-8 1933 ... [Bunker family]
Bunker, Paul D.
G BUN 1690
6 p.
1933
Typescript.

Bunker address book
Bunker, O.L.
G BUN 1705
1945
Typescript.

Bunker family history and genealogy
Bunker, O.L.
G BUN 1707
1, 92, 27 p.
1945
Typescript.

The Bunnell family [William Bunnell of New Haven Conn.]
G BUN 2180
Various pagings.
Typescript.

A record of the Bunnell family our branch...
McAvoy, Mary Jane Bunnell.
G BUN 2185
16 p.
1894-1911
Typescript.

The ancestors and descendants of Havilah and Dorcas Gale Bunnell
Andrews, Adele, 1902-.
G BUN 2190
83 p.
1936
Typescript.

Buntin lineage (Bunten and Bunton)
Holman, Winifred Lovering, 1899-1989.
G BUN 2255
29 p.
1931
Typescript.

Burdick - Tucker - Pope 1630-1932 ancestral lines
Pope, Russell Howard, 1894-.
G BUR 1086
27, 1 p.
1932
Typescript.

Supplement to descendants of Robert Burdick of Rhode Island
Johnson, Nellie Willard, b. 1875.
G BUR 1088A
231 p.
1953
Typescript.

Genealogy of Burt (or Burtt) family residing in northeastern Mass. and southern N.H. and some descendants elsewhere
Burt, Richard Bartlett.
G BUR 12484
8, 9 p.
1930
Typescript.

Burger Joris 1612-1671
Flint, Martha Bockee, 1841-1900.
G BUR 1660
6 p.
1897
Typescript.

Burgess lineage
Holman, Winifred Lovering, 1899-1989.
G BUR 1697
5, 95 p.
1957-1958
Typescript.

Burgess lineage for Mrs. Farnsworth Loomis
Holman, Winifred Lovering, 1899-1989.
G BUR 1697
Typescript, 94 p.
1958

A history and genealogy of Isaac and Sarah Burgess
Nielsen, Eugene Jay.
G BUR 1699
2, 100 p.
1961
Typescript.

Burgess genealogy ... from ... Thomas Burgess at Sandwich, Massachusetts ... the common progenitor ... to Ella Maude Burgess Cobleigh born ... 1885 ...
Cobleigh, Arthur Monroe.
G BUR 1701
1, 121, 4 p.
1964
Typescript.

The Burbeck family
Burbeck, Allan Beal.
G BUR 210
29, 85, 3 p.
1959
Typescript.

The Burbeck family
Baltzer, Madelon Burbeck.
Burbeck, Allan Beal.
G BUR 210
29, 85, 3 p.
1959
Typescript.

The Burkett story
G BUR 2240
39 p.
Typescript.

Descendants of Jehu Burket ...
Burkett, John Martin, 1876-.
G BUR 2250
1, 10 p.
1940
Typescript.

Genealogical notes on the lines of Hon. Micajah Currier Burleigh and his wife Mary Frances Russell ... with a sketch of Hon. John Holmes Burleigh his younger brother
Boyer, Charlotte Russell Burleigh.
G BUR 2420
246 p.
1928
Typescript.

Notes for revision of the Burley genealogy brought down to 1894
Burleigh, Charles, b. 1855.
G BUR 2725A
1894
Typescript.

Dr. William Burnet and his sons Jacob Isaac and David a chart of their forefathers and descendants in America 1640-1938
Burnet, Isabella Neff, 1885-.
G BUR 3715
c1938
Typescript.

War records and experiences beginning with World War 2 of the Burnet and Neff kin
Burnet, Isabella Neff, 1885-.
G BUR 3717
33, 4 p.
1953
Typescript.

Burnett genealogical data. Report of the genealogical records committee District of Columbia D.A.R.
G BUR 3925
156, 6 p.
1951-1952
Typescript.

Robert Burnham the emigrant who settled at Dover N.H. and his descendants
G BUR 4248
10 p.
Typescript.

Asa Burnham [1787-1875]. Biographical sketches diaries descendants ...
G BUR 4275
28 p.
1945
Typescript.

Some descendants of Josiah and Margaret (Wood) Burnham of Montague, Mass. whose branch [was] not included in the pub. geneal. of Thomas Burnham of Hartford Conn.
Stoughton, Ralph M.
G BUR 4280
178 p.
1950
Typescript.

A short history and partial genealogy of the Burpee family in America
Burpee, John S.
G BUR 4830
Various pagings.
1950
Typescript.

Descendants of Jerusha Beardsley Burr and John Burr Erie Co. Ohio ...
Weeks, Frank Edgar, 1857-1946.
G BUR 4985
3 p.
1932
Typescript.

Burchard or Birchard genealogy
Burchard, Nathan.
G BUR 550
1876-1887
Blueprint.

Dr. John Henry Burchsted of Lynn Mass. and his descendants
Alexander, Winthrop, 1861-1941.
G BUR 650
59 p.
1924
Typescript.

Burdakin family ... some of the descendants of James ... who settled in New Bedford about 1785
Barker, John Herbert, 1870-1951.
G BUR 850
40 p.
1928
Typescript.

Genealogy family of Bushnell Francis in N.E. 1643 Guilford, Connecticut
Porter, George S.
G BUS 1750
7 p.
Typescript.

Some Bushnell genealogical records contained in letters from Geo. E. Bushnell of Cookeville Tenn. to Clarence A. Torrey of Dorchester Mass. Apr. 1937
Bushnell, George Eleazer, 1873-1945.
G BUS 1765
7 p.
1937
Typescript.

Buswell records
G BUS 31
1969
Typescript.

Descendants of Thomas Buttolph of Boston Mass. genealogy in preparation
Eldridge, William H. (William Henry), 1873-1943.
G BUT 1008
2, 48 p.
Typescript.

The Butler genealogy [descendants of Eleazer ... from the files of the "Yarmouth Herald" of November 1 and 8 1898]
Brown, George S.
G BUT 20
11 p.
1898
Typescript.

An account of some of the descendants of Robert Butt of the southern branch of the Elizabeth River in the county of lower Norfolk Virginia
Butt, Marshall Kingfield.
G BUT 270
1957
Typescript.

Descendants of John and Ralph Butler of Essex Mass. Nathaniel Butler of Newburyport Mass. Philip and John Butler of Newburyport and Lieut. Wm. of Ipswich and Butler families of Essex Salem Marblehead and Danvers
G BUT 3
Various pagings.
Typescript.

Benjamin Butterfield and descendants
G BUT 395
3, 2 p.
Typescript.

Butterfield notes [Benjamin Butterfield b. probably in England about 1610 died in Chelmsford Mass. 1661]
Holman, Mary Campbell (Lovering), 1868-1947.
G BUT 428
7 p.
1928
Typescript.

One branch of the Butterfield family in America
Carlson, June H.
G BUT 432
7, 4 p.
1941
Typescript.

Descendants of Clement Moore Butler D.D. ...
Falkner, Roland Post, 1866-.
G BUT 50
34 p.
1933
Typescript.

Brief Buxton notes
Holman, Winifred Lovering, 1899-1989.
G BUX 110
1, 10 p.
1949
Typescript.

Byam family [George Byam of Salem 1640]
G BYA 1
6 p.
Typescript.

The ancestors of Mylo Newton Byington and Susan Eliza Ann (Throop) Byington with some notes regarding related families ... list of descendants
Smalley, H.R.
G BYI 4
1, 45 p.
1931
Typescript.

Title*Byrne and Kelly notes*
Byrne, Daniel, Mrs.
G BYR 625
94 p.
1968

Callender [family of Bristol County, Mass.]
Holman, Mary Lovering, 1868-1947.
G CAL 4625
Typescript.
1928

Genealogical notes on the families of Ellis and George Callender of Boston, Mass., and John Callender of Rehoboth and Attleborough, Mass.
Holman, Mary Campbell (Lovering), 1868-1947.
G CAL 4625
22 p. + iv.
1928
Typescript.

Extracts concerning the Carter family from the parish registers of Hinderclay, which commence 1568 [baptisms, marriages, burials.]
G CAR 10293
Typescript.

Carpenter lineage
Holman, Winifred Lovering, 1899-1989.
G CAR 6397
181p.
1960
Typescript.

Job Caswell (b. 1766) and his wife Theodora Godfrey of Taunton, Mass., and Poland, Maine, some of whose children settled in Warren and Windsor, Maine, and Boston, Mass., etc.
Adams, Charles F.
G CAS 5530
8 p.
1958
Typescript.

Sidney Edwards and Elizabeth B. (Miller) Chase's descendants
Maly, George J., Mrs.
G CHA 12461
16 p.
Typescript.

Champlin Memorial: a record of the descendants of Geoffrey Champlin of Newport, R.I., in 1638, and of Westerly in 1661
Champlin, John D.
G CHA 5870
1903?
Typescript.

The house of Champlin: by one of the sons
Champlin, Frederick D.
G CHA 5880
1933
Typescript.

Duxbury Chandler notes
Holman, Winifred Lovering, 1899-1989.
G CHA 7256
Typescript, 20p.
1930
Typescript.

A sketch of the history and genealogy of the Chipman family (particularly the branch which is settled in Nova Scotia) descended from John Chipman
Gordon, G. S.
G CHI 4541
1 + 10 + 3 p.
1907
Typewritten from mss. of 1832.

The Clark family tree: continuation of ancestry of Mary Foster, generation 12, Perley chart A ...
Lempert, Leon H.
G CLA 1509A
20 charts.
1931
Typescript.

William Coddington (1603-1678), governor of Rhode Island. Bound with a correction and an addition.
Morrison, J. H.
G COD 8
4 p. + 2 p.
Typescript.

Colby data: Maine families, miscellaneous notes
Calder, Philip R.
G COL 70
1932
Typescript.

A copy of the complete list of the name of Cole found in Bristol County [Mass.] probate records
Cole, Harriet D.
G COL 908
7 p.
1928
Typescript.

One branch of the Colby family
Colby, Eugene C.
G COL 96
3 + 34 p.
1900-1950
Typescript.

Combes of Warwickshire
G COM 75
Typescript.

The family of Shubael Conant of Connecticut
Conant, William Shubael.
G CON 31
1945
Typescript.

Coray and Lusk family history
Weeks, Jennie Noel, 1902-
G COR 310
1960
Typescript.

The Cossart family
Cossairt, Joseph Arthur.
G COS 220
4 + 90 p.
1935
Typescript.

Crockett family of New England, 1632-1943. Isaac Crockett of Fox Islands, Penobscot Bay, and some of his family
Crockett, Leon O., b. 1882.
G CRO 120; G CRO 125
7 p.; 11 p.
1949; 1950
Typescript.

Ancestors of Ella Fuchs (Baird) Burdakin, widow of Henry Gilbert Burdakin. Crosby family
Barker, John Herbert, 1870-1951.
G CRO 1450
Typescript.

The Cromwellian Crowells and allied families, traditions and genealogy
Crosby, Lillian Crowell.
G CRO 5048
Typescript.

Higgins Crowell deeds and estates, Barnstable County probate
Lewis, S. A., Mrs.
G CRO 5057
6 p.
Typescript.

Daby - Dorby data. [Thomas Derby of Stow, Mass.]
G DAB 1025, 1025A
430 p.
1963, 1967
Typescript.

Our family: Daly - Sullivan, Callaghan - McAnally, Christian - Virden, Juelfs - Wagner
Cosgrove, T. B., Mrs.
G DAL 3120
47 + 1 p.
Typescript.

Genealogical record of Marion Adelaide Morse Davis
G DAV 2018
Typescript.

Samuel Dean of Jamaica, Long Island
Holman, Winifred Lovering, 1899-1989.
G DEA 895
34 p.
1927
Typescript.

The Dennis line compiled for Mrs. S. Westray Battle of Asheville, NC.
Holman, Winifred Lovering, 1899-1989.
G DEW
51 p.
1943
Typescript.

Dunham manuscript genealogy
Young, Lizzie (Conant).
G DUN 2632
11 + 2 p.
1931
Typescript.

Dunn family records: descendants of Joseph of England
Gildersleeve, Jessie A. (Reynolds).
G DUN 4410
2 p.
1929
Typescript.

Dunsmoor notes, compiled for Mrs. Homer Pierce Clark
Holman, Winifred Lovering, 1899-1989.
G DUN 5700
85 p.
1959
Typescript.

Dunton family: will of John [Dunton] of St. Dunstan, Stepney, co. Middlesex, England, 1744
Dunton, John.
G DUN 6550
27 p.
Typescript.

Eveleth family
Holman, Winifred Lovering, 1899-1989.
G EVE 15
5 p.
1957
Typescript.

Farmer notes, compiled for Frank W. Abrams, Esquire
Holman, Winifred Lovering, 1899-1989.
G FAR 1088
42 p.
1960
Typescript.

Thomas Farr of Harpswell, Maine, and his descendants
Sinnett, Charles Nelson, 1847-1928.
G FAR 2812
30 p.
1923
Typescript.

The Farr genealogy, with index to the names
Sinnett, Charles Nelson, 1847-1928.
G FAR 2818
137 p.
1929
Typescript.

Genealogy of one line of the Fish families whose ancestors settled in the state of Connecticut about 1651, or possibly earlier,
Ames, J.M., (Jennie M.), b. 1869.
G FIS 110
"2 p. 1, 30 (i.e. 33) numb. 1, 3 l."
1941
Typescript.

Robert Fletcher of Concord, Massachusetts, 1637. A study of his life and family from the New England records, compiled for Henry Fletcher, Esquire of New York City
Holman, Winifred Lovering, 1899-1989.
G FLE 242
77 p.
1930
Typescript.

Forbes of Monymusk and Pitsligo, 1460-1880
Forbes, Louisa Lillias.
G FOR 28
1 v.; 88 x 88 cm.
1880
Chart bound into a volume.

Foskits of Staffordville, Conn. and their New England ancestry
Chapman, Grace Olive.
G FOS 50
26 p.
1943
Typescript.

An historical sketch and genealogical record of the Fowlers of Milford, Conn.
Fowler, John W.
G FOW 260B
5 p.
1887

Francis, Frances, Ffrancis, Ffranciss, family records from the Barbour Collection of Connecticut vital records, 1634-1868, for the town of Wethersfield
G FRA 2718
"p. 109-114."
Typescript.

Copies of records of the Franklin family, taken from the parish registers of the parishes of Offwell and Widworthy, Devon, England
G FRA 4360
6 p.
Typescript.

French lineage
Holman, Winifred Lovering, 1899-1989.
G FRE 6191
174 p.
1955
Typescript.

Some of the descendants of Thomas Fuller of Dedham, Mass.
Fuller, Stephen Palmer.
G FUL 262
7 p.
1892
Typescript.

Descendants of Edward Fuller of the Mayflower, 1620-1929
Riker, Mignonette de la Force, M.
G FUL 326
8 p.
1929
Typescript.

Fuller notes, compiled for Miss. C.M.C. Clark, 1945
Holman, Winifred Lovering, 1899-1989.
G FUL 340
18 p.
1945
Typescript.

William 1st and his children; court records, deeds, land grants
Furbish, Frederick Baker.
G FUR 50
119 p.
Typescript.

Gage genealogy: descendants of Thomas
Harwood, Olive Harriet.
G GAG 20
7 p.
1922
Typescript.

Some descendants of Abraham Gates of Ashby, Mass.
G GAT 60
8 p.
Typescript.

Pedigree of Gavey of Mausant, St. Saviours, Jersey
Curtis, S. Carey.
G GAV 62
Chart, 45 x 42 cm.
1932

Pedigrees concerning the ancestry of Frederick Lewis Gay, b. 1856
Gay, Frederick Lewis, 1856-1916.
G GAY 38
Typescript.

John Geib and his seven children
Gildersleeve, Alger C.
G GEI 5
23 p.
1945
Typescript.

Gerry genealogy: descendants of Thomas
G GER 575
11 p.
Typescript.

Gifford - Mitchell family record
Casebeer, Harriet
G GIF 215
1959
Typescript.

Gilman notes, compiled for Albert Boyden
Holman, Winifred Lovering, 1899-1989.
G GIL 1192; G GIL 1212
37 p.; 24 p.
1927; 1961
Typescript.

John Gillett [and descendants]
Brainerd, Homer W.
G GIL 765
6 p.
Typescript.

Peter Ginther's family. [Descendants of Peter Ginther, 1740-1814.] WITH [Supplement 1] Elizabeth Billman. [Supplement 2] W. T. Fry
Stewart, Jennie Elizabeth, b. 1878.
G GIN 850, 850A
208 p. + xvii
1938
Typescript.

Gist family: descendants of Christopher
Cockey, Charles J.
G GIS 340
10 p.
1884
Typescript.

Gleason family history
Truesdell, Miriam Gleason.
G GLE 300
23 p.
1900
Typescript.

Glover and related families: the ancestry of Laura Jane Glover
Arthur, Robert
G GLO 330; G GLO 330A, 330B
7 + 88 p.
1952; 1955; 1957
Typescript. Pt. 1 lineage, Pt. 2 American family.

Glover cousins: a chart index of the some of the descendants of Colonel Joseph Glover (1719-1785) and Anne Wilson (Doughty) (1730-1807)
McConnell, Richard B.
G GLO 335
88 + 25 p.
1965
Typescript.

Record of the Goehring family, descended from Wolfgang Wilhelm Goehring, born about 1638 in Albisheim, Germany
Goehring, John M.
G GOE 200
26 p.
1911
Typescript.

Goelet (Jacobus) who came to New York in 1676, with descendants to 1911
G GOE 375
Chart 40.5 x 52.1 cm.

Going family: descendants of Robert of Lynn, Mass.
Bolton, Ethel Stanwood, 1873-1954.
G GOI 124
Typescript.

Golds of West Stafford, Connecticut and their New England ancestry
Chapman, Grace Olive.
G GOL 324
29 p.
1943
Typescript.

Goldsmith family records copied from an old book belonging to Judge Harry H. Atwood of Worcester, Mass.
Sawyer, Edward Everett, Mrs.
G GOL 605
2 p.
1942
Typescript.

Gooch notes: original copy [more complete than in The Stevens-Miller Ancestry, vol. 2]
Holman, Winifred Lovering, 1899-1989.
G GOO 105A
23 p.
1952
Typescript.

Additions to THE GOODRICH FAMILY IN AMERICA by Lafayette Wallace Case, M.D. (1889), from the fly-leaf of Goodrich family of Minerva Delinda Goodrich (#1689)
Case, Lafayette Wallace, b. 1845.
G GOO 1724A
1 + 3 p.
Typescript.

Certified copy of Goodwin and Perkins family records, as found in the Bibles of Lovina A. Goodwin Clowe of Columbus, Ohio, and Charles A. Perkins of Hoopeston, Illinois
G GOO 2250
5 p.
1930
Typescript.

Daniel Goodwin vs. Daniel Goodwin: a study of conflicting claims made in application papers submitted to the National Society, Sons of the American Revolution
Patten, C. Wesley.
G GOO 2252
1 + 86 + 11 p (8 p. folded).
1939
Typescript.

The Goodwin genealogy, 1665-1942. Descents of Elizabeth Edith Goodwin of Epping, N.H., 1942, from Edward Goodwin, Philip Fowler, George Martin, and others
G GOO 2254
1942
Typescript.

History of the Goold family of Hull, Massachusetts, Lyme, Connecticut, Orleans County, N.Y., Jackson County, Mich., Los Angeles County, Calif.
Goold, Harriet.
G GOO 2733
8 + 1 p.
Typescript.

Rev. Leonard Stillman Goodell of Staffordville, Tolland County, Conn., his ancestors, descendants and some other relatives
Chapman, Grace Olive.
G GOO 710
90 p.
1942
Typescript.

Genealogy of Gordon family taken from family Bible of Benoni Gordon (marriage Sept. 10, 1807)
G GOR 268
4 p.
Typescript.

Noah Grant (President Grant's grandfather): his forebears and family
Hook, James W. (James William), 1884-1957.
G GRA 1245
26 p.
1951
Typescript.

The Graves families of Maine
Sinnett, Charles Nelson, 1847-1928.
G GRA 1400
32 p.
1922
Typescript.

Genealogy of William Gray (1722-1778) of Barrington, N.H., son of James Gray, who was stationed at Her Majesty's Fort William and Mary, Newcastle, N.H., in July, 1708
Gray, Irving H.
G GRA 1563
1 + 24 p.
Typescript.

Genealogical record of the Gray and allied families, including Leland, Brockway and Holmes
G GRA 1568
8 p.
Typescript.

Record of the Gray family, taken from Mass. vital records
Gray, Norman Clay
G GRA 1608
1918
Typescript.

Ancestors and descendants of Eli and Simeon Gray. Compiled for the Gray Family Association
Gray, Norman Clay
Gray Family Association.
G GRA 1618
16 p.
1941
Typescript.

Jonas Latham Gray and his wife Lucy Spicer Gray: their ancestors, their descendants
Williams, Garford Flavel.
G GRA 1628
24 p.
1956
Typescript.

Our Gray line bulletin. [Vol. 2, no. 2.]
Gray Family Association.
G GRA 1640
1963
Typescript.

Ancestors and descendants of John Calvin Gray, 1841-1930, and his wife Ruth Ellen Patterson, 1846-1912
Bloom, Raymond Roll.
G GRA 1652
5 + 61 p.
1971
Typescript.

Lineage of Martha Young Graham, National No. 123742, from Robert Millions, from Joseph Waterhouse, Sr., from Capt. Caleb Graffam, and from Joseph Waterhouse, Jr.
G GRA 606
4 p.
Typescript.

Graham family records
Seaver, J. Montgomery (Jesse Montgomery), b. 1890.
G GRA 623
"2 p. l., 3-101 p."
1929
Typescript.

The Graham family of Virginia. [Descendants of Christopher Graham, d. 1744/1745, of Virginia.]
Barr, Lockwood Anderson, b. 1883.
G GRA 642
7 p.
1948
Typescript.

The genealogy of the Grahame family with some of their descendants
Thompson, Henry Graham.
G GRA 650
11 p.
1864
Typescript.

The Greegor family, history and directory, Jacob Bocher Greeger branch
Greegor, R. D.
G GRE 155, 155A
14 p. (1932). 14 p. (1933).
1932, 1933
Typescript.

English genealogical notes on the parentage of Robert Greenough of Rowley, Mass.
Lubbe, George Anthony, Mrs.
G GRE 1970
9 p.
1928
Typescript.

Greenough: Robert Greenough of Rowley, Massachusetts, 16__-1718, and his descendants
Priest, Alice L. (Alice Lucinda), 1866-1954.
G GRE 1974
17 p.
1931
Typescript.

Greeley genealogy: compiled from genealogy by George H. Greeley (Greele - Greely and Greeley, 1905)
Cordley, Henry Gridley.
G GRE 237
2 + 12 p.
1940

Greathouse family: a history. [Descendants of Harmon Greathouse, 1676-1743]
Nelson, Mary Alice Winters Greathouse.
G GRE 25
23 p.
1949
Typescript.

The Greer family from County Down, Ireland, to America 1818
Ashcraft, Walter E., Mrs.
G GRE 2818
6 p.
Typescript.

Gregg - NH. Part 1: autobiography of Samuel Gregg (1739-1808). Part 2: addenda to section I. Notes on Hugh Gregg of New Boston; section II notes on descendants of Capt. James Gregg of Londonderry
Holman, Winifred Lovering, 1899-1989.
G GRE 2949
2 + 11 + 5 p.
1933
Typescript.

Some Gregg lines
Arthur, Robert
G GRE 2961, 2961A
1 + 42 p (1952), 1 + 55 p. (1958).
1952, 1958
Typescript.

Some Gregg records: records of birth, marriages and deaths, etc., of the members of Fairfax Monthly Meeting at Waterford, Loudon County, Virginia, from 1740 to 1880
Marine, Harriet.
G GRE 2966
29 + 2 p.
1963
Typescript.

Gregg [family] ·
Arthur, Robert
G GRE 2968
1964
Typescript.

Maternal ancestors of Katherine Mills, Bertha Louise, Lucy Garrison, William and Dorothy Green of 2501 R Street, Lincoln, Nebraska
G GRE 530
Typescript.

Dr. Ezra Green (1746-1847): genealogical notes
Wood, Robert Fellows, b. 1883.
G GRE 603
3 p.
1940
Typescript.

The Green family, dynasty of printers: the descendants of Bartholomew and Elizabeth Green of Cambridge, Mass., through seven generations, extending to Connecticut, Vermont, New Hampshire, Nova Scotia, Maryland and Virginia
Kiessel, William C.
G GRE 608
29 p.
1949
Typescript.

Green notes: original copy, more complete than given in the printed version in vol. 2 of The Stevens-Miller Ancestry
Holman, Winifred Lovering, 1899-1989.
G GRE 613A
23 p.
1952
Typescript.

The Greene family of Watauga, and family Bible record of John Henry and Sarah Ellen Moore of Mt. Jackson, Virginia
Greene, G. W.
G GRE 640
13 p.
Typescript.

Greene family record: children and grandchildren of Jonathan (b. 1776) and Catharine (Bentley) Greene of Saratoga Co. and Rush, N.Y.
G GRE 648
2 p.
Typescript.

The Greene family in England
Greene, Howard, 1864-1956.
G GRE 700
1 + 21 p.
1941
Typescript.

The Greene family of Ryal Side, Beverly - Salem, Mass.
Greene, Harriet Frances.
G GRE 705
11 p.
1946
Typescript.

The Grinnell family
G GRI 1000
3 p.
1902
Clippings from Taunton Herald News, Sept. 3, 1902.

Griffin's journal: index of names and places
Griffin, Charles Francis.
G GRI 200A
1934
Typewritten index to Augustus Griffin's journal, published in 1857.

Notes on the Griffins of Ipswich and Annisquam, from different sources
Davis, Arthur F.
G GRI 230, 230A
26 p.
1932, 1941
Typescript.

Memorials of Paul Griffith and his wife Margaret Burden, of Nelson, Madison County, N.Y., with an account of some of their descendants
White, Minnie L.
G GRI 470
2, 8, 1 leaves
1943
Typescript.

Descendants and known ancestors of William Jerry and Henrietta Harmon (Lybarger) Grimwood; maternal grandparents of Henrietta Jones Darby.
Darby, Henrietta (Jones), b. 1895.
G GRI 970
33 p.
1963
Typescript.

The genealogy of Jefferson C. Grinnalds
Grinnalds, Jefferson C.
G GRI 990
Typescript.

The Grinnell family
G GRI 995
9 p.
Typescript.

*Notes on the Groat family: reprints and clippings
from Boston Evening Transcript, July 5, 11-12,
November 22, 1935*
Groat, B. F.
G GRO 100
6 p.
1935
Typescript.

*Genealogical notes of Isaac Gross and his
descendants*
Spear, Maud E. (Maud Elsie Harris), 1890-1974.
G GRO 960
7 p.
1957
Typescript.

Grubb family ... reunion at Saratoga Park ...
G GRU 34
5 p.
1910
Mounted clippings from "News," Pottstown,
Pennsylvania.

*The descendants of Abraham Tourtelotte Andrews
and his wife Miranda Lurinda Guild*
Shiner, Harry Lawrence.
G GUI 118
1918
Typescript.

*Descendants of Hendrick Gulick, born about
1678*
Huntley, Helen Gulick.
G GUL 488
2 + 21 p.
Typescript.

One line of Guptill descent
Barlow, Claude W., (Claude Willis), 1907-1976.
G GUP 60
9 p.
1963
Typescript.

*Early ministry on the Kennebec: Robert Gutch,
the pioneer, and some descendants*
Thayer, Henry Otis, b. 1832.
G GUT 75
24 p.
1895
Paper read before Maine Historical Society, 22
November 1895.

Hadley genealogy: descendants of Anthony
Bucknam, Wilton Francis, 1861-1917.
G HAD 1935
98 p.
Typescript.

*Hadley: descendants of George Hadley of
Ipswich, Mass., and especially of his great-
grandson, Samuel Hadley of Massachusetts and
New Hampshire*
Priest, Alice L. (Alice Lucinda), 1866-1954.
G HAD 1952
21 p.
1932
Typescript.

*Biographical sketches of Rev. Joseph B. Hadden
and others, his relatives*
Baker, Nathan Martin.
G HAD 575
Typescript.

*Haines genealogical data: also Lamb, and some
Rangeley Plantation, Maine, marriages*
Lamb, Frances A.
G HAI 645
3 p.
1951
Typescript.

*Descendants of William Haliburton and Lusanna
(Otis) Haliburton of Nova Scotia*
Weis, Robert Lewis
G HAL 1060
25 p.
1967
Typescript.

*The Halls of Fairfield County, Connecticut:
Francis and Elizabeth Hall, the immigrant
ancestors of 1639 and their descendants*
Hall, David Brainard, b. 1812.
G HAL 1218
122 p.
Typescript.

*Rev. David Hall (August 6, 1704 - May 8, 1789):
selections from his diary (November 5, 1740 -
February 21, 1789), sermons; some of his
ancestors and descendants*
Kent, Daniel.
G HAL 1267
1 + 27 p.
1902
Typescript.

*Hall family of Connecticut: descendants of John
of New Haven and Wallingford, Conn.*
Browne, William Bradford, b. 1875.
G HAL 1289
4 p.
1921
Typescript.

*Hall genealogy: families of Taunton, Mass.,
Suffield, Stafford and Somers, Conn.*
Kibbee, James Allen.
G HAL 1295, 1295A
5 p.
1929
Typescript. [1295A is a negative photostat copy.]

A Hall genealogy
Hall, Frank Nelson, 1902-.
G HAL 1366
3 + 32 p.
1965
Typescript.

*Genealogy of a portion of the Halladay family of
Suffield, Connecticut, and Marlboro, Vermont*
Wheeler, Daniel M.
G HAL 1500
55 p.
1901
Typescript.

*A branch of the Hallett - Messer family of
Belgrade and West Waterville, now Oakland,
Maine*
Demers, Mabel Gould.
G HAL 1599
8 p.
Typescript.

Halley family notes
McPike, Eugene Fairfield, b. 1870.
G HAL 1750
11 p.
1902
Typescript.

*Hale, Houghton, Morrison and Brocklebank
families: the ancestry of Addie Jane Hale (Mrs.
William A. Robinson), with maternal line of Mr.
William A. Robinson*
Robinson, (Addie Jane Hale)
G HAL 386
1932
Typescript.

Hamlin (Hamblin) family
Clemmer, Virginia Rowe.
G HAM 1336
37 p.
1967
Typescript with annotations.

*Benjamin Hammatt and some of his descendants,
1712-1903*
Rogers, George Edward.
G HAM 1900
25 p. + pp. 27-46 (additions, 1929, by W. L.
Holman)
1904, 1929
Typescript.

*Records from the Hamblett Bible, published in
1841 at Cooperstown, N.Y.*
G HAM 250
4 p.
Typescript.

*Hammon Bible records: family of Thomas (b.
1737) and Alice (b. 1738), his wife*
Claypool, Edward A., 1854-1916.
G HAM 3100
5 p.
Typescript transcription.

*Genealogy of the Hamel family of Amherst,
Lorain County, Ohio*
Hamel, Claude Charles.
G HAM 420
Various pagings.
1951
Typescript.

*David (Dick) Hamilton of the Bathgate family and
some of his descendants*
Eaton, Arthur Wentworth Hamilton, 1849-1937.
G HAM 512
1884-1905
Typescript.

*Genealogy of Mary Gore (Child) Hamlen of
Augusta, Maine*
Hamlen, Mary Gore (Child).
G HAM 710
21 p.
1934
Typescript.

*The genealogies of the Hanscom family and the
Libbey family*
G HAN 1200
45 p.
Typescript.

Hanson family of Windham, Me.
Goold, Nathan, 1846-1914.
G HAN 1260
11 p.
1899
Newspaper clippings, mounted.

*Handy family: descendants of Richard of
Sandwich, Mass.*
Lewis, Ella May Swint, b. 1877.
G HAN 500
14 p.
1925
Typescript.

*The Hank family (Pennsylvania, Virginia, and
West Virginia)*
Rudolph, Myra Hank.
G HAN 700
14 p.
1930
Mounted newspaper clippings

The Hanks family of Maryland
Chidsey, A. D., Jr.
G HAN 703
22 p.
1932
Typescript.

Hart family genealogy
Carley, William H., Sr.
G HAR 10505
19 p.
Typescript.

*Descendants of Noble Augustus Hartshorn, b.
1843... and his wife, Mary Susan Yinger, b. 1844*
Shiner, Harry Lawrence.
G HAR 10800
5 p.
1918
Typescript.

Haring, 1660; Herring, 1650 families
Ackerman, Herbert Stewart, b. 1875.
G HAR 1115
257 p.
1952
Typescript.

*A line of Harwoods by families, and excerpts from
the will of John James of Goshen, Mass.*
Scholl, John William.
G HAR 14518
7 + 5 p.
Typescript.

*James and Nancy Gray Harkness; a colonial
family history, 1700 to 1850*
Michaels, Paul Wallace, b. 1905.
G HAR 1550
18 leaves.
1953
Typescript.

*A record of Sergeant William Harlow, the pioneer
of the Harlow family in America, and some of his
ancestors*
Harlow, Louise Denton.
G HAR 2004
19 p.
1902, 1912
Typescript.

Brief Harmon notes
Holman, Winifred Lovering, 1899-1989.
G HAR 2236
1 + 6 p.
1949
Typescript.

Henry Harper of Randolph County, Virginia
Grant, Howard B.
G HAR 2523
19 p.
1934
Typescript.

*Harrington family, early settlers in Otsego
County, New York*
G HAR 2890
4 p.
Typescript.

*Corp. Benjamin Harrington of Enfield,
Connecticut, and Blandford, Massachusetts*
Priest, Alice L. (Alice Lucinda), 1866-1954.
G HAR 2896
5 p.
Typescript.

*Miscellaneous notes of the Harrimans of
Bucksport, Maine, and vicinity*
G HAR 2965
17 p.
Typescript.

*The descendants of Robert Harrington, who
settled Watertown, Massachusetts, in 1642*
Harrington, Valentine F.
G HAR 3065
1939
Typescript.

*The descendants of Dr. John Harrington (1752-
1802) [and his wife Deborah Wakefield] of
Brookfield, Vt, including his lineage from the
original American immigrant*
Harrington, Charles A.
G HAR 3092
87 p.
1961
Typescript.

*Vital records of the Harris family of Connecticut,
photostated from the "Barbour Collection," Town
of New London, pp. 138-145, in the Connecticut
State Library*
G HAR 4255
Typescript.

*Records of the Harris family, descended from
Francis Harris, born 1721, Watertown*
Brooks, Virrell I. Harris.
G HAR 4260
5 p.
Typescript. Ms. additions inserted 29 Aug. 1957.

*Genealogy: family of Harris, Thomas,
Charlestown, Mass. 1630*
Porter, George S.
G HAR 4300
7 + 4 p.
Typescript.

*Ancestry of Lieut. George Harris of Canaan, New
Hampshire, and some of his descendants*
Sheldon, Sidney R.
G HAR 4304
31, 1 p. + supp.
Typescript with additions and corrections.

*Some ancestors of Philip Spooner Harris and
Diantha Baker (Brown) Harris, his wife, with
their descendants to date: reminiscences and
sketches*
Harris, Henry Lucius.
G HAR 4379
1913
Typescript.

Wills of Thomas[2] Harris... Richard[3] Harris... Jonathan[4] Harris... genealogical data of these three families ... index of children and names of their husbands and wives
Harris, Henrietta Corson.
G HAR 4415
1929
Typescript.

The descendants of four soldiers of the American Revolution: the Harris brothers of Marblehead, Mass. (Robert, Mason, John, and William).
Neilson, Gertrude A.
G HAR 4439
6 p.
1934
Typescript.

John Harris of Charlestown, Mass., and North Yarmouth, Maine, 1685
Harris, Philip H.
G HAR 4455
16 + 232 + 28 p.
1941
Typescript.

Burial records of the Harris families, Turner, Me ... with additional genealogical references
Bowley, Raymond F.
G HAR 4460
5 p.
1948

Ancestors and descendants of Benjamin and Lucretia (McGuire) Harris, with an addenda [sic] containing much other data concerning Harris
Gonseth, Winifred (Thomson) (Argersinger).
G HAR 4462
58 p.
1948
Typescript.

A genealogy of Lovell Harris of Harrisville, N.H., and his descendants
Spear, Maud E. (Maud Elsie Harris), 1890-1974.
G HAR 4470
1 + 5 p.
1957
Typescript.

The descendants of Seth Harrison
Robbins, Frank Eggleston.
G HAR 6062
14 p.
1950
Typescript.

Harding family of Henrico Co., Virginia
G HAR 680
4 p.
1881
Copied from The Richmond [Va.] Standard

Harding ancestry, compiled for Edwin E. Cox of Los Angeles
Holman, Mary Lovering, 1868-1947.
G HAR 702
22 p.
1924
Typescript.

Record of the Hardy family who have lived in East Bradford and Groveland [Massachusetts]
Ladd, William B.
G HAR 956
135 p.
1931
Typescript.

The Hardys, probably related to the Thomas Hardy family of Bradford, Mass.
Millner, Frank L.
G HAR 965
6 p.
1945
Typescript.

Bible records: Nathan Hardy Bible records, Edwin N. Stevens Bible records and Stevens genealogy
G HAR 970
1947
Typescript transcription.

Hardy of Virginia
Arthur, Robert, 1886-.
G HAR 977
7 p.
1952
Typescript.

*Family Bible of the Hastings family of Hastings
Hill, Suffield, Conn., and Feeding Hills, Mass.*
G HAS 1498
4 p.
Typescript.

*Genealogy of the Hasty tribe from the year 1700.
[Daniel-1 Hasty from Ireland to Rye, N.H., then
to Scarboro, Maine, 1731]*
G HAS 1585
33 p.
1946
Typescript.

*Genealogically: a brief history of Richard
Haskins and his descendants, referring to their
births, marriages, residences, deaths, etc.*
Haskin, Joseph Adolph.
G HAS 412A
121 + 17 p.
1962
Typescript.

*Haskin - 1655 to 1965: a brief history of John and
Richard Haskins and some of their descendants*
G HAS 412B
1965
Typescript. Revision of DeWitt Clinton Haskins's
1890 compilation.

*Family history of Mary Ann Haseltine of
Plaistow, NH: a genealogical record of the
Bradley, Chase, Follansbee, Haseltine, Huse,
Kimball, Noyes, Peaslee, Putnam and Snow
families*
Sawyer, Mary Ann (Haseltine).
G HAS 80
1966
Typescript.

*Parnel Hatheway Bible record (Parnel, b. 1732,
daughter of Ebenezer and Parnel (King)
Hatheway of Suffield, Conn.*
G HAT 1000
5 p.
1946

*Our sturdy Hathorne families of Maine, with
ancestry*
Sinnett, Charles Nelson, 1847-1928.
G HAT 1680A
106 p.
Typescript with annotations by J.I. Coddington..

*Hathaway: records of intention of marriage,
Rochester, Mass.*
G HAT 535
5 p.
Typescript.

*Hathaway family: descendants of Asa-6, b. in
Freetown, Mass., 1744*
Smith, Zilpha D.
G HAT 583
15 p.
1925
Typescript.

*Haven - Parker records copied from an old family
Bible record, now in possession of Maud H. Bixby*
G HAV 115
Typescript transcription.

*Amos Champlin Havens: his family and some of
his ancestors*
Ireland, Mark L.
G HAV 117
11 p.
Typescript.

Hawthorne - Gardner - Blanchard
Warner, L. Murle.
G HAW 1250
Typescript.

*Abstracts of English wills, chancery suits, etc., of
the name of Hawes*
Fothergill, Gerald.
G HAW 318
Typescript.

*Edward Hawes of Dedham, Massachusetts, and
some of his descendants, for seven generations*
Hawes, Frank Mortimer, 1850-1941.
G HAW 322
306 + 19 + 13 p.
Typescript.

Edmund Hawes of Yarmouth, Massachusetts, and some of his descendants
Hawes, Frank Mortimer, 1850-1941.
G HAW 355
266 p. (irregular pagination).
1935
Typescript.

Hawkins family records
Seaver, J. Montgomery (Jesse Montgomery), b. 1890.
G HAW 760
18 p.
1928?
Typescript.

Captain Abner Hawley, 1739-18__, of Haddam, Connecticut, Austerlitz and Victor, N.Y.: ancestry and descendants
Huftalen, Sarah L. (Gillespie).
G HAW 965
165 p.
1943
Typescript.

Copy of Bible record of Elisha Hayward and Lois (Albee) Hayward
G HAY 1170
2 p.
1928
Typescript transcription.

Haynes and Haines genealogies. Introduction: the seven ancestors in America
Sinnett, Charles Nelson, 1847-1928.
G HAY 862
2 + 35 p.
1922
Typescript.

The Haynes family: Jonathan Haynes, son of William Haynes and his wife Sarah Ingersol of Salem, Mass.
Himes, Nina, Mrs.
G HAY 879
6 p.
1959
Typescript.

Haynie family of Northumberland County, Va: Capt. John Haynie (ca. 1624-post 1894 [sic]) to ... Lucy Haynie (1782-1801), wife of John Mills (1748-1812) of Ludenbury [sic] County, Va and Wilkes County, Ga
G HAY 924
37 p.
1949
Typescript.

The Head family: a preliminary outline to be used as a basis for further genealogical research; miscellaneous selected data from various sources
G HEA 100
4 p.
Typescript.

Heard family in Arkansas 1830, 1840, 1850, 1860, 1870 and 1880: United States census records of Arkansas
Heard, Harold
G HEA 608
14 p.
Typescript.

Foundation of a genealogy of the Heard family of New Jersey, 1710-1922
Lilly, Julius Whiting, b. 1842.
G HEA 625
13 p.
1922
Typescript.

The ancestry and descendants of John Hearndon of Scituate, R.I., and a supplement containing some of the descendants of his five brothers Benjamin, Joseph, William, Thomas and Isaac
Eddy, Ruth Story Devereux, 1875-1958.
G HEA 720
1944
Typescript.

The Hearndon line, compiled for Mrs. J. M. Morrison
Holman, Winifred Lovering, 1899-1989.
G HEA 725
12 p.
1944
Typescript.

Descendants of Elias Heath, Jr., of Woodbury, Vermont
Wells, Charles Henry, Rev.
G HEA 933
3 p.
1922
Typescript.

Heath family history as it relates to Isabel Alsop (Holmes) Lamoreux and Ellis Bertram Holmes
Holmes, Ellis Bertram.
G HEA 950
1 + 8 + 2 p.
1945
Typescript.

The descent of the Cooks, Jones, Mase and Draper families from the first permanent white settler of Canada, Louis Hebert
Cooke, Robert G.
G HEB 680
3 p.
1959
Typescript.

A Hedley line
Clark, Bertha W. (Bertha Winifred), 1875-1965.
G HED 520
5 p.
1955
Typescript.

Heilman, Hallman, Holman notes
Holman, Mary Campbell (Lovering), 1868-1947.
G HEI 84
1 + 12 p.
1954
Typescript.

The Helmershausen family
Helmershausen, Adella, b. 1867.
G HEL 420
22 p.
Typescript.

The Henry family, 1766-1910. [Alexander Henry family.]
G HEN 1595
19 p.
Mounted newspaper clippings.

The family of John Henry of Coleraine
G HEN 1600
45 p.
Typescript.

Bits of genealogy of the Henry family and connections
Henry, William Gilmore.
G HEN 1605
35 p.
Typescript.

William Henry [Henry family data; also Ballard and Cutler]
Rountree, Scott, Mrs.
G HEN 1608
9 p.
Typescript.

Hero, first mail carrier, Leicester, Massachusetts. [Henshaw family] [Mass. DAR genealogical records.]
G HEN 1798
6 p.
Typescript.

Hendley genealogy
Tallmadge, Edith May Hendley.
G HEN 645
10 + 24 p.
1936
Typescript.

Genealogy of the descendants of Benjamin Herendeen of Providence, R.I.
Burnham, L. F.
G HER 200
124 p.
1927
Typescript.

The Hewins family in Maine
Lilly, Georgiana Hewins.
G HEW 460
49 p.
1937
Typescript.

Hickling genealogy: descendants of William
G HIC 400
Typescript.

Ancestry of Charles Nelson Hickok
Hickok, Charles Nelson, 1879-1945.
G HIC 445
Typescript.

Ancestry of John A. Hicks and his wife, Ada E. Rowe of Auburn, Maine
Hicks, Susan E.
G HIC 540
4 + 210 p.
1952
Typescript.

Reverend Samuel Hide and some of his descendants
Holman, Mary Campbell (Lovering), 1868-1947.
G HID 175A
33 p.
Typescript with annotations.

Miscellaneous notes on the Higgins family, particularly Cornelius Higgins of New York
G HIG 712
1 + 25 p.
1930
Typescript.

Some additions to "Richard Higgins and his descendants" in the line of Stephen and Ann Maria Higgins
Benham, Frederick W., Mrs.
G HIG 718
3 p.
Typescript.

Family of Jesse Higgins, born Georgetown, Maine, June 23, 1766, died in Monmouth, Maine, March 20, 1825
Hill, Mary Pelham, 1865-1943.
G HIG 720
4 p.
1941
Typescript.

The Hillyer family of Connecticut, Ohio and Florida from 1640 to 1933: a genealogy of ten generations...with records of 14 allied families
Heck, Pearl Leona.
G HIL 1800
65 p.
1933
Typescript.

The Hillyer family
Pollock, Mabel Clare Hillyer.
G HIL 1810
4 + 12 p.
1954
Typescript.

Some descendants of John-1 Hill of Guilford [Conn.]
Stratton, Harriet Russell.
G HIL 303
6 p.
Typescript.

John Hill, Dorchester, Mass. 1633: also some of the families intermarried with his descendants and colonial and revolutionary records pertaining to them
Hill, Lew Cass.
G HIL 352
35 p.
1898
Typescript.

Ancestry of William Carroll Hill of Boston, Mass., showing genealogies of Hill, Mills and McKean families, identified with the history of southern New Hampshire towns
Hill, William Carroll, 1875-1949.
G HIL 372
25 p.
1919
Clippings, mounted.

Some descendants of Peter Hill who came to Saco, now Biddeford, Maine, 1653
Cushman, Sara E.
G HIL 376
72 + 10 p.
1920
Typescript.

One branch of the Hinckley family in America, showing the Mayflower line from Patience Brewster
Hinckley, Mabel Gould Demers, b. 1887.
G HIN 130
8 p.
1960

Wills of Isaac³ Hite, Abraham³ Hite, and Joseph Hite of Louisville, Ky, 1794, 1832 and 1831, supplementing the Hite genealogy published in "Some Prominent Virginia Families," by Louise Pecquet du Bellet et al., 1907
G HIT 1105
1928
Typescript transcription.

Hitchborn family: copy from chart compared by John F. Anderson, Esq., of Portland": the descendants of Thomas Hitchborn of Boston, Mass.
Anderson, John F.
G HIT 700
9 p.
Original mss. copy (60.5" x 200.5") in SG HI

Lineage of Augustus Hitchcock. [Bound with "Excerpts from the Hitchcock genealogy" by H. G. Cleveland, 1886]
Hitchcock, Augustus.
G HIT 933
1886
Clippings from Seymour (Conn.) Record, Nov. 26, 1886.

Hoag genealogy: data relative to the descent of Sara H. Sterns from John Hoag, 1643-1728
G HOA 150
18 p.
Typescript.

Ancestry of Charles C. Hobbs of South Berwick, Me: a paper written and read by Charles C. Hobbs, Esq., before a meeting of the local history department of the Berwick Women's Club, held at the home of Miss Mary R. Jewett, Jan. 14, 1902
Hobbs, Charles C.
G HOB 254
6 p.
1902
Typescript.

Copy of memoranda found in the family Bible of Shebuel Hobart, Jr. [Cambridge, Vt?]
G HOB 43
5 p.
1927
Typescript transcription.

Some of the descendants of Edmund Hobart of Hingham, Mass.
G HOB 50
39 p.
1933
Typescript.

Bible records and genealogical data concerning the family of Noah and Abigail (Hazelton) Hobart
Fant, Luella Margarette Bancroft, b. 1861.
G HOB 59
10 + 1 p.
1935
Typescript transcription.

Descendants of Gershom and Peter Hobart of NH
Driscoll, Marion Lang.
G HOB 65
19 p.
1946
Typescript.

Hodgkins genealogy: chiefly the descendants of David and Mary (Spiller) Hodgkins of Ipswich, Mass.
Callender, Ruby Hodgkins.
G HOD 743
119 + 8 p.
1970
Typescript.

Hodgman family
G HOD 825
362 p. (pp. 260-300 blank).
Typescript.

*The descendants of Robert Hoge or Hogg, of
Tuscarora Valley, Pa, including the families of
Lytle, McCullough, McKee, Sturgeon, Dunbar,
Graham, Vance, Robinson, Stitt, Harnish, Potts,
McBride*
Egle, William Henry, 1830-1901.
G HOG 206
1921
Typescript.

*Adventures of Park Holland, surveyor, in the
wilds of Maine*
Mitchell, Hinckley Gilbert.
G HOL 3025
8 p.
Typescript.

*Holbrook: the first three generations of the
Holbrook family in New England, from 1632 to
1696*
G HOL 500
14 p.
Typescript.

*Rev. Obadiah Holmes: his ancestry, children, and
neighbors...*
Salter, Edwin, 1824-1888.
G HOL 5326
6 p.
1888
Clippings from Monmouth Democrat.

*The ancestry, and some of the descendants of
Sylvanus Holbrook of Uxbridge, Revolutionary
soldier*
Bonsall, Grace Pratt (Grace Pratt Miller), 1898-
1989.
G HOL 536
17 p.
1950
Typescript.

*Ancestors and descendants of Adeline Bethiah
Holt (1835-1880), who married 30 April 1863
Samuel Alexander Sargent (1826-1887)*
Wadland, Beatrice Flagg.
G HOL 5826
23 p.
1961
Typescript.

*Homer -- Stevens notes compiled for Mrs. Homer
Pierce Clark*
Holman, Winifred Lovering, 1899-1989.
G HOM 120
40p.
1948
Typescript.

*Copy of Bible records of the families of William S.
Honeywell and Adam Grove*
G HON 260
2 p.
1929
Typescript transcription.

*The Hoopes - Killough family Bible records,
Chester and Lancaster Counties, Pennsylvania*
Bell, Albert Dehner, 1911-.
G HOO 1455
4 leaves
1948?
Typescript.

*Hoover's kin all Quakers: genealogical notes on
the family of Herbert C. Hoover, presidential
nominee*
Petrers, Marjorie.
G HOO 2050
4 p.
1928
Mounted clipping from Boston Herald,

*Hopkins: the first three generations of the
Hopkins family who came to this country before
the year 1692*
G HOP 122
10 p.
Typescript.

Hopkins ancestry of John-4 Stevens, b. 1896
Stevens, John.
G HOP 132
Typescript.

Hopkins genealogy: ancestry of Mrs. Carrie Inman Wood through William Hopkins of Roxbury, Mass.
Wood, Carrie (Inman).
G HOP 214
3 p.
1919
Typescript.

The Hosley family, 1649-1934
Porter, Harold F., Jr.
G HOS 450, 450A
7 p. (1934), 29 p. (1935).
1934, 1935
Typescript.

Houston family
Shirk, Ida Morrison Murphy, b. 1860.
G HOU 1221
15 p.
1911
Typescript.

How notes, compiled for Albert Boyden
Holman, Winifred Lovering, 1899-1989.
G HOW 30
21 p.
1927
Typescript.

Rev. John Hull and family. Compiled for Mrs. S. Westray Battle of Asheville, N.C.
Holman, Winifred Lovering, 1899-1989.
G HUL 542
65p.
1941
Typescript.

Notes on the Humphrey family
Ferry, F. G.
G HUM 718
16 + 3 p.
1909, 1952
Typescript.

The Humphrey family in America
Cobb, Gertrude Humphrey.
G HUM 900
15 p.
Typescript.

English genealogy: Hunt of Boreatton
G HUN 2080
1933?
Typescript.

Hutchings of Kittery, Maine
Crane, Alexander.
G HUT 340
8 p.
Typescript.

Notes concerning Richard Ingraham and some of his descendants [Supplementary to "Notes on the Ingraham genealogy" by Dr. J. B. Nichols, 1898]
Jones, Matt Bushnell, 1871-1940.
G ING 1525
10 p.
1904
Typescript.

Edward Ingraham of York, Maine, and descendants
Sinnett, Charles Nelson, 1847-1928.
G ING 1530
8 p.
1923
Typescript.

Genealogy of the descendants of Edmund and Francis Ingalls (who settled in Lynn in 1629) ... together with some account of the descendants of Maudit, James and Barnet Ingles
Ingalls, Walter Renton, b. 1865.
G ING 308
7 + 150 p.
1933
Typescript.

Families of the names of Ingalls or Ingles or Engs originating in Boston
Ingalls, Walter Renton, b. 1865.
G ING 308A
22 p.
1938?
Typescript.

The genealogy of the Ingersoll family of Washington County, Maine, descendants of Elizabeth (Knowles) Ingersoll
Ingersoll, Heman N.
G ING 576
3 p.
1925
Typescript.

The Ingham family
Ingham, Henry L.
G ING 710
[1931]
Newspaper clippings and marriage certificate

Some additions and corrections to "Joseph Ingham and his descendants" by Hon. Samuel Ingham (1871), and to the reprinted and enlarged edition of 1933, by Charles S. Ingham
Putnam, Charles F.
G ING 714A
1953
Typescript.

The children of Jonathan Ingham and their relation to the Halls and Knipes
Mansur, Frank L.
G ING 720
17 + 1 p.
1963
Typescript.

The descendants of Jonathan Ingham
Mansur, Frank L.
G ING 720A
20 p.
1963
Typescript.

The descendants of Jonathan Ingham
Mansur, Frank L.
G ING 723
20 + 4 p.
1967
Typescript.

A complete record of the family of George and Jessie MacQueen Innes, immigrants to Maine 1873
Gregory, Margaret Innes.
G INN 1770, 1770A
3 + 8 p. (1770), 25 + 4 p. (1770A).
1965
Typescript.

Ireland lineage of Mark Lorin Ireland
Ireland, Mark L. (Mark Lorin).
G IRE 480
7 p.
1960
Typescript.

Irish family of Rhode Island
Wood, Carrie (Inman).
G IRI 710
4 p.
1919
Typescript.

Ancestry of Linda M. Ivers
Harris, Roger D.
G IVE 450
1958
Typescript.

J'ellison, Jellison, Gillson, Gillison, Ellison [With supplement: Nicholas Jellison of Maine - new material to supplement material on file and establish new lines with any corrections that may have been necessary]
Hinckley, Mabel Gould Demers, b. 1887.
G JEL 1060, 1060A
18 p. + 2 p. (1948), 2 + 42 + 2 p. (1963).
1948, 1963
Typescript.

Family records and letters pertaining to John H. Jacobs, born in Avon, Maine
G JAC 1025
11 p.
Typescript.

*The New England ancestry of John Clark Jacobs,
born in _____, Ohio, May 4, 1835; died in
Garland, Texas, Jan. 28, 1923*
G JAC 1045
18 p.
1959
Typescript.

*Descendants of Thomas Jacocks who died in 1692
in Perquimans District, NC*
Jacocks, William Picard, b. 1877.
G JAC 1575
89 leaves.
1957
Typescript.

*Genealogic notes and charts of the Jackson
family and some allied lines*
Jackson, Fred Kinney, b. 1874.
G JAC 683
1 + 30 p.
1938
Typescript.

*Descendants of John Jackson and Martha
Judson; includes also the family of Judson,
Jackson, and Smith*
Jackson, Eliza Ann Nichols, b. 1872.
G JAC 720
14 + 3 p.
1956
Typescript.

*James family of Marblehead, Mass, including
brief note on Richard Craft of Marblehead and
Ambrose Gale of Marblehead*
Holman, Winifred Lovering, 1899-1989.
G JAM 298
39 p.
1932

The Jan Albertse Jansen family
Wiles, Harriett M.
G JAN 1740
4 p.
Typescript.

*Jasper notes: original copy, more complete than
in the printed version in vol. 2 of The Stevens -
Miller ancestry*
Holman, Winifred Lovering, 1899-1989.
G JAS 250
2 + 3 p.
1952
Typescript.

Jay family of Westchester Co., N.Y.
G JAY 100
11 p.
Typescript.

*Ancestry of Jayne family of Long Island and
Smack family of New York*
Jayne, Edward H.
G JAY 250
26 p.
Typescript.

Genealogy of Simon Jefferds and his descendants
G JEF 250
8 + 4 p.
Typescript.

The Jefferis family
Cope, Gilbert, 1840-1928.
G JEG 500
14 p.
1870
Typescript.

Jellison (Gillison) family
Hill, Mary Pelham, 1865-1943.
G JEL 1050
3 p.
1938
Typescript.

*Histories of the Jelly family and the Hulpiau
family*
Irvine, Esther L., 1906-.
G JEL 1250
91 p.
Typescript.

Very brief Jenner notes
Holman, Winifred Lovering, 1899-1989.
G JEN 1530
9 p.
1947
Typescript.

*Descendants of John Jenney of Plymouth, Mass
[copy of the typewritten pages taken from the
manuscript working notes by Mrs. Susan Cotton
Tufts], with index by Frederick G. Jenney*
Tufts, Susan Browning (Cotton), 1869-1958.
G JEN 2026, 2026A
656 p., bound in 2 parts (2026). Index (2026A).
1941
Typescript.

Jenney genealogy
Tufts, Susan Browning (Cotton), 1869-1958.
G JEN 2028
3 + 60 p.
1947-1948
Typescript.

*John Jenney of Plymouth [Mass.] and his
descendants to the seventh generation, with
especial emphasis upon the line of John I, Samuel
II, John III*
Clark, Bertha W. (Bertha Winifred), 1875-1965.
G JEN 2030
146 leaves.
1958-1959
Typescript.

*The Jenney family of Norfolk and Suffolk in
England*
Jennings, Herman Winslow.
G JEN 2040
50 leaves.
1965
Typescript.

*The story of the family of Joshua Cushman Jenney
and their descendants from Pilgrim John Jenney
of Plymouth Colony, 1623*
Jenney, Mildred Edna Brownell.
G JEN 2045
1967
Typescript.

*Jennings family, descended from Beriah and
Eunice (Stebbins) Jennings of Springfield and
Ludlow, Mass.*
Jennings, Alice.
G JEN 2180
26 p.
1928
Typescript.

Living record of the Jensen family
Jensen, Charles C., et al.
G JEN 2752
1927
Typescript.

*Samuel Jenison, Tehama County, California:
marriage records, Tehama County, California*
Cheever, Herbert Milton.
G JEN 3350
6 p.
1948-49
Typescript.

Notes and wills of Jenkins family of England
G JEN 640
5 p.
Typescript.

*Jenkins genealogy: descendants of John of
Barnstable and Falmouth, Mass., 1855-1859*
Jenkins, John.
G JEN 650
1859
Typescript.

*Aaron Jenkins of Frederick County, Virginia, and
his descendants*
Johnson, Maude Horne.
G JEN 700
23 p.
1963
Typescript.

Jenkins and Speight families
Carruth, Margaret Ann (Scruggs).
G JEN 715
32 leaves.
1969
Typescript.

Notes on the history and genealogy of the Jenks family of Lynn, Mass. and Pawtucket, R.I.
Forshee, Archibald A.
G JEN 994
Typescript.

Timothy and Abigail Jerome of Meriden, Conn., and their son Zerubbabel Jerome of Bristol, Conn.
Shepard, James.
G JER 520
24 p.
Typescript.

Jerome history and genealogy, and the ancestry of Sarah Noble. Bound with *additional data on the descendants of Timothy Jerome*
Jerome, Samuel Bryan.
G JER 525
40 + 2 + 9 p.
1896, 1940
Typescript.

Family Bible record of Addison Gardner Jerome of New York City (b. Pompey [N.Y.] 1811)
Shepard, Elmer I. (Elmer Irwin), 1878-1966.
G JER 529
3 p.
1942
Typescript transcription.

Jerome family: descendants of Timothy
Dunston, Harry C.
G JER 532
40 p.
1947?
Typescript.

Record of the family of Charles Jesup and Abigail Sherwood. Includes Hull and Sherwood families
G JES 500
Typescript.

Jewell genealogical data, including inscriptions from the Jewell and Currier burying ground at Wonalancet, N.H.
Morton, Albert N.
G JEW 180
1950
Typescript.

Descendants of Moses Jewett: a continuation of number 2996 in "The history and genealogy of the Jewetts of America."
G JEW 410A
5 p.
Typescript.

An ancestral record of my paternal grandfather, Albion Norton Jewett, a descendant of Joseph Jewett, a founder of Rowley, Massachusetts, in 1639, and many other early American colonists who settled in Massachusetts in the 1600s
Prescott, Lucy Ada (Jewett)
G JEW 490
33 leaves.
1971
Typescript.

The Johanson family of Sweden and the upper Midwest
Eck, Aimee May (Huston), 1907-.
G JOH 100
9 leaves.
1951
Typescript.

The Johonnot family: descendants of Daniel Johonnot, 1668-1749
Buckminster, Mary Alice Edwards Miller.
G JOH 1165
153 + 15 p.
1964
Typescript.

The Johnes family of Southampton, L.I., 1629-1886
Johnes, Edward R., b. 1852.
G JOH 153
46 p.
1886
Typescript.

Genealogy of the Johns family of Huntington, Vermont
Johns, Dorothy Mae.
G JOH 215
18 p.
1961
Typescript.

Capt. John Johnson and Capt. Isaac Johnson of Roxbury, Mass., and their families
G JOH 402
4 + 1 + 1 + 4 + 5 p.
Typescript extracts.

Johnson notes
Holman, Winifred Lovering, 1899-1989.
G JOH 403
5 p.
Typescript.

Some descendants of Capt. Edward Johnson, founder of Woburn, Mass.
Johnson, Davis B.
G JOH 404
15 p.
Typescript.

Moses Johnson of Salisbury, New Hampshire, a Bunker Hill soldier: some of his ancestors and descendants
Johnson, William H., Dr.
G JOH 526
28 p.
1923

The Johnson - Berg - Westheim and Christopherson families: being a record of the paternal and maternal lines of Gena Berg Berry
Berry, Charles Jerome, b. 1892.
G JOH 532
iv, 151 p.
1930
Typescript.

Living record of the Olaus Johnson family, compiled by children and grandchildren of Oley M. Johnson
Johnson, Anna, b. 1892.
G JOH 543
57 leaves.
1927
Typescript.

Abraham Johnson and descendants
Davis, Annie Dent.
G JOH 577
1939
Typescript.

John Johnson and other Johnsons
Johnson, William E.
G JOH 588
1940
Typescript.

Very brief Johnson notes
Holman, Winifred Lovering, 1899-1989.
G JOH 598
1 + 13 p.
1947
Typescript.

Descendants of Elisha Moses Johnson, a soldier in the Revolution
Slate, Paul Johnson, b. 1899.
G JOH 609
149 p.
1952
Typescript.

Genealogy of the descendants of Captain Edmund Johnson (ca. 1741-1812)
Johnson, Edmund Roe.
G JOH 612
8 + 72 p.
1954
Typescript.

Ancestry of Maro Johnson and of his sister, Eliza Love Johnson
Johnson, Maro.
G JOH 613
1 + 246 p.
1954
Typescript.

Johnson records: with records of associated families, the Warnes and the Suttons
Biedel, Helen C.
G JOH 614
97 p.
1955
Typescript.

*The family and descendants of Jesse and
Elizabeth (Harris) Johnson of Enfield, N.H.*
Roberts, George McKenzie, b. 1886.
G JOH 625
3 + 26 p.
1957
Typescript.

*The descendants of James Theron Johnson and
Frances Agnes Cowdery*
Johnson, Kimball.
G JOH 647
1965
Typescript.

*The ancestry of Catherine (Kate) Johnson of
North Andover, Massachusetts, who was born
February 11, 1831, and died June 24, 1918, from
facts collected from various sources*
Rockwell, Samuel Forbes.
G JOH 651
333 + 14 p.
1965, 1966
Typescript.

Johnson ancestral roots
Johnson, Richard Schofield.
G JOH 666
3 + 84 p.
1972
Typescript.

*Thomas Johnston, painter, engraver, japanner,
organ builder, escutcheon maker. Compiled for
Mrs. Homer P. Clark*
Holman, Winifred Lovering, 1899-1989.
G JOH 830
1946
Typescript.

The Johnstons of Boston
Coburn, Frederick William, b. 1870.
G JOH 830
10 p.
Typescript.

*Northampton, Mass., vital records 1663-1846:
Jones [family]. From original record book in
possession of the New York Genealogical and
Biographical Society*
G JON 415
2 p.
Typescript.

*Genealogy of some of the descendants of Isaac
Jones, who was born in England*
McMillan, Richard F.
G JON 430
4 p.
Typescript.

*The correct ancestry of Samuel Minot Jones,
donor of Jones Library, Amherst, Massachusetts*
Warner, Frederick C. (Frederick Chester), 1886-
G JON 432
2 p.
Typescript.

Memorial of the Jones family from 1648 to 1876
Kidder, Frederic, 1804-1885.
G JON 438
1876
Typescript.

*Jones notes: Robert Jones, born in England
probably about 1600, died in Hingham, Mass.,
1691*
Holman, Mary Campbell (Lovering), 1868-1947.
G JON 555
20 p.
1928
Typescript.

Jones, Easter, Black, Foster family records
Jones, David Tracy, b. 1900.
G JON 560
43 leaves.
1930
Typescript.

*Jones family: descendants of Joseph or Joel Jones
of South Carolina and Alabama*
G JON 566
1931
Typescript.

Preliminary report on descendants of Snow Jones, with genealogical data on families related to them by blood or marriage
Bell, Albert Dehner, 1911-.
G JON 592
40 leaves.
1947
Typescript.

A genealogy of the Jones family of Needham, Mass., descendants of William Jones of Portsmouth and Dover, NH, to present time 1640-1959, with some descendants of the Harris family of Salem, N.H.; of the Jillson family of Cumberland, R.I.
Jones, Frederic A.
G JON 620
1959
Typescript.

Griffith Jones of Springfield, Mass 1614-1676, and his descendants of the name. Part 2: 1796-1960, descendants of Thomas Jones, 1796-1878
Jones, Edward T.
G JON 624
206 p.
1960
Typescript.

Descendants of Thomas Jones and Mary Horton who settled in vicinity of Guysborough, Nova Scotia, 1770-1962, with historical data
Jones, Frederick A.
G JON 630
1962
Typescript.

Descendents [sic] and known ancestors of Zardus and Catharine Antoinette (Hoskins) Jones; paternal grandparents of Henrietta Jones Darby
Darby, Henrietta (Jones), b. 1895.
G JON 632
20, [4] leaves
1962
Typescript. Includes bibliographical references.

Jones, Richardson, Duhamel and allied families of Maryland
Thompson, Laura Moody Johnson, 1910-
G JON 633
8 + 572 p.
1962
Typescript.

European ancestry: Cranston, biographical sketches. "This is an extension of the Jones - Locklin - Lamson - Ainsworth 'American Ancestry' to the European ancestry of one member, Gov. John Cranston of R.I."
Jones, Edward Thomas.
G JON 634A
6 vols.
1965
Typescript.

Jones
Martin, David Kendall, 1933-
G JON 636
1963?
Typescript

The descendants of Cornelius Jones, son of Benjamin Jones of Stratham, New Hampshire
Callender, Ruby Hodgkins.
G JON 640
81 p.
1965
Typescript.

Some other Joneses: descendants of Increase Jones[3], 1752-1825, of Minerva, N.Y. (Elijah J[ones][2], Cornelius J[ones][1])
Jones, Mabel (Merryfield).
G JON 645
viii + 263 leaves.
1967
Typescript.

Jordan family
Holman, Mary Campbell (Lovering), 1868-1947.
G JOR 18
3 p.
1928
Typescript.

Jordan, Jermain genealogical notes, descended from French and Italian families of Jourdain, Jourdaine, Jourdanie in French lines and the Giordanie family of Italy
Huling, Caroline Alden.
G JOR 20
14 + 58 p.
1929
Typescript.

The Jordan line. [Francis Jordan of Ipswich, Mass.] Compiled for Mrs. S. Westray Battle, Lexington, Mass.
G JOR 28
2 + 11 p.
1940-1943
Typescript.

Ancestors and descendants of Benjamin Joslyn of New Braintree, Worcester County, Massachusetts and Chesterfield, Cheshire County, New Hampshire
Chapman, Grace Olive.
G JOS 160
30 p.
1940
Typescript.

Joy family data: a copy of a letter concerning the marriage of Bethia[5] Sprague Joy, from Harry L. Foster to Society of Mayflower Descendants, 15 November 1951
Foster, Harry L.
G JOY 25
5 p.
1951
Typescript.

The Thomas Judd family, 1797-1960, pioneers of Marshall County, Illinois
Judd, Roland D.
G JUD 100
50 p.
1960
Typescript.

Patrick Judge of Boyle, Ireland [and] Twin Falls, Idaho
Eldridge, William Henry, 1873-1943.
G JUD 175
26 p.
1932
Typescript.

Judson - Burr genealogy. Part first - Judson ancestry and descendants of James Clarke Judson, who married Betsy Burr, with Clarke genealogy. Part second - Burr. Ancestry and genealogy of her connections on the female side, of Betsy Burr, who married James Clarke Judson. Collateral lines: Barlow, Beardsley, Booth, Curtis, Sherman, Wakeman, Warde
Weeks, Frank Edgar, 1857-1946.
G JUD 382
22 + 64 + 2 p.
1938
Typescript.

Genealogical records of the Judd family from various sources
Molyneux, Nellie Zada Rice.
G JUD 72
19 p.
Typescript.

Brief Judd notes, compiled for Mrs. J. M. Morrison
Holman, Winifred Lovering, 1899-1989.
G JUD 95
34p.
1947
Typescript.

The Swiss family Kaiser
Kaiser, Roland Glenn.
G KAI 125
1 + 151 p.
1962
Typescript.

Persons of the name of Kasson listed in the master index to the Vermont vital records (early file, to 1870), State House, Montpelier [Vt.]
G KAS 148
Typescript.

Copy of records from the Bible of Emily A. Kathan of Churchville (Sweetsburg), P.Q.
G KAT 100
4 p.
Typescript transcription.

Family letters (typed copies) of Keefer, Onderdonk and Hotaling families, mostly addressed to Mr. Peter Keefer, Esq., Albany City, New York State
G KEE 228
17 letters.
1911
Typescript.

Keeler family of Norwalk
Patterson, David Williams, 1824-1892.
G KEE 350
1884
Typescript.

Keeler family
Coleman, Minnie Lincoln Crow.
G KEE 359
7 + 3 p.
1933
Typescript.

The Keeners and allied families. A memorial to Ann Maria Keener
Wilson, Letitia Pinnell (Johnson), b. 1856.
G KEE 700
[76] leaves.
1923
Typescript.

The descendants of William and Rachel Keener
Lacy, Lawson Keener.
G KEE 712
2 + 154 leaves.
1964
Typescript.

The Keith family
Seaver, Jesse Montgomery, b. 1890.
G KEI 770
146 p.
1930
Typescript.

The Keith families of West and North Auburn, Maine
Adams, Charles F.
G KEI 798
10 p.
1958
Typescript.

Ancestry chart to eight generations of the family of Henry Louis and Rose Standish Mills Kellogg, with the sources from which the data were obtained
G KEL 1020
Chart + 5 p.
Bound chart with explanatory material.

The Kelly and Woodring families of Worth Township, Centre County, Penna.
Bell, Raymond Martin, 1907-1999
G KEL 1240
5 p.
1944
Typescript.

James Kelly of Letterkenny twp., Franklin Co., Penna., and his descendants
Bell, Raymond Martin, 1907-1999
G KEL 1252
3 p.
1957
Typescript.

Kelso of Kelsoland (Scotland), 910-1910
Kelso, Clarence C.
G KEL 1450
19 + 3 p.
1930
Typescript.

Andrew Foster Kelso: history and descendants
Davidson, Marie (Arrington) 1919-.
G KEL 1470
5 + 52 + 5 leaves.
1957
Typescript.

Kelso families: chiefly that branch of the family whose ancestors were Alexander Kelso and his wife Anna (McMasters) who resided in Londonderry, N.H., beginning 1719
Morton, Harriet E.
G KEL 1474
4 + 103 p.
1959
Typescript.

The Kelty family
Kelty, Elaine.
G KEL 1810
72 p.
Typescript.

Genealogy of the Kelley family, allied with Buckingham, Dudley, Howe, Hussey, Manning, and Wheeler families
Wheeler, H. M.
G KEL 923
1906
Typescript.

Kelly, Kelley, Killey, O'Killia: descendants of David O'Killia who took the oath of fidelity as an inhabitant of Yarmouth, Barnstable County, Plymouth colony (Massachusetts Bay province after 1692) 1657
Priest, Alice L. (Alice Lucinda), 1866-1954.
G KEL 935
9 leaves.
1937
Typescript.

David O'Killia of Cape Cod and some of his Kelley descendants
Driscoll, Marion Lang.
G KEL 950
11 + 3 p.
1945
Typescript.

Some ancestors and descendants of Oliver Parry Kennard of Portsmouth, N.H., 1786-1870
Kennard, Frederic Hedge.
G KEN 1310
1 + 47 + 1 p.
1935
Typescript.

Some ancestors and descendants of Oliver Parry Kennard of Portsmouth, N.H., 1786-1870
Kennard, Frederic Hedge.
G KEN 1310A
1935
Typescript.

The American ancestry of Yvonne Odette Kennedy
Kennedy, Glenn Alvin.
G KEN 1572
27 leaves
1942
Typescript.

The American ancestry of Yvonne Odette Kennedy
Kennedy, Glenn Alvin.
G KEN 1595
Unpaginated.
1962
Typescript.

Kennicot - Kinnicutt family: an outline of the early generations in New England, copied from a manuscript in the possession of Mrs. Rebecca Newton Kinnicutt Francis
Kinnicutt, Lincoln Newton.
G KEN 1830
Typescript.

Some ancestors of Daniel Kent
Kent, Georgia Tyler.
G KEN 1957 1-3
3 vols.
1917
Typescript. Vol. 1: Kent genealogy. Vol. 2: thoughts.

Genealogy of the family of Nathaniel Kenyon
Herrington, Byron M.
G KEN 2318
75 + 12 p.
1961
Typescript.

The Kendall family, descended from John Kendall of Accomac County, Virginia, with notices of the related families of Rodd, Fischbeck, Gray, Irwin and Ely
Kendall, John Smith.
G KEN 365
Typescript.

Index register of the Kendall family
Kendall, Winthrop Reed.
G KEN 370
Typescript.

American ancestors of Winthrop Reed Kendall and Kendall family bibliography
Kendall, Winthrop Reed.
G KEN 397
28 + 12 p.
1913
Typescript.

Ancestors and descendants of Capt. Isaac Lewis Kendrick of East Harwich, Cape Cod, Mass
Chapman, Grace Olive.
G KEN 850
37 p.
1943
Typescript.

Keppel family history, Holland to America
Toal, Helen Marie (Keppel), b. 1913.
G KEP 70
iv, 65 leaves.
1964
Typescript.

Information on the Kerley, Cearley, and Carley families of the South
Carley, William Henry, b. 1867.
G KER 235
128 p.
1945
Typescript.

The Kerr family and related lines
Somers, Chester Lincoln, 1917-.
G KER 680
15 p.
1949
Typescript.

Ketcham family Bible record
Bethfield, Anne Slater
G KET 150
6 p.
Typescript transcription of original Bible record.

A partial record of the family of John Ketcham who removed from Long Island to Orange County, N.Y., about 1750
Humphrey, W. Guy.
G KET 160
25 p.
1945
Typescript.

The name Kewley
Martin, David Kendall, 1933-.
G KEW 100
35 l.
196-
Typescript.

Ancestral charts of Fredelle Carolyn Keyes and her brother George Bacon Keyes, and description of the persons mentioned
Keyes, Charles Hubbard, b. 1884.
G KEY 126
[2, 55], 66 leaves.
1931
Typescript.

Record of the family of Thomas Kezartee of Ashtabula County, Ohio
Rogers, Clifford C.
G KEZ 25
2 p.
1928
Typescript.

Kezer (Kezar, Kesar, Keyser) genealogy. In memoriam Albert W. Bachelder, 1850-1934, Sarah E. Kezer Bachelder... 1846-1939
Whiting, Mabel (Robins).
G KEZ 425
32 p.
Typescript.

Genealogy of Edwina Elizabeth Kibbe Stalker's branch of the Kibbe family, 1611-1917
Stalker, Edwina Elizabeth (Kibbe).
G KIB 75
30 + 4 p.
1917, 1925
Typescript.

A Kidder chronicle: descendants of Camillus Kidder
Truslow, Arthur.
G KID 170
26 p.
1932
Typescript.

Kierstead family of New Jersey, with Bush, Cook and Mowerson descendants
Pryor, William Y.
G KIE 1100
1953
Typescript.

Kilbourn - Evans records
G KIL 15
14 p.
1949
Typescript.

Decendents [sic] of Thomas Kilner, believed to be a brother of James Kilner
Kilner, Charles Frances Thomas, b. 1880.
G KIL 385
5 leaves.
1949
Typescript.

Kilby notes
Holman, Winifred Lovering, 1899-1989.
G KIL 95
4 + 41 + 4 p.
1950
Typescript.

Kimball ancestry of my mother Eureka Kimball Goddard
Goddard, Charles Austin, b. 1872.
G KIM 110
7, [1] leaves.
1937
Typescript.

The Newton, N.H. branch of the Kimball family in America: a record of the direct lineal ancestors and descendants of Amos M. Kimball, including the ninth and tenth generations born in Newton, N.H.
G KIM 134
1958
Typescript.

Kimzey family history: Kimzey and Kimsey family records
Kimzey, Herbert Bennett, b. 1909.
G KIM 480
A-G, 28 p.
1949
Typescript.

A Kimball line
Kidder, Antoinette Kimball.
G KIM 55
4 p.
Typescript.

Abner Kingman (seventh generation) and his descendants. Supplementing "Descendants of Henry Kingman" by Bradford Kingman
Kingman, Robert, M.D.
G KIN 1023A
8 p.
Typescript.

The Kingman family
Eastwood, Sidney Kingman, b. 1890.
G KIN 1064
1965
Typescript.

Records of the births, marriages, deaths of relations from the grandparents of Rhoda Kingsbury, down as long as this record may be continued
Kingsbury, Rhoda.
G KIN 1250
4 p.
1827
Typescript transcription.

Kingsbury - Bush American ancestry
Kingsbury, Forrest Alva, b. 1883.
G KIN 1280
1958
Typescript.

Kingsley and other ancestry of the Espenscheid - Kingsley family of New York City
Espenschied, Lloyd, b. 1889.
G KIN 1568
[2], 8, [3] leaves.
1944
Typescript.

Memoirs of George Blackburn Kinkead, to which is prefixed the genealogy and a brief historical account of those from whom he is lineally descended
Kinkead, George Blackburn.
G KIN 1710
180 p.
1921
Typescript.

The Kinney family
Beitzell, Edwin Warfield, 1905-.
G KIN 2218
15 p.
1948
Typescript.

Family of Kincannon
Ravenscroft, Ruth Thayer, 1903-1991.
G KIN 225
1 + 31 p.
1960
Typescript.

Genealogical history of William Henry Kinnison 1853-1933 of Angus, Nickolls County, Neb.; related families Kincannon, Day, Dykes, Norwood, Taylor, Palmer
Kinnison, Don E.
G KIN 2525
74 p.
1956
Typescript.

Kinsley forebears: the genealogy of one line of descendants of Stephen Kinsley of Braintree and Milton, Massachusetts, 1598-1970, with some biographical notes
Hargrave, Helena M. Goodale.
G KIN 2800
25 + 1 p.
1970
Typescript.

The Kinsman family: genealogical record of the descent from Robert Kinsman of Ipswich, Mass., to and the descendants of Aaron B. and Louisa (Hatch) Kinsman
Kinsman, Raymond M.
G KIN 2860
60 + 4 p.
1961
Typescript.

King bibliography
G KIN 515
1915
Typescript.

Adrian Jansen Konninck and his descendants: an historical record of the King family
Robinson, Drew King, Mrs.
G KIN 520
9 + 23 p.
Typescript.

The King family of Althone, Purleigh, Burnham, Maldon, Southminster, Tillingham, and Much Baddow, co. Essex
Morrison, George Austin, Jr.
G KIN 525
1912?
Typescript.

The King families of King's Langley, co. Herts, England
Morrison, George Austin, Jr.
G KIN 531
1912?
Typescript.

The King families of Jamaica, West Indies
Morrison, George Austin, Jr.
G KIN 534
1912?
Typescript.

The King families of co. Suffolk, England
Morrison, George Austin, Jr.
G KIN 537
1912?
Typescript.

The King family of Thame, co. Oxon., and Worminghall, co. Bucks, England
Morrison, George Austin, Jr.
G KIN 540
1912?
Typescript.

Various King families of ... Scotland, ... Essex, ... Cornwall, ... Dorset, ... Sherburne, ... Hereford, ... Suffolk, ... Yorkshire, ... Ireland, ... Somerset, ... Staffordshire, ... Surrey, ... Warwick, ... Wilts
Morrison, George Austin, Jr.
G KIN 544
1912?
Typescript.

King family
Morrison, George Austin, Jr.
G KIN 612
1911
Typescript.

The King family of Beckenham and Bromley, Kent, England
Morrison, George Austin, Jr.
G KIN 613
1912?
Typescript.

The King family of Scituate, Mass.
Morrison, George Austin, Jr.
G KIN 613
1911
Typescript.

The Kips
Jones, Frank Lawrence.
G KIP 5
10 p.
Typescript.

Richard Kirby of Sandwich, Dartmouth and Oyster Bay
Clark, Bertha W. (Bertha Winifred), 1875-1965.
G KIR 15
10 p.
1955
Typescript.

Kistler families descended from George Kistler, Jr., of Berks County, Pennsylvania
Sprague, Floride M. (Kistler), b. 1872.
G KIS 200
2, 46 p.
1944
Typescript.

Kitzmiller families of Pennsylvania: Lancaster County family
Bishop, J. C.
G KIT 1250
1 + 7 + 6 p.
1953
Typescript.

The Kitzmiller family in Pennsylvania before 1800
Bishop, J. C.
G KIT 1252
1 + 14 + 1 p.
1959
Typescript.

Kittrell family
Whitley, Edythe Johns Rucker, b. 1900.
G KIT 750
12 leaves.
1936
Typescript.

The Kleckner Fessler families in Berks, Schuylkill, Northampton, and Lancaster Counties, Pennsylvania
Jenkins, David Spurgeon, b. 1898.
G KLE 75
54 leaves.
1957?
Typescript.

Klock - Clock genealogy
Williams, Helen Laura Clock, b. 1876.
G KLO 175
a-c, 103, 40 p.
1952?
Typescript.

Ancestors and descendants of Nathaniel Kennard of Bridgeton, Maine
Chandler, Willis H.
G KN 1300
50 p.
1928
Typescript.

Descendants of Aaron Knap
Bowley, Raymond F.
G KNA 475
9 p.
1947
Typescript.

Het geslacht Knape
Dek, Adriaan Willem Eliza, 1924-.
G KNA 590
58 leaves.
1955
Reproduction of typescript.

Knapp: descendants of Roger Knapp, who came to New England in 1630
McSweeny, John.
G KNA 737
18 p.
1939
Typescript.

Alfred Metcalf Knapp (1805-1885) family Bible record
Janowski, Rina Knapp.
G KNA 742
7 p.
1941
Photostat of mss. copy.

My mother's family, the Knapps
Sherman, Grace A., b. 1878.
G KNA 745
1945-1952
Note: Cover "The Knapp tree."
Typescript.

George Knapp of England, and some of his descendants in America
Knapp, Alfred Averill, b. 1868.
G KNA 760
16 l. + 2. Mimeo. Second copy filed with SG KN.
1952
Typescript.

Job Knapp and some of his descendants
Knapp, Alfred Averill, b. 1868.
G KNA 762
1962
Typescript.

The Knapp family: CT, NY, Ohio
Neff, Tilla Hughes.
G KNA 765
2 + 51 + 5 p.
1953
Typescript.

A Knapp line back to Adam with Huguenot, Crusade, and Magna Charta connections
Knapp, Alfred Averill, b. 1868.
G KNA 778
10 leaves.
1960

Daniel Knarr and Lucinda Ault
Reeser, Nellie Wallace, b. 1883.
G KNA 900
106 p.
1955
Typescript.

Kneeland - Brown family records, consisting of excerpts from genealogies and town histories
G KNE 295
40 p.
Typescript.

Kneeland, Neeland, Neland et[c]. variants
Holman, Winifred Lovering, 1899-1989.
G KNE 315
30 p.
1956
Typescript.

Kniss and allied families
Van Duzee, Frederic Pierce, b. 1895.
G KNI 1320
55 p.
1965
Typescript.

Knight notes
Barker, John Herbert, 1870-1951.
G KNI 468
131 p.
Typescript.

Genealogy of the Knight, Walton, Woodson, Lamaar, Daniel, Benning, Cobb, Jackson, Grant and other Georgia families, including biographies of many distinguished members
Knight, Lucian Lamar, 1868-1933.
G KNI 490
3, 251 leaves.

Knight family records: a history of the long ago, to the present time, 640-1951
Knight, Sarah Ann.
G KNI 515
1951
Typescript.

Knight family: also Albertson, Bennett, Gardner, Harding, Schultz, Thorn and Wisner families
Knight, Ray Roberts, 1881-.
G KNI 518
1952?
Typescript.

Pedigree charts showing ancestors of John Benton Knox, born: Wallingford, Conn. - 1899; presently of: Madison, Conn.
Knox, John Benton, Jr.
G KNO 860
11 p.
1969
Typescript.

Ludwig Koch: a genealogical footnote
Rubincam, Milton, 1909-1997.
G KOC 225
5 p.
1964
Typescript.

The Kole and Kamphuis families
Lartigue, Carrie Louise (Teats), b. 1912.
G KOL 175
125 p.
1962
Typescript.

The Koogler family of Virginia and allied families of Austin, Good, Hahn, Heatwole, Hemp, Knicely, Martin, Rhodes, Rodes, Showalter, Snead, Taylor and Witmer
Whitney, Virginia Koogler, b. 1927.
G KOO 125
85 leaves.
1968
Typescript.

Krom - Krum family: or Gysbert Crum of Ulster County, New York, and his descendants. Vol. 1: First four generations. Part 2: Fifth generation carried down in the male line with notes on later Kroms
Zimm, Louise Seymour Hasbrouck, b. 1883.
G KRO 125
41 + 10 p., 38 + 12 p.
1941, 1944
Typescript.

Genealogical notes on the Kuykendall and Hardin families
Fullerton, Jane Hardin.
G KUY 130
1 + 60 p.
1964
Typescript.

Kymboulde, Kemball notes from England
Kemball, Charles Gordon.
G KYM 650
2 + 26 p.
Typescript.

La Barre and Houck family record
Metzer, Beverly.
G LAB 210
56 p.
1968

Genealogy of the families Laboissiere or Labossiere, Claude or Glaude - Labossiere
Claude-Laboissiere, Alphonse.
G LAB 810
127 p.
1957
Typescript.

Matthew Lackey of Upton and Shrewsbury, Mass., and his family
G LAC 250
41 p.
Typescript.

Lackey family history
Lackey, Richard S., 1941-1983.
G LAC 256
27 leaves.
1962
Typescript.

The Lackor family
Middleton, Mary M.
G LAC 610
1965
Typescript.

Amasa Ladd of Pittsford, Vermont
Eldridge, William Henry, 1873-1943.
G LAD 20
23 p.
1932
Typescript.

Pierre Ladue, 1662-1713, Huguenot, New Rochelle, NY
Ladue, Pomeroy.
G LAD 200
21 p.
Typescript.

The Ladd family: a genealogical and biographic al memoir. One branch of the direct descendants of Daniel Ladd, 1633-1953, ten generations of a New England family in America
Ladd, Samuel Appleton, Jr.
G LAD 35
2 + 4 + 79 p.
1953
Typescript.

Lair: a Huguenot family from near Lyons, France, 1752; landed in New York and settled in New Jersey
Priest, Alice L. (Alice Lucinda), 1866-1954.
G LAI 110
1937
Typescript.

The Lake family of Derby, Conn. and Greene Co., N.Y.
Gibson, Helen Lake.
G LAK 50
22 p.
1921-1931
Typescript.

Facts regarding one Joseph Lake of Staten Island, New York
Van Name, Elmer Garfield, b. 1888.
G LAK 68
6 leaves.
1940
Typescript.

George Lamberton of New Haven
Jones, Edward Thomas.
G LAM 1155
28 + 12 + A-F p.
1963
Typescript.

La Motte genealogy: descendants of Jean Henri de la Motte (1705-1794)
G LAM 2310
12 + 16 p.
Typescript.

Family history of Sir Curtis W. Lampson, baronet, and wife, Lady Jane Walter Lampson, of London, England
Wright, J. W.
G LAM 2550A
1958?
Typescript.

Facimiles of letters sent to Frank B. Lamb relating to the Lamb family
G LAM 600
Typescript.

Lamb genealogy: descendants of Anthony
G LAM 605
Typescript.

The Lamb family in Massachusetts, 1630-1939
Albion, Robert J.
G LAM 640
7 p.
1939
Typescript.

Lamb - Bonney: records copied from the genealogical charts belonging to Mabel Lamb Merrill
Lamb, Merrick Bonney.
G LAM 646
17 p.
1947
Typescript.

William Lamb of Delaware County, New York, and his descendants
Gundry, Eldon P.
G LAM 652
46 p.
1957
Typescript.

Lambe - Lamb: nine generations from Thomas Lambe, 1609-1646, to Charles Hamilton Lamb, 1876-1927; includes over 299 allied and contemporary names
Minard, Marion Brownlee Dixon.
G LAM 710
11 + 19 p.
1968
Typescript.

Lane summary: Cornelius Lane of Somerset Co., N.J.
G LAN 1444
13 p.
Typescript.

Genealogy of the Lane family from 1693 to 1894
Lane, A. Maria.
G LAN 1450
37 p.
Typescript.

William[1] Lane of England and Dorchester and Hingham, Mass., Bay Colony, born England?, died Hingham 1654: James[5] Lane (1749-1819), Hingham, Mass., Kent's Hill, Maine
Lane, Frank C.
G LAN 1510
3 + 2 + 6 p.
1917-1946
Typescript.

Captain Daniel Lane
Bailey, Rosalie Fellows, 1908-1991.
G LAN 1515
1938
Typescript.

Lane family history
Lane, Edgar C.
G LAN 1522
7 p.
1964
Typescript.

*Lang - Harvey lines, Strout - Mooers lines,
genealogical notes*
Strout, Mary S. Lang.
G LAN 1860
47 + 16 p.
1932
Typescript.

*Descendants of Solomon Langston of Laurens
County, South Carolina, through his son Bennett*
Langston, Carroll Spencer, b. 1903.
G LAN 2500
[48] leaves.
1942
Typescript.

*Langdon - Langton: Samuel Langton (or
Langdon) of Boston [Mass.]*
Kingsbury, Anna Chandler, 1870-1943.
G LAN 2575
19 + 49 p.
1932
Typescript.

*Geneology [sic] and history: Lanphear,
Lamphier, Lamphere, and related families in
America*
Lanphere, Edward Everett, b. 1897.
G LAN 3130A
264 p.
1967
Revised
Typescript.

*Concerning John Lapham and some of his
descendants: a copy of an article published in
1948 in THE AMERICAN GENEALOGIST, with
corrections and additions*
Peckham, Mary W.
G LAP 215
1948?
Typescript.

*Morphology of Larwood genealogy: being a
prefatory tabulation of the relationships and
descents of members of the Larwood family in
America since circa 1720; preparatory to a full
account of the history and nomenclature of the
name in England since circa 1300, with its
transitions through De La Wode, Larwood
(Delawood), Larawode, Larrawood to Larwood*
Larwood, James, b. 1903.
G LAR 2350
1, ii, 15 (i.e. 14) leaves.
1933
Typescript.

*Larzelere family and collateral lines of Elkinton,
Stockton, Brigham, Carpenter*
Du Bin, Alexander.
G LAR 2510
20 leaves.
1950
Typescript.

*A transcription of notes to 1958, relating to the
American ancestry of David Chapman Lash and
his wife Emma Shrives Lash*
Lash, David C.
G LAS 220
2 + 114 + 1 + 29 p.
1958
Typescript.

*The Latour family: being the second in a series of
sketches concerning the ancestral families of
Nancy Lee Walter and Norman Winslow Walter*
Walter, William Adolph.
G LAT 1000
16 p.
1947
Typescript.

*The Lord's vineyard: including the life of E.C.
[Eli Chambers] Latta, 1831-1909*
Latta, F. F.
G LAT 1090
6 + 91 p.: map.
1940
Typescript.

Our family, the Lattimores
Lattimore, Alida.
G LAT 1125
6 leaves.
1936
Typescript.

Latham genealogy
G LAT 310
26 p.
1920
Typescript.

Corrections of certain errors made in the Lathrop family memoir, and a few additional notes
Huntington, B., Rev.
G LAT 653
13 p.
1917
Typescript.

Genealogy of Candace Elah (Sawyer) Laubach and others
Laubach, Candace Elah (Sawyer).
G LAU 110
2 + 44 p.
1912
Typescript.

A list of the married great-grandchildren of Samuel Davis Laughlin (1797-1849) and Rebecca Dunlavy (1799-1849) and their descendants ... [supplement to "Genealogical record of Anthony Dunlevy III" (1922)]
Laughlin, Kendall, b. 1890.
G LAU 620
10 p.
1953
Typescript.

A memorable note wherein is conteyned the names in part of the cheefest kendred of Robert Launce late of Medfeild in the county of Susse[x], deceased, collected faithfully out of an old booke of his owne hande writing by Thomas Fella of Hollisworth
Fella, Thomas.
G LAU 710
Typescript.

Descendants of Daniel Lawrence, son of Enoch Lawrence and grandson of John Lawrence of Watertown, Mass. Bound with Lawrence, John S., *Memorandum*
G LAW 655
Typescript.

The descent of the Danvers Pages from the Lawrences of Groton, Mass.
Moriarty, George Andrews, 1883-1968.
G LAW 680
14 p.
1926
Typescript.

The British and colonial ancestry of Esther Lawrence, wife of Capt. Samuel Ransom of the Continental army
Hoyt, Sophia (Hayward).
G LAW 684
42 p.
1931
Typescript.

A genealogical bibliography of the Lawrence family
Lawrence, Schuyler.
G LAW 692
5, 4 leaves.
1935
Typescript.

Lazenby: being such account as I have been able to collect of the families in the United States bearing the name
Lazenby, Mary Elinor.
G LAZ 848
3, 59, 5 p.
1942
2nd ed.
Typescript.

Record of the main branch of the Leavens family from A.D. 1716
Leavens, Erastus Wilkinson.
G LEA 2095
20 p.
1850
Typescript.

Notes on Dudley - Leavitt lineage, July-August, 1928, compiled for Henry Fletcher
Holman, Winifred Lovering, 1899-1989.
G LEA 2676
73 p.
1928
Typescript.

The Leavitt genealogy through the family of Deacon John Leavitt of Hingham, Massachusetts, and some of its branches, including the following allied families: Gilman, Johnson, Hobart, Gold, Sherwood, Bennett, Bliss, Madison, Greene
Hildenbrand, Leora Mae Greene, b. 1887.
G LEA 2688
2 + 55 + 1+ 56 p.
1938
Typescript.

Memorial of Francis Le Baron, of Plymouth, Mass., with genealogical records of his descendants
Goodwin, Nathaniel, 1782-1855.
G LEB 206
1 + 164 p. + additions to 40, 40a and 40b. (3 p.).
1872
Typescript.

Ledbetter family of Virginia
Tillman, James D., Jr.
G LED 75
7 + 9 p.
1931
Typescript.

Some notes on the ancestry and descendants of my parents Budd L. and Minnie-May (Havens) Lee (in preparation)
Remington, Helen Elizabeth (Lee).
G LEE 232, 232A
Typescript.

Genealogy of the Lee family: the Lees of Marblehead and Manchester, Mass.
Dearborne, Hannah Swett (Lee).
G LEE 240
18 p.
1860?
Typescript.

Lee genealogy: descendants of Samuel Lee of Watertown, Massachusetts, and Killingly, Connecticut
Priest, Alice L. (Alice Lucinda), 1866-1954.
G LEE 362
9 p.
1930
Typewritten with manuscript additions.

Descendants of Isaac and Elizabeth Pruitt Lee
Flowers, Develand.
G LEE 419
3 + 97 p.
1967
Typescript.

The Lees family
McCullough, Charles R.
G LEE 650
23 + 2 + 9 p.
Typescript.

Le Fort or Fort: Huguenot pedigrees
Lart, Charles Edmund.
G LEF 720
6 p.
Reproduced manuscript, hectograph.

Lehmann of Neuchatel
Shepard, Elizabeth Dwight Garrison, b. 1901.
G LEH 525
Geneal. table.
1949
Typescript.

The Leiby - Lambert lineage. [Part 1: Leiby.]
Rupp, Margaret (Glanding), b. 1890.
G LEI 100
1952
Typescript.

Lineage of Reuben Leighton, Barrington, N.H. 1770, Newbury, Vt. 1842, descendant of Thomas Leighton, Dover, 1633
Leighton, Martha E.
G LEI 530
1 + 22 p.
1959
Typescript.

Lenfest real estate deeds from Guernsey Island ... the last three are wills and court decisions of the parents of Peter Lenfest, a first settler in Lewiston, Maine
Lenfest, Bertram Augustus, b. 1867.
G LEN 294
Photostat and blueprint.

Lenfest wills in probate records in counties of Essex, Middlesex, Norfolk and Suffolk, commonwealth of Mass. Bound with *births, marriages and deaths in Mass., as collected in State House, Boston.* Bound with *Lenfest transfers of real estate, guardianships, etc. in Essex, Middlesex and Suffolk Counties, Mass. ...* Bound with *births, marriages and deaths of Lenfests, as collected by the State Health Dept., Augusta, Maine.*
Lenfest, Bertram Augustus, b. 1867.
G LEN 296
5 leaves + 9 p. + 7 p. + 8 p.
1941
Typescript.

Genealogy of the Lenfest family in America
Lenfest, Bertram Augustus, Dr., b. 1867.
G LEN 297
22 leaves.
1931?
Typescript.

The Lenfest genealogy in Guernsey, carrying back the ancestry of Peter Lenfest (Pierre Lenfestey) to about 1475, as verified by Guernsey records and old papers, and to before 1400 by another genealogy of a fair degree of accuracy
Lenfest, Bertram Augustus, b. 1867.
G LEN 298
Blueprints.
1938
Typescript.

John Leonard of Springfield, Mass., and some of his descendants
Leonard, Constance, 1785-1855.
G LEO 549
62 + 16 p.
1929
Typescript.

Some ancestors and descendants of Avery Leonard of Seneca County, Ohio
Blaine, Harry Stanley, b. 1880.
G LEO 558
2, 42 leaves.
1933
Typescript.

Leonards of Stafford, Tolland County, Connecticut, and their New England ancestry
Chapman, Grace Olive.
G LEO 571
86 p.
1944
Typescript.

Leonard genealogy
Leonard, Ralph Y.
G LEO 582
5 + 25 p.
1951
Typescript.

The Lester family of New London and Groton
Parkhurst, Charles Dyer, 1849-1931.
G LES 1096
32 + 1 p.
Typescript.

My life to date: with genealogical notes
Lester, J. William
G LES 1119
38 p.
1935
Typescript.

Andrew Lester and his descendants
Lester, J. William, Sr.
G LES 1122
1 + 32 p.
1937
Typescript.

Notes on the Lesuer family [Philip Lesuer, at Mendon, Mass. by 1712]
Tillotson, E. Ward.
G LES 1525
Typescript.

Meet the Lesh family
Rupp, Clarence, Mrs.
G LES 560
36 + 1 p.
1956
Typescript.

Genealogy of the family of Henry Lewis (son of Evan Lewis) who emigrated from Wales in 1682, also brief genealogies of the families of Humphrey Scarlet and Edward George
G LEW 1004
3 + 121 p.
1951

Lewis genealogy: line of Olin Bailey Lewis
G LEW 904
16 p.
Typescript.

Family record of Nathaniel C. Lewis and descendants
Worthing, Edah F.
G LEW 914
2 p.
Typescript.

A genealogical record of the Lewis and Wilkinson families, and twenty other families; a genealogical record of the ancestors of Mrs. Sarah Lewis Vaille, wife of Dr. Henry R. Vaille, and mother of Mrs. Andrew B. Wallace
Dunning, Sarah L.
G LEW 939
3 + 96 + 25 p.
1900
Typescript.

Ancestry of J. Frances Lewis of Dorchester and West Somerville, Mass., and Naugatuck, Conn.
G LEW 976
22 p.
1940
Typescript.

A genealogy of the John Lewis family 1640-1944 and the Parsons line
Stearns, Abby Catherine (Lewis).
G LEW 985
16 p.
1944
Typescript.

The royal house of Liechtenstein: a historico-genealogical memoir
Wallace, Raymond.
G LIE 150
1 + 26 leaves.
1951
"No. 8 of 31 copies".
Typescript.

The descendants of Samuel Lightfoot and Rachel Milhous
Milhous, Dorothy Z.
G LIG 225
208 p.
1966
Typescript.

A compilation of the known descendants of Thomas and Rhoda (Patterson) Lillard, a pioneer family of Missouri, Illinois, and Iowa
Lillard, Gerald Francis, b. 1904.
G LIL 220
vii + 44 leaves.
1950
Typescript.

Genealogy of the southern Lilly family. From the year 1566, county of Staffordshire, England
Lilly, Julius Whiting, b. 1842.
G LIL 949
11 leaves.
1916
Typescript.

George Lilly and his descendants
Lilly, Georgiana Hewins.
G LIL 964
39 + 2 p.
1945
Typescript.

The Lindesays of Loughry, county Tyrone:
abstract from a manuscript book, written early in
the nineteenth century and presented to his
nephew, John Lindesay.
Lindesay, Frederick.
G LIN 1320
14 p.
1951
Typescript.

A sketch of Thomas Lincoln and some of his
descendants
Lincoln, Arba N.
G LIN 258
71 p.
Typescript.

Lindamood family history
Harpine, Jacob William, b. 1881.
G LIN 3080
109 p. + iv.
1965
Typescript.

Barney Lincoln of Taunton, Mass. and Onondaga
Hill, Onondaga County, New York
Stevens, Frank Lincoln, 1871-1934.
G LIN 326
11 + 2 p.
1917
Typescript.

Lincolns of New England: an alphabetical list of
descendants of early settlers of New England by
the name of Lincoln NOT included in the history
of the Lincoln family. An account of the
descendants of Sam[uel] Lincoln
Lincoln, Waldo, 1849-1933.
G LIN 338
428 p.
1926
Typescript.

Part 1: Adam Linn, Revolutionary War pension
record 5023. Part 2: James Sargent, Sr., Pike
County, Ohio
Fullers, Forest S.
G LIN 5148
19 + 13 p.
Typescript.

The genealogy of Joseph Linnell, a soldier of the
American Revolution
Linnell, Mary Belle, b. 1888.
G LIN 5230
1963?
Typescript.

Genealogical tracing of the Linneman family in
Denmark from 1450 to 1759, with part of the
Danish family and full American record from
1759 to 1889.
Prescott, C. D.
G LIN 5425
82 p.
1889
Typescript.

The Linscott family in Maine
Sinnett, Charles Nelson, 1847-1928.
G LIN 6250
14 p.
1922
Typescript.

Connecticut Linsleys. The six Johns: being the
history, so far as known, of the descendents [sic]
of the first of the name in Connecticut
Linsley, Ray Keyes, 1875-1949.
G LIN 6780
144 leaves.
1949?
Typescript.

The Littlefield family of Rhode Island
Moriarty, George Andrews, 1883-1968.
G LIT 1050
Typewritten.
1912
Typescript.

History of the ship Tuscany and one of her
masters, Captain Clement Littlefield, including
his descendants
Foster, Harry Littlefield.
G LIT 1065
4 + 127 p.
1956
Typescript.

Anthony Littlefield of NY and Michigan and his descendants
Gundry, Eldon P.
G LIT 1068, 1068A
1st ed.: 58 p. Rev. ed.: 4 + 103 p.
1958, 1965
Typescript.

Ancestor William Littlejohn and his descendants
Sinnett, Charles Nelson, 1847-1928.
G LIT 1438
5 p.
1922
Typescript.

Ancestor Robert Lithgow of Topsham, Maine, and his descendants
Sinnett, Charles Nelson, 1847-1928.
G LIT 510
7 p.
1922
Typescript.

Genealogical notes of the family of Isaac William Littell, 3rd.
Owen, Ruth (Littell).
G LIT 626
4 p.
1929
Typescript.

Record of the descendants of Doty Little, of Castine, Maine, and Mercy and Hannah, his wives
Little, Edward Porter.
G LIT 819
19 p.
1885
Typescript.

Notes on the Livingstone family of Lanark, Scotland, and Detroit, Michigan, and related families
Clark, David Sanders.
G LIV 1035
1966
Typescript.

Genealogical register of Carlton Coolidge Case: on mother's side, taken from John Alden and John Livermore, whose respective ancestors [sic] were united in marriage...
Rivermore, Joseph M.
G LIV 304
1901
Typescript.

Généalogie de François Xavier Lizotte
Drouin, Joseph.
G LIZ 1420
2 + 234 p.
Typescript.

Lineage of the Lloyd and Carpenter family ... bound with Addenda.
Smith, Charles Perrin, 1819-1883.
G LLO 304
(1870): 88 p. 1875 Addenda: 24 p.
1870, 1875
Typescript.

Our family tree: descendants of John Loch, Revolutionary soldier, and his wife Mary Ann Raider Loch
Miller, Grace (Linson).
G LOC 210
1946
Typescript.

The Lord - Locke genealogy
Lord, Edward Locke.
G LOC 442
5 + 24 + 66 + 25 + 11 p.
1956
Typescript.

Lockhart genealogy: descendants of James Lockhart of Horton, Nova Scotia
Kimber, Sidney A. (Sidney Arthur), b. 1866.
G LOC 700
229 p.
1914
Typescript.

Isaac Locklin, 1781-1844, and his descendants of the name
Jones, Edward T.
G LOC 820
2 + 89 p.
1961
Typescript.

Rev. Clark Lockwood, 1805-1892, [and] his descendants
Downs, Arthur Channing, b. 1930.
G LOC 935
58 p.
195-
Note:"Library copy #24."
Typescript.

Logan family. Some items of family history and family papers concerning a number of early settlers of Maryland named Logan
Mills, Harry Willard, b. 1898.
G LOG 129
16 leaves.
1942
Typescript.

Our Logan history
Doyle, Ora Ellen (Logan).
G LOG 140
167 + 22 p.
[1966]
Typescript.

The Logues in America and related families
Hopkins, Mabel (Logue), b. 1893.
G LOG 440
1955
Typescript.

Ancestry of Henry Wadsworth Longfellow
G LON 1000
2 p.
1883
Clipping from Boston Evening Transcript, 1 December 1883.

John Long and his descendants
G LON 498
8 + 1 p.
Typescript.

Ancestor Joel Long of Bluehill, Maine, and descendants
Sinnett, Charles Nelson, 1847-1928.
G LON 512
18 p.
1923
Typescript.

Long family of Dorchester, Mass. and Conn., and allied families
Bates, Mary Wood, b. 1854.
G LON 527
55 p.
1931
Typescript.

Long and Lahiff biblibyography [sic] as a compliment to the relatives of Joshua or John Mary (Logan) Long
Vought, Dora Elvin (Breiner), b. 1889.
G LON 545
104 p.
c1953
Typescript.

The descendants of Stephen Loomer of New London, Conn, comprising the first to and including the ninth generation
Shepard, Addie Eugenia (Loomer), b. 1880.
G LOO 340
1960
Typescript.

The descendants of David Lopez and Priscilla Moses, and Jacob De Leon and Hannah Hendricks
Moffat, Abbot Low, 1901-.
G LOP 20
9 + 19 p.
1932

Chronicles ... of the Loring family of Massachusetts Bay, in four parts exhibiting the genealogy of the four sons of Dea. Thomas Loringe of Devonshire, England 1634. With index.
Loring, James Spear, 1799-1884.
G LOR 1100, 1100A
460 + 69 p.
Typescript.

Lorings: heads of families. Descendants of Dea. Thomas Loring
Pope, Charles Henry, 1841-1918.
G LOR 1110, 1110A
8 p.
1917, 1971
Typescript.

Rising Sun, Indiana, cemetery. [Records and notes concerning the family of Ezekiel H. Loring of Sudbury, Mass. and Indiana.]
Dickor,, Marie Paula.
G LOR 1112
3 p.
1946
Typescript.

Nathan Lord family of Kittery, Maine [to and through Samuel Lord and his descendants]
Lord, Ralph Edwin.
G LOR 434
41 + 8 p.
1932, 1967
Typescript.

Patching together records from legal sources to secure vital statistics regarding Lord - Pennock - Hoyt family relationships
Fitts, Ralph Corydon.
G LOR 445
9 p.
1958
Typescript.

Lovering lineage
Holman, Winifred Lovering, 1899-1989.
G LOV 1456
49p.
1933
Typescript.

The Lovewell family in America, volume one: the descendants of Joseph and Deborah (Morse) Lovewell
Lovewell, Samuel Harrison.
G LOV 1560
909 p.
1932-1950
Typescript. Material brought up to 1950.

A partial history of the Lovejoys
Lovejoy, Benjamin.
G LOV 603
7 p.
1928
Typescript.

A supplement to the Lovejoy genealogy by C. E. Lovejoy (1930)
MacKechnie, Horace Knight, 1909-.
G LOV 607A
Phys. Desc.3 p.
1960
Typescript.

Lovelace - Loveless [family]
G LOV 946
6 p.
1952?
Typescript.

Lowry and Breedlove notes
Byrne, Daniel, Mrs.
G LOW 1710
139 p.
1967
Typescript.

Low genealogy: the descendants of Seth Low and Mary Porter
Moffat, Abbot Low, 1901-.
G LOW 532
1, 60, 14 leaves.
1932
Typescript.

James Russell Lowell's maternal ancestors
Trail, Robert.
G LOW 754
3 p.
1957
Typescript.

The Mayflower lines of Russell Healey Lucas, Esq.
Scott, Walter Glenn.
G LUC 125
52 p.
1947-1952
Typescript mimeograph.

Luce family [copied from] Connecticut vital records
G LUC 490
3 p.
Typescript.

Luce [family]
Ferrey, F. G.
G LUC 495
12 p.
1908, 1952
"Revised, rewritten, checked 1952."
Typescript.

Geneological [sic] notes re: the American lineage of one branch of the Luce family principally residing on Long Island, N.Y., from Henry (1) Luce of Martha's Vineyard, Mass. (1670) to Herbert Pratt Luce of New York City, N.Y.
G LUC 515
1950
Typescript.

Ludden - Porter - Kinne families
G LUD 200
14 p.
1926
Typescript.

Lufkin - Haskell lines of Abigail Lufkin of Gloucester, Mass., who married Benjamin Allen Richardson (Book 1). Book 8: Family Group IX
Kluegel, Helen Richardson, b.1893.
G LUF 250
1966
Typescript.

Lufkin families in America: known vital records of male descendants
Smith, Arthur Wellington, Jr.
G LUF 257
46 + 56 p.
1973
Typescript.

Descendants of John Lukens of Horshan, Montgomery County, Pa.
Cooper, Theodore.
G LUK 300
Geneal. chart, folded and bound.
1900

American ancestors and descendants of Abraham Tennis Lukens
Edwards, William Lukens.
G LUK 325
26 leaves.
1957
Typescript.

The Lumbard lineage (sometimes written Lombard)
Harwood, Olive Harriet.
G LUM 465
4 p.
1922
Typescript.

The Lupfer - Bealor - McKeehan genealogy
McKeehan, D. O.
G LUP 315
9 + 16 p.
1960
Typescript.

The Luter - Davis and allied families: Luter - Davis - Burkhalter - Smart - Perkins, and others
Upton, Marie (Luter).
G LUT 210
2 + 141 p.
1959
Typescript.

History of the Lybarger family
Lybarger, Donald Fisher, b. 1896.
G LYB 80A
122 l.
1959
Typescript.

The light of other days: recollections of boyhood and youth [Lybarger family]
Lybarger, Donald Fisher, b. 1896.
G LYB 82
41 p.
1962
Typescript.

Historical and genealogical notes of and about the family Lycan
Dane, Harold John.
G LYC 100
1959?
Typescript.

The Lyde family of Boston and Halifax. Notes copied from [SG-EAT-1-92]
Eaton, Arthur Wentworth Hamilton, 1849-1937.
G LYD 1
Typescript.

Lyman genealogy: descendants of Timothy Lyman and Experience Bardwell of Chester, Mass.
Lyman, Joseph Bardwell, Rev.
G LYM 72
19 p.
1931
Typescript.

Lyon, Wells, Shurtleff, Fairfield, Thurber, [and] Wardwell families
McPike, Eugene Fairfield, b. 1870.
G LYO 102
43 leaves.
1934
Photostat.

The Samuel Lyon family, descendants of Samuel Lyon (1795-1884) and Catherine Hamilton (1799-?)
Lyon, Charles J.
G LYO 126
10 p.
1950
Typescript.

A listing of the descendants of Henry Lyon of Connecticut, who settled in the township of Falmouth, Nova Scotia, in 1760
Duncanson, John V. (John Victor), 1918-
G LYO 130A
5 p.
1961
Typescript.

Lyon family notes
Lyon, G. W. A. (George William Amos), b. 1854.
G LYO 68
1901-2
Typescript.

The lineage of Edward Nevill McAllister
G MacA 430
10 p.
Typescript.

Descendants of William Brownlow McLellan
McClellan, Aubrey Lester, b. 1894.
G MacC 3415; G MacC 3415A
26 p.; 109 p.
1946; 1966
Typescript.

Descendants of "honest" John McClinch of Boston Mass.
Whitney, Richard Skinner, b. 1840.
G MacC 3625
44 p.
Typescript.

Ancestry of the children of Andrew McClure of Montgomery County Kentucky
Owings, Donnell MacClure, 1912-.
G MacC 4028
1, 9 p.
1937
Typescript.

The McConnell family of N.Y. and Franklin Co. Pa. taken from wills and letters
Vosburgh, Genevieve Vail.
G MacC 4705
8 p.
Typescript.

McCoy genealogy
McCoy, George M. Jr.
G MacC 6045
3, 175 p.
1952
Typescript.

Fragmentary records of the McCullough and connected families
McCullough, George Grant.
G MacC 7058
54 p.
1918
Typescript.

"The family tree" or what I know about the McCutcheons. Compiled from records by Byron McCutcheon and his brother Lewis McCutcheon
McKee, Florence McCutcheon, b. 1860.
G MacC 7600
110 p.
1924
Typescript.

Macdonald - McDonald genealogy (... also spelled McDonnell or McDaniel)
G MacD 8490
12 p.
Typescript.

McDougal genealogy [1748-1954] the known descendants in the [U.S.] of Robert McDougal of western Scotland (1748-1832)
McDougal, Donald, 1904-.
G MacD 9350
55 p.
1954
Typescript.

[Additions & corrections for] McDougal genealogy: the known descendants in the [U.S.] of Robert McDougal ...
McDougal, Donald, 1904-.
G MacD 9350A; G MacD 9350B
2, 6, 7 p.
1956; 1964
Typescript.

McDuffee [genealogical records New Hampshire]
G MacD 9730
9 p.
Typescript.

MacEachern genealogy [misc. ref. to the family in America and Scotland]
Russell, George Ely, 1927-.
G MacE 9610
7 p.
1951
Typescript.

Family records the McElroy family
G MacE 9758
9 p.
1955
Typescript.

Mace. Reuben of Kittery Andrew of Gosport Reuben of Newcastle. Notes on Harraden Quarles. Hannah of Ipswich and Isles of Shoals. Notes on Lewis Gibbon Edgecomb Hibbert
Gathemann, Mabel S.
G MacE
1943
Typescript.

Three central Pennsylvania families McFarland of Blair Co. Weston of Huntingdon Co. Gates - Getz of Centre Co.
Bell, Raymond Martin, 1907-1999
G MacF 11090
5 p.
1948
Typescript.

MacGregor: Rev. James MacGregor 1676 or 7-1729 first minister of Londonderry N.H.
Priest, Alice L. (Alice Lucinda), 1866-1954.
G MacG 12402
2 p.
1932
Typescript.

The McHard papers [relating to James McHard of Haverhill who died in 1772 and to Philip Godfrid Kast of Newburyport [Mass.] who married Sarah daughter of James McHard]
Ketchum, Silas.
G MacH 13150
8 p.
Typescript.

The MacIntyre McIntyre and McIntire clan of Scotland Ireland Canada and New England
McIntire, Robert Harry, 1915-.
G MacI 14165
372 p.
1949
Typescript.

The clan and family of Mac Kay - Mac Coy whose ancestors were of the clan Aoidh or Mac Aoidh
McCoy, Benjamin Franklin.
G MacK 14870
21 p.
Typescript.

The Macomb genealogy [John Macomb from Ireland to America by 1775 to Albany N.Y. then to Detroit]
Burton, Clarence Monroe, 1853-1932.
G MacO 21002
19 p.
1901
Typescript.

Genealogical memoranda of the McPike family
McPike, Eugene Fairfield, b. 1870.
G MacP 22145
8 p.
1902
Typescript.

McSweeny - Day and related families
McSweeny, John.
G MacS 23489
127 p.
1946
Typescript.

Magevney family. Descendants of Michael McGivney (or Magevney) ca. 1769-1854 of Sessiah, Co. Fermanagh, Ireland
Coddington, John Insley, 1903-1991.
G MAG 250
16 p.
1933
Typescript.

Maine - Maine genealogy
Aspinwall, Algernon Aikin, 1845-1923.
G MAI 210
57 p.
1911 or 1941
Typescript.

The Mallery family descendants of Mathew and Mary Mallery and their son Isaiah
Wiles, Harriett M.
G MAL 3025
25 p.
1953
Typescript.

A brief genealogy and history of the Mann family Cambridge (or Wrentham) branch
Mann, William Leake.
G MAN 1335
15, 33 p.
1954
Typescript.

Descendants of John and Mary (Perkins) Manning of Lebanon Conn.
G MAN 1804
28, 7 p.
Typescript.

Manning family of Salem and Ipswich Mass. Maternal pedigree of Nathaniel Hawthorne
Emmerton, James A. (James Arthur), 1834-1888.
G MAN 1806
Geneal. table; 22 x 28 cm.
1880

Overflow letters from the Genealogical and biographical history of the Manning families of New England [1902]. For the use of later compilers.
Manning, William Henry, 1852-1928.
G MAN 1834
1, 77 p.
1924
Typescript.

The Manning family. The Roller family
Boyd, Scott Lee, b. 1882.
G MAN 1854
14, 29 p.
1954
Typescript.

The Reverend Samuel Man A.B. (1647-1719)
Holman, Winifred Lovering, 1899-1989.
G MAN 33
48 p.
1933

41 first cousins a history of some descendants of Jean Many French Huguenot
Many, Dorothy (Jones), 1930-.
G MAN 5110
71 p.
1961
Typescript.

The story of Benjamin and Annabel Manifold and their environments and descendants
Manifold, Jesse Benjamin, b. 1881.
G MAN 880
79 p.
1953
Typescript.

Desc. of Nathaniel Manley[2] son of William Manley[1]
Manley, Rufus.
G MAN 954
4 p.
Typescript.

The Manley family of Dorset Vt.
Fletcher, Robert Howe, b. 1884.
G MAN 984
6 p.
1944
Typescript.

Ancestors and descendants of William Manley of Connecticut
Foulk, Eleanor Gould.
G MAN 986
Various pagings.
1964
Typescript.

The John Mannen genealogy
Huggins, Mabel Irene.
G MANN 1530
iii, 53 p.
1968
Typescript.

... one line of the Maris family in direct descent from George Maris who came from New England in 1683
Garside, Winnifred A.
G MAR 1670
8 p.
Typescript.

Genealogical charts of Archie Leslie Marble
Verrill, A. H., Mrs.
G MAR 425
9 charts.
Typescript.

Samuel Marsh family master index
Marsh, Warren L., 1918-.
G MAR 4345
6, 35 p.
Typescript.

Marsh family Bible property of Daniel Benjamin Marsh ordained at Poughkeepsie N.Y. 1790
Coleman, Minnie Lincoln Crow.
G MAR 4399
8 p.
1934
Typescript.

The Marsh family of southern Indiana...
Marsh, William Edgar, 1883-.
G MAR 4408
7 p.
1936
Typescript.

Marsh - Evans records
G MAR 4430
13 p.
1949
Typescript.

Samuel Marsh ancestors and some descendants
McMillan, Bertha Lee.
G MAR 4440
44, 5 p.
1955
Typescript.

John Marshall of Billerica [Mass.] and his descendants
Marshall, Grace Merle.
G MAR 4652
11 p.
Typescript.

The Marshall family tree Rufus Marshall and Suzanna George branch
Marshall, Grace Merle.
G MAR 4669
18 p.
1940
Typescript.

Jeremiah Marshall of Colchester, New London County, Connecticut and Warren, Herkimer County, New York also his children and grandchildren
Chapman, Grace Olive.
G MAR 4672
36 p.
1941
Typescript.

The Marshalls ... descendants of John Marshall of Billerica Mass. chiefly in the line of Joseph Marshall of Weare N.H.
Marshall, Grace Merle.
G MAR 4680
2, 11, 6 p.
1943
Typescript.

Marshall family of Pennsylvania records 1650-1952
Marshall, Joseph Bowman.
G MAR 4698
33 p.
1952
Typescript.

The Marsters family Manchester Massachusetts together with the Conant Dodge Porter Leach Allen and Vail lines
G MAR 7510
1958
Typescript.

Marston [source of the name the family in England the family in America]
G MAR 8050
11 p.
Typescript.

Some descendants of Thomas Martin (b. Beekman Dutchess Co. N.Y. 1752) and Charity Hurd married 1778
G MAR 8205
6 p.
Typescript.

Some account (genealogical and otherwise) of some of the descendants of Col. George Martin of the County Belfast Dublin and Sirinam [sic]
Payson, Edward.
G MAR 8248
65 p.
1925
Typescript.

George Martin of Salisbury Mass. and his descendants. Also of the probably related lines of Samuel Martin of Francestown N.H. his brother Jesse Martin of Francestown N.H. of Richard Martyn of Portsmouth N.H. and Ephraim Martin of Goffstown N.H. and Bradford Vt.
Watson, Elliot Burnham, b. 1859.
G MAR 8256
1, xxiii, 293 p.
1929
Typescript.

Ancestors and descendants of George Castor Martin
Martin, George Castor, b. 1885.
G MAR 8288
25 p.
1950
Typescript.

John Martindell (or Martindale) cordwainer of Philadelphia[Pa.] and some of his descendants. Compiled from material collected by Harry H. Martindale
Cleveland, Marjorie Seward.
G MAR 8325
103 p.
1953
Typescript.

Toilers of the sea the Martinis family
Hutchinson, C.J.
G MAR 8530
31 p.
1947
Typescript.

Martyn - Martin genealogy
Caleff, George O. F.
G MAR 8720
Various pagings.
1936
Typescript.

Part B the David Massa family
Massa, David John.
G MAS 1200
7, 38 p.
1957
Typescript.

Marriages births and deaths from the family Bibles of Benjamin and Sarah (Mason) Plant of New Hartford N.Y. [Records of Mason Coman Plant & Hosford families]
G MAS 653
7 p.
Typescript.

A double Mason line from Major John Mason deputy-governor of Connecticut to new cadet John Mason Kemper West Point 1931
Bulkeley, Caroline (Kemper).
G MAS 741
3, 2-9, 1 p.
1932
Typescript.

A genealogy of the Mat(t)hews family with chapters on the related families of Archer Boots Brewer Busher Daniel Funkhauser Hybart Norris Paul Roberts
Boots, John R., 1939-.
G MAT 1257
iv, 377 p.
1968
Typescript.

Descendants of Coll Mathews and Catherine Campbell [of North Yarmouth Me.] with allied lines
Newborg, Bernice O.
G MAT 425
12, 664 p.
1944
Typescript.

The ledger of Charles Mathews of Lincolnville Maine 1792-1830 [b. 1759 Plainfield Conn. d. 1844 Lincolnville Maine]
Newborg, Bernice O.
G MAT 425A
3, 46 p.
1945
Typescript.

A Mathewson lineage including the descendants of John and Lois (Hicks) Mathewson
Mathewson, Louise Clark, 1884-.
G MAT 450
1, 29, 2 p.
c1941
Typescript.

The Maurer family Pennsylvania pioneers a brief history ... with ... all known descendants of Jacob Maurer 1791-1863 and ... Maria Polly Hilbisch 1793-1861 of Snyder County
Dunkelberger, George Franklin, 1879-.
G MAU 1650
242 p.
1954
Typescript.

Maxwell families in Maine
Sinnett, Charles Nelson, 1847-1928.
G MAX 821
10 p.
1922
Typescript.

John Maynard of Sudbury, Mass. and some of his descendants
Gould, William Edward.
G MAY 1625
39 p.
1914
Typescript.

Ancestor Noah Mayo of Harpswell Me. ancestry and descendants
Sinnett, Charles Nelson, 1847-1928.
G MAY 1847
4 p.
1923
Typescript.

Descent of Edward Leonard Mayo from Rev. John Mayo
Holman, Winifred Lovering, 1899-1989.
G MAY 1852
98 p.
1927
Typescript.

Ancestor Hon. Robert Means and descendants.
Sinnett, Charles Nelson, 1847-1928.
G MEA 1058
14 p.
1929
Typescript. Includes index.

Descendants of Robert Meares of Boston Mass.
Morse, Theoda Mears, b. 1876.
G MEA 1210
1, 324 p.
1919-1950
Typescript.

Some descendants of John and Lucy Rockwell Mears of Windsor Conn.
Healy, Helen E.
G MEA 1425
1, 116 p.
1960
Typescript.

Descendants of Robert Mears of Billerica Mass.
Morse, Theoda Mears, b. 1876.
G MEA 1427
139 p.
1961
Typescript.

Mears families of Virginia and Georgia vol. 1 descendants of Bartholomew Mears of Eastern Shore Va. vol. 2 descendants of William Mears of Everton England Georgia and Pennsylvania
Morse, Theoda Mears, b. 1876.
G MEA 1428
113 p.
1962
Typescript.

Allen Mead soldier 1812 wife Sally Scarlett. William Scurlock soldier 1812 wife Sarah Humphrey
Firestone, Eva Oma Mead, b. 1900.
G MEA 205
Typescript.

Brief Mead notes
Holman, Winifred Lovering, 1899-1989.
G MEA 263
1, 13 p.
1949
Typescript.

Lineage of Jeremiah Mead Jr. of Greenwich Connecticut soldier of the American Revolution
Sawers, Mary Beeler, 1903-.
G MEA 273
50 p.
1958
Typescript.

Genealogical and historical sketches of John Meader and some of his descendants
Meader, Alvin A.
G MEA 513
81, 243 p.
Typescript.

A genealogical and historical sketch of John Meader and some of his descendants
Meader, Alvin A.
G MEA 520
87, 3 p.
1928
Typescript.

Ancestry and descendants of Captain Robert M. Meader 1743-1815
Herrington, Byron M.
G MEA 530
1, 49 p.
1966
Typescript.

Bible and family records of several New Hampshire families inc. desc. of two Revolutionary soldiers Jeremiah Meacham - Ezekiel Wells. Family records of William and Alba Johnson of Norwich Vt.
G MEA 60
Various pagings.
1951
Typescript.

The descendants of Jonas and Frances Meador of Essex Caroline and Cumberland Counties Virginia
Nunnally, Major Perkins.
G MEA 681
4, 45 p.
1968
Typescript.

The Meakins lineage
Holman, Winifred Lovering, 1899-1989.
G MEA 825
18 p.
1960
Typescript.

The descendants of James Meek and Susannah Byers 1758-1942
Allison, James B.
G MEE 650
2, 1, 73 p.
1942
Typescript.

Kith and kin of the John Megee family and descendants of Indian River Hundred Sussex County Delaware
Megee, Caleb R. (Caleb Rodney), b. 1888.
G MEG 325
A-B, iv, 331, 59 p.
1963
Typescript.

Meigs lineage compiled for Henry Fletcher of New York City ...
Holman, Winifred Lovering, 1899-1989.
G MEI 402
75 p.
1929
Typescript.

Record of the descendants of Vincent Meigs who came from Dorsetshire England to America about 1635
Meigs, Henry Benjamin, 1844-.
G MEI 410
2, 230 p.
c1935
Typescript.

Meisinger family tree
Meisinger, Eldon, 1928-.
G MEI 610
176 p.
1962
Typescript.

A record of the Mellen family of Pelham [now] Prescott Mass. up to Jan. 1 1853 with recent additions
Mellen, David.
G MEL 1340
49 p.
Typescript.

*Melcher family notes ... Joseph Melcher of
Brunswick Maine & his son Josiah Melcher*
Hill, Mary Pelham, 1865-1943.
G MEL 566
9 p.
1931
Typescript.

The Melendy genealogy
Melendy, A.
G MEL 820
6 p.
1942
Typescript.

*Records from the Bible of William Meriam of
Ashburnham Mass.*
G MER 1200
2 p.
1929
Typescript.

*Descendants of Henry Merryfield of Dorchester
Mass.*
Laimbeer, William.
G MER 2710
35, 7, 2 p.
Typescript.

Merrill [records]
G MER 2954
9 p.
Typescript.

*James Merrill of New Gloucester and Lee Me.
and his descendants*
Sinnett, Charles Nelson, 1847-1928.
G MER 3004
20 p.
1923
Typescript.

*Merrill. Moses 5 Merrill (Peter 4 & 3 Nathaniel 2
& 1) 1738 - and his descendants.*
Priest, Alice L. (Alice Lucinda), 1866-1954.
G MER 3017
7 p.
1931
Typescript.

80 immigrants our Merrill Covell pedigree
Parsons, Gladys Merrill Covell, 1916-.
G MER 3058
iv, 146 p.
1969
Typescript.

Merriman family data
G MER 3240
11 p.
Typescript.

*A part of genealogical and ancestral notes series
2 ancestors of Mary Elizabeth Billard [Merriman
family no. 2-1]*
Edwards, William Hopple
G MER 3260
21, 4 p.
1959
Typescript.

*Henry Merritt of Harpswell Me. ancestry and
descendants*
Sinnett, Charles Nelson, 1847-1928.
G MER 3613
10 p.
1923
Typescript.

*Family Bible record of Elder Albert Merry of
Pittsfield Savoy and Williamstown Mass.*
Shepard, Elmer I. (Elmer Irwin), 1878-1966.
G MER 3775
3 p.
1944
Typescript.

*Genealogical outline of Charles L. Merwin family
of East Palestine Ohio. Notes to Genealogical
outline of the Charles L. Merwin family*
Merwin, Charles Lewis, 1912-.
G MER 4338
10 p.: geneal. tables
1959
Typescript.

Messenger Andrew the first settler of the name in America
Messenger, Winthrop.
G MES 1189
3 p.
1927
Typescript.

Henry Messenger of Boston Mass. brief notes subject to more exhaustive research
Holman, Winifred Lovering, 1899-1989.
G MES 1205
9 p.
1947

The paternal lineage and some of the descendants of Isaac Messenger of Connecticut
Wood, Anne Farrell Higgins
G MES 1221
2 v. in 1.
c1964
2nd
Typescript.

The Messenger family in Portage and Geauga Counties Ohio New Connecticut
Reniger, Jerilyn Jacklin.
G MES 1225
8, 339 p.
1966
Typescript.

Genealogy of the Messer family and descendants of Richard Mercer and Hannah Satchwell of Haverhill Mass.
Young, Marjorie Eleanor.
G MES 1275
6, 83 p.
Typescript.

Genealogy of the Meseroles of Greenpoint [N.Y.]
Meserole, Adrian.
G MES 425
Chart 52 x 66 cm, bound.

Pedigree of Metcalf
G MET 120
3 p.
Typescript.

The descendents [sic] of Johann Heinrich Gottleib [sic] Meyer
Meyer, Camden B.
G MEY 128
105, 11 p.
1956
Typescript.

Mickles - Dorwin Bible records family of Nicholas Mickles and Sarah Dorwin of N.Y.
Coleman, Minnie Lincoln Crow.
G MIC 220
Typescript.

The Mighill kindred of America
Wakefield, George Mighell.
G MIG 75
1935
Typescript.

William Jackson Mikesell and the Mikesell family
Mikesell, Jerome B.
G MIK 215
101 p.
1966
Typescript.

West with the Milhous and Nixon families a story of the forebears of Richard Milhous Nixon
Bell, Raymond Martin, 1907-1999.
G MIL 1245
4, 17 p.
1954
Typescript.

Rev. John Miller of Roxbury
G MIL 2463
2 p.
1877
Typescript.

The Miller family
Miller, George Norton.
G MIL 2526
31 p.
1925
Typescript.

*Millers of England ... Wrothan co. Kent
Chiddingly ... Kensing ... Seale co. Kent Laughton
co. Sussex Lewes ... West Peckham*
Miller, Spencer, 1859-1953.
G MIL 2527
1925
Typescript.

*Martin Miller the pioneer with many of his
ancestors and descendants*
Scott, Nellie Stewart.
G MIL 2538
Various pagings.
1927-1932
Typescript.

Some notes pertaining to Miller genealogy
Miller, William Norton.
G MIL 2542
7, 5, 2 p.
1930
Typescript.

*The Miller and Davis families. [Record of the
descendants of Peter Miller and Catherine
Sheeler and Thomas Davis and Rebecca Tribby]*
Gall, Fenton, 1862-1948.
G MIL 2578
iv, 83 p.
1948
Typescript.

The Reverend John Miller
Holman, Winifred Lovering, 1899-1989.
G MIL 2590
2, 3 p.
1956
Typescript.

*Miller genealogy Griffen Garten Miller and his
descendants*
Rogers, Wilmot Polk, 1889-.
G MIL 2598
1, 14 p.
1958
Typescript.

Millett genealogy
Millett, Laurence.
G MIL 2675
104 p.
1936
Typescript.

*Abstract of the genealogy of the Mills family from
a manuscript of Polly Mills Slocum late of
Tolland Mass. deceased*
G MIL 3076
6 p.
1904
Typescript.

The Mills family of Orange Co. Vt.
Driscoll, Marion Lang.
G MIL 3112
12 p.
1945
Typescript.

*A genealogy of the Mills families of Needham
with chart of the Fuller families with historical
data 1619-1953*
Jones, Frederick A.
G MIL 3125
74 p.
1958
Typescript.

*Amos Mills b. June 29 1732 - d. April 19 1775
some interesting facts about Amos and his home
now at 264 Weston Rd. Wellesley [Mass.]*
Jones, Frederick A.
G MIL 3128
3 p.
1955
Typescript.

The Milward - Millard family
Giddings, Franklin Henry, 1855-1931.
G MIL 3945
Typescript.

Genealogical history of the Joseph Mills family
Miles, Byrd E.
G MIL 942
170, 18 p.
1948
Typescript.

Minta genealogy
Cordley, Henry Gridley.
G MIN 2340
2 p.
1942
Typescript.

1346-1881 Miner name how acquired
Tenney, E.A.
G MIN 730
1881
Typescript.

Notes on the Mitchell family [sons and daughters of Joseph & Joanna (Couch) Mitchell of Kennebunk Me.]
G MIT 125
3 p.
Typescript.

Ancestors and descendants of Lowell Mitchell of Carthage Me. together with genealogies of Lois Story wife of Lowell Mitchell Persis Lowell wife of John Mitchell Keziah Libby wife of Jonathan Mitchell
Winter, Frank.
G MIT 173
1927
Typescript.

Descendants of Jacob Moak of New Scotland
MacCormick, Elizabeth Janet, 1880-.
G MOA 75
118 p.
1942
Typescript.

Mohler - Moler genealogy particularly from George Adam and Eve Moler
Moler, Charles Clyde.
G MOH 115
101 p.
1954
Typescript.

Monfort [Montfort] family [also] Ray and McChesney families
Knight, Ray Roberts, 1881-.
G MON 1240
10 p.
Typescript.

Genealogies of Isaac Monroe and William Monroe soldiers of the Revolutionary War and descendants of William Munroe of Lexington Mass.
Monroe, Lee.
G MON 2360
18 p.
Typescript.

Genealogy Richard Montague - emigrant ancestor
G MON 2630
11 p.
Typescript.

Guidex genealogical index to materials for research on the Montgomery family
G MON 3240
9 p.
Typescript.

The Tennessee colony
McMurray, Rhuy K. Williams.
G MON 3320
3, 195 p.
1966
Typescript.

Genealogy of a branch of the Moore family
G MOO 1060
45 p.
Typescript.

John Moore Jr. of Virginia Georgia and Alabama
Jones, Kathleen Paul.
G MOO 1146
32, 3 p.
1931
Typescript.

The Moore line [William Moore of York Me]
Holman, Winifred Lovering, 1899-1989.
G MOO 1178
2, 13 p.
1943
Typescript.

Moore notes
Holman, Winifred Lovering, 1899-1989.
G MOO 1189A
2, 17 p.
1952
Typescript.

Moore genealogy
Moore, Marcella Werlau, 1928-.
G MOO 1196
17 p.
1962
Typescript.

The Moore's [sic] of Mecklenburg County
Moore, James Ballagh, 1920-.
G MOO 1206
96 p.
1967
Typescript.

Descendants of John Moodie of Roxbury Massachusetts and Hartford Connecticut
G MOO 630
14 p.
1928
Typescript.

The ancestry of Albert Nowell Morton, being the ancestry of each of his four grandparents [Albert Morton Cynthia Kimball Waldron Ebenezer S. Nowell Abra D. Wentworth]
Morton, Albert Nowell.
G MOR 1575
1, 167, 31, 3 p.
Typescript.

Additions & corrections to "George Morton of Plymouth Colony" 1908
Morton, Albert Nowell.
G MOR 1577A
9 p.
1948
Typescript.

Genealogy of John Morton Henrico County Virginia and his descendants
Johnson, Beulah Jeannette.
G MOR 1588
50 p.
1939
Typescript.

Robert Morgan of Beverly Mass. and his descendants also allied families
Bassett, Abbot.
G MOR 227
500 p.
Typescript.

Some collected notes regarding the early Essex County Morgans descendants of Robert Morgan of Beverly [and] the early New Hampshire Morgans
Yates, Edgar (Edgar Allan Poe), 1856-1929.
G MOR 232
Typescript.

The Morgan family in America
Sinnett, Charles Nelson, 1847-1928.
G MOR 259
1917
Typescript.

Morley family notes [descendants of Thomas ... 1769 ... 1813]
G MOR 355
3 p.
Typescript.

John of Kittery [Me.] a Morrell memorial
Morrill, Philip.
G MOR 472
14 p.
Typescript.

Morris family [also] Arnold Barrett Clark Hill Keaton Nicholson Page Pool Pritchard Prather Shattuck Symons [and] White [families]
Knight, Ray Roberts, 1881-.
G MOR 680
7 p.
1952?
Typescript.

Morse descendants of James Morse 1782-1840 of Calais Vermont
Priest, Alice L. (Alice Lucinda), 1866-1954.
G MOR 924
1932
Typescript.

Morse genealogy dealing with the Guilford (Conn.) stay of that branch of the family of Samuel Morse (emigrant ancestor) represented by Seth⁴ Morse of Guilford Conn. and John of Leete's Island
Davis, Marion Morse.
G MOR 930
Various pagings.
1934-1941
Typescript.

Morse notes original copy more complete than in the printed version in vol. 2 of the Stevens-Miller Ancestry
Holman, Winifred Lovering, 1899-1989.
G MOR 950A
66, 70 p.
1952
Typescript.

Genealogies Morse Mason Lyon Pengra
Pengra, Ray.
G MOR 956
2, 37 p.
1959
Typescript.

Moses - Carley and related families
Moses, Pearl (Carley).
G MOS 1044
211 p.
1957
Typescript.

Mosher notes
Holman, Winifred Lovering, 1899-1989.
G MOS 1418
4, 13 p.
1957
Typescript.

Mosely family
Card, Lester.
G MOS 800
1943?
Typescript.

Genealogy of the Mott family
Armstrong, Harold Rodney.
G MOT 1140
177, 5 p.
Typescript.

William Mottern family of Turkeytown East Tennessee (Elizabethton Carter County)
Mottern, Hugh Henry.
G MOT 1450
1962
Typescript.

Mottier family Gentle family Trailor (Trailer) (Traylor) family Butts (Butt) family
Mottier, Charles Helvetius, 1888-.
G MOT 1500
1966
Typescript.

Notice genealogique sur la familie [sic] Mottin de la Balme
G MOT 1550
7 p.
1924
Typescript.

A memorial of the Mountfort family of Boston
Chase, Marion Monks.
G MOU 1328
66 p.
1937-1938
Typescript.

Philip Mowry his ancestors and descendants. After 1880 the descendants used the spelling Morey. This is the Philip Mowry in the Nathaniel line who was born in Smithfield Rhode Island 1734 and removed to Madison County N.Y. about 1800
Gundry, Eldon P.
G MOW 684
41 p.
1961
Typescript.

Problems in Mudd
Mudd, Richard Dyer, 1901-.
G MUD 50
9 p.
Typescript.

Petition requesting a declaration of innocence or a new trial for Dr. Samuel Alexander Mudd
Mudd, Richard Dyer, 1901-.
G MUD 95
13, 6 p.
1968
Typescript.

The story of Joseph Mueller of Council Bluffs Iowa and of his German forebears and American descendants
Mueller, Ralph Scott, b. 1877.
G MUE 450
1, iv, 1, 139 p.
1936
Typescript.

Muir genealogies 150 American families 1550-1943
Muir, Ophelia.
G MUI 150
1943
Typescript.

Ancestors and descendants of Roy Garland Munroe through Garland Lobel Munro Dean and Loring lines
G MUN 3252
13 p.
Typescript.

Known ancestors and descendants of Ralph Waldo Muncy
G MUN 530
15, 81 p.
1959
Typescript.

The Mundell (Mundle) family descendants of James Mundell and his wife Margaret (Garrett) Mundell of New Castle County Delaware and Greene County Pennsylvania and the migration of their children into Kentucky Ohio West Virginia Indiana Illinois Iowa Kansas and other western states
Barry, Ruby Mundell.
G MUN 830
1, 128 p.
1968
Typescript.

Genealogy Murphy Flynn Feeney Gustin
Gustin, Charles.
G MUR 1150
2, 42 p.
1967
Typescript.

Ancestors of John Herbert Murphy and Kathleen Ann Murphy
Murphy, Beulah Bernhard.
G MUR 1156
28 p.
1973
Typescript.

Timothy Murray and descendants
G MUR 1520
6 p.
Typescript.

Descendants of Robert Murray
Murray, Harold Griffith.
G MUR 1540
45, 6 p.
1940
Typescript.

Jonathan Murray of East Guilford Conn. vol. 2 no. 3
Murray, W.B.
G MUR 1548
1948
Typescript.

Descendants of James Murray and Jemima Morgan of Baltimore County (1704-1964)
Barnes, Robert.
G MUR 1555
3, 24 p.
1964
Typescript.

Kings and commoners [Murdock family of South Carver Plymouth County Mass.]
Murdock, W.B.
G MUR 40
6 p.
Typescript.

Pibroch a story of the Murdocks of South Carver Plymouth County Massachusetts
Murdock, William Bartlett.
G MUR 60
1, 27 p.
1935-1936
Typescript.

Genealogy of James Musso and his descendants
G MUS 1800
1937
Typescript.

Musick family. Proceedings of the second annual reunion held at Weaver's Creek Russell County Virginia Sunday August 24 1958
Musick, Grover Cleveland, b. 1891.
G MUS 925
1958
Typescript.

For [sic] Myers Family Association with allied lines of Mudge Whelan Breed Herron Aldrich
Keeler, Grace C.
G MYE 135
66 p.
1955
Typescript.

The Mynatt history
Hubbs, Ferol Frost.
G MYN 375
Various pagings.
1941
Typescript.

Neale lineage, compiled for William Forrester Neale, Esq.
Holman, Winifred Lovering, 1899-1989.
G NEA 458
150p.
1953
Typescript.

Needhams of Wales, Massachusetts and Stafford, Connecticut, adjoining towns
Chapman, Grace Olive.
G NEE 160
93 p.
1942
Typescript.

Nicholson family [miscellaneous notes mostly of Md. and Va]
G NIC 1050
11 p.
Typescript.

The history of a Nickels family Alexander Nickels (1691-1758) and his descendants
Nickels, Walter G.
G NIC 1420
6, 52, 1 p.
1941
Typescript.

Nickerson the family in England and ... America
G NIC 1675
40 p.
Typescript.

Nichols marriages in New England before 1750
Torrey, Frederic Crosby.
G NIC 505
1, 7 p.
1934
Typescript.

Noble [family data Lt. Col. Arthur Noble b. prob. Ireland abt. 1695 d. Grand Pre Can. 1747]
G NOB 145
8 p.
Typescript.

*[Descendants of George Oakes of Lynn Mass.
1657]*
Calder, Philip R.
G OAK 30
9, 4 p.
1932
Typescript.

*Descendants of Thomas and Sarah (Tufts) Oakes
of Cambridge Mass, 1689-1843*
Lowell, Mary Chandler, b. 1863.
G OAK 8
12 p.
Typescript.

[Oakes - Carsley lines of Maine]
Lowell, Mary Chandler, b. 1863.
G OAK 8A
3 p.
Typescript.

Genealogy of the Ober family
Loring, Katharine Peabody
G OBE 175
123 p.
1941
Typescript.

A history of the O'Hanlons
Hanlin, Monroe H.
G OHA 125
4, 1, 66, 4 p.
1954
Typescript.

*Extracts from the parish registers of St. Ann's
Garrison St. Michaels and Christ Church and
other records at Bridgetown in Barbados dealing
with the families of Oistin (Austin) and James*
Connell, Neville.
G OIS 50
3, 6 p.
1956
Typescript.

*The first two hundred years of the Oldham family
in America*
Eddy, Ruth Story Devereux, 1875-1958.
G OLD 645
1939
Typescript

*Notes relating to Thomas Oliver and his children
... especially to ... his son Richard and to Richard
Oliver's close family relationship with Elizabeth
wife of George Carr of Salisbury Massachusetts*
Crawford, Alice I.
G OLI 548
9 p.
1941
Typescript.

*The Oliver family of Albany N.Y. a genealogical
problem*
Hall, William K. (William Kearney), 1918-.
G OLI 556
2, 24 p.
1948
Typescript.

*Family tree of Hans and Karen Olson ... 1839 to
... 1948*
Henryson, Henry T., 1865-.
G OLS 325
1A-92A, 1B-92B p.
1948?
Typescript.

*Family researches at Wesel with mss. of
researches by James Riker of Harlem N.Y.*
Riker, James, 1822-1889.
G OPD 1
5 p.
Typescript.

*Whipple pedigree first few generations of the
Whipple family of Bocking Eng. and Ipswich
Mass.*
Bartlett, J. Gardner (Joseph Gardner), 1872-1927.
G or TP WHI 1109
Chart; 25 x 54.5 cm.
1924

*Orcutt (Urquhart) family from published and
unpublished records census records wills deeds et
cetera*
Hinckley, Mabel Gould Demers, b. 1887.
G ORC 80
36, 1 p.
1963
Typescript.

Our branch of the Ordway family in America
Fales, Raymond D.
G ORD 400
4, 7 p.
1931-1936

The early history of the Orm or Ormsby family
Ormsbee, J.L.
G ORM 648
5 p.
Typescript.

The Osborn family. A genealogy of the descendants of Richard Osborn who emigrated from London Eng. in 1634 and settled in Fairfield Conn. about 1650
Osborn, George Wakeman.
G OSB 386
60, 1 p.
1903-1913
Typescript.

Osborn family direct lineage ancestry of Thomas Osborn Sr. tanner of New Haven Conn. and East Hampton L.I. N.Y.
Osborne, Willard E.
G OSB 400
Various pagings.
1959
Typescript.

Supplement to the history of John Christopher and William Osgood. Additions to and corrections of the history published in 1894
Osgood, Frank Storey.
G OSG 130A
1937
Typescript.

Osgood and Silsby families
Jarvis, May Tibbetts, b. 1864.
G OSG 160
45 p.
1941
Typescript.

The descendants of Mannasseh and Anna (Buxton) Osgood of Westford Vermont
Rodgers, Robert H. (Robert Howard), 1944-
G OSG 170
41 p.
1965
Typescript.

Otis family
Laird, Frederick Jewell.
G OTI 142
25 p.
1903
Typescript.

... Owens - Grubbs families of Viginia and Kentucky
Barr, Lockwood Anderson, b. 1883.
G OWE 204
41 p.
1940
Typescript.

John Owen of Windsor Conn. and some of his descendants 1622-1924
Owen, William A.
G OWE 73
56 p.
Typescript.

Records of the Owen family copied from the Surrogate's office and the County Clerk's office Onondaga New York
Coleman, Minnie Lincoln Crow.
G OWE 76
3 p.
Typescript.

Ancestor William Owen of Braintree Mass. and descendants in Maine
Sinnett, Charles Nelson, 1847-1928.
G OWE 81
63 p.
1922
Typescript.

Packer family descendants of John b. (1626)? - d. 1689
G PAC 570
5 p.
1936
Typescript.

The Paine family in America chart no. 1. The Paine family of Rehoboth Mass. chart no. 2
G PAI 448
10 p.
Typescript.

The Pardee family in America
Adams, William H.
G PAR 1518
2, 5 p.
1936

Correspondence and records concerning the Mayflower ancestry of Samuel Eugene Parker of Shelter Island N.Y. in the Cooke line
Parker, Samuel Eugene.
G PAR 3723
Typescript.

Records of Parker Historical and Genealogical Association organized December 21 1909
Parker Historical and Genealogical Association.
G PAR 3798
Various pagings.
1916
Typescript.

Histories of the families of Archibald Parker Lettie Parker and of Joseph Thomas
Thomas, Ray C., 1898-.
G PAR 3845
3, 3-24 p.
1940
Typescript.

John Parker of Sagadahoc and his descendants
G PAR 3865
23 p.
1948
Typescript.

Ancestor John Patten of Bedford New Hampshire and his descendants
Sinnett, Charles Nelson, 1847-1928.
G PAT 1514
51, 13 p.
Typescript.

Patten genealogy
Sinnett, Charles Nelson, 1847-1928.
G PAT 1532
2 v.
1922
Typescript.

Notes on the American families of Paul or Paull
Paul, Edward Joy, 1858-1911.
G PAU 147
1903
Typescript.

Pedigree of the family of Pemberton in connection with St. Albans with genealogical notes
Moriarty, George Andrews, 1883-1968.
G PEM 265
13, 2, 3 p.
Typescript.

The Penrose family of Wheldrake Yorkshire England and of Ballykean County Wicklow Ireland together with an account of their known descendants in the British Isles and the United States of America to the year 1861
McCracken, George Englert, 1904-1986.
G PEN 3870
49 p.
1961
Typescript.

Some notes on the early family history of the Peppers of Philadelphia with genealogical charts to date
Watts, William Carleton.
G PEP 962
26, 6 p.
1948
Typescript.

English and American ancestry of the Perkins of Hampton N.H. Eastport and Calais Maine
Marston, Maude L. Swett.
G PER 1505
7 p.
Typescript.

Genealogy of the Pettit families in America descendants of John Pettit 1630-1632 [sic] first of that name in America
Van Wyck, Katherine Louise (Wood), 1857-.
G PET 2055
3, 80 p.
1936
Typescript.

The Polly lineage
Holman, Winifred Lovering, 1899-1989.
G POL 1925
1960
Typescript.

Genealogical chart of the known descendants of Micajah Pope 1808-1867 with an outline of his American ancestors 1634-1844
Guthrey, William Morris, b. 1901.
G POP 164
Chart folded to 52 p.
1972

Prince family [descendants of John son of Rev. John Prince rector of East Stafford Berkshire England who came to New England in 1633 and settled in Watertown]
G PRI 2435
5 p.
Typescript.

Notes [Pulsifer family of Gloucester Mass]
Hardon, Henry Winthrop, 1861-1934.
G PUL 1500
6 p.
Typescript.

Qua genealogy descendants of William of County Armagh Ireland
G QUA 50
Typescript.

Records of the Quint family of Maine and New Hampshire ... from family records deeds wills vital statistics etc.
Dunn, Marion L.
G QUI 1050
134 p.
Typescript.

Isaac Quintard (1794-1883) and his wife Clarissa (Hoyt) Shaw (1793-1871) both of Stamford Connecticut and their ancestors and descendants
Poole, Herbert Armstrong, b. 1877.
G QUI 1224
320, 77 p.
1950
Typescript.

The genealogy of the family of de Quincy and Quincy of England and the United States of America
Bellen, George.
G QUI 985
6 v.
1934-1937
Typescript.

Enoch Rector - his fore-fathers and descendants
Rector, Thomas G.
G REC 310
21, 3 p.
Typescript.

Ancestors and descendants of Lucius Redfield with collateral branches
McIntyre, Irma Redfield.
G RED 3140
138 p.
1942
Typescript.

Reynolds and Austin family records copied from Bibles and cemeteries
Gildersleeve, Jessie A. (Reynolds).
G REY 118
4 p.
1929
Typescript.

*The Rhodes line, compiled for Mrs. J. M.
Morrison*
Holman, Winifred Lovering, 1899-1989.
G RHO 245
35 p.
1945
Typescript.

*The Richardson family [descendants of Thomas of
West Mills Eng.]*
G RIC 1238
15 p.
Typescript.

Samuel Rich of Sutton Mass.
Eldridge, William Henry, 1873-1943.
G RIC 332
13 p.
1932
Typescript.

Persons by the name of Rich at Salem Mass.
Eldridge, William Henry, 1873-1943.
G RIC 343
16 p.
1940
Typescript.

Rice family descendants of William
Jenkins, May Rice.
G RIC 52
16 p.
1923
Typescript.

Richmond genealogy descendants of Seymour
Raymond, Ralph Leigh.
G RIC 6018
13 p.
1921
Typescript.

*The Richard genealogy ... Charles and Jacob ...
and all their known descendants*
Berry, Charles Jerome, b. 1892.
G RIC 708
iv, 176 p.
1926
Typescript.

*Humphrey and John Richards of Boston and
Newbury, Mass.*
Holman, Winifred Lovering, 1899-1989.
G RIC 924
18 p.
1947
Typescript.

*Record of Worcester County probate deeds of
Joseph Richards and heirs 1732-1768*
Holman, Winifred Lovering, 1899-1989.
G RIC 930
4 p.
1954
Typescript.

Richards lineage
Holman, Winifred Lovering, 1899-1989.
G RIC 935
1956
Typescript.

Ringo reunion in print [v. 1 no. 1]
Society of Ringo Descendants in America.
G RIN 6710
1934
Typescript.

*Genealogy of families related to George Litch
Roberts and his wife Hinda Barnes Roberts*
Roberts, George Litch.
G ROB 1590
228 p.
Typescript.

*Roberts family descendants of Joseph of
Monmouth Co. N.J.*
Gildersleeve, Jessie A. (Reynolds).
G ROB 1625
4 p.
1929
Typescript.

The Robbins family Hon. Levi Robbins
Robbins, William Randolph.
G ROB 940
19, 3 p.
Typescript.

The family tree of Mary Haselton Rossiter
Haselton, Mabel.
G ROS 3150
122 p.
Typescript.

The Shadrach Roundy ancestry
Warner, Jesse Lenard.
G ROU 1100
1971
Typescript.

*Some German English Irish French Dutch
Scottish and American ancestors of Raymond
Robert Ruppert Jr. and William Hunter Ruppert*
Ruppert, Elizabeth Miller (Hunter), 1909-.
G RUP 725
46 p.
1959
Typescript.

Sage notes
Holman, Winifred Lovering, 1899-1989.
G SAG 310
12 p.
1932
Typescript.

James Sands [& his descendants]
G SAM 2150
3 p.
Typescript.

*Sargent genealogy: William Sargent and his
descendants to the children of the sixth
generation*
G SAR 935
388 p.
c. 1951
Typescript.

*Descendants of Phineas E. Sawyer of Elliotsville
Piscataquis County Maine*
Sawyer, Fred E. (Fred Ellis), 1910-.
G SAW 1150
1943
Typescript.

*Ancestry of Fred Ellis Sawyer son of Albert &
Elsie Luella (Trenhaile) Sawyer*
Sawyer, Fred E. (Fred Ellis), 1910-.
G SAW 1153
8 p.
1943
Typescript.

Brief Scofield - Merwin notes
Holman, Winifred Lovering, 1899-1989.
G SCO 420
8, 4 p.
1949
Typescript.

The Scott line, compiled for Mrs. J. M. Morrison
Holman, Winifred Lovering, 1899-1989.
G SCO 870
27 p.
1943
Typescript.

Scribner notes, compiled for Albert Boyden
Holman, Winifred Lovering, 1899-1989.
G SCR 1055
21 p.
1927
Typescript.

*Scriptures of Connecticut. Coventry, Willington,
Stafford*
Chapman, Grace Olive.
G SCR 1936
44 p.
1943
Typescript.

Searls family notes
G SEA 2545
33 p.
Typescript.

*American ancestry of Warren Hooper Sears:
Sears - Hooper - Dunham - Gurney and allied
families*
G SEA 2827
Typescript.

Record of four generations of the descendants of Capt. Robert Seeley
Morse, Willard S.
G SEE 852
260 p.
1916
Typescript.

The Seibert family Wolfersweiler Saar Tulpehocken Pennsylvania Clear Spring Maryland Martinsburg West Virginia
Bell, Raymond Martin, 1907-1999
G SEI 150
54 p.
1959
Typescript.

American Seymour family. [The seven charts represent #1 common ancestry from Richard the settler the other six charts represent the descendants of David Seymour and Nancy Nichols ...]
Seymour, N. Gilbert.
G SEY 832
7 charts, 34.3 x 45.7 cm each.
1938
Typescript.

The John Shackford family in the U.S.A.
Pearson, N. A., Mrs .
G SHA 1125
8 p.
1952
Typescript.

The descendants of William Sharrard who emigrated to U.S.A. from England in 1760 U.E.L. came to Canada after the American war of independence. Died in 1823.
Phillips, Edward Horace, b. 1878.
G SHA 4190
1, 9 [i.e., 11], 5a-5b p.
1944
Typescript.

Family of Sherburn of Portsmouth N.H.
G SHE 14555
6, 31 p.
Typescript.

Chart showing the descendants of Hon. Henry Sherburne born at Portsmouth N.H. ... 1709 died there ... 1767 and Sarah Warner born at Portsmouth N.H. ... 1722 ... died there ... 1814.
Whittemore, Bradford Adams.
G SHE 14569
Chart, 28.4 x 35.2 cm, bound.
1957

Census probate and land records of the Sherwood family of Onondaga Co. N.Y.
Coleman, Minnie Lincoln Crow.
G SHE 16035
7 p.
1934
Typescript.

Shewbrooks, the names spelled also Shoobrooks, Shoebrooks, Sherbrooke
Chapman, Grace Olive.
G SHE 20140
29 p.
1950
Typescript.

The Shelburne family and the Shelburne family maternal genealogy
Shelburne, Robert Craig, 1912-.
G SHE 5810
5, 4 p.
1951
Typescript.

The Shelburne family
Shelburne, Robert Craig, 1912-.
G SHE 5814
5 p.
1952
Typescript.

Simpson - Trow and Pierce - Swartz family history
Swartz, Edith Evelyn (Trow).
G SIM 3400
24 p.
1961
Typescript.

*Slate family. William Slate of Windham and
Mansfield, Connecticut and some of his
descendants*
Chapman, Grace Olive.
G SLA 1700
33 p.
1941
Typescript.

*The descendants of Nathaniel Smith Jr. (1827-
1901) and his wife Mary Elizabeth Phillips (1829-
1910) their ancestors and the ancestries of the
following who married their descendants Frances
Lyman Willard Edward Stone Adams John Alden
Trott John Seymour Nicholl and James Otis
MacMillin*
Nicholl, J. Seymour Jr.
G SMI 275
22 p.
Typescript.

*Captain Matthias Smith his ancestors and
descendants*
Peacock, Mrs. George B.
G SMI 282
3, 53 p.
Typescript.

*Genealogical record of Verla-Lou Smith of
Greybull Wy.*
Smith, Louis Marshall.
G SMI 780
1938
Typescript.

*The Smith line, compiled for Mrs. J. M. Morrison,
Towanda, Pa.*
Holman, Winifred Lovering, 1899-1989.
G SMI 802
53 p.
1943
Typescript.

*Friend G. Smith of Wales, Massachusetts and his
New England ancestry*
Chapman, Grace Olive.
G SMI 822
29 p.
1948
Typescript.

Smith notes, compiled for Mrs. James S. Smith
Holman, Winifred Lovering, 1899-1989.
G SMI 871
92 p.
1958
Typescript.

Thomas Snell of Bridgewater 1625-1725
Long, Hallock P. (Hallock Porter), b. 1891.
G SNE 660
6 p.
1958
Typescript.

Southwick notes
Barker, John Herbert, 1870-1951.
G SOU 3424
48 p.
Typescript.

Spencer family descendants of Daniel
Walcott, George W.
G SPE 2553
3 p.
Typescript.

Spragins pedigree will of Thomas Spragins 1794
G SPR 520
3, 3, 1 p.
Typescript.

*Cemetery inscriptions. Hillside Cemetery,
Stafford, Tolland County, Connecticut [with
genealogical notes]*
Chapman, Grace Olive.
G STA 14
57 p.
1939
Typescript with mounted photos.

The Stansel family
Stansel, Edwin Nathaniel.
G STA 7360
59, 3 p.
1969
Typescript.

The descendants of David Steere and Phebe Milhous
Milhouse, Dorothy.
G STE 1865
258, 4, 50, 3 p.
1962, 1964
1st and 2nd.
Typescript.

The Stevens genealogy and family history Richard of Taunton Mass. Henry of Stonington Conn. and their descendants in N.C. Ind. and N.Y. including some named Stephens
Stevens, Clarence Perry.
G STE 4630
93 p.
1950
Typescript.

Stevens progenitors, compiled for Mrs. Charles Stinson Pillsbury
Holman, Winifred Lovering, 1899-1989.
G STE 4640
93p.
1957
Typescript.

Story genealogy descendants of Elisha
G STO 16238
11 p.
1922
Typescript.

Stokes - 1000 years
Stokes, William E., Jr.
G STO 4128
1958
Typescript.

Sumner lineage, compiled for Dana Ripley Bullen, 1932
Holman, Winifred Lovering, 1899-1989.
G SUM 1366
46p.
1932
Typescript.

John Sweet of Salem & Providence
Eldridge, William Henry, 1873-1943.
G SWE 1045
28 p.
1932
Typescript.

Taylor family manuscript
Brainard, Homer Worthington, 1864-1947.
G TAY 1768
11 p.
Typescript.

Jane Taylor Joy's history of the Taylor family descendants of Richard of Yarmouth Mass. and the Billingtons of Plymouth Mass.
Joy, Jane Taylor.
G TAY 1775
27, 6 p.
Typescript.

Genealogy of the Taylors of Campton N.H. traced through East Haddam Conn. (Colchester) to Barnstable Mass.
Taylor, Edith Winthrop (Mendall)
G TAY 1899
11 p.
1921
Typescript.

Descendants of Samuel Taylor Burlington County N.J.
Furman, Robert, 1863-1944.
G TAY 1954
2, 67 p.
1940
Typescript.

Prince Taylor genealogy including Taylor families of Middle Haddam Conn. Chatham Conn. Coventry Conn. Hartland Conn. Middletown Conn. Lee Mass. Tyringham Mass. Claridon Ohio ...
Russell, George Ely, 1927-.
G TAY 1980
5 p.
1951
Typescript.

Memoir of the Hon. Peter Thatcher of Cleveland Ohio
Briggs, Samuel, b. 1841.
G THA 320
8 p.
1883
Typescript.

Thayer - Danforth problem with photostat copy of John Thayer's will and codicil 1823
Russell, Allen Danforth, 1897-1984.
G THA 523
8 p.
Typescript.

Ancestors of Nathaniel Thayer
Thayer, Nathaniel.
G THA 528
Whitmore's Ancestral Tablets, 16 p.
1885

Thayer [Richard Thayer born in Thornsbury England came to Massachusetts in 1630 and settled in Braintree]
G THA 622
32 p.
1957
Typescript.

The Thompson line
Holman, Winifred Lovering, 1899-1989.
G THO 1148
13 p.
1948
Typescript.

Thwing
Holman, Winifred Lovering, 1899-1989.
G THW 275
13 p.
1947
Typescript.

Judge Nathaniel Thwing of Boston Mass. and Woolwich Me. and descendants in Maine
Sinnett, Charles Nelson, 1847-1928.
G THW 298
18 p.
1922
Typescript.

Notes on the Thwing family
Thwing, Leroy L.
G THW 310
Various pagings.
1939
Typescript.

Extract of Tidball genealogy prepared 1885-1899 by John Caldwell Tidball (1825-1906) supplemented by his son William Tidball (born Dec. 18 1875)
Tidball, William, 1875-.
G TID 50
67 p.
1945
Typescript.

Joshua Tobey 1772-1814 of Hudson New York and his descendants
Peck, I. Heyward.
G TOB 420
5 p.
1949
Typescript.

Prerogative Court of Canterbury list of Twiner wills and admons, from 1600 to 1750
G TUR 625
Typescript.

Turner lineage, compiled for Mrs. Homer Pierce Clark
Holman, Winifred Lovering, 1899-1989.
G TUR 704
109 p.
1957
Typescript.

Signatures of the Indian chief Uncas and those of his sons also epitaphs of some of Uncas' descendants at Old Norwich and Norwichtown Conn.
G UNC 450
2 p.
Typescript.

Upham genealogy. Preliminary unarranged on printed pages
G UPH 200
60 p.
Typescript.

A brief genealogy of the Usher family in New England and elsewhere showing the line of the direct descent of J.M.C. Usher
Usher, J.M.C.
G USH 255
18 p.
1920
Typescript.

Family of Value in America being the descendants of Monsieur Jean Pierre Victor Value de la Voute embracing genealogies of the families of Chapin Chase Latham Stackpole Thompson Value
Chapin, Howard M. (Howard Millar), 1887-1940.
G VAL 820
1, 9 p.
1910?
Typescript.

Heirs of Jacobus J. Van Nuys and Rachel Howell his wife
Van Nuys, Archie Clifford.
G VAN 11118
3 p.
Typescript.

History of the Van Pelt family
Tilden, Mrs. Ella Ellora (Van Pelt), 1865-.
G VAN 11585
1, 32 p.
1930
Typescript.

New Netherland families Van Sise family the first five generations
Ledley, Wilson V.
G VAN 13275
21 p.
1959
Typescript.

Van Tassel ... Van Texel. The descendants of Jan Cornelissen Van Texel 1625-1704 a family history
Van Tassel, Dan.
G VAN 13600
41 p.
Typescript.

Van Vredenburgh family to John Schureman Vredenburgh who removed to Sangamon Co. Ill. 1835 and his descendants
G VAN 15150
12 p.
Typescript.

Family Bible record of the Van Wyck family contained in a Dutch Bible ... 1690 ... and copied down in line of Jacob T. Van Wyck to 1895
G VAN 16530
3 p.
1933
Typescript.

Van Bresteede - Braisted - Brested - Breasted etc. lineage
G VAN 1850
2 p.
1924
Typescript.

The Van Buskirk family of Buskirk Rensselaer County New York
Thomas, Milton Halsey, 1903-
G VAN 2375
3, 7 p.
1922
Typescript.

New Netherland families Van Cleef Van Cleve and Van Cleave families the first five and some later generations
Ledley, Wilson V.
G VAN 2720
69 p.
1960
Typescript.

Lucas Dircksen Vanderburgh of New Amsterdam and his son Dirck progenitor of the Vanderburgh family of Dutchess Co. NY. Genealogical data compiled from notes of Richard Schermerhorn Jr. & family records of Ida, Thomas ...
Thomas, Howard A.
G VAN 3925
14, 2 p.
1951
Typescript.

Some descendants of Isaac Vandercook b. 1682 d. 1720 through Michael Vandercook member of the Committee of Safety soldier of the Revolution Albany militia collateral lines
Neikirk, Floyd E., b. 1890.
G VAN 4035
53 p.
1953
Typescript.

New Netherland families Vanderhoef family first five generations
Ledley, Wilson V.
G VAN 4420
40 p.
1959
Typescript.

Genealogy of the van de Sande family [copied from the original written by Daniel Frederick Georg van de Sande and revised by his daughter Mary Frolich van de Sande by Caroline Sinker Winslow]
Van de Sande, Daniel Frederick Georg.
G VAN 5675
51, 2 p.
Typescript.

Van Dyke - Welch 1652-1898 with references
Welch, Emma Finney
G VAN 6840
39, 4 p.
1898
Typescript.

Christian Barentsen van Horn and his descendants
Williams, C. S.
G VAN 8372
1, 136 p.
1911
Typescript.

Joris Janzen van Horne and his descendants
Williams, C. S.
G VAN 8475
1, 75 p.
1911
Typescript.

Jan Cornelis van Horne and his descendants
Williams, C. S.
G VAN 8479
1, 89 p.
1912
Typescript.

An account of Barent Baltus the progenitor of the Van Kleeck family in the United States and Canada in Holland
Van Benthuysen, Alvin Seaward, b. 1884.
G VAN 8818
5 p.
Typescript.

Varick [Rev. John Varick from Holland and Hackensack N.J.]
G VAR 1720
8 p.
Typescript.

Some descendants of George Veasey of Stratham New Hampshire
Walker, Martha Brackett.
G VEA 550
64 p.
1932
Typescript.

Genealogy and biography of Flora (Smith) Verrill wife of Professor Addison E. Verrill of Yale U.
Verrill, George E.
G VER 3265
1, 14 p.
Typescript.

Verdon family [Thomas 4 bapt. Brooklyn N.Y. 1683]
Holman, Winifred Lovering, 1899-1989.
G VER 980
8 p.
1945
Typescript.

Copy of a printed genealogy of the Vestal family from 1683 to 1839 issued in 1893 and now in possession of Elizabeth Vestal Stroud
G VES 1025
5 p.
Typescript.

Vick of Vicksburg
Arthur, Robert, 1886-.
G VIC 150
1, 69 p.
1953
Typescript.

The Vickery family of Marblehead Mass.
Holman, Mary Campbell (Lovering), 1868-1947.
G VIC 475
35 p.
1926
Typescript.

Vidito John Vidito of New York City and his descendants a Huguenot founder of an American family
Priest, Alice L. (Alice Lucinda), 1866-1954.
G VID 250
43 p.
1932
Typescript.

Lineages of Margaret Inez Viele
Stanton, Margaret Inez Viele.
G VIE 415
about 100 p.
1946?
Typescript.

Genealogical notes on the English branch of the Violet family
Bramble, Percy.
G VIO 500
Various pagings.
Typescript.

Family Bible record of Paulina von Schneidau (Mrs. Eugene Murray Jerome) of New York City and Williamstown
Shepard, Elmer I. (Elmer Irwin), 1878-1966.
G VON 2075
2 p.
1942
Typescript transcription.

Genealogical record of the family of John Vosmus 1747-1819
Vickery, Mrs. Guy Orison.
G VOS 2150
3 p.
1940
Typescript.

Vosburgh genealogy and records [descendants of Hendrick of Kinderhook N.Y.]
G VOS 360
12 p.
1935
Typescript.

Annals of the Vreeland family
Vreeland, Louis Beach, 1884-.
G VRE 465
78 p.
1950
Typescript

Edward Walker Sr. of North Carolina and his descendants
Burns, Annie Walker, 1894-1966.
G WAL 3640
Typescript.

Captain Joshua Walker: the Woburn Minuteman and his descendants through Capt. Joshua Walker Jr. of Woburn, Mass., and Rindge, N.H.
Mann, Charles Edward, b. 1857.
G WAL 3665
19 p.
[1896]
Typescript.

Wallace genealogical data suggestions for a Wallace family association a national Wallace family reunion and a complete Wallace genealogy
Seaver, Jesse Montgomery, b. 1890.
G WAL 4695
37, 1 p.
1927
Typescript.

Walcott genealogy
Walcott, George W.
G WAL 785
Typescript.

Walcott - Joslin Hungerford notes [typescript]: gathered from various sources to prove Revolutionary soldier ancestor of Mrs. Marjorie Hungerford Cook and Mrs. Miram Hungerford Ritenour
Cronbaugh, Lois W.
G WAL 805
38 p.
1958
Typescript.

Samuel Wark of Hopkinton and Upton Mass.
Pratt, Mrs. Roy P.
G WAR 4320
28 p.
Typescript.

Genealogical account of a branch of the descendants of Mark Warner grandson of William Warner who came from England to Ipswich Massachusetts in the year 1637]
Warner, Oliver, 1818-1885.
G WAR 4869
13 p.
1872
Typescript.

Joseph Warner 1725-1788 of Sudbury Vt. and Capt. Joseph Little 1732-1817 of Springfield & Sudbury Vt.
Eldridge, William Henry, 1873-1943.
G WAR 4920
10 p.
1932
Typescript.

Warner records of New Hampshire and Vermont
Warner, Everett.
G WAR 4934
3, 113 p.
1936
Typescript.

Warner genealogy [descendants of Andrew Warner and some data concerning William Tuttle and his descendants]
Burt, Jayne Llewellyn.
G WAR 4942
13, 2 p.
1942
Typescript.

Warner family a condensed and revised version of the Westmoreland Warners ...
Warner, Everett.
G WAR 4948
9, 1 p.
1947
Typescript.

Warner and allied families
Warner, Josephine S.
G WAR 4951
2, 99 p.
1948
Typescript.

Some more descendants of John Warner the immigrant of Farmington Conn. through Daniel [5] Warner (Dr. Benjamin [4] Dr. Ebenezer [3] John [2] John [1]) who was killed at the battle of Bennington

Sandiford, Edward Raymond.
G WAR 4968
1, 5, 3, 1 p.
1956
Typescript.

The family of Nathan Smith Warner and Sarah Gilbert Powers
Mentzer, Edna G.
G WAR 4970
5, 355 p.
1963
Typescript.

"Kinsmen all" descendants of Wettenhall Warner and related families
Williams, E. Russ.
G WAR 4975
1, 5, 702 p.
c1964
Typescript.

Genealogy of Warnick family (to June 1 1951) also embracing the families of Butcher and Drake and other pioneer families of Va. who migrated west of the Allegheny Mts. year of 1894 and prior thereto
Warnick, Gorman Clyde.
G WAR 5470
1951
Typescript.

The name history of Warren
G WAR 5483
1, 31, 1 p.
Typescript.

[*Records from old family Bible belonging to Jonas Warren.* Also copy of an article in the *Rutland Herald & Globe Tuesday* August 5 1884 entitled "Celebrating her centennial birthday." Birth of Mrs. Hannah (Warren) Holland.]
G WAR 5990
3 p.
Typescript.

Warren genealogical records (John Warren line of Watertown)
McCreery, Marguerite C.
G WAR 5993
22 p.
Typescript.

Warren family gathering at Newburgh N.Y. July 1871
G WAR 6007
4 p.
1871
Typescript.

Charles Warren. Report on search of Waltham church records Waltham City Hall
Holman, Winifred Lovering, 1899-1989.
G WAR 6099
2 p.
1943
Typescript.

Miscellaneous documents relating to the Ward family of Newton Massachusetts descendants of William Ward of Sudbury
G WAR 753
Typescript.

Index to Ward family descendants of William Ward by A.H. Ward 1851
Ward, Paul Theodore Bliss.
G WAR 780A
50 p.
1910
Typescript.

Ancestral families of the Wards a genealogical study
Ward, Anna Daneker, 1886-
G WAR 876
587 p.
1950
Typescript.

Thomas Ward and his descendants a genealogical study
Ward, Frank Anthony II.
G WAR 895
1963
Typescript.

Record of the ancestry of George Washington
G WAS 1348
39 p.
Typescript.

The Wass family
Wass, Walter Preston, b. 1884.
G WAS 3150
1945
Typescript.

Pedigree Margarette Chase (Small) Washburn paternal side
Washburn, Margarette Chase (Small).
G WAS 888
5 p.
Typescript.

A genealogical history of the Washburns of Huron Co. Ohio
Parkinson, Mildred Jane (Smith), b. 1892.
G WAS 974
92 p.
1954
Typescript.

The lineage of Lucy Waterman Hewitt and George Washburn
Wilcox, Philip Alan.
G WAS 985
36 p.
1964
Typescript.

*The Waterman line ... also some brief notes on
Samuel Winsor*
Holman, Winifred Lovering, 1899-1989.
G WAT 1035
1, 18 p.
1946

*Family record of John Waters of Williamstown
Mass. [b. Hebron Conn. 1757] from a framed
family record*
Shepard, Elmer I. (Elmer Irwin), 1878-1966.
G WAT 1275
2 p.
1944
Typescript.

*[Watkins genealogical material concerning
Andrew Watkins of Charlestown and Roxbury
Mass.]*
G WAT 1535
6 p.
Typescript.

*Watson [Foreman family records Delaware and
Pennsylvania]*
Holman, Winifred Lovering, 1899-1989.
G WAT 2098
7 p.
1932
Typescript.

Watson - Low and allied families
Lamb, Frank Bird, 1863-1955.
G WAT 2107
24 p.
1937
Typescript.

*... Thomas and Rebecah (Moorman) Watson and
their descendants*
Watson, Estelle Osborn Clark, b. 1888.
G WAT 2112
23 p.
1940
Typescript.

*A history and some biographies of the following
families Watson Pendell Curry Bliss Hazard
Bogardus*
Watson, Joseph M.
G WAT 2123
5, 93, 6 p.
1969
Typescript.

The Wattles family of Connecticut (John 1)
Gottschalk, Katherine Cox, b. 1880.
G WAT 2948
16 p.
Typescript.

Waterhouse family
Chapman, Leonard B. b. 1834.
G WAT 755
18 p.
1903
Typescript.

*Descendants of Richard Waterhouse of
Portsmouth N.H. with notes on the descendants of
Jacob Waterhouse of New London Conn. Joshua
Waterhouse of New Jersey and others. Also a
sketch of the Waterhouse in England*
Waterhouse, George Herbert, 1862-.
G WAT 770
3 v.
1934
Typescript.

*Descendants of Alvin Mayberry Waterhouse (6)
and Elizabeth Fitts (Howe) Waterhouse (Nov. 15
1951) supplementary to Descendants of Richard
Waterhouse of Portsmouth N.H. (Feb. 5 1934)*
Noyes, Frank H.
G WAT 770A
18 p.
1951
Typescript.

*Supplement to vol. 2 p. 921-922 of Geneal. of the
Waterhouse Family*
Noyes, Frank H.
G WAT 770B
9 p.
1952
Typescript.

Some desc. of Jeremiah and Rachel (Franklin) Weatherhead of Guilford Vt.
Stoughton, Ralph M.
G WEA 1090
54 p.
1949
Typescript.

The Wead family and its relation to Malone
Wead, Charles K.
G WEA 110
21 p.
1905
Typescript.

Weare notes original copy more complete than given in the printed version in vol. 2 of the Stevens - Miller ancestry
Holman, Winifred Lovering, 1899-1989.
G WEA 792A
40 p.
1952
Typescript

The Webber records from a collection of notes made by the late E.P. Webber of Westport Maine of the U.S.R.C.S.
Webber, E.P.
G WEB 246
186 p.
Typescript.

The Webber family of Maine data collected by the late Alice Webber Child
Champine, Emojene (Demarist).
G WEB 285
36, 2 p.
1940
Typescript.

Webber and allied family history records
Webber, Thomas Hoppel, 1893-.
G WEB 293
172 p.
195-
Typescript.

Notes on the Webber family of Maine
Hinckley, Mabel Gould Demers, b. 1887.
G WEB 296
1, 23 p.
1963
Typescript.

A family of Webb of Virginia ancestry
Leckey, Howard Louis, b. 1892.
G WEB 30
6 p.
1936
Typescript.

Webster line of Philip H. Cummings
Source "Some of the descendants of John Webster of Ipswich Massachusetts 1634" by John C. Webster M.D. Chicago 1912.
G WEB 627
3 p.
Typescript.

The ancestry of Benjamin Howard Webster a descendant of Thomas Webster of Hampton N.H.
Lord, Vivian Sutherland.
G WEB 629
2, 22 p.
Typescript.

Genealogy of the Webster family to which Daniel Webster belonged
G WEB 666
38 p.
1927
Typescript.

Webster notes and Tamworth [N.H.] marriages
Holman, Winifred Lovering, 1899-1989.
G WEB 690
1, 3 p.
1945
Typescript.

Webster lineage, compiled for Edward Sibley Webster, Esq.
Holman, Winifred Lovering, 1899-1989.
G WEB 693
171 p.
1946
Typescript.

The Webster family. Part I. The descendants of Thomas Webster of New Hampshire. Part 2 [sic]. New Hampshire descendants of John Webster of Ipswich Mass. Pt. 3 [sic]. Unclassified Webster data ...
Driscoll, Marion Lang.
G WEB 696
46, 67, A-O p.
1947
Typescript.

Genealogy of the Weddington family
Weddington, Andy Simmons, b. 1889.
G WED 205
115 p.
1960
Typescript.

One line of Weed ancestry with connections with Stevens and Disbrow families
Simmons, Frederick Johnson, b. 1884.
G WEE 120
5, 18 p.
1953
Typescript.

Frances [sic] Weekes and one line of his descendants from his son Samuel to the present day also collateral branches Bowne Cooke Cornell De Forest Emery Feake Fones Fowler Freeman Goodwin Hoag Ireland Kip Montagne Mosher Reddocke
Weeks, Frank Edgar, 1857-1946.
G WEE 799
70 p.
1936
Typescript.

Genealogical notes on the Weeks family
Bowman, Sumner Eli.
G WEE 884
6 p.
1902
Typescript.

Genealogy of the Francis Weeks (Weekes) family of Oyster Bay L.I. also bringing in connecting families of Anne Jan (Bogardus) Cornell Hoag Kipp Sands Sutton Thorn etc.
Weeks, Frank Edgar, 1857-1946.
G WEE 892
4, 69 p.
1931
Typescript.

Otis S. Weeks his ancestors and allied families of Vt and Utah
Newby, Louise W.
G WEE 935
1968
Typescript.

The genealogy of the Weitkamps
Weitkamp, Arthur Robert, 1917-.
G WEI 80
3, 51 p.
1941
Typescript.

The English ancestry of Gov. Thomas Welles of Conn.
Welles, Lemuel Aiken.
G WEL 1830
73 p.
Typescript.

Wellman genealogy
Wellman, Merritt H.
G WEL 2625
21 p.
Typescript.

A limited genealogy of the Wells family of the Colchester Conn. branch
Wells, Heber.
G WEL 3691
7 p.
1923
Typescript.

A history of the family of Joseph Wells
Bleistein, Elizabeth Wells.
G WEL 3736
10 p.
1940
Typescript.

The Wells family
Wells, Chester A.
G WEL 3755
98 p.
1954
Typescript.

The Wells lineage
Holman, Winifred Lovering, 1899-1989.
G WEL 3760
86 p.
1960
Typescript.

The ancestry of Mary (Welton) Van Wagnen in the paternal line of Welton and in the three collateral lines of Upson Buck and Cossett and the four allied lines of Andrews Porter Holcomb(e) [and] Sherwood
Van Wagnen, Frank Leslie
G WEL 4295
60, xlii p.
1948
Typescript.

Welton
Clapp, Ada Welton.
G WEL 4309
5, 24, 4 p.
1972
Typescript.

Ashbel Welch
Bogart, John.
G WEL 475
54 p.
Typescript.

Welch - Dalton deeds Parsonsfield York Co. Maine
G WEL 480
20 p.
Typescript.

Weld [pedigree descendants of William of Eton Cheshire England and his wife Margaret Bostock]
G WEL 725
8 p.
Typescript.

Weld - Faxon notes
White, Charles F. (Charles Frederick).
G WEL 744
3 p.
1928
Typescript.

Weld directory
Weld, Paul Ashworth.
G WEL 765
27 p.
1941
Typescript.

Weld records part one [descendants of Zebina Weld Sr. ... b. Cornish N.H. May 22 1793 d. Plainview Minn. June 9 1865]
Weld, Paul Ashworth.
G WEL 769
23 p.
1942
Typescript.

The descendants of Henry Wenzel of Braintree and Boston
Wenzel, John.
G WEN 2450
25 p.
1939
Typescript.

Wenban a short history and commentary on the origin and occurrence of the name in its earlier form
G WEN 400
26 p.
1948
Typescript.

Three Wessels families of New Netherland with an appendix on the Beeck family of New Amsterdam
McCracken, George Englert, 1904-1986.
G WES 1065
15 p.
1957
Typescript.

Some Revolutionary soldiers of Athol and vicinity.
#12. Benjamin Wesson of Templeton
Smith, Clare E.
G WES 1380
11, 2 p.
Typescript.

Francis West of Duxbury and his descendants in
Stafford Conn. also showing Cushman connection
Cole, Gertrude S.
G WES 1630
16, 2 p.
Typescript.

Osborn family in The West and Osborn families
Osborn, Byrle Jacob.
G WES 1678
1-78, 6 p.
1938
Typescript.

The descendants of Edward West of Lexington
Kentucky
Andrews, Mrs. Forrest.
G WES 1700
41 p.
1966
Typescript.

Sketch of the family group of Anthony Westbrook
of Canada
Westbrook, William E.
G WES 2340
35 p.
1938
Typescript.

The record and family of Nehemiah Westbrook
Westbrooke, William Edward, b. 1898.
G WES 2360
45 p.
1964
Typescript.

Westbrook and allied families: Foster Barker
Fort Sandeful Lambert Hanson
Jones, Blair.
G WES 2365
167 p.
1967
Typescript.

Westmorland lineage and descendants of Thomas
Westmoreland [sic] the immigrant to Virginia
Claypool, Edward A., 1854-1916.
G WES 5250
37 p.
1908
Typescript.

The Weser family
Beitzell, Edwin Warfield, 1905-.
G WES 675
15 p.
1948
Typescript.

Families from village Wetheral
Wetherell, Frank E.
G WET 1055
2 v.
1948-1950
Typescript.

Tables which show in part the descendants of
Christopher Wetherill 1672-1882
Wetherill, Charles.
G WET 1225
3, 33 p.
1882?
Typescript.

Descendants of John Wetherbee [of Boxboro
Mass.]
Harris, Ida A.
G WET 850
6 p.
1934
Typescript.

Descendants of Israel Wetherbee (1756-1813) of
Stow Boxborough and Ashby Mass.
Wetherbee, David Kenneth.
G WET 852
iv, 213 p.
1963
Typescript.

Weyerhaeuser [sic] 15 p Moon 6 p Olin 12 p
Seager 10 p.
G WEY 425
Typescript.

*Probable English ancestry of the Concord
Wheelers*
G WHE 1530
6 p.
Typescript.

*A line of descendants of George Wheeler of
Concord thru William Wheeler of Canton Mass.*
Wheeler, Merrill D.
G WHE 1534
11 p.
Typescript.

*Genealogical supplements ... descendants of
Thomas Wheeler ... Wheeler Holmes Smith Buck
Cutting families*
Wheeler, C. H.
G WHE 1564A
3, 170, 1 p.
Typescript.

*Wheeler notes [Thomas Wheeler b. in England
about 1610 died in Boston Mass. 18 May 1654]*
Holman, Mary Campbell (Lovering), 1868-1947.
G WHE 1576
18 p.
1928
Typescript.

*Some descendants of Richard Wheeler of Dedham
(later Medfield) and later of Lancaster Mass.*
Wheeler, L. W.
G WHE 1579
7 p.
1928
Typescript.

*Wheeler [deeds of Joseph and Hannah (Adams)
Wheeler at Pomfret Conn.]*
Holman, Winifred Lovering, 1899-1989.
G WHE 1598
2 p.
1945
Typescript.

*George Wheeler of Concord Mass. [and some of
his descendants]*
Swan, Mrs. Alton.
G WHE 1610
12, 3 p.
1951
Typescript.

*The Wheeler family of Charles County Maryland
a history and genealogy of John Wheeler 1630-
1693 immigrant to Maryland in 1652 and some of
his descendants*
Ball, Walter V. (Walter Vancion), 1901-.
G WHE 1625
108 p.
1966
Typescript.

Eleazer Wheelock and some of his descendants
Waite, Marcus Warren.
G WHE 1720
Typescript.

*Ancestors and descendants of Henry Francis
Wheelock*
Argersinger, Winifred (Thomson).
G WHE 1730
24, 2 p.
1932-1940
Typescript.

*Sketch of the life of Deacon Jonathan Wheelock of
Cavendish Vermont*
Wilgus, Gertrude Bernadette.
G WHE 1742
3, 74 (i.e., 75) p.
1942
Typescript.

*Wheelock genealogy [descendants of Rev. Ralph
Wheelock who was born in Shropshire England in
1600 and came to New England in 1637 settling
at Dedham Mass.]*
Wheelock, Carlyle C.
G WHE 1755
353 p.
1955
Typescript.

John Whelan of Brandon Vt. and descendants
Whelan, Marion E.
G WHE 2250
1935
Typescript.

Sherborne Abbey [copy of the complete list of entries in our registers relating to the Whetcombe family from 1605 to 1732]
G WHE 2900
2 p.
Typescript.

Whittemore [data copied from Bibles & records in possession of Lyman Whittemore Rhodes a native of Fitzwilliam N.H.]
Rhodes, Lyman Whittemore.
G WHI 10172
9 p.
1923
Typescript transcription.

Charles Whittemore Nottingham West (now Hudson N.H.) his ancestors and some of his descendants Mayflower descendants to Chelmsford - Harvard branches
Ross, C. Aileen.
G WHI 10185
1947
Typescript.

Whitten and allied families
Alexander, Virginia Wood.
G WHI 10250
iii, 304 p.
1966
Typescript.

Whipple genealogy [descendants of John and Sarah]
G WHI 1045
5 p.
Typescript.

A brief genealogy of the Whipple family comp. for Oliver Mayhew Whipple esq. of Lowell
Boutelle, John H.
G WHI 1060
36 p.
1857
Typescript.

Whipple notes part of Deering Whipple manuscript collections
Holman, Mary Campbell (Lovering), 1868-1947.
G WHI 1120
Various pagings.
1934
Typescript.

Genealogy of Whipple Paddock Bull families in America 1620-1970
Kapphahn, Ruth Whipple, 1901-.
G WHI 1138
69 p.
1969
Typescript.

Abstracts of Whistler family probate records originals found in Connecticut State Library
Shaw, Margaret Race.
G WHI 1350
7 p.
1946
Typescript.

Whittlesey genealogy
Patterson, David Williams, 1824-1892.
G WHI 13779
19-382 p.
1879
Typescript.

Whitton notes [James Whitton born probably in England about 1620 d. in Hingham Mass. 26 April 1710]
Holman, Winifred Lovering, 1899-1989.
G WHI 13925
2 p.; 3 p.
1928; 1959
Typescript.

The Whitaker chart by Ephraim Seward Whitaker genealogist 1900 Dec. 31st
Whitaker, Ephraim Seward.
G WHI 1590
90 p.
1929

Joseph Whitaker family of Sterling Mass.
Cheever, Herbert M.
G WHI 1607
4 p.
1955
Typescript.

Descendants of Bailey Harrison Whitcher and Ordelia De Lozier
McElroy, Wilman Whitcher.
G WHI 2253
101 p.
1960
Typescript.

Whitcomb family notes 3 letters from Samuel Whitcomb of Springfield Vt. concerning Whitcomb family written probably before 1830
Whitcomb, Samuel.
G WHI 2668
5 p.
Typescript.

John White of Nelson N.H. Revolutionary soldier born Norton Mass. Sept. 18 1757 died Nelson N.H. Dec. 21 1846
Bonsall, Mrs. George H.
G WHI 3002
6 p.
Typescript.

The White family
White, Henry Bowen.
G WHI 3010
3, 102, 7 p.
Typescript.

Miscellaneous notes on the White family chiefly the descendants of Thomas White of Weymouth Mass.
G WHI 3018
Typescript.

White genealogy [descent of Malcolm P. White from Nicholas]
G WHI 3022
3 p.
Typescript.

[Nicholas White family]
White, Jane Smith.
G WHI 3032
1, 71 p.
Typescript.

Notes on the Cornelius White family of Taunton
Davol, E. Russell.
G WHI 3180
7 p.
1911?
Typescript.

One wing of the house of White
Davol, E. Russell.
G WHI 3182
3 p.
1911?
Typescript.

Mayflower ancestry and descendants of Daniel White of Marshfield Mass. (and Winterport Maine?)
Jewett, Abbie.
G WHI 3183
1, 15, 3 p.
1911
Typescript.

White family Enoch White's memorandum 1854 [descendants of John of Eng. and Hadley Mass.]
White, Enoch.
G WHI 3220
9 p.
1928
Typescript.

Genealogy of the White family furnished from the family record book
Magee, Elizabeth F. (White).
G WHI 3235
3, 2 p.
1937-1938
Typescript.

Descendants of one line of Capt. Thomas White of Weymouth through the Whites of Mendon Uxbridge Northbridge Sutton and Millbury Mass.
White, William T.
G WHI 3239
6 p.
1937
Typescript.

Our ancestors [Ambrose family]
Brann, Mildred Carolyn (White), 1898- .
G WHI 3246
1 v.
1940
Typescript.

Our ancestors
Brann, Mildred Carolyn (White), 1898- .
G WHI 3246
1 v.
c1940
Typescript.

The White line compiled for Mrs. S. Westray Battle of Asheville, N.C.
Holman, Winifred Lovering, 1899-1989.
G WHI 3250
5 p.
1943
Typescript.

Thomas White, compiled for Mrs. Horatio Ford, Mayfield and Richmond Roads, South Euclid, Ohio.
Holman, Winifred Lovering, 1899-1989.
G WHI 3255
70 p.
1943
Typescript

Genealogy of Nancy Compton White's ancestors and descendants 1664 to 1955
White, Perry S.
G WHI 3259
47 p.
1944
Typescript.

The William White line, compiled for Mrs. J. M. Morrison, 1946
Holman, Winifred Lovering, 1899-1989.
G WHI 3265
8 p.
1946
Typescript.

The White genealogy a history of the descendants of Matthew and Elizabeth (Given) White of County Tyrone Ireland and Albany New York
Durant, William, 1846-1914.
G WHI 3270
233 p.
1951
Typescript.

William White co-founder of Salisbury Conn.
Wiles, Harriett M.
G WHI 3282
47 p.
1955
Typescript.

A genealogy of the descendants of Giles White and Sarah Dodd
Briggs, Aubrey Roy.
G WHI 3285
8, 240 p.
1958
Typescript.

History of the William Pinkney White family
McDivitt, B. Olive.
G WHI 3287
1, 6, 40, 10 p.
1959-1964
Typescript.

James and Bessie (Black) White and their descendants
Barnes, Milford Edwin, b. 1883.
G WHI 3292
3, 34 p.
1961
Typescript.

A sketch of Thomas White of Weymouth Massachusetts and certain of his descendants
White, Herbert Warren.
G WHI 3294
56 p.
1961
Typescript.

Descendants of Alex White from Stephenville Crossing Nfld. 1963-1964 [sic] a genealogy of five living generations
White, Richard Andrew, 1828-.
G WHI 3304
vi, 73 p.
1965
Typescript.

Whitehouse families in Maine ancestor Andrew Whitehouse Topsham Me. with descendants. Ancestor Benjamin Whitehouse Oxford Me. with ancestry and descendants
Sinnett, Charles Nelson, 1847-1928.
G WHI 4225
8, 10 p.
1923
Typescript.

A brief history of the family of the Rev. Pinkney Alexander Whitener and Dicey Mariah Brendle Whitener their ancestors and descendents [sic]
Whitener, Russell Pinkney, 1890-.
G WHI 4425
39 p.
1962
Typescript.

Whitfield history and genealogy of Tennessee
Whitfield, Vallie Josephine Fox, 1922-.
G WHI 4515
237 p.
1964
Typescript.

Whitfield McKeel Fox Schiefer families
Whitfield, Vallie Josephine Fox, 1922-.
G WHI 4515A
614 p.
1965
Typescript.

Genealogical notes of the Whiting family [descendants of William of Hartford Conn.]
Whiting, Andrew Fuller.
G WHI 4947
8 p.
1888
Typescript.

Ancestry and descendants of Samuel and Elizabeth St. John Whiting
Whiting, Charles F.
G WHI 4966
13 p.
1946
Typescript

Whitlock and others families included Bowne Cool Cortelyou Crawford Denise Fanshaw
Brush, Grace L.
G WHI 5225
1930
Typescript.

Whitmarsh - Reed data
Whelan, Florence Spencer
G WHI 5840
5 p.
1949
Typescript.

Ancestry of Louis L. Whitney
Whitney, Louis L.
G WHI 6889
Typescript.

A brief account of the descendants of John and Elinor Whitney of Watertown Mass.
Whitney, Henry Austin.
G WHI 6890
26 p.
1857
Typescript.

Who carried the alarm to Watertown April 18 1775?
Whitney, William H.
G WHI 6930
4 p.
1897
Typescript.

*A Whitney farm in eight generations. A memorial
of the Whitney family*
Whitney, William H.
G WHI 6934
5, 150, 8 p.
1898
Typescript.

*Abizer Whitney of Lisbon Me. and descendants
also ancestor John Whitney of New Meadows
Brunswick Me. with index.*
Sinnett, Charles Nelson, 1847-1928.
G WHI 6952
11, 6 p.
1929
Typescript.

*Whitney genealogy of the brothers Judge Joshua
and Gen. William Whitney of Binghamton N.Y.*
Weeks, Frank Edgar, 1857-1946.
G WHI 6956
3, 34 p.
1932
Typescript.

*James Whitney of North Craftsbury Vt. his
ancestry and his descendants*
Whitney, Gertrude C.L.
G WHI 6969
1, 28, 1 p.
1939
Typescript.

*Whitney lineage compiled for Grace (Whitney)
Hoff*
Holman, Mary Campbell (Lovering), 1868-1947.
G WHI 6973
14 p.
1939
Typescript.

*Some more descendants of John and Elinor
Whitney*
Sandiford, Edward Raymond.
G WHI 6977
1, 8, 2 p.
1941
Typescript.

*Wiggin genealogy. A combination of manuscripts
in the library of the New Hampshire Historical
Society by Arthur C. Wiggin Agnes P. Bartlett
Alexander Lincoln. Volume 1 seven generations*
Lincoln, Alexander.
G WIG 1265
195, 39 p.
Typescript.

*Copy of a record [Wiggin family of Stratham
N.H.]*
Wiggin, William H.
G WIG 1270
21 p.
Typescript.

*Wiggin Bible records from family Bible in
possession of Mrs. Blanch M. (Glidden) Peach of
Wadley's Falls Lee N.H.*
G WIG 1305
2 p.
1925
Typescript transcription.

*Wiggin - Brackett record descendants of Barker
Wiggin and Deborah Brackett*
Chamberlain, George Walter, 1859-1942.
G WIG 1309
4 p.
1929
Typescript.

Copy of the pension of John Wight
Holman, Winifred Lovering, 1899-1989.
G WIG 2504
23 p.
1947
Typescript.

*Copy of various documents relating to the
Revolutionary War pension claims of John Wight
& wife Olive of Penobscot Me.*
Holman, Winifred Lovering, 1899-1989.
G WIG 2504
Typescript.

*Ancestors and descendants of Rev. Oramel
Eleazer Wightman late of Mohawk N.Y.*
Gates, Frederick, b. 1848.
G WIG 3000
17 p.
1935
Typescript.

Wigton
Reeve, Mary Eliza (Wigton), 1879-.
G WIG 3810
169 p.
1961
Typescript.

John Wilcox of Hartford Conn.
Johnston, Harry Ferris.
G WIL 1040
62 p.
Typescript.

*Willey - Sanborn Robinson - Holgate Robinson -
Kellogg*
Ball, Helen Willey.
G WIL 10415
Typescript.

*Some additions and corrections to "Isaac Willey
of New London Conn. and his descendants" by
Henry Willey (1658) [sic] of New Bedford Mass.*
Putnam, Charles F.
G WIL 10442A
12 p.
1949
Typescript.

*Elnathan Wilcox (1734-1825) of Simsbury
Connecticut West Stockbridge Massachusetts and
East Bloomfield New York and some of his
descendants*
Hebel, Ianthe Bond, b. 1884.
G WIL 1085
19, 1 p.
1937
Typescript.

[Roger Williams and descendants]
G WIL 12492
7-41 p.
Typescript.

*Descendants of John Williams of Newbury and
Haverhill Mass. 1600-1674*
Williams, Cornelia Bartow, 1854-1921.
G WIL 12500
228 p.
Typescript.

*William D. Williams and his wife Martha. Wales
to Portage County Ohio 1832*
G WIL 12503
3 p.
Typescript.

*[Genealogical pedigree of the descendants of
Samuel Williams son of Robert]*
G WIL 12509
Chart; 39 x 97.5 cm

*[Genealogical pedigree of the descendants of
Stephen Williams third son of Robert b 1640]*
G WIL 12514
Chart; 44 x 111 cm

*The ancestry and some of the descendants of
Theophilus Williams and his wife Ruth Brown of
Providence R.I.*
Carter, Marion Williams Pearce, b. 1867.
G WIL 12519
8 p.
Typescript.

*Lost Creek memories a book about two Quaker
families of Tennessee and how they got together
in the little log meeting house at Lost Creek*
Dixon, Ben.
G WIL 12521
2, 40, 3 p.
Typescript.

*Benjamin Williams (1744-1835) of New Ipswich
N.H. and his descendants*
Denio, Francis Brigham, b. 1848.
G WIL 12592
82 p.
1895
Typescript.

Williams genealogy descendants of Robert and Sarah of Boston
Williams, Horace Perry.
G WIL 12644
11 p.
1909
Typescript.

Ancestry and posterity of Richard Williams of Taunton Mass.
Williams, Charles Crosby, 1855-.
G WIL 12712
2 v., 800 p.
1924
Typescript.

The Williams family the ancestry of Jane Williams Selby mother of Mrs. A.J. Ralston (Clara Williams Selby) and Prentiss Selby of California
Schmidt, Esther Skolfield.
G WIL 12730
4 p.
1927
Typescript.

[Williams family descendants of Robert the Puritan of Roxbury Mass. line of Col. Judah of Williamstown Mass.]
Getman, Mabel Gertrude.
G WIL 12734
4, 20 p.
1928
Typescript.

The ancestry and some of the descendants of Theophilus Williams of Providence R.I.
Carter, Marion Williams Pearce, b. 1867.
G WIL 12742
8 p.
1931
Typescript.

[William Williams Groton and Ledyard Conn.]
Williams, John Oliver, b. 1866.
G WIL 12751
17 p.
1932
Typescript.

Emmanuel Williams of Taunton Mass. a genealogy of some of his descendants
Williams, John Oliver, b. 1866.
G WIL 12765
2, 35 p.
1934
Typescript.

John Williams descendants
Wallwork, Emma L.
G WIL 12780
5 p.
1943
Typescript.

English ancestry of Richard Williams and his wife Frances (Deighton) Williams
Holman, Winifred Lovering, 1899-1989.
G WIL 12785
41 p.
1945
Typescript.

We three Henry Eddie and me [Henry Smith Williams Edward Huntington Williams Harriet Williams Myers]
Myers, Harriet Williams.
G WIL 12788
2, 145, 1 p.
1945
Typescript.

Roger Williams (brief notes)
Holman, Winifred Lovering, 1899-1989.
G WIL 12796
19, 4 p.
1951
Typescript.

John Hooker Williams his ancestors and descendants as compiled by his granddaughter
Cass, Elizabeth Carol.
G WIL 12799
94 p.
1952
Typescript.

A history of our descent from Robert and Marjary Williams of Boston with a sketch of the lives of Robert Williams 1753 Robert Pearce Williams 1788 and Alexander Williams 1818
Williams, Alexander.
G WIL 12802
1952
Typescript.

American ancestry of Pryor Williams the story of a Quaker heritage
Dixon, Ben F. (Ben Franklin), b. 1892.
G WIL 12820
18 p.
1959
Typescript.

The family history of John and Mary Williams Quaker pioneers of Wayne County with four generations of their descendants
Bercich, Maude McCorkindale, b. 1896.
G WIL 12827
6, 79 p.
1963
Typescript.

These are mine: one Williams family lineage
Williams, Irene, 1901-.
G WIL 12832
149 p.
1964
Typescript.

Captain Isaac Williams and his grandchildren the story of a fighting Quaker and three generations of Indiana pioneers
Dixon, Ben F. (Ben Franklin), b. 1892.
G WIL 12839
6, 71 p.
1967
Second.
Typescript.

The ancestors and descendants of Warren Thomas Williams of Osage City Kansas 1850-1922
Williams, M. Coburn.
G WIL 12847
47 p.
1971
Typescript.

A century's record of the descendants in America of Daniel Williamson Jr. of Cromarty Scotland and of Putnam N.Y.
Edes, Grace Williamson, b. 1864.
G WIL 14254
84 p.
1908
Typescript.

The Williamson family
Sanders, Walter R. (Walter Ray), 1910-.
G WIL 14262
6 p.
1945
Typescript.

Descendants of William Wilcoxson of Derbyshire England and Stratford Connecticut
Wilcox, Thomas, 1889-.
G WIL 1538A
xix, 335 p.
1963
Typescript.

Genealogy. Family of Willoughby, Francis Charlestown Mass. 1638
Porter, George Shepard.
G WIL 15456
3 p.
Typescript.

Notes of the Wills family of Newburyport Mass.
Kelton, Mrs. R.H.C. (Edith Russell Wills)
G WIL 15870
116 p.
1916
Typescript.

Genealogical record of the Willson family
G WIL 16120
22 p.
Typescript.

The Wilmarth family of Newport New Hampshire
G WIL 16925
9 p.
1936
Typescript.

Wild - Wilde - Wildes abstracts of all wills and administrations in the Prerogative Court of Canterbury 1600-1675
G WIL 1920
Typescript.

Wild genealogy
Jackson, Edward Evarts, b. 1868.
G WIL 1930
13 p.
1905
Typescript.

The name history of Wilson
G WIL 19674
2, 30, 6 p.
Typescript.

Wilson genealogical data and suggestions for a Wilson family association a national Wilson family reunion and a complete Wilson genealogy
Seaver, J. Montgomery (Jesse Montgomery), b. 1890.
G WIL 19780
60 p.
1927
Typescript.

The Wilson lineage of Miss Clara M. Wilson Berkley California ...
Ware, Josephine Grozier Sandford, b. 1865.
G WIL 19794
7 p.
1934
Typescript.

Wilson - Willson family [descendants of Samuel]
Wilson, James J.
G WIL 19798
8 p.
1934
Typescript.

William Wilson and his descendants [of Kent Co. Delaware] 1708-1946
Thoesen, Edythe Wilson.
G WIL 19813
6-13, 4-13, 63 & 64 p.
1944
Typescript.

Willson - Willsons of Massachusetts and New Hampshire
Tallmadge, Grace H.
G WIL 19824
1957
Typescript.

The Wilson family ancestry of Matthew James Wilson (1830-1924) of Oxford Chester County Pennsylvania with brief notes concerning his descendants to the present day
Haley, James Bayard, b. 1890.
G WIL 19835
1964
Typescript.

Genealogy of the Wilbour and allied families
Wilbour, Benjamin Franklin, 1887-1964.
G WIL 305
2, 409 p.
1936
Typescript.

Copy of family record of Clark W. and Pede (Robbins) Wilder married June 5 1811 at Orwell N.Y.
G WIL 3555
22.3 x 36.5 cm
1940
Typescript.

Wilder genealogy [from Nicholas to Elmira (Wilder) Bryant 1829-1907]
Manning, James Elmer, 1909-.
G WIL 3610
17 p.
1948
Typescript.

The Wilkes chronology: an historical and genealogical document
Wilkes, Charles Denby.
G WIL 5355
17 p.
1950
Typescript.

A genealogical history of the family of Wilkinson
G WIL 5520
1863
Typescript.

Samuel Willard of Sanford Me. and some of his descendants
Ackerman, Arthur W.
G WIL 6194
14 p.
1922
Typescript.

Twigs & branches a Willard descendant tells of her family in America
Wolfe, Frances Cora (Ward), 1896-.
G WIL 6218
A-J, 100, K-Z p.
1948-1952
Typescript.

The family of Stephen Franklin Willard Wethersfield Connecticut seven generations removed from Major Simon Willard settler of Concord Massachusetts
Willard, Stephen F., Jr.
G WIL 6222
1960
Typescript.

The Willards of Illinois records of descendants of William and Jane (Cooke) Willard of Virginia Tennessee and Illinois
Willard, Robert Irving.
G WIL 6225
9, 138 p.
1964
Typescript.

More Willards: descendants of Jonathan Willard(6)
Lyon, Lorene Jones.
G WIL 6229
1, 44 p.
1968
Typescript.

The Wilcombe line, compiled for Mrs. S. Westray Battle of Asheville, N.C.
Holman, Winifred Lovering, 1899-1989.
G WIL 850
18p.
1943
Typescript.

History of Wiltberger family
Magoun, Ellen Sampson.
G WILL 22500
15 p.
1936
Typescript.

Genealogy of the Winegar family as written by Ira Winegar of Middlebury Indiana in ... letters addressed to Caleb Winegar of Union Springs N.Y.
Winegar, Ira.
G WIN 2132
1, 2, 17, 2 p.
1859
Typescript.

The Winans family in America. 1939 minus 1664 equals 275 years
Winans, Charles Augustus.
G WIN 242
46 (i.e. 56) p.
1939
2d.
Typescript.

Tabulated ancestry of Martha Parker (Winkley) Suter as far as known
Suter, Martha Parker.
G WIN 3859
13 p.
1915
Typescript.

Magnificent men: a Winkley genealogy
Jesch, Lillian Winkley.
G WIN 3869
1, 3, 123 p.
c1966
Typescript.

Winn lineage compiled from notes in the possession of Dana Ripley Bullen
Holman, Winifred Lovering, 1899-1989.
G WIN 4220
56 p.
1931
Typescript.

The Winn lineage
Holman, Winifred Lovering, 1899-1989.
G WIN 4240
2, 95-104 p.
1958-1960
Typescript.

Brief sketch of our Winn family and connecting lines for 1960 reunion
Buck, Martha F.
G WIN 4244
19 p.
1960
Typescript.

The children of Edward Winslow of Drotwich [sic] Worcester Co. England
G WIN 5920
2 p.
Typescript.

Winsley - Winslow (Samuel of Salisbury Mass.)
G WIN 5930
4 p.
Typescript.

Winslow family Farr ancestry
Stone, Merlin Jones, b. 1853.
G WIN 5965
1 p.
1898
Typescript.

Winslow - Morris genealogy
Winslow, Fred E.
G WIN 6025
91 p.
1953
Typescript.

Genealogy of Isaac Winston and descendants
Hendrick, Elizabeth Winston Campbell.
G WIN 6542
c1899
Typescript.

Descendants of William Winchester
Farrell, Louis, 1878-1950.
G WIN 850
1, 47, 6, 12 p.
Typescript.

The Winchester family descended from William Winchester of Westminster Md. 1710-1947
Kendall, John Smith.
G WIN 880
28 p.
1947
Typescript.

History of a family named "Wise" also "Penninger" "Thomas" "Lawhon" "Howard" "Massie."
Wise, Holly L.
G WIS 635
2, 28 p.
1958
Typescript.

The Witham family of New Gloucester Maine
Titus, Anson, 1847-1932.
G WIT 1030
5 p.
1913
Typescript.

Genealogy of the Witherspoon family
Sibbet, Jessie Laing, b. 1884.
G WIT 3460
20, 3 p.
c1954
Typescript.

Woodhouse [family of several English counties]
G WOO 2255
245 p.
1957-1958
Typescript.

Wood of Tiverton Devon showing descent of Sir Mathew Wood Bart.
Rudkin, H.R.E.
G WOO 416
Chart 35.8 x 160.4 cm
1937

The genealogy of the Wood family and other families connected by marriage [Thomas of Rowley Mass.]
Wood, Nora A. (Piper).
G WOO 425
1937
Typescript.

Thomas Wood and his sons (Brookfield Massachusetts) in the American Revolution
Wood, Robert Franklin.
G WOO 430
1, 26 p.
1939
Typescript.

Biography of Gilbert Wood (1822-1850) writing teacher and daguerreotypist ...
Wood, Robert Franklin.
G WOO 432
3, 40 p.
1939
Typescript.

Stephen Wood 1749-1835 (b. Seneca Montgomery Co. Md.) [and John Fry and Susan Wood Fry (m. Oct. 27 1808 Fayette Co. Ky.)]
Evans, Donald Grover.
G WOO 445
6 p.
1944
Typescript.

Descendants of Josiah Wood through his son David Wood Albemarle County Virginia
Wood, McFarland Walker.
G WOO 455
6 p.
1947
Typescript.

The Rev. James Woodside of Brunswick Me. and his descendants
Sinnett, Charles Nelson, 1847-1928.
G WOO 4585
106 p.
1922
Typescript.

Descendants of Edmund Wood in America
Halverson, Frank Douglas, b. 1900.
G WOO 465
1, 11 p.
1949
Typescript.

Descendants of Robert Woodward of Scituate Mass.
Woodward, Frank Ernest, 1853-1921.
G WOO 5401
139 p.
Typescript.

Woodworth genealogy showing some of the ancestors of Penelope Potter wife of Nathaniel Patrick
Benson, Fred W.
G WOO 6004
8 p.
Typescript.

Benjamin Woodworth [son of Walter Woodworth of Scituate Plymouth Colony in New England]
Holman, Winifred Lovering, 1899-1989.
G WOO 6008
13, 2 p.
Typescript.

Life and descendants of Selah Woodworth 1750-1823
Brown, Leon R. (Leon Robertson), b. 1886.
G WOO 6028
1, 41 p.
1940
Typescript.

Benjamin Woodworth
Holman, Winifred Lovering, 1899-1989.
G WOO 6032
13 p.
1941
Typescript.

Woolcot notes
Holman, Winifred Lovering, 1899-1989.
G WOO 6620
7 p.
1960
Typescript.

[Works family Bible] five generations 1807 to 1946 copied from a Bible presented to the Me. Hist. Society by Charles Fremont Bowie ...
G WOR 1234
4 p.
Typescript.

The Worrall family ... containing some data of the Worralls of Marple in Chester Co. (now Delaware Co.) Pa. ... [also the Taylors of Chester Co. Pa. & Burnights of Lebanon Pa. & Marion Co. Ind.]
Jarvis, May Tibbetts, b. 1864.
G WOR 3355
1940
Typescript.

The Work family of Ashford and Stafford Connecticut
Chapman, Grace Olive.
G WOR 929
93 p.
1946
Typescript.

The record of the family of Wright of County Monoghan Ireland from 1615 to 1922
G WRI 398
56 p.
Typescript.

Nathaniel Wright of Moose Mountain Hanover N.H. and some descendants
Dickore, Marie Paula.
G WRI 408
2 p.
Typescript.

Benjamin Wright of Rhode Island and his descendants
G WRI 452
55 p.
1912
Typescript.

"The Wrights" [descendants of Richard]
Wright, Eugene A., 1890-1973.
G WRI 493
1924
Typescript.

Nicholas Wyeth of Cambridge Mass. and some of his descendants
Barker, John Herbert, 1870-1951.
G WYE 950
17 p.
1929
Typescript.

Wyeth some notes on the Wyeth family 1595-1940 giving eight generations of the descendants of Nicholas Wyeth who came to America about 1645.
Barker, John Herbert, 1870-1951.
G WYE 960
3, 71 p.
1940
Typescript.

Additional genealogical notes on the Wyman family. Arranged from memoranda kept by Harland P. Wyman of Swansea Mass.
Bowman, Sumner Eli.
G WYM 174
6, 3, 3 p.
1904
Typescript.

Ancestors and descendants of Lizzie Luella Yeaton (Mrs. Warren L. Gazzam) 1868-1942
Earling, Roy B.
G YEA 1975
5 p.
1959
Typescript.

Some descendants of two brothers Jonathan and Ezekiel Yeomans
Cocheu, Lincoln C. (Lincoln Chester), b. 1876.
G YEO 375
29, 5 p.
1947
Typescript.

Descendants of Joel B. Younker (1809-1879) and Sarah (Stiffler) Younker (1813-1893). A genealogy listing 325 descendants of a pioneer family of Pennsylvania "Dutch" ancestry married in New Philadelphia Ohio migrated to Iowa and back treked [sic] to Geneseo Illinois
Stiffler, R. Ewing.
G YOU 2050
a-j, 30 p.
1947
Typescript.

Kindred of John Young a chief of Hawaii
Stokes, John F.A.
G YOU 330
16 p.
Typescript.

A genealogy of Robert Young his family and descendants
Rice, Sarah Drury.
G YOU 410
75 p.
1914
Typescript.

John Young of Eastham Massachusetts descent to Elkanah Young of Eastham and Mt. Desert Maine and his known descendants
Young, Elizabeth S. Ridgely, 1908-.
G YOU 462
4, 234, 33 p.
1950
Typescript.

Descendants of Jeremiah and Betsey (Needham) Young and ancestry of Betsey Needham
Packer, Warren M.
G YOU 466
14, 22, 8 p.
1953
Typescript.

New England in the Georgia census of 1850
Hawes, Frank Mortimer, 1850-1941.
GA 12 20
Typescript.

Six hundred Revolutionary soldiers living in Georgia in 1827-1828
Houston, Martha Lou.
GA 16 20
5 + 34 p.
1932
Typescript.

Cemetery records of Georgia [1771-1944]
GA 27 50
22 p.
Typescript.

List of Revolutionary soldiers and widows of Revolutionary soldiers in Georgia prior to 1836, together with county in which they resided
Nelson, Thomas Forsythe.
GA 30 32
Typescript.

Abstracts of court records of Bryan County, Georgia
Wilson, Caroline Price.
GA 115 10
16 p.
1929
Typescript.

Marriage records from the oldest record book of Fannin County, Georgia
Revill, Janie.
GA 145 30
21 p.
Typescript.

Eleventh Land District of Habersham County, Georgia
Kimzey, Herbert B.
GA 168 2
1946
Typescript.

Early Baptist laymen leaders in Habersham County, Georgia
Kimzey, Herbert B.
GA 168 5
1946
Typescript.

Tenth Land District, Habersham County, Georgia
Kimzey, Herbert B.
GA 168 6
1946
Typescript.

Twelfth Land District, Habersham County, Georgia
Kimzey, Herbert B.
GA 168 8
1947
Typescript.

Cemetery records, Hancock County, Georgia
Genealogical Society of Utah.
GA 170 70
48 p.
Typescript.

*Rock Creek Baptist Church Cemetery records,
Monroe County, Georgia (near Forsyth)*
Genealogical Society of Utah.
GA 202 5
Typescript.

Cemetery records, Pulaski County, Georgia
Genealogical Society of Utah.
GA 216 5
Typescript.

*Beulah Church Cemetery records, Wheeler
County, Georgia (near Glenwood)*
Genealogical Society of Utah.
GA 253 5
4 p.
Typescript.

*Westover Memorial Cemetery records: Augusta,
Richmond Co., Georgia*
GA AUG 10
Typescript.

*Cemetery records: Bainbridge, Decatur Co.,
Georgia*
GA BAI 10
Typescript.

*Cemetery records; Fayetteville, Fayette Co.,
Georgia*
GA FAY 10
Typescript.

*Berea Cemetery records: Hampton, Henry Co.,
Georgia*
GA HAM 10
18 p.
Typescript.

*Thomas Hill Cemetery records, Hinesville,
Liberty Co., Georgia*
GA HIN 10
5 p.
Typescript.

*Andrews Chapel Cemetery records: Newnan,
Coweta Co., Georgia*
GA NEW 10
Typescript.

*Cemetery records: Stapleton, Jefferson Co.,
Georgia*
GA STA 10
7 p.
Typescript.

Cemetery records: Carey, Blaine Co., Idaho
Carey (Idaho) Ward Genealogical Committee.
IDAHO CAR 10
17 p.
Typescript.

Shelley, Bingham County, Idaho cemetery records
Young, Veola
Genealogical Society of Utah.
IDAHO SHE 10
8 p.
1940
Typescript.

Death records for Illinois [1803-1944]
ILL 70 75
Typescript.

*Marriages, Book A, Edinburgh, Dane County,
Illinois (now Christian County, with Taylorville
as the county seat)*
Daughters of the American Revolution. Illinois.
ILL 91 15
1 + 121 p.
[1955]
Typescript.

*Marriage licences issued in Gallatin County,
Illinois, from 1813 to 1838*
Bender, Lucy
ILL 110 70A
Typescript.

Census [1830] Gallatin County, Illinois
Bender, Lucy
ILL 110 70B
Typescript.

*Gallatin County, Illinois delinquent tax lists,
1817-1828*
Bender, Lucy
ILL 110 70C
1 + 33 p.
Typescript.

*Some early records of estates settled in Gallatin
County, Illinois from 1821 to 1838*
Bender, Lucy
ILL 110 70D
Typescript.

*Illinois: early settlers of Gallatin County, with a
brief history of Gallatin County, road petitions,
constable petitions and miscellaneous lists*
Bender, Lucy
ILL 110 70E
Typescript.

*Addenda to volume V, Early settlers of Gallatin
County, Illinois: constable petitions*
Bender, Lucy
ILL 110 70E
1936
Typescript.

*A brief history of Shawneetown and Gallatin
County, Illinois, with maps and views from the air
of Shawneetown and locality*
Bender, Lucy
ILL 110 70F
1936
Typescript.

Index to Early Settlers of Illinois, 1803-1840
Bender, Lucy
ILL 110 70G
1936
Typescript.

*State of Illinois. Daughters of the American
Revolution, cemetery records: La Salle and
Livingston Counties, Ill.*
ILL 130 15
2 + 75 p.
Typescript.

*State of Illinois, Daughters of the American
Revolution: family records from Bible and other
written records, tombstone inscriptions of old
cemeteries in Vermilion Co.*
ILL 172 10
5 + 90 + 35 + 35 p.
Typescript.

*State of Illinois, Daughters of the American
Revolution: Vermilion County, Illinois, wills
(record book 6)*
ILL 172 25
1 + 91 p.
1955
Typescript.

*Baptist Cemetery records: Washburn, Woodford
Co., Illinois*
ILL 182 10
Typescript.

*History of Christ Church, Chicago, Protestant
Episcopal 1855-1874, Reformed Episcopal 1874-
1920*
Cheney, Charles E.
ILL CHI 91
4 + 39 p.
Typescript.

*A list of debts of debts supposed good, estate of
Thomas E. Craig [Gallatin Co., Ill.]*
Bender, Lucy
ILL 110 70D
Typescript.

*List of marked graves in Ostend Cemetery,
McHenry Township, McHenry County, Illinois*
ILL MacH 25
6 p.
Typescript.

Marengo, Illinois records
Higgs, L. Gertrude
ILL MAR 4
Typescript.

The cemeteries of Marengo, McHenry County, Illinois
Higgs, L. Gertrude
ILL MAR 6
169 p. (p. 112 missing)
Typescript.

Cemetery records (miscellaneous), Indiana, bound with obituary records of Indiana
Pierson, Albert O.
IND 45 5
4 + 10 p.
Newspaper clippings copied by Albert O. Pierson

The pioneer families of Clark County [Indiana] by W. H. McCoy (1886), copied and indexed
Hayward, Elizabeth.
IND 89 45
1947
Typescript.

The pioneer families of Clark County
McCoy, W. H.
IND 89 45
14 p.
1886
Typescript.

Granville cemetery records, Delaware County, Indiana
IND 97 50
Typescript.

Grant County, Indiana marriages
Mayse, Myra E.
IND 106 71
Typescript.

Cemetery records: Franklin, Johnson Co., Indiana. Nineveh, Johnson Co., Indiana
IND 120 35
18 p. + 28 p.
Typescript.

Wayne County, Indiana cemetery records
IND 168 20
Typescript.

Cemetery records; Beech Grove, Marion Co., Indiana
IND BEE 10
Typescript.

Capitol Hill Cemetery records. Olive Branch Cemetery records. Pleasant Hill Cemetery records. Ridge Cemetery records. Cambridge City, Wayne Co., Indiana
IND CAM 10
18 + 11 + 2 + 15 p.
Typescript.

Cemetery records; Dublin, Wayne Co., Indiana
IND DUB 10
27 p.
Typescript.

Cemetery records; Economy, Wayne Co., Indiana
IND ECO 10
Typescript.

Gravestone records from the Sickler Cemetery, near Elston, Indiana
Perkins, Charles A.
IND ELS 69
1929
Typescript.

Cemetery records: Goshen, Elkhart Co., Indiana
IND GOS 10
31 p.
Typescript.

West Lawn Cemetery records; Hagerstown, Wayne Co., Indiana
IND HAG 10
1946
Typescript.

Cemetery records: Jacksonburg, Wayne Co., Indiana
IND JAC 10
23 p.
Typescript.

*Milton Cemetery records, Milton, Wayne Co.,
Indiana (south of town) Quaker Cemetery
records, Milton, Wayne Co., Indiana*
IND MIL 10
13 + 2 p.
Typescript.

*Iowa Society Daughters of the American
Revolution: Muscatine County, Iowa: gravestone
inscriptions, Brockway Cemetery. Names of heads
of families, 1840 first census, Washington County,
Iowa, from National Archives, Washington, D.C.
Marriages, 1864-1869, Washington County, Iowa*
IOWA 50 25
1 v.
1959?
Typescript.

*Long Grove Cemetery, 1774-1958, Long Grove,
Iowa*
Daughters of American Colonists, Davenport
Chapter
IOWA LON 20
1964
Typescript.

*Abstracted notes from Mt. Vernon and Lisbon,
Linn County, Iowa, 1903-1950*
Cronbaugh, Lois W.
IOWA MOU 10
Typescript.

*Marriage record of Russell County, Kansas,
1873-1883*
Evans, Mae Nichols.
KAN 184 30
9 p.
Typescript.

*Inscriptions on tombstones, etc. in cemeteries at
Russell, Kansas*
Ruppenthal, J. C.
KAN RUS 25
7 p.
1933
Typescript.

*Abstracts of pensions of soldiers of the
Revolution, War of 1812 and Indian wars, who
settled on the Kentucky side of the Ohio River*
McGhee, Lucy Kate.
KY 22 12
3 vols.
Typescript.

*Abstract of early Kentucky wills and inventories.
Copied from original and recorded wills and
inventories*
King, J. Estelle Stewart (Junie Estelle Stewart)
KY 22 16
298 p.
1933
Typescript.

*Revolutionary War soldiers and pensioners who
settled and lived in Kentucky counties*
Burns, Annie Walker, 1894-1966.
Ky 25 25
1932
Typescript.

*Record of marriages in Adair County, Kentucky
for the period of years 1801 to 1851 inclusive*
Burns, Annie Walker, 1894-1966.
KY 81 10
1932
Typescript.

*Record of Revolutionary War pension papers of
soldiers who settled in Kentucky Counties: Adair
County: Columbia: Kentucky*
Burns, Annie Walker, 1894-1966.
KY 81 12
1933
Typescript.

*Record of wills in Adair County, Kentucky for the
period of years 1801 to 1851 inclusive*
Burns, Annie Walker, 1894-1966.
KY 81 16
43 p.
1933
Typescript.

*Record of marriages in Anderson County,
Kentucky, for the period of years 1827 to 1851
inclusive*
Burns, Annie Walker, 1894-1966.
KY 83 10
1932
Typescript.

*Marriage records, 1835-1860, Anderson County,
Kentucky*
KY 83 12
Typescript.

*Record of deaths, births and marriages in Ballard
County, Kentucky for the period of years 1852 -
1862 inclusive*
Burns, Annie Walker, 1894-1966.
KY 84 10
1932
Typescript.

*Record of marriages in Barren County, Kentucky
for the period of years 1852 to 1862 inclusive*
Burns, Annie Walker, 1894-1966.
KY 85 15
19 p.
Typescript.

*Record of marriages, births and deaths in Barren
County, Kentucky for the period of years 1852 to
1862 inclusive*
Burns, Annie Walker, 1894-1966.
KY 85 15
47 p.
1932
Typescript.

*Record of births in Barren County, Kentucky for
the period of years 1852 to 1862 inclusive*
Burns, Annie Walker, 1894-1966.
KY 85 15 [Mss Project Entry)
103 p.
Typescript.

*Bath County, Kentucky. Record of marriages,
births and deaths for the period of years 1852 to
1862 inclusive*
Burns, Annie Walker, 1894-1966.
KY 86 10
37 p.
1932

Record of wills in Bath County, Kentucky
Burns, Annie Walker, 1894-1966.
KY 86 11
67 p.
1936
Typescript.

Record of wills in Bath County, Kentucky
Burns, Annie Walker, 1894-1966.
KY 86 11
67 p.
1936
Typescript.

*Record of marriages, Bourbon County, Paris,
Kentucky*
Burns, Annie Walker, 1894-1966.
KY 89 10
58 p.
1931
Typescript.

*Record of marriages in Bracken County,
Kentucky for the period of years 1796 to 1851
inclusive*
Burns, Annie Walker, 1894-1966.
KY 92 15
52 p.
1932
Typescript.

*Record of marriages, births and deaths for the
period of years 1582 to 1862 inclusive*
Burns, Annie Walker, 1894-1966.
KY 93 15
52 p.
Typescript.

*Record of abstracts of wills in Warren County,
Kentucky*
Burns, Annie Walker, 1894-1966.
KY 93 41
37 p.
1936
Typescript.

Third census of the United States (year 1810)
County of Caldwell, State of Kentucky
Bell, Annie B.
KY 96 75
15 p.
1935
Typescript.

Record of marriages in Clay County, Kentucky
for the period of years 1807 to 1851 inclusive
Burns, Annie Walker, 1894-1966.
KY 106 16
62 p.
1932
Typescript.

Revolutionary War pensions of soldiers who
settled in Fayette County, Kentucky
Burns, Annie Walker, 1894-1966.
KY 114 10
121 p.
1936
Typescript. Includes index.

Condensed history of Fleming County, Kentucky
Fischer, Dan T.
KY 115 25
16 pp.
1908
Typescript.

Floyd County KY marriages, from the formation
of the county, 1800 to 1844 inclusive
Burns, Annie Walker, 1894-1966.
KY 116 10
51 p.
Typescript.

Vital statistics of Floyd County, Kentucky for the
period of years 1852 to 1862 inclusive
Burns, Annie Walker, 1894-1966.
KY 116 12
67 p.
1931
Typescript.

Marriages, Franklin Co. KY, at Frankfort . . .
1852 to 1862
Burns, Annie Walker, 1894-1966.
KY 117 16
46 p.
Typescript.

Births, Franklin County, Kentucky, 1852 to 1862
Burns, Annie Walker, 1894-1966.
KY 117 20
86 p.
Typescript.

Deaths, Franklin County, Kentucky, 1852 to 1862
Burns, Annie Walker, 1894-1966.
KY 117 25
40 p.
Typescript.

Record of marriages in Franklin County,
Kentucky for the period of years 1794 to 1851
inclusive
Burns, Annie Walker, 1894-1966.
KY 117 31
71 p.
1931
Typescript.

Record of marriages in Harlan County, Kentucky
for the period of years as follows: 1818 to and
including 1851, 1863 to and including 1870
Burns, Annie Walker, 1894-1966.
KY 128 20
22 p.
1931
Typescript.

Record of marriages in Henry County. Kentucky
for the period of years 1798 to 1851 inclusive
Burns, Annie Walker, 1894-1966.
KY 132 15
64 p.
1932
Typescript.

Records of Hopkins County, Kentucky. Marriages
Ganrud, Pauline.
KY 134 31
29 p.
Typescript.

Record of deaths, marriages and births for the period of years 1852 to 1862 inclusive, in Jackson County, Kentucky, McKee-Kentucky
Burns, Annie Walker, 1894-1966.
KY 135 15
17 p.
1932
Typescript

Genealogical data, Jefferson County, Kentucky
Anchorage High School Genealogical Society
KY 136 9
31 p.
1949
Typescript.

Record of deaths, marriages and births in Laurel County, Kentucky for the period of years 1852 to 1862 inclusive
Burns, Annie Walker, 1894-1966.
KY 143 15
69 p.
1932
Typescript.

Letcher County, Kentucky marriages, births and deaths for the period of years 1852 to 1862 inclusive
Burns, Annie Walker, 1894-1966.
KY 147 31
42 p.
1931
Typescript.

Marriages in Letcher County, Kentucky for the period of years beginning with the formation of the county, 1842 to 1852 inclusive
Burns, Annie Walker, 1894-1966.
KY 147 33
5 p.
1931
Typescript.

Record of marriages in Lewis County, KY for the period of years 1806 to 1851 inclusive
Burns, Annie Walker, 1894-1966.
KY 148 10
60 p.
1932
Typescript.

Record of marriages in Lincoln County, Ky. for the period of years 1780 to 1851 inclusive, except for the period of years 1827 to 1837
Burns, Annie Walker, 1894-1966.
KY 149 10
76 p.
1931
Typescript.

Record of marriages in Livingston County, Ky. for the period of years 1798 to 1851 inclusive
Burns, Annie Walker, 1894-1966.
KY 150 15
87 p.
Typescript.

Record of marriages in Madison County, Kentucky for the period of years 1783 to 1851 inclusive
Burns, Annie Walker, 1894-1966.
KY 153 20
187 p.
1932
Typescript.

Record of marriages in Mason County, Kentucky for the period of years 1788 to 1851 inclusive
Burns, Annie Walker, 1894-1966.
KY 161 10
202 p.
1932
Typescript.

[Record of wills in the county of Mason, Maysville, Kentucky, 1813-1823]
Burns, Annie Walker, 1894-1966.
KY 161 11
2 vols.
Typescript.

Record of births in Mercer County, Kentucky (1852 to 1862)
Burns, Annie Walker, 1894-1966.
KY 164 15
61 p.
Typescript.

Cemetery records, Mercer County, Kentucky
Harrodsburg Historical Society
KY 164 30
4 vols.
1969-1971
Typescript.

Record of births, marriages and deaths in Montgomery County, Kentucky for the period of years 1852 to 1862 inclusive
Burns, Annie Walker, 1894-1966.
KY 167 14
42 p.
1932
Typescript.

Record of marriages, births and deaths in Morgan County, Kentucky for the period of years 1852 to 1862 inclusive
Burns, Annie Walker, 1894-1966.
KY 168 15
119 p.
1931
Typescript.

Marriage records of Nelson County, Kentucky for the period of years 1780 to 1815 inclusive
Burns, Annie Walker, 1894-1966.
KY 169 31
31 p.
Typescript.

Record of abstracts pension papers: soldiers of the Revolutionary War, War of 1812 & Indian Wars who settled in the county of Nelson ... State of Kentucky
Bell, Annie B.
KY 169 9
22 p.
1934
Typescript.

Record of wills in Nelson County, Kentucky for the period of years 1780 to 1851 inclusive
Burns, Annie Walker, 1894-1966.
KY 170 10
195 p.
1933
Typescript.

Record of marriages in Nelson County, Bardstown, Kentucky, for the period of years 1780 to 1851 inclusive
Burns, Annie Walker, 1894-1966.
KY 170 12
99 p.
1932
Typescript

Record of Wills in Nicholas County, Kentucky
Burns, Annie Walker, 1894-1966.
KY 170 76
84 p.
1936
Typescript.

Record of marriages and settlement of estates in Nicholas County, Kentucky
Burns, Annie Walker, 1894-1966.
KY 170 77
101 p.
1936
Typescript.

Record of wills in Nicholas County, Kentucky
Burns, Annie Walker, 1894-1966.
KY 171 76
56 p.
1936
Typescript.

Kentucky vital statistics: record of marriages in Ohio County, Kentucky for the period of years 1799 to 1851 inclusive
Burns, Annie Walker, 1894-1966.
KY 172 15
1 + 46 p.
Typescript.

Record of marriages in Oldham County, Kentucky for the period of years 1823 to 1851 inclusive
Burns, Annie Walker, 1894-1966.
KY 173 10
25 p.
1932
Typescript.

Record of marriages in Owen County, Kentucky for the period of years 1819 to 1851 inclusive
Burns, Annie Walker, 1894-1966.
KY 173 15
26 p.
1931
Typescript.

Pike County, Kentucky marriages, births and deaths compiled in alphabetical order
Burns, Annie Walker, 1894-1966.
KY 177 31
57 p.
1931
Typescript.

Record of marriages in Pulaski County, Kentucky
Burns, Annie Walker, 1894-1966.
KY 179-180 40
2 vols.
1936
Typescript.

Abstract of wills in Pulaski County, Kentucky
Burns, Annie Walker, 1894-1966.
KY 180 20
25 p.
Typescript.

Record of marriages and wills in Pulaski County, Kentucky
Burns, Annie Walker, 1894-1966.
KY 180 40
67 pp.
Typescript.

Record of deaths, marriages and births in Rockcastle County [Kentucky] for the period of years 1852 to 1862 inclusive
Burns, Annie Walker, 1894-1966.
KY 182 15
53 p.
1932
Typescript.

Record of marriages in Spence County, Ky. for the period of years 1824 to 1851 inclusive
Burns, Annie Walker, 1894-1966.
KY 185 12
15 p.
1938

Record of marriages in Scott County, Ky. for the period of years 1837 to 1851 inclusive
Burns, Annie Walker, 1894-1966.
KY 185 5
20 p.
1931
Typescript.

Copies of names on invitations to funerals and burials in Scott and Fayette Counties, Kentucky, 1821 -- 1898
Dickore, Marie Paula.
KY 185 8
20 p.
1942
Typescript.

Record of marriages Trigg County, Kentucky for the period of years 1820 to 1851 inclusive
Burns, Annie Walker, 1894-1966.
KY 191 10
50 p.
1932
Typescript.

Record of marriages in Trimble County, Kentucky for the period of years 1837 to 1851 inclusive
Burns, Annie Walker, 1894-1966.
KY 192 15
12 p.
1932
Typescript.

List of people buried in the cemetery of the Long Run Baptist Church [near Boston, Jefferson Co., Ky]
KY Bos 3
4 p.
Typescript.

Louisiana cemetery records, volume III, Bienville, Webster, Winn and Lincoln parishes
Louisiana Society N.S.D.A.R.
LA 65 20
220 p.
1954-1957
Typescript.

*Deaths of Maine veterans of rhe Revolutionary
War, taken from various newspapers*
Lilly, Georgiana Hewins.
ME 52 16
36 p.
Typescript.

Maine records. [Piscataway-Winslow, Me.]
ME 60 45
c. 1936
Typescript.

The History and Romance of Eastern Maine
Tewksbury, John.
ME 70 59
1924

*[Taylor family] Part I. Misc. Bible records ...
Part II. cemetery insc. ... Part III. Genealogies ...*
ME 100 23
1951
Typescript.

*Revolutionary soldiers of Hillsdale Co.,
Michigan: their lives and lineages*
Moore, Vivian Lyon.
MICH 109 69
96 + 23 p.
Typescript.

*Dubois Cemetery records, Ingham Co., Mich.
(near Lansing). Rockwell Cemetery records,
Ingham Co., Mich. (near Lansing). Strickland or
Phillips Cemetery records, Ingham Co., Mich.
(near Lansing)*
MICH 112 50
7 + 3 + 2 p.
Typescript.

*Index of persons mentioned in Pioneer History of
Ingham County [Mich], by Mrs. Franc Adams,
published 1923*
Foster, Theodore G.
MICH 112 63a
48 p.
1933
Typescript.

*Ingham Co., Mich: United States census of 1840.
Free white persons, including heads of families*
Montgomery, M.
MICH 112 74
19 p.
1934
Photostat and typescript.

*Index to D.A.R. records, Lenawee County,
Michigan*
MICH 125 24
ca. 1945
Typescript.

*Livingston County, Michigan: marriages 1836 to
1850*
MICH 126 1
1 + 70 p.
Typescript.

Cemetery records: Michigan
MICH 65 5
5 p.
Typescript.

Early settlers in Berrien Co., Michigan
MICH 90 62
18 p.
Typescript.

*Mt. Olivet Cemetery records, Battle Creek,
Calhoun Co., Michigan. Johnson Cemetery
records, Marengo twp., Calhoun Co., Michigan.*
MICH 92 15
48 + 7 p.
Typescript.

*Stone School records, Franklin township,
Lenawee Co., Michigan*
Whelan, Florence S.
MICH FRA 3
67 p.
1944
Typescript.

1839-1900 church records of the West Rome Baptist Church, Rome township, Lenawee County, Michigan
Beck, Imogene Mable Zook, 1908-1979.
MICH ROM 75
37 p.
1963
Typescript.

Tipton, Lenawee County, Michigan: monument erected, 1866, commemorating the service of the men of Franklin township in the Civil War
MICH TIP 3
Typescript.

Minnesota house and senate [index and biographical accounts of members]
MINN 18 10
Mounted newspaper clippings.

Records of burials from Layman's Cemetery, Minneapolis, Minnesota, 1860-1880, from 15 years of age
Benedict, Walter L., Mrs.
Daughters of the Founders and Patriots of America.
MINN MIN 50, 50a
122 + 1 p. 50a: index, n.d. 64 p.
Typescript.

Old Sweetwater Cemetery record, Copiah Co., Mississippi
MISS 115 5
6 p.
Typescript.

History of Hinds County, Mississippi, 1821-1922 ... comm[emoration] of the centenary ... of Jackson the capitol of the state
Rowland, Eron O.
MISS 125 5
63 p.
1922
Typescript.

Cemetery records: Holmes County, Mississippi
McNees, L. L.
MISS 126 25
[4] + 187 p., map.
1955
Typescript.

Lincoln County, Mississippi cemetery records: Macedonia Cemetery records, Brookhaven, Route 3. Ben Salem Cemetery records, Caseyville. Cemetery records, New Hope. Cemetery records, Old Macedonia.
Red Star Branch, Southern Mississippi District.
MISS 143 5
10 + 5 + 7 + 3 p.
Typescript.

Harmony Cemetery records, Tate County, Mississippi (south of Strayhorn)
MISS 168 5
5 p.
Typescript.

Mt. Olivet Cemetery records, Mechanicsburg, Yazoo Co., Mississippi Ogden Cemetery, Yazoo Co., Mississippi
Thomas, Pearl M.
MISS 181 5
10 + 10 p.
Typescript.

New Englanders in the census of 1850 for Mississippi
Hawes, Frank Mortimer, 1850-1941.
MISS 58 15
15 + 2 p.
Typescript.

Mississippi cemetery records. Mississippi death records.
MISS 65 15
33 + 8 p.
Typescript.

Friendship Church Cemetery records, Route #3, Baldwyn, Lee Co., Missisippi
MISS BAL 10
6 p.
Typescript.

Batesville, Panola Co., Missisippi cemetery records. Black Jack Cemetery records, Batesville, Panola Co., Mississippi
Genealogical Society of Utah.
MISS BAT 10
43 + 10 p.
Typescript.

*Cemetery records: Decatur, Newton Co.,
Mississippi*
MISS DEC 10
12 p.
Typescript.

*Hattiesburg, Mississippi, cemetery records:
Chappell Cemetery records. Glendale Cemetery
records. Greens Creek Cemetery (copied by Pearl
M. Thomas). Old Providence Cemetery records*
Thomas, Pearl M.
MISS HAT 10
6 + 12 + 15 + 15 p.
Typescript.

Cemetery records: Liberty, Amite Co., Mississippi
Thomas, Pearl M.
MISS LIB 10
25 p.
Typescript.

*Cemetery records: Whynot, Lauderdale Co.,
Mississippi*
Hall, Ida M.
MISS WHY 10
10 p.
1941
Typescript.

*Jackson County, Missouri marriage records,
1827-1910*
Genealogical Society of Utah.
MO 117 10
8 + 44 p.
Typescript.

*Early history of Versailles and Morgan County,
Missouri*
Moser, Mrs. Royce.
MO 140 50
7 p.
1957
Mounted newspaper clippings from the Leader -
Statesman, Versailles, Missouri.

Iberia, Missouri Cemetery
Daughters of the American Revolution. Miangua
Chapter
MO IBE 25
11 p.
Typescript.

*[Chatham graves - recorded in The Boston
Evening Transcript August 20, 22, 23, 24, 27, 29,
and 31, 1934 and September 4, 1934]*
Hudson, Chester E.
MS 70 CHA 71
6 leaves.
1934
Containing transcriptions from the North
Cemetery and South Cemetery.

*Inscriptions from gravestones in Baptist Cemetery
in Cheshire, Mass.*
MS 70 CHE 30
5 leaves.
This cemetery is located on the left hand side of
Jenks Road to Stafford Hill, a short distance from
junction of Harbour Road and Jenks Road.

*Tombstone inscriptions of the cemeteries of
Chesterfield, Massachusetts 1773-1940*
Lederer, Max, Mrs.
MS 70 CHE 50
106 leaves.
1940
Contents: Center Cemetery, Robinson Hollow
Cemetery (S. Worthington Rd.), First Highland
St. Cemetery (S. Worthington Rd.), Second
Highland St. Cemetery (S. Worthington Rd.),
"The Mount" Cemetery (northwest of West
Chesterfield), "Bofat" Cemetery (toward
Westhampton), Private Cemetery (Old
Huntington Rd.), Huntington Hill Cemetery (Old
Huntington Rd.), and index.

*Tombstone records of East Street Cemetery,
Chicopee Falls, Massachusetts*
Smith, Claire E.
MS 70 CHI 11
44 leaves.
1937
Contents: East Street Cemetery (earliest burial
1741). [D.A.R.]

[Inscriptions from Clarksburg, Massachusetts cemeteries]
MS 70 CLA 1
17 leaves.
Contents: Clarksburg Cemetery (this cemetery is located on the East Rd. to Stamford, Vt., a short distance off the main road from North Adams, Massachusetts); Old Cemetery [this small cemetery situated about one quarter of a mile from the four corners, on the old North Adams - Stamford road. It is off the road in back of an old barn and cannot be seen from the road. [D.A.R.]

Inscriptions from the burial grounds of Cohasset, Mass. from 1705, the earliest date, to 1877
MS 70 COH 1
221 leaves.
1903
Contents: Central Burying Ground, Beechwood Cemetery, North Cohasset Cemetery, Cedar Street Cemetery, Jerusalem Road Cemetery (north side and south east side). [D.A.R.]

[Inscriptions from Chandler Hill Cemetery, Colrain, Massachusetts]
MS 70 COL 10
18 leaves.
1927
Typescript.

[Inscriptions from the Branch Cemetery, and Farley Burial Yard in Colrain, Massachusetts]
MS 70 COL 12
31 leaves.
1923
Typescript.

The inscriptions of gravestones in North River Cemetery, Colrain, Massachusetts
Cram, Katherine H.
MS 70 COL 13
26 leaves.
1922
Typescript.

[Inscriptions from the Christian Hill Cemetery and Fulton Cemetery in Colrain, Mass.]
Cram, Katherine H.
MS 70 COL 14
1920
Typescript.

Colrain, Massachusetts cemetery records
Stetson, Oscar Frank, 1875-1948.
MS 70 COL 16
170 leaves.
Contents: Chandler Cemetery, Branch Cemetery, Brick Cemetery, North River Cemetery, Christian Hill Cemetery, Fulton Cemetery, Pickett Cemetery, Pennel Hill Cemetery (Halifax, Vt), Bell Cemetery (Halifax, Vt.), Heath (Mass.) Cemetery, North Heath (Mass.) Cemetery, Charlemont (Mass.) Cemetery, and Greenfield (Mass.) Meadows Cemetery. Alphabetical [descriptions included]

[Plan of West Branch Cemetery, Colrain, Massachusetts]
MS 70 COL 18
Blue print plan of cemetery.

[Inscriptions from the Main Street Cemetery and Old Hillside Cemetery in Concord, Massachusetts]
MS 70 CON 1
103 leaves.
1909
Typescript.

Tombstone inscriptions - Conway, Massachusetts
Lederer, Inez Stevens, 1882-.
MS 70 CON 22
263 leaves.
1950
Contents: Howland Cemetery, Royden and Lee Cemetery, Pine Grove Cemetery, Cricket Hill Cemetery, Allis District Cemetery, Poland District Cemetery, Private Cemetery - Burnett Place, Private Lot of Charles Boyden, Maynard Cemetery, Pumpkin Hollow Cemetery, and North Shirkshire Cemetery. [descriptions included] [D.A.R.]

Tombstone inscriptions from Main Street Burying Ground in Concord, Massachusetts
MS 70 CON 3
22 leaves.
1937
Typescript.

[Gravestone records of Dalton Cemetery and Roman Catholic Cemetery in Dalton, Massachusetts]
Hosmer, James
MS 70 DAL 1
237 leaves.
1905
Typescript.

[Cemetery records of Dalton, Massachusetts]
MS 70 DAL 3
17 leaves.
1950
Typescript.

[Inscriptions from the East Main Street Cemetery, Dalton, Massachusetts]
MS 70 DAL 5
13 leaves.
1938
Typescript.

[Inscriptions from the First Parish Cemetery and South Parish Cemetery in Dedham, Massachusetts]
MS 70 DED 1
202 leaves.
1919
Typescript.

[Inscriptions of the Old Hall Burying Ground, Dennis, Massachusetts]
MS 70 DEN 1
1909
Typescript.

[Inscriptions from the Paddock Burial Ground, East Dennis, Massachusetts]
MS 70 DEN 2
11 leaves.
1909
Typescript.

Tombstone inscriptions Dennis, Massachusetts
MS 70 DEN 5
31 leaves, and index.
Contents: Howes Cemetery (1706), Quivet Neck Cemetery (1823), Homer Cemetery (1688) East Dennis, and Indian Burial Ground (Rte. 6).
[descriptions included] [D.A.R.]

Dennis Cemetery (oldest section) near the Federated Church, Dennis [Massachusetts]
Sprague, Waldo Chamberlain, 1903-1960.
MS 70 DEN 8
31 leaves.
1957
Typescript.

[Inscriptions from the Centre Street Grave Yard in Dighton, Massachusetts]
Bowman, John Elliot, 1866-1933.
MS 70 DIG 1
12 leaves.
1913
Typescript.

Burial Grounds Dighton, Mass.
Bowman, John Elliot, 1866-1933.
MS 70 DIG 2
1914
Typescript.

[Cemetery inscriptions from Dighton, Massachusetts]
Sprague, Waldo Chamberlain, 1903-1960.
MS 70 DIG 3
27 leaves.
1957
Contents: Briggs and Trafton Cemetery (1796), Center St. Cemetery (corner of Briggs St.), Gooding Cemetery (Center St., near Somerset Ave.), Old Cemetery (at the site of the First Church, Elm St. and Brook St.), Jones Cemetery (1808) (Williams St.), Manchester Cemetery (1802 (Williams St.), Phillips and Simmons Cemetery (1804) (Main St., near Williams St.), Ware and Church (1794)

Dorchester South Cemetery, Dorchester Ave., near Dorchester Lower Mills
Sprague, Waldo Chamberlain, 1903-1960.
MS 70 DOR 7
1952
Typescript.

*Dracut, Mass. Old Ground, Varnum Ave.;
Woodbine Cemetery; Pawtucket Graveyard;
Garrison House Burial Ground; New Boston
Burying Ground; East Dracut Burying Ground;
New East Dracut Graveyard; Hildreth Ground;
Varnum Burying Ground, East Dracut; Oakland
Cemetery*
Parker, P. Hildreth (Pearl Hildreth), 1880.
MS 70 DRA 1
1906
Typescript.

*Dunstable, Mass. epitaphs. Meeting House
Burying Ground; Swallow Burying Ground;
Rideout Burying Ground*
Parker, P. Hildreth (Pearl Hildreth), 1880.
MS 70 DUN 1
1907
Typescript.

*Tombstone inscriptions, Private Cemetery,
Dunstable, Massachusetts*
Massachusetts DAR Genealogical Records
Committee.
MS 70 DUN 2
1942
Typescript.

*Meeting House Hill Cemetery and Central
Cemetery, Dunstable, Mass.*
MS 70 DUN 2
1911
Typescript.

*The Old Cemetery, Chestnut St., South Duxbury,
Massachusetts*
Lane, Margie Brewster
MS 70 DUX 1
1899
Typescript.

Duxbury, Mass. epitaphs
MS 70 DUX 5
2 v.
1911
Typescript.

*Record of deaths and burials in the East Harwich
Cemetery Cape Cod Mass. from the Cemetery
Association Secretary's Book*
Chapman, Grace Olive.
MS 70 EAS 190
1938
Typescript.

*East Harwich Massachusetts Church Yard
Inscriptions*
Chapman, Grace Olive.
MS 70 EAS 191
1940
Typescript.

*Inscriptions Old Church St. Cemetery, Easton,
Mass.*
Sprague, Waldo Chamberlain, 1903-1960.
MS 70 EAS 312
1948
Typescript.

*Memoranda of Graves. Center Street near the end
of Short Street and Short Street opposite Lyman
Wheelock Road, Easton, Massachusetts*
Ross, J. Clifford, Mrs.
MS 70 EAS 340
1956
Typescript.

*The epitaphs of the Cedarville Cemetery at East
Sandwich, Massachusetts*
Elwell, Levi Henry, 1854-1916.
MS 70 EAS 400
1905
Typescript.

Easton, Connecticut cemetery
Card, Lester.
MS 70 EAS
Typescript.

*Edgartown, Mass. cemetery inscriptions from
Pease's Point Way Cemetery*
Pease, Harriet Marshall.
MS 70 EDG 1
1909
Typescript.

Tombstone inscriptions in Southern Berkshire towns of Egremont, Monterey, and Mount Washington
Massachusetts DAR Genealogical Records Committee.
MS 70 EGR 10
1942
Typescript.

Inscriptions "Town Hill Cemetery" Egremont (Berkshire Co.) Mass.
MS 70 EGR 7
1945
Typescript.

Essex, Mass. epitaphs
MS 70 ESS 1
1903
Typescript.

Valentine Cemetery, North Main St., Fall River, Mass.
Sprague, Waldo Chamberlain, 1903-1960.
MS 70 FAL 10
1957
Typescript.

Falmouth, Mass. Inscriptions from the Falmouth Enterprise, October 17, 1903. Old Burying Ground and East End Burying Ground
MS 70 FAl 40
1903
Typescript.

Private burial lot, situated in West Falmouth, east side of Main St., on property of Arthur and Eva E. Underwood. Known as the Crowell lot
MS 70 FAL 45
1941
Typescript.

Inscription from stones in the Old South Street Cemetery, Fitchburg, Massachusetts
MacLea, Florence
MS 70 FIT 1
1927
Typescript.

Gravestone inscriptions in Park Street Cemetery, (Florence) Northampton, Mass.
Massachusetts DAR Genealogical Records Committee.
MS 70 FLO 1
1941
Typescript.

Foxborough, Mass. epitaphs
MS 70 FOX 1
1910
Typescript.

Framingham, Mass. epitaphs
Stone, George S.
MS 70 FRA 1
1903
Typescript.

Framingham, Mass. epitaphs. Old South Cemetery; Edward Cemetery, Saxonville; Church Hill Cemetery
MS 70 FRA 2
1910
Typescript.

Edgell Grove Cemetery epitaphs, Framingham, Mass.
MS 70 FRA 3
1919
Typescript.

Inscriptions from cemeteries opposite and also back of the First Christian Church, Assonet - Freetown, Mass.
Sprague, Waldo Chamberlain, 1903-1960.
MS 70 FRE 10
1955
Typescript.

Terry Cemetery, Hathway Cemetery, Freetown and the Brown Cemetery - Pembroke, Mass.
Sprague, Waldo Chamberlain, 1903-1960.
MS 70 FRE 12
1957
Typescript.

*Old cemetery in rear of Congregational Church,
Gardner, Mass.*
Massachusetts DAR Genealogical Records
Committee.
MS 70 GAR 1
1937
Typescript.

Gosnold, Mass. epitaphs
Hale, W. A.
MS 70 GOS 11
1899
Typescript.

*Gravestone records from the Old Burying
Ground, Grafton, Mass.*
Hale, Sarah A.
MS 70 GRA 1
1908
Typescript.

North Cemetery, Granby, Mass.
Massachusetts DAR Genealogical Records
Committee.
MS 70 GRA 11
1947
Typescript.

*Gravestone records from the Burying Ground at
Farnumville, in the town of Grafton, Mass.*
Flagg, Charles Allcott, 1870-1920.
MS 70 GRA 2
1908
Typescript.

*Harvard, Mass. [The Old Burial Ground;
Bellevue Cemetery; Shaker Cemetery]*
Massachusetts D.A.R. Old Concord Chapter
MS 70 HAR 30
5 leaves.
1938
Typescript.

*Inscriptions Island Pond Cemetery, Harwich,
Mass.*
Chapman, Grace Olive.
MS 70 HAR 40
72 leaves
1943
Typescript.

*Inscriptions Harwich Center Church Yard,
Harwich, Mass.*
Chapman, Grace Olive.
MS 70 HAR 45
95 leaves.
1944
Typescript.

*Old cemetery behind First Baptist Church, West
Harwich, Mass.*
Sprague, Waldo Chamberlain, 1903-1960.
MS 70 HAR 46
12 leaves.
1957
Typescript.

*Harwichport, Massachusetts cemetery
inscriptions*
Chapman, Grace Olive.
MS 70 HAR 51
58 leaves.
1942
Typescript.

*Copy of inscriptions on stones in Main Street;
Hill Burying Ground; West Hatfield; West Farms;
and West Brook Cemeteries, Hatfield, Mass.*
Hatfield Historical Club
MS 70 HAT 15
1 v.
1899
Typescript.

*West Parish Cemetery of Haverhill,
Massachusetts*
Betsy Ross Chapter N.S.D.A.R.
MS 70 HAV 2
34 leaves.
1942
Typescript.

*Inscriptions on stones in Carleton St. Cemetery,
Haverhill, Massachusetts*
Massachusetts D.A.R.
MS 70 HAV 6
5 leaves.
1953
Typescript.

Heath, Massachusetts records
MS 70 HEA 1
1v.
Typescript.

Inscriptions from gravestones in Hinsdale, Mass.
Hosmer, James
MS 70 HIN 25
184 pp.
1905
Typescript.

Inscriptions High St. Cemetery, Hingham, Mass.
Sprague, Waldo Chamberlain, 1903-1960.
MS 70 HIN 5
15 leaves.
1947
Typescript.

Inscriptions from Hingham Cemetery (Old part) Hingham, Massachusetts
Sprague, Waldo Chamberlain, 1903-1960.
MS 70 HIN 6
15 leaves.
1947
Typescript.

Inscriptions Fort Hill Cemetery, Fort Hill St., West Hingham, Mass.
Sprague, Waldo Chamberlain, 1903-1960.
MS 70 HIN 7
3 leaves.
1947
Typescript.

Inscriptions Hingham Center Cemetery
Sprague, Waldo Chamberlain, 1903-1960.
MS 70 HIN 8
17 leaves.
1947
Typescript.

Union Cemetery, Holbrook, Mass.
Jackson Edward E.
MS 70 HOL 1
59 pp.
1909
Typescript.

The inscriptions on the tombstones in Holliston, Massachusetts
Batchelder, John M.
MS 70 HOL 30
287 p.
1899
Typescript.

Lake Grove Cemetery epitaphs, Holliston, Mass.
MS 70 HOL 31
169 leaves.
1919
Typescript.

Holliston, Mass. epitaphs [Lake Grove and Old North Cemeteries]
Batchelder, John M.
MS 70 HOL 32
1 v.
Typescript.

Holliston, Mass. epitaphs. [North, South, East, West, Braggville and Central Cemeteries]
MS 70 HOL 33
1 v.
1919
Typescript.

Inscriptions Union Cemetery, Holbrook, Mass.
Sprague, Waldo Chamberlain, 1903-1960.
MS 70 HOL 4
30 leaves.
1941
Typescript.

Inscriptions in the Rock Valley Cemetery, Holyoke, Massachusetts
Massachusetts DAR Genealogical Records Committee.
MS 70 HOL 40
5 leaves.
1935
Typescript.

Inscriptions Wendell Cemetery, So. Franklin St., Holbrook, Mass.
Sprague, Waldo Chamberlain, 1903-1960.
MS 70 HOL 6
7 leaves.
1941
Typescript.

Hopkinton, Mass. epitaphs [The Glebe; Mount Auburn; Congregational Church; East Hopkinton; and Woodville Cemeteries]
MS 70 HOP 16
1 v.
1919
Typescript.

Inscriptions on gravestones near the First Congregational Church, Hopkinton, Massachusetts, not in the printed Vital Records of 1911
C.K.B.
MS 70 HOP 18
1 v.
1942
Typescript.

South Hopedale, Massachusetts and South Burying Ground, Upton, Massachusetts epitaphs
MS 70 HOP 3
1 v.
1919
Typescript.

Main Street Cemetery, Hudson, Massachusetts epitaphs
MS 70 HUD 1
158 leaves.
1919
Typescript.

Norwich Hill Cemetery, Huntington, Massachusetts
Lederer, Max, Mrs.
MS 70 HUN 1
44 leaves.
1954
Typescript.

Kingston, Massachusetts epitaphs [Kingston Cemetery and Evergreen Cemetery]
MS 70 KIN 1
1 v.
1911
Typescript.

Lancaster, Mass. epitaphs [Lancaster; The Old Common; Chocksett; Middle; North; North Village; and Shaker Cemetery]
MS 70 LAN 1
1 v.
1919
Typescript.

Cemetery inscriptions from Lanseboro, Massachusetts
Frost, Josephine C., 1864-1942.
MS 70 LAN 10
1910
Typescript.

Records of Bellevue Cemetery, Lawrence, Massachusetts. Burials: May 13, 1847 - December 31, 1866 (#1 - #2989)
MS 70 LAW 10
Vol. 1 of 4
1940
Typescript.

Records of Bellevue Cemetery, Lawrence, Massachusetts. Burials: January 1, 1867 - December 31, 1877 (#2990 - #6196)
MS 70 LAW 10A
Vol. 2 of 4
1941
Typescript.

Records of Bellevue Cemetery, Lawrence, Massachusetts. Burials: January 1, 1878 - December 31, 1888 (#6197 - #10001)
MS 70 LAW 10B
Vol. 3 of 4
1943
Typescript.

Records of Bellevue Cemetery, Lawrence, Massachusetts. Burials: January 1, 1889 - December 31, 1899 (#10002 - #14496)
MS 70 LAW 10C
Vol. 4 of 4
1947
Typescript.

Leicester, Mass. inscriptions in Eliot Hill Burying Ground
May, John Joseph, 1813-1903.
MS 70 LEI 1
4 leaves.
Typescript.

Tombstone inscriptions, Leicester, Mass. [Quaker; Eliot; Rawson Brook; and Baptist Cemeteries]
Massachusetts D.A.R.
MS 70 LEI 3
36 leaves.
1938
Typescript

David Lynde Cemetery, Leicester, Mass.
Cheever, Herbert M.
MS 70 LEI 5
6 leaves.
1955
Typescript.

Inscriptions from the cemetery near Toby Road, Leverett, Mass.
Dods, Agnes M.
MS 70 LEV 3
10 leaves
1940
Typescript.

A Transcript of the epitaphs in the burying grounds at Lexington, Mass., namely the Old Burying Ground in the centre of the town and that of the Rollins family in the East Village
Brown, Francis H. (Francis Henry), b. 1835.
MS 70 LEX 1
322 leaves
1902
Typescript.

Lincoln, Mass. inscriptions from Old Cemetery, Triangle Cemetery, New Cemetery.
MS 70 LIN 1
1 v.
1909
Typescript.

Three Cornered, Triangle or Arbor Vitae Cemetery, Lincoln, Mass. epitaphs.
Massachusetts D.A.R.
MS 70 LIN 4
46 leaves
1947
Typescript.

Old Burying Ground epitaphs, Lincoln, Mass.
Massachusetts D.A.R.
MS 70 LIN 5
15 leaves
1947
Typescript.

Center Cemetery - Old Training Field Cemetery, Lincoln, Mass.
Massachusetts D.A.R.
MS 70 LIN 6
37 leaves
1947
Typescript.

Tombstones inscriptions Longmeadow Cemetery, Longmeadow, Mass.
Massachusetts D.A.R.
MS 70 LON 2
100 p.
1938
Typescript.

Old English or Number One Burying Ground, Lowell, Massachusetts (This is the cemetery in which the early mill help were buried)
MS 70 LOW 1
137 p.
1907
Typescript.

Gravestone inscriptions in the East Yard, also known as Red Bridge Cemetery, Ludlow, Mass.
Moore, R. L. G.
MS 70 LUD 8
1 v.
1933
Typescript transcription.

Lynnfield, Mass. epitaphs
MS 70 LYN 12
1 v.
1903
Typescript transcription.

Lynnfield Center Cemetery, Lynnfield, Mass.
Massachusetts D.A.R.
MS 70 LYN 74
1956
Typescript.

Epitaphs Bell Rock Cemetery, Malden, Mass.
Massachusetts D.A.R.
MS 70 MAL 3
7 p.
1942
Typescript transcription.

Old Cemetery, Mansfield, Mass. epitaphs
Massachusetts D.A.R.
MS 70 MAN 31
1938
Typescript.

Old Burying Hill, Marblehead, Massachusetts
MS 70 MAR 2
73 p.
1937
Typescript.

Marlboro, Massachusetts epitaphs (Rocklawn or Chipman; Brigham; Spring Hill; and High School Cemetery]
MS 70 MAR 20
1 v.
1919
Typescript.

Maplewood Cemetery, Marlboro, Massachusetts on Pleasant St.
Massachusetts D.A.R.
MS 70 MAR 22
68 p.
1951
Typescript.

Tombstones inscriptions, Marshfield, Mass. (Winslow; Cedar Grove Cemetery on Ocean St.; Marshfield Hills on Main St.; Centre Cemetery Marshfield on Ferry St.; Plainville Cemetery on Plain St.; Two Mile Cemetery on Union St., North Middleboro)
Massachusetts D.A.R.
MS 70 MAR 40
1 v.
1938
Typescript.

St. Michael's Church Yard, Marblehead, Mass. epitaphs
Massachusetts D.A.R.
MS 70 MAR 8
17 p.
1938
Typescript.

Cemetery at East Medway (now Millis) Massachusetts
MS 70 MED 22
1 v.
1909
Typescript.

Mendon, Mass. epitaphs (Taft Family Cemetery on Robinson Farm; Pine Hill Cemetery; Swandale Cemetery)
MS 70 MEN 5
68 p.
1919
Typescript.

Middlefield, Mass. epitaphs (General Cemetery; Mack Cemetery; cemetery at Bell Tavern; Wright Cemetery; cemetery at old Howard Smith farm)
MS 70 MID 11
40 p.
1906
Typescript.

Purchase St. Cemetery Milford, Mass. epitaphs
MS 70 MIL 1
32 leaves.
1919
Typescript.

*The Armory Village Cemetery in Millbury
(formerly Sutton) Massachusetts*
Massachusetts D.A.R.
MS 70 MIL 120
11 p.
1940
Typescript.

*Old Church yard Cemetery (formerly East
Medway) now Millis, Mass.*
MS 70 MIL 543
152 leaves
1919
Typescript.

*Millville, Mass. epitaphs. (Old Millville
Cemetery; Darlings Repose Cemetery; Sweede
Burying Ground; Gifford Family Cemetery;
Wilson Cemetery; Aldrich Cemetery; Quaker City
Cemetery; Millville Incorporated Cemetery;
Chestnut Hill Cemetery in Blackstone, Mass; and
Quaker Burying Ground in Blackstone, Mass.)*
MS 70 MIL 762
158 leaves
1919
Typescript.

Inscriptions from Milton Cemetery, Milton, Mass.
Sprague, Waldo Chamberlain, 1903-1960.
MS 70 MIL 932A
25 leaves
1946
Typescript.

The First Burial Yard of Monson, Massachusetts
Titus, Anson, 1847-1932.
MS 70 MON 10
48 p.
1904
Typescript.

*Inscriptions from the Butler District Cemetery
and Gage Cemetery District, Monson, Mass.*
Barlow, Claude W., (Claude Willis), 1907-1976.
MS 70 MON 12
9 p.
1947
Typescript.

Pitcher Street Cemetery, Montgomery, Mass.
MS 70 MON 51
5 p.
1932
Typescript.

*Gravestone inscriptions in the town of Mount
Washington, Berkshire Co., Mass. (North of
Hughes Farm Cemetery; Center Cemetery near
church; City Cemetery*
Keith, Hebert F.
MS 70 MOU 21
1 v.
1900
Typescript.

Nahant, Mass. epitaphs
MS 70 NAH 1
30 leaves
1903
Typescript.

*Natick, Mass. epitaphs. (Indian Burial Ground;
Eliot Square Burial Ground)*
MS 70 NAT 1
1 v.
1903
Typescript.

*Natick, Mass. epitaphs (North Natick Cemetery;
Eliot Church Cemetery; Border Lane Burying
Ground; Glenwood Cemetery)*
MS 70 NAT 2
1 v.
1919
Typescript.

Dell Park Cemetery, Natick, Mass. epitaphs
MS 70 NAT 3
281 leaves
1919
Typescript.

*Old Needham Cemetery, Needham, Mass.
epitaphs*
MS 70 NEE 1
182 leaves
1919
Typescript.

New Ashford, Mass. records. (New Ashlord Cemetery; family records; and military records)
MS 70 NEW 1
1 v.
1917
Typescript.

Griffin Street Cemetery, New Bedford, Mass. epitaphs
Massachusetts D.A.R.
MS 70 NEW 14
1938
Typescript.

New Lenox, Mass. cemetery inscriptions
Massachusetts D.A.R.
MS 70 NEW 51
6 leaves
1938
Typescript.

North Adams First Baptist Church record of members who joined before 1860
Gray, Mary
MS 70 NOR 195
1940
Typescript.

Inscriptions at the Old Phillips Cemetery and North Church Street Cemetery, North Adams, Mass.
MS 70 NOR 3
28 leaves
1903
Typescript.

Gravestone inscriptions in West Farms Cemetery, Northampton, Mass.
Estabrook, Florence Dickinson
MS 70 NOR 40
21 leaves
1941
Typescript.

Revolutionary Soldiers buried in Northampton, Mass. Bridge Street Cemetery
Massachusetts D.A.R.
MS 70 NOR 43
3 leaves
1951
Typescript.

Inscriptions on tombstones in the Old Burying Ground at North Andover, Mass.
Kitteredge, Mary
MS 70 NOR 50
37 p.
1869

Tombstone inscriptions Ridgewood Cemetery, North Andover, Mass.
MS 70 NOR 52
273 p.
1938
Typescript.

South Burying Ground of the North Parish of Andover and North Andover, Mass, and Holy Sepulchre Cemetery of North Andover, Mass.
Massachusetts D.A.R.
MS 70 NOR 53
74 leaves
1941
Typescript.

Louisiana cemetery records, Vol. III: Bienville, Webster, Winn and Lincoln parishes
LA 65 20
1954-1957
Typescript.

Maine Daughters of the American Revolution, 1938-1939 miscellaneous volume: cemetery records, Bible and family records, miscellaneous data
ME 100 3
1938-1939
Typescript.

Some Maine veterans of the American Revolution. Items from newspaper files, concerning deaths of veterans in or from Maine, 1792-1857
Bowman, John Elliot, 1866-1933.
ME 51 11
1932
Typescript.

Biographies - Revolutionary soldiers marked by Mary Kelton Dummer Chapter, D.A.R., Hallowell, Maine. During Years 1928-1929
Lilly, Georgiana.
ME 51 19
1928-[1931]
Typescript.

Deaths of Maine veterans of the Revolutionary War, taken from various newspapers...
Lilly, Georgiana.
ME 51 5
Typescript.

Old Maine churches
Thurston, Clara Poole.
ME 53 9
Typescript.

Bibliography of the State of Maine
Willis, William, 1794-1870.
ME 57 5
1860
Typescript.

1812: grave locations of two hundred sixty-six 1812 service men
ME 59 15
1955

Maine Deaths: 1790-1810. Items, alphabetically arranged from Boston newspapers of the period
Bowman, John Elliot, 1866-1933.
ME 60 28
1928
Typescript.

Maine Deaths: Items from the files of the Columbian Centinel, 1816-1820
Bowman, John Elliot, 1866-1933.
ME 60 29
1930
Typescript.

Maine deaths reported in the Columbian Centinel, 1811
ME 60 30
c. 1930
Typescript.

Maine deaths: alphabetically assembled from File or Christian Mirror, Portland, Maine, 1827
Bowman, John Elliot, 1866-1933.
ME 60 31
1933
Typescript.

Maine marriage records performed by Enoch M. Fowler
Page, Rodney G.
ME 60 32
1936
Typescript.

Maine deaths: from Portland Advertiser, 1807
Bowman, John Elliot, 1866-1933.
ME 60 33
1930
Typescript.

Copy of record of persons baptized, marriages solemnized and funerals attended by the late Isaac Lord, Jr., of the Maine Conference, Methodist Episcopal Church, from 1827 to 1884. Also data regarding the Lord and Curtis families
Hodgdon, Myrtle H.
ME 60 35
c. 1934
Typescript.

Cemetery inscriptions of Central Maine
Hall, Mabel Goodwin.
ME 60 40
1939
Typescript.

List of microfilms of Maine town records: Maine State Archives
ME 79 10
c. 1969
Typescript.

Androscoggin County, Maine. Twenty one cemeteries in Leeds, Livermore, and on Route 136 South from Auburn [and Turner]
Wirth, Dorothy.
ME 81 12
2 v.
c. 1962
Typescript.

1812 pensioners. Maine, Androscoggin Co.
ME 81 8
c. 1935
Typescript.

Twenty cemeteries copied in the spring of 1960 in the counties of Cumberland and Lincoln and Waldo in Maine
Wirth, Dorothy.
ME 83 14
1960
Typescript.

1812 pensioners. Maine, Cumberland Co. (Incomplete)
ME 83 8
c. 1935
Typescript.

[Cemeteries of Franklin County, Maine]
Wirth, Dorothy.
ME 84 15
5 v.
1960
Typescript.

Inscriptions in some Hancock & Penobscot County cemeteries
ME 85 22
c. 1939
Typescript.

[Cemeteries of Kennebec County, Maine]
Wirth, Dorothy.
ME 86 25
3 v.
1961
Typescript.

Index: Revolutionary pensioners of Knox County, Maine
Gould, Edward Kalloch, b. 1865.
ME 87 51
1935
Typescript.

List of 653 Revolutionary soldiers of Knox County, Maine, with genealogical notes on some of their descendants
Gould, Edward Kalloch, b. 1865.
ME 87 51A
c. 1935
Typescript.

Gleanings of Knox County Maine soldiers of Revolution (continued)
Gould, Edward Kalloch, b. 1865.
ME 87 52
1937
Typescript.

Pension list - Revolutionary soldiers of Lincoln County [Maine]
ME 88 12
Typescript.

Commissioners records, 1759-1777. Lincoln County [Maine]
Lilly, Georgiana.
ME 88 6
Typescript.

Twenty eight cemeteries in Somerset County, Maine
Wirth, Dorothy.
ME 93 30
1960
Typescript.

Records of marriages certified by ministers of the gospel -- State of Maine: index. commissioners records -- Waldo County
Lilly, Georgiana.
ME 94 4
1934-1935
Typescript.

List of direct taxes assessed against the inhabitants of the eight district of the State of Massachusetts composed of the County of York Maine, in the Year 1813 for the support and expense of the War of 1812, under the Acts of Congress, assessed by Daniel Wood Esq. of Lebanon principal assessor and under Josiah W. Seaver Esq. of So. Berwick the revenue collector of said district
ME 96 12
1940
Typescript

Cemeteries in York County, Maine
Hill, Ethel.
ME 96 14
1946
Typescript.

William Henry Manning papers
Manning, William Henry, 1852-1928.
Mss 1
3.5 linear ft.
Consists of bound and unbound notes pertaining to genealogy, land surveys in Cambridge, Mass., and probate records from various Massachusetts towns, mainly Chelmsford, Concord and Groton. The genealogical notes are arranged alphabetically by family, Series A being the unbound notes and Series B the bound. The surveying notes are arranged alphabetically by family (Series A) and by location (Series B) with a small miscellaneous section (Series C). The probate records are also arranged alphabetically, by location, with general notes, those without a single identifying location placed at the end. A large photograph of the Manning family tree was placed at the end of the collection.

Horace Lee Washington papers, 1894-1937
Washington, Horace Lee, 1864-1938.
Mss 2
1.5 linear ft.
Unpublished finding aid in the library.
The papers contain Washington's manuscript and typescript correspondence for both his diplomatic activities as a member of the United States State Department, 1892-1929, and his private activities. His service in the diplomatic corps were at Cairo, 1894-1896; Alexandretta, 1896-1899; Geneva, 1900-1905; Capetown, 1905-1906; Marseilles, 1908-1909; Liverpool, 1909-1924; and London, 1924-1928. The Majority of letters date between 1914-1917, while Washington was Consul-General at Liverpool. His superior and chief correspondent at this time was Frederic C. Penfield, American Ambassador of the Embassy of the United States at Vienna, 1913-1917.

George Sydney Horace Lee Washington papers, 1907-1951
Washington, George Sydney Horace Lee, 1910-.
Mss 3
4 linear ft.
Unpublished finding aid in the library.
The papers contain manuscript and typescript letters and notes pertaining to the Washington and Lee genealogies written between 1928 and 1951. There are several copies of Washington's compiled work, though all are incomplete. There are 136 illustrations including photographs, negatives, and postcards, 1907-1925, and six printer's blocks. Other papers concern personal and financial matters.

John Hannibal Sheppard papers, 1791-1873
Sheppard, J. H. (John Hannibal), 1789-1873.
Mss 4
4 linear ft.
Unpublished finding aid in the library.
Consists of John Sheppard's business and personal correspondence concerning his activities in the East Indies, West Indies, and Europe; letters and household accounts of his wife, Sarah Collier Sheppard (d.1818) and daughters, Harriet Helen (1791-1817), Frances (d.1814), Ann Augusta (d.1824), and Sarah Louisa (1806-1833), who jointly operated a school for children at Hallowell, Portland, and Wiscasset ME, after Sheppard's death; and correspondence and travel journals of two other Sheppard children, George Albert (1792-1834) and William Wallace (1807-1835). The largest group of material is the papers of John Hannibal Sheppard (1789-1873), a lawyer and writer active at Hallowell and Wiscasset ME, and Boston MA. These items include letters received or written by Sheppard, chiefly concerning family matters, between 1834-1846, the settlement of his father-in-law, Abiel Wood's, estate, his diaries, original essays and poems, and an account book.

Joseph W. Jamieson papers, 1931-1948
Jamieson, Joseph W., 1874-1948.
Mss 5
4 linear ft.
Unpublished finding aid in the library.
Research notes on the Bradford family primarily focused on MA and ME, but include all of New England, NY, PA, MD, VA, and New Brunswick. The collection is separated into five categories: genealogical notes and correspondence; vital records; historical notes; alphabetical listings from city directories; and card index file by generations (through 12th). The work was begun in 1931, but started in earnest by 1944 until his death in 1948.

Higgins collection, 1741-1925
Higgins family.
Mss 6
9 linear ft.
Unpublished finding aid in the library.
Consists of the letters and diaries of Milton Prince Higgins (1842-1912), a mechanical engineer, industrialist, and pioneer in technical education, and his wife, Katharine Elizabeth Chapin Higgins (1847-1925), dating from 1859-1925. These documents reflect her education at Manchester, NH; their courtship, engagement, and marriage, family life, and social activities; and his duties as superintendent of the Worcester Polytechnic Institute and President of several manufacturing firms in the city, including the Norton Emery Wheel Co. There is also a large group of correspondence concerning Higgins' eldest son, Aldus Chapin Higgins (1872-1948) and his wife, Edgenie Gertrude Brosius Higgins (1870-1911). These letters, written between 1880-1911, concern his law studies and employment in the U.S. Patent Office at Washington, D.C.; her education at Vassar College and work as a high school teacher in the nation's capital; their European travels, courtship, marriage, and domestic relations.

Benjamin Franklin Copeland papers, 1835, 1851-1853
Copeland, Benjamin Franklin, 1798-1863.
Mss 7
127 items.
Unpublished finding aid in the library.
The bulk of this collection consists of materials received by Benjamin Franklin Copeland (1798-1863), a Boston merchant and Justice of the Peace for Roxbury, Mass., as Chairman of a Massachusetts political committee promoting the nomination of Daniel Webster for President of the United States in 1851-1852. The most significant items among the papers are letters written by prominent state congressmen, lawyers, and merchants discussing campaign tactics, the growth of the Free Soil Party in Massachusetts, and other political matters. Correspondents include George Ashmun (1804-1870), Alexander Hamilton Bullock (1816-1882), George Ticknor Curtis (1812-1894), Edward Dickinson (1794-1865), Levi Lincoln (1782-1868), and Tappen Wentworth (1802-1868). Also includes petitions gathered from various Mass. towns listing the names of local supporters; lists of delegates selected by the towns to attend a "Webster Convention" held at Boston on November 25, 1851; and notes, memoranda, and receipts.

Diary of Mary Alice Jackson Litchfield, 1871-1919
Litchfield, Mary Alice Jackson, 1853-1926.
Mss 8
39 v. (2 linear ft.)
Unpublished register in the library.
The collection of diaries was written by two sisters, Mary Alice and Lydia Jackson. Mary Alice started hers in 1871, when she worked in a factory, as a seamstress, and also a maid. After her marriage to Horace Litchfield (1845-1903), a carpenter, her diary details her life as a housekeeper and made extra money sewing. In the late 1880s when Horace prospered, they moved from Scituate to Egypt, a section of North Scituate. There, she ran a livery service and boarding house with the help of her sister Idella and others. Her diaries end in January of 1919. There are gaps in the series. The younger sister, Lydia, started her diary in 1884. Her entries were laconic. She kept house, discussed her social life which centered around the churches of Scituate. Her relationship with husband seems to have been somewhat unsatisfactory. He does not seem to have a fixed occupation, and would leave her overnight without explanation. Lydia's diaries stop at the end of 1891.

Paine collection, ca. 1764-1890
Paine family.
Mss 9
1 linear ft.
Unpublished finding aid in the library.
Contains correspondence, deeds, depositions and other legal documents, estate records, account books, bills and receipts, and other papers relating to Ebenezer Paine (1722-1795), his sons, Isaac (1759-ca. 1830) and Seth (1777-1851), and Seth's three sons, Seth, Jr. (1810 - 1850), Joshua Hopkins (1813-1834), and James Simeon (1817-1891) of Harwich, Mass. Of these papers, those concerning Seth and James Paine are the most numerous. Seth Paine Sr's papers include documents relating to his duties as town constable between 1809-1811 as well as correspondence and deeds while James Paine's consist of general correspondence, case files, estate records, War of 1812 pension claims, and personal accounts (chiefly reflecting his service as a local Justice of the Peace, tax collector and executor).

Juhan collection
Coy, Betsey Frank Tanner.
Payzant, Marion M.
Mss 10
2 linear ft.
Consists mostly of correspondence sent by Betsy Frank Tanner Coy to Marion M. Payzant in order to obtain information on the Jess, Juhan and Payzant families. These families were French Huguenots who settled in Pennsylvania. Also includes military records of Alexander Juhan and material concerning John James Juhan and Oliver Hayard Perry Juhan.

Charles Norris papers, 1794-1819, 1831-1832
Mss 11
ca. 575 items.
Unpublished finding aid in the library.
Consists of business correspondence received by Charles Norris between 1807-1818. These letters are chiefly from printers, publishers, booksellers, paper makers, and other individuals associated with the book trade in New England towns, especially those in NH and MA and in NYC and Phila. Also included among the correspondents are several authors, editors, and clergymen, notably Amos Jones Cook, a minister of Fryeburg, ME; Dudley Leavitt, an almanac editor; Abraham Maxim, the editor of music books and other publications; and Rufus Porter, future founder of the journal, Scientific American. These items outline the nature and range of Norris' business activities and, in part, reflect the impact of the War of 1812 on New England's economy. The correspondence is complemented by bills and receipts indicating sums paid by Charles Norris & Co. for paper, skins, binding, and other trade-related supplies and services between 1809-1816.

South Congregational Church records, 1823-1887
South Congregational Church (Boston, Mass.)
Mss 12
689 items.
Unpublished finding aid in the library.
Consists of records relating to two major functions of the South Congregational Church (Boston, Mass.): its sizeable Sunday-school library and the South Friendly Society. The South Friendly Society was a women's charitable organization devoted to supplying indigent female church members with material to make into saleable clothing and to assisting needy people in general. Included in the records are several business letters written by Edward Everett Hale (1822-1909), minister of South Congregational Church from 1856-1909, and by other church officials between 1838-1887, and annual reports by the South Friendly Society. The bulk of the collection, however, is composed of financial records, 1823-1882, including treasurer's accounts, bills listing books purchased for the Sunday-school library, and receipts for sums spent to support charitable causes.

Thomas Child collection, 1771-1819
Child, Thomas, 1731-1787.
Mss 13
168 items.
Unpublished finding aid in the library.
Consists of correspondence written or received by Thomas Child (1731-1787), a merchant and Custom House official at Falmouth ME, four of his children, and several relatives by marriage between 1771-1819. Most notable among these materials are letter book drafts of Thomas Child's epistles to Arthur Savage (1731-1801), Francis Waldo (1728-1784), John Wentworth (1737-1820), and other colonial officials. Dating from 1771-1787, these letters reflect Child's service as a Custom House official before and during the American Revolution as well as after the war, when customs regulations were adjusted to meet the needs of an independent nation. Thomas Child, Jr. (1782-1851) is represented by correspondence written between 1802-1807 which principally concerns his numerous mercantile ventures at Falmouth and Portland ME. This correspondence is complemented by personal letters, 1800-1815, from two uncles, Enoch Freeman (1750-1832) and Samuel Freeman (1742-1831), both prominent merchants and magistrates in the state.

Grace S. Bischof papers, 1962-1978
Bischof, Grace S., 1922-1980.
Mss 15
5 linear ft.
Unpublished register in the library.
A genealogical study of the residents of Swan's Island, Maine, 1623-1978, including genealogical notes on 154 families, bibliographic file, correspondence, and transcriptions. These transcriptions are of the vital records for the town and a card file of cemetery inscriptions from Harbor Island, Hock Head, Irish Point - Seal Cove, Stockbridge Hill, Old North, and Atlantic burial grounds. There are 18 photographic negatives of gravestones.

Gilbert Harry Doane papers, 1925-1979
Doane, Gilbert Harry, 1897-1980.
Mss 16
18 linear ft.
Unpublished finding aid in the library.
About two-thirds of the collection reflects his genealogical research which centered on Fairfield, Vermont, families, with card files, and focused on the Hungerford family, starting with the immigrant, Thomas Hungerford (ca. 1602-1663), of New London and Hartford, Connecticut. The remaining one-third includes correspondence as the Director of Libraries at the University of Wisconsin at Madison, 1937-1966; as historiographer of the Episcopal Diocese of Milwaukee, 1945-1967; and notes as the biographer for Bishop Jackson Kemper.

Simeon Doggett papers, 1638-1830
Doggett, Simeon, 1738-1823.
Mss 17
353 items.
Unpublished finding aid in the library.
The papers chiefly relate to land dealings and to service as town officials for seven generations of the Doggett family of Marshfield and Middleboro, Mass., 1638-1830. The papers include documents of Thomas Doggett (1607-1692); John Doggett (1642-1718); Samuel Doggett (1652-1725); Thomas Doggett (1676-1736/7); John Dingley; William Ford; Thomas Doggett (1706-1788); John Fuller; Simeon Doggett (1738-1823); Josiah Edson; David Pratt; John Doggett (1729-1754); Thomas Doggett (1761-1831); Elkanah Doggett (1762-1789); Simeon Doggett (1765-1852); Abigail Doggett Weston (1775-1830); John Doggett (b. 1761); Thomas Doggett (1810-1865); Stephen Ashton; Margaret Bennett; Ichabod Morton; Samuel Ransome; and Thomas White. These documents include correspondence, bills, receipts, constable records, carpenter and joiner records, lawsuit over land holdings in Maine, estate papers, papers describing unhappy experiences as a Loyalist during the Revolution, and student and tutor life at Rhode Island College (now Brown Univ.).

Some related lineages of early New England
McIntosh, Mary Charlotte Stephens, 1914-.
Mss 19
424, 7, 43 leaves; 28 cm.
1984
Typescript genealogies (generally two to three leaves in length) followed by a couple of leaves with a paragraph or two on allied families. Although most of the lineages range between the 1620's and the late 1700's or early 1800's, several extend back to England circa the 1500's or earlier and a few extend forward to the early 1900's.

Henry Augustus Peirce papers, 1629-1866
Peirce, Henry Augustus, 1801-1886.
Twenty Associates of the Lincolnshire Company Record
Mss 20
2 linear ft.
Unpublished finding aid in the library.
The collection consists of correspondence, deeds and other records of land transfer, surveyor's plans, bills, receipts, and a diary. The main part of the collection is the papers of Joseph Peirce (1745-1828) and his son Joseph Hardy Peirce (1773-1832) who were agents of the Twenty Associates Land Company (officially called the Twenty Associates of the Lincolnshire Company) disposing of 100,000 acres of land in Maine centered on Camden and Hope. These records start with a grant in 1629, the founding of the Company in 1719, and chiefly between 1791 and 1832 when the Company was actively selling land. Another part contains the papers of Henry Augustus Peirce (1808-1886), son of Joseph Hardy Peirce, who was a trader in the Pacific, diplomat, and had dealings with a cotton plantation in Mississippi in 1866.

Coert du Bois papers, 1897-1961
du Bois, Coert, 1881-1960.
Mss 21
3 linear ft.
Unpublished finding aid in the library.
The official papers, 1804-1961, of Coert du Bois mainly consists of letters, notes, and diaries reflecting du Bois' career in the United States Army as a lieutenant and Chief of Engineers with the 10th Engineers in France, 1917-1918; in the State Department as Consul to Naples, 1920, and to Port Said, 1922; as administrator of the Visa Office in Washington, D.C., 1924-1927; as Consul general at Batavia, Java, 1927-1930; as foreign service inspector at Naples, Italy, 1931-1937; as a member of the President's Anglo-American Caribbean Commission, 1942-1944; and as a United States delegate to the United Nations Security Council's Committee of Good Offices, Java, N.E. Indes, 1948. Among du Bois' private papers is correspondence between du Bois and his wife, Margaret, and some papers of his daughter, Jane. In addition, there is an incomplete manuscript of du Bois' autobiography. The collection also includes 126 personal photographs, 1897-1960, and a book of sketches drawn by du Bois between 1909 and 1955.

Drinkwater family papers, 1814-1848
Drinkwater family.
Mss 22
460 items.
Unpublished register in the library.
The Drinkwater papers, 1814-1848, are primarily those of Theophilus Drinkwater. They include correspondence (those addressed to Theophilus Drinkwater are from his brothers and sisters, while his letters are to his wife, instructing her on household and business affairs) followed by some ships papers, bills and receipts. Includes a small group of papers belonging to Theophilus' brother Allen, Jr. This material is also comprised of correspondence followed by miscellaneous bills and receipts.

Stowell Family Association records, 1854-1965
Stowell Family Association.
Mss 24
1 linear ft.
Unpublished finding aid in the library.
Consists of correspondence, 1854-1965, primarily between Mildred Pearson Stowell Coffin and Stowell relatives, a group of documents such as army vouchers and membership certificates, 1881-1908, for various Stowell family members, an alphabetical membership file of the Stowell Family Association, and 108 photographs of Stowells and relatives, 1890-1965.

Linnell collection, 1335-1968
Linnell, Arthur E., 1862-.
Mss 25
3 linear ft.
Unpublished finding aid in the library.
Consists of genealogies, arranged in alphabetical order. At the end of this section are several notebooks which contain genealogical data of related families. The genealogies are followed by a section of vital records, principally cemetery transcriptions of Cape Cod towns. Concluding the collection is a group of 17 photographs and 12 glass plate of families in the collection, the majority of which is the Linnell family.

Francis Apthorp Foster papers, 1891-1963
Foster, Francis Apthorp, 1872-1966.
Mss 26
3 linear ft.
Unpublished finding aid in the library.
Consist in large part of Foster's diary, from 1915 through 1963, continuous 1921-1963, in 46 volumes. The diaries record the weather, gardening activities, walks taken, birds seen and meetings attended of a quiet, well-to-do, public-spirited bachelor who seldom recorded his feelings. The diaries will be of interest chiefly to historians of ornithology and of natural history. The papers consist largely of membership certificates and certificates of award from various patriotic and historical societies to which Foster belonged. There are also written speeches which Foster gave before some of these societies. At the age of 91, he granted an interview to a reporter from the Japan Times, which is the only autobiographical statement in the collection. The other papers consist of the genealogical information which Foster compiled in this country and which he paid J. Gardner Bartlett, a professional genealogist to compile for him in England.

Francis Charles Foster papers, 1844-1915
Foster, Francis Charles, 1829-1915.
Mss 27
3 linear ft.
Unpublished finding aid in the library.
Consist chiefly of diaries, kept from 1857 until just before his death in 1915. They record few personal feelings, but are a meticulous account of the weather, personal expenses and unobtrusive charities. Most of the letters are from the period of his Grand Tour in Europe (1854-1856). They include some sent to him by his father. There are also a few letters by Francis from other periods of his life and material on his Harvard career. At the end of the collection is a group of photographs of Foster, his wife and children.

William Foster, Junior papers 1734-1879
Foster, William, Junior, 1777-1863.
Mss 28
3 linear ft.
Unpublished finding aid in the library.
First are the papers of William Foster, Senior which include ten scattered years of his diary. The papers of the next generation are arranged by the families of William Foster, Senior's children, in order of birth. Sally Foster, 1770-1836, married Harrison Gray Otis, prominent Federalist politician of Boston and had eleven children. Letters from two of her daughters, Elizabeth Gray Otis Lyman, 1791-1824, and Sophia Otis Ritchie, b. 1799, and Sophia's husband Andrew Ritchie are included. Grace Foster, 1774-1795, and Mary Foster, b. 1774, married in succession, John T. Apthorp of Boston. The four children of Charles Chauncy Foster, 1785-1874, are not represented here. Leonard Foster, 1787-1855, had three children: Francis Charles, 1829-1915, whose papers now comprise Mss 27, Mary Grace, 1834-1922 and William Leonard, 1837-1915, whose letters are here. The youngest child with papers in this collection was Charlotte Willis Foster, 1792-1833, who married Dr. Jeremiah Van Rensselaer.

Henry James Tudor papers, 1819-1849
Tudor, Henry James, 1791-1864.
Mss 29
170 items.
Unpublished finding aid in the library.
Consists chiefly of one hundred and fifty-five letters from family members written between 1819 and 1849. There is also one memo book dated 1827-8 and some undated reports on experiments in salt making conducted by Henry James Tudor. There are as well about fifteen letters addressed to other members of the Tudor family. There is a watercolor and lithograph portrait of Henry J. Tudor and a sketch of the family burial plot with annotations by Henry. Includes some social letters to Harry Tudor, medical advice for him and four letters concerning William Tudor.

Merton Taylor Goodrich papers, 1903-1978
Goodrich, Merton Taylor.
Mss 30
22 linear ft.
Unpublished finding aid in the library.
The first part of the collection concerns the genealogy of the Goodrich family. Included in this group is an alphabetical arrangement of material on Goodrich descendants in America. In addition, the collection contains Goodrich genealogical correspondence and research notes about families allied to the Goodriches, as well unrelated families. Of the 709 families represented, those most extensively researched are Austin, Hall, Thyng, and Walker. Aside from genealogical material, the collection includes a few historical articles on Loyalist activities in New Hampshire, which Goodrich was commissioned to write by Professor Bradley D. Thompson, 1945. Following these articles is correspondence and notes, much of it with librarians and editors at NEHGS. There is also a small amount of personal correspondence. Includes 14 photographs, 1870-1910, of various family members Goodrich researched.

Atkinson - Lancaster papers, 1795-1964
Atkinson, John, 1828-1888.
Mss 31
6 linear ft.
Unpublished finding aid in the library.
The first part consists of Atkinson family papers, beginning with material of John[5] Atkinson (1740-1811) through the children of John[7] (1795-1924). The material is a mixture of letters and legal papers, mostly deeds. It is very scanty until the papers by the children of John[6] (1771-1855). John's[8] (1828-1888) material extends from 1844, when he graduated from high school in Newburyport, to his death in 1888. The loose letters are mostly to his children. The business letters, which cover 1850 to 1853 and 1876 to 1888, are so blurred as to be almost illegible. Most of the other letters are business letters written to him in India. Bills and receipts are complete for 1853 only. There are partnership agreements with American merchants both in India and at home. The travel journals are of particular interest. His wife Elizabeth left letters, brief travel diaries of European trips and dance cards and valentines from 1840 to her death in 1914. John's[8] brothers and sisters left little written material.

Bertha Ellis Walsh papers, 1969-1981
Walsh, Bertha Ellis, 1906-.
Mss 32
5 linear ft.
Unpublished finding aid in the library.
Consists of research on Cape Cod families, 1620-1981. Of the 150 families represented, those most extensively researched are Ellis and Nickerson. There are vital records and cemetery transcriptions on these families followed by a group of mimeographed applications for membership in the Cape Cod Genealogical Society. These applications contain genealogical data on the applicants. There is an indexed transcript of Vernon R. Nickerson's book on Harwich and Chatham records which Mrs. Walsh prepared. Concluding the collection is a series of miscellaneous genealogical notes on New England families.

Thomas Noyes papers, 1651-1768
Noyes, Thomas, 1648-1730.
Mss 33
130 items.
Unpublished finding aid in the library.
Chiefly military papers, 1684-1719, of a colonel of the colonial militia of Newbury, Mass. fighting under the authority of Governor Joseph Dudley against the French and Indians. There are 14 items concerning the town of Newbury, Mass. including papers on the town ferry in 1669 and 1698, setting off a new parish in 1714 and town meeting warrants of 1722 and 1728. In addition, there are 13 items including deeds, personal financial documents and contracts or agreements dating between 1651 and 1721.

Harold Reed Hibbs papers, 1940-1974
Hibbs, Harold Reed, 1897-1978.
Mss 34
6 linear ft.
Unpublished finding aid in the library.
Consists of three sections. The first, which contains the majority of the documents, is Harold Hibbs' research on Hibbs and related families. This material includes research on the descendants of William Hibbs (1652-1696) as well as related families. Of the 380 allied families represented, the research on the Craft and Ross families is the most extensive. The research on William Hibbs also contains vital records principally from the middle Atlantic and middle west regions. The second section consists of Hibbs descendants in America not related to William Hibbs. Some of the material in this group was contributed to Hibbs by Sylpha Snook. The final section is a group of 22 photographs and 4 negatives of some descendants of William Hibbs and related families.

Adair collection, 1418-1976 (bulk: 1934-1976)
Adair, Richard Porter.
Mss 35
1 linear ft.
Unpublished finding aid in the library.
Contains material on American descendants of the Scotch-Irish Adair family followed by some census records. There is also material on allied families, many of whom are from Connecticut. Includes a small group of letters to Richard and Leo Adair. Most of the letters are concerning genealogical matters, while there are some from libraries acknowledging the donation of Leo's book.

Davies collection, 1925-1973
Davies, Daisy Hitch, 1877-1938.
Mss 36
7 linear ft.
Unpublished finding aid in the library.
About half of the collection is the papers of Daisy Hitch Davies. Her papers contain genealogical correspondence and research notes on Hitch and allied families, 1925-1938, personal correspondence, and a scrapbook of childhood and teaching experiences in New York. There are also diaries of the patriotic societies, wills and birth certificates. The papers of Daisy Davies son Wallace Evan Davies contain genealogical research notes, many of which are a continuation of his mother's work. In addition, he did extensive research on the Gayer (Geare) family, of Cornish descent. Wallace Davies' personal papers contain letters to his parents, 1932-1937, scholastic articles he wrote between 1926 and 1935, souvenirs, family wills, and deeds. The collection contains a small group of papers belonging to Richard P. Davies, husband of Daisy and father of Wallace, including letters written to Daisy, 1905-1907, and scholastic certificates, 1899-1932.

Joshua Coit papers, 1773-1854
Coit, Joshua, 1758-1798.
Mss 37
132 items.
Unpublished finding aid in the library.
Letters of congressman Joshua Coit, written to his brother Daniel Lathrop Coit between 1773 and 1798; correspondence of the family of Joshua Coit, 1794-1854.

Frank Waterman Stearns papers, 1683-1956
Stearns, Frank Waterman, 1856-1939.
Mss 38
3 linear ft.
Unpublished finding aid in the library.
The first group of material is on the Stearns family, beginning with documents of Richard H. Stearns and ending with material by Foster Stearns. Most of these papers are from Frank W. Stearns including Amherst College material and personal scrapbooks, 1900-1928. This material includes a group of papers on families connected with the Stearns family: Clark, Richards, Waterman and Cushing. The next group of is some material on the Sprague and Frost families. The R.H. Stearns Company documents are almost entirely concerned with real estate. There is nothing concerning the every day running of the store. Foster Stearns' genealogical notes make up another group of material. He traced his ancestry and that of his wife, Martha Genung Stearns, in the direct line back to England. There is more general information on the following families: Clark, Cowell, Genung, Phinney, Sanderson, Smith, Sprague, Stearns and Waterman. The last group consists of photographs, including some of the R.H. Stearns building.

Joseph Brown Read papers, 1830-1926
Read, Joseph Brown, 1830-1903.
Mss 39
3 linear ft.
Unpublished finding aid in the library.
Autobiographical account of Joseph B. Read, 1830-1903 and the personal papers of Joseph Read's son, William Alfred Read. A lawyer in Washington, D.C., William Read recorded two volumes of memoirs of his family, beginning where his father stopped in 1903. He also included miscellaneous comments on court cases as well as personal notes. Concluding the collection is a volume of genealogical notes on Read and allied families which William Read prepared between 1900 and 1910. He also researched allied families of Dean, Smith, Williams, Cushing and Barker.

Charles Carleton Coffin papers, 1861-1890
Coffin, Charles Carleton, 1823-1896.
Mss 40
2 linear ft.
Unpublished register in the library.
37 addresses or chapters of books by Coffin on patriotic and historical subjects, ca. 1870-1890. Also Confederate material collected by Coffin during his career as a war correspondent. This material, which includes correspondence, battle reports, government documents, and letters to newspapers, was primarily gathered in Richmond, Virginia during 1865.

Hayward family papers, 1816-1971
Hayward, William Pitt Greenwood, 1848-1922.
Mss 41
7 linear ft.
Unpublished finding aid in the library.
Chiefly correspondence by the family of William Pitt Greenwood Hayward (1848-1922) of Roxbury, Mass. and Denver, Colorado and his daughter Gertrude Hayward Mead (1883-1969) of Denver, Colorado and Greenwich, Connecticut. The papers of William P.G. Hayward includes a diary kept the summer of 1872, when he worked as a cowboy in Kansas. The papers of Henry Clay Moffett (1832-1863), brother of William P.G. Hayward's wife Susan Moffett, includes correspondence and a diary with an account of his trip from San Francisco to Batavia, N.Y. in 1857. Moffett's Civil War letters provide vivid and concise descriptions of combat, particularly around Shiloh, and of life on the march through Tennessee as a member of Sherman's army. Collection concludes with 659 photographs, of which there are 22 daguerreotypes, 10 ambrotypes, 18 tintypes, and a miniature painting on ivory of Mary Langdon Greenwood.

Sidney Stevens Williston papers, 1273-1944
Williston, Sidney Stevens.
Mss 42
22 linear ft.
Unpublished finding aid in the library.
Composed of historical and genealogical material. Chiefly, it pertains to the Stoddard and Williston families of Hampshire County, Massachusetts, the Breese and Stevens families of Oneida County, New York, and the Hawkins, Tucker, and Huntington families of Chicago, from 1760 to 1944. Eleven of the collection's twenty-two feet contain family papers, mostly correspondence, with some documents and business papers. The correspondence includes the diplomatic papers of Colonel John Wilson, whose daughter-in-law, Edith Huntington Wilson, was a cousin of Sidney A Stevens Williston. Most of Col. Wilson's papers are letters written as United States Consul to Brussels from 1860s-1880s. The remaining papers reflect genealogical research by Sidney A. Stevens Williston, most prepared between 1930-1937. The research on the Breese, Stevens and their allied families (especially Forman and Burrows) precede the genealogies of the Tucker, Hawkins and allied families.

Howlett collection, 1627-1969
Mss 43
4 linear ft.
Unpublished register at the library.
Contains correspondence and research notes on the descendants of Andrew Elliot (bap. 1627-1703), who immigrated to Beverly, Massachusetts from England in 1668. The notes includes extracts from Bible records, state census records, ships' lists, wills and deeds. This is followed by a series of vital records of New England and Quebec on Elliot descendants. There is also research on 155 families allied to the Elliot family and a small amount of material on Elliots not related to those who descend from Andrew Elliot.

Earl Carnes Munn papers, 1670-1981
Munn, Earl Carnes, 1910-.
Mss 44
40 items.
Unpublished register in the library.
Genealogical correspondence and research notes on the Munn, Meserve (also spelled Meservey, Meservy), and allied families, particularly those of Carnes, Casey, Clayton, and Webster, 1670-1981. Research on the Meserve, Carnes, and allied families dates from Clement Meserve, who immigrated to Portsmouth, New Hampshire from England in 1670.

William Sohier Bryant papers, 443 B.C. - 1957
Bryant, William Sohier, 1861-1956.
Mss 45
8 linear ft.
Unpublished finding aid in the library.
Bryant's professional papers reflect his position as a surgeon in the Spanish and American War, his medical service with the Red Cross in the first World War, and his scholarly interests as an active member of numerous medical societies and author of several medical works. The personal papers includes Bryant's genealogical research on the Bryant and allied families of Mason, Smith, and Sohier. Most of the research is in the form of correspondence and notes, 1902-1935, between Bryant and George W. Chamberlain. Following the genealogical research is biographical material and family papers on Bryant's immediate family, especially his grandfather, John Bryant, and his father and mother, Henry and Elizabeth Brimmer (Sohier) Bryant, with less material on Bryant's brothers, John and Henry. Collection concludes with 380 photographs and 2 pictures, 1853-1952, of William S. Bryant, his relatives and friends.

Ella Florence Elliot papers, 1620-1956
Elliot, Ella Florence, 1868-1962.
Mss 46
2 linear ft.
Unpublished finding aid in the library.
Genealogical correspondence and research notes compiled between 1897 and 1947. The research, centering on New England Families, 1620-1947, is in part the ancestry of Ella Elliot, including the families of Drake, Elliot, Hicks,Tucker, Ring, Urann and Spencer. Most of the material, however, is unrelated to Miss Elliot's ancestry, and reflects genealogical research of a professional nature. This material includes vital records of New York and New England, particularly Massachusetts and New Hampshire. The collection also includes a small amount of family papers, principally 18th century correspondence. In addition, there are 43 photographs, 1892-1942. Most of the photographs are of Miss Elliot's ancestors and descendants and are assembled at the end of the collection.

Frank H. Noyes papers, 1630-1960
Noyes, Frank H.
Mss 47
3 linear ft.
Unpublished finding aid in the library.

Reid Dana Macafee papers, 1572-1963
Macafee, Reid Dana, b. 1888.
Mss 48
2.5 linear ft.
Unpublished finding aid in the library.
Genealogical and historical research notes of Reid Dana Macafee on his ancestry and that of his wife, Edith Hazel Cushing, which includes the Sherman, Fairman, Gates, Morse, Davis, Gray and allied families. Macafee also researched the pioneer families of Bradford County, Pennsylvania. Complementing Macafee's genealogical material is a comprehensive alphabetical index of families traced by him including the 50+ lines of Macafee's ancestry, the 180+ lines of his wife's ancestry, and the 315 pioneer families who settled at Bradford County, Penn.

John G. Metcalf papers, 1839-1932
Metcalf, John G., 1839-1932.
Mss 49
8 items.
Unpublished finding aid in the library.
Manuscript genealogy, notes, and photographs, nearly all prepared by John G. Metcalf during research on descendants of Michael Metcalf, 1587-1644. Additional entries were provided after Metcalf's death by interested family members until 1932. The heart of the collection is a large manuscript volume, 115 pages of which are filled with transcriptions from newspapers, followed by 250 pages of annotated Metcalf genealogy over eight generations.

Charles Granville Way papers, 1854-1928
Way, Charles Granville, 1841-1912.
Mss 50
5 linear ft.
Unpublished finding aid in the library.
Genealogy, records, notes, correspondence and 18 photographs concerning descendants of Henry Way (d. 1667), of Dorchester MA, and allied families. Includes the lines of George Way (d. 1690) in CT, John Way (fl. 1660) and Robert Way (c. 1623-1697) in MA, James Way (d. 1685) in NY, Nathaniel Way (fl. 1725) in NC, Robert Way (d.1725) in PA, Aaron Way (d. 1688) in SC, and Edward Way (d. 1744) in VA.

Royal forefathers of Vera Joyce Fox Kvamme
Gunderson, Carl M. Ringen.
Mss 51
13 v. in 11 (681 p.): ill.; 29 cm.
Typescript: v.1 Royal descent from the Caesars Charlemagne -- v.2 Royal Spanish lines -- v.3 Royal Norwegian-Swedish lines -- v.4 Royal French-Spanish- English lines -- v.5 [without special title] v.6 Royal Plantagenets-Welsh- Scotch-Ireland -- v.7 The Le Blount line -- v.8 The Plumpton and Sherburne lines -- v.9 The Fiennes-Brienne - Danmartin - Mortimer - Sherburne lines -- v.10 Saxon-German lines -- v.11-12 King Olav II, the Saint, various royal connections -- v.13 [without special title] (bound with v. 5)

Norwegian forefathers of General George Washington: a direct descendant of the royal Yngling family of Norway, King Harald Haarfagre of Norway, King Trond Haraldson of Norway ....
Gunderson, Carl M. Ringen.
Mss 51
xiii, 67 leaves: ill.; 29 cm.
1981
Typescript.

Nathaniel B. Blackstone papers, 1082-1979
Blackstone, Nathaniel B., 1911-.
Mss 52
2 linear ft.
Unpublished finding aid in the library.
Notes and genealogical forms for 912 Blackstones of various spellings, and 881 in-laws; compiled chronologically, geographically, and alphabetically. There are also some notes on Blaichestun Manor inEngland and the founding of the Blakeston School in Cleveland, Ohio in 1973.

Thomas Durfee papers, 1740-1801
Durfee, Thomas, 1706-1784.
Mss 53
83 items.
Unpublished finding aid in the library.
Private and public legal documents of Thomas Durfee and his son Oliver Durfee (1754-1798), of Portsmouth and Middletown, Rhode Island. The elder Durfee described himself at various times as a vinter and yeoman. Among his deeds and leases, there is a complaint against a neighbor for selling rum without a license in 1772, and a later itemization of property losses to British troops in 1776. Oliver Durfee's manuscripts fall in two parts. First are 33 private deeds, contracts, public notes etc. These are followed by 27 warrants issued by Durfee as Justice of the Peace in Middletown. Finally, there are 8 miscellaneous deeds and military petitions that cannot be attributed directly to father or son, but were probably kept by Oliver in his official capacity.

Katherine Hobson Osborn papers, 1930-1977
Osborn, Katherine Hobson, 1905-.
Mss 54
2 linear ft.
Unpublished finding aid in the library.
Genealogies, correspondence, notes, etc. concerning the descendants of John Osborn (1607-1686) of Weymouth, Mass., and William Hobson (1626-1659) of Rowley, Mass., with allied families of Brown, Gale and Page.

Harvey Frank Ammidown papers, 1636-1936
Ammidown, Harry Frank, 1885-.
Mss 55
9 linear ft.
Unpublished finding aid in the library.
The bulk of the collection consists of vital records compiled from town records, Bible entries, church records and gravestone inscriptions. Entered on 70,000 cards, the data is concentrated around the Worcester County towns of Charlton, Dudley, Southbridge and Sturbridge for the period 1636 to 1924. There is Ammidown and allied family genealogies, notes and correspondence, 1727-1936, followed by some family papers including property records, estates, business papers, lawsuits and bonds, 1779-1881. Includes tax lists, road subscription and plats for Dudley and Southbridge, Mass., 1801-1842, and First Baptist Church in Southbridge records, such as minutes, contracts, deeds and treasurer's accounts, 1816-1865.

William Calneck papers, 1690-1890
Calneck, William, 1822-1892.
Mss 56
105 items.
Unpublished finding aid in the library.
Biographical and genealogical sketches of 105 families in Annapolis County, Nova Scotia. Noting the origins of each (English, Scotch, etc.), each sketch includes information about related families as well.

Marie Whitmore Roberts papers, 1580-1971
Roberts, Marie W.
Mss 57
25 items.
Unpublished finding aid in the library.
Genealogies, vital records, correspondence and 15 photographs pertaining to the Vermont Winslows descended from Kenelm Winslow (1599-1681) and the Lymans descended from Richard Lyman (1580-1640).

Josiah Smith papers, 1836-1874
Smith, Josiah, 1789-1876.
Mss 58
30 items.
The present collection provides only fragmentary evidence of Smith's long and varied career. His 1812 service appears through his pension application, accompanied by a few letters from the pension office. All that remains of his militia activities are some orders issued in the 1870's, his bills for music performed at drills between 1830 and 1874, four manuscript music pieces, and newspaper clippings. Most of the evidence is contained in an account book kept between 1825 and 1832, which records both his cobbler's and musician's fees. Another small volume records the auction sale of Smith's Lexington farm in 1862. Smith's Maine land investment and its accompanying bankruptcy proceedings can be followed through a small number of documents, bills, receipts and statements brought together in 1842.

Mary E. Boudreau papers, 1838-1959
Boudreau, Mary E.
Mss 59
100 items.
Unpublished finding aid in the library.
The bulk of this collection reflects the activities of the Hitchcock family, particularly the elder Roswell D. Hitchcock and his immediate descendants. His own papers consist of scattered correspondence, sermons, and programs generated by a career as a Congregational clergyman and educator. There is still less material for his children: Bradford D. Hitchcock (1861-1918), Mary B.H. Emerson (b. 1853), and Roswell D. Hitchcock (b. 1845). In addition to some genealogical correspondence, notes and clippings, the children left occasional family papers. Most notable is a series of letters from the younger Roswell while an officer on the U.S.S. Pensacola, 1880-1885. Allied to the Hitchcocks by marriage, the Brayton and Emerson families left similar records. There are sermons by Brown Emerson (1778-), genealogical notes by Daniel H. Emerson (1854-1939), and general family papers through Samuel F. Emerson (1854-1939) and his wife, Mary B.H. Emerson (1853-). Includes 8 photographs.

William R. Brink papers, 1929-1956
Brink, William R.
Mss 60
1.5 linear ft.
Unpublished finding aid in the library.
The collection traces North American descendants of Lambert Huybertse Brink (1635-1702) through his four sons: Pieter Lambertsen Brink (1670-1746), Huybert Lambertsen Brink (1656-), Cornelius Lambertsen Brink (1661-1726), and Matthew Brink (1695-). Also included are several allied families, particularly the Webb family through William Henry Webb (1815-1878). In addition to genealogies, Mr. Brink accumulated large quantities of research notes and correspondence documenting his investigation of numerous public and private records. Most of the material concentrates in New York, New Jersey and parts of Pennsylvania, between 1630 and 1956.

Bain collection, 1819-1983
Bain, Helen Q.
Mss 61
1 linear ft.
Unpublished finding aid in the library.
Magazine and newspaper articles on American presidential families (from Adams to Reagan), as well as those of European and Asian royalty. The material on the European and Asian royalty is in three parts. The first and largest is the English royal family, beginning with Queen Victoria, and carrying slightly beyond the marriage of Elizabeth II's son Philip. The second and third groups contain material on European and Asian royalty, each in alphabetical order by country.

James Freer Faunce papers, 1420-1982
Faunce, James Freer, 1908-2000.
Mss 62
1.5 linear ft.
Unpublished finding aid in the library.
Genealogies, questionnaires, correspondence, notes and photographs pertaining to the descendants of John Faunce (1602-1653) in England and America. English research in Essex was performed by hired genealogists, including Florence G. Main, Frederick G. Emmison and Phillimore & Co., Ltd. The reports by the professional genealogists often included copies of pertinent documents. In the United States, Mr. Faunce collected existing informal genealogies and conducted extensive correspondence with relatives around the country. The numerous replies included letters, forms, research notes, clippings, and photographs. The source material was filed geographically, while the digested data was entered on forms filed by generations one to nine.

Frank M. Hutchings papers, 1836-1955
Hutchings, Frank M., 1913-1981.
Mss 63
6 linear ft.
Unpublished finding aid in the library.
Correspondence, diaries, Bible records, reminiscences, genealogies, notes, portraits, photos, including ambrotypes, daguerreotypes, tintypes, and cartes de visite, and other papers, relating to the Hutchings and Miller families and 52 allied families including Bridgen, Brinkerhoff, De Witt, Hardenburgh, and Vermilye, chiefly of New Jersey and New York. Includes recollections of Gertrude H. Stewart reflecting pioneer life in Wisconsin; journals (1833) of Elizabeth C.L. Hutchings, a Presbyterian missionary's wife, serving with her husband in Ceylon; correspondence (1836-1855) between David Hardenburgh and his wife, Maria B. Hardenburgh, concerning his activities as a civil engineer and their social life in the Middle West; information detailing travel of family members in Europe in the early 1890s; and materials pertaining to First Congregational Church, Riverside, Calif., and relatives who were Reformed Dutch clergyman. Persons represented include Anna B. and John De Witt and Caroline G.L. Hutchings.

Wendell B. Cook papers, 1966-1982
Cook, Wendell B., 1932-.
Mss 64
3 linear ft.
Unpublished finding aid in the library.
Genealogies, notes and correspondence generated through personal and commissioned research, and activities in genealogical organizations. His personal research primarily deals with the descendants of Josiah Cook (d. 1732) of Eastham, Mass., including allied families. Prominent among the latter are Badlam, Gale, Pratt, Tolman, and Waymire families. Cook's records as a university level teacher of genealogical methods includes many of his administrative records such as his course proposal, the University's support, course descriptions, tests and evaluations.

Hiram Webb papers, 1789-1898
Webb, Hiram, 1816-1879.
Mss 65
25 items.
Unpublished finding aid in the library.
Genealogy, records, notes, correspondence, and six photographs concerning the descendants of Christopher Webb (d. 1678), who came from England to Braintree, Mass. Particular attention is paid to the allied families of Crowell and Elkins as well.

Frederick Haynes Newell papers, 1694-1975
Newell, Frederick Haynes, 1862-1932.
Mss 66
4 linear ft.
Unpublished finding aid in the repository.
Includes family and professional papers of his grandfather, Artemas Newell (1807-1871), lawyer, of Brookline MA, father, Augustus W. Newell (1832-1919), merchant and speculator, of Bradford PA, and his son, John M. Newell (1904-1971), a student at Cornell University who became a biochemist with U.S. Dept. of Health, Education, and Welfare, and later worked with the rehabilitation of the blind in Washington, D.C., and other family members including a justice of the peace in Brookline, and a teacher in a freedman's school in Mississippi; lists (1777) of marriages in Dorchester MA; commissions signed by Thomas Mifflin and John Hancock; and information concerning social life in Newton and West Roxbury MA, in the late 1880s and family travels in Europe. Persons represented include Alexander G. Bell, Noah Clap, Edward E. Dutton, Ann P. Haynes, Annie H., Josiah, Phebe L., Roger S., Sarah, and Thomas Newell, Gifford Pinchot, Theodore Roosevelt, and John Sherman.

Clarence V. Shumway papers, 1817-1940
Shumway, Clarence V., 1852-1933.
Mss 67
1 linear ft.
Unpublished finding aid in the repository.
Correspondence, personal and financial papers, notes, charts, marriage and baptismal records, and genealogical materials, chiefly relating to Shumway, his family and its emigration from England to Massachusetts, and 25 allied lines including Harvie, Johnston, Pollard, and Schofield. Includes personal ledger (1903-1923) and records reflecting Shumway's activities with Wear Wrench Company; correspondence and business papers (1817-1871) of Joseph Schofield (1785-1852), wool merchant in Dudley MA; and materials pertaining to Marino Wool Factory Co.

Ivory Hovey papers, 1732-1798
Hovey, Ivory, 1714-1803.
Mss 68
28 items.
Unpublished finding aid in the repository.
Correspondence, sermons, ecclesiastical council decisions, church records, vital records, and other papers, relating to family affairs and Hovey's congregations. Includes letters from his sons, Dominicus (b. 1740), Ivory III (b. 1748), and Samuel (b. 1750), written from Massachusetts and New York during the Revolution, describing the evacuation of New York (1783), Siege of Boston (1775-1776), reading of the Declaration of Independence to troops in New York, and the American retreat from Ticonderoga; letter (1781) from his daughter, Olive (Hovey) Pope (b. 1746), of Wells, Me., detailing wilderness life; notations of marriages and baptisms performed by Hovey in Plymouth; and records and registers of First Congregational churches in Mattapoisett and New Bedford, Mass., Second Congregational Church in Plymouth, and United Church of Christ, Little Compton, R.I. Other persons represented include Othnaiel Campbell, Israel Cheever, Hovey's father, Ivory Hovey (1682-1759), Jonathan Moore, and Chandler Robbins.

Roderick Heffron papers, 1897-1981
Heffron, Roderick, 1901-1983.
Mss 69
300 items.
Unpublished finding aid in the repository.
Correspondence, genealogies, charts, notes, and photos, relating to the Heffron family and its allied lines including the Abbott, Chapman, Crumb, Murray, and Salisbury families.

Marjorie S. Dows papers, 1978-1982
Dows, Marjorie S.
Mss 70
68 items.
Unpublished finding aid in the repository.
Transcripts of gravestone inscriptions, with indexes and notes on conditions of cemeteries concerned, taken from cemetery surveys done as part of a project of the Daughters of the American Revolution, by Dows, her husband, Robert H. Dows, and Virginia Moscrip. Includes inscriptions from 68 cemeteries, in Centerville, Mass., and Allegany, Livingston, Monroe, Ontario, and Steuben Counties, N.Y., giving particular attention to veterans' graves.

Wigglesworth family papers, 1657-1794
Wigglesworth family.
Mss 71
25 items.
Unpublished finding aid in the repository.
Correspondence, deeds, estate papers, poetry, and other papers, of three generations of Wigglesworth family members, chiefly of Michael Wigglesworth (1631-1705), Congregational clergyman, of Malden and Edward (ca. 1693-1765) and Edward (1732-1794) Wigglesworth, professors of divinity at Harvard College. Includes records of estate settlements of Sewall and Coolidge family members, records of property exchanges in Cambridge, and letter from John Erskine (1721-1803) to Edward Wigglesworth (1732-1794).

Samuel Smith papers, 1814-1815
Smith, Samuel, 1752-1839.
Mss 72
44 items.
Unpublished finding aid in the repository.
Correspondence, powers of attorney, records of prize sales, shares, and articles of agreement, relating to the disposal of goods taken by the privateer schooner Mammoth, sailing out of Portland, Me., June 23-Oct. 31, 1814, as settled by agents of Smith and his partners, crewmen, and Portland officials. Two auctions are recorded for the prize.

Nicholas Wyeth papers, 1650-1695
Wyeth, Nicholas, 1595-1680.
Mss 73
10 items.
Unpublished register in the library.
Deeds, bonds, powers of attorney, etc. of Nicholas Wyeth, of Cambridge, Mass., a mason, and his son William, also of Cambridge, a yeoman and husbandman. The deeds of Nicholas Wyeth involve transfers of land in Charlestown and Cambridge, some being fully executed and recorded, others are unsigned drafts. The deeds concerning William Wyeth involve land in Cambridge.

Joseph Cooledge papers, 1696-1735
Cooledge, Joseph, 1666-1737.
Mss 74
62 items.
Unpublished finding aid in the library.
Consists of the business and personal papers of Deacon Joseph Cooledge, a tailor in Cambridge, Mass. The papers include bonds, deeds for Cambridge property, powers of attorney, an apprenticeship indenture, a tax gatherer's commission, and miscellaneous bills and receipts. The documents include important names, particularly Brattle and Wyeth.

Jeffrey Bedgood papers, 1709-1762
Bedgood, Jeffrey, 1677-1757.
Mss 75
45 items.
Unpublished finding aid in the repository.
Bills of lading for goods shipped between Boston and Jamaica; bonds given by Bedgood; and will, estate inventory, and other papers relating to the administration of Bedgood's estate by John Fayerweather (1695-1760) and his son, Thomas Fayerweather (1724-1805), executor.

Thomas Hubbard papers, 1740-1791
Hubbard, Thomas, 1702-1773.
Mss 76
157 items.
Unpublished finding aid in the repository.
Materials concerning Hubbard's mercantile activities, chiefly information relating to his business dealings with English merchants and accounts and receipts detailing warehouse charges and ship turn-around times at his wharf; papers pertaining to the settlement of his estate, administered by Thomas Fayerweather and William B. Townsend, including property settlements extending into Connecticut and England; and estate papers of Edward Jackson (1708-1757), Boston merchant, administered by Hubbard and Samuel Sewall.

Joseph Dudley papers, 1755-1774
Dudley, Joseph, 1732-1767.
Mss 77
146 items.
Unpublished finding aid in the repository.
Chiefly bills and receipts (1750-1767) and other papers, relating to Dudley's personal and professional activities; and records of the settlement of his estate by Thomas Fayerweather (1724-1805), Boston merchant, including information concerning disposal of Dudley's real estate, household inventory, and list of contents of his library. Persons represented include Joseph Russell.

John Leverett papers, 1628-1726
Leverett, John, 1662-1724.
Mss 78
66 items.
Unpublished finding aid in the repository.
Papers concerning the administration of Leverett's estate, three Natick (Massachuset) Indian apprenticeships issued by Leverett as judge of Massachusetts Superior Court of Judicature, documents concerning argument with the Crown over the Massachusetts Colony charter, lease of land in Kingston, R.I., reports reflecting his activities as administrator of Indian lands in Rhode Island, and other papers; together with papers of family members, including deeds of Sarah Leverett (1700-1727) and Mary Leverett Dennison (1701-1756) pertaining to the transfer of property in Cambridge to Edward Wigglesworth (1693-1765). Other family members represented include John Leverett's father, Hudson (1640-1694), and his grandfather, Gov. John Leverett (1616-1679), and Margaret D. Leverett (1664-1720).

John Fayerweather papers, 1729-1761
Fayerweather, John, 1685-1760.
Mss 79
16 items.
Unpublished finding aid in the repository.
Account books (5 v.), receipts, three letters of Edward Shipping, of Philadelphia, Pa., and papers relating to Fayerweather's son, Thomas Fayerweather's (1724-1805) settling of his father's estate. Account books contain entries concerning both business and personal affairs including the recording of wagers made by the elder Fayerweather.

Thomas Fayerweather papers, 1737-1818
Fayerweather, Thomas, 1724-1805.
Mss 80
5 linear ft.
Unpublished finding aid in the repository.
Correspondence, business and personal financial records, accounts, photos, and other papers, relating to Fayerweather's business and personal affairs, including his involvement in U.S. coastwise and international shipping trade, chiefly with Nova Scotia, West Indies, England, and Europe, ventures in Maine lands and a copper mine in Smithfield, R.I., privateering, whaling, and the family farms in Beverly, Dorchester, and Westborough MA Includes business correspondence with Arthur Savage, William Shippen, and Samuel Smith; papers of his wife, Elizabeth (Phillips) Fayerweather (b. 1734), documenting her experiences in Oxford MA, during the Siege of Boston (1775-1776); and information pertaining to social activities and Fayerweather's duties as head of a large family. Other persons represented include Thomas Botineau, Elias Jarvis, and Scammon Rodman.

Charles Ewer papers, 1821-1853
Ewer, Charles, 1790-1853.
Mss 81
1 linear ft.
Unpublished finding aid in the repository.
Correspondence and genealogical papers relating to the descendants of Henry Ewer (b. 1537), of Sandwich, Mass., European ancestors, and a number of allied families including Howard, Minot, and Turrell; account books and other papers reflecting Ewer's business interests, chiefly the development of Boston's South Cove and affiliation with South Cove Corporation, with minor records of his bookstore and insurance operations; and personal papers including two 18th century poems: one an epitaph (1778) honoring a British officer thought to have been written by Stephen Hall, loyalist, of Medford, Mass., and the other, an attack on Daniel Barrett, Harvard student, accompanied by his reply. Persons represented include Ebenezer Turrell and John and Mary Wolcott.

Samuel Webster papers, 1790-1850
Webster, Samuel, fl. 1836-1850.
Mss 82
500 items.
Unpublished finding aid in the repository.
Business correspondence with merchants in New Hampshire and Massachusetts, relating to grass seed, trees, mittens, lumber, casks, and other subjects; Barnstead town records reflecting Webster's activities as selectman, including tax, road, militia, and poor records; and correspondence, petitions, lists of names, and collection lists, pertaining to his duties as sheriff of Belknap County, N.H. Includes suit by the town of Center Harbor, N.H., against Barnstead, concerning the support of a pauper.

Herman A. Parsons papers, ca. 1940-1983
Parsons, Herman A., 1907-1983.
Mss 83
300 items.
Unpublished finding aid in the repository.
Manuscript genealogy, notes, charts, and other papers, relating to the descendants of Jeffrey Parsons (1631-1689), early resident of Gloucester, Mass., and the allied families of Alden, Bridgham, Griggs, McLane, Millett, Morrill, Rust, and Willard.

Florence B. Lyman papers, 1575-1967
Lyman, Florence B., b. 1891.
Mss 84
27 items.
Unpublished finding aid in the library.
Genealogy and notes pertaining to the descendants of Jonathan Morrison (fl. 1823), the descendants of Simeon Lyman (1730-1809) and 25 allied families of Northfield, Mass.

William J. Harrison papers, 1530-1981
Harrison, William J., 1904-.
Mss 85
1 linear ft.
Unpublished finding aid in the repository.
Correspondence, genealogies, charts, records, notes, and other papers, of Harrison and his wife, Helen B. Harrison (1906-1973), relating to the Harris, Balf, and 31 allied families including Gerst, Hachman, Musselman, and Truax, chiefly residing in New Jersey and Pennsylvania.

John Marshall Raymond papers, 1953-1983
Raymond, John Marshall, 1894-1984.
Mss 86
2 linear ft.
Unpublished finding aid in the repository.
Correspondence, genealogies, charts, records, notes, and other papers, relating to the Raymond, Teel/Teele, and Thomas families, chiefly of Middleboro, Marshfield, Worcester, and Plymouth County, Mass., and 19 allied lines including Ames and Swan. Persons represented include Ethel B. Gould, George Raymond (d. 1651), Benjamin Swan (1787-1842), his daughter, Ellen Maria Swan (1824-1907), John William Teele (b. 1841), William Teele (1660-1719), David Thomas (1620-1689), John Thomas (1621-1691), and William Thomas (1573-1651).

William L. Ulrich papers, 1920-1980
Ulrich, William L., 1885-1932.
Mss 87
500 items.
Unpublished finding aid in the repository.
Correspondence, genealogy, applications for memberships in patriotic societies, charts, notes, research papers, card file, and other papers, compiled by Ulrich with the assistance of his daughter, Harriet U. Fish, of Carlsborg, Wash.

Charles M. Wales papers, ca. 1904-1911
Wales, Charles M., 1862-1930.
Mss 88
1.5 linear ft.
Unpublished finding aid in the repository.
Card files (2500 cards), indexes, and genealogical lists, tracing the descendants of Nathaniel Wales (1586-1661), of Dorchester, Mass., containing vital statistics for the Wales and its allied families.

William Eben Stone papers, 1016-1937 (bulk 1450-1881)
Stone, William Eben, 1845-1921.
Mss 89
1.4 linear feet.
Unpublished finding aid in the library.
Bulk of the collection consists of genealogical pedigree charts for the Stone and allied families, especially Jackson, Neville, Whitney, and Wright. Includes supporting documentation such as newspaper clippings, genealogical notes, and correspondence. There is also a ms. genealogy on the descendants of Gregory Stone of Great Bromley, Eng. and Cambridge, Mass. and a few documents. Some items of particular interest include the 1777 will/inventory and the 1779 appeasement of Silas Stone's estate, and the 4 March 1672 petition of Daniel Stone to the Mass. Court of Assistants for compensation for the care he provided eight survivors of a shipwreck.

Albert M. Dunham papers, 1733-1984
Dunham, Albert M., 1871-1965.
Mss 90
1 linear ft.
Unpublished finding aid in the repository.
Correspondence, genealogies, records, charts, and notes, relating to the descendants of John Dunham (1588 or 9-1670), of Plymouth MA, including descriptions by female relatives documenting early life and events in Brattleboro VT; correspondence, deeds, auction records, and other papers (1733-1950) concerning Albert Dunham's administration of properties owned by the heirs of George O. Dunham in Attleboro MA; and photos, chiefly of Dunham and Thayer homes in Attleboro. Family members represented include Lydia Carpenter (fl. 1774) and Joseph Dunham (1778-1828), his wife, Esther W. (Barrows) (1777-1825), their son, Gardner (1807-1895), and Marjorie M. Dunham (b. 1910).

Howard Parker Moore papers, 1927-1959
Moore, Howard Parker, b. 1868.
Mss 91
1 linear ft.
Unpublished finding aid in the repository.
Biographical sketches, genealogies, charts, family records, and other papers, pertaining to Richard Moore (1614-1674), of Salem MA, the Moore family, and its allied families including Dutch, Hollingsworth, Hunter, and Knowlton.

Henry A. Phillips papers, 1877-1977
Phillips, Henry A., 1852-1926.
Mss 92
5 linear ft.
Unpublished finding aid in the repository.
Correspondence, mss. of writings, genealogies, notes, charts, biographical materials, and other papers, relating to the descendants of George Phillips (1593-1644), of Watertown, Mass., and allied families, compiled by Henry Phillips as an updating of Albert M. Phillips's Phillips Genealogies (1885).

Elizabeth M. Booth papers, 1440-1979
Booth, Elizabeth M., 1906-1986.
Mss 93
1 linear ft.
Unpublished finding aid in the repository.
Correspondence, genealogies, notes, charts, and other papers, relating to the family of John Spring (b. 1589), of Watertown, Mass., including materials (1440-1851) concerning family members in Great Britain. Correspondents include genealogist Gary B. Roberts.

Maude E. Taylor papers, 1840-1966
Taylor, Maude E., b. 1884.
Mss 94
2 linear ft.
Unpublished finding aid in the repository.
Correspondence, research notes, charts, genealogies, and other papers, prepared by Taylor with the assistance of her husband, Benjamin F. Taylor, relating to the descendants of Duncan Stewart (1623-1717), early resident of Rowley, Mass., and approximately 109 allied families, some settling in Maine, including the Burrill, Clark, Cooke, Crane, Howland, Pease, Steward/Stewart, and Taylor lines. Persons represented include Martha A. Bosworth (1854-1940), Lucius Cook (1846-1924), Charlotte M. Howland (fl. 1936), Abraham Taylor (1656-1729), and Samuel C. Worthen (fl. 1915).

John Wingate Thornton papers, 1086-1884
Thornton, John Wingate, 1818-1878.
Mss 95
2 linear ft.
Unpublished finding aid in the library.
Genealogical, historical, business and personal papers of the Thornton and 37 allied families of Saco ME, and North Hampton NH. In addition to his own, those families given special attention by Thornton include Bowles, Coggswell, Cutts, Dane, Gilbert, Gookin, Lake and Wingate families. These include papers of Thomas Cutts (1736-1820), a merchant of Saco ME (ca. 300 items), and political correspondence of Nathan Dane (1752-1835) (28 items), concerning the Ordinance of 1787, its application to Michigan statehood, slavery and other issues. Thornton's articles and books on New England local history are represented by scattered letters, newspaper reviews, and photographs taken in Saco. There is also correspondence pertaining to genealogy, politics and personal affairs, often with notables of his day.

A listing of the index of deeds in Andover, Massachusetts up to 1799
Mss 96
2 vols.
Typescripts. Grantors and grantees (5794 names).

Ralph H. Bowles papers, 1718-1846.
Bowles, Ralph H., 1757-1813.
Mss 97
300 items.
Unpublished finding aid in the library.
Correspondence, documents, accounts and receipts, and other papers of Bowles and his sons, Lucius Q.C. Bowles (1789-1843) and Stephen J. Bowles (1794-1846), relating to the family lumber business, chiefly operated by Ralph H. and Stephen, Bowles's activities as postmaster and local official, and Lucius Q.C. Bowles's service as Maine state senator.

Thomas G. Thornton papers, 1787-1851
Thornton, Thomas G., 1768-1824.
Mss 98
2 linear ft.
Unpublished finding aid in the library.
Materials relating to Thornton's activities as U.S. marshal (1804-1823), chiefly regarding the War of 1812 and his concerns with prisoners of war, enemy aliens, privateering, prizes and the collection of fees, and sales of confiscated foods and tax delinquent land; and a small group of private papers including correspondence, bills, deeds, and estate papers.

Daniel Dunbar papers, 1749-1911
Dunbar, Daniel.
Mss 99
35 items.
Family record, will of Mary A. Dunbar, and deeds of Bridgewater MA property.

Alexander Wessel Shapleigh papers, 1939-1984
Shapleigh, Alexander W. (Alexander Wessel), 1918-.
Mss 100
1 linear ft.
Unpublished finding aid in the library.
Family history (2 v.), heraldic notes, charts, genealogies, and photos, relating to the family of Alexander Shapleigh (1561-1650), founder of Kittery ME Includes papers of Shapleigh's grandfather, Alfred L. Shapleigh (1862-1945); and memorials contributed by his father, A. Wessel Shapleigh, Sr. (1890-1972), and Ralph S. Bartlett.

First Congregational Society records, 1844-1872
First Congregational Society (Somerville, Mass.)
Mss 101
2 vols.
Minutes, admissions, baptisms, births, etc.

Albert C. Aldrich papers, 1896-1955
Aldrich, Albert C., 1871-1963.
Mss 102
49 items.
Unpublished finding aid in the library.
Correspondence, charts, genealogies, notes, and other papers, of the family of George Aldrich (1605-1682), of Mendon MA, and the allied families of Boyden, Hatch, and Phelps.

Calvin C. Davis papers, 1910-1958
Davis, Calvin C., 1866-1958.
Mss 103
18 items.
Unpublished finding aid in the library.
Manuscript genealogies (two versions) prepared by Davis tracing the descendants of Dolor Davis (1593-1673), carpenter, who moved around New England, eventually settling in Barnstable, Mass.; and correspondence and notes. Other persons represented include Samuel Davis (1639-1720) and Simon Davis (1636-1713).

Mary A. Lucas papers, 1482-1940
Lucas, Mary A.
Mss 104
23 items.
Notes, charts, clippings and scattered family papers of the Lucas and allied families of Denison, Gross, Hunt, Russell, and Wadhams in Connecticut.

Samuel B. Mayo papers, 1840-1981
Mayo, Samuel B., 1916-1982.
Mss 105
1 linear ft.
Unpublished finding aid in the library.
Correspondence, charts, genealogies, notes, family papers, portraits, photos, and other papers, relating to the Mayo family and its allied lines including Chandler, Claflin, Kendrick, and Wyman. Includes correspondence of Thomas Chandler (1772-1866), U.S. representative, of Bedford, N.H., describing state and national political affairs; Benjamin Franklin Kendrick (b. 1827), a forty-niner, relating to his trip across the Great Plains, Pawnee Nation, and gold mines in California; and Roxana (Mayo) Williams (1794-1861), of Illinois, reflecting her voyage (ca. 1847) on the Allegheny River on the steamboat America, while on a trip from Baltimore, Md., to Cincinnati, Ohio. Family members represented include Mary A. Mayo (1812-1893).

Dorothy L. Crawford papers, 1979-1983
Crawford, Dorothy L., 1910-1986.
Mss 106
1 linear ft.
Unpublished finding aid in the library.
Genealogical materials of five generations of the family of John Heywood (ca. 1612-1701), of Concord MA Includes information relating to 140 Heywood families, chiefly of Massachusetts, and also of Maine, New Hampshire, Vermont, New York, and Ohio.

Clarke G. Dailey papers, 1842-1962
Dailey, Clarke G., 1879-1964.
Mss 107
88 items.
Unpublished finding aid in the library.
Correspondence, genealogies, notes, records, and other papers, relating to the Dailey and thirteen allied families. Other families represented include Cary, Clark, Fuller, and Michaux.

Frederick Lewis Weis papers, 1930-1963
Weis, Frederick Lewis, 1895-1966.
First Church of Christ (Lancaster, Mass.)
Mss 108
2 linear ft.
Unpublished finding aid in the library.
Correspondence, genealogies, biographies, charts, notes, and other papers, relating to the families of Weis and his wife, Elizabeth W. (Stone) Weis (b. 1904), chiefly residents of Lancaster, Sterling, Sudbury, and Athol MA, including ancestors in England and elsewhere in New England, and 119 allied families including Atherton, Blake, Brown/Browne, Kendall, Little, Pierce, Richardson, Southworth, Wheelock, and Whitcomb; and records of First Church of Christ, Lancaster MA, reflecting Weis's duties as clergyman and its affiliate, Chocksett Church. Persons represented include Christopher Browne (d. 1519), Samuel Kendall (1682-1764), Thomas Little (d. 1672), Robert Pierce (d. 1665), Benjamin Richardson (1732-1821), Thomas Southworth (1616-1669), Constant Southworth (1614-1679), Ralph Wheelock (1600-1684), and Asa Whitcomb (1718-1804).

John Samuel Hill Fogg papers, 1682-1831
Fogg, John Samuel Hill, 1826-1893.
Mss 109
5 vols.
Minutes, admissions, baptisms, marriages, etc., of three Kittery, Maine churches (1st Church, Lower Parish, and 2nd Church), 1714-1831, as well as town records, 1682-1821.

Kenneth E. Creed papers, 1881-1985
Creed, Kenneth E., 1921-1985.
Mss 110
7 linear ft.
Unpublished finding aid in the library.
Correspondence, genealogical materials, charts, computer printouts and disks, photos, and other papers, relating to the Creed and allied families, chiefly of New England, and Creed's wife's Nyce, Van Etten, and Westbrook lines of New York and Pennsylvania; and materials pertaining to families researched professionally by Creed: Buland, Fix, Hawkes, Munroe, and Stambaugh. Includes information concerning Maine history and the Blake family home in Dorchester MA; and letters of family members serving during the Civil War. Persons and other families represented include James Blake (1644-1700), William Creed (1807-1844), Mary R.P. Hatch, Frank R. Knowlton (1847-1933), John F. Knowlton, and Eleanor Lexington and the Bass, Blake, Drew, Gould, Hooten, Huddleston, Pennell, Rosencrans, Schoonover, and Whitney families.

[Leavitt family]
Leavitt, William Hunt, 1834-.
Mss 111
705 p.: ports.; 27 cm.
1900
Ms. genealogy with photos and clippings on the descendants of John Leavitt (1608-1691) of Hingham MA. Includes an envelope with three pictures of John Hooker Leavitt (one 1877 & the other two from ca. 1902), and an image of the house John H. Leavitt's lived in from 1871-1906).

John D. Beal papers, 1972-1983
Beal, John D., 1909-
Mss 112
4 linear ft.
Unpublished finding aid in the library.
Correspondence, public and private records, genealogies, extracts of published materials, and other papers, relating to all bearers of the name Beal and its derivatives. Includes 90,000 names of family members, chiefly of Massachusetts and Maine, but also residing in New York State, Pennsylvania, South Carolina, Tennessee, Nova Scotia, England, and other places.

Agnes E. Dodge papers, 1844-1969
Dodge, Agnes E., 1883-1973.
Mss 113
147 items.
Unpublished finding aid in the library.
Correspondence, two partial genealogies, and notes, relating to Richard Dodge (1602-1671), of Wenham, Mass., and Phineas Dodge (1662-1704), of Rowley, Mass., and their descendants from Massachusetts to Illinois, Washington, and Wyoming, and the allied families of Gray and Robinson; private papers including constitution of South Boston Anti-slavery Society and minutes (1844) of a meeting of Friends of the Slave, reflecting the abolitionist interests of William B. Dodge (1813-1871) and an account (1864) written by his son, James H. Dodge (b. 1845), describing his activities as a soldier during the Civil War and garrison duty and prisoners at Fort Independence in Boston; and over 90 photos, including personal portraits (1860-1960) and subjects of family interest including a memorial in Council Bluffs, Iowa, dedicated to Ruth Anne (Brown) Dodge. Other family members represented include Henry L. Dodge (b. 1843).

An index to the records of the First Church of Stonington, Connecticut
Williams, Edward H. Jr.
Mss 114
1 v. (235 p.)
Ms. abstracts of genealogical information from original record for 1674-1874.

Vital records of the town of Southampton, Massachusetts 1740-1940
Lederer, Inez Stevens, 1882-.
Mss 115
1 v. (488 p.)
Typescript transcription of the original record.

The Hayward family of Acton and Boxborough, Mass.
Hayward, Herbert Nelson, 1853-.
Mss 116
471 p.
c. 1890
Ms. genealogy on the descendants of George1 Hayward (d. 1671) of Concord, Mass.

Notices and indexes of births, marriages and deaths published in the St. Croix Courier of St. Stephen, New Brunswick, 1865-1935
Chase, Melvin W.
Mss 117
1,211 leaves; 28 cm.
Typescript transcriptions.

[Margaret Geddes Morgan ancestry]
Morgan, Margaret Harriet Geddes, 1905-.
Mss 118
226 leaves; 28 cm.
c. 1985
Photocopy of original ms. charts and notes pertaining to the Geddes and allied family ancestors of the author.

Chronicle of the Larkin family of the town of Westerlie and colony of Rhoade Island
Larkin, William Harrison, Jr., 1871-1936.
Mss 119
205, 135 p.; 28 cm.
Typescript with pencil illustrations and includes a 1995 computer typescript done by author's grandson, Richard Fessenden Larkin.

Looking backward: a brief study of more than 50 generations of one American family's ancestors
Cook, William Grant, 1905-.
Mss 120
vi, 144 leaves: coats of arms, geneal. tables; 28 cm.
1981
Typescript. Letter by the author dated November 10, 1985 in the first folder states that "a considerable part" of this work was "rendered false by two articles in the Spring 1980 issue of The Genealogist": "The Children of Joan, Princess of Wales" by William Addams Reitweisner and "Ravens or Pelicans: Who was Joan de Harley?" by John G. Hunt and Henry J. Young. "This double blow knocks out, for the time being anyway, the pretensions of our Parke-Thompson clan, among others, to links with Plantagenets, some Scots kings, some Companions of William the Conqueror at Hastings and other assorted earls, margraves, dukes, comtes and barons. But we are left with some Gallo-Roman nobles, a set of Ripuarian Franks, the founders of the Scots and English kingdoms, a cross-section of landed gentry...and of course our own American colonial founders."

Genealogy of the Mayo family
Mss 121
210 p.; 26 cm.
S.l.: s.n
Handwritten genealogy on the descendants of John Mayo (d. 1676) of Yarmouth MA, and allied families for nine generations, 1638-1937.

Jerome M. Carley papers, 1911-1946
Carley, Jerome M., 1877-1947.
Mss 122
ca. 260 items.
Unpublished finding aid in the library.
Correspondence, genealogical materials, newspaper clippings, notes, and other papers, relating to the family of William Kerley (1637-1670), of Sudbury, Mass., including members of the Carley, Clark, and Welles families and 22 allied families; historical articles concerning Framingham, Mass., written by Walter Adams, Charles A. Esty, George F. Marlowe, and John M. Merriam; and materials pertaining to Carley's genealogical research, chiefly done on vacations. Includes "vacation journal" describing visits to New York and New England (1911-1944) and photos (1939) of the Baptist Church, Wilton, N.H.

Harvey L. Williams papers, 1375-1908
Williams, Harvey L., 1875-.
Mss 123
180 items.
Unpublished finding aid in the library.
Genealogies, charts, notes, records and correspondence pertaining to the Williams and 29 allied families.

Alma B. Chamberlain papers, 1599-1953
Chamberlain, Alma B.
Mss 124
6 in.
Chart, general notes, correspondence, family papers and photographs pertaining to the Anable, Chamberlain and Anderson families.

House and property, 1835-1957, East Brewster, Mass.
Crosby, Albert.
Mss 125
212 items.
Deeds, survey, bills, auction agreement and pictures of "Sawaseutha" and its property.

The Union Club of Boston records, 1863-1976
The Union Club of Boston.
Mss 126
3 linear ft. (44 vols.)
Unpublished finding aid in the library.
Records of the Executive Committee (1863-1905), House Committee (1904-1907), annual meetings (1901-1905), and thirty-eight scattered club yearbooks (1867-1953) which include annotated membership lists, constitution, and by-laws.

Howard L. Baldwin papers, 1415-1966
Baldwin, Howard L., 1883-1969.
Mss 128
500 items.
Unpublished finding aid in the library.
Four hundred family record sheets, charts, notes, reference materials, and other papers, relating to the family of Joseph Baldwin (d. 1684), of Hadley, Mass., English ancestors, and related families of Hutchings, Lathrop, Leffingwell, Moore, and Palm.

Porter papers, 1777-1961
Porter, Emma E., 1874-1961.
Mss 129
500 items.
Unpublished finding aid in the library.
Correspondence, genealogies, charts, Bible records, research notes, scattered family papers, and other materials, relating to the descendants of John Porter (ca. 1586-1676), of Danvers, Mass., and allied lines including Boies, Holm, and Hooper. Includes letter (1777) of Sgt. Samuel Smith (1731-1777) to his wife, Rachel, in Hopkinton, N.H., describing the early stages of Burgoyne's Saratoga campaign and military life. Persons represented include Ernest (1848-1889), Frederick W. (1836-1894), John (ca. 1586-1676), and Smith A.M. (b. 1848) Porter.

John P. Reynolds papers, 1634-1910
Reynolds, John P., 1859-1909.
Mss 130
231 p.
Genealogy, notes and correspondence pertaining to the descendants of Robert Reynolds (d. 1659) of Boston, Mass.

Edith Clara Welch papers, 1872-1954
Welch, Edith C. (Edith Clara), fl. 1936-1980.
Mss 131
1.5 linear ft.
Unpublished finding aid in the library.
Genealogies compiled by Welch and Casimir P. Stevens, notes, vital records, and other papers, relating to the descendants of James (b. 1691), Tamson, and William (1722-1778) Gray, of Portsmouth, Newington, and Barrington, N.H., and the allied families of John Hurd (1643-1689), Kittery, Me., and Philip Welch (b. 1643), of Londonderry, N.H.

Fredericka Milander Towns papers, 1975-1985
Towns, Fredericka M. (Fredericka Milander), 1921-.
Mss 132
500 items.
Unpublished finding aid in the library.
Correspondence, wills, deeds, census records, genealogies, and other papers, chiefly relating to the family of Town's mother, Clara L. (Primm) Milander (1888-1982), of Waco, Tex., and its allied lines including Bell, Dillard, Laine, Love, Primm, Taylor, and Webb, chiefly residing in North Carolina, Tennessee, Texas, and Virginia; and lesser materials concerning her father, Frederick A. Milander (1874-1941), an immigrant from Stuttgart, Germany, his emigration to Texas, and other Milander family members. Persons represented include Franklin D. (fl. 1929), Robert A. (fl. 1955), and Thomas (1766-1844) Love, and Alicia Crane Williams (b. 1947).

Virginia Dorothy Rodefer papers, 1861-1981
Rodefer, Virginia D. (Virginia Dorothy), 1920-.
Mss 133
10 items (2200 p.).
Unpublished finding aid in the library.
Genealogies (typewritten) and indexes relating to the descendants of Jacob Snyder (b. 1754), chiefly settling in Jermyn and Greenfield Township, Lackawanna County, Pa., and the allied families of Cobb, Copperthwaite, Decker, Dings, Lee, McLaughlin, Moon, Pierce, and Vail.

Births, marriages and deaths recorded in Charlotte County, N.B., 1790-1980
Chase, Melvin William.
Mss 134
17 items.
Typescript transcription of the inscriptions from the Ledge Church Cemetery, United Church Cemetery in Dufferin, Hill Family Cemetery, Richardson Private Cemetery in Lawrence Station, Lynnfield Cemetery on Lynnfield Road, Moores Mill Church Cemetery on Oak Hill Rd., Old Oak Bay Cemetery off St. Davids Ridge Rd., Cemetery by the Church on St. David Ridge, and the Scotch Ridge Cemetery. Includes transcriptions of records from the First Methodist Church in Eureka (births 1864-1943 & marriages 1870-1946), Kirk McColl Church (baptisms 1795-1846 & burials 1807-1829), Oak Bay United Church (births 1840-1961, marriages 1923-1964 & funeral/deaths 1869-1872, 1924-1961), and Wesleyan Methodist Church (births 1846-1905 & Marriages 1856-1907).

Descendants of Lt. Thomas Fuller of Dedham; English notes, 1899
Fuller, Francis H., (Francis Henry), 1846-1913.
Mss 135
106, 435 leaves; 27 - 30 cm.
1898
"English Notes Francis Henry Fuller 1899" comprised of notes, records and correspondence pertaining to the descendants of John Fuller (d. 1559) of Redenhall, England [1 folder, 106 leaves]. Followed by a typescript genealogy on the descendants of Thomas Fuller (d. 1690) for ten generations.

Mildred N. Jaques papers, 1856-1968
Jaques, Mildred N., 1895-1976.
Mss 136
159 items.
Unpublished finding aid in the library.
Correspondence, genealogical notes, and photos, relating to Foster, Hersey, and Jaques family members. Includes diary (1856) of Mary F. Hersey (1829-1897), of Brookline, Mass., describing the first month of her marriage. Persons represented include Abbie N. Jaques.

Henry C. Bigelow papers, 1855-1908
Bigelow, Henry C., 1834-1902.
Mss 137
221 items.
Unpublished finding aid in the library.
Correspondence, business records, diaries, genealogical materials, household accounts, and other papers, of Bigelow and his family. Includes rhymed account of a family vacation (1899) at Starlake, Wis.; requests for financial assistance from relatives in Clinton and Shirley, Mass., who later moved to a farm in Bismarck, N.D.; business papers of Bigelow, including diaries relating to inspection trips (1865) in New England and the South made for his principal employer, Home Insurance Company, New Haven, Conn., and appraisals of agents and their markets; and genealogical materials, pertaining to the ancestors of Samuel Bigelow (b. 1653), of Watertown, Mass. Persons represented include genealogist Mildred N. Jaques, of South Hadley, Mass., and her ancestor Ada B. Noyes.

William Prescott Holden papers, 1609-1964
Holden, William Prescott, 1911-1968.
Mss 138
69 items.
Bible record, genealogical notes, photographs and some correspondence.

Charles Lockhart Fillmore papers, 1733-1977
Fillmore, Charles L. (Charles Lockhart), 1901-1980.
Mss 139
ca. 300 items.
Unpublished finding aid in the library.
Correspondence, veterans' records, genealogies, censuses, pension records, family Bible records, notes, and other papers, chiefly relating to the 19th and 20th century descendants of John Fillmore (1676-ca. 1711), of Ipswich and Beverly, Mass., who settled in California, Connecticut, Illinois, Massachusetts, Michigan, New Brunswick, and Nova Scotia. Fillmore/Filmore family members represented include Herman C. (1893-1977), Millard (1800-1874), and William F. (b. 1894) Fillmore.

The C. M. Kuhns family record
Kuhns, Harry R.
Mss 140
90 leaves; 28 cm.
June 1984.
Typescript.

Outline of the direct and collateral family lines (in the United States) of Engelhardt Riemenschneider (1815-1899)
Riemenschneider, Edwin A.
Mss 141
133 leaves: geneal. tables; 28 cm.
1978
Updated & corrected 1987
University Microfilms copy of Mein Lebensgang ["My life story"] by Engelhardt Riemenschneider (originally published in 1882). Patrons should note that the text is in German. This is followed by typescript family group sheets with supplemental information (compiled August 1978, revised September 1, 1983 and up-dated & corrected September 1987). Includes addendae to the Tristram and Williams family genealogy consisting of thirty-four photocopied ms. geneal. tables.

Charles Frederick Quincy papers, 1670-1931
Quincy, Charles F. (Charles Frederick), 1856-1927.
Mss 142
300 items.
Unpublished finding aid in the library.
Persons represented include Edward M. Bacon, Anson Burlingame, William Gordon, Dorothy Q. and John Hancock, Henry Hill, Samuel G. Howe, Thomas P. Ives, the Marquis de Lafayette, John Lovell, Edward Manwaring, William Plumer (1757-1850), William Plumer (1789-1854), Henry C. Potter, Thomas Prince, James Savage, Samuel Shaw, Lysander Spooner, and John W. Thornton, and Hannah H. Josiah (1710-1784), Josiah (1802-1882), Josiah P., Katherine, Mary Samuel (1735-1816), and Samuel (1764-1816) Quincy.

John C. Noble papers, 1858-1965
Noble, John C., 1840-1920.
Mss 143
71 items.
Unpublished finding aid in the library.
Correspondence, diaries, deeds, estate papers, business records, certificates, burial records, and other papers, relating to Noble, other family members, and Goodrow and Leary relatives. Includes three letters from Samuel Hampton (d. 1864), a Union soldier serving in Maryland and Washington, D.C., detailing Army life and expressing his appreciation for Noble's assistance during the time of the death of Hampton's child; information concerning fruit cookery and plum puddings; and diary (1919) of Noble's son, Frederick A. Noble (1866-1925), describing his father's death.

[Pearson family genealogy]
Pearson, John M., 1845-1941.
Mss 144
[8], 86, 822 leaves; 28 cm.
Contains the typescript "Pearson Family History" by Jonathan Pearson III (May 1983) which is described by him in the preface as "a digest of the full genealogy. This history limits itself to the direct line of descent of the Schenectady, New York branch of the family from its American founder, John Pearson of Rowley, Massachusetts." [8 leaves]. This is followed by the index to the [Pearson family genealogy] [86 leaves] which is followed by the typescript genealogy, itself. The [Pearson family genealogy] is a typescript on the descendants of John Pearson (d. 1693) of Rowley, Mass. for ten generations.

Frances Howard Ford Greenidge papers, 1940-1960
Greenidge, Frances Howard Ford, 1905-.
Mss 145
650 items.
Unpublished finding aid in the library.
Correspondence, genealogies, notes, family documents, reminiscences, and other papers, relating to the families of the grandparents of Greenidge and Raymond O. Ford (b. 1901): Ford, Gilliss, Oakley, and Raymond, and 250 allied lines, chiefly residents of New York State and Vermont. Persons represented include William Ford (fl. 1666-1667), Thomas Gilliss (d. ca. 1685), Miles Oakley (1645-1682), and Richard Raymond (1602-1692).

Eva Louise Garnsey Card papers, 1834-1971
Card, Eva Louise Garnsey, 1893-1985.
Mss 146
380 items.
Unpublished finding aid in the library.
230 Photographs and 130 annotated clippings gathered during preparation of the Garnsey - Guernsey Genealogy, 1963 edition.

Charles Hansen Toll papers, 1782-1972
Toll, Charles Hansen, 1882-1972.
Mss 147
2 linear ft.
Unpublished finding aid in the library.
Correspondence, genealogies, biographies, charts, notes, photos, portraits, and other papers, relating to the descendants of Hanse C. Toll (ca. 1630-1685), a Norwegian immigrant who settled in Albany, N.Y., and over 200 allied families, many Dutch Americans, residing in New York State, including the Caldwell, Martin, Mayes, Wingfield, and Wolcott lines. Includes correspondence and other papers of Toll's father, Charles H. Toll (1850-1901), lawyer, of Del Norte, Colo., describing his law practice, the town's gold rush in the 1870s, social life, and daily events between 1875 and 1878; letters (1841-1842) of Samuel Wolcott (1813-1886), pertaining to his service with American Board of Commissioners for Foreign Missions as a missionary in Beirut, Lebanon; and information concerning students at Nine-Partners' Boarding School, Washington, N.Y. Persons represented include Toll's wife, Mayes M. Toll (b. 1888), and Truman Mitchell.

Joseph Davis papers, 1880-1909
Davis, Joseph, b. 1840.
Mss 148
1 linear ft.
Unpublished finding aid in the library.
Research correspondence, genealogies, biographies, family papers, deeds, receipts, charts, notes, and other papers, relating to Davis, his wife, Sarah A. Davis (b. 1843), the Davis family, and over 30 allied lines including Fellows, Heath, Riggs, and Ruggles. Includes papers of or concerning William Davis (1617-1683), who emigrated from Wales to Plymouth, Mass., in 1640 and settled in Roxbury, Mass.; Aaron Davis (1709-1777), patriot, and his son, Aaron (1744-1823), who fought in the Battle of Lexington; Augustus P. Davis (b. 1835), Civil War officer; and Abijah Davis (1804-1872) who migrated to Jerseyville, Ill., from Middlesex County, N.J., in 1838, reflecting frontier life and attempts to assist relatives remaining in New Jersey; and information pertaining to agricultural conditions and daily life of relatives in Henderson, Ky.; apprentices in South Brunswick, N.J.; slavery in Kentucky and New Jersey; and a shipping merchant of Philadelphia, Pa., involved in trade with Cuba.

Henry James Young papers, 1975-1984
Young, Henry James, 1908-.
Mss 149
6 linear in.
Unpublished finding aid in the library.
Correspondence, genealogies, charts, notes, and photos, tracing the families of John Blackman (d. 1675), of Dorchester, Mass., and George Eldridge (1821-1879), of Chatham, Mass.; and materials relating to 16 allied families including the Besford, Corbet, and Harley lines. Includes information concerning English ancestors; and correspondence with John G. Hunt, of Arlington, Va. Other persons represented include George Blackman (1811-1892), of Scio, N.Y., George Eldridge (1821-1879), his wife Eliza J. (Nickerson) Eldridge (1824-1902), and Maris D. Smith (1817-1873).

Maude Blaisdell Perry papers, 1864-1965
Perry, Maude B. (Maude Blaisdell), 1880-1975.
Mss 150
1 linear ft.
Unpublished finding aid in the library.
Correspondence, research notes, genealogies, and other papers, relating to the Belden family and 65 allied lines including the Card family. Includes family papers of the descendants of Samuel Belden (1629-1713), of Hatfield, Mass., including two letters from Clarissa B. Janes (1828-1910), of Lima, N.Y., discussing tuberculosis treatment by Dr. Robert S. Newton (1818-1881) in Rochester, N.Y., in 1864 and teaching in a freedman's school in Nashville, Tenn., in 1865; and papers pertaining to the family of John Belden (1773-1851), originally of Farmington, Conn., many members settling in the Midwest, including recollections (1957) of family traditions by Vera B. Wagner, of Midland, Mich. Persons represented include David Belding.

William O. Goss papers, 1872-1984
Goss, William O., 1907-1982.
Mss 151
5 linear ft.
Unpublished finding aid in the library.
Correspondence, research papers, vital records, genealogies, indexes, biographical materials, photos, and other papers, relating to the descendants of Thomas Whitehouse (d. 1707), chiefly of Dover and Rochester, N.H., elsewhere in the state and Maine and Massachusetts; and papers pertaining to the allied families of Bickford, Bull, Downing, Ham, Hanson, Hayes, Pearl, and Sanborn. Includes information concerning Henry G. Whitehouse (1870-1966) and First Free-Will Baptist Church, Rochester, N.H.

Trella M. Hall papers, 1783-1985
Hall, Trella M., 1910-1985.
Mss 152
18 linear ft.
Unpublished finding aid in the library.
Subjects include childhood in Illinois, farm life in Watertown, Wis., forest fires in Washington State, frontier life and women pioneers in the Pacific Northwest, Irish Americans in Kansas, travel in Oregon, women in agriculture, destruction and pillage in Illinois during the Civil War, and historical events in Iowa, Missouri (1867-1880), and Illinois (1856-1866). Persons and families represented include Vera P. Alker, Hugh S. Austin, Stanley R. Belden, Virginia S. Chapelle, Mary L. Duncan, George P. Hall, Ethel O. Haugenberg, Beatrice V. Hunter, Hattie James, Elizabeth B. Jones, Mary O'N. Kent, H.E. Kimmell, Bruce A. Kindig, Quantrille D. McClung, Martha A. McPartland, Harry M. Parker, Nell W. Reeves, Clarence W. Robertson, Grace M. Schenk, Darle D., Dorothy L., Frederick C., John, Lennig, and William E. Sweet, Estella Toll, Ruth B. Norbert, Delight Trent, Karl Truesdale, and Milton P. Youmans; and Members of the Andrews, Barnett, Garrison, Humphrey, Jacobs, Kindig, Newland, Nelwin, Parker, Prior, Rose, Steele, Tilton, Truesdale, Warner, Wells, Wooley, Wright, and Youmans.

Charles Edward Lord papers, 1829-1940
Lord, Charles Edward, b. 1858.
Mss 153
1 linear ft.
Unpublished finding aid in the library.
Correspondence, genealogical materials, drafts of Lord's The Ancestors and Descendants of Lt Tobias Lord (1913) and working notes, photos, and other papers, relating to the Lord family, prominent in Boston, Mass., shipping and international trade throughout the 19th century. Includes Charles E. Lord's childhood letters (ca. 1860); descriptions of travel in Europe, South America, the Middle East, and New Orleans, La., by Charles H. Lord (1825-1892) and his wife, Lucy L.H. Lord (1826-1899), including discussion of business and social affairs; letters of George Lord (1791-1861) reflecting the political situation in Maine in the 1850s; business records of George C. Lord & Co., Boston shipping merchants; and information pertaining to the capture of Fort Fisher, N.C. (1865), the role of women during the Civil War, and the personal trials of a French family during World War I.

Ancestral charts and sources of 400 direct lines
Doherty, Thomas P., 1940-.
Mss 154
57 p.
1987
Computer typescript.

Walter Hubbell papers, 1881-1915
Hubbell, Walter, b. 1851.
Mss 155
1 linear ft.
Unpublished finding aid in the library.
Correspondence, genealogies, wills, deeds, vital records, Stratfield Cemetery, Bridgeport, Conn., cemetery records, photos, and other papers, compiled by Hubbell for inclusion in his History of the Hubbell Family (1881 and 1915), relating to the descendants of Richard Hubbell (1627-1699), early settler of New Haven and Killingly, Conn.; and miscellaneous items reflecting Walter Hubbell's interests in poetry and spiritualism. Persons represented include William B. Hincks.

Bradt - Bratt genealogy
Getty, Innes.
Mss 156
235, [9] leaves; 28 cm. + 1 index (15 leaves).
[1945]
Photocopy of a typescript. Includes "Notes on the Bradt family Bible" by the donor.

Thomas E. McLaughlin collection, 1857-1963
Boston (Mass.). School Committee.
Mss 157
21 linear ft.
Unpublished finding aid in the library.
Manuscript results of the Superintendents' examinations for teacher certifications and admissions to the Boston Teachers College.

Grace Garfield McFadden papers, 1575-1968
McFadden, Grace Gertrude Garfield, 1876-1968.
Mss 158
33 items.
Genealogies, notes, clippings, correspondence and four photographs concerning the Garfield, Kennard, McFadden and allied families. Includes the following typescript genealogies by the "Descent of Grace Gertrude Garfield from Edward Garfield and allied families" (194 leaves); "Descent of Grace Gertrude Garfield from Edward Kennard and allied families" (218 leaves); "Descent of Fay McFadden from Stephen McFadden, Thomas Whedon and allied families" (226 leaves).

Result of researches into the transactions of the first settlers of the town of Hampton in the State of New Hampshire, with notices of the early history, from its settlement in 1638
Toppan, Edmund W.
Mss 159
360 leaves; 28 cm.
1845
Photocopy of a handwritten transcription by Edmund B. Dearborn, Esq. of Boston, in July 1845, of the original (handwritten by Edmund W. Toppan).

Early lines of Ensign Moses Chase[2] of Newbury, Mass.: a brief study of Aquila Chase1
Gould, William Edward.
Mss 160 v.1
191 leaves: ill., coat of arms, ports., photographs.
1912
Typescript.

The Chase migration from Newbury, Mass. to Sutton, Mass.: being volume II in studies of Chase lines
Gould, William Edward.
Mss 160 v.2
148 leaves: ill., coat of arms, maps, ports., photos
1913
Typescript.

Diary of Charles J. Devereaux, 1864-1921
Devereaux, Charles J., 1842-1921.
Mss 161
7 v. (1907 p.); 21 cm. x 17 cm. (vol. 6: 26 cm. x 20 cm.)
Household activities, social life and customs in Jamaica Plain, Boston and Arlington, Mass.

Some of the descendants of Alexander Balcombe of Portsmouth, R.I.
Balcomb, Frank Wippich, 1902-.
Mss 162
261 p.
Typescript.

Some of the descendants of Henry Balcombe of Charlestown
Balcomb, Frank Wippich, 1902-.
Mss 162
187 p.
Typescript.

[Research, England and America, 1973-1981]
Threlfall, John Brooks, 1920-.
Mss 163
2.5 in.
Records, notes and correspondence pertaining to the Daniels, Darrel, Gooch, Mantell and Verin families, 1226-1938.

Ancestry of Blanche Butler Ames
Ames, Blanche Butler, 1847-1939.
Mss 164
[xv], 148, 29, 17, 21 leaves; 28 cm.
Photocopy of family group sheets, typescript genealogies and charts concerning the Ames, Brooks, Butler and Lyman families, 1285-1922. Includes "Ancestral tablets Blanche Butler Ames" (29 leaves), "Genealogy of Harriet Lyman Brooks" (17 leaves), and "Glnealogy [sic] of Adelbert Ames" (21 leaves) both by Blanche B. Ames.

[Ancestry of Ruth Burell-Brown]
Burell-Brown, Ruth, 1931-.
Mss 165
xlv, 687 leaves: geneal. tables; 28 cm.
Photocopy of family group sheets.

The humbler Bostonians: genealogy of John and Philip Langdon of Boston
Van Agt, Louise L.
Mss 166
478 leaves; 28 cm.
Typescript with genealogical and biographical detail of family mercantile and diplomatic activities, 1647-1963.

Lincolnshire wills & admons
Smith, Walter Henry.
Mss 167
2 v. (564, 584 p.)
1887, 1894
Handwritten transcription of original record. Volume I covers A.D. 1521 to A.D. 1821. Volume II from A.D. 1368 to A.D. 1827.

An index of Buckinghamshire wills, 1483-1659
Woodman, Arthur Vere, 1884-1966.
Mss 168
[334] p.
1953
Handwritten transcription of original record. [From Preface]: "This index contains a list of the wills at Somerset House of the Archdeaconry of Buckingham. Its purpose is to show at a glance what wills - or fragments of wills for many are defective - actually exist for any particular family before the year 1660. References to wills that no longer exist have been ignored."

Genealogical history and biographical sketches of the descendants of John Lee of Agawam (Ipswich), Massachusetts, in 1635
Lee, William, 1841-1893.
Mss 169
xx, 609 leaves.
1877.
Handwritten genealogy.

James Ferdinand Morton papers, 1898-1940
Morton, James F. (James Ferdinand), 1870-1941.
Mss 170
0.5 linear ft.
Unpublished finding aid in the library.
Correspondence, notes, genealogies, charts, reminiscences, and other papers, relating to the Huggins family. Includes recollections of General E.L. Huggins (1842-1929) pertaining to his childhood on the frontier in Minnesota, including experiences with Indians there; and reminiscences (1899) of Jane S. Holtisclaw describing a family trip from Ohio to the West which was led by Alexander G. Huggins (1802-1866) in 1845.

William Fitzhale Abbot papers, 1150-1915
Abbot, William Fitzhale, 1853-1922.
Mss 171
1.5 linear ft.
Unpublished finding aid in the library.
Genealogical, private and business papers concerning the Abbott and related families, including Hale, Harris, Fiske, Larcom, Ellingwood, and Woodbury. Filed after the genealogical charts and notes are many original wills and deeds. Especially interesting are the Larcom documents, dating back to the 17th Century, which show the acquisitions of Cornelius Larcom and his son, David. There are two notebooks compiled by Mr. Abbot from original records and documents. One contains valuable genealogical information on the Lawrence and Larcom families. The other lists the military services of ancestors who fought in the Revolutionary War and other 18th century battles. The personal and professional papers include a collection of poems written by Fanny Abbot (William Abbot's mother) for her father, Henry Larcom. Mrs. Abbot was also the grandniece of Nathan Dane, Congressman, who was influential in passing the North-West Ordinance of 1787.

Eunice B. Dean papers, 1604-1953
Dean, Eunice Wetmore Bonney, 1897-.
Mss 172
28 items.
First item is a typescript genealogy called "Ancestry of Eunice Wetmore Bonney with biographical sketches" compiled and typewritten by Charles Collyer Whittier of Boston in 1922 (138 + [54] leaves). There are also notes and correspondence (1949-1987) pertaining to the Bonney and allied families of Wetmore and Fales.

Account books of Moses G. Chamberlain, 1877-1918
Chamberlain, Moses G.
Mss 173
26 items.
Account books, bills (15 items, 1883-1915), correspondence (3 items, 1910-1914) and six photographs concerning a Union and Milton Mills, N.H. merchant. The first account book covers 1877-1917 (274 p.). A second account book covers 1905-1915 (204 p.).

Yarmouth, Nova Scotia: Yarmouth Herald genealogies - 1896-1902
Brown, George S. (George Stayley).
Yarmouth Herald (Yarmouth, N.S.)
CS88/N64/Y37 also Mss 174
239, 5, [2] leaves; 29 cm.
19--

Ephraim Abbot papers, 1615-1870
Abbot, Ephraim, 1779-1870.
Mss 175
229 items.
Unpublished finding aid in the library.
Correspondence and notes of Abbot and his cousin Abiel Abbot (1765-1859), relating to their book, A Genealogical Register of the Descendants of George Abbot of Andover (1847); ms. of the book; and correspondence and notes of Ephraim Abbot's daughter, Lucy M.B. Abbot (b. 1832). Includes materials pertaining to several Massachusetts and Connecticut branches of the family as well as the allied lines of Cotton, Hall, and Whiting.

Lucille K. Fales papers, 1936-1976
Fales, Lucille K., 1896-1983.
Mss 177
0.5 linear ft.
Chiefly deeds, wills, and other records transcribed from public sources, genealogies, biographical information, notes, and research correspondence, relating to the family of John Benjamin (1598-1645), of Watertown, Mass., and his descendants in New England and New York; and the family of Abraham (d. 1680), Jacob (d. 1699), James (d. 1700), Joseph (d. 1690), and John (d. 1667) Parker, chiefly settling in Maine. Persons represented include Martha Parker Libby (1815-1885) and Martha Libby Benjamin (b. 1875).

William F. Hamel papers, 1852-1984
Hamel, William F., 1932-.
Congregational Church (Goffstown, N.H.)
Mss 178
1 linear ft.
Unpublished finding aid in the library.
Correspondence, genealogies, indexes, and research papers relating to the descendants of Thomas Hanscom (d. 1695), of Maine and Samuel Thorp (1644-1728), of Wallingford, Conn., chiefly residents of Maine, Connecticut, and other New England states, including Thorp family materials prepared by Patricia M. Hamel (b. 1935); and family Bible records, official documents, cemetery records, gravestone readings, and other church records of the Goffstown Congregational Church, Goffstown, N.H., and St. Peter's United Church of Christ, West Seneca, N.Y., primarily a German congregation active between 1873 and 1921. Includes information relating to Moses Brown, Amelia Clifford, Frank P. Martin, John Pattee, Eliphalet Richards, Mary J. Savoy, and members of the Brown, Clifford, Pattee, and Richards families.

Don Howard Wheeler papers, 1949-1965
Wheeler, Don Howard, d. 1967.
Mss 179
1 linear ft.
Unpublished finding aid in the library.
Correspondence, genealogies, notes, and other papers, relating to the family of William Bentley (ca. 1645-1720), of Kingston, R.I., and its allied lines including Bennett, Coryell, Harvey, Holbert, Ives, Laing, and Parks. Includes correspondence between Wheeler and Virginia F. Murray concerning family news, his treatment in New York and Ohio veterans' hospitals, and other subjects. Persons represented include Ezekiel (1738-1834) and Greene W. (1741-1823) Bentley.

Lawrence W. Trowbridge papers, 1935-1987
Trowbridge, Lawrence W., 1899-1987.
Mss 180
1 linear ft.
Unpublished finding aid in the library.
Genealogies, chart, and other papers, relating to the ancestors of Trowbridge, his wife, Eleanor (Daboll) Trowbridge (b. 1904), and their son, Theodore D. Trowbridge (b. 1935), tracing separate lines beginning with John Trowbridge (ca. 1590-1623), of New Haven, Conn., and Robert Deeble (Daboll) (fl. 1635), of Dorchester, Mass.

Robert Merrill Hubbard papers, 1870-1966
Hubbard, Robert M. (Robert Merrill), 1909-1988.
Mss 182
0.5 linear ft.
Unpublished finding aid in the library.
Correspondence, genealogies, notes, charts, photos, and scattered private papers, relating to the descendants of Nathaniel Merrill (ca. 1610-1654), of Newbury, Mass., and eleven allied families including Hall, Hubbard, and Kingsley. Persons represented include Robert H. Merrill (1881-1955).

John Ford papers, 1765-1878
Ford, John, 1740-1822.
Mss 183
1 linear ft.
Unpublished finding aid in the library.
Military, financial, and legal papers concerning Ford's activities during the Revolution, Shays' Rebellion, and business in Chelmsford, Mass., including muster rolls, orders, orderly book (1776) at Ticonderoga, N.Y., warrants and prison lists (1786-1787), and deeds, bonds, bills, and receipts, relating to properties owned in Chelmsford and Lowell, Mass., the family farm, and other business affairs; and papers of the Corliss family of Lowell, Mass., chiefly of Horatio G.F. Corliss (1813-1873), military officer and lawyer who resided in Ford's boardinghouse in Lowell, including personal correspondence (1829-1862), deeds, bonds, court summonses, and business papers reflecting Corliss's public and legal activities. Includes materials pertaining to Chelmsford during the Revolution, Massachusetts Militia, U.S. Continental Army, 15th and 27th Massachusetts Regiments, schools in Lowell, and the activities of John F. Corliss (husband of John Ford's daughter Sarah), a carpenter in Haverhill, Mass. and later an owner of a sawmill at Pawtucket Falls in Chelmsford, Mass.

Charles Newton Kimball papers, 1785-1986
Kimball, Charles N. (Charles Newton), 1911-.
Mss 184
0.5 linear ft.
Unpublished finding aid in the library.
Correspondence, notes, genealogical materials, parish records, government documents, and other papers of the Sharkey family and the allied families of Coyle, Hennigan, McNeely, and Teeling, Irish Americans, of the Boston, Mass., area and New Brunswick and the Lunney family who settled in Leadville, Colo. Persons represented include Joan F. Curran, Shirley H. Redden, and James R. Sharkey.

Carolyn W. Knibbs papers, 1849-1985
Knibbs, Carolyn W., 1937-.
Mss 185
0.5 linear ft.
Unpublished finding aid in the library.
Correspondence, Bible records, certificates, family papers, photos, and genealogical materials, relating to the Whitford family of Maine and Knibbs family of Michigan, and nine allied lines including Butler, Fernald, Huntress, and Ricker. Includes autobiographical sketch of Dr. Edwin P. Whitford (b. 1852) pertaining to his childhood and training in Ohio and subsequent practice in Minnesota; letter from George Gilman reflecting pioneer life in La Harpe, Ill., in 1838; correspondence of Simon Huntress (1832-1885) describing army life at Gloucester Point, Va., in 1864; and information concerning black soldiers during the Civil War. Persons represented include Moses Butler, Herbert B. Fernald, James Gilman, and Porter Gilman.

Albert Harrison Hoyt papers, 1751-1920
Hoyt, Albert H. (Albert Harrison), 1826-1915.
Mss 186
2 linear ft.
Unpublished finding aid in the library.
Correspondence, biographical sketches, genealogies, Bible records, public documents, notes, photos, and other papers, reflecting Hoyt's genealogical and historical interests and his activities with Office of the Paymaster General and Massachusetts Treasury Office. Includes materials relating to the Freeman, Hoyt, Marshall, McClenachan, Randolph, and Stuart families; journal (1751-1753) of William Smith (b. 1702) describing duty on Sable Island, N.S.; information pertaining to the safety measures taken by the British merchant marine, the Massachusetts and Connecticut boundary, financial affairs during the American Revolution, and Portsmouth, N.H., branch of Bank of the United States; and letters from Admiral Asa Walker discussing the outbreak of the Philippine Insurrection in 1899, Alexander Hamilton concerning U.S. Dept. of the Treasury matters, and John C. Calhoun pertaining to military pensions. Other persons represented include Timothy Bigelow, Mary Billingham, Greenfill Blake, Joshua Brackett.

Charles Wesley Tuttle papers, 1221-1897 (Bulk 1847-1897)
Tuttle, Charles Wesley.
Mss 187
1 linear ft.
Unpublished finding aid in the library.
Little appears from Tuttle's legal career, represented here by a Harvard Law School certificate and scattered references in personal correspondence. The genealogical material consists of correspondence, primarily concerning the Tuttle and Merrow families. The historical material includes notes, documents and correspondence pertaining to Francis Champernowne, Christopher Kilby, and Joseph Bean, as well as the Piscataqua Region and White Mountains of NH. The astronomical material, primarily notes and computations, deals with Mr. Tuttle's interest with the star Sirius and D'Arrest's comet. There is also some correspondence concerning the Prince Society. Mr. Tuttle's diaries for 1852, 1854, 1855 and 1861 describe trips to Philadelphia and England, as well as spontaneous trips from Boston to the White Mountains. Accompanying the collection are 49 photographs. Most are CDV portraits along with four printer's blocks of European scenes.

Timothy Farrar papers, 1775-1856
Farrar, Timothy, 1788-1874.
Mss 188
160 items.
Unpublished finding aid in the library.
Correspondence, court records, and other papers, of Farrar and his father, Timothy Farrar (1747-1842), also a lawyer and judge, reflecting their legal, political, and personal activities. Includes information relating to Farrar's activities as trustee of Dartmouth College and his law practice with Daniel Webster (1813-1816), the selection of a court clerk, banking in the U.S., impeachments, newspaper publishing in Boston, presidential elections, counterfeiting in Groton, Mass., travel in Maryland and Pennsylvania, the study of medicine, Phillips Exeter Academy, 1807 embargo, U.S. diplomacy during the War with Algeria, 1815, causes of the 1798-1800 war with France, and campaigns of the War of 1812. Correspondents of Timothy Farrar (1747-1842) include William Gordon, Edward S. Livermore, Simeon Olcott, John Phillips, and Jeremiah Smith; correspondents of his son include Charles Burroughs, Nathan Hale, Reuben D. Mussey, Thomas W. Thompson, and Levi Woodbury.

Recollections of a boyhood in a New England town (1922-1932): Rockport, Massachusetts
McLane, Merrill F., 1917-.
Mss 189
224 p.
1988.
Typescript autobiography.

Account book of Daniel Gammon, 1756-1846
Gammon, Daniel, 1760-1826.
Mss 190
172 p.
Account book for a general store in Gorham and Scarborough, ME.

Abiel Moore Caverly papers, 1700-1871
Caverly, Abiel Moore, 1817-1879.
Mss 191
150 items.
Unpublished finding aid in the library.
Photocopy of original manuscript questionnaires, notes and correspondence pertaining to a history of
Pittsford, Vt.

Charles Beers Gault papers, 1927-1988
Gault, Charles Beers, 1911-.
Mss 192
1.5 linear ft.
Unpublished finding aid in the library.
Correspondence, genealogies, charts, notes, documents, photos, and other papers, relating to the Gault and
109 allied families, residing in North Carolina, New England, and throughout the U.S. Other families
represented include Ashe, Beers, Bell, Burr, Davis, Doughtie, Hill, Jones, LaMotte, Lane, Lillington,
Meeker, Moore, Swann, and Willard.

Elsie A. Parry papers, 1845-1985
Parry, Elsie A., 1898-1985.
Mss 193
89 items.
Unpublished finding aid in the library.
Correspondence, charts, Bible records, photos, and other genealogical materials, relating to the Welsh
American family of Elias Parry (1782-1873), early settler of Taunton and later Fall River, Mass., and the
allied families of Barrett, Betencourt, Preston, Putnam, Smith, and Tinkham. Includes information pertaining
to Elias Parry's brother, John (1775-1841), clergyman of Welsh Calvinistic Methodist Church in Chester,
England, on the Wales border; and letters (ca. 1930s) of Rev. Thomas Roberts, of Chester, written to Elsie
Parry, including several small Welsh translations of religious works. Other family members represented
include Harvey E. Parry (1893-1968).

Bucknam allied families
Bucknam, Bettina, 1910-.
Mss 194
0.5 linear ft.
Unpublished finding aid in the library.
Ms. notes pertaining to 103 families allied to that of Bucknam, 1632-1979, an extension of Wilton F. Bucknam's family genealogy. Particular attention was given to the families of Buxton, Dexter, Drinkwater, Green, Lynde, Sargent, Townsend, Tufts, Usher, Waite and Williams.

Lawton M. Patten papers, 1783-1985
Patten, Lawton M., 1905-1992.
Mss 195
127 items.
Unpublished finding aid in the library.
Correspondence, diaries, mss. of writings, genealogies, financial records, photos, and other family papers relating to the descendants of William Patten (d. 1668), of Cambridge, Mass., and the allied lines of Mikell and Taylor. Includes diaries, poems, songs, and other papers of Col. George W. Patten (1808-1882), sometimes called "Poet Laureate of the Border" reflecting his service with 2nd U.S. Infantry Regiment in Mexico (1846-1847); accounts and sermons of Rev. William Patten (1763-1839), clergyman of Second Congregational Church, Newport, R.I.; and diaries (1837-1944) of family members in Seattle, Wash., detailing the local fishing trade. Persons represented include William E. Mikell (b. 1894), Elizabeth F. (b. 1805), Hudson T. (1877-1957), James H. (1801-1877), William S. (1800-1873), and William S. (1852-1932) Patten, and Hudson Taylor (b. ca. 1825).

Diary of Nathaniel Brett, 1751-1777
Brett, Nathaniel, 1704-1779.
Mss 196
2 v. (214 p.); 16 x 10 cm.
Interleaved almanacs of memoranda by a town clerk of Bridgewater, Mass.

Henry E. Cottle papers, 1898-1976
Cottle, Henry E., 1873-1966.
Mss 197
500 items.
Unpublished finding aid in the library.
Correspondence, typewritten genealogy with ms. annotations, working papers, charts, and other papers, relating to the families of Cottle and his wife, Ella L. (Chase) Cottle (1874-1966), and the allied families of Barker, Belcher, Mann, Place, and Robie, chiefly of Connecticut, New Hampshire, and other New England states; and notes of collection donors, Charles A. and Louise C. Barker, added after Cottle's death. Persons represented include Harriet A. Belcher and Edward Cottle, progenitor.

Diary of Gilman Joslin, 1870-1872
Joslin, Gilman, 1850-1872.
Mss 198
2 v.
Entries concern work in father's globe shop and social activities.

Joseph Wright papers, 1793-1942
Wright, Joseph, 1736-1813.
Mss 199
170 items.
Unpublished finding aid in the library.
Correspondence, estate papers, wills, deeds, photos including tintypes and daguerreotypes, and genealogical materials, of and relating to Wright, his family, and the allied families of Blodgett, Prescott, Sunbury, and Trowbridge, chiefly of Westford, with the exception of the Sunburys who also lived in Michigan (1920s-1930s). Persons represented include Ezra Prescott (1756-1789), and Abiel (1770-1841), Bela (1796-1859), Jeptha (1728-1813), and Oliver (1759-1834) Wright.

Elmer Herbert Cram papers, 1900-1948, 1988-1989
Cram, Elmer Herbert, 1865-1947.
CS71/C89/1996 Microfilm also Mss 200
Original papers restricted, use microfilm
6 microfilm reels (3 linear ft.)
Unpublished finding aid in the library.
The papers, created from 1900 to 1947, contain both manuscript and typescript material. The typescripts are usually a final version of the manuscript copy though not a verbatim transcript. The papers include genealogical family group sheets, correspondence, miscellaneous notes and clippings. The Cram family is traced from German and English origins from 1181 to the American immigrant, John Cram (d. ca. 1682) of Muddy River (now Brookline, Mass.) and Hampton Falls, N.H. The papers document the family as it grew through the generations and includes Mormon and California Gold Rush Crams. Other families prominently mentioned are Edgerly, Flanders, Gove, Hackler, Philbrick, Sanborn, Steele, Webster and many others. In 1988, an addendum by Lorraine N. (Francis Lorraine Naquin) Tyler (b. 1930) was added [as folder 413]. The processor of the collection, Ardis D. (Ardis Donetta Gardiner) King (b. 1911), created a complete, all-name index to the papers in 1989 that encompasses 407 pages.

Phyllis Gillingham Hansen papers, 1822-1984
Hansen, Phyllis G. (Phyllis Gillingham), 1912-1986.
Mss 201
255 items.
Unpublished finding aid in the library.
Correspondence, genealogies, autobiographical materials, notes, charts, photos, and other papers, relating to the descendants of Yeamons Gillingham (d. 1722), of Frankford (part of Philadelphia), Pa., many of whom settled in Gillingham, Richland Center, and other Wisconsin towns. Includes Hansen's correspondence with publishers relating to out of print genealogical works and the publication of The Descendants of Thomas Gillingham (1972) by William Elmer Gillingham; and recollections (1900-1970s) contributed by many female relatives concerning life in the Middle West and other western states and frontier life in Montana. Persons represented include Virgil Drake and Harrold E. Gillingham and members of the Hansen, Marshall, Morris, and Truesdale families.

Capers, Gamewell, Thornton & Williams family journals
Konov, Patricia Jenkins, 1935-.
Mss 202
159, 70 p.
Typescript transcription of genealogical and biographical notes of the Gamewell and allied families (Capers, Thornton & Williams families), with transcripts of supporting documents.

Alden genealogy
Alden Kindred of New York City and Vicinity.
Mss 203
282 leaves; 28 cm.
1935-1945
Typscript genealogy.

Samuel Conant papers, 1842-1940
Conant, Samuel, 1808-1883.
Mss 204
76 items.
Unpublished finding aid in the library.
Correspondence of Conant family members in Vermont with their Ball, Carroll, Metcalf, Poland, Richmond, Stevens, and White relatives, chiefly concerning family affairs. Includes Conant's description of a trip to Du Quion, Ill., carpentry work found there, and conditions in a colliery run by a Metcalf cousin in 1854; information relating to the family farm in Vermont; and correspondence of Harriet Carroll White (1796-1880), of Boston, Mass., and other Carroll and White family members pertaining to daily events.

Elisabeth D. Whittaker papers, 1710-1986
Whittaker, Elisabeth D.
Mss 205
91 items.
Unpublished register in the library.
Miscellaneous family papers for the period 1710-1986 including estate settlements, deeds, receipts, genealogical notes and photographs. Practically all of the material concerns Dickinson and Graves families in Hatfield and Whatley, Massachusetts.

Aaron Hobart papers, 1767-1929
Hobart, Aaron, 1803-1880.
Mt. Vernon Congregational Church (Boston, Mass.)
Mss 206
3 linear ft.
Unpublished finding aid in the library.
Chiefly correspondence of Hobart, his wife, Anna M. (Brown) Hobart (b. 1817), their children, his brother, Henry (1790-1862), state legislator, and other family members, residing in Abington, Boston, Bridgewater, and Wrentham, Mass., relating to family activities, social events, trips taken, state and national politics, and public opinion during the Civil War. Includes records of Mt. Vernon Congregational Church, Boston; acrostics done by family members; estate papers; information concerning Aaron Hobart's dry goods business; and political correspondence with Nathaniel P. Banks, George S. Boutwell, Lewis Cass, David T. Disney, Benjamin F. Hallett, Marcus Morton, and Richard Rush. Other persons represented include Eunis Everett, Albert (b. 1792), Deborah W. (1767-1834), Nathaniel (1758-1838), and Noah (1767-1854) Hobart, Edward N. Kirk, and members of the Felt, Herschel, Richardson, and Watson families.

Lillian H. Walker papers, 1930-1986
Walker, Lillian H., 1880-1975.
Mss 208
2 linear ft.
Unpublished finding aid in the library.
Correspondence, genealogies, charts, records, photos, and other papers, relating to the descendants of Walter Haynes (1583-1665), of Sudbury, Mass., and the allied lines of Brown, Carter, Fuller, Goodnow, and Taylor. Includes views (1900-1950) of family homes in Leominster, Newton Center, and Saxonville, Mass., and album containing autographs and photos reflecting Walker's attendance at the Pan-American Exposition in Buffalo, N.Y., 1901.

Cowley genealogy
Lamb, George, 1834-1913.
Mss 209
409 p.; 29 cm.
1897
Ms. genealogy on the Cowley and allied families of Connecticut and New York, 1630-1897.

William B. Derby papers, 1942-1984
Derby, William B., 1904-1988.
Mss 210
5 linear ft.
Unpublished finding aid in the library.
Correspondence, genealogies, indexes, name check lists, charts, copies of public and private records, notes, biographical materials, reminiscences, and other papers, relating to Derby's research on the Derby and allied families of Ballard, Campbell (his wife's family), and Miner, many of New England. Persons and other families represented include Sally Buell, Asahel Derby, Howard W. Derby, William M. Derby, Belinda Ives, Elizabeth B. Satterthwaite, and Frances M. Wood and Lewis and Maris families.

Dorothy K. Fairbanks papers, 1841-1981 (bulk 1935-1981)
Fairbanks, Dorothy K., 1919-.
Mss 211
3.5 linear ft.
Unpublished finding aid in the library.
Genealogy (3 v., typewritten) and research materials relating to the Bennett family of Massachusetts, New York, Rhode Island, and Virginia and its allied lines of Atkinson, Brown, Clough, Conant, Horton, Peck, Royce, Spencer, Whitman, and 55 additional families; corrrespondence pertaining to Fairbanks's research; scattered family papers including certificates and deeds to properties in Abington, Bridgewater, and East Bridgewater, Mass.; and 145 photos, chiefly daguerreotype and tintype portraits. Includes diary (1841-1843) of John A. Conant (1820-1845), pharmacist, of East Bridgewater, Mass., describing his employment and social activities; and photographic scenes of East Bridgewater and Andover, Mass. Persons represented include Joseph, Mary, and Woodbridge Brown, Sarah A. Conant, Benjamin H. Horton, Nathaniel Howe, and Asa and Daniel Whitman.

Account book of George H. Fullerton, 1860-1861
Fullerton, George H.
Mss 212
618 p.
Account book for a general store in Waitsfield, Vermont.

Sons of Temperance (Shakespear Division, no. 46) records, 1847-1861
Sons of Temperance. Massachusetts Chapter.
Mss 213
16 items.
Records books and misc. papers of the Shakespear Division, no. 46.

Walter Merriam Pratt papers, 1086-1945 (bulk 1798-1956)
Pratt, Walter Merriam, b. 1880.
Mss 214
9 items.
Genealogy, charts, correspondence, records, and photographs concerning the Pratt family of Pratville in Chelsea, Mass., and allied families. Includes the "Ancestry of Walter Merriam Pratt with coats of arms & illustrations" traced by Mellen Chamberlain, Walter Kendall Watkins and Florence MacLea 1928 (1 v. (227 p.): ill., maps, ports., plates, coat of arms, geneal. tables, photographs; 35 cm.). There is also a tabular pedigree for Walter M. Pratt (printed form completed in ms.; 48 x 60 cm. folded to 31 cm.) and a Guest Book (spine W.M.P. Guest Book 1915).

Chester Milton Smith papers, 1635-1989
Smith, Chester Milton, 1884-1971.
Mss 215
4 v.
Handwritten genealogies and notes pertaining to the Smith family of Newport, Mass., and allied families. The first volume is specifically on the descendants of Joseph Pike and Hannah Smith and the second volume focuses on the descendants of John and Rebecca (Poore) Smith.

John Ward Dean papers, 1741-1900
Dean, John Ward, 1815-1902.
Mss 217
2.5 linear ft.
Unpublished finding aid in the library.
Because of Mr. Dean's extensive association with this Society, more than half of the collection was removed to the Archives as official papers of the Register Department, 1859 to 1902. There is no doubt that some of the papers in each collection belong in the other. There is compiled material on the descendants of many new England Dean(e) families as well as notes, clippings, charts and documents. He also concerned himself with many collateral lines including Bridge, Frye, Gilman, How, Kingsbury, Leonard, Lord, Somerby, Tappan and Woodbridge families.

Winthrop Wetherbee papers, 1923-1985
Wetherbee, Winthrop, 1863-1949.
Weatherbee Family Association.
Mss 218
1 linear ft.
Unpublished finding aid in the library.
Correspondence, genealogy, notes, Weatherbee Family Association newsletter entitled Weatherbee Round-up, and other papers, compiled by Wetherbee and his daughter, Alice W. Badger (Mrs. Theodore L. Badger), documenting the descendants of John Witherby (Wetherbee), chiefly residing in Sudbury, Marlborough, and Stow, Mass. Other family members represented include Carl Weatherbee and David K. Wetherbee.

Reminiscences and traditions of Boston: being an account of the original proprietors of that town, & the manners and customs of its people
Crocker, Hannah Mather, 1752-1829.
Mss 219
1 v. (478 p.); 32 cm.
ca. 1829

James Harris Gilbert papers, 1854-1930 (bulk 1895-1930)
Gilbert, James H. (James Harris), b. 1844.
Mss 220
134 items.
Unpublished finding aid in the library.
Correspondence, charts, genealogies, records, and scattered family papers relating to the descendants of Jonathan Gilbert (1618-1682), of Middletown, Conn., and 18 additional lines including Butler, Dale, Johnson, Ranney/Renney, Slack, and Turnbull families. Includes diary by Ebenezer Dale (1812-1871) describing a tour of Italy in 1865; wills of family members living in Columbia County, N.Y.; and correspondence and military commissions of Charles N. Turnbull (1832-1874) including a letter commenting on the climate and general conditions in New Orleans, La., Sept. 1854. Persons represented include Joseph Byingham, Ebenezer Dale (d. 1834), Katherine L. Frick, Nathaniel Gilbert, Serina P. Johnson, Maria P. Turnbull, and Caroline M. Young.

Henry Mason Whiting papers, 1936-1967
Whiting, Henry Mason, 1881-1967.
Mss 221
500 items.
Unpublished finding aid in the library.
Group sheets and ancestral charts relating to Whiting's family and the allied lines of Briggs, Gallup, and Wheeler.

Justin Coy Bugbee papers, 1594-1986
Bugbee, Justin Coy, 1902-1992.
Mss 222
1.2 linear ft.
Unpublished finding aid in the library.
Genealogical materials and notes relating to eleven generations (chiefly of New England) of the family of Edward Bugbee (1594-1669), early settler of Roxbury, Mass. Includes genealogies compiled by Charles Marshall Bugbee (1868-1942), Edgar Curtis Bugbee (1883-1957), Edwin Holmes Bugbee (1820-1900), Wallace Lyman Bugbee (1858-1933), and other family members. Places represented include Woodstock, Conn., where early relatives settled.

Wyeth Funeral Service records, 1904-1964
Wyeth Funeral Service (Cambridge, Mass.)
Mss 223
2 linear ft.
Unpublished finding aid in the library.
Account records including death dates, age of deceased, cause of death, parentage, and type of funeral arrangements made. Persons represented include Benjamin Franklin Wyeth, owner.

George Henry Milbank Hersey papers, 1814-1950
Hersey, George Henry Milbank, 1854-1951.
Mss 224
1 linear ft.
Unpublished finding aid in the library.
Chiefly notes compiled for genealogical clients and personal research, genealogies, an original Bible record, and photos, relating to the Budlong, Dyer, Hersey, Milbank, and Upham families.

Chester Garst Mayo papers, 1907-1973
Mayo, Chester Garst, 1881-1985.
Mss 225
1 linear ft.
Unpublished finding aid in the library.
Genealogies, bonds, deeds (chiefly to lands in Roxbury and Franklin County, Mass.), estate papers, indexes, and other papers, documenting the descendants of Rev. John Mayo (1598-1676), of Barnstable, Mass., John Mayo (1630-1688), of Roxbury, Mass., the Mayo brothers, of Virginia, and family members in Canada; together with papers relating to other families in which Chester Mayo was interested. Persons represented include Capt. Thomas Mayo (1713-1792).

Dolen family history and genealogy, and that of related families
Dolen, Louis.
Mss 226
6 v.
1987
Photocopy of typescript genealogy.

The ancestry of Reuben N. Perley, Jr.
Perley, Reuben N., 1915-1989.
Mss 227
815 p.

Hildegard Snow Daffin papers, 1913-1973
Daffin, Hildegard S. (Hildegard Snow), 1904-1975.
Mss 231
8 linear ft.
Unpublished finding aid in the library.
Other persons and families represented include Melvin O. Adams, John Atwood, Nathaniel Atwood, Fred. Carlisle, Berilla S. Cherry, Elvira W. Cobb, Rufus Gilmore, John M. Masury, Fannie P. Monroe, Achsa S. Parker, Edgar M. Snow, and Lorenzo Snow and the Gilmore and Twining families.

Stuart Giddings Waite papers, 1804-1974
Waite, Stuart G. (Stuart Giddings), 1910-1979.
Mss 232
1 linear ft.
Unpublished finding aid in the library.
Correspondence, genealogies, Bible records, and other papers, relating to the Waite family and the allied lines of Harmon, Horner, Lancton, and Morgan, including correspondence between Waite and fellow genealogist Edythe (Wilson) Thoesen. Persons represented include Benjamin Harmon (1711-1794) and Miles Morgan (1616-1699), of West Springfield, Mass.

Joseph Lyle McCorison papers, 1925-1985
McCorison, Joseph Lyle, 1900-1985.
Mss 233
1 linear ft.
Unpublished finding aid in the library.
Correspondence, notes, charts, and genealogical materials, compiled by McCorison with the assistance of his son, Marcus Allen McCorison (b. 1926). Persons represented include Jotham Ward Curtis (1765-1823), David Husted (1741-1835), Luther Mead (1790-1876), Jared Parker (ca. 1764-1827), and members of the Andrews, Boughton, and Carpenter families.

Eastman family
Rix, Guy S. (Guy Scoby), 1828-1917.
Mss 234
14 items.
1894-1901
Genealogies, notes, records and correspondence pertaining to the Eastman and allied families.

Twenty generations of ancestors
Steele, Frederick M., 1851-
Mss 235
311 leaves; 33 cm.
1913
Typescript genealogy.

Hosea Starr Ballou papers, 1815-1938
Ballou, Hosea Starr, 1857-1943.
Mss 236
2.3 linear ft.
Unpublished finding aid in the library.
Personal papers include correspondence, documents, financial records, genealogical records and notes, poems, receipts, school records and sermons of the Goodell, Foskett and Ballou families. The records of the Starr Family Association are comprised of announcements, brochures, clippings, correspondence, genealogical charts and notes, letterbook, membership lists, minutes, photographs, receipts, records reports and speeches from 1905-1915 and 1937-1938. Mr. Ballou's business records include correspondence and miscellaneous items relating to the H.S. Ballou & Co. from 1904-1925.

Notes on the military history of the Turner family
Turner, Thomas L., 1812-1897.
Mss 237
8 v.
1869.
ms.

Ruth Avaline Hesselgrave papers, 1852-1989
Hesselgrave, Ruth Avaline, b. 1897.
Mss 238
4.5 linear ft.
Unpublished finding aid in the library.
Correspondence, autobiography, diaries, genealogies, church, military, and Bible records, charts, vital statistics, census records, photos, and other papers, compiled by Hesselgrave, assisted by Polly Upson (Wright) Brown Kahler (b. 1929), tracing the family of Thomas Hesselgrave (1780-1856) and his wife, Mary (Pacy) Hesselgrave (1779-1862), English immigrants who settled in Saint Lawrence County, N.Y., and the allied lines of Braithwait, Burse, Freeman, Gates, Olsen, Pierce, and Tait, many members of which moved to Minnesota, Wisconsin, and other western states. Includes minutes (1852-1976) of Daily Ridge Church, a Reformed Presbyterian congregation in Potsdam, N.Y.; interview and reminiscences of Louis F. Deans (1888-1971) and Margaret I. Deans (1861-1960), of River Falls, Wis., describing rural life and the tuberculosis deaths of several family members; diary of William B. Hesselgrave (1839-1904), farmer, of Winona County, Minn., reflecting daily life and social affairs.

Pinkerton family genealogy
Pinkerton, Samuel S. S., 1840-1918.
Mss 239
xciii, 280 p.
1883-1918
Photocopy of a typescript.

Herbert Leslie Buzzell papers, 1890-1931
Buzzell, Herbert Leslie, 1865-1931.
Mss 240
2 linear ft.
Unpublished finding aid in the library.
Genealogical materials and indexes relating to the Buzzell/Bussell/Buswell family and its allied lines. Other families represented include Abbott, Annable, Avery, Ayer, Baker, Barstow, Batchelder, Bean, Boswell, Brown, Cook, Curtis, Davis, Demerritt, Evans, Flanders, Goodspeed, Hallett, Hathaway, Hoyt, Jones, Kimball, Leighton, Merrill, Morrill, Randall, Rollins, Saltmarsh, Sanborn, Smith, Spencer, Spooner, Stevens, Taber, Tasker, Watson, West, White, Wilcox, and Willey.

Robert Waiden Coggeshall papers, 1779-1988
Coggeshall, Robert Walden, 1912-1988.
Mss 241
3 linear ft.
Unpublished finding aid in the library.
Correspondence, wills, deeds, biographies, and other genealogical materials, relating to the family of John Coggeshall (1601-1684), of Newport, R.I., chiefly settling in New England and South Carolina, English ancestors, Norwegian American family members, the family of Robert W. Coggeshall's wife, Ellie M. (Thomas) Coggeshall (1909-1985), and many allied lines including Alston, Benter, Berg, Boren, Caldwell, Chaplin, Hansen, Johnson, Lide, Pawley, Pennington, Prince, Skaalbones, Thomas, Toomer, Walden, and Wilds. Includes correspondence and other papers of Henry A. Thomas (1850-1912, known as Heck Thomas), Confederate soldier and later a frontier peace officer in Lawton, Okla., and comments by family members relating to a television program about his life; papers collected by Beulah W. Coggeshall (1880-1968), Julien T. Coggeshall (b. 1875), and Octavia Y. Walden (1889-1981), including list of slaves (1779-1864) owned by Peter A. Wilds and other family members on their plantation in Mechanicsville, S.C.

Helen M. Persuitte papers, 1377-1990 (Bulk 1880-1990)
Persuitte, Helen M., 1915-.
Mss 242
12 items.
Charts and diary pertaining to the Moore and allied families.

Bible and family records, volume 1, collected by the Florida Society for Genealogical Research, Inc.
Boyer, Dorothy Marvelle.
Mss 243
24 items.
Photocopy of typescript transcriptions.

Eli J. Whittemore papers, 1590-1985 (Bulk 1892-1985)
Whittemore, Eli J., 1824-1914.
Mss 244
22 items.
Genealogies, notes and correspondence pertaining to theWhittemore and Jones families.

Correspondence to Marjorie Cutler Burgess, 1963-1989.
Burgess, Marjorie Cutler, 1915-.
Mss 245
45 items.
Letters from Cutler and allied family members, generated by publication of the Cutler genealogy.

William Gardner Spear papers, 1613-1916
Spear, William Gardner, 1852-1916.
Mss 246
5 linear ft.
Unpublished finding aid in the library.
Research notes, clippings, photographs and correspondence dealing with Spear/Spears/Speer/Spare families, including some African-American families, mostly families in the New England area, 1613-1916. Mr. Spear intended to publish a Spear genealogy from this research, but there is no evidence that he ever did. He used a system of hand written question sheets that he sent to most correspondents, and took extensive notes from various family, public and published sources. But their value is somewhat diminished by a difficult and sometimes careless handwriting. Much of the data collected has been transferred to small notebooks and individual family data sheets, generally arranged in an inconsistant genealogical format without a numbering system. The strength of this collection is the volume of first-hand information from unpublished family records and what appears to be handwritten oral interviews.

Albert Henry Silvester papers, 1730-1976 (bulk 1892-1976)
Silvester, Albert H. (Albert Henry), 1859-1946.
Mss 247
1 linear ft.
Unpublished finding aid in the library.
Genealogy, notebooks containing vital records, directory abstracts, data from town histories, and correspondence; and charts, obituaries, notes, and family papers, collected by Silvester with the assistance of his sister, Caroline F. Silvester, and daughter, Evelyn Silvester, relating to the descendants of Richard Silvester (d. 1663), of Weymouth and Marshfield, Mass., and the allied lines of Buxton, Curtis, Dexter, French, Kirke, Oliver, and Sylvester. Includes information pertaining to local history and churches in Weymouth and records of properties owned by family members in Leicester, Mass. Persons represented include Gilbert Nash (1825-1888).

Robert M. Search papers, 1859-1970 (bulk 1959-1970)
Search, Robert M., 1906-1970.
Mss 248
2 linear ft.
Unpublished finding aid in the library.
Correspondence, Bible records, probate records, deeds, pension records, and other genealogical materials, compiled by Search, assisted by his wife, Helen C. Search (b. 1907), and Frederick C. Church (1885-1966), professor at University of Idaho, tracing the family of Search's mother, Elizabeth Monroe Church (1864-1936) and over 70 allied lines including Carver, Cleaver, Davis, Monroe, and Search, chiefly residing in Connecticut but also in Maine, Massachusetts, Ohio, Pennsylvania, and Vermont. Includes letter (1859) from Miss J.C. Ray to Lucinda Church, of Kingston, Pa., describing the writer's experiences at lyceums and her opinion of author Bayard Taylor. Persons represented include Daniel (1707-1799), Daniel (b. 1752), Joel W. (1752-ca. 1852), John (1709-1806), John (1758-1839), Samuel (d. ca. 1728), and Truman T. (1804-1892) Church, and Abigail Franklin (b. ca. 1784).

Charles D. Burt papers
Burt, Charles D., 1938-.
Mss 249
.5 linear ft.
Unpublished register in the library.
Charts, notes, records, file lists and photographs concerning the Burt and allied families.

John Walley papers, 1669-1826
Walley, John, 1677-1746.
Mss 250
127 items.
Unpublished finding aid in the library.
Business, legal, and private papers of Walley family members in Barnstable and Boston, Mass., including merchants' accounts, shipping orders, receipts, bonds, insurance papers, powers of attorney, and estate papers, chiefly of Walley, John Walley (ca. 1642-1711), and Thomas Walley (b. 1725). Includes contracts for operation of a farm in Roxbury, Mass., and several detailed estate inventories of personal and commercial properties in Barnstable and Boston. Persons represented include Mary Mico (d. 1733), John Walley (b. 1725), and Thomas Walley (1616-1678).

Bryce Metcalf papers, ca. 1902-1915
Metcalf, Bryce, 1874-1951.
Mss 251
1 linear ft.
Unpublished finding aid in the library.
Genealogical card files and notes tracing the family of Michael Metcalf (1587-1664), of Dedham, Mass., and the allied lines of Betts, Cutting, and Tiffany. Persons represented include Michael Metcalf's wife, Sarah (Ellwyn) Metcalf (1598-1644).

Thomas Henry Sherborne papers, 1941-1952
Sherborne, Thomas Henry, 1898-1952.
Mss 252
1 linear ft.
Unpublished finding aid in the library.
Card files containing over 3000 entries and supporting research papers including charts, records, notes, newspaper clippings, and scattered correspondence, relating to descendants of Michael Metcalf (1587-1664) and Sarah (Ellwyn) Metcalf (1598-1644), of Dedham, Mass.

Hackney pedigrees compiled from wills and court rolls
Howard, Joseph Jackson, 1827-1902.
Mss 253
2 v.
1856
Copied from the "Tyseen" mss., with additions.

American pedigrees
Amory, Thomas C. (Thomas Coffin), 1812-1889.
Mss 254
3 v.
1882
ms.

Genealogy and history of the Adams family of Newbury, Mass.
Mss 255
3 v.
1903
ms.

Ship-money returns, 1636
Mss 256
259 leaves.
ms. transcription.

Brewster family
Lamb, George, 1834-1913.
Mss 257
307 p.
c. 1898
Ms. notes and records on the Brewster family of New York, 1560-1898.

Wyman genealogy
Wyman, Thomas Bellows, 1817-1878.
Mss 258
3 v.
c.1866-187
Ms.

Arthur H. Bond papers, 1930-1958
Bond, Arthur H., 1891-1979.
Bailey, Brenda B., 1902-1978.
Mss 259
0.5 linear ft.
Unpublished finding aid in the library.
Alphabetical file of Bond families (arranged by surname), notes, vital records, bibliography, and other genealogical materials, chiefly relating to family members residing in Massachusetts and New York State, compiled by Bond as an addition to Henry Bond's Genealogies and History of Watertown (1855). Includes separate portion on women in the family and information produced by Brenda B. Bailey (b. 1902) and Florence B. Chance (b. 1906), concerning Samuel Bond (1692-1783) and Herbert T. Bond (b. 1873). Other persons represented include Peter Bond (d. 1705) and Ann Sharples (1708-1786).

Henry Bond papers, 1631-1859
Bond, Henry, 1790-1859.
Mss 260
4.5 linear ft.
Unpublished finding aid in the library.
Research materials gathered by Bond in preparation of his Genealogies of the Families and Descendants of the Early Settlers of Watertown, Massachusetts (1860), chapter drafts, and transcripts of vital statistics, church records, and town records, of Watertown, Waltham, and Weston, Mass., for 1631-1819; history of New England Historic Genealogical Society; and correspondence between Bond and contemporaries such as Charles Browne, Samuel G. Drake, James Savage, and Horatio G. Somerby, discussing Bond's book, genealogy, Massachusetts state politics, elections, anti-slavery, and personal matters. Persons represented include Jonathan B. Bright, Jonathan B. Felt, Thaddeus W. Harris, John G. Locke, and members of the Bond, Saltonstall, and Stearns families.

Edmond E. Ilsley papers, 1968-1979
Ilsley, Edmond E., 1887-1979.
Mss 261
1.5 linear ft.
Unpublished finding aid in the library.
Correspondence, genealogical charts, notes, reminiscences, indexes, photos, and other papers, relating to the Ilsley/Insley family, chiefly descendants of William Ilsley (1608-1681), early resident of Newbury, Mass., and the families of Isaac (1652-1704), Joseph (1648-1724), Elisha (1643-1690), Benjamin (1771-1856), and William (1685-1766) Ilsley, principally settling in the Newbury area but also in Maine and Vermont.

John Hale Chipman papers, 1927-1974
Chipman, John Hale, 1896-1974.
Mss 263
3.5 linear ft.
Finding aid in the repository.
Correspondence, public records, forms, charts, research papers, indexes, notes, photos, and other genealogical materials, relating to the family of John Chipman (1620-1708), of Barnstable and Sandwich, Mass., and its allied lines, including relatives in Canada and Australia, compiled by Chipman in the preparation of his book A Chipman Genealogy (1970). Persons represented include Harold E. Chipman (b. 1929) and Hope Howland (1629-1683).

Mrs. Page I. Tharpe papers, 1813-1988 (bulk 1970-1988)
Tharpe, Page I., Mrs.
Mss 264
1.5 linear ft.
Unpublished finding aid in the library.
Correspondence, genealogies, charts, notes, vital records, cemetery inscriptions, and other papers, tracing the Wadleigh, Wadley, and Wadlin families, chiefly of Maine, New Hampshire, and Georgia, including materials generated by Albert P. Wadleigh (b. 1886), of Merrimac, Mass., who was interested in the descendants of John Wadleigh (ca. 1605-1671), an immigrant from Bristol, England, who settled in Wells, Me.; and genealogy compiled by Sadie W. Capehart relating to family members originally of New Hampshire who moved to Georgia before the Civil War. Includes account of Benjamin D. Wadleigh (1784-1851), describing his service as a gunner on the privateer schooner Decatur in 1813; and information concerning the sawmill operations in Monroe County, Ga., owned by brothers Daniel R. (1819-1883), Dole (1824-1891), and William M. (1813-1882) Wadley. Other persons represented include Mary Ely (fl. 1627), Hollis M. (1914-1972) and Moses (1822-1887) Wadley, and members of the Goodsoe family.

Arthur Whitcomb Buell papers
Buell, Arthur Whitcomb, 1879-1970.
Mss 265
356 p.
1990
Copy of ms. notes resulting from research conducted for friends who had no relationship to the Buell family.

Epitaphs. Pearl St. and New Cemetery, Stoughton, Mass.
Kingman, Bradford, 1831-1903.
Mss 266
26 v.
ca. 1903
Handwritten transcription of the inscriptions on tombstones in the Pearl St. Cemetery and New Cemetery of Stoughton, Mass.

A collection of letters mostly relating to the genealogy of the family of Richard Baker, one of the early settlers of Dorchester
Baker, Edmund James, 1804-1890.
Mss 267
307 items.
1858
Ms.

Eben W. Jones papers, 1790-1951
Jones, Eben W., 1854-1940.
Mss 268
0.5 linear ft. (468 items).
Unpublished finding aid in the library.
Correspondence, property descriptions, deeds and other land records, genealogical materials, photos, and other papers, relating to the history of Sharon, N.H., including lot descriptions accompanied by original and transcribed agreements tracing changes in ownership and use, land surveys, and photos of local buildings (1926-1930); genealogical notes concerning nine families; and four town histories. Includes boyhood reminiscences of Nicholas F. Herbert (1848-1934), epitaphs (1795-1902) from local cemeteries; census records (1790); and notes concerning military service of residents.

Harold Everdell Curtis papers, 1940-1986
Curtis, Harold Everdell, 1905-1998.
Mss 269
4.5 linear ft.
Unpublished finding aid in the library.
Genealogies, chiefly compiled from vital and census records by Curtis with the assistance of Helen F. Emery (b. 1912), of Wayland, Mass., tracing the descendants of Thomas (1619-ca. 1706), Richard (ca. 1621-1693), and William (b. ca. 1627) Curtis, early residents of Scituate, Mass.

A list of all the names of the Protestant house-keepers in the severall baronies of Dunluce Walke: returned by William Forrester, hearthmoney coll. under the inspection of Gustavus Henderson Supervisor of Londonderry survey ann[o] 1740
Kernohan, J.W., (Joseph William), 1869-1923.
Great Britain. Exchequer.
Mss 270
1 v. (458 p.); 29 cm.
1740, 1918
Handwritten transcription of the original record by J.W. Kernohan, Secretary of the Presbyterian Historical Society of Ireland. Concerns a list of Protestant Housekeepers in counties Antrim, Derry, Donegal, and Londonderry, Ireland in 1740.

Joseph A. Nickerson papers, 1763-1966 (bulk 1930-1966)
Nickerson, Joseph A., 1892-1979.
Mss 271
1 linear ft.
Unpublished finding aid in the library.
Correspondence, deeds, wills, genealogies, reminiscences, and other papers, tracing the Westchester County, N.Y., descendants of William Nickerson (1640-ca. 1689) and his wife, Ann (Busby) Nickerson (d. 1686), of Chatham, Mass., and many allied lines including Adams, Dann, Dobbin, Hunt, James, Owen, Pugsley, Teller, Thorpe, and Upson. Includes genealogical research by Alberta M. Trethewey (b. 1871); correspondence of Nickerson's sister, Martha A. Morris (1893-1946); papers of Emily M. Perry, of Tomkins Corners, N.Y., including history of the local Methodist Episcopal Church; correspondence and reminiscences of General Hugh W. Dobbin (1763-1853) describing life on the New York State frontier; information concerning the immigration of Irish settlers to New York State, history of Cape Cod, Mass., and daily life in New York during the American Revolution; and genealogies contributed by Chauncey K. Buchanan, Grenville C. Mackenzie, and Cora B. Peck.

Abstracts Delaware County, Pennsylvania wills, 1789-1826
Swift, R. G.
Mss 272
2 v.; 28 cm.
Handwritten transcription of original record.

Robert Sheldon Trim papers, 1940-1989
Trim, Robert S. (Robert Sheldon), 1914-1988.
Mss 273
5 linear ft.
Unpublished finding aid in the library.
Correspondence, genealogies, charts, notes, public and private records, photos, and other papers, relating to over 7000 Trim family members, including British ancestors, the first American ancestor, Benjamin Trim (1755-ca. 1830), and other progenitors such as Christopher Trim (fl. 1700), of Dorchester, Mass., Ezra Trim (1750-1834), of New York State, and George W. Trim (1818-1869), of Illinois; and some related lines including Eisenlord, Peabody, Peck, and Stafford. Includes information contributed by Wilbur B. Beckwith, Emma T. Daly (b. 1874), Laura T. Drury (1873-1948), and Susan T. Stone (b. 1958). Persons represented include Mary Rose (d. 1825) and Godfrey Trim (d. 1808).

Elizabeth A. Gumm papers, 1635-1931
Gumm, Elizabeth A.
Mss 274
32 items.
Charts, notes, correspondence and photographs concerning the Austin and allied families (Dean, Freeman, Gilman, Goff and Larcom families).

Lyon J. Hoard papers, 1330-1974
Hoard, Lyon J.
Mss 275
112 items.
Documents, records, notes and correspondence pertaining to the Hoard family in England.

William Henry Eldridge papers, 1911-1942
Eldridge, William H. (William Henry), 1873-1943.
Mss 276
4.5 linear ft.
Unpublished finding aid in the library.
Correspondence, genealogy, diaries, autobiography, research papers, reminiscences, photos, and other papers, tracing six generations of the family of Samuel Eldred (1620-1677), of Kingston, R.I., and his sons, Daniel (d. 1726), John (1670-1741), and Thomas (1648-ca. 1726), chiefly settling in Maine, Massachusetts, New York, Rhode Island, and Vermont; papers of other Eldred/Eldredge/Eldridge lines including the families of William Eldred (d. ca. 1679), of Yarmouth, Mass., Robert Eldred (d. ca. 1683), Chatham, Mass., and Thomas Eldred (d. 1740), of Surry County, Va.; and of many allied lines including Atwood, Austin, Barnum, Bates, Bissell, Brown, Brownell, Buttolph, Champion, Collins, Cox, Douglas, Emery, Fuller, Greeley, Greene, Henry, Jennison, Ladd, Lilly, Little, Maverick, Rich, Rood, Singletary, Smith, Treadway, Warner, Watts, and Wells. Includes descriptions by Charles W. Eldredge (1811-1883) of a trip through New England and Canada in 1833; recollections of Mormons and early pioneer life in Utah by Joseph U. Eldredge (1843-), and Lemuel B. Eldredge's recollections of the New Haven River Flood that struck Vermont in 1830.

Diary of Sarah L. Wadley, 1859-1886
Wadley, Sarah L., b. 1844.
Mss 277
3 v. (654 p.)
Typ. transcription of orginial diary. Louisiana, Mississippi and Georgia.

The Wilmarth family: the ancestors and descendants of Everett Balcom Wilmarth
Van Pelt, Robert Howard, 1934-.
Mss 278
282 p.
Photocopy of typescript.

Alvin E. Ivie papers, 1938-1947
Ivie, Alvin E., 1872-1954.
Mss 279
0.5 linear ft.
Unpublished finding aid in the library.
Correspondence (1938-1944) relating to genealogical research, genealogy, public records, and other papers, pertaining to the Ivie family and the allied lines of Creighton, Green, and Perry, chiefly immigrants from Waterford County, Ireland, who settled in New York State.

Edward J. Wheeler papers, 1066-1930
Wheeler, Edward J., 1864-1930.
Mss 280
1 linear ft.
Unpublished finding aid in the library.
Genealogies, charts, notes, records, correspondence and photographs concerning Wheeler and allied families in England, Connecticut, Massachusetts, New Jersey, and New York. Among the allied families treated, those of Valentine, Wilcox and Yale received the most attention.

Collection of Connecticut vital records to 1850
Barbour, Lucius Barnes, 1878-1934.
F93/C72 Microfilm also LOAN also Mss 281
Access to original papers restricted; Use preservation photocopy in Reference Library or microfilm
14 linear ft.
Unpublished finding aid in the library.
Typescript transcription of vital records for 137 of 160 towns (in 1850, there are now 172) in Connecticut copied from 1918 to 1928. Each town is bound in one volume except for Hartford and Middletown which are in two volumes. Each volume is an alphabetical list of vital events for that town. The listings start at or near the founding of the town and come down to the present stopping between 1846 to 1868, and four cases between 1810 and 1840. Eighteen towns had separate publishments of their vital records. Eight of these are duplicated in the Barbour Collection (marked with *). The separate publications are for the towns of Bolton, Coventry, East Granby, Granby*, Lyme*, Mansfield, Middlebury*, New Haven, Norwich, Salisbury*, Saybrook, Seymour, Simsbury*, Suffield*, Vernon, Windham*, and Woodstock. Norwich and Woodstock have continuations transcribed as a part of the Barbour Collection.

Notes on the American families of Paul or Paull
Paul, Edward Joy, 1858-1911.
Mss 282
6 v. (178, 138, 164, 206, [81], 187 leaves): ports.; 33 cm.
1897-1903
Typescript genealogy on the descendants of "William Paul of Taunton, in the Colony of Plymouth. Volume 1 covers generations I, II, III, and IV, volume II has the fifth generation, volume 3 has the sixth generation, volume 4 has the seventh generation, and volume 5 has the eight and ninth generations. Volume 6 contains "notes concerning divers persons and families named Paul or Paull, which have been gathered incidentally to work upon the history of William Paul of Taunton in the Colony of Plymouth and his descendants".

Family records of Abbe, Bradford, Church, Clark, Crane, Dewey, Fitch, Hebard, Huntington, Learned, Leavens, Pettis, & allied lines of New England families: ancestors and their families of Marian Hebard Pettis, Edward Fitch Pettis, Dorothy Bradford Pettis, Donald Lathrop Pettis, [and] Jean Pettis McDonald Woldt, Grace Shaw.
Mss 284
383 leaves: ports., geneal. tables; 28 cm.
1987
Computer typescript genealogy with pedigree charts and family group sheets with photocopies of some source documents including family records, obituaries and correspondence (typescript transcription and photocopies of the original letters).

Some descendants of the Belchertown, Mass. Willsons
Willson, Frederick Roosevelt, 1941-.
Mss 285
226 leaves; 28 cm.
1990
Computer typescript.

Ralph Clymer Hawkins papers, 1900-1976
Hawkins, Ralph Clymer, 1887-197?
Hawkins Association.
Mss 286
2 linear ft. (664 items).
Unpublished finding aid in the library.
Chiefly correspondence between Hawkins and other family members relating to his genealogical research and the publication of his A Hawkins Genealogy: 1635-1939 (1939); and notebooks, research notes, charts, newspaper clippings, genealogies, newsletters, and photos, tracing the descendants of Robert (d. 1704) and Mary (b. 1611) Hawkins and their sons, Joseph (1642-1682) and Zachariah (1639-1699), of Charlestown, Mass. Includes materials of Hawkins Association, a family genealogical organization, of which Ralph C. Hawkins was co-founder. Other persons represented include Ada Sanford Hallock, Charles W., Ernest C., and Israel G. Hawkins, and Abigail Holbrook.

Descending genealogy: Tetreau / Tetreault / Tatro / etc. family [and] list of marriages
Tatro, Eugene R., 1945-.
Mss 287
461 p.
Typescript.

Albany Reformed (Holl Soc)
Kenney, Arthur C. M.
Mss 288
776 p.; 28 cm.
c. 1990
Typescript transcription of Albany Reformed Church marriages and baptisms, 1683-1807.

Genealogy of the Richard Snow family
Snow, George Burwell, 1835-1923.
Mss 289
691 p.
c. 1923
Typescript genealogy for eleven generations.

William Augustus Mowry papers, 1644-1909
Mowry, William A. (William Augustus), 1829-1917.
Mss 290
1.3 linear ft.
Unpublished finding aid in the library.
Records, notes, correspondence and documents used in preparation of Mowry genealogies. The documents include deeds, notes, memoranda, clippings, and similar material dating from 1661 to 1863, concerning or originally belonging to various Mowrys.

Vital records of the town of Brooksville, Hancock County, Maine, incorporated as a town June 13, 1817,
from parts of Castine, Penobscot and Sedgwick. Part of Penobscot set off to Castine
Bush, Anne Rainsford French.
Mss 291
4 v. (321, 53, 23, 53 leaves); 21-28 cm.
1948-1951
Typescript transcription. Volume two is on "Marriages in Brooksville, Hancock County, Maine 1847-1893."
Volume three is on "Brooksville, Hancock County, Maine: A list of ministers, justices of the peace, and
others officiating at marriages in Brooksville 1847-1893. Index for marriages in Brooksville 1847-1893."
Volume four is on "Brooksville, Maine, Deaths 1892-1929."

The town book of Bow, New Hampshire: town meetings 1767-1820, genealogy 1710-1890
Hammond, Priscilla.
Mss 292
1 v. (341 leaves); 28 cm.
1933
Typescript transcription of the original record.

Hollis Street Church, Boston: records of admissions, baptisms, marriages and deaths, 1732-1887
Codman, Ogden, 1863-1951.
Mss 293 a
Access to original papers restricted: Use F73.25/C59/1998.
479 leaves; 28 cm.
1918.
Photocopy of handwritten transcription of original record.

Records of Hollis Street Church, 1732-1789
Gay, Frederick Lewis, 1856-1916.
Mss 293 b
1 v. (175 leaves); 27 cm.
Handwritten transcription of the original record.

Pedigree of Joseph Bolles
Ayers, Augustine H.
Mss 294
379 leaves: geneal. tables; 28 cm.
Computer typescript.

John Stanley Howard papers, 1628-1850
Howard, John Stanley, 1885-1946.
Mss 295
6 v.
Handwritten records of Howard, Hayward and Haywood families in New England and New York, 1628-
1850. Includes a typescript transcription and index prepared by John S. Howard, Mabel H. Kingsbury,
Margery H. Orem and William E. Weihrouch.

Winifred LeBoutillier Tyer papers, 1850-1890
Tyer, Winifred LeBoutillier, b. 1900.
Mss 296
4.75 linear ft.
Unpublished finding aid in the library.
Correspondence, diaries, genealogy, sketches and photographs concerning the Hopkins, Wait, and LeBoutillier families. The correspondence, 1850-1990, covers four generations of Mrs. Tyer's family. The main correspondents are Mrs. Tyer's great-grandparents (Mary Tyrell Hopkins Wait and Heman Keyes Hopkins Jr.), her grandparents (Mary Eliza Hopkins Wait and William Augustus Wait), her grandmother's brother (Stephen DeForest Hopkins), her parents (Elsie Wait LeBoutiller and Addison Brayton LeBoutillier), her mother's sisters (Winifred and Bertha Wait), her husband (Henry G. Tyer), her brother (George Tyrell LeBoutillier) and Mrs. Tyer. The diaries, 1854-1930, are by Mary Eliza Hopkins Wait and Bertha Wait. The graphics include photographs of family members and family homes and sketches drawn by Addison B. LeBoutillier and George T. LeBoutillier.

Palmer family in America. [Vol 2]
Palmer, Horace Wilbur, 1878-1953.
Mss 297
0.9 linear ft. (8,220 p. in 13 bound volumes); 28 cm.
Unpublished register in the library.
1915-1953
Carbon copy typescript genealogy on all Palmer families who immigrated to the United States from the 1600s to the 20th century. The data is generally cited to its sources, a method usually not practiced in this era.

Index to the Horace Wilbur Palmer papers in the New England Historic Genealogical Society's R Stanton Avery Special Collections Department
Buss, Karen.
New England Historic Genealogical Society
CS71/P175/1998a also LOAN also Mss 297 Index
vii, 925 p.; 29 cm.
1998

Marriages, deaths and ordinations from newspapers in the city library, Springfield, Massachusetts 1812-1850
NSDAR Mercy Warren Chapter.
Mss 298
18 v.
1941-1964
Typescript.

Long Island, N.Y. cemetery inscriptions
Frost, Josephine C., 1864-1942.
Mss 299
10 v.
Typescript transcription.

Ana Byrd Hall papers, 1919-1924
Hall, Ana Byrd, 1852-1924.
Mss 300
2.7 linear ft.
Unpublished register in the library; Ardis D. King's *Guide and Index to the Ana Byrd Hall papers: ca. 1919 1924* (Boston: NEHGS, 1995) call number CS71/H177/1995 also LOAN.
Genealogies, notes, records and correspondence pertaining to the descendants of William Seavey (1601 1688) and Thomas Seavey (1627-1708/9) and allied families (Abbott, Bean, Drake, Hall, Odiorne Pickering).

David Thomas Marvel papers, 1904-1937
Marvel, David T. (David Thomas), 1851-1931.
Mss 301
64 items.
Unpublished finding aid in the library.
Correspondence, deeds, wills, genealogies, state and local records, and other papers, relating to the family of John Marvel (1632-1707) and the allied lines of Jefferson, Pepper, Phillips, Spencer, and Warrington, chiefly residents of Delaware, Maryland, and Virginia. Persons represented include Mary Robinson (fl. 1883-1884). Unfortunately, the collection does not include evidence of his varied and interesting career.

Philip Kirkham Allen papers, 1856-1981 (bulk 1897-1981)
Allen, Philip K. (Philip Kirkham), 1910-1996.
Mss 302
1.5 linear ft.
Unpublished finding aid in the library.
Correspondence, diaries, genealogies, and other papers, chiefly gathered by Carroll Dunham (b. 1858), of Irvington, N.Y., relating to the Dunham family and its allied lines including Fleming, Johnson, Lawrence, MacGregor, Metcalf, Parker, Rigg, Scott, and Skinner. Includes papers of Edward W. Dunham (1794-1871), merchant, of New York, N.Y., and diary (30 v., 1856-1891) of his son, Edward (b. 1819), cashier of Corn Exchange Bank, reflecting business and family affairs; diary (1 v., 1950-1955) of Allen's mother, Anne L. (Kirkham) Allen (b. 1877), of Walpole and Watertown, Mass.; diary (1864) of Ann L. Coleman (b. 1832), of New York, N.Y., describing social events and a trip to New Hampshire; and papers of Charles D. Deshler and Ann S. and Azariah Dunham, of New Brunswick, N.J., pertaining to daily life and activities there.

Kenneth E. Northrop papers, 1323-1992
Northrop, Kenneth E., 1899-.
Mss 303
148 items.
Unpublished finding aid in the library.
Genealogies, notes, records, correspondence and photographs concerning the Northrop, Bates, Brush and allied families, in particular, the Hall and Loveland families. Includes 17 items concerning Mr. Northrop's uncle, Dr. Henry B. Northrop (1860-1966), whose graduation from the McLean Hospital nursing program made him the first male graduate nurse in America. The photographs include family portraits and 13 reels of moving picture film of trips and trains in the 1970's and 1980's.

Mcclure Meredith Howland papers, 1941-1977
Howland, Mcclure Meredith, 1906-1985.
Mss 304
1 linear ft.
Unpublished finding aid in the library.
Correspondence, genealogies, articles, notes, and other papers, relating to 69 families including Brice, Dulaney, Herrman, Howland, Southworth, and Stansby, including research on English genealogy and ancestors. Includes unpublished article by David H. Kelley containing information pertaining to the ancestry of Eve of Leinster (fl. 1170). Persons represented include Richard de Clare, Augustine Herrman, and Judith Verleth.

James Swift Rogers papers, 1572-1905 (bulk 1894-1905)
Rogers, James S. (James Swift), 1840-1905.
Mss 305
8 linear ft.
Unpublished finding aid in the library.
Correspondence, genealogies, military and town records, obituaries, newspaper clippings, indexes, photos, and other papers, tracing the family of James Rogers (1615?-1687), of New London, Conn., and 22 other "root" families, including English and Irish ancestors and family members residing in the South. Includes annotated version of Rogers's book entitled James Rogers of New London, Ct., and his Descendants (1902). Persons represented include Charles (d. ca. 1810), Eli (1769-1849), George (d. 1740), Hope (d. 1749), James (d. ca. 1652), James (1686-1755), John (1572?-1636), John (d. ca. 1661), John (1630-1684), John (1684-1755), Nathaniel (1701-1775), Philip (1727-1810), Robert (1650-1682), Samuel (1740-1789), Simon (ca. 1615-1680), Smith (d. 1819), Stephen (d. 1785), Thomas (d. ca. 1621), Thomas (d. 1736), and William (d. ca. 1656) Rogers.

Henry Tibbetts of Dover, New Hampshire and some of his descendants
Jarvis, Mary T., 1864-.
Mss 306
2 v. (692 leaves); 28 cm. + index (362 p.)
Ardis D. King's Index to Henry Tibbetts of Dover, New Hampshire and some of his descendants.
1937-1939
Typescript.

Wayne Charles Hart papers, ca. 1580-ca. 1991
Hart, Wayne Charles, 1925-1991.
Mss 307
8 linear ft.
Unpublished finding aid in the library.
Genealogies, computer printouts, indexes, ancestral charts, and other papers, relating to over 800 colonial families who settled in Farmington and elsewhere in Connecticut, including early residents of Windsor, Conn., who were descendants of passengers on the ship Mary and John, compiled by Hart with the assistance of Burton Wells Spear (b. 1924). Persons represented include John Cowles (ca. 1598-1675), Julius Gay (1834-1918), Stephen Hart (d. 1682 or 3), Thomas Judd (ca. 1608-1688), Joseph Loomis (d. 1658), Richard Seymour (d. 1655), John Warner (fl. 1592-1593), and members of the Porter family.

The Josiah Closson family of New England, including the allied William Olin family
Closson, William G., 1880-.
Mss 308
xvi, 392 p.
1947
Typescript.

Glenn E. Roberts papers, 1595-1992
Roberts, Glynn E., 1926-.
Mss 309
539 p.
Computer typescript genealogy on the descendants of John W. Roberts of Kentucky and allied families.

Frederick William Prince papers, 1580-1988
Prince, Frederick W., 1829-1907.
Mss 310
1.25 linear ft.
Unpublished finding aid in the library.
Genealogies, family papers, notes, records, correspondence and photographs concerning the Prince and allied families.

Augustus Wylie papers, 1847-1925 (Bulk 1854-1870)
Wylie, Augustus, 1826-1905.
Mss 311
ca. 400 items.
Unpublished finding aid in the library.
Photocopies of family correspondence and scattered documents pertaining to the Wylie and allied families in New Hampshire, Vermont and the midwest. Principal topics addressed include crops, farming, weather, travel, family and friends, and health reports. In all 22 relatives supplied letters; however, five were especially prolific and together accounted for almost 70% of the total. These five were Mason Wheeler (74 letters), Minerva Wylie (69 letters), Arvilla (Wheeler) Crary (44 letters), Mary Wylie (41 letters), and Huldah Wheeler (38 letters).

The descendants and families of Jacob Doten 1361
Berg, Robert H., 1915-.
Mss 312
iv, 222 leaves; 28 cm.
1991.
Computer typescript.

The family of David Cook(e)
Brown, Vera H. (Vera Helen), 1909-.
Mss 313
[658] leaves: ill., ports., geneal. tables; 29 cm.
1992
Photocopy of typescript.

Descendants of Richard Curtis (1610-1681) of Dorchester, Mass. and Wallingford, Conn.
Curtis, Harlow Dunham, b. 1883.
Mss 314
390 leaves; 28 cm.
Photocopy of a typescript.

Edgar Whittemore papers, 1066-1955
Whittemore, Edgar, 1891-1955.
Mss 316
6 linear ft.
Unpublished finding aid in the library.
Genealogies, correspondence, clippings, etc. pertaining to the Whittemore and allied families in America.

Winifred Carpenter Gates papers, 1897-1973
Gates, Winifred Carpenter, 1883-1980.
Mss 317
1 linear ft.: photographs.
The bulk of the collection is a set of file cards documenting the descendants of Stephen Gates of Hingham and Lancaster, Mass., with assigned numbers that conform to Charles O. Gates' book on the family published in 1898, though these cards carry forward to 1943. There are letters dated 1918 to 1919 from Mrs. Gates to her mother describing her husband's appointment to the University of Guelph, finding a house, the Spanish Flu epidemic, and his preparing of an exhibit of bee related products. A second group of letters by Mrs. Gates dated 1963 to 1973 are her reminiscences of the Carpenter family home at Amherst, Mass. There are 138 photographs, ca. 1860-1973, of relatives, mostly Carpenter and Gates, 10 views of ancestral homes, and a 40-page album, 1894-1900. Also, there are bankbooks from Worcester, Mass., 1898-1909, and an autograph album, 1863-1865.

John Hutchinson Cook papers, 802-1976
Cook, John Hutchinson, 1921-1994.
Mss 318
8 linear ft.
Unpublished finding aid in the library
Genealogies, charts, notes, correspondence and photographs concerning the Cook and allied families of New Jersey, 1375-1976; and notable families in America, Europe and Asia, 802-1960. Among these, English lines receive the most attention, followed by French, German and Italian. A major part of this section consists of newspaper articles mounted in scrapbooks, for the period 1918-1939. John Insley Coddington (1902-1991) provided considerable information and comment, most of it in the form of correspondence, 1947-1973.

Nathan Holbrook Glover papers, 1647-1982 (bulk 1686-1744, 1793-1927)
Glover, Nathan Holbrook, 1856-1945.
Mss 319
1.67 linear ft.
Unpublished finding aid in the library.
A collection primarily of business papers, 1647-1982, concerning the Glover family which includes the related families of Clough and Holbrook. The papers contain land deed and/or tenant matters in Boston, Braintree, Dorchester (especially including Neponset), Hull (especially including Point Allerton), Marshfield and Quincy all in Massachusetts, and other towns. The bulk of land business matters are of Nathan Glover, 1881- 1935. Other documents are estate papers (especially wills, 1702-1958), mortgages (1845-1935), indentures (1647-1931), a pre-maritial agreement (1737), powers of attorney (1869-1926), court cases (1719-1853, including a paternity suit, 1853), receipts (1726-1810), slave deeds (1704, 1744), and miscellaneous papers. There are two account books for Point Allerton (Hull, Mass.) land, 1881, and Neponset (Dorchester, Mass.) land, 1906.

Robert Wilson Tirrell papers, ca. 1600-1977
Tirrell, Robert Wilson, 1898-1977.
Mss 320
14 linear ft.
Unpublished finding aid in the library.
Genealogies, charts, notes, records, clippings, correspondence and photographs concerning the Tirrell and related families.

Andrew Brian Wendover MacEwen papers, 1961-1972
MacEwen, Andrew B.W. (Andrew Brian Wendover), 1939-
Mss 321
0.2 linear ft.
Notes and correspondence concerning the Lounsbury family with some compiled genealogy. There is some information on the allied family of Prosser.

Paul Wesley Prindle papers, 1591-1991
Prindle, Paul Wesley, 1903-1991.
Mss 322
18 linear ft.
Unpublished finding aid in the library.
Genealogies, charts, records, notes, articles, correspondence and photographs concerning the Prindle and allied families, as well as professional client research gathered by Prindle as an amateur and later professional genealogist, from about 1921 to 1991. The largest section is his research on various families focusing geographically on Stamford and Greenwich, CT; colonial Plymouth Co MA; Palatine and Mohawk families of New York and Virginia. A second, smaller section of research on various families is geographically arranged. It focuses on the Dutch, Palatine and Mohawk families of New York; Palatine families of PA; Schoarie Valley families of New York; and Mayflower families. Prindle's interest in royalty concentrated on the English. His research files centered on New York topics. His general correspondence files with 72 genealogists were in addition to the specific correspondence kept with the familial and geographical files. He had charts on royal and American ancestry.

The descendants of John Maccoon of Cambridge, Mass. and Westerly, Rhode Island
Lines, Maxine Phelps, 1909-.
Mss 323
841 leaves.
1991
Typescript genealogy.

John Adams Comstock Jr. papers, 1595-1945
Comstock, John Adams, Jr., 1883-1970.
Mss 324
13.3 linear ft.
Unpublished finding aid in the library.
Genealogy, correspondence, records and photographs regarding descendants of William Comstock (ca. 1595- ca. 1683) who emigrated from England to Watertown, Mass. circa 1635, settled in Wethersfield, Conn. and died in New London, Conn.

Katherine Ruth Kimmerle Follett papers, 1940-1991 (bulk: 1960-1991)
Follett, Katherine R. (Katherine Ruth Kimmerle), 191
Mss 325
Access to original papers restricted; Use microfilm copy.
0.6 linear ft.
A genealogical study of the descendants of John Follett (1669-1718) is the focus of the collection. There are smaller sub-groups for the descendants of Benjamin Follett (1789-1870); Ezekiel Follett (d. 1817); John Follett of Kittery, Me.; and William Follett (ca. 1745-1808). There are two photographs in the collection.

Herbert Holton Holmes papers, 1973-1993
Holmes, Herbert Holton, 1911-1993.
Mss 326
1.5 linear ft.
Unpublished finding aid in the library.
Typescript genealogy concerning the possible British ancestry and American descendants through nine generations of John Holmes (ca. 1583 - ca. 1667), the "messenger of the Plymouth Court", of Plymouth Colony.

Bible records, Westchester County, New York State
NSDAR Pierre Van Cortlandt Chapter.
Mss 329
360 leaves; 28 cm.
1991.
Photocopy of a typescript transcription.

Brief genealogies of and historical notes on the Walden, Vermont, branches of the Elkins, Farrington, Foster, Gilman, Perkins, Rogers, Sanborn and Webster families
Farrington, Julia Agnes, 1868-.
Mss 330
8 items.
ca. 1951
Photocopy of handwritten genealogy "copied and presented by Charlotte Marjorie (Farrington) Fithian to Donald G. Farrington. Indices prepared and added by Donald G. Farrington (1992)."

The Teney, Tenney, Tenneyson, Tennison, Tiney, Tinn, Tinne, Tinney, Tinneyson, Tinning, Tinnison, Tinny and some variations
Tinney, Thomas Milton, 1941-.
Mss 331
1,008 leaves.
1975
Typescript.

Nathan Warren and Persis Sumner and their children of Vermont, New York and Ohio
Cooke, Raeola Ford, 1925-.
Mss 332
ca. 330 leaves; 28 cm.
1995 Mar.
The manuscript is broken up into chapters, each deals with a different child, but starting with Nathan Warren (ca. 1758-1827). Nathan lived in Wells, Vt., then moved on to Jay, N.Y., and finally to Thompson, Gauga Co., Ohio. Each chapter contains a descendancy genealogy is a modified "Register" form down to the present.

Some descendants of Silas (4) Taft [Stephen (3), Benjamin (2), Robert (1)] and Elizabeth Cruff
Todd, Neil B. (Neil Bowman), 1936-.
Mss 333
2 v.
Photocopy of a typescript genealogy.

Anson Titus papers, 1600-1935
Titus, Anson, 1847-1932.
Mss 334
Access to original papers restricted; Use microfilm.
3.5 linear ft.
Unpublished finding aid in the library.
Genealogies, records, notes, articles, correspondence and photographs concerning the Titus, Sabin and allied families.

The descendants (to 1941) of President James Marsh of the University of Vermont, and Lucia and Laura Wheelock, his first and second wives and their sons President Sidney Harper Marsh and Professor Joseph Walker Marsh of Pacific University...
Marsh, William Parmelee, 1867-1948.
Mss 335
126 leaves: ill., ports., geneal. tables, photographs; 28 cm.
1941
Typescript.

Family record Foster
Foster, Howell, 1864-1949.
Mss 336
1 v. (343 leaves): ill., coats of arms, ports.; 28 cm.
1909, 1993
Typescript transcription of family records, letters, account books and reminiscences on the descendants of Reginald Foster, who emigrated in 1635 from England to America and settled in Ipswich, Mass., and allied families of Howell, Brown, Young, etc. Includes newspaper clippings and photographs.

Bible record for the James Richards family, 1661-1714
Richards, James, fl. 1665.
Mss 337
Access restricted: Extremely fragile.
2 p.
Original record without title page concerning the Richards family of Hartford, Connecticut.

The cemeteries of Raymond [N.H.]
Hoffman, Ruth Brooks.
Mss 338
313 leaves: maps; 28 cm.
1975
Typescript transcription of the inscriptions in the Batchelder, Batchelder family, Bean, Brown, Dearborn, Dudley-Tucker, Green, Ham, Holman, Lane, Launier, Lovering, Moulton, Oak Hill, New Pine Grove, Old Pine Grove, Prescott, Prevere, Scribner, Town Line, Tucker, the cemetery between Winter and Green Roads, and the cemetery off Nottingham Road in back of Underhill farm close to Folsom Farm.

Lebourveau family tree
Le Bourveau, Allen E., 1950-.
Mss 339
320 leaves; 28 cm.
1984
Photocopy of family group sheets concerning the descendants of John Lebourveau.

Dwan and Ogle families, Wayland, Mass., 1743-1987
Barnes, Shirley M., 1922-.
Mss 340
0.5 linear ft.
Family group sheets concerning the Dwan and Ogle families with source documents (photocopies or transcriptions) including charts, notes, correspondence and photographs.

The Shaws of ... [Ohio, Pennsylvania, Rhode Island, Kansas, Idaho, Kentucky, Virginia, New York]
Chew, Emma Mae.
Mss 341
356 leaves: maps, ports.; 28 cm.
1992
Photocopy of a typescript genealogy.

Arthur (1) Howland of Marshfield, Massachusetts and some of his descendants
Atwood, Howland Fay, 1918-.
Mss 342
545 leaves: ports., maps; 28 cm.
1992
Photocopy typescript genealogy. Includes 1997 Jul 30 revision.

Index to deaths in the Massachusetts Centinel and the Columbian Centinel, 1784-1840
American Antiquarian Society.
REF F73.25/A45 also MT also Mss 343
Access to original restricted; Use photocopy version in Reference Library
12 v. (3.125 linear ft.)
Unpublished finding aid in the library.
Carbon copy of the original typescript index. NEHGS has a complete bound set of the original issues of the Massachusetts Centinel and Columbian Centinel. Only in rare instances does the original issue contain more information than does this index.

A further contribution to the history of that branch of the Wilders who immigrated to Massachusetts about 1638 by enlargement, extension and correction of Book of the Wilders ... by Rev. Moses Hale Wilder
Wilder, Edwin Milton, 1871-1963.
Mss 344
1,273 leaves: ill., ports.; 28 cm.
1961-1979
Photocopy of a typescript genealogy originally started by E.M. Wilder of Sacramento, Calif. The project was completed in 1969 by Harold K. Wilder.

Allyn Stephens Brown papers, 1597-1983
Brown, Allyn S., 1916-1993.
Mss 345
12 items.
Item 1 is two letters from Homer W. Brainerd of Hartford, Conn. to Mrs Elwin H Johnston of Ulster, Penn. dated Dec 3 and Dec 17 1927 [6] p. concerning the Abell family. Item 2 is a handwritten transcription of an Abell family record. Item 3 is a typescript ["Descendants of Thomas Allyn"] by Henry Gladys Allyn [51] leaves. Item 4 is a photocopy of a typescript called ["The Allyn Family"] [10] leaves. Item 5 is an assortment of records, correspondence, charts, notes etc. concerning the William Best family of Ireland and Quincy, Ill. Item 6 is a text descendancy chart by Allyn S. Brown Sr. with the heading "Descendants of Nicholas Brown" (1778-1843) [7] p. Item 7 is a typescript with annotations called "Brown-Stephens Genealogy" by Allyn S. Brown, Sr. [15] leaves. Item 8 is a computer printout witht he heading "Brown-Stephens Genealogy" [36] leaves. Item 9 has photocopies concerning the Benjamin Clark family [20] leaves.

George Allen of Weymouth, Mass., 1635, of Lynn, Mass., 1636, and of Sandwich, Mass., 1637-48, together with some of his descendants
Allen, John Kermott, b. 1858.
Mss 346
1 v. (252 leaves); 28 cm.
1924
Typescript.

Allen genealogical data ... supplemental to George Allen of Weymouth, Mass. ... by John Kermott Allen 1924
Warner, Mabel A.
Mss 347
13 leaves; 28 cm.
1952
Typescript.

Ralph Allen of Sandwich, Massachusetts, and some of his descendants
Allen, John Kermott, b. 1858.
Mss 348
1 v. (349 leaves); 28 cm.
1924
Typescript genealogy through nine generations.

Genealogical records for some of the early pioneers and immigrants in P.E.I. lots 61, 63 and 64, and their descendants
Johnston, Harry.
Mss 349
7 in.
1992
Computer typescript

Some of the descendants of Asaph Phillips and Esther Whipple of Foster, Rhode Island
Faig, Kenneth W.
Mss 350
xxv, 332 leaves; 28 cm.
1993
Typescript. Includes bibliographical references and index.

Corrections and additions for some of the descendants of Asaph Phillips and Esther Whipple of Foster, Rhode Island: originally published, 1993
Faig, Kenneth W.
Mss 350
23 leaves: ill.; 28 cm.
1994

John Mayhew genealogy
Stebbing, Elwynne Lincoln, 1906-.
Mss 351
213 leaves: maps, ports., coat of arms; 28 cm.
1986
Family group sheets with copies of some source documents.

Maine records
Hill, Mary Pelham, 1865-1943.
Mss 352
128 leaves
1928
Typescript and handwritten transcriptions of miscellaneous Bible records, cemetery inscriptions, family records and vital statistics collected by D.A.R. chapters in Maine. The family records concern the Ames, Brown, Fairfield, Garcelon, Haley, Hartwell, Hinckley, Kendall, Martin, Minot, Odiorne, Patten, Philoon, Powers, Smith, Sprague, Springer, Stinson, Sylvester, Towne and Webber families. The cemetery records (many concerning the stones for Revolutionary War soldiers) are for the Bangor area, Bingham, Brunswick, Bucksport, Troy and Concord. The Bible records are for the Bacon, Chamberlin, Crawford, Creech, Dennison, Fitts. Larrabee, Lindsay-Lindsey, Linscott, Merryman, Mitchell, Moody, and Moses families. These are followed by cemetery records for Lewiston, Moose River, Moscow, Old Orchard (Biddeford, Limerick), & Portland (Deering, Stroudwater) and the records of the Society for building a meeting house in Bingham. Baptisms, marriages & deaths in Sanford.

The genealogy of Johannes Wallkamm, 1688-1990
McCord, Yvonne DeBow.
Mss 353 a
355 p.: maps, ports., geneal. tables, photographs.
Typescript genealogy.

Some ancestors of Dorre Marie Koesel, wife of John G. Walcom
McCord, Yvonne DeBow.
Mss 353 b
27 p.: port., maps; 28 cm.
1991
Typescript.

The Scottish ancestors of Carrie Taylor, wife of John Jackson Walcom
McCord, Yvonne DeBow.
Mss 353 c
62 p.: geneal tables, ports., maps; 28 cm.
1991
Typescript.

The ancestry of Rev. Harvey Colcord Wood, direct descendant of Edward Wood of Charlestown, Mass.
Bates, Mary Wood, b. 1854.
Mss 354
159, 214 leaves: coat of arms; 28 cm.
1937
Typescript.

George Washington Spencer papers, 1873-1953 (bulk: 1907-1936)
Spencer, George W. (George Washington), 1860-1939.
Mss 355
0.2 linear ft.
A family collection of 156 letters, 13 postcards, 54 leaves of notes and documents, and 15 photographs which deal with the estranged family of George W. Spencer. He was a real estate agent in Worcester, Mass., by 1902 while his wife and children lived in Warwick, R.I. The earliest letters are concerning his wife, then Nancy Edna Sarle while at Greenwich Academy Preparatory School, and the postcards from their son William Spencer during World War I while in Europe. There is a very small amount of material being collected for a Spencer genealogy, though one was never published.

Crary family records
Crary, Charles Judson, b. 1881.
Mss 356
1 v. (235 leaves); 28 cm.
1956
Typescript.

Abbott genealogy
Abbott, Clifford Nelson, 1931-.
Mss 357
716 p.
1992
Typescript family group shhets with photocopies of source material concerning the Abbott family of Andover, Mass. and Fryeberg, Me., 1470-1992.

Fuller genealogy
Brakebill, Margaret J., 1924-.
Mss 358
351 p.: coat of arms, maps, geneal. tables, ports.; 28 cm.
c.1992
Typescript.

James Spear, Sr. / Esther Colton
Parent, Kenneth W.
Mss 360
160 p.; 28 cm.
1992
Typescript notes, transcriptions and photocopies of family papers and correspondence, etc. collected during research concerning James Spear of Newbury, Vt., 1772-1992.

Maine name indexes
Mss 361
1,767 leaves.
c. 1991
Ms. name indexes for Hon. Edward Wiggin's History of Aroostock, Charles Morrow Wilson's Aroostook: Our Last Frontier, Bob Considine's It's the Irish, Vinal A. Houghton's The Story of an Old New England Town [Lee, Me.], Ava H. Chadbourne's Maine Place Names and the Peopling of its Towns, Dana Willis Fellows' History of the Town of Lincoln Maine 1822-1928, and William B. Lapham and Silas P. Maxim's History of Paris, Maine from Its Settlement to 1880.

Nathan Wyman and Samuel Eames papers, 1688-1834, 1928-1988
Wyman, Nathan, 1696-1778.
Mss 362
2.5 linear in. (102 items).
Unpublished finding aid in the library.
Legal documents particularly pertaining to probate matters. The information is divided into three main sections concerning the Wyman family of Woburn, Eames family of Woburn and the Rebecca Stalcup letters. The Wyman family material, 1688-1834, includes deeds, wills and miscellaneous documents (quits of claim, receipts of payment, a work order, a request of services to Nathan as highway surveyor, and an inventory of the possessions of Nathan Wyman at the time of his death). The Eames family material includes deeds, bonds and miscellaneous documents 1693-1761. Rebecca Stalcup letters, 1809-1816, include several letters written by Rebecca Stalcup of Maryland to her daughter Henrietta Higgins Eames (Ames) of Woburn, Mass. Also enclosed in this section is a letter written by James Parker (son-in-law to Stalcup) to Jacob Eames/Ames, Henrietta's husband. The letters primarily discuss family matters and religious beliefs.

Halifax (Mass.) records, 1748-1866
Halifax (Mass.) Town officers.
Mss 363
1 linear ft.
The Town papers contain mostly tax records from 1748 to 1866 probably created by the tax collector as he received it and from which the official town copy was made. There also are highway maintenance records, 1823-1865; Overseer of the Poor records, 1805-1859; marriage records involving Halifax residents in other towns, 1734-1798 copied later; special enanctments, 1781-1859; and an expenditure book called "Tax Book No. 3," 1782-1828.

Robert Frank Collins papers, 1603-1982
Collins, Robert Frank, 1901-1983.
Mss 364
11 linear ft.
Unpublished finding aid in the library.
Generation information on sixteen major Collins lines from 1603 to 1982, each has been traced to its English Collins ancestors. The collection includes card and/or sheet indexes for many of these lines. Mr. Collins maintained an active correspondence with a large number of Collins descendants worldwide. That too has been indexed on cards. Later in his genealogical work, Mr. Collins developed an activity which he called the "Collins Clearing House". He advertised its existence offering free help for anyone with a Collins research problem who was willing to send him a return envelope. This also generated a large volume of correspondence, about half the size of the earlier files. Allied families in a variety of geographical locations were also investigated but in a more limited manner.

Richard Sears of Yarmouth and his descendants: with an appendix containing some notices of other families by the name of Sears
May, Samuel Pearce, b. 1828.
Mss 365
2 v. (846 p.); 28 cm
1913
Revised & corrected
Bound typescript genealogy.

Edith Phemister Ferguson papers, 1964-1988
Ferguson, Leonard Wilton, 1912-1988.
Ferguson, Edith Beverly Phemister, 1913-.
Mss 366
1 linear ft.
Unpublished finding aid in the library.
Register of some early Provincetown and Truro (Provincetown related) families. The husband and wife team gathered information on these families and recorded it on 5x8 inch index cards. The information recorded was gleaned from vital records, numerous Bible records and church records at the Unitarian Church and Methodist Church in Provincetown, several family genealogies, cemetery records, federal census records, and town reports. Family group sheets were created and arranged alphabetically by surnames. Large, newspaper-sized pages were used to construct family trees. Non-Provincetown residents were included if they were related to local families. The general time period covered was 17xx to 1850, though information beyond that time is given to complete a family group. A dictionary format is used to present the final data, which is also cross-referenced under the spouses name.

Edith Wilcox Holton papers, ca. 1920-1943
Holton, Edith Wilcox, 1868-1950.
F63/H65/1989 Microfilm also Mss 367
Access to original papers restricted, use microfilm copy.
6.25 linear ft.
Unpublished finding aid in the library.
This is a collection of genealogical notes compiled during her years of research. The files are arranged alphabetically by family names which number just under 500. The families all lived in Suffolk, Barnstable, Plymouth and Essex Counties, Mass. The major families include: Allerton, Atwood, Bradford, Brewster, Brown, Chilton, Cooke, Doty, Fuller, Hopkins, Howland, Parker, Pratt, Rogers, Sampson, Smith, Soule, Thomas, Warren, White, Wood, and Wright. The Mayflower families are covered in great detail including female lines.

Joseph (1) Merry (1607-1710) and some of his descendants through 1994
Sasson, Hilda Edna Anderson, 1924-.
Mss 368
256 leaves: geneal. tables, ports.; 28 cm.
1994
Photocopy of typescript family group sheets with copies of a few source documents and photographs.

Maclain Warren McLean papers, ca. 1880-1988 (bulk 1959-1988)
McLean, Maclain W. (Maclain Warren), 1906-1990.
Mss 369
16..35 linear ft.
The collection's primary focus is of compiled genealogies of southeastern New England families. The most well known is that of the Sandwich, Mass., families. There are large amounts of material on the Crosby, Ellis and Gifford families. Much less, but worth noting are the Bourne, Dimmock, Fish, Gibbs, Handy, Howland, Landers, Nye, Parker, Perry, and Swift families. He had lengthy correspondence with Bernice Bengel, Lydia Brownson, and Helen Joy Lee. There is a series of transcriptions of Wareham and Yarmouth, Mass., and Plymouth County, Mass., vital records. McLean also compiled the ancestry of his mother, Marion Louise (McLean) Schultz.

Jaques family genealogy: an omnibus genealogy of several immigrant ancestors bearing Jaques, Jacques, Jakway, Jaquish, Jaquith, Jaqua, Jaku and similiar names
Jaques, Roger Alden, 1941-.
Mss 370
436 leaves: ill., ports., maps, geneal. tables, coat of arms; 28 cm.
1988
Typescript.

Descendants of William Berry and Jane of Strawberry Bank, to and including the fifth generation
Berry, June, 1925-.
Mss 371
v, 73, v, 127, v, 122, vi, 152, vi, 128, vii, 306 leaves
1992
A descendancy genealogy of the Berry family for five generations that is split into seven books, the children of the immigrant. The books are compilations of family group sheets as follows: (1) John Berry and Susanna; (2) James Berry and Eleanor Wallis; (3) William Berry and Judith Locke; (4) Joseph Berry and Rachel; (5) Rachel Berry and John Marden; (6) Elizabeth Berry and John Locke; (7) Mary Berry and John Foss [not yet published].

Howard A. Thomas papers, 1951-1981
Thomas, Howard A.
Mss 372
0.2 linear ft.
A collection compiled from various authors concerning the Timson family is America. The focus is on Robert Timson (1754-1839), but material relating to Benjamin Timson (ca. 1750-ca. 1804), Thomas Timpson (1765-1856), and Timsons from Virginia, New Hampshire and England can be found. There are two "compiled" items which contain indexes. The other half of the collection is notes and correspondence between Thomas and Lindsley Bailey (1904-1985), Jan Reid in England, Belle Horton Davis Smith (1903-1989), and Helen Eaton Timson (1924-1991).

Henry Watson Gore papers, 1876-1962 (bulk 1876-1890)
Gore, Henry W. (Henry Watson), 1842-1917.
Mss 373
3 linear ft.
Unpublished finding aid in the library.
The focus of the collection is on the Gore and Crafts families. The Crafts material was used in the Craft genealogy written in 1893. Bible records, deeds, diaries, commissions, receipts, estate papers, letters, tax receipts, wills, poems, jokes, and photographs genres can be found here. Gore was involved in the First Independent Corps of Cadets for Massachusetts during the Civil War. There are two diaries, a transcript kept by Elizabeth Howe (1769-1853) describing life in Brookline, Mass., from a young women's perspective from 1783 and 1791; and the diary of Samuel Doggett (1794-1856) describing his business trip to England in 1831 for his carpet making company. A group of 17 letters from Francis D. Crafts describing his voyage to the gold rush area of California shortly before his death. There are genealogical works on Davis, Doggett, Gardner, Litchfield, Spooner, and White families. There are many photographs of portraits and views. Further description can be found in the unpublished register in the library.

The Dearborn family [descendants of Godfrey], vol. 1
Dearborn, Edmund B. (Edmund Batchelder), 1806-1886.
CS71/D285 Microfilm also Mss 374
Access to original papers restricted, use microfilm copy.
1 microfilm reel; 35 mm. (409 p.)
1880?

Artig family history
Artig-Swomley, Gretchen, 1958-.
Mss 375
ca. 150 pages: facsim., geneal. tables; 28 cm.
1994 Apr.
5th ed.
The ancestry of the Artig family, but include related families of Bouck, Dye, Healy, Hinkley, Londsdale, McCann, and McNally. Reproductions of family photographs and genealogical charts fill this unpaginated work.

Charles Frederic Farlow papers, 1879-1895
Farlow, Charles Frederic, 1848-1900.
Mss 376
2.5 linear ft.
The papers are research notes and transcriptions of deeds and probates for the Ballard, Blanchard, and Harris families. There are extensive descendancy genealogies for William Ballard (ca. 1603-ca. 1641), William Ballard (d. 1689), and John Harris who are all early New England immigrants. The Ballard families lived in Andover and Lynn, Mass. The collection contains one map of Massachusetts towns cut into its counties and annotated with dates of incorporation.

Barbara McKee Damon Doyle papers, 1623-1994
Doyle, Barbara McKee Damon, 1925-1994.
Mss 377
1 linear ft.
Unpublished finding aid in the library.
Genealogies, records and notes pertaining to descendants of Duncan Stewart of Ipswich, Newbury and Rowley, Mass. Includes Barbara Doyle's expansion of a genealogy by George Sawim Stewart as it appeared in Stewart Clan Magazine, 2:6 [1923 Dec] to 6:8 [1928 Feb]. The intention was to produce a guide to the family rather than a scholarly genealogy. This is a compiled genealogy for nine generations, numbered 2-887. Most of the sources are family genealogies and are so marked in the collection, the originality lying with the extension of women's lines for two generations and the correction of a few errors that were found in George S Stewart's genealogy. There is also a table on the descendants of William Parker McKee (1862-1933).

John Augustus Downs papers, 1974-1994
Downs, John A.
Mss 378
0.8 linear ft.
Unpublished finding aid in the library.
Consists of several compiled Down(e)(s) genealogies with a small amount of correspondence from family members and photocopies of vital records. Mr. Downs based his work on the genealogical work found in the William Ephraim Daniel Downes papers housed at NEHGS. Includes the typewritten bound mss "Thomas Downs of Dover, New Hampshire and Ebenezer Downes of Dover, Newhampshire and some of his descendants" (1991), "Robert Downs and his son, Benjamin Robert Downes and descendants" (1980) and "William Downe of Boston, Massachusetts and some of his descendants" (1981).

Charles Lansing Bacon papers, 1967-1992
Bacon, Charles L. (Charles Lansing), 1924-1992.
Mss 379
5 linear ft.
Unpublished finding aid in the library.
The papers detail the descendants of Michael Bacon (1579-1648), especially through Samuel Newton Bacon (1829-1889). Other related families are Fitch, Gibbs, Lansing, and Mather. Also, Bacon researched his wife's family, including Blish, Maclay and Tinsley. The Amherst (N.H.) Conservation Commission; letters between the Fitchs of New York and Gibbs of Georgia, 1852-1913; transcription of diary (1861-1863) by Andrew Adrian Mather (1812-1903), as a sheriff; Lansing family letters of their travel in Europe between 1892-1893; Leonard Gibbs Sanford (1839-1912) journals of his experience as a whaler, U.S. Consul in Peru, and travel in Ecuador are represented in the papers. A majority of the 383 images depict family, though this collection include 101 views, most of Garrattsville, Loundonville, and Rensselaerville, N.Y.

Verna Maxine Baker Banes papers, 1983-1994
Banes, Verna Baker (Verna Maxine Baker), 1920-.
CS71/V367/1995 Microfilm also Mss 380
Access to original papers restricted, use microfilm copy.
1 microfilm reel (5.2 linear ft.)
Unpublished finding aid in the repository.
1995
The papers are a collection of data on the Vaughan surname which formed the basis for the "Vaughan, etc. newsletter" published between 1983-1989. The focus is on Vaughans in the southern United States from Texas to Virginia from the mid-18th to the early 20th centuries. This is not the descendants of a specific immigrant, though there are several compiled genealogies, namely: Francis Vaughn Spencer (Vera Francis Vaughn), b. 1926, "Vaughan family genealogy" (1992) [which is the descendants of Littleton Vaughan, 1800-1849]; Mickey Vaughan Cullum (Michelle Denise Vaughan), b. 1956, "The Charles Henson Vaughan [1821-1884] family" (1992); Kenneth G. Vaughn (Kenneth Gwyn), b. 1925, "Descendants of James Vaugh'a'n [ca. 1760-ca. 1850];" and other untitled works. The bulk of the collection is the correspondence files of 542 people. The first folder is a 15,000 name index to these files. The collection contains a complete run of the "Vaughan, etc. newsletter," 1983-1989; as well as "The Vaughan/Vaughn report", 1978-.

Joshua Wyman Wellman papers, 1720-1918
Wellman, J. W. (Joshua Wyman), 1821-1915.
Congregational Society (Cornish, N.H.)
Mss 381
7.83 linear ft.
Unpublished finding aid in the library.
Collection of the genealogical writings, notes and correspondence amassed by the Rev. Joshua Wyman Wellman during the creation of the Wellman genealogy. Includes original deeds, wills, vital records, accounts, receipts, town and church records, diaries, military records, photographs and copper printing plates. Writings detail religious views, controversies in Sutton, Mass., and Cornish, N.H. Personal records reflect the barter economy of Massachusetts and New Hampshire and contain many societal records of Cornish, N.H.

Bennett Franklin Davenport papers, 1636-1923 (bulk 1876-1880)
Davenport, Bennett Franklin, 1845-1927.
CS71/D247/1998 Microfilm also Mss 382
Access to original papers restricted, use microfilm copy.
6 microfilm reels (4.25 linear ft.)
Unpublished finding aid in the library.
1998
Correspondence constitutes the bulk of the papers. While there is some correspondence to and from Henry Davenport (1811-1898), it is primarily between Bennett F. Davenport and his relatives, members of related families, town clerks and historical societies. The majority of this relates to Thomas Davenport (ca. 1604-1685) and Richard Davenport (ca. 1606-1665) and their descendants. This is the continuation of his published work. Some of the correspondence with individuals from allied families is concerned with those related families including the Hagar, Coolidge and Sturtevant families. There is correspondence and genealogical works by others; original documents, 1636-1697; and many photographs.

Charles Deering papers
Deering, Charles.
Mss 383
Correspondence, family group sheets and copies of public records concerning the Deering and allied families. Much of the correspondence was with Emily Wilder Leavitt of Brookline, Eben Putnam, S.W. Watson of the Maine Historical and Genealogical Recorder, and General William D. Whipple. The largest collection of allied family data is for the Whipples, including again much research by E.W. Leavitt and a Whipple pedigree chart from J. Gardner Bartlett of NEHGS. A separate collateral family, Barbour, is represented by letters, family groups, and charts from Mrs. E. Russell Barbour (Carrie F.) of Portland, ME. The collection includes the original typescript "Ancestry of Barbara (Deering) Danielson" prepared by Mary Lovering Holman. In 1929, T.R. Marvin published "Abstracts of English Records" dealing with the English Deering-Whipple ancestry, based on research done for Charles Deering by Messrs Stevens & Brown, London. This research is represented by four typescript volumes, "Deering Reports."

Mary Elizabeth Way papers, 1959-1986
Way, Mary Elizabeth, 1897-1986.
Mss 384
7.9 linear ft.
Unpublished finding aid in the library. Card files
A collection of research by Mary Elizabeth Way, who built upon the previous research of Charles Granville Way (1841-1912), from 1959 to 1986, and focusing mainly on the Stinson and Way families (especially John Way, ca. 1698-1760), though including 180 allied families. The papers contain research notes and correspondence that include genealogical charts; typescript genealogies or reference works by Harriet L. Angelich (b. 1921), Gloria S. Bullock (b. 1931), Iva Virginia Way Feathers (1921-1989), Consuelo Furman, Robert Furman (1863-1944), Glenn Charles Way (1881-1969), Harry Abel Way (1873-1940), and Henry W. Way (1800-1867); photographs; Bible records for Davidson, Stinson and Douglass - Wilson families; reminisences; scrapbook; newspaper clippings; and transcriptions of various original records.

Earl Morgan Savage Photograph Collection, 1900-1956 (bulk 1937-1940)
Savage, Earl Morgan, 1907-1986.
Mss 385
5.4 linear ft.
Unpublished finding aid in the library.
Photographs, negatives and glass plate negatives pertaining to historic Massachusetts buildings, the 1930 Boston Tercentenary Parade, the Hingham Bethlehem Shipyard, the 1926 Washington D.C. Ku Klux Klan March, various Boston street scenes, the 1951 Boston Veterans Seabee Convention, the Massachusetts National Guard (1934-1939), Massachusetts towns, New England churches and railroad tour books with photographs of New England.

Emigrants to New England before 1650
Banks, Charles Edward, 1854-1931.
Mss 386
Access to original papers restricted: use published book version.
2 v. ([3], 375, 81 leaves); 34 cm.
This work is most likely the work of Charles Edward Banks. The last typed entry's reference is 1928. The bookplates of Alfred Trego Butler, a colleague of Banks, are present. It is Butler who likely wrote the manuscript annotations from 1929 to 1945. The work does contain improved, or more detailed, references for some entries of the dictionary, otherwise the published book accurately relates the same information.

Deacon Jacob Burgess and the Noppett
Burgess, Edward S. (Edward Sandford)
Mss 387
2.5 linear inches.
Typescript

Martha G. Campbell papers
Campbell, Martha G.
Mss 388
7.08 linear ft.
Draft finding aid in the library.
Collection of data on the Plymouth Colony, Plymouth County, the Town of Abington and Indian deeds and names. For Plymouth Colony, there are photocopies of deed and probate records with transcriptions, transcriptions of the Colony laws, judicial acts, and copies of historical data taken from the Leila Gurney papers. For Plymouth County, there are transcriptions of county deeds, indexed. The material on the town of Abington includes transcriptions of reports 1713-1840, tax valuations 1785+, direct federal tax 1798, land grants, a typescript "Abington in the Revolution," a list of adult males in Abington prior to 1712 a notebook of historical and genealogical data by William Coughlan; and a hand-written copy of the account book of Samuel Porter. Finally, in addition to the Indian deeds in the Plymouth Colony records, there is a card file of Indian place and personal names, with some information on spouses and children.

Virginia DeJohn Anderson papers, 1560-1699
Anderson, Virginia DeJohn.
Mss 389
2 linear ft.
Unpublished finding aid in the library.
Contains abstractions of baptism, marriage and burial records found in the parish register of Framlingham, County Suffolk, England, and family group forms created by Dr. Anderson from the information in the parish records. Due to the varable spellings of the time, surnames are grouped together when they appear to be the same name with a different spellings; however, researchers should allow for many possible spellings of a surname.

Raymond David Wheeler papers
Wheeler, Raymond David, 1931-1994.
Mss 390
14.16 linear ft.
Collection of genealogies on the descendants of Thomas Wheeler (ca. 1560-5 - 1634/5). Thomas Wheeler had 10 children and Thomas, his eldest son, was born ca. 1591 in Cranfield, Bedfordshire and died in 1654 in Fairfield CT. He is known as Thomas Wheeler of Fairfield CT, and it is with him that the American Wheeler and allied family genealogy begins. The genealogical charts trace the Wheeler and allied families up until about the turn of the 20th century.

Verne Raymond Spear papers
Spear, Verne Raymond, 1917-
Mss 391
15.5 linear ft.
Draft finding aid in library.
Family group sheets providing the genealogy of the descendants of George Spear, miscellaneous other Spear families, and the allied Alderman and Hasting families.

Ian Michael Watson papers, 1242-1984 (bulk: 1666-1900)
Watson, Ian Michael, 1970-
Mss 392
3 linear ft.
Unpublished finding aid in the library.
Consists of the materials collected and compiled by Ian Watson between 1982 and 1987 while researching the Pasco family and solving the problem of three women with the name of Mary Pease in Salem, Massachusetts, one of which was the second wife of Hugh Pasco. The bulk of the collection concerns Hugh Pasco and his descendants. Material relating to Abel Pasco and his descendants is a separate section of the collection. The source files for the Hugh and Abel Pasco genealogies, located separately under each line, include photocopies and transcriptions of census, probate, court, land, military, church, cemetery and vital records with notes from histories, newspapers and some correspondence. Of particular interest is a transcription of Seymour Pasko's diary, a soldier in the 96th Regiment NY Volunteers.

Descendants of David Ackerman of 1662
Ackerman, Herbert Stewart, b. 1875.
Mss 393
4 volumes (1158, 60, A-N p.); 29 cm.
1944 - [1953]
One of five carbon copies of the first three volumes continuously paginated. The fourth volume is a mimeograph copy supplement made nine years after the earlier volumes. The first volumes were the culmination of over 25 years of research.

Mildred Mosher Chamberlain papers, 1558-1995
Chamberlain, Mildred Frances Mosher, 1915-2001.
Mss 394
7 linear ft.
Unpublished finding aid in the library.
Consists primarily of the research materials, compilations and correspondence collected by Mrs. Chamberlain during her research for the book she co-authored with Laura McGaffey Clarenbach, "The descendants of Hugh Mosher and Rebecca Maxon through seven generations" (1990). The research includes material on the allied families of Allen, Macomber, Manchester and Pratt as well as research on the unrelated Chamberlain family, Spielmacher family, and the Capt. Josiah Dodge family of Nova Scotia. Most of the photos are of Moshers and allied families, but there is a good representation of Chamberlains and allied families.

Brotherton Indian collection
Ottery, Rudi (RuEllen Serina Hjella), 1927-1992.
Mss 395
33 linear ft.
Unpublished finding aid in the library.
Consists of records on the Brotherton Indian tribe including tribal rolls, censuses, descendancies from Brotherton progenitors, and enrollment files collected from individuals of Brotherton descent wishing to be placed on the Brotherton Indian rolls (as part of a larger effort to petition the federal government for formal recognition as an Indian tribe). The enrollment files include supporting documentation such as notes, family group sheets, correspondence, vital records, newspaper articles, land records and some photographs. The collection contains historical records consisting of photocopies of treaties, deeds, government reports, powers of attorney, letters and other documents primarily concerning the tribes land dealings as well as applications made by New York Indians (Oneida, Stockbridge, Brotherton) and their descendants for compensation from the federal government for the Kansas lands which were promised in the treaty of Buffalo Creek, N.Y., January 15, 1838.

Elinor Reed Clark papers
Clark, Elinor Reed, 1906-.
Mss 396
2.9 linear ft.
Consists of correspondence with genealogists along with Mrs. Clark's research notes and charts. There are materials gathered for submission to the Society of the Colonial Dames of America, the National Society of Women Descendants of the Ancient and Honorable Artillery Company, and Revolutionary Ancestor Honor Rolls. Of particular interest in the family papers is a transcript of excerpts from the diary of Edward Bacon Burgess (1833-1905) on a cruise from Maui to New Bedford, Mass., 1859-1860.

Algernon Aikin Aspinwall papers
Aspinwall, Algernon Aikin, 1845-1923.
Mss 397
3.17 linear ft.
Register style format of 22 out of 23 Mayflower heads of families through sixth generation, fully compiled but undocumented.

Woodbury genealogy
Woodbury, Ruth A.
Woodbury Genealogical Society.
Mss 398
v, [1], 1215, [145] leaves; 28 cm.
1957
Typescript genealogy of John Woodbury (ca. 1579-1642) of Salem, Mass. Includes an introduction with a history of the Woodbury Genealogical Society.

Eben Putnam papers
Putnam, Eben, 1868-1933.
Mss 399
38 linear ft.
Unpublished finding aid in the library.
Genealogies, records, notes, documents, correspondence, and graphics pertaining primarily to the descendants of John Putnam (1580-1662), who settled in Salem, Mass. In addition, the collection contains extensive research on Putnam families in New York's Mohawk Valley, as well as lesser amounts concerning southern lines. Mr. Putnam also did varying amounts of research, often on commission, for many allied families including the Bixby, Converse and Holden families. Putnam's personal papers consist of scattered family correspondence, a diary, some political material concerning Democratic activities in Danvers and Salem at the turn of the century, and records of his military service. Finally, the collection has 133 photographs of individuals or groups, 34 views of homes and places, as well as 2 photographs of family furniture.

Sally Stone Cook Fiske papers
Fiske, Sally Stone Cook, 1932-.
Mss 400
2.5 linear ft.
Draft register in the library.
Family group sheets (with some documentation), genealogies, and research notes for Cook, Stone, and numerous allied families. Mrs. Fisk's primary interest was in documenting her direct ancestry, rather than compiling comprehensive genealogies of descendants, and her lines are traced to their earliest known American progenitors.

Peter Roger Knights papers, 1961-1995
Knights, Peter R. (Peter Roger), 1938-1995.
Mss 401
7 linear ft.: maps, photographs.
Unpublished finding aid in the library.
Research material on language in 17th century; history and power of the newspapers and their editors; and the effects of the telegraph. Migration is an underlying theme, as well as documenting this and the effects of railroads. The focus of the papers is a study of the migration patterns of Boston from 1830 to 1870. There is a large card file of data. Two books have been written from this material. There are photographs of Knights and negatives of maps for Boston, 1831-1855.

Harry Clifford Belcher papers, 1944-1997
Belcher, Harry Clifford, 1923-.
Mss 403
2.5 linear ft.: coat of arms, geneal. tables, photographs.
Compiled descendancy genealogy of Gregory Belcher of Braintree, Mass., in text and on index cards and a compiled descendancy genealogy of Jeremiah Belcher of Ipswich, Mass., on index cards.

John Frederick Mason papers, ca. 1885-1990
Mason, John Frederick, 1913-1991.
Mss 404
1.7 linear ft.
Genealogical correspondence and research notes on Arms, Mason, Stockton, and Williams families. Also contains material from Jean MacNeish Rand (b. 1922) and Pamela Jean Leslie Jeglinski (b. 1941). Stockton material contains descendants of Richard (d. 1707) and Robert (1699-1744) and the Williams material on descendants of Alexander Stephen Williams (1847-1928). Collection includes many photographs from ca. 1885 to 1947.

Dorothea Bates Cogswell papers, 1647-1975 (bulk: 1710-1853)
Cogswell, Dorothea Bates, 1908-1996.
Mss 405
2 linear ft.
Unpublished finding aid in the library.
Collection contains applications to the Society of Stukely Wescott Descendants of America from 1937-1975, ancestral charts and notes compiled by Dorothea's mother (Theodora Cogswell), grandfather (Edward Russell Cogswell), and E.R.C's uncle (Edward Russell). Collection includes 139 original documents dating from 1647 to 1864 including original accounts, agreements, appointments, bonds, church covenants, commissions, correspondence, court orders, deeds, minutes, mortgages, photographs, probate records, receipts, resolutions and returns, shares and slave bills of sale which have been handed down from the intertwined families of Cogswell, Russell and Northend of Gloucester, Ipswich and Rowley, Mass.

Settlement and ethnicity in Lunenburg, Nova Scotia, 1753-1800: a history of the foreign-protestant community
Paulsen, Kenneth S. (Kenneth Stuart), 1962-.
Mss 408
0.2 linear ft.: charts, maps.
This thesis details the settlement and ethnicity in Lunenburg, Nova Scotia, 1753-1800, and is a history of the foreign protestant German and Swiss community with maps and charts illustrating the division of land based on ethnic groups. The appendices include a list of Lunenburg Twp. master and genealogical charts of Lunenburg's leading families: Rudolph, Kaulbach, and Zwicker. Genealogies with details of places of origin for Jean-Louis Deladeray (d. 1757), Casper Meisner (1715-1792), Casper Friedrich Saltzmann (ca. 1746-1832), Andreas Volker (1713-1799), and Johann Adam Weinacht (1707-176?) are included. The Volker family daughters out to the Weil, Hauptman, and Hatt families.

Genealogical records of early settlers in Malden, Commonwealth of Massachusetts, 1640-1800
Chamberlain, George Walter, 1859-1942.
Mss 409
4 v. (1034 p.); 29 cm.
c 1997
Typescript.

Voyage of Sir Francis Drake, Knt., around the world
Drake, Francis, Sir, ca. 1540?-1596.
Mss 410
[4], 557, [4] leaves, bound; 22 cm.
1844 handwritten copy.
The voyage of Sir Francis Drake, Knt., including the world encompassed, published in London by Nicholas Bourne, 1628, and the famous 1589 voyage handcopied by and with notes by Samuel Gardner Drake (1798-1875).

Descendants of William Fifield
Wells, Peter Fifield, 1937-.
Mss 411
[3], 360 p.: 28 cm.
1992 Aug.
1992 computer ed.
Descendancy genealogy of William Fifield (ca. 1612-1700), of Hampton, N.H., to the 13th generation.

Legacy of dissent: religion and politics in revolutionary Vermont, 1749-1784
Smith, Donald Alan, 1943-.
Mss 412
ix, 949 p.: charts; 25 cm.
1980
1996 photocopy ed.
A bound photo-reduced thesis which examines the internal rebellion by Vermonters against New York's jurisdiction over the state and an external revolt from Britain which resulted in the creation of the independent State of Vermont.

The genealogy of Gilman Pilsbury Beverly and John Winn Maxwell: with related families: Jones, Mitchell, Winn, and Littlefield
Martin, Alan W. (Alan Wayne), 1947-.
Mss 413
v, 199, 18, [2] p.; 28 cm.
1992
A bound typescript ancestry of Gilman Pilsbury Beverly (1845-1914) and John Winn Maxwell.

Autobiography of Alexander Francis Adams
Adams, Alexander Francis, 1865-1943?
Mss 414
239, 10 p.; 24 cm.
1943?
Autobiography that highlights the author's strong interest in music throughout his life. There are several sections after the autobiography: accidental falls of Adams, music associations, residences and jobs, historic street names in Boston, geographical name changes (mostly in New England, but not very extensive), original settlements in Massachusetts with current names, and compiled genealogies of ancestral families (most notable are Adams, Call, Manning, especially Jonathan Call Manning (1795-1859)).

The life and times of Colonel William Lamb, 1835-1909, Norfolk, Virginia
Lamb, William.
Mss 416
[137] p.: 28 cm.
[1989]
Photocopied typescript with annotations in first section. Includes two copied letters about publishing manuscript.

The genealogy of George Lane Dodge
Martin, Alan W. (Alan Wayne), 1947-.
Mss 417
x, 276, 37, 23, 21, 26, 3 p., bound: ills., maps; 28 cm.
1991
1991 typescript ed.
Genealogy of the ancestry and descendants of George Lane Dodge (1871-1952) and the allied families of Beverly, Lane, Leavitt, Dole, Nelson, Conant, Edwards, and Fiske. Work contains a fair about of photocopies from published works and of original documents.

Early families of Boxborough, Massachusetts
Pettingell, John (John Mason), 1890-1972.
Mss 418
3 v.; 29 cm.
Bound typescript ed.
The title page was added to this work before it was bound into three volumes. The first page says "Boxborough, Mass. - A Genealogical history of early settlers" with a sub-title of "Histories of some families residing in district of Boxborough before 1798." The families include: Batchelor, Blanchard, Brown, Cameron, Chester (a negro), Cobleigh, Coolidge, Crouch, Davis, Farr, Fletcher, Fox, Graham, Hartwell, Hayward, Holt, How, Jennings, Kidder, Lawrence, Mead, Patch, Phillips, Raymond, Robbins, Sargent, Sawyer, Stearns, Stevens, Stone, Taylor (2), Whitney, Wheeler, Willard, Wood (2), and Wyman. The work is mostly typescripts with some thermofax copies. There are a few maps and two photographs.

Gustavus Adolphus Hinckley papers, 1883-1905
Hinckley, Gustavus A. (Gustavus Adolphus), 1822-1905
Mss 419
4.6 linear ft. (35 v.)
The papers include transcripts of the Barnstable, Mass., town records [including vital records; v.6 has family records], 1640-1866, in 11 volumes plus a 1-volume index copied by Abbie L. Hinckley; Barnstable County, Mass., probate records, 1685-1742, in 7 volumes plus a 1-volume index; and the "Bourne Papers" [John, Melatiah (1722-1778), Richard (1739-1826) and Silvanus (b. 1731) Bourne], a letterbook covering 1748-1790, extracts from the log book of William Parker on board the Derby (ship), 1813-1814, Bible record of Silvanus Bourne (1694-1763) in 253 pages. The last few pages contain a listing of many people and how they were sick, likely of smallpox, referring to inoculation, and a copy of a survey of Jonathan Bourne's land at Roxbury, Mass., in 1774. Barnstable, Mass., births and marriages, 1634-1756, is attributed to Gustavus A. Hinckley, though the handwriting is different. There are Old Colony records relating to the town of Barnstable, 1633-1691.

James Bolard More papers
More, James Boland, 1907-1993.
Mss 420
3.3 linear ft.
Draft finding aid in the library.
Genealogical notes, pedigrees and typescripts on the More, Bolard, Innes, Brennesholtz and other allied families. There are many photocopies of deeds, wills and other records from American and Scottish sources as well as 102 photographs.

Stedman Shumway Hanks papers, 1903-1974
Hanks, Stedman Shumway, 1889-1979.
Mss 421
2.1 linear ft. (12 v.)
This collection is in three parts. The first part is biographical notes, 1903-1947 is further divided into volumes entitled: (1) Groton and Harvard, 1912; (2) American Embassy, London, 1913; (3) Dept. of State, 1916; (4) Aviation Signal Corps, 1919; (5) Mass. Aeronautics Comm., 1936; (6) N.Y. Stedman Hanks & Co. Airports, 1940; (7) Army Air Corps, 1941; (8) Europe-Airlines, I.C.A.O., 1947; (9) U.S. Congress, 1947; (10) Army Air Forces, 1948. The second part is a "catalogue of political and historical collections" (1961) including literature, donations (this one and to other institutions), memorials, miniatures, daguerreotypes, portraits, works of art, and tombstones. The third part is "notes" or draft for a proposed book "Making of an American" (1974). There are two genealogical charts (1967, 1969 rev.) on the Hanks family and allied family ancestry. Many of these volumes contain charts and mounted photographs.

Hanks family papers [notes]
Hitchcock, Caroline Hanks, b. 1863.
Mss 422
0.4 linear ft. (3 v.)
This collection contains the Hanks Family Notes in one volume (1938) and supplement in two volumes (1946). This work has a large section devoted to Nancy Hanks Lincoln, mother of Abraham Lincoln. The first volume states that "the original papers are loaned to Dr. Louis A. Warren, Director, Lincoln National Life Foundation, Fort Wayne, Indiana. The following papers with additional notes were used by Mrs. Susan C. Tufts, in preparing the article on the Hanks family which was published in the Register of the New England Historical and Geneaological [sic] Society, dated January, 1932. Gift of Stedman Shumway Hanks, Manchester-by-the-Sea, Massachusetts." (t.p.) The first volume is a photoreproduction.

Genealogy of Francis Weekes ... and collateral lines, Bowne, Burrowes, Carpenter, Cooke, Cornell, Davenport, De Forest, Emery, Feake, Fones, Freeman, Goodwin, Fowler, Hoag, Ireland, Jansen, Kierstede, Kip, Montagne, Mosher, Paddy, Reddocke, Sands, Stevenson, Sutton, Taber, Thorn, Warren, Winthrop
Weeks, Frank Edgar, 1857-1946.
Mss 423
4 p. l., 183, 183 1/2-411, 411 1/2-497, 499-746 n
1938
Typescript with illustrations, plate, portraits, maps, plans and facsimiles that are mounted.

A Caswell encyclopedia
Haler, Noreen Ellen Smith, 1922-.
Mss 424
5 v. (2321, 369 p.); 29 cm.
c1998

The Hickok genealogy: descendants of William Hickocks of Farmington, Connecticut
Hickok, Charles Nelson, 1879-1945.
Mss 425
1 v.; 28 cm.
1936-1938
This typescript was created between March of 1936 and April of 1938 which contains a Register-style family group sheet for each individual descendant who is assigned a number. That number is the "page number" given in the upper right-handed corner of the page. Each page has a header with the month and year of its creation.

Joel Warren Norcross papers, 1882-1887
Norcross, Joel Warren, b. 1821.
Mss 426
3 v. (456, 335, 264 p.)
The author has written two genealogies. The first one, "Norcross genealogy, descendants of Jeremiah and William" was written at Lynn, Mass., in 1882 which is bound in two volumes. The second one, "Fay family, descendants of John of Marlborough, Mass." was written at Boston, Mass., in 1887 which is also bound.

Rough genealogical notes for the Tilden and related families
Brown, Farwell T. (Farwell Tilden), 1910-.
Mss 427
[589] p.; 28 cm.
This work includes photocopies of typescript notes, letters, photographs, books, and manuscripts concerning the Tilden family of New England, with references to Briggs, Emerson, Cooper, Warren and Powers families. Particular attention is given to Rochester, Vt.

Genealogical notes on the Dimick families in North America
Dimick, Alan R. (Alan Robert), 1932-.
Mss 428
[6], 2, 1, 3, 7, 16, 35, 55, 59, 54, 44, 43, 18, 2, 9, 23, 24, [73] p.; 28 cm.
1997 July
1997 rev. ed.
This work is the descendants of Thomas Dimick of Barnstable, Mass., for 13 generations. There is a file of "unconnected" Dimocks arranged geographically.

Frank Storey Osgood papers, 1923-1931
Osgood, Frank Storey.
Mss 430
3 v. ([73, 4, 120, 92, [4] p.): facsim.; 29 cm.
Three typescripts on the Caldwell family. Vol. 1 is the descendants of "Alexander Caldwell of Litchfield, New Hampshire and his descendants" (1923). Vol. 2 is "The History of Joseph Caldwell and his descendants" (1926). Twenty-five copies were made of this volume distributed by Wilders Genealogical Bookshop, Somerville, Mass. Vol. 3 is "William Caldwell of Londonderry and Chester, N.H., and his descendants" (1931).

Account book of Moses Copeland, 1764-1787
Copeland, Moses, 1741-1817.
Mss 432
[3], 13-193, [1] leaves; 31 cm.
Moses Copeland was born in Milton, Mass., and during the time period of the account book, was a resident of Saint George and later Warren, Maine. On leaf 193, Moses started a brief biography of his life with about one note per year from 1758 to 1774. The first half of the book is of entries between 1764 to 1772 with some continuation at the bottom of these pages from 1780-1787. The second half of the volume contains accounts mainly from the 1770s. The binding is in very poor condition.

Records of the people of Athens, Somerset County, Maine
Prince, Elaine Bush (Elaine Louise Bush), 1922-.
Mss 433
147, 79, 210, 20, 18, 22, 18, 13, 12, 14, 18, [1], 17, [13] p.; 28 cm.
This is a collection compiled by the author from 1988 to 1998. It is made up of three main section labelled "Obituaries," vital records, and "Miscellany." The first section is transcriptions from modern newspapers of the area. The second section is in two parts. Part one is vital records from several source including the town records. This includes births, 1900-1944, marriages, 1807-1820, 1829-1899, and deaths, ca. 1900-1996. Part two is deaths from town reports, 1900-1944, state vital records [ie. 1892+], and data from cemeteries in Athens. The third section is in seven parts. The main themes are extracts from newspapers, materials relating to Somerset Academy and other schools, and history of the town.

William Herbert Wood papers 1876-1953 (bulk 1933-1952)
Wood, W. Herbert (William Herbert), 1888-1953.
Mss 435
6 linear ft.

Louise Redfern Pells papers
Pells, Louise Redfern (Louise Mildred Redfern), 1908
Mss 436
4.5 linear ft.
Draft finding aid in library.
Consists of notebooks of transcribed data collected on research trips and folders of family group charts for the Barrett, Brady, Brides, Burke, Callahan, Clarkin, Costello, Curran, Delany, Dowling, Fay, Flaherty, Grace, Haslam, Kelleher, Kellett, Leonard, Lucey, Lynch, McCaffrey, McDonald, McEntee, McGowan, McMahon, Nathan, Pells, Plunkett, Smith, Victory, and Whelan / Whelen families. Includes photocopies and transcriptions of source data – amounts vary from family to family.

Janna Lee Jones Kalina papers
Kalina, Janna Lee Jones, 1942-1995.
Mss 437
1.5 linear ft.
Draft finding aid in the library.
Consists of the ahnentafel of Kalina's grandfather Howard Seneca[10] Smith (1889-1979) back to James[1] Smith (d. 1676) of Weymouth, Mass. as well as the descendants of Joseph[7] Smith (1792-1842). The Kinney genealogy consists of the descendants of Mary Almina Kinney (1834-1887) who married Charles Deming[8] Smith (1830-1895). Janina attempted unsuccessfully to relate her Kinneys to Henry Kinne (1624-1696) who married Ann Howard (1632-1680) and to Andrew Kinny who married Ariantje Bennet (b.1773) of Brooklyn, N.Y. There are many photographs of family and friends particularly in Gouverneur and Watertown, N.Y. but many of these are unidentified.

Arthur Morse Jones papers
Jones, Arthur Morse, 1875-1943.
Mss 438
3.9 linear ft.
Draft finding aid in library.
Genealogy on the descendants of Cornelius[1] Jones of Stamford, Conn. Contains information on a number of other early New England Jones families, especially on the families of Robert (b. ca. 1633) of Salisbury, Mass., Thomas (d.1654) of Guilford, Ct., and William (1624-1706) of New Haven. There are genealogies on many allied families, in particular , the families of Robert Harrington (1616-1707); John Hoyt (d.1687/8); Job Judkins (d.after 1672); and John Leavens (c.1581-1647). The Morse genealogy concerns the descendants of the brothers Anthony (1607-1686) and William (1614-1683) as well as the descendants of Mark Morse of Marblehead, Mass. who married Christian Hoyle in 1699. The bulk of the source material consists of Cambridge Land Records with many maps.

Session Book [Aghadowey, Co. Londonderry, Ireland], 1702-1725
Kernohan, J.W., (Joseph William), 1869-1923.
Mss 439
1 v. (131 leaves); 35 cm.
Handwritten transcription of the original by J.W. Kernohan, Secretary of the Presbyterian Historical Society of Ireland. The first fifteen pages were not transcribed since they were missing (book begins with session 25). Includes letters (tipped in after the records) between Mr. Kernohan and the donor concerning the transcription of these records (fees etc.). The donor wrote that they were particularly interested in obtaining the records concerning James McGregor, a Pastor at Aghadowey (ordained 25 June 1701) who emigrated to America with some of his Scots-Irish Congregation and settled Londonderry, NH in 1719.

John Insley Coddington papers
Coddington, John Insley, 1903-1991.
Mss 440
Linear ft.
Draft finding aid in library.

Thomas Nixon papers, 1777-1800 (bulk 1777-1780)
Nixon, Thomas, 1736-1800.
E263/M4/N59/1995 Microfilm also Mss 441
Access to original papers restricted, use microfilm copy.
2 microfilm reels (7 orderly/return books; 1 letter)
Unpublished finding aid in the library.
The papers, 1777-1780, are comprised mostly of orderly books for the 6th Massachusetts Regiment while under his command. Also part of the collection is two return books for the same period, one letter book from 1779, and an account book which contains five pages of the inventory of Thomas Nixon's estate likely by his executor. This collection is not complete by any means. However, some known material in other repositories, as researched by Bob McDonald, will give a more complete picture (see inventory).

The records of ye second church in Berwick, Maine
Second Church (Berwick, Me.)
Mss 443
Access to original record restricted; Use published version.
1 vol. (148 p.); 31 cm.
Additional form: transcribed version; published as *Records of the First & Second Churches of Berwick, ME.*
Maine Genealogical Society Special Publication No. 33 (Rockport, ME: Picton Press, 1999)
Original record book of the Second Church of Berwick, Maine (also called the Blackbury Hill Church).
Records include "members in full communion in this church" (1755-1794), "catalogue of members owning the covenant and having liberty to offer themselves and children to baptism, both male and female" (1756-1767); male/female "children brought to baptism by their parents one or both of them or by those who had the care of their education" (1755-1822) and a list of marriages that "were found elsewhere recorded by the Revd Mr John Morse first pastor of this church and are entred here in the book by me Matthew Merriam Pastor" (1755-1843). The verso of the last page also has a list of marriages from 1856.

Ledger of Daniel Browne, 1762-1776, 1778-1801
Browne, Daniel, 1739-ca. 1801.
Van Vleck, Teunis, 1784-1857.
Mss 444
1 vol.; 37 cm.
Entries relate to tailoring; however, the entries by Daniel's son-in-law, Teunis Van Vleck, also include accounts of the weather. Includes computer typescript transcription by the donor of the inside cover and one of the end sheets which identifies the book as belonging to Daniel Browne. The donor also provided computer typescripts concerning a short history of Daniel Browne and his ledger, an index of the names within the ledger and pedigree charts for Daniel Browne and family.

Faith Adams Griefen papers, 700-1988 (bulk 1800-1934)
Griefen, Faith Adams, 1915-
Dickinson, John, 1732-1808. -- The liberty song.
Gale, Wakefield, 1797-1881.
Mss 445
3.75 linear ft.
Unpublished finding aid in the library.
Collection is comprised of a wide range of original documents including correspondence, a Bible record, deeds, diaries, family registers, marriage intentions, newspaper clippings, probate records, recipes, receipts and wills. There are numerous poems, stories, lectures and addresses written by various family members. The graphics, many of which are identified, include daguerreotypes, ambrotypes, tintypes, and a miniature portrait. Collection focuses on the family of William Sydney and Elizabeth Inglesbee (Hallett) Fisher and the family of their daughter and son-in-law, Edward Payson and Ellen (Fisher) Adams. The Hallett and Fisher families lived in Yarmouth and Barnstable, Mass. Born in Castine, Maine, Edward Payson Adams lived on the Sandwich Islands (now Hawaii) for twenty years before returning to Cambridge, Mass. in 1885. Of particular interest is a record of marriages by Rev. Wakefield Gale from 1826-1880. Ellen Fisher Adams' involvement with the Women's Suffrage Movement is represented in this collection by a few letters to government officials and the editor of the Herald as well as a typescript list of "Songs for a Women Suffrage Rally". The collection also has a hand written musical score for "Blessed are the poor in spirit" and a 6 July 1768 letter from John Dickinson (1732-1808) in Philadelphia to James Otis (1725-1783) in Boston includes the revised lyrics for Dickinson's The Liberty Song. There are diaries written by three generations of women -- Elizabeth's mother Mehetable Davis (Cobb) Hallett, Elizabeth Inglesbee (Hallett) Fisher herself, and Elizabeth's daughter Ellen (Fisher) Adams. Finally, the collection has several handmade children's books either hand written or a typescript with hand drawn illustrations including Rollo's Reminiscences, The bunnie nonsense book (dated 1898), and The Last Leaf of Lettuce.

Indenture, 1826 October 21
Hayward, Edward.
Hayward, George.
Hayward, John.
Hayward, William.
Rogers, John.
Mss 447
1 leaf; vellum; 58 x 77 cm.
Deed between William Hayward of Ashford & others (John, George and Edward Hayward) and Richard Greenhill to surrender copyhold deed of the manor of Ashford by way of mortgage for securing 350 pounds and interest (William Haywood owed Richard Greenhill 200 pounds and borrowed another 150 pounds). Witnessed by Jn Rogers. Verso has receipt signed by William Hayward that he received the 150 pounds owed him. There is also a note dated 2d Aug 1842 stating that Mr Wm Hayward & others to Mr Greenhill further charge for securing 200 pounds interest.

Register for the parish of Newchurch, 1574-1813
Newchurch (Pendle, England)
Mss 448
1 v. (484 leaves); 33 cm.
Transcription of original record. Includes alphabetical list of baptisms 1574-1813 (225 leaves), marriages 1582-1813 (108 leaves), and burials 1574 to 1813 (151 leaves).

Tucker family of Clay County, Illinois
Priebe, Kathleen.
Mss 449
0.25 linear ft: ill., maps, ports., coat of arms, geneal. tables; 28 cm.
1992
Photocopy of original record comprised of family group sheets and individual data sheets with accompanying documentation including obituaries, census records, vital and family records, etc.

Lapham genealogy: descendants of John Lapham (1635-1710)
Kitson, Phyllis S., 1924-.
Mss 450
878 p.; 28 cm.
1994
Typescript.

Genealogy of the family Wolf of Brensbach, Germany: immigrated 1832 to the United States of America
Lundberg, Charles William, 1934-.
Mss 451
500 p.: geneal. tables, maps; 28 cm.
1999
Typescript.

The Howards of Brooksville, Maine
Brownell, Richard J.
Mss 452
288 leaves; 28 cm.
[1989]
Typescript.

The Warner heritage: Washington Wright Warner descendants, 1827-1991
Parsons, Charlette Warner, 1919-.
Mss 453
2 v.: ill.; 28 cm.
1991
Typescript.

Hutcheson - Hutchinson
Dean, Joseph Lynn, 1918-.
Mss 454
417, 8, 79 p.; 28 cm.
1994 revised ed.
Typescript originally produced 1988, revised 1993 and 1994.

Reed family tree
Mss 455 [Location: Mss flat storage]
1 photograph: geneal. tables; 26 x 35 cm.
Photograph of a four generation descendancy chart for Nathan Parker Reed and Ella May Burgess depicted using a colored family tree motif.

Gene loqie des Pelchat branche de Rene familles des numeros ... inclus avec la Gaspesie
Mss 456
[259] leaves; 28 cm.
1971?

Smith - Bartholomew family papers
Mss 457
0.5 linear ft.
Unpublished finding aid in the library.
Personal correspondence of the Bartholomew and Smith families. In addition to typical topics such as social activities, illnesses, and family matters, the letters often record the writer's great concern with personal salvation, piety, and submission to the will of God. Woodward Bartholomew's letters describe life as a traveling book salesman in the southern states during the 1830s. Letters between Sarah Jane Bartholomew and Ira Smith chronicle their courtship and marriage, their subsequent health problems and recuperation at Massachusetts General Hospital, and the emotional and psychological struggles of a man who became a clergyman but felt unworthy of his calling. Correspondence from the Kansas Territory in the 1850s and 60s discusses illnesses, troubles between the Unionists and Secessionists, roaming guerrilla parties, preparations for war, and concerns about the Indians. There is also a small amount of poetry written by Sarah Jane Bartholomew.

The Aldrich family genealogy: descendants of George Aldrich of Mendon, MA
Aldrich, Ralph Ernest, 1902-1984.
Mss 458
1.85 linear ft.; 28 cm.
[1998 typescript ed.]
Photocopy of computer typescript genealogy. Part A. George and Katherine (Seald) Aldrich and their children -- Part B. Joseph (2) and Patience (Osborne) Aldrich and their descendants -- Part C. John (2), His wives, Sarah (Thomson), and Sarah (Leach) Aldrich, and their descendants -- Part D. Peter (2) and Mehitable (Swazey) Aldrich and their descendants -- Part E. Jacob (2) and Huldah (Thayer) Aldrich and their descendants.

Howard family papers, 1860-1910
Howard, Stanley, b. ca. 1839.
Mss 459
0.25 linear ft. (ca. 160 items).
Consists of letters written by four brothers - Stanley, Charles, Henry, and Edward Howard - to their sister Ella and/or their parents in Leeds, a section of Northampton, Mass. Corporal Stanley Howard served with Co. G 27th Regt Mass. Vol. from 1861-1865 and wrote from such locations as Camp Hampshire, Newbern and Washington NC; Annapolis and Baltimore MD; York PA; and Julians Creek VA. Charles A. Howard was at Carver Hospital, Washington D.C. early in the War, and later at Ft. Ellsworth VA, Newport Barracks, Annapolis MD, and Plymouth NC. Henry N. Howard served with Co. D, 10th Reg. MA Volunteers and was wounded at Malvern Hill. His letters are from, among other places, Camp Brightwood, Washington D.C.

Zephaniah Buffinton papers, 1787-1871
Buffinton, Zephaniah, b. 1771.
Mss 460
0.5 linear ft.
Unpublished finding aid in the library.
The bulk of the collection is business-related documents from about 1800 through 1850, including real estate transactions and memoranda relating to property in Bristol and Berkshire Counties, Massachusetts; financial notes, receipts, and accounts; legal notes and depositions; miscellaneous memoranda; and a few letters.

The American family Way
Way, Harry Abel.
Mss 461
5 v. (1210, 804 p.); 28 cm.
[1999]
Printout from Microsoft Works 3.1 Database compiled from The Way family of Nantucket by Mary Elizabeth Way (1969); Descendants of Robert and Hannah Hickman Way by D. Herbert Way (1975); The Connecticut Way Family by Harry A Way (1989); The New York Way Family by Harry A Way (1995); The South Carolina Way Family by Harry A Way (1996); United States Census Records 1790 thru 1850; United States Soundex Films 1880 thru 1920; and Ontario, Canada Census Films 1851 thru 1901. The first three volumes are records for individuals of the Way family organized alphabetically by given name: Volume I A thru George; Volume II H thru Nottie and Volume III O thru William. The last two volumes contain census records organized alphabetically by state: Volume IV Alabama thru Montana and Volume V Census Nebraska thru Wyoming and Ontario, Canada.

[John C. Leighton] family register, 1805-1854
Mss 462 [Mss flat storage]
1 sheet: col. ill.; 25.5 x 36 cm.
Hand colored lithograph (c.1846) printed by N. Currier completed in ms. for the Leighton family of Addison, Me.

[Leonard Enos] family register, 1820-1905
Enos, Leonard, 1820-1905.
Mss 463 [Mss flat storage]
1 sheet; col. ill.: 25.5 x 36 cm.
Hand colored lithograph (c.1847) printed by F.R & E.C. Kellogg completed in ms. for the Enos family of Smyrna, N.Y.

Account book of David Chamberlain, 1809-1861
Chamberlain, David.
Mss 464
1 v. (ca. 534 p.); 33 cm.
Account book for a tavern kept by David Chamberlain in Jefferson, N.H. Entries include purchases of whiskey and/or gin along with some food items such as potatoes, rye, oats, sugar, etc.

William Burnham & Sons account book, 1844-1849
William Burnham & Sons.
Mss 465
1 v. (357 p.); 35 cm.
Account book for a general store in Cherryfield, Maine. Entries concern the purchase of items like sugar, vinegar, molasses, flour, pork, corn, tea, tobacco, nails, silk, gloves etc.

Day book, 1808-1818
Mss 466
412 p.; 40 cm.
Day book for a country store in Bath, Maine. The first eleven sheets were torn in half. Entries concern a large number of products including sugar, tea, veal, tobacco, grog, clams, eggs, nails, hops, brandy, snuff, rye, pork, vinegar, molases, candles, rum, chocolate, beef, coffee, etc.

Day book, 1798-1801
Bradford, William.
Mss 467
367 p.; 39 cm.
Day book for a country store in Connecticut (Glastonbury, East Hampton, and Marlborough are mentioned). Entries concern purchases of goods such as rum, cloth, flannel, snuff, buttons, gamblet, hose, tea, sugar, brandy, molasses, potatoes, hat, comb, tobacco, ginger, wine, silk etc.

Day book, 1800-1801
Mss 468
[455] p.; 41 cm.
Day book for a country store in Lebanon, Maine. Entries include purchases of rum, sugar, corn, wine, snuff, tobacco, molasses, tea, silk, raisins, brandy, nails etc.

Day book, 1815-1816
Mss 469
1 v.
Day book for a country general store/tavern in New Gloucester, Maine. Entries include purchases of items such as rum, tobacco, coffee, gin, fish, crackers, tea, eggs, butter, cider, shovel, cotton, sugar, powder, brandy, indigo, etc.

Day book 1840-1841
Richardson & Co.
Mss 470
254 p.; 41 cm.
Day book for a store in Medway, Massachusetts. Entries include the purchase of sugar, tea, molasses, coffee, sugar, mackerel, scythe, butter, shoes, oil, etc.

Nahum Sawin Cutler papers, 1538-1685, 1883-1939
Cutler, Nahum Sawin, b. 1837.
Mss 471
0.25 linear ft.
Unpublished finding aid in the library.
Extracts from English parish registers and transcriptions of English wills concerning the Cutler family, 1538-1685. Includes correspondence and clippings sent to Nahum S. Cutler from 1883 to 1939. The bulk of the letters were received after he published the Cutler Memorial in 1889 and concern errors, additional information, requests for copies, etc.

Holsen roots: Cisel, Holste (1803), Holze (1829), Holtz (1849), Holtsen (1850), Holsen (1860), Kniep-Keneipp, Kühn-Keen
Holsen, Paul J. (Paul Jennings), 1940-.
Mss 473
1 v. (various pagings): ill.; 28 cm.
c 1994
Computer typescript.

Andrew Edward Richardson family register, 1813-1866
Mss 474 [Mss flat storage]
1 sheet: col. ill.; 26 x 36 cm.
1845
Hand colored family register lithograph by N. Currier (c1845) completed in ms. for the Andrew Edward Richardson family of Dorset, VT.

Joseph Prescott family register, 1808-1940
Mss 475 [Mss flat storage]
1 sheet: col. ill.; 29 x 40 cm.
Hand colored lithograph by D.W. Kellogg & Co. completed in ms. for the Joseph and Harriet (Marshall) Prescott family of Natick, Mass.

Rockwell & Newcomb genealogies: American & Canadian, (1630) - (1760)
Rockwell, Warren Ayres.
Mss 476
1 v. (various pagings): ill., ports.; 30 cm.
Typescript (photocopy)

Stoddard genealogy
Stoddard, Oliver Hazard Perry, 1844-1901.
Mss 477
233 leaves; 28 cm.
Annotated typescript genealogy on the descendants of John Stoddard (d. 1661) of England and Hingham, Mass. for nine generations.

Rawson family Bible
Mss 478
Access to original Bible is restricted; Use transcription in *Register*, 39[1885]:59 or photocopy.
1620?
Original family Bible.

The self-interpreting Bible: containing the sacred text of the Old and New Testaments: translated from the original tongues, and with the former translations diligently compared and revised, to which are annexed, marginal references and illustrations, an exact summary of the several books, a paraphrase on the most obscure or important parts, an analysis of the contents of each chapter, explanatory notes, and evangelical reflections
Brown, John, 1722-1787, ed.
Mss 479
Access to original Bible is restricted; Use preservation photocopy, Mss A 728
[1046] p., [17] . of plates: plates, map; 43 cm.
M.DCC.XCII
Original family Bible.

[William Putnam] family register, 1755-1828
Mss 480 [Mss flat storage]
1 sheet; 41 x 35 cm.
Oval shaped printed family register completed in ms. for the William and Submit (Fisk) Putnam family of Upton and Buckland, Mass.

Julie Overton papers
Overton, Julie.
Mss 481
2.2 linear ft.
The collection includes family group sheets for the descendants of Peter Twiss (1654-1743) of Salem, Mass., as well as other Twiss and Twist family members and allied families. In addition, there is correspondence between Julie Overton and Twiss/Twist family members, and source data such as cemetery records, census data, and military service records from the Revolutionary War and Civil War.

George and Sarah Marshall diaries, 1860-1908
Marshall, George Lester, 1833-1882.
Marshall, Sarah Larkin, 1838-1908.
Mss 482
2.5 linear ft.
Original diary consisting of 22 volumes dating from 1860 to 1882 written by George Marshall, a farmer in Tolland, Mass. His entries include brief descriptions of the weather, what he did that day, and sometimes a brief note concerning local or national events. There is also the diary written by his wife Sarah (Larkin) Marshall consisting of 29 volumes written between 1883 and 1908. Her entries include descriptions of the hard work of a farmer's wife as well as the activities of friends and relatives. Includes typescript genealogies on the Bentley and Marshall families as well as photographs, including daguerreotypes and tintypes, of family members.

Thorndike family papers
Mss 483
2.58 linear ft.
Draft finding aid in the library.
Collection of documents that were either created by or relate to the Thorndike family. Most of the documents focus on the families of John Prince[7] Thorndike (1784-1865) and John's son, George Quincy[8] Thorndike (1827-1886). The bulk of the documents are the business papers of John Prince and George Quincy Thorndike including papers relating to ropewalk lands, bonds, contracts, correspondence and deeds concerning stores and other property in Boston, Mass. The personal papers include a marriage certificate, correspondence, Sarah Hill Thorndike's diary of a voyage to Europe circa 1847, and Capt. J.F. Thorndike's Log of the siege of Charleston, 1864. In addition, there are charts and a genealogical information on the descendants of John Thorndike (1603-1668) and extracts of Thorndike family information from various English sources.

Richard Andrew Pierce papers
Pierce, Richard Andrew.
Mss 484
4.33 linear ft.
Unpublished register in the library.
Over three-quarters of this collection consists of research conducted by R. Andrew Pierce for clients. Most of the folders contain copies of correspondence by Mr. Pierce to the client, correspondence from the client to Mr. pierce and various supporting documentation either supplied by the client or researched by Mr. pierce. Over 80% of the research done by Mr. Pierce centers on finding the ancestors or documentation for individuals and families of Irish and New England descent. The second subgroup contains mostly documents, original and copies and notes. Over half of the folders in subgroup II pertain to Mr. Pierce's own ancestry. There are also three folders containing information pertaining to the lineage of former United States of America Presidents, John F. Kennedy, Ronald W. Reagon, and William J. Clinton.

[Patrick Kiernan] family register, 1845-1852
Mss 486 [Mss flat storage]
1 sheet: col. ill.; 22 x 29 cm.
Lithograph by Kelloggs & Comstock handcolored and completed in manuscript for the Patrick and Sarah Keirnan family of Rhode Island.

[William F. Dame] family register, 1828-1946
Mss 487 [Mss flat storage]
1 sheet: col. ill.; 26 x 36 cm.
Lithograph by Currier & Ives (c1852) handcolored and completed in manuscript for the William F. and Betsey C. Dame family of Dover, NH.

[Peter Nichols] family register, 1803-1914
Mss 488 [Mss flat storage]
1 sheet: col. ill.; 26 x 36 cm.
Lithograph by Currier & Ives (c1864) handcolored and completed in ms. for the Peter and Lucretia Nichols family.

[James M. Eaton] family register, 1832-1886
Mss 489 [Mss flat storage]
1 sheet: col. ill.; 26 x 36 cm.
Lithograph by N. Currier handcolored and completed in ms. for the James M. and Nancy (Balentine) Eaton family.

[Nathaniel Gammon] family register, 1808-1894
Mss 490 [Mss flat storage]
1 sheet: col. ill.; 26 x 36 cm.
Lithograph by Kellogg handcolored and completed in ms. for the Nathaniel and Edel Gammon family of Phillips, Me.

[Horace A. Davis] family register, 1819-1869
Mss 491 [Mss flat storage]
1 sheet: col. ill.; 26 x 36 cm.
Lithograph by Kellogg & Comstock handcolored and completed in ms. for the Horace A. and Harriett N. Davis family of Northfield, Vt.

[Aaron Varney] family register, 1767-1860
Mss 492 [Mss flat storage]
1 sheet: col. ill.; 26 x 36 cm.
Lithograph by Kelloggs & Comstock handcolored and completed in ms. for the Aaron and Anne (Clemens) Varney family.

[George Hall White] family register, 1815-1855
Mss 493 [Mss flat storage]
1 sheet: col. ill.; 26 x 36 cm.
Lithograph by Kellogg handcolored and completed in ms. for the George Hall and Eliza Morgan White family of Elba, NY and Chicopee, Mass.

[Jeremiah Ward] family register, 1774-1847
Mss 494 [Mss flat storage]
1 sheet; 38 x 29.5 cm.
Lithograph by "H. Fe" [note: the rest of the surname is missing but was probably Hiram Ferry] completed in ms. for the Jeremiah and Hannah Ward family of Buckland, Mass. A 12 x 15 cm. section of the lower right corner is missing.

Edmund Swett Rousmaniere papers, 1869-1941
Rousmaniere, Edmund Swett, 1858-1926.
Rousmaniere, Abigail Whitmore Swett, 1820-1895.
Rousmaniere, Sophie Knight, 1865-1944.
Mss 496
1.1 linear ft.
Unpublished finding aid in the library.
Primarily correspondence from Edmund Swett Rousmaniere to his mother, Abigail Whitmore Swett Rousmaniere, or his wife, Sophie Knight Rousmaniere, and vice versa. The letters generally concern family matters (travel, health and activities of friends and relatives) but some of Edmund's letters to his mother were written during an 1885 trip to Europe. Much of the correspondence to Edmund during 1895 concerns the death of his mother and many of the letters from 1899 concern Edmund accepting the call to Grace Church in Providence. Includes some class notes and adresses written by Edmund and a few photographs.

Essex County Deed collection, 1697-1825
Mss 497
1.67 linear ft.
Draft calendar in the library.
Collection of miscellaneous deeds from Essex County, Mass.

Ames & Fobes Company account book, 1794-1836
Ames & Fobes Company (Oakham, Mass.)
Mss 498
1 v. (434 p.); 33 cm.
Original account book for a innkeeper and merchant in Oakham, Mass. Entries includes items such as rum, brandy, molasses, sugar, cider, tobacco, butter, cheese, nails, buttons, shoes, cloth, seeds, and bushels of potatoes, corn and/or rye, etc.

Proprietors of Charles River Bridge records, 1785-1842
Proprietors of Charles River Bridge.
Mss 499
1 v. (288 p.); 33 cm.
Record of the meetings for the Proprietors of Charles River Bridge, a corporation and body politic incorporated by the state legislature for the purpose of building a bridge in the place where the ferry between Boston and Charlestown was then kept and maintaining the same for 40 years (extended for an additional 30 years in 1792).

Letterbook of Thomas Fitch, 1714-1717
Fitch, Thomas.
F73.4/F58 Microfilm also Mss 500
1 microfilm reel. Orginial is 1 v. ([348] p.); 37 cm.
Access to original is restricted: Use microfilm.

Karen Buss papers, 1485-1997 (bulk 1610-1966)
Buss, Karen, 1941-1988.
Mss 501
1.3 linear ft.
Unpublished register in the library.
Genealogical notes, charts, maps, correspondence, photographs, and photocopies of documents concerning the Buss, Prentice and Wise families. The Buss line is traced from William Buss of England through descendants in Mass., N.H., and Ohio to Karen Buss of California. The Prentice line covers from Ireland (ca. 1816) to Canada, California and Ohio while the Wise family line goes from England (ca. 1816) to California. Limited research was done concerning twenty-three allied families. Although the collection includes 868 will abstracts, many dealing with Delaware and Pennsylvania families, it is not readily apparent how this material relates to the rest of the collection.

Corydon L. Ford papers, 1604-1894 (bulk 1621-1870)
Ford, Corydon L., (Corydon La), 1813-1894.
Mss 502
1.9 linear ft.
Unpublished finding aid in the library.
Consists of 19 notebooks with handwritten notes, transcriptions, etc. by C.L. Ford. Some of these notebooks represent early genealogical data gathering efforts, and others are more finished works based on the earlier research notes. Collection includes correspondence written to C.L. Ford in response to his solicitation for information regarding the Ford family in America. Most of these letters are from Ford family members, and give as much information as they knew about their own family history. C.L. Ford incorporated this information into his Ford family notebooks. In 1900, Susan Blanchard Kidder compiled the "Index to Ford genealogy," a bound typescript every name index, arranged by notebook, for the first 18 notebooks.

Francis Sedgwick Watson correspondence, 1879-1881
Watson, Francis Sedgwick, 1853-1942.
Mss 503
67 items (250 p.)
Letters written to family and friends while studying medicine and traveling in Europe.

Donald G. Farrington papers
Farrington, Donald G.
Mss 504
11.67 linear ft.
Genealogical notes, family group sheets, etc. on the descendants of Edmund and John Farrington, miscellaneous other Farrington families and allied families.

The Abell family of America
Abell, Horace A. (Horace Avery), b. 1883.
Abell, lewis Parker, b. 1873.
Mss 505
2 v.: coat of arms, photographs, ports.; 28 cm.
[1926]
Carbon copy typescript genealogy concerning the English ancestry and American descendants of Robert Abell of Rehoboth, Mass.

The Bottomly and allied lines
Foskett, Marion Martin.
Mss 506
0.25 linear ft.
2000
Family group sheets and photocopies of some source documents for the Bottomly family of Worcester, Mass. Includes sheets, generally one to two per family, for 24 allied families.

Van Wart genealogy
Van Woert, Irving.
Mss 507
[39], 478 leaves: ill.; 28 cm.
[1952?]
Typescript genealogy (photocopy).

Alden family letters, 1832-1883 (bulk: 1832-1844)
Mss 508
Approx. 85 letters; 28-31 cm.
Correspondence of Albert, Caleb H., Timothy, and Martin L. Alden, sons of the Rev. and Mrs. Martin Alden (Mary Kingman Alden) of West Barnstable, Mass. The sons resided at Barre, West Barnstable, Lancaster, and Lynn, Mass. Most letters date from the second quarter of the nineteenth century, and cover typical family and domestic subjects. There are also numerous references to Timothy Alden's efforts to perfect a type-setting machine. A brief evaluation of his work appears in a front-page article in "The World" (a New York newspaper), dated 23 August 1868. Other items in the collection include an advertising card for the Alden Type Setting & Distributing Machine Co., and several miscellaneous letters to Alden family members.

Howe genealogies update: vol I supplement #2 vol II supplement #2
Duane, Edward Howe, 1920-.
Mss 509
0.25 linear ft.: ill., maps, geneal. tables, photographs
2001
Typescript genealogy on the John Howe family of Marlborough and Sudbury, Mass. (Vol I Suppl. #2) and the Abraham Howe family of Roxbury, James Howe family of Ipswich, Abraham Howe family of Marlborough, Edward Howe family of Lynn, and an appendix of various Howe families who do not fit into any of the above family linages.... (Vol II Suppl. #2). Includes copies of some source documentation and tipped in photographs.

The ancestry of Samuel, Freda and John Warner. [Warner - Harrington]
Warner, Frederick C. (Frederick Chester), 1886-
Mss 510
5 v. (937 leaves): ill.; 28 cm.
1949
Typescript.

Standish, Maine births, marriages and deaths 1759 to 1900
Mss 511
1 v. (135, 23, 19, 12 leaves); 33 cm.
Handwritten transcription of original records.

Hopkinton Mass. records
Fitch, Elijah, 1746-1788.
Hopkinton (Mass.)
Mss 512
1 v.; 32 cm.
Handwritten transcription of original records including cemetery inscriptions (leaves 1-77), personal records (leaves 1-162), accounts of Deacon Elijah Fitch for attending funerals and digging graves, 1833-1840 (leaves 163-171), Hopkinton Rebellion Records (leaves 1-15), and church records, 1724-1838 (leaves 1-194).

American ancesters [sic] of interest to the descendants of either John(1) Smart of Exeter NH (-1652) [or] Patrick Kincaid of Brunswick Me. (1747-1821) and the various families certain their descendants have married into through the years
Norton, James A.
Mss 513
.25 linear ft.; 29 cm.
1953-63
Typescript genealogy.

Account book of Samuel Sewall, 1670-1728
Sewall, Samuel, 1652-1730.
Mss 514
Access to original record is restricted; Material extremely fragile.
1 v. (210 p.); 36 cm.
Original account book recording debits and credits. Besides the names of numerous individuals, there are entries concerning "Gratuities", "Connecticut contribution," "Point-Judith of Narragansett," "Commissioners for the Indian Affairs," "an account of books lent," "Council of Massachusetts" and "Arguments for reprinting the Bible in the Indian Language."

Early records of families in Andover
Abbott, Charlotte Helen, 1844-1921.
Mss 515
1.7 linear ft. (14 v.)
Photocopy of typescript genealogy, notes, correspondence, etc. on early settlers of Andover, Mass.

Genealogies of four early Massachusetts families: Balch, Bridge, Browne, and May
Browne, Charles, 1793-1856.
Mss 516
0.25 linear ft.
Handwritten genealogies treating the descendants of John and Margery Balch of Salem, 1626; John Bridge of Cambridge, 1631; Abraham and Lydia Brown of Watertown, 1636; and John May of Roxbury, 1628. Balch material includes correspondence from the 1840s, and a small notebook of data "copied verbatim from a memo prepared by Benj Balch of Salem." Bridge material includes correspondence from the 1840s. Brown material includes a printed chart, dating from the mid nineteenth century, showing several generations of descendants from Abraham and Lydia Brown.

Descendants of Joseph Baldwin of Connecticut and Massachusetts
Dodd, Thomas C., b. 1818.
Mss 517
0.25 linear ft.
Handwritten genealogies of the descendants of John Lothrop of Barnstable, Mass., and Joseph Baldwin of Milford, Conn., and Hadley, Mass. Also brief genealogies of several allied lines: Uriah Cutler of New Jersey; Nicholas Byram of Weymouth, Mass.; John Alden of Plymouth, Mass.; and Daniel Moore of Bridgehampton, N.Y.

Barnstable, Massachusetts transcribed records of marriages and births
McLaughlen, James.
Mss 518
6 v.; 29 cm.
Handwritten transcription of original record bound into volumes: Vol. 1 pt 1 has Aalto-Bystrom, Vol. 1 pt 2 has Cabral-Cusick, Vol 2 pt 1 has Dahiel-Guyer, Vol 2 pt 2 has Haddaway-Hynes, Vol 3 pt 1 has Imberg-Kwiatkowski, Vol 3 pt 2 has La Bayer-Lyons, Vol 3 pt 3 has Macey-Nye, Vol 4 pt 1 has O'Brien-Rider, Vol 4 pt 2 has Sabins-Tyska, Vol 4 pt 3 has Valli-Zuccari. Vol 5 pt 1 has marriages 1637-1916 Abbey-Fuller, Vol 5 pt 2 has marriages 1637-1916 Gage-Otis, Vol 5 pt 3 has marriages 1637-1916 Paddleford-York, Vol 6 has marriages 1917-1938, and Vol 7 Sketches and descriptions of Houses.

Beardsley genealogy
Beardsley, Josiah, 1833-
Mss 519
1 v.; 27 cm. + 1 photograph.
Handwritten genealogy on the Beardsley family of Connecticut and the allied families of Bingham, Cogswell, Curtis and Fitch. Includes photograph of the Beardsley homestead in Kent, Conn.

Source book of Lynn history from newspapers, diaries, Bibles, and other sources
Ward, William G.
Mss 520
1 linear ft. (9 v.); 24-28 cm.
Typescript transcription from various sources concerning the town's history. Also includes genealogical information on Lynn [Mass.] families.

Index of Revolutionary veterans buried in Maine
Maine Old Cemetery Association.
Mss 521
0.25 linear ft. (computer printout: 30 x 39 cm.)
1978-
Computer print out list produced from card index held in Special Collections, Fogler Library, University of Maine at Orono.

Correspondence and miscellaneous papers relating to Briggs family
Briggs, H. G. (Herbert G.)
Mss 522
0.25 linear ft.
Manuscript and typescript material relating to various Briggs individuals and families; also some material that may relate to allied families. Correspondence is grouped into five categories: letters to Herbert G. Briggs from various correspondents; letter to Briggs from Wilford J. Litchfield, compiler of a Litchfield genealogy; letters to Briggs from Mary S. P. Guild of Cambridge, Mass.; a letter from Briggs; and miscellaneous correspondence neither to nor from Briggs.

Richard Austin of Charlestown, Mass., his descendants, and allied families
Austin, Frances Adeline, b. 1878.
Mss 523
0.25 linear ft.; 28 cm.
Manuscript-typescript genealogy of Richard Austin of Charlestown and his descendants. Includes information on allied lines.

Holway - Rich families and allied lines
Holway, E. F. (Ernest Fletcher), b. 1881.
Mss 524
6 v. in 3 (119, 146, 69, 118, 136, 94 leaves): photographs; 29 cm.
19??
Typescript genealogy with two tipped in photographs. Vol. 1 Joseph Holway and some of his descendants. Vol. 2 Richard Rich and some of his descendants. Vol. 3 William Bassett and some of his descendants. Vol. 4 Henry Cobb and some of his descendants. Vol. 5 William Carpenter and some of his descendants. Vol. 6 William Carpenter (finished).

Bouton - Boughton family papers
Mss 525
0.25 linear ft. (56 items); 26-58 cm. folded to 30 cm.
Photostats of documents relating to the Bouton - Boughton family of Connecticut and New York. Each photostat, or "panel," is numbered in pencil and keyed to a typescript item-level catalog. The 13-leaf catalog includes an index of names, places, and dates. Documents date from 1732 to 1851, and include deeds, indentures, notes, receipts, a will, church-related items, executions, bonds, and an inventory.

Descendants of Giles Badger and other Badger families
Badger, John Cogswell.
Mss 527
3 v. (404, 404, 400 p.): photographs; 36 cm.
ca. 1930
Manuscript genealogies of the descendants of Giles Badger of Newbury, Mass., in particular the descendants of his grandsons John and Nathaniel, as well as other Badger families. These volumes may have served as the basis for the author's published genealogy of 1909, or perhaps provide corrections and supplemental material. Also an oversize photograph of Mr. and Mrs. Harris G. Badger and family.

Wadleigh chronicle
Mss 528
0.42 linear ft.
Typescript with extensive ms. annotations.

Benjamin family papers, 1785-1899
Mss 529
0.25 linear ft.
Material relating to the Benjamin family of Lincoln and Lexington, Mass. Includes original deeds (27 items, 1785-1879); receipts (9 items, 1838-1879); documents concerning a dispute over flooding of land (13 items, 1810-1865); wills and notes (2 items: William Benjamin 1843; William O. Benjamin 1899), and miscellaneous papers (2 items: transfer of church pew, 1851; pasturing cattle, 1871). Other families involved in these transactions include Abbott, Blaisdell, Brown, Child, Goodale, Hoar, Simonds, Walcott, and White.

Bowdish of Rhode Island
Lamb, Frank Bird, 1863-1955.
Mss 530
0.25 linear ft.: geneal. tables, photographs.
Manuscript and typescript genealogy of the descendants of William Bowdish of Salem, Mass., and Newport, R.I. Also two extensively annotated carbon copy typescripts entitled "Bowdish Family Records". Correspondence arranged chronologically.

Genealogy of the Bowen family
Paine, Royal.
Mss 531
2 v. (286, 148 p.); 32 cm.
Manuscript genealogy and notes on Bowen families, including descendants of Griffith Bowen. Pamphlets, numerous newspaper clippings.

The Reg Auckland papers: social and historical story of Sandridge, Hertfordshire, a Domesday village
Auckland, R. G. (Reginald George)
Mss 532
373 leaves: ill., maps, geneal. tables; 28 cm.
2001
Typescript.

Records of the town of Princeton, Massachusetts: births, deaths, marriages 1759-1842 with a few additional records of earlier and later dates. Intentions of marriages, 1760-1816
Blake, Francis E. (Francis Everett), 1839-1916.
Princeton (Mass.)
Mss 534
1 v. (32, 371, 56 p.); 35 cm.
Handwritten transcription of original town records.

Account book for the sloop Oliver Wolcott, 1817-1822
Avery, Frederick A.
Proprietors of Sloop Oliver Wolcott.
Mss 535
1 v. (300 p. only 50 p. used); 33 cm.
Cover has "Sloop Oliver Wolcott & Owners Ledger December 8th 1817". Entries are true copies of meeting minutes, agreements, bills, etc. written by Frederick A. Avery, Agent for the Sloop Oliver Wolcott [of Norwich] and Owners in Preston, Conn.

Account book of Daniel B. Potter, 1814-1851
Potter, Daniel B., 1804-1844.
Mss 537
1 v. (300 p.); 34 cm.
Original leather bound account book recording debts and credits. End sheet has "Daniel B Potters ledger 1814". Entries concern the use of his horse and various kinds of waggons as well as purchased commodities such as corn, pork, sand paper, rye, etc. Includes seven pages with "Geneology [sic] of the Potter family".

State prison, physician's records No. 4, 1816-1817
Clark, Robert.
Massachusetts State Prison.
Mss 538
1 v. (300 p.); 25 cm.
Leather-bound volume with handwritten record of the medical treatment provided to inmates at the Massachusetts State Prison in Charlestown. End sheet has "Robert Clark Esqr Records commencing Jan 1816". Most entries just list the date, surname and treatment although a few provide more detail.

Subscription book for Carter and Hendee, 1832-1834
Carter and Hendee.
Mss 539
1 v.; 35 cm.
Account book with handwritten lists of purchasers of titles published by Carter and Hendee.

Roll of original and hereditary members of the Society of the Cincinnati in the State of New Jersey. [Taken from the official roster]
Society of the Cincinnati in the State of New Jersey
Mss 540
45 leaves; 28 cm.
1874?
Typescript. Bound with rolls for DE, NY and PA.

Roll [of original members] of the State Society of the Cincinnati of Pennsylvania
State Society of the Cincinnati of Pennsylvania.
Mss 540
33 leaves; 28 cm.
1890?
Typescript. Bound with rolls for DE, NY and NJ.

List of [original] members of the New York State Society of the Cincinnati
New York State Society of the Cincinnati.
Mss 540
13 leaves; 28 cm.
1880?
Typescript. Bound with rolls for DE, NJ and PA.

Names of the original members of the Rhode Island State Society of the Cincinnati, alphabetically arranged
Society of the Cincinnati in the State of Rhode Island.
Mss 540
16 leaves; 28 cm.
1874?
Typescript. Bound with rolls for CT, MA, and NH. Includes "Names of members admitted in right of their deceased fathers," "Honorary members," and "Officers of the Rhode Island State Society of the Cincinnati."

List of original and hereditary members of the Massachusetts Society of the Cincinnati
Massachusetts Society of the Cincinnati.
Mss 540
87, 5 leaves; 28 cm.
1875?
Typescript.

[List of] original members of the North Carolina Society of the Cincinnati
North Carolina Society of the Cincinnati.
Mss 540
4 leaves; 28 cm.
1880?
Typescript.

List of the [original and hereditary] members of the South Carolina Society of the Cincinnati
South-Carolina State Society of Cincinnati.
Mss 540
24 leaves; 28 cm.
1880?
Typescript.

List of [original] members of the Maryland State Society of the Cincinnati
Society of the Cincinnati of Maryland.
Mss 540
8 leaves; 28 cm.
1880?
Typescript.

Roll of the [original] members of the New Hampshire State Society of the Cincinnati
Society of the Cincinnati in the State of New Hampshire.
Mss 540
4 leaves; 28 cm.
1878?
Typescript. Bound with rolls for CT, MA, and RI.

Roll of the [original] members of the Delaware State Society of the Cincinnati [Taken from the original parchment roll of the Delaware Society]
Delaware State Society of the Cincinnati.
Mss 540
3 leaves; 28 cm.
1880?
Typescript.

Roll of the [original] members of the Georgia State Society of the Cincinnati
Society of the Cincinnati. Georgia.
Mss 540
5 leaves; 28 cm.
1881?
Typescript.

Roll of the [original] members of the Virginia State Society of the Cincinnati. [Supplemented from list in possession of the New York Society]
Society of the Cincinnati. Virginia.
Mss 540
14 leaves; 28 cm.
1802?
Typescript. Bound with rolls for GA, MD, NC, and SC.

Roll of the [original] members of the Connecticut State Society of the Cincinnati
Connecticut Society of the Cincinnati.
Mss 540
27 leaves; 28 cm.
1855
Typescript. Bound with rolls for MA, NH, and RI.

Avery family collection, 1638-1936 (bulk 1815-1912)
Avery family.
Mss 541
3.2 linear ft.
Unpublished finding aid in the library.
Comprised of family photographs, including some daguerreotypes, ambrotypes, and tintypes. The collection also contains miscellaneous correspondence, documents and some genealogical research. Allied families include Abel, Byles, Emmons, Fuller, Hinckley and Lord.

Account book of John Winthrop and Asa Taylor, 1786-1803
Winthrop, John, 1747-1800.
Taylor, Asa.
Mss 542
1 v. (440 p.); 33 cm.
Vellum bound account book for Boston merchant John Winthrop with debit and credits concerning goods purchased from Winthrop's rope walk. Entries include tattow, coil spun yarn, cordage of different sizes, wormline, etc. Paste down has "John Winthrop's October 1786." Pages one through five, two-thirds of pages six/seven, and pages ten/eleven are missing. Since the accounts continue (in a different hand) for three years after John Winthrop's death, the account book was obviously given to a business partner or to one of his sons prior to its acquisition by Asa Tyler.

Account book of Samuel Woodbridge, 1753-1799
Woodbridge, Samuel.
Mss 543
2 v. (ca. 400, 9 p.); 29-33 cm.
Leather bound account book kept by Samuel Woodbridge of Somerworth, NH (1753-1766) and Andover, Mass (1767-1799). Entries include making or mending jackets, briches, coats, etc. Second volume is a typescript index (9 p.) by Lenora White McQuesten called "Account book of Samuel Woodbridge, tailor, of Somersworth, N.H., 1753-1766, & Andover, Massachsuetts, 1767-1799: index."

Account book of Trueworthy Dudley and Ebenezer Straw, 1750-1832
Dudley, Trueworthy.
Straw, Ebenezer, 1751-1820.
Mss 544
1 v. (470 p.); 31 cm.
First page has "Trueworthy Dudley book Jan 29 1754. Trueworthy Dudley of Exeter in New England his ledger begon in the year 1754". His entries involve the mending or selling of chisels, sythes, axes, hatchets, etc. Inside cover has "Ebenezer Straw of Epping 1781". Entries include making cider, cord of hemlock bark, bushels of corn, ploughing, flax, rye, pork, veal, etc. Pages 467-9 have entries concerning the birth, marriage and deaths of Ebenezer Straw's family.

Journal and account book of John Cooper, 1823 January 1-1829 January 18
Cooper, John, 1765-1845.
Mss 547
1 v. (267 p.); 40 cm.
Debts and credits interspersed with journal entries. The entries include descriptions of the weather as well as town and church proceedings including the names of those elected to town offices, baptisms, those admitted to the church, etc.

Gershome A. Clark Jr. family register, 1818-1884
Mss 548 [Mss flat storage]
1 sheet: col. ill.; 26 x 36 cm.
Partially printed family register lithograph, hand colored and completed in ms. for the Gersham A. and Olive A. (Rigby) Clark family of Chenango and Tioga County, NY. Includes a hand drawn chart of the ancestors of Harold Junior Bradley, a descendant of Gersham and Olive Clark.

Descendants of Richard Waterhouse of Portsmouth, New Hampshire: with notes on the descendants of Jacob Waterhouse of New London, Connecticut, Joshua Waterhouse of New Jersey and others, also a sketch of the Waterhouse family in England
Waterhouse, George Herbert.
Mss 549
3 v. (1594, 199 p.): plates; 30 cm.
1934
Typescript genealogy.

McCorrison, McCorison, MacCorison genealogy: the descendants of William McAllister of Gorham, Maine, and Scotland - Ireland
McCorrison, Paul C., b. 1948.
Mss 550
[1404] p.: ill. (some col.), geneal. tables, ports. (some col.), maps; 28 cm.
1999
Photocopy of a computer-generated genealogy comprising descendancy charts and family group records with commentary and documentation. Scattered throughout are copies of vital records. Includes a list of sources. The appendix contains photocopies of manuscript and typescript correspondence; extracts from published works; military records; transcriptions of deeds; newspaper clippings; census records; and pedigree charts.

Genealogy of the Binney family in the United States
Binney, Charles J. F. (Charles James Fox), 1806-1888.
Mss 551
[640] p.: ports., plates, geneal. tables, photographs; 23 cm.
1886
A printed genealogy, extensively annotated and updated in manuscript by Amos Binney, of the descendants of John Binney of Hull, Mass. (Amos's widow, Julia S. Binney, apparently continued updating to about 1940.) Includes notes from the manuscripts of Charles J. F. Binney and Henry P. Binney. Pedigree charts and genealogical notes are bound in the volume; photographs, autographs, newspaper clippings, correspondence, and a manuscript family register dated 1817 are tipped in. There is also information on other Binney families in the United States, England, Scotland.

Diary of Rebecca Bolyston Clark, 1804-1808, 1822-1823
Clark, Rebecca Boylston, 1784-1825.
Mss 552
Access to original record is restricted: Material extremely fragile; Use preservation photocopy.
4 v.; 16-30 cm.
Diary of a young woman living in Brookline, Mass. Entries include descriptions of the health of family, friends and acquaintances as well as specific notices of births, baptisms, engagements, marriages and deaths. Describes local events in Brookline such as the construction of a new meetinghouse, celebrations, etc. Of particular interest is the insight Clark's entries provide concerning the activities of a young woman from a prominent Massachusetts family living during the early 19th century. These activities include listening to sermons on Sundays, attending lectures, and social visits (often for tea). Rebecca also provides detailed accounts of some of the literature she has read and some descriptions of the weather.

The confessions of diverse propounded to be received and were entertained as members, ca. 1635-1640
Shepard, Thomas, 1605-1649.
F74/C1/S54/1980 Microfilm also Mss 553
Access to original record is restricted: Material fragile; Use microfilm
1 microfilm reel. Original is 1 v. (98 leaves)
Additional form: Transcription of the confessions by George Selement and Bruce C. Woolley; published as "Thomas Shepard's Confessions" in *Publications of the Colonial Society of Massachusetts*, Vol. 58 (Boston: The Society, 1981).
Contains the relations of the experience of persons admitted as members to the church: Edward Hall, Francis Moore, Goodman Luxford's wife, George Willdoe, John Sill, John Sill's wife, Mr. Eaton, Christopher Cane, Goodman Daniell, Mr. Sparhawke, Mrs Sparhawke, Mr. Sanders, John Stedman, Goodwife Holmes, Mr. Collins, John Stansby, Barbary Cutter, Goodman Manning, Mrs. Ruggles maid Katherine, John Stedman's wife, John Trundle, Mr. Andrews, our brother Jackson's man Richard Eagles, Mrs Green, B. Jackson's mayd, Golding Moore, William Hamlet, Brother Collin's wife, B. Moore's wife, B. Parrish's wife, B. Crackbone's wife, Hannah Brewer, Robert Homes, old Goodwife Cutter, B. Winshop's wife, Goodwife Willdoes, B. Greene's wife, Mr. Dunster, Mr. Haynes, Goodman Shepard, Goodman Fessington, Mr. Richard Cutter, Goodwife Usher, Widow Arrington, Goodwife Grizzell, Goodwife Champney, Goodman With, Sr. Jones, and Goodman Funnell. Beginning at the other end of the book are some abstracts of sermons by Mr. Cotton (Revel. 4:1:2; Revel. 5:12,13), Mr. Cott (Revel. 5:13), Mr. Ward (Isaj. 42:18-21), Mr. Cotto (Revel. 6:1,2), J.C. (Revel. 6:1,2), Seale 4: (Revel. 7.8), Seale 5. (Revel. 6:9,10,11; Acts: 13:48), Mr. Ward (Nehem. 8:10), Mr. Chancy (John 1:12), Mr. Ward (Hab. 3:16), Mr. Huit (1 Cor. 12:ult.; Ezek. 47:11), and Mr. Bur (Isaj. 30:20,21). Then follows the confession of "Will: Ames."

Ancestry of Ruth L. C. Child
Mss 554
0.25 linear ft.
Manuscript and typescript material relating to the ancestry of Ruth L.C. Child. Includes allied families Gerry, Joy, Patch, Sawtelle, Sawyer, Stone, and Tower.

Genealogical notes on the Folger, Parker, and Monroe families
Grant, Fannie Louise Folger, b. 1899.
Mss 555
0.25 linear ft.: geneal. tables, photographs.
Miscellaneous manuscript genealogical notes. Newspaper clippings concerning individuals surnamed Folger. Correspondence, 1925-1949, most addressed to Fannie Folger Grant. Photographs of family members, residences, and gravestones. Two manuscript charts showing the ancestry and descendants of Ebenezer Parker and wife Dorcas Monroe of Lexington, Mass.; and the descendents of Charles Folger and wife Bethia Parker of Maine and Massachusetts.

Notes on Codman and Belknap ancestral families
Codman, Arthur Amory, 1833-1896.
Mss 557
0.25 linear ft.: maps, coat of arms, photographs.
Volume of manuscript notes on the ancestry of Arthur Amory Codman and wife Mary Elizabeth Belknap, with information on English origins; newspaper clippings (obituaries and other items); and manuscript correspondence. Surnames include Amory, Belknap, Cartwright, Codman, Green, Haven, Livermore, Robison, Standbridge, and Willard. Also three files of loose items, including correspondence and notes.

Ancestry of Harriet Frances Greene, Bridgton, Maine
Greene, Harriet Frances, b. 1880.
Mss 558
[445] leaves; 28 cm.
Typescript genealogy of the ancestral families of Harriet Frances Greene, daughter of Henry Eugene Greene and Florence Adelaide Knight.

Genealogy: Crocker family
Crocker, Alvah, b. 1858.
Mss 559
0.25 linear ft.
Typescript and manuscript notes on Capt. John Crocker of Boston and Newburyport, Mass., wife Mary Savage, and their ancestors and descendants. Original and transcribed correspondence (1898-1901, 1904, 1929-30); many of the earlier letters are from Josephine Crocker Smith or Anson Titus. Also an original manuscript report (1899) by researcher Anson Titus concerning the ancestry of the Crocker and Savage families.

Bayley - Bailey genealogy: John of Salisbury branch. Account of John Bayly of Salisbury, Mass., and some of his descendants
Bailey, Hollis R. (Hollis Russell), 1852-1934.
Mss 560
2 v. (885, 89 leaves); 28 cm.
1932
Typescript.

Correspondence, 1863-1880
Chester, Joseph Lemuel, 1821-1882.
Mss 561
2 v.; 23 cm.
Manuscript correspondence (1863-1880) from Joseph Lemuel Chester, England, to William H. Whitmore, Boston, Mass., concerning Chester's genealogical research in England.

The Baldwin family: records compiled from New England vital statistics
Baldwin, Aubrey Haines, Jr.
Mss 562
1 v. (43, 59, 72, 108, 33, 131, 170 leaves); 28 cm.
1967
Typescript.

Power of attorney for John Ellery, 1708 March 27
Ellery, John, 1681-1742.
Mss 563 [Mss flat storage]
1 ADS; 38 cm.
Handwritten document by which John Ellery of Newport, RI assigns power of attorney to Benjamin Ellery. Includes the seal of John Ellery. Witnessed by John Ward and William Coddington and recorded by William Wanton Jr.

Plan of Crown Point Fort, 1762
Mss 564 [Mss flat storage]
1 sheet; 37 x 31 cm.
Hand drawn map of the fort illustrating the location of various bastions, barracks, the guard house, ravelin, well, gateway, trenches, drain, places for arms, flagstaff, sally ports, etc. Drawn to a scale of 90 ft to an inch.

Plan of Fort Hill Fort in Boston
Mss 565 [Mss flat storage]
Access to original record is restricted: Material fragile.
1 sheet; 34 x 31 cm.
Hand drawn sketch of the Fort Hill Fort in Boston indicating the location of the well, guard house, etc.

An elegy upon the death of master John George Washington Hancock, the only son of the Hon. John Hancock, Esq., who departed this life Jan. 27, in the ninth year of his age
Dorr, Samuel Adams, 1775-1855.
Mss 566 [Mss flat storage]
1 sheet; 37 x 46 cm.
Hand drawn and colored mourning piece signed "Samuel Adams Dorr scripsit 1787 South School Pleasant Street."

Military commission certificate for Oliver Barron, 1758 March 13
Pownall, Thomas, 1722-1805.
Mss 567 [Mss flat storage]
Access to original record is restricted: Material fragile.
1 DS; 35 x 40 cm.
Partially-printed document completed in ms. appointing Oliver Barron Second Lieutenant in Col. Joseph William's Regiment of Foot raised for a general invasion of Canada.

Military commission certificate for Joseph Barrett, 1732 March 6
Belcher, Jonathan, 1682-1757.
Mss 568 [Mss flat storage]
Access to original record is restricted: Material fragile.
1 DS; 32 x 42 cm.
Partially-printed form completed in ms. whereby Joseph Barrett is appointed Captain Lieutenant of the Foot Company of Concord, Mass. in the Regiment of Militia commanded by Col. John Flynt.

Deed, 1665 December 17, Cambridge, Mass. to Charles Chauncey
Andrew, Samuel, 1620-1701.
Mss 569 [Mss flat storage]
Access to original record is restricted: Material extremely fragile.
1 ADS; 32 x 39 cm.
Deed by Samuel Andrewe (son and heir of the late William Andrewe), Samuel's wife Elizabeth Andrewe, and Reana Daniels (relict of William Andrewes) to Charles Chauncy concerning 250 acres of land in Cambridge for 200 pounds. Acknowledged before Edward Goffe and Thomas Danforth 17 December 1655 and recorded by Thomas Danforth in liber 2 page 2.

Blodget - Blodgett descendants of Thomas of Cambridge
Thompson, Bradley DeForest.
Mss 570
6 v. (1204 p.); 30 cm.
1952-54
Typescript. Vol. 1 covers generations 1-6, vol. 2 has generation 7, vol. 3 has generation 8, vol. 4 has generations 9 & 10, vol. 5 has generation 11 & 12 + unidentified, vol. 6 additions and corrections.

Ball genealogy and family history
Murray, James E. (James Ellis), 1898-.
Mss 571
1 v.; 30 cm.
c. 1961
Typescript.

Our Belding family in America
Cummings, Lawrence Belding, 1881-1947.
Mss 573
1 v.: ill., maps, ports., facsim., photographs; 29 cm.
1929
Typescript.

The Benham family in America
Randall, Georgiana H. (Georgiana Hathaway), b. 1893.
Mss 574
3 v. (736 leaves); 29 cm.
1954
Carbon copy typescript with ms. additions.

Five Bogert families
Ackerman, Herbert Stewart.
Mss 575
2 v. (875, [117] p.); 29 cm.
1950?
Typescript. Vol. 1 on The Bogardus family; descendants of Evert Bogert, of Jan Laurenez Bogert, of Cornelis Bogert, of Guysbert, and of Dr. Harmense Myndertse Van de Bogert. Vol. 2 has More Bogert families.

The Bewley heritage
Parker, Donald Dean, b. 1899.
Mss 576
1 v. illus., maps 28 cm.
1947
Typescript.

Military commission certificate for William Loud, 1742 February 19
Shirley, William, 1694-1771.
Mss 577 [Mss flat storage]
Access to original record is restricted: Material fragile.
1 DS: vellum; 28 x 30 cm.
Handwritten document appointing William Loud of Boston Lieutenant of "his Majesty's Snow Prince of Orange".

The American ancestors and descendants of Willard William and Cora Dunham Boyd, 1620-1928
Boyd, Cora Dunham, 1860-.
Mss 578
440 p.: front., plates, ports., facsim.; 29 cm.
1928
Mimeograph typescript.

Bonham, 1631-1973: Letters, quotations, genealogical charts, military record, directory index
Smith, Emmet Lincoln, 1865-1920.
Mss 579
506 leaves: ill., col. coat of arms, port.; 29 cm.
1973
Revised by Elmer B. Hazie
Typescript.

King's grant Annapolis County Nova Scotia, 1803
Williams, Alicia Crane.
Mss 580 [Location: mss flat storage]
2 photostats (28 x 46 cm.) + [4] leaves
Photostat and typescript transcription of original land grand by King George III to inhabitants of Annapolis County, Nova Scotia, 1803 July 4.

A history of the Dustin family in America
Dustin, Charles E.
Duston-Dustin Family Association.
Mss 581
9 v.; 29 cm.
1933-
Carbon copy typescript with some ms. annotations. Vol I generations 1-6, vol II generations 7-9, Vol III generations 9-11 + index to vols 1-3. Vol IV corrections and additions, bibliography of Hannah Duston, the names Durston and Duston, English Durstons, generations 4-8. Vol V corrections and additions generation 8-12. Vol VI-VII additions and corrections generation 5-12, incomplete line of John Dustin + index to vol 6-7. Vol VIII additions and corrections geneation 5-13 + index to vol 8. Vol IX is an index to vols 4-5 by Harriet B (Kilgore) Curtis bound separately.

Genealogy of the Foss family of America
Rix, Guy S. (Guy Scoby), 1828-1917.
Mss 582
505, lxxxvi leaves; 29 cm.
1944?
Typescript.

Brockway records: data on descendants of Wolston Brockway
Brockway, Florence M. (Florence May), b. 1869.
Mss 583
1 v. (408, 22, [92] leaves); 29 cm.
1949
Typescript.

Blake Parker family register, 1806-1854
Parker, T. D.
Mss 584 [Mss flat storage]
1 sheet; 30 x 31 cm.
Hand drawn and painted family register for the Blake and Mary (Clark) Parker family of Southboro, Mass. The names of the family members forms a ring around the outside edge of the register with a color image of presumablely their house in the center of the piece. "Done at Medfield School March 15, 1854 by T.D. Parker."

The Davis family, 1640-[1924]
Davis, Samuel Austin, 1857-1924.
Mss 585 [Mss flat storage]
64 leaves: ill., coat of arms; 41 cm.
1924
Photocopy of a handwritten pedigree (with two images of the residence of Edward S. Davis of Danbury, Conn. and newspaper clippings) on the Davis family of New Jersey.

Marriage certificate for Charles Rich and Nettie Campbell, 1878 November 21
Boughton, C. M.
Mss 586 [Mss flat storage]
1 sheet: photographs; 28 x 35 cm.
Certificate of marriage form published by John Gibson (c. 1873) and completed in ms. for Charles F. Rich and Nellie Campbell by Rev C. M. Boughton, Pastor, Methodist Protestant Church at Sand Bank, N.Y. The center of the document has two photographs: one of Charles Rich and one of Nellie Campbell.

Portrait of Mr. and Mrs. James W. Converse, ca. 1870
Mss 587 [Mss flat storage]
1 photograph; 46 x 39 cm.

Account book of John Cabot, 1712-1722
Cabot, John, 1680-1742.
Mss 588
1 v. (360 p.); 36 cm.
Vellum bound account book for a merchant of Salem, Mass. Cover has "Book No 2. 1716". Entries include cotton, linen, thread, Mohair, buckram, silk, corn, molasses, rum, butter, sugar, tobacco, oil, etc.

Stephen Paschall Sharples papers, 1595-1900 (bulk 1634-1897)
Sharples, Stephen Sharples, 1842-1923.
Mss 589
9.9 linear ft.
Unpublished finding aid in the library.
Consists of source and draft material collected by Professor Sharples and Leonard A. Morrison in preparing for their comprehensive work, *History of the Kimball Family in America From 1634 to 1897,* published in Boston in 1897 by Damrell and Upham. This book traces the descendants of Richard Kimball (1595-1675), and his wife, Ursula (Scott) Kimball, who emigrated from Ipswich, England, April 10, 1634, on the ship *Elizabeth*, and settled in Watertown, Mass.

Nathan Brewer family register, 1784-1832
Mss 590 [Mss flat storage]
1 sheet; 42 x 34 cm.
Black and white family record lithograph engraved by E.C. Tracy and printed in Cooperstown (N.Y.). This family record has written entries concerning the Nathan Brewer family of Massachusetts and New York. (Donor information: Nathan bought land in Middlefield, Otsego County, NY -- near Cooperstown -- on 29 Mar 1813 then removed back to Mass. around 1840).

Alpheus Nichols family register, 1742-1821
Mss 591 [Mss flat storage]
1 sheet; 42 x 34 cm.
Black and white family record lithograph engraved by E.C. Tracy and printed in Cooperstown (N.Y.). This family record has written entries concerning the Alpheus Nichols family of Framingham, Mass.

Joel Brewer family register, 1752-1847
Mss 592 [Mss flat storage]
1 sheet; 42 x 34 cm.
Black and white family record lithograph engraved by E.C. Tracy and printed in Cooperstown (N.Y.). This family record has written entries concerning the Joel Brewer family of Southborough, Mass.

Peter Brewer and Nathan Newton family register, 1750-1800
Mss 593 [Mss flat storage]
1 sheet; 42 x 34 cm.
Black and white family record lithograph engraved by E.C. Tracy and printed in Cooperstown (N.Y.). This family record has written entries concerning the Peter Brewer and the Nathan Newton families of Southborough, Mass.

Peabody ancestry and related families of Daniel Putnam Peabody, and his children Daniel Putnam Peabody, Jr., Carol Peabody Greenway, Elizabeth Peabody Johnson
Peabody, Orline White, 1900-.
Mss 594
274 leaves: geneal. tables; 28 cm.
1980
Typescript genealogy.

Diary of Helen M. Warner, 1850-1852
Warner, Helen M., 1834-.
Mss 595
3 v. (678 p.); 20 x 17 cm.
Diary written by a young lady of Boston, Mass. attending Normal school in Newton, Mass. Entries include descriptions of the author's studies and social activities.

Abstract of Middlesex court files from 1649 [to 1675]
Wyman, Thomas Bellows, 1817-1878.
Mss 596
2 v.; 26-28 cm.
Handwritten transcription of original records: Vol. 1 1649-1664; Vol 2 1664-1675.

Reading, Mass. families
Bucknam, Wilton Francis, 1861-1917.
Mss 597
2 v. (216, 296 p.); 26-27 cm.
Notebooks with handwritten genealogical notes on families that lived in Reading, Mass. from 1635 to 1870. The records in vol. one begin on pg 34 since pgs 1-33 has a list of attendees to "Union System Meeting June 23 1907".

Hyde Park deeds: being deeds of land in what is now the town of Hyde Park, Massachusetts, and recorded in the Registry of Deeds for Norfolk County
Jenney, Charles Francis, 1860-1923.
Mss 598
4 v.; 26 cm.
Handwritten transcription of original records: Vol. 1 covers Lib. 1-20, Vol. 2 covers Lib 21-40, Vol. 3 Lib 41-60, & Vol. 4 covers Lib 61-80.

[Alden] Family annals
Alden, John Eaton, 1835-1910.
Mss 599
1 v. (560 p.): ill., maps, coat of arms, geneal. tables
Handwritten genealogy circa 1896 on the Alden and allied families.

Account books of John Hull, 1669-1687
Hull, John, 1624-1683.
Bodge, George M. (George Madison), 1841-1914.
Mss 600
Access to original record is restricted: Material fragile; Use microfilm.
1 microfilm reel. Original is 5 v.; 36 cm.
Conservation and microfilming (by NEDCC) funded in part by the Society of Colonial Wars in the Commonwealth of Massachusetts and a grant by the Massachusetts Cultual Council.
The first account book covers 1669-1687 and has entries that include goods purchased from Hull such as indigo, bushels of wheat, whalebone, canvas, cotton, callico as well as money loaned and interest due. The second (1675-1676), third (1675-1677) and fourth (1677-1680) account books, known as the "colony journal" contain the expenses of the Colony of Massachusetts during King Philip's War – kept by John Hull as treasurer (1676-1680) of the Colony of Massachusetts. Fifth volume is an "Index to the Ledger of John Hull, Treasurer of Massachusetts Colony..." collected and arranged for NEHGS by George Madison Bodge...the work was begun October 10th 1881...until February 10th 1882 at which time it was completed."

Bristol County, Massachusetts court records, 1749-1903
Stetson, Oscar Frank, 1875-1948.
Mss 601
1078 leaves: maps; 28 cm.
Typescript transcription of original records.

Correspondence to Maria Mehitable Eastman Child, 1847-1848
Mss 603
0.25 linear ft.
Group of letters written to Maria Mehitable (Eastman) Child of Manchester, NH and Boston, Mass. from various correspondents. Many of the letters written from Jan 1847 to Feb 1848 were sent to "Mehitable Eastman", publisher of "The Voice of Industry", a weekly newspaper "devoted to the elevation and improvement of the industrial classes, etc.". In Feb 1848, Ms. Eastman switched jobs and worked for the Prisoner's Friend Office; however, the letters from this time on primarily concern family matters.

Scrapbook about the U.S. Navy, 1862-1864
Mss 604
1 v.: ill, maps, photograph; 30 cm.
Scrapbook with clippings of the "Naval Records" section of a Boston(?) newspaper. Includes some of the illustrations from the paper concerning satirical cartoons, battles, ships, etc. The reports cover a wide range of topics from Congressional resolutions, to reports of new ships being built and launched, the movement of ships at sea, obituaries, historical notes (such as an account of the first iron plated ship), accounts of battles, appointments, resignations, dismissals, etc. There is a map of Beufort Harbor, S.C. and Santa Rosa Island with Ft. Pickens. There were several CDV photographs throughout the scrapbook, however, all except one were removed.

Distribution of prize money to the officers and crew of the Chesapeake for merchandise captured from the Brig Liverpool Hero, 1814
Mss 605 [Mss flat storage]
Access to original record restricted: Material fragile; Use transcription.
18, [13] p.; 27-39 cm.
Handwritten record of the money distributed to the officers and crew. Entries are arranged by rank and include the men's names, signatures (only some of the men signed), witness and amount. Includes 13 p. transcription of the original document.

Commission certificate for John Walley, 1700 June 11
Addington, Isaac, 1665-1715.
Mss 606 [Mss flat storage]
Access to original record is restricted: Material fragile.
1 ADS: vellum; 27 x 46 cm.
Handwritten document by which John Walley Esq. is commissioned to be one of the Justices of the Superior Court of Judicature in the Massachusetts Bay. Verso has note that Walley took the oath of office on July 5 1700 Boston, Mass.

A record of the marriages, births and deaths in the family of Capt Jonathan Woodbury and Hannah his wife of the State of Massachusetts County of Worcester & town of Sutton
Mss 607
Access to original record is restricted: Material fragile.
1 sheet: col. ill.; 30 x 38 cm.
Handwritten and colored family register. Top half of the register has an image of bird in an olive tree and the bottom half has the handwritten entries. Nineteen of the entries are in the same hand with the last date of 1807. The remaining thirteen entries are in a different hand and range from 1814 to 1853.

Benjamin Harden Gaylord papers
Gaylord, Benjamin Harden, 1927-2000.
Mss 608
6.88 linear ft.
Besides the Gaylord and Warren genealogies, the collection contains genealogical data on many allied families, and also some families which proved not to be related to his own ancestry. The source material includes correspondence with genealogists and Gaylord family members, photocopies of wills and deeds, and applications to patriotic societies. The graphics include Gaylord family members, photos of cemetery markers and sites relating to the family

William Miller family record, 1756-1847
Mss 609 [Mss flat storage]
1 sheet: ill.; 35 x 29 cm.
Hand drawn and colored family register listing the birth as well a couple of the marriage and death dates for the William and Paullina Phelps Miller family.

American ancestry: Jones Locklin Lamson Ainsworth
Jones, Edward Thomas.
Mss 610
10 v.; 29 cm.
1963
Typescript. Vol 1 introduction, ancestral names, ships, status and geographical index. Vol 2 ancestral sketches 0-01 to 7-47. Vol 3 ancestral sketches 7-49 to 9-183. Vol 4 ancestral sketches 9-193 to 10-295. Vol 5 ancestral sketches 10-305 to 11-49. Vol 6 ancestral sketches 11-57 to 11-619. Vol 7 ancestral sketches 11-621 to 11-783. Vol 8 ancestral sketches 11-801 to 12-1219. Vol 9 ancestral sketches 12-1221 to 13-3707. Vol 10 ancestral charts (indexed). Vol 11 general index.

Harvard diploma of William Clark, 1759 July 18
Harvard University.
Mss 612 [Mss flat storage]
Access to original record is restricted: Material fragile.
1 sheet: vellum; 36 x 35 cm.
Handwritten diploma with a decorative initial letter.

Military commission certificate for Thomas N. Wiesenthal, 1814 December 10
Madison, James, 1751-1836.
Crowinshield, Benjamin W., 1772-1851.
Mss 613 [Mss flat storage]
Access to original record is restricted: Material fragile.
1 DS: parchment; 45 x 34 cm.
Partially printed document completed in ms. designating Thomas N. Wiesenthal surgeon's mate in the U.S. Navy. Also signed by Benjamin W. Crowinshield.

An answer to Richard Ways reasons of appeal from the judgement of the county court held at Boston the 30th of July 1667, tendered by Ephraim Hunt and John Bicknell now defendants
Hunt, Ephraim.
Bicknell, John.
Rawson, Edward, 1615-1693.
Mss 614 [Mss flat storage]
Access to original record is restricted: Material extremely fragile.
1 DS; 40 x 31 cm.
Handwritten copy attested by Rawson.

Roll and muster of the light infantry company, 8th Massachusetts Regiment, commanded by Colonel Michael Jackson, 1783 April
Armstrong, Samuel, 1754-1810.
Barber, W.
Burnham, John.
Mss 616 [Mss flat storage]
Access to original record is restricted: Material fragile.
1 sheet; 47 x 38 cm.
Partially printed form completed in ms. Has columns for ranks, names, term of enlishtment, casualties, mustered, time since last muster or inlistment, and altercations since last muster. Certified by Capt. John Burnam (April 1783) and Major W Barber (March 1783) that the above roll is the true state of the company.

Roll and muster of the 7th Company, 8th Massachusetts Regiment, commanded by Col. Michael Jackson, 1783 April 24
Armstrong, Samuel, 1754-1810.
Barber, W.
Wade, Abner.
Mss 617 [Mss flat storage]
Access to original record is restricted: Material fragile.
Partially printed form completed in ms. Has columns for ranks, names, term of enlistment, casualties, mustered, time since last muster or enlistment, and altercations since last muster. Certified by Capt. Abner Wade (April 1783) and Major W Barber (March 1783) that the above roll is the true state of the company.

A muster roll of part of the company in His Majesty's service under the command of Capt. Enoch Bayley, 1755
Mss 618 [Mss flat storage]
Access to original record is restricted: Material fragile.
1 sheet; 38 x 47 cm.
Lists men from the the Boston area and the North Shore. "1755" written at head of form. Includes columns for men's names, quality, names of fathers, at what per month, days travel, time of entrance in service, dead/deserted/or discharged, time of return from captivity, until what time in the service, whole time in service, wages due to each man, for arms not returned, what each man received of the Captain, what each man received of the Commissary of the Regiment, what each man received of the Commissary-General, and balance due.

Family record of Dean Sparrow, 1821-1873
Sparrow, Dean, b. 1821.
Charles Shober & Co. (Chicago, Ill.) Engravers.
Mss 619 [Mss flat storage]
1 chart; 50 x 60 cm.
Lithograph black and white chart designed by Rollin H. Trumbull, engraved by Charles Shober & Co., Chicago, published by Trumbull & Cruver, Chicago, and calligraphied by J. N. Macomber & Son, South Dartmouth, Mass., on 1872 Jan 1 with one addition in 1873. This family record is of Dean Sparrow and his children.

New England Genealogies
Binney, Charles James Fox, 1806-1888.
Mss 620
0.63 linear ft.
Handwritten genealogical records and notes on various New England families.

George Henry Preble papers, 1791-1873
Preble, George Henry, 1816-1885.
Mss 621
3.83 linear ft.
The bulk of the collection consists of ships' journals--most from ships upon which George Henry Preble sailed. These journals contain daily log entries, ships' procedures, lists of ports visited, lists of armament, sketches, etc. All of the journals contain a list of officers attached to the ship, with all but the USS Pensacola containing watch bills and quarter bills listing the men on board. The journals for the USS St. Louis, the USS Katahdin, and the USS State of Georgia contain complete descriptive lists of all the sailors on board. A number of items in the collection consist of naval documents, including correspondence, acts, and general orders. Certain volumes are dedicated to the orders of a single officer--John Dahlgren, in one case, and David Porter in another. Accounts of an 1839 court martial case against Preble are included. George Henry Preble's research interests are also represented in this collection by his notes on the Boston Navy Yard, the history of steam navigation, the American flag, the study of spherics and nautical astronomy, and Preble family genealogy.

Abbe (Abbey), Brown, Burch, Hulbert families
Burch, Edwin Welch, b. 1869.
Mss A 1
11 p.; 28 cm.
1943 typescript ed.
Carbon copy typescript, being a copy by Ray G.
Hulburt from the original typescript by Edwin W.
Burch made on 1943 Oct.

One line of descent from John Albro of
Portsmouth, Newport County, R.I.
Beck, Imogene Zook (Imogene Mable Zook),
1908-1979.
Mss A 10
[26] p.; 28 cm.
[1965?]

Rial D.W. Lathrop Bible record, 1819-1918
Dean, Judah B., 1850-1918.
Mss A 100
[3] leaves; 29 cm.
Original record of Rial D.W. Lathrop (b. 1819)
lacking title page, 1819-1866. Another leaf
concerns the Judah B. Dean (1850-1918) family
which may be a separate item.

Coat of arms of the Bullard family
Mss A 1000
[2] p.: coat of arms (col.); 26 cm.
1938
Color plate of the Bullard family coat of arms.
Description, in French, on verso.

Ancestry of David Almon Bushee
Mss A 1001
11 p., [8] leaves: geneal. tables; 28 cm.
Manuscript notes on David Almon Bushee's
ancestral families, including Danforth, Bridge,
Livermore, Schweitzer or Switzer, and Olds.
Pedigree charts for Switzer, Bridge, Livermore,
Ball, Olds, and Brooks.

Bible record for the William Louis Sharon family,
1899-1935
Mss A 1002
[5] p.; 27 cm.
Original Bible record (with title page) concerning
the William Louis Sharon family of Springfield,
Mass. and New Hampshire.

Material relating to the Campbell family of
Scotland
McGregor, John.
Mss A 1003
[81] leaves; 27 cm.
Photostats of pages (331-366, 371-416) from the
original John McGregor manuscript, vol. 35, of
the Campbells of Glenorchy, later Earls of
Breadalbane from 1432 to 1811.

Perpetual family record and genealogical tables:
a new method for recording genealogies
Cooke, N. B.
Mss A 1004
2 v.: geneal. tables; 26-29 cm.
1863
Descendants of Richard Bullock of Rehoboth,
Mass. Volume 1 contains printed genealogical
tables completed in manuscript. Volume 2 is
entirely in manuscript, but follows the format of
volume 1.

Genealogical data copied from manuscript of
Herbert Jester(9) Robinson entitled record of
more than eighty immigrant ancestors of Charles
Kendall(8) Robinson traced through their
descendants to Herbert Kendall(10) Robinson
Robinson, Herbert Jester, 1881-.
Mss A 1005
1 v. (53 p.); 27 cm.
Handwritten genealogy on the Robinson and 17
allied families.

Cahoone-Cohoon-Calhoun memoranda
Greenlaw, William Prescott, 1863-1945.
Mss A 1006
[340] p.; 28 cm.
1916
Genealogical data on members of the Cahoone,
Cohoon, and Calhoun families. Information is
entered by hand onto printed forms, which are
ordered alphabetically.

Ledger of marriages performed by Daniel D. Smith, 1828-1851
Smith, Daniel Drown, 1807 or 8-1878.
Mss A 1007
1 v. (35 p.); 21 cm.
Handwritten account of marriages performed in and around Gloucester and Haverhill, Mass. and Portland, Me.

Partial supplement to Calhoun genealogical material
Flint, William W.
Mss A 1008
[5] leaves; 17 cm.
1923
Manuscript letter which corrects and supplements W. P. Greenlaw's data concerning Daniel Cahoon of Lyndon, Vt., and his descendants. (See "Mss A 1006".)

The descendants of George Lawton of Portsmouth, Rhode Island
Lawton, Elva, b. 1896.
Daughters of the American Revolution. New York.
Mss A 1009
iii, 121, 6, 30 leaves; 29 cm.
1977
Photocopy of a typescript genealogy.

Abraham Hubbell Bible record, 1786-1868
Hubbell, Abraham, 1786-1819.
Mss A 101
[3] leaves; 26 cm.
Original Bible record lacking title page.

Bible record for the Fanning and Faulkner families, 1745-1801
Mss A 1010
1 v. ([4] p., [1] leaf); 27 cm.
Original record (without title page) for the families of Thomas and Elizabeth (Capron) Fanning, and Thomas and Susannah (Faulkner) Fanning, all of Connecticut. This material is incorporated in Walter Frederic Brooks's "History of the Fanning family".

Brooks family of Concord, Mass.
Tolman, George, 1836-1909.
Mss A 1011
1 v.; 21 cm.
Manuscript genealogy of the descendants of Thomas and Grace Brooks of Concord, Mass. Walter Frederic Brooks has made additions and corrections.

The descendants of Thomas Brooks who settled at Watertown, Mass., 1631 and Concord, 1638
Brooks, Walter Frederic, b. 1859.
Mss A 1012
1 v.; 28 cm.
1894
Manuscript genealogy of the descendants of Thomas and Grace Brooks of Watertown and Concord, Mass. Also some notes on other Brooks lines.

Genealogical records of the Bradford, Merwin, Fox, and Dailey families
Mss A 1013
30 items: ill., coat of arms, geneal. tables; 28 cm.
Manuscript genealogies and notes concerning the Bradford, Merwin, Fox, and Dailey families of Connecticut, descendants of James Fitch Bradford and wife Mary Merwin. Also photocopies of newspaper clippings and three descendant charts.

Ancestors of Caroline Elizabeth (Williams) Briggs
Briggs, William Churchill, 1853-1939.
Mss A 1014
1 v. (309 leaves): geneal. tables; 29 cm.
1917
Typescript genealogy with annotations.

Ancestors of William C. Briggs: Briggs - Churchill - Williams & Crane families
Briggs, William Churchill, 1853-1939.
Mss A 1015
1 v. (510 leaves): geneal. tables; 29 cm.
1918
Typescript genealogy with annotations.

Genealogy of the Cable family of Connecticut
Banks, Charles Edward, 1854-1931.
Mss A 1016
1 v.; 24 cm.
1895
Manuscript genealogy of John Cable of
Connecticut and his descendants.

Record of the Byram family
Byram, Aaron G.
Mss A 1017
1 v. (125 p.); 25 cm.
Manuscript genealogy of the Byram family.
Draws from Mitchell's "History of the early
settlement of Bridgewater, in Plymouth County,
Massachusetts..." for the early generations, then
incorporates new material on the descendants of
Ebenezer and Abigail (Alden) Byram of
Bridgewater, Mass., and Mendham, N.J.

*The houses of Howe and Faxon: links with the
past*
Palmer, Alice Howe.
Mss A 1018
61, [31] p.: ill., geneal. tables, maps, ports.; 28
cm.
c1999
Typescript genealogy.

Barnard and Wilcox: family history and writings
Palmer, Alice Howe.
Mss A 1019
1 v.: ill., facsims., geneal. tables, ports.; 28 cm.
c1999
Typescript genealogy.

*Bamp: Biographical sketch of Edmund Lawson
who is known by his family as Bamp*
Lawson, Edmund, 1906-.
Mss A 102
23, [3] p.; 28 cm.
1981? typescript ed.
Photocopied typescript of the biographical sketch
of Edmund Lawson (b. 1906).

*The family of Edward Gardner Howe I & Mary
Elizabeth Barnard Howe*
Palmer, Alice Howe.
Mss A 1020
1 v.: ill., facsims., ports.; 28 cm.
c1999
Typescript genealogy.

Genealogy of the Isaac Buswell family
Mss A 1021
[28] leaves; 28 cm.
Photocopies of a manuscript genealogy of Isaac
Buswell of Salisbury, Mass., and his descendants.
Photocopies of corresponence concerning
donations Mrs. Bernice R. Wentworth, a Buswell
descendant, made to the Minnesota Historical
Society and to the Smithsonian Institution.

Business of the 4th Auditor's office
Etheridge, John.
Mss A 1022
419 p.; 26 cm.
Handwritten history of the creation of this office
followed by a list of "Books and records of the
4th Auditor's Office," a transcription of "An Act
for the better government of the Navy of the
United States" [April 23, 1800], and "Laws, rules
and regulations governing the settlement of
accounts of pursers, Fourth Auditors Office,
Treasury Department."

*Marriages Linton, Cambridge[shire], England:
[Part I] 1559-1753. Part II 1599-1812 from
transcripts*
Genealogical Society of Utah.
Mss A 1023
81, 73 leaves; 29 cm.
1945
Typescript transcription.

*Marriages Quainton, Buckinghamshire, England
1599-1900: Part one pp 1-85, Part two pp 85-108
(Note: all surnames arranged alphabetically)*
Genealogical Society of Utah.
Mss A 1024
108 leaves; 29 cm.
1945
Typescript transcription.

Marriages Woodchester, Gloucestershire, England 1563-1837
Genealogical Society of Utah.
Mss A 1025
72 leaves; 29 cm.
1945
Typescript transcription.

Inventory of goods and chattles [sic] of Sarah Calif.
Mss A 1026
1 notebook ([5] p.); 21 cm.
Original manuscript estate inventory dated 18 February 1835, listing items room by room and estimating their values. Also copies of newspaper clippings from the Boston Transcript, April 22 and 29, 1907, concerning the Calef family.

Account book of Amos Jones, 1794-1824
Jones, Amos, 1776-1846.
Mss A 1027
1 v. ([30] p.); 16 cm.
An account book kept by blacksmith Amos Jones of Ipswich, Mass., son of Thomas and Hannah Jones. Entries concern accounts, payments, travel, deliveries, and work schedule of Jones and others. The volume also contains more than 30 scattered vital records for family members and acquaintances, mostly deaths but including several births. Many of the deaths occurred at Ipswich, according to the town's published vital records. Several entries are for the Smith family, likely relatives of Jones's wife, Elizabeth Smith.

H. Fox Davis letters
Cummings, Henry A.
Mss A 1028
6 items; 21 cm.
Six manuscript letters, 1885-1887, addressed to Mr. H. Fox Davis of Manchester, N.H., naming the heirs of Mary J. (Campbell) Worthley. These heirs, all nieces and nephews, were surnamed Cummings, Campbell, and Reccord, and were living in Thetford, Vt.; Volga City, Iowa; Lebanon, N.H.; East Livermore, Me.; North Wayne, Me; and Fayette, Me.

Robert Campbell [and] George Campbell of Townsend, Massachusetts
Priest, Alice L. (Alice Lucinda), 1866-1954.
Mss A 1029
1 v. (79, [21] p.); 26 cm.
1929
Manuscript genealogy of Robert and George Campbell, both of Townsend, Mass., and their descendants.

Carman family genealogy
Sarter, Emilie.
Mss A 1030
[102] leaves; 28 cm.
1944-1946
Typescript genealogy of Adam Carman of Long Island, N.Y., fifth-generation descendant of John Carman of Hempstead, Long Island. Traces his descendants to the twelfth generation in some lines. The genealogy appears to be a continuation of a previously compiled work, possibly Tredwell's "John Carman(1) of Hempstead, Long Island" (see "Mss C 4987"). Also typescript notes on the surname Carman and extracts from published sources citing the name; transcriptions of newspaper articles about Carman family reunions in 1881, 1916, and 1919; and miscellaneous transcriptions of deeds, wills, petitions, and marriage records.

Account book of Eliphalet Pond, 1718-1765
Pond, Eliphalet, 1704-1795.
Mss A 1031
1 v. (100 p.); 31 cm.
Original account book with entries concerning the sale of timber, keel-piece, floore timber, rudder, etc. as well as cyder, beef, veal, etc. Includes signed notes written in the book by individuals employed by Pond stating that they received their salary.

A brief sketch of some of the Carpenter family in New England
Carpenter, Harvey, b. 1819.
Mss A 1032
1 v. ([1] leaf, 86 p., [1] leaf); 22 cm.
1881
Manuscript genealogy tracing the direct descent of the author from the emigrant William Carpenter of Weymouth. The bulk of the volume, however, comprises manuscript poems written by the author and mounted clippings of his published poetry and articles.

Genealogical records of the Carr family
Mss A 1033
[23] leaves: coat of arms, geneal. tables; 28 cm.
Typescript and manuscript genealogy of the descendants of Thomas Carr of England and wife Mary Dabney of Virginia, including Dabney Carr who married Martha Jefferson, sister of Thomas Jefferson. Also information on the allied Overton family.

Letters concerning the Carruth family, 1894-1895
Rogers, Elizabeth S.
Mss A 1034
[77] p.; 21 cm.
Letters to Hayden Carruth showing proof of the fraudulent coat of arms of the Carruth family -- see Carruth genealogies by Arthur J. Carruth and by Harold B. Carruth. Also a letter from John Carruth Campbell.

Genealogical records of the Carman family
Mss A 1035
[5] leaves; 26 cm.
Photocopies of several pages from a manuscript genealogy in the New York Public Library concerning Gabriel Carman, his wife Hannah Le Strange, and their descendants.

Records of the descent of Annie Wilkins Carroll
Mss A 1036
[46] leaves; 20 cm.
Records of the descent of Annie Wilkins (Mrs. Charles H. Carroll), showing her eligibility for membership in various patriotic and hereditary societies. Ancestors include: Daniel Wilkins of Amherst, N.H.; Bray Wilkins of Salem and Dorchester, Mass.; Anthony Morse of Newbury, Mass.; Ralph Hill of Plymouth and Woburn, Mass.; William Trask of Salem, Mass; Thomas Putnam of Lynn, Mass.; Edward Converse of Charlestown and Woburn, Mass.; and Nathaniel Merrill of Newbury, Mass.

Notes on Carskaddan genealogy
Bishop, J. C. (Jerome C.)
Mss A 1037
[13] leaves; 28 cm.
1950
Typescript genealogy of some descendants of Robert Carskaddan of Ulster Co., New York.

Carter: some descendants of Rev. Thomas Carter of Woburn, Mass.
Parks, Charles Wellman, b. 1863.
Mss A 1038
1 v. (353 leaves): ports., photographs; 23 cm.
1922
Manuscript and typescript genealogy of some descendants of Thomas Carter, minister of the First Church, Woburn, Mass.

Cartland clan in America
Cartland, George L. (George Lindley), b. 1900.
Mss A 1039
[31] leaves: geneal. tables; 28 cm.
1935
Typescript genealogy of the descendants of John Cartland of Durham, N.H. Manuscript and typescript correspondence (1906-1934 and undated) and miscellaneous handwritten notes concerning the Cartland family.

The Pilgrim fathers: their history and associations at Scrooby and Austerfield
Mss A 103a
34 p.; 28 cm.
Typescript essay written in the early 1900s describing the life and history of the Pilgrim fathers in the years preceding their voyage to Amsterdam in 1608.

Pilgrim father documents just discovered
Mss A 103b
[21] leaves; 28 cm.
Twenty-one sheets pasted with newspaper clippings and other documents including a copy of the letter signed by John Robinson and Bridget, his wife, written prior to the death of Robinson in 1625. Most of the sheets consist of newspaper accounts of the Mayflower Tercentenary in England in 1920. This series of articles most likely appeared in a British newspaper in September, 1920.

Plymouth: Pilgrim father memories
Mss A 103c
[11] leaves; 28 cm.
Clippings of articles and photographs published at the time of the Mayflower Tercentenary in 1920.

13 Generations of the family of John Gay of Dedham, Mass., 1612-1996
Gay-Taylor, Linda (Linda Louise), 1937-.
Mss A 104
[4], 135, [51] leaves: ill.; 28 cm.
1996
Typescript genealogy of the John Gay (ca. 1612-1688) family of Dedham, Mass. Included are photocopies of photographs of Jesse L. Gay (1840-1909) and David MCLellan Gay (1864-1938) and an ancestral charts for Linda Louise Gay (b. 1937).

Notes on the Adams, Hasey, Hanson, Greenleaf, Whittier, and Stone families
Mss A 1040
[23] leaves; 36 cm.
Miscellaneous manuscript and typescript notes on various New Hampshire families; some material is unidentified. Also a typescript explanation of a Dover Neck map.

Bible record for the James D. T. Cudworth family, 1744-1943.
Mss A 1041
[10] p.; 15-29 cm.
Original record with title page for the James D. T. and Martha Y. (Leach) Cudworth family of Providence, RI.

Account book, 1740-1748
Mss A 1042
1 v. (121 p.); 26 cm.
Original leather bound account book for an unidentified merchant or merchants of Boston, Mass. Entries include many clothing items such as necklaces, gloves, shoes, beaver hat, etc. but also miscellaneous goods such as flour, Psalm books, fish, pig iron, bohea tea, etc.

William Henry Chaney (1821-ca. 1902)
Mood, Fulmer, b. 1898.
Mss A 1043
5 leaves; 28 cm.
1932
Typescript genealogy and biographical sketch of William Henry Chaney, born at Chesterville, Me., son of William and Betsey (Linscott) Chaney.

Account book of Rev. Samuel Wigglesworth, 1710-1753, 1767-1768
Wigglesworth, Samuel, 1689-1768.
Mss A 1044
Access to original record is restricted: Material extremely fragile.
1 v. (68 p.); 29 cm.
Additional form: List of marriages published by Spaulding, S.J. "Marriages in Hamilton, Mass., by Rev. Samuel Wigglesworth, 1714-1733" *NEHG Register* 26[1872]:386-388.
Vellum bound account book. Cover has "Rev(d) Sam(l) Wigglesworth account book." The earliest entries, 1710-1712, are for charges for medical care provided by Samuel Wigglesworth as a physician during the short time he practised medicine before entering the ministry. Includes a statement of the terms for his settlement in Ipswich as well as the following entries: "An account of what I have expended about my house, barn, garden, fences, well, little house, etc." and "Account of my salary for the year" 1715-1753. There are four loose account book pages in the back of the book dated 1767-1768.

Genealogy of David Tolles Chamberlin of Weathersfield, Vt., Belton and Waco, Texas, and an account of his children
Chamberlin, Jessie Cora.
Mss A 1045
[1], 404, [1] leaves; 27 cm.
Typescript genealogy.

Ancestors and descendants of Darius Case of North Canton, Conn.
Jones, Edward Payson, 1866-1953.
Mss A 1046
21 leaves; 28 cm.
Typescript genealogy tracing Case's ancestry to John Case of Simsbury, Conn. Case's descendants are traced in both male and female lines.

Two roads from East Hartland to North Canton, Ct., and Cases and Jones who lived on them, 1850-1875
Jones, Edward Payson, 1866-1953.
Mss A 1047
38 leaves; 23 cm.
1949
Typescript memoir containing historical and genealogical data.

Charts of descendants of John(1) Case, Simsbury, Ct.
Jones, Edward Payson, 1866-1953.
Mss A 1048
8 charts: geneal. tables; 22 x 56 cm. folded to 22 x 16 cm.
1949
Eight manuscript charts on graph paper.

Chandlers, collected by Dr. George Chandler of Worcester, not descendants of William and Annis Chandler of Roxbury of 1637; Griffins and Stedmans of Hampton, Conn.
Chandler, George, 1806-1893.
Mss A 1049
[206] p.: geneal. tables; 28 cm.
Correspondence and genealogical notes on various Chandler families. Also genealogies of the Griffin and Steadman families of Hampton, Conn.

A Record of the persons interred in the grave yard on Libby Hill in Gardiner, Maine, 1857-1898
Libby, Ebenezer, d. 1890.
Mss A 105
1 v. ([38] leaves); 20 cm.
Bound manuscript with handwritten entries of 195 individual burials at the Libby Hill graveyard, Gardiner, Maine, 1857 - 1898. Entries were made in large part by Ebenezer Libby (d. 1890), who identifies himself as "Superintendent of [the] Burying Ground." There are 38 leaves filled with writing and the remainder are blank. There are two typewritten pages included from the seller describing the volume.

Bible record for the James A. Rea family, 1841-1991
Mss A 1050
[12] p.; 16-32 cm.
Original record, with title page information, concerning the James A. Rea family of Ohio, Illinois and Oklahoma. Includes photostat copy (a positive and negative copy of the same leaf) of a page from a Bible for the Frederick K. Bowman family, 1847-1882.

A study of the Thomas Allyn family group in Rehoboth, MA (c1722-1850) resulting from the discovery of a cluster of Allyn tombstones in Newman Cemetery, Rumford, RI.
Allyn, Christopher L.
Mss A 1051
11 p.: ill., maps, geneal. tables; 28 cm.
2001
Computer typescript.

Account book of John and Thomas Greenwood, 1709-1804
Greenwood, John, 1673-1737.
Greenwood, Thomas, 1696-1774.
Stone, John.
Mss A 1052
1 v. (ca. 200 p.); 31 cm.
Vellum bound account book for John Greenwood, Thomas Greenwood, and John Stone. First page has "John Stone His Book 1778" below which is "John Greenwood His Book of account" which was x'ed out. The earliest entries by John Greenwood of Newton, Mass., 1709-1734, are business records concerning the weaving of flanel, sheeting, blankets, etc. His records as Justice of the Peace for Middlesex County, Mass. cover 1733-1749. The records of Thomas Greenwood as Justice of the Peace for Middlesex County, Mass. cover 1696-1774 and the records for Justice John Stone cover 1778-1804.

Governor Theophilus Eaton of New Haven, Connecticut, and his ancestry
Ullmann, Helen Schatvet.
Mss A 1053
9 leaves; 28 cm.
2001
Computer typescript genealogy in Register format.

Partial supplement to George Chandler's The Chandler family
Chandler, William Wallace, 1821-1896.
Mss A 1054
28 p.; 26 cm.
1876
Manuscript genealogy that draws largely on the information found in George Chandler's book. Adds some biographical information on William Brown Chandler and wife Electa (Owen) Chandler, daughter of Joel Owen and Mary Gillett.

Our line from William (1) and Hannah (Eaton) Jones of New Haven, Connecticut
Ullmann, Helen Schatvet.
Mss A 1055
21 leaves; 28 cm.
2001
Computer typescript genealogy in Register format.

Baptisms, marriages, & burials Weston-on-Trent, Derbyshire, England: 1565-1799
Genealogical Society of Utah.
Mss A 1056
141 leaves; 29 cm.
1945
Typescript transcription.

Baptisms, marriages, burials Walton-on-Trent, Derbyshire, England 1586-1799
Genealogical Society of Utah.
Mss A 1057
108 leaves; 29 cm.
1945
Typescript transcription.

Record data from the family Bible of Samuel Howard Gerrish and Sarah Jane Rogers
Adams, Douglass Graem, 1950-.
Mss A 1058
[14] leaves; 28 cm.
2001
Computer typescript transcription of original record.

Genealogy of Emmaline Catlin (Mrs. Mark Harmon Pike) of New Marlborough and Sheffield, Mass.
Chamberlin, Jessie Cora.
Mss A 1059
160 leaves; 28 cm.
1915
Typescript genealogy of her ancestral families.

Account of the deaths and marriages since 1853
Mss A 106
1 v. (57 p.); 19 cm.
A handwritten record of the deaths and marriages that occurred in Kennebunk, Maine, from 1853 to 1879. The volume contains 57 pages filled and the remainder are blank.

Genealogy on my mother's side
Hovey, Horace Carter, 1833-1914.
Mss A 1060
1 v. (51, [45] p.): geneal. tables; 19 cm.
Manuscript genealogy of 1853 (revised 1914)
showing the ancestry of Mary Carter Hovey,
daughter of Ezra Carter and Martha Ellsworth.
Includes notes on the descendants of Dr. Ezra
Carter and wife Ruth Eastman of New
Hampshire, and on the descendants of Franklin
Hubbard Carter.

*A journal of the proceedings on board H. M. Ship
Hind, Wm Young Esqr Commander from 11th of
Augt 1779 to the 26th of Feby 1782 kept by Jas
Cox*
Cox, James.
Mss A 1061
1 v. ([240] p.); 20 cm.
Leather bound diary with "James Cox / Journal
book / Hind" on the cover. Entries concern the
date, winds, and remarks. The remarks include a
general description of the weather (wind strength,
direction), his activities (knoting yarns, etc.), the
activities of the crew (lowered top gallant yards,
soundings, etc.), the food received and expended,
and brief notices of who came on board the ship.
The journal covers a trip from England to Quebec
and the return trip.

Journal of Joshua Green, 1770-1774, 1776
Green, Joshua, 1731-1806.
Mss A 1062
1 v.; 18 cm.
Entries interleaved among almanacs. The
almanacs were bound together in the following
order: 1776, 1770-1774.

*Record of marriages by Rev. Angelo Hall:
(ordained as regular Unitarian minister at
Turners Falls, town of Montague, Mass., Dec 9,
1897)*
Hall, Angelo, 1869-1922.
Mss A 1063
1 v. (97 p.); 20 cm.
Handwritten record (on pages 1-13) of marriages
performed in Montague, 1898-1900, and
Andover, 1901-1902. Entries include date, name
of bride and groom, place of residence, age,
occupation, number of marriage, birth place and
the names of their parents. Hall also noted when
the intentions of marriage were entered into the
town records. Page 67 has "Record of
Christenings" dated June 11, 1899. Pages 75-78
have "Record of Funerals" for Montague, 1896-
1900, and Andover, 1900-1903. These entries
include at least some of the following: name, age,
death date and place, funeral date and place, and
place of burial. The rest of the pages are blank.

Slate genealogy
Mss A 1064
1 v. (31 p.); 20 cm.
Handwritten genealogy on the Slate family of
Norwich, Conn. and Bernardston, Mass.

Joseph Richards family genealogy, 1762-1905
Mss A 1065
1 v. (50 p.); 24 cm.
Handwritten genealogy on the Joseph and
Elizabeth (Nichols) Richards family of Wales.
End sheet has "Mary C. Richards 1906" and
inside front cover has stamp for "St. Andrew's
Abbey, So. Newbury, Vermont 05066."

Account book, 1868-1883
Independent Order of Good Templars. Lodge No.
291.
Mss A 1066
1 v. (195 p.); 17 cm.
Leather bound account book with a running
account of credits, debits and the balance in the
treasury.

Account book of Isaac Davis, 1829-1853
Davis, Isaac.
Mss A 1067
1 v. (128 p.); 20 cm.
Entries concern the renting of rooms, houses or
stores on Green, Hanover, Staniford and
Washington Streets in Boston, Mass.

Rice Edwards of Salem, Wenham and Beverly
Massachusetts Bay Colony 1615-1683
Kenney, Donald S.
Mss A 1067
[9] leaves; 28 cm.
2001
Computer typescript on Rice Edwards which
refutes that Rice Edwards' wife was named Joan
or Joanna.

Cash book of William Donnison, 1827-1832
Donnison, William.
Mss A 1069
1 v. (161 p.); 19 cm.
Account book with hand written tally of cash
received verses expenses and the balance.
Includes monthly lists of general expenses,
"expenses of every kind paid," "charges on real
estates in Boston," repair, insurance, taxes, etc. on
estates in Boston," and bank account balance.

Barrows family papers, 19th or early 20th
century
Barrows family.
Mss A 107
[54] leaves; 7-22 cm.
Handwritten notes and papers of the Barrus,
Barrows, Barrett families of Mass. and N.H.
Included are a bound notebook containing notes
on the family of Abraham Barrus (1714-1789) of
Attleboro, Mass., and obituary for Hannah M.
Barrows (1843-1932), and a Bible record for the
family of Samuel A. Barrus (b. 1845).

Receipt book of John and Mary Gillespie, 1767-
1797
Mss A 1070
1 v. (110 p.); 17 x 10 cm.
Leather bound account book (missing front cover)
with hand written notices dated and signed by
various merchants, constables, etc. stating that
they received payment from John and Mary
Gillespie of Boston and Cohassett, Mass.

Catalog of books owned by A. D. W. French
French, Aaron Davis Weld, 1835-1896.
Mss A 1071
1 v.; 16 cm.
Leather address book with a list of books, chiefly
genealogical.

Receipt book of Jane Ivers, 1750-1775
Mss A 1072
1 v.; 14 x 17 cm.
Leather bound account book with hand written
notices dated and signed by various merchants,
etc. stating that they received payment from Jane
Ivers of Boston, Mass.

Our heritage [Brooks]: parts I and II
Adair, Carolyn Brooks, b. 1876.
Mss A 1073
37, 33 leaves: geneal. tables; 20 cm.
1954
Mimeographed typescript tracing the ancestors
and descendants of Samuel Brooks and wife
Dorothy Stevens Leonard. Ancestral families,
most from Massachusetts, include Brooks, Dean,
Deming, Fenner, Leonard, Rice, Stone, Swetland,
Willard, and Woods.

Autograph album of William Mason Cornell, ca.
1846-1882
Cornell, William Mason, 1802-1895.
Mss A 1074
Access to original record is restricted: Material
fragile.
1 v.; 13 x 20 cm.
Autograph album with the autographs of college
presidents, clergymen, lawyers, doctors,
professors, librarians, antiquarians, congressmen,
representatives, governors, etc.

Orderly book for a Rhode Island artillery
regiment, 1776-1779
Mss A 1075
1 v.; 20 cm.
Contains an incomplete record of the orders
issued at various times and places by George
Washington (Commander-in-chief), General
Sullivan (commander of the forces in Rhode
Island), and William Perkins. Perkins was a
commander of a Rhode Island artillery regiment.
The orderly book was trimmed at some point
(with the loss of some text) and bound.

Commonplace book of John Dane, 1682
Dane, John, ca. 1612-1684.
F74/I6/D36/1978 Microfilm also Mss A 1076
Access to original record is restricted: Material
fragile; Use microfilm copy.
1 microfilm reel: positive; 35 mm. Original is 1
(132 p.); 15 cm.
Additional form: Transcribed version of the prose
narrative published as *A declaration of
remarkable providences in the course of my life*
(Boston, Mass.: Samuel G. Drake, 1854)
Vellum bound book with a lappet. Contains two
narratives, one in rhyme and one in prose, some
religious meditations, and advice to the author's
children in rhyme. The record contains some
notes on sermons by Mr. Dennison, Mr. Hubbard,
and Mr. Gerrish. There is also some short hand.
The narratives provide the author's recollections
of his childhood in England, his life as a taylor's
apprentice while a young man in Herford
(England), settling in New England, and life in
Ipswich, Massachusetts.

The genealogy of Frothingham in New England
Wyman, Thomas Bellows, 1817-1878.
Mss A 1077
168, 3 p.: coat of arms, geneal. tables; 21 cm.
1850
Handwritten genealogy on the ancestors and
descendants of William Frothingham of
Charlestown, Mass. There are hand drawn charts
for the English and Scottish branches as well as
diagrams for the Frothingham families in
Charlestown, Boston, Cambridge, Salem,
Newburyport, and Danvers, Mass. The diagrams
are followed by "an alphabetical arrangement of
the Frothingham family". Includes presentation
letter to Richard Frothingham.

*In memoriam M. R. K. [Matilda Rockwell Kent]
born May 5th 1832 died Oct 20th 1863*
Kent, V. T.
Mss A 1078
[50] p.: ill.; 17 cm.
1882
Memorial on Matilda Rockwell Kent written for
her children (Rockwell, Alice, Frederick and
Percy Kent) by V. T. Kent. The family lived in
Brooklyn, NY.

*Transcript of the diary of the Rev. Samuel
Chandler while at York, Me., and at Gloucester,
Mass., 1745-1746, 1749-1764*
Chandler, Samuel, 1713-1775.
Mss A 1079
1 v. ([510] p.); 26 cm.
Manuscript transcription by Dr. George Chandler
of Worcester, Mass., of portions of Samuel
Chandler's diary. Typical entries include sermon
texts and topics; locations where Chandler
preached; accounts of ministerial activities such
as visits to parishioners; daily weather; travels;
farm chores and family life; and financial
accounts. There are also occasional yearly lists of
deaths in the parish, and lists of scholars whom
Chandler taught.

*Bible record of the Abraham G. Wyman family,
1801-1890*
Wyman, Abrahahm G., 1801-1868.
Mss A 108
[5] p.; 28 cm.
Original record with title page concerning the
Wyman family of New Hampshire and
Massachusetts.

Diary of Josiah Williston, 1808-1814
Williston, Josiah.
Mss A 1080
Access to original record is restricted: Material
fragile.
1 v. ([266] p.); 16 cm.
Diary of a man living in Boston, Mass. circa the
War of 1812. Entries concern brief notes on the
weather, deaths and some marriage notices, as
well as local and national events: fires, the
election of James Madison and proclamations by
the president, town meetings, ordinations, arrival
of ships into Boston harbor, processions of
various regiments and brigades, and news of the
embargo.

Caldwell, William and Joseph and James Caldwell, perhaps brothers, natives of Scotland, emigrants to Ulster. Certainly immigrants to New Hampshire by 1721, 1726, and 1736
Priest, Alice L. (Alice Lucinda), 1866-1954.
Caldwell, Lucinda King, 1798-1889.
Mss A 1081
1 v.: plates, ports., maps (some col., 1 folded), ports.; 28 cm.
1932-1933
Typescript genealogy, extensively annotated by hand, primarily concerning James Caldwell of Londonderry and Windham, N.H., and his descendants. The work also traces the descendants of William Caldwell of Londonderry and Chester, N.H., and Joseph Caldwell of Portsmouth and Nottingham West (Hudson), N.H.

Estes family chart
Estes, Charles, b. 1849.
Mss A 1082
1 item: geneal. tables; 28 x 30 cm.
1888
Reduced image (mounted) of a hand-drawn tree showing descendants of Richard Estes and wife Elizabeth Beck of New Hampshire and Massachusetts.

Charter relating to Simon Fiske
Mss A 1083
Access to original record is restricted: Material fragile; Use preservation photocopy
2 items; 28 cm.
Charter (1440) relating to Simon Fisk. Also a letter (19 November 1946) from Roundell P. Sanderson to G. Andrews Moriarty.

Ye Atte Wode annals, October 1929, giving English history, descendants of Harman, Henry, John, Philip, Stephen, Thomas of Ipswich and Thomas of Wethersfield ...
Atwood, Elijah Francis, b. 1871.
Mss A 1084
1 v.: ill., maps, ports., photographs; 25 cm.
1930
Genealogical data on the Atwood family in England and America. Manuscript annotations by the author.

Notes concerning the family of William Chapman of Ipswich, Mass., and his son John of Ashford, Conn.
Rose, Henry N., Mrs.
Mss A 1085
[25] leaves; 25 cm.
1937
Typescript genealogy.

Great Stambridge parish register, 1559-1750
Great Stambridge (England)
Mss A 1086
[96] leaves; 42 cm folded to 30 cm.
Photocopy of original register recording the baptisms, marriages (note 1584-1599 missing), and burials in the parish of Great Stambridge. Two pages of the original were copied onto a single leaf.

Cobb family of Massachusetts
Mss A 1087
[8] leaves; 26 cm.
Manuscript genealogy of some descendants of David Cobb and wife Lucy Bickford of Massachusetts, in particular the children and grandchildren of Elisha Bickford Cobb of Hingham, Mass.

Descendants of Henry Collins
Mss A 1088
9 leaves; 18 cm.
Brief manuscript genealogy of some descendants of Henry Collins and wife Ann who immigrated in 1635.

Genealogical data of the Cobb and Candler families
Cobb, George W., b. 1895.
Mss A 1089
132 leaves: geneal. tables; 28 cm.
Typescript genealogy tracing the ancestry of George W. Cobb and wife Margaret L. Henderson of New York City and Old Greenwich, Conn.

Compilation of pedigree charts from the Sheboygan County, Wisconsin, Sesquicentennial
Sheboygan County Genealogical Society.
Mss A 109
x, 278, [6] p.: charts; 28 cm.
1990
Typescript collection of pedigree charts compiled by the Sheboygan County Genealogical Society for their sesquicentennial celebration.

Account book for the Boston Express (Red Top Wagons), 1845-1846
Pollard, Henry, 1810-1852.
Mss A 1090
1 v. (280 p.); 20 cm.
Entries list the customer's name, who/what was transported, delivery location, and the cost. Newspaper clippings were pasted over some pages. Includes some company advertisements.

Genealogical material on Cogswell families
Cogswell, Edward Russell, 1841-1914.
Mss A 1091
17 v. (ca. [272] p.); 21 cm.
Manuscript genealogies and notes, unattributed, but likely the work of Edward Russell Cogswell. Genealogies include the descendants of Jonathan Cogswell and wife Elizabeth Wade of Ipswich, Mass. (vols. 1-5); descendants of John Cogswell and wife Elizabeth (vol. 9); and descendants of Nathaniel Cogswell and wife Judith Badger of Ipswich and Haverhill, Mass. (vols. 10-15). The remaining volumes (6-8, 16-17) contain miscellaneous notes on Cogswells of Westford, Concord, Marlborough, and Bedford, Mass., and Londonderry, N.H.; extracts from Middlesex deeds and probate records; and relevant gravestone inscriptions from the burying ground at Essex, Mass.

The war-time diary of Walter Lindsay Avery, 1917 January 2-1918 October 2
Avery, Walter Lindsay, 1892-1978.
Mss A 1092
ii, 85, 12 p.; 22-28 cm.
Typescript transcription of orginal record along with some photocopies of newspaper articles concerning Walter L. Avery. Includes a few copies of newspaper articles on Walter Avery's father, Frank Elmer Avery as well.

Partial supplement to Howard M. Chapin's Life of Deacon Samuel Chapin, of Springfield
Chapin, Howard M. (Howard Millar), 1887-1940.
Mss A 1093
[11] leaves: plates, geneal. tables; 24 cm.
Manuscript letter (11 August 1909) in which the writer conveys additional information on the Chapin family of Devon, England. Also six plates from Chapin's "Life of Deacon Samuel Chapin of Springfield."

Receipt book of Edward Russell, 1798-1810
Mss A 1094
2 v.; 10 x 16, 10 x 20 cm.
Account books with hand written notices dated and signed by various merchants, etc. stating that they received payment from Edward Russell of Yarmouth, Mass.

Chandler
Clarke, Mary Stanton Blake.
Mss A 1095
1 v. ([122] p.): geneal. tables; 26 cm.
1858
Manuscript genealogy of descendants of William Chandler and wife Annice of Roxbury, Mass.; of William Ward and wife Elizabeth of Sudbury and Marlborough, Mass.; and of Daniel Clark of Windsor, Conn.

A history of the Chubb family, 1609 to 1942
Bixby, Stedman G.
Mss A 1097
[79] leaves: geneal. tables; 29 x 21 cm.
[1942?]
Typescript genealogy of the descendants of Thomas Chubb of Salem and Beverly, Mass.

Descendants of Richard Church, of Plymouth
Mss A 1098
1 v. ([264] p.); 27 cm.
Manuscript genealogy to nine generations, through about 1892.

Commonplace book of Samuel Brown, ca. 1700-1812
Brown, Samuel, 1687-1749.
Mss A 1099
Access to original record restricted: Material fragile.
1 v.; 13 cm.
Small notebook with transcriptions of sermons (by Mr. Alling, Crary & Mitchel), Biblical passages in Latin and Greek, and family records recording the births of family members. Also includes the following entries: "The Rhetorick of Farnabe translated" [Thomas Farnaby's "Index Rhetoricus"] , "Joseph Brown his book ye 1790," "Value of silver money per the ounce" from 1705-1747, "Josiah Brown Eqr liber anno domini may 2 1760," and Samuel Brown's "A memorandum of the remarkables of my life."

Eliab Alden, fourth in descent from John Alden the Pilgrim and his descendants
Alden, Charles Henry, 1836-1906.
Mss A 11
[i, 23] p.; 27 cm.
1904.
An alphabetical listing of the descendants of Eliab (5) Alden to the ninth generation. This is a manuscript copy made by Henry Shaw of Beachmont (Revere), Mass., on 1904 Feb 23 from the original.

Log Book, 1804-1809
Watts, [Edward?], d. ca. 1815.
Mss A 110
[68] leaves: ill.; 18 cm.
Ship's log book kept by an officer in the American navy during a voyage of the ship Fisgard along the coast of South America. Includes data on making ordnance and lights, also watercolor illustrations of the country and some of its inhabitants.

Register of births for the William Smith family, 1780-1804
Mss A 1100
[1] p.; 16 cm.
Handwritten record of the births of William Smith's children. Smith lived in Buxton, Maine. Record appears to be just the bottom half of the original.

Chipman - Parker genealogical records
Trethewey, Alberta Mary Parker, b. 1871.
Mss A 1101
[18] leaves; 28 cm.
1951
Manuscript and typescript material supplementing Alberto Lee Chipman's "The Chipman family, a genealogy of the Chipmans in America".

Diary of William Otis Rockwood, 1878
Rockwood, William Otis.
Mss A 1102
1 v.; 15 cm.
Contains short entries concerning Rockwood's activities and business dealings in the railroad industry.

Orderly book 3d troop 2nd Regt Lt Dragoons commanded by Capt Jero Hoogland, 1782-1783
Hoogland, Jeronimus.
Purketh, Henry, ca. 1755-1846.
Mss A 1103
Access to original record restricted: Use published transcription.
1 v. (172 p.); 16 x 21 cm.
Additional form: Transcribed version by Salvatore Tarantino and John T. Hayes; published as *Soldiering On, 1782-1783: a revised and annotated edition of the orderly book of the Third Troop, Second Continental Light Dragoons as kept by Captain Jeronimus Hoogland and Sergeant Henry Purketh* (Fort Lauderdale, Fla.: Saddlebag Press, 2001)
Record of the general, regimental and troop orders issued to the Third Troop Second Continental Light Dragoons. The orders were recorded by Jeronimus Hoogland and Henry Purketh during 1782 and 1783. Includes accounts of the provisions given to the soldiers including clothing, equipment and food.

Diary and account book of Capt. William Sweat, 1758-1771
Sweet, William.
Mss A 1104
1 v. (ca. 220 p.); 16 cm.
Diary contains a narrative of the expedition against Ticonderoga during the French and Indian War.

John Rodgers Jewitt: the descendants from 1840 to 1940
Jewitt, Frank Henry, b. 1880.
Mss A 1105
69, xviii p.; 18 cm.
1940
Typescript genealogy of the descendants of John Rodgers Jewitt of Boston, England; Boston, Massachusetts; and Middletown, Conn., who married Hester Jones of Bristol, England.

Genealogy of the Deane family: descendants of Walter Deane of Chard, Somersetshire, England and Taunton, Massachusetts
Dean, Walter.
Mss A 1106
[1], 105 leaves; 28 cm.
1924
Typescript genealogy for up to nine generations. Supplemental material added on 12 February 1941.

Inscriptions from Tarrytown Dutch Church Cemetery, Westchester County, New York
Miller, Robert Brown, 1856-1915.
Mss A 1108
[208] leaves; 26 cm.
1915
Typescript transcription.

More than 300 Foggs
Sauers, Grace Harrison.
Mss A 1109
[1], xxvi leaves: geneal. tables; 28 cm.
Twenty-six manuscript charts showing the descendants of Samuel Fogg of Hampton, N.H.

Knowlton family Bible record, 1805-1882
Mss A 111
[5] leaves; 28 cm.
Photocopy of original records from a Bible, lacking title page. Includes photocopies of newspaper death and marriage notices.

Some genealogical notes and charts [including Dean, Hathaway, White, Hammond, Sisson, Putnam, Oliver, and Warner families]
White, Louie Dean, b. 1860.
Mss A 1110
[153] leaves: geneal. tables, facsim.; 28 cm.
1938
Typescript genealogy of some descendants of Walter Dean of Taunton, Mass.; Nicholas Hathaway of Taunton; Thomas White of Weymouth, Mass.; Benjamin Hammond of Sandwich, Mass.; Richard Sisson of Rhode Island and Massachusetts; Thomas Putnam of Danvers, Mass.; Launcelot Oliver of Barre, Mass.; and Andrew Warner of Hadley, Mass. Also pedigree charts completed by hand.

Descendants of Jessee [sic] Fletcher: dates of deaths, marriages, etc., up to the year 1895
Fletcher, Clifton, b. 1823.
Mss A 1112
1 v. ([46] p.); 21 cm.
1895
Manuscript genealogy of the descendants of Jesse Fletcher and wife Patience Hobart of Brookline and North Groton, New Hampshire.

Ancestry of the Taylor family: Part I ancestry of Joseph and Betsey (Green) Taylor; Part II ancestry of Nathan and Mary (Walton) Tylor
Taylor, Arthur O. (Arthur Orison), 1858-1948.
Mss A 1113
86 leaves; 29 cm.
Typescript genealogy. Leaves 1-4 and 45-46 contains information on the Taylor family while the remaining 80 leaves concern allied families.

A complete system of family registration [Hill ancestry]
Shattuck, Lemuel, 1793-1859.
Mss A 1114
1 v. ([70] p.): geneal. tables; 26 cm.
1841
Printed forms onto which the ancestry of Charlotte "Lottie" Farnsworth Hill has been entered. Ancestral families include Farnsworth, Fogg, Hill, Leach, Lowe, and Thayer. Children are enumerated for some families, including Philip Ellis Hill and wife Louisa Packard, and James Delap Farnsworth and wife Rebecca Miller Thayer Fogg.

Jenney - Jennings family
Jennings, Herman Winslow.
Mss A 1115
[26] leaves: photographs, facsim.; 28 cm.
Typescript genealogy of the descendants of Henry Jennings and wife Meribah Dexter of Monroe County, N.Y. Also facsimiles of marriage certificates, photocopies of newspaper clippings, and facsimiles of Jennings and Whitney Bible records.

Account book of Colonel Jonathan Kingsbury, 1787-1803
Kingsbury, Jonathan, 1751-1806.
Mss A 1116
1 v. (150 p.); 16 cm.
Small account book without a cover. The bulk of the entries concern sawing done by Kingsbury for various customers. Near the end of the book is a section with the title "Memorandum book" that has entries concerning the meetings of the West Company militia in Needham.

Proceedings of the Committee on Necklands, 1823-1829
Boston (Mass.). Committee on Necklands.
Mss A 1117
1 v. (80 p.); 21 cm.
Records of the committee to supervise the Necklands. Includes accounts of cash received, cash paid, bills approved by the committee, and meeting sumaries.

Genealogy of the Jewett family
Bradlee, Arthur E., 1854-1916.
Mss A 1118
1 v. (75 p.): coat of arms; 22 cm.
Manuscript genealogy of some descendants of Edward Jewett of Bradford, West Riding of Yorkshire, England, whose sons, Maximillian and Joseph, settled at Rowley, Mass., in 1639.

Account book of William Parker Jr., 1732-1739
Parker, William, 1703-1781.
Mss A 1119
1 v. (80 p.); 19 cm.
On first page is "William Parker Jun his book of acco(ts) begun March the first anno domini 1732/3 at Portsmouth in New Hampsh(re) in New England to March 1739." Entries concern fees for cases, producing or copying various documents and forms such as power of attorney, deed, writs, indentures, petitions, etc.

Gillis family Bible record, 1779-1857
Mss A 112
[2] leaves; 28 cm.
Photocopy of original Bible records, lacking title page.

Genealogical notes on the Jewett family
Bradlee, Arthur E., 1854-1916.
Mss A 1120
34 items: geneal. tables; 28 cm.
Manuscript notes on various Jewett families descended from Maximillian and Joseph Jewett, brothers who settled at Rowley, Mass., in 1639. Includes correspondence from Joshua Jewett (1856) and H.L. Jewett (1899); a manuscript history (ca. 1860) by Joshua Jewett concerning the brothers James, Jonas, and Nathan Jewett who settled in Solon, Me.; several family records; notes from published works; newspaper obituaries; and miscellaneous notes. Also two certificates of commendation (1802, 1806) for Lucy Baldwin.

The Clark family: some facts relative to Arthur Clark and his descendants principally collected previous to the year 1858
Clark, George Faber, 1817-1899.
Mss A 1121
1 v. (289 p.); 26 cm.
Manuscript genealogy.

General record of deaths in Hingham, 1837-1877
Mss A 1122
1 v. (58 p.); 20 cm.
Handwritten list that includes the date, name (many entries have son, daughter, or wife of...), their age, place of death if not in Hingham, and a few entries note how the individual died. Despite the title, there are numerous individuals listed who were from other communities, e.g. "of Boston," etc. -- though sometimes formerly of Hingham.

Account book of rents paid by tenants of Peck Lane House, 1838-1840
Mss A 1123
1 v. (75 p.); 20 cm.
Entries record the date, customer's name, duration of rent, room number, payment and the cash received. Verso of front cover has "Plan of Peck Lane House".

Clarke connections
Clarke, George S. (George Sharp), b. 1884.
Mss A 1124
1 v. ([190] p.); 15 cm.
Manuscript notes on Clarke's ancestral families, including Babcock, Barker, Borden, Cherry, Clarke, Coggeshall, Dungan, Latham, Peckham, Sage, Slocum, Star, and Wicks.

Clayton and related families of New Jersey and [the] eastern United States, 1650-1850: (a preliminary study)
Clayton, James Wilbur, 1905-.
Mss A 1125
[39] leaves; 28 cm.
1942
Typescript genealogy and notes; copies of newspaper genealogical columns.

Memorial of ancestry [Coffin family]
Mss A 1126
1 v. ([14] p.); 18 cm.
Manuscript genealogy of the descendants of Tristram Coffin of Salisbury, Haverhill, Newbury, and Nantucket, Massachusetts.

Genealogy of the family of Dr. John Clarke
Clark, William, 1670-1742.
Mss A 1127
[8, 6] p.: geneal. tables; 25 cm.
Manuscript statement (copied from original by F.M. Harris) concerning the ancestry of William Clark of Boston, Mass., son of John Clark and Martha Whittingham. Surnames of his ancestral families include Clark, Saltonstall, Whittingham, and Hubbard. The full statement is published in the N.E.H.G. Register 33[1879]: 19-20. Also includes six manuscript items: three relating to the Clark family above; two relating to the descendants of John Clark and Mary White; and one relating to the the descendants of John Clark and wives Sarah Shrimpton and Elizabeth Hutchinson.

Bible record of the Ralph and Fanny (Bartlett) Clapp family, 1795-1928
Mss A 1128
[20] p.: col. maps; 23 cm.
Original Bible record (with title page) for Ralph and Fanny (Bartlett) Clapp of Westhampton, Mass., and descendants.

Bible record of the Charles C. and Sarah M. (Bryant) Clapp family, 1874-1928
Mss A 1129
[15] p.; 29 cm.
Original Bible record (with title page) for Charles Carroll and Sarah Maria (Bryant) Clapp and children.

Tirrell family Bible record, 1824-1927
Mss A 113
[5] leaves; 28 cm.
Photocopy of original records and title page from a Bible.

Bible record of the Sylvanus and Charity (Pierce) Clapp family, 1764-1862
Mss A 1130
[6] p.; 27 cm.
Original Bible record (with title page) for Sylvanus and Charity (Pierce) Clapp and children, perhaps of Westhampton, Mass.

Bible record of the Ralph and Fanny (Bartlett) Clapp family, 1795-1905
Mss A 1131
[24] p.: ill.; 23 cm.
Original Bible record (with title page) for Ralph and Fanny (Bartlett) Clapp of Westhampton, Mass., and descendants.

Genealogical material on the Kimball and Clapp families
Mss A 1132
[13] leaves; 28 cm.
Manuscript notes and correspondence concerning Ebenezer Kimball and wife Keziah W. Harris, and Ellery Channing Clapp.

Clark family letters, 1832-1897
Clark, Leander, b. 1828.
Mss A 1133
27 items.
Routine correspondence between various members of the Clark family of Massachusetts, New York, and Pennsylvania, concerning general family matters, health, weather, daily activities, and work. While many of the letters contain indirect genealogical information, only two (from 1897) have genealogy as their primary topic: (1) Typescript transcriptions of five letters (1832-1851; one original is in the collection) from Otis Clark of Lee, Dalton, and Stockbridge, Berkshire Co., Mass., to his brother, Eleazer Clark.

The Clark family of New Hampshire
Mss A 1134
1 v.; 19 cm.
Genealogical record of some descendants of Amos Clark of Hampstead, N.H., through his son, Moses Clark, who married Molly Gile, daughter of Jonathan Gile and wife Lydia Colby. Includes a brief account of Molly (Gile) Clark's life, death, and character, written probably by her son Amos. Information is given on several of her children, in particular her son Amos Clark who married Betsy Hardy. Amos's children are recorded, as are his grandchildren through sons Roswell L. and George W. Clark. Vital statistics on other Clarks are scattered throughout the volume.

Bible record of the Cheever family, 1719-1876
Mss A 1135
1 v. ([4] p.): ill.; 27 cm.
Original Bible record (without title page) for Samuel Cheever and descendants.

Hood family of Lynn, Mass.
Mss A 1136
[2] p.: geneal. tables; 20 x 26 cm.
Genealogical chart showing some descendants of Richard Hood, Quaker, of Lynn, Mass. Includes allied families Phillips, Rich, and Bassett.

Ancestors of the Jones family of Oakwood, Oakland Co., Michigan
Jones, Melvin E.
Mss A 1137
1 item: geneal. tables; 65 x 54 cm. folded to 23 cm.
Blueprint tabular pedigree showing the ancestors of Melvin E. Jones. Compiled in 1927 and revised several times through 1931.

Stephen Hopkins of the Mayflower and some of his descendants
Hopkins, Timothy, b. 1859.
Mss A 1139
[83] leaves; 28 cm.
Typescript genealogy (beginning with the seventh generation) of descendants of Stephen Hopkins of the Mayflower. This unpublished material is a continuation of an article that appeared in the *N.E.H.G. Register* 102[1948] through 105[1951].

Tirrell family Bible record, 1801-1856
Mss A 114
[4] leaves; 28 cm.
Photocopy of original records and title page from a Bible.

Halliday records copied from those owned by Edith Halliday Jennelle, daughter of Edwin Warner Halliday, fourth son of Samuel Halliday
Mss A 1140
1 v. ([84] p.); 22 cm.
Manuscript genealogy of the descendants of Alexander Halliday and wife Jean of Scotland, whose sons emigrated to Ohio in 1818-20. Also genealogy of the descendants of William Parker and wife Betsey Wyatt of Massachusetts and Ohio.

Stephen Hopkins of the Mayflower and some of his descendants
Patch, Miriam A., b. 1883.
Mss A 1141
10 leaves: geneal. tables; 28 cm.
Manuscript genealogy. Also two pedigree charts showing the author's ancestry.

William Hamblet, with descendants and others with the name of Hamblet [Hamlet]
Blake, Marion E.
Mss A 1142
[432] p.; 19 cm.
Typescript genealogical data on descendants of William Hamblet and wife Sarah (Paige) Hubbard. Each individual's information is entered on a looseleaf sheet, then filed alphabetically by first name.

Ancestors of many names: direct progenitors of John Milton Gregory, LL.D., and Julia (Gregory) Gregory, his wife
Gregory, Grant, b. 1864.
Mss A 1143
[174] leaves: geneal. tables; 28 cm.
1945
Typescript genealogy of the ancestral families of Grant Gregory. Includes pedigree charts.

Some Gregg lines
Arthur, Robert, b. 1886.
Mss A 1144
[1], 55 leaves; 28 cm.
1958
Typescript genealogy of the descendants of David Gregg or MacGregor of Scotland; William Gregg of Delaware; Greggs of Pennsylvania; Robert Gregg of Ireland; James Gregg of New Hampshire; and Greggs of South Carolina.

Bible record for the Rufus Rose family, 1783-1827
Mss A 1145
[4, 2] p.; 26-28 cm.
Original record, without title page information, concerning the Rufus Rose family of Granville, Mass. and Sherburne, NY. Includes a two page typescript transcription of the original record.

Diary of Mabel MacGregor Watt, 1896-1902
Watt, Mabel MacGregor.
Mss A 1146
3 v.; 17 x 10 cm.
Diary of a young woman living in South Ontario (in Guelph?). Watt was attending college and although she does note going to school and attending lectures, the entries tend to focus on her social activities after class or while at home.

Some of the ancestors of Frank Rockwood Hall
Hall, Mary Elizabeth Farnsworth.
Mss A 1149
1 v.: ill., ports., coat of arms, geneal. tables; 26 cm.
1878
Manuscript genealogy of the ancestral families of Frank Rockwood Hall, son of Samuel Hall and wife Harriet Bridge. Includes an original first communion certificate (1872) for Hall's wife, Florence May Macisaac.

Martin family Bible record, 1739-1790
Mss A 115
[1] leaf; 28 cm.
Photocopy of original Bible record lacking title page.

Crooke: Elmendorf - Rutger line
Kinkead, George B.
Mss A 1150
[20] leaves; 28 cm.
1937
Typescript genealogy of the descendants of John Crooke of New York, through Petrus Edmundus Elmendorph and Rutger Bleeker.

Genealogy of the Barrell family: dealing more especially with those descendents of George Barrell, died in Boston, Massachusetts, September 2, 1643, who have borne the surname of Barrell
Barrell, Joseph, 1869-1919.
Mss A 1151
185 leaves: ill., ports., coat of arms, photographs; 28 cm.
1915
Typescript with photographs glued on various pages. Includes additional information by the author's son.

Account book and diary of Alexander Kirkwood, 1751-1757
Kirkwood, Alexander.
Mss A 1152
1 v. (100 p.); 16 cm.
Access to original record restricted: Material fragile.
Account book with brief diary entries primarily concerning the arrival/departure from various ports in North America (Boston, Philadelphia, etc.) and Europe (London, Cadus, etc.). The first eight pages and front cover are missing. Entries include lists of things bought or sold such as wheat, corn, beans, fox skins, codfish, tobacco, beef, etc. as well as a crew list and a 1755 list of indentured servants for four years.

Account book of William Brown, 1835-1836
Brown, William.
Mss A 1153
1 v. (50 p.); 21 cm.
Original account book for a manufacturer of bonnetts in Boston, Mass. Front paste down has "Mrs Wlt & GS Montague Boston Mass New England 1835" and "Wm Brown's book 1835."

Account book of Henry Quincy, 1770-1773
Quincy, Henry.
Mss A 1154
1 v. (134 p.); 20 cm.
Vellum bound account book. Entries include the sale of charcoal, tobacco, indigo, rum, etc.

Account books of Josiah Quincy Jr., 1831-1840, 1850-1851
Quincy, Josiah, 1802-1882.
Mss A 1155
3 v.; 20-21 cm.
First volume has "acct of labor &c. upon the city lands," 1831-1839. Most of the entries simply have the date, a list of individuals and how much they were owed. A few of the later entries indicate the work they had done such as sawing timber, recording deeds, etc. There are also entries for "Virginia Rail Roads," "Massachusetts Rail Roads," "New York Rail Roads" and "Estimated cost of filling South Cove as pr plan of Jany 25 1837." Many of the entries for 1837 concern wharfs leased to various merchants.

Names of the descendants of William and Mary (Earle) Corey who settled early at Portsmouth, R.I.
Mss A 1156
[57] leaves; 28 cm.
Newspaper clippings from the Boston Evening Transcript (1904). Also typescript sheets listing Coreys whose ancestors are unknown.

Account book of Joshua Pico, 1764-1784
Pico, Joshua.
Mss A 1157
1 v. (50 p.); 20 cm.
Vellum bound account book for a Boston merchant. Entries include the sale of oil, blubber, fish, etc.

Coston family
Butler, Charles, Mrs.
Mss A 1158
[92] leaves: ill., coat of arms, geneal. tables; 29 cm.
Typescript genealogy of the descendants of Ebenezer Coston of New Hampshire. Includes allied families Skinner, Leonard, Hale, and Stevenson.

Descendants of Nicholas Cottrell
Cottrell, Ellen Rowland, 1870-1929.
Mss A 1159
[156] leaves; 28 cm.
1952
Manuscript genealogy of Nicholas Cottrell of Newport and Westerly, R.I., and Taunton, Mass., and his descendants.

History of the family of Perkins
Perkins, Horatio N. (Horatio Nelson), 1808-1883.
Mss A 116
29 p., [131] leaves; 24 cm.
1842
Genealogical data on the descendants of John Perkins (1590-1654) of Ipswich, Mass., handwritten in ink and pencil, bound. Includes correspondence and clippings.

Receipt book for Stanton and Spelman, 1814-1815
Mss A 1160
1 v. (200 p.); 11 x 21 cm.
Account book with hand written notices dated and signed by various merchants stating that they received payment from the firm Stanton and Spelman of Boston, Mass. for various services provided or goods sold.

Account book of Samuel Pears, 1692-1731
Peirce, Samuel.
Mss A 1161
1 v.; 9 x 15 cm.
Access to original record restricted: Material fragile.
Small leather bound account book (leather stretched over wooden boards) with entries concerning the receipt of goods by Mr. Pears and purchases of yards of cloth, mending, etc. from Mr. Pears.

Davis reunion: 5 mo. 28 1903
Cranor, Henry Downes. The Davis family.
Mss A 1162
1 v.: ill., photographs; 22 cm.
Manuscript minutes of a reunion (28 May 1903) of descendants of John Davis, son of Samuel Davis of Plymouth, Philadelphia County, Pa. Volume includes transcriptions of speeches given at the reunion and names of attendees. One of the speeches, "The Davis Family" by Henry Downes Cranor, was printed, and a copy is bound with this volume. Also bound with the volume is an original deed from 1803.

The Cowells of Boston and Wrentham, Mass., being a compilation of documentary evidence tracing the line between them
Cowell, Samuel.
Mss A 1163
1 v.: coat of arms, geneal. tables; 25 cm.
1888
Manuscript genealogy of the descendants of Edward Cowell.

John Rickerson on the Lexington alarm from Connecticut and his descendants
Edes, Grace Williamson, b. 1864.
Mss A 1164
[139] leaves; 28 cm.
Typescript genealogy.

Chronicles of the Bement family in America for Clarence Sweet Bement
Leach, Josiah Granville, 1842-1922.
Mss A 1166
[2], 3, 399; 29 cm.
1928
Carbon copy typescript.

The genealogy of the Jacob Barrickman family from Pennsylvania, Kentucky to Franklin, Ripley and Marion Counties, Indiana
Shoemaker, Vivian (Barrickman), 1903-1959.
Mss A 1167
17 leaves; 28 cm.
1967
Mimeographed typescript genealogy.

Record of the family of Adam Barger, son and 8th child of Philip Barger - Eve Clements, of Blacksburg, Va.
Barger, G. J. P. (Gervase James Patterson), b. 1882.
Mss A 1168
[1], 37 leaves; 22 x 28 cm.
[1962
Mimeographed typescript genealogy.

Time scale chart of family tree of William Barger, Sarah Ann Zeck
Barger, G. J. P. (Gervase James Patterson), b. 1882.
Mss A 1169
[1], 27, [4] leaves; 22 x 28 cm.
1959
Mimeographed typescript genealogy.

Andrew Wallace Wadsworth's descendants, 1844-1997
True, William Wadsworth, 1925-.
Mss A 117
15 p.; 28 cm.
1998
Typescript genealogy of the descendants of Andrew Wallace Wadsworth (1844-1930) of Lincolnville and Camden, Maine, for five generations, including female lines, no index. It is an update of an addendum compiled by the same author in 1981 to the book: Two Hundred and Fifty Years of the Wadsworth Family in America by Horace Andrew Wadsworth (Lawrence, MA: Printed at the Eagle steam job printing rooms, 1883). Also, includes four Mayflower ancestries for individuals in the genealogy.

An early Barrickman line in the State of Kentucky
Barekman, June Beverly, 1915-.
Mss A 1170
8 leaves; 28 cm.
1969
Photocopied typescript genealogy of the descendants of Jacob Barrickman.

The Bardin genealogy
Bardin, Howard Gay, b. 1884.
Mss A 1171
[1], 11, [2] leaves; 28 cm.
1957
Typescript genealogy of Joel Bardin, his siblings, and their descendants.

Some Bible records on a family named Barackman, Barekman, Barickman, Barkman, Barrackman, Barrickman, Bergman; from Germany to the Colonies: Va., W. Va., Ind., Penna., Ky., Ill., Md., and Ohio, "with a bit of family information."
Barekman, June Beverly, 1915-.
Mss A 1172
19 leaves; 28 cm.
1967
Mimeographed typescript concerning Peter Bergmann or Barrickman and his descendants, including son Jacob Barrickman of Maryland, Pennsylvania, Kentucky, and Indiana.

The boughs of the Baneck family tree
Gnacinski, Janneyne Longley.
Mss A 1173
39 p.: ports.; 28 cm.
1970
Mimeographed typescript genealogy of the descendants of Frederick Baneck and wife J. Wilhelmina Liebrantz, Prussian immigrants to Wisconsin.

Atwater
Mss A 1174
13 leaves; 28 cm.
1947
Typescript genealogy tracing ancestors and descendants of Fred Atwater of Bridgeport, Conn.

Archibald
Cappers, Elmer Osgood, 1902-.
Mss A 1175
14 leaves; 28 cm.
1970
Typescript data tracing the descent of Dorothy Higgins from David Archibald of Londonderry, Ireland, and Nova Scotia. Also data on Alexander Kent Archibald, wife Janet Harvie, and their descendants. Includes photocopies and a transcription of an Archibald family Bible.

An Austin yuletide
Giffin, Viola Austin.
Mss A 1176
[8] leaves; 22 x 28 cm.
1914
Photocopy of a printed reminiscence concerning the Hazelton, Haile, and Austin families of Vermont.

Baptiste: collateral lines: Boucquet, Kierstede, Ryckman
Baptiste, Eugene Leonard, 1901-.
Mss A 1177
[2], 16, [3] leaves: ill.; 28 cm.
[1968?]
Mimeographed typescript genealogy of the descendants of Jerome Boucquet of Holland and New York City. Also photocopied material concerning the Boucquet, Kierstede, and Ryckman families.

Ancestry of Lydia Ballou Almy, [b.] 1881
Mss A 1178
[26] leaves; 28 cm.
Carbon copy typescript concerning the ancestry of Lydia Ballou Almy, daughter of Leonard Ballou Almy and wife Caroline Stowell Webb.

The ancestry of Lawrence Bathurst of Pennsylvania, 1757-1845
Bathurst, John.
Mss A 1179
7 leaves; 28 cm.
[1968?]
Photocopy of a typescript genealogy.

A biographical history of the ancestry of Julian Carroll Sampson: embracing that of his wife Bertha Sylvester Sampson, including all data obtainable by those who are connected in these two direct lines of William and Obediah Sylvester and Abraham Samson
Sampson, Gertrude Sylvester, 1842-1925.
Mss A 118 a-b
[296] p.: ill., photographs; 24-28 cm.
An original personal family history, handwritten in ink in a fragile binding with numerous photographs and postcards, pasted throughout the text, depicting family members, their houses, and areas where they lived. This was written circa 1904 through 1916, with additions to 1925. Traces some of the descendants of Abraham Samson, who was in Duxbury, Mass., between 1630 and 1686, and Richard Sylvester, who was in Weymouth, Mass., between 1630 and 1668. A typescript transcription by Frank Hollis Billeter, with photo reproductions of the illustrations accompanies the original in folder B. There is no index.

Bayha genealogy
Barner, Martha Clapp.
Mss A 1180
60, [2] leaves: geneal. tables; 28 cm.
1972
Typescript genealogy of the American descendents of brothers Blasius Frederick Bayha and Johann Ludwig Bayha, sons of Johann Ludwig Bayha and wife Christina Siegle. The brothers settled in Wheeling, W. Va. Includes allied families Loeffler, Imhoff, and Prager.

Genealogy of Urbanus E. Baughman, Jr., and son William Edmund Baughman, and wife Ruth Yessel Baughman
Baughman, Urbanus Edmund, 1905-.
Mss A 1181
[1], 22 leaves: geneal. tables; 28 cm.
1965
Carbon copy typescript genealogy.

Ancestor table of John Woodbridge Beal Jr., David Dean Beal, Thomas Howes Beal, Philip Cushing Beal
Beal, Eugenie.
Mss A 1183
[49] leaves, various pagings: maps; 28 cm.
1971
Photocopy of a typescript genealogy tracing the ancestry of four Beal brothers.

From merrie England to "old Mizzou": a genealogy of the Beale-Terrill, Christian-Terrill, Blackford-Yager and Lampton-McKinsey families, together with several allied lines
Bealmer, Mary Beale McKinsey, 1909-.
Mss A 1184
[45] leaves: coat of arms; 27 cm.
1964
Mimeographed typescript genealogy.

The Tansill, Bender, Callan, Holmead, and other early American families
Tansill, Xavier Bender, 1897-.
Mss A 1185
18 leaves: ill., ports., geneal. tables, photographs; 28 cm.
[1971]
Photocopy of section two (the Bender family) of the complete genealogy. Concerns descendants of Jacob Bender who came to the United States from Germany ca. 1740-50.

Boynton family: a family scrapbook of genealogy notes
Flagg, Glenna Beatrice Towner.
Mss A 1186
19 leaves; 28 cm.
1960
Typescript genealogy of the ancestors of Emma Florence Boynton Towner. Also notes from various sources on the Boynton family.

A Sutherland - Stephenson family history in New England, New Brunswick, Wisconsin and Minnesota: includes details of Scotsmen who served in the King's army during the American Revolution and Kenneys and Kimballs in Nova Scotia who supported the patriots
Fuller, Carol M.
Mss A 1187
31 p.: ill., maps; 28 cm.
2002
Typescript.

Notes taken from pastors book of Albert Francis Newton, 1877-1886
Newton, Albert Frances, 1848-1917.
Mss A 1188
[16, 1] leaves; 28 cm.
2001
Typescript transcription of original record.
Includes one leaf of biographical information.

Appendix I: genealogical data of the Bradlee, Tisdale, and Goddard families
Morris, Charles R.
Mss A 1189
17 leaves; 28 cm.
1971
Photocopy of a typescript genealogy and notes.

Bart S. Scribner Bible record, 1820-1942
Scribner, Bart S., 1820-1892.
Mss A 119
[5] leaves; 19-26 cm.
Original Bible record lacking title page with two Bible leaves and three additional leaves. Family lived around the Montpelier, Vt., area.

Bradstreet genealogy
Olson, Cecil Franklin, b. 1906.
Mss A 1190
[15] leaves: coat of arms; 28 cm.
1970
Carbon copy typescript genealogy of various Bradstreet families, beginning in the late 1400s.
Also photocopied material and correspondence.

These are your ancestors: it is because of them you are here
Atkins, Edith Whitehead.
Mss A 1191
[169] leaves: ill., ports.; 28 cm.
2000
Computer typescript. Consists primarily of laser printed images of photographs on the right hand pages with the identification of family members in the images on the left hand pages.

The Dutcher - Vanosdall ancestors of Bette Jean "Dutcher" Creager (1931-2000)
Creager, Bette Jean.
Mss A 1192
131, 105 leaves; 29 cm.
2001
Typescript.

Barlow and allied families
Hawkins, Laura Campbell.
Mss A 1195
3 p. leaves, 217 (i.e. 225), [41] p.; 28 cm.
1930
Typescript.

Notes on Jacob Bressman - Brussman - Brossman, 26 March 1830-11 January 1896: his ancestors and descendants and his life journey from Lebanon County, Pa., to Fremont County, Iowa, to Ruby Valley, Nevada
Brossman, Schuyler C.
Mss A 1196
[5] leaves; 28 cm.
1971
Photocopy of a typescript genealogy.

Baldwin family records: early Baldwin immigrants to America ...
Baldwin, Aubrey Haines, Jr.
Mss A 1197
1 v. (5, 12, 45, 265 leaves) 28 cm.
1970
Carbon copy typescript.

The Brintnalls
Brintnall, Kenneth W., 1902-.
Mss A 1198
5 leaves; 27 cm.
1967
Photocopy of a typescript genealogy tracing some descendants of Thomas Brintnall of Sudbury, Mass.

Brittain - Britton
Scheffel, Iva, b. 1891.
Mss A 1199
20 leaves; 28 cm.
1964
Carbon copy typescript data concerning the Brittain or Britton family of Pennsylvania and Iowa.

Alden genealogy: five generations including the problems relating to these early generations
Alden, Edward Smith, b. 1875.
Mss A 12
134 p.; 28 cm.
Arranged in alphabetical order by Alden given names. Each family group starts on a new page. If the head of the family is of another surname, search down for the Alden wife, which is the given name that that page is arranged by.

Flint - Garland - Ferguson Bible record, 1823-1909
Mss A 120
[2] leaves; 29 cm.
Original Bible record lacking title page. Majority of entries are in two different inks.

Genealogical record of Brooks family: 1509 in Holland, to 1600 in London, England, to 1870 in America
Brooks, Ella Augusta, b. 1870.
Mss A 1200
[22] leaves: geneal. tables; 28 cm.
1956
Manuscript genealogy of some descendants of Hans Harold Brookes and wife Ione Chester of Holland, including descendants who came to America on the Mayflower in 1620.

Brossman pioneers in America
Brossman, Schuyler C.
Mss A 1201
[6] leaves; 28 cm.
1964
Mimeographed typescript. Notes on early Brossmans, mainly in Pennsylvania.

Supplement to a Brown genealogy
McAllister, Ruth Brown, b. 1898.
Mss A 1202
[1], 23 p.; 28 cm.
1971
Typescript notes, additions, and corrections.

A genealogy of a part of the family of Bryant in Plympton, Massachusetts
Bradford, Lewis.
Mss A 1203
17 leaves; 28 cm.
1964
Photocopied typescript of the original, updated by Dorothy Bryant Makas.

The family history of Benjamin Brownell of Westport [Mass.], 1755
Jenney, Mildred Edna Brownell.
Mss A 1204
[14] leaves; 28 cm.
1960
Mimeographed typescript genealogy.

Descendants of Dannell Blacke (Daniel Black)
Black, George Leonard, 1899-.
Mss A 1205
[70] leaves; 28 cm.
1968
Mimeographed genealogy of the descendants of Daniel Black of Scotland who settled at Rowley or Boxford, Mass., ca. 1660. Many of his descendants settled throughout Maine.

Blair genealogy: descendants of Alexander Blair of Augusta County, Virginia, and allied families Downey, McPheeters, Walker, Campbell; also Whitaker and Holloway
Bryan, Mary Bates.
Mss A 1206
[44] leaves; 28 cm.
1936
Typescript genealogy.

Material relating to Seth Blanchard
Mss A 1207
[6] leaves; 28 cm.
Photocopies of correspondence and a newspaper obituary relating to Seth Blanchard of Mansfield, Mass., and California. Includes information on some descendants.

Our family: as compiled from letters and papers of the late Rowland B. Bliven, the family Bible, and the more recent data of the present generation
Bliven, Mary.
Mss A 1208
12 leaves; 27 cm.
1962
Typescript genealogy of some descendants of Coddington Bliven and wife Sally Babcock of Rhode Island. Also notes on the Bliven ancestry.

Additions to History of the Bower family by Oscar Bower, 1970
Hahn, Margaret.
Mss A 1209
[39] leaves; 28 cm.
1970
Mimeographed typescript additions to a published genealogy of the descendants of Michael Bauer of Northumberland Co., Penn.

Orson Perkins Bible record, 1749-1916
Perkins, Orson, 1802-1882.
Mss A 121
1, 6 leaves; 28 cm.
Photocopy of original Bible record lacking title page. The record starts at Orson Perkins' grandparents. This is one leaf that delineates a descent from Robert Taft.

Ancestry charts of Harriet Allen Bensen
Mss A 1210
[3] leaves: geneal. tables; 28 cm.
Three charts showing the paternal ancestry of Harriet Allen Bensen, daughter of Henry A. Allen.

Chamberlin genealogy: one branch in the lineage from Richard Chamberlin of Braintree, Mass., 1642
Chamberlin, Glenn.
Mss A 1211
[13] leaves; 28 cm.
1965
Reproduced typescript genealogy and notes.

Jacob Brown Chase, a colonist of 1854
Feighny, John Patrick, Mrs.
Mss A 1212
8 leaves; 28 cm.
1961
Typescript genealogy showing the ancestry and some descendants of Jacob Brown Chase of Newbury, Mass. Also transcribes a brief account by Chase concerning several years he spent in Topeka, Kan.

Record of the line of descent of one segment of the Child family in America
Wells, Catherine Helene, 1903-.
Mss A 1213
14 leaves; 28 cm.
1966
Mimeographed typescript genealogy of some descendants of William Child of Watertown, Mass.

Descendants of William Clapp and Priscilla (Otis) Clapp of Scituate, Massachusetts
Weis, Robert Lewis
Mss A 1214
ii, 32 p.; 28 cm.
1969
Mimeographed typescript genealogy.

Clapp family lineage from Thomas Clapp, 1597-1684
Melvin, Jeneve M.
Mss A 1215
8 leaves; 28 cm.
1962
Typescript genealogy tracing the ancestry of Sarah Lillian Clapp, wife of George Allen Clapp, to Thomas Clapp of Scituate.

Clarke / Clarke families in early Connecticut
Glazier, Prentiss.
Mss A 1216
6 leaves; 28 cm.
1973
Mimeographed typescript genealogy and notes.

A record of the Samuel Browning and Emily Nichols line
L'Amoureux, Harold Dane.
Mss A 1217
[1], 5 leaves; 28 cm.
1966
Carbon copy typescript supplementing "Genealogy of the Brownings" by Edward Franklin Browning. Includes Samuel Browning's direct Browning lineage; data on some descendants of Samuel Browning and wife Emily Nichols; and a transcription of information entered in Dorcas (Morwy) Browning's family Bible.

Genealogy of the John Bryant family
Mosher, Austin, b. 1893.
Mss A 1218
7 leaves; 28 cm.
1964
Typescript genealogy of some descendants of John Bryant of Scituate, Mass.

Buck, DeBuk, DeBeck, DeBuck, Debeck, etc.
Hinckley, Mabel Gould Demers, b. 1887.
Mss A 1219
2, 24 leaves; 28 cm.
1971
Revision of a 1962 work.
Typescript genealogy and notes concerning descendants of Samuel Debeck and wife Alice Harris of Trenton, Maine.

Some descendants of Thomas Moulton, of York, Me.
Clarke, Charles L.
Mss A 122
[2], 13 p.; 28 cm.
1913 Apr.
Typescript copy of a 1901 genealogy transcribed by Augustus F. Moulton. A photocopy made for patron use.

The Buffington lineage of James Buffington, 1867-1954
Sears, Francis Richmond.
Mss A 1220
38, [2] leaves; 28 cm.
Photocopy of a typescript genealogy concerning some descendants of Thomas Buffington of Salem and Swansea, Massachusetts. Also a one-page carbon copy typescript addendum, updating the genealogy to 1969.

The Bush family
Johnson, Stanley F.
Mss A 1221
8 leaves; 28 cm.
1967
Photocopy of a manuscript genealogy concerning some descendants of John Bush of Cambridge, Mass.

Bulkeley - Andrus family charts
Andrus, Lucius B., (Lucius Buckley), 1875-1947.
Mss A 1222
4 items: coat of arms, geneal. tables; 28 cm.
[19--?]
Typescript, printed material, and charts concerning the ancestry of the author. Includes Bulkeley, Andrus, and other families.

Some descendants of Thomas Burnham of Massachusetts and New York
MacCormick, Elizabeth Janet, 1880-.
Mss A 1223
3 leaves; 28 cm.
1948
Photocopy of a typescript genealogy concerning the Burnham and Wicks (Weeks) families.

A problem in genealogy
Cabaniss, Allen, 1911-.
Mss A 1224
9 leaves; 28 cm.
1960
Carbon copy typescript concerning the Cabaniss family of Virginia and Alabama.

Goodhue line, Kendall line
Cady, Ethel Crandall Smith, b. 1892.
Mss A 1225
6 leaves; 28 cm.
1969
Photocopy of a typescript genealogy concerning some Wisconsin descendants of William Goodhue of Ipswich, Mass. Includes information on the allied Moore and Kendall families.

Ancestry and descendants of Timothy Augustus Stacy of Newmarket, N.H., and Groveland, Mass.
Mss A 1226
[17] leaves; 28 cm.
1962
Mimeographed typescript genealogy. Includes information on allied families Carleton, Patterson, and Smith.

The Carscaden - Skaden families of New York and Pennsylvania in the 18th century
Bishop, Jerome C.
Mss A 1227
14 leaves; 28 cm.
1968
Mimeographed typescript genealogy.

The Calhoun - Cohoon - Cahoon family of Massachusetts, Virginia, North Carolina, and South Carolina
Johnston, Hugh Buckner.
Mss A 1228
13 leaves; 28 cm.
Mimeographed typescript genealogy.

Clifford genealogy
Clifford, Stewart H., 1900-.
Mss A 1229
[17] leaves; 28 cm.
1967
Mimeographed typescript genealogy of the descendants of B. B. Clifford and wife Ruth N. George of Concord, N.H., and Chelsea, Mass. Includes information on some descendants of John Bailey of Newbury and Salisbury, Mass., one of whom was Brigadier General Jacob Bailey.

Harrison Bancroft Bible record, 1830-1913
Bancroft, Harrison, 1830-1897.
Mss A 123
[2] leaves; 19 cm.
Original Bible record lacking title page regarding the Bancroft family.

Samuel Cluff or Clough of Alfred, Maine, and some of his descendants
Sweet, N. Josephine, 1872-.
Mss A 1230
9 leaves; 28 cm.
[19--]
Typescript genealogy.

Ancestors of Jeanne Coan
Mss A 1231
[3] leaves; 28 cm.
Carbon copy typescript.

Descendants of Alexander Cockrell I of Dallas, Texas, as shown on my original chart dated April 1, 1944, with extensions to April 1, 1960
Cockrell, Monroe F. (Monroe Fulkerson), b. 1884.
Mss A 1232
5 leaves; 28 cm.
1960
Mimeographed typescript genealogy.

Cohee family
Chance, Hilda Nancy Ersula Snowberger, 1909-.
Mss A 1233
[14] leaves: geneal. tables; 28 cm.
[1967]
Mimeographed typescript genealogy concerning the Cohee and Collison families of Maryland, Pennsylvania, and Delaware, and descendants.

Grantor and grantee index to deeds in Rockingham County, New Hampshire, 1648-1863, relating to members of the Colcord family
Colcord, Timothy A.
Mss A 1234
44 leaves; 27 cm.
1965
Carbon copy typescript.

Grantor and grantee index to deeds in York County, Maine, 1760-1885, relating to members of the Colcord family
Colcord, Timothy A.
Mss A 1235
12, 10 leaves; 27 cm.
1966
Carbon copy typescript.

Bible record for the Collier and Thurlow families, 1775-1909
Mss A 1236
5 leaves; 28 cm.
1968
Typescript transcription (including title page) concerning the families of Thomas Tucker Collier and David Thurlow.

John Collins, shoemaker, of Boston, Mass., and the English connections of Dea[con] Edward Collins, of Cambridge
Hulbert, Edward P.
Mss A 1237
21, v, leaves; 28 cm.
Typescript with notes.

Some Connecticut ancestors of Robert George Cooke of St. Paul, Minnesota
Cook, Ross Keely.
Mss A 1238
[12] leaves: coat of arms; 28 cm.
1965
Typescript genealogy. Includes Fenn, Hart, Leaper, Lee, Lord, Palmer, Shepard, Stanton, Upson, and Welton families.

Collison family
Chance, Hilda Nancy Ersula Snowberger, 1909-.
Mss A 1239
7, [3] leaves: geneal. tables; 28 cm.
1967?
Mimeographed typescript genealogy.

Descendants of Alexander McDonald
MacDonald, Donald R. G. (Robert Gordon), 1941-1997.
Mss A 124
11 p.; 28 cm.
1997
Computer typescript genealogy of Alexander McDonald (1800-1889) of Quebec City, Quebec, Canada.

Johannes (H.) Gohn or John Coon, our emigrant ancestor, and some of his offspring
Robison, Charles K., 1902-.
Mss A 1240
[1], 22 leaves: photographs; 24 cm.
1971
Typescript genealogy of the descendants of Johannes Gohn (John Coon) who settled in Philadelphia, Pa., in 1738.

Anthony (1) Coombs of Maine
Tallmadge, Webster, Mrs.
Mss A 1241
[72] p.: maps; 28 cm.
Typescript genealogy of the descendants of Anthony or Alister Coombs and wife Dorcas Worden who settled at New Meadows, Me., by about 1665.

The records of the Coomer - Comer - Commor family
Kelty, Dan, Mrs.
Mss A 1242
12 leaves; 28 cm.
[19--]
Typescript genealogy of the descendants of John Comer.

Cooke - Hopkins - Perkins - Johnson - Henry
Davis, Lucile H., 1900-.
Mss A 1243
[21] leaves; 28 cm.
[196-?]
Mimeographed typescript genealogy of some descendants of Francis Cooke of Plymouth, Mass.

History of the Debos in America
Tilden, John Leslie, b. 1897.
Mss A 1244
[47] leaves: geneal. tables; 28 cm.
1973
Photocopy of a typescript genealogy of the Debo family.

Records of the Denison, Harris, and Thompson families at Horton, Nova Scotia
Osborne, Esther W.
Mss A 1245
[8] leaves; 28 cm.
1963
Photocopy of typescript information extracted from records in the Public Archives of Canada at Ottawa.

Denslow "namesakes" and other miscellaneous items
Roberts, George McKenzie, b. 1886.
Mss A 1246
71 leaves; 28 cm.
1971
Photocopy of a typescript compilation of miscellaneous data on persons surnamed Denslow. Includes individuals whose first or middle name is Denslow.

The Dexters of Liverpool and Brooklyn, Nova Scotia
Gardner, George O.
Mss A 1247
12 leaves; 28 cm.
1958
Carbon copy typescript genealogy of some descendants of Thomas Dexter of Lynn and Plymouth, Mass.

Cornforth, Morrison, Keith, Lovejoy families: Readfield and Chesterville, Maine
Lovejoy, Frederick Collins.
Mss A 1248
[6] leaves; 28 cm.
1971
Photocopy of a typescript genealogy of some descendants of Robert Cornforth.

The Henry Cowan family of Virginia
Lamb, Frank Bird, 1863-1955.
Mss A 1249
43 leaves; 28 cm.
[19--]
Carbon copy typescript genealogy.

Chubbuck family in North America
MacDonald, Donald R. G. (Robert Gordon), 1941-1997.
Mss A 125
[211] p.; 28 cm.
1997
Computer typescript genealogy of the descendants of Thomas Chubbuck (d. 1676) of Hingham, Mass.

Some descendants of Edward Cowell, 1616-1691, Boston
Barnes, Roger.
Mss A 1250
33 p.; 28 cm.
1972
Mimeographed typescript genealogy.

The Cowells of Wrentham
Barnes, Roger.
Mss A 1251
11 p.; 28 cm.
1972
Mimeographed typescript genealogy on the descendants of Joseph Cowell of Hingham and Wrentham, Mass.

Richard Crockett
Crockett, J. Shiles.
Mss A 1253
16 leaves; 28 cm.
Typescript genealogy of Richard Crockett of Maryland and his descendants.

The Baldwin genealogy from 1500
Baldwin, C. C. (Charles Candee), 1834-1895.
Mss A 1254
84 leaves; 29 cm.
1967
Typescript.

*Adam's Eves; historical and genealogical
information about the Banks, Bruce [and]
Overton families, and the Ellis, Cain, Bell [and]
Banks relationships of Susan Mourning Cain
(Bell)*
Harmon, Francis Stuart, 1895-.
Mss A 1255
77 p. illus., facsims., geneal. tables., maps (part
fold.), ports. 29 cm.
1964
Typescript

First Banning genealogy
Banning, Pierson Worrall, 1879-.
Mss A 1256
[390] leaves: ports.; 30 cm.
1908
Typescript. Endsheet has newspaper clippings
from the Transcript.

*A Crossman - Kennedy family tree and its various
branches*
Crossman, Ward O., b. 1888.
Mss A 1257
[27] leaves: geneal. tables; 28 cm.
Mimeographed typescript genealogy and notes
concerning Josiah Allen Crossman and his
descendants.

Danforth, Rugg, and King families of Vermont
Thompson, Jeanette Forsyth, b. 1905.
Mss A 1259
13 leaves: geneal. tables; 28 cm.
1970
Typescript family group charts.

*Blackman genealogy: descendants of John of
Dorchester, Mass.*
Watkins, Walter Kendall, 1855-1934.
Mss A 126
[65] leaves; 28 cm.
1990 annotated photocopy
Photocopy version of original missing 1928
manuscript with annotations by Julie Helen Otto.
Original work was donated 1928 July 5.

*Earle: Ralph Earle of Exter, England and
Portsmouth, Rhode Island; Patience Stafford
Earle of Dutchess County, New York, Perquimans
County, North Carolina*
Rehfeldt, Martha Nellie Cooper, 1887-.
Mss A 1260
13 leaves; 28 cm.
1953
Photocopy of a typescript genealogy.

A little of my father's and mother's life
Bell, Anne Dransfield, 1872-.
Mss A 1261
9 leaves; 28 cm.
1960
Mimeographed typescript genealogy of some
descendants of Richard B. Dransfield and wife
Ann Broadbent, and of Jacob Bell and wife Mary
Gawthrop.

Bigelow
Mss A 1262
2 leaves; 28 cm.
Typescript genealogy of some descendants of
John Bigelow and wife Mary Warren of
Watertown, Mass.

*Name index to Something about the Dulaney
(Dulany) family by Benjamin Lewis Dulaney*
Jennett, Carolyn F.
Mss A 1263
11 leaves; 28 cm.
1967
Typescript.

Bible record for Doughty families, 1788-1913
Mss A 1264
9 leaves; 28 cm.
Typescript transcription of Bible records
concerning the families of Nathaniel, Enoch, and
Baker Doughty. Also typescript extracts
concerning Doughty families from Friends
records of Flushing, New York.

Genealogy of the Doty - Williams families
Mss A 1265
8 leaves; 28 cm.
1968
Photocopy of a typescript genealogy concerning some descendants of William Doty of Westchester County, N.Y., and of Nathaniel Williams and wife Mary Pierson, of Newark, N.J.

A collection of genealogical data and references for Argene Wellington Dominy, 1882-1962
Sikes, Thomas W.
Mss A 1266
34 leaves: geneal. tables; 28 cm.
1968
Reproduced typescript genealogy and pedigree charts concerning Argene Wellington Dominy of Laurens County, Ga.

Some of the descent of Robert Danks of Northampton, Massachusetts
Barnes, Frederick R.
Mss A 1267
[46] leaves: maps; 28 cm.
1939
Carbon copy typescript genealogy. Appears to be a working draft, as it is annotated and corrected by hand.

My ancestors, the Dana's
Nesja, Michael S.
Mss A 1268
[14] leaves: maps; 28 cm.
1966
Photocopy of a typescript genealogy concerning ancestors and descendants of Richard Dana of Cambridge, Mass.

Ancestry & descendants of Frere Edey
Jenkins, John Jay, 1910-.
Mss A 1269
85 leaves: ill., geneal. tables; 28 cm.
[1972?]
Reproduced typescript genealogy of Frere Edey of Barbados and Brooklyn, New York.

A history of the Charles W. Tidd family: c. 1600-1995
Tidd, J. Thomas (Joy Thomas), 1926-.
Mss A 127
[5], 22, [39] p., bound: ills.; 28 cm.
1995 Jun.
Ancestry and descendants of Charles W. Tidd (1892-1935) which includes many illustrations through photocopies of letters, epitaphs, obituaries, wills, and photographs. There are five separate leaves containing corrections and omissions.

The American descendants of Richard (Thomas) Ellard, born 1791 in England, with other Ellard lines
Burnham, Walter Jefferson, 1920-.
Mss A 1270
1 v.: geneal. tables; 28 cm.
1968
Mimeographed typescript genealogy.

Family of Ellers, Hart, Higgins
Chance, Hilda Nancy Ersula Snowberger, 1909-.
Mss A 1271
7 leaves: geneal. tables; 28 cm.
[1967?]
Mimeographed typescript genealogy concerning families of Delaware, Maryland, and Pennsylvania. Chart of the descendants of James Ellers and wife Margaret A. Downey of Maryland.

Genealogical data re the Ellis family, 1852 to 1963
Breck, Grace Marion, b. 1885.
Mss A 1272
12 leaves; 28 cm.
1963
Typescript genealogy concerning descendants of Richard Ellice of Dedham, Mass., particularly in the eighth through twelfth generations.

Enoch family research
Roberts, Harry Durward, 1906-.
Mss A 1273
10 leaves; 28 cm.
1970
Mimeographed typescript genealogy.

Eustis genealogy: descent from Eustace, Earl of Boulogne
Mss A 1274
9 leaves: coat of arms; 28 cm.
Carbon copy typescript genealogy.

Descendants of George Harvey Everett 7 and a summary of the direct line of descendants as found in The descendants of Richard Everett of Dedham, Massachusetts, by Edward Franklin Everett
Everett, Arthur Wilson, b. 1902.
Mss A 1275
10 leaves; 28 cm.
1966
Photocopy of a typescript genealogy.

Partial supplement to Arthur Wilson Everett's Descendants of George Harvey Everett
Righter, Leah Wilson.
Mss A 1276
[5] leaves; 28 cm.
[1968?]
Photocopy of a typescript and correspondence relating to descendants of John Shinn of New Jersey, and the Everett family.

The family history of Asa Albert Fairchild and his wife Helen May (Graves) Fairchild which is supplemental and part of the Fairchild genealogy
Corning, Herbert I.
Mss A 1277
5 leaves; 28 cm.
1968
Photocopy of a typescript genealogy.

Fancher family record: descendants of Edmond Meade Fancher & Jane Gates Fancher
Fancher, Ward B.
Mss A 1278
34 [i.e. 32] p.; 28 cm.
1963
Mimeographed typescript genealogy.

James Fanning of Hopkinton, Mass., and some of his descendants
Stafford, Frederic Luther, 1906-.
Mss A 1279
8, [52] leaves; 22 cm.
1971
Mimeographed typescript genealogy.

Henry M. Davis Bible record, 1861-1868
Davis, Henry M.
Mss A 128
[2] leaves; 27 cm.
Original Bible record lacking title page regarding the Davis family of Springfield, Mass.

Genealogical notes on the Hardie family of Alabama
Mss A 1280
[6] leaves; 28 cm.
Carbon copy typescript of some Hardie gravestones at Thornhill, Talladega County, Alabama. Also one letter with data relating to the Hardie family of Alabama.

An abstract of the family record of William James Barber and Elizabeth Hutcheson Barber: Edinburgh, Scotland, and their descendants from 1775 to 1961
Barber, Hugh Leslie, 1884-.
Mss A 1281
1 v.; 28 cm.
[1961]

Aaron Bartlett of Brookfield, Revolutionary soldier, with some of his descendents
Bartlett, Nellie Allen, 1875-.
Mss A 1282
8, [95], [18] leaves: ports., coat of arms, 27 cm.
1931
Mimeograph typescript.

The Bonham family
Bonham, Samuel Jeremiah, b. 1892.
Mss A 1283
101 leaves: ports., geneal. tables.; 29 cm.
1955

Breazeale kin, 1643-1880
Plotts, Lois Davis.
Mss A 1284
1 v. (in various pagings): coat of arms, geneal. tables; 28 cm.
1965
2d ed.
Mimeograph typescript.

Genealogy of the Kellogg family: allied families, Beecher, Hitchcock, Tuttle, others
Kellogg, Joseph M. (Joseph Mitchell), b. 1885.
Mss A 1285
1 v. (472 leaves): ill., coat of arms, photographs; 28 cm.
1928?
Typescript with some ms. additions.

Additional information to Deacon Samuel Haines and his descendants in America
Graves, John Kimball, 1912-.
Mss A 1286
10 leaves; 28 cm.
1961
Typescript data supplementing the published genealogy.

Hackett
Hackett, Lewis Wendell, b. 1884.
Mss A 1287
29, 10 leaves; 28 cm.
Photocopy of a typescript genealogy concerning the descendants of Jabez Hackett of Lynn and Taunton, Mass. Includes Mayo, Paddock, and Bryant families. Photocopies of additional manuscript notes by Margaret Zeller Garrett, and data from the town clerks of Yarmouth and Middleborough, Mass.

The Green(e) ancestry of Vashti (Green) Miller, 1813-1881
Miller, Malloy M.
Mss A 1288
16 leaves; 28 cm.
1968
Photocopy of a typescript genealogy tracing the descent of Vashti (Green) Miller from John Greene of Quidnessett (Kingstown), R.I.

Descendants of Nathan Benedict Gregory and Fannie Arthur Gregory
Pollett, Jeanne, 1920-.
Mss A 1289
30 leaves: ports.; 28 cm.
1970
Photocopy of a typescript genealogy.

Descendants of Reverend Samuel (5) Cotton of Litchfield and Claremont, New Hampshire
Kugler, Lee Kinraide (Ethel Leona Kinraide), 1916-20.
Mss A 129
30, iii p.; 28 cm.
Descendancy genealogy of Samuel Cotton (ca. 1737-1818) giving three more generations. It was written between 1984 and 1993.

The Halsell story
Bullock, Joseph Floyd.
Mss A 1290
22 leaves; 28 cm.
1963
Mimeographed typescript genealogy of the Halsell family, in particular the ancestors and descendants of Elizabeth (Halsell) Bullock Frost of Mississippi and Arkansas.

History of the Gratto family
Gratto, Isabel C.
Mss A 1291
5 leaves: geneal. tables; 28 cm.
1956
Mimeographed typescript genealogy of some descendants of George Gratto, emigrant from France, who settled at Lunenberg and Tatamagouche, Nova Scotia.

New Fairfield (Sherman) Conn. early days and the life of a pioneer woman, Abigail Wakeman Gorham
Halstead, Vera Colton.
Mss A 1292
18, [3] leaves: geneal. tables ; 28 cm.
1971
Photocopy of a typescript genealogy and a manuscript chart.

Descendants of Robert Goold who came to America in the year 1665
Goold, Howard R.
Mss A 1293
[20] leaves; 28 cm.
[1961?]
Mimeographed typescript genealogy.

*Descendants of Solomon Goewey (Gowey) of
Lansingburgh, N.Y. and Arlington, Vt.*
Thomas, David L.
Mss A 1294
1 v.: geneal. tables; 28 cm.
1971
Photocopies of family group sheets.

*Descendants of Jacob Godfrey of New York and
Noble County, Indiana*
Godfrey, Jack Montgomery, 1918-.
Mss A 1295
22 leaves; 28 cm.
[1958]
Typescript genealogy of the descendants of Jacob
Godfrey and wife Rebecca Douglas.

The Goadby family in America
Bloom, Elsie Goadby, 1917-.
Mss A 1296
8 leaves; 28 cm.
1967
Photocopy of a typescript genealogy concerning
the descendants of William Goadby of England
and Pennsylvania, and wives Catherine Masters
and Mary Dawson.

*Genealogical and historical notes on the Giles
family of Devonport and Plymouth, Devon,
(Portsmouth, Hants.), London, and Australia*
Best, Evan C., 1937-.
Mss A 1297
9, 6 leaves; 39 x 26 cm. folded to 20 x 26 cm.
1968
Photocopy of a typescript genealogy in two
sections. Section I, published in 1966 and revised
in 1968, relates to the Giles family. Section II
(Addenda) concerns the connections between the
families Giles, Linzee, Smith, and Shea. It also
includes notes on Captain John Shea, R.M.

The Gilcreast genealogy, 1748-1973
Gilcreast, Harriet J., 1911-.
Mss A 1298
22 leaves; 28 cm.
1973
Mimeographed typescript genealogy of
descendants of John Gilchrist of Methuen and
Dracut, Mass.

*Gifford: ancestors and descendants of Enos and
Hannah (Palmer) Gifford*
Morgan, Alice Vera Gifford Curtis, b. 1887.
Mss A 1299
17 leaves; 28 cm.
1960
Carbon copy typescript genealogy.

Aldrich family
Aldrich, George T.
Mss A 13
8 p.; 28 cm.

*Scrapbook of hairweavings given to Hellen
Marion Adams of Fair Haven, Vt., 1843*
Mss A 130
[30] leaves; 17 cm.
A scrapbook of hairweavings given to Hellen
Marion Adams (1834-after 1893), of Fair Haven,
Vt., in 1843. Her father Joseph Adams (1802-
1878) sold his business in 1843 and moved to
Racine, Wis. He returned to Fair Haven in 1845.
The bulk of the hairweaving are from Fair Haven
or Whitehall, N.Y. Other towns covered are West
Haven, Vt., Hampton and Granville, N.Y., and
Bolton, Canada East.

*Pedigree of Barbara Budsell Getzler thru great-
grandparents George Edwin Loring (1854-1932)
and Jennie Libby Clark (1855-1943) and
Mayflower ancestors*
Loring, Frank Veazie.
Mss A 1300
[19] leaves: geneal. tables; 28 cm.
Photocopies of pedigree charts.

The Ferry family of early Granby, Massachusetts.
Hook, James W. (James William), 1884-1957.
Mss A 1301
13 leaves; 27 cm.
1951
Carbon copy typescript genealogy of the
descendants of Charles Ferry of Springfield,
Mass.

*Supplementary notes to Ancestry and posterity of
a certain John Flagg by M. L. Driscoll*
Drew, Gwendolyn Flagg.
Mss A 1302
3 leaves; 27 cm.
[1964?]
Typescript notes concerning John Flagg of
Boston, Mass., and his heirs.

*Field genealogy: taken from vol. 1 and 2 by
Frederick Clifton Pierce, Chicago, Illinois, 1901*
Pierce, Frederick Clifton, 1855-1904.
Mss A 1303
18 leaves; 28 cm.
[1973?]
Mimeographed typescript genealogy of the Field
family, in particular the descendants of Seth and
Lucy (Mix) Field of Northfield, Mass., and
Geneva, N.Y. Includes extracts from family
letters from the 1840s through the 1880s.

The Samuel Ford family of Rowe, Massachusetts
Stewart, Elizabeth Cobb.
Mss A 1304
7 leaves; 28 cm.
1965
Photocopy of a typescript genealogy.

*A Fraser of Lovat genealogy: the Fraser-Lovett
families of Scotland and England*
Ward, Maud E.
Mss A 1305
[3], 11 leaves; 28 cm.
1968
Photocopy of a typescript genealogy.

*French family record: genealogy of Mabel
French Taylor (Mrs. Norman Ingraham Taylor)
of Burnside, Pulaski County, Kentucky*
Taylor, Mabel French, 1880-1966.
Mss A 1306
[24] leaves; 28 cm.
[1956?]
Photocopy of typescript family records
concerning the ancestors of Mabel French Taylor,
born in New Hampshire, daughter of Alonzo
Currier French and wife Martha Jane Locke.

*Genealogy of a branch of the Frohlich family
which emigrated from Hesse-Cassel (now the
Prussian province of Hesse-Nassau), Germany, to
America in 1855*
Hamel, Claude Charles.
Mss A 1307
8 leaves; 27 cm.
1948
Carbon copy typescript of the descendants of
George Frohlich and wife Anna Christina Zimmer
of Ohio.

*The Frye family, being a record of the
descendants of Stephen Frye of Keokuk, Iowa &
Sheridan Co., Kansas (1841-1917)*
Frye, Marian McCauley.
Mss A 1308
[25] leaves: facsim.; 28 cm.
1969
Mimeographed typescript genealogy.

*One branch of the Fuller family of Dedham,
Needham and Wellesley*
Jones, Frederic A.
Mss A 1309
14 leaves: maps, geneal. tables, photographs;
1960
Photocopy of a typescript genealogy.

Genealogy of a branch of the Beebe family
Mss A 131
4, 2 p.; 28 cm.
Typescript ed.
Photocopy of typescript of Beebe lineal descend
for ten generations from Alexander Beebe to Asa
Secord Beebe.

*The Gamble family of Butler Township, Knox
County, Ohio: Section II, narrative*
Martin, William Gamble.
Mss A 1310
23 leaves; 28 cm.
1962
Mimeographed typescript. Intended as a
supplement to Section I (chart).

*The early generations of George Gardiner of
Newport*
Mss A 1311
20 leaves; 29 cm.
Carbon copy typescript genealogy.

One branch of the Halletts showing Messer alliance, Belgrade and West Waterville, Maine
Hinckley, Mabel Gould Demers, b. 1887.
Mss A 1312
12 leaves; 28 cm.
1971
Typescript genealogy of some descendants of Jonathan Hallett, compiled for Old Colony Trust Company, Boston, Mass., in connection with settling the Messer estate.

Harrington
Ford, Nel W.
Mss A 1313
7 leaves; 27 cm.
1965
Typescript notes and genealogy concerning descendants of Charles Harrington of North Carolina.

A Hartshorn (Hartson) genealogy
Hartson, Louis Dunton, b. 1885.
Mss A 1314
19 leaves; 28 cm.
1967
Typescript genealogy of descendants of Thomas Hartshorn of Reading, Mass.

The Healy family
Healy, Ruth Stanton.
Mss A 1316
[43] leaves: maps, photographs; 28 cm.
1966
Photocopy of a typescript genealogy concerning the Healy family of Fall River, Mass., and Lisbon, Me.

Descendants of John Heard, Sr. of Wilkes Co., Ga.
Heard, Harold, 1903-.
Mss A 1317
19 p.; 28 cm.
[197-?]
Mimeographed typescript genealogy.

Agrippa Henderson and Letha Eytcheson Henderson: their decendants and ancestors
Curray, Roy Ernest, b. 1889.
Mss A 1318
A-N, 32 leaves: maps, geneal. tables; 28 cm.
1971
2nd ed.
Reproduced typescript genealogy of the descendants of Agrippa Henderson and wife Letha Eytcheson of North Carolina and Iowa.

Who is William Hess?: a sketch of the family of Apollos Hess who came from Shelby County, Kentucky, before 1819 to Floyd and Clark Counties, Indiana; being the lineage of, as far as possible of [sic] one son, William Hess, whose later kin are found in Washington and Knox Counties, Indiana
Barekman, June Beverly, 1915-.
Mss A 1319
20 leaves; 28 cm.
1971
Mimeographed typescript genealogy.

Isaac Babson Bible record, 1806-1921
Babson, Isaac, 1806-1874.
Mss A 132
[3] leaves; 28 cm.
Typewritten explanation and manuscript transcription of Bible record probably by Leslie Sanders.

The descendants of George Lewis Heston and Roseanna Jane Schnebly
Heston, Paul M.
Mss A 1320
23, v leaves; 28 cm.
1960
Mimeographed typescript genealogy. Includes George Lewis Heston's line of descent from ancestor Zebulon Heston and wife Dorothy Hutchinson.

The Hichborn family and some of their descendants
Favor, Elizabeth Savage, b. 1887.
Mss A 1321
21, [3] leaves: geneal. tables, photographs; 28 cm.
1940
Rev. and updated ca. 1970
Photocopy of a typescript genealogy of the descendants of David Hichborn and wife Catherine of Boston, Mass.

Hicks family of Maine, New Hampshire, Ohio, Massachusetts
Hicks, Robert B. (Robert Boyd), 1943-.
Mss A 1322
[23] leaves: ill., maps, ports., coat of arms; 28 cm.
1971
Photocopied typescript genealogy of descendants of Dennis Hicks and wife Sarah Deering.

Material for a genealogy of the Hill family of Biddeford - Saco, Maine
Greene, Harriet Frances.
Mss A 1323
[1], 6 leaves; 28 cm.
1961
Reproduced typescript genealogy.

Some of the descendants of William Hill of Boston, Massachusetts, and Brunswick, North Carolina, and his wife, nee Margaret Moore
Gault, Charles Beers, 1911-.
Mss A 1324
21 leaves; 28 cm.
1969
Typescript genealogy.

Genealogy of one branch of the Hill family
Hill, Norman P.
Mss A 1325
35 leaves; 28 cm.
1973
Photocopy of a typescript genealogy concerning descendants of Valentine Hill of Boston, Mass., and New Hampshire.

A Hinckley family
Hinckley, Robert Carman.
Mss A 1326
16, [2] leaves; 28 cm.
1971
Photocopy of a typescript genealogy concerning descendants of Samuel Hinckley and wife Sarah Soule of Barnstable, Mass.

Supplemental material to Henry Hoisington's American family Hoisington
Voss, Beatrice Velma, 1905-.
Mss A 1327
7 leaves; 28 cm.
1970
Typescript material concerning the descendants of Bert Monroe Hoisington and wife Myrtle J. Hendryx.

Holts, other than from New England, who served in the American Revolution
Holt, Everett G.
Mss A 1328
13 leaves; 28 cm.
1961
Carbon copy typescript.

"Piety is peace": the story of the descendants of John Hopkins in Niagara County, N.Y.
Townsend, Ruth Truesdale, 1913-.
Mss A 1329
[2], 46, 26 p.: maps, geneal. tables; 28 cm.
1971
Mimeographed typescript genealogy concerning descendants of John Hopkins of Hartford, Conn., in particular the descendants of Daniel Dewey Hopkins of Vermont and Niagara County, N.Y.

Eben Vaughan Bible record, 1818-1898
Vaughan, Eben, 1818-1889.
Mss A 133
[2] leaves; 28 cm.
Typescript transcription of Vaughan Bible record from a two-volume "Cottage Bible" edited by William Patton [whose first Bible was printed in 1833].

Correspondence and notes on Hubbell and Smith families
Field, Ruth Marie.
Mss A 1330
[24] leaves; 28 cm.
Photocopies of typescript notes and transcribed correspondence concerning Seth Hubbell and son Benjamin Hubbell; Andrew Smith and son Moses Smith; and their families of New York and New Jersey.

History of the Hughes family
Boles, Iva.
Mss A 1331
21 leaves; 28 cm.
ca. 1965?
Carbon copy typescript concerning the descendants of Thomas Hughes and wife Elizabeth Williams of North Carolina and Jefferson County, Indiana.

Genealogical charts and data concerning ancestors of Ray G. Hulburt
Hulburt, Ray G. (Ray Garland), b. 1885.
Mss A 1332
[3] charts, 29 leaves: geneal. tables; 28 cm.
1936
Mimeographed charts and ancestral data. Includes pedigree charts for Dorwin Hulburt, Elizabeth Fanny Sherwood, and India Siloam Rogers.

James family letters, 1777
Mss A 1333
32 leaves; 28 cm.
Typescript transcriptions of letters of the James family of Scituate, Mass. Written from various locations during the Revolution, including Scituate; and Ticonderoga, Saratoga, and Albany, N.Y.

Jayne family of Nicholson, Pennsylvania
Williams, Garford F.
Mss A 1334
30 p.; 29 cm.
1970
Mimeographed typescript genealogy of some descendants of William Jayne of New Haven, Conn., and Brookhaven, N.Y.

Jacques
Merrill, Howard Weld, 1921-.
Mss A 1335
10 leaves; 28 cm.
1966
Photocopy of a typescript genealogy concerning the descendants of John Jacques and wife Elizabeth Rountree of Nova Scotia.

The name of Ingham in some Yorkshire church records
Mansur, Frank L.
Mss A 1336
12 leaves; 28 cm.
1967
Typescript transcription of extracted entries (1539-1891), the purpose of which was to trace the ancestry and descendants of Jonathan Ingham of Yorkshire.

English research regarding the Ingalls family of Lincolnshire, England, and Lynn, Massachusetts (advancing the theory that Edmund Ingalls was not an original settler of Lynn in 1629)
Gibbs, Rosalyn Davenport.
Mss A 1337
28 leaves: maps, facsim.; 28 cm.
1973
Carbon copy typescript.

Hutchins family notes
White, H. Bowen.
Mss A 1338
[3], 18 leaves: photographs; 28 cm.
1971
Typescript genealogical notes on various ancestral families, including Hutchins, Corliss, Page, Child, Dwight, Hurd, Estabrook, Leavitt, Harrington, and others.

First draft of genealogy of George Huntress of Newington, N.H.
Hunt, Robert Parker.
Mss A 1339
[31] leaves; 28 cm.
1973
Photocopy of a typescript genealogy of descendants of George Huntress and wife Mary Nott. Manuscript corrections and additions.

Some descendants of Peter Sim of Peabody, Massechusetts [sic], USA
MacLeod, Judith (Judith Sim)
Mss A 134
1 chart; 21 x 53 cm.
Descendancy genealogical chart of Peter Sim (1832-1897) who emigrated from Scotland to Peabody, Mass., in ca. 1849. Includes a letter from author explaining her intention and that the source of the chart is information from a group of letters her possession from Peter Sim to his brother Duncan Sim, who settled in New South Wales, Australia.

Genealogy of Harold Dudley Hussey, a descendant of Richard Hussey
Hussey, Harold Dudley, b. 1888.
Mss A 1340
18 leaves: geneal. tables; 28 cm.
1966
Typescript genealogy of the descendants of Richard Hussey of Dover, N.H. Includes allied lines Batcheller, Bradstreet, Dudley, and Peabody.

Pension records of the Hurd family
Norton, Theodore E.
Mss A 1341
[3], 80, [4] leaves; 28 cm.
Photocopy of typescript abstracts from pension files at the National Archives, Washington, D.C., concerning Hurds in the Revolutionary War and the War of 1812.

Some descendants of Joseph Langdon and Susannah Root who were married in Farmington, Conn., December 24, 1712
Mss A 1342
[99] leaves; 27 cm.
[1952?]
Carbon copy typescript.

The Larson and related families
Magarian, Agnes Town.
Mss A 1343
39, 16 leaves; 28 cm.
1969
Photocopy of a typescript genealogy concerning the Larson family of Sweden and Iowa, as well as the ancestry and descendants of Salem Town of Illinois.

The American descendants of James Latta
Latta, Emmitt Girdell, b. 1849.
Mss A 1344
26 leaves; 28 cm.
1904
1932 typ. ed.
Carbon copy typescript genealogy of James, Samuel, and Moses Latta of New York State, sons of James Latta of Ireland.

Some Launders, Landers and Landrus descendants
Robison, Charles Karmin.
Mss A 1345
63 leaves: photographs; 25 cm.
1971
Typescript genealogy of some descendants of Thomas Launders of Sandwich, Mass.

Lee
Smith, Robert Chandler.
Mss A 1346
8, [2] leaves: geneal. tables; 28 cm.
1959
Reproduced typescript genealogy of the Lee family of Connecticut, in particular Orlando Bridges Lee, his siblings and descendants.

Lemaster family, U.S.A., 1959
Lemaster, Howard Marshall, b. 1897.
Mss A 1347
[29] leaves: ill., geneal. tables; 28 cm.
1959
Mimeographed typescript genealogy.

Ancestry & descendants of James Jenkins, 1787-1834, hardware merchant of New York
Jenkins, John Jay, 1910-.
Mss A 1348
[64] leaves: ill., geneal. tables; 28 cm.
1971
Photocopy of a typescript genealogy.

Jennings: genealogy of a Jennings family of Moravia, New York, and the adjoining town of Venice
Luther, Leslie L. (Leslie Leon), 1886-1976.
Mss A 1349
15 leaves; 28 cm.
1968
Mimeographed typescript genealogy of the descendants of Oliver Jennings.

Avery family Bible record, 1685-1835
Miller, Karen Avery.
Mss A 135
[17] leaves; 28 cm.
Photocopy of original Bible record lacking title page (though N.T. t.p. present) regarding the Avery family plus a transcription of the text by Karen Avery Miller dated 1998 Jan.

Genealogical history of the ancestors of Harold M. Jones and Margaret J. Bartram
Jones, Harold M. (Harold Marshall), 1882-.
Mss A 1350
5 leaves; 28 cm.
1965
Photocopy of a typescript genealogy. Includes Bright, Brown, French, and Jones families.

Adah Beebe Segar notes on Joslyn - Moon (Moore) research
Segar, Adah Beebe.
Mss A 1351
5 leaves; 28 cm.
Typescript notes.

A branch of the Karns family
Norweb, Evelyn L.
Mss A 1352
[19] leaves; 28 cm.
1967
Mimeographed typescript genealogy of some descendants of Lewis Karns and wife Eleanor of Pennsylvania and West Virginia.

Some ancestors of Lavinia Lloyd Kaufman, first wife of James Amory Sullivan of Boston, Massachusetts
Nickerson, Vernon Roscoe, 1933-.
Mss A 1353
11 leaves; 28 cm.
1968
Typescript genealogical notes showing Lavinia Lloyd Kaufman's descent from the following families: Bachman, Bombaugh, Buttall, Cadwalader, Croasdale, English, Heaton, Jarrett, Jones, Kaufman, Kenderdine, Knight, Lambert, Lloyd, Lukens, Masters, Paul, Peacock, Pearson, Reehm, Robert, Roberts, Stoner, Walker, Worth, Wynne, and Young.

The Keane family of Millstreet, Co. Cork, & Massachusetts
Keane, Leonard M., 1940-.
Mss A 1354
[9] leaves; 28 cm.
1969
Photocopy of a typescript genealogy. Includes royal descent of the Keane family from Rurik the Varangian; royal descent of the Keane family from Edward I.

The descendants of Alice Maud Walker (1882-) and Alexander McMillan (1869-1949) and the descendants of Usena Abigail Walker (1878-1950) and Chester Kellogg (1879-1933)
Keeling, Robert, 1938-.
Mss A 1355
15 p.: geneal. tables; 28 cm.
1971
Mimeographed typescript genealogy.

The ancestors and descendants of Charles Samuel Keeling (1854-1918) and Cassie Amelia Walker (1865-1942)
Keeling, Robert, 1938-.
Mss A 1356
26 p.: geneal. tables; 28 cm.
1970
Mimeographed typescript genealogy.

Kelleher family, of Knockraheen, Carriganimma, Macroom, Co. Cork, Ireland (and Australia and U.S.A.)
Kelleher, Bryan J.
Mss A 1357
1 v.: ill., maps, coat of arms, geneal. tables, photographs; 26 cm.
1970
Photocopied genealogy comprising typescript, manuscript, and published material.

Keney, Kenney, Kinney: a monograph
Hinckley, Mabel Gould Demers, b. 1887.
Mss A 1358
25 leaves: geneal. tables; 28 cm.
1968
Typescript genealogy of some descendants of John Kenney and wife Sarah Cheever of Newbury, Mass., in particular descendants of Israel Kenney and wife Susannah Hood of Topsfield, Mass., and Maugerville, New Brunswick. Allied families include Dwinnell, Potter, and Shaw.

The Kenney - Kinney family: a monograph
Hinckley, Mabel Gould Demers, b. 1887.
Mss A 1359
20 leaves; 28 cm.
1969
Typescript genealogy of some descendants of John Kenney and wife Sarah Cheever of Newbury, Mass.

Chester Bill Bible record, 1725-1922
Robinson, Belle (Fanny Belle Hurlbutt), 1923-.
Mss A 136
4, [9] leaves; 28 cm.
Photocopy of original Bible record lacking title page. Includes a transcription by Belle Robinson.

Notes for a speech delivered at a King family reunion in 1911, Somerset County, Pennsylvania
Critchfield, Norman Bruce, b. 1838.
Mss A 1360
7 leaves; 28 cm.
Typescript genealogy of the descendants of Philip King of Belgium and Pennsylvania. Also a photocopied biographical sketch of Critchfield.

The Kingsbury family and related families: a family scrapbook
Flagg, Georgia M.
Mss A 1361
27 leaves: geneal. tables; 28 cm.
1961
Typescript genealogy of some descendants of Joseph Kingsbury and wife Millicent Ames. Allied families include Boynton, Eaton, Flagg, Judson, Morse, Sargent, Towner, and Wadland.

Bible record for the Kinnear and White families, 1749-1909
Mss A 1362
4 leaves; 28 cm.
Carbon copy typescript transcription, without title page information, concerning the Kinnear and White families of Newcastle, N.H. Includes families of John Kinnear and wife Margaret; William Kinnear and wife Mary; Charles White and wife Frances Kinnear.

Bible record for the Kipp and Van Etten families, 1702-1817
Mss A 1363
6 leaves; 28 cm.
1962
Carbon copy typescript transcription, without title page information, concerning the Kipp and Van Etten families of New York.

The ancestry of Harriet Elizabeth King, wife of LaFayette Norris
Norris, George.
Mss A 1364
15 p.: ill., photographs; 21 cm.
1963
Printed genealogy; two inserted photographs.

Kirk of Virginia
Barekman, June Beverly, 1915-.
Mss A 1365
24 leaves; 29 cm.
1972
Reproduced typescript research covering the period ca. 1790-1815.

The Klinger family
Klinger, M. Robert B.
Mss A 1366
[8], 28, iv leaves: ports., coat of arms; 28 cm.
[1969]
Reproduced typescript genealogy of the ancestry and descendants of Alexander Klinger of Pennsylvania.

A partial record of the descendants of William Knipe of Ducklington
Mansur, Frank L.
Mss A 1367
15, 5 leaves; 28 cm.
[1969]
Typescript genealogy of the descendants of William Knipe and wife Jane Hall of Ducklington, Oxfordshire, England. Jane (Hall) Knipe came to America in 1853 and lived in Maine and New Hampshire. Also information on the Hall family, in particular John Hall.

The New England descendants of Cornelius Kollock of Delaware
Hill, Joseph Bennett, 1891-1991.
Mss A 1368
10 leaves; 28 cm.
1961
Reproduced typescript genealogy of the descendants of Cornelius Kollock and wives Jerusha Billings and Hannah Billings.

The Lacy family: some historical notes and the descendants of James Lacy (1829-1888) and Annah McCormick
Lacy, Ruth Barrett.
Mss A 1369
59 leaves: ill., maps, coat of arms, geneal. tables; 28 cm.
1970
Rev. ed.
Photocopy of a typescript genealogy concerning the Lacy family of Ireland and New York. Extensive notes on the Lacy family in Great Britain and Ireland; copies of published material.

Sam'l Wilcok's His book of names: The Names of every offesor [sic] in Col. Parsons' Regt.
Gilman, Frances M.
Mss A 137
[1, 15] p.; 28 cm.
1991
Typescript transcription with a photocopy of the original listing of the officers in Col. Samuel Holden Parsons' Regiment (created by the Connecticut legislature on 1775 May 1 and disbanded 1775 Dec. 10) as recorded by Samuel Willcox, of the regiment's 8th company.

Immigrant ancestors of Charles C. Lamb
Mss A 1370
6 leaves; 28 cm.
Mimeographed typescript list.

Brief history of the Nathan Lamb, Sr., family
Lamb, LeRoy Eugene, b. 1895.
Mss A 1371
13 leaves; 28 cm.
1972
Photocopy of typescript notes and genealogy concerning Nathan Lamb of Franklin Co., Vermont, and Ohio, and his descendants.

Descendants of Asa R. and Hannah D. Lippincott
Lippincott, Elizabeth R. (Elizabeth Roberts), 1888-1
Mss A 1372
27, 3 leaves; geneal. tables; 28 cm.
1960
Mimeographed typescript genealogy of the descendants of Asa Roberts Lippincott and wife Hannah Dudley Thorne, many of whom remained in Burlington and Camden Counties, N.J. Includes summary information on the Lippincott and Thorne ancestry, and a 3-page supplement dated 1964.

Myrtle M. Lewis descent for Order of Americans of Armorial Ancestry
Mss A 1373
8 leaves; 28 cm.
Typescript showing line of descent. Surnames include Fulwood, Gunne, Tomes, Welles, Judson, Lewis, and Mosher.

*Leibundgut family [in] church records [in]
Switzerland (1650-1750)*
Livengood, Charles A.
Mss A 1374
25 leaves; 28 cm.
1952
Reproduced typescript of extracts from church
records.

*The Lincoln ancestry of Mary (Lincoln) Paddock,
1815-1883*
Miller, Malloy M.
Mss A 1375
22 leaves; 28 cm.
1967
Photocopy of a typescript genealogy of some
descendants of Thomas Lincoln of Hingham,
Mass.

Genealogy of the Edmund Lewis family
Mosher, Austin, b. 1893.
Mss A 1376
3 leaves; 28 cm.
[1964?]
Typescript genealogy of some descendants of
Edmund Lewis and wife Mary of Lynn, Mass.

Jonathan Lamson
Jones, Edward Thomas.
Mss A 1377
9 leaves; 28 cm.
1963
Typescript genealogy concerning Jonathan
Lamson of N. Brookfield, Mass.; Randolph, Vt.;
and Jefferson Co., N.Y. Includes data on his
wives (Sally Morton and Anna Cobb) and
children.

A Lane genealogy
Hall, Frank Nelson, 1902-.
Mss A 1378
19 leaves; 28 cm.
1965
Mimeographed typescript genealogy of some
descendants of William Lane of Dorchester,
Mass.

Lane
Gault, Charles Beers, 1911-.
Mss A 1379
13 leaves: geneal. tables; 28 cm.
1969
Typescript genealogy of the descendants of Levin
Lane and wife Margaret Moore Hill of North
Carolina.

*Baptist Church of Christ (Raynham, Mass.)
records, 1780-1795*
First Baptist Church of Raynham (Mass.)
Mss A 138
[15] leaves; 17 x 21 cm.
Contains entries of baptisms, admonishments,
marriages, and removals. Last five leaves are
blank.

Lundy genealogy, 1741-1945
Poole, Lilly Blackwell Lundy.
Mss A 1380
12 leaves; 28 cm.
1945
1962 typ. ed.
Typescript transcription of the original
genealogical work concerning descendants of
Richard Lundy of Bucks Co., Pa. Includes data on
the ancestors of Catherine Shannon Lundy.

*Descendants of Henry Lyon of Falmouth, Nova
Scotia*
Duncanson, J. V.
Mss A 1381
2 leaves; 28 cm.
1961
Carbon copy typescript genealogy.

*A Lovett genealogy: emigrant ancestor John
Lovett of Beverly, Massachusetts, landed from
England prior to 1639, and allied families of Rea,
Jordon, Thorndike, Larkin, Woodbery, Dodge,
Proctor, Hale, Hall*
Hall, Frank Nelson, 1902-.
Mss A 1382
1 v.: maps; 28 cm.
1965
Reproduced typescript genealogy.

Lyon
Mss A 1383
5 leaves; 28 cm.
Unattributed typescript genealogy of some
descendants of William Lyon and wife Sarah
Ruggles of Roxbury, Mass.

*Supplement to genealogical survey of the Lyon
family prepared by Charles J. Lyon in 1948*
Meade, Charlotte Lyon, 1903-.
Mss A 1384
17 leaves; 28 cm.
1964
Carbon copy typescript with additional data on
the Lyon family.

*Benjamin Lyon, Revolutionary War soldier: his
antecedents and descendants*
Lyon, Lorene Jones.
Mss A 1385
[67] leaves; 28 cm.
1971
Reproduced typescript genealogy.

Longwood connections
Howell, Margie Ellis, 1918-.
Mss A 1386
[40] leaves; 28 cm.
[1970]
Photocopies of typescript and manuscript notes
and genealogies concerning Longwood families.

History of the Loutzenhiser family
Loutzenhiser, P. V.
Mss A 1387
15 leaves; 28 cm.
1894
Typescript transcription of original.

Ahnentafels
Lord, Charles Melville, b. 1895.
Mss A 1388
20, 4 p.; 28 cm.
1961
Mimeographed typescript showing the ancestry of
Charles M. Lord and wife Laura V. Harnsberger.

Royal and noble lines
Lord, Charles Melville, b. 1895.
Mss A 1389
22, [1] p.; 28 cm.
1961
Mimeographed typescript showing royal lineages
of Charles M. Lord and wife Laura V.
Harnsberger.

Foster - Gould Bible record, 1770-1882
Mss A 139
[4] leaves; 17-28 cm.
Original Bible record lacking title page with one
leaf being a photocopy of the original. Two leaves
are actual Bible pages on the Foster family
(written in one hand and ink) and the other two
are leaves possibly inserted into the Bible on the
Gould family that intermarried with the Foster
family.

*Notes on the Loye family: concerning some
descendants of William Loye, b. 1790 in England,
d. 1835 in Chatham, N.B., Canada*
Loye, Percival Elliot.
Mss A 1390
10 leaves: photographs (col., mounted); 28 cm.
1966
Reproduced typescript genealogy.

*Family of Robert Livingston, first lord of the
manor of Livingston*
Mss A 1391
28 leaves; 28 cm.
Typescript genealogy concerning the descendants
of Robert Livingston and wife Alida Schuyler of
New York.

*Pedigree of George Lloyd, bishop of Sodor and
Man, 1600-04, and of Chester, 1604-15*
Mss A 1392
[2] leaves: geneal. tables; 28 cm.
Typescript pedigree extracted from records of the
College of Arms, London.

Data concerning the Lockwood family
Davis, Genevieve Lockwood.
Mss A 1394
[3] leaves: facsim.; 28 cm.
Three facsimiles of manuscript and typescript data concerning the Lockwood family: correspondence from 1951 and 1955, and a certified transcript from New Milford, Conn.

David Long, shipwright, of Somerset and Anne Arundel Counties, Maryland
Long, John D.
Mss A 1395
8 leaves; 28 cm.
1960
Reproduced typescript data concerning David Long, son of Jeffrey Long and wife Mary Sewell of Maryland. Includes extracts from deeds, wills, vital records, and accounts.

References to genealogical fan chart of Horace K. and Prudence S. MacKechnie
MacKechnie, Horace Knight, 1909-.
Mss A 1396
[30] leaves: geneal. tables; 28 cm.
1960
Mimeographed typescript notes concerning their ancestors. Genealogical fan chart (61 x 91 cm. folded to 21 x 23 cm.; dated 1960) of Horace K. and Prudence S. MacKechnie inserted at end.

Descendants of John McIntosh
McIntosh, Florence M. (Florence Moulton), b. 1881.
Mss A 1397
12 leaves; 28 cm.
[194-?]
Mimeographed typescript genealogy of some descendants of John McIntosh of Dedham, Mass. "From Dedham records examined in 1907 and from information supplied by members of the family. Added to by Dr. George E. Emery and his son, George I. Emery (descendants of Nancy McIntosh)."

The first three generations of the McEwen family on Prince Edward Island
McEwen, Andrew Brian Wendover, 1939-.
Mss A 1398
[17] leaves; 28 cm.
1961
Carbon copy typescript genealogy of the descendants of Duncan McEwen of Scotland and Prince Edward Island. "Based on the notes of Harvey David McEwen."

Notes on the McDuffie family
Sherman, John MacDuffie.
Mss A 1399
4, 2 leaves; 28 cm.
1968
Reproduced typescript notes and genealogy concerning the McDuffie family, in particular descendants of John and Martha McDuffie of Ireland. Several of their children came to America about 1720 and settled in New England.

The Reverend William Armstrong of Killashandra, county Cavan, Ireland and his wife Jane Irwin and their descendants in America
Poole, Herbert Armstrong, b. 1877.
Mss A 14
25, [8] p., bound; 29 cm.
[1954?]

George F. Adams Bible records, 1911-1933
Adams, George F., fl. 1911-1930.
Mss A 140
[2] leaves; 30 cm.
Original Bible record lacking title page. The family was from Stowe, Vt.

McDaniel family research
Roberts, Harry D.
Mss A 1400
50 leaves; 28 cm.
1968
Mimeographed typescript notes concerning McDaniel families throughout the United States.

Account book of Lieut. Joel Pratt, 1777-1780
Pratt, Joel.
Mss A 1401
Phys. Desc.1 v. (100 p.); 15 x 19 cm.
Account of supplies from various companies to "military stores." Entries list date, by whom received, and a tally of the number of guns, bayonets, belts, scaboards, gunslings, ramrods, c. boxes, etc. A large portion of record is devoted to lists of the casualities among the various companies of the 4th Mass. Regiment. Also includes various receipts and promissory notes.

Copy of a receipt book kept by Samuel Sewall, 1680-1721
Sewall, Samuel, 1652-1730.
Mss A 1402
100 p.; 10 x 17 cm.
Handwritten transcription of original record. Original record was a folio volume of 83 leaves though the first four leaves were missing when it was copied by Drake in 1854. Most of the entries are in the hand of Samuel Sewall, the society's commissioner and disbursing agent. The entries note missionary payments paid out of the "Indian Stock," primarily missionary and teacher salaries, and other expenses. Many entries were signed by the recipient of the payment. Also included is a copy of the 1704 commission to Sewall and others authorizing them to be commissioners for Indian work for that year.

Griffith Jones of Springfield, Massachusetts 1614-1676 and his descendants of the name
Jones, Edward T.
Mss A 1403
1 v. (206 leaves); 29 cm.
1960
Typescript.

Our Baildon family in England
Cummings, Lawrence Belding, 1881-1947.
Mss A 1404
1 v.: ill., maps, ports., coat of arms, geneal. tables; 29 cm.
1929
Typescript.

The ancestry of Barbara Allen Butler
Andrews, Elliott Morrison, 1886-1970.
Mss A 1405
1 v.: geneal. tables; 29 cm.
1952
Typescript.

The ancestry of Burnham Clark Benner embracing the following families
Benner, Winthrop Ellsworth.
Mss A 1406
1 v. (177 leaves): coat of arms; 29 cm.
1922
Typescript.

Early settlers of Rowley, Mass: including all who were here before 1700 with several generations of their descendants
Blodgette, George Brainard, 1845-1918.
Jewett, Amos Everett, b. 1862.
Mss A 1407
1 v. (631 leaves); 29 cm.
1924
Typescript with annotations and corrections.

Horne family of Dover, New Hampshire
Ham, John Randolph, 1842-1920.
Mss A 1408
1 v. (80 leaves): photograph; 27 cm.
1902
Handwritten genealogy on the descendants of William Horne of Dover, NH. Includes typescript preface and index by the donor.

Curtis Stevens Bible record, 1790-1913
Stevens, Curtis, 1821-1903.
Mss A 141
[6] leaves; 27 cm.
Original Bible record lacking title page with 3 leaves of mounted obituaries on the Stevens and Qumiby families, descendants of the early settlers of Saint Johnsbury, Vt.

Genealogy of the McCrum family
McCrum, Ephraim Banks.
Mss A 1410
19, [1] leaves: geneal. tables; 28 cm.
1965
Reproduced typescript genealogy concerning descendants of Henry McCrum of Ireland; New Jersey; and Milford, Juniata Co., Pa.

The Merrill family: a genealogical sketch of one line of one branch of the Merrill family, traced by "family units" in America directly descendent from Nathaniel Merrill, immigrant progenitor of this branch of the Merrill family within the United States, May 4, 1601 to December 1, 1958
Randolph, Frank Peiro, b. 1881.
Mss A 1411
9 leaves; 28 cm.
1958
Mimeographed typescript genealogy.

Genealogy of Willoughby and Susannah Wood Micklethwaite (Mickelwait) and their descendants
Lingenfelter, Keith E.
Mss A 1412
iii, 57, [9], 2 leaves: maps, ports., photographs; 28 cm.
1973
Photocopy of a typescript genealogy.

Memorial of the family of Nathan (1) Lord of Kittery, Me.: the emigrant settler at Kittery, Maine [and] freeman 16 Nov 1652
Lord, Henry Dutch.
Mss A 1413
33 leaves; 26 cm.
1895
Handwritten genealogy.

Account book of Seth Wiley, 1833-1849
Wiley, Seth.
Mss A 1414
1 v. (ca. 100 p.); 21 cm. + 1 photograph.
Original account book for a tanner near Fryeburg, Me. Entries included tanning sheep or calf skins and horse hides as well as preparing leather for boots, harnesses, etc. Includes a tintype identified as "your little granddaughter Lula May?"

The Millers of Roxham: with the ancestry of John Wesley Miller, Jr. and Blanche Ethel Wilson
Miller, John Wesley, 1941-.
Mss A 1415
[38] leaves: ill., maps; 28 cm.
1958
Mimeographed typescript genealogy.

Miller genealogy
Miller, Blandina Dudley.
Mss A 1416
[26] leaves; 28 cm.
Photocopy of a typescript genealogy on some descendants of John Miller of Easthampton, Long Island.

Jeffrey Minshall, migrant to the Eastern Shore
Stewart, Charles Leslie, b. 1890.
Mss A 1417
8 leaves; 28 cm.
1964
Reproduced from typescript genealogy.

The Marsh interlude, 1642-1970: ten generations
Marsh, Ian Dawson.
Mss A 1418
45 p.: coat of arms; 28 cm.
1970
Mimeographed typescript genealogy of some descendants of William Marsh and wife Elizabeth Yeomans.

A genealogical and biographical record of the Marshall family of Massachusetts and Vermont, 1722-1972
Catts, Florence M., 1916-.
Mss A 1419
[29] leaves (various pagings); 28 cm.
1972
Mimeographed typescript genealogy of some descendants of Peter Marshall and wife Sarah Davis.

James Alfred Dennison Bible record, 1813-1936
Dennison, James Alfred, 1846-1900.
Mss A 142
[4] leaves; 26-30 cm.
Original Bible record lacking title page which concerns the Dennison and Dudley families of Johnstown, N.Y.

Mattoon family in Europe and early America
Mattoon, Lillian G.
Mss A 1420
50, [4], 4, [11] leaves: ill., maps, geneal. tables; 28 cm.
1971
Reproduction of a typescript genealogy.

Mattoon family genealogy
Mattoon, Lillian G.
Mss A 1421
15 p.; 28 cm.
1965
Mimeographed typescript additions to "A genealogy of the descendants of Philip Mattoon of Deerfield, Massachusetts."

Our branch of the Maynard family
Davis, Genevieve L.
Mss A 1422
[35] leaves: photographs; 28 cm.
Carbon copy typescript genealogy of some descendants of John Maynard of Sudbury, Mass.

One line of the Moody family of Maine, descendants of William Moody of Ipswich, Mass.
Simmons, Frederick Johnson, b. 1884.
Mss A 1423
16 p.; 28 cm.
1966
Typescript genealogy.

The Galusha royal descent
Mss A 1424
[8] leaves; 28 cm.
Carbon copy typescript showing the descent of the children of Daniel Galusha and wife Sarah Warren from Edward I of England. Also a genealogy of some descendants of Daniel Galusha and wife Hannah Gould of Chelmsford, Mass.

Moore genealogy
Moore, Marcella Werlau, 1928-.
Mss A 1425
17 leaves: coat of arms; 28 cm.
1962
Mimeographed typescript genealogy of some descendants of Andrew Moore and wife Sarah Phelps of Connecticut.

Genealogical notes on the Gallup family of Guilford, Vt.
Stoughton, Ralph M.
Mss A 1426
[20] leaves; 23 cm.
1949
Typescript genealogy of some descendants of Richard Gallup of Rhode Island.

Some of the descendants of Alpheas A. Morse of Essex County, New York
Burnham, Koert DuBois.
Mss A 1427
[2], 8 leaves: geneal. tables; 28 cm.
1970
Mimeographed typescript genealogy concerning descendants of Alpheas Morse, son of Ebenezer Morse of Dorset, Vt.

Ancestors and descendants of Frederick T. Moses, Carl A. Moses, Kathleen E. Moses (Woodward)
Moses, Frederick T.
Mss A 1428
12 leaves: coat of arms; 28 cm.
1958
Reproduced typescript genealogy.

Ancestors and descendants of Jarrett Mutchner: Randolph & Wayne Counties, Indiana [and] Darke County, Ohio
Hawkins, Carl H., 1906-.
Mss A 1429
17 p.: geneal. tables; 28 cm.
1971
Mimeographed typescript genealogy.

Percy Adelbert Ellenwood Bible record, 1902-1919
Ellenwood, Percy Adelbert.
Mss A 143
[1] leaf; 29 cm.
Original Bible record lacking title and death page regarding Ellenwood family.

Genealogy of the Tressa (Burgess) Nau family
Bowers, Glenn.
Mss A 1430
7 leaves; 28 cm.
1963
Mimeographed typescript genealogy of the descendants of Tressa Burgess, daughter of George Washington Burgess and wife of Jacob Nau.

The Neely family with related genealogies
Neely, Charles Batcheller, 1909-.
Mss A 1431
[73] leaves; 28 cm.
1971
Photocopy of a typescript genealogy concerning descendants of Alexander Neely and wife Lydia of New York and Illinois. Includes numerous allied families.

Pioneer settlers: Reverend John A. Nelms, Methodist minister, and wife Mary Belle Crain Nelms and their descendants of Bonham and Ector, Fannin County, Texas, in the Red River Valley
Herriage, Vivian Newingham, 1947-.
Mss A 1432
20 leaves; 28 cm.
1968
Mimeographed typescript genealogy.

What's in a name? [Nevers family]
Mss A 1433
[12] leaves: ill., geneal. tables; 28 cm.
Photocopies of miscellaneous notes on Nevers families and on Nevers, France.

The descendents [sic] of Thomas M. Neville and Theresa Nevin
Jones, Ruth D. Neville, 1913-.
Mss A 1434
14 leaves; 28 cm.
1970
Mimeographed typescript genealogy of the descendants of Thomas Neville of Ireland and Brooklyn, N.Y.

Luther Nile (1837-1897): an account of a successful Maine farmer who was the grandson of a real pioneer, his ancestors, his relatives, and a genealogy of his several lineal descendants through four generations
Nile, Abbott Howe, b. 1901.
Mss A 1436
6 leaves; 28 cm.
1956
Mimeographed typescript genealogy of the descendants of Luther Nile (born Luther Hoar), son of Joseph Hoar and wife Hannah Brackett, and wife Aribelle Peary Abbott.

The history of the Ole Njos family
Twomey, Charles J.
Mss A 1437
28 leaves; 28 cm.
1968
Rev. ed.
Mimeographed typescript genealogy of the descendants of Ole Njos and wife Synneva Henjum of Norway and South Dakota.

Norwood lineage
Winters, Catherine Norwood.
Mss A 1439
[1], 4 leaves: coat of arms; 28 cm.
1966
Photocopy of a typescript tracing the Norwood lineage of Leon Charles Norwood of Keene, N.H.

Haynor family record, 1847-1870
Mss A 144
[1] leaf; 16 cm.
A family record apparently written at one time of Haynor sibling births between 1847 to 1870.

The family of Ethel Rita Landau (Voorhis)
Voorhis, Harold Van Buren, b. 1894.
Mss A 1440
7 leaves; 28 cm.
1960
Mimeographed typescript genealogy of the descendants of Dennis O'Leary.

The Calvin Newlin Bible record and the White family Bible record, with some records of the connections to the Hollingsworth family, Quakers of Indiana and Illinois
Ewers, Dorothy Wood, 1910-.
Mss A 1441
9 p.; 28 cm.
1965
Mimeograph typescript transcription and notes concerning some descendants of Calvin Newlin and wife Rebecca Hadley, and of James White and wife Sarah Cosand. Record includes data on allied Maris, Trueblood, and Cosand families. Date span of the Bible record is approximately 1776-1955; supplemental historical material on the Cosand family begins ca. 1732.

The Orr history
Arnold, Gladys, 1905-.
Mss A 1442
69 leaves; 28 cm.
1967
Mimeographed typescript genealogy of the descendants of Robert Orr and wife Susan Hughes of Ireland and Wellington Co., Ontario, Canada.

Orr family genealogical notes
Todd, Margaret, 1902-.
Mss A 1443
9 leaves; 28 cm.
1963
Typescript notes on the surname Orr and its Scottish origins.

Outland genealogy
Nicholson, Mary Ann.
Mss A 1444
[5] leaves; 28 cm.
1972
Typescript genealogy of some descendants of Cornelius and Elizabeth Oudelant, including those surnamed Outland of Virginia and North Carolina.

The probable Paddock ancestry of Sarah Louisa (Paddock) Miller, 1848-1920
Miller, Malloy M.
Mss A 1445
[15] leaves; 28 cm.
[196-]
Photocopy of a typescript genealogy.

The name and family of Pain(e)
Media Research Bureau.
Mss A 1446
10 leaves; 27 cm.
[19--]
Typescript giving general information on the surname in England and early America.

Record of marriages performed by Lucius Bradford, 1855-1877
Bradford, Lucius.
Mss A 1447
1 v. (ca. 118 p.); 19 cm.
Small notebook with 25 handwritten entries (on 12 pages) recording the marriages by Lucius Bradford throughout Androscoggin County, Maine. Entries list the couple's names, residence, and the date and location of the marriage.

Record of the Smith family of Rehoboth and Mansfield, Mass.
Foster, Nancy.
Mss A 1448
[10] leaves: photographs; 28 cm.
1960
Typescript genealogy concerning two lines of descent from Henry Smith of Hingham and Rehoboth, Mass.

Smith family of Fleming County, Kentucky; Peoria County, Illinois; [and] Linn County, Oregon, being descendants of Robert Smith who died 1798 in Fleming County, Kentucky
Hall, William K. (William Kearney), 1918-.
Mss A 1449
14 leaves; 28 cm.
[1961?]
Carbon copy typescript genealogy.

John Lindsay DeLong Bible record, 1823-1907
DeLong, John Lindsay, 1823-1901.
Mss A 145
[2] leaves; 30 cm.
Original Bible record lacking title page regarding the DeLong family.

Staples family from Deer Isle, Maine, town records
Hinckley, Mabel Gould Demers, b. 1887.
Mss A 1450
4 leaves; 28 cm.
1954
Carbon copy typescript extracts.

Wells, Maine epitaphs 1700-1921
Durrell, Harold Clarke, 1882-1943.
Mss A 1451
1 v. (42 p.); 23 cm.
1922
Handwritten transcription of tombstone
inscriptions.

Ayres family of Brookfield
Whitmore, William Henry, 1836-1900.
Mss A 1452
41 p.; 20 cm.
Handwritten genealogy on the descendants of
John Ayres (d. 1676) of Ipswich, Mass.,
especially the Brookfield, Mass. branch of the
family. Title originally had "Hind family of
Brookfield", however, the surname "Hind" was
crossed out and Ayres written in.

Gifford genealogy
Mss A 1453
276 p.; 20 cm.
ca. 1881
Handwritten genealogy on the descendants of
William Gifford of Sandwich, Mass., 1758-1881.

*Commonplace book of Reverend Seaborn Cotton,
1650-1752*
Cotton, Seaborn, 1633-1686.
Cotton, John, 1658-1710.
Gookin, Nathaniel, 1687-1734.
Mss A 1454
Access to original record restricted: Material
fragile.
1 v. (ca. 130 p.); 12 cm.
Additional form: Partially transcribed version by
Samuel Eliot Morison published as "Rev Seaborn
Cotton's Commonplace Book" in Publications of
Colonial Society of Massachusetts 32:320.
Small leather bound commonplace book that
belonged to the Rev. Seaborn Cotton of Hampton,
N.H., to his son and successor, the Rev. John
Cotton, and to the latter's son-in-law and
successor, the Rev. Nathaniel Gookin. Entries
include copies of songs, ballads, and prose
extracts written while Seaborn was in college
(1648-1651) as well as church records (including
meetings, admissions, list of members, baptisms,
etc.) written while minister in Hampton. Includes
Seaborn Cotton's family records and John

Cotton's family records 1687-1710 followed by
misc. family records 1710-1752. Book also
includes Hampton church records written by
John Cotton and some ballads, poetry and
astrological entries by "D.C." – perhaps
Seaborn's wife Dorothy (Bradstreet) Cotton.

The Peairs family
Mss A 1455
24 leaves; 28 cm.
Typescript genealogy of some descendants of
Richard Pearse of Newport, R.I.

The ancestors of Samuel Pearsall
Anderson, Adrienne E.
Mss A 1456
[5] leaves: geneal. tables; 28 cm.
1982
Photocopy of a typescript genealogy concerning
some descendants of Henry Pearsall of
Hempstead, Long Island.

Pease
Mss A 1457
4 leaves; 28 cm.
Typescript genealogy of some descendants of
Robert Pease of Salem, Mass.

Descendants of John Peckham of Newport, R.I.
Hill, Allen D.
Mss A 1458
7 leaves; 28 cm.
1959
Mimeographed typescript genealogy concerning
one line of descent to Ethel B. Peckham Haswell
of Petersburg, N.Y.

*Captain William Peirce, "ancient planter" and
early settler of Mulberry Island in Virginia*
Vollertsen, Dorothy F.
Mss A 1459
13, [4] leaves; 28 cm.
1970
Reproduced typescript biographical sketch.

List of deaths in Clinton, Conn., from January 1, 1809, to January 1, 1878
Hurd, Aaron G.
Mss A 146
[14, 11] leaves; 24-28 cm.
[1878?]
With this chronologically published list is a typescript alphabetical list prepared in the 1950s for the Clinton Historical Society. Clinton set off from the town of Killingworth in 1838. Barbour vital records for Clinton cover 1838-1854.

Record book for Lenox Church, 1900-1903
Hoyt, William H.
Lenox Church (Boston, Mass.)
Mss A 1460
1 v. (175 p.); 27 cm.
Account book kept by Clerk William H. Hoyt with the following written on the end sheet "No. # Two - Record Book Jany 1900" with "to October 1903" added in pencil. Contains handwritten copy of the constitution (p.12-25) followed by Church meeting minutes and reports. Includes a plan of cemetery lot 877 in Mount Hope Cemetery and a list of members from 1889-1902 (p. 39-42).

Account book and diary of John Tileston, 1761-1775
Tileston, John, 1735-1826.
Mss A 1461
1 v. (75 p.); 15 cm.
Vellum bound account book for a school teacher in Boston, Mass., 1761-1765. Entries concern fees for schooling, pens and ink, and books. Includes "An account of contribution money for my pew" [No. 42] (1768-1775), pew No.56 (1762-1763), "F[ir]e M[one]y -- fees paid by students to heat the school(?) (1761-1765), and brief diary entries scattered among the last twenty pages, 1761-1766.

Diary of Dr. Ezra Green, 1777 November 1-1778 September 27
Green, Ezra, 1746-1847.
Mss A 1462
Access to original record restricted: Material fragile; Use transcription.
1 v. (38 p.); 18 cm.
Additional form: Transcribed version by George Henry Preble published as "Diary of Dr. Ezra Green..." in *NEHG Register* 29[1875]:13-24.

Diary of a surgeon under Capt. John Paul Jones during the cruise of the Continental Ship of War Ranger.

Perkins of Western Virginia and North Carolina: a New England emissary branch
Perkins, Dow W.
Mss A 1463
45 leaves; 28 cm.
1970
Photocopy of a typescript genealogy linking pioneer Perkins families of the south and west to earlier New England ancestry.

Rachel Perne, the female of the species, 1618-, late of Gillingham, Dorset, England, and Newbury and Boston, Massachusetts
Slade, W. W.
Mss A 1464
14 leaves; 28 cm.
[1972?]
Mimeographed typescript. Biographical sketch of Rachel Perne, wife of Edward Rawson, and her family.

Some descendants of Philip Phetteplace of Portsmouth, Rhode Island
Chapman, Grace Olive.
Mss A 1465
49 leaves: geneal. tables; 28 cm.
[1959]
Carbon copy typescript genealogy. One manuscript chart.

The descendants of Major William Phillips and his wife Martha Jerusha Medearis
Rehfeldt, Martha Nellie Cooper, 1887-.
Mss A 1466
9 leaves; 28 cm.
1957
Photocopy of a typescript genealogy. Phillips and his wife were natives of North Carolina.

A biographical sketch and the complete total genealogy of Captain George Pierce, Jr. of Greenfield, Mass., 1830-1915
Pierce, Richard L. (Richard Lewis), 1947-.
Mss A 1467
15 leaves; 28 cm.
1969
Photocopy of a typescript genealogy.

Pineo
Jackson, Harold Pineo.
Mss A 1468
9 leaves; 28 cm.
1968
Mimeographed typescript genealogy concerning some descendants of James Pineo of Bristol, R.I., and Lebanon, Conn.

Early generations of original landowners of Clinton, Connecticut
Gilman, Frances M.
Mss A 147
55, [4]: maps, charts; 28 cm.
1992 July
Plaisted family records
Mss A 1470
2 leaves; 28 cm.
Carbon copy typescript concerning some descendants of Roger Plaisted of Kittery, Me., in particular the family of John Plaisted and wife Thankful Babb of Limington, Me.

Descendants of William Dodman Plumb and Evelyn Howland Crandon
Plumb, William D.
Mss A 1471
8 leaves; 28 cm.
1966
Photocopy of a typescript genealogy concerning some descendants of early immigrant John Plumb of New London, Conn.

Mathematical textbook, ca. 1800
Mss A 1472
Access to original record restricted: Material fragile.
1 v. (100 p.): ill.; 20 cm.
Handwritten mathematical textbook with sections on geometry, trigonometry, surveying, navigation (dated November 4, 1800), and dialing.

Potter genealogical notes
Hanna, Doreen Potter, b. 1899.
Mss A 1473
24, [7] leaves; 28 cm.
1969
Carbon copy typescript genealogy concerning some descendants of Nathaniel Potter of Rhode Island, in particular the descendants of Elias Champlin Potter and Lucien Bonaparte Potter.

Cash book of F[rancis] Jackson, 1830-1848
Jackson, Francis.
Mss A 1474
1 v. (100 p.); 20 cm.
Cash book for Francis Jackson, Land Commissionerfor Boston, Mass. Entries concern cash received for rent or taxes. Includes a small group of loose receipts.

Marriages 1538-1650 at Littleham, North Devon
Banks, Charles Edward, 1854-1931.
Mss A 1475
35 p.; 20 cm.
1924
Transcription of original record.

Letterbook of Mather Byles, 1727-1784
Byles, Mather, 1707-1788.
Mss A 1476
Access to original record restricted: Material extremely fragile.
1 v. (ca. 200 p.); 20 cm.
Leather bound account book with "A collection of the original copies of several letters" written by Mather Byles, Congregational minister and Tory. The letters were written to Alexander Pope (1688-1744), Ezra Stiles (1727-1795), Benjamin Franklin (1706-1790), Andrew Oliver (1731-1799), Isaac Watts (1674-1748) and others. Includes letters by his daughters, Mary and Catherine Byles, 1778-1784.

Record of marriages performed by Warren Emerson, 1828-1857
Emerson, Warren, 1796-1882.
Mss A 1477
Access to original record restricted: Use transcription in the Register.
1 v. (48 p.); 21 cm.
 Additional form: Transcribed version by Warner Dumas published as "The Rev. Warren Emerson's Marriage Records" in *NEHG Register* 116[1962]:255-260.
Handwritten account of the marriage ceremonies performed by Rev. Emerson of the Methodist Episcopal Church throughout Central and Eastern Massachusetts, Connecticut and Rhode Island. Entries list date, name of the groom and bride, town of residence and location of marriage.

Mellen family: comprising the descendants of Richard Mellen of Charlestown and various allied families from the manuscript of Mariette Mellen Woolford
Woolford, Mariette Mellen.
Mss A 1478
1 v. (360 p.); 21 cm.
1902
Handwritten transcription of original record by Wilton F. Bucknam.

Diary of James Price, 1792
Price, James, b. 1766.
Mss A 1479
1 v. (45 p.); 15 cm.
Diary by a Boston merchant recording a voyage and visit to France.

Diary of a proper young Bostonian, 1883/ transcribed by Robert E. Chaloner
Chaloner, Louis E., b. 1863.
Mss A 148
[93] p.: ill.; 28 cm.
1989
Photocopy of typescript transcription with illusions and table of contents added by transcriber.

Shropshire wills in the Perogative Court of Canterbury, 1700-[1709]
Adams, Arthur, 1881-1960.
Mss A 1480
1 v.; 21 cm.
Transcription of originial record.

Pratt family records: Shutesbury [Mass.]
Simmington, Theodore, Jr.
Mss A 1481
[19] leaves; 28 cm.
1965
Photocopies of typescript extracts from Shutesbury, Mass., vital records concerning the Pratt family.

The family of James McCall (Mycall, Mackll) of New England
McCall, Charles D.
Mss A 1482
118, [43], xv leaves: geneal. tables; 28 cm.
Typescript genealogy on the descendants of James McCall of Braintree, Mass. Includes 43 leaves of charts and an addendum of 15 leaves.

Thomas Pratt of Watertown, Mass., and a few of his Framingham and Oxford descendants, 1635-1816
Pratt, Stephen D.
Mss A 1483
[8] leaves: maps; 28 cm.
1970
Reproduced typescript genealogy.

Notebook, ca. 1815-1825
Mss A 1484
Access to original record restricted: Material fragile.
1 v. (162 p.): ill.; 19 cm.
Notebook with handwritten exercises in arithmetic, grammar, logic and interest. A page with an exercise in latin is dated "Cambridge Oct 2 1815," the logic notes include several dates in 1822 and one for "July 1825."

Receipt book of Andrew Sigourney, 1803-1811
Sigourney, Andrew.
Mss A 1485
1 v. (50 p.); 10 x 17 cm.
Account book with hand written notices dated and signed by Andrew, Daniel or Elisha Sigourney stating that they received the rent for the lobby of the Boston Theatre. The rent by paid by Stephen North from 1803 to 1809 and by Eben Oliver from 1809 to 1811.

Account book of Samuel Treadwell and James Kimball, 1838-1845, 1848-1864
Treadwell, Samuel.
Mss A 1486
1 v. (ca. 145 p.); 21 cm.
The entries for Treadwell, a cobbler, date from 1838 to 1845 and concern the mending shoes, boots, etc. The entries for Kimball begin at the other end of the book and range from 1848 to 1864. Most of Kimball's entries relate to work he did for Martha Lawrence or her estate.

Genealogical workbook re Purdum
Ewers, Dorothy Wood, 1910-.
Mss A 1487
[28] p.: ill.; 28 cm.
1965
Mimeographed typescript genealogy concerning several families surnamed Purdum.

Registry of ancestry showing how the Broughton and Proctor families of Marblehead came together
Proctor, Joseph R.
Mss A 1488
[8] leaves; 28 cm.
1972
Mimeographed typescript genealogy.

Account book of Joseph Tuck and Simeon Drake, 1789-1827
Tuck, Joseph.
Drake, Simeon.
Mss A 1489
1 v. (80 p.); 19 cm.
An end sheet has "Joseph Tuck's booke bought November 25th 1791 of Ebenezer Larken Jurs Cornhill." Tuck's entries include making a chest, hinges, raising a house frame, making squares of glass. The entries for Drake concern various sorts of farm labor including planting, hoeing, mowing, cutting logs, fencing, etc.

Diary of Helen B. Hall Harding, 1898
Harding, Helen B. Hall, b. 1864.
Mss A 149
1 v. ([123] p.); 15 cm.
Boston social register lady whose diary in a pre-printed volume in which not each day is filled. She and her family lived at 77 Marlborough St. in the Back Bay section of Boston, Mass. They summered at Marblehead, Mass. Rough notes of diary entries are written by the donor, Marcia B. Wood, and volunteer Kathy Wilensky.

Letters concerning the Butler and Price families of Ireland
Younge, Katharine E., b. 1859.
Mss A 1490
[23] leaves; 27 cm.
1937
Typescript transcriptions of letters written by Katharine E. Younge of Queen's Co., Ireland, concerning the Butler and Price families. Two letters are addressed to Ethel Butler of Ireland and England; three are addressed to Annie Leavenworth Price of Scranton, Pa.

Biographical notes, 1910
Clarke, George Kuhn, 1858-1941.
Mss A 1491
1 vol.
Supplementary biographical and genealogical typescript notes to George Kuhn Clarke's Epitaphs from graveyards in Wellesley (formerly West Needham), North Natick, and Saint Mary's churchyard in Newton Lower Falls, Massachusetts (privately printed 1900).

Prior - Pryor genealogy
Morgan, Alice Vera Gifford Curtis, b. 1887.
Mss A 1492
[28] leaves; 28 cm.
1962
Carbon copy typescript genealogy concerning the Prior family of England and America, in particular the descendants of Thomas Prior of Scituate, Mass.

The descendants of James Quaif(e) [Quaif - Quaife]
Brownyard, Theodore Lucius.
Mss A 1493
21 leaves; 28 cm.
1968
Mimeographed typescript genealogy concerning the descendants of James Quaif and wife Mary Beal of England and Calhoun County, Mich.

Account book of Capt. James Tisdale, 1781-1783
Tisdale, James.
Mss A 1494
1 v. (80 p.); 15 x 20 cm.
Account book concerning Captain Tisdale's company in the 3rd Massachusetts Regiment. Entries include lists for the clothing issued to each soldier with columns for when delivered, coats, vests, briches, W overalls, shirts, L Overalls, hats, blankets, shoe buckles, knapsacks, canteen, socks, etc. There are also lists for the arms and accountiments issued to each soldier with columns for when delivered, firelocks, baynets, c. boxes, g. sling, swords, flints, cartridges, etc. In the reverse direction is "A size roll of Capt James Tisdales Company in the 3d Mass Regiment in the United States Novr 9th 1781." Only the men's names were filled in, the rest of the columns were left blank.

The ancestors of Alfred and Harriet Quaif
Brownyard, Theodore Lucius.
Mss A 1495
5 leaves; 28 cm.
1966
Mimeographed typescript genealogy concerning the ancestry of Alfred Quaif and wife Harriet Lawrence of Michigan.

Poems addressed to Phebe Ann Bunker, 1835-1838
Mss A 1496
1 v. (33 p.); 20 cm.
"Album" published by C.F. Gleason of Boston with handwritten poems written to Phebe Ann Bunker of Nantucket, Mass. by her friends.

Amos Purington of Bowdoinham, Me.
Johnston, Dorothy Daggett.
Mss A 1497
[19] leaves: geneal. tables; 28 cm.
1969
Photocopy of a manuscript and typescript genealogy concerning Amos Purington of Bowdoin, Me., and his descendants.

Account book of Chandler Tucker, 1835-1851
Tucker, Chandler.
Mss A 1498
1 v. (80 p.); 21 cm.
Account book for a stone worker(?) in Boston, Mass. Entries concern paving, setting grates, plastering or building chimneys, doorways, furnaces, sidewalks, vaults, and/or tombs. Work locations include house of industry, court house, rail road, banks, schools, South Cove, Charlestown Meeting House, and buildings/homes.

A glance at the Power house
Power, Jane Dale.
Mss A 1499
[9], 36 leaves: geneal. tables; 28 cm.
1972
Rev. ed.
Reproduced typescript genealogy concerning the ancestors and descendants of Jane Burgess Dale, wife of William Whiteman Power.

Arnold's of Braintree
Jackson, Edward Evarts, b. 1868.
Mss A 15
31, [1] p.; 28 cm.
Title taken from label on acidic covers which were discarded. Written between 1939 and 1947.

Diary of William Charles Dustin Grannis, 1847
Grannis, William Charles Dustin, 1826-1898.
Mss A 150
[25] leaves; 15 cm.
This is a photocopy (2 original pages per leaf) of a daily diary kept by a Woodstock, Vt., store clerk.

Our American forefathers, 1633-1874
Kinnison, Don E., 1915-.
Mss A 1501
[26] leaves; 27 cm.
1972
Photocopy of genealogies and notes on various ancestral families. Surnames include Day, Dykes, Hitt, Kincannon, Kinnison, Norwood, Palmer, and Taylor.

Genealogy of a branch of the Zimmer family, from Robens Housa, Hesse - Cassel (now the Prussian province of Hessen - Nassau)
Hamel, Claude Charles.
Mss A 1502
5 leaves; 27 cm.
1960
Carbon copy typescript genealogy concerning siblings Anna Christina (Zimmer) Frohlich and Margaretha (Zimmer) Adams, both of whom lived in Vermilion, Erie Co., Ohio.

Preston genealogy: Begun Sept. 1, 1908
Preston, Harry Longyear, 1877-1930.
Mss A 1503
1 v. (200 p.); 29 cm.
1931?
Handwritten genealogy on the descendants of Samuel Preston, 1651-1738, of Andover, Mass. The genealogy is written on 35 pages scattered throughout the volume.

One line of descent from Hans Zaug of Berne, Switzerland
Beck, Imogene Mable Zook, 1908-1979.
Mss A 1504
12, [1], 3 leaves; 28 cm.
[1964]
Carbon copy typescript concerning a branch of the Zaug or Zook family, descendants of Moritz Zaug who immigrated to Pennsylvania in 1742. Includes data on allied families Stowe, Kaufman, and Mentzer.

Random researches into the family of (Sir) John Young(e) (-1691) of the Massachusetts Bay Colony, New England, 1628; from Devonshire, England to Massachusetts in 1628 and at Salem, Plymouth, and Eastham; associate lineages, wills, biographical sketches
Young, James Kimble, Jr.
Mss A 1505
[vi], 35 p.; 28 cm.
1960
Original and carbon copy typescript material concerning the Young family.

Record of marriages solemnized by George H. Hosmer, 1867-1899
Meek, Henry M.
Mss A 1506
1 v.; 22 x 28 cm.
1881
Partially printed notebook to be completed in ms. with columns for "no.," "date of marriage," "names of the groom and bride," "color (other than white)," "Place of marriage," "Residence of each at time of marriage," "age of each," "occupation," "what marriage 1st, 2d, etc.," "birthplace of each", "names of parents," "signature, official station, and residence of person by whom married," and "date of record".

Woodruff geneology [sic]
Woodruff, Julius E.
Mss A 1507
8 leaves; 28 cm.
Reproduced typescript notes on the Woodruff family of Connecticut.

The Woodford family: the ancestors and descendants of Solomon Woodford (1751-1808) of Northington Parish (now Avon), Hartford Co., Conn. and Cato, Cayuga Co., N.Y.
Parsons, Gerald James, 1924-.
Mss A 1508
[32] leaves; 28 cm.
1962
Carbon copy typescript genealogy. Includes references throughout.

Volume sixteen - historical collections: consisting of families supposed to be descendants of Phinehas (or Phineas) and Mary (Priest) Pratt, of Weymouth and Charlestown, Mass. Born England 1590 died in Charlestown, Mass. 1680, aged 90 years
Bucknam, Wilton Francis, 1861-1917.
Mss A 1509
1 v. (201 p.); 22 cm.
Notebook with a handwritten genealogy on the descendants of Phineas Pratt.

Indorf / Endorf genealogy manuscript
Landis, Mark Emerson.
Mss A 151
3 p.; 28 cm.
Three generation descendancy of Herman C. Endorf (1851-1929) who was a German immigrant that lived at Dayton, Ohio. This is likely written by Mark Landis probably in 1998.

A historical sketch of the town of Halifax, Plymouth County, Massachusetts
Thomson, Ignatius, 1774-1848.
Mss A 1510
1 v. (399 p.); 27 cm.
Incomplete handwritten copy by Sue Frances Sylvester of a manuscript history of Halifax, Mass. with genealogical notes. The ms. was owned by Calvin J. Phillips of South Hanover, Mass.; however, an illness prevented Miss Sylvester from finishing the copy (this being about two thirds of the original) before Mr. Phillip's death -- the text in this volume ends on page 132.

Diary of J. H. Knott, 1868-1870
Knott, J. H.
Mss A 1511
1 v. (197 p.); 16 cm.
"Clergyman's pocket diary and visiting book 186_" (New York: Carlton & Porter, c1860) arranged by James Porter. Includes sections for "pastor's report," "funerals attended," "Sermons preached," "official members," "alphabetical list of members," "alphabetical list of probationers," "Alphabetical list of friends not members," "record of baptisms," "record of marriages""subscribers for periodicals," "cash account," "general accounts," "general memoranda," and "diary, 186_."

Trafford families
Trafford, Perry D.
Mss A 1512
1 v.: ports.; 29 cm.
1952
Typescript genealogy (239 leaves + 27 photostats) on the Trafford family in England and America, 1212-1952.

Wood genealogy
Oakes, Edward F.
Mss A 1513
7 leaves; 28 cm.
1912
Typescript genealogy of the descendants of Joshua and Esther Wood of Keene, N.H.

Runlet - Ranlett
Ranlett, Seth Alonzo, 1840-1905.
Mss A 1514
Restrictions: cannot be photocopied: pages fragile.
1 v. (126 p.); 22 cm.
ca. 1882
Handwritten genealogy on the descendants of Charles Runlett (d. 1709) of Exeter, NH., 1675-1882.

Genealogical record of the descendants of William Wood who came to America in 1629
Wood, Ethan Allen.
Mss A 1516
1 v.; 28 cm.
[189-?]
Photocopy of a manuscript genealogy.

George Adam Wittman (Whitman)
Baudler, Anne.
Mss A 1517
3 leaves; 28 cm.
1960
Typescript genealogy of the descendants of George Adam Wittman of Robeson, Berks Co., Pa.

Genealogies of Wise and allied families
Mss A 1518
[39] leaves; 28 cm.
Mimeographed typescript concerning Wise families. Also data on allied families, including Howard, Massie, Penninger, and Thomas.

The Williams names copied from the parish records of St. Mary, White Chapel 1558-1643, of London, England
Mss A 1519
11 leaves; 28 cm.
Typescript extracts.

Ancestors and descendants of Richard Thayer of Cambridge, Mass.
Thayer, James Henry, 1814-1881.
Mss A 152
32, [1] p.; 23 cm.
Genealogy focuses on Richard Thayer (1772-1821), his children, and grandchildren as written by his son James H. Thayer probably before 1876. A note likely written by James' son Farwell J. Thayer explains that the remainder of this manuscript is missing.

Descendants of James Wills of Maine, Revolutionary War patriot
Smith, Danny D.
Mss A 1520
20 leaves; 28 cm.
1973
Photocopy of a typescript genealogy concerning some descendants of James Wills of Belgrade, Me.

Descendents [sic] of James Wilder and Susan Wilmarth
McGregor, Hattie.
Mss A 1521
17 leaves; 28 cm.
1959
Mimeographed typescript genealogy concerning the Wilder family that settled in Ohio.

Notes on the genealogy of the Bethel, Vermont, Wilson family
Wilson, Harold F. (Harold Fisher)
Mss A 1522
20 leaves; 28 cm.
1948
Mimeographed typescript genealogy concerning the ancestry and descendants of Samuel Wilson of Barre, Mass., and Bethel, Vt.

Ancestry of Donald Whiston and wife Mae Elizabeth Christie
Whiston, Mae Elizabeth, 1915-.
Mss A 1523
[1] leaf: geneal. tables; 28 cm.
1970
Photocopy of a genealogical chart completed in manuscript.

Bible record for the Richard C. Christie family, 1821-1933
Mss A 1524
[4] leaves: ills.; 28 cm.
1970
Photocopy of an original record, with title page, concerning the Richard C. Christie family of New Brunswick, Canada, and Massachusetts.

History of the Wetteroth family of Millstadt, Illinois
Buecher, Robert.
Mss A 1525
[16] leaves: geneal. tables; 28 cm.
[1969?]
Mimeographed typescript genealogy.

Descendants of George Francis Weld, 1866-1933
Plumb, Marjorie Weld.
Mss A 1526
8 leaves; 28 cm.
1967
Photocopy of a typescript genealogy.

Some of the descendants of George Way (1614-1684) and Elizabeth Smith, b. abt. 1630
Way, Glenn Charles, 1881-1969.
Mss A 1527
52 leaves; 28 cm.
[19--]
Reproduced typescript.

Annie Elizabeth Holt Warner
Warner, Jesse Lenard.
Mss A 1528
13 leaves; 28 cm.
1969
Mimeographed typescript genealogy concerning the ancestors and descendants of Annie Elizabeth Holt, wife of John Fox Warner.

James Warren's fifty acre grant, Kittery, 15 July 1656: the Warrens who dwelt thereon and some of their neighbors
Warren, Vanetta (Hosford), b. 1894.
Mss A 1529
17, [4] leaves: maps, photographs; 28 cm.
1966
Typescript genealogy concerning immigrant James Warren of Scotland and Kittery, Me., and his descendants.

Letter, 1909 Apr. 26
Brown, Elizabeth (Elizabeth Lucinda Merrill), b. 183
Mss A 153
1 item ([8] pages); 18 cm.
Letter written by "Aunt" Elizabeth Brown, of Compton, Quebec, to Mrs. Charles E. (Edna) Curtis, of Woodstock, Vt., discussing the Merrill family of Compton, Quebec. The envelope is included and a newspaper clipping noting Charles E. Curtis' death in 1937.

Genealogical notes on Wallis, Buckeridge, McLallen and allied families
Hanna, Doreen Potter, b. 1899.
Mss A 1530
19 leaves; 28 cm.
1969
Carbon copy typescript genealogy concerning descendants in England, Canada, and America of William and Mary (Buckeridge) Wallis. Includes notes on the allied McLallen family.

The descendants of William Wakefield of Pontefract, England, who died in 1466
Wakefield, Robert S., 1925-.
Mss A 1531
8 leaves; 28 cm.
1965
Mimeographed typescript genealogy.

Wakefield family
Rowell, Evelyn P.
Mss A 1532
7 leaves; 28 cm.
1967
Reproduced typescript genealogy and notes concerning some descendants of Jonathan and Anna (Wheeler) Wakefield. Supplements the Wakefield memorial by Homer Wakefield.

Pedigree of Suzanne Louise Willett
Willett, Suzanne Louise, 1944-.
Mss A 1533
7 leaves; 28 cm.
[1971?]
Reproduced typescript.

Family Bible record of Howard Augustine Willett
Mss A 1534
6 leaves; 28 cm.
1966
Reproduced typescript transcription of original record (with title page information) for the Howard A. and Martha (Rogers) Willett family of Kentucky, 1854-1965.

Genealogical record of some of the Sterling [Mass.] descendants of Thomas Wilder, immigrant from England in 1630
Wilder, Katharine A., b. 1901.
Mss A 1535
3 leaves; 28 cm.
1965
Typescript genealogy.

White
Martin, David Kendall, 1933-
Mss A 1537
[32] leaves; 28 cm.
[1965?]
Mimeographed typescript genealogy of the descendants of George and Nathaniel White, brothers who emigrated from Ireland and settled in Rensselaer County, N.Y.

The Whitfields and Blackwells of Mortlake and those of New York
Mss A 1538
10 leaves; 28 cm.
[19--]
Carbon copy typescript concerning the Whitfield family of Surrey, England, and America. Also mention of allied families Blackwell, Manning, Fitch, and Ludlow.

Simeon White, 1769-1846, East Randolph, Massachusetts
Poole, Joseph R.
Mss A 1539
[14] leaves: ill., geneal. tables, photographs; 28 cm.
1969
Family group sheet, ancestry chart, photocopies of deeds, and other miscellaneous information relating to Simeon White.

John Higgins Nichols Bible record, 1828-1898
Nichols, John Higgins, 1828-1898.
Mss A 154
[2, 1] leaves; 29 cm.
Also includes a certificate of marriage (issued by New Hampshire) for a ceremony at Wilmington, Mass., in 1860.

Mark White (1690-1758) of Acton, Mass.: the search for his ancestry
Sherman, Robert Moody, 1914-1984.
Mss A 1540
6, [19] leaves: geneal. tables; 28 cm.
[1974?]
Photocopies of typescript research report and background materials.

Genealogy of the Napoleon Senesac family
Senesac, Arthur Thomas, b. 1892.
Mss A 1542
28, [7] leaves: photographs; 28 cm.
1968
Reproduced typescript genealogy concerning the ancestry and descendants of Napoleon Senesac of Quebec and Illinois.

Sell genealogy
Sell, Anna May, 1921-.
Mss A 1543
27 leaves; 28 cm.
1958
Mimeographed typescript genealogy concerning the descendants of Abraham Sell of York County, Pa.

The family of Samuel Murray Seavey (1847-1899) through 1963
Owen, Ruth Seavey, b. 1901.
Mss A 1544
[8] leaves; 28 cm.
[1963?]
Typescript genealogy concerning Seavey's ancestry and descendants.

Vital records of Windsor, Mass., 1742-1912
Galusha, Hattie B.
Windsor (Mass.)
Mss A 1545
2 v.; 28 cm.
1912
Handwritten transcription of original records by Hattie B. Galusha: Vol. 1 has "Records of deaths in Gagesborough - Windsor, Mass. from 1794-1850" (p. 22-45) and "Baptisms, deaths and marriages in Gagesborough, Windsor, Mass. from 1771-1851 copied from church records" (p. 1-20). Vol 2 has "Windsor, Mass. epitaphs and births, marriages and deaths" (p. 1-43) and "Windsor Massachusetts Berkshire Co. Bible records".

One branch of the Short family of Hart County, Kentucky and surrounding area
Short, Conrad L.
Mss A 1546
7 leaves; 28 cm.
1965
Mimeographed typescript genealogy of some descendants of Aaron and Elizabeth (Boler) Short.

Lineage of Lucille Mary Irons (Mrs. Chester D. Slocum)
Slocum, Lucille Irons, 1902-.
Mss A 1547
8 leaves; 28 cm.
[1961?]
Typescript showing Mrs. Slocum's lines of descent from Henry Adams, Walter Haynes, Ralph Hemenway, Edward Howe, Thomas Oliver, and John Perse (Pierce).

Some descendants of John Slafter and his wife, Persis (Grow) Slafter
Hanna, Doreen Potter, b. 1899.
Mss A 1548
11, [5] leaves; 28 cm.
1969
Carbon copy typescript genealogy concerning the Slafter family of Vermont and Michigan.

The descendants of Joshua Simmons
Simmons, Richmond H., 1925-.
Mss A 1549
17 leaves; 28 cm.
1961
Mimeographed typescript genealogy concerning the descendants of Joshua and Hannah (Macomber) Simmons, early settlers of Livonia Township, Wayne Co., Mich.

Simon Jenness family Bible record, 1787-1933
Jenness, Simon, 1792-1870.
Mss A 155
[8] leaves; 28 cm.
Photocopy of original with title page with includes the Jenness and Garland families.

The Abraham J. Siebert family record
Cooper, Lydia (Eck), b. 1891.
Mss A 1550
ix, 93 p.; 28 cm.
1959
Reproduced typescript genealogy concerning the ancestry and descendants of Abraham Siebert, a Mennonite of Poland. Allied families include Unruh and Schmidt. Many of Siebert's descendants settled in Canada and the United States.

Diary of Burr Beach, 1858-1861
Beach, Burr.
Mss A 1556
1 v.; 21 cm.
Diary written by a young man living in Lawrence, Mass. who attends Harvard University. Entries concern his studies and chemistry experiments, notes on the activities of friends and family, and descriptions of short trips to Boston, Andover, etc. There are brief notes on local and national events -- a day for a national fast to preserve the union and a factory explosion in Lawrence, etc. -- as well as a meteorological register for January-March 1858.

Diary of Robert Allen Hayden, 1832-1856
Hayden, Robert Allen, 1807-1856.
Mss A 1557
1 v. (62 p.); 17 cm.
Diary written by a man living in Braintree and Quincy, Mass. End sheet has "Robert A Hayden's record including thermometer rec." At the end of the diary going in the reverse direction is a "Family record by R.A. Hayden commencing with Robert Hayden of Braintree & Huldah Cleverly of Quincy who were married on February 2, 1803." Diary entries concern birth, marriage and deaths of family, friends, etc. as well as accounts of his activities and local events.

Hannah T. Garland Bible record, 1814-1917
Garland, Hannah T., b. 1852.
Mss A 156
[4] leaves; 28 cm.
Photocopy of Bible with title page that includes Garland and Brown families, though there is no marriage page.

Pratt - Palmer family record, 1752-1844
Mss A 157
[3] p.; 18 cm.
A manuscript transcription possibly from a Bible record for the Pratt and Palmer families.

Bible record for the Isak Norton family, 1863-1991
Mss A 1570
[8] p.; 29 cm.
Original record (with title page information) concerning the Isak Axel and Wandla (Allbeck) Norton family of Boston and Gardner, Mass. Includes entries for the allied Kuniholm family.

D'Oyly family: pedigree of Nathaniel Goddard of Boston
Grew, Jane Norton Wigglesworth, b. 1836.
Mss A 158
1 v. 27 cm.
Primarily a lineal descend of Nathaniel Goddard (1767-1853) from Edward Goddard and the descendants of Nathaniel Goddard for four generations. It seems that this is a transcription made after 1896 from a source written after 1893. The transcriber is likely Jane N. Grew (b. 1836). This family marries into the families of Oliver Wendell Holmes and John Pierpont Morgan.

Record of marriages in Boston by Thomas Baldwin, pastor of the Second Baptist Church, 1790-1826
Baldwin, Thomas, 1753-1825.
Mss A 1586
Access to original record restricted: Use transcription in Register.
1 v.; 24 cm.
Additional form: Transcribed version published as "Marriage records of the Rev. Thomas Baldwin, Pastor of the Second Baptist Church, Boston, Massachusetts" in NEHG Register 125[1971]:99-109, 214-223, 287-294 & 126[1972]: 64-68, 141-145, 204-209.
Handwritten list with the date, name of the groom and bride and the fee.

Diary of Woodbury Marsters, 1849 January 6-April 16
Marsters, Woodbury, 1822-1882.
Mss A 1587
1 v. (59 p.); 16 cm.
Account of a ship passage from Newburyport, Mass. to San Francisco.

New Jersey marriage records
Bass, Clarissa Taylor, 1863-1939.
Mss A 159
8, 2 p.; 28 cm.
This transcript abstracts records of the Taylor family in Monmouth Co., N.J., 1795-1830, and a couple miscellaneous sources.

Arnolds in Michigan
Boughton, Willis A. (Willis Arnold), 1885-1977.
Mss A 16
15 p.; 28 cm.
Written between 1946 and 1950.

Answer to the Cary Society Bulletin #9, May 1810: 1733 Barnabas Cary 1788
Cary, Luther F.
Mss A 160
[3], 8, 4, 75, [3], 8, [2], 4, [2], 7 p.; 28 cm.
1968 Jan.
This is a typescript supplement to the book "John Cary: The Plymouth Pilgrim (Boston, 1911)" for section 28-A, Barnabas Cary (1733-1788), the majority of this work, section 63-B, Samuel Cary (1758-1843), and section 63-C, Benjamin Cary (1763-1830).

The Genealogy of the Gannett family
Gannett, William Wyllys, 1839-1903.
Mss A 161
pages 1-48; 28 cm.
Mimeograph ed.
This is a genealogy of the descendants of Matthew Gannett (ca. 1617-1694). This edition includes dates to 1951 and annotations to 1952. The copy's ownership, and seemingly the annotations, are those of Michael Ross Gannett (b. 1919).

Diary of Clarence W. Dunham, 1943-1947
Dunham, Clarence W.
Mss A 1611
1 v. (370 p.); 14 cm.
Diary written by the pastor of the Pilgrim Congregational Church in Boston, Mass. Includes a list of books read.

Randolph vital records, Book 1 - Births (and several publishments) also record of births from diary of Dr. Jonathan Wales (1798-1850), Randolph, Mass. (Spear family)
Bonsall, Grace Pratt (Grace Pratt Miller), 1898-1989
Mss A 162
16, [5] p.; 28 cm.
1938
Typescript.

Stafford, Connecticut directory, 1891-1892
Fuller, Marjorie.
Mss A 1629
173 leaves; 22 cm.
1973
Typescript transcription of original record.

Descendants of John Grover Stone and Grace Ball Stone (with addresses)
Stone, Frank B. (Frank Bush), 1913-.
Mss A 163
14 p.; 28 cm.
1994 Jul
Photocopy of computer typescript.

Some notes on the children and grandchildren of John William and Sarah Ann Elvira (Johnson) Marshall of the parish of St. Joseph, Barbados; Granville Ferry, Nova Scotia and Saint John, New Brunswick
Murphy, Peter.
Mss A 164
[6] p.; 28 cm.
Typescript ed.
Descendancy genealogy covering the Marshall, Cox, and Hyson families of Barbados; Granville, Nova Scotia; and Saint John, New Brunswick. This work was likely written in 1993.

Some descendants & ancestors of the Northampton Hunts, 1550-1994: including branches in Michigan & Texas with biographical sketches
Hunt, Sanford Beebe, 1915-.
Mss A 165
40, [4] p.; 28 cm.
1994 Oct
Typescript.

William Little, Jr., of St. George Parish and Burke County, Georgia, 1753-1800
Lotz, Eleanor Little, 1935-.
Mss A 166
46 p.; 28 cm.
1994

Ogilvie: Descendants of William Ogilvie (1767-1847) and his wife Nancy (Phelps) Ogilvie (1789-1858), of Bedford County, Tennessee
Ogilvie, Helen Jacobsen, 1923-.
Mss A 167
[57] leaves: ill.; 28 cm.
1993
Contains many genealogical charts and photocopies of a variety of material.

Women property owners in four Massachusetts towns: using an index to the 1798 tax list
Avery, Judith Caroline, 1938-.
Mss A 168
iv, 111 p.; 28 cm.
1994
A Master's thesis studying women landowners listed in the Direct Tax of 1798 for Chatham, Dracut, Northfield, and Sutton, Mass.

John Hill Bible record, 1790-1849
Budd, Nancy J.
Mss A 169
[7] leaves; 28 cm.
Photocopy of original Bible record with title page. Includes a family group chart on John Hill's family constructed by donor, Nancy J. Budd.

Arnold, Redway and Earle families: notes, records, letters, copies of original manuscripts
Boughton, Willis A. (Willis Arnold), 1885-1977.
Mss A 17
[35] p.; 28 cm.
Notes and letters from 1883 to 1944.

Robert Edwin Hill Bible record, 1790-1963
Budd, Nancy J.
Mss A 170
[20] leaves; 28 cm.
Photocopy of original Bible record with title page covering 5 leaves. Includes material inserted into Bible such as obituaries, typed records, and one family group chart created by Nancy J. Budd.

Memorandum kept by Samantha G. Sprague, Highland, Minnesota, 1863
Sprague, Samantha G.
Mss A 171
23, [10] p.; 12-21 cm.
Journal starts on 1863 Feb. 19 to Sept. 21 with several leaves of written obituaries while living at Highland, Wabash Co., Minn. This is continued in 4 loose leaves from 1863 Sept. 11 to Dec. 31 which outlines her trip back to Vermont. The last leaf lists places which are possibly stops on the trip out or back to Vermont.

Taylor family tree: roots in England & branches in America
Taylor, Richard B. (Richard Blackburn), 1929-.
Mss A 172
1 chart; 22 x 66 cm.
Genealogical chart starting with John Taylor (b. ca. 1699), but it is actually the descendants of George Taylor (b. 1752), in Lincolnshire, England, for six to eight more generations, who mostly live in the United States, but a few in England and Rhodesia. The front side is a chart with names only. On the verso, the descendants are listed by their assigned numbers, name, birth place and date, death date, and wife's name.

Notes on the Bonney family in New York State
Bonney, Wilbert L.
Mss A 173
4 p.; 28 cm.
1930
Photocopy of original typescript.

Plan of Monhegan Cemetery, Monhegan Island, Maine
Nelson, Editha H.
Mss A 174
[2], 15, 6,[3] leaves: maps, geneal. tables; 22-28 cm.
1994 ed.
This work contains a transcription of Monhegan Cemetery, Monhegan Island, Me., with map of the cemetery, a descendancy chart of Henry Trefethen, and a 1994 May addendum.

Union Church records, 1870-1876
Parsons, Henry M. (Henry Martyn), 1823-1913.
Mss A 175
[41] p.; 28 cm.
Photocopy of minister's records for the Union Church, Columbus Ave., Boston, Mass. There are three other items. One being a list of ministers and the other two are printed church circulars from First Church of Christ, Springfield, Mass., 1886 and 1911. The latter mentions Parsons term from 1854 to 1870.

Reflections, my family IV
Reed, William Maxwell, 1922-.
Mss A 176
[115] p.; 28 cm.
1994
Covers the Reed family of Boothbay, Me.; Morrill family; and Shattuck family.

Reuel Colt Gridley (1829-1870) of Hannibal, Missouri; Austin, Nevada; Stockton, Ca.; and Paradise, Ca.
Boslooper, Thomas David, 1923-.
Mss A 177
iv, 137 p.; 28 cm.
1994
Ancestors and descendants of Reuel Colt Gridley (1829-1870).

Hackett lines from William (1) Hackett
Peterson, Jim (James Warren), 1923-1994.
Mss A 178
4, 14, 4, [2], 4, [5], [3] p.; 28 cm.
1993 ed.
The several sections including Hacketts in the 1790 census; the Potter Co. Pa. family; Vermont families; a family record of Vermont and New York; and Peterson family who descend from a Hackett. Not all material was written by Peterson, and only one section was dated, that being 1993 Aug. 11. All material is photocopied.

Jabez1 Hackett lines
Dunn, Marion L.
Mss A 179
6, [7], [11] p.; 28 cm.
Typescript ed.
Three separate copied items concerning Jabez1 Hackett; one by Marion L. Dunn and copied by Mrs. John Linsey Jr., one by Lewis Wendell Hackett with additions by Margaret Zeller Garrett, and the last one the author is unknown.

The Arnold family of early Haddam and East Haddam
Hook, James W. (James William), 1884-1957.
Mss A 18
41 p., bound; 28 cm.
1952 Sep.

Hackett family research
Peterson, Jim (James Warren), 1923-1994.
Mss A 180
7, 9, [2], 6, 5, 16 p.; 28 cm.
1949-1993
Six different copied items regarding different research issues. One item is on the descendants of Emery Hackett (1807-1869) by Jim Peterson (1923-1994); Hacketts of Vermont by O. Milton Hackett in 1989 and revised in 1992; corrections to Mary Elizabeth Smith's manuscript possibly by Jim Peterson; descendants of John Hackett possibly by Jim Peterson; a William Hackett piece by Beverly Hovanec with additions of Gary I. Hackett; and partial genealogy of the Hacketts, Moodys and allied families by Esmer M. Saxton in 1949. All material written between 1949 and 1993.

One Ober family of Beverly, Essex Co.,
Massachusetts, and allied families
Woodman, Avis Elsie Jones, 1911-1999.
Mss A 181
57 p.; 28 cm.
1993
Typescript.

Nathaniel Bowman Brown family record, 1737-
1828
Mss A 182
[1] leaf; 28 cm.
Photocopy of family record in the possession of
Robert Edgar Gilbertson in 1991.

Josiah Jenison Bible record, 1771-1849
Jenison, Josiah, 1778-1861.
Mss A 183
[6] p.; 28 cm.
Photocopy of the original Bible with title page.
On fly: "The Property Of Josiah And Susanna
Jenison, Shrewsbury, Vt., Aug. 24th 1830."

Artemas S. Hubbard Bible record, 1809-1905
Hubbard, Artemas Slack, 1809-1903.
Mss A 184
[5] p.; 28 cm.
Photocopy of original Bible record with title page.

Elledge descendants of Thomas and Betsy Huff:
Early Mormon converts
Hough, Granville W.
Mss A 185
4, 40 p.; 28 cm.
This work is in two parts. The first is four pages
of "Thomas and Elizabeth Huff, Mormons in
Search of Truth" by Granville W. Hough. The
second is forty pages of the descendants of
Thomas Richardson Elledge (1822-1887) who
married Bethena Huff by Harry and Betty Brown.
Both were probably written in 1991 or 1992.

Sanborn Cemetery, West Baldwin, Maine
Paddock, Norman D.
Mss A 186
4 p.: maps, photographs; 28 cm.
1995
Contains a scanned photograph of the cemetery
and a map of the layout with the transcripts of
epitaphs. Almost all epitaphs are for the Sanborn
family.

Descendants of Lewis DeS. Ford
Jackson, Ellen Ives Ford, b. 1879.
Mss A 187
101, [2], 3 p.: ill.; 28 cm.
1953?
Photocopy of a genealogical scrapbook of the
Ford family with a lineal descent from William[1]
Ford to Lewis DeSaussure Ford (1801-1883),
then all his descendants. This work contains color
photocopies of photographs and genealogical
charts that fold out. There are annotations to
1973. The second page of the index missing.

England to Ecorse: Goodell ancestors patriot
puzzles
Goodell, Peter Alexander.
Mss A 188
30, [4] p.: ills.; 28-36 cm.
1998 July
2nd ed.
Two works on the Goodell family in England to
Encorse, Mich. It includes photocopies of maps
and texts from other sources, and show a lineal
descend.

Jonathan Cobb Bible record, 1800-1856
Cobb, Jonathan, 1800-1845.
Mss A 189
[2] leaves; 28 cm.
Two color photocopies of the original Bible
record lacking title page. The date is derived from
the lithograph date on the second leaf. This record
concerns the Cobb family.

Ancestry and descendants of John Chambers
Arnold and Mary Elizabeth (Shepard) Arnold
Regan, Marjorie Organ, fl. 1967-1970.
Mss A 19
ii, 36, [16] p., bound; 29 cm.
[1967]
16-page section entitled "Batten Addition" was
received on 1968/06/24 without an index. Notes
suggest a 7-page addition on the Crawford family
produced on 1970/08/06, though is not bound in
this volume.

Cemetary inscriptions from the Thing Cemetary in the woods off Rowell Road, Brentwood, N.H. [sic]
Gilman, Gregory S. (Gregory Stewart)
Mss A 190
[1] leaf; 28 cm.
Transcription of inscriptions at the Thing Cemetery in Brentwood, N.H.

The Woodford family tree
Forbes, Elizabeth B. (Ida Elizabeth Bryan), 1906-1980.
Mss A 191
120, [2] p.; 28 cm.
1978 typescript ed.
Typescript genealogy of the descendants of Luther and Nancy (Bell) Woodford of Licking Co., Ohio, which apparently is based on research by Charles Franklin Coombs (b. 1874) and a surname index created by Norman G. Patterson in April 1994.

A family record of the descendants of Bennat and Tirzah (Ivey) Champion who came from County Cornwall, England, in 1843
Patterson, Norman George, 1911-.
Mss A 192
215, [3] p.; 28 cm.
1993
Typescript genealogy on the descendants of Bennat Champion.

Bible record collection of Sofia Fillmore Taylor, 1803-1996
Taylor, Sofia Fillmore (Sofia Emily Fillmore), 1930-.
Mss A 193
78 p.; 28 cm.
Photocopies of three original Bible records with title pages including William Courtland Fillmore (1818-1902), 1818-1996; Sanborn - Parmelee families, 1803-1996; and William Dampier (1823-1882), 1869-1993, Bible records. The Taylor family is also strongly represented, as well as the places of California, Quebec, and Vermont. These records were offered to the Florida DAR Genealogical Records Committee.

Jonathan Bartlett Bible record, 1809-1987
Bartlett, Jonathan, 1809-1859.
Mss A 194
[7] p.; 28 cm.
Photocopy of original Bible record with title page concerning the Jonathan Bartlett family. The last two pages are a typescript transcription.

Bowers - Simonds - Parker family record, 1796-1822
Mss A 195
[3] leaves; 21 cm.
Original family record on the leaves of a sermon book published in 1746.

Caleb Goodwin Bible record, 1822-1926
Goodwin, Caleb, b. 1822.
Mss A 196
[5] leaves; 28 cm.
Photocopy of the original Bible records of Caleb Goodwin (b. 1822).

Evan J. Beaumont Bible record, 1840-1905
Beaumont, Evan J., 1840-1894.
Mss A 197
[3] leaves; 30 cm.
Original Bible record with title page concerning the Beaumont family.

Allen E. Hoxie Bible record, 1877-1934
Hoxie, Allen E., b. 1877.
Mss A 198
[5] leaves; 30 cm.
Original Bible record with title page concerning the Hoxie family.

Edward Hughes Bible record, 1759-1897
Hughes, Edward, 1759-1828.
Mss A 199
[6] leaves; 14-27 cm.
Original Bible record with title page concerning the Hughes family with a fragmented family record, a poem, and painted image of a flower.

Isaac Brockway's book: Haverstraw, Jan 1st 1865
Brockway, Florence M. (Florence May), b. 1869.
Mss A 2
18, [2] p.; 28 cm.
Typescript copy of family record of John Abrams (1758-1829) as transcribed by Isaac Brockway (1821-1891) in 1840, 1865 and 1875 which had additions to 1933 by an unknown author and more additions by Florence M. Brockway of Dorchester, Mass., to 1948. The records are of Abrams and Brockway families of Newburgh, Orange Co., N.Y., and surrounding area.

The Arrowsmith - Kenton family record book, with data of allied families: Anno, Bayles, Cleland, Clemens, Cone, Darbyshire, Haller, Harbor (Harbour), Jarboe, Patterson (Paterson), Potter, Rose, Stewart, Talbott and Wilson
Newbold, Mary Ruth Cherry, b. 1897.
Mss A 20
[23], 87 leaves, bound: geneal. tables; 29 cm.
1927.
Typescript.

Harvey Folts Bible record, 1847-1945
Folts, Harvey, 1824-1906.
Mss A 200
[10] leaves; 28 cm. + 3 tintypes + 4 albumen prints. Photocopy of original Bible record with title page concerning the Folts family including tintypes, albumen photographs, and a funeral remembrance card.

Lewis Johnson Bible record, 1863-1952
Johnson, Lewis, d. 1912.
Mss A 201
[5] leaves; 28 cm.
Photocopy of original Bible record with title page concerning the Johnson family.

Henry L. Allen Bible record, 1814-1919
Allen, Henry L., 1826-1897.
Mss A 202
[6] leaves; 28 cm.
Original Bible record with title page concerning the Allen and Gates families.

William F. Thompson Bible record, 1883-1948
Thompson, William F.
Mss A 203
[3] leaves; 29 cm.
Original Bible record with title page concerning the Thompson family.

Sumner Warner Bible record, 1800-1968
Warner, Sumner, 1835-1914.
Mss A 204
[11] leaves; 28 cm.
Photocopy of original Bible record with title page concerning Warner and Cowling families.

Letter, 1881 Dec. 22, New York City [to] H. A. Jones
Edsall, Thomas Henry.
Mss A 205
1 ALS; 18 cm.
Letter to uncle inquiring about their grandfather Burt.

Letter, 1917 Mar. 26, Trempealeau, Wisc., [to Angelo Guscetti, Loyalton, Calif.
Guscetti, Matthew, b. ca. 1864.
Mss A 206
[2] ALS; 27 cm. + 1 envelope.
Letter addressed to "uncle" discussed the family of Ferdinand Guscetti, brother to the addressee.

Henry H. Collamore Bible record, 1865-1919
Collamore, Henry H., 1841-1918.
Mss A 207
[2, 5] leaves; 28 cm.
Photocopy of original Bible record with title page concerning the Collamore family. There are two leaves of transcript included.

The Magners of Hingham, Massachusetts
Shannon, Christopher P.
Mss A 208
[36] p.; 28 cm.
1995
Final ed.
The descendants of John and Bridget (Hanley) Magner of Hingham, Mass., for seven generations in all lines.

Young family record, 1714-1818
Mss A 209
[13] leaves; 28 cm.
Photocopy of original family record with title page concerning the Young, Gardiner, Strong, Brewster, Carpenter, Tuthill, Reeve, Rachet, and Little families. It was suggested that these families were from Oxford, Blooming Grove Twp., Orange Co., N.Y.

Tophats and broadbrims: [ancestral lines of Blanche West (Walter) Arter]
Arter, Blanche W. (Blanche West Walter), 1890-1974.
Mss A 21
2 v. ([2], 83, [2], 162 leaves); 28 cm.
[1951?]
Volume I contains: Bidgood, Burroughs, Child, Heath, Kirkbride, John Roberts, Sotcher and Stacy families. Volume II contains: Allen, Almy, Bachiler, Barter, Lippincott, Mayhew, Paine, Potts, Revell, Shattuck, Shinn, Snowden, Watson, West and Wing families.

Joseph Allen Bible record, 1806-1844
Perry-Hooker, John H. (John Hollister), 1923-.
Mss A 210
[1] leaf; 28 cm.

Bodwell family Bible record, 1834-1931
Mss A 211
[3] leaves; 19 cm.

Henry William Kennedy Cutter Bible record, 1871-1918
Cutter, Henry W. K. (Henry William Kennedy), 1849-.
Mss A 212
[6] leaves; 28 cm.

Memorandum of the Sherburne family
Sherburne, Joseph, b. 1769.
Mss A 213
[20] leaves; 20 cm.
1822 Oct.

The Heirs of James Van Nostrand Suydam (1844-1928)
Sheedy, Stuart R. (Stuart Rockwood), 1918-.
Mss A 214
24 p.; 28 cm.
1998
Typescript ed.
This work contains a lineage from the emigrant down to James Suydam's father, Henry[6] Suydam (1806-1858), and from that point following all descendants in all lines through the eleventh generation.

Photographs, 1872-1896
Cook, Lemuel Wallace, Photographer.
Highland Gallery (Boston, Mass.), Photographer.
Mss A 215
4 photographs; 11-17 cm.
Photographs from two Boston, one Brockton, and one Fall River, Mass., photographers. Three are cartes-des-visite (with two identified as Herb Bragg and Will Bragg), and one cabinet photograph. These items were created between 1872 and 1896.

The Genealogy of the Adams family from the first of the name that came to America about the year sixteen hundred & thirty Illustrated by Rev. Charles S. Adams, Hillsdale, Mich., 1869
Adams, Charles S. (Charles Shaw), 1797-1873.
Mss A 216
[14, 4] leaves; 28 cm.
A photocopy of a manuscript family record written on printed pages concerning the lineal descent from Henry[1] Adams through to the next generation after the author. There is one page of annotations to 1907. This lineal is not carried fully in the Henry Adams genealogy published in 1898. There is a typescript transcription of this work by Robert J. Bergman.

Extracts from the church registers of Betley
Mss A 217
[25] leaves; 21 cm.
Manuscript transcription of the Betley parish records from 1538-1700, though probably incomplete. This work was possibly authored by the donor in 1907.

Banton family letters, 1789-1868
Banton family.
Mss A 218
[21] items.
These letters and associated items deal with the family and ancestry of William[1] Banton, a school teacher born at Manchester, Lancashire, England, who came to Charlestown and Chelsea, Mass., about 1792, moving later to coastal Maine. Other families mentioned were Gillum and Hartley. There is a four-page letter being a diatribe against the South for provoking the Civil War and a scrip valued at 20 centavos from a Spanish-speaking country signed and dated 29 July 1866. There is a typescript calendar of items with the identity of each person by David Curtis Dearborn (b. 1949).

Nipher notes and Bible record
Nipher, Francis Eugene, 1847-1926.
Mss A 219
3 p.; 28 cm.
Photocopy of genealogy discussing the Wurttemburg immigrant M. Niver who lived on Livingston Manor, New York. Most of the record is that of a Bible record, 1746-1882, of Michael Nipher (1746-1826). This was written between 1907 and his death in 1926.

Pearce notes from 1853 and Bible record, 1814-1830
Mss A 22
[4] items; 18 cm.
Three items are an inquiry into a baptism at Rushall, Norfolk, England and one leaf of a Pearce Bible record, 1814-1830, with no title page. These items were the contents of an antique box purchased at a New England shop.

Teape: A genealogy
Day, Jesse H. (Jesse Harold), 1916-1989.
Mss A 220
104, 11, [12, 3] p.; 28 cm.
1982 [ie. 1983]
Descendants of John and Mary Teape whose only child Ellen, married James Bunce (ca. 1757-1829). An index in two parts (starting on page 77) is followed by 12 addenda. That is followed by "A Family Chronology" written by Douglas William Teape (1810-1885) circa 1870 added as another addendum in 1987 with an index.

Nichols genealogy: Line of James Nichols (1719-1804) who married Hannah or Mary Mann (1739-1827)
Jackson, Eliza Ann Nichols, b. 1872.
Mss A 221
13 p.; 28 cm.
1957?
Typescript ed.
There is a lineal descend down to John[3] Nichols (1821-1905), and then following all descendants who lived predominantly in Utah and Idaho. The author was the daughter of John[3].

Memoranda and letter book of William Lambert, 1759-1820
Lambert, William, b. 1743.
Mss A 222
[6], 188 p.; 28 cm.

Nichols: The families of Daniel and Levi Nichols of Leominster, Massachusetts
James, Elias Olan.
Mss A 223
5 p.; 28 cm.
1953?
Typescript ed.
Lineal descent through Daniel Nichols (1731-1790), his son Levi Nichols (1763-1817), and his grandson Levi Nichols (1789-1864).

Record book of the sextons of the First Presbyterian Church of Elizabethtown, New Jersey
Cleveland, Edmund Janes, 1842-1902.
Mss A 224
201 p.; 26 cm.
Inscriptions and list of old settlers with the first 20 pages being a reprint from the New England Historical and Genealogical Register, 1890-1891. The source is the sexton's records and the cemetery found there.

Early Wells Taylors: Collated notes, showing descendants of Joseph Taylor of Wells 1692 for four generations, and including all who are named in town records in that vicinity before 1800 as well as many later
Yates, Edgar (Edgar Allan Poe), 1856-1929.
Mss A 225
65, [8] p.; 28 cm.
1915
This typescript contains annotations and has an appendix concerning the Taylor family of Exeter, N.H.

Marlow, NH: An unfinished manuscript on the history of Marlow
Allen, Patricia A. (Patricia Ann), 1946-.
Mss A 226
[128], 22 p.; 28 cm.
1996
This is a photocopy of the original typescript by Elgin Jones which was indexed by Patricia A. Allen. There are sections on cemeteries, churches, industries, military histories, residents, roads, schools, stores and taverns.

Gerrish family
Adams, Douglass Graem, 1950-.
Mss A 227
[5] p.; 28 cm.
1998 July
Transcription of a ledger of Benjamin Gerrish of Salem, Mass., from the original at the Phillips Essex Library, Salem, Mass. From the inside from cover: "Materials for a genealogy of the Gerrish family written out Jany 31, 1863 by Benj. F. Browne, a descendant through Nathl. Higginson & his wife Hannah, daughter of Benjm. Gerrish."

Genealogical studies on Harvey & Glynn families of Waltham, Mass.; Fitzgerald & O'Connor families of Nova Scotia, Holyoke and Melford; Groff & Eagland families of Rome Vienna, New York
Jenkins, Gael Ann Harvey, 1944-.
Mss A 228
1 linear inch.

Diary of Daniel Lamson, 1750 Dec. 24 - 1751 Apr. 27
Lamson, Daniel, 1723-1757.
Mss A 229
[2], 14 p.; 28 cm.
1930? typescript ed.
Anonymous typescript transcription of a diary of Daniel Lamson, possibly a lawyer or businessman from Orange, N.Y., travelling from New York City to London. Lamson was accompanied by John Condit (ca. 1701-ca. 1783).

Orson Perkins Bible record, 1725-1916
Mss A 23
6 leaves; 28 cm.
Handwritten transcription of original material in the possession of the donor with title page lacking.

Michigan marriages records, 1870-1887, [and] the Coulter family records
Coulter, Cyrenius N. (Cyrenius Newton), b. 1834.
Minnesota DAR Genealogical Records Committee.
Mss A 230
[8], 6 p.; 28 cm.
1951
Mimeograph ed.
Transcription of a book of records kept by Coulter in Michigan, 1870-1887. He also started a genealogy of the descendants of John[1] Coulter (d. 1789) from Ireland through six generations.

Saginaw County, Michigan, cemetery inscriptions
Northern States Mission Saginaw Branch.
Mss A 231
22, 13 p.; 28 cm.
Typescript ed.
Transcriptions of a cemetery at Brant, Mich., and the Oakwood Cemetery, Saginaw, Mich. Each list is alphabetically arranged.

*Land warrants for service in War of 1812 –
1814; Muster rolls and pay rolls in War of 1812-
1814; [and] Muster rolls, Militia, Erie Co., N.Y.,
1837-1838*
Haynes, Myrte Rice.
New York DAR Genealogical Records
Committee.
Mss A 232
[16] p.; 28 cm.
[1943?]
Material was transcribed by Myrte Rice Haynes.

*Some New York veterans of the American
Revolution*
Bowman, John Elliot, 1866-1933.
Mss A 233
34 p.; 28 cm.
1929
An alphabetical arrangement of 200 death notices
in a variety of newspapers.

*The townships of Mother Cumberland, including
Bedford, Blair, Centre, Cumberland, Franklin,
Fulton, Huntingdon, Juniata, Mifflin and Perry
Counties, Pennsylvania*
Bell, Raymond Martin, 1907-1999.
Mss A 234
21 p.: maps; 28 cm.
1943
Mimeograph copy of a series of maps detailing
the boundary changes of townships and counties
from 1750 to 1800.

Norcross family
Fisher, A. Helen N. (Alice Helen Norcross), b.
1881.
Mss A 235
[5] p.; 28 cm.
Typescript notes from New Jersey sources and
three pages on Norcross family in Michigan. The
author was alive in 1963.

*Barney Lincoln of Taunton, Mass., and Onondaga
Hill, Onondaga County, New York*
Stevens, Frank Lincoln, 1871-1934.
Mss A 236
11, 2 p.; 28 cm.
Typescript.

*Green - Greene families in New England from
records and authorities on the various families*
Bucknam, Wilton Francis, 1861-1917.
Mss A 237
182 p.; 26 cm.
There is a list of Green immigrants to New
England, though the focus is on the descendants
of Thomas[1] Green of Malden, Mass., to the fifth
generation.

*A Genealogical and historical report on the
family of James Webb, pioneer settler of York
County, Pennsylvania, and Harford County,
Maryland, and allied lines*
Dows, Arthur P.
Mss A 238
[52] p.; 28 cm.
1962
Typescript.

Connecticut descendants of John Winton
Winton, Orrin C. (Orrin Craig), 1952-.
Mss A 239
63 p.; 28 cm.
1997
This work is a computer generated one first
entered in Personal Ancestral File and printed out
using GenBook, thus the biographical notes
appear as source notes and not true text. The work
focuses on the Connecticut branch of the John[1]
Winton family which starts with John[3] Winton, of
Fairfield, Conn., and goes down to the 11th
generation.

By the name of Grover
Grover, Richard Baxter, 1851-1928.
Mss A 24
ix, 6, 72 p., pages 33, 38-41, 65-67; 28 cm.
The first part is the descendants of Edmund
Grover (d. 1682) for five generation fully and
notes to some lines to the ninth. This part has
annotations to 1994. The second part is the largest
section that is mostly an appendix of notes on
Edmund Grover. The third and smallest part
concerns the allied families of Haskell, Tibbet,
Witham, Somes, Babson, and Bangs, though
nothing authoritatively written. Seemingly, this
was written by Grover in 1909 with minor
additions to 1916. It is not determined who made
the additions to 1994 on the last page of part one.

Thomas Gardner and his Nantucket descendants
Greene, Howard, 1864-1956.
Mss A 240
73 p.: geneal. tables; 28 cm. + 1 chart.
[1917]
Typescript transcription of a series of articles published in the "Nantucket Inquirer" in 1862 by William C. Folger. The two articles, numbers 13 and 14 published in 1863, are not included. There is a large genealogical chart of the descendants now [1998] in many pieces. This chart, and the additions to the above, were made by Howard Greene.

Califf - Calef family
Califf, Charles Carter, 1883-1969.
Mss A 241
[16] p.: geneal. tables; 28 cm. + 5 photographs
1938?
Mimeograph ed.
Research at Stanstead Church, Glemsford, Stanstead, Suffolk Co., England, for the ancestry of Robert Calef (b. 1648). It includes transcriptions of baptisms, etc., and photographs of the church. A 1960 letter from the College of Arms concerning the pedigree of Calef is included.

Calkin lines
Sherling, Marjorie Oulton Calkin, 1894-1973.
Mss A 242
56, [1] p.; 28 cm.
[1961?]
Typescript ed.
Bound carbon copy typescript of descendants of Hugh Calkin (d. ca. 1690) that traces 23 lineal descents from the immigrant. The work was created in 1960 or 1961.

Cemetery inscriptions from North Egremont, Race Graveyard, Tuller Graveyard, South Egremont, Town Hill, South Egremont and Mt. Everett Cemeteries, Berkshire County, Massachusetts
Fiske, Arthur D., d. 1996.
Mss A 243
32 p.; 28 cm.
[1996]
This is a reprint edition. The original was published by the author, himself, no later than 1973.

Westport Island, Maine cemeteries
Mss A 244
ca. 128 p.: maps; 28 cm.
1996?
Table of contents to cemeteries, location maps, and a list of deaths from vital records, 1892 to present.

Lucretia Hunt (1798-1879), wife of Darius Burnham of Windham County, Connecticut & Madison County, Ohio & some of her ancestors, descendants & kin
Heider, Loraine Miller, 1916-.
Mss A 245
104 leaves; 28 cm.
1997

Union Cemetery, 33 So. Main Street, South Carver, Mass.: list of names by lot numbers with alphabetical index
Shaw, John A.
Mss A 246
57 p.: ill. (some col.); 29 cm.
c1997

The early Hunt families of Sharon, Connecticut and surrounding areas of Litchfield County: where they came from and where they went
Hunt, Mitchell J. (Mitchell Jerry), 1918-.
Mss A 247
Phys.Desc.:pages 108-133; 28 cm.
1985 July
Photocopied typescript of the Hunt work.

Merrill in America.
Merrill, Virginia T.
Mss A 248 a-b
2 v. ([3, 5], 389, 46 p.); 28 cm.
[1989?]
Photocopy typescript spiral-bound work on descendants of Nathaniel1 Merrill (1601-1655) of Newbury, Mass., for six generations.

James Caldwell of Londonderry and Windham, New Hampshire, and his descendants: Vital records only, also a few other Caldwell vital records
Priest, Alice L. (Alice Lucinda), 1866-1954.
Mss A 249
35 leaves, bound; 28 cm.
1933
Typescript genealogy with manuscript additions of James[1] Caldwell through five generations fully, and some lines through seven generations. A second section concerns itself with the descendants of William[1] Caldwell of Londonderry, N.H. A third section contains a list of marriages in New Hampshire and Vermont vital records not placed in either genealogy.

Woodward genealogy
Woodward, LeRoy Albert, 1916-.
Mss A 25
2 p.; 28 cm.
[1996]
Computer typescript of additions to published genealogy.

Abner Smith Bible record, 1794-1892
Mss A 250
[3] leaves; 28 cm.
Photocopy of original Bible record with title page lacking concerning the Abner Smith family.

Ebenezer Bradford Bible record, 1796-1946
Mss A 251
[8] leaves; 28 cm.
Photocopy of original Bible record with title page lacking concerning Ebenezer Bradford's family.

A Memorandum of the line of Fishers
Fisher, Samuel, 1777-1856.
Mss A 252
10 leaves; 28 cm.
Photocopy of typescript notes of the Fisher family made by Rev. Samuel Fisher with some additions after his death which starts with Anthony Fisher of Dedham, Mass.

The les Etudiants de Dieu Class of the West Somerville Congregational Church
[Smith, Lermond S. (Lermond Smalley), 1916-]
Mss A 253
[67] p.; 28 cm.
1996
Les Etudiants de Dieu is a group of children organized at the West Somerville Congregational Church [Mass.], often called "Eds," formed in 1936. This work is a brief biography on each member of this group.

Pieter Quackenbos and his descendants
Sussell, Mildred Shores, 1917-.
Mss A 254
[9], 46, [2] leaves; 28 cm.
1996
Typescript copy of this Dutch family which settled in Albany, N.Y., which includes a one-page addenda.

General William Warren of Erie County, New York (1784-1879)
Cooke, Raeola Ford, 1925-.
Mss A 255
[1], 12, [103] p.; 28 cm.
Photocopies of typescript notes, documents, family group charts regarding William Warren, his four children, and grandchildren.

Deed, 1842 Feb. 8
Hill, Thomas P.
Mss A 256
1 ADS; 35 x 22 cm.
Original deed signed between Thomas P. Hill to Sally H. Silver, widow of James, all of Sanbornton, N.H. Other names mentioned in the deed are Peter Burley, John Crockett, Daniel T. Morrison, and witnessed by Noah Eastman, Justice of the Peace.

Moses Silver family record, 1777-1881
Mss A 257
[1] leaf; 20 x 22 cm.
Original family record written at one time which lists Moses and Polly (Rust) Silver and their children, births and deaths.

Diary of Zenas Doane Bassett, 1807-1816, commenced upon his 21st birthday (Oct. 14th 1807)
Bassett, Zenas Doane, 1786-1864.
Mss A 258
[57] leaves; 28 cm.
This is a photocopy of a daily diary up to 1808 Jan. 1. Then the diary is filled with several poems he wrote. The next entry is dated 1809 Jan. 10, though very sparse all the way through 1810 Apr. 2. There are only a couple of entries for 1812 before continuing an almost daily journal on 1813 Jan. 1 through Apr. 8 (during the war). The diary entries are very sporadic to 1816 July 28. Bassett lived at Barnstable, Mass. The works last seven pages contains photocopies of photographs of Bassett, his wife Mary Palmer (Howland) Bassett (1788-1863), and his daughter Emmeline Watson (Bassett) Bacon (1809-1887). Also included is some genealogical data on the family written by Phebe Bacon (Case) Burnham (b. 1920).

Page - Coombe Bible records, 1782-1943
Mss A 259
[8] leaves; 28 cm.
Typescript transcription of a Bible record with title page information lacking. The main families concerned Page, Coombe, and Ketler.

Descendants of Orlando Bridge Lee
Smith, Robert C. (Robert Chandler), 1925-.
Mss A 26
[82] leaves: geneal. tables; 28 cm.
[1959?]

James G. Coombe Bible record, 1837-1937
Coombe, James G., 1810-1883.
Mss A 260
[8] leaves; 28 cm.
Photocopy of original Bible record with title page. Coombe is the main family entered in this Catholic Bible, and includes one page of newspaper clippings.

The Forgotten Flagg family of pre-revolutionary Boston
Drew, Gwendolen Flagg, 1902-1973.
Mss A 261
[69] leaves: photographs; 29 cm.
1961
Typescript of the Flagg family of Boston with mounted photographs.

The Crumpacker family: from Pennsylvania to Maryland, 1733 to 1800
Poling, Virginia Smith, 1911-1997.
Mss A 262
17, [7] p.; 28 cm.

The Descendants of George Marshall Fellows and Ellen Maria Emmons
Fellows, Clara Louise Kelley, 1909-.
Mss A 263
[33] leaves: geneal. tables, photographs; 28 cm.
1996
This work is a continuation of one line from the "Fellows family history and genealogy," a 5-volume work by George Marshall Fellows. This starts at the eighth generation bringing it down to the twelfth generation (in 1996).

Signor family: Sickner, Signer, Signor
Signor, Clarence E. (Clarence Edmund), 1888-1975.
Mss A 264 a-b
63, 86 p.; 28 cm.
This work is on the descendants of Johan Jacob[1] Sickner of Rhinebeck, Dutchess Co., N.Y., through eight generations. This is a Palatine emigrant who arrived in 1710. The original work was create on 1946 Apr. 15, and the indexed transcript on 1998 Oct.

The Ancestry of John Dodge, pioneer of New Castle, Maine
Ames, Carolyn S., 1922-.
Mss A 265
9, [4] leaves: maps; 28 cm.
1998
Photocopy of a typescript work analyzing the identification of John Dodge (1787-1831) of Newcastle and Edgecomb, Maine. The work contains four maps.

Josiah F. Whitney Bible record, 1825-1934
Mss A 266
[7] leaves; 15-30 cm.
Original Bible record with title page concerning the Whitney family of Solon, Somerset Co., Maine.

Joseph M. Gilson family record, 1786-1899
Gilson, Joseph M. (Joseph Mansfield), 1826-1892.
Mss A 267
[10] leaves; 12-37 cm.
Photocopy of original Bible title page, but the original inserted family record here on the Gilson family. The Bible was inscribed "Joseph M. Gilson, a Memorial of Mrs. Eliza Susan Quincy from Josiah Quincy, 5 Sept. 1850." Gilson was the Quincy family's coachman. The original Bible is with the donor. The papers include an original 1813 marriage certificate written and signed by the minister.

James Cole Letters, 1634-1650
Cole, James.
Mss A 268
[19] leaves; 28 cm.
Photocopy from microfilm of letter book in the British Library, London, England, of letters to and from James Cole concerning issues of religious strife in England, legal issues for Cole in England, and an account of the Civil War in England. This collection includes 10 letters.

Stires family lines: with various spellings, Stiers, Styers, Stire, Steyr, Steer, Steyer, Steiermark, Stoehr, Steirs, Steier, Steeres, Stehr, Stohr, Stiuer, and others!
Stires, William Dennis, 1939-.
Mss A 269
[2], 41 p.; 29 cm.
1979 Jun.
Photocopy of work on the descendants of John[1] Stires of New Jersey.

John Finlay Bible record, 1755-1799
Mss A 27
[4] leaves; 28 cm.
Photocopy of original record and title page from volume with a typescript transcription by donor/owner.

Taylor family tree: roots in England & branches in America
Taylor, Richard B. (Richard Blackburn), 1929-.
Mss A 270
1 chart; 22 x 66 cm.
1999 Jan.
3rd ed.
Genealogical chart starting with John Taylor (b. ca. 1669), but it is actually the descendants of George Taylor (b. 1752), in Lincolnshire, England, for six to eight more generations, who mostly live in the United States, but a few in England and Rhodesia. The front side is a chart with names only. On the verso, the descendants are listed by their assigned numbers, name, birth place and date, death date, and wife's name.

Provisional family tree: descendants of John Taylor, 1742, Wootton, Lincolnshire
Taylor, Richard B. (Richard Blackburn), 1929-.
Mss A 271
1 chart; 28 x 43 cm.
1998?
The chart details the descendants of James Taylor (1789-1856) of Georgia and beyond for six generations. There are ten photographs reprinted with another of a Taylor house. On the verso, there is a chart of George Taylor (b. 1752) giving the probably connection between the James Taylor on the other side to this English ancestry. This side reprinted two photographs and one of a church in England.

Grovenor T. Anderson Bible record, 1838-1922
Anderson, Grovenor T., 1838-1911.
Mss A 272
[4] leaves; 20 cm.
Original Bible record with transcribed title page concerning the Anderson family of Grosvenor Dale, Conn.

George W. Shumway Bible record, 1832-1963
Shumway, George W., b. 1832.
Mss A 273
[4] leaves; 30 cm.
Original record with transcribed title page concerning the Shumway family of Webster, Mass.

Lucy Ann (Wells) McKeen Bible record, 1814-1869
McKeen, Lucy Ann Wells, b. 1837.
Mss A 274
[5] leaves; 27 cm.
Original record with transcribed title page concerning the Wells family of Littleton, N.H., and some McKeen entries.

Lorenzo West Bible record, 1726-1899
West, Lorenzo, 1820-1899.
Mss A 275
[7] leaves; 23 cm.
Original record with title page concerning the West family of Petersham, Mass. Included is a family record which transcribes the Bible record, and also details the family of Caleb West (1726-1816), Roger West (1755-1824), and Oren West (1795-1872). This is the lineal ancestry for Lorenzo West. There are several newspaper clippings that have been photocopied onto a single page.

Williams family Bible record, 1758-1899
Mss A 276
[5] leaves; 26 cm.
Original record with transcribed title page concerning the Williams family of Hubbardston, Mass. Included is a family record of Asa Stearns (1755?-1795).

Birthday book, 188?-1962
Parker, Nellie M. King, 1872-1962.
Mss A 277
1 v.; 19 cm.
Nellie lived in Greenwich, Mass., until about 1929, when she moved to Peabody, Mass. She entered the births and deaths of friends in this "Longfellow Birthday Book" which is missing the title and first two pages, though all the recording area in there. The book itself is in extremely poor condition. There are many newspaper clippings inserted into the volume. The book was published after 1882.

The Russells of Dartmouth, N.S., linked to those of Boston, Mass.
Flint, Susan.
Mss A 278
[13] leaves; 30 cm.
1994?
Typescript ed.

Pease family papers, 1851-1897
Mss A 279
[6] ADS; 11-32 cm.
Several mounted documents in the back of the Pease genealogy (1869).

Commodore Charles Green, 1812 - 1888
Nichols, Sally Starr, d. 1983.
Mss A 28
25 p.; 28 cm.
[1983]
"... compiled from family letters found in my mother's attic." The author sent some family papers to the New London Historical Society in Connecticut which may be the same letters. This typescript was submitted to American Heritage and accepted before 1983 Aug. 28. This is a photocopy of that 1983 typescript detailing Charles Green's life and experiences in the U.S. Navy.

Family history of the Arzbergers from Marktredwitz in Bavaria to Davenport, Iowa
Mss A 280
[3] leaves; 28 cm.
Photocopy of a computer typescript that presents a lineal descent from Michel Arzberger to Hugo August Arzberger (1891-1970). The author is a child of the latter.

Record of births, marriages and deaths, town of Hannibal, Oswego Co., N.Y., 1847-1850
Mss A 281
[34] leaves; 36 x 21.5 cm.
Photocopy of original manuscript record of earliest officially required vital records for New York State.

Driots de navigation
Mss A 282
[1] DS; 18 cm.
1825 Feb.

Six per cent. stock of 1813
United States. Massachusetts Loan Office.
Mss A 283
[1] DS; 29 x 15.25 cm.
1813 Jul.
Note issued to William Payne of Boston, Mass., for $22,000.

Desendents (sic) of Thomas Penny of Wells, Maine
Campbell, LeRoy Archer, 1902-.
Mss A 284
24 p.; 28 cm.

Comments on Elmer Hough's book, "The Hough Genealogy," privately published in 1936
Hough, Granville W.
Mss A 285
9 leaves; 28 cm.
1993 Nov.
Typescript ed.
Corrections to Elmer Hough's genealogy that is apparently filled with errors.

Stearns - Vincent family
Bridge, Carl J. (Carl James), 1922-1996.
Mss A 286
[5] leaves; 28 cm.
1995
Typescript ed.
Details the descendants of Jonathan Stearns (b. 1793) mainly through his great great-daughter Anne Stearns Sebastian (1921-1970) who married John Furlone and Ralph Fletcher Vincent. The 20th century family lived between Bellows Falls, Vt., and Keene, N.H.

56 Main Street: A History - genealogy of the Stearns and Killmaster families of Port Rowan
Hughes, Jane.
Mss A 287
49 leaves: ill.; 28 cm.
1994
Typescript ed.
A history of a house and the two families that lived there. The two immigrants the start the genealogies are John Killmaster (1771-1861) and Austin Stearns (d. by 1823).

Thomas James Cheetham (1832-1909): his forebearers & descendants of his first family
Bratton, Jeanne Beverly Morrow, 1935-.
Mss A 288
ca. 125 p.; 28 cm.
Typescript ed.
This work is divided into twelve "books" of descendants which are individually indexed. All descendancy is through Thomas James Cheetham, though the family daughtered out in the next generation to the surnames Rodman and Ware. Both daughters were adopted separately before they married.

The Descendants of John Watson (c. 1805-1850)
Levy, Ann Hinckley (Ann Chamberlain Hinckley).
Mss A 289
44 leaves; 28 cm.
1994
Typescript ed.
Computer typescript of seven generations of the descendants of John Watson from Ireland and Chipman, New Brunswick.

ADS, 1863-1918 (bulk: 1863-1865)
Kidder, George Edwin, 1841-1918.
Mss A 29
[12] items; 24-30 cm.
Documents chronicle the U.S. Naval career of Kidder, a boy from East Boston, Mass., who was buried in the San Francisco National Cemetery. Documents include various orders, discharge and pension (#21173) papers.

History of Healing Springs Baptist Church of Barnwell Co., S.C.
Shuck, Lewis Hall.
Mss A 290
28 leaves; 28 cm.
This photocopy of a typescript written perhaps in 1960 from a small book in 1866 and "published" in 1867. Only the first two pages are a history of the church. The remainder is a descendancy genealogy of Nathaniel Walker (1724-1794) from England and Healing Springs, S.C.

The Robinett(e)s, 1744-1992
Robinette, William James, 1964-.
Mss A 291
[62] leaves; 28 cm.
1992?
Photocopy of computer printout from
genealogical program of the descendants of Zoro
Robinette (1744-1795) of Ireland, though most of
his descendants came to the Boston, Mass., area.

The Kuehle family of Duderstadt, Germany
Kaufholz, C. Frederick (Charles Frederick), 1915-
.2000.
Mss A 292
41 p.: geneal. tables; 28 cm.
1990 Oct.
Rev. English ed.
This work was originally published in German by
The Breitenbach Leisner Family Association in
May of 1976. This is the descendants of Hans von
Kule for twelve generations.

Die Familie Thüringer in Grafenberg
Kaufholz, C. Frederick (Charles Frederick), 1915-
.2000.
Mss A 293
v, 13 p.; 28 cm.
1993
Typescript ed.

*Die Familie Brandstetter von Tischardt,
Württemberg*
Kaufholz, C. Frederick (Charles Frederick),
1915-. 200
Mss A 294
24, vii leaves; 28 cm.
1993
Typescript ed.

Lowman families, Book 1
Foshee, Velma Lowman (Velma Jean Lowman
Frank), 1923
Mss A 295
146, 9, 6, 108 leaves, bound; 29 cm.
1993 Apr.

Descendants of John Muchmore, 1640-1700
Muchmore Family Association.
Mss A 296
44 p.; 28 cm.
Photocopy of a computer generated
primogeniturally arranged genealogy of the
descendants of John Muchmore (1640-1700) for
thirteen generations.

Descendants of John Muchmore, 1670-1717
Muchmore Family Association.
Mss A 297
13 p.; 28 cm.
Photocopy of a computer generated
primogeniturally arranged genealogy of the
descendants of John Muchmore (1670-1717) for
twelve generations.

A Branch of "Dennett" family
Holmquist, Helen Dennett (Helen Campbell
Dennett), 1
Mss A 298
3 p.; 22 cm.
1967
The author compiled the information on the
Dennett family of New York City from an old
family Bible and a diary of Arthur Clark Dennett
(1870-1913).

Wilson family Bible record, 1811-1937
Mss A 299
[4] leaves; 27 cm.
Original record with title page concerning the
Wilson family. The bulk of the record in 1871
was seemingly written at one time by one person.

Adams family genealogical notes
Eustis, Caroline Bartlett, fl. 1878-1879.
Mss A 3
[25] p.; 25 cm.
Excerpts from the *New England Historical and
Genealogical Register*, v. 33 (1879) with
manuscript additions on the family of John
Adams of Plymouth, Mass.

The Bedell family: part one: the New Jersey descendants of Robert Bedell of Hempstead, Long Island, NY, through John Bedell of New Providence, NJ, to the fifth generation
Burwell, Gale S. (Gale Simons), 1934-.
Mss A 30
13, 7 p.; 28 cm.
1996
Computer typescript, This is part one of two.

Tombstone inscriptions: Several small cemeteries, Mass. and N.H.
Starkey, Louis, Mrs.
Massachusetts DAR Genealogical Records Committee.
Mss A 300
[42] leaves, bound; 29 cm.
1953
Typescript transcription of the New Boston Cem., Winchendon, Mass.; Baptist Common Cem., Templeton, Mass.; several cemeteries in Winchester and Chesterfield, N.H.; "Hemenway" and "Harty" Cem., Hubbardston, Mass.; Ainsworth Cem., Phillipston, Mass.; Wheeler Cem., Chesterfield, N.H.; Old Cem., Fitchburg, Mass.

Massachusetts records
Mss A 301
[8] leaves, bound; 25 cm.
Mounted newspaper clippings of gravestone inscriptions at Dighton, Mass.; marriages at New Salem, Mass., 1787-1793; Old Burial Ground, North Rehoboth, Mass.; Old Center Cem., Sandisfield, Mass.; Bow Wow Cem., Sheffield, Mass.; and Calderwell Cem., Rutland, Mass. These clippings probably from the Boston Evening Transcript were likely assembled in 1936.

Inscriptions on the old gravestones at the northern end of the Abington Cemetery, Mass.
Faxon, Walter.
Mss A 302
34, [2] leaves, bound; 28 cm.
Manuscript transcription of the older stones at the Abington Cem., Abington, Mass. Volume in poor condition.

Acton, Mass., epitaphs
Reed, Reuben L.
Mss A 303
[44] leaves, bound; 16 cm.
1900
Manuscript transcription of an old burying ground in the north end of Acton, Mass.

Agawam, Hampden County
Hastings, Judson W.
Mss A 304
[104] leaves, bound; 29 cm.
1900
Manuscript transcription of the cemeteries of Agawam, Mass., that includes North Burial Ground, Agawam, Old (Feeding Hills), Feeding Hills (new one on Springfield Street), Maple Grove, and Ferre family cemeteries.

Epitaphs from the gravestones in the Old Burial Ground, Pleasant Street Arlington Mass.
Fowle, Frederick E.
Mss A 305
[173] pages, bound; 28 cm. + 7 photographs.
1902
Manuscript transcription of the gravestones of the Old Burial Ground on Pleasant Street, Arlington, Mass.

Tombstone inscriptions, Alford, Massachusetts
Morse, G. C., Mrs.
Massachusetts DAR Genealogical Records Committee.
Mss A 306
31, [12] leaves, bound; 29 cm.
1936-1937
Typescript transcription of the cemeteries of Alford Mass., that includes "Town-owned Cemetery One," "Town-owned Cemetery Two," "Corson," "Willoughby," "Lester-Church," "Calkins," "Holmes," and "Andrews" cemeteries.

Alford, Massachusetts, tax records, 1815-1816
Mss A 307
8, 7, 8, 6, 8, 7 leaves; 28 cm.
Typescript transcription of the Tax Records for Alford, Mass., from the original copy at the Berkshire Athenaeum, Pittsfield, Mass.

Inscriptions from Ashby, Mass.
Albree, John, b. 1859.
Mss A 308
[47] leaves, bound; 28 cm.
1903 May 1
Typescript ed.
Typescript transcription of the gravestones that date prior to 1850 in the West Ground, Ashby, Mass. Also included are newspaper clippings of the Kendall family of Ashby, Mass., and manuscript of original transcriptions by G.S. Shaw.

Burial Ground at Ashby, Massachusetts: Old Village Yard
Bowman, John Elliot, 1866-1933.
Mss A 309
112, [1] p., bound; 28 cm.
1921-1922
Manuscript transcription of the Old Village Yard Burial Ground, Ashby, Mass.

The Bedell family: Part Two: The New Jersey descendants of John Bedell of New Providence, NJ, beginning with the fifth generation, including a list of "unplaced Bedells"
Burwell, Gale S. (Gale Simons), 1934-.
Mss A 31
[78] p.; 28 cm.
1996
Computer typescript with rough table of contents to part of the work. This is part two of two.

Gravestone records from the Old Yard Ashby, Massachusetts
Fowle, Richard Jaquith, 1912-1972.
Mss A 310
12 leaves; 29 cm.
1937
Typescript transcription of the Old Yard Cemetery, Ashby, Massachusetts.

Ashland, Mass., epitaphs
Mss A 311
162, 51 leaves, bound; 26 cm.
Typescript transcription of the cemeteries of Ashland, Mass., that includes the Old Burying Ground, Ashland Churchyard "near Congl Church," and Wildwood cemeteries.

Revolutionary markers placed by the Margery Morton Chapter, D.A.R. Athol, Mass., in the fall of 1930 and spring of 1931.: Also 3- War of 1812 markers and 1 Confederate marker
Massachusetts DAR Genealogical Records Committee.
Mss A 312
[4] leaves; 28 cm.
1930-1931
Typescript transcription of the American Revolutionary, War of 1812, and Confederate veterans in the cemeteries of Athol, Mass., that include Old Highland, Mt. Pleasant, Chestnut Hill, Highland, and Silver Lake cemeteries.

Cemetery records: Attelboro - Rehoboth, Mass.
Carter, Marion Williams Pearce, b. 1867.
Mss A 313
11 leaves, bound; 29 cm.
1928
Typescript transcription of the cemeteries of Attleboro and Rehoboth, Mass. that includes Burial Hill, Conant Burying Ground, Briggs Corner, and Oak Knoll cemeteries.

Inscriptions Avon, Mass., formerly East Stoughton, until 1888
Sprague, Waldo Chamberlain, 1903-1960.
Mss A 314
5, [1] leaves; 29 cm.
1936 Oct.
Typescript transcription of the cemeteries of Avon, Mass., that includes Page Street and Old East Main Street (North of East Spring Street) cemeteries.

Greenlawn Cemetery, Town of Baldwinville, County of Worcester, Commonwealth of Massachusetts
Bishop, Enos R., Mrs.
Massachusetts DAR Genealogical Records Committee.
Mss A 315
83 leaves, bound; 28 cm.
1946
Carbon copy typescript transcription of the Greenlawn Cemetery, Baldwinsville, Mass., likely created in the same year it was donated.

Bellingham, Mass., South Bellingham Cemetery
Mss A 316
[24] leaves; 28 cm.
Manuscript transcription of the South Bellingham
Cemetery, Bellingham, Mass.

*Inscriptions from the graveyard at the Fox
cemetery in Berkeley, Mass., nearly two miles
from "Centre."*
Crane, C.T.
Mss A 317
16 leaves, bound; 28 cm.
Manuscript transcription of the cemteries in
Berkeley, Mass., that includes Fox and the Town
[on Berkeley Common] cemeteries.

*Gravestone inscriptions in private cemetery in
Berkeley, Mass., on road from Myricks to
Berkeley Center*
Winthrop, Alexander.
Mss A 318
[3] leaves; 28 cm.
1910
Typescript transcription of the private cemetery
(on road from Myricks to Berkeley Center),
Berkeley, Mass.

*Inscriptions from Old or Fox Cemetery, Berkeley,
Mass.*
Sprague, Waldo Chamberlain, 1903-1960.
Mss A 319
31 leaves; 29 cm.
1955
Manuscript transcription of the Fox (or Old)
Cemetery, Berkeley, Mass.

Luna Pope Bible record, 1798-1867
Mss A 32
[1] leaf; 28 cm.
Typescript transcription of original record before
auction at Bradford, Vt.

Cemetery north of the common at Berkeley, Mass.
Sprague, Waldo Chamberlain, 1903-1960.
Mss A 320
22 leaves, bound; 28 cm.
1955
Manuscript transcription of the cemetery north of
the common, Berkeley, Mass.

Dean Cemetery, Assonet Neck, Berkeley, Mass.
Sprague, Waldo Chamberlain, 1903-1960.
Mss A 321
4 leaves; 28 cm.
1956
Manuscript transcription of Dean Cemetery,
Berkeley, Mass.

Caswell and Clark Cemetery, Berkeley, Mass.
Sprague, Waldo Chamberlain, 1903-1960.
Mss A 322
[2] leaves; 28 cm.
1957
Manuscript transcription of the cemeteries of
Berkeley, Mass., that includes Caswell and Clark
cemeteries.

Cemeteries of Blandford, Massachusetts
Massachusetts DAR Genealogical Records
Committee.
Mss A 323
[125] leaves, bound; 29 cm.
1936-1937
Typescript transcription of the cemeteries of
Blandford, Mass., that include Centre (Hill),
Family Burials, Hastings, Blandford Centre (Old
Burying Ground), Stannard, and North Blandford
cemeteries.

Cemetery inscriptions in Boxford, Mass.
Peabody, A. B.
Mss A 324
76 leaves, bound; 27 cm.
Manuscript transcription of the cemeteries of
Boxford, Mass., that includes Harmony and West
Boxford (New) cemeteries. The first part
collected by Rev. A.B. Peabody and Grace I.
Peabody, and copied by Lucie A. Peabody. The
second part written by Laurissa C. Ladd in 1900.

*Inscriptions of Elm St. Cemetery, Braintree,
Mass.*
Sprague, Waldo Chamberlain, 1903-1960.
Mss A 325
16 leaves; 29 cm.
1941 Aug.
Typescript transcription of the Elm St. Cemetery,
Braintree, Mass., copied from a list made by
Edward E. Jackson, of Braintree, in 1904 and
checked with the originals in 1941 and made
additions.

Inscriptions, Plain St. Cemetery, Braintree, Mass.
Sprague, Waldo Chamberlain, 1903-1960.
Mss A 326
5 leaves; 29 cm.
1941 Oct.
Typescript transcription of the Plain St. Cemetery, Braintree, Mass. Many burials of soldiers from Post 87 G.A.R. which has a large granite monument. Also other unmarked graves from the town poor.

Records of Brewster Cemetery, Brewster, Massachusetts
Howes, Maude M.
Massachusetts DAR Genealogical Records Committee.
Mss A 327
97 leaves, bound; 29 cm.
1946 Jan.
Typescript transcription of the Brewster Cemetery, Brewster, Mass.

Records of Burying Ground of the First Parish (Unitarian) Church, Brewster, Massachusetts
Howes, Charles William, Mrs.
Massachusetts DAR Genealogical Records Committee.
Mss A 328
26 leaves; 29 cm.
Typescript transcription of the Burying Ground of the First Parish Church of Brewster, Mass.

First Parish Church Cemetery, Brewster, Mass.
Archambault, Phyllis Shillaber Dillingham, b. 1891.
Mss A 329
20, [10] leaves; 28 cm.
1949
Typescript transcription of the cemetery of the First Parish Church, Brewster, Mass.

Family of Atkinson - Button and allied names
Ravenscroft, Ruth Thayer, 1903-1991.
Mss A 33
[1], 42, [2] p.; 28 cm.
1960.

Dillingham Cemetery, Brewster, Mass.
Archambault, Phyllis Shillaber Dillingham, b. 1891.
Mss A 330
5, [2] leaves; 29 cm.
1949
Typescript transcription of the Dillingham Cemetery, Brewster, Mass.

Brookline, Mass., inscriptions: Walnut Street Cemetery
Watson, Mary.
Mss A 331
42 leaves, bound; 29 cm.
1903
Manuscript transcription of the Walnut Street Cemetery, Brookline, Mass.

Brookline, Mass., epitaphs
Mss A 332
16, 28 leaves, bound; 29 cm.
Manuscript transcription of epitaphs from unnamed cemeteries of Braintree, Mass., in two different recording bound together. It was probably created in the year it was given.

Inscriptions in Precinct Burying Ground, Burlington, Mass.: September, 1894
Mss A 333
[138] leaves, bound; 29 cm.
Typescript index and manuscript transcription of the Precinct Burying Ground, Burlington, Mass., bound together.

Inscriptions of Proprietors Burying Ground + Episcopal Churchyard, Washington St., Canton, Mass.
Sprague, Waldo Chamberlain, 1903-1960.
Mss A 334
3, 30, [1] leaves; 29 cm.
1948 Jul.
Manuscript transcription of the cemeteries of Canton, Mass., that include Proprietors Burying Ground, Old Episcopal Church (Canton?) Cemetery, and Gridley Burying Ground.

*Central Burying Ground, Carlisle,
Massachusetts, Middlesex County*
Burrell, W. Alden, Mrs.
Massachusetts DAR Genealogical Records
Committee.
Mss A 335
[18] leaves; 29 cm.
1946 Aug.
Typescript transcription of the Central Burying
Ground, Carlisle, Mass.

*Inscriptions in Old Burying Ground, Carlisle
Centre, Mass.*
Wilkins, Martha F. (Martha Adelia Fifield), 1879-
196
Mss A 336
[10] leaves; 28 cm.
1936 Sept.
Manuscript transcription of the Old Burying
Ground, Carlisle, Mass.

*Charlemont, Mass., epitaphs, church and private
records*
Mss A 337
[131] leaves, bound; 28 cm.
Manuscript transcription of the cemeteries of
Charlemont, Mass. that include [Nelson], Tea
Street, Village, [River Road and Railroad
Station], [Tower Place], Warner Family, Leavitt,
Zoar, The "Old" Cemetery, and East Charlemont
Cemeteries. Also includes records of the First
Congregational Church; a membership list of the
Methodist Church, Charlemont and Rowe Circuit;
Baptist Church records; Church of Christ records;
the Niles family records; the Rice family records;
and vital record from a pamphlet entitled
"Charlemont as a Plantation." These records were
the source for gravestone and church records in
the published Charlemont vital records book. The
listings were compiled between 1910 and 1913.

*Epitaphs on Old Burial Hill (Phipps Street Burial
Ground), Charlestown, 1622 to 1952*
Griffin, William R. J.
Mss A 338
[126] leaves, bound; 28 cm.
1952
Typescript transcription of the Phipps Street
Burial Ground (Old Burial Hill), Charlestown,
Mass.

*Charlestown Burying - Ground: Charlestown
Chronicle excerpts, Sept. 1873 - Oct. 1873*
Mss A 339
[10] leaves, bound; 28 cm.
Mounted newspaper clippings of the Charlestown
Chronicle covering inscriptions of the
Charlestown Burying Ground, Charlestown,
Mass.

*Some descendants of Joseph Ashley of Rochester,
Massachusetts*
Dennis, Walter W., fl. 1929.
Mss A 34
3 p.; 28 cm.
1929.

*Webster Cemetery, Algerine Road, Berkeley,
Mass.*
Sprague, Waldo Chamberlain, 1903-1960.
Mss A 340
[2] leaves; 28 cm.
1957
Manuscript transcription of the Webster Cemetery
of Berkeley, Mass.

*Bridgewater, Mass., records, Vol. 1: Bible
records, town of Bridgewater*
Hewett, E. A.
Mss A 341
[151, 70, 42, 82, 81] pages, bound; 28 cm.
1910
Manuscript transcription of private, Bible, and
church records used as a source in the published
vital records of Bridgewater.

Bellingham, Mass., epitaphs
Mss A 342
[5, 24, 14, 104] leaves, bound; 26 cm.
Manuscript transcription of the cemetery
inscriptions of Scott's Crossing Cem., South
Bellingham, and Bellingham Center Cem. using a
self-made form. Title was derived from the spine
label.

Brockton, Mass., epitaphs
Mss A 343
[597] pages, bound; 28 cm.
Manuscript transcription of the Coweeset Cem., Plymouth Rock Cem., North End or Ashland Cem., Union Cem., Melrose Cem., Thayer Cem., Old Cem., and a private cem., all in the town of Brockton, Mass. This volume was used as a source for the published vital records of Brockton. The title was dervied from the spine label.

Attleboro, Mass., epitaphs
Thacher, Susan.
Mss A 344
[92, 107] leaves, bound; 28 cm.
Manuscript transcription of the Hill Burying Ground, Briggsville, Mass., and Old Kirk Cem., Attleboro, Mass. The first section is attributed to the authors given. The second section is a different arrangement and hand. Title derived from spine label.

Old Braintree, Mass. (Braintree, Quincy, Randolph, and Holbrook), all cemeteries laid out before 1850 except St. Mary's R.C. Cemetery in West Quincy
Sprague, Waldo Chamberlain, 1903-1960.
Mss A 345
[5, 16, 2, 5, 11, 30, 7, 4, 4, 33, 50, 10] leaves, bound; 29 cm.
1940-1942
Manuscript and typescript transcriptions of the Dyer Hill, Lakeside, and Pond St. Cem., South Braintree; Elm St., and Plain St. Cem., Braintree; Union (or East) and Wendell Cem., Holbrook; Christ Church Episcopal and Hancock Cem., Quincy; Hall Cem., West Quincy; Central and Oakland Cem., Randolph. The first two cemetery transcriptions are copies from work done by Edward E. Jackson, of Braintree, in 1904 with additions.

Bridgewater, Mass., records, vol. 2
Crane, Joshua E. (Joshua Eddy), b. 1850.
Mss A 346
[210, 52, 16, 4, 10, 1] pages, bound; 21-31 cm.
Manuscript and typescript transcriptions of the Mt. Prospect Cem., Bridgewater, Mass., by Clara S. Washburn; "Record of Interments in the South Precinct Burying Place made by Lieut. John Washburn, 1739-1797" copied from the original

by Joshua E. Crane and this copy by Florence Conant Howes in 1913; and the "Records of the Trinitarian Congregational Church, Bridgewater, Mass." now called the Central Square Church; "Records of the Church of the New Jerusalem, Bridgewater"; "Copy of Names of Persons Buried in Scotland Grave Yard, 1753-1840"; and "Record Book of the Church In Scotland, Bridgewater, Mass., Now Known as the Scotland Trinitarian Congregational Church, Bridgewater." These records were used as a source in the published vital records for Bridgewater.

Billerica epitaphs
Bowman, John Elliot, 1866-1933.
Mss A 347
ca. 150 leaves, bound; 29 cm.
Manuscript transcription of the South Burial, Old Corner, and Hill Burial Grounds, Billerica, Mass., copied in 1898 and recopied in 1902.

Burials in Ashby, Mass., Old Yard
Hodgman, Arthur Winfred, b. 1869.
Mss A 348
347, [3] pages, bound; 26 cm.
1947 Aug.
Manuscript transcription of the Old Yard, Ashby, Mass. The transcription appears on the right-hand side. The left-hand side is a genealogical write-up of that same person giving sources. There is an addendum created from work of Richard Jaquith Fowle in 1937.

Graveyard records, town of Chelmsford, Massachusetts
Parker, P. Hildreth (Pearl Hildreth), 1880.
Mss A 349
[466] pages, bound; 28 cm.
1906
Manuscript transcription of the Forefather's, Heart Pond, Riverside, West Chelmsford, School Street Cemeteries in Chelmsford, Mass.

Rollin Atkins Bible record, 1764-1935
Mss A 35
[5] p.; 28 cm.
Photostat of original lacking title page. Record first created sometime after 1856. Included was a single leaf of an earlier Bible record of Austin Bishop, father of Rollin Atkins' wife, which appears to be a transcription.

Genealogical records of persons buried in Cambridge Old Burying Ground at Harvard Square, Cambridge, Massachusetts
Massachusetts DAR Genealogical Records Committee.
Mss A 350
[5], 192, [3] leaves, bound; 29 cm.
1940
Typescript transcription of the Old Burying Ground at Harvard Square, Cambridge, Mass., with genealogical additions. This is a DAR transcription of an early W.P.A. Project sponsored by the Cambridge Public Library and in their care.

Tombstone inscriptions from that portion of Mt. Auburn Cemetery situated in the city of Cambridge, Massachusetts
Massachusetts DAR Genealogical Records Committee.
Mss A 351
2 v. (353, [7, 25, 7, 26] leaves): maps; 28 cm.
1936
Typescript transcription of all persons listed as owners of lots, the numbers of which are less than 6000, were taken from the "Catalogue of Lot Owners in Mt. Auburn Cemetery" (1891).

[Old] Abington, Mass., epitaphs
Mss A 352
328 pages, bound; 28 cm.
Manuscript transcriptions of the Mount Vernon Cem., Old Cem. (near church on Washington St.), Abington, Mass.; Maplewood Cem., Spring St. Abiah Reed Cem., Samuel Reed Cem., Old Cem. (Liberty St.), Lane Cem., Beal Cem., Mount Pleasant Cem., Rockland, Mass.; High St. Cem., Small Pox Cem., Mt. Zion Cem., Colebrook Cem., Whitman, Mass.

Inscriptions from the headstones of three (sic) cemeteries in Ashburnham, Mass.
Brainerd, John B. (John Bliss), 1859-1926.
Mss A 353
[12], 143, [12], 87 leaves, bound; 28 cm.
1906
Manuscript transcription of the Meeting House Cem., Roman Catholic Cem., Russell Cem., Fairbanks Cem., and New Cem., Ashburnham, Mass.

Old Burial Hill, Charlestown
Mss A 354
[1, 26], 215 leaves, bound; 26 cm.
Manuscript transcription of the Old Burial Hill Cem., or Phipps' Place Burying Ground, Charlestown, Mass. Also includes a single Boston Transcript newspaper clipping of early gravestones found buried near the monument to John Harvard in Charlestown.

Prescott, Massachusetts, vital record prior to 1850
Massachusetts DAR Genealogical Records Committee.
Mss A 355
4, [150] leaves; 29 cm.
1970
Carbon copy transcript transcription of the vital record of Prescott, Mass., a "drowned" town located where the Quabin Reservoir was built in 1938.

Greenwich, Massachusetts, vital record prior to 1850
Massachusetts DAR Genealogical Records Committee.
REF F74/G87/D2 also Mss A 356
4, [150] leaves; 29 cm.
1962
Carbon copy transcript transcription of the vital record of Greenwich, Mass., a "drowned" town located where the Quabin Reservoir was built in 1938.

Graveyard records of Chester, Mass.
Mss A 357
[355] leaves, bound; 22 cm.
Manuscript transcription of the Chester Center Cem., Huntington Street Cem., Pine Hill Cem., Littleville Cem., Ingell Cem., North Chester Cem., Round Hill Cem., Fisk Cem. (at Littleville), and private cemeteries: Moor Lot, Bell Lot, Bromley Lot, Horatio Lyman Lot, Tomb Lot, and Kenney Brook Lot, all in Chester, Mass. This was a source for the published vital records for Chester.

Epitaphs in South Attleboro Cemetery
Whitehill, John.
Mss A 358
[258] pages, bound; 22 cm.
1900
Manuscript transcription of the South Attleboro Cem., Attleboro, Mass.

Ashland, Mass., epitaphs
Mss A 359
2, 27, 113 leaves, bound; 28 cm.
Manuscript transcription of the Old South Island Cem., Congregational Church Cem., and Wildwood Cem., in Ashland, Mass. Title derived from spine label.

Atkins family: [Part 1] of Massachusetts, [Part 2] of Connecticut
Atkins, Susan Herod Winter, b. 1872.
Mss A 36
[12] p.; 28 cm.
[1935]

Entries from the Skinners' Company London
G. E. C. (George Edward Cokayne), 1825-1911.
Mss A 360
115 leaves, bound; 21 cm.
1894
Manuscript transcriptions of the company's apprenticeships, 1496-1515, 1547-1694, and freedoms, 1500-1694. This was published in the *Miscellanea genealogica et heraldica*, 3rd series, vol. 1.

The Posterity of Benjamin (2) Taft (Robert 1), 1684-1768
Todd, Neil B. (Neil Bowman), 1936-.
Mss A 361 a-b
ca. 80, 120 leaves; 28 cm.
Part 1 is the families of his, Benjamin[2] Taft, children and grandchildren (ie. the third and fourth generation in that branch). Part 2 is the families of his great grandchildren (ie. the fifth generation). This work is a photocopy of a typescript written in the Register format of genealogy except in regard to numbering the entries. There is no pagination.

Diary of Thomas Scott Burnell, 1848 Oct. 23 - 1849 Feb. 26
Burnell, Thomas Scott, 1823-1899.
Mss A 362
76, [2] pages; 26 cm.
This diary records the Congregational missionaries to Ceylon and India that sailed out of Boston harbor on the ship Bandich in the fall of 1848. Two additional pages written by Muriel B. Willey in 1999 further describe the manuscript.

Dart
Mss A 363
[1] leaf; 25 cm.
A newspaper clipping of a short genealogical record of the descendants of Richard Dart of New London, Conn., that was published in "The Seymour Record" in Seymour, Conn., on 1884 Feb. 8.

The Abraham Nutting family of Westminster, Vermont: Some ancestors and some descendants
Nutting, Edmund Washburn, 1923-.
Mss A 364
50 leaves: geneal. tables, photographs; 28 cm.
Winter 1998 ed.
This work traces the direct line from the immigrant John Nutting to Abraham (6) Nutting (1770-1833), and then all descendants of Abraham to the 12th generation. Included are reproductions of other works, photographs, and documents. Most of the information is presented through a series of genealogical charts.

Brooks Edge Tool Manufacturing, Brooksville, Vermont: Nineteenth century tool production for a nation growing westward
Brooks, Ralph Edison, 1929-.
Mss A 365
114 p.: ill., maps, facsim., photographs; 28 cm
1998
Typescript.

Marriage certificate of Joseph L. Jellerson and Mary B. Bradbury
Mss A 366
[6] items.
The marriage certificate of Joseph L. Jellerson and Mary B. Bradbury, with invitation, envelope, name cards, photocopy of newspaper clippings announcing marriage.

Day family: Descendants of Ralph
Skofield, Perley F.
Mss A 367
4 leaves; 28 cm.
Lineal descent from Ralph(1) Day to Ebenezer (5) Day.

A Short genealogical record of John and Alice Darby of Marblehead, Mass., and their descendants in the male line
Derby, Samuel Carroll, 1842-1921.
Mss A 368
118 leaves, bound; 25 cm.
Includes an appendix detailing other Darby - Derby families unconnected to this one.

Some seventeenth - century New England settlers: John Ayer, John Aires, Moses Eayers, Richard Ayres, Robert Ayars, Samuel Ayres, Simon Eyre, and others, extended four generations
Graves, John Kimball, 1912-.
Mss A 369
[52] leaves, bound; 29 cm.
1963
Typescript genealogies of the various Ayer families with an appednix of unplaced Ayers through four generations in a modified "Register" style which has the citations at the end of each family.

The Descendants of Samuel Wilson (1779-1863)
Lyon, Norman W. (Norman Wilson), 1903-.
Mss A 370
108 leaves; 28 cm.
1976
Mimeograph ed.

James (5) Eno (Enos) 1743-1812 of Leicester, VT and Israel (6) Fitts 1759-1815 of Leicester, VT
Eldridge, William H. (William Henry), 1873-. 1943.
Mss A 372
[5] leaves; 28 cm.
1932 manuscript ed.
Carbon copy manuscript copy of lineal descent from James[5] Eno through to the children of his sons Abner[6] and Parley[6]. Information is also provided on the family of Isreal[5] Fitts. Material includes a hand drawn chart of the ancestors of Israel Fitts[7] Enos, a son of Parley[6] Eno.

Samuel (4) Atwood 1725-1796 of Bennington, VT.
Eldridge, William H. (William Henry), 1873-.1943.
Mss A 373
[13] leaves; 28 cm.
1932 manuscript ed.
Carbon copy manuscript copy of the lineal descent from Samuel(4) Atwood through Paul(5), Roswell Paul(6), and George(7). There are separate entries for some of Samuel's other children including Samuel(5), David(5), Prudence(5) and Sally(5) as well as two children of Paul(5), Levi(6) and Almon(6). The file also contains a typescript transcription of the Bennington Declaration of 1775 from the original at the Vermont Historical Society.

Bible record for the Edward Sargent family, 1791-1811
Sargent, Edward, fl.1791.
Mss A 374
[2] leaves; 28 cm.
Photocopy of original record with title page concerning the Sargent family of Boston, Mass.

Bible record for the John Sanborn family, 1776-1877
Sanborn, John, 1776-1868.
Mss A 375
[3] leaves; 28 cm.
Original record with title page concerning the Sanborn family.

Bible record for the Thomas Elwell family, 1792-1903
Elwell, Thomas, 1792-1874.
Mss A 376
[6] leaves; 28 cm.
Photocopy of original record with title page and a typescript transcription

Bible record for the Elwell family, 1841-1941
Elwell, Ellen Momeny, d.1893.
Mss A 377
[8] leaves; 28 cm.
Photocopy of original record in the possession of the donor with title page concerning the Elwell family of Sandusky County, Ohio. Includes typescript transcription by the donor.

Bible record for the Freeman Remick family, 1756-1885
Remick, Freeman, 1756-1826.
Mss A 379
[3] p.; 28 cm.
Original record with title page.

Vermont deaths: from newspaper files
Bowman, John Elliot, 1866-1933.
Mss A 38
38, 16 p.; 28 cm.
1930
This is an alphabetical list of death notices of people who died in Vermont, or were formerly of Vermont. The first section is from a variety of cited newspapers from Massachusetts and Vermont. The second section is from the Columbian Centinel, 1811-1815.

Bible record for the William H. Heath family, 1793-1864
Heath, William H., 1793-1860.
Mss A 380
[5] p.; 23 cm.
Original record with title page concerning the Heath family of Hillsboro, New Hampshire. Includes photocopy of a newspaper clipping concerning the death of Albert M. Heath along with the poem "The Dying Soldier" from the paste-down.

Bible record for the Martha Ann Knowles Rumery family, 1827-1896
Rumery, Martha Ann Knowles, 1832-1864.
Mss A 381
[8] leaves; 28 cm.
Photocopy of original record with title page concerning the Rumery and Moulton families of North Hampton, New Hampshire. Includes computer typescript transcription by the donor.

Bible record for the Robert Henry White family, 1845-1983
White, Robert Henry, 1845-1922.
Mss A 382
[6] leaves; 28 cm.
Photocopy of original record lacking title page concerning the White family. Includes computer typescript transcription by the donor.

Bible record for the Lynde Walter family, 1767-1898
Walter, Lynde, 1767-1844.
Mss A 383
[22] leaves; 28 cm.
Photocopy of original record with title page concerning the Walter family of Boston, Massachusetts. Includes computer typescript transcription by the donor.

Bible record for the John Parmele family, 1778-1816
Parmele, John b. 1778.
Mss A 384
[1] leaf; 28 cm.
Computer typescript of original record.

Bible record for the Henry Sherman family, 1806-1866
Sherman, Henry, b. 1806.
Mss A 385
[4] leaves; 17 cm.
Original record with title page concerning the Sherman family. The notes were written on the back of three maps within Erodore's *Conversations on the Bible* (1829).

Bible record for the James J. Lynch family, 1898-1917
Lynch, James J.,
Mss A 386
[6] leaves; 29 cm.
Original record with title page concerning the Lynch family of Holyoke, Massachusetts. Includes a penmanship lesson of Thomas Jerome Lynch during his first year of high school (1917).

Bible record for the Nathaniel Stickney family, 1755-1895
Stickney, Nathaniel, 1792-1873.
Mss A 387
[6] leaves; 26 cm.
Original record with title page.

Bible record for the Natt Stickney family, 1847-1874
Stickney, Natt, b. 1822.
Mss A 388
[7] leaves; 18-29 cm.
Original record with title page concerning the Stickney family of Dracut, Massachusetts.

A genealogical history of the Parr family of Ashland and Richland Counties, Ohi
Kelley, Michael Garhardt Roosevelt, 1943-.
Mss A 389
1 v. 80, [2], 4, 5 leaves: port; 29 cm.
1980
Includes The origins of the Parr family in New Jersey; the John Parr (1775-1843) family of Sussex Co., NJ, Beaver Co., PA & Ashland Co., OH; the Jesse Parr (1799-1860) family of Ashland Co., OH; The Abram/Abraham Parr (1801-1839) family of Beaver Co., PA; Mrs Nancy (Parr) Paxton (1803-1880?) of Ashland Co., OH; The Andrew Helford/Helfeard Parr (1807-1876) family of Ashland Co., OH; & Smith Family Notes.

A Record of some of the Attwood - Atwood family for three centuries with several of the allied lines: 1635-1945
Attwood, Mary Frances Harris Shaw, 1860-1957.
Mss A 39
[1], 60, [3] leaves; 28 cm.
1945?

Isaac Leonard of Middleboro, Mass. and Bowdoinham, Maine: his ancestors and some of his descendants
Merrow, Leta Leonard, 1915-.
Mss A 390
6 leaves; 28 cm.
Typescript genealogy of the lineal descent from James (1), Benjamin (2), Joseph (3-4-5) to Isaac (6) Leonard and from that point following through Isaac (7) to George William (8) Leonard.

The Descendants of William Brown of Ancient Dover, Oyster River Parish, New Hampshire
Burell-Brown, Ruth, 1931-.
Mss A 391
52 leaves; 28 cm.
1991
Typescript.

[Lathrop] family record
Mss A 392
1 item ([2] p.).
Original handwritten record of the Mebane and Lydia (Peck) Lathrop family. Both were born in Norwich, Conn. and were married in Lebanon, N.H.

Diary of Julia Cecilia Moses 1859 Jan. 1 - Sept. 23
Arnold, Rhodes F.
Mss A 393
68 leaves; 28 cm.
1997
Typescript transcription of the original diary of Julia Cecilia Moses written in 1859 while living and working in Boston. The entries include comments on the weather, social visits, and activities such as reading, sewing or work. Provides a list of cash accounts (leaves 51-7) and bills payable (leaves 58-9). The diary also includes 1935 entries made by Julia's daughter, Mrs. Stephen M. Wirts. The donor provided a list of sunames in the Julia Moses Diary (leaves [60-4]), a list of other names & words (leaves [65-6]), and Arnolds listed in Boston Directory 1849-1852-1854-1860.

Payment order: Newport, to Benoni Waterman, 1754 Jan. 15
Wanton, J. (Joseph), 1705-1780.
Mss A 394
1 ADS; 16 x 9 cm.
Original document requesting that John Potter Esq. be paid seventy pounds for dues in the office. Verso has note of receipt by John Potter dated 1754 Feb. 22.

Biography of the Kaple family
Mss A 395
1 leaf; 25 x 20 cm.
Original record of the Edward Kaple family of Massachusetts with a brief outline of his ancestry (Orlando, John, Thomas). Includes additional notes added in another pen in 1966 by Bob Chapman.

Records of the Antislavery Aid Society founded in Hudson, Massachusetts on October 6, 1853
Spofford, John Eliot.
Anti-slavery Aid Society of Hudson (Mass.)
Mss A 396
15 leaves; 28 cm.
1998 typescript ed.
Typescript transcription of original record.

Rawson Journals: George S. Rawson's Journal of travel in New York, Vermont & Canada Apr. 7, 1847 Volume 1st and Sarah B. (Burnham) Rawson's journal from April 8, 1847 to October 22, 1848
Spofford, John Eliot.
Mss A 397
146, 10 p.; ill., ports.; 28 cm.
c1998
Typescript transcription of original journals along with a catalog of books in George S. Rawson's library.

Some Webster families of Penobscot Bay in Maine
Fellows, W. A.
Mss A 398
29 leaves; 28 cm.
1968
Photocopy of typescript with the lineal descent from Thomas Webster of Ormesby, Norfolk County, England through Thomas(1), John(2) to Andrew(3) and then through the descendants of the three Deer Island (Me.) "pioneers" Andrew (1746-1807), Ebenezer (1749-) and Daniel Webster (1751-) for two to four generations.

Bible record for the Wilson Swift family, 1802-1942
Swift, Wilson, 1806-1894.
Mss A 399
[12] leaves; 28 cm.
Photocopy of original record with title page. Several pages were intentionally repeated with faded writing traced to make it legible. Last page is a photocopy of a stiched bookmark.

One line of Adams ancestry: being complete descent from Benjamin Adams, George Adams and Charles Frederick Adams
McCleary, Helen C., fl. 1944.
Mss A 4
11 p.; 28 cm.
Carbon copy typescript with pencil and ink additions to June of 1944.

Information about the Austin family
Grant, Ethel Austin, b. 1880.
Mss A 40
[10] leaves; 28 cm.
1941?

Morans, Stantons, Blackmores: Ixonia, Wisconsin families
Druse, Joseph L.
Mss A 400
47 p.: maps; 28 cm.
1998.
Typescript.

Our Blodgett line: Especially descendants of Levi(6) Blodgett [Timothy(5), Samuel(4), Thomas(3), Samuel(2), Thomas(1), Robert(A)]
Ullmann, Helen Schatvet.
Mss A 401
71, [3] leaves; geneal. tables; 28 cm.
1999
Computer typescript genealogy.

Hodsdon family record, (ca 1760-1879)
Kirk, Marshall K. (Marshall Kenneth), 1957-.
Mss A 402
[3] leaves; 28 cm.
Computer typescript transcription of John A. Hodsdon's (of Lewiston, ME) family record.

This is the family history of Leonard and Adriana Heerschap - Hascup
Anderson, Karen Sue, 1941-.
Mss A 403
30 leaves: ill.; 28 cm.
1992
Typescript.

Bible record for the John P. Dane family, 1844-1966
Dane, John P., 1844-1906.
Mss A 404
[5] p.; 29 cm.
Original record with title page.

Bible record for the Elzaphan I. Barker family, 1834-1956
Barker, Elzaphan I., b. 1834.
Mss A 405
[4] p.; 29 cm.
Original record with title page concerning the Barker family of New Hampshire and New York.

Bible record for the Jacob Cook family, 1803-1896
Cook, Jacob, b. 1851.
Mss A 406
[7] leaves; 23 cm.
Original record with title page. Includes handwritten genealogical notes on the Cook family from the donor and an obituary for Nicholas Jansen.

Bible record for the Samuel Frost Davis family, 1789-1875
Davis, Samuel Frost, 1789-1849.
Mss A 407
[5] leaves; 28 cm.
Photocopy of original record with title page.

Bible record for the William Bliss Abell family, 1795-1912
Abell, William Bliss, 1795-1853.
Mss A 408
[9] leaves; 28 cm.
Photostat of original record with title page and a typescript transcription on the back of each copy. Includes a typescript genealogy with sources on the William Bliss Abell and Mary McCarthy family of Duanesburgh and Esperance, New York.

Kemp and allied families
Kellogg, Lucy Jane Cutler, b. 1866.
Mss A 409 a-c
220, [51] leaves; 28 cm.
[1947?]
Photocopy of typescript genealogy with corrections consisting of the lineal descent from Samuel (1) Kemp through Zerubbable (2), John (3), Lawrence (4-5), Horace (6), and William Sumner (7) to William Sumner (8) Kemp, Jr. Varing amounts of genealogical information on sixty-one allied families is also provided (often just a single family -- see "Notes" field). Folder C contains [51] leaves of correspondence primarily

to and from Lucy Cutler Kellogg consisting of source material for the typescript.

The Averys, 1700-1959, of Groton
Jones, Norma, fl. 1966.
Mss A 41
[1], 24, [4] p.; 28 cm.
1966?

Bible record for the James D. Litchfield family, 1806-1909
Litchfield, James D., b. 1806.
Mss A 411
[10] leaves; 22-27 cm.
Original record with title page. Includes two baptism certificates and a hand colored partially printed family register for the James D. Litchfield and Elisabeth A. Thurston family (trimmed to fit the Bible -- "died" column missing).

Bible record for the Frederick J. Logan family, 1829-1967
Logan, Frederick J., 1835-1871.
Mss A 412
[11] leaves; 11-28 cm.
Original record with title page concerning the Logan family of Connecticut and Massachusetts.

Bible record of the Anna C. Seaquist Bergman family, 1849-1924
Seaquist, Anna C. (Anna Christina), b. 1892.
Mss A 413
[12] leaves; 28 cm.
Photocopy of original record with title page. Includes typescript "Interpretation of initials in Bible record of Anna C. Bergman" by Stanley R. Clark, great nephew of Anna C. Bergman.

Bible record for the David Ames, Junior, family, 1791-1903
Ames, David, Jr., 1791-1883.
Mss A 414
[3] leaves; 28 cm.
Photostat of original record with title page concerning the Ames family of East Bridgewater and Springfield, Mass.

Bible record for the Almy family, 1788-1843
Mss A 415
[2] leaves; 28 cm.
Photostat of original record lacking title page
concerning the Almy family of Dartmouth
[Mass.?].

Arnold family records, 1495-1888
Mss A 416
1 item: Coat of arms; 17 x 24 cm.
Photostat of early records of the Arnold, Browne
and Haviland families with Arnold family coat of
arms.

*Bible record for the James Adams family, 1770-
1865*
Adams, James, 1770-1803.
Mss A 417
[4] leaves; 28 cm.
Photostat of original record with title page
concerning the Adams family of Grafton (Vt.) and
New York. Includes page on the Kinney family of
Sackets Harbor (N.Y.) and Chicago (Ill.).

*Bible record for the Nathan Dillingham family,
1759-1896*
Dillingham, Nathan, 1759-1836.
Mss A 418
[7] leaves; 28 cm.
Photocopy of original record with title page.

*Bible record for the Alve Hotchkiss family, 1741-
1936*
Hotchkiss, Alvie, b. 1781.
Mss A 419
[7] leaves; 26 cm.
Original record with title page.

Aulls - Bryan and allied families
Bryan, Leslie A. (Leslie Aulls), 1900-1985.
Mss A 42
[2], ii, 156 p.; 28 cm.
1966 Sep.

*Bible record for the Nathan W. Miller family,
1816-1927*
Miller, Nathan W., 1819-1889.
Mss A 420
[3] leaves; 27 cm.
Original record with title page.

*Bible record for the James Arthur O'Leary
family, 1854-1878*
O'Leary, John Arthur,
Mss A 421
[4] leaves; 28 cm.
Photocopy of original record lacking title page.
Includes a photocopy of a marriage record for
John and Elizabeth (Lynch) O'Leary and a copy
of two photographs. The first photo is appearently
of a Fourth of July celebration in Canton and the
second photo is of John and Elizabeth (Lynch)
O'Leary and their son Michael O'Leary taken
early 1900s.

*Bible record for the John Harmon Allen family,
1807-1962*
Allen, John Harmon, 1848-1900.
Mss A 422
[3] leaves; 28 cm.
Photocopy of handwritten transcription of the
original record with title page information.

*Statement of Oliver Brown describing his
participation in the American Revolution, 26 June
1839*
Brown, Oliver, 1760-1845.
Mss A 423
[2] leaves; 24 cm.

*Photograph of the coat of arms on Jabez Bowe's
gravestone in the Old Newman Cemetery,
Rumford, R.I.*
Mss A 424
1 photograph; 14 x 9 cm.
Since the focus of the photo is the coat of arms,
only a portion of the inscription is captured by the
image: "In Memory/LABEZ BOWE/Of
Providence/Who departed this Life".

*Bible record for the Thomas Baldwin Jr. family,
1730-1861*
Baldwin, Thomas, Jr., 1755-1834.
Mss A 425
[4] leaves; 24 cm.
Photostat of original record lacking title page
concerning the Baldwin family of Westminster
and Coventry, Vt.

Bullard family records, 1635-1864
Bullard, Cullen, 1806-1883.
Mss A 426
[7] leaves; 26 cm.
Photostat of a handwritten genealogical record by
Dr. Cullen Bullard concerning the lineal descent
from John(1), Joseph(2), Ebenezer (3),
Hezekiah(4), Benjamin(5) to Cullen(6) Bullard.
The information was taken from "Morse's
genealogy and a record left by Dr. Benj[amin]
Bullard of New Haven, Vt" (Dr. Cullen's father).
Includes a photostat of Benjamin(5) Bullard's
genealogical record followed by notes from
Ebenezer's fourth child, Ward(6) Bullard, with
information on his maternal ancestry, especially
the Ward family.

*Bible record for the John Burtt family, 1690-
1822*
Burtt, John, 1692-1746.
Mss A 427
[2] leaves; 38 cm.
Photocopy of original record lacking title page.
The Bible was purchased in Amsterdam Jan
1716/7.

*Bible record for the Benjamin Brown family,
1720-1849*
Brown, Benjamin, 1720-1802.
Mss A 428
[2] leaves; 29 cm.
Photostat of original record lacking title page. The
record includes a note that Benjn Brown
purchased the Bible in 1784.

*Record of the Nathan and Elizabeth (Fish)
Brownell family*
Freeborn, Jonathan.
Mss A 429
[1] leaf; 25 cm.
Photostat of original record written by Rev.
Freeborn "This is to satisfy that Nathan Brownell
of Portsmouth...And Elizabeth Fish...was Married
by me." Includes a listing of Nathan and
Elizabeth's children and their date of birth.

*Notes relating to the allied families of Avery,
Foster, Edes, Gardner, Haliburton, and Trescott,
[1592-1911]*
Sawyer, Jacob Herbert, 1837-1913.
Mss A 43
2, [1], 41 leaves; 28 cm.
[1913]

*Bible record for the William Bradford family,
1789-1928*
Bradford, William, b. 1815.
Mss A 430
[7] leaves; 21 cm.
Photostat of original record lacking title page.

*Registre de l'eglise protestante episcopale
Francaise du Sain-Sauveur Philadelphia*
'Eglise Sain-Sauveur (Philadelphia, Pa.)
Mss A 431
217 leaves; 28 cm.
Photocopy of original record with entries for
baptisms, confirmations, marriages and funerals.
Includes By-laws of the church St Sauver (p.162)
and Recettes de L'eglise du Sain Sauver a partir
1872-1898 (p.162-217).

*The Welsh ancestry of Owen Owens Williams and
Rebecca Pierce*
Troemner, Deborah Williams.
Mss A 432
13, [1] p.; geneal. tables; 28 cm.
[1999]
Computer typescript genealogy of the descent
from Owen Williams (fl.1761) through Owen
(1767-1809), Owen Owens (1802-1881) to
William Pierce (2) Williams (1840-1908).
Includes information on the John Owen Williams
(1783-1872) family. Page six covers the lineal
descent from Griffith Pierce (fl.1756) through
William Pierce (1768-1847) to Rebecca Pierce
(1807- after 1870). Includes descendancy chart
for Owen Williams and a second chart for Griffith
Pierce.

Bible record for the C. C. Hudson family, 1856-1982
Hudson, C. C., 1856-1902.
Mss A 433
[6] leaves; 28 cm.
Photocopy of original record with title page concerning the Hudson family of Bosque County, Texas. Some of the entries on the "Memoranda" page are cited as being written by Beulah Ann Johnson.

Bible record for the Henry Barbour family, 1793-1853
Barbour, Henry, b. 1793.
Mss A 434
[3] p.; 26 cm.
Original record with title page concerning the Barbour family of Canton Center, Connecticut.

Bible record for the Samuel Haines family, 1792-1898
Haines, Samuel, 1792-1842.
Mss A 435
[7] p.; 28 cm.
Original record without title page. Includes a [5] page handwritten genealogy called "Holmes family formerly of Plymouth, Mass." by F. Holmes and Agnes Holmes Fuller.

Bible record for the Samuel Webster family, 1781-1913
Webster, Samuel, 1759-1804.
Mss A 436
[4] p.; 27 cm.
Original record with title page concerning the Webster family of Salem, New Hampshire. Includes two hand stiched bookmarks - the first one has the name "Gracie Webster" in red yarn with a blue border and the second one has "Holy Bible" in pink and green yarn. Also includes a copy of Dea. Samuel Webster's will dated 2 April 1804 in which he bequeaths his property to son (Thomas), wife (Lydia, also named as the Executrix), and daughters (Elizabeth, Ruth, Lydia, Hannah and Sarah).

Record of the Edward Parks family, 1767-1865
Parks, Edward, 1741-1807.
Mss A 437
Restrictions: Material fragile; use photocopy.
[4] leaves; geneal. tables; 26-28 cm.
Original record concerning the Park(s) family of Milton and Dorchester, Mass. Includes a photocopy of a tabular pedigree chart of the descendants of Edward Parks for three generations by the donor.

Bible record for the Ward Jackson family, 1792-1889
Jackson, Ward, 1768-1845.
Mss A 438
[2] leaves; 27 cm.
Original record lacking title page concerning the Jackson family of Spencer, Massachusetts. The donor identified the birth, marriage and first three death records as being in the hand of Ward Jackson, the great, great grandfather of the donor and original owner of the Bible.

Bible record for the Joseph Brown family, 1763-1921
Brown, Joseph, 1763-1837.
Mss A 439
[6] leaves; 28 cm.
Photocopy of original record with title page concerning the Brown family of Bennington, Underhill and Jericho, Vermont. Some family members went to New York (state) and Canada.

Notes on the genealogy of the Averys (Dedham branch) of Lubec and Machias, Washington County, Maine
Avery, Myron Haliburton, fl. 1923-1925.
Mss A 44
119, [5] leaves, bound; charts, coat of arms; 28 cm.
1923-1925.

Record of the Moses Flanders family, 1737-1866
Flanders, Moses, b. 1737.
Mss A 440
[1] leaf; 27 cm.
Original record by A.B.H.(?) listing the birth dates for Moses and his wife Elizabeth along with their children. Additional information was added in pencil in another hand along with a note in black ink.

Record of the Moody Bean family, 1752?-1835
Bean, Moody, ca. 1752-1834.
Mss A 441
[3] p.; 26 cm.
Original record listing the birth and death dates for the Moody Bean family along with the marriage date for Moody and his wife, Sarah. Page two includes the death dates for John and Mary Adams (parents of Sarah?).

Correspondence to Joel Reece of Pratt, KS
Mss A 442
[36] p.; 20-28 cm.
Original correspondence primarily from cousins providing genealogical information on Reece or allied families of Hastings or Elliott. Includes typescript called "Reece Genealogy" consisting of the lineal descent from J. Reece (1) through Francis (2), John (3), to Nathan (4), John (4), and Daniel (4) including Nathan and Daniel's children.

Poor/Poore family notes, 1936-1999
Poor, Edward A.
Mss A 443
[57] leaves.
Photocopy of original notes and correspondence concerning the Poor/Poore family. First leaf is a 29 April 1999 letter from Bernice B. Gunderson of Long Beach, CA to Ed concerning a David Poore and Jane Martin. Leaves 2-4 is a letter 17 Nov 1936 from Louise Robinson of Burlington, VT to Mr Edward A. Poor concerning Lydia Poor. Leaves 5-9 is a letter 19 March 1936 from Mary (Poor) Webster of Walden, MA to Edward with Mary's recollections of members of the Poor family. Leaves 10-13 is a 7 Jan 1938 letter from Lee [Sherman] Chadwick of Cleveland, OH to his sister. Mr. Chadwick discusses family matters, climbing the Rocky Mountains, quotes Leigh Hanes' "Mountains," offers his opinions on the

lazy nature of the unemployed and discusses the Depression. Mr. Chadwick writes that Washngton needs to follow some plan of "Balanced Employment" outlined in his books of 1931 and 1930. Leaves 15-51 contain genealogical notes on Poor and allied families.

Bible record for the Anson Burgess family, 1791-1963
Burgess, Anson, 1791-1863.
Mss A 444
[7] leaves; 28 cm.
Photocopy of original record lacking title page concerning the Burgess and allied families of Massachusetts. The donor also provided a typescript transcription of the death records and a photocopy of the Family Record page from Gleason's Pictorial Drawing-room Companion (information was only added to the deaths column).

Bible record for the Joel Hamblen family, 1792-1897
Hamblen, Joel, 1809-1888.
Mss A 445
[6] leaves; 28 cm.
Photocopy of original record lacking title page. Includes typescript transcription by the donor.

Petition, 1789 Dec. 15, to the New Hampshire Senate and House of Representatives by the inhabitants of Chesterfield
Mss A 446
[2] leaves; 29 cm.
Photostat of original record in which the subscribers from Chesterfield petition for incorporation of a body corporate to erect a seminary of learning.

Lineage of Charles Henry Snedeker of Aurora, Ill
Waters, Isaac Snedeker.
Mss A 447
[8] leaves; 28 cm.
Typescript providing the lineal descent from Jan (1) Snedeker through Gerret (2), Isaac (3), Abraham (4), Elbert (5), Abraham (6), Ferdinand Sutphin (7) to Charles Henry (8) Snedeker.

The genealogy of Ralph Olin Jenkins
Jenkins, Juline E. Hitchcock.
Mss A 448
[ii, 18] leaves; 28 cm.
1975
Typescript providing the lineal descendants from
Joel (1) Jenkins through Obadiah (2), Joel (3),
Obadiah (4), David (5-6), Edmund (7-8),
Frederick Henry (8) to Ralph Olin (8) Jenkins
including his children. Excerpts from The Bixby
Genealogy Part 1-2 by Willard G. Bixby (1914)
concerning the Jenkins family are followed by
some correspondence to the donor relating to
individuals covered in this genealogy. Final two
leaves have the heading "Jenkins genealogy
additional memoranda."

Lounsbury genealogy
Coleman, Edith Agnes.
Mss A 449
48 leaves; 28 cm.
[1975]
Typescript genealogy of eleven generations on the
Bethany Branch of the Lounsbury family (i.e. the
descendants of Josiah (3) and Ruth Lounsbury
who settled in Bethany, Connecticut).

*Salisbury, Goshen, Ripton, Hancock, Granville,
Waltham & Leicester, Addison County, Vt.:
Inscriptions copied from gravestones arranged
with genealogical notes and an index*
Spies, Francis F. (Francis Ferdinand), 1871-1934.
Mss A 45
245 p.; 28 cm.
1931.
Typescript copy of cemetery inscriptions with an
index. Includes list of Revolutionary War
soldiers. Cemeteries in this volume include:
Salisbury: Washington St. Cem., Village Cem.,
Thomas Family Cem., West Salisbury Cem.;
Goshen: one unnamed cem.; Ripton: Village
Cem., North Branch Cem., Bread Load Cem.,
Kirby Family Cem.; Hancock: Bread Loaf -
Hancock Cem., Old Village Cem., New Village
Cem., Ford Family Cem.; Granville: Yard #1,
Yard #2; Waltham: one unnamed cem.; Leicester:
one unnamed cem.

*Bible record for the Alexander Trowbridge
family, 1799-1948*
Trowbridge, Alexander, 1803-1882.
Mss A 450
[4] p.; 28 cm.
Photocopy of original record lacking title page.

*Bible record for the Elison Ely Duncan family,
1782-1967*
Duncan, Elison Ely, 1817-1897.
Mss A 451
[5] leaves; 28 cm.
Photocopy of original record with title page.

*Bible record for the Elizabeth Waring family,
1768-1883*
Waring, Elizabeth, 1768-1845.
Mss A 453
[1] leaf; 28 cm.
Typescript transcription of original record with
title page information.

*Bible record of the Russell Wheeler family, 1783-
1887*
Wheeler, Russell, 1783-1861.
Mss A 454
[1] leaf; 28 cm.
Typescript transcription of original record with
title page information.

New York cabinetmaking prior to the revolution
Johnson, J. Stewart.
Mss A 455
108 leaves; 28 cm.
1964
Typescript

*The Dennis family, specifically, the descendants
of Thomas Dennis of Ipswich, Massachusetts,
born about 1638*
Dennis, Frank G.
Mss A 456
[3], 49 leaves; 28 cm.
1998
Decendancy charts produced from a GEDCOM
file covering six generations.

Some descendants of John Fenno
Edgecomb, Dana E.
Mss A 457
34, [5] leaves; 28 cm.
1996
Computer typescript genealogy formatted in a
Register style covering eight generations.

*Ancestral lines of Jean Deering McCollom
Everett*
Everett, Harold Hutchinson, 1913-.
Mss A 458
1996
"This work, using largely secondary references, is
unashamedly a database creation, without any
word-processor manipulation to make it more
readable. The sole intent is to create a family of
ladders, leading from one individual in this
generation, Jean Deering McCollom Everett, back
to all traceable immigrant ancestors (through her
father), responsible for her being here."--from
"Introduction" p.[1]. The author "designed the
lineage form used to show easily the name (and
arbitrary code number) of each immigrant
ancestor, his emigration date from (mostly)
England, and the town in New England where he
settled."--from "Notes on methodology" p.[4]. A
total of 76 lines are recorded.

*Peter Brown of the Mayflower and Peter Brown
of Windsor, Connecticut: Father and Son?*
Everett, Harold Hutchinson, 1913-.
Mss A 459
16 leaves; 28 cm.
1996
Computer Typescript.

*Addison County, Vt., Bridport, Shoreham, Orwell:
Inscriptions from gravestones arranged with
genealogical and historical notes, list of
Revolutionary Soldiers & Index*
Spies, Francis F. (Francis Ferdinand), 1871-1934.
Mss A 46
302 p.; 28 cm.
Typescript copy of cemetery inscriptions with an
index. Includes list of Revolutionary War
soldiers. Cemeteries in this volume include:
Bridport: one unnamed cem.; Shoreham: Lake
View Cem., Goodrich Farm Cem., Callender
Farm Cem., Russell Farm Cem., Doolittle Farm
Cem., Atwood Cem., Bowker Cem., Rich Family

Tomb, Richville Cem., Pliny Smith Farm Cem.;
Orwell: Old Grounds, New Grounds.

*McHarg and Craven family correspondence,
1807-1968 (bulk: 1860-1864)*
Mss A 460 a-b
57 items.
Folder "a" contains McHarg family
correspondence concerning family matters (1856-
1907). Includes three letters from John McHarg to
his wife, Martha Whipple (Patch) McHarg; ten
letters from William McHarg to his son, Rufus
King McHarg; five letters from Mrs. Henry
McHarg (Martha W. McHarg) to her son, Rufus
King McHarg and thirteen letters to Henry King
McHarg from various relatives. Folder "b"
contains Craven/Hamill correspondence of a
genealogical nature which includes a chart (1807-
1919) and Orr/Macklin family notes and chart
(1968 Oct 15- Nov 19).

*Index to Virginia court records in Pennsylvania
(District of West Augusta)*
Waldenmaier, Inez Raney
Carnegie Museum.
Mss A 461
54 p.: map; 29 cm.
c1957

The descendents of Melancton and Clarissa Hurd
Hurd, John Coolidge, b. 1888.
Mss A 462
[11] p.; 28-56 cm. folded to 28 cm.
Descendency chart for the Melancton and Clarissa
Hurd family. Includes the letter sent "to cousins"
along with the chart, the addresses of recipients of
the Hurd family chart, the Bruce line of
ancestry/descent in America, and an earlier chart
produced in 1928 by George A. Hurd (donor's
uncle) with the title "A partial list of ancestors of
the Hurd and other related families compiled in
the hope that it will encourage further
researches."

Bible record for the Rufus Gay family, 1770-1923
Gay, Rufus, 1770-1852.
Mss A 463
[4] leaves; 28 cm.
Photocopy of original record lacking title page concerning the Gay family of Gardiner, Maine. Includes some entries for allied families especially the Worcester and Dearborn families.

Hurlbut family of Roxbury, Connecticut
Jacobus, Donald Lines, 1887-1970.
Mss A 464
[4] leaves; 28 cm.
1910
Photocopy of hand drawn decendancy chart for Thomas and Sarah Hurlbut of Saybrook and Wethersfield, Conn. focusing upon the Hurlbuts living in Roxbury, Conn.

Bible record for the James Potter family, 1773-1886
Potter, James, 1773-1850.
Mss A 465
[5] leaves; 28 cm.
Photocopy of original record with title page.

Bible record for the Abner Weeks family, 1766-1968
Weeks, Abner, 1766-1846.
Mss A 466
[7, 2, 1] leaves; 28 cm.
Photocopy of original record lacking title page concerning the Weeks family of China, Maine. Includes [2] leaf Register style genealogy called "Abner Weeks of China, Maine" and a single leaf with the heading "A twig from the family tree of Gerald Goss Weeks" both by the donor.

Bible record for the Josiah Fellows family, 1757-1852
Fellows, Josiah, 1757-1852.
Mss A 467
[6] leaves; 28 cm.
Photocopy of original record with title page concerning the Fellows family of NH. Includes typescript transcription of the original Bible record, of excerpts from the will of Jonathan Fellows of Kensington, N.H., 1752 (Grandfather of Josiah), and a copy of a sketch done by

Margaret (Fellows) White of Jonathan Fellows' tombstone.

Bible record for the Jonathan Bridgman family, 1781-1900
Bridgman, Jonathan, 1781-1851.
Mss A 468
[6] leaves; 18 cm.
Photostat of original record with title page.

Bible record for the Jorras Baker family, 1747-1895
Baker, Jorras, 1747-1829.
Mss A 469
[4] leaves; 28 cm.
Photostat of original record lacking title page concerning the Baker family. Includes entries for the allied Francis Blood family.

Cornwall & Whiting, Addison County, Vt.: Inscriptions copied from the gravestones arranged with genealogical notes, list of Revolutionary Soldiers and an index
Spies, Francis F. (Francis Ferdinand), 1871-1934.
Mss A 47
225 p.; 28 cm.
1931.
Typescript copy of cemetery inscriptions with an index. Includes list of Revolutionary War soldiers. Cemeteries in this volume include: Cornwall: Church Cem., Payne District Cem., South Cem., Lemon Fair Bridge Cem.; Whiting: one unnamed cem.

Bible record for the Reuben Brooks family, 1770-1890.
Brooks, Reuben, 1770-1844.
Mss A 470
[4] leaves; 28 cm.
Photostat of original record lacking title page.

Old English Quaker records of Gregory, Post, Fogg & Row families
Larrabee, Frank R.
Mss A 471
Photocopy of original ms. Most leaves have family records of births and or deaths. The eighth leaf is a letter dated 21 April 1704 which describes the arrest of Valintine and Gabriel Gregory "called in scorn quakers" for not paying their tithes.

Bible record for the Nehemiah Beardsley family, 1745-1877
Beardsley, Nehemiah, 1745-1804.
Mss A 472
[2] leaves; 28 cm.
Photocopy of original record lacking title page from two Bibles, the first was printed in 1818 and the second in 1828, concerning the Beardsley family of Tompkins County, N.Y.

Bible record for the Joseph Bartlett family, 1762-1840
Bartlett, Joseph, 1762-1835.
Mss A 473
[5] leaves; 28 cm.
Photostat of original record lacking title page concerning the Bartlett family of Plymouth, [Mass.?].

Bible record for the David Justus Bennett family, 1790-1936
Bennett, David Justus, 1790-1886.
Mss A 474
[4] leaves; 28 cm.
Photostat of a typescript transcription of the original record concerning the Bennett, Chamberlain and Whitehead families. David J. Bennett was a Baptist Minister serving at Altay, Bradford and Tyrone, New York.

Bible record for the John S. Bristow family, 1795-1878
Bristow, John S., b. 1795.
Mss A 475
[4] leaves; 26 cm.
Photostat of original record lacking title page.

Bible record for the Paul Brown family, 1792-1931
Brown, Paul, b. 1792.
Mss A 476
[4] leaves; 28 cm.
Photostat of original record lacking title page concerning the Brown family of Quincy, Mass.

Bible record for the Elisha Bradford family, 1719-1797
Bradford, Elisha.
Mss A 477
[2] leaves; 22 cm.
Photostat of original record with title page.

Bosworth family records, 1672-1801
Mss A 478
[4] leaves; 22 cm.
Photostats of original records. First is a deed dated May 1672 between John Wodsone and Jonathan Bosworth, both of Rehoboth, Mass. for a tract of meadow called the Mill Run. Second is of the will of Jonathan Bosworth dated 24 Feb 1686/7. Third is a deed dated 13 April 1725 between Joseph Bosworth and Nathaniel Bosworth concerning a twelve acres of land at the south end of their late Father's Estate. Includes a photostat of an agreement dated 10 January 1801 in which Ammi Bissell, Apelles Slocomb and Apelles Slocomb Jr. all of Sharon, Conn. are to build a meeting house in the town of Berlin for the sum of $3800.

Photograph of the gravestone for Susanna Brownson
Mss A 479
1 photograph; 6.5 x 9 cm.
Black and white photograph of Susanna Brownson's tombstone in Landaff, N.H. Inscription reads "Widow Susanna Brownson,/was born August 3, 1699/and died June 19, 1802/ aged 103 years." There is a passage below which reads, in part, "To God her Spirit" but the rest is too faint to read.

Vital records: items from files of Burlington (Vt.) Free Press, June 1830 - June 1832
Bowman, John Elliot, 1866-1933.
Mss A 48
199 p.; 27 cm.
1919.
Originally copied in October of 1916 from author's files and recopied and bound for this edition in alphabetical order.

Bible record for the Job Frederick Brooks family, 1764-1879
Brooks, Job Frederick, 1764-1822.
Mss A 480
[5] leaves; 28 cm.
Photostat of original record with title page.

Bible record for the Solomon Bell family, 1738-1892
Bell, Solomon, 1738-1825.
Mss A 481
[2] leaves; 28 cm.
Photostat of original record with title page.

Bible record for the William Brooks family, 1764-1928
Brooks, William, 1806-1880.
Mss A 482
[5] leaves; 28 cm.
Photostat of original record with title page concerning the Brooks family of New Hampshire and Minnesota. The Bible was presented to Louisa A. Swan by her "affectionate Father Joseph Swan" June 20, 1886.

Bible record for the James Booker family, 1796-1875
Booker, James, 1796-1860.
Mss A 483
[2] leaves; 28 cm.
Photostat of a handwritten transcription of the original record lacking title page information.

Bible record for the Jeremiah Barnard family, 1751-1879
Bernard, Jeremiah, 1749-1835.
Mss A 484
[4] leaves; 28 cm.
Photostat of original record lacking title page concerning the Barnard family of Amherst, N.H. Includes entries for the allied Clarke, Eaton and Henchman families.

[Radway family] cemetery markers
Radway, Merton.
Mss A 485
Photocopy of typescript with extracted genealogical information from Radway family tombstones in Amber and Truxton, New York and the Dipping Hole Cemetery in Putney, Vermont.

Bible record for the Jonathan French family, 1760-1912
French, Jonathan, 1760-1841.
Mss A 486
[7] leaves; 28 cm.
Photocopy of original record with title page.

Genealogical notes concerning the Pickering family
Benton, Madelon Chandler, b. 1897.
Mss A 487
[7] leaves; 10-28 cm.
Photostat copy of ms. family record dated Dec. 1, 1853 and signed by Sam[ue]l Pickering Jr. concerning the children and grandchildren of Charles Pickering, Sr. (d. 1786). Includes a note by the author dated 22 June 1975 on the children of Rev. Geo. Pickering. Photostat of a typescript transcription of an original ms. by the author with the heading "Pickering Descendants -- U.S. Colonists" and a photostat of three file cards concerning the ancestors of the author is followed by a leaf with a five generation ancestral chart for the author.

John Chewe, some descendents in Virginia, Maryland, and Ohio
Chew, Dorothy Clendenin, 1914-
Mss A 488
26 leaves; 29 cm.
[1982]
Computer typescript concerning the descendants of John Chewe (1590-1668) who came to Jamestown, Va. in 1621 from England. Covers the lineal descendants from John (1) through Samuel (2-3), Nathaniel (4), Joseph (5-6), William (7), Ezekiel (8), Amon (9), Mahlon Mattison (10) to Mahlon Hopkinson (11) Chew.

The Sallows - Solas - Sollis - Sollace family with notes on allied families of Becket, Bingham, Durkee, Fuller, King, Moulton, Needham and Perry
Arthaud, John Bradley, 1939-
Mss A 489
8 leaves; 28 cm.
2000
Computer typescript genealogy in Register format which supplements the article by the author "The Sallows-Solas-Sollis-Sollace Family, Mariners of Salem and Beverly, Massachusetts," published in *The American Genealogist* 72[1997]:1-14 and 115-134. While the original article covered the first six generations of the agnate lines of this family in Massachusetts, this typescript consists of another four generations with some cursory comments about some of the early female lines.

Carpenter Cemetery, Guilford, Vermont
Akeley, N. M. P. (Nettie May Pomeroy), 1862-
1934.
Mss A 49
4 p.: 27 cm.
1926?
Typescript transcription of cemetery inscriptions
arranged in alphabetical order.

*Chapman genealogy, being the descendants of
John Chapman of Yorkshire, England the first
settler, of Stonington, Conn. U.S.A. who married
Sarah Brown down ten generations from 1610 -
1931*
Chapman, Emilas Ravaud, b. 1870.
CS71/C466/1931 also LOAN also Mss A 490
2 p. l., 2-19 numb. l.: illus. (port.); 24 cm.
1931
Typescript

James Davis of Haverhill, MA
Rouse, Richard Gammons, 1927-
Mss A 491
9 leaves; 28 cm.
1997
Typescript genealogy in Register style concerning
eleven generations of descendants for James
Davis, Sr. (1585/6-1678). The earlier generations
often have information on a single lineal
decendant but more recent generations cover all
children.

Emmanuel Rouse of Rhode Island
Rouse, Richard Gammons, 1927-
Mss A 492
7 leaves; 28 cm.
1997
Computer typescript supplement, in Register
format, to the article by the author called
"Emmanuel Rouse of Rhode Island, ca. 1673-
1739 and some of his descendants" in Rhode
Island roots [Warwick, R.I.: Rhode Island
Genealogical Society, 1993, p. 70-82].

Reuben Rouse of Voluntown, CT
Rouse, Richard Gammons, 1927-
Mss A 493
3, [1] leaves; 28 cm.
1997
Computer typescript genealogy for three
generations in Register format.

Colonel Phillip Wheeler
Rouse, Richard Gammons, 1927-
Mss A 494
8, [2] leaves; 28 cm.
1997
Computer typescript genealogy, in Register
format, focusing on the descent from Colonel
Philip Wheeler through Aaron (2), Asaph (3),
Walker (4), Shubeal Goff Wheeler (5), Henrietta
E.S. (Wheeler) Davis (6), Alice Bertha (Davis)
Gammons (7), Ruth Alice (Gammons) Rouse (8)
to Richard Gammons Rouse (9) and his children,
Deborah, Sharon, Elizabeth and Richard (10). The
earlier generations often have information on a
single lineal decendant but more recent
generations cover all children.

Descendants of William Gammons
Rouse, Richard Gammons, 1927-
Mss A 495
56, [9] leaves; 28 cm.
1997
Computer typescript genealogy in Register format
for ten generations.

Record of the Jabez Backus family, 1781-1904
Backus, Jabez, 1788-1854.
Mss A 496
[6] leaves; 20-23 cm.
Photostat of original record concerning the
Backus and allied families of Connecticut. Allied
families include Lathrop, Call and McCall
families.

*Military commission certificates, 20 Oct 1775, 1
Aug 1776*
Mss A 497
2 items (2 leaves); 17 x 25 cm.
Photostat of original documents. The first
certificate has Bartholomew Barratt (also spelled
Barritt) being commissioned Second Lieutenant
of the 4th Company of Foot in the 9th Regiment
Albany County (N.Y.) Militia, 1775 Oct. 20. The
second certificate has Bartholomew Barratt being
commissioned as Captain of the same Company,
1776 Aug. 1.

A Morton line: from Richard (1) Morton of Hatfield, Massachusetts through Richard (5) Morton of Athol, Massachusetts, and Orwell, Vermont
Ullmann, Helen Schatvet.
Mss A 498
15 leaves; 28 cm.
2000
Typescript genealogy in Register format.

The Yates family
Harrison, David.
Mss A 499
6 leaves; 28 cm.
Typescript of genealogical notes on Amariah Yates and his children especially concerning Amariah's activities while in Smithfield, R.I. and both his and his children's activies once they removed to Apalachin, a post-village in Owego, Tioga Co., N.Y.

William Joseph Adams Bible record, 1833-1877
Adams, William Joseph, 1802-1866.
Mss A 5
[4] p.; 28 cm.
Copied by donor on 1944 Jun 15. Fly leaf inscribed "Deborah F. Chickering from her mother August 26, 1833."

Bible and other records of Greensboro, Vt.
Allen, Louise R.
Mss A 50
[26] p.; 28 cm.
1933.
Typescript copy that includes Bible records on the following families (several are Scotish): Batten, Cuthbertson, Cutler, Fotheringham, Howard, Ingalls, Kinney, Logan, Olin, Patterson, Tolman, and Young. Also contains cemtery inscriptions in Greensboro for the people mentioned in the Bible records and the entire grand (tax) list (names only) for the town in 1830.

Military discharge certificate for Richard Aylward, 1864 Nov 7
Mss A 500
1 item; 28 cm.
Photostat of original record in which Corporal Richard Aylward is discharged from his service in the First Regiment of the Volunteer Massachusetts Cavalry. Record includes a physical description of Mr. Aylward, his age, place of birth (Ireland), and his occupation.

Description of her participation in the "American Army of Two" in Scituate, Massachusetts during the War of 1812
Bates, Rebecca W., 1793-1886.
Mss A 501
[3] leaves; 8.5 cm.
Photostat of original record in which Rebecca Bates accounts how she and her sister, Abigail Bates, prevented two American vessels from being taken and their crew imprisoned by the British. Includes the cover letter sent by the donor describing the record.

[Watson family] cemetery markers
Mss A 502
[3] leaves; 28 cm.
Photocopy of a typescript transcription of Watson family tombstone inscriptions in the Port Kent Cemetery of Chesterfield, New York.

Robert McFadden: linen weaver of Armagh, Ireland and farmer of Ontario, Canada and some descendants
Natirboff, Miriam Ann Cady.
Mss A 503
12 leaves; ill., ports.; 28 cm.
1995
Computer typescript genealogy for three generations.

The witch of Newburyport
Morse, Stafford-Ames.
Mss A 504
6, [6] leaves; ill., maps; 28 cm.
1999
Computer typescript concerning the site of the home of William and Elizabeth Morse of Newburyport, Massachusetts. Elizabeth Morse was accused of being a witch in 1679. Includes [2] leaves on "William Morse" and [4] leaves on "Other Lands of Morse in Newbury and Newburyport, Essex County, Massachusetts."

Coxe chronicles: our immigrant ancestors and their ports of entry
Coxe, Simeon O. 1877-1955.
Mss A 505
11, [78] p.: ill., maps, geneal. tables; 28 cm.

Lott family of New York and New Jersey
Furman, Robert, 1863-1944.
Mss A 506
[2], iii, 46, 1, [4] leaves; 28 cm.
1940
Typescript genealogy for six generations.

Gowing family notes
Gowing, Henry Augustus, b. 1834.
Mss A 507
[2], 42 p.; 25 cm.
Handwritten genealogical notes taken from town, church and family records concerning the Gowing family of Massachusetts, New Hampshire and Vermont. Includes computer typescript index by the donor.

Journey from Hamilton to the State of Ohio April 4th 1825
Cutler, Temple, 1782-1857.
Mss A 508
1 vol. (63 p.); 17 cm.
Beginning April 4, 1825, Temple Cutler travels from Hamilton (Mass.) to Boston by stagecoach. He traveled from Boston to New York City on the steamship Connecticut and then to [New] Brunswick, NJ by the steamship Legislature. After a "dusty passage" via stagecoach through Princeton (NJ), Trenton (NJ) and Bristol (Penn.) to Philadelphia, Mr. Cutler took the steamship Congress to Newcastle (Del.), a stage to Frenchtown (MD) followed by the steamship United States to Baltimore (MD). The journey continued by stagecoach via the Great National Road through Hagarstown (MD), Cumberland (MD), and Uniontown (Penn.) to Wheeling (WV) where he boarded the steamship Herald to Marietta (OH). In Marietta, Temple borrowed a horse to ride to his Brother's house in Warren, arriving on April 14th, 1825.

Dalton family history
Sullivan, Robert John Michael, Jr., 1956-.
Mss A 509
162 p.; ill., coat of arms, ports., geneal. tables; 28 cm.
1997
Typescript genealogy in Register format focusing on the John Thomas(4), John Michael(3), Richard(2), William(1) Dalton line. Includes information on the ancestors and descendants of the following individuals of allied families: Roseanne Bernadette (Rose) Egan, Anne Eugenia Soulier, Kathryn Cecilia O'Connor, Michael Edward Aloysius Kennally and Thomas Rice Dickerson.

A Record of gravestones and their locations in the Kibling Cemetery, 1788 - 1962
Bassingthwaighte, George E.
Mss A 51
[9] p.: Maps; 28 cm.
1964
Mimeograph typescript transcription of inscriptions for the Kibling Cemetery alphabetically arranged. Includes map of cemetery with location of gravestones.

Family stories
Miller, Dorothy D.
Mss A 510
18 leaves; 28 cm.
2000
Typescript

Irish aid for our early immigrant ancestors: the first Thanksgiving
LaRocca, Mary Catherine, 1922-.
Mss A 511
13, [1] p.; 28 cm.
1999
Computer typescript which attributes the arrival the ship "Lion" in 1631 with flour from Ireland as the impetus behind the first Thanksgiving Day celebration. Explains how the consequences of the King Philip's War prompted further aid from Ireland called the "The Irish Donation" of 1676; thus, the second Thanksgiving in late November 1676. Also includes "The Legacy of Captain Thomas Wheeler" and "Brief Pedigree of Mary C. Brown La Rocca."

Searl families of Lewis County, New York
Searl, Edwin Noyes.
Mss A 512
44 leaves; ports., geneal. tables; 28 cm.
1995

Searl record
Towser, Clara, b. ca. 1866.
Mss A 513
[25] p.; 28 cm.
1953
Photocopy of handwritten family record. The record begins with Eliphaz(5) Searl; however, the primary focus is upon the Luke(6) Searl family, especially, Luke's children and grandchildren. Includes the author's personal reminiscences of relatives.

List of officers and soldiers belonging to Amherst, NH who lost their lives in the Revolutionary War
Wilkins, Robert Bradford, 1751-1832.
Mss A 514
[2] p.; 28 cm.
Photocopy of a letter written by Lt. Robert Bradford Wilkins to be published in the New Hampshire Patriot and State Gazette, August 24, 1829. Mr. Wilkins, a native of Amherst, was in the third New Hampshire Continental Army from 1775 to 1783. Many of the names are listed in Daniel F. Secomb's History of the Town of Amherst, Hillsborough County, New Hampshire...(Concord, NH: Evans, Sleeper & Woodbury, 1880). However, Robert Wilkins' list includes the cause of death.

Correspondence to Henry Mirick, 1855-1902 (bulk: 1855-1866)
Decker, Jefford M.
Mss A 515
11 items (p.); 20-28 cm.
This collection consists of ten letters sent to Henry and one business letter Henry wrote (dated May 23 1901) to William [Harvey] Jones of Columbus, Ohio. Mr. Jones was a lawyer who worked in the Law Firm of Booth, Keating, Peters & Butler. There are five letters from Henry's Mother, Caroline (Pritchard) Mirick, written between 1855-1866; a May 21, 1863 letter from Henry's Father, Charles Mirick, and a Dec 12 1865 letter from his Brother, George Mirick, all concerning family matters. There are two letters

by J[efford] M. Decker [Lt. Col. 10th Regt.] (dated April 21 1861 and May 27 1861) sent to Adj Henry concerning Companies A and B. Finally, there is a business letter to Henry (dated April 7, 1902) from T[homas] J. Keating of Columbus, Ohio. Mr. Keating was a Partner of the law firm Booth, Keating, Peters & Butler.

Licences to pass from England beyond the seas
Fothergill, Gerald.
Mss A 517
[70] p.; 22 cm.
"These supplement the list made by John Camden Hotten of those sailing for America and are those licenced as settlers in Europe [ca 1631-1638]. Many went to Holland for a time probably because it was easier to get leave for there than to America. They are obtained from the records of the Exchequer, King's Remembrancer, No. 16."

My family history: direct maternal and paternal genealogical lines as compiled by author
Loop, Janet Glendenning, 1933-.
Mss A 518
[18] p., 12, 83, 3, 18 leaves; 28 cm.
1980
Ancestor charts and corresponding family group sheets (bound together with library binding) for the author's maternal (Langill) and paternal (Glendenning) families.

Genealogical notes on the Perham, Harvey, Ellis and Cox families
Kanetzky, Lois.
Mss A 519
1 vol. (304 p.); 24 cm.
Account book with genealogical notes on the Perham (p.1-52), Harvey (p.53-66), Ellis (p.67-86), and Cox (p.87-106) families. Pages 107 to 290 are blank. Pages 291-293,295 and 303 have names and addresses of "Ancestors" (i.e. relatives/contacts?). Includes maps cut from unidentified publications.

Epitaphs and inscriptions copied from the old cemetery at Sheddsville, Vermont
Hayden, Arthur B.
Mss A 52
32 p.; 28 cm.
Typescript transcription of cemetery inscriptions arranged in alphabetical order.

Great Missenden Parish Church register, 1575-1682
Great Missenden Parish Church (England).
Mss A 520
1 vol. (77, [44] leaves); 28 cm.
Photostat of handwritten transcription bound into a book. Includes Baptisms, Burials & Marriages for 1575/1576, 1594/1595, 1603-1664, 1671-76, 1677, and 1680-82. Includes similar copies for entires on the Baldwin family from the Bishop's Transcripts for Little Missenden, Great Kimble, Linslade, Chilton, Chalfont St Peters, Langley Parish and "other papers including eleven sheets relating to an ancient Book of Wills. Other surnames mentioned in the records are often listed.

Sheriffs of Northumberland, England 1154 to 1811: Under sheriffs of Northumberland, England 1689 to 1811; Knights of the shire for the county of Northumberland Eng. 1298 to 1808; Members of Parliament for the borough of Morpeth 1553 to 1807
Whinfield, Hattiebell.
Mss A 521
23 leaves; 27 cm.
1931
Typescript transcription of original record. Includes index.

The Gloucester family of Dollivers: from Peter of 1707
Dolliver, William Henry, 1831-.
Mss A 522
207 leaves, 29 cm.
[1890?]
Photocopy of the original handwritten genealogy. Includes two leaves tipped in after the genealogy with photocopies of newspaper clippings concerning the Dolliver family.

A schoolgirl of the fifties: a daughter of old Vermont
Utterback, Helen Tappan.
Mss A 523
93 leaves; 28 cm.
1973
Photocopy of a typescript transcription of Harriet Ann Tappan's diary, kept at Fort Edward Institute, 1855. Includes a history of Panton, Vt., brief histories of the Tappan and Shepard families

and a description of the Fort Edward Institute prior to the transcription of the diary. Also includes transcriptions of an account of Harriet's expenditures (p.51-53), a listing of "Public Exhibitions" (Saturday morning lectures) (p.55-57), thirty-seven compositions (p.58-73), and "Instructions in the art of ornamental leather pelisse work" (p.90-93). Pages 81-89 discusses the death of Harriet, age nineteen, due to tuberculosis.

Copy of the records of the Congregational Church in Gilmantown. Being the records kept by Isaac Smith, Pastor of the Old Smith Meeting House et al.
Follansbee, Katie M.
Mss A 524
150 leaves; 28 cm.
1912
Typescript transcription of original church records from 1774 to 1819. Includes baptismal, marriage, death and admittance records.

The Scullys
Mss A 525
14, [4], 5 leaves; 28 cm.
Photocopy of a typescript genealogy on twelve generations of the James Scully family of Tipperary, Ireland.

Genealogy of Johnathan [sic] Bailey's family of Groton, New London Co., Conn.
Bailey, Frank M. (Frank Myron), 1867-1926.
Mss A 526
45 leaves; 29 cm.
199-
Photocopy of author's composition book ms.

Record of the Reppucci family of Chiusano, Province of Avellino, Italy
Mss A 527
[4] sheets; 44 cm. folded to 28 cm.
Photocopy of a handwritten genealogy.

Thomas Varney of Boston and descendants
Varney, George W.
Mss A 528
96 leaves; 28 cm.
1995
Computer typescript genealogy in Register format. This unedited ms. version is more extensive than the author's article: Varney, George W. "Thomas Varney of Boston and Some of his descendants," *New England Historical and Geanealogical Register*, Volume 149 (Jan., April, July: 1995): 3-27, 141-154, 244-264.

Bible record for the Jared Foote family, 1770-1850
Foote, Jared, b. 1770.
Mss A 529
[4] leaves; 28 cm.
Photocopy of original record with title page. Includes an account by Jared concerning where he was born and the towns he lived in as well as "a few words of councel or advice" for his son.

South Fairlee (Ely) Cemetery, Fairlee, Vermont: with genealogical notes on Carpenter, Heath, Kibbey
Neal, Philemon C., Mrs.
Massachusetts DAR Genealogical Records Committee.
Mss A 53
17 p.; 28 cm.
1955.
Carbon copy typescript transcription of the Ely (or South Fairlee) Cemetery with genealogical notes added and an index.

Bible record for the Elias Lester family, 1794-1885
Lester, Elias, b. 1836.
Mss A 530
[6] leaves; 28 cm.
Photocopy of original record with title page concerning the Lester family of Seneca Falls, N.Y. Includes entries for the Foote, Strong, Bacon and Clark families.

Bible record for the William Day Chamberlain family, 1818-1934
Chamberlain, William Day, b. 1818.
Mss A 531
[5] p.; 29 cm.
1818-1867,
Original record with title page concerning the Chamberlain family of Lynn, Mass.

Bible record for the Leach and Damon families, 1797-1934
Mss A 532
[4] leaves; 28 cm.
1871?
Photocopy and typescript transcription of original record with title page information. Includes 10 January 1934 letter from Lillian D. Leach to D. Bradford Damon of Worcester, Mass. providing genealogical information concerning her family.

Bible record for the Samuel Neal family, 1764-1886
Neal, Samuel, 1770-1856.
Mss A 533
[13] leaves; 28 cm.
Photocopy of original record with title page concerning the Neal family of Alstead, N.H. Includes entries for the Chandler and Huntoon families.

Family genealogy of Massasoit Ousamequin
Brady, Philip.
Mss A 534
[4] leaves; 28 cm.
1995
Computer typescript.

Bible record for the Luther Hastings family, 1775-1950
Hastings, Luther, 1775-1860.
Mss A 535
[4] leaves; 28 cm.
Photocopy of original record with title page. The donor transcribed the entires on the back of each leaf since the entries are faded.

The family tree of the Wilckens family (1897) by Fannie Tillessen Translation, transcription and additions by Jan Alexander Koso with Jerome Anderson
Koso, Jan Alexander, 1960-.
Mss A 536
[29] leaves; 28 cm.
1995
Computer typescript transcription in Register format of the genealogical information from a family tree (chart) originally in German.

Joel Carter and Sidney Holman Agreement, 1854 May 8
Small, Aaron.
Millbury (Mass.) Fence viewer.
Mss A 537
1 ADS; 26 cm.
Document written by the fence viewers of Millbury, Aaron Small and Abijah Gleason, settling a dispute between Joel Carter and Sidney Holman concerning a fence between their property.

Deed, 1860 November 16
Wheeler, Jonathan, 1792-1872.
Mss A 538
[3] leaves; 18 cm.
Quitclaim deed in which Jonathan Wheeler sells land in Athol to Hollon Farr, Chester Bancroft, Daniel Davies (all of Athol, Mass.) and Elisha Davies (of Warwick) for $1000. Verso states that "The foregoing is a true copy of record recorded in the Registry of Deeds Book 631 Page 537 Attest Alex H Wilder, Regr".

Account book of Clark Perry, 1828-1842
Perry, Clark, 1800-1843.
Mss A 539
Access to original record restricted access; use published version first.
1 vol. (ca. 170 p.); 19 cm.
Additional form: Transcribed version by George Freeman Sanborn, Jr. published as "Vital records kept by the Rev. Clark Perry of Newbury, Vermont," *Vermont Genealogy*, Volume (January 1996): 11.
Account book of the marriages performed by Rev. Clark Perry in Newbury, VT (1828-1836); Wethersfield, VT (1835-1836); Standish, ME (1838-1840); and Lancaster, NH (1841-1842).

Record of Births in Newbury, VT for 1829 (only five entries) and Records of Deaths in Newbury, VT 1832-1835. Includes a list of expenses 1866-1872 and a list of "Donations for benevolent objects made by the Congregational Church and Society" 1833-1835.

Inter-state journal index
Miller, J. Wesley (John Wesley), 1941-.
Mss A 54
48 p.; 28 cm.
1969
Mimeograph copy typescript index to the Inter-state Journal and Advertiser and its successor Inter-state Journal published from April, 1900, to December, 1905, at White River Junction, Vt., in 55 issues.

Civil War letters of James Andrew Mansfield, 1863 Jan 27-April 7
Mansfield, James Andrew, 1819-1875.
Mss A 540
[4], [4], [2] p.; 20-25 cm. + 5 tintypes.
Three letters written to "My Dear Wife" [Mary Ann (Whitney) Mansfield] by James Mansfield while at Camp Parapet in Carrollton, Louisana. In the letter dated January 27 1863, James asks for more letters and describes New Orleans, Camp Parapet, his pay raise and their order to take charge of 2000 contrabands to build a fort and extend the parapets to New Orleans. In his letter dated March 11, 1863, James again requests more letters especially from his children. He describes how many of the soldiers have "ground itch". After writing that he will send money once he is paid, James expresses his desire to better clothe and house his family. In the letter dated April 7 1863, James writes about the creation of a negro regiment. He describes a 8 PM to 2 AM march during which they surprised a Negro camp and took 67. He reassures his wife that he will not reenlist and requests money since he wont be paid until he is discharged.

Family record of Joseph S. Jones, 1790 to 1870
Hall, G.
Mss A 541
1 sheet; 46 x 36 folded to 28 cm.
1873
Photocopy of original record concerning the Jones family of Sutton, Mass. Provides the names of his parents, and the parents of his wife, Nancy H. Putnam, as well as the birth (sometimes the death) of their children.

Taverner of Limerick, Ireland, showing descent from the End family of Mallow, Co. Cork: 1630-1823
Melnick, Louis Daniel, 1934-.
Mss A 542
[4] leaves; 28 cm.
1994
Computer typescript pedigree and accompanying notes.

The Gridley & Ely heritage of Gerald R. Ford
Boslooper, Thomas David, 1923-.
Mss A 543
iv, 50 leaves: ill., maps, coat of arms; 28 cm.
1993
Typescript.

Capt. Charles Vernon Gridley: United States Navy. Hero of the battle of Manila Bay, the Spanish American War May 1, 1898
Boslooper, Thomas David, 1923-.
Mss A 544
93 leaves: ill., maps, ports.; 28 cm.
1993
Computer typescript.

The Cook / Taylor heritage
Boslooper, Thomas David, 1923-.
Mss A 545
40 leaves: ill., maps; 28 cm.
1993
Computer typescript.

The Boslooper / Devries heritage
Boslooper, Thomas David, 1923-.
Mss A 546
43 leaves: ill., maps; 28 cm.
1985
Computer typescript.

Thomas Loomis of Buffalo, New York: #8702 [in] The Loomis family in America. His heritage and descendants
Boslooper, Thomas David, 1923-.
Mss A 547
iii, 74 leaves: ports.; 28 cm.
1993
Computer typescript.

Bible record for the Joel Bacon family, 1755-1898
Bacon, Joel, 1766-1830.
Mss A 548
[9] leaves; 28 cm.
1828
Photocopy of original record with title page.

The Deering family of Southern Maine
Jones, Susan D.
Mss A 549 also CS71/D3135/1979
v, 4, 172 leaves: geneal. tables; 28 cm.
1979
Photocopy of computer typescript genealogy on the descendants of Roger Deering for ten generations.

Rutland Co., Vt., epitaphs
Spurling, Fannie Smith, b. 1876.
Mss A 55
58 p.; 28 cm.
1946?
Mimeograph copy typescript of three cemetery inscriptions, each alphabetically arranged. Cemeteries in this volume include: Evergreen Cem., Pittsford, Vt.; St. Alphonsus Cem., Pittsford, Vt., and Bump Cem., North Chittenden, Vt. Also, transcribed from the Pittsford town records, a list of persons born before 1880 who have been buried since 1940.

The ancestors and descendants of William Gage Brown and Harriet Alice Wolfe of Urbana, Illinois
Brown, William Jay Jr., 1918-.
Mss A 550
1 v. ([25] leaves): ill.; 28 cm.
1995
Computer typescript. "Tributaries" section covers allied families of Doane, Dodge, Fellows, Gage, Sharples, Iddings, Stickney and Warren (generally just 1-2 leaves per family).

Jonah Austin of Taunton, Massachusetts: sailed on Hercules of Sandwich in March 1634-5
Austin, William Wallace.
Mss A 551
101 leaves in various foliations (some folded); 28 cm.
1973
Photocopy of original typescript. "English ancestry and early generations in this country" may be found in *New England Historical Genealogical Register* volume 67, pg 161-169."

Jacobus Spira
Krauthausen, Udo, 1935-.
Mss A 552
[16, 13, 5] p.; 28 cm.
19--
Computer typescript transcription of a German genealogical work on the descendants of Jacobus Spiera, last Abbot from the monastary Sponheim, followed by an English translation. Includes some information on Johann Wilhelm Spira, who immigrated to Pennsylvania in 1753.

From Scottish borders to New York's frontiers, 1772: the Bells, Blakes and Telfords
Tilford, Ernest H.
Mss A 553
8 leaves; 28 cm.
1988
Computer typescript.

Bible record for the Ransom Whitney family, 1785-1880
Whitney, Ransom, 1785-1871.
Mss A 554
[6] leaves; 28 cm.
Photocopy of original record lacking title page concerning the Whitney family of Pennsylvania and Ohio. Includes typescript transcript of the Bible record and one leaf of
genealogical / historical information on Ransom Whitney both by the donor.

Bible record for the George Dearborn Tewksbury family, 1812-1931
Tewksbury, George Dearborn, 1812-1927
Mss A 555
[2] p.; 27 cm.
Original record lacking title page.

Virginia - Massachusetts Lincoln Letter 1856-1867: with listing of descendants of Enos Lincoln of Petersham, MA. Letters from or about the grandchildren & great grandchildren of Enos Lincoln
Davies, David L.
Mss A 556
[ii], 16 leaves: geneal. tables; 28 cm.
1995
Computer typescript transcription of Lincoln family correspondence written in Broadford and Marion, Virginia. The bulk of the letters are by Charles Francis Lincoln (nine letters) and his first wife, Martha Jane Woodward Lincoln (six letters). There are also two letters written by Charles' second wife, Harriet Clark Lincoln and one letter written by his mother, Laura Graves Lincoln. Most of the letters were written to either "Mother", Laura Graves Lincoln, or to "Sister", Ellen Maria Lincoln Stone. The donor included a list of the descendants of Enos Lincoln with individuals mentioned in the letters listed in bold-face and another chart of the ancestors of Enos Lincoln.

Six generations of the family of Warren Ferris Hitchcock
Gilman, Frances M.
Mss A 558
30, [12] p.; 28 cm.
1995
Computer typescript.

Bible record for the Robert Bridges family, 1721-1832
Bridges, Robert, fl. 1785.
Mss A 559
[7] leaves; 28 cm.
Photocopy of original record with title page. Includes entries for the Brown (difficult to read) and Stearns families.

Vermont marriages: compiled from newspaper files
Bowman, John Elliot, 1866-1933.
Mss A 56
14 p.; 28 cm.
1930
This is an alphabetical list of marriage notices of people who were married in Vermont between 1830 and 1848. The first section is from a variety of cited newspapers from Massachusetts and Vermont. The second section is from the Columbian Centinel, 1811-1815.

Bible record for the John Merrow family, 1802-1932
Merrow, John, 1802-1877.
Mss A 560
[5] leaves; 28 cm.
Photocopy of original record with title page concerning the Merrow family of Eaton, New Hampshire.

Parish register St. Michael's Church, Bishop's Stortford, Co. Herts, England
Glascock, J. L., Jr.
St. Michael's (Church: Bishop's Stortford, England)
Mss A 561 a-c
3 v.; 30 cm.
192?
Photostat of handwritten transcriptions of original parish register by J.L. Glascock, Jun. Volume one [folder "a"] contains baptisms 1561-1652 (117 leaves); volume two [folder "b"] Marriage and Burials 1561-1712 (120 leaves); volume three [folder "c"] is an index compiled by Spencer Miller.

Bible records of Massachusetts families
Daughters of the American Revolution.
Massachusetts.
Mss A 562
148 p.; 29 cm.
1945
Typescript.

Genealogical records of Austin Bearse (or Bearce) of Barnstable, Cape Cod, Massachusetts ... 1638 to 1933: a record of his descendants under six different spellings of the name ... and other data secured
Meadows, Fanny Louisa Steed.
Mss A 563
390, 100 leaves; 30 cm.
1933
Typescript.

Supplement to genealogical records of Austin Bearse (or Bearce) of Barnstable, Cape Cod, Massachusetts, U.S.A. A.D. 1638 to 1933: a record of his descendants under six different spellings of the name ... and other data secured
Meadows, Fanny Louisa Steed.
Mss A 564
49, 17 leaves; 29 cm.
1939
Typescript.

The boke of moysteres of the kyngs: mte is tennentes and tynn(r)s of his man(r)s w(t)yn wrytyn and of the stayn(r)es of Blakemo(a) and ffowymo(a) as by the same more playnly appereth
Banks, Charles Edward, 1854-1931.
Mss A 565
1 v. ([85] leaves); 27 cm.
1923
Typescript transcription of original record. "This militia list is a bound book of paper leaves 71pp. being one of a lot of County Musters. Temp. Henry VIII but they are all undated. Some have been identified as about 1538 and the writing of the Cornwall Muster is consistent with that date. I would place it not later 1540. There are about 36 County Musters altogether. The reference is Exchequer, Treasury of the Receipt. Vol. 53."

Marriage certificate for Harry A. Rogers and Mary F. Brigham, 1874 September 17
Putnam, Richard F.
Mss A 566
1 leaf; 28 cm.
Record for the marriage of Harry A. Rogers and Mary F. Brigham at St. Mary's Church in Newton Lower Falls, Massachusetts.

Genealogy of Lent family
Bundy, Meta Lent, b. 1874.
Mss A 567 a-b
1 vol. (300 p.); 27 cm. + 1 photograph.
1917?
Ms. genealogy (some pages were cut and many are blank) written ca. 1917 with annotations written ca. 1925. Includes an albumen print of Maide Van Wegen, Edmund Lent, Phebe Lent, Emma Van Vegen, Dan Van Wegen and Fred Van Wegen with an annotation on the back of the photograph identifing each person, their date of birth and page in the Lent genealogy with information concerning these individuals. The donor also provided a typescript transcription of a letter to Anna Smith Lent by Alice Ransom concerning the "Ryker-Lent families Holland and German."

Genealogical information relevant to the Robertson family of Thornton, New Hampshire
Robertson, John Hugh, 1933-.
Mss A 568
[4], 6, 20 leaves: geneal. tables; 28 cm.
1996
Computer typescript, text descendancy chart and a name sorted list.

The Granville Jubilee: celebrated at Granville, Mass., August 27 and 28, 1845
Cooley, Timothy Mather, 1772-1859.
First Church of Christ (Granville, Mass.)
Mss A 569
37, [4] leaves; 28 cm.
1845
Typescript transcription of work printed at Springfield, Mass. In cludes a list of "Names of the native emigrants from East Granville, now living" and "Names of the Representatives to the General Court from Grandville."

Elderkin wills and deeds
Alt, Joseph D. (Joseph Douglas), 1921-.
Mss A 57
[3], 51 p.; 28 cm.
1997 July
Photocopy of computer printout typescript of transcriptions of Elderkin family deeds and wills from horton, Nova Scotia, and Brookhaven, N.Y., and indentures from Brookhaven, N.Y.

Second Church of Christ, Grandville, Massachusetts: records
Robbins, Muriel E. (Muriel Edna Taylor), 1923-
Mss A 570
31 leaves; 28 cm.
1965
Typescript copy of Mrs. Joseph Duris' manuscript transcription of the original record.

Account book of Christopher Sanborn, 1834-1853
Sanborn, Christopher, b. 1803.
Mss A 571
1 vol. (172 p.); 19 cm.
Entries concern building [stone] walls, ploughing, shingling, hewing timber, chopping wood, taking animals to pasture, haying, butchering animals, planting and harvesting crops.

Genealogy of the Henry Hayward family of Nova Scotia and New Brunswick
Franks, Eunice Marion Hayward, 1922-.
Mss A 572
[91] leaves; 28 cm.
1995?
Computer typescript of the author's research from 1981 to 1995 on the descendants of Henry Hayward.

Prince, outstanding members of the Prince family, 1600-1950's
Prince, Louise M. (Louise Marguerite), 1908-.
Mss A 573 a-b
235, 47 leaves: ill.; 29 cm.
1975

Ancestors and descendants of Reverend Samuel Terry: born March 26, 1690 Enfield Mass and his wife Margaret (Coffin) Hall-Wilson born June 10, 1689 Nantucket Mass.
McCraw, Carol J McCune.
Mss A 574 a-b
89, 67, [19] leaves; 28 cm.
28 cm.
Typescript.

*Thomas Davenport of Dorchester, Massachusetts:
his descendants in Sidney, Maine (1762-1995)
and their families: Reynolds, Bacon, Dyer, Field,
Benson, Bragg, Blaisdell, and others*
Reynolds, Beatrice Kay.
Mss A 575
vi, 34 leaves; 28 cm.
c1995
Typescript.

*John Hastings of Cambridge, Massachusetts
(1643): six generations of his descendants from
Mathew and (Mary Battelle) Hastings: early
settlers of Maine*
Reynolds, Beatrice Kay.
Mss A 576
viii, 90 p.; 28 cm.
c1995
Typescript.

*Richard Park of Newton, Massachusetts (1635)
and his descendants in Sidney, Maine including
ancestral lines from Dix (Dikes, Deekes), Miller,
Black, Blaisdell, Stowers, Sprague, Goffe
(Gough), Viall (Vvall), Simpson, Stimpson, Cole*
Reynolds, Beatrice Kay.
Mss A 577
viii, 52 leaves; 28 cm.
c1995
Typescript.

*Nathaniel and Mary (Tolman) Reynolds, IV of
Bridgewater, Massachusetts*
Reynolds, Beatrice Kay.
Mss A 578
xi, 106 leaves; 28 cm.
c1995
Typescript.

*Daniel Townsend, Sr.: early settler of Sidney,
Maine (1764) and his descendants*
Reynolds, Beatrice Kay.
Mss A 579
35 leaves; 28 cm.
c1995
Typescript.

Redden family Bible record, 1890-1968
Mss A 58
[8] p.: 28 cm.
Photocopy of original records and title page from
a Bible.

*The Labrecque family: a history from its
approximate beginings in 1657 France to the
current generation living around the north shore
area of Massachusetts*
Labrecque, Patricia Wolfe.
Mss A 580
18, [5] leaves; 28 cm.
Typescript.

*The Poffenberger family: dealing chiefly with
those of this name (in its many variations) as
found in Frederick and Washington Cos. in
Maryland*
Randall, Georgiana H. (Georgiana Hathaway), b.
1893.
Mss A 581 a-b
v, 308 leaves; 28 cm.
1979
Photocopy of original record.

*Isle La Motte (Vineyard) Vermont: Historical and
genealogical data 1791-1860*
Hayden, Harold B.
Mss A 582
[146] leaves: maps; 28 cm.
1928
Typescript.

*The ancestry of the sons of Henry Hill Pierce, and
his wife, Katharine Curtis Pierce*
Pierce, William Curtis, 1906-.
Mss A 583
202 leaves; 28 cm.
1980?
Typescript.

1792-1866 / as a western Maine lawyer saw it
Pierce, William Curtis, 1906-.
Mss A 584
v, 315 .: ill., ports., maps; 28 cm.
197-
Typescript.

Yankee wanderer Josiah Pierce 1827-1913
Pierce, William Curtis, 1906-.
Mss A 585
ii, 130 leaves: ill., ports.; 28 cm.
19??
Typescript.

Henry Hill Pierce
Pierce, William Curtis, 1906-.
Mss A 586
140 leaves: ill., ports.; 28 cm.
1991
Typescript.

Squire Pierce 1756-1830
Pierce, William Curtis, 1906-.
Mss A 587
99 leaves: maps; 28 cm.
1989
Typescript.

Two hundred years of pioneering
Slichter, Charles Sumner, b. 1864.
Mss A 588
17 leaves; 28 cm.
1935?
Photocopy of original typescript.

Some descendants of John Flye of the Isle of Shoals, Maine
Pinkham, Steven R.
Mss A 589
17 leaves: geneal. tables; 29 cm.
[1980]
Typescript (photocopy)

Daniel Collins, 1648-1690, of Enfield, Conn.
Eldridge, William Henry, 1873-1943.
Mss A 59
[9], 16 p.: 28 cm.
1932.
Carbon copy manuscript copy of lineal descent from Daniel(1) Collins through Daniel(2), Nathan(3), Daniel(4). There are separate entries for Nathan(5), Daniel(5), and David(5), and one child each of the latter two. The file contains another computer typescript of this item done by Jonathan Paul Foulkes in 1991 that contains an index to names and places for this version.

Our history is our future: a genealogical outline of the Pangborn / Pangburn / Pangman family in Canada and the United States
Byram, Thomas Leslie, 1931-.
Mss A 590
181, xlvii p.; 28 cm.
[1994]
Typescript. "Not proofread or edited draft: September, 1994."

Carleton - Carlton forebears: a genealogy of some descandants [i.e. descendants] of Edward Carleton, proprietor of Rowley, Mass., 1639-1648: with some bibliographical notes
Hargrave, Helena M. Goodale.
Mss A 591 also microfiche
84, 24, 4 leaves: ill., coat of arms, maps, geneal. tables; 29 cm.
1977

The Favor / Favour family of America: given name index
Brady, Philip.
Mss A 592
164 leaves; 28 cm.
1944 [i.e. 1994]

The Favor / Favour family of America: surname index
Brady, Philip.
Mss A 593
[157] leaves; 28 cm.
1944 [i.e. 1994]

Ancestral tablets: a collection of diagrams for pedigrees, so arranged that eight generations of the ancestors of any person may be recorded in a connected and simple form
Whitmore, William Henry, 1836-1900.
Mss A 594
16 p.: geneal. tables; 31 cm.
1890
8th ed.
Printed geneal. tables completed in ms. with the genealogy of John Hooker and Elisabeth (Wood) Packard.

Public health and personal ideology: the commission and reception of Lemuel Shattuck's 1850 Report for the promotion of public and personal health
Chin, Amy Wen-I, 1974-.
Mss A 595
[iv], 112 p.: facsim.; 28 cm.
1996
Typescript thesis (B.A.) – Harvard University, 1996. Includes bibliographical references (p. 95-112).

Jacobsen: descendants of Tord Jacobsen (c. 1720-1809) and his wife Ingeborg (Knudsen) Jacobsen (1758-1826) of Niehuus (Neuhaus, or Nyhus), Bov Parish, Denmark
Ogilvie, Helen Jacobsen, 1923-.
Mss A 596
[106] leaves: ports., facsim., geneal. tables; 28 cm.
1994
Photocopy of family group sheets and charts with copies of some source material including correspondence, certificates, and obituaries.

Our Irish kinfolk book no. 2: a Pierce family saga
Overbo, Clara Pierce Olson, 1916-.
Mss A 597
200 leaves: ill., ports.; 28 cm.
1993
Computer typescript genealogy and "memories" on the following families: James Pierce, Katherine Pierce (Emmett-Gardner), William Pierce, John Pierce, Mary Pierce (Kienast), Matthew Pierce, and Ellen Pierce (O'Brien).

Index of wills, Greene Co., NY, 1803-1873
Barber, Gertrude A. (Gertrude Audrey)
Mss A 598
58 leaves; 28 cm.
1973
Photocopy of original typescript.

Virginia DAR Genealogical records Committee report. District V Bible records project
Daughters of the American Revolution. Virginia.
Mss A 599 a-b
1 v. (unpaged): facsims.; 29 cm.
1994
Typescript with facsims. of original records covering AL, AR, CA, FL, GA, KY, LA, MD, MS, NC, NY, PA, TN, TX, VA.

Joshua Adams (1779-1846) of Falmouth, Gray and Raymond, Maine, and some of his descendants
Adams, Charles F., b. 1889.
Mss A 6
9 p.; 28 cm.
1957.

Congregational Church Cemetery, Truro (Barnstable County), Massachusetts
Massachusetts DAR Genealogical Records Committee.
Mss A 60
67 p.: 28 cm.
1951.
Carbon copy typescript transcription of cemetery inscriptions in order by gravestone's physical location.

Town of Danvers survey of gravestone inscriptions
Dumke, James, 1928-.
Danvers (Mass.) Preservation Commission.
Mss A 600
[69] p.; 28 cm.
1997 Jan. printing.
Apple II computer generated list from a database in two sections. The first is an index to the cemeteries: Endicott, Goodale, High, Leach, Locust, Nurse, Old Settler's, Pope, Preston, Prince, Putnam, Russell and Swinerton, Holton (in two parts) and Wadsworth cemeteries followed by full transcriptions. Note that there are other cemeteries in Danvers not included in this survey and the records only include people whose names are engraved on markers, not everyone who is buried in each cemetery. The second list is organized by surname. Includes two indexes with 17 sections variously paginated. This data was gathered for the Commission by Jim and Penny Dumke.

Richard Lowden of Duxbury and Pembroke Center, Mass. and some of his descendants
Vincent, Vernon Delano.
Mss A 601
[17] leaves; 28 cm.
Typescript

The Bird family: a genealogy of the two branches of the Bird family of Stoughton, Massachusetts and vicinity descended from Thomas Bird of Dorchester, Massachusetts who was born about 1613 in England
Mann, Ralph Herman, Jr.
Mss A 602
iii, 27, [21] leaves; 28 cm.
1945, 1950
Typescript genealogy that follows the lineal descent from Thomas (1) Bird through Thomas (2) to Benjamin (3) before tracing multiple descendants of Benjamin (4). Part two begins with the linear descent from Thomas (1) Bird through John (2), to Samuel (3) before tracing multiple descendants of Samuel (4).

John Somers Esq. of Gloucester County, New Jersey, and some of his descendants
Mss A 603
[12] leaves; 28 cm.
Typescript genealogy on the life of John Somers with a list of his children and some information concerning the family of his son James (2).

John Clawson: a contemporary of Roger Williams in Rhode Island
Greene, Welcome Arnold, 1795-1870.
Mss A 604
[53] leaves; 28 cm.
1924
Typescript biographical sketch on John Clawson who was murdered at Providence, R.I. in 1660.

Ancestors and descendants of David Finzer: compiled from the notes of his grandson, Vinton Finzer
Nickerson, Vernon Roscoe, 1933-.
Mss A 605
16 leaves; 28 cm.
1968
Typescript genealogy for five generations. Although there is some information on the family in Kappelen bei Aarberg, Switzerland, the focus is on the family after they migrated to America in 1853.

The early Tryon, Jones, Harris, Lay families of Saybrook, Connecticut
Hook, James W. (James William), 1884-1957.
Mss A 606
58 leaves; 28 cm.
1952
Typescript.

Major Daniel Gookin: Boxborough pioneer
Pettingell, John (John Mason), 1890-1972.
Mss A 607
10, [9] leaves: maps; 28 cm.
Typescript.

Two early histories of Pembroke, Maine
Sprague, Donald R.
Mss A 608
35, [3] leaves; 28 cm.
1969
Typescript. Includes Sidney A. Wilder's "An account of the town's early settlement by English-speaking white men" and "Annals of Pembroke" (1768-1924).

The descendants of William Goodrich of Wethersfield, Connecticut through his 6th great grandson William Homer Goodrich of Beerston, New York
Goodrich, Victor B., (Victor Burton), 1928-.
Mss A 609
iii, 88 leaves; 28 cm.
1994
Typescript genealogy on the lineal descent from William (1) Goodrich through William (2-3), Elnathan (4), Isaac (5), Charles (6), Harry (7), Smith H (8) to William Homer (9) Goodrich then continues through William Homer (9) Goodrich's children, grandchildren and some great-grandchildren.

Family of Fall
Lord, Henry Dutch, 1829-1900.
Mss A 61
[59] leaves: 26 cm.
1898.
Manuscript on the lineal descent from John(1) Fall (d. 1746), of Kittery and Berwick, Me., to Charles Gershom Fall (b. 1845), of Boston, Mass.

Thurber family genealogical index: a work in progress
Martin, Joanne E.
Mss A 610
1 v. (various pagings); 29 cm.
1995

Wood family of Shelf, Halifax Parish, Yorkshire, England, Massachusetts, Connecticut, Long Island, N.Y., and Canada
Wood, Casey A. (Casey Albert), 1856-1942.
Mss A 611
39 leaves; 30 cm.
1920

The descendants of Edward Munyan, 1677-1647
Guadagni, Sally.
Mss A 612
iv, 149 p.; 29 cm.
1994

The Reverend William Worcester and his background: 1595-1662
Worcester, Dean K.
Mss A 613
ii, 20 leaves; 28 cm.
c1992
Includes memorandum dated April, 1995 (6 leaves) concerning the Reverend William Worcester of Salisbury, Massachusetts (d.1662).

History of the Philip Larkin family: with three associated lines, Hadley, Lawrence, Prescott
Plummer, Helen Regan Sleeter, b. 1900.
Mss A 614
1 v. (various pagings): photographs; 28 cm.
1965
Photocopy of original typescript with mounted photographs.

The Powers of Woodstock, Vermont
Powers, Duane Gordon.
Mss A 616
[30] leaves; 28 cm.
1994

Some ancestors & descendants of Alexander Beebe
Seger, Adah Beebe, 1881-.
Mss A 617
20 p.; 28 cm.
1958

Miscellaneous Beebe data
Whelan, Florence S.
Mss A 618
11 leaves; 28 cm.
1949

The Flaggs in South Carolina: the Colonial years
Nord, Barbara K.
Mss A 619
47 p.: ill., maps, ports., geneal. tables; 28 cm.
1982

Barnard, Vt., epitaphs and fragmentary births, marriages and deaths
Newton, William Monroe, b. 1864.
Mss A 62
[50], 42 p.: 28 cm.
1916, 1922
1916-1927 typescript ed.
Carbon copy typescript transcription of cemetery inscriptions in Barnard, Vt., which include: Methodist Cem. (14 p.), Nye Cem. (4 p.), Perkins Cem. (2 p.), Moore Family Burying Ground (1 p.), Chamberlain Family Cem. (1 p.), "Clapp" Graveyard (1 p.), East Barnard Cem. (13 p.), and South Barnard Yard (11 p.). These records are arranged in rough alphabetical order within each cemetery. A second section is called "Fragmentary births, marriages and deaths in Barnard". It is a genealogical compiling of vital records (includes some from neighboring towns of Pomfret and Royalton) and cemetery inscriptions, though seemingly not complete. Starting on page 28, there is a list of marriages that were not used in the first part. The marriages, perhaps, may be complete.

The Flagg family in South Carolina: from the Revolution to 1801
Nord, Barbara K.
Mss A 620
ii, 59 p.; 28 cm.
1984

The Flagg family in South Carolina: the nineteenth century
Nord, Barbara K.
Mss A 621
102 p.; 28 cm.
1984

The Flagg family in New England: the ancestry of Dr. Henry Collins Flagg
Nord, Barbara K.
Mss A 622
78 p.: geneal. tables; 28 cm.
1988

Bible record for the George W Shattuck family, 1793-1909
Shattuck, George, 1833-1909.
Mss A 623
[6] p.; 26-28 cm.
Original record with title page concerning the Shattuck and Jackson families.

Bible record for the Augustus Merritt family, 1603-1919
Merritt, Augustus, b. 1827.
Mss A 624
[14] p.; 28 cm.
Original record with title page concerning the Merritt, Wyman, Hills, Byram, Hoar families. Includes written pedigrees of the Wyman and Hunt families.

Bible record for the William Hall family, 1805-1965
Hall, William, ca. 1785-1832.
Mss A 625
[9] p.; 27 cm.
Original record with title page concerning the Hall family of Litchfield, Connecticut and North East, Erie Co., Pennsylvania. Includes a photocopy of an obituary for William Hall's daughter Louisa (Hall) Ross.

Bible record for the Azariah Hunt family, 1779-1847
Hunt, Azariah, ca. 1777-1821.
Mss A 626
[6] p.; 27 cm.
Original record with title page concerning the Hunt family of Lamberton and Spring Hill Farm near Bordentown, [NJ].

The Putnam family 1355-2000
Thomas, Robert Alan.
Mss A 627
[25] p.: ill., maps, ports., coat of arms; 28 cm.
2000
Typescript.

Lucius Henry Packard: born, Stoughton, Mass. 15th August 1840 died, Montreal, Que. 6th March 1914
Packard, Lucius Henry, 1840-1914.
Mss A 628
53, 119, 7 p.: ill., ports.; 28 cm.
1999
Computer typescript transcription of Lucius Henry Packard's (1840-1914) four diaries, 1861-1866, preceeded by 53 pages of biographical information on LHP including the transcription of "a number of original letters written to or from family members...newspaper clippings...snippets of business and personal papers" and photographs of family members. The first two diaries run from 1st Jan 1861 to 9th Jul 1862 and provide a "glimpse of life in the South during the Civil War" (quote from donor's cover letter). There is a gap until 23rd Oct 1863 when the third diary begins with a review of the past few months including his arrest in Sept 1863 for providing "aid and comfort to the enemy" (the charges were dimissed for lack of evidence), his assignment to Co. K (his name is spelled Packyard in the records), his desertion and eventual return to Stoughton. The fourth diary opens on 27th Dec 1865 and consists of an account of a business trip to Chicago and St. Louis and another trip to Buffalo.

Bible record for the Samuel Shaw Jr. family, 1827-1879
Shaw, Samuel, Jr., b. 1827.
Mss A 629
[5] leaves; 28 cm.
Photocopy of original record with title page.

Fairfax, Vermont, town records: Births, marriages and deaths
Hitchcock, Alison B.
Mss A 63
56 p.: 28 cm.
Typescript transcription of vital records to the year 1860.

Bible record for the Charles Atkinson Pearson family, 1805-1991
Pearson, Charles Atkinson, 1805-1878.
Mss A 630
[11] leaves; 28 cm.
Photocopy of original record with title page concerning the Pearson, Shippy and Harwood families of Mississippi and California.

Letter, 1840 July 22, Lexington, Mass. [to] Rev. David Damon, West Cambridge, Mass.
Damon, H. M., (Hannah Motley), 1823-1901.
Mss A 631
[3] p.; 25 cm.
Original letter with the heading "What I did during a normal year at the normal school." Provides a list of studies and texts used at the first State Normal School in the United States, founded in 1839 at Lexington, Mass.

A line from John (1) Bouton of Connecticut: a thoroughly documented account
Ullmann, Helen Schatvet.
Mss A 632
22 leaves; 28 cm.
2000
Typescript genealogy for seven generations in NEHG Register format.

Bible record for the Joseph Cassander Cromack family, 1836-1893
Cromack, Joseph Cassander, 1836-1908.
Mss A 633
[11] p.; 27 cm.
Original record with title page concerning the Cromack family of Williamstown, MA and Bennington, VT. Donor included photocopies of five records concerning the Joseph Cassander Cromack family from Vermont Vital Records to 1870 and 1871-1908 used along with the Bible record to write a one page genealogical sketch on the family.

Descendants of Jeffery and John Staple of Weymouth, Massachusetts, circa 1638
Staples, James Courtenay, 1928-
CS71/S793/1978 also Mss A 634
xiii, 431 p.: ill.; 28 cm.
1978
Typescript.

Account book of Robert Cook, 1722-1742
Cook, Robert, 1670-1756.
Mss A 635
Access to original record restricted; Use transcription in Register.
1 v. ([44] p.); 16 cm.
Additional form:
Transcribed version; published as "Account book and family record of Robert Cook of Needham, Massachusetts" in *NEHG Register* 155[2001]:391-396.
Account book of Robert Cook of Needham, Mass. with the following written on the first page: "Robert Cook His Book for Debt and Credit." Page nine has "The Children of Robert and Submit Cook", 1694-1714, and page eleven and twelve has records concerning Robert's son, Eliakim Cook dating from 1734 to 1822. Includes accounts of what Robert Cook's daughters received at marriage.

Marriage records, 1851-1894
Mss A 636
1 v. (20 p.); 19 cm.
Record of marriages performed by D. Bosworth of Hampton, VT from 1851 Feb 18 to 1894 Feb 12. Locations include Hampton, Shrewsbury, Mt Holly, Newton, Bristol, New Haven, E Wallingford, Burlington, Waterbury, Cuttingsville, and Brandon, VT and Whitehall, NY.

Descendants of Levi Weston
Caulfield, Robert N.
Mss A 637
12 p.; 28 cm.
2000
Computer typescript genealogy for three generations.

[John Felt] family register, 1798-1887
Felt, John, 1798-1887.
Mss A 638
1 sheet; col. ill., 25.5 x 36 cm.
Color photocopy of original record. Hand colored lithograph published by T. Baillie (118 Nassau St, NY) completed in ms. for the John Felt family of Jaffrey, NH and Stowe, Mass.

Charles Burgess Hawkins family information
Pope, Elizabeth Harris.
Mss A 639
[54] leaves: port.; 28 cm.
2000
Typescript with information on the Charles Burgess Hawkins family of Cranston, RI, Southborough, Mass., and Mansfield, Conn. Includes photocopies of source material (census and vital records, transcribed gravestone inscriptions, military service records and newspaper articles).

Bristol, Vermont
Spies, Francis F. (Francis Ferdinand), 1871-1934.
Mss A 64
64 p.: 28 cm.
1935.
This work was retyped by Mrs. Franklin E. Scotty in 1935 from the author's work compiled in 1905-1906. This typescript transcription lists the inscriptions from the Bristol Cem. and the Hill Cem., to which other genealogical data is added, possibly from vital records. There are sections of copied birth, marriages and deaths, however it looks as though they are not complete, especially the deaths. It may be that these lists are of events not covered by listings in the two cemeteries. A list of Revolutionary soldiers is given. Includes an index to the cemeteries lists.

Bible record for the Ebenezer Plum Pitcher family, 1815-1922
Pitcher, Ebenezer Plum, 1821-1877.
Mss A 642
[7] leaves; 28 cm.
Photocopy of original record, with title page, concerning the Pitcher family of Mount Holly, Northampton Twp., NJ. The donor's cover letter includes some information on Ebenezer from the 1850 Federal Census and New Jersey Death Records. Donor also notes that Ebenezer's occupation (stone cutter)"obviously led directly into the sculptured calligraphy Pitcher employed in writing the entries in his family Bible".

Sebago families as mentioned in the 1850 census
Taylor, Robert.
Mss A 643
[39] leaves; 28 cm.
Photocopy of a typescript which provides genealogical information on the families listed in the 1850 U.S. census for the town of Sebago, Maine.

Our Waite line in Portsmouth, Rhode Island, and Hatfield, Massachusetts
Ullmann, Helen Schatvet.
Mss A 644
17 leaves; 28 cm.
2000
Computer typescript genealogy in Register style for four generations.

Strong & Parsons
Farnsworth, James D., (James Delap), 1793-1854.
Mss A 645
1 v. (95 p.); 15.5 cm.
1840
Ms. genealogy on the Strong and Parsons families, in particular, the Northampton MA branches. The author's wife, Rebecca Miller Thayer Fogg, daughter of the late Dr. Daniel Fogg, was a lineal descendant of both families.

Samuel Goddard family record, 1705-1867
Hall, G.
Mss A 646
2 sheets; 36 cm. folded to 28 cm.
Color photocopy of original 46 x 36 cm. family record for the Samuel Goddard family of Sutton and Royalston, Massachusetts. Provides the names of his parents, and the parents of his wives, Elizabeth King and Catharine Parker Parks, as well as the birth, marriage and deaths of their children.

Inscriptions from the Stannard Mountain Cemetery, Greensboro Bend
Cutler, Edwin B. (Edwin Burton), 1925-.
Mss A 65
[3] leaves: maps; 28 cm.
1964
Typescript transcription of cemetery inscriptions with a map showing the location of the cemetery and a diagram of the cemetery.

Bible record for the Daniel Columbus Stice family, 1804-1990
Stice, Daniel Columbus, 1851-1916.
Mss A 651
[9] leaves; 28 cm.
Photocopy of original record (with title page but no date of publication) concerning the Stice family of California. Leaves seven and eight are from a family record that have come down through the donor's side of the family. Although the family record was not originally with the Bible record, the donor included a copy since it deals with the same family.

Bible record for the Thomas Vercoe family, 1827-1859
Vercoe, Thomas, b. 1827.
Mss A 652
[3] leaves; 28 cm.
Photocopy of original record with title page concerning the Vercoe family of California.

Bible record for the George Washington Sharrer family, 1828-1921
Sharrer, George Washington, b. 1828.
Mss A 653
[11] leaves: ports.; 28 cm.
Photocopy of original record with title page concerning the Sharrer and Gulick families of Clipper Mills near Brownsville, California. Includes a transcription of the record by the donor and a photo of the Sharrer family.

Bible record for the Orville S. Harmon family, 1838-1901
Mss A 654
[11] p.; 28 cm. + 2 photographs.
Original record with title page concerning the Harmon family of Gloversville and Brooklyn, New York. Includes newspaper clippings (photocopied) and two photographs. The first photograph is of Mrs Anno O Harman [sic Ann O Harmon] holding a child. The second photo is a stereoview of the 1869 Harmon family reunion in Downers Grove, IL.

Durkee / Poor family documents, 1783-1937
Mss A 655
[23] leaves; 28 cm.
Photocopies of an assorted group of records concerning the Durkee and Poor families. The first item (leaves 1-4) is a letter to Capt Benjamin Durkee at New London written by Joseph Burham of Ashford March 15, 1783. The second item is (leaves 5-6) is a "receipt for curing ring-bone on horses" by Solomon Durkee. Leaves 7-12 are four letters from 1853, 1854 and 1856 concerning the Revolutionary War pension claim of Captain Benjamin Durkee. The seventh item (leaves 13-19) is a copy of the John and Electa (Scofield) Poor family record, 1808-1926. John Poor and family lived in Morristown and Stowe, Vermont. Reminiscences of Mary E (Poor) Webster written down on Nov 7 1937 (by the donor?) is the last item (leaves 20-23).

Town of Burlington [Connecticut]
Hart, J. C.
Mss A 656
1 v. (128, [2] p.); 22 cm.
1871
Ms. history of Burlington, Connecticut "as it was 65 or 70 [years] ago & later". The first 94 pages is a survey, following the roads of the town, of the houses with notes on their owners. The survey of houses and owners is followed by a list of some occupations (ministers, deacons, justice of peace, town clerks, lawyers, doctors, military captains, mayors, school teachers) and under each occupation is a list of men from the town who practiced these vocations. The list is accompanied by short biographies of some of the men (pages 95-120). Finally, there is a section with the title "Untimely Deaths in Burlington" (pages 121-124) followed by notes on waggon making, bridges, and meeting houses.

Account book of Isaac Litchfield, 1791-1812
Litchfield, Isaac, 1777-1852.
Mss A 657
1797
Small handmade ms. account book. "Scituate April the 28 1797 Isaac Litchfield his book" is written on the first page (his name is repeated a couple of times followed by "Scituate November the 9 day 1797 Isaac Litchfield"). Pages two through five have measurements of pieces of furniture including a desk, bedstand and table. Pages six to nine are blank. Page ten lists the births of Isaac (the author), Sally (Isaac's wife) and Enoch Litchfield (Isaac's son). The final two pages has some notes on the health of Isaac's son Enoch and the marriage of Isaac's sister-in-law, Elisa[beth] Litchfield, to Bernard Litchfield.

Account book of Joseph Edwards, 1806-1832 (bulk 1806-1811)
Edwards, Joseph.
Mss A 658
1 v. (111 p.); 20 cm.
Entries include purchases (including corn, wood, sundry items, whiskey etc.) and labor performed. There are also several entries concerning the use of his horse, "schooling", and payments for a "subscription". "Ledger C Begun March 1806 By Joseph Edwards in his senior year at college and in the 23d year of his age" is written on the last page.

Manning family of Plainfield, NJ: pioneer settlers of Plainfield and vicinity
Leonard, Oliver B.
Mss A 659
37 leaves; 28 cm.
Typescript genealogy extracted from a scrapbook of newspaper clippings cut from a Plainfield, New Jersey newspaper dated 1886 from internal evidence. These articles were reprinted or perhaps rewritten in 1917 in other New Jersey newspapers. The genealogy is presented in Register format with Leonard's biographical data placed after the name.

Burgin family Bible record, 1805-1877
Mss A 66
[3] leaves: 26 cm.
Original record with N.T. title page. Found in auction lot at Bradford, Vt., in July, 1997, from the Harmon estate of Newbury, Vt.

Bible record for the Asa Waterhouse family, 1784-1877
Waterhouse, Asa, 1784-1849.
Mss A 660
[4] leaves; 28 cm.
Photocopy of original record with title page concerning the Waterhouse family of Detroit, Scarboro, and Parsonfield, Maine.

Bible record for the William Barrett family, 1804-1877
Barrett, William, b. 1822.
Mss A 661
[4] leaves; 28 cm.
Photocopy of original record with title page.

Reunion of the Birkett family at the Birkett house Tyringham, Massachusetts 3 October 1993
Birkett, Georgia Hoyt, 1913-
Mss A 662
[14] p.: ports.; 28 cm.
Typescript Birkett family genealogy with miscellaneous papers. The papers include a list called "Genealogical Societies of the Richard Elmer Birkett Family" and photocopies of newspaper articles and/or pictures concerning the Richard Elmer Birkett family.

Bible record for the Dwight Toogood family, 1839-1950
Marshall, Dora May Toogood, 1872-1950.
Mss A 663
[15] leaves; 28 cm.
Photocopy of original record with title page concerning the Toogood and Marshall families of Minnesota, South Dakota, and Washington. Includes typescript transcription of the record by the donor. Donor states in the transcription that most of the entries were made by Dora May (Toogood) Marshall.

The Floyds from Porter, Maine
Floyd, Leo Asa, Jr., 1934-.
Mss A 664
31 p.: ports.; 28 cm.
1995
Typescript genealogy. Provides the lineal descendants from Michael Floyd, who is recorded living in Parsonfield, Maine at the time of the first U.S. census in 1790, through Henry (2), William (3), Moses (4), Asa Joseph (5) to Leo Asa Sr. and Jr. (6-7).

Bible record for the Daniel Clark family, 1772-1887
Clark, Daniel, 1812-1884.
Mss A 665
[4] leaves; 28 cm. + 1 photograph.
Photocopy of original record lacking title page. Includes a reprint of an ambrotype of Daniel Clark's mother, Selina (Beardsley) Clark.

The King family register
King, Walter.
Mss A 666
61, [3] p.; 28 cm.
Photocopy of a ms. family register "opened 15 February 1845 by Walter King containing miscellaneous information relative to the family of that name from the first ancestor who landed on our shores to the present time forward. This information herein inscribed is derived from a book borrowed by me of Uncle Walter King of Utica, New York which record he commenced in the year 1817." Quote is from the first page. The register was indexed by the donor.

Donovan family
Ogg, Joan Elizabeth Little, 1954-.
Mss A 667
[70] leaves: ill., ports.; 28 cm.
1995
Typescript genealogy for eight generations on the descendants of Dennis Donovan of Ireland and Lowell, Mass.

Bible record for the George Evans family, 1794-1875
Evans, George, 1797-1867.
Mss A 668
[6] leaves; 28 cm.
Photocopy of original record lacking title page.

Guyton
Ford, Nel W.
Mss A 669
[9] leaves; 28 cm.
1965
Typescript on the Joseph Guyton family of Laurens County, S.C.

Chase family Bible record, 1833-1935
Mss A 67
[3] leaves; 18 cm.
Original record with title page. Found in trash at a Warren, N.H. auction.

Chase family Bible record, 1798-1935
Mss A 68
[3] leaves; 21 cm.
Original record with title page. Found in trash at a Warren, N.H. auction.

Beers family history: beginning with Joseph Beers, 1968?
Beers, G. Pitt (George Pitt), 1883-1970.
Mss A 69
[48] leaves: geneal. tables; 21-28 cm.
Typescript and carbon copies from several different versions with no clear indication of which is complete. There are eight letters, 1935-1968, and one genealogical chart. This is a genealogy of the descendants of Joseph Beers (1750-1817).

Some of the descendants of John Adams (1789-1867) and Dorcas (Gerald) Adams (1785-18??) who settled in Canaan, Maine, about 1815-1816
Andrews, Elliott Morrison, 1886-1970.
Mss A 7
[28] p.; 28 cm.

Letter, 1825 Jan. 23, Burlington, Mass. to Thomas Winship, Hartford, Conn.
Winship, Phoebe, b. 1814.
Mss A 70
1 ALS; 30 cm.
Letter from Phoebe Winship, of Burlington, Mass., to brother Thomas Winship, of Hartford, Conn., where she talks about her schooling, family and local news. They are the children of Joel and Phebe Winship.

Inscriptions from gravestones at Chesterfield, Massachusetts
Kent, Mabel Wood.
Mss A 700
[15] leaves; 28 cm.
Typescript transcription.

Journal of Leonard Christopher Rudolf, 1710-1752
Rudolf, Leonard Christopher.
Mss A 701
6 leaves; 28 cm.
Typescript transcription of original journal (transcriber unknown) of Leonard Christopher Rudolf of Illesheim, Germany and Lunenburg, Nova Scotia.

Peter Blinn of Wethersfield
Bonsall, Grace Pratt (Grace Pratt Miller), 1898-1989
Mss A 702
12 leaves; 28 cm.
Typescript genealogy for four generations.

Records of Jonesboro, Maine
Ashe, Margaret Kelley.
Mss A 703
44, 27 leaves; 22 cm.
Carbon copy typescript transcription of original marriage (44 leaves) and birth (27 leaves) records found by the transcriber in the old books in the town clerks home in 1937. "Recopied and alphabetized as a service to those interested in the records of Washington County, Maine".

Pamlico County abstracts: samplings of land transfers, 1767-1872 from records of Beaufort and Craven Counties
Mss A 704
14 leaves; 28 cm.
Photocopy of typescript abstract of original records.

Pamlico County marriage bonds, 1782-1861
Mss A 705
15 leaves; 28 cm.
Photocopy of typescript abstract of original record providing names, date, witness and page.

Partial supplement to William H. Manning's Genealogical and biographical history of the Manning families of New England and descendants
Hagman, Carman Mae Greenstreet, 1928-.
Mss A 706
10 leaves; 28 cm.
Photocopy of a typescript providing genealogical information for an additional three generations of descendants from Clarence Manning Greenstreet, #2612 in William H. Manning's book (CS71/M283/1902) (page 469).

William H. Ritter and family
Mss A 707
1 item: ports.; 14 cm.
1910
Postcard with an image of the William H. Ritter family of Philadelphia on the front. Image includes his wife (Selma Holly Ritter), son (William Ritter) and two daughters (the eldest is mentioned in the genealogy, Theresa Louisa). Verso has "8/29/10 Flett--1517 Boardwalk Atlantic City N.J. a17029 August 29 1910 Wm H. Ritter & family".

A new Langstroth genealogy
Oakley, David R., (David Robert), 1929-.
Mss A 708
[106] p.; 28 cm.
1994
Computer typescript genealogy for fifteen generations created using Family Origins computer software package (Cedar Rapids, IA: Parsons Technology). Based on and including a copy of The Annals of the Langstroth Family by Clifford Barnes Langstroth, M.E., July 1958.

Notes on Rev. John Mayo, the immigrant
Mayo-Lakotas, Jean.
Mss A 709
[35] p.: geneal. tables, maps; 28 cm.
1994
Summary of the research by the compiler on the ancestry of Rev. John Mayo in England (Thorpe-Mandeville, Farthinghoe Parish, and Slapton) and on his life in New England (Barnstable and Boston).

Susan Maria Sparrow Diary, 1857
Sparrow, Susan Maria, 1833-1910.
Mss A 71
26, [3] p.: maps; 28 cm.
1997
Transcribed from original by Jean Mayo-Lakatos, Naugatuck, Conn., who added notes on the family at the end. Ms. Sparrow lived at Orleans, Mass.

Research notes on Susan Allen (Littlefield?Ham) Stevens
Miller, Philip DeHaven.
Mss A 710
ca. 90 p.: geneal. tables, maps; 28 cm. + 7 photographs
Summary of research by author (dated 1981 and 1982) on Susan Allen Stevens of Kennebunkport, Maine and Alameda, California who married Charles Waldon Ham in 1844. Includes investigation of the possibility that Susan first married a Littlefield. Researchers should note that the author put the subject's married names in parenthesis and not her maiden name.

Bible record for the Moses Stevens family, 1764-1861
Stevens, Jessica W.
Mss A 711
[3] leaves; 28 cm.
Transcription of original record including title page concerning the Stevens family of Danville, Vt. Includes annotations by Jessica W. Stevens providing further information on this family from published town histories, vital records, and family genealogies.

The family of Cyrus David Foss
Wood, Helen Foss, b. 1872.
Mss A 712
51 leaves: ports.; 28 cm.
1946
Typescript.

The family of James and Mary Ann Canfield Robertson
Wood, Helen Foss, b. 1872.
Mss A 713
94 leaves; ill., coat of arms; 28 cm.
1945
Typescript.

Ancestry of one branch of the Wilkins family: from Bray Wilkins and Hannah Way, Salem Village, Massachusetts
Wilkins, Dana P., (Dana Parker), 1931-.
Mss A 714
71 leaves; geneal. tables; 28 cm.
1993
Computer typescript genealogy in Register format for thirteen generations. Prior to the ancestral charts for John Wilkins & Harriot Hemenway (leaves 64-65), the author explains (leaf 63) that "Our genealogy centers around John and Harriot, at least from the point of their descendants forming the essence of the Wilkins Family Association." Thus, the typescript provides the lineal descent from Bray (1) Wilkins through Thomas (2), Ithamer (4), Zadock (5), Asaph (6) to John (7) then follows multiple branches.

Bible record for the Otis Leander West family, 1790-1909
West, Otis Leander, 1816-1897.
Mss A 715
[10] leaves; 28 cm.
Photocopy of original record with title page.

Bible record for the Peter P. Armstrong family, 1845-1947
Armstrong, Peter P., b. 1845.
Mss A 716
[6] leaves; 28 cm.
Photocopy of original record lacking title page concerning the Armstrong family of Adams County, Ohio.

Thurber family record, 1671-1869
Mss A 717
[5] leaves; 28 cm.
Photocopy of original record concerning the families of John Thurber who left Great Britain in 1671 and settled in Barrington (RI) and James Thurber, son of John, who came to America in 1672 and settled in Rehoboth, Mass.

Bible record for the Jabez Fitch Jr. family, 1751-1893
Fitch, Jabez, Jr., 1794-1876.
Mss A 718
[5] leaves; 28 cm.
Photocopy of original record with title page concerning the Fitch family of New York.

New Haven, Vermont: vital statistics prior to 1857 (including Haywards elected)
Rodgers, Robert H. (Robert Howard), 1944-.
Mss A 719
60 p.; 28 cm.
1984
Computer typescript transcription.

Genealogical chart of the Clement family of Livingston and Crittenden Counties, Ky.
Clement, Coleman C., fl. 1963-1976.
Mss A 72
1 Geneal. chart 123 x 62 cm.
1976.
[5th] rev. ed.
Blueprint copy of the descendancy and ancestry chart of Isham Clement (1781-1856?) and his wife Sally Rudd (1785-1857), of Virginia. There are two maps showing migratory routes and two charts of statistics.

Bible record for the Isaac Davis family, 1770-1899
Davis, Isaac, b. 1824.
Mss A 720
[1] leaf; 21 cm.
Transcription of original record lacking title page.

Bible record for the William Weir family, 1761-1926
Weir, William, 1788-1827.
Mss A 721
[18] leaves; 28 cm.
Photocopy of original record with title page concerning the Weir family of Boston and Concord, Mass. Includes a copy of a family record.

Bible record for the Squire family, 1806-1936
Mss A 722
3, [9] leaves; 28 cm. + 1 chart (42 cm. folded to 28 cm.)
Photocopy of original record with title page concerning the Squire(s) family of Indiana and Ohio. Donor provided a typescript transcription of the original record and a six generation pedigree chart showing the donor's descent from Isaac Squire (b. 1810).

Bible record for the Burley Batchelder family, 1793-1909
Batchelder, Burley, b. 1793.
Mss A 723
[2] p.; 28 cm.
Photocopy of original record lacking title page.

Bible record for the John R. Young family, 1827-1893
Young, John R., b. 1827.
Mss A 724
[2] p.; 28 cm.
Photocopy of original record lacking title page.

Moody Bible record
Allbright, Noble.
Mss A 725
1 sheet; 28 cm.
[1994?]
Typescript transcription of original Samuel Moody family Bible record with title page information.

Bible record for the Allen Sperry family, 1760-1849
Sperry, Allen, 1761-1843.
Mss A 726
[21] p.; 13-26 cm.
Original Bible record written within the book "The new and complete life of our blessed Lord and Saviour, Jesus Christ...". Entries concern the Sperry family of Connecticut and Camden, N.Y. as well as two obituaries (photocopied for preservation).

Peter Lurvey of Massachusetts, Vermont and New York and some of his descendants
Lurvey, Joan.
Mss A 727
[15] leaves; 28 cm.
2000
Typescript genealogy on Peter(4) Lurvey [Eliezer(3), Peter(1-2)], his children and some of his grandchildren. Supplements "The Peter(2) Lurvey family of Essex County, Massachusetts, Maine, and Vermont" by John Bradley Arthaud and Ernest Hyde Helliwell III in the *NEHG Register* 155:69-90 (note that the Arthaud / Helliwell article begins in *Register* 154:387-409 and ends in 155:167-188).

Bible record for the Gilbert Aspinwall family, 1708-1982
Mss A 728
Access to original Bible restricted; Use this preservation photocopy.
7, [9] leaves; 28-41 (folded to 28) cm.
Photocopy of original Bible record with title page concerning the Aspinwall family of New York. Includes entries concerning the allied families of Van Buren and Kearny and some of the recorded events took place in Zanesville, Ohio. Donor provided a typescript transcription.

Bible record for the Joseph Bartlett family, 1790-1874
Bartlett, Joseph, 1757-1829.
Mss A 729
[5] p.; 27 cm.
Original Bible record with title page concerning the Bartlett family of Warner, NH.

Vestus Parks Bible record, 1805-1934
Parks, Vestus, 1805-1889.
Mss A 73
[4] p.: 28 cm.
Photocopy of original record with title page lacking.

Our Fairchild line in Fairfield County, Conn.
Ullmann, Helen Schatvet.
Mss A 730
13 leaves; 28 cm.
Computer typescript genealogy in Register style for four generations.

Bible record for the Charles Medbury family, 1810-1910
Mss A 731
[6] leaves; 28 cm.
Photocopy of original Bible record without title page concerning Medbury family of New Berlin and Pittsfield, NY.

Longley
Farnsworth, James D., (James Delap), 1793-1854.
Mss A 732
2 v. (60, 33 p.); 16 cm.
1840
Ms. genealogy on the descendants of William Longley of Groton. The author was a great, great grandson.

History of the Imlay family of Monmouth County, New Jersey
Hutchinson, Charles Robbins, 1838-1927
Mss A 733
1 v. (76 leaves); ill.; 27 cm.
1886
Carbon copy typescript genealogy. Includes a letter dated 14 Oct 1931 from Mary Imlay Taylor of Mamaroneck, N.Y. to "Grandfather" accompanied by a photograph of "our ancestral home in Limerick County, Ireland".

Deed, 1729/30 January 2
Manning, Samuel, ca. 1665-1755.
Mss A 736
[2] p.; 31 cm.
Deed by which Sam[ue]l Manning of Windham, Conn. transfers ownership of a parcel of land to his son, John Manning, also of Windham, Conn. The deed was recorded in lib. G folio 80.

Bible record for the John Bissell family, 1761-1913
Mss A 737
[5], [6] p.; 3-28 cm.
Original Bible record with title page (five pages) concerning the Bissell and Chapel families of Litchfield, Conn. Includes fragments of documents (four items, six pages) found in the Bible.

Letter, [15 Sept. 1862], [South Mountain, MD], to "parents"
Brown, C. W., (Charles W.), b. 1840.
Mss A 738
[2] leaves; 28 cm.
Photocopy of a letter written by Charles Brown, a soldier in Company K, 35th Regiment of the Massachusetts Volunteers, to his parents the day after the Battle of South Mountain which took place 14 Sept. 1862. He describes the battle and the wounding of Col. [Edward A.] Wild and the death of [Joseph W.] Cobb.

Bible record for the George Batterson family, 1758-1898
Mss A 739
[8] leaves; 28 cm.
Photocopy of original Bible record with title page concerning the Batterson and Griswold families of Fairfield and Warren, Conn.

Jacob Maby (1796-1861) and some of his descendants
Maby, Ernest Conway, 1919-.
Mss A 74
32 p.: 28 cm.
1993 Jun.
Computer typescript copy with footnotes and appendix.

Gerhart Gottfried (Gerald Godfrey) and Jean (Blackman) Otto family register, 1892-1991
Otto, Julie Helen, 1954-.
Mss A 740
[1] leaf; 28 cm.
2000
Handwritten record of the Blackman and Otto families of New York and California.

Roger and Martha (Freeman) Hovey family record, 1759-1841
Mss A 741
1 v. ([5] p.); 16 cm.
Small handmade ms. book in which the birth, marriage and deaths of the Roger and Martha (Freeman) Hovey family of Hanover (NH) were recorded. Entries also include the towns of Berlin (VT), Mansfield (CT), Manchester (NH), and Norwich (VT).

Lyman Draper's Hoisington papers
Follini, Maida Barton, 1930-.
Mss A 742
96 p.; 28 cm.
Typescript transcription of 136 letters, memos, notes, etc. concerning the Hoisington family from the Lyman Draper collection at the State Historical Society of Wisconsin. These items were sent to or created by Lyman Copeland Draper (1815-1891), Secretary of the State Historical Society of Wisconsin and genealogist, in response to numerous letters of inquiry sent by Draper in the 1860s and 70s to relatives, town clerks, etc.

Bible record for the John Loring family, 1697-1876
Loring, Abigail Thomas, 1773-1853.
Mss A 743
[12] leaves; 28 cm.
Photocopy of original Bible record with title page concerning the Loring, Thomas and Sherman families of Plymouth and Plympton, Mass.

The Ward family: A genealogy and history of the descendants of the George and Rebecca (Newcomb) Ward family of Eastham, MA who removed to Gorham, Maine
Ward, Linton Briggs, 1919-1998.
Mss A 744
105 p.; 28 cm.
1990
Typescript.

Meetinghouse Road Cemetery, Orleans, MA, corner of Meetinghouse Road and Main Street 1812-1892
Snow, Bonnie M.
Mss A 745
[6] leaves; 28 cm.
2000
Computer typescript transcription of tombstone inscriptions.

Rogers Cemetery, Orleans, MA, between Routes 28 and 39
Rogers-Eldredge, Saraetta Crowell.
Mss A 746
[6] leaves: maps; 28 cm.
1935
Typescript transcription of tombstone inscriptions. Includes a photocopy of an newspaper article, "Orleans through the years", in the *The Cape Codder* describing "our burial grounds".

Orleans Center Cemetery (Old Methodist Cemetery), Orleans, MA, corner of Route 6A and Main Street 1818-1989
Snow, Bonnie M.
Mss A 747
[10] leaves; 28 cm.
2000
Computer typescript transcription of tombstone inscriptions.

Orleans Cemetery, Orleans, MA, between Tonset Road and Main Street: gravesites of Orleans' veterans, Revoltionary War, War of 1812, Mexican War, Spanish American War, World War I, World War II, Korean War, Vietnam War
American Legion. Massachusetts. Post no. 308, Orleans.
Mss A 748
[21] leaves: maps; 28 cm.
1990
Photocopy of hand drawn maps indicating the location of gravestones in the nine sections of the Orleans Cemetery. Includes "Veteran graves map" of the whole cemetery (39 x 50 cm. folded to 28 cm.).

Robert Morgan of Beverly, Mass. and his descendants
Bassett, Abbot, b. 1845.
Mss A 749
1 v. (264 p.); 27 cm.
1908?
Nine generation handwritten genealogy tracing the descendants of Robert Morgan to 1907 (one entry has 1908 and another has 1923 but the latter is in a different pen).

Diary of Charles Greenwood Brett for 1864 [and 1865]
Piper, Richard K. (Richard Kenneth), 1931-.
Mss A 75
74, 73 p.: 28 cm.
1991, 1997
Computer typescript transcription from the original diaries loaned to the transcriber. The diarist was part of the 39th Massachusetts Infantry Regiment stationed in Virginia during the Civil War. Annotations by the transcriber are made as footnotes.

Sargent record: taken from compilation of Edwin Everett Sarent of St. Johnsbury, Vt. with additional data concerning the generation of Moses F. Sargent VII (page 136 no.623 by E.E. Sargent), Robert S. Sargent VIII (page 198 no.1082 by E.E. Sargent) and his children of the IX generation
Sargent, Benjamin Felton, b. 1892.
Mss A 750
8, [1] leaves; 28 cm.
1920
Typescript genealogy providing supplemental information to Edwin Everett Sarent's "Sargent record" (1899) concerning the lineal descendants from William (1) Sargent through William (2), Philip (3-5), Robert (6), Moses (7), Robert (8) to Benjamin Felton (9) Sargent.

Cash book of Stephen Crooker, 1815-1824
Crooker, Stephen, ca. 1786-1824.
Mss A 751
[1], 29 leaves; 28 cm.
Typescript transcription of original cash book used by Stephen Crooker, an attorney in Merrimack, NH, to record cash receipts and expenditures. The donor provided some biographical information on Stephen Crocker on the first leaf.

Bible record for the William Jones Hastings family, 1765-1891
Mss A 752
[5] p.; 26 cm.
Original Bible record with title page concerning the William J. and Elizabeth (Rawson) Hastings family.

Brief notices of the family of the Johnsons in Woburn & Burlington: being an appendix to a sermon of Revd Samuel Sewal, preached on the death of Mrs Elizabeth Skelton, who died May 23d 1831 aged 90 yrs
Mss A 753
[15] p.; 21 cm.
Handwritten genealogy providing the lineal descent from Edward (1) Johnson through William (2) to Ebenezer (3) Johnson and Ebenezer's children, including his daughter Elizabeth who married Thomas Skelton.

A record of the birth, marriage and death of the family of Joseph Smith; A record of the birth, marriage and death of the family of Col. Jeremiah Folsom
Mss A 754
1 v. (11 p.); 20 cm.
Handwritten family register, 1694-1803, bound with pins and string into a little book with part of a 1796 newspaper as a cover. As noted in the title, this register records the birth, marriage, and deaths for the Col. Joseph & Sarah (Glidden) Smith and Col. Jeremiah & Mary (Hersey) Folsom families of Newmarket, NH. The register continues with the John and Elizabeth (Smith) Folsom family and then their son John's family.

Record of births for the Henry Stodder family, 1723-1768
Mss A 755
[2] leaves; 28 cm.
Handwritten family record recording the births of Henry and Abigail Stodder along with the births of their children. Includes typescript transcription.

Seaverns family records, 1736-1904
Seaverns, Luther, 1773-1825.
Mss A 756
2 v. ([6], 21 p.); 14-20 cm. + [1] sheet.
1787, 1788
Two small handmade books with records concerning the birth, marriage and deaths of the Samuel and Lucy Seaverns family followed by records for the Luther and Mary (Parker) Seaverns and allied Winchester family. The Seaverns family lived in Weston and Roxbury, Mass. An additional sheet of paper has records for the Joseph Dudley and Sarah Payson (Seaverns) Gould family.

New light on the history of the Sampson family: with special reference to the line of descent through Jane Sampson to her granddaughter Marietta Wood Todd
Todd, Edwin S.
Mss A 757
10 leaves; 29 cm.
1939
Typescript genealogy (photocopy).

The ancestry of Robert Browne Fraser (1899-1963) of Cape Breton, Nova Scotia and Amesbury, Massachusetts
Fraser, Marise Lowell Castelhun, 1928-.
Mss A 758
vii, 107 p.: ill., maps, ports., geneal. tables; 28 cm.
1997
Typescript genealogy.

Correspondence with Frank Ashenden of Soltau, Germany
Brown, Katherine Dickson, b. 1904-.
Mss A 759
[5], iii, 108 p.: geneal. tables; 28 cm.
1991
Photocopy of genealogical correspondence between Katharine Brown of Henniker, NH and Frank Ashenden of Soltau, Germany. Includes a manuscript genealogy on the Ashenden family by Frank Ashenden and E. Batha called "Five hundred years of a family of Kent".

Joseph Glines and his descendants
Glines, William, b. 1806.
Mss A 76
8 p.: 28 cm.
1887 Apr.
Photocopy of original (whose location is unknown) manuscript that measures 24 x 15 cm. concerning the Glines family of Marietta, Ohio.

Dicksoune, Dickson, Dickson, Dixon: the ancestors and descendants of Edward Dixon of Nantucket
Brown, Katherine Dickson, b. 1904-.
Mss A 760
[11, 87] p.: maps, coat of arms, geneal. tables; 28 cm.
2000
Photocopy of genealogical correspondence between Katharine Brown of Henniker NH and Robert E. Dixon of Lancaster KY. Includes a 1987 typescript genealogy on the Dixon family by Robert E. Dixon called "The antecedents and descendants of Edward Dixon of Nantucket".

*Ashenden: the English background of Harry
Burton Ashenden*
Brown, Katherine Dickson, b. 1904-.
Mss A 761
[134] p.: ill., maps, geneal. tables; 28 cm.
1992, 1999
Photocopy of ms. genealogy.

[Ichabod H. Wentworth] family record
Mss A 762
1 sheet: col. ill.; 22 x 29 cm.
Hand drawn and colored record of the births,
marriages and deaths for the Ichabod H. and
Peace (Varney) Wentworth family of Milton,
N.H.

John Gooch family record, 1749-1818
Mss A 763
1 leaf; 20 cm.
Handwritten register of the births and marriages
for the John and Mary (Whidden) Gooch family
of Portsmouth, NH.

*Mug shots of criminals arrested by the Boston
Inspector's office, 1895-1897*
Boston (Mass.). Inspector's Office.
Mss A 764
9 photographs: cartes de visite; 10.5 x 6.5 cm.
Photographs for police "mug book" of criminals.
The verso of each photograph notes the
individual's name, alias, crime, age, birthplace,
trade, marital status, height, build, weight, hair
color, eye color, nose, face, complexion,
detective/officer, date of arrest, and remarks.

Tukesbury family register
Mss A 765
1 v. (20 p.); 15.5 x 9.5 cm.
Small handmade book with hand sown pages and
a cover made from wallpaper. The register
records the birth, marriage and deaths for the
Thomas Tewksbury and Ebenezer and Mary
Farrington families. The register continues with
the Peter and Anna (Farrington) Tukesbury
family.

*Book of records of ages of Francis Felton, his
wives, and children, also their deaths: recorded
in the town of Marblehead books*
Felton, Hannah Turner, 1734-1805.
Mss A 766
1 v. (8 p.); 19 x 15.5 cm.
Handmade book recording the births, marriages
and deaths of the Francis Felton family of
Marblehead, Mass. with his first wife, Mehetabel
(Kimball) Felton, and his second wife, Hannah
(Turner) Felton.

A register of the family of Samuel & Betty Woods
Mss A 767
[1] leaf; 26 cm.
Handwritten register of the births, marriages and
deaths of the Samuel and Betty Woods family of
Lancaster, Mass. and Fairlee, VT. Entries cover
1759-1856.

*Vital records of Plaistow, New Hampshire:
compiled from the town's original record books
1726-1871 and other sources. Earliest and latest
dates recorded 1652-1905*
Hammond, Priscilla.
Mss A 768
1 v. (291 leaves); 28 cm.
1937
Typescript transcription.

The Vermont Lurvey's
Lurvey, Mason Scott, 1958-.
Mss A 769
1 v. ([253] p.): ill., maps, ports., facsim., geneal.
tables; 28 cm.
1993
Typescript genealogy tracing the descendants of
Peter Lurvey for eleven generations. Includes
photocopies of source documents.

Joel L. Pixley Bible record, 1763-1953
Pixley, Joel L., 1817-1890.
Mss A 77
[14] p.: 28 cm.
Second generation photocopy of original Bible
record with title page and transcription by owner.
Also includes photocopies of several clippings
found within Bible.

Bible record for the Henry Gray family, 1757-1843
Mss A 770
[3] p.; 28 cm.
Original Bible record with title page concerning the Henry and Minerva (Loomis) Gray family of Vermont. Page [4] only has birth dates being subtracted from death dates but no names and page [5] is blank.

Edmund Lewis of Stratford, Connecticut, his father Benjamin, of Wallingford and Stratford, and his possible ancestry
Ullmann, Helen Schatvet.
Mss A 771
21 leaves; 28 cm.
2001
Typescript genealogy in Register format.

A short line from Thomas (1) Graves of Hartford, Conn., and Hatfield Mass., with extensive documentation
Ullmann, Helen Schatvet.
Mss A 772
23 leaves; 28 cm.
2001
Typescript genealogy in Register format covering "the families of Thomas (1), his son John (2) and his son John (3) Graves".

Bible record for the Benjamin Medbery Jr. family, 1741-1875
Mss A 773
[7], [3] leaves; 28 cm.
Photocopy of original Bible record with title page for the Benjamin Jr. and Nancy (Davis) Medbery family of New Berlin, NY. Includes computer typescript transcription by the donor.

Journal of Elihu Benton Baxter
Baxter, Elihu Benton, 1787-1874.
Mss A 774
Access to original record restricted: Material fragile; Use preservation photocopy.
48, 12 p.; 19 cm.
Journal of Elihu Benton Baxter regarding his missionary labors for the Congregational Church in Vermont and New York. Describes preaching, revival lectures, seeking converts, attending meetings, etc. The only vital statistic information provided concerns his own children. Pages 1, 2, 49 and 50 are missing. Includes a twelve page computer typescript transcription by the donor.

A family record kept by Elisha Robinson, a son of Seth Robinson
Robinson, Elisha, 1820-1899.
Mss A 775
64, 4 p.; 21 cm.
Handwritten register of birth, marriage and deaths for the families of Micaiah & Sarah (Ballard) Robinson [author's grand-parents]; Seth & Martha (Field) Robinson [author's parents]; the author's children by wives Elisabeth and Asenath Robinson, and the author's grand-children. Includes entries for the allied Field and Mathewson families. The entries date from 1737 to about 1895, with a few entries made by other family members since then (1957 the latest). The entries were recorded on the first 18 pages of a 64 page notebook with colored (blue-green), blue-lined paper. Includes a four page computer typescript transcription by the donor.

The descendants in New England of Joseph Holland, 17th century cloth-worker of London, England
Schwartz, Frederick Earl, 1949-.
Mss A 776
74, [6] leaves; 28 cm.
1988
Computer typescript genealogy for eleven generations. Includes some correspondence (6 leaves) the author sent to the NEHGS Publications Department.

Some male lines from Edmund Grover of Salem and Beverly (Mass.) 1633-2000
Grover, Charles Wyman, 1928-.
Mss A 777
iii, 187 p.: ill., maps, ports.; 28 cm.
2000
4th ed.
Typescript genealogy.

James Harvell of Massachusetts and his descendants
Dow, Paul C., Jr.
Mss A 778
13 leaves: ill.; 28 cm.
2001
Computer typescript genealogy to the sixth generation.

Bible record for the Joseph Birkett Sr. family, 1780-1988
Mss A 779
[8] leaves; 28 cm.
Photocopy of original Bible record with title page concerning the Joseph and Martha (Beers) Birkett Sr. family of Ferrisburgh, Vt.

Ebenezer Berry Bible records, 1835-1936
Berry, Ebenezer, 1835-1890.
Mss A 78
[10] leaves: 18-29 cm.
Original record with title page. Concerns Berry and Sanborn families, and includes original marriage certificate from Jersey City, N.J., in 1855; two school report cards from Bergen City, N.Y., in 1870; and two funeral receipts (1870, 1900).

Bible record for the Joseph Chilson family, 1735-1814
Mss A 780
[7] p.; 28 cm.
Photocopy of original Bible record with title page concerning the Joseph and Elizabeth (Myers) Chilson family of Ferrisburgh, Vt. Includes entries for the Jackson family and a page listing the genealogical societies of the Richard Elmer Birkett family in 1995.

Bible record for the Joseph Birkett Jr. family, 1780-1933
Mss A 781
[4] p.; 28 cm.
Photocopy of original Bible record with title page concerning the Joseph and Louisa Birkett family of Ferrisburgh, Vt.

Bible record for the William Davis Sanders family, 1746-1936
Elliott, Cornelia Sanders, 1852-1933.
Mss A 782
[8] leaves; 35 cm. folded to 27 cm.
Photostat of original Bible record with title page information concerning the William Davis and Cornelia Ruth (Smith) Sanders family of Cleveland, Ohio and Jacksonville, Ill. Includes entries for the related Clark and Elliott families. Record includes a note that most the entries were written by Cornelia Sanders Elliott.

Elijah Partridge (1763-1814) and Prudence Brown (1761-1844) and some of their descendants
Whitehouse, Martha L.
Mss A 783
63, [4] leaves: Ill., ports., facsim., geneal. tables; 28 cm.
2001
Typescript genealogy in Register style for six generations.

Account books of the Cushing family, 1747-1816
Cushing, Hezekiah, 1703-1790.
Mss A 784
5 v. (40, 32, 54, 24, 40 p.); 16-21 cm.
The first record is a small handmade day book for Hezekiah Cushing of Hingham, Mass. The entries are dated between 1745-1750 and primarily concern sawing done by Hezekiah for various customers. The record also contains a few entries by Hezekiah's son Matthew Cushing dating from 1753-1759. The second record is a small handmade day book for Jacob and Isaac Cushing. The entries, which date from 1768-1769, concern heeltapping of shoes, etc.

The Carter T. and Mary (Coberly) Black family of Bates County, Missouri
Arthaud, John Bradley, 1939-.
Mss A 785
iii, 7 leaves; 28 cm.
2001
Computer typescript genealogy.

Account books of William Donnison, 1790-1833
Donnison, William.
Mss A 786 a-b
2 v. (76, 62 p.); 24 cm.
The first account book [Mss A 786 a] concerns "Repairs on real estate in Boston of Wm Donnison consisting of house & shop No 1 Marlborough Street, house & shop No 2 Marlborough Street, house & shop No. 9 Marlborough Street, grocery store on Winter Street & two small houses and land on Grove Street 1790-1833". The second account book [Mss A 786 b] concerns "Rent book from 1796 and repairs of houses and stores". Includes some properties located on Washington Street, all in Boston, Mass.

Indenture, 1708 October 28, between Benjamin Smith of Boston and Michael Dwight of Dedham
Mss A 787
1 ADS; 27 cm.
Original record in which Benjamin Smith became an apprentice of Michael Dwight for six years in consideration of sufficient meals, lodging, apparel etc.

Stock certificates, 1826
Boston and Canton Manufacturing Company.
Mss A 788
1 v. (58 p.); 24 cm.
Contains 15 completed forms recording the purchase of shares by Willard Phillips, Benjamin C. Ward, Sarah Blake, Samuel D. Ward, Samuel Sneling Jr., Thomas A Dexter, George W. Sturgis, William Hill, Holbrook L. Dexter, Jonathan Amory, Aaron Dexter, Benjamin Guild, Samuel Snelling, Anthony Olney, Aaron Hill, Seth Boyden, and 43 blank forms. There are also three loose stock certificates for shares purchased by John G & John Rogers.

Genealogical data connected with the name of George
Hills, Thomas, 1828-1910.
Mss A 789
1 v. (443 p.): photos; 26 cm.
1909
Handwritten collection of genealogical information concerning the George family including John(1) of Boston and some of his descendants [for three generations], Richard(1) of Boston and some of his descendants [for two generations], John(1) of Watertown and some of his descendants [for three generations], John(1) of Charlestown and some of his descendants [for three generations], Nicholas(1) of Dorchester and some of his descendants [for eleven generations] followed by "The partial lines that follow are groups of two or more generations that can not be traced to an English immigrant."

Blair and Dickey Bible records, 1810-1954
Blair, John, 1810-1848.
Mss A 79
[11] leaves: 24-30 cm.
Two original Bible records, one with title page. The larger, newer Bible belonged to Silas M. Dickey (1850-1886), of Nova Scotia, and Lowell, Mass. The smaller one without a title page was inside the first, and probably belonged to John Blair (1810-1848). The latter has a preservation photocopy of the original.

Account book of Joseph Hills, 1627-1679, 1708-1718
Hills, Joseph, 1602-1688.
Hills Family Genealogical and Historical Association
Mss A 790 a-b
2 v. (354, 120 p.); 15-22 cm.
The first volume is the original account book kept by Joseph Hills of Malden, Mass. The entries concern business accounts, contracts, transactions, payments and receipts. The account book was continued in the 18th century by Joseph Hills' son, Samuel, who brought the book with him to Leominster from West Newbury in 1774. The entries by Samuel Hills include calculations and figures for church rates, work, dues, etc. in the spaces unused by his father. The second volume is a handwritten transcription of parts of the original record by the Hills Family Genealogical and Historical Association with an introduction William Smith Hills. The transcription was sent to Thomas Hills of Boston, Mass. in 1895.

Bible record for the Job Coon family, 1751-1855
Lowe, Esta Etta.
Mss A 791
[3] leaves; 28 cm.
Photocopy of a handwritten transcription of the original record, without title page information, concerning the Job and Ama (Colegrove) Coon family of New York (the family later moved to Indiana). The transcription was made in April 1910 by Esta Etta Lowe when the Bible was in the possession of Alva Thompson.

Bible record for the Thomas and Rebecca Powel Schumo family, 1705-1914
Schumo, Rebecca Powel, 1806-1880.
Mss A 792
[7, 4] leaves; 20-28 cm.
Original Bible record with title page concerning the McClean, Charlesworth, Powel, Schumo, Porterfield and allied families of Pennsylvania. Includes typescript transcription by the donor. End sheet has "Rebecca M. Schumo Williamsport Octo 6/49."

Orderly book of Jotham Ames, 1775
Ames, Jotham, 1743-1812.
Mss A 793
1 v. (180 p.); 21 cm.
Record of the orders issued by General Artemas Ward from 1775 August 22 to 1775 December 17 copied by Jotham Ames, a Sergeant in Capt. Daniel Lothrop's (Artillery) Company, Col. John Bailey's Regt. Includes copies of orders from Generals Washington and Sullivan.

Deaths in Leicester, Mass., 1820-1855
Mss A 794
1 v. (59, 34 p.); 21 cm.
Lists date, cause of death, and age of deceased.

Account book of Elias R. Hitchcock, 1845
Hitchcock, Elias R., 1826-1881.
Mss A 795
1 v. (48 p.); 16 cm.
Entries concern lists of students(?) with the headings "Remainder of No.1 Class". Includes lists for the No. 2, No. 4, No. 5, & No. 6 classes as well. The account book was also used as a notebook by Elias Hitchcock's son, Andrew Earl Hitchcock.

Bible record for the Simon Davis family, 1617-1887
Mss A 796
[4] p.; 41 cm. folded to 20 cm.
Original Bible record (with title page) and ancestry of Simon Davis Jr. (1781-1850) of Thompson, Conn. Simon Davis Jr.'s ancestry is provided through a handwritten genealogy tracing the lineal descent from William(1) Davis through John(2), Samuel(3), Daniel(4), Simon(5) to Simon Jr. (6). The record then continues with the issue of Simon Davis Jr.'s daughter and son-in-law, James Nathaniel and Anne Dorinda Brown (Davis) Granger.

Miscellaneous documents concerning the Wyman family
Wyman, Merrill, Jr.
Mss A 797
10 items (44 p.); 25 cm.
First item is a 17 pg hand written family register (1617-1846) for the Wyman and Cutter families with a page on the Hall family. The second item is a 3 page letter, dated 8 Nov 1895, from Merrill Wyman Jr. of Cambridge, Mass. to Geo. A. Gordon, NEHGS Secretary, with information concerning the Francis and John Wyman family. The third item is a 8 pg letter, dated Feb 25 1857, from Thos Wyman Jr of Charlestown, Mass. to Mr. Boutelle concerning the descendants of David and Francis Wyman. Fourth item is 4 pgs of notes on the descendants of William Wyman of Woburn. Fifth item is a page on the Wyman surname.

The Chou's family from China: original inhabitants of the village of ZhouHan, town of JiangShanzhen, county of YinXian, province of ZheJiang (in traditional Chinese)
Chou, Thomas Tsu-teh.
Mss A 798
ii, 42 leaves; 28 cm. + 13 col. photographs.
2001
Computer typescript genealogy.

The Bibler family tree
Mss A 799
31 leaves: port.; 28 cm.
195-?
Typescript (photocopy).

*The Ailman family of Newport, R.I. about 1764-5
to Dec. 1932*
Waterman, Katherine Minerva Utter, b. 1872.
Mss A 8
45 p.; 29 cm.
1934?
There are two indexes, though they only cover
part of the work.

*Grandchildren of John More living at time of the
first family reunion in Sept. 1890*
Mss A 80
[1], 8, [1] p.; 18-28 cm.
Manuscript notes found inside our library book
entitled "History of the More family, and an
account of their reunion in 1890" with dates as
late as 1918.

The Clapp family in Connecticut, 1710-1790
Adams, Douglass Graem, 1950-.
Mss A 800
[19] leaves; 28 cm.
2001
Computer typescript genealogy providing
corrections and supplemental information to
Ebenezer Clapp's "The Clapp Memorial" for
some of the descendants of Capt. Roger(1) Clapp,
Thomas(1) Clapp, and George Gilson(1) Clapp.

Little Compton, Rhode Island Wills
Wilbour, Benjamin Franklin, 1887-1964.
Mss A 801
1 v. (314 leaves); 29 cm.
1945
Typescript transcription of the probate of wills at
Taunton, Mass. where the Little Compton, R.I.
wills are recorded until 1747 and all of the wills
from the Little Compton, R.I. probate from 1747
to 1875.

*Photograph and brief biography of the Rev.
Horatio Alger Sr., with a photograph of his
residence in Marlborough, Mass.*
Mss A 802
1 item: ill., ports., photograph; 28 cm.

*Transcribed documents relating to John Alden of
Boston and John Dunham of Plymouth, Mass.*
Mss A 803
[8, 13] p.; 20-27 cm.
Handwritten transcription of seven original
documents (13 p.). Includes five letters (1905
March 14-October 19, [8] p.) written by Mrs.
Orinda C. Alden, the first to Mr. Lord and the rest
to William Prescott Greenlaw, both of Boston,
Mass., in which Mrs. Alden discusses selling
some autographs.

*Eliab Alden, fourth in descent from John Alden
the Pilgrim, and his descendants, with husbands
and wives*
Alden, Charles Henry, 1836-1906.
Mss A 804
2 v. ([24] leaves); 27 cm.
1904
Two notebooks containing a handwritten
genealogy of the descendants of Eliab(4) Alden
for five generations.

Cookson family
Allen, John K. (John Kermott), b. 1858.
Mss A 805
Correspondence and handwritten notes on the
Cookson family.

York family
Allen, John K. (John Kermott), b. 1858.
Mss A 806
ca. 123 p.; 18-28 cm.
Correspondence and notes on the Abra[ha]m
York family of Maine.

Was John (5) Harris a bigamist?
Arleigh, Sylvia-Lee Harris, 1931-.
Mss A 807
[48] leaves; 28 cm.
2001
Computer typescript genealogy (leaves 1-3) on whether the John(5) Harris who married Abigail Edson in 1787 is the same John Harris who married Lydia Bates at Claremont, NH in 1833. Includes photocopies (leaves 4-48) of some of the documentation for the genealogy including military documents, a marriage record, and Bible records.

Descendants of John Vickery
Cafferky, Michael Edwin, 1950-.
Mss A 809
[12] leaves; 28 cm.
2001
Computer typescript genealogy to the seventh generation.

James Brotherton Bible record, 1801-1921
Mss A 81
[6] leaves; 28 cm.
Photocopy of original records and title page from a Bible.

Bible record for the Joseph Kirby family, 1798-1909
Mss A 810
[12] leaves; 28 cm.
Photocopy (leaves 1-7) of the original record including the title page for the Joseph and Sally (Corbin) Kirby family. Includes entries for the allied Humphrey and Medbury families. A typescript transcript (leaves 8-12) of the original record was provided by the donor.

Bible record for the Curtis family of Connecticut, 1779-1844
Mss A 811
[2] leaves; 28 cm.
Photocopy of original record (without title page) for the Curtis family of Danbury, Bristol, and Cornwall, Connecticut.

Bible record for the Samuel Tenney family, 1815-1965
Mss A 812
[4] leaves; 28 cm.
Photocopy of the original record (without title page) for the Samuel and Elizabeth Tenney family. Includes entries for the allied Adams and Mayers families. A few of the entries note locations such as Boston MA, Paris France, and Columbus Ohio.

Vital records of Waterville, Maine, to the year 1892: births
Lang, Sara Drummond, b. 1863.
Mss A 813
118 leaves; 29 cm.
1949

Vital records of Waterville, Maine, to the year 1892: deaths
Lang, Sara Drummond, b. 1863.
Mss A 814
[130] leaves; 29 cm.
1949

Jean 11 Poitevin dit Laviolette & Rose Otis & Rene, Desrivieres
Potvin, Annette, 1916-.
Mss A 815
68 p.: ill., maps, geneal. tables; 28 cm.
The author notes in the dedication that this typescript genealogy is an English translation of the second chapter of her family history created for those who are not fluent in French.

Choosing cultures: the captivity story of Grizel and Margaret Otis of Dover, New Hampshire
Nash, Alice.
Mss A 816
20 p.; 28 cm.
Typescript.

Bible record for the Joseph Dayton Price family, 1750-1900
Mss A 817
[4] p.; 28 cm.
Original record (without title page) for the family of Joseph Dayton Price and his three wives, Elizabeth W. Furman, Abby W. Crane and Susan Cooper. Record includes entries for the allied Cooper family of New Jersey.

Ashby family notes
Graham, Mary Ashby.
Mss A 818
[41] leaves: photographs; 28 cm.
Typescript information relating to the Ashby
family of Virginia, particularly Thomas Ashby,
his descendants, and the allied family Mauzey.
Includes transcriptions of a will and an indenture.
There are also typed transcriptions of
correspondence between Mary Graham and staff
at Colonial Williamsburg concerning a watch
presented to Captain John Ashby (1707-1797) by
the Virginia House of Burgesses. Ms. Graham
donated this watch to Colonial Williamsburg.
Other transcriptions of correspondence have to do
with Ms. Graham's efforts to erect a tablet in
Christ Church, Winchester, Virginia, in memory
of Captain Ashby.

Arnolds of Braintree
Jackson, Edward Evarts, b. 1868.
Mss A 819
[33] leaves; 26 cm.
Handwritten genealogical record of the
descendants of Joseph and Rebecca Curtis Arnold
of Braintree, Mass., showing up to eight
generations in some lines. "Mss A 15" appears to
be a typescript of this manuscript.

Melvin - Wisner family record, 1758-1894
Mss A 82
[11] leaves: ill.; 28 cm.
Photocopy of computer typescript transcription of
family records for Jonathan Melvin and James
Wisner. They likely include Bible records. Also
includes a photocopy of a photograph of Milan
Morrel Melvin's family circa 1883.

Appleby, Applebee: descendants of James
Appleby of Providence, Rhode Island, who died
there December 21 1716...
Priest, Alice L. (Alice Lucinda), 1866-1954.
Mss A 820
8 v. (180 p.); 27 cm.
1928
Eight handwritten notebooks containing a
genealogy of the family of James and Anne
(Clemence) Appleby of Providence, Rhode
Island; with notes on the Appleby families of
Durham, New Hampshire, and York County,
Maine.

Genealogical records of the Arey and Hammond
families of Massachusetts
Arey, Lisa Treat
Mss A 821
[57] p.: geneal. tables; 20-28 cm.
Typewritten and handwritten notes, pedigree
charts, and correspondence on some descendants
of Richard and Elizabeth (Crouch) Arey of
Martha's Vineyard, Mass. and of Thomas
Hammond of Cambridge, Mass.

Descendants of Robert Amory, b. ca. 1600
Mss A 822
10 leaves; 26 cm.
Typescript.

Abstracts of Allen records from Barre, Mass. vital
records
Cook, Clinton C.
Society of Descendants of Walter Allen.
Mss A 823
[1], 9 leaves; 24-27 cm.
Allen family entries from the vital records of
Barre, Mass.: births (1754-1837) grouped by
family; marriages (1772-1843) arranged
chronologically; deaths (1789-1844) arranged
chronologically. A printed report ([4] p.) on the
annual meeting of the Society of Descendants of
Walter Allen, 1898. A printed report ([2] leaves)
on a meeting of the executive committee of the
Society, 1899.

Allens in the 1850 census for Ellisburg and
Brownville, Jefferson Co., N.Y.
Hills, Frank J.
Mss A 824
[25] file cards; 8 cm.

Genealogy of the early generations of the Coffin family in New England
Macy, Sylvanus J. (Sylvanus Jenkins), b. 1833.
Mss A 825
1 v. ([39] p.); 24 cm.
1870
A printed genealogy showing several generations of descendants from Peter Coffin of Brixton, co. Devon, England, whose widow Joan (Thember) and children immigrated to Salisbury, Mass., in 1642. The Coffin family lived also at Haverhill and Newbury, Mass. This genealogy is reprinted from the *N.E.H.G. Register* 24[1870]:149-154 and 305-315. Brief annotations by William Sumner Appleton appear on the printed pages themselves; his more extensive annotations are handwritten on interleaved pages. Additional printed material on the Coffin family, taken from the *Register* of October 1848, appears in the back of the volume, and includes some data on the English Coffin family.

Ames
Mss A 826 a-b
[331] leaves: geneal. tables; 15 cm.
Handwritten manuscript containing notes on numerous families that apparently were in the unknown compiler's pedigree. Families are ordered alphabetically, and include, among others, Ames, Allen, Benjamin, Brewer, Chapman, Clark, Cleves, Fuller, Fox, Gates, Hamilton, Mitten, Partridge, Power, Rayner, Rowland, Savage, Sherwood, Symonds, Tyng, Weld, Wentworth, Whiting, Wilson, and Woodward. The notes are largely extracts from published works or transcriptions of original documents, and range in length from a sentence or two to a fuller genealogy with descendants to several generations. Sources are named, and are often evaluated.

The Altnows and their descendants: a family history
Altnow, Randall D. (Randall Dayton), 1905-.
Mss A 827
[3], 31 leaves; 29 cm.
1933 typ. ed.
Background information on the Altnow surname and Altnow ancestors in Germany. Genealogy of the first American immigrants, brothers Heinrich Wilhelm Altenau and Ferdinand Ludwig Altenow, and their descendants.

Report on the Adams family
Chamberlain, George Walter, 1859-1942.
Mss A 828
[3] leaves; 28 cm.
Handwritten genealogy and notes on Deacon John Adams of Framingham, Mass., and some of his descendants.

John and Margaret Abrams family record, 1737-1819
Mss A 829
[2] leaves; 27 cm.
Birthdates for the children of John and Margaret Abrams, 1737-1751; the children of William and Anna Abrams, 1770-1790; and the children of unidentified Abrams parents, 1765-1775. This last family is recorded in two versions: an older incomplete fragment and a transcription dated 14 May 1833. The complete Abrams record was perhaps written on this date. Four deaths from 1777 to 1819 are also recorded. The original records, measuring 9 x 19 cm., 11 x 13 cm., and 8.5 x 9.5 cm., have been glued to two larger leaves.

Samuel Tripp Bible record, 1764-1892
Mss A 83
[2] leaves; 28 cm.
Typescript transcript of Bible record found in Grace Church Archives, Newton Corner, Mass.

One branch of the Abell family showing allied families: descendants of Jonathan Abell, who came from Connecticut and settled in Schnectady County, New York
Abell, Horace Avery, b. 1883.
Mss A 830
134, [40] p.: ill.; 28 cm.
1930
Carbon copy typescript tracing some descendants of Robert Abell and wife Joanna of Rehoboth, Mass., in particular, the line of Jonathan Abell who married Lucy Treadway. Handwritten annotations and corrections throughout.

A record of the Aspinwall family of Muddy River (now Brookline, Mass.)
Bowen, Edward Augustus, 1847-1926.
Mss A 831
[2], 80 leaves; 26 cm.
1891
A manuscript genealogy tracing the descendants of Peter and Remember (Palfrey) Aspinwall of Brookline, Mass. Peter was an ancestor of the compiler's maternal grandmother. The compiler notes that the record of Capt. Joseph Aspinwall (the "New York branch") is very imperfect.

Allyn family
Allen, Francis Olcott, 1840-1909.
Mss A 832
1 v. (70 p.); 21 cm.
Transcriptions of marriages and christenings (1545-1630) relating to the Allen family from parish records at Braunton, Devonshire, England. These were obtained in the course of a search for Samuel Allen of Windsor, Conn.

Alden family: Vol. 1 Gen 1, 2, 3, 4, pt. of 5
Mss A 833
1 v. (77 p.); 21 cm.
Handwritten genealogy of John and Priscilla (Mullins) Alden and their descendants for five generations.

Baker families of New England
Chamberlain, George Walter, 1859-1942.
Mss A 834
[17] leaves; 28 cm.
Handwritten notes on 17th- and 18th-century Baker families in Connecticut, Vermont, and Massachusetts. The Baker family of Canterbury, Conn., is prominent.

Baker, Vose, Wyman, and Cleaveland families
Wyman, Theodore C.
Mss A 835
[15] leaves: maps, coat of arms; 29 cm.
Photocopied typescripts showing the direct descent of Lydia May (Baker) Wyman (b. 1864) from Richard Baker (d. 1689) and Robert Vose (d. 1683), and the direct descent of Mary (Cleaveland) Wyman (b. 1842) from Moses Cleaveland (d. 1702). Photocopied typescript of selected Baker, Vose, Wyman, May, and King monuments in Canton Cemetery, Canton, Mass.

Photocopies of Baker, Vose, Wyman, and Cleaveland coats of arms with descriptions. Reproduction of a small map showing the southeast corner of England near the Strait of Dover; a handwritten note on the reverse states that Francis and John Wyman came from West Mill, England, in the late 1630s and settled in Woburn, Mass.

Letter, 1910 March 19, Sturbridge [Mass.], to Emma
Upham, Betsy.
Mss A 836
1 p.; 18 cm.
A one-page original letter in which Mrs. Upham states that her Grandmother Corey was the sister of a woman named Adams. A newspaper obituary for Mrs. Upham accompanies the letter.

Family of Henry Adams who emigrated from England to this country and settled in Braintree, Mass.
Shattuck, Lemuel, 1793-1859.
Mss A 839
1 v. ([12] p.); 29 cm.
Notebook containing a handwritten genealogical record of the descendants of Henry Adams (d. 1646) of Braintree, Mass. Several sheets of additional notes are interleaved. An accompanying letter, from "J.A." of Townsend, Mass., to Lemuel Shattuck of Boston, is dated 25 March 1854; Shattuck is probably the compiler of this manuscript.

Ancestry and descendancy of Charles Morrison (1836-1902): Lighthouse Keeper, Amet Island, Cumberland County, Nova Scotia in memory of his daughters: Eliza, Sara and Elvira
Love, Barbara Manchester, 1933-.
Mss A 84
[1], 40, [4], 17 p.: photographs, maps; 28 cm.
1996
Typescript of descendancy of Charles Morrison (1836-1902), with excerpts from History of the Morison or Morrison Family by Leonard A. Morrison, published in 1880. Included are John W. Morrison (1806-1842) family Bible record and a map of the Remsheg Grant in Malagash, N.S. The last seventeen pages are a reminiscence of life on Amet Island, N.S., written by Sara Bethia Morrison Manchester in 1948.

Copy of genealogical records
Hall, Samuel, Jr., Mrs.
Mss A 840
1 v. (145 p.); 27 cm.
Manuscript genealogy of the descendants of Henry Adams (d. 1646) of Braintree. Includes historical notes and vital records on various families, probably entered about 1879 and updated periodically thereafter. Much of the historical material appears to have been transcribed from other sources. There are also loose sheets of information and newspaper clippings scattered throughout the notebook. Allied families are Hoar of Massachusetts and New Hampshire, and Brooks of Massachusetts.

Children and later descendants of John(4) Alden of Bridgewater son of Isaac(3), son of Joseph(2) who was son of the pilgrim
Alden, Hattie L.
Mss A 841
1 v. (100 p.); 28 cm.
1910?
This manuscript volume appears to be a supplement to a published genealogy (perhaps the "Alden Memorial"?), as it begins with John Alden of the fourth generation and his second wife, Rebekah Nightingale. Their descendants, in New England and elsewhere in the United States, are traced for several generations. Ten loose pages of additional data have been inserted.
Accompanying material includes two manuscript notebooks (indexed) of 13 pages each with further Alden information, and an 8-page typescript recounting the story of Seth Alden's shipwreck in 1840.

Alden genealogy five generations: including the problems relating to these early generations (Aalden, Alden, Aldin, Aldine, Aldon, Allden, Alldin, Aulden, Auldin, Auldine, Olden)
Greenlaw, William Prescott, 1863-1945.
Mss A 842
[137] p.; 28 cm.
Vital statistics and biographical data for John Alden's descendants and their spouses. The information has been entered by hand onto printed genealogical forms; sources are generally given. The forms are in alphabetical order by name of the Alden spouse. This material may be related to "Mss A 12".

A history of Temple, Maine: its rise and decline
Pierce, Richard Donald, 1915-1973.
Mss A 843
ix, 210 . mounted port., mounted facsims., mounted maps.
1946

The Fitch family: a copy of the records
Fitch, Silas Hedding.
Mss A 844
240 leaves; 28 cm.
[197-?

Data on the descendants of Andrew Turnbull of Paisley, Scotland and Tariffville, Connecticut
Greer, Agnes Fulton Philpot.
Mss A 845
12, [7] leaves: ill., ports.; 28 cm.
1976

An index of Albany County records: covering materials within the dates 1630-1930
Gale, Lydia Hammond, 1879-1949.
Mss A 846
137 leaves; 28 cm.
1933

Geographic consequences of the location of some New England town commons and greens
Brodeur, David Dallin, 1932-.
Mss A 847
207 leaves: ill.; 28 cm.
1963
Typescript.

The Johnson family: Solomon the First of Sudbury, Mass., 1639
Kimball, Luella A. (Johnson)
Mss A 848
74 leaves; 29 cm.
1943

The Heards of Ipswich, Massachusetts
Hanson, Edward W. (Edward William), 1951-.
Mss A 849
1 v. (336 leaves); 29 cm.
1975
Photocopy of a typescript genealogy.

Sutton - Dudley, 1380-1649: A (partially) corrected pedigree
Kirk, Marshall K. (Marshall Kenneth), 1957-.
Mss A 85
[5] p.; 28 cm.
[1997]
Typescript partially corrected pedigree of the Sutton-Dudley family beginning with Sir John Sutton, Lord of Dudley, 1380-1406. Includes Dudleys of Atherington / Northumberland, some unplaced but probable Sutton-Dudleys, Dudley daughters, and Dudleys of Yanwath.

James Roberts family record, 1779-1928
Mss A 850
1 v.; 10 x 17 cm. + 6 sheets.
Records (primarily birth dates but also some death dates) concerning the James and Amy (Lamb) Roberts family written in an autograph book. There are also entries for the allied Ellsworth, Gay, and Gould families. Contains hair clippings from Elizabeth Moody and her daughter Elizabeth Folsom Hunt. The autograph book is followed by six sheets originally folded into the book which contain additional records for the families mentioned above.

Letter, 1914 March 3, Malden, Mass. to John P. Roberts, Anson, Me
Roberts, Frank A.
Mss A 851
[12] p.; 17 cm.
Original letter in which Frank Roberts informs his uncle about the health of friends and relatives. However, the bulk of the letter deals with Frank's concern that "Romanism" [Roman Catholism] is "the greatest problem this country has every had aside from the Rebellion and Civil War...The Romish church is doing every thing in their power to strengthen their forces by letting in all the ignorant forces from the old countries". As an example, he describes Polish factory workers who can't read or write and complains that "The Irish Catholics have ruined Boston, morally, socially and politically".

Layn genealogy: Edmund and Jane (Hussey) Layn of Dover, New Hampshire and their descendants in the 18th and 19th centuries
Skinner, Alfred L. (Alfred Loring), 1924-.
Mss A 852
45 p.: ports.; 28 cm.
2001

Extracts from the account book of Thomas Hobbs, Jr. of Berwick, Maine from 1757-1773
Hobbs, Thomas, Jr.
Mss A 853
1 v. (121, 5 p.); 28 cm.
Typescript extract from original record.

Bible record of the Daniel Eddy family, 1768-1847
Mss A 854
[13] p.; 18-28 cm.
Original record (single loose page thus no title page information) concerning the Daniel and Elizabeth Eddy family of Spencer and Jamaica, Vermont. There are also two documents which provide some provenance information, three photocopies from the Bible that the loose Eddy record was kept in, and the letter from the donor with a summary of the provenance information and original record.

Bible record of the Thomas C. Hale family, 1739-1906
Mss A 855
[10, 5] p.; 28 cm. + 2 photographs.
Original record for the Thomas C. and Ellen (Murray) Hale family of Nashville, Greenfield, and Saratoga Springs, NY. Includes typescript transcription of the original record by the donor and two unidentified photographs.

Extracts from various authors concerning the science of heraldry
Child, Isaac, 1792-1885.
Mss A 856
193 p.: col. ill., coat of arms; 24 cm.
1810-1840
Handwritten extracts and drawings from Francis Nichols' *The Irish Compendium...* (London: 1745); *The Baronetage of England...* (London: 1720); M.A. Porny's *The Elements of Heraldry* (London: 1795); explanation of the device for the arms of the Commonwealth of Massachusetts; "coats of arms of many of the distinguished families of New England copied from sketches and partly finished 'coats' done while colonies of England by John Gore, brother of the Christopher Gore, Governor of Massachusetts;" and some 1865 Heraldic Journal articles.

Linn County, Iowa cemetery records, with a few pages of miscellaneous records, as noted
Cronbaugh, Lois W.
Mss A 857
95 leaves; 30 cm.
1960
Typescript transcription.

Linn County cemetery records, 16 cemeteries
Daughters of the American Revolution. Iowa.
Mss A 858
198 p.: ill.; 29 cm.
1959
Typescript transcription.

Notes on the genealogy of the Averys of Washington County, Maine
Avery, Myron Haliburton, fl. 1923-1925.
Mss A 859
1 v. ([63] leaves)
Notes on the Avery family of Nova Scotia; Dedham, Mass.; and Washington Co., Maine (Machias, Lubec). Includes abstracts from early English records, with an emphasis on heraldry. See also Mss A 44, an expanded and revised second edition of this work.

Letters, 1929, 1953
Johnson, Charles D.
Mss A 86
[11] leaves; 27-28 cm.

Letters to Mrs. C. Fred Thornburg: A letter from Charles D. Johnson gives the descendancy of William Stacy (1733-1804) who married Sarah Day in 1750; and a letter from Arthur W. Jordan which gives the descendancy of Nymphas Stacy (1764-1837).

Atkins
Greenlaw, William Prescott, 1863-1945.
Mss A 860
[105] p.; 28 cm.
1928
Vital statistics and biographical data relating to the Atkins family of Cape Cod, beginning with Henry Atkins. Descendants bearing the surname Atkins are traced. Information is entered by hand onto printed genealogical forms ("Ashburton Forms.

Biographical sketches of Theodore Atkinson, Sr. and Jr.
Mss A 861
[1] sheet; 47 x 59 cm. folded to 24 x 15 cm.
Brief handwritten sketches of the lives of Theodore Atkinson of Boston, Mass., and New Castle, N.H., and his son Theodore, President of the Council of New Hampshire. The second sketch is incomplete.

The ancestry descendants and collateral kindred of James Trecothick Austin with biographical sketches etc. prepared from authentic family papers etc.
Austin, Ivers James, 1808-1889.
Mss A 862
1 v. ([21] leaves, 102 p.): geneal. tables; 26 cm
A handwritten biographical sketch of James Trecothick Austin, Harvard College Class of 1802, prepared in 1871 in response to a request by John Langdon Sibley. Provides extensive information on Austin's ancestry, which includes the Austin, Barbour, Ivers, Sprague, Trecothick, and Waldo families. Austin's wife, Catherine, was the daughter of Elbridge Gerry, a signer of the Declaration of Independence and fifth Vice President of the United States; some information is given on her ancestry. The sketch concludes with details on James Trecothick Austin's descendants and various collateral relations.

Atwell (or Attwill)
Mss A 863
[4] p.; 25 cm.
Handwritten genealogy of John Atwell of Casco Bay, Maine, and Lynn, Mass., showing his descendants in one line for six generations.

John Ayer of Haverhill
Mss A 864
1 v. ([22] leaves); 20 cm.
Handwritten genealogical record of John Ayer of Salisbury and Haverhill, Mass., and his descendants.

Buckley family
Bartlett, J. Gardner (Joseph Gardner), 1872-1927.
Mss A 865
[19] leaves: geneal. tables; 29 cm.
Typescript transcription of a letter from J. Gardner Bartlett to the Rev. George Winthrop Sargent, Wellesley, Mass., concerning the identity of a portrait purported to be of the Hon. Peter Bulkeley. Notes on various Buckley family members. Charts of the Buckley and Oliver families.

Family of Ayer
Porter, George S.
Mss A 866
4 leaves; 27 cm.
[1920?
Typescript genealogy of John Ayer of Newbury, Salisbury, and Haverhill, Mass., and his descendants.

Material relating to the Bosworth family
Bosworth, George Frederick, b. 1859.
Mss A 867
22 p.: ill.; 17-28 cm.
Correspondence between George F. Bosworth and Mary Bosworth Clarke, compiler of a Bosworth family genealogy. Incomplete copy of the Bosworth Bulletin, no. 23.

Burrage and Mills Bible record.
Martin, George Castor, b. 1885.
Mss A 868
[2] leaves; 29 cm.
Typescript of an original record concerning the Burrage and Mills families of Pennsylvania, 1782-1879.

Burdick family photograph
Mss A 869
1 photograph; 22 x 28 cm.
[188?-1900
Photograph (reproduction) of seven Burdick sisters: Margaret, Louise, Elizabeth, Seraphine, Jane C., Mary L., and Ann. A typescript note on the back gives the years of their births and deaths.

Richard Smith of Bristol, Rhode Island: being a genealogy of the descendants of Richard Smith of Bristol, Rhode Island
Smith, Benjamin Francis, 1841-1926.
Mss A 87
[2], i, 79 p.; 28 cm.
[1997]
Computer typescript transcription of a genealogy of the descendants of Richard Smith (1643-1696) written originally by Benjamin Francis Smith and this copy by Claire Benson.

Burrill lineage: John Burrill. John Burrill 1658-1731. John Burrill 1694-1756. John Burrill 1719-. John Burrill 1752-1842. Jacob Burrill 1818-1891. John Henry Burrill 1842-1906
Burrill, Paul C. (Paul Colburn), b. 1881.
Mss A 870
[24] p.; 23 cm.
1919
Mimeographed typescript genealogy of John Burrill of Weymouth, Mass., and his descendants.

Genealogy: Backus-Alden
Stevens, Isaac.
Mss A 871
1 v. ([34] p.); 17 cm.
Handwritten genealogy of the Samuel and Elizabeth (Tracy) Backus family of Connecticut and the allied Alden family. The genealogy is an 1897 copy by Mary Colony Adams from a book written by and belonging to her grandfather, Isaac Stevens. Includes a 13 leaf typescript transcription.

The Ballard family
Thruston, R. C. Ballard (Rogers Clark Ballard), 1858
Mss A 872
[21] leaves; 27 cm.
ca. 1898
Typescript genealogy of the Ballard family of Virginia and Kentucky, and allied Piety and Cox families.

Bible record for the Jacob Bacon family, 1810-1866
Bacon, Jacob, 1788-1865.
Mss A 873
[3] p.; 23-28 cm.
Original Bible record of the family of Jacob Bacon of Plymouth, Mass., son of David Bacon, and wife Nancy Withington of Dorchester, daughter of Lemuel Withington. Family names include Bacon, Baker, Carpenter, Jones, Warren, and Withington. Included with this record are two letters dated 1803 April 23 and April 30.

Bible record for the Joseph Allen Sterling family, 1822-1927
Mss A 874
[4] p.; 19 cm.
Original record (without title page) for the Joseph Allen and Henrietta (Dowling) Sterling family.

Bible record for the James Sterling family, 1761-1829
Mss A 875
[4] p.; 26 cm.
Original record (without title page) for the James and Sarah (Tomlin) Sterling family.

Bible record for the Joseph Henry Sterling family, 1854-1905
Mss A 876
[4] p.; 23 cm.
Original record (without title page) for the Joseph Henry and Blanche (Groesbeck) Sterling family of New York City.

Baldwin family: heads of families in 1850 U.S. census
Baldwin, Aubrey Haines, Jr.
Mss A 877
1 v. (214 leaves); 29 cm.
1974
Typescript.

Marriages and deaths January 2, 1847 - December 25, 1847 copied from Springfield Republican
Hayes, Daniel W. Mrs.
Clark, William C., Mrs.
Daughters of the American Revolution. Mercy Warren Chapter (Springfield, Mass.)
Mss A 878
1 v. (214 leaves); 28 cm.
1960
Typescript transcription.

Some early records of the town of Springfield, Maine in Penobscot County
Jones, Priscilla Alden Fortier.
Springfield (Me.)
Mss A 879
1 v.; 29 cm.
1967
Typescript transcription of original records including history of Springfield and of the Bingham Penobscot purchase; marriages 1834-1890; intentions published 1834-1891 of marriages not recorded; a short sketch of Company D Eleventh regiment Maine Infantry Volunteers, War of the Rebellion with enlistments from Springfield; names and births of the inhabitants residing in the town at the time of its organization 27 March 1834 and births after; early settlers and their families with genealogies, etc.

Ainsworth family Bible record, 1811-1909
Mss A 88
[2] leaves; 28 cm.
Typescript of Bible record copied at a Bradford, Vt., auction sale in March of 1997.

Record of deaths 1749-1850 in Middleborough, Raynham, Bridgewater, Taunton and Norwich kept by Rev. Isaac Backus and in Titicut kept by Joseph A. Backus
Backus, Isaac, 1724-1806.
Mss A 880
163 p.; 27 cm.
Handwritten transcription of original records by George S. Stewart and Mary E. Stickney. Includes discussion of unusual deaths, accidents and earthquakes.

Records of ancestry of Deacon Edmund Rice
Smith, May Hart.
Mss A 881
1 v. (ca. 90 leaves); 28 cm.
1930
Typescript genealogy tracing the ancestors of Edmund Rice back to Adam.

Seth Thomas, Yankee clockmaker
Wiley, Keith Brahe, 1912-1955.
Mss A 882
1 v. (50, [14] leaves); 29 cm.
Typescript.

Miscellaneous genealogical notes on the Bacon family
Davis, Marion Morse.
Mss A 883
20 p.; 24 cm.
Miscellaneous typescript and manuscript notes on the Bacon family in England and America.

Geneology [sic] of the Barker family: extract from an address written for the Pembroke Female Reading Society
Barker, Hannah.
Mss A 884
[37] leaves; 21 cm.
Small notebook with an 1835 address by Hannah Barker that was transcribed by an unknown individual. The address concerns Francis Barker of Massachusetts, his descendants, and the Garrison House of 1628 at Pembroke, Mass.

The John and Anne (Broome) Routledge family of England, Ohio, Missouri, and Kansas 1813-1978
Arthaud, John Bradley, 1939-.
Mss A 885
[4] leaves; 28 cm.
2001
Computer typescript genealogy in Register format.

Pedigree of Marcia Godfrey Boudreau
Boudreau, Marcia Godfrey, b. 1906.
Mss A 886
[24] leaves: coat of arms, geneal. tables; 28-36 cm.
Typescript pedigree. Typescript material concerning the Whitney family.

Bible record for the Charles Sefrit family, 1823-1933
Mss A 887
16 p.: Col. ill., photo; 4-28 cm.
Original record (without title page) for the Charles and Elizabeth (Everett) Sefrit family followed by a hand drawn and colored family record (contains much of the same info as is in Bible record). Entries include notices concerning the allied Martindale, Cropp and Robinson families. There are also photocopies of newspaper obituaries for Rebecca May (Cropp) Martindale, William Alexander Cropp and Mary Stewart Lochrie as well as a clipping concerning the wedding of Marrietta Cropp to J.H. Robinson.

Inscriptions Horsemeadow cemetery, Haverhill, N.H.
Pickwick, Harold Curtis, b. 1897.
Mss A 888
1 v. (118 p.); 28 cm.
1954
Carbon copy typescript transcription.

Hodgdon, Maine -- cemetery records
Skofield, Perley F.
Mss A 889
1 v. (34 p.); 28 cm.
1962
Typescript transcription.

Hannah Cushman?: Which Hannah Cushman? A study of the Lineage, History and Descendants of Hannah Cushman and her husband Lawton Barker
Wadhams, Charles H. (Charles Hastings), 1926-.
Mss A 89
8, [36] p.: geneal. tables; 28 cm.
1994
Typescript of the search for the identity of Hannah Cushman (1773-1857) who married in 1794 to Lawton Barker (1772-1860), with a computer generated ahnentafel chart of Hannah's corrected ancestry including the Cushman and Barker families. Also included are a decendancy chart for Hannah and Lawton Barker to six generations and a photocopy of the Bible record for Samuel Penfield Goodsell (1791-1872).

North Swansea cemetery records: a copy of names and dates to 1900
Carter, Marion Williams Pearce, b. 1867.
Mss A 890
1 v. (36 p.); 28 cm.
Typescript transcription.

Monuments of the Allens of Vermont: including the "mystery" of Ira Allen's grave
Carter, Joseph C.
Mss A 891
1 v. (ca. 200 p.): ill., maps, geneal. tables, photographs; 29 cm.
1974
Annotated typescript in which the author seeks (according to the introduction) to "record and comment upon the creation and placement of the epitaphed memorials of the illustrious family of Allens...show how historians...have narrated the details of the deaths, burials and monuments of Generals Ethan Allen and Ira Allen" and "present, in a year-by-year chronology, a compact documentary account of some details of the personal activities of the Allens, through nearly two centuries, narrated against the backdrop of township, state, national, and world history."

Genealogical sketch of the Barber family
Barber, Lucius I. (Lucius Israel), 1806-1889.
Mss A 892
18 leaves; 28 cm.
Carbon copy typescript genealogy of Thomas Barber of Windsor, Conn., and his descendants. Material on the early generations, taken from Lucius I. Barber's "Sketch," is occasionally annotated by Lucius George Fisher. Fisher has then carried the genealogy several generations further in his own line.

History of the Metropolitan District Police, Commonwealth of Massachusetts: 1894-1954
Hendrickson, Charles H.
Mss A 893
1 v.: ill., ports., photographs; 25 cm.
1959
Typescript. Includes a photograph of the author.

General notes on residents of Waldoborough, Maine
Bolton, Charles Knowles, Mrs.
Mss A 894
1 v. (ca. 170 p.); 25 cm.
Miscellaneous handwritten notes.

Town meetings 1817-1850: Brooksville, Hancock County, Maine. The town of Brooksville was incorporated June 13 1817, from parts of Castine, Penobscott and Sedgwick. Part of Penobscott was set off to Castine
Bush, Anne Rainsford French.
Brooksville (Me.)
Mss A 895
321, 11 leaves; 29 cm.
1949
Typescript transcription.

Greenfield, Mass., Gazette and Courier July 9, 1844-November 3, 1879: Marriages
Stetson, Oscar Frank, 1875-1948.
Mss A 896
1 v. (166 leaves); 29 cm.
Typescript transcription.

Ancestry of the Searsport and Monroe Putnams and related families
Putnam, Robert Conrad, 1914-.
Mss A 897
1 v. (90 leaves): geneal. tables, fasicm.; 29 cm.
Bound photocopy of a typescript genealogy with copies of source documents, letters, pedigree charts, family group sheets, etc. concerning the Putnam and allied Mitchell and Pattee families.

Dover-Foxcroft cemeteries: Dover section
Mss A 898
1 v. (100 leaves); 28 cm.
1939?
Typescript transcription of epitaphs in the Old Dover Village, Brown, Lander & Bassett, Poole, East Dover, South Dover, Pine Grove and McAllister cemeteries.

Dover-Foxcroft cemeteries: Foxcroft section
Mss A 898
1 v. (80 leaves); 28 cm.
1939?
Typescript transcription of epitaphs in the following cemeteries: Rural Grove, Gray, Southeast Burying Ground, North Cant, Hazeltine and Jefferds.

Russell genealogy
Mss A 899
3 v.; 29 cm.
Typescript genealogy (with annotations) on the Russell family beginning with William Russell, who came to Salem, Essex County, Mass., in 1673. Vol 1 covers 1st-5th generations, vol. 2 the 6th and 7th generations, and Vol 3 covers the 8th-10th generations.

Lineage of John Albee (7) of Wiscassett, Maine, and his descendants to 1951
Spear, Maud E. (Maud Elsie Harris), 1890-1974.
Mss A 9
5, 8 p.; 28 cm.
[1951]
Second section entitled "The following is a complete record of all the descendants of Edward Alonzo Albee and Ellen Lorinda Danforth to February 1951."

The Descendants of Robert Hale: in Ellery, N.Y.
Mower, Lyman, 1927-.
Mss A 90
40 p.; 28 cm.
1997.
Genealogy in two parts, the first a transcription of a 1932 narrative by Claude Parker, and the second a re-formatted rendition of the same material with some additional data, by Lyman Mower, in 1997, which is called an appendix.

Our Adams line, through Henry(1) Adams of Braintree, Massachusetts
Ullmann, Helen Schatvet.
Mss A 900
57 p.; 28 cm.
1998
Typescript genealogy in Register format that follows the line from Henry[1] Adams through John[2-4], Joseph[5], John[6], Asa Sibley[7], Adin Townsend[8] to Lilla Lucretia[9] Adams.

The Roes: material sent to Miss A. Jessie Roe, Milton, N.Y. by her cousin A. J. Roe, 173 Broadway, N.Y.
Roe, A. J.
Mss A 901
1 v. (23 leaves); 28 cm.
1883?
Typescript.

Genealogical data on families of Steuben, Millbridge, Cherryfield, and Harrington in Washington County, Maine
Colton, Margeret Kelley Ashe, b. 1896.
Mss A 902
1 v. (ca. 250 p.); 26 cm.
1930-1955
Handwritten transcription of original records.

Descendants of Thomas Blanchard of Charlestown, Mass.
Bucknam, Wilton Francis, 1861-1917.
Mss A 903
2 v. (100, [4], 62 p.); 21 cm.
Manuscript geneabgy of Thomas Blanchard of Charlestown, Mass., who died in 1654, and his descendants.

Vital records of Maine(?) families
Haskell, Jessica J.
Mss A 904
[78] p.; 15 cm.
Small memorandum notebook in which are
entered extracted vital records of Maine(?)
families. No discernable genealogical
organization. No sources. Surnames include:
Ballard, Barton, Blaisdell, Blish, Brackett, Bragg,
Brown, Burgess, Capen, Childs, Clark, Colby,
Collins, Crosby, Cross, Doe, Fairfield, Faught,
Fletcher, Gazlin, Getchell, Jackson, Johnson,
Kelly, Longley (Langley), Lovejoy, Marchant
(Marchand), Moody, Packard, Pullen, Redington,
Robinson, Seavard, Smiley, Snow, Stedman
(Steadman), Storer, Stuart, Taber (Tabor), Taylor,
Thurston, Warren, Webber, and Wing.

Blake family
Mss A 905
[4] p.; 26 cm.
Manuscript genealogy showing descendants in
one line from Jasper and Deborah (Dalton) Blake
of Hampton, N.H.

*Mayflower descent of Lucinda (Clapp) Bosworth
and her descendants*
Bosworth, George F. (George Frederick), b. 1859.
Mss A 906
72 leaves; 30 cm.
1953
Manuscript genealogy tracing the descent of
Lucinda (Clapp) Bosworth from John Alden.
Includes the Alden, Bass, Adams, Wild,
Wetherell, Clapp, Lincoln, and Field families.
Also traces descendants of George and Lucinda
(Clapp) Bosworth of Petersham, Mass.

*A family record containing the ancestry of Elisha
Brigham and Sukey Thayer with notes on the
Anthony Fisher and William Cary families
together with notes bearing on the ancestry of the
above in the Morse, Peirce, Fay, Barron,
Shattuck, Avery and other families...*
Fisher, Philip A.]
Mss A 907
1 v. ([132] p.): geneal. tables; 21 cm.
1893
Manuscript genealogy of Elisha Brigham and
wife Sukey Thayer Brigham. Includes the allied
families of Avery, Barron, Cary, Eager, Fay,

Fisher, Lane, Morse, Peirce, Rice, Shattuck, and
Warren, all of which had Massachusetts origins.

*Memorial to Samuel Warren Barrington, William
Barrington: their descendants, allied families,
and other Barringtons*
Verrill, A. H., Mrs.
Mss A 908
176, [15] leaves; 22 cm.
1948
Family group sheets for Barrington and allied
families, with an alphabetical index for the
Barrington surname only. Also a 15-leaf
supplemental index, unalphabetized, for all
surnames.

*Thomas Barber (or Barbour) and some of [his]
descendents [sic] especially [the] line of Thos of
Rehoboth Mass. and Townshend Vt.*
Stoughton, Lewis H., b. 1867.
Mss A 909
1 v. (103 p.); 21 cm.
1935
Manuscript genealogy of Thomas and Mary
(Munt) Barber of Boston, Mass., and their
descendants, in particular Thomas and Hannah
(Millard) Barber of Rehoboth and Warwick,
Mass., and Townshend, Vt.

Tupper family photographs, 1853-ca. 1940
Mss A 91
1 v. (7 b&w photographs) + 1 card (10 x 15 cm.)
Photographs (annotated on reverse) of John Robb
Tupper family, with index card citing pages in
Tupper Genealogy (CS/71/T93/1972) where
subjects of photos and their ancestors can be
found.

*Bible record for the Flora Jane Beardsley
Sanford family, 1819-1850*
Mss A 910
[1] leaf; 17 cm.
Original record (without title page) for the A. and
Flora Jane (Beardsly) Sanford family.

Decendants [sic] of James Barrett of England, one of the first settlers in Charlestown
Barrett, Artemas.
Mss A 911
1 v. ([86] p.); 21 cm.
1865
Genealogy of the James Barrett family of Massachusetts, including descendants with surnames other than Barrett. The back portion of the notebook contains summaries of real estate transactions that may have to do with family members.

Descendants of Abraham Parker of Woburn and Chelmsford, Massachusetts, and ancestors of Benjamin Franklin Parker
Lee, Charlotte E., 1925-.
Mss A 912
[16] leaves; 28 cm.
1965
Carbon copy typescript genealogy.

Preliminary compilation data: Burnham genealogy
Burnham, D. E. (D. Edmund)
Mss A 913
178 p.; 19 cm.
1940
Carbon copy typescript of data gathered in 1939-40, with additions in September 1942 and August 1943. This material is a compilation of occurrences of the surname Burnham, as found in hundreds of sources in Canada, the United States, and the British Isles. The sources span several centuries. When an occurrence is not cited verbatim either partially or in its entirety, an abstract is supplied.

Supplement to Borden genealogy; lineage and descendants of James Barker of Rhode Island
Moriarty, George Andrews, 1883-1968.
Mss A 914
[19] leaves; 28 cm.
Typescript supplement to George Andrews Moriarty, "The Bordens of Headcorn, Co. Kent," in the *N.E.H.G. Register* 84[1930]:70-84 and 225-229. Typescript notes on the Borden family of Portsmouth, R.I., and on the lineage and descendants of James Barker, Deputy Governor of Rhode Island.

Record of Mathew [sic] M Atherton and his decendents [sic] in the Merrill line
Mss A 915
1 v.; 21 cm.
Handwritten genealogy of some descendants of Matthew Atherton of Bolton, Mass., and Royalton, Vt., who married as his second wife Jemima Pelton. Their daughter, Phoebe Atherton, married Robert Merrill of Landaff, N.H. Also included are handwritten transcriptions of family records from two Bibles: the C. R. Merrill Bible and the Henry M. Merrill Bible.

Petition of the inhabitants on the Kennebec River for protection
Mss A 916
[2], 12 leaves; 25 cm.
Manuscript transcription of a petition for protection dated 22 April 1775 from inhabitants on the Kennebec River, now in the State of Maine. A transcription of the petition was published in the *N.E.H.G. Register* 44[1890]:202-208.

Descendants of Thomas Blanchard of Braintree
[Blanchard, Darwin Currier, b. 1839]
Mss A 917
4 sheets: geneal. tables; 46 cm., folded to 23 x 20 cm.
Miscellaneous genealogical material. Photostat of a typescript entitled "Genealogy of Mr. David Blanchard and his children," by Darwin C., and Rufus G. Blanchard, tracing descendants in one line from Thomas Blanchard of Braintree, d. 1654. Photostat of a letter concerning the Blanchard family, dated 7 January 1882 and written by Darwin Currier Blanchard to an unidentified cousin (possibly Rufus G. Blanchard). A photostat of the letter's reverse side shows a manuscript genealogical chart again tracing descendants in one line from Thomas Blanchard of Braintree. A one-page original typescript by Raymond White Blanchard and Pauline (Ayres) Blanchard adds information to the chart of 1882.

Descendants of Capt. Joseph Horton of Rye, New York, son of Barnabas Horton of Southold, N.Y.
Bristol, Theresa Hall.
Mss A 919
3 v.; 29 cm.

Typescript genealogy.
Milliken family Bible record, 1773-1921
Mss A 92
[5] leaves; 28 cm.
Photocopy of original records and title page from a Bible, found in auction lot at Charlestown, N.H., in 1997.

Derbyshire - genealogy: Bancroft family
Drury, Gertrude Martha Gilbert, b. 1886.
Mss A 920
1 v. (17 leaves); 29 cm.
1953
Typescript genealogy on the ancestry of Thomas Bancroft of Dedham and Reading.

A scrapbook of memories
Legg, Caroline E (Caroline Ella), b. 1887.
Mss A 922
1 v. (85 leaves): photographs; 29 cm.
1960
Typescript autobiography with tipped in photographs.

Travel tales: on and off "O. B."
Legg, Caroline E (Caroline Ella), b. 1887.
Mss A 923
1 v. (155, 2, 17, [4] leaves): photographs; 29 cm.
1961
Typescript autobiography focusing on the author's travels (1918-1949) -- personal and on "official business" for the U.S. Department of Labor, Children's Bureau. Includes tipped in photographs.

Bible record for the William and Abigail (Bradford) Barrett family, 1758-1803
Mss A 924
[6] p.; 26 cm.
Original Bible record with title page for the William and Abigail (Bradford) Barrett family of Boston, Mass. Includes families of John Spooner and Rebecca (Swier) Barrett, Benjamin and Rebecca (Swier) Barrett Burrows.

James Stuart Holmes: a biography and family history
Wallis, Gertrude Stuart Steel-Brooke, 1889-.
Mss A 925
iii, 295 leaves; 29 cm.
1965

Typescript biography.
Bartlett and Raitt family photographs
Bartlett, Ralph Sylvester, b. 1868.
Mss A 927
17 items: photographs; 5 x 8 cm.-23 x 17 cm.
Fourteen black-and-white photographs (thirteen reproductions, one original) of various members of the Nathan Bartlett and John Raitt families of Eliot, Maine. Also three black-and-white photographs (reproductions) of the Sylvester Bartlett home in Eliot, Maine. There is a typescript inventory, and each photograph is numbered and identified on its reverse.

Ancestry of Laura Herbert Bailey of Brookline, Mass.
Bailey, Laura Herbert.
Mss A 928
1 v. (300 p.): ill., coat of arms, ports.; 26 cm.
1929
Manuscript notes on New England ancestors of Laura Herbert Bailey. Surnames include: Alcock, Bagley, Bailey, Baker, Barnes, Barstow, Brewster, Brown, Bulkley, Clap, Colby, Cotton, Cowen, Cushing, Dennis, Dennison, Emerson, Fogg, Giddings, Gill, Hanscom, Harraden, Harvey, Hasty, Hatch, Hawke, Hawkrit, Hewes, Hobart, Hoyt, Hubbard, King, Langer, Lawrence, Libby, Lincoln, Litchfield, Otis, Perkins, Randall, Rogers, Rositer, Sargent, Shaw, Stockbridge, Turner, Ward, Warner, Wells, White, York.

Dr. Walter Baily and my earlier articles
Horton-Smith, Lionel Graham Horton.
Mss A 929
62 leaves; 28 cm.
1948
Typescript, extensively corrected and annotated by hand, concerning the genealogy of Dr. Walter Bailey, physician to Queen Elizabeth I.

Genealogy of the early Irish kings
Verrill, Ruth (Lida Ruth Shaw), b. 1900.
Mss A 93
[1], 13, 27 p.: geneal. tables; 28 cm.
Manuscript genealogical charts extracted from typescript copy of The History of Ireland by Abbe' Mac-Goeghegan (included), and explanatory letter.

Familia Bardi nobile di Firenzi venuta a Genova l'anno 1350.
Mss A 930
[1] item: ill., coat of arms, geneal. tables; 105 x 71 cm., folded to 28 x 20 cm.
Hand-drawn and colored tabular pedigree of the Bardi family of Genoa tracing the family from 1350 through the eighteenth century. Includes watercolor coat of arms.

The Pennell family in Brunswick, Maine
Phinney, Clara Pennell.
Mss A 931
2 v. (259 leaves); 29 cm.
Typescript (photocopy) genealogy.

Phineas Taylor Barnum: his decent [sic] from Rev. Peter Bulkeley
Bulkeley, R. E. (Roger Edward), b. 1916.
Mss A 932
[6] p.: ports.; 22 cm.
1957
Manuscript notes on the ancestry of Phineas Taylor Barnum ("P. T. Barnum") of Connecticut. Woodcuts of P. T. Barnum; his wife Charity; his mother Irena; and Phineas Taylor. Also pedigree charts for Roger Bulkeley, Peter Bulkeley, and Phineas Taylor Barnum.

Barnard ancestors of Alexander James Harper, Jr.
Mss A 933
[104] leaves; 28 cm.
Carbon copy typescript tracing the ancestry of Alexander James Harper, Jr. Surnames include: Adams, Barnard, Battles, Bent, Bowers, Brigham, Bush, Chadwick, Draper, Frary, French, Garfield, Goddard, Harrington, Harvey, Howe, Hunt, Laughton, Lee, Low, Milford, Mixer, Morse, Osgood, Paul, Phillips, Pierce, Puffer, Stewart, Stone, Trowbridge, and Wood. Descendants are traced for some families.

Bright family of England and allied families
Mss A 934
1 v. (83 p.): geneal. tables; 28 cm.
Manuscript genealogical records of the Bright family of England and allied families Cage, Dawtrey, Luther, Osborne, Salter, and Tirrell or Tyrrell. Records include pedigrees, transcriptions of wills, records of college admissions, and numerous extracts from English parish registers.

Genealogy of George Barbour who came from England to America in 1635 and settled in Medfield, Mass.
Barber, George W. (George Warren), 1835-1886.
Mss A 935
1 v. ([276] leaves): photographs; 26 cm.
1886?
Manuscript genealogy of George Barbour of Medfield, Mass., and his descendants. Includes an autobiography of the author, and a first-person account of his experience in the battle of Fredericksburg, Virginia, in December 1862, during which he was wounded and had an arm amputated.

Ancestors and descendants of Moses Peirce
Leatherbee, Ethel Brigham, b. 1878.
Mss A 936
1 v. (222 leaves): ill., ports., geneal. tables, photographs; 29 cm.
1937
Typescript genealogy. Peirce ancestral families include: Bartlett, Benjamin, Bullard, Dana, Eaton, Ferguson, Gates, Hagar, King, Livermore, Norcross, Nye, Oldham, Rice, Robinson, Spring, Stubbs, Traine, and Wheeler.

Ancestors and descendants of Elijah Sparhawk Brigham, son of Elijah Brigham and Sophia Houghton, & Moses Peirce, son of Abel Peirce and Susanna Spring
Leatherbee, Ethel Brigham, b. 1878.
Mss A 937
1 v. (8, [72] leaves): geneal. tables; 29 cm.
1916
Typescript genealogies with numerous corrections and additions. Brigham ancestral families include: Allen, Houghton, How, Hurd, Jackson, Johnson, Moore, Rice, Taylor, Trowbridge, Ward, Wheelock, and Willis. Peirce ancestral families include: Bartlett, Bemis, Benjamin, Brooks, Bullard, Cassel, Clary, Dana, Dix, Ferguson, Fuller, Gates, Hagar, Hase, Johnson, King, Livermore, Norcross, Oldman, Perry, Rice, Sherman, Spring, Stratton, Stubbs, Traine, Vassall, Wheeler, and White.

Bartlett
Mss A 938
1 v. ([82] p.); 17 cm.
Notebook of manuscript extracts concerning the Bartlett family from unidentified church records to about 1850. Location may be Newbury, Mass., or New Hampshire. Also family registers for Caleb and Dorothy (Sargeant) Moody; Josiah and Sally (Moody) Bartlett; and Josiah Moody Bartlett and Mary Stetson (Bowers) Bartlett.

Bible record for the William Robins family, 1821-1875
Mss A 939
[3] p.; 27 cm. + 2 photographs.
Original record with title page information concerning the William and Ann Robins family. Includes a photograph of Miss Carrie Robins of Kingston NY and a second photo of an unidentified male.

Lewis family Bible record, 1768-1853
Mss A 94
[3] leaves; 27 cm.
Original record with title page.

Bible record for the James Allen family, 1755-1848
Mss A 940
[3] leaves; 28 cm.
Original record with title page information concerning the James and Betty Allen family.

Goldsmith genealogy: descendants of Richard Goldsmith of Wenham, Mass.
Radasch, Arthur Hitchcock, b. 1898.
Mss A 941
1 v ([118] leaves); 29 cm.
1959
Typescript genealogy with annotations.

Genealogical records of the Barker family of Rhode Island, including allied families of Shaw, Holmes, and Paine
Paine, Hannah Sherman, b. 1836.
Mss A 942
[16] p.; 21-28 cm.
Typescript genealogy of the family of Joshua and Hannah (Shaw) Barker of Newport, R.I., whose descendants married into the Holmes family of Nantucket, Mass., and the Paine family of

Plymouth, Mass. Material includes a manuscript record of the family of John Sampson and Deborah (Holmes) Paine, and a letter written by Hannah Sherman Paine, the first ordained female Baptist minister in America.

Genealogical data on the Barrows family
Greenlaw, William Prescott, 1863-1945.
Mss A 943
[480] p.; 28 cm.
1922
Vital statistics and biographical data relating to the Barrows family. Descendants bearing the surname Barrows are traced. Information is entered by hand onto printed genealogical forms ("Ashburton forms"), and the forms are arranged alphabetically.

Edward Howard Brigham, M.D., and his paternal ancestry
Leatherbee, Ethel Brigham, b. 1878.
Mss A 944
1 v. (115, [9] leaves): ill., ports., geneal. tables, photographs; 29 cm.
1932
Typescript genealogy compiled by Dr. Brigham's daughter, Ethel. Ancestral families include: Farrar, Gates, Hill, Houghton, Jackson, Linton, Maynard, Moore, Rice, Stodder, Taylor, Trowbridge, Water, Whale, Wheelock, Whitcomb, Willis. Material in this volume includes photographs and silhouettes from the early 1860s through 1917; letters written from Maryland and Virginia as a prisoner during the early years of the Civil War; war discharge papers; certificates of appointment as a hospital steward; and Masonic lodge certificates.

The ancestors and descendants of David Bishop
Leasure, Virginia Miller.
Mss A 945
1 v. (58 leaves): ill., coat of arms; 29 cm.
1969
Typescript (photocopy) genealogy.

Random notes on the Toothaker family
Smith, Ellen A.
Mss A 946
1 v. (52 leaves); 27 cm.
Handwritten transcription of original records at Maine Historical Society, town of North Yarmouth, Town of Harpswell, Cumberland County Registry of Deeds, Town of Bruswick as well as notes from some published histories and vital records. Records include an account book, gravestone inscriptions, town records, church records, a will, deeds and a Bible record.

Typescript of account books kept by William Ross [at] Sterling, Massachusetts between 1775-1815
Ross, William, b. 1749.
Sterling (Mass.) Bicentennial Committee.
Mss A 947
1 v. (vii, 85 leaves); 29 cm.
1975
Typescript transcription of original record. William Ross was a farmer who hired out oxen, horses and farm equipment and who was frequently hired for digging graves.

Genealogies of Barrett families
Mss A 948
[26] p.; 21-25 cm.
Genealogies of Barrett families, including William Barrett, born 1630; and John Barrett of Chelmsford, Mass. Miscellaneous notes on the Barrett family of Littleton, Mass.

Barnes, King and related families of Chenango County, New York
Barnes, Raymond Curtis, b. 1899.
Mss A 949
[68] leaves; 29 cm.
c1962
Mimeographed typescript genealogy of Raymond C. Barnes, whose ancestry includes the Barnes, Cook, Dakin, Fenner, King, Phillips, Reed, Roberts, Sage, Sanders, Thompson, Wade, Warren, and White families.

Burroughs family Bible record, 1748-1843
Mss A 95
[2] leaves; 28 cm.
Photocopy and typescript transcription of original Bible record. Title page lacking.

Ancestry of Arthur Thomas Bond in America
Bond, Arthur Thomas, 1852-1936.
Mss A 950
[79] leaves: ports., photographs; 28 cm.
1932
Typescript genealogy of the Bond family of Maine and Massachusetts, descendants of Nicholas Bond who died in 1703. Also some information on Bonds in England.

The Borden family of Nova Scotia: extracted from the Borden genealogy published July 1899 by Hattie Borden Weld...
Kimber, Sidney A. (Sidney Arthur), b. 1866.
Mss A 951
[44] leaves: maps; 25 cm.
1917
Manuscript genealogy of the descendants of Richard Borden of Rhode Island, in particular the line of Perry Borden who settled in Kings County, Nova Scotia, in 1760.

Booth genealogical fragments
Booth, John T.
Mss A 952
[71] leaves; 22-28 cm.
1877
Manuscript genealogy of the descendants of Richard Booth of Stratford, Conn.

Records of Bassett family association
Bassett Family Association of America.
Mss A 953
1 v. ([36] p.); 27 cm.
Manuscript and typescript records of the first and second annual meetings of the Bassett family association, held at Boston, Mass., in 1897 and 1899. List of association members.

Ancestral charts for Waldo F. Bates
Bates, Waldo F. (Waldo Francis), b. 1889.
Mss A 954
[11] charts: ill., ports., geneal. tables; 21-26 cm
19--
Photostats of fan charts for the grandparents of Waldo Francis Bates: Daniel Johnson Bates, Mary Barnes Bearce, Alfred Clapp, and Abigail Brooks Merritt. Also pedigree charts for the Franklin and Lincoln families, showing Bates's relationship to Benjamin Franklin and Abraham Lincoln.

Beebe genealogical data
Whelan, Marion E.
Mss A 955
[128] leaves; 28 cm.
1951
Typescript data on Beebe families of Vermont,
Connecticut, New York, and Michigan.

William Bassett of Lynn, Mass., son of Roger
Bassett of Docking, England...
Bassett, Abbot, b. 1845.
Mss A 958
361 p.; 27 cm.
1922
Manuscript genealogy of William Bassett of
Lynn, Mass., and his descendants. Includes
branches at Boston, Chelsea, Lynn, and
Marblehead, Mass.; New Hampshire; New Jersey;
and Rhode Island, as well as unplaced Bassetts
and allied families.

Notes of the Bassett family descended from
William Bassett...
Bassett, Abbot, b. 1845.
Mss A 959
330 p.: coat of arms; 27 cm.
1922
Manuscript genealogy of William Bassett of
Plymouth, Mass., and his descendants.

Rideout family Bible record, 1795-1852
Mss A 96
[1] leaf; 28 cm.
Photocopy of original records from a Bible,
annotated, lacking title page.

Marriage and death records 1820-1828 (copied
from newspapers): Hancock Gazette [of] Belfast,
Maine, published every Thursday by Fellowes &
Simpson July 6, 1820-Decmber 7, 1821. Hancock
Gazette & Penobscot Patriot [of] Belfast, Maine,
published every Thursday by Fellowes & Simpson
December 14, 1820-May 10, 1821 and on
Wednesdays, starting May 21, 1821-June 21,
1826. Belfast Gazette [of] Belfast, Maine,
published Wednesday by, E. Fellowes June 28,
1826-1828
Jones, Priscilla Alden Fortier.
Mss A 960
1 v. (53, 74 p.); 29 cm.
Typescript transcription.

Baptisms, marriages and burials of Leonard
Stanley, Gloucestershire, England 1570-1876
Genealogical Society of Utah.
Mss A 961
146 leaves; 29 cm.
1945
Typescript transcription.

Manning Manse tavern book 1753-1797
Manning, William.
Mss A 962
1 v. (36 p.); 29 cm.
1925
Typescript transcription of original record.

Genealogy of Daniel C. Brown
Brown, Daniel C., b. 1814.
Mss A 963
[44] p.: photographs; 28 cm.
1867
Manuscript account of the ancestry of Daniel C.
Brown. Includes the descendants of George
Brown of Salisbury, Mass.; Hugh Gunnison of
Kittery, Me.; Samuel Colcord of Kingston, N.H.;
and David Clifford of Brentwood, N.H. Also
several notes and items of correspondence from
the 1860s, 1870s, and undated. Four of the
unidentified photographs are probably of Brown
himself. The photograph of an unidentified
woman is perhaps his wife. Includes two earlier
versions of this manuscript: "Genealogy of my
family as full and correct as I am able to make it
with my present information" [dated at Boston, 5
August 1856] and "Genealogy of Daniel C.
Brown" [dated at Boston, 1864]

Lineages for the ancestors of Ruth Minerva Potter
Potter, Ruth Minerva, b. 1894.
Mss A 964
1 v. (ca. 80 p.); 29 cm.
1932
Lineage record for the *Compendium of American*
Genealogy for Ruth Minerva Potter followed by
typescript genealogy providing lineages of her
ancestors back to the immigrant.

Boehme: Boehme, Behme, Beam, Beem, Bream, Ream, Roam, Roan, Been, Bean, Baum, Peame, Doehne, Deem
Russell, J. L.
Mss A 965
[30] leaves: ill., maps; 28 cm.
Typescript and manuscript material concerning the Boehme family of Pennsylvania. Includes transcriptions of or extracts from various legal documents such as deeds, releases, letters of administration, and wills. Also several letters.

A thousand ancestors
Bouwens, L. H.
Mss A 966
1 v. ([54, 44], 129 p.): ill., geneal. tables; 22 cm.
1935
Published ancestry of the Bouwens and de Grey families. Genealogical tables comprise the first half of the volume; the second half contains extensive notes on ancestral families, arranged alphabetically by surname.

Partial supplement to Harry Alexander Davis's The Junkins family, descendants of Robert Junkins of York County, Maine
Benton, Marion A., b. 1890.
Mss A 967
[6] leaves; 19 cm.
1950
Manuscript letter in which the writer corrects and adds to information on the Junkins, Ford, and Benton families of Maine.

Beach, 1643: line of descent from Richard Beach, b. 1615 prob. England
Mss A 968
1 v.; 22 cm.
Miscellaneous manuscript genealogical data on Beach families, including John and Richard Beach of New Haven, Conn.

Boardman
Mss A 969
1 v.; 18 cm.
Manuscript genealogy of Boardman familes, in particular Samuel Boardman of Ipswich, Mass., and Connecticut and his descendants. Also in the same volume, a manuscript genealogy of the descendants of Thomas Tyler of Budleigh, Devonshire, England, and Boston, Mass.

Diary of Alexander Warren, 1818-1827
Warren, Alexander, 1789-1878.
Mss A 97
[28] leaves, bound; 10 cm.
Diary of Alexander Warren of Kennebunk, Maine spanning years 1818-1827 (entries from 1818-1824 retrospective). Entries only for Sundays, predominantly scripture citations, but also notices of deaths and marriages.

Diary of cornet Noah Chapin of Somers, Conn., April 18, 1775 to July 17, 1775, while in the army at Roxbury
Chapin, Noah, d. 1790.
Mss A 970
14 leaves; 21 cm.
Manuscript transcription by Mary W. Davis of a diary her grandfather kept during the Revolutionary War. The brief entries record troop movements; skirmishes and enemy fire; daily activities and duties of an enlisted man; punishments meted out for offences such as stealing, swearing, or firing without orders; and occasionally the names of men injured or killed. Some genealogical data is also appended.

Diary of John Bliss, 1799-1804
Bliss, John, 1775-1804.
Mss A 971
1 v. ([176] p.): ill.; 24 cm.
Diary of John Bliss of Brimfield, Mass., kept from 1799 to 1804, recording his activities as a farmer until he was killed in a plow accident. Includes pencil sketches of unidentified buildings. Later entries are a short Bliss genealogy, and a 65-page family reminiscence written in 1882 by Bliss descendant A. F. Bridgman.

Marriages of Tring, Hertfordshire, England 1566-1837
Genealogical Society of Utah.
Mss A 972
228 leaves; 29 cm.
1945
Typescript transcription.

Bible record for the Bowditch and Gerould families, 1729-1884
Mss A 973
Access to original record restricted: Material fragile; use preservation photocopy.
[4] p.; 26 cm.
Original record (without title page) concerning the Bowditch and Gerould families.

Parish register of Spondon, Derbyshire, England: Volume 1 1653-1741, Volume 2 1726-1812
Genealogical Society of Utah.
Mss A 974
259 leaves; 29 cm.
1945
Typescript transcription.

Descendants of Richard Browne and wife Edith Holt of Boston, 1634
Clark, Carolyn B. H.
Mss A 975
10 p.; 27 cm.
1962
Manuscript genealogy and notes.

Letter concerning the Browne family of England and Virginia
Bryan, J. R.
Mss A 976
[5] leaves; 21 cm.
1873
Manuscript transcription of information concerning the English background of the Browne family, as found on the reverse of a portrait of Sir Anthony Browne. Genealogical notes on the Browne family of Massachusetts and Virginia.

Marriages of Plymstock, Devonshire, England 1591-1812
Genealogical Society of Utah.
Mss A 977
166 leaves; 29 cm.
1945
Typescript transcription.

Brown genealogy
Mss A 978
[5] p.; 21 cm.
Manuscript genealogy of the descendants of Daniel Brown and wife Ruth Morrill of Kingston, N.H., and Brunswick, Me., including Sarah Brown who married Benjamin Abbot.

The Lovett family: a temporary arrangement of the first five generations of the Lovett family of Beverly, Mass.
Brooks, Lucille E.
Mss A 979
13 leaves; 28 cm.
1944
Typescript carbon-copy genealogy of the descendants of John Lovett and wife Mary of Salem and Beverly, Mass.

Hebb family Bibles
Plassmann, Elizabeth Hebb, 1928-.
Mss A 98
[20] leaves; 28 cm.
1996 July
Typescript of the descendancy of Elijah Hebb (1858-1940). Included is a photocopy from Elijah Hebb's Bible, 1879-1979, imprinted at Philadelphia or New York in 1897. Also included are two pages photocopied from Elijah Hebb's Bible, 1880-1889, imprinted at London, no date.

Forty five immigrant ancestors of Lucille Eastman Brooks through her maternal grandfather Eliphalet Eastman Kinsman of Heath, Holliston, and Natick: including the lines of Putnam, Morse, Battle, Snow, Perkins, Draper, Frary, Fisher, Roberts, Hendricks, Harriman, Swan, Day, Acie, etc.
Brooks, Lucille E.
Mss A 980
[45] leaves; 28 cm.
Carbon copy typescript tracing ancestral lines of Lucille E. Brooks.

Bowen family epitaphs
Hawes, Harriet J.
Mss A 982
[3], 11 leaves; 25 cm.
1914
Manuscript transcription of Bowen family
epitaphs in Rumford, R.I., once a part of
Rehoboth, Mass.

Bradford family
Bray, Susan M., b. 1860.
Mss A 985
1 v.; 27 cm.
1904
Manuscript genealogical notes on some
descendants of Governor William Bradford.

Genealogies of the Bradstreet and Fuller families
Bradstreet, J. Fuller.
Mss A 986
[45] leaves, 7 items: photographs; 28 cm.
1931
Typescript genealogy of the descendants of Sir
John Bradstreet of Ipswich, Mass., and wives
Judith Hale and Abigail Glidden. Includes allied
families Foye, Fuller, Hutchins, Jacques, Knight,
Lowell, Plumer, and Swett. Also a photostat of
the family record of Eben Hale Bradstreet.

*Bible record for the John Bolton family, 1762-
1890*
Mss A 987
[8] p.; 6-29 cm.
Original Bible record (with title page information)
for the John and Tryphine (Strange) Bolton
family of Freetown, Mass. Includes entries for the
allied Mixter family.

Bradford records
Mss A 988
[20] p.; 25 cm. + 2 ports. (24 cm.)
Manuscript genealogy of some descendants of
Gov. William Bradford. Also 2 portraits of
Deacon Lewis Bradford, cut from a published
volume.

Bradford genealogy
Mss A 989
1 v.; 20 cm.
Manuscript genealogy of some descendants of
Gov. William Bradford.

*Photographs concerning Lawrence Brainerd, ca.
1900-1925*
Mss A 99
[4] photographs; 29 cm.
Photograph of Lawrence Brainerd (1874-1925)
and three photographs of his apartment at 3
Concord Avenue, Cambridge, Mass.

*The history of the Brainerd family from the first
man of the name ever known in New England,
collected from every accessible mean [sic] of
information, chiefly in the year of our Lord 1785*
Brainerd, Elijah, 1757-1828.
Mss A 990
1 v. ([42] p.); 18 cm.
Manuscript genealogy of some descendants of
Elijah Brainerd of Connecticut.

*The descendants of William Bolton of Reading,
Mass.*
Bolton, Charles Knowles, 1867-1950.
Mss A 992
1 v.: ports.; 24 cm.
1888
Printed genealogy of the descendants of William
Bolton of Reading, Mass., with manuscript
annotations and additions. Bound with manuscript
material on the Bolton family in England and
New England, including mounted portraits of
Charles Edward Bolton, Franklin E. Bolton, and
William Bolton.

*Bible record for the Henry Carlton family, 1794-
1905*
Mss A 993
[5] p.; 28 cm.
Photocopy of the original record (with title page
information) concerning the Henry and Elizabeth
(Fogg) Carlton family of Maine and New York
City.

The Salter saga
Salter, Leonard M.
Mss A 994
8 leaves: ports.; 28 cm.
Computer typescript.

The Margeson family in the colonial period: a chronological account
Whitson, Norris Margeson.
Mss A 995
30 leaves: ill.; 28 cm.
2001
Computer typescript.

Old hundreds: first census of Mississippi valley
Waldenmaier, Inez Raney.
Mss A 996
[15] leaves; 28 cm.
Carbon copy typescript compilation of information from several published sources concerning genealogical notes on families living in "Green Bay (now Wisconsin) District" circa 1785, "Americans living at Spanish Port of Natchez 1788-1790", "Galvez (now Galvestown-Galveston) roster of first militia Co. of Galvez, 27 June 1779" and "census 26 Sept 1774 of slave owners in Natchitoches".

Brereton genealogical data
Watson, A. J.
Mss A 997
[1], 5 leaves: geneal. tables; 26 cm.
[1932?]
Manuscript transcription of English data on the Brereton family, extracted from Davy's Suffolk Collections, Vol. XLIV, Additional Ms. 19120, folios 112 and 112v.

Genealogical notes
Swaim, E. D.
Mss A 998
1 v. ([28] p.); 20 cm.
Manuscript genealogical notes concerning Thomas Bunce of Hartford, Conn., and his descendants, and the Skinner family of Woodstock, Conn. Also a manuscript transcription of a Bible record, 1778-1899, concerning two families: Samuel and Elizabeth (Ross) Budd, and Thomas and Mary (Budd) Swaim.

The descendants of William Busby of Brington Parish, Old Weston, Huntingtonshire, England: with related families of Goodman, Symons, Meadows, Taylor, Woodward, and Stringer
Busby, Gladys J.
Mss A 999
20 leaves; 28 cm.
1944
Carbon copy typescript concerning the Busby family and allied families, all of which have English origins.

Settlers of Martha's Vineyard
Banks, Charles Edward, 1854-1931.
Mss A B32
25 v.
1922
Mounted records and clippings on families of Martha's Vineyard.

Census of Martha's Vineyard
Banks, Charles Edward, 1854-1931.
Mss A B32.1
2 v.; 28 cm.
1915-1922
Holograph abstract of decennial census of Martha's Vineyard 1790-1850. Some typescript leaves added. Vol. 1 includes 1790-1840 and vol. 2 includes 1850.

Account book of Eliphelet Bartlett, 1799-1852
Mss A B35
4 v.

Claude Barlow collection
Barlow, Claude Willis, 1907-1976.
Mss A B37
Correspondence with clients, records, and much of Barlow's genealogical work on Massachsuetts and Connecticut families: Box 1: Barlow, Archer & Ashburton. Box 1a: Warner, Whitney, Whitcomb, Whipple, Williams. Box 2: Bartlett, Belchertown, Beswick, Biographical Records of Tolland & Windham Co., Blair & Blake. Box 3: Blood, Bowman, Boylston CT, Buell, Carmen, Chamberlain, Chapman & Chedel. Box 4: Civil War letter, Clark, Coney CT Cemeteries, CT Soc. of Genealogists, Cook, Crystal Lake Cemetery, Dimmock, Divoll, Dresser & Durante. Box 5: Eastford CT church, Fox-Legg, Gardner, Gates & Grover. Box 6: Hampden Co. MA, Hartman, Hope Cemetery, Horton, Humes, Jennings & Neff. Box 7: Jepherson, Jones, Lawrence, Messenger, Moffit, Monson burial grounds, Moose Meadow Cemetery, Mosely, Clark, Peck, Neff & Newell. Box 8: Nicholls, Piper, Pratt & Prouty. Box 9: Sawyer, Scripture & Snow. Box 10: Sprague, Stacy, Sterling, Swansea MA vital records. Box 11: Utley, Walter, Weller & Weston-Adams. Box 12: Wyllys, Woodstock CT, Worcester Co. Probate & Miscellaneous #1-9. Box 13: Miscellaneous #10-29. Box 14-16: Miscellaneous.

Letterbooks (1771-1773), account books (1729-1782) and cash book (1815-1825) of Henry Bromfield
Mss A B38
24 v.

William Bollan papers, 1749-1757
Bollan, William, 1710-1782.
Mss A B62
19 folders (100 items)
Letters, petitions and memorials sent by Bollan to the British government on behalf of the colonists concerning the sugar trade, colonial boundaries, the Louisburg Expedition, and British military forces in America.

Boutelle genealogical collection
Boutelle, John Alonzo, 1811-1880.
Mss A B67
19 v.; 21-33 cm.
Unpublished finding aid in the library.
Genealogical records and notes on various New England families: Abbott, Adams, Aldrick, Alvord, Bacheller, Bacon, Bailey, Bancroft, Beard, Belcher, Belknap, Bentley, Blake, Blanchard, Bond, Boutelle, Bouton, Bowman, Bowtwell, Brigham, Bright, Brooks, Brown, Bruce, Bryant, Bucke, Buffington, Burke, Burnham, Burt, Chace, Chase, Cheny, Choate, Church, Clark, Cleaves, Coburn, Cole, Colson, Cooper, Cragin, Cummings, Curtis, Cushing, Cutter, Daland, Damon, Day, Dodge, Dow, Dupee, Earle, Eaton, Estes, Favor, Fay, Felton, Fenwick, Field, Flanders, Foster, Fowle, Fox, French, Frothingham, Fuller, Gage, Gleason, Goldthwait, Gould, Gove, Hall, Hamlen, Hart, Haynes, Hill, Hix, Holden, Holt, Hopkins, Hovey, Huntington, Hutchinson, Jacques, Jarvis, Jenks, Johnson, Jones, Kelly, Kendall, Kimball, Lane, Lewis, Livermore, Locke, Loomis, Lund, MacIntire, Manning, March, Marston, Morse, Nason, Newhall, Nicholas, Nick, Osgood, Packer, Parker, Parks, Patch, Potter, Prescott, Priest, Reed, Reeves, Rhodes, Rice, Richardson, Robbins, Roberts, Rogers, Sawyer, Shaw, Shedd, Smith, Spalding, Stowers, Sutton, Swan, Symmes, Symonds, Tarbell, Teel, Tewksbury, Thayer, Thomas, Thompson, Tidd, Trueworthy, Trull, Tufts, Turner, Varnum, Wade, Walker, Warren, Weld, Wetherbee, Whipple, White, Whitney, Wild, Wilson, Wing, Winn, Wood, Wyer, Wyman, York & Youngman.

Account book of Edward Bucknam, 1812-1871
Bucknam, Edward, 1789-1880.
Mss A B8
3 v.
Account books for a land surveyor and carpenter of Stoneham, Mass. Includes some brief journal entries.

Chapman collection
Mss A C53
ca. 100 letters.
Approximately 100 letters from Rufus Chapman, Union soldier, to his wife Catherine Chapman of Acton, Maine, dated 1861-1865. Most were written from the South. Also includes: document signed by Abner Coburn, Governor of Maine, and sent to Mrs. Chapman in 1863; several letters to Mrs. Chapman from members of her family; and a letter dated 1860 to Rufus Chapman from A. Brinaird of Greenfield.

William Clark papers, 1759-1815
Clark, William, 1740-1815.
Mss A C6
2 linear ft.
Includes 56 journals; 9 copy books (consisting mainly of items from London newspapers in the 1780's); 4 ecclesiastical documents (certificates of ordination and licenses to preach) dated 1768; and Clark's Harvard diploma dated 1759.

William Croswell papers, 1797-1833
Croswell, William.
Mss A C76
3 boxes.
Draft inventory in the library.
Papers and diaries of William Croswell, early American educator.

Naval journals of John B. Dale, 1831-1846
Dale, John B., 1814-1848.
Mss A D32
7 v.
Volumes 1-2 Journal of a cruise on the Vincennes. Volume 3 Journal of a cruise on the USS Constitution. Volume 4 Journal kept on board the Porpoise. Volumes 5-6 Private journals. Volume 7 Dale's commission signed by Martin Van Buren.

Elizabeth B. Hall collection
Hall, Elizabeth B.
Mss A D33
1 box + 1 flat archival box.
Draft finding aid in the library.
Papers pertaining to families of Barnstable County, Mass., especially the Dolliver, Wing, Holway, and Hoxie families. Mostly deeds and wills. A few concern Essex County, Mass.

Reverend Joseph Eckley papers, 1772-1810
Eckley, Joseph, 1750-1811.
Mss A E3
6 linear ft.
743 ms. sermons, 4 letters, 2 commonplace books.

Eastman family letters, 1830-1841
Mss A E37
1 box.
Letters written by members of the Samuel Eastman family of Strong, Maine. Contains information of life in that part of Maine at that time.

Elwell family genealogical notes, 1887-1960
Elwell, Levi Henry, 1854-1916.
Mss A E55
4 boxes + 6 v.
Draft finding aid in the library.
Notes and correspondence concerning the Elwell family in America. The bulk of the material was gathered by Levi Henry Elwell (1854-1916). Also notes compiled by the Reverend Jacob T. Elwell, Charles H. Pope, and Walter Corbin (compiled between 1948 and 1957). An index to the 5 bound volume work by Walter E Corbin was compiled in 1993 by June D. Brown.

The Gedney family records surveyed to 1974
Gedney, Edwin Kemble, 1904-.
Mss A G43
6 v. in 10 bks.: maps, coat of arms, geneal. tables Photocopy of printed family record charts completed in ms. with typescript genealogies, charts, notes, etc. and some copies of source documents.

Thomas Theodore Goff papers
Goff, Thomas Theodore.
Mss A G64
34 boxes, 1 v. typ., + 57 boxes of index cards.
Genealogical correspondence, notes, etc. on the
Goff family.

Luther Metcalf Harris papers, 1693-1885
Harris, Luther M. (Luther Metcalf), 1789-1865.
Mss A H3
2 linear ft. (950 items).
Draft finding aid in the library.
The bulk of the collection deals with the Harris
family of Brookline, Mass. and the Metcalf
family of Dedham, Mass., and includes 18th
century wills, deeds, inventories, tax receipts and
legal papers. There are several bound volumes
including an incomplete Harris family
diary/almanac (1788 July 4 - 1789 Jan 8); the
account book of John Harris (1755-1791); and
Lydia M. Harris' notebook (19th century) of
poetry. Also includes the correspondence, school
and professional records and genealogical notes
of Luther M. Harris.

Thomas Hibbard family correspondence
Mss A H53
1 box.
Mostly correspondence to and from Thomas
Hibbard, including letters by Mrs. Herbert
Walters, Mr. Charles Walters, and a letter from
Franklin D. Roosevelt, 28 March 1918, written
while Assistant Secretary of the Navy.

Winifred Lovering Holman papers
Holman, Winifred Lovering, 1899-1989.
Mss A H63
24 linear ft. (37 boxes, 32 vols.)
Unpublished finding aid in the library.
Boxes 1-35 contain notes on (usually) one line of
descent from over 1200 (mostly) New England
immigrants, 1620-1650. These notes include
detailed summaries, abstracts or transcriptions of
all probate and land records for each head of
family. Boxes 36-37 contain transcripts and
photostats of 17th-19th century wills, inventories,
and related probate documents, which may not be
abstracted or fully copied. New England families
predominate, but the collection also contains
material pertaining to the Middle Atlantic states
and Virginia. The work was done for clients by

Winifred L. Holman [Dodge] and, to a lesser
extent, by her mother Mary Campbell Lovering
Holman (1868-1947). Accompanying these 37
boxes are 27 separate volumes of genealogies
prepared for clients and 5 volumes of various
bibliographical aids and source records. In
addition, Mrs. Dodge and her mother contributed
numerous typescripts and extensive separately
catalogued manuscripts on the Bentley, Claflin,
Fletcher, Lovering, Merrill and Rice families.

Genealogy of the Horton family from John (4)
Horton through the tenth generation
Horton, Byron Barnes, 1873-1941.
Mss A H67
21 v.
Typescript with ms. annotations, additions and
revisions.

Descendants of John Johnson of Roxbury, Mass.
Johnson, William Edward, 1867-1937.
Mss A J65
4 v.
Typescript genealogy tracing the male lines from
1630 to 1937. Includes index.

Ketcham's New Hampshire Biography
Ketcham, Cyrus
Mss A K48
6 boxes.
Papers compiled by Cyrus Ketcham intended to
be used for a dictionary of New Hampshire
Biography which was never completed or
published.

Account book and daybook of David Legro, 1791-
1837
Legro, David, ca. 1759-1835.
Mss A L44
11 v.

Nahum Mitchell papers, 1670-1862
Mitchell, Nahum, 1769-1853.
Mss A M62
70 items.
Largely deeds and wills relating to the Mitchell
and the Hayward families of Bridgewater, Mass.
and to the Hearsey family of Hingham. Some of
Nahum Mitchell's personal papers are included.

Gilbert Nash papers, ca. 1830
Mss A N3
3 v.
Includes descriptions of the history, inhabitants, and houses of Abington, Mass. during the 18th and 19th centuries.

Warren Sears Nickerson papers
Nickerson, W. Sears (Warren Sears), b. 1880.
Mss A N55
3 boxes.
Collection of genealogical notes, papers, charts and correspondence on the Nickerson and Eldridge families. Includes documents concerning Jonathan Eldridge (1747-1837).

Nathan Eric Niles papers
Niles, Eric Nathan, 1847-1930.
Mss A N56
1 box.
Papers, correspondence, genealogical material and diary.

New England Mississippi Land Company records, 1790-ca. 1850
New England Mississippi Land Company.
Mss A N66
13 v.
Most of the volumes comprise a parallel series of minutes of meetings of the company's proprietors and directors. There is a continuous series from 1796-7 to 1817, with the proprietors' minutes being items 1, 2A and 8, and the directors' minutes being items 3A, 7/9 and 5. There is a break from 1817 to 1832, after which there is a volume of proprietors' minutes from 1832 to 1847 (item 5A) and a combined volume of minutes for both bodies for 1848 to 1865 (item 4A). There are four other volumes recording the various financial transactions of the company: a share register (item 9A), two dividend registers (items 4 and 6), and a book of accounts (item 3). Lastly, the most interesting volume is a book of miscellaneous records (item 2). This contains all the basic agreements of the company, and various other letters and legal instruments. On page 39 of this volume is a copy of the 26 January 1795 deed by which the company purchased its land from the Georgia-Mississippi Company.

Olmsted Family Association records, 1911-1941
Olmsted Family Association.
Mss A O54
8 linear ft.
Correspondence, genealogical papers and card file, photographs, copper photographic plates (including plates for family coat of arms), family reunion material, and clippings relating to the Olmsted family in America. Principle correspondents include Frank Lincoln Olmsted, Edward Olmsted, George K. Ward, and Henry Buckland Olmstead.

Alexander Parris papers, 1812-1853
Parris, Alexander, 1780-1852.
Smith, Nathaniel, b. 1807.
Mss A P37
1 box.
68 letters written to Parris while he was Superintendent of Artificers, U.S.A., Sacketts Harbor, Plattsburg, NY. Also 5 letters from later period; 12 interleaved almanacs kept by Parris' nephew, Nathaniel Smith, containing diaries and weather reports for the years 1839 and 1845-1853. Many of the entires concern Parris' business activities.

Phelps Stokes collection
Stokes, Olivia Egleston Phelps, 1847-1927.
Stokes, Caroline Phelps, 1854-1909.
Mss A P54
2 boxes.+ 6 v.
Collection of genealogical and family papers belonging to Olivia Egleston Phelps Stokes and Caroline Phelps Stokes, philanthropists and grandaughters of Anson Green Phelps (1781-1853) and sisters of Anson Phelps Stokes (1838-1913). Includes information on other families, especially the Dudley, Woodbridge, Trumbull and Harlakenden families.

Pepperrell family papers, 1689-1764 (bulk 1710-1755)
Pepperrell, William, 1646-1734.
Pepperrell, William, 1696-1759.
Micro B/6/9-10 also Mss A P5
Access to original papers restricted; Use microfilm copy.
2 reels (35 mm.); (2 linear ft., ca. 950 items).
Chiefly business and personal papers of Col. William Pepperrell (1646-1734) and his son, Sir William Pepperrell, Bart. (1696-1759). Also includes documents relating to the capture and occupation of Louisburg, Cape Breton Island, Nova Scotia in 1745. Principal correspondents include Benjamin Clarke, Silas Hooper, Thomas Kerby, Robert Oram, Andrew Pepperrell (son of Sir William), Nathaniel Sparhawk, Andrew Tyler, and William Tyler. There is also some correspondence dealing with Thomas Cushing, William Shirley, Peter Warren, and Benning Wentworth.

Notes on the Russell and Andrews families
Mss A R18
1 box.
Ms. and newspaper clippings. Includes transcriptions of late 19th century letters.

Lemuel Shattuck collection
Shattuck, Lemuel, 1793-1859.
Mss A S53
7 boxes.
Draft inventory in the library.
Deeds, wills, genealogies and materials relating to Shattuck's History of Concord, Mass.

Sermon collection
Mss A S87
3 boxes.
Collection of ms. sermons written and preached by Boston area clergy. Also included are sermon notes and a few personal and legal papers of Rev. Job Wight of Medfield, Mass.

Sutherland collection
Sutherland, Minnie Sarah.
Mss A S88
5 boxes.
Draft inventory in the library.

Papers relating to Hartford, Connecticut, 1729/30-1770
Mss A T32
ca. 90 items.
Largely receipts, business invoices, and correspondence of John, Samuel and Richard Edwards and Jonathan Williams of Hartford, Conn. Also numerous court orders for the settlement of debts in Hartford.

Names and dates of the descendants of John Thurber who settled in Swansea, Massachusetts in 1664
Thurber, Alfred Edward.
Mss A T58
720 leaves; 28 cm.
Photocopy of original index cards (two cards copied per leaf).

Account book of Samuel Townsend, 1739-1775
Townsend, Samuel.
Mss A T69
4 v.
Account books for a general store in Oyster Bay, NY.

Frederick Whitcomb Wead papers
Mss A W44
12 boxes & 30 v.
Personal, family, and genealogical papers. Includes Samuel Whitcomb's papers, Wead's genealogical library, and correspondence with other prominent genealogists.

Edwin B. Worthen Jr. papers
Mss A W67
1 box, 1 v., 1 chart.
Papers concerning the Worthen family. Includes material relating to the Heal, Parker, Stickney, Jameson, Fernald, McKenney, Mathews and Burroughs families.

Metcalf family record
Mss A H3, Folder 42
1 leaf.
1732
This record is dated at Dedham, Mass., and contains the names of the descendants of Michael Metcalf for three generations. Birth years are included for the second generation only. This record has undatable additions to the original.

News room records kept by Samuel Gilbert, 1810-1811
Mss B 05
5 v.
Account books kept in the news room of the Old Exchange Coffee House in Boston (burnt down in 1818) established by Samuel Gilbert to record incoming news and vessels in Boston Harbor.

Account book, 1836 Sept 15-1839 June 6
American Stationers' Company (Boston, Mass.)
Mss B A6
Vol. 1 credit. Vol. 2 sales.

Bay State Association of Democratic Young Men records, 1838 Nov 27- 1843 Oct
Bay State Association of Democratic Young Men.
Mss B B38
Vol. 1 Constitution and dues records. Vol. 2 Minutes. Vol. 3 Accounts.

Records, 1798 – 1799
Mss B B5
Historical note: The frigate "Boston" was built by subscription then transferred to the U.S.
Vol. 1 Ledger book showing subscribers. Vol. 2 Account book.

Boston Phrenological Society records, 1832-1838
Mss B B65
Vol. 1 Meeting records. Vol. 2 Correspondence. Vol. 3 Council records.

Boston Sea Fencibles records, 1817-1835
Mss B B68
2 v.

Boston Water Power Company records, 1834-1873
Mss B B69
Vol. 1 Time book and pay roll, 1834. Vol. 2 Time book, 1834. Vol. 3 Stock ledger and index, 1848-1859. Vol. 4 Dividends, 1873. Vol. 5 Accounts, 1868.

Papers, 1685-1787
Company for the Propagation of the Gospel in New England and parts Adjacent
Mss B C40
3 boxes.

Draft finding aid in the library.
Box 1 Commissioner's book. Box 2 Account books and Notes & Minutes on the meetings of the Commissioners in Boston. Box 3 Contains individual items: letters, deeds, receipts, etc. Collection also includes several oversize documents.

Dorchester Antiquarian and Historical Society Papers, 1630-1874
Mss B D46
Draft finding aid in the library.
Note: Currently being processed [4/2002]
Consists of records created by the Society itself as well as documents collected by the Society that relate to the town and/or people of Dorchester, Mass. The Society records include notifications and minutes of meetings, committee reports, member nominations, a visitor's book, notes and a draft version the history of Dorchester that the Society published in 1859, and correspondence concerning the celebration of the 225th anniversary of the settlement of Dorchester. The original documents fall into several general groups: church, financial, marriage intentions, military, real estate, school, and town records as well as the records of several societies, clubs, associations of Dorchester. The church records include proprietor meeting minutes, correspondence concerning the Second Parish controversy, and programs of services, exercises, etc. The financial records include tax lists, bills, receipts, lists of payments and contributions, etc. The military records include alarm lists, muster roll, soldier lists, documents relating to Castle William (i.e. Fort Independence), and an orderly book for the First Regiment, First Brigade of the Massachusetts Militia. The political records consist primarily of party tickets and broadsides announcing future rallies, meetings, etc. The real estate records are primarily deeds from the 18th century and copies of a few 17th century deeds. The school records include notes on town meetings concerning school issues, supplies, teacher applicants and resignations, student lists, documents concerning Milton Academy, and the North School District in Medfield, Mass. The town records include notices of town meetings, lists of voters, warrants, etc.

*Papers concerning the history of Dedham,
Massachusetts and in particular, the Farrington
family of Dedham*
Mss B D43
1 box.
Mostly legal papers, accounts, etc. 17th and 18th
century.

Records, 1852 – 1856
Granite Club No. 1 (Boston, Mass.)
Mss B G7
2 v.

*Direct tax list of 1798 for Massachusetts and
Maine*
F63/M343/1978 also LOAN also Mss B M35
[134]
18 microfilm reels + a published index and guide.
Original is 20 folio volumes + 2 suppl. volumes
totaling nearly 16,000 pages
Access to original records restricted: Use
microfilm copy.
An economic survey conducted in 1798 of all
property holders and renters residing in
Massachusetts (Maine at that time was part of
Massachusetts). The assesors who compiled the
lists determined owners and tenants of land,
amount of acreage, number of dwellings, relative
boundaries, current valuation, and taxes due.
Portions of the original volumes were lost or
destroyed, most of which relate to Maine
townships in volumes one to four, are noted in the
printed guide.

*Vital records of Middlesex County,
Massachusetts, 1635-1791*
Mss B M54
2 v. (650, 677 p.)
1896.
Transcription of the original ms.

*Old School Boys Association of Boston records,
1880-1925*
Old School Boys Association of Boston.
Mss B O58
Vol. 1 Minutes, 1880-1918. Vol. 2 Minutes,
1919-15. Vol. 3 Scrapbook and notes on
members. Vol. 4 Newspapers clippings
concerning members. Vol. 5 Applications for
memberships, 1912-1913.

Israel Litchfield diary, 1774 Nov. 4-1775 Aug. 25
Litchfield, Israel, 1753-1840.
Mss C 1
[48] p.; 33 x 21 cm.
Litchfield, of Scituate, Mass., describes
establishment of minuteman company in Scituate,
the reaction to the Lexington Alarm, and the
guarding of the coast. Also chronicles day-to-day
life. Includes biography on inside front cover and
poem written by grandson Paul Brooks Merritt,
circa 1833, that was printed on silk cloth and
mounted on back cover.

*Letter, no date, [Boston, Mass. to Joseph Eckley,
Boston, Mass.]*
Channing, William Ellery, 1780-1842.
Mss C 10
[1] leaf; 17 cm.
Channing's letter dated "Saturday" written from
Boston to Joseph Eckley, of Boston, Mass.,
requesting Eckley to substitute preach for
Channing. Eckley added notes to the letter.

*List of men belonging to Engine No. 2, Boston,
1780 June 16*
Mss C 100
1 p.; 19 cm.
Handwritten list provides the men's names and
their salary.

*Letter, 1895 February 4, [to] George A. Gordon,
Recording Secretary, NEHGS*
Abbott, Lemuel Abijah, 1842-1911.
Mss C 101
1, 5 leaves; 25 cm.
Describes parentage of George Abbott of Rowley.

*Additions and corrections to Savage's
"Genealogical Dictionary" concerning Abby,
Adams, Allen, Amey, Angier, Armitage, Avis,
Nevill, Snell and Walley families*
Alger, Arthur Martineau, b. 1854.
Mss C 103
14 p.; 20 cm.

Miscellaneous papers concerning the Ames family
Mss C 105
8 p.; 17-36 cm.
Includes handwritten copy of the "Ames pedigree" by W.B. Frank showing the descendants of Richard Ames of Bruton, England; a handwritten transcription of an obituary for Nabby L. Ames (1771-1854); handwritten transcription of "Sketch of the pioneer family of the late Judge Sylvanus Ames, ancestry etc. prepared by A.B. Walker and submitted to the [Pioneer] Association July 4 1871"]; and a hand drawn pedigree chart for the Ames family.

Lieutenant Samuel Armstrong diary, 1777-1778
Armstrong, Samuel, 1754-1810.
E263/M4/A76 Microfilm also Mss C 1058
Access to original diary restricted; Use microfilm copy.
1 microfilm reel (35 mm.); Original is 1 v. (80 p.); 17 cm. x 10 cm.
    Additional form: transcribed version (with historical footnotes) published as "From Saratoga
to Valley Forge: The Diary of Lt. Samuel Armstrong" by Joseph Lee Boyle in *The Pennsylvania Magazine of History and Biography*
vol. CXXI, No. 3 (July 1997) p. 237-270.
Diary covers the experience of Lt. Armstrong while serving in the 8th Mass. Regiment. Describes the capture of Burgoyne and the encampment at Valley Forge. Also contains a number of songs.

Armstrong genealogy
Mss C 107
[108] p.: coat of arms; 25-33 cm.
Extract of a will, recollections, handwritten notes, letters, and drafts of compiled genealogies on the Armstrong and allied Bass family.

Original, unpublished documens relating to the Alden family discovered by R. Randall Hoes in Duxbury, Mass. 1879
Hoes, Roswell Randall, 1850-1921.
Mss C 108
1 v. (46 p.); 22 cm.
Handwritten transcription of original record including a "genealogy of the Aldens", a family

record and two deeds. Only 13 of the 46 pages were used.

Letter, 1816 May 27, Portland, Me. [to] [Elnathan] Duren, Boston, Mass.
Freeman, Betsey Ilsley Jones, 1754-1831.
Mss C 11
[1] leaf; 32 cm.
As "B. Freeman, of Portland, Me.," a letter to her son [-in-law] Elnathan Duren, of Boston, Mass., which focuses on death of children, family and community news. Duren's wife, Freeman's daughter, died in 1815.

Genealogical data relating to the Amos Ames, Eber Parker, Wild and Goldthwait families
Parker, Russell J.
Mss C 111
11 p.; 33 cm.
Typescript transcription of original family records.

Memo[randum] of the Jacquelin and Ambler family now in Virginia, 1690-1798
Ambler, Jacquelin, 1742-1798.
Mss C 112
1 p.; 21 x 33 cm.
Handwritten pedigree with the families of Edward and Martha (Cary) Jacquelin (author's maternal grandparents), Richard and Elizabeth (Jacquelin) Ambler (author's parents), the author's own family as well as the families of John and Mary (Jacquelin) Smith and Edward and Mary (Cary) Ambler. Verso has "note the within was commenced in Aug 1773 Mrs Martha Jacquelin gave the principal information to J. Ambler."

Ashley genealogy
Miller, Albertine Cornelia Hull, 1872-
Mss C 114
[2] leaves; 28 cm.
Typescript genealogy on the descendants of Mary Ashley Van Alstyne of Schodack Landing, NY.

Bible record for the Moody Austin family, 1791-1883
Mss C 115
[3] p.; 25 cm.
Original record without title page for the Moody and Ann (Carter) Austin family.

Tabular pedigree for Sarah Ann Atherton with notes
Atherton, Sarah Ann, 1813-1889.
Mss C 117
25 p.

Letter, 1928 July 5, Chicopee Falls, Mass., to [William Prescott] Greenlaw, NEHGS, Boston, Mass.
Hendrich, Charles T.
Mss C 118
1 ALS; 28 cm.
Handwritten letter with a transcription of the Bible record for the David Adams family of Moultonboro, N.H., 1769-1830.

Daniel Allen family record, 1754-1775
Mss C 119
[6] p.; 14 cm.
Loose pages apparently removed from a small account book (on the back of each sheet is the page number: 10, 12, 14). Entries concern the births and a few deaths for the Daniel and Mary (Holman) Allen family of Sutton, Mass.

Houseville, Lewis County, New York, Cemetery
Goff, Arthur James, b. 1881.
Mss C 12
11 p.; 28 cm.
Typescript transcription of cemetery inscriptions. Author compared his results against those of the DAR transcription and they agree. Goff added genealogical data to entries.

The descendants of Richard Ambler of Stamford, Connecticut for eight generations]
Ambler, Alice M.
Mss C 120
16 p.; 28 cm.
Partially-printed family group sheets completed in ms. providing the lineal descent from Richard (1) Ambler through Rev. Abraham (2), John (3-5), Peter (6), Silas (7), to Samuel H. (8) Ambler.

Bible record for the Samuel Rogers Andrew family, 1787-1858
Mss C 121
[3] p.; 28 cm.
Original record (without title page) for the Samuel R. and Mary (Daggett) Andrew family of Woodbury, Conn.

Notes on the Alexander and Whitaker families from the Bibles of Ebenezer Alexander and Nathaniel Howland Whitaker of Boston
Alexander, Winthrop, 1861-1941.
Mss C 122
11 leaves; 28 cm.
Typescript transcription of original record.

Bible records from old Bibles owned by the Onondaga Historical Association: Austin, Baker, Clement, Greene, Kirkpatrick and Mercer families
Coleman, Minnie Lincoln Crow.
Mss C 123
1 v. (ca. 50 p.); 23 cm.
Handwritten copy of original Bible records on the Ezekiel and Ann Austin, Charles A. and Maria (Wood) Baker, Tobias and Sally (Lee) Clement, Nowal D. Greene, William and Nancy (Dunscomb) Kirkpatrick and John Mercer families.

Copy of the old Bible records of Joseph Atkins of Orleans, Mass...
Mss C 124
6 p.; 22 cm.
Handwritten transcription of original record.

Evidence identifying Joshua Austin, who married Tryphena Hatheway at Suffield Connecticut, July 10, 1747, as Joshua the son of Anthony 2nd and Abigail (Holcomb) Austin. Also identifying Elijah, Ruth and Shadrach as children of Joshua and Tryphena
Austin, Alpheus Elijah, b. 1867.
Mss C 125
5 leaves; 28 cm.
1930
Typescript with ms. annotations.

Ancestry of Ozro Daniel Adams
Priest, Alice L. (Alice Lucinda), 1866-1954.
Mss C 126
2 leaves; 28 cm.
Typescript genealogy providing lineal descent from Henry (1) Adams through Ensign Edward (2), Elisha (3), William (4-5), Elisha (6), James (7), Elijah Watkins (8) to Ozro Daniel (9) Adams of Northfield, Mass.

Record conerning the Joseph Ames family
Mss C 127
[2, 1] p.
Handwritten note describing how Joseph Ames of Bridgewater, Mass., prior to being married for the third time in 1768, distributed "almost the whole of his real estate to his sons" in order "to do justice to his family". Includes a page with biographical information by the donor.

Record on the death of Carlton L. Allen
Mss C 128
1 p.; 28 cm.
Single sheet from a Bible -- the "births" side is blank and there is a single entry on the "deaths" side for Carlton L. Allen with a newspaper clipping on Mr. Allen's marriage.

Ancestry of Oliver Ames
Mss C 129
1 p.; 10 x 16 cm.
Small hand drawn chart showing the ancestors of Oliver Ames. Chart only has names, no dates, etc.

Pine Hill Cemetery, Mendon, Mass.
Daniels, Joan J.
Mss C 13
[20] p.; 28 cm.
Typescript transcription of cemetery inscriptions arranged in alphabetical order.

Angier family of Framingham
Mss C 130
11 p.
First item is "Angiers of Framingham, Mass." (typescript notes taken from Temple's History of Framingham). Second item is a hand written pedigree chart for Gardner Everett Angier. Third item is a letter by Philip A.M. Brooks, 1903 Dec 13, Chestertown Md., to G. Everet Angier. Fourth item is a letter, 1822 Nov 23, Framingham [Mass.], to Ann A Haven, Boston [Mass.]. Final item is a letter, 1869 Aug 28, New York to G. E. Angier from H.G.B.

Bible record for the John Axtell family, 1778-1858
Reynolds, Charles W.
Mss C 131
2 leaves; 28 cm.
Typescript transcription of original record (with title page information) for the John and Rebecca (Wate) Axtell family.

Alden and Reynolds deaths: as found in the old family Bible of the late Rutillus Alden of Winthrop, Maine
Reynolds, Charles W.
Mss C 132
4 leaves; 28 cm.
Typescript transcription of original record without title page information.

Supplement to "The Ladd Family" by Warren Ladd (New Bedford, Massachusetts: E. Anthony and Sons, 1890)
Ladd, Bessie Ruth, b. 1899.
Mss C 134
1 p.; 28 cm.
Typescript genealogical information on the family of Daniel Bartlett (6) Ladd of New Hampshire.

Bible record for the Daniel W. Allen family, 1825-1931
Mss C 135
1 p.; 28 cm.
Typescript transcription of original record (with title page information) on the Daniel W. and Elizabeth Allen family.

Bible record for the Samuel Alley family, 1735-1843
Mss C 136
2 leaves; 28 cm.
Typescript transcription of original record (with title page information) on the Samuel and Deborah (Breed) Alley family of Lynn, Mass.

Extract from the Atkinson - Stevens Bible recently owned by Mrs. Stevens of the old Bartlett - Atkinson house, 3 Market Street, Newburyport
Mss C 137
2 leaves; 28 cm.
Typescript transcription of original record (without title page information) for the John and Sarah (Crooker) Atkinson family and the Samuel and Sarah C. (Atkinson) Stevens, Jr. family.

Bible record for the Frank L. Ames family, 1844-1929
Mss C 138
1 p.; 28 cm.
Typescript transcription of original record for the Frank L. and Genevieve (Keizar) Ames family of Corinth, Maine.

Births, deaths, & marriages at Westmoreland, N.Y., January 1853 - April 1855, as recorded in the diary of Adelaide Julia Clark, aged 11 to 13
Clark, Adelaide Julia.
Mss C 139
1 p.; 28 cm.
Typescript abstract of genealogical data from original diary.

Letter, 1850 May 6, Flemington, N.J., [to] John Hayward
Higgins, Samuel M.
Mss C 14
[1] leaf; 25 cm.
Higgins, of Flemington, N.J., to John Hayward writes about the California Gold Rush story of James W. Marshall, of Hunterdon Co., N.J., who arrived there in 1845 and now in partnership with John Sutter.

Atherton records copied from the Atherton Bible
Mss C 140
2 leaves; 20 cm.
Typescript transcription of original record for the Jonathan and Nancy (Bridge) Atherton family of Harvard, Mass. and Cavendish, Vt.

Notes on the Austin, Allen, Arnold, Babcock, Barker, Easton and Hall families
Clarke, George S. (George Sharp), b. 1884.
Mss C 141
1 v. (ca. 100 p.)
Small notebook with handwritten notes on the Austin family of RI and the allied families of Allen, Arnold, Babcock, Barker, Easton and Hall. Most of the notes are from published RI vital records with a little additional information.

Bible record for the Gabriel Abrams family, 1750-1841
Mss C 142
2 leaves; 28 cm.
Typescript transcription (with title page information) of original Bible record for the Gabriel and Rebekah (Loveberry) Abrams family of Pennsylvania.

Bible record for the James Augustus Adams family, 1827-1906
Mss C 143
1 leaf; 28 cm.
Typescript transcription (without title page information) of original Bible record for the James Augustus Adams family of Newburyport, Mass.

Letter, 1794 Oct. 4
Boylston, Thomas.
Mss C 15
[3] letters; 23-38 cm.
Business letter sent to Greffuthe [?] Monty & Co., Bankers at Paris, by Boylston, formerly of Boston, Mass., saying he was a citizen of the United States that is residing in London, England, and thus should not have his assets confiscated because of the war between England and France. This being a follow-up letter with a copy of the first letter and a copy of Thomas Pickney, Minister Plenipolentiary [?] of the United States at the Court of Great Britain attesting to Boylston's claims. Another letter of the same date was written to Richard Codman asking him to deliver the letters to Paris when Codman went there.

A Hymn for America
Whitney, Peter, 1744-1816.
Mss C 16
[1] leaf; 20 cm.
Autograph manuscript of undated poem. Reverso reads "Hymn for America by the Revd. Mr. Peter Whitney."

[Roxbury Camp song], 1775 Dec. 31
Mss C 17
[1] leaf; 20 cm.
Five stanza song on America's preparation for war before the American Revolution.

The Glutton: A tale
Mss C 18
[1] leaf; 19 cm.
A poem on gluttony.

Diary of Lieutenant Samuel Armstrong, 1777-1778
Armstrong, Samuel, 1754-1810.
E263/M4/A76 Microfilm also Mss C 1058
Acess to original diary restricted; Use microfilm 1 microfilm reel (35 mm.); ms. 17 cm. x 10 cm., Diary covers the experience of Lt. Armstrong while serving in the 8th Mass. Regiment. Describes the capture of Burgoyne and the encampment at Valley Forge. Also contains a number of songs.

Lovering family: Descendants of John Lovering of Dover, New Hampshire, 1657
Lovering, Wentworth R. (Wentworth Reynold), 1912-
Mss C 19a
9, 28 p.; 22 cm.
1978 Oct.
Photocopy of a genealogy formatted in a Register-style numbered outline list.

Lovering family: Descendants of John Lovering of Dover, New Hampshire, 1657
Lovering, Wentworth R. (Wentworth Reynold), 1912-.
Mss C 19b
32, [2] p.; 22 cm.
1980 Oct.
Photocopy of a genealogy formatted in a Register-style numbered outline list.

Census of the east ward in Framingham taken as of the 1st of May 1837
Mss C 2
[20] p.; 20 x 8 cm.
Census of Framingham, Mass., lists heads of house, number in family, and totals in east, southwest, and northwest wards.

Trumansburg: A list of former residents who attended the Centenniel Reunion, 18-19 August 1897, Trumansburg, N.Y.
Fisher, Carl W.
Mss C 20
[6]; 28 cm.
[19--?]
Typescript copy from The Free Press and Sentinel newspaper's 21 August 1897 issue.

Typewritten copy of "A Family Account Book" handed down by James Haney Bevans to James Lung Bevans
Bevans, James Lung, b. 1869.
Mss C 21
111, [17] p.; 21 cm.
1920.
Transcript of an account book assumed to kept by John Bevans and covering from 1763 to 1812.

Exemplication of the will for Henry Bromfield Esquire, 1833 January 1
Mss C 22
8 p.: ill.; 41 cm.
Handwritten extract by Foller and Sons of the original record including drawn tax stamps and seals. Includes statement by Notary Public that this is a true copy.

Bible record for the James Harvey Thompson family, 1783-1910
Mss C 23
[2] leaves; 28 cm.
Typescript transcription of the original record for the James Harvey and Harriet Eliza (Birch) Thompson family of Gouverneur, NY. Includes letter from donor with information concerning the provenance and description of the handwriting.

Letter, 1824 July 2, Paris [France], to Capt.
Allyn of the Cadmus
Lafayette, Marquis de, 1757-1834.
Mss C 24
1 ALS; 23 cm.
Original letter in which Lafayette discusses the
date of his passage to the United States. Includes
a newspaper clipping from 2 March 1888
concerning "The claim of Captain Allyn, which
calls up an interesting incident of the visit of
Lafayette".

Extracts from the account book of Ebenezer
Chase, 1825-1843
Chase, Ebenezer, 1796-1882.
Mss C 25
2 leaves; 36 cm.
Typescript extract of the original account book of
Ebenezer Chase of Mendon and Blackstone,
Mass. The transcription provides the first date the
name is listed in the original and for recurring
names, the year of the last entry in the book as
well.

A geneological [sic] synopsis of the name
Brainerd, beginning at the root Mr. Daniel
Brainerd
Brainerd, Elijiah.
Mss C 26
1 v. (46 p.); 17 cm.
Handwritten genealogy in a small handmade
book.

Handwritten transcription of a letter by Richard
Saltonstall, 1636, to John Winthrop, Governor of
Connecticut
Saltonstall, Richard, 1610-1694.
Mss C 27
[2, 1] p.; 25 cm.
Two page handwritten copy of original letter
concerning Mr. Saltonstall's complaint that "there
has been some abuse...done me by Mr. Ludlowe
& others of Dorchester who would not suffer
Francis Styles & his men to impayle grounds
where I appoynted them at Connecticut".... Third
page has the "Order of march at the funeral of
Governor Leverett, who died 16 March 1678, and
was buried the first of the next year, 25 March
1679".

Notebook of Jose Winthrop, 1683
Winthrop, Jose, 1666-1702.
Mss C 28
1 v. (56 p.); 20 cm.
First page has "Jose Winthrop his booke Anno
1683. Entries include "To make French Bisket,"
"Princes Bisket," "To preserve quinces," "To
stench bleeding," "for a prick under the nail," "to
stay bleeding at the nose," "for weakness of the
sight," "elixir salutis," and in the reverse direction
"the form of a will," "An interpretation of
difficult words" and "The law given at Sinai."

Twenty four country dances for the year 1782:
with proper directions to each dance as they are
performed at court almacks bath pantheon and all
public assemblies
Mss C 29
1 v. (24 p.); 15 cm.
Handwritten guide to country dances recorded in
a little handmade book. Dances include "Was not
that Provoking," "Rakes of Cashell," "Goddess of
the Chace," "Just the Thing," "The Great Devil,"
"Garret Election," "Rochester Rakes," "Margate
Whim," "Pert as a Pearmonger," "Pretty Peggy of
Darby," "Trip to Cork," "Prince De la Cour,"
"The Sooner the better," "millers Wedding," "St
James's Park," "Trip to Aberdeen," "Margate
Wash," "Vestrie Figg," "Rakes of Dublin," "Trip
to the Nore,"(?) "Porcupine Dance," "Trip to
Cumberland," "Vauxhall Walk," and "Begin the
Dance."

Explanation of the New Testament
Mss C 3
80 p.; 21 cm.
Bound notes of lectures "taken by a young lady"
delivered by Rev. O.B. Frothingham at Boston,
Mass., in 1846 discussing the Book of Matthew.

To the English Nation
Mss C 30
2 p.; 31 cm.
An open letter to the citizens of Great Britain and America written by "A field labourer". The first 19 lines attacks the taking of African children as slaves. The remaining 48 lines, however, concerns the "ruined state" of Great Britain and the colonies due to debt as well as the corruption caused by pride and luxury. The author claims that "if wee were but all willing to live as the Gospel teaches all publick debts may be discharged in a few years" then offers some examples. In a nine line post script, the author adds that instead of reforming, Great Britain and America "get to fighting".

Promissory note, 17--[torn] October 4, Boston, to Adam Winthrop, Boston
Prentice, Thomas, 1677-1730.
Mss C 31
1 DS; 28 cm.
Original note promising to pay 23 pounds for a servant named James Dougherty. Verso contains receipt by Adam Winthrop dated 1730 May 26 stating that the estate of Thomas Prentice paid the balance he was owed.

Bond, 1780 March 18, to be paid to Nathaniel Greenough
Appleton, Nathaniel, 1731-1798.
United States. Massachusetts Loan Office.
Mss C 32
1 DS; 11 x 21 cm.
Original bond (no. 299) for twelve dollars payable after thirty days to Nathaniel Greenough for interest due on money borrowed by the United States. Signed by F. Hopkinson, Treasurer of Loans, and countersigned by Nathaniel Appleton, Comissioner of the Continental Loan-Office in the State of Massachusetts. The verso has a note by Nathaniel Greenough to pay the contents to Duncan Ingraham Jr.

The Paslay family genealogy
Paslay, Robert Buckingham, 1916-1982.
Mss C 3269
5, 9, 39, [3] p.; 35 cm.
1958
Carbon copy typescript genealogy of the Peasley, Paslay, Paisley family in Massachusetts and Virginia with a brief introduction of the family in England, Ireland and Scotland.

Cash book of Elias R. Hitchcock, 1840
Hitchcock, Elias R., 1826-1881.
Mss C 33
8 p.; 32 cm.
Original handmade book recording debits and credits from 1840 January 2 to June 15.

The Arthaud family of Bourbonne-les-Bains and Langres, Department of Haute Marne, France with related families of Gascard, Gautherot, Lauzanne, Liegault, Mutinot and Walferdin and one immigrant branch in the United States
Arthaud, John Bradley, 1939-.
Mss C 3305
xlii, 123 p.: facsim., charts; 28 cm.

Boaz Brown (16412-1724) of Concord, Stow and Dedham, Massachusetts
Sprague, Eleanor Robbins, 1927-.
Mss C 3348
[2], 18 leaves; 28 cm.

The Saga of the Oberns Orbens: A Journey from the Palatinate to California
Obern, A. Gaylord (Alfred Gaylord), 1921-.
Mss C 3349
47 p.: ports., geneal. tables; 28 cm.
1996.

[Memorandum of agreement ... new meeting house at Kittery, Maine ...], 1727 Jul. 23.
Pearson, Moses, fl. 1727.
Mss C 3350
1 ADS.
Memorandum of agreement for painting the new meeting house in Kittery, Maine, between the Committee: Timothy Gerrish, William Pepperell, Jr., Richard Cutts, Hercules Farnald [sic] and John Wells and the painters: Moses Pearson and Isaac Ensly. Describes the colors of paint to be used.

Bunker and Wood family Bible record, 1781-1899
Bunker, David, 1818-1890.
Mss C 3351
[5, 5] leaves
Color inkjet reproductions of scanned original pages. A transcription was downloaded from the donor's web page and included in the folder.

[Middletown, Delaware County, New York, town record book, 1789-1815]
Middletown (N.Y.). Town clerk's office.
Mss C 3352
1 v. ([59] p.)
Photocopy of original records copied by the donor at the town clerk's office. This is a complete copy of the first town record volume.

Correspondence, 1860-1869
Wyszinski, Eustace, 1840-1870.
Mss C 3353
10 letters ([31] leaves); 28 cm.
Photocopies of eight letters and a typescript transcription of each. Included are photocopies several documents relating to Wyszinski. Letters were written while Wyszinski was aboard the whaling ship Atlantic, out of New Bedford, Mass., 1860-1862, and the USS Vandalia, 1866-1869, to his parents, Aunt Adeline and sister Julia. There were alledgedly more letters that were destroyed in the Chicago fire of 1871.

Geneology [sic]: William Eager born Scotland ca. 1639
Rushforth, Dorothy Mae Gould, fl. 1943-1996.
Mss C 3354
[66] p.; 28 cm.
Photocopy of the desendancy of William Eager through genealogical family group charts. Includes three ancestral charts for Ethel Melissa (Eager) Rushforth (1896-1958), mother-in-law of the author.

Some additions and corrections to the family record of Nathan and Hannah Austin of Methuen, Massachusetts
Austin, John Michael, 1956-.
Mss C 3355
[5] p.; 28 cm.
Computer typescript copy.

A List of men from Methuen[,] Massachusetts[,] who served in militia units during the French and Indian War (1755-1763)
Austin, John Michael, 1956-.
Mss C 3356
[11] p.; 28 cm.
Computer typescript transcription of original records at the Massachusetts State Archives and Massachusetts Historical Society with citations back to the original record with biographical data added to an alphabetical list of all men at the end.

A List of marriages performed by Rev. Christopher Sargent [sic] in Methuen[,] Massachusetts[,] from 1730-1788
Austin, John Michael, 1956-.
Mss C 3357
[15, 7, 7, 7] p.; 28 cm.
A partial computer typescript transcription of Rev. Sargeant's Commonplace book (Ms. S-40), the original notebook located at the Massachusetts Historical Society with photocopies of the original included. The list of 325 marriages is then repeated and compared to the Methuen vital records, showing all decrepancies. The list is then repeated two more times, first in alphabetical order by the bride's name and second by the groom's name.

Jeffrey Massey, Planter[,] of Salem, Massachusetts (1591-1676)
Sparks, Caroline Massey, 1920-.
Mss C 3358
17, [30] p.: ill., maps; 28 cm.
Photocopy of typescript that includes document, map, illustration and photographic reproductions.

The Original Massey family genealogy: Descendants of Jonathan Massey (1747-1830)
Sparks, Caroline Massey, 1920-.
Mss C 3359
143, [20] p.; 28 cm.
Photocopy of a typescript transcription with additions.

The Eaton family: descendants of David Eaton of Tremount, Illinois[,] a seventh generation descendant of John and Anne Eaton of Salisbury and Haverhill, Massachusetts[,] through thirteen generations based upon data collected
Dixon, George David, 1936-.
Mss C 3360
109 p.: facsim.; 28 cm.
Photocopy of typescript which contains fascimiles of pages from the "Report of the Sixth Annual Reunion of the Eaton Family Association held at Boston, August 19th, 1890".

The Dixon family: Descendants of John Wesley Dixon of Dakota County, Minnesota[,] and Los Angeles, California[,] through six generations based upon data collected from the now living descendants
Dixon, George David, 1936-.
Mss C 3361
82 p.: ill., facsim.; 28 cm.
Photocopy of typescript which contains reproductions of various photographs and illustrations.

The Vennerstrom family: Descendants of Ole Vennerstrom of Battle Lake, Minnesota
Dixon, George David, 1936-.
Mss C 3362
205 p.: ill., facsim.; 28 cm.
Photocopy of typescript with photoreproductions of photographs.

Genealogical notes on Caleb (7) Bates, Master mariner and merchant of Massachusetts
Bates, Constance S. (Constance Sumner), 1919-.
Mss C 3363
2, 11, [6] p.: facsim.; 28 cm.
Holograph with some parts being a photocopy, which include a photocopy of six pages from "Memoirs of members of the Social Circle in Concord" (Cambridge, Mass.: Riverside Press; Third Ser., 1907).

Joseph French Bible record, 1662-1944
French, Joseph, 1770-1841.
Mss C 3364
[12] p.; 28 cm.
Photocopy of original Bible records and secondary title page which includes several loose pages within Bible. This family is originally from Chesterville, Me.

Jerome family genealogy: [10 generations of the family of Timothy Jerome, the immigrant]
Gay-Taylor, Linda (Linda Louise), 1937-.
Mss C 3365
[12], 48, [19] p.: geneal. tables; 28 cm.
Dot matrix printout of descendancy genealogy that includes several ancestral genealogical charts of research conducted from 1990 to 1996.

A Record of marriages, baptisms, admission to the communion and funerals, 1822-1835
Hull, Lemuel B. (Lemuel Beach), 1792-1843.
Mss C 3366
1 item (80 p.); 10 x 15 cm.
These minister's records are from when Hull was at the Christ's Church (Redding, Conn.) and the St. James Church (Danbury, Conn.) and include marriages, 1823-1828, 1834-1835 (9, 2 p.); admissions, 1823-1827 (1 p.); baptisms, 1823-1828 (9 p.); and funerals, 1822-1828 (8 p.) which cover the Connecticut towns of Danbury and Redding primarily, but also Bridgeport, Brookfield, Brooklyn, Newtown, Norwich, Pomfret, and Weston. The last page says Hull commenced officiating at both parishes on Oct. 19th 1823. This volume was part of the Thelma K. Frazee and Marie P. Lemley Papers which were donated to the National Society of the Daughters of the American Revolution Library, in Washington D.C., on 1996 Jun 27.

Hesselgrave families in the 1881 census index – Yorkshire
Hesselgrave, G. F. D.
Mss C 3367
1 item ([10] p.); 28 cm.
Dot matrix printout in alphabetical order.

Manheimer family tree: Descendants of Israel and Hannah
Luftman, Alvin S. (Alvin Stanley), 1927-.
Mss C 3368
4 charts: geneal. tables; 28 cm.
Photocopy of computer generated genealogical descendancy charts.

Luftman family tree: Descendants of Wolf and Sarah Luftman
Luftman, Alvin S. (Alvin Stanley), 1927-.
Mss C 3369
5 charts: geneal. tables; 28 cm.
Photocopy of computer generated genealogical descendancy charts.

Reinstein family tree: Descendants of Henry and Sarah
Luftman, Alvin S. (Alvin Stanley), 1927-.
Mss C 3370
3 charts: geneal. tables; 28 cm.
Photocopy of computer generated genealogical descendancy charts.

George W. Duffy Bible record, 1800-1866
Mss C 3371
[8] leaves; 19-28 cm.
Original record (with title page) of two leaves with a marriage certificate (1830); dismissal from the Friends [Quakers] (1831); two funereal poems (undated); and one newspaper clipping (undated, photocopy) regarding the Duffy and Wilson families.

Joseph Newbold Bible record, 1766-1873
Mss C 3372
[4] leaves; 28 cm.
Original records with title page.

Caleb Newbold Bible record, 1680-1897
Mss C 3373
[9] leaves; 12-28 cm. + 1 silhouette + 2 ribbons
Original record with title page which also has mounted clippings. It contains a genealogical descendancy of Michael Newbold for four generations, listing the fifth as children. Also strongly treated are the Stockton and White families. There are two orange ribbons with "68" on each; one unidentified silhouette; 3 clippings; and one holographic copy of address by Cotton Mather.

Judith Haden Bible record, 1791-1875
Mss C 3374
[3] leaves; 29 cm.
Original record (with title page) belonging to Judith Haden dated August of 1800 at Boston, though only lists members of the Sullivan family.

Asa Bugbee Bible record, 1790-183
Mss C 3375
[5] leaves; 27-28 cm.
Original record with one family record form leaf blank and including decorative presentation on front paste-down.

James Molineux Bible record, 1829-1908
Mss C 3376
[5] leaves; 14-27 cm.
Original record with title pages and a note on a smaller piece of paper .

John Gould Bible record, 1772-1890
Mss C 3377
[4] leaves; 29 cm.
Original record with title pages which includes a fly leaf that has an attached note from the donor.

William Ellison Bible record, 1762-1820
Mss C 3378
[6] leaves; 30 cm.
Original record with title pages.

Mary Barnard Bible record, 1765-1872
Mss C 3379
[5] leaves; 28 cm.
Original record with title pages and fly leaf with name of owner.

Samuel Wells Hunt Bible record, 1763-1889, 1914
Mss C 3380
[5] leaves; 27-29 cm.
Original record with title pages and fly leaf with name of owner. Also includes one typed letter (1914) and one undated newspaper clipping.

Simon Pettee Jr. Bible record, 1788-1855
Mss C 3381
[5] leaves; 28 cm.
Photocopy of original record with title page with one family record form page being blank. The original is located in the Rare Book collection.

Sarah Palmer Bible record, 1742-1797
Mss C 3382
4 items ([12] p.); 22 x 28-36 cm.
Photocopy of original records and title page from a Bible. Also included are photocopies of three broadsides: "Dr Anderson's Famous Scots Pills" (printed Philadelphia, ca. 1787); "An Epistle from Our Yearly Meeting Philadelphia ... 1812"; and "At a Quarterly Meeting of Friends ... Philadelphia ... 1850", which were found inside the Bible.

John Haacke: A Pioneer of Markham Township, York County, Upper Canada
Haacke, E. Mark.
Mss C 3383
19 p.: 28 cm.
Computer typescript with letter at the end.

Frank B. Coleman papers, 1897-1992?
Coleman, Frank B., 1864-1952.
Mss C 3384
13 leaves: ill.; 8-21 cm.
Two letters (ALsS, 1897, 1911) discuss descendancy from William Brewster, but focus on the descendancy of Ozias Coleman (1765-1843). Included are three leaves of undated data and one photograph (1992?).

Beale family papers, 1785-1915 (bulk 1785-1820)
Beale family.
Beale, George Washington, 1815-1870.
Brewster, Benjamin Emmons, 1851-1935.
Warren, James, 1757-1821.
Mss C 3386 a-c
[4] items; 21-31 cm.
The first folder contains a diary written by James Warren (1757-1821) from 1788 Oct. 2 to 1789 Apr. 9. These 16 pages were folded at the bottom to fit into a bound book. A separate leaf describes Warren as a schoolmaster in the family of Capt. Benjamin Beale at Summer Hill, Squantum [a village in the town of Quincy, Mass.] and the verso has a mounted bill for the passage of Benjamin Beale, his family, and cargo. The second folder in a letterbook, 1785-1820, of 24 letters to Benjamin Beale (1741-1825) from family and businessmen. Beale was employed by Thomas Smythe & Co., of Liverpool, England. The flyleaf has an ink drawing of Capt. Benjamin

Beale's residence at Edge Hill in Liverpool sketched by George Washington Beale (1815-1870) in 1838 [the date of the letterbook's creation?] and a color ink "copy of a drawing by a sailor" of the ship "Betty" of Liverpool commanded by Capt. Beale, 1771. Also, a single letter of 13 pages written by George Washington Beale likely at Burlington, Iowa, in 1863 to his sister Ann.

Family record: Holmes & Snow
Holmes, Nellie M. (Nellie Marina Ford), b. 1874.
Mss C 3387
[24] p.; 28 cm.
Family record created by a mother and daughter-in-law on the Holmes and Snow families.

Jonathan Thing
Mss C 3388
[2] leaves; 35 cm.
Undated, anonymous work on the Thing family starting with Jonathan[1] Thing for four generations.

The only Protestant burial ground in South Boston
Hills, Thomas, 1828-1910.
Mss C 3389
10 p.; 32 cm.
Manuscript transcript of the Emerson Street burial ground, now [1901] called the Hawes Cemetery in South Boston between L and M Streets.

Genealogy of William Ham and his descendants
Ham, Samuel F. (Samuel Franklin), b. 1833.
Mss C 3390
186 p.: photographs; 36 cm.
1900 Jan.
Descendants of William[1] Ham of Portsmouth, N.H., through nine generations. It includes a photograph of the author in the front.

Diary, 1840 Mar. 23-1841 Apr. 15
Smith, Shelton, 1817-1872.
Mss C 3391
[27] leaves; 22 x 36 cm.
Photocopy of the diary of Shelton Smith, of
Oxford, Conn., later a blacksmith, carpenter, and
general store owner. There is a one leaf
genealogical account of everyone mentioned in
this diary by Emily Frances Adams, Shelton
Smith's great great grandchild.

Notes on the LeRoy family, 1855-1938
Mss C 3392
[6, 11] leaves; 16-36 cm.
Mounted information contained within the book
"Nicholas LeRoy et ses descendants" by J-
Edmond Roy (1897).

*Genealogy of the most ancient family of Ashe of
co. Devon, Somerset, Ireland, etc.*
Ashe, Gordon.
Mss C 3393
128 leaves; 36 x 22 cm.
Photocopy of manuscript of the Ashe family.

*Genealogy of the most ancient family of Ashe of
co. Devon, Somerset, Ireland, etc., original
manuscripts by Gordon Ashe*
Molar, Janet.
Mss C 3394
[73] leaves; 28 cm.
Typescript ed.
Photocopy of typescript of the Ashe family with
additions.

*Inscriptions from the Old Cemetery in Bradford,
Mass., 1680-1898*
Woodbury, Louis A. (Louis Augustus), 1843-
1916.
Mss C 3395
80 leaves, bound: photographs; 34 cm.
1895
Typescript transcription of the old cemetery in
Bradford, Mass. Also contains several mounted
photographs.

Account book, 1825-1827
Mss C 34
7 p.; 20 cm.
Portion of an original account book for a
cordwainer(?) in Conway, Mass. - many of the
entries concern the making or repair of shoes.

Daniel Alden Bible record, 1725-1824
Alden, Daniel, -1790.
Mss C 3527 [project entry]
3 p.
Typescript.

*Appointment, 1794 February 14, Rockingham
County, N.H.*
Pearson, Joseph, 1737-1822.
New Hampshire. Governor (1793-1794: Bartlett)
Mss C 36
1 ADS; 19 x 31 cm.
Original partially-printed document completed in
manuscript. Signed by Josiah Bartlett, Governor
of New Hampshire, as a witness and Joseph
Pearson as Secretary. Verso has note that Josiah
Bartlett, Jr. took the oath of allegiance and office
1794 April 1.

*Three Boxford, Massachusetts marriage intention
documents, 1761, 1767*
Wood, Aaron.
Boxford (Mass.). Town Clerk.
Mss C 37
3 DS; 6-13 cm.
First document is a notice of the intent of Joshua
Cleaves of Beverley to marry Huldah Perley of
Boxford, 1761 April 6. Second item is a notice of
the intent of Thomas Cross of Bradford to marry
Lucy Hovey of Boxford, 1767 Nov. 23. Third
item is a notice of the intent of Dudley Foster of
Boxford to marry Rachel Steel of Andover, 1767
Dec 19. All three documents are signed by Aaron
Wood, Town Clerk of Boxford.

Tax bill for David Slaton, 1806 October 1
Smith, William.
Boston (Mass.) Tax collector.
Mss C 38
1 DS; 14 x 17 cm.
Partially printed form completed in manuscript by
William Smith, Collector, with the assessment for
David Slaton.

Letter, 1872 Feb. 28, Concord, Mass. to Thomas G. Appleton
Emerson, Ralph Waldo, 1803-1882.
Mss C 4
[1] leaf; 18 cm.
Letter from Emerson at Concord, Mass., to Thomas G. Appleton thanking him for his gift of a book, probably Appleton's "Faded Leaves."

Concord [Mass.] directory: containing the names of the legal voters and householders in town with their occupations, offices, etc. for the year 1830
Mss C 40
22 p.; 23 cm.
Handwritten lists arranged by surname and by occupation.

Samuel Perry family register, 1754-1810.
Mss C 41
[1] p.; 17-28 cm.
Handwritten register recording the births for Samuel and Penelope Perry family as well as two entries concerning the death of two of their nine children. Includes typescript transcription of the original record by the donor.

Goods on hand at the furnace 1804: stock & book debts, etc.
Mss C 43
36 p.; 31 cm.
Historical note: [Henry Griffith's *History of the town of Carver, Massachusetts* (New Bedford, Mass.: E. Anthony & Sons, printers, 1913)]: The federal furnace was established in 1793 on the Cranebrook by Gen. Silvanus Lazell et. al. Originally known only as the furnace, it produced hollow ware including pots, kettles, pans and irons, etc. However, during the War of 1812, the then idle plant was leased by Benjamin Ellis to produce cannon balls, etc. for the U.S. government (thus it became known as the federal furnace). Operations ceased in 1841.
Original account book with inventories of farming utensils, house furniture, blacksmith shop, tools, and iron left on hand at the federal furnace in Carver, Mass. for April & May 1804. Includes a list of "debts and credits on books at furnace".

Some Orcutt homesteads
Bates, Frank E.
Mss C 4361
16 leaves; 28 cm.
1990, 1904

Journal of our voyage to Cape Briton, 1745 March 6-September 18
Cleaves, Benjamin, Jr., 1722-1808.
Mss C 44
Access to original record restricted: use Register transcription.
36 leaves; 13 cm.
Additional form: transcribed version published in *NEHG Register* 66[1912]:113-124.
Original account of the English campaign against the French fort at Cape Briton. Cleaves was the clerk for the company commanded by Capt. Benjamin Ives, Jr., in Col. Hale's Fifth Massachusetts Regiment. Includes a roll of Capt. Ives' company.

Charles Cohoon family record
Mss C 45
[1] p.; 28 cm.
Typescript transcription of original record (with title page information) for the Charles and Pheobe (Foster) Cohoon of Port Medway, Nova Scotia.

Bible record for the Nathan Bryant family, 1767-1876
Mss C 46
[3] leaves; 28 cm.
Typescript transcription of original record (with title page information) for the Nathan and Sally Bryant family of Dorchester, Billerica and Bedford, Mass.

Genealogy of the Hutchinson family in England and America from 1282-1893
Hutchinson, George Hunt, b. 1861.
Mss C 4622
145 p.: geneal. tables; 35 cm.
1897
A handwritten genealogy of the Hutchinson family that begins with a compiled account from Perley Derby (1823-1897). Also includes an ahnentafel for Anne Louise Hutchinson (1933-1986?) and typed genealogical chart for the Alter family.

Transcription of three letters written by Joseph Bass to Gillam Bass, 1776-1780
Bass, Joseph.
Mss C 47
[2, 2, 2] p.
Handwritten copy of original letters by Joseph Bass dated 1776 October 19 (Camp Mount Independence), 1776 November 9 (Camp Mount Independence), and 1780 July 15 (West Point) to his brother Gillam Bass, Northborough, Mass.

Glimpses of the past
Vroom, James.
Mss C 4752
250 p.; 28 cm.
1892-1895.
[1945 typescript ed.]

Hernly - Hershey - Snavely family Bible, 1747-1931
Mss C 4753
[16] p.; 28 cm.

Armer Fred Earwood Bible record, 1843-1992
Earwood, Armer Fred, 1921-.
Mss C 4754
[6] p.; 28 cm.

Josiah S. James Bible record, 1819-1930
James, Josiah S., b. 1819.
Mss C 4755
[4] p.; 28 cm.

Joseph Daniels Bible record, 1775-1825
Daniels, Joseph, b. 1775.
Mss C 4756
3 leaves; 26.5 cm.

Hammond family Bible record, 1696-1877
Mss C 4757
[19] p.; 43 cm. folded to 21.5 x 28 cm.

Brewster Bible record, 1869-1952
Mss C 4758
1 leaf; 35 cm.

Joseph Odell Bible record, 1793-1839
Odell, Joseph, b. 1796.
Mss C 4759
5 leaves; c 18 cm.

Bennet, Burrows, Crane, Fox, Greenly, Hull, Kelsey, Lewis, Paddock, Pike, Prior, Root, Stannard, Stevens, Sturges Bible records, 1764-1920
Mss C 4760
[20] p.; 28 cm.

Merrill Bible record, 1818-1823
Merrill, Abraham, 1737-1821.
Mss C 4761
1 leaf; 23 cm.

William O. Jones Bible record, 1837-1880
Jones, William O., b. 1837.
Mss C 4762
[4] p.; 28 cm.

Tibbetts - Felt Bible record, 1803-1960
Felt, Ephraim, 1803-1851.
Mss C 4763
[5] p.; 28 cm.

William Stone Bible record, 1772-1820
Stone, William, b. 1772.
Mss C 4764
[5] p.; 28 cm.

Thomas Minard Bible record, 1779-1901
Mss C 4765
[1] p.; 28 cm.

Solomon Robards Bible record, 1733-1819
Mss C 4766
[1] p.; 28 cm.

Main - Blodgett Bible record, 1792-1836
Mss C 4767
[7] p.; 28 cm.

Asa Taft Bible record, 1794-1921
Wikoff, Helen Lyons.
Mss C 4768
[2] p.; 28 cm.

Coolidge family Bible record, 1702-1862
Mss C 4769
[2] leaves; 28 cm.

Research on the Burdick family in England
Burdick, James Alan.
Mss C 4770
[24] leaves; 28 cm.
Photocopy of typescript at the Library of
Congress.

Joseph Bailey Bible record, 1777-1906
Bailey, Joseph, 1777-1850.
Mss C 4771
[1] p.; 28 cm.
Typescript transcription by donor of Bible sold at
auction in Bradford, Vt., on 1996/03/02.

*The descendants of Ethel Davis Born: 1756
Derby, Connecticut[;] Died 1801 Westport, Nova
Scotia*
Davis, Frank B. (Frank Bancroft), 1938-.
Mss C 4772
[i], 4 p.; 28 cm.
Computer typescript descendancy chart.

Hercules Mooney genealogy
Mss C 4773
8 leaves; 14 x 18 cm.
Ms. genealogy originally on 4 leaves which have
since torn in two along the fold.

[Daniel Moore family papers]
Griffin, Robert, fl. 1772-1773, seller.
Mss C 4774
Access to original records restricted; Use
photocopies within same folder.
2 leaves.
One bill of sale (ADS), 1773, which includes
Bristo, a negro slave, from Robert Griffin, of
Bedford, N.H., to Daniel Moore, of Bedford N.H.;
two page genealogy of Daniel Moore. Service
photocopies created for all original material.

Family records not previously printed
Pierce, George E. Mrs.
National Society Daughters of the American
Revolution
Mss C 4775
[7] p.
Photocopy of typescript which includes pages 79
to 82 for Triangle Chapter of the Daughters of the
American Revolution.

*Pig iron furnace cemeteries of the Hanging Rock
Iron region*
Ramsey, Virgil.
Mss C 4776
[iii], 93 p.: ill., maps; 28 cm.
Photocopy of typescript detailing the history of 32
furnace and transcribing inscriptions of their
associated cemeteries in the Hanging Rock Iron
region of Ohio.

Walter Leslie Hubbard papers
Hubbard, Walter Leslie, 1872-1942.
Mss C 4777
[61] leaves; 28 cm.
Photocopy of manuscript written sometime
between 1905 and 1942.

Hermanssen family Bible record, 1878-1916
Mss C 4778
1 item ([4] p.): 28 cm.
Photocopy of original record lacking title pages
and typescript transcription of original.

Ephraim Cutter Bible record, 1767-1864
Cutter, Ephraim, 1767-1841.
Mss C 4779
1 item (3 leaves); 28 cm.
Photocopy of original record and title page.

Descendants of Abial Beadel of Limerick, Maine
Clark, Kenneth Alton, 1967-.
Mss C 4781
[8] leaves; 28 cm.
1993.

*Partial supplement to Samuel Bradlee Doggett's
A history of the Doggett-Daggett family*
Clark, Kenneth Alton, 1967-.
Mss C 4782
[10] leaves: ports.; 28 cm.
[1993]

*Partial supplement to Marlene Hinkley's
Genealogy and family history of the descendants
of John Clarke of Wenham, Massachusetts and
Exeter, New Hampshire*
Clark, Kenneth Alton, 1967-.
Mss C 4783
[13] leaves: ports.; 28 cm.
[1993]

The Ryan family of Edgecomb and Belfast, Maine
Clark, Kenneth Alton, 1967-.
Mss C 4784
[12] leaves: ports.; 28 cm.
[1993]

Genealogy of the Farrow / Farrar family of Maine
Clark, Kenneth Alton, 1967-.
Mss C 4785
17 leaves; 28 cm.
1993.

Descendants of Edward Dwyer of St. Stephen, New Brunswick
Clark, Kenneth Alton, 1967-.
Mss C 4786
[13] leaves: ill.; 28 cm.
1993.

The Duplisea family of New Brunswick and Maine
Clark, Kenneth Alton, 1967-.
Mss C 4787
[15] leaves; 28 cm.
1993.

Partial supplement to J. W. Penney's A genealogical record of the descendants of Thomas Penney of New Gloucester, Maine
Clark, Kenneth Alton, 1967-.
Mss C 4788
[10] leaves: ports.; 28 cm.
[1993]

John Long, Taunton, Mass.
Boyd, Richard G.
Mss C 4789
[121] p: facsims.; 28 cm.
1992
A genealogical letter dated 1851 from David Long, 1761-1852, son of John Long, to Aaron Long Jr., his nephew; continued in 1968 by Paul M. Long, with miscellaneous letters by other family members. Photocopies of original letter interleaved with dot-matrix printer transcription.

Ten generations of Roberts, 1675-1992: Virginia, Tennessee, Kentucky
Fobister, Alice Roberts, 1916-
Mss C 4790
112 p.: ill., maps, facsims.; 28 cm.
[1992]

(John) Bernhard Seibert, Shenandoah County, Virginia, 1717-1801
Bell, Raymond Martin, 1907-1999
Mss C 4791
7, [3] p.: geneal. tables; 28 cm.
1982
Photocopy of typescript which include one genealogical table.

The Seiberts of Saarland, Pennsylvania and West Virginia
Bell, Raymond Martin, 1907-1999
Mss C 4792
44 p.: geneal. tables; 28 cm.
1982
Photocopy of typescript with place name and surname (other than Seibert) index. There is no index to Seibert forenames and the maps contained in original typescript are not present.

Denton ancestors: of Stephen Reynolds, who married Lydia Bartlett
Mss C 4793
[3] leaves; 33 cm.
[1959?] typescript ed.
Carbon copy typescript of lineal descent of Rev. Richard Denton (1586-1663).

Henry Wood of Middleborough, 1959
Wood, J. Sumner, (John Sumner), 1902-1987.
Mss C 4794
[1], 21 p.; 33 cm.
Discussion of the life and times of Henry Wood (d. 1670), analyzing genealogical evidence.

Reminiscences, 1837-[1859]
Abell, Alfred, 1772-1859.
Mss C 4795
[3] journals: col. ills.; 31-32 cm.
Three handwritten and illustrated journals by
Alfred Abell. The first entitled "The family
records of Alfred Abell, Goshen, New
Hampshire," 1837-1859 (one of several "titles"),
memorializing his parents, siblings, and children.
The second entitled "Abell's life memorials" was
started in December of 1837 detailing his
childhood and another part describing his
religious experiences from childhood at Lempster,
Acworth, and Goshen, N.H. The third entitled
"The Pilgrim harp," the largest of the journals at
112 numbered pages, is religious hymns and
poetry. All three journals have color illustrations,
especially the second journal. Each are bound in
stiff newsprint covers bearing the year 1848.

*Second division of Annapolis Township,
Annapolis County, Nova Scotia*
Spurr, Vernon Morse, 1929-.
Mss C 4796
i, 39, [1] p.: maps, charts; 28 cm.
1993 Jan.
Computer typescript ed.
Study of the the grantees by lot within the second
division of the township of Annapolis with this
overlaid on a topographical map.

*Letter, 1825 Dec. 28, Roxbury, Mass. [to] Mrs.
Anstis Tower*
Stratton, Thankful, b. 1764.
Mss C 4797
1 item; 31 cm.
Original letter from Thankful (Rich) Stratton
expressing how happy she was to receive a letter
from her "Dear Daughter".

*Bible record for the Clara Anna Rumery Moulton
family, 1827-1978*
Moulton, Clara Anna Rumery, 1859-1929.
Mss C 4798
[9] leaves; 30 cm.
Photocopy of original record lacking title page
(there is a photocopy of N.T. title page)
concerning the Moulton and Rumery families of
North Hampton, New Hampshire. Includes
computer typescript transcription by the donor.

*Private letters written during the war of the
American Revolution*
Mss C 48
[12] leaves
Handwritten copy of seven letters: two letters by
Stephen Badlam dated 1775 June 25 (Roxbury,
Mass.) and 1776 May 14 (Shamble) to Mary
Badlam, Milton, Mass.; a letter by Lt. John Noyes
dated 1776 July 7, Horns Hook, to Capt. Ezra
Badlam, New York; a letter by Loammi Baldwin
dated 1777 February 4, Woburn, Mass., to Capt.
Ezra Badlam; and two letters by Patience Badlam
dated 1777 June 4 and 1777 June 11, Drchester,
Mass. to Maj. Ezra Badlam, Albany, N.Y.; and a
letter by John Bailey dated 1777 November 23,
White Marsh Camp, to Lt. Col. Ezra Badlam.

Bible record for the Mott family, 1753-1907
Mss C 4800
[10] leaves; 28 cm.
Photocopy of original record with title page.

Brooks genealogy
Brooks, Ralph Edison, 1929-.
Mss C 4801
67 leaves; 29 cm.
[1995]
Typescript concerning the direct line from
Benjamin (ca. 1726-) and Ruth (Davis) Brooks to
Thomas (b.1925) and Ralph (b.1929) Brooks
families (white sheets), other branches (canary
sheets).

*The Summits of colonial America and the United
States: the descendants of Johannes Frantz
Sammet of Lincoln County, North Carolina*
Summit, Glen Scott, 1967-.
Mss C 4802
137 leaves; 28 cm.
[1999]

Stranaghan family, Co. Down 1800-1950
Allen, Frederick.
Mss C 4803
126 p.; maps; 30 cm.
1990

Smith family records, 1865-1936
Smith, Lilian Mercedes.
Mss C 4804
26 leaves; 33 cm.
1944 typescript ed.
Photocopy of typescript transcription of some original material concerning her Smith family ancestry. An account by Sarah Bellona Ferguson called The American colonies emigrating to Brazil - 1865 comprises the bulk of the typescript. Sarah, a daughter of Alfred Iverson Smith, recounts in 1936 her families' emigration (Nov 1865-Aug 1866) from Spring Hill, Navarro Co., Texas along with other Southern families who were going to the Frank McMullen-Bowen Colony in Brazil, the three years spent by the head waters of the Juquia, a tributary of the Ribeiro, and their removal to a town near Sao Paulo. Also includes "Our Pedigree" by Mrs. A.I. Smith and "Smiths show up by the hundreds" copied from a letter by Mary Smith.

A Maciora family memoir
Maciora, Joseph G. V., 1959-.
Mss C 4805
3 p.; 30 cm.
1999
Additional information on the Maciora family which supplements the donor's book Maciora and Mik families Genealogy (1982). Provides information on the donor's grandparents, great grandparents and great great grandparents of Turosl, Lomza, Poland. The handwritten memoir is an English translation, by the donor, of information located in 1991 by a private researcher in Poland.

Some descendants of Joseph Parkhurst (1629-1709) of Chelmsford, Mass.
Sheedy, Stuart R. (Stuart Rockwood), 1918-.
Mss C 4806
53 p.; 28 cm.
1999

A compilation of the line of descent of the Warren family and a short bit of the Hopkins line, compiled with reference to the Bigelow line
Howe, Gilman Bigelow, 1850-1933.
Mss C 4807
5 leaves; 28-34 cm.
Photocopy of original document. Includes photocopy of T.A. Hopkins' invitation dated 1849 Jan. 13 to Henry Shorter's hanging at the Erie County Prison in Buffalo, NY.

Bible record for the Lewis Smith family, 1844-1925
Smith, Lewis, d. 1847.
Mss C 4808
[6] leaves; 28-36 cm.
Photocopy of original record with title page concerning the Smith family of Randolph and Spencer, Massachusetts.

Bible record for the David Ames, Sr. family, 1760-1890
Ames, David Sr., 1760-1847.
Mss C 4809
[4] leaves; 33 cm.
Photostat of original record with title page concerning the Ames family of Bridgewater and Springfield, Mass.

Will of James Mackall, 1753 November 6, Lebanon, Conn.; Inventory, 1755 Jun 23
Mackall, James, 1690-1755.
Mss C 4810
[9, 8, 4] leaves; 33 cm.
Photocopy of original records in which James bequeaths land and movable estate to his wife (Hannah), sons (Archippus, Ebenezer, Elijah, John, Joseph, James, Benajah), daughters (Olive and Rachel), grandsons (Nathanial, Benjamin) and granddaughter (Rachel). Includes typescript transcription of will by the donor.

Will of John Eaton, 1695 March 16, Reading, Mass.; Inventory, 6 January 1696
Eaton, John, d. 1695.
Mss C 4811
[6] leaves; 33 cm.
Photocopy of original record in which John Eaton bequeaths land and moveable estate to his wife (Elizabeth), sons (William, John) and daughters (Elizabeth, Rebekah, Martha, Tabitha, Abygail, Hephsobah, Hannah).

A eulogy on the life and character of John Quincy Adams, delivered at the request of the Legislature of Massachusetts, in Fanueil Hall, on the 15th of April 1848
Everett, Edward, 1794-1865.
Mss C 4812
1 vol. (42 p.); 32 cm.
Holograph with corrections. Includes letter, 17 April 1848, Cambridge (Mass.) to [Jos. Buckingham, Samuel Doane, John Fray, Ezra Wilkinson and David Dewey] from Edward Everett acknowledging receipt of a letter requesting a copy of the eulogy for publication.

Pension file relating to the Civil War service of Zephaniah Howard
Mss C 4813
[14] leaves; 36 cm.
Photocopy of original record (certificate no. 217771) which includes the Death Certificate for his wife, Certificate of Record of Marriage, Neighbor's Affidavit, General Affidavit, Declaration for Pension and Declaration for Invalid Pension.

Pension file relating to the Civil War service of Dwight Hayward
Mss C 4814
[16] leaves; 36 cm.
Photocopy of original record (certificate no. 192558) which includes Pensioner Dropped record, Evidence of Proof documents, Declaration for Original Pension of an Invalid, General Affidavit and Certificate of Disability for Discharge.

Genealogy of the Thaxter family, for my sisters Cushing and Hazelton
Parks, Frederick Thaxter, 1855-1940.
Mss C 4815
[6] leaves; 32 cm.
[192?]
Handwritten copy of a genealogy tracing the lineal descendants from Deacon Thomas[1] Thaxter through John[2], Samuel[3-6] to Samuel[7] which was signed and dated as being written by Samuel Thaxter[8] on 24 Sep 1855. The copyist, Frederick Thaxter Parks (information supplied by the donor, the Grandson of Frederick), then starts back with Samuel[6] on the third leaf and continues through Samuel[7-8], Lucy Jackson[9] (Thaxter) Parks, Frederick Thaxter[10] Parks, to Hope[11] Thaxter and Ward Jackson[11] Parks. The fifth leaf lists the children for Abigail Smith (Thaxter) Hazelton and Sarah Holland (Thaxter) Cushing, both daughters of Samuel[7] Thaxter. The final leaf is blank.

Record of deaths for the John Jacob Lothrop family, 1813-1855
Mss C 4816
1 leaf; 36 cm.
Original record listing the death dates and often the sermon for the John J. Lothrop family and relatives of Cohasset, Massachsuetts.

[Ezekiel M. Brown] family register, 1781-1858
Brown, Ezekiel M., 1782-1858.
Mss C 4817
[1] leaf; 36 cm.
Photocopy of partially-printed lithograph by N. Currier with information concerning the Ezekiel M. Brown family of Brunswick, Topsham and Bowdoinham, Maine.

Appointment, 1753 Sept. 14, Boston, Massachusetts
Shirley, William, 1694-1771.
Mss C 4818
1 sheet: 47 x 28 cm. folded to 23 x 28 cm.
Photostat of original record designating William Pepperrell, Jacob Wendell, Thomas Hubbard, John Winslow, and James Bowdoin Commissioners to act on behalf of the Commonwealth of Massachsuetts at the Fort at St. George's River concerning a treaty with the Indians of the Penobscot and Norridgewock tribes in order to establish and confirm the peace.

John Disbrow of Hackney, Esquire 1608-1680: A brief introduction and a transcipt of his will
Johnson, Eddis, 1901-.
Mss C 4819
7, [3] leaves; 28 - 51 cm. folded to 32 cm.
1973
Typescript biography on John Disbrow (leaves 1-3) and a typescript transcription of John Disbrow's will signed 26 March 1678 and probated 20 September 1680 (leaves 4-7). Includes a photocopy of the original will.

A genealogy of the Philbrick family from their first settlement in America about 1640 to the present time, 1843: Collected from various records and other sources
Philbrick, John.
Mss C 4820
[45] leaves; 28-36 cm.
Photocopy of original ms.

Bible record for the Henry Kipp family, 1774-1913
Kipp, Henry, b. 1803.
Mss C 4821
[7] leaves; 28-36 cm.
Photocopy of original record with title page.

Family record of Ammi Ruhmah Robbins and his wife Salome Robbins of Colebrook and Norfolk, Conn., 1791-1818
Mss C 4822
[2] leaves; 35 cm.
Photocopy of original record.

Lineage of George R. Raub (b. 1895) from William Henry Bowen (1825-1897)
Raub, George R., b. 1895.
General Society of the War of 1812.
Mss C 4823
Typescript with the heading "Genealogical Data" by George R. Raub, Sr., District Deputy President General of the General Society of the War of 1812. The typescript is on paper with the Society of the War of 1812 letterhead. Includes photostat of a letter signed by Mary Torbert at Lycoming dated 8 Sept. 1837 to Mr. Henry Bowen Mansfield, Ohio which provides information concerning George R. Raub's lineage from William Henry Bowen.

Bible record for the Samuel Barrett family, 1792-1891
Barrett, Samuel, 1792-1872.
Mss C 4824
[5] leaves; 36 cm.
Photocopy of original record lacking title page concerning the Barrett family of Wardsborough, Vt. and Jamestown, N.Y.

Bible record for the Peabody Bradford family, 1758-1937
Bradford, Peabody, b. 1758.
Mss C 4825
[3] leaves; 46 cm.
Photostat without title page of original "Family Register" lithographs by D.W. Kellogg concerning the Bradford family. Includes a register for the Charles Bradford (son of Peabody Bradford) and Samuel Gooding families.

Marriage covenant of Stephen Bowen and Esther Shove, Salem, Mass., 11 November 1819
Mss C 4826
1 sheet; 58 x 45 folded to 29 x 23 cm.
Photostat of original marriage record between Stephen Bowen of Newport, RI and Esther Shove of Danvers, Mass. "before the monthly meeting of the people called Quakers in Salem" [Mass.]. Includes the signatures of fifty-seven witnesses.

Journal of Daniel Emerson (partial), 1836-1845
Emerson, Daniel, b. 1810.
Mss C 4827
[6] leaves; 21 cm.
Photocopy of original ms. (two original pages per leaf) which refer to Rev. Emerson's ministry while in Northborough, Mass. The Rev. Emerson later served in East Whiteland Twp., Chester Co., Pa. and the English Presbyterian Church, York, York Co., Pa. Records include "Items of my History" (1810-1836); "Ordination - Marriage" (Aug.-Dec. 1836); "Commission-temperance-Middlesex Conference" (Dec. 1836-Apr. 1837); "Deacons-Weddings-Installation-H. Missions" (Apr.-June 1837); "List of Marriages solemnized by me Danl H. Emerson Minister of the Gospel" (1836-1840); "Baptisms of Children Northborough, Worcester Co., Mass." (1837-1842); and "Northborough Admissions to Church" (1837-1839).

Orderly Book of the Washington Rifle Corps, 1815-1832
Massachusetts. Militia. Fifth Division, Second Brigade, Fourth Regiment, Light Infantry Company
Mss C 4828
Photocopy of original records kept from 9 June 1815 to 22 Oct 1832 by the "Washington Rifle Corps" of Attleboro, Mass. organized June 9, 1815 and disbanded June 1, 1841. Records include the petition to the Governor and Council to establish the Corps; the Grant, the raising of the Corps, rules and regulations of the Corps; description of the Uniform of the Corps; and record of company meetings with notes of the admission, dismssion and death of members. Includes copies of letters concerning the Corps' disbanding.

Account book of Jason Newell, 1811-1830
Newell, Jason, 1784-1853.
Mss C 4830
1 vol. (81 p.); 33 cm.
Records include an account of schooling and a record of tuition for a school in Cumberland, [R.I.] 1811-1812; a list of creditors to the estate of Ruffus Arnold of Cumberland, RI; Report on the appraisal, division and partitioning of the real estate of Joseph Jencks late of Cumberland April 2 1817; plot of land divided between widow and heirs of Welcome Jillson late of Cumberland by Jason Newell surveyor; account of debts due the estate of Rufus Arnold late of Cumberland deceased 5 Feb 1816; day book records for a mill at Poughkeepsie, [N.Y.] 1823-1825; Agreement 29 April 1831 between Nathan Whipple and Daniel Bloodgood of Poughkeepsie and Henry Wheeler; Letter to "Uncle" [Jason Newell] by Whipple Newell of Stamford; letter 19 February 1813 to Jason Newell of Cumberland by William Newell and a Letter 12 March 1830 to Jason Newell in Poughkeepsie, NY from E.J. Metcalf concerning business equipment.

James Edward Warne family documents, 1900-1952
Mss C 4831
[9] leaves; 15-36 cm.
Contains original and photocopies of documents concerning James Edward and Sarah Kate (Commerford) Warne family of Brookyln, N.Y.

First item is a certificate of Holy Matrimony between James and Sarah. Second leaf is a Certificate and Record of Birth for Winifred Lavinia Warne. Third leaf is a deed between Ellen L. Warne and James Edward Warne followed by an Affidavit of Interest and two Certificates of Redemption from Tax Sale. The seventh item is a photocopy of the Certificate of Death for Sarah Warne with the seal of the Recorder on the eighth leaf. The final leaf is a photostat of the Certificate of Death for Edward Warne.

Pedigree charts for Doris Estelle Starkweather
Starkweather, Doris Estelle, 1819-1997.
Mss C 4832
[45] leaves; geneal. tables; 36 cm.

Isaac Little family documents, 1699-1718
Mss C 4833
First item is a photo negative of a portrait (ca. 1710 artist unknown) of Mrs. Bethiah (Little) Barker, the youngest child of Isaac and Bethia (Thomas) Little of Marshfield. The second item is a photostat copy of the Inventory of Isaac Little's estate dated 17 January 1699. The third item is a deed dated 20 June 1718 between Isaac Barker and Gilbert Winslow. Bethiah (Thomas) Little and her daughter, Abigail Little, were witnesses.

Estelle Hutchins Gough's family data
Mss C 4834
[23] p.; 28-36 cm.
First item is a handwritten genealogy concerning the lineal descendants of Enoch[1] Hutchins through Jonathan[2], Joseph[3], John Carr[4], Stephen[5], Alphonso[6] to Estelle Hutchins[7]. Second item is a typescript genealogy concerning the lineal descendants of Howland and Polly (Waterman) Otis through Howland, Jr. to Lizzie Mary Otis (Estelle's mother). Third item is an 1897 application from Clara A. Otis (Estelle's aunt) for membership to the National Society of the Daughters of the American Revolution. Fourth item is a letter from Estelle to the King's Daughters Home, Inc in St. Albans, Vt. The last item is a typescript genealogy called "The Waterman Family of Scituate" on the descendants of Robert Waterman.,
Indenture, 1821 May 11, between Joseph Townson of Westmorland County, New Brunswick and Charles C Carter.

Carter, Charles C.
Mss C 4835
[2] p.; 31 cm.
Indenture by which Joseph Townson of
Westmorland County, New Brunswick bound
himself to Charles C Carter for the sum of $600.
Witnessed by Watson King.

Deed, 1811 March 27
Sawyer, Enoch, 1776-1857.
Mss C 4836
[2] leaves; 32 cm.
Deed by which Enoch Sawyer sold 25 acres of
land in Alton, NH to Ephraim Hanson for $150.
Witnessed by Elijah Hanson and Lemuel Hayes.
Verso has release of Eleanor Sawyer, wife of
Enoch. Deed is recorded in Lib. 68 fol. 280.

Agreement, 1865 May 31
Coates, Hood.
Mss C 4837
[3] p.; 31 cm.
Agreement to settle a boundry dispute between
the heirs of the late Samuel McCully and Hood
Coates of Cumberland County, Nova Scotia.
Witnessed by Robert Moffit and signed by J
McCully, Hood Coates, Wm McCully and R
McCully. Second ADS concerns William
McCully & others vs. Joseph Coates in
Cumberland County, N.S. Supreme Court Case
20 November 1865.

Deed, 1852 July 31
Miller, Thomas.
Mss C 4838
[1] leaf; 36 cm.
Warranty deed in which Thomas Miller sells
fifteen acres of land in Athol, Mass. to Jonathan
Wheeler in consideration of $214. Witnessed by
Isaac Stevens. Recorded in the Registry of Deeds,
Book 503 Page 171.

Robert Gass family record
Gass, Lizzie Janette Oakes, 1852-1918.
Mss C 4839
1 sheet; 43 x 36 cm. folded to 22 x 35 cm. + 1
photograph.
1909?
Hand drawn chart (ca. 1909?) concerning the
descendants of Robert Gass organized into two
columns with the headings "name," "born,"

"died," "married," "husband or wife," and
"children." Includes annotations to 1918 plus a
photograph of Lizzie Oakes Gass.

*The Salisburg Bonds, 1643-1995: with Captain
Joseph Bond of Wilmington, Massachusetts, b.
1761, d. 1840, his ancestors and descendants*
Eisenhart, George Bond, 1934-.
Mss C 4840
[22] leaves; ill., geneal. table; 36 cm.
[1997?]
Computer typescript. Includes ms. transcription of
Bond family members listed within the "Index to
Philadelphia Deaths" from 1860 to 1905.

Account book, 1813-1816, 1819-1821
Mss C 4841
1 v. (ca. 186 p.); 32 cm.
Account book for a general store in Newbury,
Massachusetts. Although most entries concern the
purchases of food items (such as molasses, coffee,
sugar, tea, tobacco, butter, rye flower, cheese and
chocolate), there are items such as nails, soap,
candles and clothing (flannel shirts, shoes etc.)

Account book of Daniel Bond, 1812-1838
Bond, Daniel.
Mss C 4842
1 v. (165 p.); 33 cm.
There are many entries relating to a cider mill
including picking apples, purchasing bushels of
apples, use of the cidermill, and buying cider.
There are also entries concerning the chopping
wood, use of a grindstone, mending fences, use of
pasture, butchering animals, etc.

Day book, 1829-1832
Mss C 4843
1 v. (ca. 172 p.); 38 cm.
Day book for a country store. Entries include purchases for items such as nails, wrapping, brandy, gin, butter, sugar, etc. and payments (often by barter). An endsheet has "DayBook No 4 1829."

Ancestors and descendants of Harry and Roberta Patten
Patten, Roberta, (Roberta Ann), 1936-.
Chesbro, Edward.
Mss C 4844
38, [68] leaves: ports., coat of arms, geneal. tables; 28 cm.
1996
Typescript. Includes photocopies of source documents.

Bolles pedigree
Mss C 4845
[12] leaves: coat of arms; 34 cm.
Negative photostat of evidences for the pedigree of the Bolles family of Osberton, Co. Notts. Includes certified copies from the College of Arms in London and extracts from the Ashmolean mss.

The Bishops' transcripts of Great Missenden parish registers [1575-1680] Buckinghamshire, Eng.: marriages, baptisms, and burials
Great Missenden Parish Church (England).
Mss C 4846
3, 38 leaves; 30 cm.
1924
Typescript.

… The [Norton] family book of origins, private and personal, with historical notes, coats of arms and photographs compiled by [Edward Crandall Norton] ….
Bailey, Frederic W. (Frederic William), d. 1918.
Norton, Edward Crandall, 1920-.
Mss C 4847
120 p.: col. ill., coat of arms, geneal. tables, photographs; 36 cm.
[c1957]
Printed geneal. tables completed in ms. with the genealogy of Edward Wadhams and Margerie May (Crandall) Norton.

Bible record for the Thomas William Pritchard family, 1828-1936
Pritchard, Thomas William, b. 1828.
Mss C 4848
[6] p.; 33 cm.
Original record with title page.

Bible record for the Smith family of Boston, 1805-1876
Smith family.
Mss C 4850
[5] leaves; 38 cm.
Photocopy of the original Bible's title page but an original ms. family record concerning the Smith family of Boston. Donor provided a transcription of the record and a Smith family genealogy concerning the lineal descent from Thomas[1] Smith through Isaac[2-3], James[4] to Eliza[5] Smith of Charlestown, Mass.

Account book of Jonathan Clark, 1790-1814
Clark, Jonathan, 1748-1815.
Mss C 4851
1 v.; 33 cm.
Account book of Jonathan Clark of Northwood, N.H. Entries concern purchases (including bushels of corn, wheat, barley, potatoes; flax; cheese, vinegar, cider, etc.) and labor (including butchering animals, mowing, plowing, chopping wood, etc.) or bording. Seventh page from the back of the book is a genealogical record for the Joseph (1719-1790) and Deborah (1718-1802) Clark family [Jonathan's parents].

Account book of Joshua Emery, 1784-1825
Emery, Joshua, b. 1766.
Mss C 4852
1 v.; 33 cm.
Account book for Joshua Emery of South Berwick, Me. Entries concern the purchase of food (corn, cider, fish, rum, pork etc.), clothing, hay, or labor performed. Many entries deal with timber, especially pine, including culling trees, cutting logs, buying boards, etc.

Account book, 1806-1807
Marsh, Lowrin.
Mss C 4853
268 p.; 39 cm.
Day book for a country store in Waterford, VT. A page in the front of the book has "Lowrin Marsh begins to trade [at] Waterford June 19 1806 for Josiah Marsh which he means to be faithful in their business if he can."

Partial supplement to Robert Wilson Tirrell's The Tirrell, Tirrill - Terrill, Tyrrell book; descendants of William Therrill
Halbrooks, Elizabeth Staples, 1918-.
Mss C 4854
[1] leaf; 36 cm.
2000
On page 197 of Robert Wilson Tirrell's book, it is stated that no further records were found for Rhoda Smith Tirrell (the donor's grandmother). This record provides the name and dates for Rhoda Smith Tirrell's husband, Charles Merion Staples, and their only child, Frederick Clifton Staples (who married Elizabeth Yerkes Flanders). Account continues with the children of Frederick and Elizabeth Staples (Frederick C. Staples, Jr. and Elizabeth Biglow Staples) and the children of Arthur Trenchard and Elizabeth Biglow (Staples) Dyer.

Day book of William Jones, 1819-1836
Jones, William.
Mss C 4855
1 v. (ca. 170 p.); 37 cm.
Day book for a tavern, country store and livery stable kept by William Jones of Lyndeborough, N.H. Entries include items such as tobacco, rum, sugar, brandy, tea, molasses, potatoes, veal, butter, rye, mutton, etc.

Day book, 1811-1817
Tinkham, Joseph.
Mss C 4856
1 v. (ca. 175 p.); 37 cm.
Day book for a general store kept by Joseph Tinkham in Winthrop, Maine. Entries include items such as sugar, rum, wine, eggs, wool, vinegar, butter, tobacco, brandy, Webster's spelling book, farmer's almanac, etc.

Account book, 1850-1854
Mss C 4857
1 v. (145 p.); 33 cm.
Account book for a butcher shop. Entries include purchases of veal, pork, beef, tripe, sausage, lamb, ham, etc.

Day book, 1854-1856
Mss C 4858
1 v. (130 p.); c 31 cm.
Day book for a tavern/general store in Norwich, CT. Entries include purchases of cigars, burning fluid, tea, soap, schnapps, gin, rum, cordial, tobacco, wine, ale, licorice, whiskey, brandy, pepermint, hair dye etc.

Documents concerning Eleazer Frary, 1782-1791
Mss C 4859
Access to original records restricted: Material fragile; use preservation photocopy.
Documents include three letters from Solomon Ensign of Hartford to Eleazer Frary of Hatfield dated 18 March 1782, 22 April 1784 and 28 March 1785. There is one undated ADS from Joseph Holmes and a copy of Eleazer Frary's will dated 7 December 1791.

Bible record for the Platt B. Smith family, 1781-1889
Mss C 4860
[36] p.; 28-32 cm.
Transcription of original record without title page information concerning the Smith, Harmon, Avery, Heacock and Hagadorn families of NY. There are transcriptions of obituary notices for Esther Maria (Smith) Harmon, Anna O. Harmon, and Lottie & Louie (i.e. Louis) Harmon. There is also a transcription of some family records and the "Reunion of the Harmon Family" copied from a Chicago newspaper dated Thursday Sept 30th 1869 No.5.

Bible record for the Jan Le Roy family, 1697-1786
Le Roy, Jan.
Mss C 4861
[9] leaves; 28-40 cm folded to 28 cm.
Photocopy of original record with title page concerning the Le Roy and Sluijter families of Amsterdam. Includes English translation.

Account book of Elijah Fox, 1802-1807, 1827-1834
Fox, Elijah.
Mss C 4862
1 v. ([124] p.); 31 cm.
Account book for a blacksmith shop. Entries concern the making, mending, and/or sharpening of various tools (plow, hoe, sythe, knife, axe, etc.), hinges, chains, etc.

Densmore, Powers and Winslow families
Winslow, I. J.
Mss C 4863
[ca. 152] p.; 22 cm.
Ms. genealogy.

Account book of Chapin Warner, 1825-1860
Chapin, Warner, 1795-1872.
Mss C 4865
117, 20 leaves; 36 cm.
Photocopy of original account book for Warner Chapin of Littleton, NH and Shrewsbury, Mass. Includes family records (pages 115-117). Several of the births were in Westmoreland (NH). Many of the entries in the account book deal with work in a saw mill though there are others concerning general labor (haying etc.)

Bible record for the Chase family, 1618-1889
Mss C 4866
[13] leaves; 27-32 cm.
Original record with title page concerning the Chase family of Sunapee and Wendell, New Hampshire. Includes letters and notes on the Remington and Sturrock family.

James Hall, 1753-1822
Mss C 4867
[3] leaves; 36 cm.
Photocopy of a handwritten biography of James Hall (1753-1822), who was born in England and died in Reading, Mass.

Bible record for the Isabella Purdie Smith family, 1827-1921
Smith, Isabella Purdie, 1827-1916.
Mss C 4868
[4] p.; 32 cm.
Original Bible record without title page concerning Smith family of Ayrshire, Scotland and Ware and Marblehead, Mass.

John Robert Young diary 1846-1859
Young, John Robert, 1820-1879.
Mss C 4869
205, [1] p.; 36 cm.
Photocopy of original record with entries for ministrial services, deaths of communicants, funerals, conversions, baptisms, admissions, dismissions, excommunications, marriages, sermons etc. Locations include Penfield, Oak's Corners, Painted Post, Baldwinsville, Keeseville and Plattsburgh, NY.

Book of the records of the church of our Lord Jesus Christ att [sic] Hassanamisco: Gather'd the 28th of December, Anno Dom: (ni 1731)
Congregational Society (Grafton, Mass.)
Mss C 4871
180 p.; 36 cm.
Photocopy of original record. Includes the foundation church covenant; lists of members (original and admissions), 1731-1774; dismissions, 1736-1773; baptisms, 1731/2-1774; minutes of meetings; public confessions; and miscellaneous items.

Pension file relating to the Civil War service of George Buisch
Mss C 4872
[128] leaves; 28-36 cm.
First eight leaves is a typescript summary of the pension records for George Buisch, a Private in Company C, 160th Regiment New York Volunteers, by the donor. The remaining [120] leaves are photocopies of the original documents in Mr. Buisch's pension file including the certificate of disability for discharge, application for invalid army pension, application for an artificial limb, widow's application for increase of pension, and depositions.

John Heald family register
Mss C 4873
1 leaf; 32 cm.
Handwritten register recording the marriages, births, and deaths of the John and Mary (White) Heald family and that of their son's family, John and Dorcas (Green) Heald. These families lived in Acton and Carlisle, Massachusetts.

The birth days and babtizeing [sic] of the children of Jeremiah Oliver Vallotton & Elizabeth Landry his wife
Vallotton, David Moses, b. 1745.
Mss C 4874
[8] p.; 37 cm.
This handwritten register records the birth, marriage and deaths for the seven children, including the author, of Jeremiah Oliver & Elizabeth (Landry) Vallotton. The final page has a similar register for the David Moses and M. (DuBois) Vallotton family (last 3-4 entries are difficult to read).

A register of the children of the family of Joseph Whitney Junr.: containing their names and ages, time when born, when died, what disease died of, etc.
Mss C 4875
[3] leaves; 30 cm.
Two copies (draft & finished copy?) of a handwritten family register for the Joseph and Abigail (Barnard) Whitney family of Shutesbury, Mass. The third leaf is a copy of the letter from the donor with provenance information.

Marriage intention for Thomas Marshall and Anne Manwaring, 1749
Mss C 4876
1 holograph; 17 x 31 cm.
Handwritten marriage intention with florishes for Thomas Marshall of Norwich and Anne Manerin (Manwaring) of New London. Thomas and Anne were married 23 March 1749 New London, Conn.

Record of marriages performed by Rev. John M. Wedgewood, 1843-1890
Wedgewood, John M., 1820-1891.
Mss C 4877
[10], [10] leaves; 36 cm.
Photocopy of original record of marriages performed by Rev. John M. Wedgewood in Berwick, Shapleigh and Wells, Maine from 1843-1856 then in Decorah, Castalia, Waukon, and Bethel, Iowa from 1858-1890. Record includes columns for "where solemnized," "names," "homes," and "date." Donor included photocopies of biographical material on Rev. Wedgewood including his entry in the 1870 census of Bloomfield Twp, Winneshiek Co., IA and Mr. Wedgewood's obituary in the Waukon Democrat.

Smith / Dinsmoor family correspondence, 1793-1833
Dinsmoor, Silas, 1767-1847.
Dinsmore, William.
Sawyer, E.
Smith, Daniel D., 1782-1825.
Smith, Samuel, b. 1788.
Mss C 4878
16 items (33 p.); 25-33 cm.
The bulk of the letters were written to either John or Robert Smith of New Chester and Bristol, NH. There are five letters, 1793-1804, by Silas Dinsmoor. The subject of Silas' letters includes the death of father, views on female education, and descriptions of his activities as Agent to the Cherokee and Choctaw Indians. There are five letters, 1808-1833, from Samuel Smith of Hinds County, Miss. The subject of Samuel's letters include the "destruction of a part of our little family by the explosion of gun powder," a cholera epidemic, and the new state constitution.

Account book of Amariah Biglow, 1784-1788
Biglow, Amariah, 1757-1790.
Mss C 4879
1 v. (ca. 41 p.); 33 cm.
Account book for Dr. Amariah Biglow of West Boylston, Mass. Entries include charges for visits, delivering children, setting bones, pulling teeth, bleedings, and medicine.

Bible record for the Joseph Seabrook Jr. family, 1761-1800
Mss C 4880
Access to original record restricted: Material fragile; Use preservation copy
[3], [3] leaves; 43 cm. folded to 28 cm.
Original Bible record with title page concerning the Joseph and Ann (Rippon) Seabrook family.

Miscellaneous documents concerning the John Leland and Ann Heaton (Simmons) Perry family of Lyme, NH, 1806-1916
Allen, Fred H. Records of the town of Lyme, NH collected 1884-85.
Mss C 4881
14 items; 9-36 cm.
The first item is a Bible record for the John Leland and Ann (Heaton) Perry family of Lyme, NH (1806-1868). Five unidentified photographs including ferrotypes are then followed by the seventh item, a marriage certificate for Henry Hale and Mary A. Perry who were married in Athol, Mass on 16 Aug 1871. The eighth item consists of two pieces a paper "A quick note from Elizabeth F. Hale" with genealogical notes followed by the nineth item, a note which states "Away and sorrow is no more from your affectionate mother Patty Simmons." The tenth item is the will of Caleb Perry of Athol, Mass., 4th May 1847 [he was the father of John Leland Perry].

Orderly book of the Battalion of Artillery, Third Brigade, First Division, 1822-1834
Massachusetts. Militia. Division 1st, Brigade 3rd.
Mss C 4882
1 v. (156 p.): ill.; 34 cm.
Original record book recording the orders for the battalion by Major Joseph E. Smith and Adjutant Charles H. Hammadt. The handwritten title page includes florishes of a griffen and a dragon and a watercolor illustration. The next page includes a florish of an eagle and two watercolor illustions -- the first is of nine men around a cannon and the second is of a battle scene showing three men firing a cannon down a hill towards an infantry company.

Col. Bond's regimental acc[oun]t book 25th regiment, 1775-1776
Bond, William.
Mss C 4883
1 v. (378 p.); 33 cm.
Original account book of William Bond, a Colonel in "Gardner's Regiment" (25th Continental Regiment). Contains records concerning the companies of Capt Harris, Capt Child, Capt Cook, Capt Fuller, Capt Hatch, Capt Draper, Capt Egery, and Capt Mayhew. There are also sections for Colonel Bond, Doctor Pitcher,

Lt. Col. Alden, Adjt Hunt, and Ensign Ward. Entries concern the receipt of supplies (blankets, firearms, ammunition, shoes, etc.) and their cost, lists of men who have arms in custody (including whether they have a bayonet, gun mark and their gun number), monthly abstracts of the number of men in each company (by rank), and some records concerning officer's pay. Locations include Prospect Hill, Albany, Crown Point and Ticonderoga.

Day book of William Brattle, 1753-1761
Brattle, William, 1706-1776.
Mss C 4884
1 v.; 32 cm.
Original day book for William Brattle of Cambridge, Mass. Cover has "Willm Brattle N Cambridge 1749" and the first page has "William Brattles book August 27th 1753." Most of the entries are "x'ed" out (indicating that the entry had been posted in an account book?). Entries include date, patient's name, and notes concerning treatments such as pills, extracting teeth, dressings, etc.

Account book of Isaac Farwell, 1773-1800
Farwell, Isaac, 1746-1792.
Mss C 4885
1 v. (ca. 150 p.); 30 cm.
Account book of retail inventories, debits and credits for a merchant in Charlestown, Mass. Includes "John Willard to the estate of Isaac Farwell deceased," "account of monies paid for the use of Abigail Farwell - widow of Isaac Farwell deceased" and "Moses Willard" as guardian to Mariam & Betsey Farwell.

Benjamin Adams & Company account book, 1829-1832
Mss C 4886
1 v. (282 p.): ill., 33 cm.
Original account book for Benjamin Adams & Company of Boston. Benjamin Adams was a merchant in business with Peter Thacher Homer, brother Caleb Adams and later with brother Charles Frederick Adams. Entries include "sundries in petty ledger", "petty ledger profit & loss", "balance of interest", "notes receivable", "merchandise to petty ledger", etc. Genealogical notes on the Adams and Homer families written by Fred E. Crowell in 1932 were also tipped in.

Bible record for the George Baker family, 1755-1927
Mss C 4887
[35] p.: col. ill.; 13-38 cm.
Original Bible record with title page concerning the Baker family of Troy, NY. Page [1] has entries for the George and Mary (Green) Baker family. Page [2] & [3] lists the children of George's parents, Joseph and Eleanor Baker. Page [4] has more entries concerning the George and Mary (Green) Baker family. Page [5] lists George Baker's grandchildren by his son, John and Gertrude Maria (Hogle) Baker. Pages [6-7] has a handwritten summery of the original record called "Chronolgy of the Baker family as per the family Bibles". Pages [8-12] is a handwritten transcription called "The Baker's Family Bible" followed by some miscellaneous notes on pages [13-20].

Genealogy of the Locke and allied families
Locke, John Goodwin, 1803-1869.
Mss C 4888
1 v. (136 p.); 37 cm.
ca. 1849
Handwritten genealogies in an account book with the cover title "Record Book No. 1." Includes information on the following families: "Merriam of Oxford" (pgs 1-10, 90-93), Gen. Joseph Locke's family" (pgs 11-13), "David Locke of Woburn" (pgs 14-17), "John Locke of Templeton" (pg 19), "Samuel Locke Prest of H.U." (pgs 23-25), "Jones" (pgs 26-37, 86-89, 111-), "William Locke of Fitzwilliam" (pgs 38-45), "Wilder" (pgs 46-53), "Jonathan Locke of Charlestown" (pgs 58-70), "Barrett" (pgs 74-78), "Withington" (pgs 79-80), [Stone] (pgs 98-103, 106), "Lord" (pgs 108-110), "Proctor" (pgs 116-121) and Ebenezer Locke son of Joshua" (pgs 124-134).

Larrabee family records, 1655-1813
Banks, Charles Edward, 1854-1931.
Larrabee, Mehitable.
Larrabee, Temperance.
Mss C 4889
5 items (26 p.); 15-32 cm.
First item is a Larrabee family register (1751-1813) recorded in a small hand made book. Second item is a loose sheet of paper from the family register which duplicates information

found in the register though it is more legitable and it has a note stating "Temperance Larrabee / her hand / ages of children". Third item is a short one pg letter written by Mehitable Larrabee. Fourth item is a 2 pg "Genealogy of the Larrabee family" tracing some of the descendants from Stephen Larrabee of Wells, Maine. The fifth item is a hand written genealogy by Dr. Chas. E. Banks called "Larrabee" on the descendants of William(1) Larrabee of Maine for three generations.

Houses in Lincoln 100 years old and over with some of their owners
Farrar, Edward Rogers, b. 1863.
Farrar, Samuel.
Mss C 4890
65 leaves, [1] leaf of plates in binder: ill., 1 map; 33 x 26 cm.
1935
Typescript (carbon copy) with photographs of houses pasted in.

Caleb Aldrich family register
Mss C 4891
[16] p.; 32 cm.
Booklet, bound with a ribbon, giving the names (only) of the children and grandchildren of Caleb and Mary (Arnold) Aldrich of Smithfield, RI, as of 7 October 1816. Also some biographical information on Moses Aldrich of Mendon, Worcester Co., Mass., and his twelve children, of whom Caleb was one.

[Alden genealogical records; line of Elisha Alden of Stafford, Conn., including allied families of Allen, Orcutt, and Shepherd]
Mss C 4892
Handwritten notes on the Alden, Allen, Orcutt, and Shepherd families. Two charts. A small (11 x 17 1/2 cm.) handsewn booklet, probably begun about 1808, listing births and deaths from 1793 to 1848 of family members.

[Genealogical records of the Alcott and allied families]
Mss C 4893
Notes (handwritten and typed) and newspaper clippings on the Alcott family and allied families Leggett, Barnum, Elwell, Telfer, Patchen, Hull, and Collyer -- some with Scottish roots.

[Griffith family]
Allen, John K. (John Kermott), b. 1858.
Mss C 4894
Correspondence and handwritten notes on the
Griffith family of Portsmouth, NH.

[Meserve family]
Allen, John K. (John Kermott), b. 1858.
Mss C 4895
Handwritten notes on Clement Meserve of Maine
and some of his descendants.

Deed, 1875 December 28
Wass, James.
Mss C 4896
[1] leaf; 36 cm.
Deed by which James and Adaline Wass of
Addison, Maine mortgages to Abraham Merritt of
Columbia, Maine 1440 acres of land in Addison
(a fourth part of the Troron purchase) for $120.
Witnessed by Christia M. Wass. Recorded by the
Registry of Deeds 1876 Jan 5 in book 141 page
232.

Deed, 1884 December 26
Thompson, Frank H.
Mss C 4897
[1] leaf; 36 cm.
Deed by which Frank H. and Rose E. Thompson
sold to Stillman Heath a parcel of land in Addison
for $20. Witnessed by E.A. Austin and F.A.
Chandler. Recorded by the Registry of Deeds
1888 December 20 in book 185 page 113.

The Harvey family
Harvey, Thomas Middleton, b. 1884.
Mss C 4898
[9] p.; 36 cm.
Typescript genealogy.

Records of the Arblaster and Leigh families
Mss C 4899
[29] leaves; 25-36 cm.
Handwritten notes on the Arblaster family of
England and the Leigh family of Essex and
Surrey, England. Includes photostats of wills and
other documents from the Public Records Office.

*Miscellaneous documents relating to Edmund
Andros*
Mss C 4900
[124] p.: geneal. tables; 34 cm.
Handwritten transcriptions of documents relating
to Sir Edmund Andros and the Massachusetts Bay
Colony. Biographical information on the Andros
family includes extracts from "Sarnia, or brief
memorials of many of her sons", published in
Guernsey in 1862. There are also copies of the
Andros grant of arms in Herald's College; the
Andros pedigree in Herald's College; and Sir
Edmund's will. The remaining transcriptions
(tracts, pamphlets, extracts from letters) have to
do with the political situation in the colony.

When was George(1) Allen born?
Brewster, Mrs. Wales C. (Margaret Isabel Fraser),
b. 1886.
Mss C 4902
[8] p.: geneal. tables; 28-36 cm.
Brief handwritten notes on George Allen who
emigrated to America in 1635 and was buried at
Sandwich, Mass., in 1648. Includes photostats of
his will (proved 7 June 1649) and the inventory of
his estate (1649).

*Ancestry and descendants of William Almy of
Portsmouth, RI*
Chamberlain, George Walter, 1859-1942.
Mss C 4903
[64, 19] leaves: geneal. tables; 28-32 cm.
Handwritten notes on William Almy (ca. 1601-ca.
1676) of Portsmouth, R.I., his wife Audry
Barlowe, and their descendants for several
generations. Notes on the English ancestry of the
Almy family, including transcribed extracts from
records at Northamptonshire and Leicestershire,
England. Genealogical tables. Typed
transcriptions of several late eighteenth- and early
nineteenth-century wills from Massachusetts and
New York.

Tabular pedigree of Robert Abell of Stapenhill, Derbyshire, Eng., and George Abell of Hemington, Leicestershire, Eng., with notes
Abell, Horace A. (Horace Avery), b. 1883.
Mss C 4904
[13] leaves: geneal. tables; 33 cm.
1928
Carbon copy typescript of selected records (complaints, wills, and an extract from the 1611 Visitation of Derbyshire) relating to the Abell family. Locations of the original records include the Public Record Office, London; the Probate Registry, Lichfield; the Prerogative Court of Canterbury; and the Principal Probate Registry, London. A chart shows the descendants of Robert Abell and George Abell.

Family group sheets for Henry Adams of Braintree (d. 1646) and his children
Colt, LeBaron C.
Mss C 4905
7 p.; 26 x 36 cm.
Negative photostats of handwritten family group sheets with source citations.

Genealogical record of the family of Robert Ashley (d. 1682) of England; Roxbury, Mass.; and Springfield, Mass.; with material relating to the Bowdoin Square Baptist Society, Boston, Mass.
Pond, Joseph Adams.
Mss C 4906
[41] p.: ill.; 20-35 cm.
A typescript genealogical record (carbon copy) of the family of Robert Ashley (d. 1682) of England; Roxbury, Mass.; and Springfield, Mass., showing descendants in one line for nine generations. These descendants include Seraph Ashley, b. 1827, who married the Hon. Joseph Adams Pond of Boston (1827-1867). Pond was affiliated with the Bowdoin Square Baptist Society, Boston, Mass., as parishioner, treasurer, and clerk.

Records of confession processes from 5 May 1787 to 22 June 1794
Avery, James, 1758-1798.
Mss C 4907
1 v. (132 p.); 33 cm.
Original record of courts held before James Avery "in a process of confession in a plea of the case". Entries record the date and location of the court proceedings, the plaintiff and defendant's names,

and the judgement. Record includes transcriptions of writs issued by James Avery to the sheriff of Lincoln County for the seizing of assets and/or arrest of delinquent defendants.

Trinity Church records, 1795-1860
Trinity Church (Litchfield, Conn.
Mss C 4908
1 v. (265 p.); 33 cm.
Original record book recording the establishment of the church, "members of the church deceased" 1796-1835 (p. 73-4), "members received anew into the church" 1795-1837 (pg. 181-2 & 175-178), "list of members received on recommendation from other churches" 1795-1836 (pgs 183-4), "list of members dismissed from this church" 1798-1799 (pgs 185-6), "register of marriages" 1795-1836 (187-193), "register of marriages in Episcopal Society" 1795-1816 (197-198). "Register of deaths Episcopal Society" 1835-6 (p. 200), "bill of motality Pr[esbyteria]n Society" 1795-1837 (pgs. 205-218), bill of mortality in Ep[iscopa]l Society" 1795-1834 (219-224), "register of baptisms in the Presbyterian Society" 1795-1836 (pgs. 225-233 & 163-164), "register of births in Preby Society," 1795-1816 (234-244), and "register of births in Ep^1 Society," 1795-1811 (250-255).

Record book of Nathan West, Justice of the Peace, Rensselaer County, New York, 1824-1834
West, Nathan.
Mss C 4909
1 v. (ca. 150 p.); 33 cm.
Original record concerning courts held before Nathan West. Entries record the date the summons and/or warrant was issued, the date and location of the court proceedings, the plaintiff and defendant's names, and the judgement.

Hanson [Mass.] family Bible records
Drew, Eric N.
Mss C 4910
57, 19 p.; 32 cm.
Handwritten transcription of original records.

1st Kansan colored vol. reg't., 1863-1865
Earle, Ethan.
E508.9/1st Microfilm also Mss C 4911
Access to original record restricted; Use
microfilm
1 v. (100 p.); 31 cm.
Original account book of Capt. Ethan Earle,
commander of First Kansas Colored Volunteer
Regiment Company F. A list of the regiment's
field, staff and line officers and the roll of soldiers
in Company F is followed by monthly lists
concerning the issue of clothing to Company F.
The lists include the men's names and notations
as to whether the men received items such as
jackets, pants, shirts, drawers, shoes, caps,
blankets, etc. Mr. Earle added a memorandum
dated "Boston January 1873" concerning his
service, a short history of the flag for Company F,
and a 28 page history of the regiment.

*A copy of the records of births, deaths, marriages,
and intentions of marriages of Northborough,
Mass.: also a copy from the church records of the
First Church in Northborough Mass. of baptisms,
admissions to the church and dismissals to other
churches also a copy of the inscriptions from the
old cemeteries in Northborough*
Howe, Gilman Bigelow, 1850-1933.
Northborough (Mass.)
Mss C 4912
152, 18, 167 p.; 36 cm.
1899
Handwritten transcription of original records.

*List of persons taxed in the precinct and town of
Northborough, Mass. from the year 1744 to 1850
so far as can be obtained from existing records
and papers in the year 1899*
Howe, Gilman Bigelow, 1850-1933.
Northborough (Mass.)
Mss C 4913
44 p.; 36 cm.
1899
Handwritten transcription of original records.

Dover, Mass. family records
Mss C 4914
30 p.; 32 cm.
Handwritten transcription of family records from
19 Bibles with records concerning families from
Dover, Mass.

*Dover, Mass. records of the First Parish Church
1812-1849*
First Parish Church (Dover, Mass.)
Mss C 4915
9 p.; 31 cm.
Handwritten transcription of original record.

*Miscellaneous documents concerning the Leander
P. Lovell family and the Fall River Iron Works,
1820-1841*
Lovell, Leander P., 1798-1842.
Mss C 4916
93 items.
Original documents including correspondence
(both business and personal), deeds, promissory
notes and receipts to and from Leander P. Lovell
as director of the Fall River Naillery, a subsidiary
of the Fall River Iron Works. The subject of the
business letters includes procuring labor, labor
costs, prices/quality of nails, operating expenses,
etc. The personal letters deal with the health of
family members, school experiences, current
events and loving sentiments. Includes draft of a
speech by Leander Lovell on the advantages of
labor saving machinery. Prominent
correspondents include Richard Borden, Francis
Henry Saltus and Leander's siblings.

*Baptisms and deaths taken from the records of the
First Congregational Church in Hanson, formerly
Pembroke, from the year 1820*
First Congregational Church (Hanson, Mass.)
Mss C 4917
7, 4 p.; 31 cm.
Handwritten transcription of original records.
Includes "Deaths taken from the records of the
Baptist Church South Hanson."

Letterbook of Thomas Goadsly, 1795-1796
Goadsly, Thomas.
Mss C 4918
1 v. (160 p.); 33 cm.
Original letter book of business correspondence
concerning the purchasing, receipt and selling of
goods, attachments, securities, opening/closing
accounts, etc.

West Stockbridge, Mass. family records
Mss C 4919
[25] p.; 27-31 cm.
Handwritten transcription of six original family records, including Bible records, a family register and an account book. Entries concern the Easland, Arnold, Cone, Moore, Edwards & Jaquins families.

Carver, Mass. records
Mss C 4920
[52] p.; 14-31 cm.
Handwritten transcription of original records concerning families of Carver, Mass.

The roll of Karlaverock: anno 1300.
Taylor, C. R.
Mss C 4921
1 v. ([32] leaves): col. ill., coat of arms; 34 cm.
Handwritten transcription of an ancient heraldic poem from a manuscript in the British Museum enumerating the barons, knights & gentlemen who attended King Edward during a campaign against the Scots in 1300. Includes hand painted decorative initials, floral rules, and coat of arms.

Inventory of all the estate of his late excellency John Hancock Esqr of which he died possessed in the County of Suffolk and Commonwealth of Massachusetts taken by order of the Hon George Minot, Judge of Probate
Mss C 4922
1 v. (18 p.); 31 cm. + 1 photograph.
Contemporary handwritten copy of the original (see historical note) bound as a small book. Note on inside cover by the donor states "This inventory was copied for Dr. Richard Perkins whose wife, Mary Hancock, was sister to Gov. John Hancock. Their children were among the heirs to the property." The back paste down has some genealogical information dated 3-1-1932 on the donor's descent from Richard and Mary (Hancock) Perkins along with a photograph of Mary Perkin's tombstone in the South St Burying Ground in West Bridgewater, Mass.

Bible record for the Aaron Sanford Sr. family, 1786-1966
Mss C 4923
[5] p.; 30 cm.
Original record (without title page) for the Aaron and Fanny (Hill) Sanford Sr. family.

Church records of Chester, Mass.
Hosmer, J.
First Church (Chester, Mass.)
Mss C 4924
1 v. (154 p.); 32 cm.
Handwritten transcription of the original records of the following churches in Chester: First Church (births, marriages & deaths 1769-ca. 1850), Second Congregational Church (deaths 1857-1897) (on pgs. 151-2) and Methodist Episcopal Church (deaths 1851-1896) (on pgs. 152-4).

Baptisms in the second religious society of Pembroke, now the First Congregational Church of Hanson: these records are in the possession of the church
First Congregational Church (Hanson, Mass.)
Mss C 4925
38 p.; 31 cm.
Handwritten transcription of original record covering 1749-1819. Last page includes one death (1819) for the Baptist Church of South Hanson, fomerly Pembroke.

Copy of births, marriages & deaths taken from Wells town books of record.
Hubbard, Joshua, 1795-1868.
Wells (Me.)
Mss C 4926 a-b
330, 117 p.; 34 cm.
Handwritten transcription of original records (1750-1830) by Joshua Hubbard in folder a. Typescript "Index to the records of the town of Wells Maine" by Stephen P. Sharples in folder b.

Genealogical record of the descendants of John and Elizabeth Baker of Charlestown and Concord, Mass., and of Killingly, Conn.
B. A. (Baker, Amos)
Mss C 4927
1 v. (39 p.); 32 cm.
Handwritten record showing five generations. John and Elizabeth Baker emigrated from England in 1721.

Bacon and Libby descent
Mss C 4928
[2] sheets: ill.; 25 x 35 cm.
Photocopy of a [handwritten?] record of the
descendants of Josiah Bacon of Barnstable,
Mass., and James Libby of Maine.

*A copy of the records of births, marriages and
deaths from the original records of the town of
Sudbury, Mass., from the first settlement of the
town 1638 to 1850*
Hunt, Jonas S.
Sudbury (Mass.)
Mss C 4930
1 v. (304 p.); 35 cm.
1884
Handwritten transcription of the original record.
Births are on pages 3 to 157, marriages pages 160
to 259 and deaths on pages 262 to 304.

*Sudbury [Mass.] records and miscellaneous
papers*
Ward, Andrew Henshaw, 1784-1864.
Sudbury (Mass.)
Mss C 4931
1 v. (356 p.); 35 cm.
Handwritten transcriptions of original records.
Includes births from 1635-1792 (pgs. 1-285) &
from 1639-1700 (pg. 287), marriages from 1639-
1806 (pgs. 1-285) & from 1717-1735 (pg. 293),
deaths from 1640-1835 (pgs. 1-285), records of
the names of the inhabitants of Sudbury and the
quantities of meadow land granted to each (pg.
286), N. Sudbury valuation 1798 (pg. 324),
miscellaneous papers (pg. 336), petition from the
inhabitants of Strawberry Bank [now Portsmouth,
NH] (pg. 340), petition Brain Pendleton &c. (pg.
341), return of sample packages to test invoices
(pg. 348), church records (pg. 344), papers of
Andrew H. Ward (pg. 353) and deaths and
marriages 1719 to 1841 (pg. 356).

Rochester, Mass.: records
First Church (Rochester, Mass.)
Mss C 4932
37, 135, 7, 47 p.; 25-34 cm.
Handwritten transcription of original records
concerning Rochester, Mass. Includes epitaphs
for cemeteries in Marion and Mattapoisett, Mass.,
family Bible records from Mattapoisett and
Rochester, Mass., two vols from the First Church,

records of the Second Church (1740-1849);
baptisms in the Third Church in North Rochester
(1794-1845); and records of marriages, births,
deaths and burials of friends belonging to the
Monthly Meeting of Dartmouth (records
pertaining to Rochester, Mass.)

*About some descendants of Samuel and Sarah
(Lamson) Bancroft of Reading, Mass.*
Mss C 4933
[42] p.; 21-32 cm.
Manuscript genealogy of the descendants of
Samuel and Sarah (Lamson) Bancroft of Reading,
Mass., with notes on other Bancroft families.

Baldwin family: working papers
Baldwin, Evelyn Briggs, 1862-1933.
Mss C 4934
2 parts ([23, 22] leaves); 29-33 cm.
1925
Carbon copy typescripts, annotated and corrected
by hand. Part 1, based on the Baldwin Genealogy
by Charles C. Baldwin, traces English
descendants from John Baldwin of the Hayle,
Buckinghamshire, England, whose will was
proved 1565-6. Includes extracts relating to the
surname Baldwin from parish registers in
Buckinghamshire, and extracts from the U.S.
Census of 1850 relating to Baldwin and other
families from various New York towns.

*Copies of documents relating to George Baldwin
of Rhode Island and Long Island, New York 1652-
1680*
Baldwin, Evelyn Briggs, 1862-1933.
Mss C 4935
[16] photostats; 21-25 cm.
Photostats of 17th-century deeds, bill of sale,
codicil, bond, divorce papers, and other
documents relating to George Baldwin of
Warwick, R.I.; and Huntington, Hampstead, and
Gravesend, Long Island, N.Y. A typed
transcription and translation of Baldwin's divorce
proceedings (original in Dutch, 1656-7) from his
first wife, Abigail, is provided.

Documents concerning Abiezer Packard of Stoughton, Mass.
Mss C 4936
13 items: ill.; 4-31 cm.
Miscellaneous papers, including receipts, promissory note, lease, license to sell alcohol, court writ, and certification to teach.

Ancestry of Asa Bacon(5)
Bacon, Erdix Newton, b. 1844.
Mss C 4937
[28] leaves; 32-39 cm.
Typescript genealogy of Asa Bacon of Wrentham, Mass., and Washington, Vt., and his descendants. Includes introductory notes on the Bacon family in England and America. Numerous handwritten annotations and corrections, and one manuscript page of additional records. This material closely parallels the published genealogy of 1915.

Bosworth genealogical records
Bosworth, Mary Ella, b. 1852.
Mss C 4938
1 v. ([26] p.): photographs; 21-35 cm.
Brief genealogy of the family of Bela and Joanna (Harlow) Bosworth of Plympton, Mass. Includes the Volunteer Enlistment form for their son, George W. Bosworth, in the Civil War. Bosworth was a captain in Company G, Sixteenth Regiment New-Hampshire Volunteers.

Brockett family of England and America
Mss C 4939
1 folder (ca. 30 items): geneal. tables; 17-36 cm.
Manuscript and typescript material relating to the Brockett family of England and America. Includes correspondence, data from English sources, and English pedigrees. There are references to the Brockett or Brackett immigrants to America: John Sr. of New Haven, Conn. and Elizabeth, N.J., and Anthony of Portsmouth, N.H.

The Barney family of America: four generations (from Rev. Jacob Barney Jr.)
Barney, William.
Mss C 4940
[16] p.; 17-32 cm.
1882
Manuscript genealogy of the Barney family of Massachusetts. Includes three letters relating to the genealogy itself.

Vital records of Bayley - Bailey family
Mss C 4941
[52] p.; 28-32 cm.
Manuscript notes from from published sources on the Bailey family of Massachusetts and Maine. Also family records for Edmund Bailey and wives Mary (Parkhorst), Abigail (Bartlett), and Prudence (Morse); and Thomas Bailey and wife Elizabeth (Himball).

Miscellaneous papers relating to Samuel K. Bailey
Bailey, Samuel K.
Mss C 4943
[6] items: geneal. tables; 22-25 cm.
Certificate (1839) confirming Bailey's election as lieutenant of a cavalry company in Massachusetts; certificate (1842) accepting his resignation. Statement (1851) concerning Bailey's height. Draft genealogical chart. Short genealogy (names only) of descendants of John Bailey who came to America in 1635. Letter (1909) having to do with the collection's provenance.

Notes on the Borden family
Mss C 4944
[13] leaves; 33 cm.
Notes on the Borden family from the Feet of Fines, Kent, 1500 to 1630.

Genealogical records of the Bean family of New Hampshire, including allied families Bohonon and Webster
Mss C 4945
[49] leaves, [62] p.; 11-36 cm.
Typescript notes on the Bean, Bohonon, and Webster families. Manuscript notes on Ebenezer Webster and son Daniel Webster. Miscellaneous manuscript notes on Bean families and others. Correspondence circa 1812-1912.

Beauclerk, Lord Vere, coat of arms
Mss C 4946
[1] item: coat of arms; 36 x 23 cm.
Black-and-white printed coat of arms, ca. 1800, of Beauclerk, Lord Vere. Cut from a printed volume.

Letter, 1630 March 14, Watertown, Mass. [to] the Barrington family et al.
Masters, John.
Mss C 4947
[7] leaves: geneal. tables; 26-30 cm.
Photostat of a letter dated 14 March 1630 from John Masters at Watertown, near the Charles River, New England, to Lady Barrington and others in England. Masters writes briefly about living conditions and his responsibilities toward the family of Sir Richard Saltonstall. An accompanying typescript transcription gives detailed information on the location and appearance of the original. There is also a brief manuscript genealogical chart of the immediate Barrington family.

Genealogical notes on the Baird or Beard family of Massachusetts
Crane, Alexander.
Mss C 4948
[18] p.: geneal. tables; 28-32 cm.
Manuscript notes on Baird or Beard families of Massachusetts, extracted from town collections of vital statistics. Genealogical charts of Baird, Beard, Bard families of Auburn, Billerica, Boston, Grafton, Leicester, Worcester, Mass., and elsewhere.

Letters pertaining to the Barnes and Reed families of Vermont
Mss C 4949
15 items ([50] p.); 21-33 cm.
Twelve letters and three miscellaneous manuscript items pertaining to the Barnes and Reed families of Bakersfield, Vermont circa 1833-1866.

The Baxters of New England: a family history
Baxter, James Phinney, 1831-1921.
Mss C 4950
1 v.: geneal. tables; 29 cm.
1921
Typescript genealogy of Simon Baxter of Martha's Vineyard, Mass., and Connecticut, and his descendants. Index to all surnames. Pedigree sheets for Mehitable Cummings Proctor, Sarah Cone, and Sarah Kimball Lewis.

Blake family: a genealogical history of William Blake of Dorchester and his descendants comprising all the descendants of Samuel & Patience (White) Blake
Blake, Samuel, 1797-1867.
Mss C 4951
1 v. (vi, 144, [8] leaves); 32 cm.
1856
Manuscript genealogy from which Blake's genealogy of 1857 was printed. Appendix and index.

Indian account book of Joseph Twitchell, 1773-1791
Twitchell, Joseph, 1718-1792.
Mss C 4953
1 v. (85 p.); 38 cm.
Original account book for the associate guardian for Natick Indians (as appointed by the General Court). First page has "Joseph Twitchells Bok of Indian accounts". Entries include debts and credits concerning the selling of property and estate settlements performed by Twitchell on behalf of the Natick Indians. Entries also include his acquisition of clothing and food.

Redway family letters
Redway, Carpus, 1791-1873.
Mss C 4954
[23] leaves; 28-34 cm.
Photocopies of original letters written by two members of the Redway family: Carpus Redway of Lanesborough, Mass.; Henderson, N.Y., and Ray and Armada, Mich.; and his son Jesse W. Redway. Carpus's letters date from 1865 to 1869. Jesse's letter is dated 1847.

Barber genealogy and miscellaneous information pertaining to the Barber family
Barber, George W. (George Warren), 1835-1886.
Mss C 4956
1 v. ([464] p.); 36 cm.
1876
Manuscript genealogical data on the Barber family. This appears to be an earlier version of A 935 (formerly "SG BAR 15"), although it contains some information that was not transcribed into that volume.

Records of the British church of Salvador, Bahia, Brazil
Fraser, Marian Foster, 1922-.
Mss C 4957
39, 16, 31, 40 leaves; 32 cm.
1980
Typescript transcription of the original record.

Account book, 1647-1650, 1666-1677
Sedgwick, Robert, 1613-1656.
Learned, Ebenezer.
Mss C 4958
1 v. (100 p.); 35 cm.
Cover has "Ledger an(o) 1671" below which is "Robt Sedgwick ??? 1642" with a line through it below which is "Eben(r) Learned's book July 1770" [Ebenezer Learned lived in Medford, Mass. circa 1782]. Entries concern the provisions, crew and cargo of the ships Unicorn of London and the Sarah of Boston. There are many entries circa 1672 concerning the sale of medical supplies obtained from Spencer Piggott of London, apothecary.

Brown family genealogical records and legal papers
Mss C 4960
16 items; 36 cm.
Manuscript genealogy of some descendants of Richard Brown of Newbury, Mass. Also legal papers of Charles H. Brown and his son, Gardner C. Brown, both of Boston, Mass.

Genealogy of some of the first settlers in Attleborough
Jillson, David, 1824-1889.
Mss C 4961
1 v. (375 p.); 35 cm.
Handwritten genealogies on Attleborough, Mass. families.; transcribed "Inscriptions from Grave Stones in Cumberland, R.I." (p. 300-334); "Bristol Co. Probate Records" (p. 335-356); "Inscriptions Gravestones at Rehoboth Centre" (p. 357-359); "Inscriptions from g.s. at North Rehoboth" (p. 360-375).

Correspondence and notes concerning the Bowditch family
Bowditch, Harold, 1883-1964.
Mss C 4962
ca. 142 items: ill., geneal. tables.
Manuscript and typescript correspondence, primarily from 1922 and 1923, in response to Mr. Bowditch's requests for information on the Bowditch family. Arrangement is chronological when possible. Also miscellaneous interspersed notes on the Bowditch family, including extracts from the Boston Directory, 1816-1920.

Account book of John Pearson, 1736-1740
Pearson, John, 1702-1784.
Mss C 4963
1 v. (300 p.); 31 cm.
Original account book for a cloth dresser - many of the entries concern the dressing, scouring, dyeing and pressing of cloth. Last page and the back pastedown has genealogical information on the John and Ruth (Hale) Pearson family.

Sir William Browne, knight, 1556-1610, and Sir Nathaniel Rich, knight, 1636: a chapter of family history
Scull, G. D. (Gideon Delaplaine), 1824-1889.
Mss C 4965
[94] leaves: coat of arms, geneal. tables; 34 cm.
1882
Manuscript history of the Brown family in England. Nathaniel Brown was an early settler at Ipswich, Mass.

Orderly book, 1841-1845
Massachusetts. Militia. Division 1st, Brigade 3rd.
Massachusetts. Militia. Division 1st, Brigade 1st.
Mss C 4966
1 v. (250 p.); 33 cm.
Cover title states "Records of the regiment of Light Infantry in the Third Brigade, First Divison; records of the 1st Regiment, 1st brigade, 1st division", the bulk of the records concerns the latter. Entries concern the general, brigade and regimental orders. Many of the orders were written into the book, although, there are also orders via letters (handwritten and printed) and pamphlets tipped in along with records concerning the choice of officers to fill vacancies.

Subscription book, 1812-1814
Bradford & Read.
Mss C 4967
1 v.; 32-34 cm.
Account book recording the names of subscribers to the American Review of History and Politics, Medical Journal, Journal of Medicine and Surgery, British Lady's Magazine, and London Medical and Physical Journal. Includes an invoice of books returned to Bradford and Read by Josiah C. Shaw June 5 1816, an account of books bought of Hillard November 1814, and "supposed account of stock of Bradford & Read Booksellers".

Copy of the town records of Yarmouth, Mass., 1657-1797
Mss C 4968
1 v. (158 p.); 35 cm.
Handwritten transcription of original record.

Lineage of the Bowens of Woodstock, Conn., copied from rough notes
Bowen, Edward Augustus, 1847-1926.
Mss C 4970
2 v.; 34-36 cm.
1895
Manuscript genealogy and notes on the Bowen and allied families. Much of this material appears in Bowen's printed genealogy of 1897.

Deaths from various sources 1700 to 1800
Copeland, Elisha Gilman.
Boston (Mass.) Committee for the Reduction of the City Debt.
Mss C 4971
1 v. (109, 47 p.); 34 cm. Note: Boston City Archives also has a handwritten version.
   Additional form: One of the sources for Robert Dunkle and Ann Lainhart's; *Deaths in Boston Medical Center1700 to 1799* (Boston, Mass.: NEHGS, 1999)
Handwritten list of people who died in Boston from 1700 to 1800 compiled from various sources. List includes the person's name, age, death date, and source. Back to front has a copy of "City of Boston. Record of the proceedings of the Committee for the Reduction of the City Debt" from 1827-1839.Refers to the building of Faneuil Hall, East Wharf, the suggestion that the city should sell land west of Charles St., etc.

[Bullock genealogical records]
Davis, John W.
Mss C 4972
[38] p.; 32 cm.
1897-99
Manuscript notes on brothers Samuel, Richard, and Israel Bullock, who settled in Rehoboth, Mass., in 1640.

The Treasurer's [Richard Russell's] account of receipts & disburs[e]ments of the Colony of Massachusetts Bay from 1645 to 1656
Russell, Richard, 1611-1676.
Mss C 4973
Access to original record restricted; Material fragile
1 v. (123 p.); 35 cm.
Original account book with entries concerning the Narragansett expedition, General Court, charge of prisoners, charge of Magistrates and Deputies, wolves killed, fines, impost of wines, Winslow's voyage for the Country, etc.

The Folger family
Folger, William Coleman, 1806-1891.
Mss C 4974
1 v. (21 p.)
Handwritten genealogy on the Folger family. Includes clippings from the Inquirer and Mirror concerning the Folger/Foulger surname and two letters written by the author to John Ward Dean, Editor of the *NEHG Register*. The early generations of this manuscript were printed in the *NEHG Register* 16[1862]:269-78.

Ledger of the Schoodic Lakes Land Company, 1844-1854
Chs Copeland & Co.
Mss C 4975
1 v. (143 p.): map; 35 cm.
Company held by Charles and Benjamin Copeland and James Wiggin. Wiggin sold his interest to Frederick Kidder in 1845. Record contains a handwritten transcription of the 1844 deed by which the company acquired the hundred thousand acres around the Schoodic Lakes in Maine from the Bingham heirs. Includes debits and credits for bills payable and receivable. Most of the entries relate to the lumber removed from their lands.

Ancestral tablets: a collection of diagrams for pedigrees, so arranged that eight generations of the ancestors of any person may be recorded in a connected and simple form
Whitmore, William Henry, 1836-1900.
Mss C 4976
1 v. ([34] p.): geneal. tables; 31 cm.
1885
Printed genealogical tables completed in manuscript with the ancestry of Freeman Josiah Bumstead and Mary Josephine (White) Bumstead, parents of Josephine Freeman Bumstead.

[Genealogical records of the Bushnell and Holt families]
Mss C 4977
1 v.; 32 cm.
Genealogical records of Stephen and Mary (Andrus) Bushnell and their descendants, and of Uriah and Margaret (Mason) Holt and their descendants. Also correspondence from the 1930s and loose manuscript notes.

[Genealogical notes on William Brown of Plymouth, Mass., 1635, and some of his descendants]
Gren, Axel Henry, b. 1892.
Mss C 4978
[4] items: geneal. tables; 17-34 cm.
1958
Genealogical material concerning some descendants of William Brown and his wife Mary Murdoch of Plymouth, Mass. Includes a report from the College of Arms, London, concerning the occurrence of the name William Brown in 17th-century visitations in England. Also several charts tracing various Brown lines.

[Genealogical records of the Brick family]
Mss C 4979
7 items: ports., geneal. tables; 32 cm.
Photostats of material concerning the Brick family of New Jersey, Mississippi, and Texas. Collection includes an illustrated family tree, marriage certificate and bonds, and newspaper clippings.

Genealogy of Governor Simon Bradstreet of Massachusetts Bay Colony
Helmershausen, Adella, b. 1867.
Helmershausen, Mary F. Bradstreet, 1841-1921.
Bradstreet, Daniel Moore, 1795-1877.
Mss C 4980
3 v.: ill., ports., coat of arms, geneal. tables, photographs; 32 cm.
1939
Manuscript and typescript genealogy of the descendants of Simon Bradstreet. Includes notes on English ancestry.

[English records pertaining to the Butler family]
Mss C 4981
[21] leaves; 33 cm.
Typescript abstracts of wills and acts of administration, 1562-1652.

[Descendants of George Cabot of Boston, Mass.]
Watkins, Walter Kendall, 1855-1934.
Mss C 4982
[96] leaves, [65] p.; 33 cm.
Manuscript genealogy of the descendants of George Cabot and his wife Abigail Marston of Boston and Salem, Mass. Miscellaneous manuscript notes and correspondence concerning the Cabot family, including extracts from 17th century French baptismal, marriage, and burial registers, perhaps from the Isle of Jersey.

[Notes on the Butler family]
Mss C 4983
[41] p.: geneal. tables; 32 cm.
Miscellaneous manuscript notes on the Butler family, perhaps from mss of Lawrence Park.

Account book of Zebulon Parker, 1800-1874
Parker, Zebulon.
Parker, Alpheus, 1814-1885.
Mss C 4984
1 v. (200 p.); 31 cm.
Original account book for Zebulon Parker of Chelmsford, Mass. The account book was also used by his son Alpheus Parker. Entries concern the sale of hay, wood, etc. and many concerning plowing or hauling materials with his oxen. Third and fourth pages lists the births of the Zebulon Parker's children, the death of his first wife and his second marriage.

*Descendants of Richard Butt and wife
Deliverance Hoppin of Dorchester, Mass.*
Mss C 4985
[209] p., [20] leaves, 11 items: photographs; 32
cm.
Collection comprises four manuscript genealogies
of Richard Butt and his descendants; manuscript
transcriptions from legal documents such as
inventories, deeds, and probate records; original
correspondence, 1840-1899 and undated (9
items); cyanotypes of tombstones (2 items); and
miscellaneous notes.

*Account book of Abner Pratt, 1857 January 15-
December 31*
Pratt, Abner.
Hitchcock, Walter Bardwell, 1861-1936.
Hitchcock, Russell Snow, b. 1893.
Mss C 4986
1 v. (433 p.); 34 cm.
Original account book for Abner Pratt, a
blacksmith and wagon builder in Greenfield,
Mass. (pp 1-172). First couple of pages has severe
glue damage and pages 13-20 are missings. Pages
174-202 have handwritten genealogical notes and
clippings (1800-1928) on the Hitchcock family of
Springfield, Mass. by Walter Bardwell Hitchcock.
Russell Snow Hitchcock made a few corrections,
in red ink, to the genealogical information.

*John Carman(1) of Hempstead, Long Island, and
some of his descendants through his son John(2)*
Tredwell, Henry Alanson.
Mss C 4987
36 leaves; 34 cm.
1946
Photostats of a typescript genealogy. Includes six
generations.

*Account book of Hananiah and Ebenezer Parker,
1685-1796*
Parker, Hananiah, 1638-1724.
Parker, Ebenezer, b. 1676.
Temple, John.
Mss C 4988
Access to original record restricted: Material
fragile.
1 v. (100 p.); 30 cm.
Original account book missing its cover. The
earlier records date from 1685-1703 and concern
money paid to various individuals and the
purchase of nails, tobacco, indian corn, laying
part of the meeting house, etc. There is a
handwritten copy of a 1709 deed from Samuel
Parker to his father Hananiah Parker. There is a
1731 list concerning "Payed to my daughter Mary
toward her portion" followed by a similar account
for daughter Rebecca. However, the bulk of the
entries are by John Temple and date from 1749 to
1796. Temple's entries concern the sale of items
such as cyder and corn and services provided like
plowing, the use of his oxen, thrashing rye, the
settlement of his father-in-law's (Ebenezer
Parker) estate, etc.

*Collections relating to the pedigree of the
Carwithen family*
Carwithen, William, b. 1783.
Mss C 4989
1 v. ([33] p.): geneal. tables; 35 cm.
Manuscript genealogical table of English
Carwithen families. Also extracts from parish
registers relating to Carwithens; transcriptions of
several monument inscriptions; and extracts from
wills and other manuscript documents. Entries
dating from the 1830s and 40s were apparently
added by the copyist.

*Facsimile of Washington's accounts, from June
1775 to June 1783*
Washington, George, 1732-1799.
Mss C 4990
66 p.: facsim.; 35 cm.
1833
Facsimile reproduction of original account book.

Cash book of Henry Worcester, 1865-1873
Worcester, Henry.
Mss C 4991
1 v. (168 p.); 33 cm.
First page has "Malden Jan 1st 1865. Cash book
of Henry Worcester. Who is about to turn over a
new leaf in life & commences by openning a set
of books for the purpose of telling how he stands
with the world, and they with him to be a correct
statement of my standing in the world, at any
time. And taking an account of my assets this day
as per inventory book I shall be able at any time
to tell what I am, how well off in this worlds
goods. I mean to know at the end of each year.
Now I have turned over this new leaf, I must see
how well I am keep it"....

Account book, 1805-1809
Mss C 4992
1 v. (116 p.); 33 cm.
Original account book for an unidentified
merchant or institution. Entries concern
attendance.

*Account book of the stores on Union Wharf,
1805-1820*
Mss C 4993
1 v.; 33 cm.
Vellum bound account book. Cover has "Stores
Union Wharf book". Entries include a list of
individuals who rented stores on Union Wharf in
Boston, fees for "wharfage", and "dockage" of
ships, etc.

*A chart of the Chadbourne families of Berwick
[Maine] and their descendants*
Chase, Enoch, b. 1792.
Mss C 4994
1 sheet: ill., geneal. table s; 26 x 196 cm., folded
to 21 x 35 cm.
A manuscript chart ("tabular pedigree") showing
the descendants of Humphrey Chadbourne of
Berwick, Maine.

[Genealogical notes on various families]
Mss C 4995
1 v. ([48] p.); 32 cm.
Short manuscript genealogies relating to various
families, including: Samuel Adams of
Pennsylvania; Samuel Barker of Virginia;
William Bell of Virginia; Benjamin Chandler of
Connecticut; John Chandler of Vermont and
Ohio; John Flanagan of Pennsylvania; David
Fouts of Virginia; Solomon Fouts; Thomas Fouts
of Virginia; Richard Gay of Boston; Titus
Gaylord of Connecticut; Hedges family of
Virginia; Robert McConnell of Pennsylvania;
Joseph Moore of New Jersey; Odell family of
Maryland; William Steel of Virginia; Sweeting
family of Maryland; Charles Wells of
Pennsylvania; and Samuel Williamson of
Pennsylvania.

*Partial supplement to George Chandler's The
Chandler family*
Chandler, Zack Anson, b. 1879.
Mss C 4996
[4] p., [6] leaves: geneal. tables; 33 cm.
Manuscript additions to Chandler's genealogy of
1883, showing descendants of James Walker
Chandler, and the ancestry and descendants of
Zack Anson Chandler.

*Account book of court judgements by James
Avery, 1785-1798*
Avery, James, 1758-1798.
Mss C 4997
1 v. (88 p.); 31 cm.
Handwritten record of judgements issued by
Justice of the Peace James Avery concerning
court cases he presided over. The records from
1785-1789 were in Lincoln County while the
records from 1790-1798 were in Washington
County.

Day book, 1789-1822
Mss C 4998
1 v. (ca. 130 p.); 32 cm.
Original day book for an unidentified merchant of
Boston, Mass. Cover has "Day Book W." Entries
concern rent for shops and the sale of Wyson tea,
tobacco, cotton, etc. There are many entries
concerning Joseph Dommison, a business
partner?, and several lists concerning a store at
Towncreek, Maryland.

Account book of Richard King, 1727-1755
King, Richard.
Mss C 4999
1 v. (225, 112 p.); 32 cm.
Vellum bound account book for Richard King, a
merchant/tavern keeper in Portsmouth, NH.
Entires include earthen ware, rum, beer, cord of
wood, beef, gingerbread, meals, etc. New
pagination begins after page 225 with the note:
"Scarborough March 24th 1754 being out of
paper whearewith to make a day book I therefore
approprieate the following part of this book to my
own use for that same purpose -- Richard King".

*Genealogy of the Hutchinson family in England
and America from 1282-1893*
Hutchinson, George Hunt, b. 1861.
Mss C 5
145 p.: geneal. table; 36 cm.
1897.
A bound, handwritten genealogy of the
Hutchinson family. It begins with a compiled
account of the family in England and America
taken from the 1870 published book, "The
Hutchinson family or the descendants of Barnard
Hutchinson of Cowlam, England" compiled by
Perley Derby (1823-1897). Included is an
ahnentafel for Anne Louise Hutchinson (1933-
1986?) and a typed genealogical table for the
allied Alter family written by Harvey Montiville
Dibble (1862-1947).

Account book, 1728-1733
Mss C 5000
1 v. (ca. 200 p.); 33 cm.
Vellum bound account book for an unidentified
merchant of Boston, Mass. Entries include "ship
building at Newport," nails, sugar, rum, pitch,
logwood, pork, beef, etc.

[Material relating to Chandler families]
Chandler, George, 1806-1893.
Mss C 5001
[122] p.: geneal. tables, photographs; 35 cm.
Correspondence (1859-1884), manuscript
genealogies, notes, and printed forms requesting
genealogical information. Also one photograph of
a child.

Account book, 1799-1803
Mss C 5002
1 v. (ca. 250 p.); 38 cm.
Leather bound account book for an unidentified
merchant in Massachusetts. Entries include
cotton, cheese, tea, sugar, pepper, indigo, nutmeg,
etc. Headings include "owners of schooner
Success," "schooner Lion," "owners of the Brig
Interprize," "store in merchant's row," land and
saltworks in Chelsea, owners of the "Schr
Bellisarius," etc.

Account book, 1850 February-June
Mss C 5003
1 v. (81 p.); 34 cm.
Leather bound account book with missing front
cover and fire damage. The first 17 pages have
newspaper clippings pasted on them including a
portion of "Letters on Emigration," "The
population of Ireland," "Mr. Ball's Evening Free
School," "The Catholics and the Evening Free
School," and several clippings concerning the
Maine liquor law among others. Under each
woman's name are entries concerning "for work
given out" (sub-divided by "overalls, skeins of
yarn, other work") and "by work returned" (sub-
divided for overalls, socks, mittens, other work").

*A collection of epitaphs written by Hanah Flagg
Gould of Newburyport, Mass. on various friends
in their lifetime: transcribed from a copy made by
Caleb Cushing of Newburyport, for Miss Mary
Townsend of Salem, Massachusetts*
Gould, Hannah Flagg, 1789-1865.
Mss C 5004
1 v. (12, 1p.); 23 x 36 cm.
Handwritten transcription of the original record.
Includes a 1876 September 20 letter from Caleb
Cushing of Newburyport to John Ward Dean of
Boston concerning the authorship of the Cushing
epitaph as well as five newspaper clippings
concerning the Cushing and Gould epitaphs.

Horace C. Hovey papers
Hovey, Horace Carter, 1833-1914.
Mss C 5005
[50] leaves; 32 cm.
Manuscript and typescript correspondence and
notes on the Carter and allied families.
Correspondence (1824-1914 and undated)
includes a transcription of a letter (25 September
1824) from William C. Carter containing much
genealogical data. There is also an original letter
(24 April 1847) from Franklin Hubbard Carter
concerning his immediate family. Horace Hovey
was a descendant of Thomas Carter of Salisbury,
Mass.

[Cochran family of Scotland]
Mss C 5006
[47] leaves; 33 cm.
Miscellaneous manuscript genealogical material
and notes.

[Descendants of Daniel Cole]
Cole, George Nathan, b. 1869.
Mss C 5007
[2] leaves; 35 cm.
1926
Manuscript letter (24 July 1926) concerning one line of descent from Daniel Cole, brother of John and Job, who settled at Eastham, Mass. Daniel's son, John, married Ruth Snow, daughter of Mayflower immigrants.

Genealogical and historical notes concerning the ancestors of Helen A. Whittier
Whittier, Helen A., b. 1846.
Mss C 5008
1 v. ([208] p.): coat of arms; 16 cm. + 22 items
A notebook containing information on the ancestry of Helen A. Whittier of Lowell, Mass., including the Chase and Whittier families. Also manuscript and typescript notes on descendants of Aquila Chase and wife Anne Wheeler of Hampton, N.H., and Newbury, Mass. A printed genealogy of descendants of Aquila and his brother Thomas of Hampton, N.H., who married Elizabeth Philbrick. Postcard views of Chase homesteads in Massachusetts and England. Photocopies of nineteenth-century newspaper articles concerning a purported fortune due Chase heirs in America. Miscellaneous material on Moore families, perhaps allied.

Jenney family record
Jenne, Fred Chadwick, b. 1873.
Mss C 5010
[13] leaves; 33 cm.
1904
Typescript genealogy of the descendants of John Jenney of Plymouth, Mass.

[Notes on families of Ipswich, Massachusetts]
Caldwell, Augustine, b. 1836.
Mss C 5011
1 v.: ill., coat of arms; 34 cm.
Scrapbook containing manuscript notes, clippings and extracts from various sources on Ipswich, Mass., and some of its families. The families include Caldwell, Foster, Heard, Henderson, Hodgkins, Jones, Newmarch, Safford, Shatswell, Smith, and others. Notes on Ipswich churches and clergy are interspersed throughout as well as transcribed vital records.

History of the Jones family [Massachusetts]
Jones, William Henry.
Mss C 5012
[4] p.: geneal. tables; 46 x 30 cm. folded to 24 x 30 cm.
1834
Printed genealogy of the descendants of Josiah Jones and wife Lydia Treadway of Watertown and Weston, Mass. Includes a chart in the "tree and branch" style.

[Records of the Hopkins family of Nova Scotia]
Mss C 5013
3 items: facsim.; 32 cm.
Photostats of vital records for Seth Hopkins and George Hopkins. Photostat of a petition (1778) from John Hopkins of Liverpool, N.S.

[Ancestry of Adelaide Haley of Saco, Me.]
Haley, Adelaide, b. 1875.
Mss C 5014
ca. 60 items: ill., maps, geneal. tables; 36 cm.
Manuscript and typescript notes on ancestral families of Adelaide Haley, daughter of John Haley and wife Abbie Batchelder. Many of these families were from Biddeford, Buxton, Saco, Wells, and York, Maine. Surnames include Barnes, Batchelder, Dearing, Googins, Haley, Lee, and Prescott. Also correspondence (1840-1923) and newspaper clippings.

Henry Hall papers
Hall, Henry.
Mss C 5015
1 folder ([64] p.); 36 cm.
Miscellaneous manuscript and typescript genealogical records and correspondence concerning various families, perhaps allied with Henry Hall of New York City. Surnames include Botsford, Foster, and Peck of Fairfield Co., Conn.; and Emery, Fry, Hagaman, Hageman, Marshall, and Owen.

[The ancestry of Oliver Cromwell, with some collateral lines]
Mss C 5016
6 items: geneal. tables; 33 cm.
Four manuscript charts, one newspaper clipping, and one page of typescript notes concerning the Cromwell family.

[Descendants of Yelverton Crowell]
Mss C 5017
1 v. (144) p.; 32 cm.
Manuscript genealogy of the descendants of
Yelverton Crowell and wife Elizabeth.

*[Genealogical records of the Haley and Gordon
families]*
Gordon, Dudley, 1766-1842.
Mss C 5018
6 items: maps, geneal. tables; 36 cm.
Manuscript notes on the ancestry of Mabel
Carena Haley, including Thomas Haley of Exeter,
N.H., and Alexander Gordon of Scotland and
Exeter, N.H.

[English records of Cox families]
Mss C 5019
[49] leaves: geneal. tables; 33 cm.
Typescript notes on English wills of Cox families:
Consistory Court of Gloucester, 1600-1650;
Consistory Court of Bristol, 1572-1699. Also
miscellaneous manuscript material.

On the ancestry of Governor Thomas Dudley
Elmendorf, George F., Mrs.
Mss C 5020
[36] leaves: coat of arms; 33 cm.
Published excerpt from *The American
Genealogist*, July 1968, together with typescript
and facsimile material used in compiling the
article.

*Copies of letters, newspaper clippings and other
data relating to Nelson Henry Benson of Heath,
Massachusetts*
Mss C 5021
[24] leaves; 36 cm.
Typescript transcriptions of documents
concerning Nelson Henry Benson of Heath,
Mass., and Troy, N.Y. Also photocopied
newspaper articles relating to Benson family
reunions in 1853 and 1869.

*Moses Dam of Newington, New Hampshire, and
some of his descendants*
Dame, George Alva.
Mss C 5022
8 leaves; 36 cm.
[1961?]
Mimeographed typescript genealogy.

Plan of homestead of Samuel Jennings
Mss C 5023
1 sheet; 39 x 31 cm.
Hand drawn land plot of Samuel Jennings' farm
in Bridgewater, Mass. Scale is ten rod to one inch.
Includes the note: "I think this is handwriting of
Benjamin Tope Esq Jan 20 1881 W. Latham."

[Morrill genealogy]
Morrill, Katherine L., 1838-1903.
Mss C 5024
[8] leaves; 36 cm.
Photocopies from a manuscript genealogy on the
descendants of Abraham Morrill with two pages
of miscellaneous material and notes.

Sawyer family
Coit, Ella Sawyer, 1867-
Mss C 5025
1 sheet; 41 x 53 cm. folded to 21 x 27 cm.
1910
Typescript chart with handwritten annotations
providing the author's lineal descent from
Thomas (1) Sawyer of Lancaster, Mass. through
Nathaniel, Lieut. Ephraim, Col. Ephraim, Josiah,
Rufus, Rollin Augustus Sawyer to Ella Sawyer.
Information on each individual is organized into
the following columns: name, born, when
married, to whom, present residence, died, names
of children, where born and remarks. Dates cover
1618-1874.

The early history of the Painter (Bender) family
Thomas, Ray C.
Mss C 5026
[7] p.: maps; 36 cm.
1963
Mimeographed typescript genealogy of some
descendants of Mathias Bender (or Painter) who
came from Germany to Philadelphia about 1720.
Includes descendants who lived in Rockingham
County, Va.

The Macys and other Nantucket families
Mss C 5027
1 v. (54 p.); 35 cm.
Reproduction (ca. 1984) of a ms. notebook
apparently written in 1825.

Putnam's direct line
Putnam, Read H., 1918-.
Mss C 5028
12 leaves: ports., geneal. tables; 36 cm.
1964
Reproduced typescript genealogy concerning the ancestry and descendants of Savannah Clarke Putnam of Mexico, Me., and Salt Lake City, Utah.

Putnam's direct line
Putnam, Read H., 1918-.
Mss C 5029
6 leaves: geneal. tables; 36 cm.
1962
Mimeographed typescript genealogy concerning the ancestry and descendants of Savannah Clarke Putnam of Mexico, Me., and Salt Lake City, Utah.

Account book of Nathaniel Leonard, 1793-1832
Leonard, Nathaniel, 1751-1833.
Mss C 5031
Access to original record restricted: Material fragile.
1 v. (100 p.); 33 cm.
Account book for a cordwainer in Middleborough, Mass. and Buckfield, Me. Received with the front cover and the first 22 pages missing. Folder two contains some loose documents including an 1803 promissory note, an 1811 letter, and a typescript list of names mentioned in the account book.

Solomon Bundy (1775-1851) of Huntington, Conn. and Oxford, N.Y. and his descendants
Bundy, Frederick McGeorge.
Mss C 5032
[41] leaves; 36 cm.
1964
Reproduced typescript genealogy and updates. Inc. additions to 1970.

A genealogy of one line of the Carpenter family, together with allied branches
Carpenter, Richard Vernon, b. 1871.
Mss C 5033
53, [2] leaves; 33 cm.
1897
Typescript genealogy tracing the author's ancestry.

The Buck family of Yorkshire
Mss C 5034
[12] leaves; 22 x 33 cm.
1965
Photocopy of typescript extracts concerning the Buck surname. Taken from Friends records at Yorkshire, England, to the year 1800.

Pension file relating to the Civil War service of William John Pentland
Mss C 5035
[220] leaves; 36 cm.
Photocopy of original record (certificate no. 323351) which includes the claim for pension incease, officer's or comrade's testimony, affidavit for neighbors' and general purpose, declaration for invalid pension, and surgeon's certificate.

Account book of John Foye, 1687-1696
Foye, John, ca. 1637-1715.
Mss C 5037
Access to original record restricted: Material fragile.
1 v. (56 p.); 32 cm.
Vellum bound account book with records concerning Foye's activities as captain of the Dolphin (ship) and the Europian (ship). Records include contract signed by crew with rate of pay and signed acknowledgements for receipt of wages. The ship Europian sailed from Boston to Jamaica and back with a cargo of lumber then rum, sugar, etc. Record includes handwritten copies of letters sent to Foye.

Shippee family genealogy
Quick, Harry Lee, b. 1883.
Mss C 5038
20 leaves; 36 cm.
1941
Mimeographed typescript genealogy of some descendants of David Shippee of Warwick, R.I., in particular the descendants of Christopher Shippee and wives Joanna Jillson and Nancy Oakes Phillips. Also some information on the allied family Jillson.

Day books for the H. D. Trask & Company, 1877-1882
H. D. Trask & Company.
Mss C 5039
3 v.; 26-40 cm.
Day books of the H. D. Trask and Company of Philadelphia, Pa. and Boston, Mass., proprietors and manufacturers of Norcross furnace governor, for all kinds of hot air furnaces. First volume is a day book (168 p.) for 1877-1879. The second volume is a day book for 1877-1878 along with a customer list for 1877-1881. The third volume is a day book (719 p. with pages 1-169 missing) for 1879-1883 [note: vol. 3 stored with oversize mss ledgers].

Letterbook of Isaac Hull, 1838 August-1839 December 6
Hull, Isaac, 1773-1843.
Mss C 5041
1 v. (520 p.); 33 cm.
Handwritten copy of letters sent to and from commodore Isaac Hull, Commander of the U.S. Navy Force in the Mediterranean. He assumed his command on 12 Sept 1838 and his flagship, the USS Ohio, arrived at Port Mahon, the headquarters of the command on 4 Jan 1839. The letters concern his assuming this command, his trip on the Ohio to Europe, and his traveling to various ports in the Mediterranean looking out for the interests of Americans, especially seamen, as well as inquiring into and reporting on the condition of American commerce.

Orderly book, 1775 October 9-December 21
Mss C 51
1 v. ([28] p.); 17 cm.
Handwritten list of who was on guard and scout duty written in a small handmade book. Last page has roll of Capt. Luke Drury's company of Minutemen.

Mary Brown her Relation April 26, 1699
Brown, Mary.
Mss C 52
Access to original record restricted: Use preservation photocopy.
1, 2 p.; 21-28 cm.
Handwritten account of Mary Brown's conversion testimony, "confession" or "public relation," in which she describes the afflications she suffered as a sinner and her effort to seek a new relationship with God. Includes typescript transcription and preservation photocopy.

Military discharge certificate for William C. Allen, 1843 September 4
Redington, Alfred.
Maine. Adjutant General.
Mss C 53
1 DS; 21 x 32 cm.
Partially printed form completed in ms. in which the Commander-in-Chief accepts the resignation of Major William C. Allen from the Second Brigade, First Division Maine Militia. Document is signed by the Adjutant General for the State of Maine, Alfred Redington, and registered in Vol 6, No. 254.

Handwritten copy of the appointment certificate for Cornet Seth Alden
Mss C 54
1 p.; 28 cm.
Handwritten transcription of the appointment of Seth Alden as Cornet of the Troop in the Regiment of Horse, in the Province of Massachusetts Bay, 1745 May 16.

State of her Majesty's Garison of Annapolis Royall under the Command of Governour Vetch as they are thiss day, 1711 June 1
Mss C 56
3 p.
Handwritten copy of original record.

Annual return of the Company of Foot commanded by Captain Hezekiah Anthony: taken from the Company Roll, as revised on the first Tuesday of May, 1815
Carter, Marion Williams Pearce, b. 1867.
Mss C 57
3 leaves; 28 cm.
Typescript transcription of original record.

Annual return of the Company of Foot commanded by Captain Giles J. Chace of Berkley taken from the Company Roll, as revised on the first Tuesday of May, 1814
Mss C 58
1 p.; 28 cm.
Typescript transcription of original record.

*Letter, 1813 June 19, Ashburton, to R[euben]
G[aunt] Beasley*
Mss C 59
2 p.; 23 cm.
Letter by 23 prisoners of war requesting that
Beasley "use every means in your power to have
us sent out of this country as soon as possible."

[Isaac Ketchum] family record, 1762-1880
Mss C 6
1 sheet: col. ill.; 30 cm. + [1] p.
Note: Used for cover illustration of *New England
Ancestors* Winter 2001 ed.
Hand drawn and brightly colored record of the
birth, marriage, and deaths of the Isaac and Anna
(Grenell) Ketchum family. Includes a piece of
paper with additonal notes on the Ketchum family
by the donor.

*A list of ye names of ye inhabitants at Blackpoint
garison Octo: 12th 1676*
Mss C 60
1 p.; 31 cm.
Handwritten list of inhabitants at the Blackpoint
garrison in Scarborough, Maine commanded by
Henry Jocelyn during King Philip's War.

*Letter, 1882 July 17, Chicago, Illinois to
W[illiam] H[arrison] Eaton*
Eaton, William Wentworth, 1811-.
Mss C 61
8 p.; 12-20 cm.
Provides genealogical information on the Eaton
family. Accompanied by a transcription of a deed
(dated 7 September 1765) in which David Eaton
of Cornwallis, N.S., transfers land to John
Burbridge and William Best.

*Acknowledgement of prisoner of war status, 1813
May 28*
Broughton, Bartholemew.
Mss C 62
2 DS; 12 x 20 cm.
Partially printed document dated May 28 1813
and completed in ms. by Bartholemew Broughton
to acknowledge his status as a prisoner of war
who should proceed directly to Boston. In the
second document dated May 28 1813, Broughton
agrees to remain in Portland.

*List of the flagg officers of the British navy, 1745
April 4*
Norris, John, Sir, 1660?-1749.
Great Britain. Navy.
Mss C 63
Access to original record restricted: Use
preservation photocopy.
1 v. (51 p.); 20 cm.
Handwritten list of the flag officers in the British
Navy followed by a list of the ships in the British
Navy including a count of their guns and men.
Both lists are written in a small handmade book.

*Handwritten copy of letters from a British army
officer under General John Burgoyne, 1777
November 17 - 1778 December 10*
Mss C 64
112 p.
Handwritten transcription.

*Accounts concerning the frigate Chesapeake,
1878-1881*
Trefethen, Benjamin, b. 1790.
Mss C 66
9 p.; 21-25 cm.
Remembrance (dated March 18, 1878) about the
damage caused by a sudden squall to the frigate
Chesapeake followed by an account (dated Sept
20, 1881) of the battle between the frigates
Chesapeake and Shannon. Several pages are
copies of the original.

*Morning report of a detachment of marines,
commanded by Captain John Hall, on board the
United States frigate Constitution, Commodore
Edward Preble, Commander*
Hall, John.
Mss C 67
1 ADS; 16 x 19 cm.
Partially printed document completed in
manuscript for 30 April 1804. Verso names the
two marines listed as sick and the marine listed as
confined.

Revolutionary War record of Francis Soucee / Brooks
Mss C 68
[3] leaves; 28 cm.
Letter from the Veterans Administration dated 1934 November 20 sent to Carrie L. Miller of Lawrence, Mass. in response to her request for the Revolutionary War record of Francis Brooks.

Revolutionary War record of John Boynton of Gilsum, NH
New Hampshire Historical Society (Concord, N.H.)
Mss C 69
[2] leaves; 28 cm.
Typescript compilation of information on the Revolutionary War service of John Boynton gathered from NH State papers, Pension papers, and Abstracts of Revolutionary Pension papers.

List of person married by Rev. Michael Eddy at the First Baptist Church, Newport, R.I., 1790-1835
Eddy, Michael, 1760-1835.
Mss C 7
[33] p.; 32 cm.
Manuscript transcription either from church records or personal record kept by the minister.

Sarah Leighton's Relation Octob(r) 1 1697; Sarah Nelson's Relation Nov. ult. 1697
Leighton, Sarah.
Mss C 70
Access to original record restricted: Use preservation photocopy.
2, 2 p.; 21-28 cm.
Handwritten account of Sarah Leighton and Sarah Nelson's conversion testimony, "confession" or "public relation," in which she describes the afflications she suffered as a sinner and her effort to seek a new relationship with God. Includes preservation photocopy.

John Roberts Jr. family records
Mss C 71
[2] leaves; 28 cm.
Typescript transcription of original record for the John and Deborah (Freeman) Roberts Jr. of Liverpool, Nova Scotia.

Commission of Joseph Buck to Ensign, Lieutenant, and Captain, 1800-1806
Mss C 72
[3] leaves; 28 cm.
Typescript transcription of original commissions for Joseph Buck to Ensign (13 October 1800), Lieutenant (19 May 1803) and Captain (19 May 1806) of the 3rd Company, 11th Regiment, Connecticut State Militia.

Miscellaneous documents relating to the Civil War service of Rinaldo Butters, 1861-1912
Mss C 73
9 DS; 19-32 cm.
First item is a 24 December 1861 commission to sergeant of 5th Vol. Company Infantry, 15th Reg. Maine Vols. Second item is an order dated "Head Quarters Camp Parapet, La. 12 July 1863" concerning "Police Instructions." Third item is a provisional commission dated 13 August 1863 in which Sgt. Butters is promoted to 2nd Lieut. of the Engineers Corps d'Afrique. There are two documents dated 14 August 1863 concerning Butters' transfer. Sixth item is the muster-in roll of Renaldo Butters 2nd Lieut E Co. 2nd La Vol. Engineers. Seventh item is an acknowledgement, dated 7 Oct 1890, of Butters' discharge from the 15th Maine regiment by the Adjutant General of Maine. Final item is a letter by Isaac Dyer dated Skowhegan Jany 31 1912 with a newspaper clipping concerning Mr. Dyer's house.

Revolutionary War record of Seth Babbitt
Mss C 74
[2] leaves; 28 cm.
Letter from the Veterans Administration dated 1938 July 1 sent to Parker Sage of Detroit, Mich. in response to his request for the Revolutionary War record of Seth Babbitt.

Warrant to Benjamin Steele to pay Col. Timothy Bigelow for rations, 1778 October 6
Mss C 75
[1] p.
Typescript transcription of original record.

Transcription of military records relating to the Buck family of Mass., 1908-1938
Mss C 76
Typescript transcription of military records concerning Charles E. Buck, Herbert W. Buck, Isaac Buck and Arthur J. Buck.

Nathaniel Brown's Relation April 18 1699; James Stewart's relation Jan(y) 23 1698/9; John Stewart's Relation Jan(y) 24 1698/9
Brown, Nathaniel.
Mss C 77
Access to original record restricted: Use preservation photocopy.
2, 7 p.; 21-28 cm.
Handwritten account of Nathaniel Brown and James and John Stewart's conversion testimony, "confession" or "public relation." Includes preservation photocopy and typescript transcription.

Sermon of Moses Parsons, 1748 June 15
Parsons, Moses, 1716-1783.
Mss C 78
8 p.; 16 cm.
Handwritten sermon on "I am a companion of all those that fear thee and of those that keep thy precepts" given to young people in Byfield.

Hall family papers, 1743-1970
Mss C 8
33 items.
Correspondence, indentures, military papers and genealogical materials relating to the Hall family of Sandwich, Mass. Stephen Hall, Charles W. Hall, Joshua Hall, and Isaac Hall are prominent names. Also contains information on the Jewett family.

Letter, 1842 September 12, Southbury, Conn., to Abel S. Beardslee
Shelton, G. P.
Mss C 80
1 ADS; 25 cm.
Handwritten letter authorizing Beardslee to exercise the powers of Sergeant in the 4th Company 12th Regiment Connecticut Militia.

Pension applications of Revolutionary soldiers of Boothbay, Maine
Reed, Elizabeth Freeman.
Mss C 81
15 p.; 28 cm.
Carbon copy typescript transcription of original record. Includes a copy of the muster roll of Capt. Israel Davis' Company, Mass. 1778.

List of Revolutionary soldiers interred in the Walnut Street Cemetery in Brookline, Mass.
Daughters of the American Revolution. Hannah Goddard Chapter.
Mss C 82
1 p.; 28 cm.
Typescript.

Military discharge certificate for Captain Sierra D. Braley, 1871 March 14
Cunningham, James A.
Massachusetts. Adjutant General.
Mss C 83
1 DS; 22 x 35 cm.
Partially printed form completed in ms. in which the Commander-in-Chief accepts the resignation of Captain Sierra D. Braley from the Third Infantry Regiment, First Brigade, First Division Massachusetts Militia. Document is signed by the Adjutant General for the State of Massachusetts, James A. Cunningham.

Select records of the Congregational Church of Bethany, Conn., 1814-1845
Chipman, Richard Manning.
Congregational Church (Bethany, Conn.)
Mss C 86
10 p.; 25 cm.
Handwritten transcription of the original record. Includes a list of members and baptisms.

Almshouse subscriptions ward no. 2, 1781 April 11
Mss C 87
[4] p.; 32 cm.
Handwritten record of a Boston town meeting on 1781 April 11 at which the Overseers to the Poor describe the needs of the Almshouse. Includes "List of subscribers for supplies to the alm's house April 1781 Ward No.2."

Petition for the paving of Atkinson Street, 1746 March
Mss C 88
1 ADS; 32 cm.
Handwritten petition "to the freeholders & other inhabitants of the town of Boston in town meeting regularly assembled" by sundry inhabitants of Boston requesting the paving of Atkinson Street.

Expenses of my education &c.
Jacques, George, 1816-1873.
Mss C 9
[39] p.; 20 cm.
Jacques detailed account of his educational expenses from 1832 to 1843. He was a 1836 graduate of Brown University who ultimately became a horticulturist in Worcester, Mass.

Letter, 1880 September 23, Boston to John Ward Dean
Allan, George Hayward, 1832-1886.
Mss C 90
8 p.: maps; 19 cm.
Describes the topography near the neckland of Boston during the American Revolution, and the location of "Brown's House". Includes a "rough tracing from Lieut Page's map (London, 1777)" showing "Canton St fortifications (British advance lines)."

Book of records for burying grounds, 1810-1813
Snelling, Josiah.
Boston (Mass.). Board of Health.
Mss C 91
1 v. (26 p.); 20 cm.
Includes handwritten copies of correspondence sent to Josiah Snelling, Superintendant of the North District, from N. Greenough, Secretary, Health Office. There are also lists of funeral undertakers appointed by the Board of Health October 1810, "sundry persons to the board of Health for the use of the car," "account of expenses for burying grounds," "Board of Health to Josiah Snelling," and "Mem. of work done on acct of Board of Health."

Request by the Catholics of Boston, Mass. for subscribers in Salem, Mass., to help build a church
Mss C 92
1 sheet; 40 cm.
Handwritten document with a list of donors and the amount of their contribution.

Map of the West Cemetery in Amherst, Mass., and names of owners of cemetery lots
Gates, Charles Otis, b. 1852.
Mss C 93
1 sheet.
1927
Hand drawn enlargement of a map of unknown date drawn by E. A. Davis.

1810 census of Boston and Chelsea, Massachusetts
Boston (Mass.)
Mss C 94
3 v. (222 p.); 25 cm.
Handwritten copy of the enumerator's records for the 1810 Boston census in three volumes labeled on cover "Book letter" A, [B], and C. Entries include the name of street, number of houses, names of heads of families, males under 10, from 10 to 16, from 16 to 26, from 26 to 45, above 45, females under 10, from 10 to 16, from 16 to 26, from 26 to 45, above 45, all other free persons except Indians, aggregate." Covers Boston wards 1-12, South Boston, Chelsea, and the Islands.

Abstract of the 1825 Boston census
Mss C 95
[2] p.
Handwritten summary of the whole number of inhabitants, white males, white females, coloured males, coloured females, and the aggregate population in the respective wards.

Record of members of United Church of Christ Disciples, Milton, Nova Scotia 1856-1913
Mss C 96
24 leaves; 28 cm.
Typescript transcription of original minute book of the church.

Testimony concerning the burning of John Creek's house in Boston, Mass., 1679 October
Mss C 97
1 p.
Handwritten transcription of original documects concerning the testimony given to Edward Rawson by witnesses.

List of deaths in Boston, Mass., 1819-1821
Mss C 98
1 v. (32 p.); 21 cm.
Handwritten compilation of individuals who died in Boston from 7 Nov 1819 to 27 July 1821. Entries just list name, date of death, and age.

Description of Capt. John Doble's land and house, purchased from Cabot 1758 February 18]
Mss C 99
[4] p.; 20 cm.
Hand drawn plot of Doble's land along with a description of the lot according to the 1758 deed by which Doble acquired the lot. Apparently written by a neighbor in a complaint that Doble's house encroaches upon his land.

Alphabet to wills, estate accounts, inventories, etc., of record in the clerk's office of the county court of Loudoun, 1852
Rogers, Arthur L.
Mss Cb 1131
[2], 324 leaves; 40 cm.
An index begun in 1852 but covering 1757 to 1871. Arranged by the first letter of the surname only, then chrononlogically, volumes A-VV, giving volume and page references.

Portrait of Paul Franklin Johnson: author of the genealogy of Captain John Johnson of Roxbury, Massachusetts
Gerrish, Charles, 1947-.
Mss Co 40
1 sheet; ports.; 28.5 x 39.5 cm.
1999
Photocopy of a photograph enlarged from the 4 x 5 in. original on a digital Canon 1000 photocopier.

Mildred Evangeline Carver Carpenter papers
Carpenter, Mildred Evangeline Carver, b. 1890.
Mss H 1
20 linear ft.
Draft finding aid in the library.
Genealogical notes, clippings, and correspondence. Most of the genealogies relate to the Carver, Brayton, and Carpenter families (boxes 2 & 3) and the Burrows family (box 5). Also notes on the Deshon, Curtis, West and Hempstead (box 1), Packer, Dennison, Shea, Rice, Wilder, Carter, Bigelow, Minard, Olney and Mason-Salsman families (box 4). Includes information about Huguenot settlers in America and Huguenot societies (especially box 6).

Percy E. Nute papers
Nute, Percy E.
Mss H 10
2 boxes + 6 v.
Genealogical papers concerning the descendants of James Nute of Dover, New Hampshire.

John Severinus Conway papers
Conway, John Severinus, 1852-1925.
Mss H 11
1 box + 1 roll of charts.
Includes 37 coat of arms painted on cardboard, genealogical notes and charts on the Conway family, and notes on heraldry.

Marion B. Tuttle papers
Mss H 13
3 boxes.
Notes and correspondence relating to the genealogy of the Tuttle family, ca. 1940-1950.

Notes used in preparation of "Ancestors and descendants of Frank Lusk Babbott, Jr., M.D., and his wife Elizabeth Bassett French."
Stryker-Rodda, Harriet.
Mss H 14
1 box.
Typescript and photocopies. Includes a partial genealogical history of Henry Short (iv, ms.).

Records, ca. 1930 - 1942
Anglo-American Records Foundation.
Mss H 15
1 box.

Fenno family papers
Mss H 17
1 box.
Papers relating to the genealogy of the Fenno family. Includes the ancestry of Margaret Fitzhugh Browne.

Papers relating to the Bruce and Arnold families
Mss H 18
1 box.
Ms., photos and typescripts.

Papers relating to the Forbes family of Milton, Massachusetts
Cunningham, Henry Winchester, 1860-1930.
Mss H 19
1 box.
Ms. and printed matter.

Genealogical notes and correspondence relating especially to the Brewster family
Greenlaw, Lucy Hall, 1869-1961.
Mss H 2
1 box.
Research done in connection with the "Genealogical Advertiser."

Bertrand A. Chapman family papers
Mss H 20
9 boxes.
Papers, photographs, and memorabilia pertaining to the Bertrand A. Chapman family of Springfield, Vermont. Includes material concerning the Smith and Klein families. 19th-20th centuries.

Loud family papers
Mss H 21
2 boxes.
Papers, notebook, and pedigrees concerning the family and descendants of William Loud.

Roderick Bissell Jones papers
Jones, Roderick Bissell, 1898-.
Mss H 3
4 boxes.
Genealogical notes and correspondence. The focus is on the Jones, Harris, and Coult (Colt) families. Also information on the Ball, Beardsley, Bissell, Cave, Clarke, Cole, Drake, Ely, Gaillard, Gonseth, Graham, Loomis, McCracken, Roberts, Rogers, Smith, Swift, Thompson, Towne, Tucker, Ward, Warren, and Waters families. Includes correspondence and typescripts of Edward Payson Jones.

Henry Winchester Cunningham papers
Cunningham, Henry Winchester, 1860-1930.
Mss H 4
10 boxes.
Collection is concerning primarily with the genealogy of the Winchester family of New England. Includes notes on the history of Manchester, Mass.

Viaux family papers, 1819-1966
Mss H 7
3 linear ft.
Unpublished finding aid in the library.
The bulk of the material in the collection is correspondence by Frederick Viaux (1882-1960) and Florence Viaux (1878-1966). Includes some correspondence from other family members and of the related families of Ballou, Farrar and Cushing.

Robert Humphrey Montgomery papers
Montgomery, Robert Humphrey, 1889-1974.
Mss H 8
2 boxes.
Family letters, copies of diaries and documents, charts and photographs concerning the Montgomery family. Includes information on the allied families of Gay and Buchanan.

Mi's (Kent) - Barming, Brenchley, Hunton, Teston
Frost, John E. (John Eldridge), 1917-1992.
Mss CS436/B258/F76/1974
1 v.; 28 cm.
1974
Typescript.

Monumental inscriptions St. Peter's, Ditton, Church of St. Peter and St. Paul, Leybourne, St. Michael's, Offham, Plaxtol Church, St. Martin's, Ryarsh, St. Giles' Shipbourne
Frost, John E. (John Eldridge), 1917-1992.
Mss CS436/D58/F76/1969
1 v.; 28 cm.
1969
Typescript.

St. Michael's East Peckham, baptisms, 1813-1836, marriages, 1813-1836, burials, 1813-1850
Frost, John E. (John Eldridge), 1917-1992.
St. Michael's Church (East Peckham, England).
Mss CS436/E257/F76/1967
1 v.; 28 cm.
1967
Typescript.

Monumental inscriptions, St. Mary's Hadlow and St. Michael's East Peckham
Frost, John E. (John Eldridge), 1917-1992.
Mss CS436/H212/F76/1967
1 v. (various pagings); 28 cm.
Typescript

Monumental inscriptions Horsmonden (Kent)
Frost, John E. (John Eldridge), 1917-1992.
Mss CS436/H83/F76/1968
64, 11 leaves; 28 cm.
1968
Typescript.

Parish register transcripts, Leigh, Mereworth, Offham, Ryarsh in Kent 1813-1837
Frost, John E. (John Eldridge), 1917-1992.
Mss CS436/L39/F76/1970
1 v.; 28 cm.
1970
Typescript.

Monumental inscriptions, St. Peter's, Pembury, All Saints, Tudeley, St. Thomas A Becket, Capel, St. Mary's, Leigh and St. Dunstan's, West Peckham
Frost, John E. (John Eldridge), 1917-1992.
Mss CS436/P45/F76/1969
1 v. (various pagings); 28 cm.
1969
Typescript.

Acton (Maine) record book
Frost, John E. (John Eldridge), 1917-1992.
Mss F29/A18/F76/1964
[1], 60, [3], 2 leaves; 29 cm.
1964
Typescript.

Alfred (Maine) record book
Frost, John E. (John Eldridge), 1917-1992.
Mss F29/A3/F76/1968
79, vi leaves; 29 cm.
1968
Typescript.

The Biddeford (Maine) record book
Frost, John E. (John Eldridge), 1917-1992.
Mss F29/B75/F76/1968
2 v.; 28 cm.
1968
Typescript.

The Buxton (Maine) record book
Frost, John E. (John Eldridge), 1917-1992.
Mss F29/B96/F76/1968
213, xii leaves; 29 cm.
1968
Typescript.

Hollis (Maine) record book
Frost, John E. (John Eldridge), 1917-1992.
Mss F29/H67/F76/1967
[1], 117, vi leaves; 29 cm.
1967
Typescript.

The Kennebunkport and Arundel (Maine) record book
Frost, John E. (John Eldridge), 1917-1992.
Mss F29/K32/F76/1965
1 v.; 29 cm.
1965

Old Limington (Maine) record book
Frost, John E. (John Eldridge), 1917-1992.
Mss F29/L65/F76/1967
ii, 107, 4, 2 leaves; 29 cm.
1967
Typescript.

Lyman and Dayton (Maine) record book
Frost, John E. (John Eldridge), 1917-1992.
Mss F29/L9/F76/1966
[2], 106 v, ii leaves; 29 cm.
1966
Typescript.

Newfield (Maine) record book
Frost, John E. (John Eldridge), 1917-1992.
Mss F29/N62/F76/1965
[2], 62, 4, 2 l.; 29 cm.
1965
Typescript.

Saco (Maine) record book
Frost, John E. (John Eldridge), 1917-1992.
Mss F29/S1/F76/1970
2 v.; 29 cm.
1970
Typescript.

Shapleigh (Maine) record book
Frost, John E. (John Eldridge), 1917-1992.
Mss F29/S5/F76/1965
[1], 42, 3, [1], 1 leaves; 29 cm.
1965
Typescript.

South Berwick (Maine) record book
Frost, John E. (John Eldridge), 1917-1992.
Mss F29/S67/F76/1967
[1], 169, x leaves; 29 cm.
1967
Typescript.

Waterboro (Maine) record book
Frost, John E. (John Eldridge), 1917-1992.
Mss F29/W27/F76/1965
iii, 117, 6, 3 leaves; 29 cm.
1965
Typescript.

York (Maine) record book
Frost, John E. (John Eldridge), 1917-1992.
Mss F29/Y6/F76/1973
1 v.; 29 cm.
1973
Typescript.

[Men of Cambridge] [Massachusetts]
Whitney, William H.
MS CAM 144
c. 1897
Typescript.

Notes from an interleaved copy of Drake's "Founders of New England" once belonging to Henry F[itz-Gilbert] Waters, A.M., and made by him
Waters, Henry Fitz-Gilbert, 1833-1913.
NE 11 3B
37 p.
c. 1947
Typescript.

Scots captured in the battle of Dunbar
NE 15 40
1922
Typescript.

A memorial to the soldiers of the American Revolution who at various periods lived in Acworth, N.H.
Allen, George Lawrence.
NH ACW 18
19 p.
1956
Typescript with corrections.

Record of the founding of the First Methodist Society in New Hampshire, copied from original clerk's offical record book
NH ALE 25
25 p.
Transcription of original record.

Inscriptions from gravestones in Crawford Cemetery at Alexandria, New Hampshire
NH ALE 5
12 p.
Typescript.

Inscriptions ... copied from gravestones in two cemeteries within the town limits of Alstead, New Hampshire
NH ALS 2
6 p.
Typescript.

Some gravestone inscriptions from Alton and West Alton, N.H.
NH ALT 40
12 p.
Typescript (incomplete).

Allen family of Sandwich Dartmouth Fairhaven ... Sherman family ...
Wright, Anna Allen, b. 1882.
Oversize G ALL 4582
1938
Typescript.

Andrews family records
Seaver, Jesse Montgomery, b. 1890.
Oversize G AND 1979
18 p.
Typescript.

Puritanism versus Quakerism. A dark page in the history of New England. [Connections of the Bakers Trumbulls and Robinsons]
Baker, Fred A. (Fred Abbott), b. 1846.
Oversize G BAK 13
8 p.
Typescript.

David Baldwin of Summit Schoharie County N.Y. his ancestors and descendants
Baldwin, Frank Boyd.
Oversize G BAL 2663
42 p.
1964
Typescript.

Bancroft family in England 1260-1587
Oversize G BAN 6
4 p.
Bound tabular pedigree.

Record of the Barnes family ... Small family ... [and] Sheldon family
Beamish, Sarah Jane (Elliott) 1908-.
Oversize G BAR 4481
162 p.
1958
Typescript.

Barber genealogy [Thomas of Simsbury Conn. and desc.]
Wilson, Oliver E.
Oversize G BAR 539
41 p.
1897
Typescript.

Barrows genealogy: descendants of John of England and Salem Mass.
Barrows, Chester Willard.
Oversize G BAR 6400A
9 p.
1928
Typescript.

English family history of the Beechers 1500-1637 Beecher family in America 1637-1690
Oversize G BEE 130
4 p.
Typescript.

Beebe - Whelan data
Seger, Adah Beebe, 1881-.
Oversize G BEE 51
10 p.
Typescript.

Beebe
Whelan, Florence Spencer
Oversize G BEE 74
8 p.
1950
Typescript.

Ancestry of Martha (Rogers) Benjamin
Oversize G BEN 2302
11 p.
Typescript.

Descendants of John Bidwell of Hartford Conn.
Higby, Clinton David, b. 1860.
Oversize G BID 22
1914
Bound charts.

Ancestors of Amos Binney
Binney, Amos, 1857-1912.
Oversize G BIN 945
31 p.
Typescript.

Blake genealogy descendants of Jasper of Eng. and Hampton N.H.
Oversize G BLA 7060
5 p.
Typescript.

Genealogical descent of Amos S. Blake of Waterbury New Haven Co. Conn.
Blake, Edwin Mortimer.
Oversize G BLA 7086
1906
Typescript.

The pedigree of Katherine Alexander (Duer) Blake
Blake, Katherine Alexander (Duer).
Oversize G BLA 7106
1925
Typescript.

Bogert family
Walker, Raymond.
Oversize G BOG 237
48 p.
Copy of a Bogert record revised, corrected and enlarged by John Nicholas Bogert ... with additions on the Bogert Walker Johnstone families by Raymond Walker

Richard Bonsall of Pennsylvania [from England in 1683] and 8 generations of descent (in one line only)
Bonsall, Grace Pratt Miller, 1898-1989
Oversize G BON 850
1945
Typescript.

Wills and inventories of Peter Bourdett and Stephen Bourdett of Hackensack Bergen Co. N.J.
Oversize G BOU 1650
12 p.
Typescript.

Bradford descendants of William of Plymouth Mass.
Oversize G BRA 3233
58, 2 p.
Typescript.

Genealogy of Moses Bradford Boardman on his mother's side
Boardman, William B.
Oversize G BRA 3294
10 p.
1923
Typescript.

Genealogy and biography of the descendants of James Breakenridge [sic] who came to America in 1727
Breckenridge, C.E.
Oversize G BRE 110
49 p.
1903
Typescript.

John Brown of Hampton
Brown, Ernest.
Oversize G BRO 5832, 5823A
3, 44 p.
1939
Typescript.

History of the Brundage family [descendants of John Brundage of Ipswich England and Rachel Hubbard his wife who settled in New England in 1633]
Brundage, Arthur N.
Oversize G BRU 1575
6 p.
1946
Typescript.

Rev. James Buckham and President Matthew Henry Buckham their families and descendants to 1941
Marsh, William Parmelee, 1867-1948.
Oversize G BUC 215
2, 4, 40, 1, 18 p.
1941
Typescript.

Records of the Bull or Buell family of America 1897
Dudley, H. C.
Oversize G BUL 110
2, 12, 1 p.
1897
Typescript.

Application for membership to the [NSDAR] of Josephine Freeman Bumstead 1925
Bumstead, Josephine Freeman.
OverSize G BUM 400
1925
Typescript.

Family record of Jonathan Bunker & of his wife Sarah Runnels who settled at Barnstead N.H. A.D. 1770 & an accurate record of four generations of the Bunker & Banchor name
Banchor, John Franklin.
Oversize G BUN 1650
28 p.
1903
Typescript.

Descendants of John Burr and Jerusha Beardsley of Ohio
Weeks, Frank Edgar, 1857-1946.
Oversize G BUR 4986
14 p.
1933
Typescript.

Burdakin notes
Barker, John Herbert, 1870-1951.
Oversize G BUR 845
48 p.
Typescript.

Notes on the Calef and Watkins families, with family records from Bartlett - Calef Bible
Robbins, Dana Watkins, b. 1875.
Oversize G CAL 1845
4 p.
Typescript.

Our lineage through the Call family and other families allied with the Calls by marriage
Mills, William Stowell.
Oversize G CAL 3568
17 p.
1896
Typescript.

Record book of William Carruth, b. 11 March 1825, Birkenhead Farm, Houston and Killalan parish, Renfrewshire, Scotland
Carruth, Blaine.
Oversize G CAR 9533
Typescript.

Certified copies of Carruth birth records in Scotland ... compiled at the General Registry Office, Edinburgh. 2 vols. Vol. 1: Jan. 1, 1855-Dec. 31, 1855. Vol. 2: Jan. 1, 1886-Dec. 31, 1915
Carruth, Harold Bertram, b. 1887.
Oversize G CAR 9543 A, B
2 vols.
1950-1955
Typescript.

Certified copies of Carruth death records in Scotland ... compiled at the General Registry Office, Edinburgh. 2 vols. Vol. 1: Jan. 1, 1855-Dec. 31, 1885. Vol. 2: Jan. 1, 1886-Dec. 31, 1915
Carruth, Harold Bertram, b. 1887.
Oversize G CAR 9547
2 vols.
1950-1954
Typescript.

Certified copies of Carruth death records in England and Wales from 1847 to 1945, inclusive, compiled at the General Register Office, Somerset House, London
Carruth, Harold Bertram, b. 1887.
Oversize G CAR 9549
1950

Memoir of the Charnock family
Charnock, Richard Stephen.
Oversize G CHA 12175
17 p.
1861
Typescript.

Partial genealogical record of the descendants of Deacon Joseph Chandler
Currier, Harvey Lear, b. 1839.
Oversize G CHA 7207
17 p.
Typescript.

Chandler. [A New Jersey line with indication of a Massachusetts ancestry.]
Mapes, Leslie Dunbar.
Oversize G CHA 7258
3 p. + iv.
1933
Typescript.

Chapman genealogical data, suggestions for a Chapman family association, a national Chapman family reunion, and a complete Chapman genealogy
Seaver, Jesse Montgomery, b. 1890.
Oversize G CHA 9662
50 p.
1927
Typescript.

Families of Clapp, Ray, and Kenyon
Oversize G CLA 1143
1925
Typescript.

The Clark genealogy, diagram 2, descendants of Elisha Clark of Kittery, Maine
Clark, Carlos T.
Oversize G CLA 1483
10 p.
1925

Clark family genealogy: descendants of Elisha of Kittery, Maine, data sheets with side lines
Lempert, Leon H.
Oversize G CLA 1489
13 p.
1925

The Clark family tree, continuation of ancestry of Mary Foster, generation 12. Perley chart A ...
Lempert, Leon H.
Oversize G CLA 1509
14 p.
1930

The Clark family tree, diagrams II, with extracts from diagram I; this book contains tabulated lists of known ancestors and descendants of John Clark and Abigail Bryant, John Perley and Mary Spaulding, Phineas Warren, Sr. and Betsy Collier, Henry Tibbetts, Jr. and Abigail Young ...
Lempert, Leon H.
Oversize G CLA 1512 A – B – C
28 charts + 24 typ. sheets
1930; 1931

Claflin genealogy: the posterity of Cornelius Claflin, son of Daniel
Claflin, Francis Gardner.
Oversize G CLA 298
32 + 1 p.
Typescript.

Clemence genealogy: descendants of Richard of Chepachet, R.I.
Raymond, Ralph Leigh.
Oversize G CLE 4135
5 p.
1921
Typescript.

Clough family Bible records. Theophilus Clough, b. 1789, m. 1814 Sarah Richards, b. 1788, of Springfield, N.H.
Oversize G CLO 2850
3 p.
Typescript.

*Genealogy of the Collier family of Cohasset,
Mass.* Bound with *The Briggs-Collier house at
"The Farms*
Tower, Gilbert S.
Oversize G COL 3714
24 p. + 5 p.
1949
Typescript.

Colton - Tucker families of Ohio and California
Colton, Charles M.
Oversize G COL 8265
1930
Typescript.

*Lewie Columbia and his descendants, from
records by Sally (Columbia) Robbins*
Robbins, Dana Watkins, b. 1875.
Oversize G COL 8450
3 p.
Typescript.

*Compton family: descendants of John and Helen
Compton of New Jersey*
Compton, Murat.
Oversize G COM 150
39 p.
1899
Typescript.

*One line of the Coolidge family from John
Coolidge of 1630 of Watertown, Mass., for 10
generations through Mass., N.Y., Wisconsin, and
South Dakota, up to March 15, 1927*
Coolidge, Walter W.
Oversize G COO 1089
15 p.
1927
Typescript.

*Cook cemetery inscriptions: families of
Watertown, Mass. and Preston, Conn.*
Phillips, Daniel L.
Oversize G COO 68
6 p.
1924
Typescript.

*Ancestor Thomas Cunningham of Unadilla, N.Y.,
and descendants; other Cunningham families;
ancestor John Cunningham of Vermont, and
descendants; John Cunningham of North
Carolina and descendants*
Sinnett, Charles Nelson, 1847-1928.
Oversize G CUN 28
1922
Typescript.

*Partial record of the descendants of Richard
Currier of Amesbury [Massachusetts]*
Currier, Harvey Lear, b. 1839.
Oversize G CUR 1656
1906
Typescript.

*Partial record of the descendants of Richard
Currier of Amesbury*
Currier, Harvey Lear, b. 1839.
Oversize G CUR 1656A
1907
Typescript.

*Descendants of Captain William Daniel of
Middlesex County, Virginia*
Heinemann, Charles Brunk, b. 1882.
Oversize G DAN 652, 656
1931
Typescript.

*Genealogie van de Nederlandse Tak van het
Geslacht Dees, Dez, geparenteerd in 1775 met de
Nederlandse Tak van het Geslacht Alvarez*
Jurry, J. E. J.
Oversize G DEE 225
33 p.
1957
Typescript.

Het Geslacht Dek
Dek, Adriaan Willem Eliza, 1924-.
Oversize G DEK 20, 20A
96 p.
1953
Typescript.

*Genealogical records of the Digges family
showing the ancestors and descendants of Gov.
Edward Digges and his son, Col. William Digges*
Oversize G DIG 525
8 p.
Typescript.

*The Dightons of the West Riding and their
descendants*
Deighton, H.
Oversize G DIG 750
5 p.
1938

*Ancestry of Warwick M. Downing, son of James
M. Downing and Nellie Summers*
Downing, Warwick M.
Oversize G DOW 4294
55 p.
1954
Typescript.

The Eells line: family of Mrs. Elva (Eells) Parker
Oversize G EEL 1
15 p.
Typescript.

Fargo - Rich family
Bicknell, Carrie Fargo.
Oversize G FAR 80
92 p. (many blank).
Bailey's Photo Ancestral Record.

*The record of my ancestry (Col. Frederick Samuel
Fish). The Fish family. Book of origins, private
and personal, with historical notes, coats-of-arms
and photographs*
Oversize G FIS 73
107 p.: coat of arms, photographs.
1915
Typescript.

*The Foster family: descendants of Reginald or
Renald Foster of Ipswich, with mss. and typed
notes taken from many printed sources pertaining
to [the] name of Foster*
Oversize G FOS 140
Typescript.

*The ancestry of Winslow Howard Foster and that
of his wife Anna Mabel (Burr) Foster of
Ludington, Michigan. Also various items of
information about the ancestry and about some of
the families connected with it*
Foster, Winslow Howard, b. 1869.
Oversize G FOS 210
1941
Typescript.

*French [Descendants of John and Joanna
French, who settled in Cambridge between 1635
and 1637.]*
Baker, Frances.
Oversize G FRE 6194
7 p.
1956
Typescript.

*Report on Frye [family: Adrian Frye m. Margaret
Bryan near Bristol, 23 July 1627]*
Oversize G FRY 55
7 p.
1927
Typescript.

*Genealogy and pedigree of the Kingston branch
of Dr. S. F. Fuller [sic], the pilgrim of the
Mayflower, 1620... to 1887... with historical notes
before and after the arrival of the Mayflower in
1620... also the arms of the different branches of
the Fuller family*
Fuller, T. B.
Oversize G FUL 256
14 p.
Typescript

The Fulkerson story
Preston, John F.
Oversize G FUL 275
99 p.
1961
Typescript.

The Gillmore saga 1720-1960, volume 1: containing a biography of Rev. George Gillmore, 1720-1811, together with a genealogical record of his descendants through his daughters and sons ... of Kings and Hants Counties, Nova Scotia
Tucker, Sidvin Frank, b. 1888.
Oversize G GIL 1094
99 p.
1960
Typescript.

Genealogy of Capt. Mastthias Gorham, who moved to Westminster, Vermont, from Yarmouth, Mass., April 1793
Gorham, David.
Oversize G GOR 700
4 p.
Typescript.

An Ohio Gott family: ancestors and descendants. The first Gotts in America
Gott, Philip Porter, b. 1889.
Oversize G GOT 312
2 p.
1940
Typescript.

Genealogy of the Graves, Farrington and Bingham families
Corning, Herbert I.
Oversize G GRA 1373
Typescript.

Graves genealogy: John Graves, Concord, Mass., 1635, to Thankful Graves, who married Daniel Woodin and died Nov. 3, 1851
Graves, John Card, 1839-1931.
Oversize G GRA 1385
12 p.
1902
Typescript.

Genealogy of Barbara Ann Grever: Crump, Grever, Heemann, Van Aken
Grever, Barbara Ann.
Oversize G GRE 6001
1966
Typescript.

Griffith family records
Seaver, Jesse Montgomery, b. 1890.
Oversize G GRI 467
21 p.
1928?
Typescript.

The journal of Jonathan Grimshaw (1818-1889), with the Grimshaw family records
Grimshaw, Jonathan, 1818-1889.
Oversize G GRI 965
19 + 5 p.
1951

Haley family
Haley, Samuel G.
Oversize G HAL 900
259 p.
1871
Typescript.

Sketch of Benjamin Harwood - "was the first white child born in Bennington, Vermont."
Oversize G HAR 14515
10 p.
Undated clipping from *Bennington Banner*.

Hatch genealogy: descendants of Thomas of England and Massachusetts
Oversize G HAT 100
1912
Typescript.

The sturdy Hathorn families of Maine
Sinnett, Charles Nelson, 1847-1928.
Oversize G HAT 1680
110 p.
1922
Typescript.

Hawes family: extracts from Bucks Co., England, records
Hawes, Frank Mortimer, 1850-1941.
Oversize G HAW 346
1926
Typescript.

Thomas Hayward of Duxbury and Bridgewater, Mass., and his family
Mapes, Leslie Dunbar.
Oversize G HAY 1175, 1175A
5 leaves.
1943
Typescript.

Sketch of the Herman family
Little, Alla Pearl.
Oversize G HER 904
13 leaves.
1939
Typescript.

The pedigree of Mary Adelaide Lochary Hoge
Oversize G HOG 215
23 + 1 p. NY Gen. & Biog. Soc. forms.
1933
Typescript.

Hoisington family
Kidder, Almon.
Oversize G HOI 300
4 + 30 p.
1900
Typescript.

Holmes family records
Seaver, Jesse Montgomery, b. 1890.
Oversize G HOL 5346
20 p.
1929
Typescript.

Genealogy of several branches of the Hosmer family
Hosmer, Charles Bridgham.
Oversize G HOS 545
7 + 4 p.
1926
Typescript.

Samuel Hotchkiss of the New Haven Colony and some of his descendants
Hotchkiss, Clarence Roland.
Oversize G HOT 78
15 p.
1939
Typescript.

Howland family of New Jersey: an article on the family tree, a list of families connected to the Howland line, and copies of wills filed in Freehold, New Jersey, and Trenton, New Jersey
Oversize G HOW 1291
9 p.
Typescript.

History of the Hubbell family in England and America., also history of the Hubbell coat-of-arms, and Stuart and Graham pedigrees
Hubbell, Walter, b. 1851.
Oversize G HUB 558
1905, 1908
Typescript.

The Hunt family of Pickins [sic] District, South Carolina
Young, Pauline.
Oversize G HUN 2082
13 p.
Typescript.

William Huston of Voluntown, Conn., and some of his descendants
Eck, Aimee May (Huston), 1907-.
Oversize G HUS 1130
6 p.
1947
Typescript.

William Brown Ide and his descendants: records secured in California, 1948-1949
Cheever, Herbert Milton.
Oversize G IDE 80
49 + 5 p.
1954
Typescript.

The Ingham family
Oversize G ING 698
23 + 78 p.
Typescript.

Pedigree chart of Betsey R. Keyes
Keyes, Betsey R.
Oversize G KEY 130
68 p.
1956
Typescript.

Pedigree charts of Kiehl/Grinnell and related families of Onondaga Co., N.Y.: a preliminary genealogical work
Kiehl, Ralph Adam, 1908-.
Oversize G KIE 820
1959
Typescript.

Miscellaneous data concerning the Kimballs of New Jersey and Pennsylvania, descendants of William and Anna (Cole) Kimball of Conn. and N.Y.
Kimball, Charles Newton, 1911-.
Oversize G KIM 53
Typescript.

The King family of Bromley, Kent, and New York
Morrison, George Austin, Jr.
Oversize G KIN 608
11 p.
1911
Typescript.

Knox genealogy
Oversize G KNO 800
Typescript.

Kreider genealogy
Duty, Allene Beaumont, 1912-.
Oversize G KRE 250
18 p.
1953
Typescript.

The Lamb family
O'Connell, Loren W.
Oversize G LAM 641
32 p.
1939
Typescript.

Genealogy of Langford and the allied families of Sweeting, Robertson, [and] Bell
Langford, George, b. 1876.
Oversize G LAN 2325
4 v. in 1. (130 p.)
1936
Typescript.

Lawrence family: descendants of John, William, and Thomas of Long Island
Walcott, George W.
Oversize G LAW 583
10 p.
1853
Typescript.

Lawrence family of New Jersey: photostat records
Lawrence, Schuyler.
Oversize G LAW 700
9 p.
1945
Typescript.

English ancestry of the Leavitt family of Hampton and Eastport, Maine
Marston, Maude L. Swett.
Oversize G LEA 2658
5 p.
Typescript.

Abstract of the title of the Lefferts farm, in the city of Brooklyn, known as the New Bedford farm, situate on the north side of the Jamaica turnpike about seventeen chains, or eleven hundred and twenty-two feet easterly from the Hunterfly road, and estimated to contain about ninty-seven [sic] or one hundred acres, and represented on the accompanying diagram
Wheeler, A. S.
Oversize G LEF 430
5 leaves.
1870
Typescript.

Pedigrees of the two Ellis Lewises, with notes
Conner, Philip Syng Physick.
Oversize G LEW 931
4 p. + 1 p.
1893
Typescript.

Lewis pedigree: the pedigree of David Lewis, Esq. of Philadelphia
Conner, Philip Syng Physick.
Oversize G LEW 932
6 + 1 + 31 + 4 p.
1894
Typescript.

*A brief sketch of the life of Joseph Limeburner,
captain of the Great Republic: his ancestors,
descendants and his kinsmen*
Limeburner, Grace M. Grindle, b. 1880.
Oversize G LIM 530
2 + 18 p.
1958
Typescript.

*The genealogy of John Lindsley (1845-1909) and
his wife Virginia Thayer Paine (1856-1941) of
Boston, Massachusetts*
Poole, Herbert Armstrong, b. 1877.
Oversize G LIN 2500
532 p. + 111.
1950
Typescript.

*Richard Long of Salisbury, killed by Indians,
September 4, 1692*
Long, Hallock P. (Hallock Porter), b. 1891.
Oversize G LON 554
5 p.
1958
Typescript with annotations.

Lowthrop of Yorkshire
Culleton, Leo.
Oversize G LOW 1730
Unpaginated.
Typescript and mss.

The record of my ancestry
Watkins, Walter Kendall, 1855-1934.
Oversize G LYM 44
69 p.
"Bailey record" of my ancestry filled in with the
genealogy of the Lyman family.

*In memoriam. [To the memory of Walter Lyon
and his wife Maria Antoinette (Giddings) Lyon,
by their daughter ...]*
Johnson, Louise Antoinette Lyon, b. 1853.
Oversize G LYO 89
1928
Typescript.

*Eliab Lyon and his descendants: with brief
accounts of Peter Lyon of Monmouth, Maine;
Henry Ware Lyon of South Paris, Maine; [and]
Laban Lyon of Hallowell, Maine*
Lilly, Georgiana Hewins.
Oversize G LYO 98
55 p.
1932
Typescript.

Peter McCormack 1772-1852 of Boyle Ireland
Eldridge, William Henry, 1873-1943.
Oversize G MacC 5312
22 p.
1932
Typescript.

*Notes on Hugh and Christiana McMillen of Loch
Eil Scotland and Stony Creek N.Y.*
Wright, Anna Allen, b. 1882.
Oversize G MacM 19559
48 p.
1939?
Typescript.

*Notes on the family history of William B. McNail
(1782-1868)*
McNail, Stanley D.
Oversize G MacN 19750
12 p.
1957
Typescript.

George McNutt and his descendants
Eaton, Arthur Wentworth Hamilton, 1849-1937.
Oversize G MacN 20975
6 p.
Typescript.

Register of the Rev. Samuel Mann &c.
Mann, Samuel.
Oversize G MAN 1300
4 p.
Typescript.

A correction of the Mapes family ancestral line
Mapes, Leslie Dunbar.
Oversize G MAP 510
6, 3 p.
1935
Typescript.

A tentative correction of the Mapes family line
Mapes, Leslie Dunbar.
OverSize G MAP 515
1, 21 p.
c1941
Typescript.

Some south Jersey descendants of Joseph Mapes a Quaker of Southold Long Island and subsequent marriages of his son's widow Mary
Mapes, Leslie Dunbar.
Oversize G MAP 518
5 p.
1944
Typescript.

The paternal and maternal ancestors of James Marshall born Landaff N.H. May 1 1789 died Kingston N.H. April 1 1858 ...
Hills, Thomas.
Oversize G MAR 4627
15 p.
Typescript.

Life of Joseph Meigs
Meigs, William M.
Oversize G MEI 380A
3, 43, 8 p.
1887
Typescript.

Descendants of Vincent Meigs born 1583 Book 1
Oversize G MEI 384
Various pagings.
Typescript.

The sturdy Melcher family of Maine
Sinnett, Charles Nelson, 1847-1928.
Oversize G MEL 560
79 p.
1922
Typescript.

Merritt family records Guilford and Killingworth Connecticut Fair Haven Benson and Georgia Vermont St. Lawrence and Allegany Counties New York Fort Dodge Webster County Iowa
Stevens, Halsey, 1908-.
Oversize G MER 3615
6 p. Typescript
1942

Mixsell family [Philip 1731-1814 Williams Twshp. Northampton Co. Pa. and allied families]
Mixsell, Raymond Boileau.
Oversize G MIX 350
79 p.
Typescript.

Moody family data
Oversize G MOO 645
3, 4 p.
Typescript.

The history of Franklin Joy Morton Esq. and his ancestors from Maine Massachusetts and Maryland [including the allied families of Joy Nason and Balch]
Morton, F. Craig.
Oversize G MOR 1619
28, 9, 17, 12 p.
1966
Typescript.

Genealogy the Munson Granniss Humiston Brockett Doolittle Dunham families with collateral branches
Munson, Dunham O.
Oversize G MUN 4256
54 p.
1925
Typescript.

Family record of the Nichols family [descendants of Levi Nichols and Eleanor Boutelle]
Oversize G NIC 450
6 p.
Typescript.

O'Carroll - Carroll.
Oversize G OCA 420
12 p.
Typescript.

Genealogy of the Ormsbee family Ormsbee Ormsby
Ormsbee, Arthur E.
Oversize G ORM 665
31, 132 p.
1952
Typescript.

The Orr genealogies
Sinnett, Charles Nelson, 1847-1928.
Oversize G ORR 65
199 p.
1922
Typescript.

Orser a genealogical record of the descendants of William Orser of Dutch origin immigrant ancestor of the Orser families of New Brunswick and New England
Turner, Daniel, 1905-.
Oversize G ORS 150
2, 37, 6.
1935
Typescript.

Genealogical notes on David Philbrook and Benjamin Philbrook among the first settlers of Hardwick Vt.
Philbrook, Mary.
Oversize G PHI 468
3 p.
1929
Typescript.

Pulsifer genealogical notes: descendants of Benedict of Ipswich Mass.
Chamberlain, George Walter, 1859-1942.
Oversize G PUL 1510
1928
Typescript.

Genealogical records relating to Nathan Henry Richardson and Martha Ann (Barber) Richardson and their ancestors and descendants
Richardson, Charles F.
Oversize G RIC 1320
85 p.
1933
Typescript.

Genealogical record of the ancestry of Henry Royds and his wife Margaret Bowne married 11 July 1848
Oversize G ROY 875
In William H. Whiteman's Ancestral Tablets

The family of Rene St. Julien and the allied families of Bullock Hoge Hume White Long (Langue) Robinson Hoover Waymire Fouts Bryan Crawford Cooper Patten Downey Beiler Besler Shryock Teagarten
Oversize G SAI 1320
1941?
Typescript.

Genealogical memoranda ... of Hon. Charles Fay Shepard of Westfield Mass. ... genealogy of the Shepard family as far back as the town of Westfield records can be traced of Jarred Shepard and his wife Esther Noble
Shepard, Charles Fay.
Oversize G SHE 11220
4 p.
1908
Typescript.

History of Simmons and Hamilton families ...
Simmons, Greenberry, b. 1901.
Oversize G SIM 2365
21 p.
1949
Typescript.

The Stinson family in Me.
Sinnett, Charles Nelson, 1847-1928.
Oversize G STI 3025
49 p.
1922
Typescript.

Story [descendants of William Story who settled in Chebacco Parish Ipswich about 1639]
Oversize G STO 16220
14 p.
Typescript.

The Tabor genealogy. Assembled with recent editions from The Tabor genealogy compiled by Charles Ayer Tabor
West, Harriet Tabor.
Oversize G TAB 1025
16 p.
1960
Typescript.

Genealogical record of Richard ("Rock") Taylor Yarmouth Mass.
Taylor, Bushrod Shedden.
Oversize G TAY 1860
13 p.
1908
Typescript.

Pedigree charts Jesse Lenard Warner b. 1916 Spanish Fork Utah Co. Utah
Warner, Jesse Lenard.
Oversize G WAR 4947
43 p.; 35.4 x 21.7 cm.
1947
Typescript.

Whipple family descendants of John Samuel Ibreck Isreal [sic] and Molly of Cumberland R.I.
Walcott, George W.
Oversize G WHI 1055
1853
Typescript.

The Wild family of Braintree Mass.
Jackson, Edward Evarts, b. 1868.
Oversize G WIL 1934
34, 6 p.
1906
Typescript.

Wilbor genealogy
Wilbor, Otis.
Oversize G WIL 90
125 p.
1903
Typescript.

The Winslow genealogy [descendants of Edward]. Copied from the original papers by J.F. Trott in 1870 and carried down to the 25 Dec. 1913 by John [Edward] Winslow.
Trott, J.F.
Oversize G WIN 5982
23 p.
1913
Typescript.

Genealogy of the State of Maine descendants of John Winter (immigrant) of Watertown Mass. together with genealogies of certain collateral branches of the family and also memoranda taken from probate
Winter, Frank.
Oversize G WIN 6564
1929
Typescript.

Genealogical record of the descendants of the Schwenkfelders...
Kriebel, Reuben, 1820-1890.
PA 40 15A
32 + 339 p.
1879
Typescript.

Descendants of Munson Hoyt Beers who originated in Fairfield Connecticut
Gault, Charles Beers, 1911-.
Pamphlet Box G BEE 1750A
1973
Revised ed.

Beedle - Simpson [pedigree chart of Lynn S. Beedle]
Beedle, Lynn S.
Pamphlet Box G BEE 285
5 p.

Pedigrees of New England families
Watkins, Walter Kendall, 1855-1934.
SG 000 2 [296]
1 ctn, 1 box.
Ms. notes and charts on numerous New England families.

Arthur Adams collection
Adams, Arthur, 1881-1960.
SG ADA 20 [37]
2 ctn, 1 box.
Genealogical collection of Dr. Arthur Adams containing records of the Adams family of New Jersey including the allied families of Baynard, Brush, Budlong, Clement, Denn, DuBois, Elkington, Grant, Ladd, Lake, Milnor, Morrison, Mungall, Seymour, Shapleigh, Somers, Spicer, Stanton, Steelman and Van Cowenhoven.

Andrew Napoleon Adams collection
Adams, Andrew Napoleon, 1830-1905 or 1908.
SG ADA 5 [70]
4 ctn, 1 box.
Genealogical data including correspondence and working papers collected by Andrew N. Adams in his compilation of "Henry Adams of Braintree and John of Cambridge and Robert Adams of Newbury".

Mary Langford Taylor Alden collection
Alden, Mary Langford Taylor.
SG ALD 11
15 boxes.
Alden, Pabodie, Snow and Soule families, Cape Cod families and miscellaneous genealogical notes.

Marcus Morton Aldrich collection
Aldrich, Marcus Morton.
SG ALD 20 [94]
1 ctn.
Papers concerning the descendants of George Aldrich through the lines of Jacob and Joseph.

Winthrop Alexander collection
Alexander, Winthrop, 1861-1941.
SG ALE 10 [38]
1 ctn.
Papers on John & George Alexander of Windsor, Conn., Alexanders of NH & VT, Alexanders of Mendon & Woburn, Mass., and Alexanders of southern Mass. and RI.

William M. Allen papers
Allen, William M.
SG ALL 12 [22]
2 ctn, 2 boxes.

Alverson collection
SG ALV 1 [79]
3 ctn.
Papers on the Alverson – Albertson and allied families of Housh, Collin, Cornwall, King, Lewis, Pentecost, Sayles, Stoutenburg.

Azel Ames papers
Ames, Azel, 1845-1908.
SG AME [214]
36 linear ft.

Henry Franklin Andrews collection
Andrews, H. Franklin (Henry Franklin), 1844-1919.
SG AND 10
9.5 ctn.
Miscellaneous papers concerning the descendants of John Andrews arranged according to his children: (#1) Direct line of H. F. Andrews. (#2-3) Descendants of John (2). (#4-17) Descendants of William (2). (#18-19) Indeces to William. (#20-21) Descendants of Elizabeth (2). (#22) Descendants of Thomas (2). (#23-29) Descendants of Joseph (2). (#30) Index to names other than Andrews. (#31) Index to records and notes wanted. (#32) Andrews family geographical index. Hamlin family records: (#33-41) Descendants of John. (#42-43) Descendants of Eleazer. (#44) Hamlins of NJ and PA. (#45) Hamlins of VA, NC, SC, MD, TN, KY, MI, TX. (#46-47) Misc. Hamlins. (#48) Fragmentary records of James (1) Hamlin. (#49) Fragmentary records of James (2) Hamlin. (#50) Post office addresses of descendants of James Hamlin, Jr. (#51) Typed copy of some fragmentary Hamlin family records. (#52) Female line. (#53) Index to Hamlin records.

Frances Eleanor Andrews collection
Andrews, Frances Eleanor, 1869-1954.
SG AND 16 [132]
2 boxes.
Genealogical notes on the Andrews and Wilkins families.

Annis collection
Fairman, Charles George, 1870-1941.
SG ANN 7 [23]
1 box.
Genealogical material on the Annis family of the U.S. & Canada. Includes Annis Annals 1638-1931, desc. of Daniel Annis of Hopkinton & Warner, Annisses of Manchester CT, Annisses of Maine, newspaper clippings, correspondence and misc. notes.

John Gould Anthony collection
Anthony, John Gould, 1804-1877.
SG ANT 1 [20]
2 boxes.
Typescript genealogies on the descendants of John[1] Anthonie who immigrated from England to Portsmouth, R.I. in 1634 (see notes field). Includes correspondence, geneal. letters & mss. received after the death of John Gould Anthony, and memo left by John Gould Anthony. Also includes information on the Gould family.

Ayer collection
Chamberlain, George Walter, 1859-1942.
SG AYE 1
4 boxes.
Papers concerning the Ayer family, five generations of descendants of John Ayer of Haverhill, Mass., also the Connecticut branch, and Ayer genealogical notes of Wiltshire, Eng.

Baker collection
Tufts, Susan Browning Cotton, 1869-1958.
SG BAK 1 [18]
3 boxes.
Baker genealogy - working notes for a revision with additional material of Nelson Morris Baker's "A genealogy of the descendants of Edward Baker of Lynn, Mass. 1630" (1867).

Samuel Weed Balch collection
Balch, Samuel W. (Samuel Weed), b. 1862.
SG BAL 1 [59]
4 CTN, 3 boxes, 3 card file boxes.
Papers concerning the descendants of John Balch who settled in Beverly, Mass. in 1623.

Jonathan Franklin Bancroft collection
Bancroft, Jonathan Franklin, 1847-1925.
SG BAN 16 [248]
1 ctn, 1 box.
Genealogical collection relating to the descendants of Thomas (1) Bancroft (1622-1691) of England and Lynn, Mass. There is genealogical correspondence to J. Franklin Bancroft, clippings, diary (multiple volumes), "The Gleaner", and original documents relating to Jonathan (4) Bancroft (1750-1815) and Ebenezer (4) Bancroft, original/typed transcriptions of letters by Timothy (5) Brancroft, 1816-1836, and a Roll of the Company of Infantry 3rd Reg 2nd Brigade, 3rd

Division for 1820/1826, 1828-1838. Includes a photocopy of a Bancroft genealogy by Ella Bancroft (Jones) Holden.

Edmund Dana Barbour collection
Barbour, Edmund Dana, 1841-1925.
SG BAR 18 [50]
1 ctn, 13 boxes.
Source material used to write Barbour genealogy (G BAR 548).

John Herbert Barker collection
Barker, John Herbert, 1870-1951.
SG BAR 21
9 boxes.
(021): Genealogical notes: Atherton, Belcher, Benjamin, Bigelow, Blood, Blowers, Browne, Church, Clark, Cooper, Danforth, Downe, Eliot, Errington, Felton, Fitch, Fowle, Francis, Gates, Gibson, Gilman, Goss, Green, Hall, Ham, Hancock, Harrington, Holmes, Lakin, Lane, Mulberry, Myrick, Newhall, Nutting, Parks, Pike, Prentice, Roberts, Ropes, Shattuck, Sparhawk, Stimson, Stubbs, Symmes, Treadway, Trowbridge, Varnum, Walker, Warren, White, Whitmore, Williams, Wilson, Wright & Wyeth.
(021A): Genealogical notes: Appleton, Belcher, Batchelder, Clark, Converse, Cutler, Danforth, Deschedde, Dunster, Eames, Eliot, Farmer, Felch (Fletch), Fletcher, Gifford, Gould, Greenough, Hildreth, Kimball, Knight, Lakin, Long, Mason, Montgomery, Morse, Osgood, Parker, Peabody, Phillips, Pierson, Pollard, Pope, Poulter, Pratt, Puffer, Richardson, Sargent, Sawtell, Scott, Symmes, Whitcomb, Whitney, Willard, Williams, Wilson, & Winship etc.

Robert Grosvenor Bartelot collection
Bartelot, Robert Grosvenor, 1868-1947.
SG BAR 60 [34]
10 boxes.
Collection of English material, mainly parish registers.

Joseph Gardner Bartlett collection
Bartlett, J. Gardner (Joseph Gardner), 1872-1927.
SG BAR 86 [146]
59 boxes, 36 card file boxes.
Genealogical material covering the ancestry of American immigrants from early English and American sources, also includes much later material. Major families: Adams, Ambrose, Austin, Baker, Baxter, Bradford, Browne, Byers, Bushnell, Cabot, Chandler, Crosby, Dowes, Eddy, Earle, Flagg, Foster, French, Gale, Gregg, Griswold, Hartshorne, Holbrook, Josselyn, Ledyard, McClain, McLean, McNeil, Marston, Massey, Matthews, Moody, Moore, Neubury, Newton, Pardee, Parker, Payne, Pomeroy, Robinson, Saltonstall, Selden, Seymour, Shedd, Sheldon, Southern, Stone, Sturgis, Talbot, Thompson, Throckmorton, Warden, White, Windsor and Woolson. Includes card index to probate records, incomplete index to Chancery proceedings time of Charles I roughly alphabetical, and place names.

Eben Pierce Bassett collection
Bassett, Eben Pierce, b. 1876.
SG BAS 12 [57]
13 CTN, 4 card file boxes.
Papers concerning the Bassett family and allied families of Veazie and Wheelden. Box 1 Classified males index & A-E; Box 2 Classified males G-K; Box 3 Classified males L-Z; Box 4 Unclassified males A-G/7; Box 5 Unclassified males G/8-M; Box 6 Unclassified males N-Z & husbands; Box 7 Husbands A-L; Box 8 Husbands M-Z; Box 9 Classified females Index & A-I; Box 10 Classified females J-Z & Unclassified females A-A/5; Box 11 Unclassified females A/6-Q; Box 12 Wives A-K; Box 13 Wives L-Z; Box 14 Unclassified females R-Z, Wives Index & Places Alabama-Mass.; Box 15 Places Montana-Foreign; Box 16 Allied families G-Veazie; and Box 17 Allied families Veazie-Wheelden.

George A.Bates collection
Bates, George A.
SG BAT 35 [75]
2 boxes.
Papers on the Bates family.

Bates collection
Davis, Marion Morse.
SG BAT 37 [2]
Correspondence and proof sheets collected in the preparation of "The Bates boys on the Western Waters" which appeared in the Western Pennsylvania Historical Magazine, 1946.

James Phinney Baxter collection
Baxter, James Phinney, 1831-1921.
SG BAX 9 [21]
1 ctn, 2 boxes.
Genealogical notes etc. on the Baxter and Proctor families used to write the "Baxter family: a collection of genealogies" (G BAX 2) and "The Baxters of New England, a family history" (G BAX 13).

Baylies collection
SG BAY 3 [103]
1 box.
Genealogical notes concerning the Baylies families of Uxbridge, Sturbridge, Dighton, Mass., Conn., Vt., N.Y., West and South.

Charles Addison Bean collection
Bean, Charles Addison, b. 1866.
SG BEA 14 [29]
1 ctn.
Notes on Lewis Bane of York, ME and his descendants in both lines; also working notes on the descendants of Robert Follett of Salem, MA.

Manly Colton Beebe collection
Beebe, Manly Colton.
SG BEE 1 [93]
1 ctn.
Papers on the Beebe and allied families incl. Blin, Holt, Keeney, and Tibbetts.

Gibson Bell collection
Bell, Gibson.
SG BEL 11 [133]
2 boxes.
Miscellaneous papers and records on the Bell family.

Bentley collection
Holman, Mary Lovering, 1868-1947.
SG BEN 20 [27]
1 ctn, 1 box.
Unfinished Bentley family manuscript. Includes
(1) Bentley vital records VT, (2) note books births
1843-1885 & vital records 1842-1890, (3) list of
persons named Bentley in the U.S., (4)
genealogical charts, (5) English Bentleys, (6) RI
1st, 2nd, 5th, 7th-9th gen., (7) males 3rd gen; 4th;
6th, (8) charts, (9) Conn.; Conn. females; Conn.
unfiled; Conn. preston etc, (10) Stonington
Bentleys, desc of George (5), (11) vital records &
probate Conn. families, (12) VT males; ancestry
not known; prob. desc. of Wm. of Lebanon; VT
females, lines not known, (13) Joseph of
Dutchess, (14) females, (15) PA, (16) Bentley,
southern, (17) Nova Scotia, Prince Edward Island
some desc. from Lebanon, (18) Bentley b. after
1800 also RI, (19) stray notes, etc, (20)
correspondence.

Beville collection
Tedcastle, Agnes Beville Vaughan.
SG BEV 1 [4]
Genealogical records, notes, etc. Includes a
typescript genealogy on the material English
ancestry of George Washington (Ball family).

The Binney family record
Binney, Charles J. F. (Charles James Fox), 1806-
1888
SG BIN 8
3 boxes.
Mss.

Blanchard collection
Blanchard, George Dana Boardman.
SG BLA 13 [68]
3 boxes.

Francis Everett Blake collection
Blake, Francis E. (Francis Everett), 1839-1916.
SG BLA 3, 3A, 3B
3 boxes.
(3): Genealogical papers concerning the Blake
family. (3A): Blake family memoranda. (3B):
17th and 18th century deeds and wills, 1621-
1704.

Isaac Dimond Blodgett collection
Blodgett, Isaac Dimond, 1828-1916.
SG BLO 5 [11]
1 ctn, 1 box.
Genealogical papers concerning the Blodgett
family.

Bolles collection
Watson, Edith Sarah.
SG BOL 25 [12]
1 box.
Includes misc. papers etc. pertaining to Bolles
family English connections.

Ethel Stanwood Bolton collection
Bolton, Ethel Stanwood, 1873-1954.
SG BOL 26 [152]
1 ctn., 1 box.
Genealogical records of the Bolton family in
England and Wales.

Bolles genealogy
Bolles, William Palmer, 1845-1916.
SG BOL 6 [9]
1916.

Clarence Winthrop Bowen collection
Bowen, Clarence Winthrop, 1852-1935.
SG BOW 9 [49]
10 ctn, 2 boxes.
Papers relating to his compilation of "The History
of Woodstock, Connecticut."

Elizabeth Hitchcock Brayton collection
Brayton, Elizabeth Hitchcock, 1865-1935.
SG BRA 21 [24]
2 boxes.
Mss. of Elizabeth H. Brayton's paternal, maternal
and misc. lines.

Horace Standish Bradford collection
Bradford, Horace Standish.
SG BRA 5
10 boxes.
Genealogical papers concerning the descendants
of Gov. William Bradford. (#1) Complete
genealogy. (#2) Genealogy on cards generation 1-
7. (#3) Genealogy on cards generation 8-10. (#4)
Misc. records.

Eva St. Clair Brightman collection
Brightman, Eva St. Clair, 1858-1939.
SG BRI 20 [19]
1 ctn.
Papers concerning Brightman and allied families.

Benjamin William Brown collection
Brown, Benjamin William, b. 1868.
SG BRO 52 [45]
4 boxes.
Brown genealogical records, John Browne of
Wannomoisett (Rehoboth) and misc. records on
various Brown family lines.

Brown - Weld collection
SG BRO 65 [15]
1 box.
Genealogical notes and charts on the Brown and
Weld families.

Wilton Francis Bucknam collection
Bucknam, Wilton Francis, 1861-1917.
SG BUC 2, 4
1 ctn., 9 boxes.
Mss. Bucknam genealogy.

John S. Burpee collection
Burpee, John S.
SG BUR 25 [10]
2 ctn.
Genealogical records of the Burpee family.

William Pelby Cabot collection
Cabot, William Pelby.
SG CAB 15 [25]
3 boxes.
Papers on the Cabot families of Salem, Mass.,
Vermont and Jersey Isle. Includes charts,
correspondence, letter books, etc.

Colin Campbell collection
Campbell, Colin.
SG CAM 31
2 boxes.
Copies of documents concerning the lands of
Finlariq, Breadalbane, and Perthshire, Scotland
1503-1680 taken from the family papers of the
Earl of Breadalbane and relating to the Campbell
family. Also includes added material on the
Campbell family of Craig and Edramuckie,
Pethshire, Scotland.

Myrtelle May Moore Canavan collection
Canavan, Myrtelle May Moore, b. 1879.
SG CAN 25 [14]
1 ctn.
Papers on the Moore, Chase, Young & Clarke
families. Also includes chart, biography of the
compiler, personal notes, correspondence and
photographs.

Barnard and Joan Capen gravestone fragments
SG CAP 5
Access to original material restricted; use
transcription in Register
1 box.
A fragment of the orginal gravestone for Barnard
and Joan Capen from the old cemetery in
Dorchester, MA. See Register 49:489 for a copy
of the inscription from the fragments and from the
renewed stone. The article states that "This is,
probably, 'the oldest Inscription to be found on
any grave stone in New England,' so far as the
date of death of Barnard Capen is concerned.-
Register iv.,165."

Leslie Albert Carter collection
Carter, Leslie Albert.
SG CAR 24 [218]
1 ctn., 1 box.
Genealogical correspondence and records of the
Carter-Cater families of Maine, N.H., Maryland
and Ohio.

Chapman collection
SG CHA 27 [33]
1 ctn., 1 box.
Misc. genealogical notes and papers on the
Chapman, Ferguson, Hamilton, and Knox
families.

John Carroll Chase collection
Chase, John Carroll, 1849-1936.
SG CHA 32-34 [31]
3 ctn., 3 boxes.
Genealogical records of the Chase family
including descendants of William Chase, Aquila
Chase, English research on Chase and other
Chase items. The 8th generation of descendants of
Aquila Chase included.

Chase - Townley correspondence
Thorne, Adela (Page) , b. 1845.
SG CHA 37 [56]
1 ctn.

George Walter Chamberlain collection
Chamberlain, George Walter, 1859-1942.
SG CHA 6
Genealogies on the following families ("of
Mass." assumed unless stated otherwise): Adams,
Barnes of CT & NY, Bass, Beebe of MA & CT,
Beekman of NY & NJ, Bennett, Blake of NH
with Eng. notes, Bonney, Booth with Eng. notes,
Bridgen of Shropshire, Eng., Burbank, Burgess,
Butler of PA, Collins, Crooks, Crowell, Dadmun,
Durham of MA & NY, Fall of ME & NH, Fiske,
Fletcher with Eng. notes, Fowler with Eng. notes,
Glidden of NH, Gorton of RI, Gould of New
England, Griffin with Eng. notes, Gurney,
Haynes, Hoar alias Hanson of New England with
Eng. notes, Hopkins with Eng. notes, Jackson of
NY, Jenkins, Kelly, Knight, Luscomb, Mace of
NC, Masters with Eng. notes, May of MA & CT,
Morgan of New England, Oliver, Osborn, Page of
NH with Eng. notes, Paine of NH, Pollard, Pratt,
Priest, Pulsifer, Rice, Shaw, Stevens, Stratford,
Trask, Trench, Webster, Weymouth of NH &
ME, & Worthen of NH.

Chase collection
Brown, Joseph Warren.
SG CHA 60 [153]
2 ctn.
Papers concerning the Chase family of Newbury,
Mass.

Arthur Howard Churchill collection
Churchill, Arthur Howard, b. 1862.
SG CHU 10 [1]
Genealogical papers of Arthur H Churchill of
Montclair, N.J. and later of Vermont, tracing his
ancestry through his maternal and paternal lines
showing his connection with the Plymouth
Churchills. Includes material concerning the
ancestry of his wife, Cora Hatch Churchill.

George Kuhn Clark collection
Clarke, George Kuhn, 1858-1941.
SG CLA 16 [85]
1 ctn., 1 box.
Papers concerning the Clarke and Kuhn families
with records of the town of Needham, MA.

Clark collection
Holman, Winifred Lovering, 1899-1989.
SG CLA 18 [71]
1 ctn., 2 boxes.
Genealogical material concerning the descendants
of William Clark: Gens. 1-4 male and female both
branches, 5th male also 5th female of Conn.
branch, V & VI females, VIth male, VII VIII IX
male, VII VIII IX female, misc. notes, Clark mss.
misc. families descendants (female), Lt. William
Clark material removed from cabinet of Dwight
Clark Washington D.C. 1935, Clark mss.

Bertha Winifred Clark papers
Clark, Bertha W. (Bertha Winifred), 1875-1965.
SG CLA 23 [223]
7 ctn.
Genealogical notes, correspondence, work sheets
and ms. genealogies on the Allen, Baker,
Congdon, Haxton, Jenney, Johnson, Scott, Smith,
and Tucker families. Includes notes and queries
from "Hartford Times" and "Geneal. & Hist."

Vernet E. Cleveland collection
Cleveland, Vernet E.
SG CLE 20 [74]
2 ctn., 1 flat storage box.
Papers on the Cleveland and allied families of
Barnes, Marsh, Shepard and Webster.

Edmund Janes Cleveland collection
Cleveland, Edmund Janes, 1842-1902.
SG CLE 21
1 ctn., 2 boxes.
Consists mainly of the original index to the 3 vol.
1899 Cleveland Genealogy; also some insets of
the addenda.

Isaac Cobb collection
Cobb, Isaac.
SG COB 5 [97]
3 boxes.
Papers concerning the ancestry of Elder Henry Cobb of London, Scituate and Barnstable and his descendants.

Henry James Coggeshall collection
Coggeshall, Henry James, 1845-1907.
SG COG 1 [310]
3 boxes, 1 flat storage box.
Mss. of Coggeshall genealogy and index.

Colburn collection
Gordon, George Augustus, 1827-1912.
SG COL 10 [32]
2 boxes.
Colburn genealogy.

Charles Clifton Colby III collection
Colby, Charles Clifton, III, 1895-1941.
SG COL 12 [83]
6 ctn., 2 boxes, 6 card file boxes.
Papers on the Colby and allied families of Annis, Bean, Currier, Follansbee, Frost, Mackentire, Putney, Ring, Rowell, Rowley, Webb, and Webster. Includes the correspondence of Roscoe E. Colby concerning the Colby and allied families as well as misc. correspondence and material from several towns and counties in NH, VT, CT, ME.

Samuel Willett Comstock collection
Comstock, Samuel Willett.
SG COM 11 [87]
2 ctn.
Correspondence, clippings, notes, etc. on the Comstock and Willett families.

Combs collection
SG COM 20 [95]
2 boxes.
Charts, reports and correspondence concerning the family of George D.A. Combs of Rockville Centre, N.Y.

Congdon collection
SG CON 10 [274]
4 ctn., 1 box, 2 card file boxes.
Notes, correspondence, photographs, charts, family group sheets, etc. concerning the Congdon and allied families.

Ancestry of Helen May Cook [and] allied families of Rhode Island and Plymouth Colony (1620-1947)
Cook, Helen May.
SG COO 25 [91]
2 boxes.
Typescript genealogy. Vol 1. A-B, Vol. 2 C, Vol. 3 D-F, Vol. 4 G-H, Vol. 5 I-L, Vol. 6 M-R, Vol. 7 S, Vol. 8 T-W, Vol. 9 charts.

Harriet Ruth Waters Cooke collection
Cooke, Harriet Ruth Waters, b. 1841.
SG COO 28 [96]
1 ctn., 1 box.
Papers on the Cooke and allied families of Brown, Chauncy, Clarke, Driver, Gaines, King and Skinner.

Frank Ethridge Cotton collection
Cotton, Frank Ethridge, 1861-1921.
SG COT 20 [253]
3 ctn, 5 boxes, 9 card files boxes.
Papers concerning the Cotton family, descendants of William.

Charles Judson Crary collection
Crary, Charles Judson, b. 1881.
SG CRA 30 [16]
1 box.
Crary family records, accumulated data and correspondence.

Crosby collection
Kelly, Emerson Crosby.
SG CRO 18 [229]
2 ctn.
Genealogy of the Crosby family, descendants of Simon Crosby. Also includes letters from the Crosby family.

Howard Crosby collection
Crosby, Howard.
SG CRO 7 [275]
1 box, 12 flat storage boxes, 5 card file boxes.
Genealogical ms. of the Crosby family.

Charles Henry Crocker collection
Crocker, Charles Henry.
SG CRO 9 [210]
4 ctn, 5 boxes, 2 card file boxes.
Papers concerning the descendants of Francis
Crocker of Marshfield, Mass. Includes Crocker,
Crooker, and Croker as well as House – Hows
lines.

Cunningham collection
Lane, Jennie T.
SG CUN 10 [185]
1 ctn., 1 box, 1 card file box.
Genealogical records and correspondence
concerning the ancestry and descendants of
Robert and Hugh Cunningham of Brookfield and
Spencer, Mass.

William Ralph Curtis collection
Curtis, William Ralph, b. 1870.
SG CUR 25 [101]
2 ctn.
Papers concerning the Curtis, Kelly, Morse,
Webster, Worth and many other familie s.

Clarence Edward Dame collection
Dame, Clarence Edward, 1886-1961.
SG DAM 5 [40]
1 ctn., 2 boxes.
Papers on the Dame - Dam families. Includes
several maps of Waterboro, ME and vicinity.

Joseph Dexter Danforth collection
Danforth, Joseph Dexter, 1876-1957.
SG DAN 6 [117]
1 ctn., 1 box.
Biographies, pedigrees and royal ancestry of the
Danforth and Chace families together with
records of the Blake, Mansfield, Munroe, Perkins,
Pollard, Porter, Thather and Wixon families.

Carlos Parsons Darling collection
Darling, Carlos Parsons, b. 1876.
SG DAR 6-6A [175]
7 ctn.
Genealogical papers concerning the Darling
family - descendants of Denice Darling of
Braintree and George Darling of Lynn. 6A
contains genealogical records showing the
ancestry of Carlos Parsons Darling through
numerous allied families, including chart of
Margaret Wyatt of Devon with ms. additions
carrying it down to Lewis Darling (1840-1916) of
Conn.

Florence Marguerite Davis collection
Davis, Florence Marguerite.
SG DAV 32 [28]
4 boxes.
Genealogical records of the Dolor Davis and
other families, also notes on Princeton, Mass. and
surrounding towns.

Milton Davidson collection
Davidson, Milon.
SG DAV 6 [92]
2 boxes, 1 tube, 1 ctn.
Papers concerning the descendants of William
Davidson and his wife Mary who came to this
country from the north of Ireland in 1728 and
settled in Woburn, Mass.

Paul Dudley Dean collection
Dean, Paul Dudley, 1878-1938.
SG DEA 25 [150]
2 ctn.
Genealogical records on the descendants of
William Dean, a settler of Boston as early as 1688
and later of Dedham, Mass. and Lebanon, Conn.

William Dean collection
Dean, William, 1830-1911.
SG DEA 50 [104]
6 ctn., 1 flat starage box.
Papers relating to Dean families in England and
New England: (1) Map 24"x 30" showing
portions of Dorset, Wilts, and Hants., Eng. (2)
Chart 20"x 30" showing descent from Richard de
Denefeld (1154-1189) of the Deane lines from
Christ Church, Holdenhurst and Sopley, Eng. (3)
Papers, wills and other documents relating to
Deanes of Chard (Somerset) and vicinity. (4)
English wills relating to Deanes and allied
families, 1631-1800. (5) Records and wills
relating to Deanes and allied families. (6-7)
Geneal. correspondence (8) "Sundry papers -
contains much of interest." (9) "Sundry
interesting memoranda & Bristol wills." (10)
Narrow parchment covered bk of items relating to
Deane families. (11) Pasteboard covered bk
"Visitation of Hampshire 1575-1622-1686,
Adenda Visitation of Dorset 1623 and sketch of
life of Sir Richard Deane. (12) Scrap bk of
clippings with Wimborn / Winster marriages. (13)
Sundry Southern wills. (14) Welch & English
notes, index English wills. (14) Lg note bks of
index & abstracts (non-wills), etc.

Samuel Carroll Derby collection
Derby, Samuel Carroll, 1842-1921.
SG DER 1 [100]
2 boxes.
Notes on the author's ancestry and on the history
of Dublin, NH.

Dickinson pedigree
SG DIC 5 [311]
1 flat storage box.
1836.
Pedigree of the family of Edward Dickinson, the
father of George Dickinson, late of New York in
America, with affidavits and extracts from
English parish registers to confirm the pedigree.

George Dimmock papers, ca. 1890-1930
Dimmock, George, 1852-1930.
SG DIM 6 [108]
9 linear ft.
Unpublished finding aid in the library.
Genealogical records, notes and correspondence
concerning the descendants of Thomas Dimmock

(ca. 1608-1680), an early settler of Barnstable,
MA and related families, especially Nash and
Sykes/Sikes. In addition, Dimmock organized
genealogies of some early Welsh, English and
French families, as well as of American
Dimmocks who, he determined in the course of
his research, were not descendants of Thomas
Dimmock.

Alfred Alder Doane papers, 1086-1927
Doane, Alfred A. (Alfred Alder), 1855-1918.
SG DOA 51 [277]
6 linear ft.
Unpublished finding aid in the library.
Genealogical correspondence and notes on which
Doane based his book "The Doane Family"
(1902). Includes 94 photographs of Doane and
related family members, Doane houses and
gravestones.

George Buckman Dorr collection
Dorr, George Buckman, 1853-1944.
SG DOR 10 [116]
1 ctn., 1 flat storage box.
1 & 1A. Genealogical notes on the Edward Dorr
family of Roxbury, Mass. 2. State legislative
service of the Hon. Samuel Dorr including notes
on men serving with him. 3a. Genealogical notes
on the Edward Dorr family and his estate at
Roxbury, Mass., 3b. the Rev'd Joseph Dorr, 3c.
Hon Joseph Dorr and notes on Nathan Buckman,
minister, 3d. Hon. Samuel Dorr-Adams, Lazinby,
Brown, house of Samuel Dorr in Boston, children
of Samuel Dorr by his first marriage + Susan,
daughter by second marriage, 3e. Notes on places
in connection with Dorr genealogy. 4. Letters
relating to Dorr genealogy. 5&6. Notes on places.
7a. Elizabeth Weld Gardner's last request to her
husband, 7b. William Ward's letter to his
grandchildren, 7c. Memo of William Ward's last
communication to the Sec. of State, Sept 25,
1819, 7d. Last will of William Ward, 7e.
Fragment from Ward genealogy (1786), 7f.
prayer, 7g. estate of Samuel Gray, 7h. Samuel
Gray's will, 7i. prayer, Mrs Gray, 7j. William
Ward's story, 7k. Misc. papers & charts.

William Ephraim Daniel Downes collection
Downes, William Ephraim Daniel, 1864-1936.
SG DOW 10 [124]
5 ctn.
Miscellaneous notes on many families collected on the compilation of the Downes genealogy and including the Downes family manuscript.

Governor Thomas Dudley Family Association collection
Trask, Warren Dudley, 1886-1958.
Governor Thomas Dudley Family Association.
SG DUD 3, 3A, SG DUD 3 (20 ctn.); SG DUD 3A (1 ctn., 1 box)
SG DUD 3: Dudley family ancestral history; mss. lineage records compiled for the Governor Thomas Dudley Family Association. SG DUD 3A: Collection of material of the Governor Thomas Dudley Association including year books, reunion reports, lineage records, membership applications, historical pamplets, publications and card catalogs.

The Durham - Russell ancestry
Russell, Allen Danforth, 1897-1984.
SG DUR 4 [134B]
1 flat storage box.
Ms. genealogy.

Dutton collection
Eustis, William Tracy, 1822-1906.
SG DUT 10 [178]
2 ctn., 2 boxes.
Typescript Dutton genealogy, descendants of John. 11A has Dutton family manuscripts collected by author in prepartion of his "Dutton genealogy".

Eames collection
Blount, Lucia Augusta Eames, 1841-1925.
SG EAM 10 [110]
2 ctn., 3 boxes.
Papers relating to the families of Thomas Eames of Dedham, Mass., his brother Robert of Woburn, Mass, and Robert of Boxford, Mass.

Fanny Isabel Kennish Earl collection
Earl, Fanny Isabel Kennish, b. 1854.
SG EAR 5 [51]
1 ctn.
Papers on the Earl and allied families.

Arthur Wentworth Hamilton Eaton papers, 1871-1927
Eaton, Arthur Wentworth Hamilton, 1849-1937.
SG EAT 1
7 linear ft.
Unpublished finding aid in the library.
Genealogies, history, vital records, notes and correspondence pertaining to Planters and United Empire Loyalists in Nova Scotia., particularly Kings and Hants Counties. The collection has material from Eaton's works on the Anglican church in Nova Scotia and the country's heritage of verse and lyrics. Eaton's church activities appear through correspondence with Phillips Brooks (1835-1893), Richard H. Newton (1840-1914), and William W. Newton (1843-1914). Eaton's tenure as an educator at the Cutler School is marked by numerous letters from former students. Eaton's private papers consist of social correspondence between 1880-1891 while Eaton was in New York which includes the poet William O. Partridge (1861-1930). In addition, there is a small collection of papers relating to the portraitist Wyatt Eaton (1849-1896).

Eaton collection
SG EAT 15
2 ctn., 1 box, 2 card file boxes.
Collection of Eaton material containing genealogical data, also Eaton Family Association correspondence.

Daniel Cady Eaton collection
Eaton, Daniel Cady, 1834-1895.
SG EAT 17 [276]
5 ctn., 1 box.
Letters and genealogical material concerning the Eaton families of England, Massachsuetts, and Connecticut, and other families, accompanied by Eaton wills, probate and town pension records.

John Eaton collection
Eaton, John, 1829-1906.
SG EAT 4 - 14
9 boxes.
SG EAT 4 [Abstracts of deeds relating to the
Eaton family]. SG EAT 5 [Wills of Eatons of
Salisbury & Haverhill, Mass.]. SG EAT 6
[Abstracts of land grants relating to the Eaton
families of Haverhill & Salisbury, Mass.;
descendants of John and Anne Eaton]. SG EAT 7
[Abstracts of deeds relating to the Eaton family of
Hancock Co., Maine]. SG EAT 8 [Abstracts of
deeds taken from the records of Hillsboro Co.
Register, wherein the name of Eaton appears]. SG
EAT 9 [Abstracts of conveyances in which the
name of Eaton appears as found in Oxford Co.,
ME registry of Deeds, Eastern District, from
1806-1885]. SG EAT 10 [Abstracts of deeds from
Rockingham Co., NH relating to the Eaton
family]. SG EAT 11 Abstracts from Strafford Co.,
NH wills and deeds in which the name Eaton
occurs]. SG EAT 13 [Miscellaneous notes and
correspondence relating to the Eaton family].

Eddy collection
Horton, Byron Barnes, 1873-1941.
SG EDD 57 [119]
1 ctn., 2 boxes.
Genealogical notes on the Eddy family including
the mss. of Dr. Charles Eddy and a collection of
Eddy notes by B. B. Horton.

Eddy collection
Avery, Clara Arlette, 1850-1937.
SG EDD 6 [109]
2 boxes.
Papers including notes, genealogical
correspondence, photographs, Bible records etc.
concerning the Eddy, Avery, and Wild family.

Henry Herbert Edes collection
Edes, Henry Herbert, 1849-1922.
SG EDE 1
1 ctn., 4 boxes.
(1) William Edes of Wells, Maine. (2)
Descendants of Edward T. Edes. (3) Needham
branch. (4) Isaiah Edes of Groton. (5) Gideon Day
Edes. (6) Generations 1-4. (7) 6th generation,
Boston. (8) 7th generation, Boston. (9) Edes tea
party. (10) Miscellaneous.

John Stetson Edmands collection
Edmands, John Stetson, 1873-1935.
SG EDM 1 [47]
1 ctn, 1 box.
Misc. records of the Edmands, Stone, Grover,
Fisher, Cutter, Hill, Bonner, Whittemore, and
Winship families.

Frank Custer Edminster collection
Edminster, Frank Custer, 1903-.
SG EDM 3 [239]
1 ctn, 1 box.
Manuscript and original reference material used
in compiling "The Edminster family in America"
published in 1965.

Charles Wallace Eldredge collection
Eldredge, Charles Wallace.
SG ELD 18 [171]
2 ctn, 1 box.
Genealogical data on (1-3). Crowfoot – Crofoot –
Crofut family; (4). Jennison family; (5).
Singletary family; (6). John Eldred of England;
Thomas Eldridge of VA, William Eldred of
Yarmouth, Robert Eldred of Yarmouth, Eldreds
of Greene Co. Ill.; (7). Eldreds, mainly of RI, CT,
NY; (8-13). Eldred – Eldridge – Eldredge, misc.;
(14). misc.; (15). 22 photstats of Eldredge
records, Chatham and Harwich, Mass.; (16). Line
of Robert Eldred of Monomoy; (17). Line of
William of armouth; (18). Ancestral charts of
C.W. Eldredge, Jackson NH.

Annie Corinne Colburn Ellison collection
Ellison, Annie Corinne (Colburn), 1862-1946.
SG ELL 25 [126]
2 ctn.
Miscellaneous genealogical material on Beals,
Colburn, Colson, Erskine, Harlow, Thayer,
Tower, West and allied families.

Emery collection
Emery Family Association.
SG EME 10 [122]
1 ctn., 3 boxes, 4 flat storage boxes.
Miscellaneous genealogical data on the Emery
family and the Emery Family Association which
was in the possession of Miss Jesse Emery,
Secretary of the Emery Family Association.

Endicott collection
Holman, Mary Lovering, 1868-1947.
SG END 12 [295]
2 boxes.
Misc. collection of Endicott genealogical
material.

William Crowninshield Endicott collection
Endicott, William Crowninshield, 1860-1936.
SG END 15 [151]
1 ctn.
Genealogical records of the Endicott, Pickman,
and Putnam families.

Warner Eustis collection
Eustis, Warner, 1865-1974.
SG EUS 11 [244]
1 ctn., 1 box.
Source material and notes accumulated by Warner
Eustis in his compilation of the Eustis families in
the United States 1657-1972 including letters,
questionaires, public records, etc.

Wynn Cowan Fairfield collection
Fairfield, Wynn Cowan, 1886-1961.
SG FAI 11 [127]
3 ctn., 2 card file boxes.
Genealogical records of the Fairfield family.

Charles George Fairman collection
Fairman, Charles George, 1870-1941.
SG FAI 7 [115]
3 ctn.
Genealogical notes, correspondence. clippings
and photographs on the Fairman and allied
families of Blackmer, Bruce, French, Gilman,
Harris and Wiggin.

Lilian Keturah Pond Farrar collection
Farrar, Lilian K. P., (Lilian Keturah Pond), b.
1871
SG FAR 12 a-d [134A]
1 flat storage box.
(a). Copy of Jacob Farrer's marriage certificate,
and of bapt. certificate of his son, Halifax, Co.
Yorkshire, Eng.; also Farrar genealogical
tabulations. (b). Parish church, Halifax, Yorkshire
(interior and exterior views), church where Jacob
Farrer was married and his son Jacob was bapt.,
the first ancestor in this country; Farrar chart; map
showing location of Ewood Hall; certificate

granted by the Royal College of Arms to Dr.
Lilian K.P. Farrar. (c). Portrait of Thomas
Wentworth Higginson. (d). Farrar family records
including those of allied families Holland,
Thayer, Gore and Goodwin.

Robert Irving Farrington collection
Farrington, Robert Irving, 1861-1948.
SG FAR 35 [262]
4 ctn., 1 card file box.
Genealogical collection relating to the Farrington,
Foster and allied families.

Lucia Idelle Russell Fellows collection
Fellows, Lucia Idelle Russell, b. 1864.
SG FEL 11 [267]
2 ctn.
Carton one has Abbott family through Fellows to
Runyon. Carton two has Russell, Sherwood
through to the Young family and glass plates.

Fewkes - Ross collection
Fewkes, Ernest Edwin, 1865-1942.
SG FEW 20
2 ctn., 1 box.
Book of Ross:. Vol. 1 [Town records A-N] Vol. 2
[Town records O-Y inclusive; deeds, probates,
military records & other matter] Vol. 3
[Appendix composed of extracts from other
genealogies & additional town and county
records] Vol. 4 [Personal histories of N.E.
Rosses...that date back in America to 1651] Vol 5
[Personal histories of N.E. Rosses... Scotch-Irish
Rosses who came mostly to Maine about 1718 to
1720. To which is added a long list of
unidentified persons by name of Ross] Vol 6
[Notes and corrections and a general index] Vol.
7 pt. 1 [Personal histories of N.E. Rosses...date
back in America to 1651] Vol. 7 pt.2 [Personal
histories of N.E. Rosses contains accounts of
Rosses in Ipswich & Boston, Mass., Falmouth &
Kittery, Me., Portsmouth, NH, and New Haven,
Conn., and notices of female lines and families of
Gleason, Allen, Bacon, Barrett, Scollay, Grover,
Hay, Russell, Eddy, Given and others] Vol 8
[Scotch-Irish families of Ross in ME and the
U.S.]

Flagg collection
Fuller, Benjamin Apthorp Gould, 1818-1885.
SG FLA 12 [58]
1 ctn.
Papers on the Flagg family.

Fletcher collection
Holman, Winifred Lovering, 1899-1989.
SG FLE 7
2 ctn, 3 boxes, 3 card file boxes.
Fletcher manuscript (descendants of Robert
Fletcher, early settler of Concord, Mass.)

Ford family genealogy
Ford, Hannibal Choate, 1877-1953.
SG FOR 21
9 v.: ill., ports., facsims.; 30 cm.
1950.
Typescript with additions and corrections in ms.
Based on the records of the Ford family compiled
by Corydon L. Ford.

Arthur Presbury Fowler collection
Fowler, Arthur Presbury, 1862-1916.
SG FOW 13 [120]
1 ctn.
Papers concerning the Fowler, Allen and De
Haviland families in England and America.
Contains correspondence references to English
records and manuscript genealogy.

Fox family collection
SG FOX 6
3 boxes.
Fox family records, mainly of Thomas Fox of
Concord, Mass.

Caleb Jay French collection
French, Caleb Jay, 1841-1924.
SG FRE 15 [62]
2 boxes, 2 card file boxes.
Papers on Caleb French and Susanna Avery of
Epping NH and their descendants from 1802 to
1918. French family by generations (descendants
of Edward). Alphabetical list of Frenches from
record of Prof. D. F. Thompson of Troy NY.
French entires from many sources. French family
wills and deeds.

George Willis Freeman collection
Freeman, George Willis, 1884-1951.
SG FRE 55 [111]
24 boxes, 10 card file boxes.
Freeman and allied family data. Male and female
lines arranged alphabetically.

William Hyslop Fuller collection
Fuller, William Hyslop, b. 1839.
SG FUL 24 [231]
9 ctn, 2 boxes, 2 flat storage boxes, 3 card file b
Ms. for proposed fifth volume of Fuller
genealogy.

Fuller collection
Cushman, Joseph Augustine, 1881-1949.
SG FUL 8 [134F]
1 box, 2 card file boxes.
Papers on the Fuller and Cushman families of
New England, in particular, the descendants (5
generations) of Samuel Fuller. Includes many
negatives and prints of Fuller and Cushman
gravestones.

Frederick Baker Furbish collection
Furbish, Frederick Baker.
SG FUR 1 [64]
2 boxes.
Papers relating to the Furbish family of Elliot,
Maine.

Lydia Hammond Gale collection
Gale, Lydia Hammond, 1879-1949.
SG GAL 52 [161]
1 ctn., 1 box.
Notes on many families.

Frederick Lewis Gay collection
Gay, Frederick Lewis, 1856-1916.
SG GAY 15
6 boxes.
Genealogical papers concerning John (1) Gay,
who came to New England about 1630 and settled
at Watertown MA, and his descendants.

Everett Lamont Getchell collection
Getchell, Everett Lamont, b. 1871.
SG GET 3 [72]
2 boxes.
Notes, correspondence, etc. on the Getchell-
Gatchell and allied families, 1636-1952.

Franklin Henry Giddings collection
Giddings, Franklin Henry, 1855-1931.
SG GID 1 [187]
1 ctn., 1 box, 7 card file boxes.
(1). Misc. data Miller, Millward, etc. (2). misc.
data Giddings, Millard, Beach, etc. & misc. data
Hungerford, Giddings, Bigelow, etc. (3). misc
data and correspondence. (4). 35 ancestral charts
(Lee, Beach, Giddings, Willey, Rust, Fuller, Day,
Ransome, Baldwin, Rowley, etc.); (5). misc. data
on the ancestry of Caroline Hungerford.

John Humphrey Grenville Gilbert collection
Gilbert, John Humphrey Grenville.
SG GIL 24 [134 G]
2 boxes.
Papers on the Gilbert family, Capt. Benjamin
Gilbert, b. Pomfret, Conn. 1767 and Betsey Pierce
Gilbert.

Gillett collection
Matthews, Mary Louisa, b. 1864.
SG GIL 51 [53]
2 boxes.
Genealogical material concerning the
Gillett/Gillette and allied families of Alvord,
Edgerton, Holley, Hotchkiss, Linsley, Porter,
Towslee, Tuttle, and Webster.

Paul Henry Goss collection
Goss, Paul Henry, 1890-1963.
SG GOS 1 [135]
2 ctn.
Genealogical papers on the descendants of Philip
Goss of Roxbury, Mass. including the allied
families of Fowler, Seward, Cooley & Hayward.

Benjamin Apthorp Gould collection
Gould, Benjamin Apthorp, 1824-1896.
SG GOU 9 [149]
2 ctn.
Genealogical papers relating to the genealogy of
Zaccheus Gould of Topsfield.

Stanley D. Gray collection
Gray, Stanley D.
SG GRA 15 [202]
2 ctn., 3 boxes, 2 card file boxes.
Genealogical collection on the Gray family of
Maine. Includes deeds of Castine, Sedgewick,
Brooksville, etc.

Grant collection
SG GRA 21
3 boxes (9 vols. - paging irregular).
Genealogical notes relating to some of the
ancestors of Patrick Grant born 1748 son of
Patrick and Rosamond (Pierce) Grant of Dedham,
Mass.

Everett Mason Grant collection
Grant, Everett Mason, 1915-1967.
SG GRA 23 [236]
2 boxes.
Deeds, probate, cemetery, Bible and genealogical
records concerning the Grant, Garnzey (Garnsey)
and Codding families of New England.

Greeley collection
SG GRE 10 [137]
2 boxes.
Notes and clippings on the descndants of Andrew
Greele (Greeley) of Salisbury, Mass. Includes
material on the allied Webster family.

Greene pedigree
Kerr, Helen Culver, b. 1896.
SG GRE 12 [312]
1 flat storage box.
Photocopy of the pedigree of Richard Gleason
Greene (b. 1926) and his sisters Helen Margaret
Greene (b.1922) and Dorothy Doris Lothian
Greene (b. 1923). Helen Culver Kerr, their
grandmother, compiled the information on charts
published by William Gordon ver Planck (1895).

Greenlaw collection
Greenlaw, Henrietta.
SG GRE 20 [46]
2 boxes.
Misc. genealogical records of the families of
Ellis, Shuttleworth, Barstow, Morton-Foster,
Weller-Field Mayflower lines and others. Also
includes real estate titles.

Annie Louise Tripp Griffith collection
Griffith, Annie Louise Tripp, b. 1879.
SG GRI 7 [169]
1 ctn., 2 boxes.
Genealogical papers on the Hinckley, Tripp and
allied families.

Anna Noyes Gurney collection
Gurney, Anna Noyes, 1875-1959.
SG GUR 10 [193]
3 ctn.
Records of the Gurney family and mounted misc. genealogical clippings from the Boston Evening Transcript.

Andrew Mack Haines collection
Haines, Andrew Mack, 1820-1898.
SG HAI 1 [257]
4 ctn., 1 box.
Genealogical material concerning the Haines family.

Mary Elizabeth Farnsworth Hall collection
Hall, Mary Elizabeth Farnsworth.
SG HAL 6 [313]
1 flat storage box.
Charts, notes, correspondence, etc. concerning the Hall family.

Henry Winthrop Hardon collection
Hardon, Henry Winthrop, 1861-1934.
SG HAR 4
2 ctn.
(A) Cole family of Stark, NH. (B) Horne family of Milan, NH. (C) Huckins family. (D) Huntress family of Newington, NH. (E) Jackson family of Stark, NH. (F) Lang family of Portsmouth NH. (G) Lord family of Berwick, ME. (H) Newington, NH families. (I) Peverly collaterals. (J) Roberts of Dover, NH. (K) Seward family of Portsmouth, NH.

Frank Mortimer Hawes collection
Hawes, Frank Mortimer, 1850-1941.
SG HAW 7 [196]
1 ctn.
Notes and proof sheets for Richard Hawes of Dorchester, Mass., Edmund Hawes and some of his descendants and Richard, Edmund, Edward and Robert Hawes including miscellaneous census, tax returns and probate records.

Elijah Haywood collection
Haywood, Elijah, 1786-1864.
SG HAY 11 [131]
1 ctn., 1 box.
Genealogical papers.

Alice Hayes collection
Hayes, Alice.
SG HAY 7 [263]
2 ctn., 2 boxes.
Miscellaneous papers on various families. ctn 1 has Alden - Hale families, ctn 2 has Hall - Way families, box 3 has Webb - Young families and box 4 has misc. notes etc.

Heald - Hale collection
Drury, Edwin, b. 1842.
SG HEA 10 [314]
1 ctn., 2 boxes.
Notes and correspondence concerning the Heald - Hale families. Includes genealogical correspondence sent to Clarence A. Torrey. There is also some material on the Baker family.

Heath collection
Heath, Jeff.
Heath Association of America.
SG HEA 19 [215]
2 ctn, 3 boxes, 3 flat storage boxes.
Heath family records of the Heath Association of America.

Hemenway collection
Cabot, George Edward, 1861-1946.
SG HEM 1 [30A]
1 box.
(1) Family genealogical record of Caroline Tileston Hemenway b. NYC 1874. (2) Collaterals of descendants of William Minns and of Thomas Tileston first settlers. (3) Hemenway and allied families: Bk 1 Parents, grandparents, great grandparents of Caroline Tileston Hemenway; Bk 2 Hemenway to Ralph of Roxbury 1633; Bk 3 Fitch to Dea. Zachary of Lynn abt. 1632 of Reading abt. 1640-44; Bk 4 Upton to John b. 1625 of Reading and Danvers; Bk 5 Browne to John, freeman of Salem 1637; Bk 6 Tileston to Thomas of Dorchester abt 1636; Bk 7 Minns to William b. 1728 of Boston 1737; Bk 8 Porter to John of Hingham 1635 of Salem 1644; Bk 9 Austin to Richard of Charlestown 1662; Bk 10 Colonial Wars and deputies Revolutionary War.

Sidney H. Herrick collection
Herrick, Sidney H.
SG HER 11 [143]
1 ctn., 1 box.
Genealogical records of the Herrick and allied families.

Waterman Thomas Hewett collection
Hewett, Waterman Thomas, 1846-1921.
SG HEW 1 [320]
3 boxes, 2 card file boxes.
Genealogical papers relating to early Mass. branch of the Hewett family by Prof. Waterman Hewett, early Connecticut branch by Judge R.A. Wheeler, and the remainder and additions by Mary C. Olmsted.

Fred Clark Hodgman collection
Hodgman, Fred Clark, b. 1864.
SG HOD 5 [194]
2 boxes.
Typ. Hodgman genealogy, partial typ. genealogy on Woolson family, correspondence relating to mss., misc. material on Hodgman and various other families and typ. material relating to Old Burying ground at Rockingham VT.

Almon Danforth Hodges Jr. collection
Hodges, Almon Danforth, Jr., 1843-1910.
SG HOD 6
5 ctn., 1 box, 5 card file boxes.
(A) 13 mss notebks for genealogy. (B) 5 mss. notebks for index. (C) Hodges in England. (D) Early N.E. Hodges. (E) Variants of Hodges. (F) Family of Almon Danforth Hodges, Jr. mss. notebk with clippings. (G) Misc. Hodges notes. (H) Vital records from journals of Almon Danforth Hodges (1819-1878). (I) Misc. genealogy and records collected in compilation of the Hodges genealogy (1896). (J) Questionaires and correspondence of Hodges genealogy. (K) Plates used in "Almon D. Hodges and his neighbors."

Mabel Augusta Curtice Holt collection
Holt, Mabel Augusta Curtice, 1877-1944.
SG HOL 1 [219]
1 box.
Curtice family history; misc. genealogical information; early settlers of Salisbury, Ipswich; Curtice and Eaton families; ancestry of Mabel Curtice Holt (patriotic services of ancestors, copies of wills, patriotic society membership data), a chronicle of my ancestors.

Eliza Winslow Eaton Holland collection
Holland, Eliza Winslow Eaton.
SG HOL 13 [212]
1 ctn., 2 boxes.
Papers concerning the Nathaniel Holland, Shaw and Fuller ancestry of Eliza W.E. Holland with related families.

David Emory Holman collection
Holman, David Emory, 1852-1924.
SG HOL 25 [69]
2 boxes.
Mss. of 2nd volume of "Holmans in America," descendants of William of Plymouth, John of Dorchester, William and Winifred of Boston, and the Southern Holmans.

Holt Association of America records
Holt Association of America.
SG HOL 32 [280]
1 ctn., 1 box, 1 tube.
Card index of the members of the Holt Assoc. of America in 1946, complete file of Holt Happenings, photographs, Holt Assoc. Bulletin & notices, misc. pamp. incl. (insc. 2 old cemeteries on the East Hill, Peterborough NH & John Holt Printer and postmaster 1920), diary of Edward H.Holt during the Civil War, old letters and pamphlets and other material, and three charts showing the genealogy of Dr. Frank Holt of Mich.

David Parsons Holton collection
Holton, David Parsons, 1812-1883.
SG HOL 41 [84]
5 ctn., 3 boxes.
Scrapbooks containing letters of the Parsons and allied families of Farwell and Winslow.

Homer collection
Stafford, Morgan Hewitt, 1873-1940.
SG HOM 1 [199]
5 boxes.
Material concerning the Homer and allied families.

Hopkins collection
Couch, Franklin.
SG HOP 16
1 ctn, 1 box.
The Hopkins family of New York, descendants of Stephen, including the allied families of Cole and Merrick.

Byron Barnes Horton collection
Horton, Byron Barnes, 1873-1941.
SG HOR 3 [281]
5 ctn., 5 card file boxes.
(1). Misc. geneal. material. (2). Desc. of Lieut. Joseph Horton. (3). Letter files. (4). Horton year books. (5). 1st 4 Horton generations, Rye, Harrison & Cortland ms. deeds and sketches. (6). Index cards, geneal. cards. (7). Desc. Capt. Joseph Horton of Rye, NY through 10th generation.

George Leonard Hosmer collection
Hosmer, George Leonard, 1874-1935.
SG HOS 10
1 ctn., 1 box.
Hosmer genealogical notes.

Benjamin Kent Hough collection
Hough, Benjamin Kent, 1875-1948.
SG HOU 5 [26]
3 ctn. + 3 boxes.
Note: Currently being processed [3/2002]
A group of geneal. papers chiefly on the family of Hough together with the Archibald, Balch, Brown, Chipman, Coues, Elwell and Hughes families. Second group of papers on the Parrott and Pearce families together with the Penhallow, Redding, Sargent, Sayward, Sawyer, Stacy and Stimpson families. A group of misc. documents (mostly membership certificates, diplomas etc) and a group of photos, clippings and notes.

Henry Herbert Howard collection
Howard, Henry Herbert, b. 1849.
SG HOW 21 [52]
1 box, 1 card file box.
Notes on the Howard and allied families.

Fisher Howe collection
Howe, Fisher, 1851-1935.
SG HOW 22 [114]
1 box.
Papers, notes etc. on the Howe family.

Pedigrees of families of Great Britain
Howard, Joseph Jackson, 1827-1902.
SG HOW 4 [81]
7 ctn., 1 box (50 vols).
Ms. pedigrees.

Frederic B. Hyde collection
Hyde, Frederic B.
SG HYD 4 [315]
1 flat storage box.
Genealogical charts, notes, etc. conerning the ancestors of Frederic B. Hyde.

Arthur Crew Inman collection
Inman, Arthur Crew, 1895-1963.
SG INM 1 [228]
2 ctn.
Genealogical notes of Arthur Crew Inman, containing his ancestry, chiefly in Georgia and Tennessee with original papers and photographs.

William Jenks papers
Jenks, William, 1778-1866.
SG JEN 20 [118]
1 linear ft.
Unpublished finding aid in the library.
Includes correspondence, outlines of sermons and addresses, and material by or about other members of his family including his father Samuel (1731/2-1801) and his sons Theodore Russell Jenks, Joseph William Jenks and Lemuel P. Jenks. There are records concerning the First Church in Bath and other institutions or benevolent societies in Maine. The material on the Green Street Congregational Church in Boston includes records of marriages which he preformed between 1827 and 1848. The records of three benevolent societies of Boston are particularly noteworthy. The Boston Marine Bible Society supplied Bibles to seamen. The Boston Society for the Moral and Religious Instruction of the Poor in the 1820s ran Sunday schools for the children of workers, services for seamen on board ships in the harbor as well as ashore and the Penitent Females' Refuge, a home for reformed prostitutes.

Frank Leonard Johnson collection
Johnson, Frank Leonard, 1852-1936.
SG JOH 2 [278]
2 ctn., 1 box.
Ms. Johnson genealogy (1932 & 1935 versions) followed by miscellaneous notes, genealogical correspondence and clippings bearing on the Johnson genealogy (working material).

Picture of the residence of Thomas Jones, great-grandfather of Edward T. Jones, Chiselville, Vermont
SG JON 10
1 photo.

Dana I. Joslin collection
Joslin, Dana I.
SG JOS 2
2 ctn.
Miscellaneous collection of correspondence and genealogical data on the Joslin family.

William John Keep collection
Keep, William John, 1842-1918.
SG KEE 6 [157]
1 box.
Ms. genealogy on the Keep family.

James Edward Kelley collection
Kelley, James Edward.
SG KEL 12 [123]
1 box.
Papers on the Kelley and allied families of Drew, Whitney, Heald, Stone and Nickery. Includes typ. of "Ancient Norembega and Acadia".

Kibbe collection
SG KIB 3 [78]
2 boxes.
Family group sheets and some correspondence on the Kibbe family.

Kidder collection
Stafford, Morgan Hewitt, 1873-1940.
SG KID 20 [230]
1 ctn.
Papers concerning the Kidder family.

Horace W. Killam collection
Killam, Horace W.
SG KIL 18 [240]
1 ctn., 1 card file box.
Papers concerning the Killam family of New England, descendants of Austin and Alice Killam and including records of the Killam family Association of Boxford, Mass.

Kingsleys and Kinsleys
Kingsley, James Luce, 1778-1852.
SG KIN 20
2 boxes.
Ms. dictionary catalog arranged in alphabetical order by given name. There are two lines of descent - from John[1] and from Stephen[1]. Descendants of John have a superscript number indicating their generation of descent while those of Stephen have a numeral preceed by the letter S.

Frank Bird Lamb collection
Lamb, Frank Bird, 1863-1955.
SG LAM 8 [266]
2 ctn.
Genealogical material concerning the Lamb
family of Maine, Mass., Conn., and New York
with the allied families (such as Cross, Goodyear,
Powers, Kingley and Smith) including the census
of 1790.

Leavitt family collection
SG LEA 29 [207]
5 boxes.
Note: Currently being processed [4/2002]
Original papers, correspondence, photographs,
etc., on the Leavitt family. Includes allied lines as
well as descent from John of Hingham, Mass.
Includes the 1865 diary of Sheldon Leavitt (1818-
1876) concerning family and war news along with
the 1864 diary of Sheldon Leavitt Jr. (1844-1921)
concerning his preparation for service with the
5th Regt. Mass. Vol. Cav. and memoranda.

Leffingwell - Alsop collection
Leffingwell, Douglas, 1863-1942.
SG LEF 1 [174]
3 boxes.
Genealogical papers concerning the Leffingwell,
Alsop and allied families.

Leighton collection
Cornman, Julia Leighton, 1852-1921.
SG LEI 5 [67]
2 boxes.
Genealogical notes, draft of the Leighton
genealogy, wills and correspondence.

James Minor Lincoln collection
Lincoln, James Minor, b. 1854.
SG LIN 5
6 ctn, 2 boxes.
Bible and family records, genealogies,
transcriptions of church & cemetery records,
Rochester Proprietors Records, town records,
pension claims, diaries, etc. Includes the papers
found in the old David Swift house in Wareham,
George Arthur Lincoln papers, Henry Philip
Lincoln papers, John Wesley Lincoln papers, and
Rufus Lincoln papers.

Wilford Jacob Litchfield papers
Litchfield, Wilford J. (Wilford Jacob)
SG LIT 2 [256]
6 record boxes + 17 card file boxes.
Unpublished guide: "Introduction to the
Litchfield Manuscripts" & index by Philip and
June Currier (1981)
Includes Wilford Litchfield's genealogical record
books where he kept his material organized in
family groups, smaller note books in which he
gathered information of a general nature to be
used at a later date or transferred into his basic
record books, a file on male Litchfields
alphabeticalized by their given name (often
refered to as the "Litchfield Collection" in his
record books), a surname file covering
descendants of female Litchfields and also some
of his ancestry.

Henry Dutch Lord collection
Lord, Henry Dutch, 1829-1900.
SG LOR 4 [258]
5 ctn., 1 box.
Ctn 1 has Lord families Adam-William & Lord
families of CT and ME 1-14. ctn 2 has Lord
families of ME 15-40 & VT. ctn 3 has allied
families Adams - Dutch. ctn 4 has allied families
Emerson-Rowell. ctn 5 has allied families
Sampson - Wright, Hist. Ipswich & Roxbury and
misc. notes. The last box has misc notes and
graphics.

Mary Chandler Lowell papers
Lowell, Mary Chandler, b. 1863.
SG LOW 17 [211]
1 ctn.
Papers concerning the Chandler and Parsons
families.

Mack genealogy scrapbook
Martin, Sophia Smith, b. 1847.
SG MAC 1 [316]
1 flat storage box.
Scrapbook with newspaper clippings and photos
concerning the Smith, Martin and allied families.

McIntire index
SG MACI 5 [317]
1 flat storage box.
Ms. genealogical notes on the McIntire family
arranged by given name.

Descendants of Dr. John McKechnie (1) and other relatives
McKechnie, Ernst.
SG MacK 10 [318]
1 flat storage box.
Ms. notes, charts.

Manning Family Association records
Manning Family Association.
SG MAN 10 [285]
11 ctn., 15 boxes.
Genealogical data and correspondence of the Manning Family Association.

Martin family papers, 1896-1927
Hay, Thomas Arthur, 1850-1927.
SG MAR 20 [260]
1 linear ft.
Unpublished finding aid in the repository.
Correspondence, genealogies, notes, and other papers, based on Hay's Martin Genealogy (1911), relating to the descendants of Samuel Martin (d. 1683), of Weathersfield, Conn., and selected allied families including Dodge, Skeel, and Wheeler. Correspondents include Frederick R. Martin (1871-1952), journalist, and Thomas S. Martin (1847-1919), U.S. senator.

Mason collection
Mason, Ralph R.
SG MAS 17 [182]
9 ctn., 1 box.
Records of many families of Williamsburg, Mass. and vicinity and some town records of Mass., Vermont, New York, and Connecticut.

Merrill collection
Holman, Winifred Lovering, 1899-1989.
SG MER 17 [30]
3 ctn., 2 boxes.
Correspondence, notes, transcriptions, etc. of genealogical material concerning the Merrill family. Includes census, vital statistics, town histories, genealogies and indexes.

Alfred Brooks Merriam collection
Merriam, Alfred Brooks, 1859-1944.
SG MER 51 [259]
1 ctn.
Genealogical collection (includes correspondence, clippings, pictures, wills, deeds, etc.) concerning

the Merriam, Hill, Hooper, Runkle-Bird, Taylor, Welbie, Wentworth, Wheeler families. Includes diary of Abraham Hasbrouck, 1707.

Mixter - Mixer collection
Bartlett, Elizabeth French.
SG MIX 10 [77]
2 ctn.
Genealogical material concerning the Mixter and Mixer family, especially, Isaac of Watertown, Mass., Conn., & Ohio. Includes records on the Woolson and Hartshorn families.

Robert Humphrey Montgomery collection
Montgomery, Robert Humphrey, 1889-1974.
SG MON 20 [249]
2 ctn.
Montgomery family of the eastern states.

Herbert Albion Moody collection
Moody, Herbert A., (Herbert Albion), b. 1877.
SG MOO 14 [170]
1 ctn., 1 box.
Genealogical records of the Moody family, principally of New England including descendants of William Moody of Newbury, Mass., John Moody of Hartford, Conn., Clement Moody of Exeter, N.H. and others.

Mary Eliza Cook Morse collection
Morse, Mary Eliza Cook.
SG MOR 16
6 ctn., 2 boxes.
(1) Townsend family records. (2) Brown-Stevens family records. (3) Robbins family records. (4) Hobart family records. (5) Van Rensselaer ancestry. (6) Ancestry of Caroline Lockett Moore. (7) Abbot, Barnard, Chandler, Cornell, Culer, Ingalls, Josselyn, Lansing, Livingston family records. (8) Mack, Schepmose, Schuyler, Stevens, Titus, Van Rensselaer, Van Schayk, Wright family records. (9) Bayard, Cuyler, Lansing, Livingston.Schuyler, Staats, Stoddard, Titus, Van Cortlandt, VanHorne, Van Rensselaer, Van Schaick, Van Schoenderwoert, Van Slichtenhorst, Vetch family records. (10) Fish family. (11) Bennet family. (12) Butts & Manchester families. (13) Baker family. (14) Taber family, (15) charts.

Morse Society records
Morse Society.
SG MOR 18 [279]
3 ctn., 1 box.
Genealogical papers and records of the Morse Society.

George Andrews Moriarty collection
Moriarty, George Andrews, 1883-1968.
SG MOR 24 [136]
4 ctn., 9 boxes.
Genealogical material concerning the ancestry of American immigrants from English and American sources, including some later material. Carton 1: Alcock, Almey, Andrews, de Arsic, Barlowe, Bassett, de Bocland, Bodge, Borden, Borrowdale, Bowditch, Brocklebank, Butler, Clarke, Cocke, Coggeshall, Crowninsheild, Cutler, Dickens, Earle, Eaton, Fiske, Fowle, and Gardiner. Carton 2: Gifford, Gilbert, Glanville, Goodspeed, Gorton, Greene, Grey, Gubion, Haskett, Hooker, Jewett, Jones, Knight, Lake, Lawrence, Littlefield, Merley. and Carton 3: Moriarty, Morse, Morteyn, Moseley, Murdoc, Manseglos, Newberry, Page, Paine, Peck, Pemberton, Poore and Reynolds. Carton 4: Sheffield, Spine, de Stuteville, Symonds, Throckmorton, Vaux, Wait, Waters, Weeden, White, Wightman, Winslow, Woodman, English research, Mass. historical articles, R.I. historical articles, Maryland papers. Also "The ancestry of George A. Moriarty, Jr. of Newport RI," with an index by William Macomber.

Nellie Morris collection
Morris, Nellie, b. 1856.
SG MOR 6 [264]
2 ctn., 1 box.
Misc. genealogical material including the families of Crittenden and Brown.

Anna Chandler Kingsbury collection
Kingsbury, Anna Chandler, 1870-1943.
SG NIC 31
4 ctn., 2 boxes.
Notes prepared for William Emery Nickerson on over 50 families (largely from Mass.)

William Emery Nickerson papers
Nickerson, William Emery, 1853-1930.
SG NIC 40 [289]
41 boxes.

Consists of note books mainly misc. families: Bangs, Bassett, Bower, Cole, Collier, Covell, Dunham, Emery, Emery-Emerson, Fitzpen alis Phippen, Howes, Howland, Hudson, Joyce, Knowles, Mayo, Miller, Mulford, Nason, Nickerson, Pray, Rich, Roberts, Rogers, Tart, Vickery, Waymouth; Provincetown V.R. 10 note bks; passengers on Fortune, Anne or Little James 1621, 1623; place index of ances. of Wm E. Nickerson, etc. Also 1 book of vital and cemetery records of Chatham Nickerson and other families.

Henry Lebbeus Oak collection
Oak, Henry Lebbeus, 1844-1905.
SG OAK 5
2 ctn.
Genealogical concerning relating to the Oak – Oaks – Oakes genealogy with many portraits and data relating to allied families.

O'Brion collection
Gatheman, Mabel Stewart O'Brion.
SG OBR 10 [102]
2 boxes.
Papers concerning the descendants of John and Abigail (Wilson) O'Brion of Kittery and Cornish, Maine. Includes notes on the allied families of Meserve, Palmer, Stewart, Wilson and other.

John Howard Paine collection
Paine, John Howard.
SG PAI 11 [222]
2 ctn.
Papers concerning the Paine and other families of Harwich, Mass. Includes geneal. notes by Josiah Paine, marriages & deaths taken from Harwich records, vol. 1 and deaths & marriages copied from Rev. Nathan Underwood's private record in 1865; scrapbook of original Harwich deeds & legal papers; genealogical notes of Harwich families; Records of the Nickerson family 1637-1900; mss relating to the "Wing Purchase"; extracts from the records of the Purchasers; original 7 share purchase 1748-1819 meadow at Swans Island; copies of papers relating to the Quason Purchase 1713-1822; Snow letters & genealogy; extracts from probate, town & church records; Letters from Rev. Fred Freeman 1869-1875.

Parkman collection
Cordner, Caroline Parkman, 1857-1940.
SG PAR 21 [43]
2 boxes.
Genealogical notes, correspondence, certificates, etc. on the Parkman family.

George Homer Partridge collection
Partridge, George Homer.
SG PAR 30 [80]
1 ctn.
Papers concerning the Patridge family 1693-1834; descendants of John Partridge of Medfield, Mass. and some notes on the Templeton and Duxbury, Mass. branches of the family. Probably ms. of his written work G PAR 13555.

Kate E. Parker collection
Parker, Kate E.
SG PAR 6 [166]
1 box, 2 card file boxes.
Miscellaneous manuscript of genealogical material, letters, notes and a chart of the Parker family.

Henry Spaulding Perham collection
Perham, Henry Spaulding, 1843-1906.
SG PER 17 [183]
1 ctn.
Manuscript genealogy on Perham and related families collected by the late Henry S. Perham of Chelmsford which includes that gathered by Dr. Lapham and Joel Perham of Maine.

Olive May Graves Percival collection
Percival, Olive May Graves, 1869-1945.
SG PER 21 [44A]
2 boxes.
Papers on the Percival and allied families.

Phillips collection
Phillips, Frederick A.
SG PHI 18 [48]
2 boxes.
Notes, charts, documents, correspondence, etc. on the descendants of Walter and John Phillips of Lynn, Mass. and allied families.

Phillips collection
Phillips, Alexander V.
SG PHI 22 [13]
7 ctn.
Papers on the Phillips family of Long Island, NY, including the allied families of Biles, Van Cleave, Van Room, Swem, Tindall, Walton and others alphabetically arranged.

Phillips collection
SG PHI 5 [283]
3 ctn.
Misc. genealogical data on the Ackerman, Bradford, Burrell, Hamlin, Hoag, Phillips, Sedgewick, Seeber, etc. 19 rolls of charts; Dutch, Flemish, English, Irish, Scottish records. Photostat records of English pedigrees; Albany NY early settlers, etc. and misc. geneal. data incl. graphs and photostats (Hoag, DePeyster, etc.).

Richard Donald Pierce collection
Pierce, Richard Donald, 1915-1973.
SG PIE 17 [247]
2 ctn.
Genealogical notes. Ctn 2 contains bound typescript sermons of Richard Pierce.

Claude Pitcher collection
Pitcher, Claude.
SG PIT 5 [241]
2 ctn.
Genealogical records concerning the Pitcher and allied families.

Maurice J. Pollard collection
Pollard, Maurice J., 1892-1972.
SG POL 10 [144]
2 boxes, 1 flat storage box.
Genealogical material concerning the history of the Pollard family.

Franklin Leonard Pope collection
Pope, Franklin Leonard, 1840-1895.
SG POP 11 [134 C]
1 box.
Collection of newspaper clippings mostly from the Berkshire Courier including Pope family records; Great Barrington MA history; early roads into Berkshire County; Western boundary of Mass.; History of Sandwich; and miscellaneous record.

Eugene Dimon Preston collection
Preston, Eugene Dimon, 1888-1926.
SG PRE 20 [198]
4 ctn.
(A). Correspondence and genealogy of families of Inman, Wood, Tucker, Galusha. Also royal ancestry of some American families. (B). Material pertaining to Tillinghast, Bowen, Brown, Sampson, Preston, Hutchinson, and Dyer families. (C). Material pertaining to Hassall, Chamberlaine, Tucker, Wood-Atwood, Galusha families. (D). The Barney family in America.

Francis D. Randall collection
Randall, Francis D.
SG RAN 10 [189]
1 ctn.
Papers concerning the descendants of Richard, Edward, Elder Benjamin, and William Randall, the Westerly line and much misc. data.

Charles Augustus Ranlett collection
Ranlett, Charles Augustus, 1804-1878.
SG RAN 11 [209]
4 ctn.
Correspondence and maritime papers of Capt. Charles Augustus Ranlett (1804-1878) of Charlestown, Mass., Mrs. Esther M. Ranlett (his wife), and children including some Elder and Dodge family papers.

Alanson Henry Reed collection
Reed, Alanson Henry, 1841-1924.
SG REE 1 [291]
4 ctn., 2 boxes, 4 card file boxes.
Letters, probate, and town records and other genealogical material.

Marion Charlotte Reed papers
Reed, Marion Charlotte, 1906-1966.
SG REE 3 [220]
15 ctn., 2 boxes.
Papers reflecting the author's research on the Budd, Caldwell, Dayton, Gardner, Hayden, Hook, Hubbard, Husselman, Linnell, Love, Millet, Reed, Slater, Spear, Stewart, Stillman, Sutton, Waugh, Wetherbee, White, and Whitcomb families.

Floyd T. Reynolds collection
Reynolds, Floyd T.
SG REY 7 [65]
1 box.
Papers concerning the Reynolds and allied families of Short, Sonderegger, Engster, etc.

Albert Edward Rhodes collection
Rhodes, Albert Edward, 1864-1937.
SG RHO 6
3 ctn., 1 box.
Genealogical papers, including English research, on the Rhodes and allied families.

Rhodes collection
Roberts, George McKenzie, b. 1886.
SG RHO 7 [179-179A]
4 ctn., 1 box.
Correspondence and material representing the complete file and records of the compiler of the Rhodes genealogy (also see G RHO 255), a series of seven genealogies. Includes the following families: Rhodes, Harrison, Place, Perqua, Sage, Jones, and Matteson.

Descendants of George and Maturin Ricker, Dover, New Hampshire, 1670
Ricker, Percy Leroy, b. 1878.
SG RIC 28 [134 E]
2 boxes, 2 card file boxes.
Handwritten genealogy.

Edmund Rice Association records
Edmund Rice (1638) Association.
SG RIC 29 [235]
5 ctn., 2 boxes, 5 card file boxes.
Genealogical records relating to the Rice family as collected by the Edmund Rice (1638) Association, Inc. Includes historical and genealogical notes from letters of John Bigelow, Brigham family, Drury lineages, Mayflower ancestry, MA vital records, family lineages, Marshall Rice, Hovey-Rice diaries, letters and pictures, Brattleboro and Canadian vital records, Coolidge, Drury vital records and Rice's for Ward's published genealogy.

Alexander Hamilton Rice collection
Rice, Alexander Hamilton, 1875-1956.
SG RIC 50 [99]
3 ctn., 1 box.
Genealogical material on Edmund Rice, who came from Berhanstead, England and settled in Sudbury, and his descendants. Includes (1) Partly typed, used material, I & II gen. (2) Male & female III, "Our John" IV. (3) IV generation. (4) Mainly probate records, negative Edmund Rice deed. (5) V A-N inclusive. (6) V Females. (7) V O-Z, VI A-E. (8) Males VI, F-Z. (9) Females VI. (10) Females VII. (11) Males VII. (12) VIII, 8th gen. (13) Females VIII. (14) John Rice of Dedham and Timothy and Richard of Concord. (15). Mass. town records. (16) N.H. Royce VT. (17) VT families. (18) Misc. "Our John". (19) General anc. (20) Rough ms. (21) Present work and English search. (22) 16 notebks, deaths, epitaphs, marriages. (23) Descendants of Orlando Rice, later Royce of VT, NY, Iowa, Kansas. (24) Finished ms (gen. I-IV).

Richards collection
Richards, John Bion, 1871-1954.
SG RIC 52 [191]
1 box.
Papers concerning mainly Huguenot families.

Lucien Moore Robinson collection
Robinson, Lucien Moore, 1858-1932.
SG ROB 16 [286]
3 ctn.
Carton one has material on the Robinson family and allied families Adams through Barrows. Carton two has allied families Bartlett through Multon. Carton three has allied families Osgood through Zouch plus records and graphics.

Avis Whitlemore Robinson collection
Robinson, Avis Whitlemore.
SG ROB 19 [195]
1 ctn., 1 flat storage box.
Ancestry of Avis Whitlemore Robinson including the families of Robinson, Mumford, Wilcox and others.

Frank Eggleston Robbins collection
Robbins, Frank Eggleston.
SG ROB 21 [192]
Genealogical records of the Robbins and Eggleston families.

Henry Stoddard Ruggles collection
Ruggles, Henry Stoddard, b. 1846.
SG RUG 2 [141]
1 ctn.
Genealogical records of the Ruggles and allied families.

Albert Brill Russell collection
Russell, Albert Brill, 1878-1940.
SG RUS 12 [200]
1 box.
Genealogical material, mainly on Russell family.

Savage collection
Park, Lawrence.
SG SAV 2 [106]
1 ctn.
Working notes of Lawrence Park used in his compilation of Major Thomas Savage of Boston and his descendants. Includes copies of family letters.

Edward W. Sawyer collection
Sawyer, Edward W.
SG SAW 10 [128]
1 ctn.
Some descendants of Edward W. Sawyer of Rowley and Ipswich, Mass. who was born in England in 1608.

Harrison Emery Schock collection
Schock, Harrison Emery, 1893-1965.
SG SCH 2 [107]
2 boxes.
Genealogical papers showing the ancestry of Harrison Emery Schock with the allied families of Allen, Emery, Barron, Harriott, Harrison, Howard, Proctor and others of New Jersey and Maine. Includes some material on the Saugus Iron Works.

Scollay collection
Tufts, Susan Browning Cotton, 1869-1958.
SG SCO 15 [232]
1 ctn.
Scollay genealogical collection, mostly James and
Deborah (Bligh) Scollay of Boston.

Henry Edwards Scott collection
Scott, Henry Edwards, 1859-1944.
SG SCO 30 [255]
1 ctn., 2 boxes.
Draft finding aid in the library
(1). Genealogy of Sir John Scott of Kent, Eng.
and John Scott of L.I. (2). Records of Sir John
Scott and wife, Anne Pympe of Kent, England
and ancestors. (3). Records of Sir John Scott,
written for Mrs. Alfred Scott of Geneoa,
Switzerland. (4). Misc. papers of Sir John Scott
and ancestry. (5). The Bull family.

Selden collection
LeBrun, M.O., (Maria Olivia Steele), 1860-1937.
SG SEL 5 [288]
4 ctn.
Charts, notes, transcriptions and documents
concerning the descendants of Thomas Selden, of
England and Hartford, Conn.

Seymour collection
Greenlaw, Lucy Hall, 1869-1961.
SG SEY 5A [181]
3 ctn.
Seymour genealogy. Richard Seamer of Hartford
and Norwalk, Conn. and his descendants.

Samuel Burnham Shackford collection
Shackford, Samuel Burnham, 1871-1934.
SG SHA 5
7 ctn., 5 boxes.
(1) Adams fam. of NH. (2) Allen fam. of NH. (3)
Amazeen fam. (4) Applebee fam. of NH. (5)
Austin fam. of ME & NH. (6) Babb fam. of NH.
(7) Bean fam. of NH. (8) Berry fam. of Strafford
Co., NH. (9) Burr fam. of Dover, NH. (10)
Canney fam. of NH. (11) Cartland fam. of ME &
NH. (12) Cate fam. of Strafford, Co., NH. (13)
Cavano – Caverno fam. of NH. (14) Chadwick
fam. (15). (16) Cloutman fam. of ME. (17)
Critchett fam. of Stratford Co., NH. (18) Dame
fam. of NH. (19) Day fam. of NH. (20) Dover,
NH streets & locations. (21) Downing fam. (22)

Bagdad neighborhood, Durham. (23) Evans fam.
of NH. (24) Felker fam. of NH. (25) Foss fam. of
Rye & Barrington. (26) Furber fam. of
Newington. (27) Gage fam. of NH. (28) Gove
fam. of NH. (29) Hale fam. (30) Samuel Hale
correspondence. (31) Ham fam. cemetery, Dover,
NH. (32) Hayes fam. (33) Heard fam. of Strafford
Co., NH. (34) Hill fam. of Strafford Co., NH. (35)
Hoit fam of Strafford Co., NH. (36) Jackson fam.
of NH. (37) Judith Johnson of Kensington. (38)
Jorgenson fam.

James L. Sherman collection
Sherman, James L.
SG SHE 2 [90]
1 ctn.
Genealogical collection relating to the
descendants of Philip and Sarah (Odding)
Sherman of Portsmouth, R.I.

John Eaton Shepardson collection
Shepardson, John Eaton, b. 1875.
SG SHE 31 [246]
1 ctn., 2 boxes.
Genealogical records.

*Clarence Bishop Smith ancestry: a history in
terms of one family*
Smith, Clarence Bishop.
SG SMI 19
6 boxes.
Typescript genealogy. England has sections 1-21
then New England has sections 1-11 followed by
historical material relating to English Counties.

Fannie Brownell Brown Smith collection
Smith, Fannie Brownell Brown, b. 1851.
SG SMI 20 [125]
1 box.
Papers on the Smith and Brownell, Brown,
Putnam, Woodruff and other families.

Alton Lincoln Smith collection
Smith, Alton Lincoln, 1867-1957.
SG SMI 21 [66]
2 boxes.
Papers concerning the descendants of Francis
Smith and allied families of Reading MA.

Horatio Gates Somerby collection
Somerby, H. G. (Horatio Gates), 1805-1872.
SG SOM 5 [154]
7 ctn.
English data on many early families in America.

Southworth genealogy
Webber, Samuel Gilbert, 1838-1926.
SG SOU 20 [250]
2 ctn., 7 card file boxes.
Ms. genealogy. Contains much in male and
female lines not in his printed volume of 1905.
Includes genealogical correspondence.

Waldo Chamberlain Sprague collection
Sprague, Waldo Chamberlain, 1903-1960.
SG SPR 17
Access to *Genealogies old Braintree families*
restricted; use microfilm or CD.
Note: *Genealogies of the Families of Braintree,
Mass 1640-1850* on CD available from NEHGS
Sales Dept.
(1) Genealogies of old Braintree families. (2)
Family genealogies: Thomas Thayer (4 vol.),
Richard Thayer (3 vol.), Nathaniel Thayer (1
vol.), Nathaniel Wales (2 vol.), Henry & Jane
Curtis (1 vol.) & Misc. Curtis material (1 vol.).
(3) Vital, church and census records of Braintree,
Quincy and Randolph, Mass. (4) Vital, church
and census records of Braintree (2 vol.), Quincy
(5 vol.), & Randolph, Mass. (3 vol.).

Standish collection
Weyman, Wesley, 1877-1931.
SG STA 4 [273]
8 ctn.
Descendants of Capt. Myles Standish, male and
female lines also material on the Bennett,
Ramsdell, and Wyman families.

Benjamin Stanton collection
Stanton, Benjamin.
SG STA 8 [186]
2 boxes.
Mss. material for a Stanton genealogy.

George Sawin Stewart collection
Stewart, George Sawin, 1870-1922.
SG STE 111 [261]
2 ctn.
Papers on the descendants of Duncan Steward of
Ipswich and Rowley, Mass., various Read
families, early New England Scotch families and
Scotch prisoners of 1651 employed in the Lynn
Iron Works.

Oscar Frank Stetson collection
Stetson, Oscar Frank, 1875-1948.
SG STE 23 [290]
4 ctn., 27 boxes, 1 flat storage box, 15 card file
boxes
Genealogies, notes, clippings, records, and card
files concerning the Stetson and allied families,
including the Dimock and Greene families.

Henry Joseph Stevenson collection
Stevenson, Henry Joseph, 1882-1962.
SG STE 38 [162]
1 ctn., 1 box, 6 card file boxes.
Genealogical papers concerning the Stevenson
family of East Boston and Wolfeboro, NH and the
Jenkins family of Andover, Mass.

Jesse Fenno Stevens collection
Stevens, Jesse Fenno, b. 1869.
SG STE 50 [63]
1 ctn, 2 boxes, 1 flat storage box.
Mss., clippings, photographs, charts etc.
concerning Richard Stephens (Stevens) of
Taunton, Mass. and some of his descendants.
Includes typescript transcription of New
Hampshire birth, marriage, and death records for
the Stevens family.

Willard Straight papers
Straight, Willard.
SG STR 3

Sutton collection
SG SUT 2 [225]
1 ctn.
Records of the Sutton and allied families;
descendants of George Sutton and Sarah Tilden
Sutton of Scituate, Mass. and their son, William
of Eastham, Mass.

Clifford Melville Swan collection
Swan, Clifford Melville, 1877-1951.
SG SWA 53 [158]
1 ctn., 3 boxes.
Genealogical papers on the descendants of Richard Swan, the immigrant, who settled in Roxbury, Mass., and inter-related families, especially the Melville family.

Robert Hale Symonds collection
Symonds, Robert Hale.
SG SYM 7 [35]
1 ctn. + 3 boxes.
Papers on the descendants of John (1) Symonds of Salem; Robert (1) Simmonds of Wenham, Mass. & Windham, Conn.; William (1) Simonds of Enfield, Conn.; William (1) Symonds of Haverhill, Mass.; Caleb (2) Simonds of Woburn, Mass.; Joseph (2) Simonds of Wobun, Mass.; & Lieut. Benjamin (2) Simonds of Woburn. Includes information on the Carr family; notes on the Simonds/Symonds family of Plymouth, Salem and Ipswich; transcribed vital statistics for N.H. and Vt.; and Symonds letters and records.

Thacher collection
Thacher family.
SG THA 4 [159]
1 ctn., 1 box.
Genealogical papers and letters on the Thacher family. Includes English and early American records.

George Linneaus Thompson collection
Thompson, George Linneaus, b. 1870.
SG THO 20 [39]
1 ctn.
Genealogical notes on the Thompson and Moulton families as well as notes on Thomas Jefferson. There are genealogical and historical notes on Abington-Whitman MA, Dighton MA, Randolph MA, New Bedford MA along with the History of the Universalist Church in Springfield, Vermont. Includes transcription of the record kept by Rev. George W. Bailey during his ministry in NH and VT from Jan 1 1860 to 1900.

Stephen Millett Thompson collection
Thompson, S. Millett (Stephen Millett), 1838-1911.
SG THO 28 [293]
1 flat storage box.
Records of the Thompson family of Piscataqua, NH, including original notes, letters, and diaries.

Thorndike collection
Stafford, Morgan Hewitt, 1873-1940.
SG THO 38 [208]
1 ctn., 3 boxes, 1 card file.
Genealogical material on the American and English Thorndike family.

Dwinel French Thompson collection
Thompson, Dwinel French.
SG THO 47 [168]
1 ctn.
Genealogical papers concerning his ancestry and that of his wife, Mary Lena Saxton, of Troy NY. Includes Miles Thompson of Kittery, ME; Edward and Thomas French of Ipswich MA; plus allied families of Saxton, Chapin, Dwinell, Cotton, and Quimby.Material also includes a little of Alcie (Thompson) Hall's supplementary work.

Ticknor collection
Hunnewell, James Melville, b. 1879.
SG TIC 10 [36]
1 ctn.
Genealogical notes and correspondence collected while compiling a Ticknor genealogy arranged as follows: personal notes, misc. data, military service & census of 1800; diretory lists; Mass. Ticknors (except Berkshire County); Berkshire County Ticknors; Southern Orray (6) & desc.; Elisha Ticknor; NH Ticknors, chiefly Lebanon; circulars received; NY Ticknors; Teachenor family (not connected); misc. data; Philadelphia families; Conn. Ticknors (except Litchfield County); Ticknors not descended from William of Scituate; research in England; misc. letters; misc. Western families; answers to circular of Aug '19; Sharon & Salisbury, Conn. Ticknors; Roswell descndants; Desc. of Amasa & correspondence.

Tilden collection
Linzee, John William, 1867-1949.
SG TIL 7 [139]
2 boxes.
Papers concerning the history of the Tilden family (10 generations). Also includes Tilden and Tylden families of county Kent, England and the John Phillips Tilden branch.

Tinkham genealogy: descendants of Ephraim Tinkham, 1614-1893
Tinkham, Horace Williams, b. 1858.
SG TIN 20
398 p.

George Tolman collection
Tolman, George, 1836-1909.
SG TOL 10
1 ctn. 1 box.
Genealogical papers including family genealogies and church and town records: (1) Adams family. (2) Barrett family. (3) Flint family. (4) Concord, Mass. families: Dutch, Heywood, Kendall, Meriam, Parkman, Parks, Sawyer and Wheeler. (5) Moore family. (6) First Church records. (7) Births and deaths, town records. (8) Miscellaneous material: Dakin chart, Moore family, Misc. Concord families, Meriam, Brown & Brooks.

Clarence Almon Torrey collection
Torrey, Clarence Almon, 1869-1962.
SG TOR 5 [147]
16 ctn.
Note: *New England Marriages Prior to 1700* on CD available from NEHGS Sales Dept.
Genealogical papers concerning the Torrey, Rob and allied families of Adams, Clark, Fairbanks, Gates, Gawkroger, Gilbert, Gilman, Heald, Whitebread, and Young. Includes English records.

Tourtellotte collection
Moore, Albert H.
SG TOU 1 [155]
1 ctn., 2 boxes, 4 card file boxes.
(1). Genealogy of the Tourtellot (Tourtellotte) family of America compiled by Albert H. Moore to 1933, (2). Tourtellot (Tourtellotte) family of America by Wm B Browne, (3). Genealogy of the Tourtellot-Tourtellotte family of America 1687-

1943 by L. Holbrook Tourtellotte of Marlboro MA, (4). Tourtellotte photographs and misc. data, (5). card index, (6). letters relating to the Tourtellotte genealogy, (7). Moore family genealogy (allied to Tourtellotte).

William Blanchard Towne collection
Towne, William Blanchard, 1810-1876.
SG TOW 3 [300]
1 flat storage box.
Towne genealogy.

Tozier - Tozer collection
Bichowsky, Francis Russell.
SG TOZ 4
1 ctn. 2 boxes, 1 card file box.
(1) 1-500. (2) 501-1000. (3) 1001-1500. (4) 1501-1750. (5) 1751-2000. (6) 2001-2250. (7) 2251-2426. Tozier index by number & name: (8) A-J. (9) K-Z. (10) Tozier index A by number; B by name; C. by wife's name. (11) Tozier index - female. (12) Toziers by location. (13) Toziers by location. (15) Tozier wives and husbands by last names, to serial no. 2408 (3x5 cards). (16) Tozier ms.

William Blake Trask collection
Trask, William Blake, 1812-1906.
SG TRA 11 [167]
12 boxes.
Papers relating to the Trask family including (1). Deeds, (2). Seaver notebook, photo of gravestone of John Trask who died 1720, copy of Capt Trask's deed to Gov. Endicott, 1648, plan of Capt Traske's mill ponds, Salem MA, (3). List of subscribers to the Register 1883, biography of Lemuel Shaw, (4). Index of Trask in the NEHG Register, (5). Miscellaneous papers and letters, (6). Two diaries and misc. material, (7 & 8). Miscellaneous genealogical material.

Alberta Mary Parker Trethewey collection
Trethewey, Alberta Mary Parker, b. 1871.
SG TRE 2 [134 D]
2 boxes.
Miscellaneous genealogical papers concerning the Trethewey family.

Larkin T. Tufts collection
Tufts, Larkin T.
SG TUF 10 [203]
2 boxes.
Tufts family genealogy, history of Peter of Malden, Mass., and such other of the name in America as have been discovered.

Susan Browning Cotton Tufts collection
Tufts, Susan Browning Cotton, 1869-1958.
SG TUF 12
23 boxes, 1 flat storage box.
Genealogical data, relating mainly to membership in the Mayflower Society, D.A.R., Colonial Dames, etc. Includes information on the following families: Abbott, Austin – Frazar, Bird, Bisbee, Blakesley, Bradleys of Concord, NH (chart), Bumstead – Thompson, Burton, Cobb – Smith, Crandall, Densmore-Denbo, Drake – Densmore - Denbo, Estell, Evans (pedigree notes, Mayflower lines), Glazier and intermarried families, Goodhue family and other names A-E, Goodhue families F-W, Graham, radio entertainer Horace Heidt, Hollingsworth-Sumner, Horton – Kimball – Byam, Hunt, Jeffries families of Conn. & Ala., Laughton – Bissell – Fitch, Lincoln, Lyman (Moses branch only), McCauley-Hale, McLead (incomplete), Marsh – Packard – Hersey, Morse- Fuller, Parra, Perry, Phillips & intermarried families, Pierce notes from Richmond VA, Ramsdell, Scott, Shepard, Smedberg, Sweet – Elliott, Tebbets – Tibbetts, Tidd – Tead, Van Swearingin, Weeks – Tedcastle, Weston, White – Campbell – Fitzpatrick, Wiggin -Meserve, Wood (Mayflower line), and Yong-Loring – Renton.

Fred Elbridge Varney collection
Varney, Fred Elbridge, 1861-1944.
SG VAR 5 [206]
2 ctn.
Vital records and other Varney family data.

John Adams Vinton collection
Vinton, John Adams, 1801-1877.
SG VIN 1, 1A, 2, 3, 4, 6
1 ctn. 2 boxes.
SG VIN 1 & 1A Vinton family manuscript. SG VIN 2 & 3 Vinton papers. SG VIN 4 letters containing genealogical matter relating to numerous families including Bisbee, Briggs, Carpenter, Curwen, Flint, Giles, Gould, Holmes, Jennison, Leonard, Lindall, Marshall, Pool, Putnam, Tarr, Upon, Very, Wait, Webb & Winthrop. SG VIN 6 Miscellaneous letters to Rev. John A. Vinton.

Walter Kendall Watkins collection
Watkins, Walter Kendall, 1855-1934.
SG WAT 23
1 ctn. 1 box.
Manuscript notes on the Watkins family.

Wedge collection
Grant, Seth Hastings, 1828-1910.
SG WED 5 [205]
2 ctn.
Papers on the descendants of Thomas Wedge (ca. 1640-1685) of Sudbury, Mass.

Eugene Francis Weeden collection
Weeden, Eugene Francis.
SG WEE 7
137 items (in 86 bound vol. + 1 ctn)
Covers families (ca.100) and transcriptions of primary sources for Berwick, Maine and Somersworth, New Hampshire.

Edward Wellington collection
Wellington, Edward.
SG WEL 13 [156]
1 ctn., 1 box.
Genealogical records of the Wellington family; descendants of Roger Wellington of Watertown, Mass. "planter" born about 1608 and his wife, Mary Palgrave.

Nathan Earl Wharton collection
Wharton, Nathan Earl, 1886-1950.
SG WHA 3 [224]
3 ctn.
Beverly Whartons, Cheshire, City of York,
County of York, English misc., English pedigrees,
English Whartons, Finley, Gillingwood, Leeds,
London, Motts and Lincolns, Ottey and Ilkley,
Wartons of Lancashire / Shropshire,
Westmoreland, Wharton emigrants, West Indies,
The House of Normandy, Boston Whartons, KY,
MD, MO and KS, NJ/ DE/CT, NY Whartons,
NC, Ohio misc., PA (Bucks Co., misc., Arthur
Wharton Sr. of Fayette Co., Phildelphia
Whartons), SC Whartons, VA (Accomack
Whartons, George the "Royalist", John of
Albermale, John of Raccoon Ford, Samuel of
Fauquier, Samuel - VA line, Thomas - VA line,
VA county genesis, VA misc., VA work sheets),
Wharton soldiers, Whartons of Royal descent,
Navy, genal. data, my own line, my line misc.,
unidentified, Barnes, Bates, Harrison and Saffle,
Johns, Lewis, Rucker, Slack, Wells records,
correspondence, Paxton letters, Hastings family,
Norman Nobility, Whartons of Wharton Manor.

George Hunt Wheeler collection
Barton, George Hunt, 1852-1933.
SG WHE 20 [188]
2 boxes.
Collection of genealogical material concerning
the descendants of Elisha Wheeler and Mary
Loring.

Charles Frederick White collection
White, Charles F. (Charles Frederick).
SG WHI 14 [269]
1 ctn., 1 box.
Genealogical collection on the Cotton, Davis,
White, Weld families and others.

Francis Beach White collection
White, Francis Beach, 1872-1948.
SG WHI 21 [160]
2 ctn., 1 box.
Genealogy, family letters, papers and photographs
concerning the descendants of Edward White of
Dorchester, and allied families. Includes the
writings of Rev. Greenough White.

William Arthur Whitcomb collection
Whitcomb, William Arthur, 1873-1946.
SG WHI 26 [204]
1 ctn. 2 boxes.
Genealogical records of the Whitcomb and allied
families of Sutton, Parks, Burghardt, and Budd
lines.

John Walter Coates collection
Coates, Walter John, 1880-1941.
SG WHI 38 [82]
1 ctn.
Papers on the Whitford family in America (Pasco
Whitford of R.I. 1680 or earlier).

Joseph Willard collection
Willard, Joseph, 1798-1865.
SG WIL 10 [238]
1 ctn. 1 box.
Bound ms. concerning the Willard family and
"The Adventures of a name" (clippings
concerning the Willard family). Includes
correspondence to the Rev. Charle Henry Pope in
relation to the Willard genealogy. Data supposed
to be incorporated in the published book.

Martha Adelia Fifield Wilkins collection
Wilkins, Martha Adelia Fifield, 1879-196
SG WIL 16 [234]
2 boxes.
Records concerning Sunday River and Riley
Plantation (Oxford County), Maine families and
various other families.

Elizabeth Josephine Wilmarth collection
Wilmarth, Elizabeth Josephine, 1858-1927.
SG WIL 26 [237]
2 ctn.
Ten generations of Wilmarth genealogical
material, descendants of Thomas, and some
miscellaneous data.

Raymond Royce Willoughby collection
Willoughby, Raymond Royce.
SG WIL 50 [180]
1 ctn.
Miscellaneous genealogical material on the
Willoughby family.

George Henry Williams collection
Williams, George Henry, 1858-1948.
SG WIL 77 [271]
1 box, 1 flat storage box, 5 card file boxes.
Genealogical records on the Richard Williams of Dorchester, Taunton; Robert Williams (2); Williams of Providence unplaced; Robert Williams misc.; Roger Williams Providence lines; Thomas family of R.I.; Thomas family; Roger Williams; Nicholas Williams; LeBlanc family; Rev. Ebenezer Williams; Davis family; William Davis A-I, J-Z & John of Roxbury; Nathaniel of Roxbury; Gloucester lines including Hutchings, Davis & Weld; Roxbury families A to D, E to N, N to Y; Thomas family of Providence, and charts (Bugbee, Davis, Hutchins, Trask, Williams).

Theron Royal Woodward collection
Woodward, Theron Royal, 1848-1906.
SG WOO 31
6 boxes.
Miscellaneous manuscripts pertaining to the Woodward family.

Emmett Huling Woodworth collection
Woodworth, E. Huling (Emmett Huling), b. 1896.
SG WOO 34 [235]
1 ctn., 1 box.
The Mayflower register, a compilation of the names of the 104 passengers of the Mayflower and of their descendants with supplementary material. Includes copies of the lineage blanks of the Alden Kindred of America.

Jay Backus Woodworth collection
Woodworth, Jay Backus, 1865-1925.
SG WOO 35 [268]
1 ctn., 2 boxes.
Woodworthiana, including the descendants of Walter Woodward and Oliver Woodworth, allied families, misc. correspondence, data and photostats. Note: The carton has Bucher through Woodworth families, Woodworthiana, notes 1-15. The next box has notes 16-35 and the final box has notes 36-43 plus graphs.

Henry Dickinson Woods collection
Woods, Henry Dickinson, 1852-1931.
SG WOO 5 [270]
2 ctn., 2 card file boxes.
Genealogical records of the Woods and allied families

Rodney Prescott Wright collection
Wright, Rodney Prescott, 1841-1920.
SG WRI 11 [298]
1 ctn., 4 boxes.
Wright genealogy (mostly Samuel of western Massachusetts).

Florence Peirce Wright collection
Wright, Florence Peirce.
SG WRI 14 [164]
1 ctn.
Genealogical papers on the Wright and Peirce families including the allied families of Alden, Tilton and others.

William Hill Young collection
Young, William Hill, 1867-1960.
SG YOU 9 [216]
1 ctn.
Miscellaneous genealogical material concerning the Young and Tucker families.

Stephen Badlam papers, 1633-1841
Badlam, Stephen, 1751-1815.
Spec. Col. 11 B 1
3 linear ft.
Unpublished finding aid in the library.
Consists of almost equal parts of legal documents and surveyors' papers. The former concerns the Badlam family and relations, being generally deeds, estate inventories, and wills. Some of these documents are linked to surveys done by Badlam, although spanning the period 1633-1841. The surveys are represented by maps, plats and field notes by Stephen Badlam, William Spurr and Mather Withington. They generally cover private and public properties in Dorchester, as well as roads between Boston, Braintree, Medford, Milton, Taunton, etc. There are 82 drawings and 13 field books in all.

Joseph G. Bell papers, 1717-1800
Bell, Joseph G.
Spec. Col. 11 B 1a
3 folders (19 items).
Unpublished finding aid in the library.
Miscellaneous papers pertaining to the Plymouth, Mass. merchants Barnabas Hedge and Isaac Lothrop, and John Winship of Lexington. There are two items concerning Barnabas Hedge involving mercantile correspondence and accounts. The Isaac Lothrop material consists of seven items including general business bonds, accounts and receipts. The ten documents concerning John Winship include militia notices, town and personal correspondence, and miscellaneous receipts.

Clark family papers, 1644-1868
Clark family.
Spec. Col. 11 C 1
400 items.
Unpublished finding aid in the library.
Consist almost entirely of miscellaneous legal and personal documents pertaining to the Clark and related families of Newton, Waltham, and Watertown, Mass. Most of the material was generated by John Clark (1766-1850), a justice of the peace in Waltham. Often called upon as an executor, his papers include estate settlements and guardianships. His own household records contain numerous references to medical and educational bills. Five other John Clarks are represented in the collection: John of Watertown and Newton (1641-1695), John of Newton (1680-1730), John of Waltham (1700-1773), John of Newton (b. 1738), and John (b. 1796). The latter was a genealogist, and his papers hold what little correspondence is to be found in the collection. Also represented are the Cutting, Dominion, Quincy, and Salter families. Again, the material is limited to scattered legal documents, most sworn before Edmund Quincy in Boston from 1772 to 1781.

Samuel Cutler collection, 1782-1822
Cutler, Samuel, 1752-1832.
Spec. Col. 11 C 2
5 items.
Two business account books chiefly of trade for the years 1782-1793; two volumes of religious memoranda; and a silhouette of the merchant. His business accounts reflect shipping and trade ventures, with investments and goods sales of spices, cloth, hardware, tea, etc. In addition, Cutler noted tranactions with the Proprietors of the Locks and Canals of the Merrimack River, of which he was a member. Cutler's religious memoranda includes prayers, obituaries, sermon transcriptions, and advice.

William P. Brechin collection, 1878-1896
Brechin, William P., d. 1899.
Spec. Col. 11 B 3
3.5 linear ft.
Unpublished finding aid in the library.
Genealogies, vital records, town records, articles, correspondence, etc., pertaining to the towns of Alyesford, Cornwallis (Wolfville), and Horton, Nova Scotia.

Richard Clarke collection, 1756-1775
Clarke, Richard, 1711-1795.
Spec. Col. 11 C 3
1 linear ft.
Unpublished finding aid in the library.
Clarke's business papers are strongest for the period 1756-1769, becoming thin and scattered until concluding in 1775. Most of the correspondence is in two letter books for 1758-1759 and 1767-1769. Mostly concerning business, they touch on his trade with London, Canada, the West Indies, and nearby coastal cities. Tea, oil, molasses, sugar, and potash figured prominently in this trade, and they are also prominent in Clarke's account books, invoices, ladings and receipts spread from 1756 to 1775.

Chase collection, 1639-1947
Chase, George Bigelow, 1835-1902.
Chase-Chace Family Association.
Spec. Col. 11 C 4a
9 linear ft.
Unpublished finding aid in the library.
Chase genealogical materials generated between 1847 and 1889 and records kept by the Chase-Chace Family Association from the year of its origin, 1899, to the year it became defunct, 1947. The first group of genealogical papers in the collection consists of Benjamin Chase's (1799-1889) correspondence. These letters, written between 1847 and 1887, were used by Chace in the course of his research on his Chase genealogy appearing in his book "History of Chester, N.H.: 1719-1869," published in 1869. The second group of genealogical papers is the correspondence and notes of John B. Chace (1816-1881), George B. Chase (1835-1902), and James F. Chase (d. 1923). Written between 1870 and 1889, the letters were used in Chase genealogical works to which these three mutually contributed. The records of the Chase-Chace Family Association consists of administrative and activity records, followed by misc. genealogical papers, circulars and newspaper articles on the Chace family.

Jeremiah Colburn collection, 1842-1892
Colburn, Jeremiah, 1815-1891.
Spec. Col. 11 C 5
3 linear ft.
Unpublished finding aid in the library.
Papers reflecting Colburn's interest in local history and numismatics with related organizational records and collected historical documents. Includes the papers of Daniel Denison Rogers (1751-1825), Boston merchant allied with Bromfield, Foxcroft and Gilman families.

Henry Wyles Cushman collection, 1679-1867
Cushman, Henry Wyles, 1805-1863.
Spec. Col. 11 C 7
16 linear ft.
Unpublished finding aid in the library.
The papers of Henry Wyles Cushman reflect virtually all aspects of his extraordinarily busy life. Included in this collection are personal, business, and political correspondence; diaries; deeds, wills, leases, contracts, estate inventories, court orders, case files, and many other legal documents; financial accounts; lectures, addresses, reports, and other writings; historical and genealogical materials; and miscellaneous scrapbooks, certificates, and plans. In addition to Cushman's own personal and business papers, particularly notable materials in this collection are records of the Mass. Committee on Pardons, directors' minutes of the Greenfield & Northampton and Connecticut River Railroads, account books of the Bernardston Union Store, and registers of both the First Unitarian Church Sabbath School and Powers Institute at Bernardston.

William Reed Deane collection, 1308-1889
Deane, William Reed, 1809-1871.
Spec. Col. 11 D 2
2 linear ft.
Unpublished finding aid in the library.
Consists of material generated by Deane's activities as a genealogist and historian, family correspondence, and scattered records of Deane, Bradstreet & Co. In large part, the collections reflects his genealogical interest in Deane and allied families from 1308 to 1866. Particularly useful are collected vital records of Mendon, Raynham and Taunton, Mass. Deane's historical researches included essays, notes and correspondence on New England religion, the textile industry, English migration to New England, literature and botany. In addition, there are scattered records of his work with Charles B. Richardson establishing the latter's "Historical Magazine" in 1857. The Deane family material consists of correspondence with Nicholas and George F. Dean from 1846-1867, and some household bills and receipts. Although even fewer, his business papers concentrate on the firm's supplying of cloth book bindings. Particulary interesting is a volume of signatures and comments, 1836-1846, and an account book for 1850.

Francis Samuel Drake collection
Drake, Francis S. (Francis Samuel), 1828-1885.
Spec. Col. 11 D 3
300 items.
Unpublished finding aid in the library.
Much of the business portion concerns the compilation and publication of his "A Dictionary of American Biography." In addition, there are notes and correspondence from Drake's work on the Boston Tea Party, and the originial membership of the Massachsuetts Society of the Cincinnati. The collection also holds a small quantity of family correspondence.

Fuller family papers, 1685-1800
Fuller family.
Spec. Col. 11 F 2,3
100 items.
Unpublished finding aid in the library.
The collection generally reflects the activities of Amos Fuller (1732-1810) and Timothy Fuller (b. 1765), both of Needham, Mass. Piecemeal and scattered, the contents consists mostly of deeds and account books, most notable Dr. Timothy Fuller's charges for medical services from 1792 to 1793. The family material includes items concerning the Kingbury family resulting from Amos Fuller's marriage to Sarah Kingsbury (1731-1810) in 1754.

Thomas Fillebrown papers, 1787-1840
Fillebrown, Thomas, 1763-1844.
Spec. Col. 11 F 4
36 items.
Unpublished finding aid in the library.
Chiefly commissions to military and civil office for Thomas Fillebrown.

Charles Pelham Greenough collection, 1648-1879
Greenough, Charles Pelham, 1844-1924.
Spec. Col. 11 G 1
250 items.
Unpublished finding aid in the library.
Miscellaneous correspondence and diary, 1770-1854, generally pertaining to American and English legal, commercial and business matters. Also includes English probate records from 1648 to 1879 including letters of administration, inventories, and wills.

William Hammond collection, 1730-1812
Hammond, William, 1740-1834.
Spec. Col. 11 H 1,4
304 items.
Unpublished finding aid in the library.
Consisting of 304 separate mss., the collection is made up of almost entirely of account books, bills and receipts for the period 1730-1812. The material is scattered, being especially thin from 1730 to 1772. This initial period contains papers of Thomas (b. 1698), John (1696-1763), Joshua (1761-1792), and Daniel (1727-1777) Hammond; primarily estate settlement receipts and totaling 24 items. The bulk of the collection was generated by William Hammond (1740-1834) from 1772 to 1812. A Boston merchant, he dealt in provisions and dry goods while making ventures into coastal and Surinam ports. He was also a military commissary during the Revolution, but the period is represented by only 20 items. The collection is strongest between 1792 and 1812, with 259 items.

John Hayward papers, 1827-1852
Hayward, John, 1781-1862.
Spec. Col. 11 H 3
12 items.
Unpublished finding aid in the library.
Twelve separate items and two duplicates. All but one, a transcript of John Adams' May 15 letter to Jedidiah Morse, were generated by Hayward's publishing and writing activities between 1821 and 1857. Most of the material concerns religious topics, in the form of opinions solicited from prominent clergy of the day. In addition, there are notes on fire-place construction, fruit growing, and geography. Contributors included the artist John Banvard (1821-1891), the publisher John Farmer (1789-1838), and the religious exhorter Joshua V. Himes (1805-1895).

Joshua Hubbard papers, 1766-1807
Hubbard, Joshua, 1744-1807.
Spec. Col. 11 H 5
455 items.
Unpublished finding aid in the library.
Legal documents (suits, bonds, powers of attorney, estates, grants, apprenticeships, marriage intentions, etc.) and correspondence derived from Joshua Hubbard's activities in and around Eliot, Maine., 1766 to 1807.

Hill papers, 1675-1760
Spec. Col. 11 H 6
48 items.
Unpublished finding aid in the library.
Military orders, commissions, correspondence, etc. of Major John Hill and Samuel Frost and Massachusetts authorities. There are 13 items dealing with Hill and Frost family affairs, notably a letter from Humphry Chadburn to John Hill describing the capture of Isle aux Noix in 1760. Finally, two apparently unrelated letters to William Pepperrell (1696-1759) appear discussing shipping ventures to Cadiz in 1733 and 1735.

Edwin R. Hodgman papers
Hodgman, Edwin R., 1819-1900.
Spec. Col. 11 H 6a
3 linear ft.
Unpublished finding aid in the library.
Genealogies, research notes, correspondence and a few scattered family papers. Primarily concerned with the Hodgman and Eaton families, it focuses on material gleaned from records in Chelmsford, Townsend and Westford, Mass., for the period 1663-1898. Many public records were transcribed as part of the collection.

Howe collection
Spec. Col. 11 H 7
1 box.

Winslow Lewis collection, 1643-1845
Lewis, Winslow, 1799-1875.
Spec. Col. 11 L 1
2 linear ft.
Unpublished finding aid in the library.
Consists mainly of court records and other legal documents, particularly bonds, deeds, executions, probates, suits, summonses, etc. There are, in addition, scattered pieces of local records, military papers, correspondence, and notes on local history.

Abner Morse collection
Morse, Abner, 1793-1865.
Spec. Col. 11 M
1 linear ft.
Unpublished finding aid in the library.
Consists principally of genealogical correspondence received by Abner Morse. Most of this correspondence is with Morse descendants and contains information from which Morse wrote his seven genealogical registers of early New England families, 1670-1865. Morse's personal papers consist of private correspondence, financial records, an address on the history of Chester, N.J. in 1832, and the journal of Jedediah Morse (1726-1819) from 1803-1805. The Jedediah Morse journal is of particular interest for its description of the origin and growth of the town of Woodstock, Conn., of which the author was an active citizen.

Pulsifer collection, 1680-1890
Spec. Col. 11 P 4
1 linear ft.
Unpublished finding aid in the library.
The collection is based on the activities of Captain Bickford Pulsifer of Ipswich, Mass. (fl. 1790) and four of his five sons; Bickford (b. 1800), Ebenezer (b. 1800), David (1802-1894), and John Stanwood (1798- 1866). Both Bickfords followed the sea, leaving small amounts of personal and business correspondence, bills, etc. Ebenezer lived in Ipswich, leaving similar material and a few records from his clerkship of the First Parish of Ipswich. The material concerning David Pulsifer consists of scattered letters and documents from his work as an assistant clerk to the Suffolk County Court, and touching also on his part in several scholarly editing and publishing ventures pertaining to early Massachsuetts history. John Stanwood Pulsifer's activity as a Presbyterian missionary in New York State and Pennsylvania are reflected in a number of journals, diaries, and reports to his sponsoring presbytery, as well as by his preserved sermons and orations.

Sewall-Shattuck collection, 1638-1844
Sewall, Samuel, 1652-1730.
Shattuck, Lemuel, 1793-1859.
Spec. Col. 11 S 1-41
525 items.
Unpublished finding aid in the library.
Principally legal papers arising from the law activities of Judge Samuel Sewall (1652- 1730) as well as similar documents collected by Dr. Lemuel Shattuck (1793-1859) for his genealogical and historical research. Court records, deeds, inventories, wills, etc. of Suffolk County, Mass. predominate, with lesser amounts from other counties. The states of Connecticut, Maine, New Hampshire, and Rhode Island are also represented to a slight degree. What small amounts of personal material contained are generally of the Blood, Bulkley, Hosmer and Sewell families.

Allen, William C., 516
Allen family, 19, 20, 106, 252, 263, 374, 443,
    444, 452, 457, 471, 475, 488, 525, 543,
    549, 561, 562
Allerton, Walter Scott, 19
Allerton family, 257
Alley, Samuel and Deborah (Breed) family, 474
Alleyne, Mary, 19
Alleyne, Rebecca, 19
Allin, Samuel, 19
Alling family, 22
Allison, James B., 109
Allyn, Captain, 477
Allyn, Christopher L., 311
Allyn, Henry Gladys, 252
Allyn, Thomas, 252
Allyn, Thomas family, 311
Allyn family, 445
Almey family, 558
Almy, Leonard Ballou and Caroline (Stowell)
    Webb, 327
Almy, Lydia Ballou, 327
Almy, William and Audry (Barlowe) family,
    500
Almy family, 374, 398
Alsop, Richard, 19
Alsop family, 556
Alston family, 19
Alt, Joseph Douglas, 417
Altenau, Henrich Wilhelm, 444
Altenow, Ferdinand Ludwig, 444
Alter family, 484, 512
Altnow, Randall Dayton, 444
Altnow family, 444
Alvarez family, 529
Alverson family, 538
Alvord family, 465, 551
Amazeen family, 562
Ambler, Jacquelin, 472
Ambler, Richard and Elizabeth (Jacquelin)
    family, 472
Ambler, Richard family, 473
Ambrose family, 141, 540
Ambrose of America, 19
Ambrose of England, 19
Ames, Adelbert, 217
Ames, Amos family, 472
Ames, Azel family, 538
Ames, Blanche (Butler), 217
Ames, Carolyn S., 380
Ames, David Jr. family, 397

Ames, David Sr. family, 489
Ames, Frank L. and Genevieve (Keizar) family,
    475
Ames, Jacob, 255
Ames, Jennie M., 55
Ames, Joseph family, 474
Ames, Jothan, 440
Ames, Millicent, 346
Ames, Nabby L., 472
Ames, Oliver family, 474
Ames, Richard family, 472
Ames, Samuel family, 20
Ames, Sylvanus, Judge, 472
Ames family, 19, 201, 217, 253, 444
Amey family, 471
Ammidown, Harry Frank, 193
Amory, Jonathan, 20
Amory, Robert family, 443
Amory, Thomas Coffin, 235
Amory family, 293
Ams family, 19
Anable family, 209
Anderson, Adrienne E., 356
Anderson, Grovenor T., 381
Anderson, Esq. John F., 71
Anderson, Hilda Edna, 256
Anderson, Karen, 396
Anderson, Madge, 46
Anderson, Mary (Brown), 46
Anderson, Virginia (DeJohn), 262
Anderson family, 209, 381
Andrew, Samuel, 295
Andrew, Samuel Rogers and Mary (Daggett),
    473
Andrewe, Samuel and Elizabeth, 295
Andrews, Abraham Tourtelotte, 20, 62
Andrews, Adele, 49
Andrews, Alfred, 20
Andrews, Amy Elizabeth, 20
Andrews, Charles Herbert, 31
Andrews, Christopher Blake, 10
Andrews, Elliott Morrison, 20, 351, 428
Andrews, Elliott Seabury, 20
Andrews, Experience Bardwell, 20
Andrews, Frances Eleanor, 538
Andrews, Henry Franklin, 538
Andrews, John, 20
Andrews, John family, 538
Andrews, Martha Susan, 20
Andrews, Mary, 20
Andrews, Miriam Lurinda (Guild), 20

Brownell, Mildred Edna, 329
Brownell, Nathan and Elizabeth Fish family, 399
Brownell family, 46, 239, 562
Brown family, 24, 36, 44-47, 89, 193, 205, 217, 220, 227, 232, 239, 250, 251, 252-253, 257, 267, 287, 305, 318, 329, 345, 367, 454, 465, 507, 509, 542, 544, 546, 554, 557, 558, 560, 562, 565
Browning, Dorcas Mowry, 331
Browning, Edward Franklin, 331
Browning, Samuel and Emily (Nichols) family, 331
Browning, Susan, 76, 539, 562, 566
Brownson, Lydia, 257
Brownson, Richard, 44
Brownson, Susanna, 405
Brownson Ernest Ray, 44
Brownsville, New York, 443
Brownyard, Lucius, 360
Brownyard, Mary Electa (Beach), 28
Brownyard, Theodore Lucius, 28, 361
Bruce family, 335, 403, 465, 522, 549
Bruen family, 20
Brumby, Myrtle (Palfrey), 47
Brundage, Arthur, 526
Brundage, John and Rachel (Hubbard) family, 526
Bruner, Catherine, 30
Bruns, Jens Nielsen, 46
Bruns family, 46
Brush, Grace, 47
Brush, Grace L., 142
Brush family, 47, 244, 537
Brussman, Jacob, 328
Bruyn family, 47
Bryan, John Neely, 47
Bryan, J.R., 462
Bryan, Leslie Aulls, 398
Bryan, Margaret, 530
Bryan, Margaret (Beeman), 47
Bryan, Mary (Bates), 329
Bryan family, 47, 398, 536
Bryant, Abigail, 528
Bryant, David, 47
Bryant, Dorothy, 329
Bryant, Elmira (Wilder), 147
Bryant, Henry, 191
Bryant, Henry and Elizabeth (Brimmer) (Sohier) family, 191
Bryant, John, 191, 331

Bryant, Lawrence, 47
Bryant, Lawrence Chesterfield, 47
Bryant, Nathan and Sally family, 484
Bryant, Nathaniel, 47
Bryant, Pattie (Sessoms), 47
Bryant, Percy, 47
Bryant, Sarah Maria, 321
Bryant, William Sohier, 191
Bryant family, 191, 329, 338, 465
Bryerhurst, Thomas, 47
Buby, Gladys J., 464
Buchanan, Chauncey K., 238
Buchanan, J.H., Mrs., 38
Buchanan family, 522
Bucher family, 568
Buck, Charles E., 519
Buck, George, 47
Buck, George M., 47
Buck, Herbert W., 519
Buck, Isaac, 519
Buck, Joseph, 518
Buck, Martha F., 149
Buck, Philander, 47
Bucke, John, Sir, 47
Bucke family, 465
Buckeridge, Mary, 365
Buckeridge family, 365
Buck family, 136, 138, 331, 510, 515
Buckham, Rev. James family, 527
Buckham, Matthew family, 527
Buckingham, Joseph, 490
Buckingham, William, 47
Buckingham family, 47, 83
Buckland, William Hingham, 48
Buckley family, 449
Bucklin, Squire, 48
Buckman, Nathan, 546
Buckman, Wilton Francis, 362
Buckminster, Mary Alice (Edwards) (Miller), 77
Bucknam, Bettina, 224
Bucknam, Edward, 466
Bucknam, Wilton F., 224
Bucknam, Wilton Francis, 62, 300, 377, 453, 542
Bucknam family, 224, 542
Budd, Mary, 464
Budd, Nancy J., 369
Budd, Samuel and Elizabeth (Ross) family, 464
Budd family, 560, 567
Budlong family, 230, 537
Buecher, Robert, 364

Fouts, Thomas family, 511
Fouts family, 536
Fowle, Frederick E., 385
Fowle, Richard Jaquith, 386
Fowle family, 465, 539
Fowler, Arthur Presbury, 550
Fowler, John W., 56
Fowler, Philip, 58
Fowler family, 56, 135, 269, 543, 550, 551
Fox, Elijah, 496
Fox, Vera Joyce, 192
Fox, Vallie Josephine, 1
Foxcroft family, 570
Fox family, 29, 142, 267, 306, 444, 465, 485, 550
Foye, John, 515
Foye family, 463
Frances family, 56
Francis, Rebecca Newton (Kennicutt), 83
Francis family, 56, 539
Franklin, Abigail, 234
Franklin, Benjamin, 358, 459
Franklin, Indiana, 155
Franklin, Rachel, 134
Franklin family, 56
Frankln family, 459
Frank, Velma Jean (Lowman), 382
Franks, Eunice Marion (Hayward), 417
Frary, Eleazar, 495
Frary family, 457, 462
Fraser, Marian (Foster), 507
Fraser, Margaret Isabel, 19, 500
Fraser, Robert Browne, 435
Frazee, Thelma K., 480
Freeborn, Jonathan, 399
Freeman, Betsey Ilsley (Jones), 472
Freeman, Deborah, 518
Freeman, Enoch, 182
Freeman, Rev. Fred, 558
Freeman, George Willis, 550
Freeman, Martha, 433
Freeman, Samuel, 182
Freeman family, 35, 135, 222, 232, 239, 269, 550
French, Aaron Davis Weld, 314
French, Abigail, 43
French, Alonzo Currier and Martha Jane (Locke), 340
French, Anne Rainsford, 241, 252
French, Caleb and Susanna (Avery), 550
French, Caleb Jay, 550

French, Elizabeth (Bassett), 521
French, John and Joanna family, 530
French, Jonathan family, 406
French, Joseph family, 480
French, Mabel, 340
French family, 56, 340, 345, 457, 465, 540, 549
French settlers, 564
Frick, Katherine L., 229
Frohlich, Anna Christina (Zimmer), 340, 362
Frohlich, George and Anna Christina (Zimmer) family, 340, 362
Frolich, Mary, 129
Frohlich family, 340
Frost, Elizabeth Halsell (Bullock), 338
Frost, John Eldridge, 523, 524
Frost, Josephine C., 6, 12, 171, 243
Frost, Samuel, 573
Frost family, 189, 544
Frothingham, Richard, 315
Frothingham family, 315, 465
Fry, John and Susan Wood, 150
Fry, W.T., 57
Frye, Adrian and Margaret (Bryan) family, 530
Frye, Marian (McCauley), 340
Frye, Stephen, 340
Frye family, 228
Fry family, 513
Fulham, Tabitha, 18
Fulkerson family, 530
Fuller, Amos, 571
Fuller, Benjamin Apthorp, 550
Fuller, Edward, 56
Fuller, Francis H., 211
Fuller, John, 183
Fuller, Marjorie, 368
Fuller, Samuel family, 550
Fuller, S.F. family, 530
Fuller, T.B., 530
Fuller, Thomas, 56
Fuller, Thomas, Lt., 211
Fuller, Timothy, 571
Fuller, William Hyslop, 550
Fuller family, 56, 205, 227, 239, 255, 257, 290, 340, 406, 444, 457, 463, 465, 550, 551, 553, 566, 571
Fullers, Forest S., 97
Fullerton, George H., 227
Fullerton, Jane (Hardin), 89
Fulton, Agnes, 446
Fulwood family, 347
Funkhauser family, 107

Haynes, Walter, 227
Haynes, William and Sarah (Ingersoll) family, 68
Haynes family, 68, 465, 543
Haynew, Myrte Rice, 377
Haynie, Capt. John, 68
Haynie, Lucie, 68
Haynie family, 68
Haynor family, 354
Hayward, Edward, 273
Hayward, Elisha and Lois (Albee) family, 68
Hayward, Elizabeth, 155
Hayward, Eunice Marion, 417
Hayward, George, 207, 273
Hayward, Henry family, 417
Hayward, John, 273, 475, 572
Hayward, Sophia, 93
Hayward, Thomas family, 532
Hayward, William, 273
Hayward, William Pitt Greenwood, 190
Hayward family, 190, 207, 467, 551
Hayward family, 267
Haywood, Elijah, 552
Haywood family, 46
Hazard family, 133
Hazelton, Abigail, 71
Hazelton, Abigail (Smith) (Thaxter), 490
Hazelton family, 326
Hazie, Elmer B., 297
Heacock family, 495
Head, Margaret, 41
Head family, 68
Heald, John and Dorcas (Green) family, 496
Heald, John and Mary (White) family, 496
Heald family, 552, 555, 565
Heal family, 469
Healy, Helen E., 108
Healy, Ruth (Stanton), 341
Healy family, 238, 341
Heard, Harold, 68, 341
Heard, Sr., John, 341
Heard family, 68, 446, 513, 562
Hearndon, Benjamin, 68
Hearndon, John, 68
Hearndon, Joseph, 68
Hearndon, Thomas, 68
Hearndon, William, 68
Hearsey family, 467
Heath, Albert M., 394
Heath, Elias, Jr., 69
Heath, Jeff, 552

Heath, Stillman, 500
Heath, William H. family, 394
Heath family, 69, 214, 374, 412, 552
Heaton, Ann, 498
Heaton family, 345
Heatwole family, 89
Hebard, Marilyn, 240
Hebard family, 240
Hebb, Elizabeth, 462
Hebb, Elijah family, 462
Hebel, Ianthe Bond, 144
Hebert, Louis, 69
Heck, Pearl Leona, 43, 70
Hecklinger, Roger S., 38
Hedge, Barnabas, 569
Hedges family, 511
Hedley family, 69
Heemann family,, 531
Heerschap, Leonard and Adriana family, 396
Heffries family, 566
Heffron, Roderick, 197
Heffron family, 197
Heider, Loraine Miller, 378
Heidt, Horace family, 566
Heilman family, 69
Helmershausen, Adella, 69, 509
Helmershausen, Mary F. (Bradstreet), 509
Helmershausen family, 69
Hemenway, Caroline (Tileston), 552
Hemenway, Harriot, 430
Hemenway, Ralph, 366, 552
Hemenway family, 552
Hemp family, 89
Hempstead family, 521
Henchman family, 405
Henderson, Agrippa and Letha (Eytcheson) family, 341
Henderson, Margaret L., 316
Henderson family, 341, 513
Hendley, Edith May, 69
Hendley family, 69
Hendrich, Charles T., 473
Hendrick, Elizabeth Winston (Campbell), 149
Hendricks, Hannah, 99
Hendricks family, 462
Hendrickson, Charles H., 452
Hendrix family, 42
Hendryx, Myrtle J., 342
Hennigan family, 221
Hennings, Herman Winslow,, 320
Henry, Alexander family, 69

Hill, Robert Edwin family, 369
Hill, Thomas P., 379
Hill, Valentine, 342
Hill, William and Margaret (Moore), 342
Hill, William Carroll, 70
Hill families, 70
Hill family, 38, 114, 223, 319, 342, 369, 379,
    458, 465, 548, 557, 562
Hills, Frank J., 443
Hills, Joseph, 439
Hills, Thomas, 439, 482
Hills family, 423
Hillyer, Mabel Clare, 70
Hillyer family, 70
Himes, Joshua V., 572
Himes, Nina, Mrs., 68
Hinckley, Abbie C., 45
Hinckley, Abbie L., 268
Hinckley, Ann Chamberlain, 383
Hinckley, Gustavus Adolphus, 268
Hinckley, Mabel Gould, 118
Hinckley, Mabel Gould (Demers), 71, 74, 134,
    331, 341, 346, 355
Hinckley, Robert Carman, 342
Hinckley, Samuel and Sarah (Soule) family, 342
Hinckley family, 71, 253, 268, 290, 551
Hincks, William B., 216
Hind family, 356
Hinkley, Marlene, 486
Hinkley family, 258
Hinman, Royal Ralph, 30
Hitch, Daisy, 188
Hitchborn, Thomas, 71
Hitchborn family, 71
Hitchcock, Alison B., 423
Hitchcock, Andrew Earl, 20, 440
Hitchcock, Augustus, 71
Hitchcock, Bradford D., 194
Hitchcock, Caroline (Hanks), 268
Hitchcock, Elias R., 440, 478
Hitchcock, Elizabeth, 541
Hitchcock, Mary B., 194
Hitchcock, Roswell D., 194
Hitchcock, Russell Snow, 510
Hitchcock, Walter Bardwell, 510
Hitchcock, Warren Ferris family, 415
Hitchcock family, 71, 194, 338
Hitch family, 188
Hite, Abraham, 71
Hite, Isaac, 71
Hite, Joseph, 71

Hite family, 71
Hitt family, 361
Hix family, 465
Hoag, John, 71
Hoag family, 71, 135, 269, 559
Hoar, Joseph and Aribelle (Peary) (Abbott)
    family, 352
Hoar, Joseph and Hannah (Brackett) family, 354
Hoar, Luther, 354
Hoard, Lyon J., 239
Hoard family, 239
Hoar family, 287, 423, 446, 543
Hobart, Aaron, 226
Hobart, Albert, 116
Hobart, Anna M. Brown, 226
Hobart, Deborah W., 226
Hobart, Edmund,, 71
Hobart, Eunis Everett, 226
Hobart, Gershom, 71
Hobart, Henry, 226
Hobart, Nathaniel, 226
Hobart, Noah, 226
Hobart, Noah and Abigail (Hazelton), 71
Hobart, Patience, 319
Hobart, Peter, 71
Hobart, Shebuel, 71
Hobart family, 94, 456, 557
Hobbs, Charles C., 71
Hobbs, Thomas, Jr., 447
Hobson, Katherine, 193
Hobson, William, 193
Hodgdon, Myrtle H., 176
Hodges, Almon Danforth, Jr., 553
Hodges family, 553
Hodgkins, David and Mary (Spiller) family, 71
Hodgkins, Ruby, 80
Hodgkins family, 20, 513
Hodgman, Arthur Winfred, 40, 390
Hodgman, Edwin R., 573
Hodgman, Fred Clark, 553
Hodgman family, 71, 573
Hodsdon, John A. family, 396
Hoes, Roswell Randall, 472
Hoff, Grace (Whitney), 143
Hoffman, Ruth (Brooks), 251
Hoge, Mary Adelaide (Lochary), 532
Hoge, Robert, 72
Hoge family, 536
Hogg, Robert, 72
Hogle, Gertrude Maria, 499
Hoisington, Bert Monroe and Myrtle J.

Johnston family, 79, 196
Johonnot, Daniel, 77
Jones, Amos, 308
Jones, Avis, Elsie, 371
Jones, Arthur Morse, 271
Jones, Benjamin, 80
Jones, Betsey Ilsley, 472
Jones, Blair, 137
Jones, Cornelius, 80, 271
Jones, David Tracy, 79
Jones, Dorothy, 105
Jones, Eben W., 237
Jones, Edward Payson, 311, 522
Jones, Edward T., 80, 98, 351
Jones, Edward Thomas, 23, 90, 302
Jones, Ella Bancroft, 539
Jones, Elijah, 80
Jones, Elizabeth B., 215
Jones, Frank Lawrence, 87
Jones, Frederic A., 80
Jones, Frederick A., 112
Jones, Griffith, 351
Jones, Griffith family, 80
Jones, H.A., 373
Jones, Harold M. and Margaret J. (Bartram)
      family, 345
Jones, Harold Marshall, 345
Jones, Henrietta, 61, 80
Jones, Hester, 319
Jones, Janna Lee, 271
Jones, Increase, 80
Jones, Isaac, 79
Jones, Joel, 79
Jones, Capt. John Paul, 357
Jones, Joseph, 79
Jones, Joseph family, 414
Jones, Josiah and Lydia (Treadway) family, 513
Jones, Kathleen (Paul), 38, 113
Jones, Lorene, 148, 349
Jones, Mabel (Merryfield), 80
Jones, Matt Bushnell, 73
Jones, Melvin, 322
Jones, Melvin E., 322
Jones, Norma, 397
Jones, Pauline Myra, 32
Jones, Priscilla Alden (Fortier), 450
Jones, Robert, 79
Jones, Roderick Bissell, 43, 522
Jones, Samuel Minot, 79
Jones, Snow, 79
Jones, Susan D., 414

Jones, Thomas, 555
Jones, Thomas, 80
Jones, Thomas and Hannah, 308
Jones, William, 495
Jones, William and Hannah (Eaton) family, 312
Jones, William Henry, 513
Jones, William O. family, 485
Jones, Zardus and Catherine family, 80
Jones family, 48, 69, 79, 80, 223, 232, 233, 302,
      322, 345, 421, 450, 465, 513, 522, 558,
      560
Jordan, Francis family, 81
Jordan family, 80, 81
Jordon family, 348
Jorgenson family, 562
Josiah, Hannah H., 212
Josiah, Josiah P., 212
Joslin, Dana I., 555
Joslin, Gilman, 224
Joslin family, 131, 555
Joslyn, Benjamin family, 81
Joslyn family, 345
Josselyn family, 21, 540, 557
Jourdaine family, 81
Jourdain family, 81
Jourdanie family, 81
Joy, Bethia (Sprague), 81
Joy, Helen, 257
Joy, Jane (Taylor), 126
Joyce family, 558
Joy family, 81, 293, 535
Judd, Roland D., 81
Judd, Thomas, 245
Judd, Thomas family, 81
Judd family, 81
Judge, Patrick, 81
Judkins, Job family, 271
Judson, James Clarke, 81
Judson, Martha, 75
Judson family, 81, 346, 347
Juelfs family, 54
Juhan, Alexander, 181
Juhan, John James, 181
Juhan, Oliver Hazard Perry, 181
Juhan family, 181
Julian, Jennie Bowen (Bourn), 39
Junkins, Robert family, 461
Junkins family, 461
Jurry, J.E.J., 529

K

A

Abington, Massachusetts
    cemetery inscriptions, 385, 391
    history, inhabitants and houses, 262, 468
    notes, 564
Accomac County, Virginia, 21, 83
Acton, Maine, 466, 523
Acton, Massachusetts, 207, 366, 385, 496
Acton, Suffolk County, England, 41
Acworth, New Hampshire, 488, 524
Adair County, Kentucky, 156
Adams County, Ohio, 430
Addison, Maine, 276, 500
Addison County, Vermont, 402, 403, 404
Agawam, Massachusetts, 37, 218, 385
Aghadowey, Ireland, 271
Alabama, 1, 2, 337
Albany, New York
    early settlers, 559
Albemarle County, Virginia, 150
Albisheim, Germany, 57
Alexandria, New Hampshire, 524
Alford, Massachusetts, 385
Alfred, Maine, 332, 523
Allegheny County, New York, 535
Allisburg, New Hampshire, 443
Alstead, New Hampshire, 412, 525
Altay, New York, 405
Althone, England, 86
Alton, New Hampshire, 493, 525
Amber, New York, 406
Amesbury, Massachusetts, 36, 435, 529
Amet Island, Nova Scotia, Canada, 445
Amherst, Massachusetts, 79, 247, 520
Amherst, New Hampshire, 309, 406, 410
Amherst, Ohio, 64
Amite County, Mississippi, 164
Amsterdam, Holland, 495
Ancient Dover, New Hampshire, 395
Anderson County, Kentucky, 156
Andover, Massachusetts
    cemetery inscriptions, 175
    early settlers, 285
    index of deeds, 203
    marriage records, 313
Androscoggin County, Maine, 177, 355
Angus, Nebraska, 86
Annapolis, Maryland, 516
Annapolis County, Nova Scotia, Canada, 193, 297
Annapolis Township, Nova Scotia, Canada, 488

Annisquam, Massachusetts, 61
Anson, Maine, 447
Anthony, Florida, 17
Antrim County, Ireland, 238
Apalachin, Owego, New York, 408
Arizona, 2
Arlington, Massachusetts, 217, 385
Arlington, Vermont, 339
Armagh County, Ireland, 121, 408
Aroostock, Maine, 255
Arundel, Maine, 523
Ashburnham, Massachusetts, 110, 391
Ashby, Massachusetts, 56, 137, 386, 390
Ashenden, Harry Burton, 436
Asheville, North Carolina, 46, 55, 141, 148
Ashford, Connecticut, 26, 151, 316
Ashland, Massachusetts, 386, 392
Ashland County, Ohio, 395
Ashtabula County, Ohio, 84
Athens, Maine, 270
Atherington, England, 447
Athol, Massachusetts
    cemetery inscriptions, 386
Attleboro/Attleborough, Massachusetts, 23, 53, 202, 314, 386, 390, 392, 491, 507
Auburn, Maine, 70
Auburn, Massachusetts, 506
Augusta, Georgia, 153
Augusta, Maine, 64
Augusta, New York, 45
Augusta County, Virginia, 21, 329
Austerfield, 310
Austerlitz, New York, 68
Austin, Nevada, 370
Avon, Connecticut, 362
Avon, Maine, 74
Avon, Massachusetts, 386
Ayrshire, Scotland, 496

B

Bainbridge, Georgia, 153
Baker, Florida, 17
Bakersfield, Vermont, 506
Baldwinsville, New York, 495
Baldwinville, Massachusetts, 386
Baldwyn, Mississippi, 163
Ballard County, Kentucky, 157
Ballykean, Ireland, 120
Baltimore County, 115
Bangor, Maine, 253
Barbados, West Indies, 19, 336, 369